Your All-in-One Resource

On the CD that accompanies this book, you'll find additiona.

The reference library includes the following fully searchable titles:

- *Microsoft Computer Dictionary*, 5th ed.
- *First Look 2007 Microsoft Office System* by Katherine Murray
- Windows Vista Product Guide

Also provided are a sample chapter and poster from *Look Both Ways: Help Protect Your Family on the Internet* by Linda Criddle.

The CD interface has a new look. You can use the tabs for an assortment of tasks:

- Check for book updates (if you have Internet access)
- Find links to helpful tools and resources
- Go online for product support or CD support
- Send us feedback

The following screen shot gives you a glimpse of the new interface.

Microsoft® Office Project 2007 Inside Out

Teresa S. Stover

PUBLISHED BY
Microsoft Press
A Division of Microsoft Corporation
One Microsoft Way
Redmond, Washington 98052-6399

Library of Congress Control Number: 2006940679

Printed and bound in the United States of America.

2 3 4 5 6 7 8 9 QWT 2 1 0 9 8

Distributed in Canada by H.B. Fenn and Company Ltd.

A CIP catalogue record for this book is available from the British Library.

Microsoft Press books are available through booksellers and distributors worldwide. For further information about international editions, contact your local Microsoft Corporation office or contact Microsoft Press International directly at fax (425) 936-7329. Visit our Web site at www.microsoft.com/mspress. Send comments to mspinput@microsoft.com.

Microsoft, Microsoft Press, Active Directory, ActiveX, Excel, Internet Explorer, MSDN, Outlook, PivotChart, PivotTable, PowerPoint, SharePoint, SQL Server, Visio, Visual Basic, Windows, Windows Live, Windows Server, Windows Server System, and Windows Vista are either registered trademarks or trademarks of Microsoft Corporation in the United States and/or other countries. Other product and company names mentioned herein may be the trademarks of their respective owners.

The example companies, organizations, products, domain names, e-mail addresses, logos, people, places, and events depicted herein are fictitious. No association with any real company, organization, product, domain name, e-mail address, logo, person, place, or event is intended or should be inferred.

Acquisitions Editor: Juliana Aldous Atkinson
Developmental Editor: Sandra Haynes
Project Editor: Victoria Thulman
Editorial and Production Services: Custom Editorial Productions, Inc.
Technical Reviewer: Brian Kennemer
Cover Design: Tom Draper Design

Body Part No. X13-24210

Contents at a Glance

Acknowledgments.........................xix
About the CD xxi
Conventions and Features Used in
This Book...............................xxiii

Part 1: Project Fundamentals
Chapter 1
Introducing Microsoft Office Project 2007.... 3

Chapter 2
Understanding Projects and Project
Management 37

Part 2: Developing the Project Plan
Chapter 3
Starting a New Project 59

Chapter 4
Viewing Project Information 105

Chapter 5
Scheduling Tasks 153

Chapter 6
Setting Up Resources in the Project........ 201

Chapter 7
Assigning Resources to Tasks.............. 235

Chapter 8
Planning Resource and Task Costs 273

Chapter 9
Checking and Adjusting the Project Plan ... 307

Part 3: Tracking Progress
Chapter 10
Setting a Baseline and Updating
Progress................................ 369

Chapter 11
Responding to Changes in Your Project 401

Part 4: Reporting and Analyzing Project Information
Chapter 12
Reporting Project Information 437

Chapter 13
Analyzing Progress Using Earned Value 489

Part 5: Managing Multiple Projects
Chapter 14
Managing Master Projects and
Resource Pools.......................... 503

Chapter 15
Exchanging Information Between
Project Plans........................... 529

Part 6: Integrating Microsoft Project with Other Programs
Chapter 16
Exchanging Information with Other
Applications 547

Chapter 17
Integrating Microsoft Project with
Microsoft Excel......................... 581

Chapter 18
Integrating Microsoft Project with
Microsoft Outlook...................... 639

Chapter 19
Integrating Microsoft Project with
Microsoft Visio......................... 653

Part 7: Managing Projects Across Your Enterprise

Chapter 20
Understanding Enterprise Project Management 675

Chapter 21
Administering Your Enterprise Project Management Solution 691

Chapter 22
Managing Enterprise Projects and Resources. 753

Chapter 23
Participating On a Team Using Project Web Access 827

Chapter 24
Making Executive Decisions Using Project Web Access 865

Part 8: Customizing and Managing Project Files

Chapter 25
Customizing Your View of Project Information. 897

Chapter 26
Customizing the Microsoft Project Interface. 967

Chapter 27
Automating Your Work with Macros 987

Chapter 28
Standardizing Projects Using Templates ... 1003

Chapter 29
Managing Project Files 1021

Appendix A
Installing Microsoft Office Project 2007 ... 1037

Appendix B
Online Resources for Microsoft Project 1049

Appendix C
Keyboard Shortcuts. 1053

Table of Contents

Acknowledgments xix
About the CD xxi
Conventions and Features Used in This Book xxiii

Part 1: Project Fundamentals

Chapter 1   **Introducing Microsoft Office Project 2007** 3
Using This Book 4
Using Microsoft Project—An Overview 6
Microsoft Office Project Standard 2007 8
Microsoft Office Project Professional 2007. 8
Microsoft Office Project Server 2007. 10
Microsoft Office Project Web Access. 10
Microsoft Office Project Portfolio Server 2007 10
What's New in Microsoft Office Project 2007 11
What's New in Microsoft Office Project Standard 2007 11
What's New in Microsoft Office Project Professional 2007 18
What's New in Project Server 2007 and Project Web Access 20
Learning As You Go 25
Working with the Project Guide 25
Getting Help. 29
Working with Project Smart Tags 35

Chapter 2   **Understanding Projects and Project Management** 37
Understanding Project Management Basics 37
What Is a Project? 37
What Is Project Management? 38
Understanding Project Management Processes. 41
Planning the Project 41
Executing the Project 43
Controlling the Project. 44

What do you think of this book? We want to hear from you!

Microsoft is interested in hearing your feedback so we can continually improve our books and learning
resources for you. To participate in a brief online survey, please visit:

www.microsoft.com/learning/booksurvey/

Closing the Project 44
Facilitating Your Project with Microsoft Project 44
Creating a Model of Your Project. 46
Working with Your Team Through Microsoft Project 49
Using Microsoft Project in Your Enterprise. 51
Working with the Project Stakeholders 52
Keys to Successful Project Management 53

Part 2:   Developing the Project Plan

Chapter 3   **Starting a New Project** **59**
Focusing the Project Vision 59
Defining Scope. 60
Understanding Product Scope and Project Scope 60
Developing the Scope Statement. 61
Creating a New Project Plan. 63
Creating a Project File. 63
Saving Your New Project 69
Scheduling from a Start or Finish Date 70
Setting Your Project Calendar. 72
Attaching Project Documentation 82
Entering Tasks. 86
Adding Tasks to Your Project Plan 88
Importing Tasks from an Excel Worksheet 89
Entering Recurring Tasks 91
Sequencing and Organizing Tasks 93
Moving Tasks 93
Inserting Additional Tasks 93
Copying Tasks 94
Deleting Tasks 95
Undoing Multiple Edits. 96
Organizing Tasks into an Outline 97
Setting Up Your Work Breakdown Structure. 99
Understanding Work Breakdown Structure Codes 99
Setting Up Work Breakdown Structure Codes 101
Adding Supplementary Information to Tasks 102

Chapter 4   **Viewing Project Information** **105**
Understanding Project Information Categories 106
Accessing Your Project Information 107
Using Views 107
Using Tables 125
Using Fields 134
Rearranging Your Project Information 138
Sorting Project Information. 138
Grouping Project Information. 140
Filtering Project Information. 142

Arranging Your Microsoft Project Window 147
    Setting Your Default View 148
    Showing and Hiding Screen Elements. 148
    Splitting a Window 149
    Switching Among Open Projects 151
Navigating to a Specific Location in a View. 152

Chapter 5   **Scheduling Tasks** **153**
Setting Task Durations. 154
    Developing Reliable Task Duration Estimates. 155
    Understanding Estimated vs. Confirmed Durations 156
    Entering Durations 157
    Understanding How Durations Affect Scheduling. 159
    Reviewing Durations. 162
    Calculating Your Most Probable Duration 162
Establishing Task Dependencies 167
    Creating the Finish-to-Start Task Dependency 169
    Understanding the Dependency Types. 171
    Delaying Linked Tasks by Adding Lag Time 173
    Overlapping Linked Tasks by Adding Lead Time. 174
    Changing or Removing Links 176
    Reviewing Task Dependencies 177
Scheduling Tasks to Achieve Specific Dates. 178
    Understanding Constraint Types 180
    Changing Constraints. 182
    Working with Flexible and Inflexible Constraints. 184
    Reviewing Constraints 185
Setting Deadline Reminders. 186
Creating Milestones in Your Schedule 188
Working with Task Calendars. 192
    Setting Up the Task Calendar 192
    Assigning a Base Calendar to a Task 194
Seeing Feedback on Scheduling Changes 195
    Highlighting the Ripple Effects of Schedule Changes 196
    Reviewing the Factors That Affect a Task Start Date. 197

Chapter 6   **Setting Up Resources in the Project** **201**
Understanding the Impact of Resources in the Project Plan 202
Adding Resources to the Project. 203
    Entering Resources in the Resource Sheet 203
    Adding Work Resources to the Project 205
    Adding Material Resources to the Project. 213
    Adding Cost Resources to the Project. 214
Removing a Resource from the Project 216
Identifying Tentative, Generic, or Budget Resources. 216
    Proposing Tentative Resources. 216
    Using Generic Resources as a Placeholder 218

Specifying a Budget Resource. 220
Setting When Resources Are Available for Work 220
Setting Working Times and Days Off for Work Resources .220
Specifying Resource Availability with Max Units 225
Adding Detailed Resource Information 228
Working with Supplemental Resource Fields. 228
Specifying Contact Information 231
Adding a Note Regarding a Resource 231
Hyperlinking to Resource Information 232

Chapter 7   **Assigning Resources to Tasks**. **235**
Assigning Work Resources to Tasks 235
Creating Work Resource Assignments. 237
Adding and Assigning Resources at the Same Time 239
Finding the Right Resources for the Job 241
Understanding Assignment Calculations 248
Assigning Material Resources to Tasks. 251
Assigning Cost Resources to Tasks 253
Reviewing Assignment Information 256
Showing Assignments by Task or Resource 256
Showing Assignment Information Under a Task View 258
Changing Resource Assignments 261
Controlling Changes with Effort-Driven Scheduling. 264
Controlling Schedule Changes with Task Types. 265
Contouring Resource Assignments. 269

Chapter 8   **Planning Resource and Task Costs** **273**
Working with Costs and Budgeting 274
Planning Resource Costs. 275
Setting Costs for Work Resources. 275
Setting Costs for Material Resources 277
Setting Multiple Costs for a Resource 278
Setting Cost Accrual 281
Entering Costs for Cost Resource Assignments 282
Planning Fixed Task Costs. 284
Reviewing Planned Costs 287
Reviewing Assignment Costs. 288
Reviewing Resource Costs 289
Reviewing Task Costs 290
Reviewing the Total Planned Cost for the Project 291
Setting Up and Reviewing a Project Budget. 292
Creating Budget Resources 293
Assigning Budget Resources to the Project Summary Task. 294
Entering Budget Values for the Budget Resources 296
Aligning Resources with their Budget Resource Type. 298
Comparing Resource Costs with Budget Resource Values. 301
Setting a Different Currency 304

Setting Up a Different Currency in Your Computer 304
Setting Up a Different Currency in Microsoft Project 305

Chapter 9   **Checking and Adjusting the Project Plan. 307**
Working with the Critical Path and Critical Tasks 309
Understanding Slack Time and Critical Tasks 311
Viewing the Critical Path 314
Bringing in the Project Finish Date 320
Viewing Finish Dates and the Critical Path 320
Checking Your Schedule Assumptions. 322
Adjusting Resource Settings to Bring in the Finish Date 327
Reducing Project Costs 331
Viewing Project Costs. 331
Checking Your Cost Assumptions. 336
Adjusting the Schedule to Reduce Costs. 337
Adjusting Assignments to Reduce Costs. 337
Adjusting Cost Resources. 337
Balancing Resource Workloads 338
Viewing Resource Workloads 339
Adjusting Resource Availability. 347
Adjusting Assignments. 347
Splitting Tasks 354
Leveling Assignments. 355
Changing Project Scope 364
Reviewing the Impact of Changes. 364
Obtaining Buyoff on the Project Plan. 365

Part 3:   **Tracking Progress**

Chapter 10   **Setting a Baseline and Updating Progress. 369**
Saving Original Plan Information Using a Baseline. 370
Setting a Baseline 372
Reviewing Baseline Information 374
Saving Additional Baselines. 377
Reviewing Multiple Baselines 378
Saving Additional Scheduled Start and Finish Dates. 379
Clearing a Baseline 381
Updating Task Progress. 382
Choosing the Best Method for Entering Actuals 383
Updating Progress with Task Scheduling Controls 386
Using Resource Work to Update Progress 390
Rescheduling the Project. 395
Updating Actual Costs. 397
Updating Actual Costs for Work Resources 397
Updating Actual Costs for Material Resources 397
Updating Actuals for Cost Resources. 398
Updating Actuals for Fixed Costs on Tasks. 398

Manually Updating Project Costs 399

Chapter 11   **Responding to Changes in Your Project 401**

Monitoring and Adjusting the Schedule 403
Monitoring Schedule Progress 404
Correcting the Schedule. 414
Monitoring and Adjusting Costs 415
Monitoring Project Costs. 416
Realigning the Project with the Budget. 423
Monitoring and Adjusting Resource Workload. 424
Monitoring Resource Workload 424
Balancing the Resource Workload 432

Part 4:   Reporting and Analyzing Project Information

Chapter 12   **Reporting Project Information. 437**

Establishing Your Communications Plan 438
Using Views to Report Project Information. 440
Setting Up and Printing Views 440
Getting Assistance from the Report Project Guide 443
Generating Text and Visual Reports 445
Working with Text-Based Reports 445
Working with Visual Reports in Excel and Visio. 448
Running Reports for Your Requirements 452
Summarizing with Overview Reports. 452
Focusing on Tasks with Schedule Progress Reports 455
Analyzing Budget Status with Cost Reports 460
Evaluating Resource Allocation with Assignment Reports. 466
Revising a Built-In Report. 474
Modifying a Text Report 474
Modifying a Visual Report. 478
Building a Custom Report. 478
Creating a New Text Report 479
Creating a New Visual Report Template 481
Saving Project Data Fields 484
Saving the Reporting Cube 484
Saving the Reporting Database 486

Chapter 13   **Analyzing Progress Using Earned Value 489**

Generating Earned Value Data. 489
Setting the Baseline 490
Specifying the Status Date. 491
Reviewing Earned Value Data 492
Working with Earned Value Tables. 492
Understanding the Earned Value Fields 495
Generating the Earned Value Text Report 497
Generating the Earned Value Over Time Visual Report 498

Part 5:   Managing Multiple Projects

Chapter 14   **Managing Master Projects and Resource Pools** **503**
Structuring Master Projects with Subprojects. 503
Setting Up a Master Project 504
Working with Subproject Information. 508
Unlinking a Subproject from its Source File 512
Removing a Subproject from the Master Project .513
Consolidating Project Information 513
Sharing Resources by Using a Resource Pool 517
Setting Up a Resource Pool. 518
Linking a Project to Your Resource Pool 520
Checking Availability of Resource Pool Resources. 523
Updating Resource Pool Information 525
Disconnecting a Resource Pool from a Project Plan 526

Chapter 15   **Exchanging Information Between Project Plans**. **529**
Linking Information Between Project Plans. 529
Linking Tasks Between Different Projects. 529
Reviewing Cross-Project Links. 534
Updating Cross-Project Links 536
Removing Cross-Project Links. 538
Copying and Moving Information Between Projects. 538
Copying and Moving Task and Resource Information 538
Copying Fields Between Projects 540
Copying Project Elements by Using the Organizer 542
Copying an Element from a Project to the Global Template. 543
Copying an Element Between Two Projects 544

Part 6:   Integrating Microsoft Project with Other Programs

Chapter 16   **Exchanging Information with Other Applications** **547**
Copying Information 549
Copying from Microsoft Project to Another Application. 549
Copying from Another Application to Microsoft Project. 551
Copying a Picture of a View 553
Embedding Information 557
Embedding from Microsoft Project to Another Application 558
Embedding from Another Application to Microsoft Project 562
Linking Information 568
Linking from Microsoft Project to Another Application. 568
Linking from Another Application to Microsoft Project. 569
Hyperlinking to Documents in Other Applications 571
Importing and Exporting Information 573
Updating Security Settings to Allow Data Import and Export 573
Importing Information into Microsoft Project 574
Exporting Information from Microsoft Project 576

Working with Microsoft Project and XML Files 578
Importing and Exporting Database Information 579

Chapter 17   **Integrating Microsoft Project with Microsoft Excel** **581**

Copying Between Microsoft Project and Excel 584
Copying Information from Excel 584
Copying Information to Excel 589
Embedding Between Microsoft Project and Excel 593
Embedding an Excel Object in Microsoft Project 593
Embedding a Microsoft Project File in Excel 597
Linking Between Microsoft Project and Excel 600
Linking from Excel to Microsoft Project 601
Linking from Microsoft Project to Excel 602
Working with a Linked Object 603
Importing and Exporting with Excel 606
Importing from Excel to Microsoft Project 606
Exporting from Microsoft Project to Excel 616
Re-Using a Previously Saved Export Map 627
Producing a Visual Report of Project Data in Excel 628
Generating a Visual Report from a Built-In Template 629
Creating and Editing Visual Report Templates in Excel 632
Configuring a Visual Report in Excel 636

Chapter 18   **Integrating Microsoft Project with Microsoft Outlook** **639**

Exchanging Task Information with Outlook 639
Adding Outlook Tasks to Your Project Plan 640
Adding Microsoft Project Tasks to Outlook Tasks 642
Building Your Resource List with Outlook 643
Sending Project File Information 644
Sending an Entire Project File 645
Sending Selected Tasks or Resources 646
Routing a Project File 649
Publishing the Project File to an Exchange Folder 651

Chapter 19   **Integrating Microsoft Project with Microsoft Visio** **653**

Creating a Visual Report of Project Data in Visio 654
Generating a Built-in Visual Report for Visio 654
Configuring a Visual Report in Visio 657
Creating and Editing Visual Report Templates in Visio 659
Presenting Microsoft Project Data with Visio 661
Showing Project Timeline Information in Visio 662
Displaying Project Information in a Visio Gantt Chart 664
Exporting Data from Visio to Microsoft Project 666
Exporting Timelines from Visio to Microsoft Project 666
Importing Visio Gantt Charts to Microsoft Project 667
Representing Project Data in a Visio Diagram 668
Using the Visio Timeline Template 668

Using the Gantt Chart Template. 670
Using the PERT Chart Template 672

Part 7: Managing Projects Across Your Enterprise

Chapter 20   **Understanding Enterprise Project Management** **675**

Who's Who in Enterprise Project Management 677
Understanding the Components of EPM. 680
    Understanding the Role of Project Server 681
    Understanding the Role of Project Professional 682
    Understanding the Role of Project Web Access. 683
    Putting the Project Server Components Together 683
Understanding the EPM Workflow 684
    Collaborating as a Project Team. 685
    Standardizing Enterprise Projects. 688
    Managing Enterprise Resources 688
    Analyzing Project Portfolios 689

Chapter 21   **Administering Your Enterprise Project Management Solution**. **691**

Logging On and Off 692
Managing Users and Permissions 692
    Understanding Groups, Categories, and Permissions. 694
    Creating a New User Account 695
    Removing a User from Your Project Server 698
    Viewing or Changing Permissions for User Groups. 699
    Creating a New Security Template. 700
    Creating a New Group 700
    Customizing Categories. 702
    Sending Automated Alerts and Reminders to Users. 704
Administering the Enterprise Resource Pool 704
    Creating the Enterprise Resource Pool 705
    Updating Resource Information 716
    Removing a Resource from the Enterprise Resource Pool 719
Establishing the Enterprise Portfolio. 720
Standardizing Enterprise Project Elements 721
    Working with the Enterprise Global Template 721
    Customizing Enterprise Project Fields 725
    Creating Calendars to Reflect Nonworking Times 730
Setting Up Team Member Work Pages 732
    What's the Difference Between My Tasks and My Timesheets? 732
    Defining the Task Progress Page. 734
    Defining the My Timesheets Page 739
Managing Pages, Views, and Reports. 741
    Creating and Managing Pages with Web Parts 742
    Integrating Project Information with Business Processes. 745
    Creating and Managing Views 746
    Customizing the Quick Launch Task Bar 748

Setting Up Project Report Cubes for Data Analysis. 749
Managing and Maintaining the Server. 751

Chapter 22   Managing Enterprise Projects and Resources 753

Connecting to Your Project Server 754
Setting Up Project Professional for Your Server. 754
Logging On via Project Professional 756
Logging On via Project Web Access. 757
Finding Your Way Around 759
Working with Enterprise Projects 763
Creating a New Enterprise Project 763
Managing Your Project Files on the Server. 767
Refining Your Enterprise Projects 773
Building Your Enterprise Project Team. 780
Finding Resources to Meet Your Needs 781
Assigning Tasks to Enterprise Resources 792
Collaborating with Your Project Team 794
Configuring Task Update Options 795
Publishing Project Information for Resources 800
Exchanging Task Progress Requests and Updates. 802
Requesting and Receiving Status Reports. 808
Tracking Billable and Nonbillable Time by Using Timesheets 811
Managing Documents, Risks, and Issues. 814
Creating Proposals and Activity Plans 820
Working with Proposals. 821
Creating an Activity Plan 825
Creating a Resource Plan for a Proposal or Activity Plan. 825

Chapter 23   Participating On a Team Using Project Web Access. 827

Getting Started with Project Web Access 828
Logging On and Off. 829
Finding Your Way Around 831
Working On Your Assignments and Updates 834
Reviewing New and Changed Assignments 834
Reassigning a Task to Another Resource. 837
Assigning Yourself to New Tasks. 838
Working with Your Assignment Information 843
Glimpsing the Big Project Picture. 846
Tracking Assignments and Submitting Progress Updates 848
Submitting Text-Based Status Reports. 852
Logging Time Using Timesheets 853
Working with Your Timesheets. 854
Copying Items Between My Tasks and My Timesheets 856
Requesting Nonproject or Nonworking Time 857
Setting Up E-Mail, Reminders, and Calendars. 858
Setting Your E-Mail Alerts and Home Page Reminders 859
Working with Project Tasks in Outlook 860

Managing Resources in Project Web Access 864

Chapter 24   **Making Executive Decisions Using Project Web Access** **865**

Getting Started with Project Web Access 866
  Logging On and Off 866
  Finding Your Way Around 868
Viewing Project Portfolio Information 869
  Working with Pages and Controls 870
  Working with Tables 871
  Understanding Fields 872
  Rearranging View Information 872
Working with the Project Portfolio 874
  Viewing the Portfolio of Projects 875
  Opening a Project in Project Professional 876
  Reviewing Program Information 877
  Project Workspaces and Documents, Issues, and Risks .877
  Creating a New Project 878
  Creating Proposals and Activity Plans 879
Working with Resource Information 883
  Viewing the Enterprise Resource Pool 883
  Viewing Resources for Specific Projects 884
  Reviewing Resource Assignments 885
  Reviewing Resource Availability 886
  Reviewing Resource Plans 887
  Requesting and Responding to Status Reports 887
Analyzing and Reporting on Project Information 891
Setting Your Alerts and Reminders 893

Part 8:   Customizing and Managing Project Files

Chapter 25   **Customizing Your View of Project Information** **897**

Customizing Views 898
  Changing the Content of a View 898
  Creating a New View 902
  Changing the Font for a View 902
  Formatting a Gantt Chart View 904
  Modifying a Network Diagram 912
  Modifying the Resource Graph 915
  Modifying the Calendar View 919
  Modifying a Sheet View 922
  Modifying a Usage View 924
  Modifying the Timescale 926
Customizing Tables 928
Customizing Fields 931
  Customizing a Field 933
Working with Outline Codes 941
  Setting Up Outline Codes 941

Assigning Outline Codes 946
Reviewing Your Tasks or Resources by Outline Code 947
Customizing Groups 948
Modifying a Group 948
Creating a New Group 951
Customizing Filters. 952
Modifying a Filter 952
Creating Filters. 955
Customizing AutoFilter Criteria. 959
Sharing Customized Elements Among Projects 961
Working with the Organizer 961
Copying Customized Elements 962
Removing Customized Elements 964
Renaming Customized Elements 964
Restoring Customized Elements to their Default State. 965

Chapter 26   **Customizing the Microsoft Project Interface** **967**
Creating and Customizing Toolbars 967
Customizing Toolbars. 968
Creating Toolbars 973
Deleting Toolbars 975
Modifying Button Images 976
Creating and Customizing Menus. 977
Creating and Customizing Forms 979
Creating Forms. 980
Editing Forms. 984
Renaming Forms 985
Displaying Custom Forms 985

Chapter 27   **Automating Your Work with Macros** **987**
Understanding Macros 987
What Is a Macro?. 987
Why Use Macros? 988
Creating Macros. 989
Understanding the Record Macro Dialog Box 989
Knowing When to Say "When" 992
Recording a Macro 992
Looking at Macro Code 996
Running Macros 998
Creating Keyboard Shortcuts 998
Creating Toolbar Buttons. 999

Chapter 28   **Standardizing Projects Using Templates** **1003**
Understanding the Template Types 1004
Working with the Project Global Template 1005
Working with Project Templates 1008
Starting a New Project Using a Template 1009

Downloading a Project Template from the Web 1013
Creating Your Own Project Template. 1014
Updating an Existing Template. 1017
Closing a Project. 1018
Analyzing Project Performance 1018
Recording Lessons Learned 1018
Saving Acquired Project Knowledge 1019

Chapter 29 **Managing Project Files** **1021**
Opening Project Files 1021
Opening a Saved Project 1021
Opening Projects Created in Previous Versions of Microsoft Project 1024
Searching for Files. 1024
Adding and Removing Project Summary Information 1025
Saving Files 1026
Saving a New Project to Your Local Computer or Network Drive 1026
Saving an Enterprise Project File. 1027
Specifying the Default Save Location 1029
Saving and Opening with Different File Formats 1030
Safeguarding Your Project Files. 1032
Saving Project Files Automatically 1032
Backing Up Your Project Files 1033
Protecting Your Project Files with a Password 1035
Responding to a Microsoft Project Problem 1036
Opening Files Safely 1036

Appendix A **1037**

Appendix B **1049**

Appendix C **1053**

Index to Troubleshooting Topics **1057**

Index **1059**

What do you think of this book? We want to hear from you!

Microsoft is interested in hearing your feedback so we can continually improve our books and learning resources for you. To participate in a brief online survey, please visit:

www.microsoft.com/learning/booksurvey/

Acknowledgments

Writing this book sometimes felt like rolling a boulder up Mount Everest. Fortunately, I had a support system of people who made sure I didn't fall tumbling backwards into the abyss.

Thanks to Brian Kennemer, enterprise project management expert, who served as my technical editor, lucky me. Thanks also to Adrian Jenkins, in the Microsoft Project product team, who provided me with enterprise project management capability and answered questions about all things Project.

Thanks to Bonnie Biafore, PMP, of Monte Vista Solutions, who helped write and update several chapters to help me stay on track. It was also a comfort to know she was out there and knew exactly what I was going through. (Please read more about Bonnie in "About the Authors.")

Thanks to Steve Adams and James Scott, who contributed to the previous edition of this book.

Thanks to Victoria Thulman and Sandra Haynes at Microsoft Press for providing guidance, resources, and especially kindness. They kept the project moving forward, sometimes against long odds.

Thanks to Megan Smith-Creed and her team at Custom Editorial Productions (CEP) for asking the right questions and paying attention to the details.

Thanks to my agent Claudette Moore of Moore Literary Agency, who offered to help in any way. "Just don't ask me to write any chapters," she said. Thanks to Patricia Snyder for making me look good.

Thanks to my family and friends to whom I repeatedly said "No, I have to work on the book." Now...let's have lunch. Or a nice long gab-fest on the phone.

Big hugs of appreciation to Craig Stover. He cooked dinners, folded the clothes, played with the dog, kept flowers on my desk, and guarded the door. In addition to being a great sounding board, he's also a living testimonial to how well project management can be done while maintaining a high level of quality.

Thanks also to you, dear reader and project manager. May you do great things with your projects, and may they all be on time and under budget.

About the CD

The companion CD that ships with this book contains many tools and resources to help you get the most out of your Inside Out book.

What's On the CD

Your Inside Out CD includes the following:

- **Bonus Content.** Here you'll find the following additional chapters that supplement the book:

  - Chapter 23, Participating on a Team Using Project Web Access. As well as being printed in the book, this chapter is provided as a separate PDF file for use by project team members, team leads, and resource managers involved with your enterprise projects.

  - Chapter 24, Making Executive Decisions Using Project Web Access. As well as being printed in the book, this chapter is provided as a separate PDF file for use by managing stakeholders, upper management, and executives involved with your enterprise projects.

- **Additional Ebooks.** In this section you'll find the entire electronic version of this title along with the following resources:

  - *Microsoft Computer Dictionary*, Fifth Edition

  - *First Look 2007 Microsoft Office System* (Katherine Murray, 2006)

  - Sample chapter and poster from *Look Both Ways: Help Protect Your Family on the Internet* (Linda Criddle, 2007)

  - Windows Vista Product Guide.

- **Extending Microsoft Project.** Here you'll find links to Microsoft Project Web sites where you can find templates, downloads, and trials. You'll also find links to other third-party tools that will help you get the most out of your software experience.

- **Product Information.** On this tab, you'll find links to demonstrations and product guides for Microsoft Office Project 2007, Microsoft Office Project Server 2007, the Microsoft Office Enterprise Project Management Solution, and Microsoft Office Project Portfolio Server.

- **Resources.** In this section, you'll find links to user assistance, discussion groups, product support, technical library, developer support, and other Project-related information.

System Requirements

Following are the minimum system requirements necessary to run the CD:

- Microsoft Windows Vista, Windows XP with Service Pack (SP) 2, Windows Server 2003 with SP1, or later operating system

- 500 megahertz (MHz) processor or higher

- 2 gigabyte (GB) storage space; a portion of this disk space will be freed after installation if the original download package is removed from the hard drive.

- 256 megabytes (MB) RAM

- CD-ROM or DVD-ROM drive

- 1024x768 or higher resolution monitor

- Microsoft Windows or Windows Vista–compatible sound card and speakers

- Microsoft Internet Explorer 6 or higher

- Microsoft Mouse or compatible pointing device

> **Note**
> An Internet connection is necessary to access the hyperlinks on the CD. Connect time charges may apply.

Support Information

Every effort has been made to ensure the accuracy of the contents of the book and of this CD. As corrections or changes are collected, they will be added to a Microsoft Knowledge Base article. Microsoft Press provides support for books and companion CDs at the following Web site:

http://www.microsoft.com/learning/support/books/

If you have comments, questions, or ideas regarding the book or this CD, or questions that are not answered by visiting the site above, please send them via e-mail to:

mspinput@microsoft.com

You can also click the Feedback or CD Support links on the Welcome page. Please note that Microsoft software product support is not offered through the above addresses.

If your question is about the software, and not about the content of this book, please visit the Microsoft Help and Support page or the Microsoft Knowledge Base at:

http://support.microsoft.com

In the United States, Microsoft software product support issues not covered by the Microsoft Knowledge Base are addressed by Microsoft Product Support Services. Location-specific software support options are available from:

http://support.microsoft.com/gp/selfoverview/

Microsoft Press provides corrections for books through the World Wide Web at *www.microsoft.com/mspress/support/.* To connect directly to the Microsoft Press Knowledge Base and enter a query regarding a question or issue that you may have, go to *www.microsoft.com/mspress/support/search.htm.*

Conventions and Features Used in This Book

This book uses special text and design conventions to make it easer for you to find the information you need.

Text Conventions

Convention	Feature
Abbreviated menu commands	For your convenience, this book uses abbreviated menu commands. For example, "Choose Tools, Forms, Design A Form" means that you should click the Tools menu, point to Forms, and select the Design A Form command.
Boldface type	**Boldface type** is used to indicate text that you enter or type.
Initial Capital Letters	The first letters of the names of menus, dialog boxes, dialog box elements, and commands are capitalized. Example: The Save As dialog box.
Italicized type	*Italicized type* is used to indicate new terms.
Plus sign (+) in text	Keyboard shortcuts are indicated by a plus sign (+) separating two key names. For example, Shift+F9 means that you press the Shift and F9 keys at the same time.

Design Conventions

Note

Notes offer additional information related to the task being discussed.

Cross-references point you to other locations in the book that offer additional information on the topic being discussed.

CAUTION!

Cautions identify potential problems that you should look out for when you're completing a task, or problems that you must address before you can complete a task.

INSIDE OUT

This statement illustrates an example of an "Inside Out" problem statement

These are the book's signature tips. In these tips, you'll get the straight scoop on what's going on with the software—inside information on why a feature works the way it does. You'll also find handy workarounds to different software problems.

TROUBLESHOOTING

This statement illustrates an example of a "Troubleshooting" problem statement

Look for these sidebars to find solutions to common problems you might encounter. Troubleshooting sidebars appear next to related information in the chapters. You can also use the Troubleshooting Topics index at the back of the book to look up problems by topic.

Sidebar

The sidebars sprinkled throughout these chapters provide ancillary information on the topic being discussed. Go to sidebars to learn more about the technology or a feature.

PART 1

Project Fundamentals

CHAPTER 1

Introducing Microsoft Office
Project 2007 3

CHAPTER 2

Understanding Projects and
Project Management. 37

Using This Book 4

Using Microsoft Project—An Overview 6

What's New in Microsoft Office Project 2007 . . . . **11**

Learning As You Go **25**

L et's say you are a supremely multitasking product specialist for a small startup company. You handle research, development, material procurement, marketing, and staff development. On top of all this, you have just been assigned the responsibility of managing the project for the launch of your company's newest product.

On the other hand, we could say that you are an accomplished project management professional who manages projects for several departments in your organization at any given time. You're responsible for managing thousands of tasks, hitting hundreds of deadlines, and assigning scores of resources. You need to plan and monitor each project, work with different managers, and make the best use of resources—some of whom might work on only one project and others who might be shared among several of your projects.

As these two scenarios illustrate, project management is a process and a discipline that can be the full focus of your career or one of many aspects of your job description.

Numerous industries rely on sound project management for their success. Here are just a handful:

- Construction
- Filmmaking
- Computer system deployment
- Logistics
- Engineering
- Publishing
- Events planning
- Software development

Regardless of the size of your organization, the scope of your projects, or even the number of projects you find yourself managing simultaneously, effective project management is vital at the start of a project. This is when you're determining what needs to be done, when, by whom, and for how much money. Effective project management is also essential after you kick off the project, when you are continually controlling and managing the project details. You frequently analyze the project—tracking the schedule, the budget, resource requirements, and the scope of tasks. In addition, you're managing the level of quality in the project, planning for risks and contingencies, and communicating with the members of the project team as well as upper management or customers.

Throughout this intricate process of planning and tracking your project, Microsoft Office Project 2007 is a smart and trustworthy assistant that can help you manage the many responsibilities associated with your project. Many software applications can help you work toward producing a specific result that you can print, publish, or post. And it's true that you use Office Project 2007 to set up a project schedule and print reports that reflect that schedule. However, Microsoft Project goes far beyond just the printed outcome. This is a tool that helps you brainstorm, organize, and assign your tasks as you create your schedule in the planning phase. Microsoft Project then helps you track progress and manage the schedule, resources, and budget during the execution phase. All this so you can achieve your real objective—to successfully achieve the goals of your project on schedule and under budget.

Using This Book

This book is designed for intermediate to advanced computer users who manage projects. Even if you have never used Microsoft Project or managed a project before, this book assumes you have experience with Microsoft Windows and at least a couple of programs in Microsoft Office, for example, Microsoft Office Word, Microsoft Office Excel, or Microsoft Office Outlook. Depending on where you are along the spectrum of project management experience, this book can help you in the following ways:

- If you are completely new to project management and Microsoft Project, this book will give you a solid grounding in the use of Microsoft Project as well as basic project management practices and methodologies. It will help you understand the phases of project management, including the controlling factors in the project life cycle.

- If you're an experienced project manager, this book integrates common project management practices with the use of the software tool. This helps you see how you can use Microsoft Project to carry out the project management functions you're accustomed to.

- If you're already an experienced Microsoft Project user, this book will help you better understand the inner workings of Microsoft Project so that you can use it more effectively to do what you need it to do. This book also introduces the new features of Project 2007, giving you ideas and tips as to whether and how you can use those features.

Regardless of your previous experience, this book will help you work with Microsoft Project as a facilitator for your project's processes and phases. Read the chapters and parts you feel are appropriate for your needs right now. Familiarize yourself with the topics available in the other chapters. Then, as you continue to manage your projects with Microsoft Project, keep the book within arm's reach so that you can quickly find the answers to questions and problems as they come up. As you achieve mastery in one level of knowledge, use this book to help you attain the next level, whether it's working with multiple projects at one time, customizing Microsoft Project, or programming Microsoft Project functions to automate repetitive activities. This book is your comprehensive Microsoft Project reference, in which you can quickly find answers and then get back to work on your project plan. The book is organized into the following parts:

- **Part 1: Project Fundamentals** If you want a primer on project management in general or Microsoft Project in particular, read the chapters in this part. Here, you find an overview of Microsoft Project, including what's new in Project 2007. There's an overview of project management processes and how Microsoft Project facilitates those processes. You also find a discussion of the various kinds of people involved in your project, as well as some keys to successful project management.

- **Part 2: Developing the Project Plan** Everything you need to know about starting a new project and creating a new project plan is found here. You get details about working with the Microsoft Project workspace, scheduling tasks, setting up resources, assigning resources to tasks, establishing costs, and adjusting the project plan to be an accurate model of your project's reality.

- **Part 3: Tracking Progress** After you create the perfect project plan, you're ready to execute it. To keep the project plan working for you, it needs to be up to date. This part provides details about setting and working with baselines so you can track and compare your progress toward deadlines. It covers important aspects of updating and tracking costs as well as adjusting the schedule, resource workload, and costs to reflect ongoing changes in your project.

- **Part 4: Reporting and Analyzing Project Information** Microsoft Project provides a wide range of options for setting up and printing views and reports. This part outlines these methods—from simply printing your current view to generating a built-in report to designing and running your own custom report. This part also describes how you can export data to Office Excel or Microsoft Office Visio to generate visual reports for analysis, as well as how you can use earned value data to analyze progress and costs.

- **Part 5: Managing Multiple Projects** As a project manager, it's likely that you're managing more than one project at a time. This part explains the concepts and practices of master projects, subprojects, and resource pools. It also explains how you can exchange information between different project plans; copy or link information; and leverage customized views, reports, groups, and other Microsoft Project elements you might have created.

- **Part 6: Integrating Microsoft Project with Other Programs** Microsoft Project is designed to work seamlessly with other programs. You can copy, embed, link, hyperlink, import, and export information. This part describes these methods in detail and also devotes chapters to the specific integration techniques for working with Excel, Office Outlook, and Office Visio.

- **Part 7: Managing Projects Across Your Enterprise** Microsoft Project helps to facilitate collaboration in project teams across your enterprise. If you're using Microsoft Office Project Professional 2007, Microsoft Office Project Server 2007, and Microsoft Office Project Web Access, you and your organization have access to robust project team collaboration and enterprise project management features. In this part, you see how you can assign tasks, obtain task progress updates, and receive status reports. This part also describes how you can set up and use the enterprise features to standardize and customize Microsoft Project and project management throughout your organization. A chapter each is devoted to the duties and capabilities of different stakeholders in the enterprise project management structure: the project server administrator or portfolio manager, the team member or team lead, and the executive or other managing stakeholder.

- **Part 8: Customizing and Managing Project Files** With Microsoft Project, you can create and customize your own views, tables, groups, reports, formulas, toolbars, dialog boxes, macros, and more. This part covers the details of these custom elements. This part also discusses methods for closing a project at the end of its life cycle and continuing to use what you learn by creating templates that can become the basis for the next project of its kind. Along these lines, this part details project file management issues, including file locations, backups, and multiple versions.

- **Part 9: Appendixes** This part includes ancillary information you'll find useful in your work with Microsoft Project. For example, there are installation guidelines and a list of online resources to expand your knowledge of Microsoft Project and project management. Also included is a handy keyboard shortcut reference.

Throughout the book, you'll find tips that provide shortcuts or alternate methods for doing certain tasks. The Inside Out tips give you information about known issues or idiosyncrasies with Microsoft Project and possible methods of working around them.

There are also Troubleshooting tips, which alert you to common problems and how to avoid or recover from them.

This book is designed to be referenceable so that you can quickly find the answers you need at the time you have the question. The comprehensive table of contents is a good starting point. Another excellent place to start finding your solution is in one of the two indexes at the end of the book. Use the special Troubleshooting index to solve specific problems. Use the master index to help you find the topics you're looking for when you need them.

Using Microsoft Project—An Overview

Microsoft Project is a specialized database that stores and presents thousands of pieces of data related to your project. Examples of such data include tasks, durations, links, resource names, calendars, assignments, costs, deadlines, and milestones.

These pieces of information interrelate and affect each other in a multitude of ways. Underlying this project database is the scheduling engine, which crunches the raw project data you enter and presents the calculated results to you (see Figure 1-1). Examples of such calculated results include the start and finish dates of a task, the resource availability, the finish date of the entire project, and the total cost for a resource or for the project.

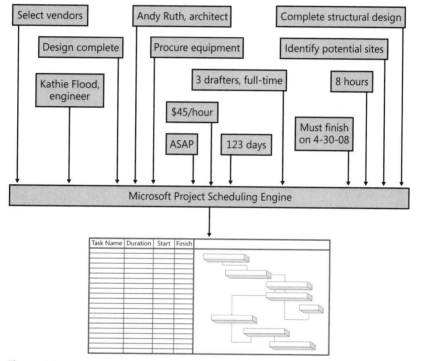

Figure 1-1 Use Microsoft Project as your database of project management information.

You can then manipulate and display this calculated data in various views to analyze the planning and progress of your project. This information helps you make decisions vital to the project's success.

You can also communicate your progress and provide the feedback necessary to keep your team and other stakeholders informed of essential project information, create and print reports for status meetings or distribution to stakeholders, and print or publish certain views or reports to your team's Web site.

There are different Microsoft Project editions and companion products available for you and your organization to get the project management features you need.

Microsoft Office Project Standard 2007

Microsoft Office Project Standard 2007 is the basic desktop edition. Office Project Standard 2007 has all the essential features for individual project management, including the following:

- Task scheduling

- Resource management

- Tracking

- Reporting

- Customization

With this substantial tool set, you can start planning, managing, and reporting your project information "straight out of the box"—that is, immediately upon installation (see Figure 1-2).

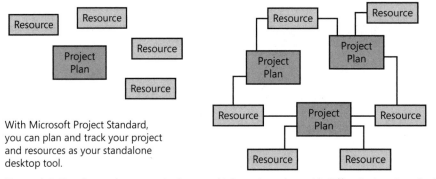

With Microsoft Project Standard, you can plan and track your project and resources as your standalone desktop tool.

Figure 1-2 Develop and execute single or multiple project plans with Office Project Standard 2007.

Microsoft Office Project Professional 2007

Microsoft Office Project Professional 2007 provides everything that Project Standard 2007 does. In addition, Office Project Professional 2007 works with Office Project Server 2007 and Office Project Web Access to provide a complete enterprise project management solution.

This includes enterprise capabilities for project standardization, resource management, team collaboration, communication, and executive analysis. With Project Professional 2007, project management is fully scalable across multiple departments and divisions in an organization (see Figure 1-3).

Chapter 1

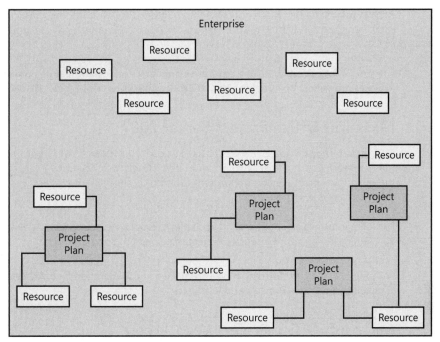

Figure 1-3 Develop and execute project plans across an enterprise with Project Professional 2007.

Project Professional 2007, as connected to Project Server 2007, includes the following features:

- Team collaboration through Project Web Access integrated with Windows Share-Point Services. From Project Professional, the project manager can submit assignments to the organization's project server and Windows SharePoint Services, and resources can view and update their assignments by using Project Web Access, the Web-based project management interface.

- Global templates, enterprise fields, and other elements, enabling your project administrator to standardize and customize the use of Microsoft Project for the way your enterprise manages projects.

- The ability to choose and manage resources from the pool of a specific group or the entire company. You can see resource availability across multiple projects and have Microsoft Project automatically find resources that will appropriately fill project team requirements.

- High-level overviews of all the projects taking place throughout the organization. With the enterprise capabilities of Project Professional, all information is gathered, organized, and reported consistently throughout the organization, providing a complete and accurate picture of all projects.

Project managers use Microsoft Project to enter, store, and update project information. They can then send project information, such as assignments or task updates, to specific resources through Project Server.

For more information about the enterprise project management features provided through Project Professional, see Chapter 20, "Understanding Enterprise Project Management."

Microsoft Office Project Server 2007

Microsoft Office Project Server 2007 is the separately licensed companion server product that works with Project Professional 2007 to provide the enterprise project management solution including team collaboration among project managers, resources, and other stakeholders.

For more information about setting up Project Server and Project Web Access, see Chapter 21, "Administering Your Enterprise Project Management Solution."

For project manager information on enterprise and collaboration features, see Chapter 22, "Managing Enterprise Projects and Resources."

Microsoft Office Project Web Access

Microsoft Office Project Web Access is the client that works with Project Professional and Project Server to provide the Web-based user interface for enterprise project management and team collaboration functions for project managers, resources, executives, and other stakeholders.

Resources and other associated stakeholders in the project can view and work with the information held in Project Server. Resources can review their assigned tasks and other project information in Project Web Access. In addition, they can add tasks, update progress information, and submit status reports through Project Server. This information ultimately updates the project plan being maintained by the project manager.

Executives can view project summary and detail information, examine projects within a particular program, analyze several projects within a portfolio for resource usage or cost, and make strategic decisions about proposed projects.

For more information about functions for resources and resource managers, see Chapter 23, "Participating on a Team Using Project Web Access." Upper managers and other stakeholders should see Chapter 24, "Making Executive Decisions Using Project Web Access."

Microsoft Office Project Portfolio Server 2007

Newly available with this release, Microsoft Office Project Portfolio Server 2007 is the separately licensed server product that can work with Project Server 2007 to provide complete portfolio management services as part of an integrated enterprise project management solution.

Chapter 1

Office Project Portfolio Server 2007 includes sophisticated tools to help organizations identify, select, and manage portfolios compatible with their business strategy. It also provides tools for resource management, billing, and invoicing. Project Portfolio Server can integrate with one or more implementations of Project Server throughout your organization. So where an implementation of Project Server might show the portfolio of all projects within a group, for example, Project Portfolio Server can provide insight into all portfolios from all groups in the entire organization.

Project Portfolio Server 2007 uses the Microsoft Office Project Portfolio Web Access client as the Web-based user interface.

Project Portfolio Server is beyond the scope of this book. However, you can get more information on the Microsoft Office Project Portfolio Server page on Microsoft Office Online at *www.microsoft.com/office/portfolioserver*.

What's New in Microsoft Office Project 2007

Microsoft Office Project 2007 includes new features and significant improvements in the following areas:

- Planning and scheduling

- Tracking resource work, costs, and time reporting

- Viewing and reporting on project information

- Collaborating within the project groups and with other business systems

As in Microsoft Office Project 2003, there are two editions of Microsoft Office Project 2007: Project Standard and Project Professional. When used as a standalone desktop project management application for a single project manager, both editions have the same features. However, with the implementation of Project Server for enterprise project management, a host of additional features becomes available in Project Professional.

This section summarizes the new features in Project Standard, Project Professional, Project Server, and Project Web Access. Cross-references indicate where these new features are covered in more detail elsewhere in this book.

What's New in Microsoft Office Project Standard 2007

Highlights of the new version of Project Standard include the ability to undo multiple edits to your project plan. Through the new Task Drivers pane and change highlighting, you have more visibility into what's happening with your schedule as you make changes. Thirty new project templates have been added to start you up and get you planning and managing your project as quickly as possible. New visual reports provide an excellent way to analyze and communicate project information.

Planning and Scheduling

You can use the following new and improved tools in Project Standard 2007 to make project scheduling more efficient and accurate:

- **Project templates** Project Standard 2007 includes 29 additional built-in project templates reflecting new product, service, or activity projects in different types of organizations (see Figure 1-4). All the templates are based on widely accepted industry standards. There are templates for business development, customer service, construction and facilities management, finance and accounting, human resources, information technology, and standards and process methodologies.

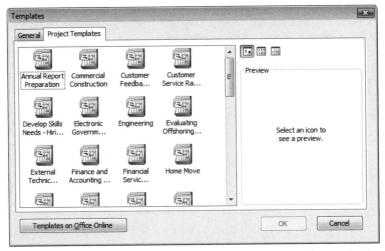

Figure 1-4 Use one of 29 new built-in project templates to quickly start the development of your project schedule. More templates are available online.

> For more information about templates, see the sections titled "Creating a New Project with a Template" in Chapter 3 and "Working with Project Templates" in Chapter 28.

- **Working and nonworking time** The methods for setting up working times and nonworking times for project, resource, and task calendars have been refined. You can now set up one-time exceptions to the normal working times, such as holidays and vacations. If needed, you can set up recurrence patterns for these working time exceptions (see Figure 1-5). You can also create any number of alternative work weeks to reflect an entirely different set of working and nonworking times that might take place on a somewhat regular basis.

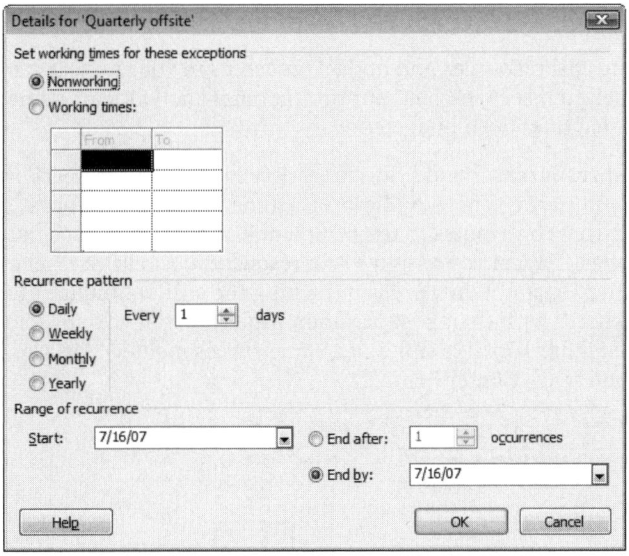

Figure 1-5 Identify working time exceptions, including recurring exceptions.

For more information about the working time calendar, see the section titled "Setting Your Project Calendar" in Chapter 3.

- **Task drivers** You can now review the list of factors responsible for the schedule, specifically the start date, of any selected task in your project. Such factors, or task drivers, might be the project start date, the project calendar, predecessor tasks, constraint date, and so on (see Figure 1-6). You can click the name of the task driver to see more details.

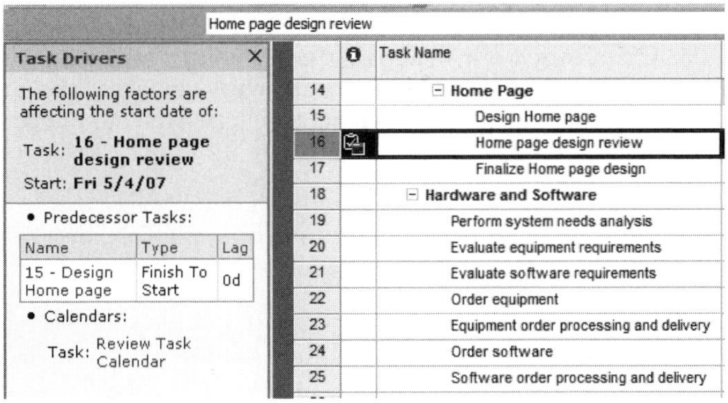

Figure 1-6 Examine the Task Drivers pane to see the factors responsible for scheduling a task's start date.

For more information about task drivers, see the section titled "Reviewing the Factors That Affect a Task Start Date" in Chapter 5.

Tracking Resource Work and Costs

Identifying cost resources and budget resources in your project can help you track costs more closely and see whether your project costs and work amounts are in line with the amounts that have been budgeted.

- **Cost resources** In addition to work resources and materials resources, the cost resource type is new in Microsoft Office Project 2007. A cost resource is a cost item that contributes to the completion of a task but does not affect the duration of a task. When you assign a cost resource to a task, or a set of tasks, you can be assured that not only are you tracking the cost of human resources or equipment resources with their cost per hour or per use, but you are also tracking the cost (see Figure 1-7). Examples of cost resources include "Airfare," "Lodging," and "Conference Center Rental."

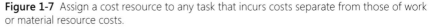

Task Name	Work	Cost
⊟ **Apply for Permits**	**40 hrs**	**$325.00**
⊟ Secure foundation permit	40 hrs	$125.00
General contractor	40 hrs	$0.00
Permit fee		$125.00
⊟ Secure framing permit	0 hrs	$200.00

Figure 1-7 Assign a cost resource to any task that incurs costs separate from those of work or material resource costs.

> For more information about cost resources, see the sections titled "Adding Cost Resources to the Project" on page 06xx and "Assigning Cost Resources to Tasks" in Chapter 7.

- **Budget tracking** You can now create a budget resource, which is used specifically to capture the high-level budgeted work or cost amount for a particular category related to the project as a whole. You create a resource that represents that project budget category, for example, "Travel Budget," "Equipment Cost Plan," or "Project Materials." Any work, material, or cost resource can be identified as a budget resource. You can then roll up work and cost amounts to the project summary task and compare them with the amounts reflected in your budget resources (see Figure 1-8).

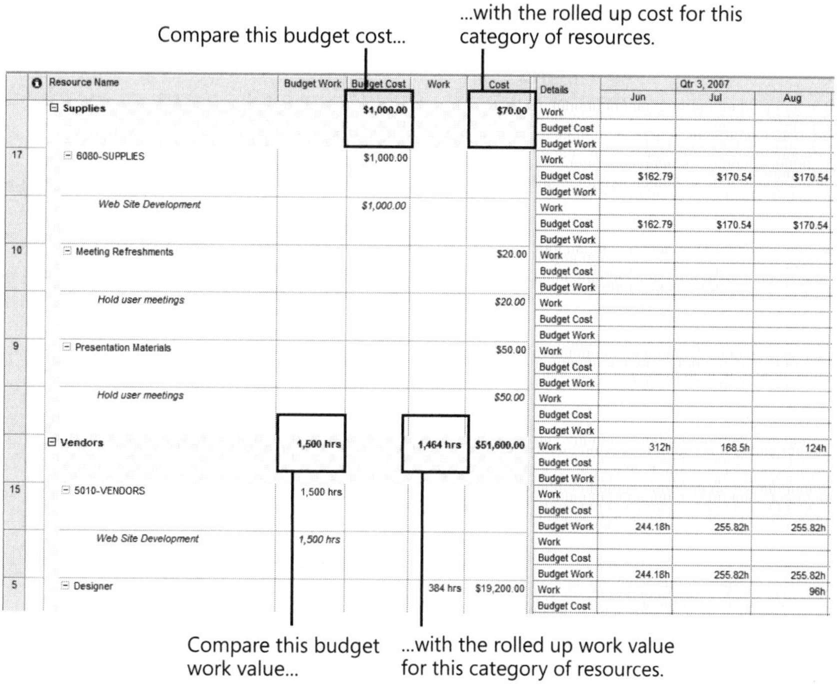

Compare this budget cost...   ...with the rolled up cost for this category of resources.

Compare this budget work value...   ...with the rolled up work value for this category of resources.

Figure 1-8 When you group your resources by their budget categories, you can quickly compare the planned costs and planned work against the budgeted costs and work as shown by the budget resources.

For more information about budget tracking, see the sections titled "Specifying a Budget Resource" in Chapter 6 and "Setting Up and Reviewing a Project Budget" in Chapter 8.

Viewing and Reporting on Project Information

Improvements to the Microsoft Project user interface help you work more effectively with project information. New methods and formats for generating project reports help you analyze and communicate project information with enhanced clarity.

> **Note**
>
> The interface in other applications such as Office Word 2007 and Office Excel 2007 has changed to include the new Ribbon across the top of the application window, replacing menus, toolbars, and most task panes. However, the Microsoft Office Project 2007 interface still uses the traditional menu bar and toolbars.

- **Multiple level undo and redo** In previous versions of Microsoft Project, you can only undo your last operation. New in Project 2007 is the ability to undo and redo multiple edits. Not only does this let you reverse changes you did not intend to make, you can also safely test what-if scenarios to see the impact of potential changes you might need to make.

> For more information, see the section titled "Undoing Multiple Edits" in Chapter 3.

- **Change highlighting** When you make a scheduling change, for example, to durations or predecessors in a sheet field, if that change affects the start or finish dates for any other tasks, the affected fields for those tasks are temporarily filled with a background color (see Figure 1-9). This change highlighting remains in effect until you make another change or save the project file. Change highlighting also shows on the Resource Sheet and other resource or assignment sheet views. Change highlighting alerts you to the impact of your changes, and you can also use it to test what-if scenarios to see the impact of potential changes you might need to make.

Task Name	Duration	Start	Finish
⊟ **Web Design**	**34 days**	**Thu 3/29/07**	**Tue 5/15/07**
⊟ **Interior Pages**	**24 days**	**Thu 3/29/07**	**Tue 5/1/07**
Design interior pages	8 days	Thu 3/29/07	Mon 4/9/07
Interior page design review	5 days	Tue 4/10/07	Mon 4/16/07
Finalize interior page design	4 days	Tue 4/17/07	Fri 4/20/07
Develop style sheets	3 days	Mon 4/23/07	Wed 4/25/07
Develop page templates	4 days	Thu 4/26/07	Tue 5/1/07
⊟ **Home Page**	**10 days**	**Wed 5/2/07**	**Tue 5/15/07**
Design Home page	3 days	Wed 5/2/07	Fri 5/4/07
Home page design review	4 days	Mon 5/7/07	Thu 5/10/07
Finalize Home page design	3 days	Fri 5/11/07	Tue 5/15/07
⊟ **Hardware and Software**	**103 days**	**Mon 3/5/07**	**Wed 7/25/07**
Perform system needs analysis	9 days	Mon 3/5/07	Thu 3/15/07
Evaluate equipment requirements	13 days	Fri 3/16/07	Tue 4/3/07
Evaluate software requirements	15 days	Wed 4/4/07	Tue 4/24/07

Figure 1-9 By reviewing the highlighted cells in a task sheet, you can see the ripple effects of scheduling changes you make.

> For more information about change highlighting, see the section titled "Highlighting the Ripple Effects of Schedule Changes" in Chapter 5.

- **Background cell highlighting and shading** In Microsoft Office Project 2003 and earlier versions, the only way to emphasize tasks in a sheet view was to change the color for task text or use a filter that highlighted tasks. In Project 2007, you can now change the background color of cells, for example, to make critical tasks in a table stand out by changing the background color to light red. With background cell highlighting, you can apply highlight colors or patterns to the cells in the view tables to make key tasks stand out.

> For more information about background cell highlighting, see the section titled "Highlighting the Background in Cells" in Chapter 25.

- **Visual reports with Excel and Visio** The new Microsoft Office Project 2007 visual reports automatically compile and export project information to either Excel or Visio. For an Excel visual report, a PivotTable is generated from which a chart, such as a column or pie chart, is drawn. A Visio visual report generates a PivotDiagram. In either case, you can display data from a different angle as needed. There are 22 templates for visual reports built in to Microsoft Project (see Figure 1-10). You can use these templates as is or edit them to fit your requirements.

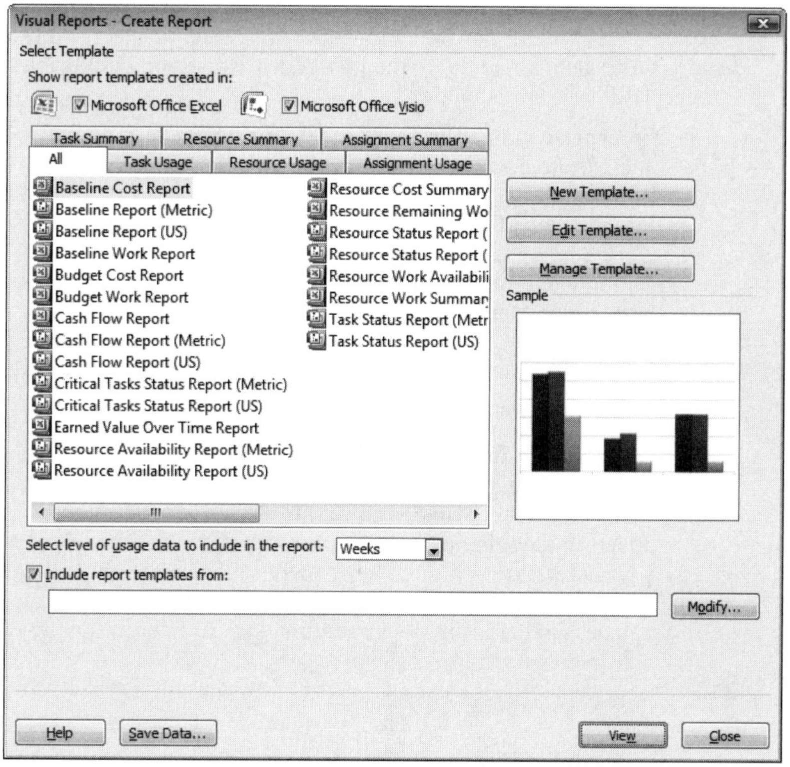

Figure 1-10 There are six categories for 22 built-in visual reports.

> For more information about visual reports, see the section titled "Working with Visual Reports in Excel and Visio" in Chapter 12.

- **Custom visual reports** You can create entirely new templates for visual reports in Excel or Visio. This is done through the use of the online analytical processing (OLAP) cube, a method for identifying the set of fields that will build the PivotTable or PivotDiagram for the resulting visual report. You can select one of six OLAP cubes, for example, Task Usage or Resource Summary, and then identify the specific fields you want to use in that cube.

> For more information about creating visual reports and defining OLAP cubes, see the section titled "Creating a New Visual Report Template" in Chapter 12.

What's New in Microsoft Office Project Professional 2007

Project Professional 2007 includes all the new features of Project Standard 2007. In addition, when Project Professional 2007 is connected to Project Server 2007, the following additional features become available.

Planning and Scheduling

You can enhance the collaboration and communication of dependencies among different projects through the ability to work with master projects and subprojects in Project Server, and also the ability to identify dependencies on deliverables between different enterprise projects, as follows:

- **Enterprise master projects and subprojects** You can now create master projects and subprojects as part of your enterprise project management solution. Using this technique, you can model a program of projects, reflecting all the projects that are being implemented under a specific program in your organization.

  For more information about inserting one project into another, see the section titled "Structuring Master Projects with Subprojects" in Chapter 14.

  For more information about programs, see the section titled "Setting Up a Program of Projects" in Chapter 22.

- **Deliverables and deliverable dependencies** New in Project Server 2007 is the ability to manage dependencies on deliverables among enterprise projects. Doing this, you can keep an eye on commitments in other projects without necessarily affecting the scheduling of your project. Likewise, you can create deliverables in your enterprise project to which others can create dependencies (see Figure 1-11). All enterprise project managers can check the status of these cross-project dependencies from within Project Professional 2007 or in the project workspace available from within Project Web Access.

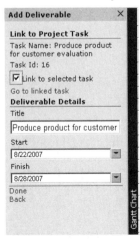

Figure 1-11 Create a deliverable associated with your enterprise project.

For more information about working with deliverables, see the section titled "Depending on Deliverables in Other Projects" in Chapter 22.

Tracking Resource Work and Time

In Microsoft Office Project 2007, you now have more flexibility in determining which resources report progress on which tasks, and which managers receive that information, as follows:

- **Assignment owners** Through the use of assignment owners, you can assign one resource to a task but make another resource the assignment owner, that is, the person responsible for submitting progress updates about the assignment to the project manager. This makes it possible for someone to submit updates for equipment resources or for human resources who do not have Project Web Access.

  For more information about assignment owners, see the section titled "Identifying Assignment Owners" in Chapter 22.

- **Status managers** Just as a resource needs to be responsible for submitting progress updates for an assignment, another person needs to be responsible for reviewing and accepting that progress information into the project plan. That person is the status manager. Although the default status manager for a task is the person who originally published the assignment to the project server, different status managers can be identified for different tasks.

  For more information about status managers, see the section titled "Assigning Status Managers" in Chapter 22.

Viewing and Reporting on Project Information

You now have more control over when project information is made available to the rest of the project team. Also, the number of custom fields that can be created for enterprise projects is now unlimited, enabling your organization to customize and standardize the project plan to reflect how it does business.

- **Publish project information** In previous versions of Microsoft Project, saving the project is the same as publishing. Now in Project 2007, saving and publishing are two different steps, giving you more control over when information becomes available to others on the project team. You explicity choose a publish command when you are ready for new or changed project information to be made public through Project Web Access. You can exclude the publication of certain marked tasks if you need to.

  For more information about publishing your project, see the section titled "Managing Your Project Files on the Server" in Chapter 22.

- **Custom enterprise fields** Although local projects impose a limit on the number of custom fields you can create, new in Project 2007 is the ability to create an unlimited number of custom enterprise fields for each field type. This includes all the custom fields including cost, text, number, date fields, and more. Custom enterprise fields are created in Project Web Access. Typically, the project server administrator or the portfolio manager creates the custom enterprise fields for the organization.

> For more information about custom enterprise fields, see the section titled "Customizing Enterprise Project Fields" in Chapter 21.

What's New in Project Server 2007 and Project Web Access

In Project Server 2007 and Project Web Access, a multitude of new features work together to facilitate planning and scheduling, resource management, and viewing and reporting on project information.

Planning and Scheduling

New features in Project 2007 provide for planning and tracking throughout the life cycle of a project, and also ensure that information is readily available whether you're working in Project Professional or Project Web Access. These features are as follows:

- **Server-side scheduling** New in Project 2007 is the ability to change project information and have task updates processed and recalculations made from within Project Web Access without having to make any "round trips" between the two.

- **Proposals and activity plans** New in Project Server 2007 is the ability to create project proposals and activity plans. With a proposal, you can set up a preproject plan (see Figure 1-12). You can create a resource plan with the proposal to help you anticipate potential resource needs without committing those resources to a project that might or might not be initiated. When the proposal is approved, it can be converted into a project. With an activity plan, you can track the routine operations that typically take place after the completion of a project. You can also use activity plans to track maintenance activities, very small projects, or even a personal to-do list.

2007 Bond

| Save | Save and Publish | Close |

⦿ Work Details ○ Summary Information

Actions ▾ | Go To ▾ |

✛ | ➡ | ➡ | 🔗 Link Tasks | 📝 Unlink Tasks | 📄 Link Document | 🏢 Build Team | 📋 Resource Plan | ✕ Delete Task | 📝 New Task |

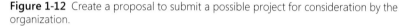

▲	♥	Task Name	Milestone	Duration	Start Date	Finish Date	% Work Comp
1		Stadium Turf and Track Upgrades	☐	6mo	1/29/2007	7/20/2007	0%
2	∞	Gifted Program Interim Housing	☐	3mo	1/29/2007	4/27/2007	0%
3	∞	Emergency Storage Sheds and Safety Equipment	☐	3mo	4/30/2007	7/20/2007	0%
4		Replace Carpet and Roof of Spring Street Elementary	☐	5mo	1/29/2007	6/22/2007	0%
5		Modernize Junior High Science Classrooms	☐	12mo	1/29/2007	1/4/2008	0%
6		Classroom Technology Systems and Equipment	☐	18mo	1/29/2007	6/20/2008	0%
7		Vine Street High School Classroom Addition	☐	24mo	1/29/2007	12/5/2008	0%
8		Elm Avenue Junior High Roof Replacement	☐	6mo	1/29/2007	7/20/2007	0%
9		Performing Arts Center remodel	☐	12mo	1/29/2007	1/4/2008	0%
10		Seismic Upgrades	☐	12mo	1/29/2007	1/4/2008	0%

Figure 1-12 Create a proposal to submit a possible project for consideration by the organization.

> For more information about proposals, activity plans, and resource plans, see the section titled "Creating Proposals and Activity Plans" in Chapter 22.

- **Task list import** If you have created a simple project or task list in Microsoft Windows SharePoint Services 3.0, you can import it to Project Web Access.

> **Note**
>
> Other new planning and scheduling features in Project Server 2007 and Project Web Access include enterprise master projects and subprojects, as well as deliverables and dependencies. These are both described in the section titled "What's New in Microsoft Office Project Professional 2007" earlier in this chapter.

Tracking Resource Work and Time

In Project 2007, team members can use the new Project Web Access timesheet to report on their time spent on billable or nonbillable activities. You can also preview the impact of an assignment progress update on the overall schedule before accepting it for integration into the plan. New resource work and time tracking features include the following:

- **Permanent task notes** If you create a note on an assignment and publish it, the assigned resource can see it and respond to it, and that response becomes part of the note as well, which shows as a permanent task note in Project Professional 2007. There can be as many additions to the note as needed.

> For more information about assignment notes, see the section titled "Reviewing Changed Assignments" in Chapter 23.

- **Outlook integration** If you use Outlook, project resources can keep track of their assigned tasks in their Outlook calendars, along with their other appointments. They can update progress on their project assignments in the calendar and report actual work on assignments back to the project server directly from Outlook. As usual, the project manager reviews and approves the updates and incorporates them into the project plan.

> For more information about integrating task assignments with Outlook, see the section titled "Working with Project Tasks in Your Outlook Calendar" in Chapter 23.

- **Updated schedule preview** When you review progress updates of actual information submitted by resources, you can now see the impact of a particular update on the schedule. A separate Web-based Approval Preview window appears with a Gantt Chart showing how the schedule would look if you accepted the update (see Figure 1-13).

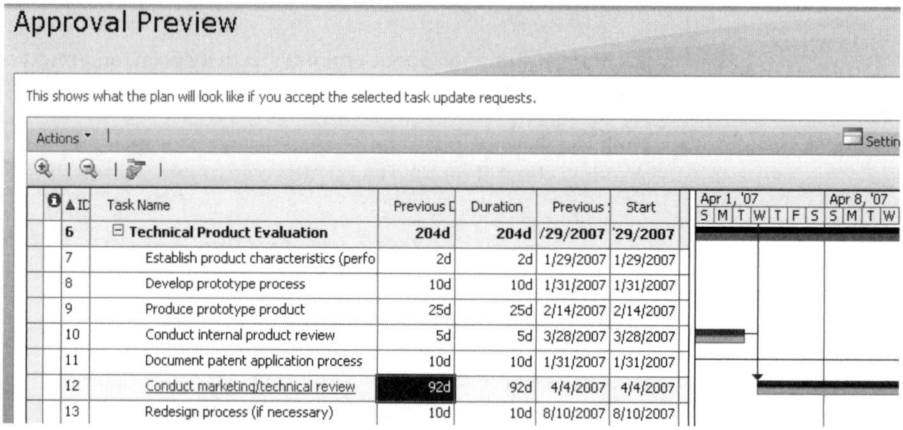

Figure 1-13 Review the Approval Preview window to see the potential impact of accepting the assignment update.

> For more information about the Approval Preview window, see the section titled "Incorporating Task Updates into the Project" in Chapter 22.

- **Timesheets for billable and nonbillable time** New in Microsoft Office Project 2007, the Project Web Access timesheet can now be used in organizations that have specific time reporting requirements. For example, use the timesheet when you want visibility into certain time categories, for example, billable and nonbillable time, scheduled and actual time, or overtime. The timesheet is especially useful when you need to integrate information about resource time with an accounting or general ledger system, particularly for client billing purposes. Using the timesheet, resources can also set up and use the administrative time feature, in which they can identify and report on instances of nonproject working time or nonworking time. Like task progress, team members submit timesheets to their designated timesheet managers on a periodic basis. Project tasks can be integrated into the timesheet, or nonproject tasks can be integrated into the project task list (see Figure 1-14).

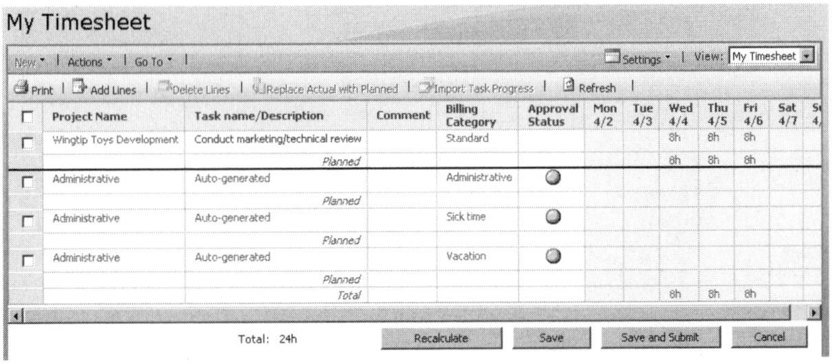

My Timesheet

	Project Name	Task name/Description	Comment	Billing Category	Approval Status	Mon 4/2	Tue 4/3	Wed 4/4	Thu 4/5	Fri 4/6	Sat 4/7	S 4
☐	Wingtip Toys Development	Conduct marketing/technical review		Standard				8h	8h	8h		
☐		Planned						8h	8h	8h		
☐	Administrative	Auto-generated		Administrative	○							
		Planned										
☐	Administrative	Auto-generated		Sick time	○							
		Planned										
☐	Administrative	Auto-generated		Vacation	○							
		Planned										
		Total						8h	8h	8h		

Total: 24h

Figure 1-14 The timesheet can include project tasks as well as nonproject tasks and non-working time for a particular time period.

For more information about timesheets, see the sections titled "Understanding the My Timesheets Page" in Chapter 21 and "Logging Time Using Timesheets" in Chapter 23.

> **Note**
>
> Other new resource management features in Project Server 2007 and Project Web Access include the assignment owner and status manager. These are both described in the section titled "What's New in Microsoft Office Project Professional 2007" earlier in this chapter.

Viewing and Reporting on Project Information

Project Server 2007 is tightly integrated with Windows SharePoint Services 3.0. It is this integration that provides for the creation of project workspaces and the availability of Web Parts to customize the pages. The use of the SQL Server Cube Building Services makes it possible for dynamic views and reports to be created for the high-level analysis of projects and portfolios. The Project Server Interface can be used to integrate your project server with other line-of-business systems throughout your organization. Specifically, the following are viewing and reporting features new in Project Server 2007:

- **Project workspace** As soon as you publish a new project, it is listed in the Project Center, and by default, a Web-based Windows SharePoint Services project workspace is created to help the team centrally manage and track project-related documents, issues, and risks. The workspace can also include announcements among team members, a calendar of upcoming events, a list of the project's deliverables, and team discussions (see Figure 1-15).

Project Web Access > Wingtip Toys Development

Wingtip Toys Development

Home

View All Site Content	Microsoft Office Project Server Workspace
Documents	
• Project Documents	**Announcements** ▾
Lists	There are currently no active announcements. To add a new announcement, click "Add new announcement" below.
• Issues	
• Risks	⊞ Add new announcement
• Deliverables	
• Calendar	**Calendar** ▾
• Tasks	There are currently no upcoming events. To add a new event, click "Add new event" below.
Discussions	
• Team Discussion	⊞ Add new event
Sites	
People and Groups	
⎙ Recycle Bin	

Figure 1-15 A project team can use the workspace for communication and collaboration. They can also use it as the repository for project documents.

> For more information about the project workspace, see the section titled "Project Workspaces and Documents, Issues, and Risks" in Chapter 24.

- **Project Web Access Web Parts** Your organization's project server administrator can use Web Parts to develop and customize Web page components in Project Web Access that convey key project information efficiently for your team or organization. Web Parts group and position all key information logically and consistently; the information is accessed through hyperlinks.

> For more information about using Web Parts to customize views, see the section titled "Creating and Managing Pages with Web Parts" in Chapter 21.

- **Project databases** Project Server 2007 maintains four databases. The Draft database contains project information that has been saved to the project server but has not yet been published for all users to see. The Published database contains project information that has been published. Typically a published project is listed in the Project Center, its tasks are submitted to the assigned resources, and its project workspace is made available for team collaboration. The Reporting database is a copy of the Published database and is used to create the Project Web Access views and project-related reports. When your project is closed, its information moves to the Archive database.

> For more information about the project databases, see the section titled "Four Versions of an Enterprise Project" in Chapter 22.

- **Interactive OLAP-based views and reports** The project server administrator or portfolio manager creates OLAP cubes, or dynamic views and reports, through the use of the Cube Building Services in conjunction with Project Server and Project Web Access. These reports are made available to Project Web Access users in the form of a spreadsheet (PivotTable) or column chart (PivotChart). These views are added to the View list of the Data Analysis page for users to select and manipulate. Users can also add, move, or delete fields in the resulting PivotTable or PivotChart.

For more information about the OLAP views and reports, see the sections titled "Setting Up Project Report Cubes for Data Analysis" in Chapter 21 and "Analyzing and Reporting on Project Information" in Chapter 24.

- **Project Server Interface (PSI)** Project 2007 has a new method for extending functionality and integrating project information with other applications. Through the new application program interface (API) called the Project Server Interface, which works with the Windows Workflow Foundation, you can integrate information between your project server and other organizational systems that interact with project management processes, such as accounting, procurement, or human resources. In fact, the means through which Project Professional 2007 and Project Web Access interact with Project Server 2007 is solely through the Project Server Interface.

For information about the Project Server Interface, the Event Modeler, and Windows Workflow Foundation, refer to the Project 2007 Software Development Kit (SDK), available at ***http://msdn2.microsoft.com/en-us/library/bb187382.aspx***.

> Note
>
> Other new viewing and reporting features in Project Server 2007 and Project Web Access include publishing project information and custom enterprise fields. These are both described in the section titled "What's New in Microsoft Office Project Professional 2007" earlier in this chapter.

Learning As You Go

As you work in your project plan, you can quickly get assistance and other information when you need it—from the Project Guide, from Help, from Office Online, and other sources.

Working with the Project Guide

When you first start Microsoft Project, the Project Guide appears in the task pane on the left (see Figure 1-16).

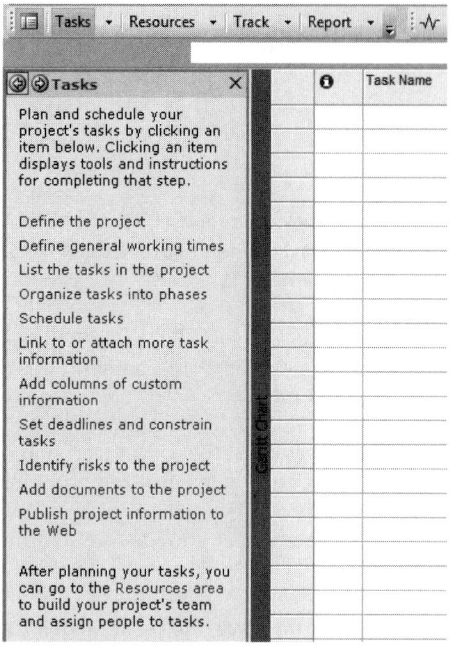

Figure 1-16 The Project Guide appears on the left side of the screen.

The Project Guide helps you work through the major aspects of defining, tracking, and reporting on your project. It provides topics, instructions, controls, and wizards that assist your current work in your plan. The Project Guide takes note of your current view and current activities and presents a list of relevant topics and tools within that context.

For example, while you're working in the Gantt Chart, the Project Guide displays the Tasks guide, which contains topics directly related to entering and scheduling tasks. If you then switch to a resource view, the Project Guide displays the Resources guide, now presenting topics and controls related to entering and assigning resources. There are also groups of topics for tracking and reporting.

You can control the content in the Project Guide by using the Project Guide toolbar just above the Project Guide pane. Use the buttons on this toolbar to display any Project Guide list or topic you want to see. You can view the Tasks, Resources, Track, or Report lists; display any topic on those lists; and toggle the display of the Project Guide pane on and off.

Show/Hide
Project Guide

> **Note**
>
> If you're concerned about the real estate that the Project Guide is taking up on your screen, you can temporarily turn the Project Guide off and then turn it on again whenever you like. Click the Close button in the Project Guide pane or click the Show/Hide Project Guide button on the Project Guide toolbar. When you want the pane back, click the button again.

When you click a topic in the Project Guide, you might find concise text about how to carry out the activity. Or you might click a control in the Project Guide, and the activity is done for you on the spot.

TROUBLESHOOTING

The Project Guide toolbar is not available

By default, the Project Guide and its toolbar are showing. You can close the Project Guide pane by using the Close button and open it when you need it by clicking any of the buttons on the Project Guide toolbar.

If the Project Guide toolbar is hidden, you can add it back. Click View, Toolbars, Project Guide.

If the Project Guide toolbar is not listed on the Toolbars menu, this means the Project Guide has been completely turned off. Click Tools, Options and then click the Interface tab. Under Project Guide Settings, select the Display Project Guide check box.

The Project Guide also includes wizards to help automate or walk you through certain processes. With a wizard, the Project Guide asks you specific questions about the activity you want to carry out. As you answer the questions, the wizard pulls together your answers and executes the task automatically, without your having to search for and work with the appropriate dialog boxes in the appropriate views. The following is a list of Project Guide wizards:

- **Define The Project Wizard** Helps you create a new project plan, either from scratch or from an existing template (see Figure 1-17). This wizard integrates all the tasks you need to create a new project: entering basic project information, setting team collaboration options, adding supporting documentation, and saving the project file.

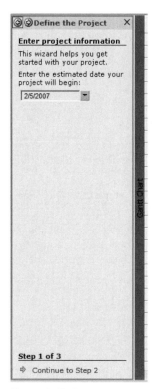

Figure 1-17 Start creating your plan with the Define The Project Wizard.

- **Project Working Times Wizard** Simplifies the methods of specifying and changing working days and hours, nonworking days and hours, and time units. You can use the Project Working Times Wizard for the project as a whole, in alternative calendars such as a weekend shift, and for specific resources.

- **Setup Tracking Wizard** Determines how you collect and enter progress information about tasks. Based on the information you provide, the Setup Tracking Wizard designs a tracking view for your specific purposes.

- **Print Current View Wizard** Sets up the current view to be printed the way you want. You can specify the length of the view to be printed as a report, preview the view as it will be printed, change the dimensions of the report, and modify the content to be included. You can also set the header, footer, and legend for the view.

> **Note**
>
> If you don't want to use the Project Guide at all, you can turn it off so it doesn't appear when you start Microsoft Project. Click Tools, Options and then click the Interface tab. Clear the Display Project Guide check box. The Project Guide and its toolbar are hidden. The Project Guide no longer opens when you start up Microsoft Project, and the Project Guide toolbar is not even listed on the Toolbars menu.

Task Drivers

In Project 2007, the new Task Drivers pane has been added to the Track guide. On the Project Guide toolbar, click the Track menu and then click See What Is Driving The Start Date Of A Task. You can also click Task Drivers on the Standard toolbar. The Task Drivers pane appears, showing the list of factors responsible for the scheduling of the current task.

Getting Help

You can find Help topics to assist you with your project plan. A large set of Help topics is installed and available with Microsoft Office on your local computer. Another set of Help topics and other forms of assistance are available on the Web through Office Online. You can:

- Search for topics using key words or phrases.

- Browse the Help table of contents.

- Browse for additional resources on Office Online.

- Join and ask questions from a Microsoft Project discussion group.

Search for a Specific Topic

Rather than going through a particular structure of topics, it's often faster to just ask a direct question and get a direct answer. If you prefer to get your help that way, search using a question or phrase as follows:

1. In the upper-right corner of the Microsoft Project window, click in the Type A Question For Help box.

   | Type a question for help | ▾ |

**Microsoft Office
Project Help**

> **Note**
>
> You can also search for Help topics by clicking Help, Microsoft Office Project Help or by clicking the Microsoft Office Project Help button on the Standard toolbar. In the Project Help pane that appears, type your question or phrase in the search box and then click Search.

2. Type your question in the box and press Enter.

   The Project Help pane appears with a list of Help topics related to your question (see Figure 1-18).

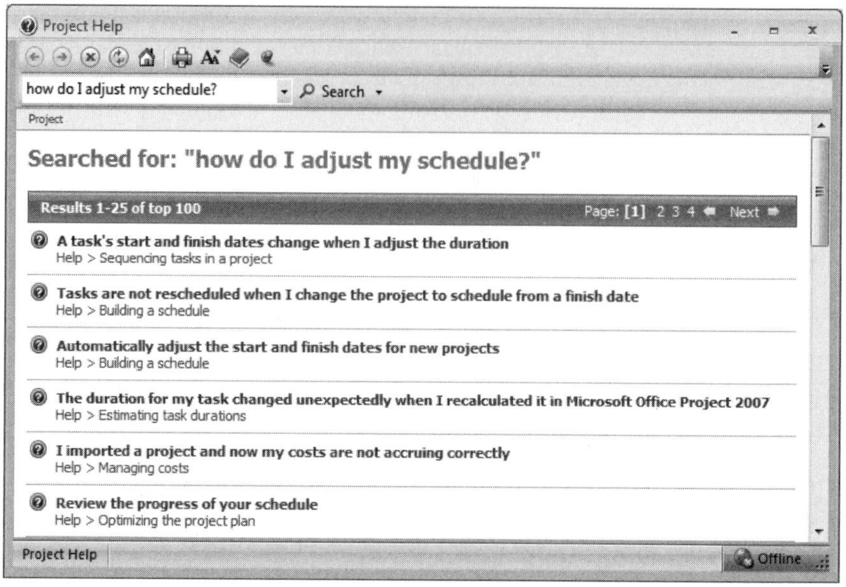

Figure 1-18 The Project Help pane lists topics related to your search question.

3.   Click a topic that matches what you're looking for and read an article or procedure about your question.

4.   To read a different Help topic that was listed, click the Back button to return to the list of topics and click the other topic.

Back

If you're connected to the Internet, you can expand your keyword search to include help available on Office Online. This way, you can access new content much more quickly than wiating for a service pack to update your offline help files. In the lower-right corner of the Project Help pane, click the Offline button.

In the menu that appears, click Show Content From Office Online. When you are connected to Office Online, Help search results appear both from your local Help topics as well as from any related topics on the Office Online Web site.

TROUBLESHOOTING

The Project Help pane is obstructing your work

When you search for help, the Project Help pane appears and floats over the top of your Microsoft Project window. Even when you click on the Microsoft Project window, the Project Help pane stays on top.

The pane is designed to stay on top like this, because you might want to follow a procedure in a Help topic while working in Microsoft Project. If this is the case, resize the Project Help pane and drag it to the side so that you can still read it, but it's out of the way of your work.

If you don't need the Project Help pane showing right this minute, but you want to keep it handy, click its Minimize button to temporarily move it out of the way.

Browsing Project Help Contents

If you want to see Help topics in a logical sequence, follow these steps:

1. Click Project Help on the Standard toolbar.

   The Project Help window appears showing a table of contents of major topics (see Figure 1-19).

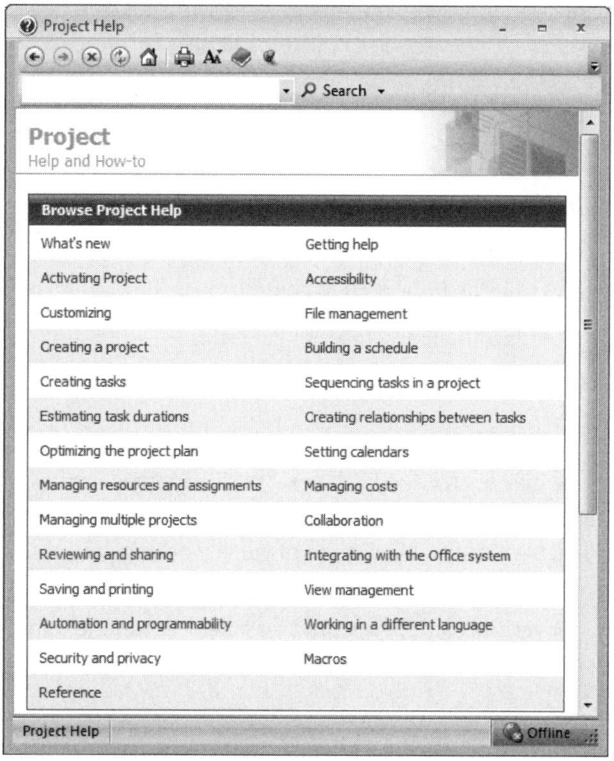

Figure 1-19 Browse through a logical sequence of categorized Help topics.

2. Click the name of the category of topics.

3. In the topic list, click a link to view the Help topic.

> **Note**
>
> In addition to clicking the Project Help button on the Standard toolbar, you can open the Project Help pane by simply pressing F1.

If you're connected to the Internet and Office Online, you see even more categories and topics listed in the Project Help pane.

> **Note**
>
> If you ever want to turn off the search for Help topics or contents on Office Online through your Project Help pane, in the lower-right corner of the pane, click the Connected To Office Online button. In the menu that appears, click Show Content Only From This Computer.
>
> **Connected to Office Online**

Getting Help for Project Fields

There is a Help topic for each and every field in Microsoft Project. One way to find such topics is by browsing the Project Help contents, as follows:

1. On the Standard toolbar, click Project Help.

2. At the bottom of the Browse Project Help categories, click Reference.

3. Click Fields Reference.

4. Click the topic for the field you want to learn more about.

   Each field reference topic includes best uses, examples, calculations if applicable, and particular issues to be aware of when working with this field.

You can also open a field reference Help topic if the field is showing in a table. Rest your mouse pointer over the column heading for a field. A ToolTip appears, indicating the name of the field as a link (see Figure 1-20). Click the field name link. The Help topic for that field appears.

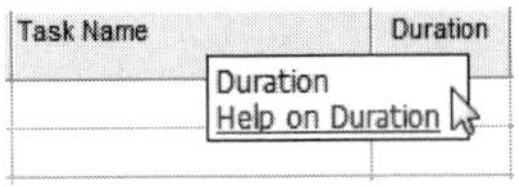

Task Name	Duration
	Duration
	Help on Duration

Figure 1-20 Click a field's ToolTip to launch the field's reference topic.

Getting Help for Dialog Boxes

Many of the more complex dialog boxes in Microsoft Project have associated Help topics. One way to find such topics is from the Help Table Of Contents, as follows:

1. On the Standard toolbar, click Project Help.

2. At the bottom of the Browse Project Help categories, click Reference.

3. Click Dialog Box Reference.

   The dialog boxes' topics are listed in alphabetical order. Each dialog box reference topic includes steps on how to open the dialog box and contains descriptions of each field and control in the dialog box.

4. Click the name of the dialog box you want to learn more about.

You can also open a dialog box reference Help topic if you already opened the dialog box. Many dialog boxes include a Help button. Click that Help button, and the topic for that dialog box appears. If a dialog box does not have a Help button, there is no associated Help topic—ostensibly because the dialog box was considered self-explanatory enough not to require a separate Help topic.

Finding Project Assistance on the Web

You have already seen how you can click the Offline button in the lower-right corner of the Project Help pane to search on a keyword or browse the contents of Project Help topics on Office Online on the Web. As long as you're connected to the Internet, you can also simply open Office Online in a full Web browser window. To do this, follow these steps:

1. In Microsoft Office Project 2007, click Help, Microsoft Office Online.

   A Web browser appears showing the Microsoft Office Online Web site. Review the various tabs available, including Products, Help And How-To, and Downloads.

2. Click the Products tab and then click Project in the side pane to see a set of Web resources having to do with Microsoft Project, including news, downloads, and articles.

3. In the side pane of this page, click Project 2007 Help to see a comprehensive list of articles and other Microsoft Project resources (see Figure 1-21). Some articles provide step-by-step instructions. Others have conceptual information about Microsoft Project features. Still others provide advice about project management solutions using Microsoft Project. There is access to information in the Microsoft Project Knowledge Base and Microsoft TechNet.

Figure 1-21 This is an example of the Project 2007 Help And How-To page that you can use to browse through articles about various aspects of Microsoft Project.

Joining a Project Discussion Group

It's often easiest to learn from your more experienced buddies. A built-in group of knowledgeable friends willing to help can be found on Office Online. There you will find a Microsoft Project discussion group that can help you find answers to your questions and also learn from questions posed by other users. To find and join a Microsoft Project discussion group:

1. On Office Online, click the Products tab.

2. In the side pane, click Project.

3. Toward the bottom of the page, under Additional Resources, click Discussion Groups.

The Discussions In Microsoft Project page appears (see Figure 1-22). You can search for a particular topic or browse through a list of topics in the General Questions, the Microsoft Project Server, or the Microsoft Project Developer discussion group.

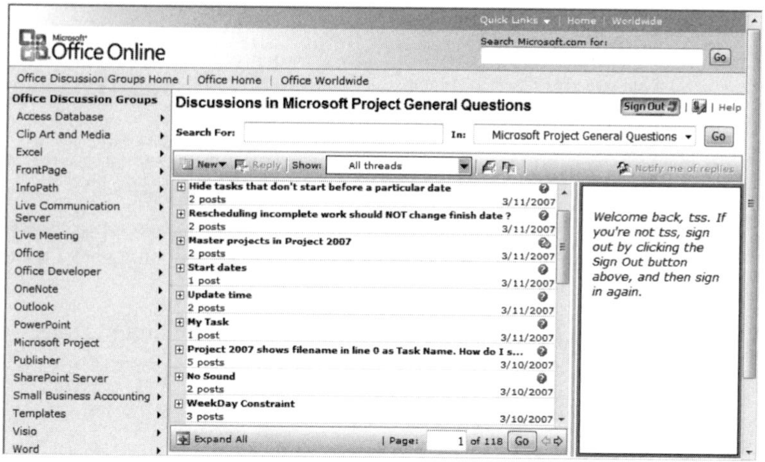

Figure 1-22 The Project discussions page represents a community of Project users and experts who ask and answer questions.

4. If you want to ask a question, first see whether your question has been asked (and answered) previously. Enter a key word or phrase in the Search For box, click the discussion group in the In box, and then click Go.

    It's a great idea to do this before posting a new question, especially if you're a newer user.

5. If you don't find anything in the archives that answers your question, click the Sign In button to sign in with your Windows Live ID. Then click New, Question. You can type your question and post it to the discussion group.

You'll find that you'll get great answers to your questions, often quite quickly. If you stick around long enough, you'll soon find that you're knowledgeable enough to answer others' questions. To reply to an existing question, click the Reply button. Enter your answer and post it to the discussion group.

Working with Project Smart Tags

When you make certain types of adjustments to your project plan, Microsoft Project can present Smart Tag indicators with option buttons (see Figure 1-23). These Smart Tags specify the action you've just taken, along with any possible implications that action might have. You get information, especially in certain ambiguous situations, to make sure that the result is really your intention. You also see options to switch to a different action if you intended a different outcome.

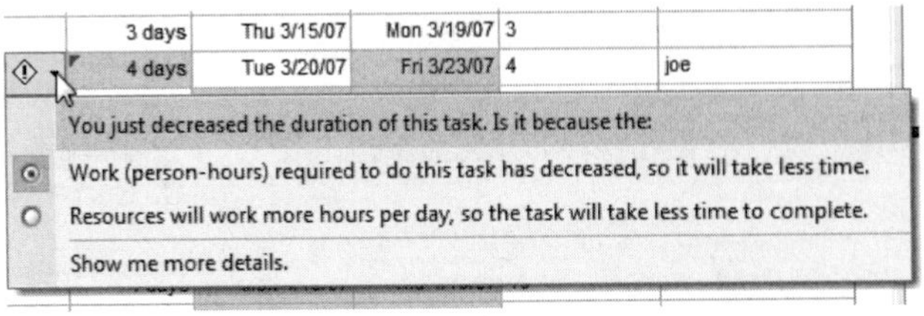

Figure 1-23 A Smart Tag is first marked with a triangle marker in the affected cell. When you move your mouse pointer over the marker, the Smart Tag indicator appears. Click the indicator, and the options appear.

There are four times at which indicators and option buttons might appear—when you are:

- Adding, changing, or removing resource assignments.

- Changing start or finish dates.

- Editing work, duration, or units.

- Deleting a task or resource in the Name column.

The indicator appears in the cell as long as the edit is available for an Undo operation. After you make a new edit, the indicator disappears.

You cannot change or create your own feedback messages in Microsoft Project.

You can turn off the display of indicators and option buttons. Click Tools, Options and then click the Interface tab. Under Show Indicators And Options Buttons For, clear the check boxes for the category of changes for which you don't need indicators.

CHAPTER 2

Understanding Projects and Project Management

Understanding Project Management Basics. **37**

Understanding Project Management Processes **41**

Facilitating Your Project with Microsoft Project **44**

Working with the Project Stakeholders **52**

Keys to Successful Project Management. **53**

You use a word processing program to create a text document. You use a spreadsheet program to calculate sales data. You use a publishing program to design and lay out a brochure. In these cases, the application helps you create the end result.

With Microsoft Office Project 2007, this isn't so. Although Office Project 2007 helps you create a *project plan*, the actual project is being executed by you and your team, who are carrying out the tasks to fulfill the overarching goals of the project. It's up to you to track and control the actual project, using the project plan as your essential road map. When effectively maintained, the project plan is a model providing an accurate picture of what's currently going on in your project, what has happened in the past, and what will happen in the future.

This chapter describes project basics and the phases of the project management process. It also outlines how Microsoft Project fits into the world of your project. You'll understand how you can use Microsoft Project as your project information system; that is, the essential tool for modeling your project and helping you efficiently and successfully manage it.

If you're new to project management, read this entire chapter. If you're an experienced project manager but new to Microsoft Project, skip ahead to the section titled "Facilitating Your Project with Microsoft Project" later in this chapter.

Understanding Project Management Basics

Although it might overlap with other types of management, project management is a specific management process.

What Is a Project?

Organizations perform two types of work: operations and projects. An *operation* is a series of tasks that are routine, repetitive, and ongoing throughout the life of the organization. Operations are typically necessary to sustain the business. Examples of operations are accounts receivable, employee performance reviews, and shipping and receiving. Employee performance reviews might take place every six months, for example, and although the names and circumstances of employees and supervisors might change, the process of preparing and conducting employee reviews is always the same.

In addition, it's expected that employee reviews will be conducted throughout the life of the organization.

On the other hand, *projects* are not routine or ongoing. That is, projects are unique and temporary and are often implemented to fulfill a strategic goal of the organization. A project is a series of tasks that will culminate in the creation or completion of some new initiative, product, or activity by a specific end date. Some project examples include an office move, a new product launch, the construction of a building, and a political campaign. It is never the same project twice—for example, this year's product launch is different from last year's product launch. There's a specific end date in mind for the launch, after which the project will be considered complete. After the project is complete, a new and unique product will be on the market.

Projects come in all sizes. One project might consist of 100 tasks; another, 10,000. One project might be implemented by a single resource; another by 500. One project might take 2 months to complete; another might take 10 years. There can be projects within projects, linked together with a master project consolidating them all. These subprojects, however, are all unique and temporary, and all have a specific outcome and end date.

What Is Project Management?

Project management is the coordinating effort to fulfill the goals of the project. The *project manager*, as the head of the project team, is responsible for this effort and its ultimate result. Project managers use knowledge, skills, tools, and methodologies to do the following:

- Identify the goals, objectives, requirements, and limitations of the project.

- Coordinate the different needs and expectations of the various project stakeholders including team members, resource managers, senior management, customers, and sponsors.

- Plan, execute, and control the tasks, phases, and deliverables of the project based on the identified project goals and objectives.

- Close the project when completed and capture the knowledge accrued.

Project managers are also responsible for balancing and integrating competing demands to implement all aspects of the project successfully, as follows:

- **Project scope** Articulating the specific work to be done for the project.

- **Project time** Setting the finish date of the project as well as any interim deadlines for phases, milestones, and deliverables.

- **Project cost** Calculating and tracking the project costs and budget.

- **Project human resources** Signing on the team members who will carry out the tasks of the project.

- **Project procurement** Acquiring the material and equipment resources, and obtaining any other supplies or services, needed to fulfill project tasks.

- **Project communication** Conveying assignments, updates, reports, and other information with team members and other stakeholders.

- **Project quality** Identifying the acceptable level of quality for the project goals and objectives.

- **Project risk** Analyzing potential project risks and response planning.

INSIDE OUT Microsoft Project and the project management disciplines

Microsoft Project supports many, but not all, of the management areas associated with project management. For example, it provides only minimal support for project procurement and project quality.

However, you can combine Microsoft Project with other tools to create for yourself the full package of project management support. Use Microsoft Project to capture the lion's share of project information including the schedule, milestones, deliverables, resources, costs, and reporting. Then draw upon other tools as needed to more fully handle responsibilities specifically associated with procurement or quality. Finally, come full circle with Microsoft Project by adding notes to tasks or resources, inserting related documents, or hyperlinking to other locations.

For example, use Microsoft Project to help estimate your initial equipment and material resource requirements. Work through your organization's procurement process and compile the relevant data. Add notes to the resources or tasks in your project plan, making the information easy to reference. Use a tool such as Microsoft Office Excel 2007, or another program especially designed for this purpose, to help track the depletion of materials to the point where reorder becomes necessary. Even though Microsoft Project can't manage every aspect of your project, it can still be the central repository for all related information.

Balancing scope, time, and money is often among the biggest responsibilities of the project manager (see Figure 2-1).

Chapter 2

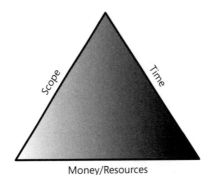

Figure 2-1 The project triangle is an effective model for thinking about your project's priorities.

If you increase the scope, the time or money side of the triangle will also be increased. If you need to reduce time, that is, bring in the project finish date, you might need to decrease the scope or increase the cost through the addition of resources.

Is It Really a Project "Rectangle?"

There's some debate about how to accurately describe the key controlling elements that make up a project. Some believe that a project is best described as a triangle—the three sides representing time, money, and resources. Others say that it's a square—with scope, time, money, and resources being the four sides, each one affecting the others. This book approaches money and resources as synonymous in this context because resources cost money. Adding resources adds money, and the only thing you'd need more money for would be resources. So in this book, the project is conceptualized as a triangle with the three sides being scope, time, and money/resources.

For information about working with the project triangle to help control your project, see Chapter 11, "Responding to Changes in Your Project."

Project Management Practices: Balancing and Integrating Competing Demands

Depending on the priorities and standards set for your project and by your organization, certain demands carry more weight than others in your project. Knowing these priorities and standards will help you make appropriate decisions about the project as inevitable issues arise. Although scope, time, and cost tend to be the most prevalent demands, the following is the full list of project controls:

- Scope
- Human resources
- Quality
- Time

- Procurement
- Risk
- Cost
- Communications

Understanding Project Management Processes

It might seem daunting when you realize that, as a project manager, you're responsible for such a tremendous balancing act throughout the life of the project. However, this responsibility can be broken down into the following four manageable processes:

1. Initiating and planning the project

2. Executing the project

3. Controlling the project

4. Closing the project

Most of the chapters in this book are structured with these four processes in mind. For each process, you use Microsoft Project in specific ways. Standard project management practices are also related to planning, executing, controlling, and closing the project. Throughout this book, the Microsoft Project procedures as well as the project management practices are described in the context of the relevant project process.

The following sections detail the key elements of each of the four project management processes.

Planning the Project

You're ready to begin the planning process after an authoritative stakeholder has decided to implement this project with you as the project manager. The outcome of this planning process will be a workable project plan and a team ready to start working the project. When planning the project, do the following:

- **Look at the big picture.** Before you get too far into the nuts and bolts of planning, you need a comprehensive vision of where you're going with your project. You shape this vision by first identifying the project goals and objectives. This practice helps you set the scope of the project. You learn the expectations, limitations, and assumptions for this project, and they all go into the mix. You also identify possible risks and contingency plans for the project.

- **Identify the project's milestones, deliverables, and tasks.** Subdivide the project into its component tasks and then organize and sequence the tasks to accurately reflect the project scope.

- **Develop and refine the project schedule.** To turn the task list into a workable project schedule, specify task durations and relate tasks to each other. You can create task dependencies, that is, a model of how the start of one task depends on the completion of another task, for example. If you have any specific dates for deliverables, you can enter them as deadlines, or, if really necessary, task constraints. At that point, Microsoft Project can start to calculate a realistic schedule for tasks in particular and the project as a whole. With this plan, you can accurately forecast the scope, schedule, and budget for the project. You can also determine which resources are needed, how many, and at what time.

- **Identify skills, equipment, materials, supplies, and services needed.** After the tasks are identified, you can determine the skills, equipment, and materials needed to carry out the work for those tasks. You obtain the needed human, equipment, and material resources and assign them to the appropriate tasks. You also factor in supplies, services, and other cost items that will be incurred, and assign those cost resources to tasks as well. You can now calculate when the project can be completed and how much it will cost. If it looks like you're exceeding the allowable deadline or budget, you can make the necessary adjustments.

> **Note**
>
> Some project managers refer to the "project plan" as the text-based document in which the broad goals and methodologies of the project are defined. Throughout this book, however, we refer to the Microsoft Project file as the project plan. Although some refer to this file as the project schedule, there's more going on in that file than the schedule. For example, it can include resource definitions, cost information, reports, and attached documents.

> **Project Management Terminology**
>
> The following is a list of terms related to project management:
>
> - **Baseline** A snapshot of key project information for tasks, such as their start dates, finish dates, durations, and costs. With baseline information, you have a means of comparison against actual progress on tasks.
> - **Date constraint** A specific date associated with a specific task. A date constraint dictates that a task must be finished by a certain date, for example, or started no earlier than a certain date.
> - **Deliverable** A tangible outcome, result, or item that must be produced to mark the completion of a project or a project phase. Often, the deliverable is subject to approval by the project sponsor or customer.

- **Dependency** The reliance of one task upon another. When one task cannot start or finish until a related task starts or finishes, the tasks are dependent upon one another, or related. Also referred to as a *task link* or *task relationship*.

- **Gantt chart** A graphic representation of a project. The left half of a Gantt chart is a table listing task names and other task-related information. The right half of the Gantt chart is a bar chart along a timeline in which each bar represents a task, its start and finish date, and its duration. Links to other tasks can also be represented.

- **Milestone** A significant event in the project, often the completion of a major deliverable or phase. Milestones are represented as part of a project's task list.

- **Network diagram** A graphic representation of a project, characterized by nodes representing tasks and link lines showing the relationship among the tasks. Also sometimes called a PERT (Program Evaluation and Review Technique) chart.

- **Phase** A grouping of tasks that represents a major stage in the life cycle of the project. The outcome of a phase is typically a major deliverable.

- **Scope** The specific work that needs to be done in a project to deliver the product or service.

- **Stakeholders** Individuals or organizations who have a vested interest in the outcome of the project and who can influence those project outcomes. Stakeholders include the project manager, members of the project team, the sponsoring organization, and customers.

Executing the Project

The second project management process is execution. At this point, you have your project plan in hand. The tasks are scheduled and the resources are assigned. Everyone's at the starting gate waiting for you to say "Go!"

You give the word, and the project moves from planning to the execution and controlling process. In the course of executing the project, you do the following:

- **Save a baseline plan for comparison.** To get good tracking information, keep a copy of certain project plan information on hand so you can compare your plan to actual progress as the project moves along.

- **Monitor the resources as they carry out their assigned tasks.** As the project manager, you keep an eye on their progress in completing their tasks.

- **Track task progress.** You can track progress in terms of percentage complete, how long a task takes from beginning to end, or how many hours a resource spends on a task. As you gather this information, you can see whether tasks and milestones will finish on time. You can also gather information about costs of resources, tasks, and the project as a whole.

Controlling the Project

While your project team is executing the tasks, you're making sure that the project stays within the prescribed deadline and budget while maintaining the scope outlined in the project goals. In project management, this process is referred to as "controlling the project." In the controlling process, you monitor all task activities, compare the plan to actual progress, and make adjustments as needed. To control the project, you do the following:

- **Analyze project information.** Analyze the information you're gathering and use this analysis to solve problems and make decisions. Often, you need to decide how to recover a slipped schedule or a budget overrun. Sometimes, you're in the happy position of deciding what to do with extra time or money.

- **Communicate and report.** Throughout the execution of the project, you will be in constant communication with your team members and other stakeholders. You need to keep upper management, customers, and other stakeholders informed of any potential problems, new decisions, and your overall progress.

Closing the Project

In the final process of the project, you have successfully fulfilled the goals of the project, and it's now complete. Before you move on to the next project, you want to capture the knowledge you gained from this one. When closing the project, you do the following:

- **Identify lessons learned.** Work with your project team and conduct a "postmortem" meeting to learn what went well and what could be improved. You can therefore articulate potential problems to avoid in future projects and also capture details of efficiencies gained.

- **Create a project template.** Save the project plan along with tasks, duration metrics, task relationships, resource skills, and the like, so the next time you or one of your colleagues manages a similar project, your wheel will not need to be reinvented.

Facilitating Your Project with Microsoft Project

Because a project involves a myriad of tasks, resources, assignments, dates, and more, it's clear that you need some kind of tool to help you keep track of the details. By using a spreadsheet or word processing program, you could create a table that lists your tasks, durations, start and finish dates, and assigned resources. In fact, that might very well get you started. But it's likely that you'll end up working harder than you have to in an attempt to make the tool work right. Such a table would not be able to perform the following functions:

- Calculate the start and finish dates for you

- Indicate whether assigned resources are actually available

- Inform you if assigned resources are underallocated or overworked

- Alert you if there's an upcoming deadline

- Understand how much material you've depleted or how much you're spending on supplies and services

- Calculate how much of the budget you've spent so far

- Draw your project tasks as a Gantt chart or network diagram so you can get a visual of your project

To do this and more, you can create a table in Microsoft Project instead. You can then use the project database, schedule calculation, and charting capabilities to help facilitate your project management processes (see Figure 2-2).

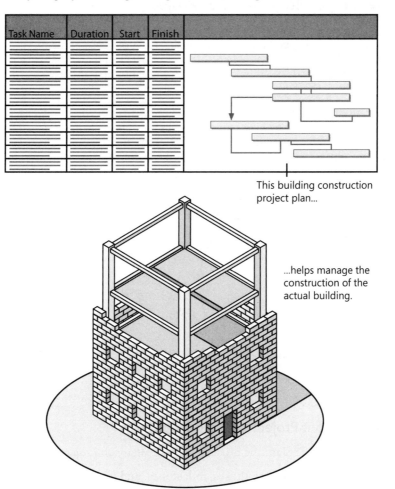

Figure 2-2 The project plan helps you manage your project.

Although Microsoft Project can't negotiate a more reasonable finish date, it can help you determine what you have to sacrifice to make that date. Although Microsoft Project won't complete a difficult and time-consuming task for your team, it will help you find extra time in the schedule or additional resources for that task. And although Microsoft Project can't motivate an uninspired team member, it can tell you if that team member is working on critical tasks that will affect the finish date of the entire project.

In short, Microsoft Project can help you facilitate all processes in the project management life cycle, from developing your scope, modeling your project schedule, and tracking and communicating progress to saving knowledge gained from the closed project. Furthermore, with Microsoft Office Project Professional 2007, project management standards can be established and disseminated throughout your enterprise.

Creating a Model of Your Project

You can use Microsoft Project to create a model of your project. This model reflects the reality of your project. You enter your tasks, resources, assignments, and other project-related information into Microsoft Project. You can then organize and manage the copious and very detailed bits of project information that otherwise can be quite overwhelming.

With all the necessary information stored in Microsoft Project, the exact project information you need at any given time is always at your fingertips. You can manipulate and analyze this information in various ways to solve problems and make decisions to successfully manage the project. As you take action and move forward in your project, you update information in Microsoft Project so that it continues to reflect reality (see Figure 2-3).

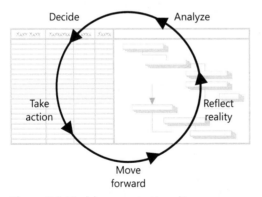

Figure 2-3 Model your project's reality.

Planning Your Project in Microsoft Project

Specifically, in the planning process, you use Microsoft Project to do the following:

- **Create your project phases, milestones, and task list.** Microsoft Project uses your task list as the basis for the project database it creates for you. You can organize tasks within phases, or subtasks within summary tasks, so you can break your project down into manageable segments.

- **Estimate task durations.** One task might take 2 hours to complete; another might take 4 days. Microsoft Project uses these durations to help build your schedule.

- **Link tasks with their appropriate relationships to other tasks.** Often, a task cannot begin until a previous task has been completed. For example, for an office move project, you schedule the "Design office space" task before the "Order new furniture" task. The two tasks are linked because the second task cannot be done until the first task is complete. Microsoft Project uses these task relationships to build your schedule. The durations and task relationships are also shown in the Gantt Chart and Network Diagram views of your project.

- **Enter any imposed deadlines or other date constraints.** If you know that you must vacate your current office space by the end of August, for example, you work with that date as one of the important constraints of your project. Microsoft Project schedules according to such constraints and informs you if there's a conflict between a constraint and the durations or task relationships you have also set.

- **Set up the resources and assign them to tasks.** Resources can be employees, vendors, or equipment that are responsible for carrying out the task. Not only does Microsoft Project keep track of which resources are assigned to which tasks, it also schedules work on assignments according to the resource's availability and lets you know if a resource is overloaded with more tasks than can be accomplished in the resource's available time. Resources can also include materials consumed or special costs incurred in the execution of a task, so you can plan for how much lumber you need, for example, or how much you're going to have to spend on travel costs throughout the life of the project.

- **Establish resource costs and task costs.** You can specify hourly, monthly, or per-use rates for the employees or equipment being used to complete tasks. You can specify the cost for consumable materials or other special costs for items such as trade show registration, printing, or travel. When your human, equipment, material, and cost resources are assigned to tasks, Microsoft Project calculates and adds these costs, so you can get an accurate view of how much your project will cost to execute. You can often use this calculation as a basis for the project budget.

- **Adjust the plan to achieve a targeted finish date or budget amount.** Suppose that your project plan initially shows a finish date that's two months later than required or a cost that's $10,000 more than the allocated budget. You can make adjustments to scope, schedule, cost, and resources to bring the project plan in line. While working through your inevitable project tradeoffs, Microsoft Project recalculates your schedule automatically until you have the result you need.

For more information about using Microsoft Project to plan your project, see the chapters in Part 2, "Developing the Project Plan."

Executing and Controlling Your Project in Microsoft Project

In the execution and control process of the project, use Microsoft Project to do the following:

- **Save the baseline plan.** For comparison and tracking purposes, you need to take a snapshot of what you consider your baseline project plan. As you update task progress through the life of the project, you can compare current progress with your original plan. These comparisons provide valuable information about whether you're on track with the schedule and your budget.

- **Update actual task progress.** With Microsoft Project, you can update task progress by entering percentage complete, work complete, work remaining, and more. As you enter actual progress, the schedule is automatically recalculated.

- **Compare variances between planned and actual task information.** Using the baseline information you saved, Microsoft Project presents various views to show your baseline against actual and scheduled progress, along with the resulting variances. For example, if your initial project plan shows that you had originally planned to finish a task on Thursday, but the resource actually finished it on Monday, you'd have a variance of 3 days in your favor.

- **Review planned, actual, and scheduled costs.** In addition to seeing task progress variances, you can compare baseline costs against actual and currently scheduled costs and see the resulting cost variances. Microsoft Project can also use your baseline and current schedule information for earned value calculations you can use for more detailed analyses.

- **Adjust the plan to respond to changes in scope, finish date, and budget.** What if you get a directive in the middle of the project to cut $10,000 from your budget? Or what if you learn that you must bring the project in a month earlier to catch a vital marketing window? Even in the midst of a project, you can adjust scope, schedule, cost, and resources in your project plan. With each change you make, Microsoft Project recalculates your schedule automatically.

  For more information about using Microsoft Project to track and control your project, see the chapters in Part 3, "Tracking Progress."

- **Report on progress, costs, resource utilization, and more.** Using the database and calculation features of Microsoft Project, you can generate a number of text-based and visual reports. For example, there are reports for project summary, milestones, tasks starting soon, over-budget tasks, resource to-do lists, and many more. The visual reports send Microsoft Project data to Microsoft Office Excel 2007 or Office Visio 2007 so you can see the data as a column chart or flow diagram, for example. You can modify these built-in reports to suit your own needs or create custom reports entirely from scratch.

  For more information about using Microsoft Project to report progress, see Chapter 12, "Reporting Project Information."

Closing Your Project in Microsoft Project

In the closing process of the project, use Microsoft Project to accomplish the following tasks:

- **Capture actual task duration metrics.** If you tracked task progress throughout the project, at the end of the project you have solid, tested data for how long certain tasks actually take.

- **Capture successful task sequencing.** Sometimes, you're not sure at the outset of a project whether a task should be done sooner or later in the cycle. With the experience of the project behind you, you can see whether your sequencing worked well.

- **Save a template for the next project of this kind.** Use your project plan as the boilerplate for the next project. You and other project managers will have a task list, milestones, deliverables, sequence, durations, and task relationships already in place that can be easily modified to fit the requirements of the new project.

> For more information about closing the project and creating templates, see Chapter 28, "Standardizing Projects Using Templates."

You can also use Microsoft Project to work with multiple projects, and even show the task or resource links among them. In the course of modeling your project in this way, Microsoft Project serves as your project information system. Microsoft Project arranges the thousands of bits of information in various ways so you can work with it, analyze your data, and make decisions based on coherent and soundly calculated project management information. This project information system carries out three basic functions:

- It stores project information including tasks, resources, assignments, durations, task relationships, task sequences, calendars, and more.

- It calculates information including dates, schedules, costs, durations, critical path, earned value, variances, and more.

- It presents views of information you're retrieving. You can specify the views, tables, filters, groups, fields, or reports, depending on what aspect of your project model you need to see.

Working with Your Team Through Microsoft Project

In addition to helping you create your project plan, Microsoft Project helps with resource management, cost management, and team communications. With Microsoft Project resource management features, you can perform the following tasks:

- Enter resources in the Microsoft Project resource list.

- Enter resources from your organization's e-mail address book, Active Directory directory service, or Project Server accounts.

- Maintain a reusable pool of resources available across multiple projects.

- Specify skills required for a task and have Microsoft Project search for available resources with those skills.

- Schedule tasks according to assigned resources' availability.

- Check for resource overload or underutilization and make adjustments accordingly.

- Book a proposed resource in your project (using Office Project Professional 2007).

> **For more information about managing resources, see Chapter 6, "Setting Up Resources in the Project," and Chapter 7, "Assigning Resources to Tasks."**

With the cost management features of Microsoft Project, you can do the following:

- Enter periodic or per-use costs for human, equipment, and material resources, including multiple rates for different task types.

- Enter costs for fees, supplies, or services that will be incurred on a task, for example, permit fees or travel costs.

- Enter fixed costs for tasks.

- Estimate costs for the project while you're still in the planning process.

- Compare planned cost variances to actual cost variances.

- Compare planned, actual, or scheduled costs against your budget.

- View cost totals for tasks, resources, phases, and the entire project.

- Analyze earned value calculations including budgeted cost of work performed (BCWP), schedule variance (SV), and cost variance percent (CV%).

> **For more information about setting and managing costs, see Chapter 8, "Planning Resource and Task Costs," and Chapter 11, "Responding to Changes in Your Project." For information about working with earned value, see Chapter 13, "Analyzing Progress Using Earned Value."**

Your communications requirements might be as simple as printing a Gantt chart or resource list for a weekly status meeting. Or, you might prefer to electronically exchange task updates with your resources every day and publish high-level project information to your company's intranet.

With Microsoft Project, you can communicate with others in just the way you need, as follows:

- Print a view as it looks on your screen

- Generate and print a predesigned text-based report

- Generate and print a predesigned visual report using Microsoft Project data in Excel or Office Visio 2007

- Create a custom view, text-based report, or visual report

- Copy a project view as a static picture in another Microsoft Office application

For more information about working with views and reports, see Chapter 12, "Reporting Project Information."

- Exchange task assignments, updates, and status reports with your team members through Microsoft Office Project Server 2007 and Microsoft Office Project Web Access

- Allow team leads to delegate tasks to other team members

- Track issues and documents through Microsoft Windows SharePoint Services, Office Project Server 2007, and Office Project Web Access

- Publish the project through Project Server and Project Web Access for review by team members, senior management, customers, and other stakeholders

For more information about working with resources across an enterprise, see Chapter 22, "Managing Enterprise Projects and Resources."

Using Microsoft Project in Your Enterprise

Through the use of Project Server, as accessed by Project Professional and Project Web Access, an entire portfolio of projects can be standardized across your enterprise. Numerous Microsoft Project elements including views, filters, groups, fields, and formulas, can be designed and included in the enterprise global template that reflects your organization's specific project management methodology. This customization and design is done by a *project server administrator*. This project server administrator is the person who sets up and manages the installation of Microsoft Project for your organization. The project server administrator knows the requirements of project management and the features of Microsoft Project well enough to design custom solutions and is often a programmer or other information technology professional. The project server administrator might also be a technically oriented lead project manager.

When your project server administrator designs a common enterprise project template, all project managers in the organization can then work with the same customized project elements that support organizational initiatives. In addition, senior managers can review summary information from multiple projects throughout the organization.

The project server administrator also sets up the enterprise resource pool, which contains all the resources available to the enterprise, from which the various project managers can draw to staff their projects. The enterprise resource pool includes key resource information such as cost, availability, and skill set.

Some organizations might divide the duties between a project server administrator and *portfolio manager*. The project server administrator can handle installation, server, network, and database issues, and the portfolio manager can be responsible for designing custom project elements, managing the enterprise resource pool, and setting up users and permissions.

For more information about enterprise capabilities, see Part 7, "Managing Projects Across Your Enterprise."

Working with the Project Stakeholders

Every project has a set of stakeholders associated with it. *Project stakeholders* are individuals or organizations who are connected to the project in one way or another and can influence the project's outcome. As the project manager, you need to be able to work with different types of stakeholders in various ways. A stakeholder can do the following:

- Be actively involved in the work of the project.

- Exert influence over the project and its outcome (also known as *managing stakeholders*).

- Have a vested interest in the outcome of a project.

There are a variety of stakeholder categories, each supported in its own way by Microsoft Project. The categories are as follows:

- **Project manager** Microsoft Project directly supports the project manager with its scheduling, tracking, and communication capabilities.

- **Team members** The project resources who are executing the project can be supported through Project Web Access, where they can view their assigned tasks, send and receive assignment progress updates and timesheets, send status reports, and review the project as a whole.

- **Team leads** Team leads can use Project Web Access to reassign and manage tasks.

- **Project resource manager** A resource manager might work in concert with the project manager to help acquire and maintain necessary resources. Through Project Web Access, a resource manager can analyze resource utilization information, build project teams, make assignments, and approve timesheets.

- **Senior managers, executives, or sponsors** People who lead the organization in implementing the project or supply the project budget or other resources can use Project Web Access to review high-level project summaries. In an enterprise environment, executives can review a summary comparing multiple projects being carried out throughout the organization.

INSIDE OUT **Project support for customers and end users**

Other possible stakeholders include customers or end users. Microsoft Project does not provide direct support for such stakeholders. However, you can provide them with Project Web Access or periodically publish a view designed for them on a Web site.

For more information about Project Web Access, see Chapter 23, "Participating on a Team Using Project Web Access," and Chapter 24, "Making Executive Decisions Using Project Web Access." For more information about publishing project information, see Chapter 12, "Reporting Project Information."

Managing stakeholders can influence the planning processes of a project and help set the expectations and assumptions of the project. Sometimes the expectations of different stakeholders conflict with one other. It's the job of the project manager to balance and reconcile these conflicts well before project execution begins.

Managing stakeholders might also impose new requirements that necessitate adjustments to the finish date, budget, or scope. Even if this happens in the midst of execution, you can use Microsoft Project to make adjustments responding to the new demands.

Keys to Successful Project Management

Being well-versed in project management processes and using a powerful tool such as Microsoft Project puts you well ahead in the project management game. For an even greater edge toward a successful project, follow these guidelines:

- **Develop the goals and objectives.** Know the overarching goals as well as the specific, measurable objectives of your project. They are your guiding principles.

- **Learn the scope.** Know the scope (including tasks, quality, and deliverables) of your project and exactly what is expected of it. The scope includes how much you're doing (quantity) and how well you're doing it (quality).

- **Know your deadlines.** Find out any deadlines—final as well as interim milestone and deliverable deadlines. If these deadlines are up to you to suggest, lucky you. But often you don't have this luxury. Often, you might propose one reasonable date only to have upper management or your customers suggest another, not-so-reasonable date. The sooner you learn about these dates, the better you can plan for them by adjusting the scope, the budget, and the resources.

- **Know your budget.** If the project finish date is not your limitation, the budget might very well be. Again, it might be up to you to tell upper management how much the proposed project will cost. But it's also likely that the budget will be imposed upon you, and you'll need to be able to fulfill the goals of the project within a specific and unrelenting dollar amount. Again, the sooner you know the definitive budget of the project, the more realistic and accurate your plan can be. You can adjust scope, time, and resources to meet the budget.

- **Find the best resources.** Gather input about who the best candidates for certain tasks are so you can get the best resources. Although the more experienced resources will likely be more expensive, they'll also be more apt to complete tasks quickly and with a higher level of quality (likewise with equipment or consumable material resources). Determine the acceptable level of quality for the project, balance this determination with your budget constraints, and procure the best you can get.

- **Enter accurate project information.** You can enter tasks and durations, link them together, and assign them to resources, making it seem like you have a real project plan. But suppose the data you entered doesn't reflect the real tasks that will be done, how much time resources will really be spending on these tasks, and what needs to be done before each task can start. Then all you have is a bunch of characters and graphics on a screen or in an impressive-looking report. You don't have a project plan at all. The "garbage-in, garbage-out" maxim applies. As you're planning the project, draw upon previous experience with a similar type of project. Solicit input from resources already earmarked for the project—they can provide excellent information about which tasks need to be done, how long they take, and how tasks relate to each other.

- **Adjust the project plan to meet requirements.** Look at the plan's calculated finish date and the total cost. See if they match your limitations for project deadline or budget. If they do not, make the necessary adjustments. This must all be done before you actually start the project—probably even before you show the project plan to any of your managing stakeholders.

- **Save a baseline and go.** After you have a project plan that solidly reflects reality, take a "snapshot" of the plan and begin project execution. This snapshot, which is called the baseline, is the means for determining whether you're on track and how far you might have strayed if you need to recover the schedule later.

- **Track progress.** Many project planners take it only this far: They enter and calculate all the tasks, durations, relationships, and resources to where they can see a schedule and budget. They say "Go" and everyone charges, but the plan is left behind. As project variables change (and they always do), the project plan becomes useless as a blueprint for managing the project. If you want the project plan to be useful from the time you first enter, assign, and schedule tasks until the time you close the project on time and on budget, you need to maintain the project plan as a dynamic tool that accompanies you every step of the way. Maintaining the plan means tracking progress information. Suppose a task planned for 5 days takes 10 days instead. You can enter that the task actually took 10 days, and the schedule will be recalculated. Your plan will still work, and you'll still be able to see when succeeding tasks should be completed.

- **Make necessary adjustments.** As project variables change during project execution, you can see whether an unplanned change affects key milestones, your resources' schedules, your budget, or your project finish date. For example, suppose that 5-day task took 10 days to complete, and it changes the project finish date and also causes the project to exceed its budget. If this happens, you can take steps well ahead of time to make the necessary adjustments and avert the impending crisis. Use the power of Microsoft Project to recalculate the project plan when actual project details vary from the plan. Then you can analyze the plan, decide on the best course of action to keep the project on track, and take action. This action might be within the project plan or outside the confines of the plan in the real world of the real project itself.

- **Communicate.** Make sure that your team members know what's expected of them and stay focused. Pay attention when they alert you to potential problems with their tasks. Keep upper management and customers informed of your progress and of any changes to the original plan.

- **Close the completed project and capture information.** When a project goes well, we're often so pleased with ourselves that amidst the congratulations and celebrations we don't think to capture all the information we should. When a project is completed with much difficulty, sometimes we're just relieved that we're done with it and can't wait to get on with the next project and forget about such an unhappy nightmare. But whether a project is simple or difficult, a radiant success or a deplorable failure, much can always be learned. Even if you're not involved in any other projects of this type, other people might be. It's important to record as much information about the project as possible. Narrative and evaluative information can be captured through a postmortem or "lessons learned" document. Project information such as tasks, resources, durations, relationships, and calendars can be recorded in a project plan itself. If the project went very well, you can even save your project plan as a template to be used for future similar projects, thereby enabling future project managers to benefit from your hard-won experience.

Chapter 2

PART 2

Developing the Project Plan

CHAPTER 3
Starting a New Project .59

CHAPTER 4
Viewing Project Information 105

CHAPTER 5
Scheduling Tasks 153

CHAPTER 6
Setting Up Resources in the Project 201

CHAPTER 7
Assigning Resources to Tasks. 235

CHAPTER 8
Planning Resource and Task Costs 273

CHAPTER 9
Checking and Adjusting the Project Plan. . . 307

Starting a New Project

Focusing the Project Vision	59	Organizing Tasks into an Outline	97
Creating a New Project Plan	63	Setting Up Your Work Breakdown Structure	99
Entering Tasks	86	Adding Supplementary Information to Tasks	102
Sequencing and Organizing Tasks	93		

Because the heart of project management is planning, it's no wonder that the planning processes of a new project has you doing a significant amount of work just to set the stage. You define the big picture and obtain stakeholder approval for the specifications of the product or service you're creating and for the boundaries defining the overall scope of the project itself.

After this vision is in place, you're ready to create your project blueprint—the project plan—using Microsoft Office Project 2007. You create a new project file and enter foundation information.

Then you break down your project goals and objectives into the actual phases, milestones, and tasks that form the backbone of your project information system. You sequence the phases and tasks, and organize them into a hierarchy that maps to your project.

If your project or organization has more specialized or advanced requirements, you can use work breakdown structure codes that organize your task list by each deliverable.

You can add your supporting documentation, such as the vision or strategy document, to the project plan. Likewise, you can add other supplementary information such as notes or hyperlinks to individual tasks, milestones, and phases. All this information makes your project plan the central repository of all project information.

Focusing the Project Vision

You might already have a clear picture in your mind of what your project is about and what it will be when it is complete. On the other hand, the project might still seem a little fuzzy, at least around the edges. It's not uncommon for other stakeholders to have a clear vision when you're not sure if you get it just yet.

And don't be surprised if one stakeholder's expectations seem clear enough, but another stakeholder's expectations sound entirely contradictory.

The challenge at this important starting point is to clearly define the project without ambiguity, so that everyone involved is talking about the same project, the same expectations, and the same results. Defining the vision clearly at the beginning prevents redirection (and the attendant wasted effort) in the middle of the project or disappointment at the end.

So how do you create a vision? You work with key stakeholders such as the customers, potential users, sponsors, executives, and project team members to get their project expectations. You might have to reconcile conflicting views and opposing agendas. Throughout this process, you'll identify the goals of the project as well as their measurable objectives. You'll identify project assumptions, spell out potential risks, and make contingency plans for those risks. You'll also identify known limitations, such as budget, time, or resources.

By the time you finish this high-level project planning and get the necessary approval, everyone involved will know exactly what they're signing up for.

Defining Scope

A defined scope articulates the vision of the product you're creating and the project that will create it. As your project is executed and issues arise, your defined scope can help you make decisions. The scope definition is your guideline for whether the direction you're considering is really the job of this project. If you don't stay focused on the agreed-upon scope of the project, you're likely to experience "scope creep," in which you end up spending time, money, and resources on tasks and deliverables that are not part of the original vision.

This is not to say that scope can't change during the course of a project. Business conditions, design realities, budgets, time, resource availability, and many other factors can make it necessary to change project scope midway through. In addition, as members of your project team work on their tasks, they are likely to generate great new ideas. Nonetheless, your scope document helps you make decisions and manage those changes so that you change in the proper direction—in line with your organization's overall strategy, the product's reason for being, and the project's goals.

Understanding Product Scope and Project Scope

There are two types of scope: product scope and project scope. First, you define the product scope, unless it has already been defined for you. The *product scope* specifies the features and functions of the product that will be the outcome of the project. The product scope might well be part of the product description in your charter. The product can be tangible, such as the construction of a new office building or the design of a new aircraft. The product can also be the development of a service or event, for example, deployment of a new computer system or implementation of a new training initiative.

Regardless of the type of product, the product scope indicates the specifications and parameters that paint a detailed picture of the end result. For example, the product scope of the construction of a new office building might include square footage, number of stories, location, and architectural design elements.

The **project scope** specifies the work that must be done to complete the project successfully, according to the specifications of the associated product scope. The project scope defines and controls what will and will not be included in the project. If there will be multiple phases of product development, the project scope might specify which phase this project is handling. For example, a computer system deployment project might specify that its scope encompass the infrastructure development and installation of the new computer system, but not the documentation and training for new system users. Or it might specify that the project handle all aspects of the product, from concept through completion of the final stage.

Developing the Scope Statement

To define the project scope and communicate it to other key stakeholders, you develop and record the *scope statement*. Depending on your organization's planning methods, certain elements of the scope statement might be defined very early, sometimes even before you've been assigned as project manager. Other elements might be defined just before you begin identifying and sequencing the project's tasks. Your scope statement should include the following:

- **Project justification.** The scope statement should define the business need or other stimulus for this project. This justification provides a sound basis for evaluating future decisions, including the inevitable tradeoffs.

- **Product description.** The scope should characterize the details of the product or service being created. The project justification and product description together should formulate the goals of the project.

- **Project constraints or limitations.** The scope should include any limiting factors to the project. Factors that can limit a project's options include a specific budget, contractual provisions, a precise end date, and so on.

> **Note**
> Because we use the term *constraints* throughout this book to mean task constraints, in this chapter we're using the term *limitations* to refer to overall project constraints.

- **Project assumptions.** The scope should list any elements considered to be true, real, or certain—even when they might not be—for the sake of being able to continue developing the project plan and moving forward. By their nature, assumptions usually carry a degree of risk. For example, if you don't know whether the building for a commercial construction project will be 10,000 or 15,000 square feet, you have to assume one or the other for the sake of planning. The risk is that the other choice might end up being correct. You can adjust the plan after the facts are known, but other project dependencies might already be in place by then.

> **Note**
>
> Although certain aspects of your scope statement might remain unchanged through the iterative planning process, that's not necessarily the case with project limitations and assumptions. As the scope becomes more tightly defined, the limitations and assumptions come to light and are better exposed. Likewise, as you continue down the road in the planning process, the entire project scope tends to become more and more focused.

- **Project deliverables.** The scope should list the summary-level subproducts created throughout the duration of the project. The delivery of the final subproject deliverable marks the completion of the entire project. This list might bring into focus major project phases and milestones, which will be valuable when you start entering tasks into your project plan.

- **Project objectives.** The scope should enumerate the measurable objectives to be satisfied for the project to be considered successful. The objectives map to the deliverables and are driven by the project goals, as described by the project justification and product description. To be meaningful, the project objectives must be quantifiable in some way, for example, a specific dollar amount, a specific timeframe, or a specific level of quality.

> **Note**
>
> Your scope statement might also address other project planning issues such as communications, quality assurance, and risk management. It can define the reporting requirements and the collaboration tools to be implemented. The scope statement can also specify the minimum level of quality acceptable, define the potential risks associated with the itemized limitations and assumptions, and stipulate methods of countering the risks.

Product scope and project scope are intricately linked. The project scope relies on a clear definition of the product scope. The project scope is fulfilled through the completion of work represented in the project plan. In the same way, product scope is fulfilled by meeting the specifications in the product requirements.

With the draft of the scope statement in hand, you have a document you can use to clearly communicate with other project stakeholders. This draft helps you flush out any cross-purposes, mistaken assumptions, and misplaced requirements. As you continue to refine the scope statement, the project vision is honed to the point where all the stakeholders should have a common understanding of the project. And because all the stakeholders participated in the creation of the vision, you can feel confident that everyone understands exactly what they're working toward when you begin to execute the project plan.

Creating a New Project Plan

You're now at the point where you can start Microsoft Project 2007 and actually create your project plan. When you create a new project file, you first decide whether you're scheduling from a start date or finish date. You set your overall project calendar that the tasks will be scheduled against. If you like, you can attach project documentation such as your all-important scope statement and possibly other project-related documents.

Creating a Project File

To begin creating your new project plan, you start Microsoft Project and choose whether you're creating a new project from scratch or from a template.

If you haven't installed Microsoft Project yet, refer to Appendix A, "Installing Microsoft Office Project 2007," for installation details and guidelines.

To start Microsoft Project, click the Windows Start button. Point to All Programs, point to Microsoft Office, and then click Microsoft Project. Microsoft Project starts (see Figure 3-1).

> Note
>
> If you're working with enterprise projects using Microsoft Office Project Professional 2007, you might first be prompted to enter your account name to connect to Microsoft Office Project Server 2007.

Chapter 3

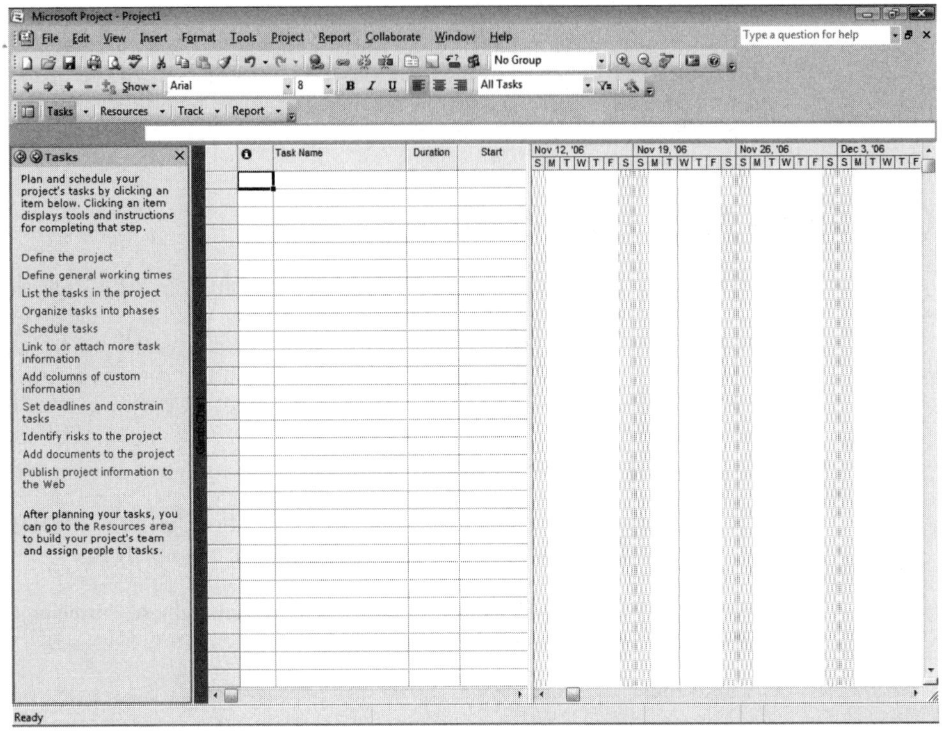

Figure 3-1 A blank project file appears in Microsoft Project.

> **Note**
>
> Depending on how you customize your setup, you might also be able to open Microsoft Project by double-clicking its icon on the Windows desktop.

The Microsoft Project workspace is called the **view**, and the view that appears by default when you first open Microsoft Project is the Gantt Chart. The Gantt Chart has a task table on the left side and the chart with Gantt bars on the right.

For more information about working with the Gantt Chart and the other views available in Microsoft Project, see Chapter 4, "Viewing Project Information."

You can use this blank project file to start creating your project plan from scratch. If you prefer to do this, skip to the section titled "Saving Your New Project."

You can also create a new project from a template. A *template* is a type of project file that contains existing project information that helps you start your project more quickly. The template usually contains a list of tasks, already sequenced and organized. The task list might be further detailed with phases, milestones, and deliverables. There might be additional task information in the template as well, such as task durations and task dependencies. You can use this task list as the basis for your project. You can add, remove, and rearrange tasks, adapting the task information as needed to correspond to your project requirements. A template can also include resource information, customized views, calendars, reports, tables, macros, option settings, and more.

The template file has an extension of .mpt, indicating that it is the Microsoft Project template file type. When you open and modify a template file, it is saved as a normal .mpp (Microsoft Project plan) file by default.

For more information about file types and project file management, see Chapter 29, "Managing Project Files."

Templates can be generated from the following sources:

- **The set of 41 templates built in to Microsoft Project.** These templates reflect various types of product, service, or activity projects in different industries (see Table 3-1). Twenty-nine of these templates are new in Microsoft Project 2007. All the templates are based on widely accepted industry standards.

Table 3-1 Project Templates

Business Development	Managing incoming request for quotes (RFQ)
	Marketing campaign planning
	Marketing event planning and execution
	New business
	New product
	New product launch
	Product development planning
	Trade show planning, execution, and wrap-up
Customer Service	Customer feedback monitoring
	Customer service ramp up
	Post-manufacturing customer service planning
Construction and Facilities	Commercial construction
	Engineering
	Home move
	Office move
	Residential construction

Finance and Accounting	Finance and accounting system implementation
	Financial service offering launch
	Preparation of an opening balance sheet at the date of transition to IFRS
General Business	Annual report preparation
	External technical readiness training
	Insurance claim processing
	Internal readiness training
	Product evaluation post launch
	Strategic merger or acquisition evaluation
	Vendor evaluation and consolidation
	Vendor request for proposal (RFP) solicitation
Human Resources	Develop skills needs – hiring plan – hiring forecast
	Evaluating offshoring strategy for HR functions
	Human resources information system implementation
	Performance reviews
Information Technology	Electronic government (e-gov) project
	Infrastructure deployment
	Security infrastructure
	Software development
	Software localization
	MSF Application development
Standards and Process	Project office
	ISO 9001 management review
	Six Sigma DMAIC cycle
	SOX compliance and technology options

- **Any previous projects you have saved as project template files.**

  For more information about using completed projects as templates, see Chapter 28, "Standardizing Projects Using Templates."

- **The templates standard to project management within your specific industry.** Professional organizations, standards organizations, and industry groups might have resources, possibly on their Web sites, which include such templates for use with Microsoft Project.

- **Templates available on Office Online.** New Microsoft Project templates are continually added to the Templates page on Office Online.

Examples of the dozens of templates available on Office Online include a comprehensive hiring plan, Microsoft Windows SharePoint Services deployment plan, training rollout initiative and plan, audit preparation plan, direct mail marketing campaign, and primary market research schedule.

> **Note**
>
> If you use the enterprise features of Microsoft Project Professional 2007, you use the enterprise global template, a different kind of template that's set up by the project server administrator. The enterprise global template can include elements such as customized views, tables, and fields that reflect the project standards for your organization.

Creating a New Project with a Template

To create a new project from a template, follow these steps:

1. Click File, New.

New

> **Note**
>
> If you just click the New button on the Standard toolbar, a new blank project is created by default, and you don't see the template choices you need in the Project Guide.

2. In the New Project task pane, under Templates, click the On Computer link.

3. In the Templates dialog box, click the Project Templates tab (see Figure 3-2).

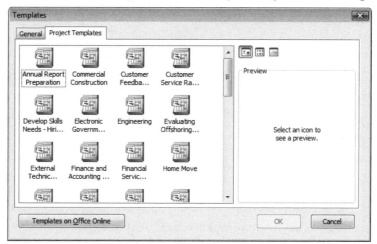

Figure 3-2 The Project Templates tab lists all templates provided with Microsoft Project.

4. Click the project template you want to use and then click OK (see Figure 3-3).

The first time you choose a template, Microsoft Project might need to install it. This takes only a few moments.

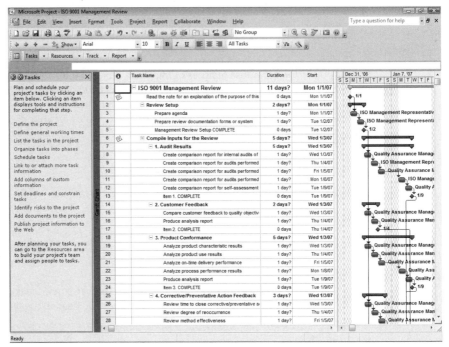

Figure 3-3 A new project file is created based on the chosen template.

Find More Templates Online

New Microsoft Project templates are continually being added to the Templates page on the Office Online Web site. These templates are created not only by Microsoft, but also by project management consultants, solution providers, and everyday users. To see these templates, first be sure that your computer is connected to the Internet. In Microsoft Project, click File, New. In the New Project task pane under Templates, click the Templates On Office Online link. The Office Online Templates page appears in your Internet browser.

Under Browse Templates, click Plans. A list of Microsoft Office planning templates appears. In the left pane, click the arrow in the Filter By Product box and then click Project. The list of plans are filtered to show only Microsoft Project plan templates. Click the thumbnail or name of a template, and a preview of the template appears. If you want to download the template, click Download Now and follow the instructions. When finished, the downloaded template is loaded into Microsoft Project as a new file based on that template.

Return to this Templates page periodically to check for new templates you can use. Other categories that contain Microsoft Project templates are Evaluations, Planners, and Schedules.

> **Note**
>
> Looking for a New dialog box? As of Microsoft Project 2002, the New dialog box is replaced by the New Project task pane in the Project Guide area. This is true even if you close the Project Guide pane and completely turn off the Project Guide.

Creating a New Project from an Existing Project

If you have an existing project that you want to use as a starting point for your new project, you can simply copy and modify it for your current purposes. You will save it under a different file name, creating a completely new file. Follow these steps:

Open

1. On the Standard toolbar, click Open.

2. Browse to the existing project file and then click Open.

Saving Your New Project

Whether you are creating a new project from scratch, from a template, or from an existing project file, your next step is to save your new project. To do this:

1. Click File, Save As.

> **Note**
>
> If you're creating a new project from scratch or from a template, you can simply click the Save button on the Standard toolbar to open the Save As dialog box.

2. In the Save As dialog box, choose the drive and folder in which you want to save the new project.

    If you're set up for enterprise project management using Microsoft Project Professional 2007 and Microsoft Project Server 2007, you'll see the Save To Project Server dialog box instead.

3. In the File Name box, enter a descriptive name for your project and then click the Save button.

    If you're working with Project Server, and you want to save the project to the server, click the Save button. Depending on how your organization has set up enterprise project management standards, you might need to add information in custom enterprise fields.

    If you want to save the project locally on your own computer instead, click the Save As File button.

> For more information about working with enterprise projects, see the section titled "Creating a New Enterprise Project" In Chapter 22.

Use the Define The Project Wizard

The Define The Project Wizard can walk you through the setup of your new project and complete the necessary dialog boxes quickly for you. To set up a new project using the Define The Project Wizard, follow these steps:

Tasks

Tasks

1. Create your new project file, either from a blank project or from a template.

2. If necessary, click the Tasks button on the Project Guide toolbar to open the Tasks pane.

3. Click the Define The Project link. The Define The Project Wizard starts in the task pane.

4. Enter the estimated start date for your project and then click the Continue To Step 2 link at the bottom of the pane.

5. Specify whether you will be collaborating via Project Server and Project Web Access, and then click the Continue To Step 3 link.

6. In the final pane, click the Save And Finish link.

7. In the Tasks pane again, click the Define General Working Times link and work through the Project Working Times Wizard.

Scheduling from a Start or Finish Date

Your first scheduling decision is whether Microsoft Project should calculate the schedule of your new project from a start date or from a finish date. Often, you have a finish date in mind, but you can still schedule from the start date and then make sure you hit the targeted finish date. You'll get more predictable results when you schedule from a start date.

For example, suppose you set up a project with 100 tasks to be scheduled from the start date. You specify task durations and sequence, link the tasks in the order they are to be done, and indicate whether any tasks have specific dates by which they must be completed. When you do not enter specific task start or finish dates, Microsoft Project schedules tasks to be done as soon as possible. Using task durations, links, and date constraints, Microsoft Project schedules the first task to start on your project start date and the remaining tasks from that point forward until the last task is completed. If that last task is done on a date that is too late for your project requirements, you can adjust the duration and sequencing, as well as the scope and resources assigned, to bring in the finish date where you need it to be.

However, you might know the project finish date but not when your project will begin because you're receiving work from another source that could be delayed. Or the project management methodology you use might require you to schedule from a finish date.

Consider that same project of 100 tasks. In a project scheduled from the finish date, any tasks that do not require a specific date are scheduled to be done as late as possible, rather than as soon as possible. Microsoft Project schedules the last task to be finished on your project finish date and works backward from that point until the first task is started. If that first task is scheduled before the current date or too early for your project requirements, you can adjust the tasks and other aspects of the schedule.

INSIDE OUT Beware of scheduling from the finish date

If you must schedule from the finish date, be aware that your task dependencies, task constraints, and leveling tools will behave differently than in a project that is scheduled from the start date.

For more information about task constraints, see the section titled "Scheduling Tasks to Achieve Specific Dates" in Chapter 5. For more information about resource leveling, see the section titled "Balancing Resource Workloads," in Chapter 9.

To set up your project plan to be scheduled from the project start date, follow these steps:

1. Click Project, Project Information.

    The Project Information dialog box appears (see Figure 3-4).

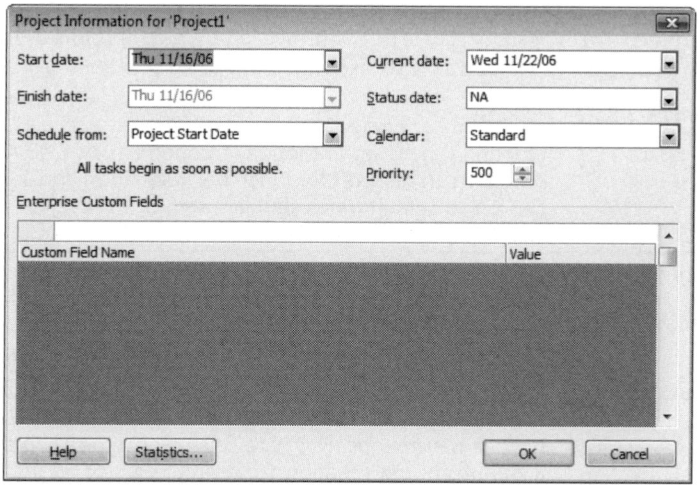

Figure 3-4 Use the Project Information dialog box to specify settings for the entire project.

1. In the Start Date box, enter the project start date.

   By default, the Start Date box shows today's date.

2. In the Schedule From box, click Project Start Date.

   Note that the date in the Project Finish Date box is grayed out so you cannot edit it. Because you have chosen to schedule from the project start date, Microsoft Project will calculate this date for you later.

To set up your project plan to be scheduled from the project finish date, follow these steps:

1. Click Project, Project Information.

2. In the Schedule From box, click Project Finish Date.

3. In the Finish Date box, enter the project finish date.

   The date in the Project Start Date box is grayed out so you cannot edit it. Because you have chosen to schedule from the project finish date, Microsoft Project will calculate this date for you later.

Setting Your Project Calendar

With the *project calendar*, you establish the working days and times for your project and its tasks. The project calendar also becomes the default calendar for any resources working on your project. The project calendar indicates when your organization typically works on project tasks and when it's off work. By setting your project calendar, you're establishing one of the fundamental methods for scheduling the tasks in your project.

You choose a *base calendar* to become your project calendar. You can create your own base calendar, or you can choose one of the three base calendars that comes with Microsoft Project. A base calendar is rather like a calendar template that you can apply to a set of resources, a set of tasks, or the project as a whole. Table 3-2 describes the working days and times specified in the base calendars provided by Microsoft Project.

Table 3-2 Base Calendars

Standard	Working time is set to Monday through Friday, 8:00 A.M. until 5:00 P.M., with an hour off for lunch between noon and 1:00 P.M. each day. This is the default base calendar used for the project, for tasks, and for resources.
Night Shift	Working time is set to an 11:00 P.M. until 8:00 A.M. night shift, five days a week, with an hour off for lunch from 3:00 A.M. until 4:00 A.M. each morning. This base calendar is generally used for resources who work a graveyard shift. It can also be used for projects that are carried out only during the night shift.
24 Hours	Working time is set to midnight until midnight seven days a week; that is, work never stops. This base calendar is typically used for projects in a manufacturing situation, for example, which might run two or three back-to-back shifts every day of the week.

Applying a Base Calendar to the Project Calendar

If you're using the Standard base calendar as your project calendar, you don't need to do much—the Standard calendar is the project calendar by default. If you want to use a different base calendar, you must select it as your project calendar. Follow these steps:

1. Click Project, Project Information.

2. In the Calendar box, select the name of the base calendar.

3. Click OK.

You can use any of the three base calendars (Standard, Night Shift, or 24 Hours) as the basis for the project calendar, resource calendars, or task calendars. In fact, you could use all three within the same project. For example, you might apply the Standard calendar to the project as a whole, the Night Shift calendar to a certain group of resources, and the 24 Hours calendar to tasks being carried out by automated equipment.

For more information about the task calendar, see the section titled "Working with Task Calendars" in Chapter 5. For more information about the resource calendar, see the section titled "Setting Resource Working Time Calendars" in Chapter 6.

Modifying a Base Calendar

You can modify your project calendar to reflect your team's normal working times and days off, including any holidays you'll all be taking and other one-time calendar exceptions. You can also specify recurring exceptions in your working times calendar.

To modify the project calendar, you change the base calendar that the project calendar is using as its starting point. Any of the base calendars can be customized to reflect specialized working days and times.

Specifying the Normal Work Week for a Base Calendar

As specified in Table 3-2 previously, the three base calendars that come with Microsoft Project have their default working days and times. You might apply one of these base calendars to your project for it to become the calendar on which your project is based. When you do this, your schedule is governed by the working days and times in that base calendar.

You can change the default working days and times of the normal work week. To do this, follow these steps:

1. Click Tools, Change Working Time.

2. In the For Calendar box, click the name of the base calendar you want to modify (see Figure 3-5).

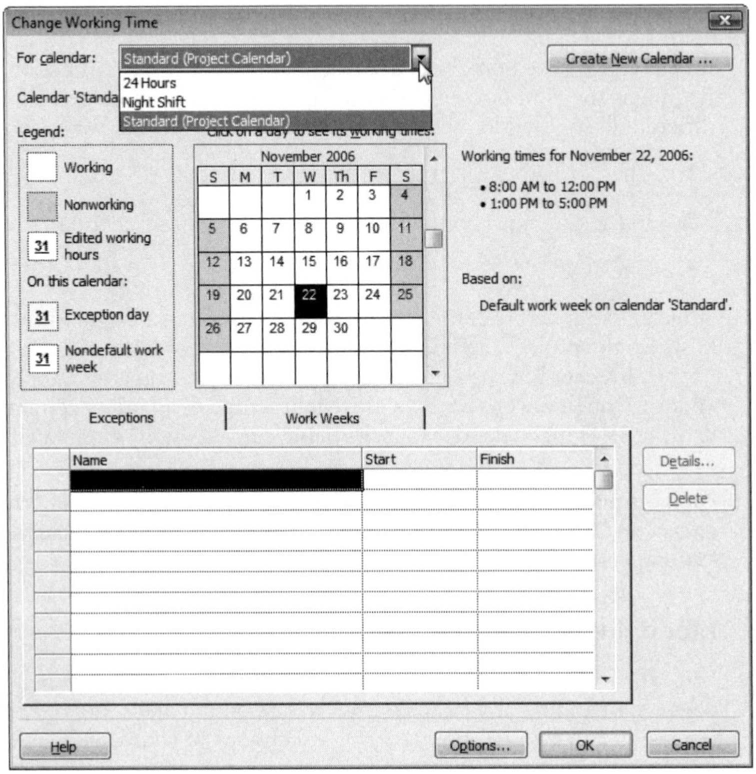

Figure 3-5 Use the Change Working Time dialog box to modify a base calendar.

3. Click the Work Weeks tab (see Figure 3-6).

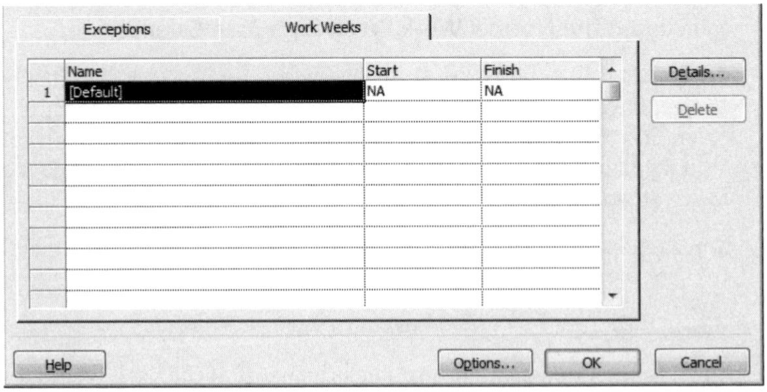

Figure 3-6 Use the Work Weeks tab to change the default work week or to create alternate work weeks.

Notice that row 1 contains the word "[Default]" with "NA" in both the Start and Finish fields. This indicates that the default working days and times are to be used whenever an alternative work week is not scheduled.

4. Make sure that the Default row is selected and then click the Details button to open the Details for '[Default]' dialog box (see Figure 3-7).

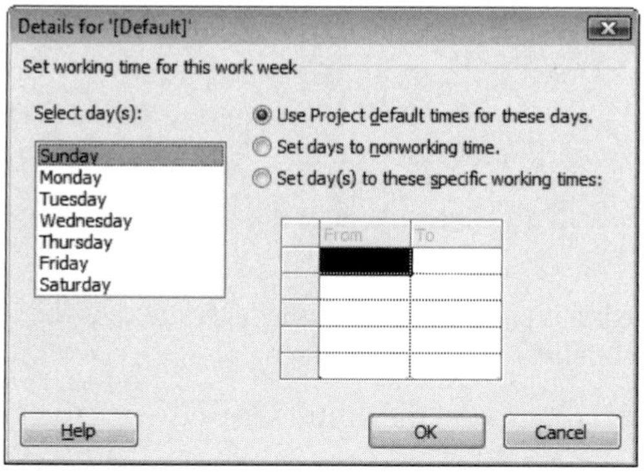

Figure 3-7 The work week Details dialog box shows the working days and times for the selected work week.

If you click a day of the week in the Select Day(s) box, its working times appear in the From/To table to the right. If no working times appear in the table, this indicates that the selected day is a nonworking day. Above the table, the Use Project Default Times For These Days option is selected.

5. In the Select Day(s) box, click the day of the week you want to change.

You can drag to select consecutive days. You can also click the first day, hold down the Shift key, and then click the last day. To select several nonadjacent days, click the first day you want to change, hold down the Ctrl key, and then click the other days.

6. To change the day(s) to nonworking time, click the Set Days To Nonworking Time option.

To change a nonworking day to a working day, or to change the working times of a working day, click the Set Day(s) To These Specific Working Times option. Then, in the From/To table, type the start and finish working times.

7. Click OK in the Details dialog box and then click OK in the Change Working Time dialog box.

Setting Up an Alternative Work Week

Your project might need an alternative work week specified for a particular period of time. One example might be a construction company working an accelerated schedule to complete exterior work before winter. Another example might be a training project in which the default work week is used for curriculum development and testing and a different, temporary work week is used when actual training is taking place.

New in Microsoft Office Project 2007 is the ability to specify any number of alternative work weeks to make sure your project scheduling reflects such situations. To specify an alternative work week, follow these steps:

1. Click Tools, Change Working Time.

2. In the For Calendar box, click the name of the base calendar you want to modify.

3. Click the Work Weeks tab.

4. Click in the next blank row below the Default row. In the Name field, type a name for the alternative work week, for example, "Roofing Week" or "Training Week."

5. Click in the Start field and enter the first date that the alternative working times should be in effect.

6. Click in the Finish field and then enter the last date that the alternative working times should be in effect.

7. With the row for the new work week still selected, click the Details button.

8. In the Select Day(s) box, click the day(s) of the week you want to change.

9. To change a nonworking day to a working day, or to change the working times of a working day, click the Set Day(s) To These Specific Working Times option. Then, in the From/To table, type the start and finish working times.

    To change the selected day(s) to nonworking time, click the Set Days To Nonworking Time option.

10. Click OK in the Details dialog box and then click OK in the Change Working Time dialog box.

> **Note**
> To delete an alternative work week, on the Work Weeks tab in the Change Working Time dialog box, click the name of the work week. Click the Delete button. You cannot delete the Default work week.

Setting Up Holidays and Other One-Time Calendar Exceptions

To make a one-time exception to an existing base calendar, follow these steps:

1. Click Tools, Change Working Time.

2. In the For Calendar box, click the name of the base calendar you want to modify.

3. Click the day in the calendar thumbnail whose working times you want to change.

When you click a day in the calendar thumbnail, information about that day's working times appear to the right. This tells you whether the day is a working or nonworking day, what the working times are, and which work week or exception and base calendar this day and calendar are based on.

> **Note**
>
> To change the working time of a day in another month, use the scroll arrow in the calendar thumbnail until you see the correct month.

4. Make sure the Exceptions tab is selected, click in the first available row in the Name column, and then enter the name of the calendar exception. Press Enter or Tab when finished.

   Although entering a name for the exception is not required, it can be useful for distinguishing the reason for the exception. Examples might include "Martin Luther King, Jr. Holiday" or "Department Offsite."

   After you press Enter or Tab, the name is entered and the Start and Finish dates are entered, defaulting to the date you clicked in the thumbnail calendar.

5. If necessary, change the date in the Start or Finish field.

   When you enter an exception for a working day, by default it changes to a nonworking day.

> **Note**
>
> By default, the Start and Finish dates are the same—the date selected in the thumbnail calendar. If the date of an exception is several months in the future, it's easier to enter the date in this field rather than scroll to it in the thumbnail calendar.
>
> Also, if the exception goes across a series of days, enter the last day of the exception in the Finish field. This can be useful for entering a two-week holiday shutdown, for example.

6. If the exception is a change other than switching a working day to a nonworking day, click the Details button to open the Details dialog box (see Figure 3-8).

Chapter 3

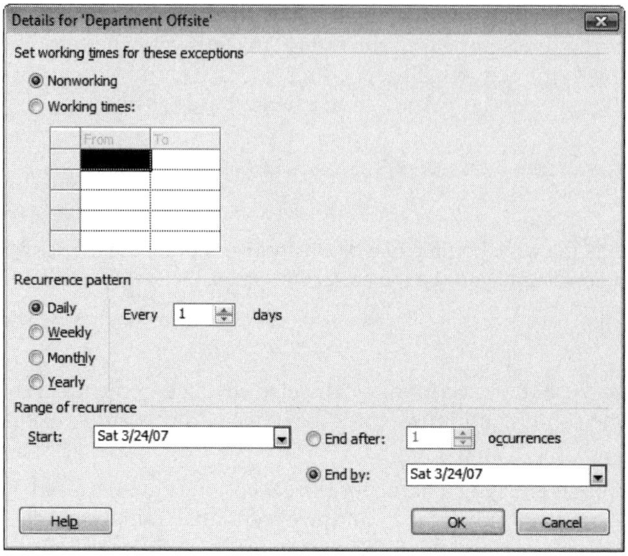

Figure 3-8 Use the Details dialog box to specify the details about the working times calendar exception.

7. If you're changing working time to nonworking time, select the Nonworking Time option.

8. If you're changing the working time to something other than the default, select the Nondefault Working Time option. Then, change the times in the From and To boxes as needed.

9. Click OK to close the Details dialog box and then click OK to close the Change Working Time dialog box.

Setting Up a Recurring Calendar Exception

You can set up a calendar exception to take place on a recurring pattern. For example, if you're developing the plan for a three-year project, you'll probably want to show that the New Year's Day holiday exception takes place on January 1 of each year, or that the Thanksgiving holidays take place on the fourth Thursday and Friday of November each year.

In the same way, if you know that no work on the project will take place from 9:00 to 11:00 A.M. on the first Monday of every month because of the monthly divisional staff meeting, you can build that into your project's working times calendar.

> ### Recurring Calendar Exceptions vs. Recurring Project Tasks
>
> If there are company or department events that will take place and affect progress on project tasks, such as meetings or offsites that don't have a direct bearing on the project work itself, it's best to handle the time for these events using a calendar exception.
>
> However, if you know you have a recurring project status meeting every Wednesday morning, for example, you can build that into your project tasks schedule and assign resources to it. For more information, see the section titled "Entering Recurring Tasks" later in this chapter.

To set up a recurring calendar exception to an existing base calendar, follow these steps:

1. Click Tools, Change Working Time.

2. In the For Calendar box, click the name of the base calendar you want to modify.

3. Click the day in the calendar thumbnail whose working times you want to change.

4. On the Exceptions tab, click in the first available row in the Name column and then enter the name of the calendar exception. Press Enter or Tab when finished.

5. If necessary, change the dates in the Start or Finish field.

6. Click the Details button.

7. If you're changing working time to nonworking time, select the Nonworking Time option.

8. If you're changing the working time to something other than the default, select the Nondefault Working Time option. Then, change the times in the From and To boxes as needed.

9. Use the controls under Recurrence Pattern and Range of Recurrence to specify the details of the recurrence.

10. Under Recurrence Pattern, specify how often the calendar exception takes place; that is, daily, weekly, or monthly.

11. Specify the details of when the recurring calendar exception is to take place during that frequency, for example, every other Thursday or the first Monday of every month.

12. Under Range Of Recurrence, specify the number of times the recurring calendar exception is to take place or the date when the recurring calendar exception is to end.

13. Click OK to close the Details dialog box and then click OK to close the Change Working Time dialog box.

Chapter 3

> **Note**
>
> To delete an exception, on the Exceptions tab in the Change Working Time dialog box, click the name of the exception. Then click the Delete button.

Set Up a Weekly Working Times Exception

In Microsoft Project 2003 and earlier, if there was a working times exception on a particular day of the week, you selected the day heading in the calendar thumbnail and then changed the working times.

To do the same thing in Microsoft Office Project 2007, you select the first day that this exception occurs and give the exception a name. Then in the Details dialog box, you specify the recurrence pattern of every week. You also specify how long that recurrence pattern takes place. If this exception will be happening throughout the life of the project, use the project finish date as a guideline.

If the project finish date changes, remember to come back to this dialog box and change this setting. In fact, it wouldn't hurt to have such recurring working times calendar exceptions overshoot the project finish date by a month or so. Then, when you need to adjust your project schedule for the inevitable changes that will take place, you'll have one less adjustment to have to worry about.

Creating a New Base Calendar

If you need to apply a common working schedule to your project, a group of resources, or a set of tasks and it isn't built in to Microsoft Project already, you can create your own base calendar.

To create a new base calendar, follow these steps:

1. Click Tools, Change Working Time.

2. Click the Create New Calendar button. The Create New Base Calendar dialog box appears (see Figure 3-9).

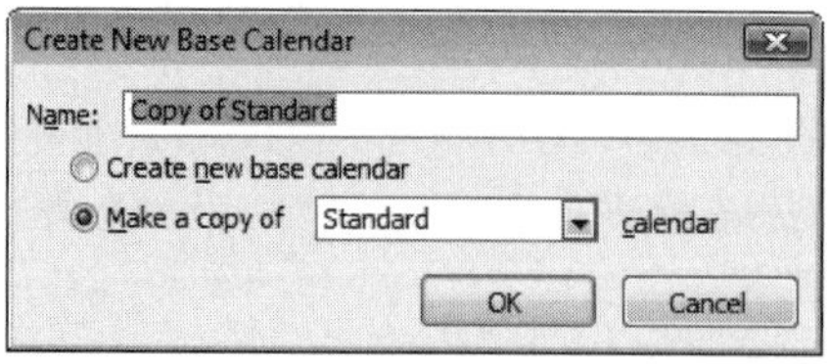

Figure 3-9 You can create a new base calendar from scratch or adapt it from an existing one.

3. In the Name box, type the name you want for the new base calendar, for example, Swing Shift.

4. Select the Create New Base Calendar option if you want to adapt your calendar from the Standard base calendar.

Select the Make A Copy Of option if you want to adapt the new calendar from a different base calendar, such as the Night Shift calendar. Click the name of the existing calendar you want to adapt and click OK.

5. Make the changes you want to the working days and times of individual days or of a particular day of every week, as needed.

6. When finished with your new base calendar, click OK.

Note

You can delete a base calendar you have created, but you cannot do it within the Change Working Time calendar. Instead, you need to use the Organizer. Click Tools, Organizer. Then click the Calendars tab. In the box on the right, you'll see a list of base calendars used by the current project. Select the base calendar you want to delete, click the Delete button, and then click Yes. Click the Close button to dismiss the Organizer dialog box.

For more information about using the Organizer, see Chapter 25.

Project, Resource, and Task Calendars

Microsoft Project uses three types of calendars as tools for scheduling the project, as shown in Table 3-3.

Table 3-3 Calendars in Microsoft Project

Project calendar	Governs when tasks are scheduled to be worked on and when resources are scheduled to work on assigned tasks. See "Setting Your Project Calendar" in this chapter.
Resource calendar	Governs when resources are scheduled to work on assigned tasks. One group of resources (for example, day shift resources) can be assigned to a different base calendar than another group of resources (for example, swing shift resources). Each resource can have his or her own individual resource calendar, which can reflect special work schedules, personal days off, and vacation time. By default, the resource calendar is the Standard calendar. See "Setting Resource Working Time Calendars" in Chapter 6.
Task calendar	Governs when tasks are scheduled to be worked on. As a rule, tasks are scheduled according to the project calendar and the calendars of any assigned resources. However, sometimes a task has special scheduling requirements that are different from the norm. For example, a task might be carried out by a machine running 24 hours a day. In such a case, it's useful for a task to have its own calendar. See "Setting Up the Task Calendar" in Chapter 5.

Attaching Project Documentation

You can make Microsoft Project the central repository for all your important project documentation. For example, you might want to attach or link your scope statement to your project plan, as well as other documents such as the needs analysis, market study, and product specifications.

Showing the Project Summary Task

To attach planning documentation to your project, the first step is to display the project summary task. Not only does the project summary task eventually provide summary date and cost information for the project as a whole, it can serve as the location for your attached or linked planning documents. To display the project summary task, follow these steps:

1. Click Tools, Options and then click the View tab.

2. Under Outline Options, select the Show Project Summary Task check box.

3. Click OK.

A summary task appears in Row 0 of the Gantt Chart (see Figure 3-10), adopting the name of the file as the project summary task name. If you want to change the name, click in the Task Name field for the project summary task. Edit the name in the entry field above the task sheet.

	❶	Task Name	Duration	Start	Finish
0		⊟ WebDev5	74 days	Mon 3/5/07	Thu 6/14/07
1		⊟ Web Structure	18 days	Mon 3/5/07	Wed 3/28/07
2		Brainstorm content categorie	3 days	Mon 3/5/07	Wed 3/7/07
3		Hold user meetings	5 days	Thu 3/8/07	Wed 3/14/07
4		Develop Web structure	3 days	Thu 3/15/07	Mon 3/19/07
5		Web structure review	5 days	Tue 3/20/07	Mon 3/26/07
6		Finalize Web structure	2 days	Tue 3/27/07	Wed 3/28/07
7		⊟ Web Design	37 days	Mon 3/5/07	Tue 4/24/07
8		Design interior pages	7 days	Mon 3/5/07	Tue 3/13/07

Figure 3-10 Use the project summary task to attach or link planning documents.

Copying a Document into Your Project File

You can include planning documents created in other programs within Microsoft Project. Although this can significantly increase your file size, you'll know that all your project information is stored in one place. To include the documents, follow these steps:

Task Information

1. With the project summary task selected, click Task Information on the Standard toolbar and then click the Notes tab. You can also double-click the task to open the Summary Task Information dialog box.

On the Notes tab, click the Insert Object button.

Insert Object

2. In the Insert Object dialog box, select the Create From File option and then click the Browse button.

3. In the Browse dialog box, select the project planning document you want to attach or embed into your project file. Click the Insert button.

4. Back in the Insert Object dialog box again, select the Display As Icon check box (see Figure 3-11).

If the document is small, consider clearing the Display As Icon check box. Clearing this check box embeds the content of the file into your project Notes box, so you can read it directly from there.

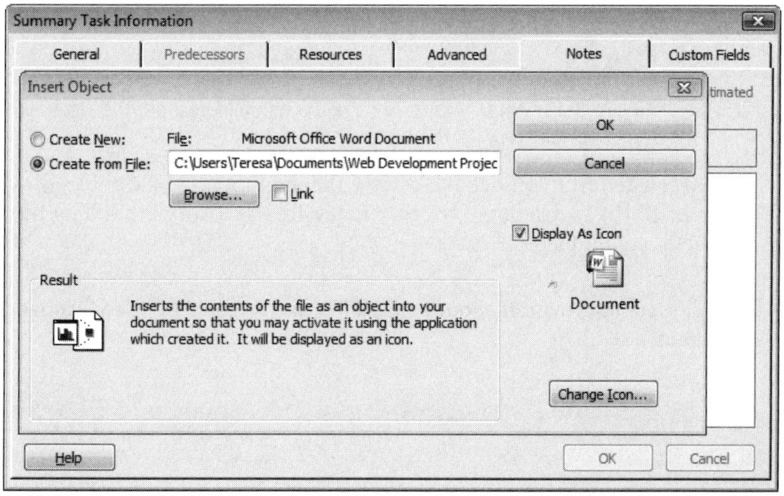

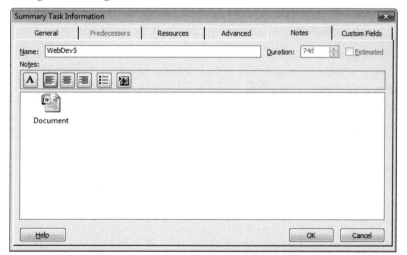

Figure 3-11 The selected document will be embedded in your project plan.

5. Click OK.

The document's icon appears in the Notes area of the Summary Task Information dialog box (see Figure 3-12).

Figure 3-12 Double-clicking the icon opens it in its originating application.

6. In the Summary Task Information dialog box, click OK.

The Notes indicator appears in the Gantt Chart (see Figure 3-13).

	❶	Task Name	Duration
0	📝	⊟ **WebDev5**	**74 days**
1		⊟ **Web Structure**	**18 days**
2		Brainstorm content categorie	3 days
3		Hold user meetings	5 days
4		Develop Web structure	3 days

Figure 3-13 When you store something in a Notes tab, the Notes indicator appears in the corresponding row of the Gantt Chart.

Now, whenever you need to review the document, just double-click the Notes indicator to open the Notes tab of the Summary Task Information dialog box. Then double-click the document icon.

For more information about embedding, see the section titled "Embedding Information" in Chapter 16.

> **Note**
>
> In addition to attaching documents to the project summary task, you can attach documents to summary tasks and individual tasks. This can be useful when you have specifications or drawings that further define the scope of a particular sub-phase or task. You can also attach deliverables or milestone reports on milestone tasks.

Hyperlinking a Document to Your Project File

Hyperlinking is another way to include planning documents with your project file. Hyperlinking is a preferred method when you want to keep your file size trimmer, and you know that your project plan and associated planning documents will always be in the same place. It's also a very efficient method for opening associated documents quickly. To insert a hyperlink, follow these steps:

Insert Hyperlink

1. With the project summary task selected, click Insert Hyperlink on the Standard toolbar.

2. In the Text To Display box, type a descriptive name for the document to which you are linking, for example, Project Scope Statement.

3. Find and select the project planning document you want to link to your project file (see Figure 3-14).

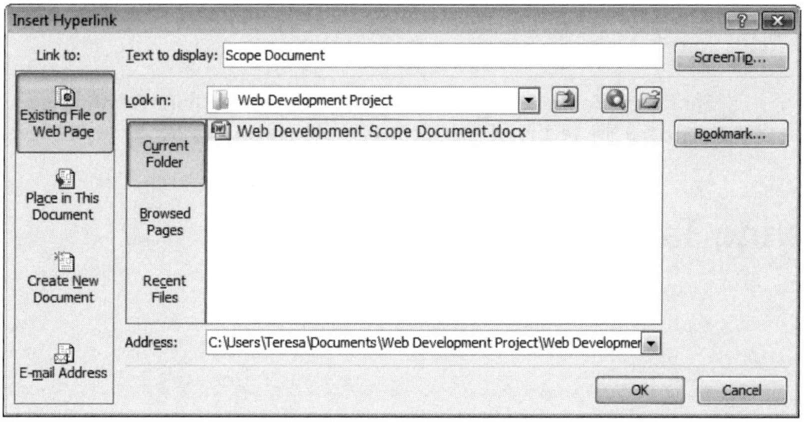

Figure 3-14 The path and name of the selected document appear in the Address box.

4. Click OK.

The Hyperlink indicator appears in the Indicators field of the Gantt Chart (see Figure 3-15).

	ⓘ	Task Name	Duration
0	🔗	⊟ **WebDev5**	**74 days**
1		⊟ **Web Structure**	**18 days**
2		Brainstorm content categorie	3 days
3		Hold user meetings	5 days
4		Develop Web structure	3 days

Figure 3-15 When you hyperlink a document to a task, the Hyperlink indicator appears in the corresponding row of the Gantt Chart.

Now, whenever you need to review the document, just click the Hyperlink indicator. The document opens in its own application window.

> **Note**
>
> In addition to hyperlinking to documents from the project summary task, you can create a hyperlink from summary tasks and individual tasks.

For more information, see the section titled "Hyperlinking to Documents in Other Applications" in Chapter 16.

If you're using Microsoft Office Project Professional with Microsoft Office Project Server for enterprise project management, the preferred method for keeping all project documents together is to use the *document library*. By setting up Microsoft Office Project Web Access with Windows SharePoint Services, you can set up and maintain a document library. This way, all your team members and other stakeholders can view the documents through their Web browsers. They can also check documents in and out, providing vital version control.

For more information about setting up a document library with Windows SharePoint Services, see the section titled "Controlling Project Documents" in Chapter 22.

Entering Tasks

Now that your project file has the foundation it needs, you're ready to get down to the real business of entering tasks.

> **Note**
>
> If you're working with a template or a copy of an existing project plan, you already have tasks in place. In this case, you can skip this section.

When entering tasks and filling in the Gantt Chart, you are essentially entering the elements and the hierarchy reflected in your work breakdown structure (WBS). There are several approaches you can take to develop your work breakdown structure. The following are some examples:

- **Brainstorming** Enter tasks as you think of them, without regard to sequence or grouping of related tasks. You can move and organize the tasks later.

- **Sequential** Think through the project from beginning to end, and enter tasks sequentially.

- **Phases** Think of the overall phases of the project. For example, in a commercial construction project, you might enter the phases of Procurement, On-Site Mobilization, Site Grading, Foundations, Steel Erection, and so on. After those phases are in place, you can add tasks and subtasks beneath them.

- **Milestones and deliverables** Consider what the project is producing in terms of the milestones and deliverables. Enter those events as tasks and then add tasks and subtasks beneath them to flesh out the project. Your scope statement can be a valuable guide in this process.

- **Team collaboration** Ask team members to list the tasks they believe will be necessary to the areas under their responsibility. This assumes, of course, that you already have team members in place and available. Team members can do this informally, for example, through e-mail. Or, team members can submit tasks and their estimated durations in a Microsoft Office Excel 2007 spreadsheet, which you can then import into Microsoft Project. If you're using Project Server, team members can send you tasks from Project Web Access and then you can incorporate them automatically into your project plan.

For more information about using tasks entered in an Office Excel 2007 spreadsheet, see the section titled "Importing Tasks from an Excel Worksheet" later in this chapter. For more information about creating new tasks through automated team collaboration, see the section titled "Assigning Tasks to Enterprise Resources" in Chapter 22.

- **Archived projects**   Review completed projects of a similar type done in your organization. With such historical information, you might find that much of the "legwork"—in terms of phases, task sequencing, resource assignments, and more—has been done for you. If the archived projects contain solid tracking information, you'll have excellent data on durations and costs.

For more information about using an old project as a starting point for a new one, see the section titled "Starting a New Project Using a Template" in Chapter 28. For more information about saving a completed project for future reference, see the section titled "Closing a Project" in Chapter 28.

- **Expert consultation**   Ask known experts what tasks are needed for various aspects of the project. This is particularly useful if you're the manager of a project in which you're not necessarily an expert. This happens frequently enough, and it's not necessarily a bad thing, but you will need dependable experts to help provide reliable task information. Even if you're well-versed in the project knowledge area, you might not know all the nitty-gritty details for each phase. Experts can come from within your own group, from stakeholders, from other groups or project managers within your organization, or from colleagues in your profession or industry.

Chapter 3

Project Management Practices: Activity Definition

The stage of the project management process in which you're entering tasks is often referred to as *activity definition*. Here, the planning team identifies the specific activities, or tasks, that must be done to produce the project deliverables and meet the project objectives as specified in the scope statement.

Activity definition is typically done with the guidance provided in the scope statement and the work breakdown structure. The deliverables, or work packages, described in the WBS are divided and subdivided into smaller tasks that can be better managed and controlled in the project.

For more information about work breakdown structures in Microsoft Project, see the section titled "Setting Up Your Work Breakdown Structure" later in this chapter.

In some organizations, the project management methodology dictates that the WBS is developed first and the task list is developed next. Other organizations develop both at the same time.

In any case, the task list must include all activities that will be performed in the project, but it does not include any activities that are not required as part of the project scope. Each task should be descriptive enough to communicate to responsible team members what is required by the task.

Adding Tasks to Your Project Plan

To enter tasks directly into your project plan, follow these steps:

1. Make sure you're working in the Gantt Chart.

You can see the name of the current view in the Active View bar that runs vertically along the left side of the view. If it doesn't say **Gantt Chart**, click View, Gantt Chart.

> You can enter tasks in any task view, of course. For more information about views, see Chapter 4, "Viewing Project Information."

2. Type the name of the task in the Task Name field.

3. Press Enter or the Down Arrow key to move to the next row.

The task name isn't recorded, and other commands remain unavailable until you press Enter.

4. To edit a task that's already entered, click the task name and then make your changes in the entry box just above the task sheet.

You can also click in the selected task name until the cursor appears and edit it directly in the Task Name field. You might have to click the task name twice to get the cursor to appear. However, do it slowly enough so that it's not interpreted as a double-click, or a dialog box will appear.

> For more information about entering durations, links, and start and finish dates, see Chapter 5, "Scheduling Tasks."

Tips for Entering Tasks

Keep the following suggestions in mind while entering tasks:

- Don't be overly concerned about sequence when first entering tasks. You can worry about that after you have a "first draft" of tasks in place.

- Enter duration estimates either at the same time you enter your new tasks or later. The default duration estimate is 1 day, and estimates are formatted with a question mark to remind you that they are not confirmed yet.

- Don't enter a start or finish date in the Start or Finish fields in the Gantt Chart, although it might be tempting to do so. In most cases, you'll want Microsoft Project to calculate those dates for you, based on other task information you'll be entering.

- Name the task with sufficient description to communicate to team members and stakeholders what the task is about. A task called simply "Review" or "Edit" might not provide enough information.

- Decide whether you want the context of the task to be understood if it's ever separated (by being in a separate view, report, filter, or grouping, for example) from its surrounding tasks. For example, you might have several tasks in different phases for "Administer contracts." But one task might relate to procurement, one to the architects, and another one to the builders.

- Note whether you have sets of tasks that are repeated in different phases of the project. You might want to give them more general names so you can copy and paste these sets of tasks under their respective phases, instead of repeatedly typing them individually.

INSIDE OUT   Don't fill in the Start and Finish fields

By default, the Gantt Chart table includes the Task Name, Duration, Start, Finish, Predecessors, and Resource Names fields as columns. A natural impulse when entering tasks is to enter project information into each of these fields. However, you can get yourself into some trouble if you enter dates in the Start and Finish fields. Not only would you be struggling to calculate start and finish dates for each task while Microsoft Project could more easily do it for you, but you'd be putting undue restrictions on your schedule and possibly creating scheduling conflicts.

The best approach is to enter the task names first and then the durations if you know them. Leave the Start and Finish fields as they are for now and let Microsoft Project calculate them for you as you add other project information. The Predecessors field is filled in for you when you start creating links between tasks. At that point, with durations and links in place, Microsoft Project calculates the Start and Finish dates. If you then need to constrain the dates, you can edit them as you need.

Importing Tasks from an Excel Worksheet

Many project managers find that they can more quickly build an accurate task list for their project plan by having others on the team develop a task list of their specific areas of responsibility. Even if a team isn't in place yet, you can still ask the advice of those with the necessary expertise. If these individuals are not Microsoft Project users, a great way to automate this process is to have them use Excel to create their task lists. You can then import the worksheets into the Microsoft Project Gantt Chart.

The standard Excel importing process involves mapping the Excel columns to the corresponding Microsoft Project columns to ensure that the right information ends up in the right places in your Gantt Chart task table. Microsoft Project comes with an Excel Task List template set up for this very purpose.

To use Excel and the Excel Task List template on the same computer on which Microsoft Project is installed, follow these steps:

The Microsoft
Office Button

1. Start Microsoft Office Excel 2007. Click the Microsoft Office Button and then click New.

2. In the New Workbook dialog box, under Templates, click Installed Templates.

3. Click the Microsoft Project Task List Import Template.

4. Click the Create button.

   The template creates a new file with columns that correspond to the default Gantt Chart in Microsoft Project (see Figure 3-16).

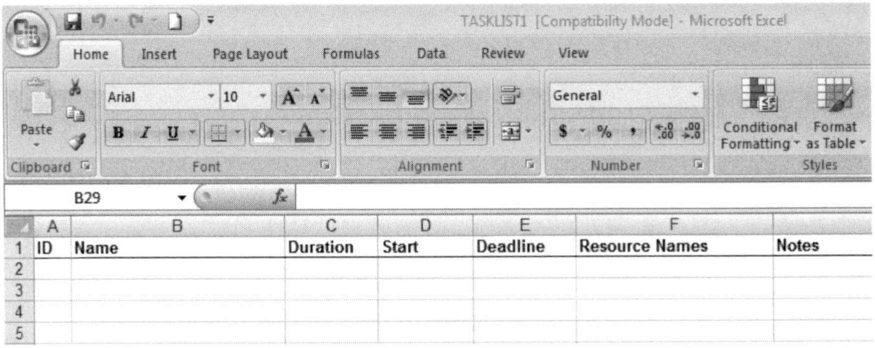

	A	B	C	D	E	F	
1	ID	Name	Duration	Start	Deadline	Resource Names	Notes
2							
3							
4							
5							

Figure 3-16 Share the Excel Task List template with your team to help build your project plan.

5. Save this file and provide it to your team members to use to enter tasks and other task information. Have them save the information and return the file to you when they're finished.

> **Note**
>
> If you're working with a version of Microsoft Office Excel 2003 or earlier, you can still use the Microsoft Project Task List Import template. Open Microsoft Office Excel 2003 and then click File, New. In the task pane, click the On My Computer link. Click the Spreadsheet Solutions tab. Double-click the Microsoft Project Task List Import Template.

When you're ready to import the task list into your project plan, follow these steps:

1. Open the project plan into which you want to import the Excel task list.

2. On the Standard toolbar, click Open.

3. Browse to the location on your computer or network where the Excel task list is saved.

4. In the Files Of Type list, click Microsoft Excel Workbooks (*.xls).

   The task list appears in the list of folders and files.

Chapter 3

5. Click the task list workbook and then click Open.

   The Import Wizard appears.

6. Click Next.

7. Click Project Excel Template and then click Next.

8. Specify whether you want to import the file as a new project, append the tasks to the currently active project, or merge the data into the active project.

9. Click Finish.

   The tasks are imported into Microsoft Project as you specified.

10. If you want to provide this template to others on your team, by default, it's located in the C:\Program Files\Microsoft Office\Templates\1033 folder, and it's named TASKLIST.XLT.

    Those who want to use this template should copy this file to the same location on their computers.

    > For more information about using Microsoft Project with other applications, see the section titled "Importing and Exporting Information" in Chapter 16, and Chapter 17, "Integrating Microsoft Project with Microsoft Excel."

Entering Recurring Tasks

You might have certain tasks that need to be scheduled at regularly occurring intervals. For example, suppose that you have a project team meeting every Thursday morning. Or perhaps you gather information and generate a resource management report the first Monday of each month. Instead of entering the same task every week or every month throughout the span of the project, you can create a *recurring task*. To do this, follow these steps:

1. Make sure that you're working in the Gantt Chart.

   If necessary, click View, Gantt Chart.

2. In the Task Name field, click in the row above which you want the recurring task to appear.

3. Click Insert, Recurring Task.

4. In the Recurring Task dialog box, type the name of the recurring task in the Task Name field, for example, Generate resource management report (see Figure 3-17).

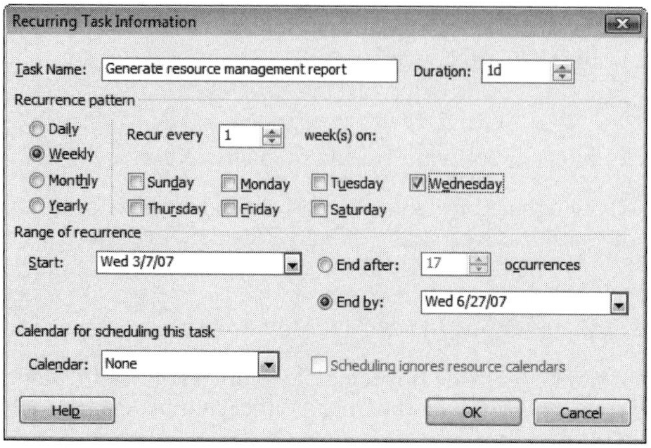

Recurring Task Information

Task Name: Generate resource management report   Duration: 1d

Recurrence pattern

- ○ Daily
- ● Weekly
- ○ Monthly
- ○ Yearly

Recur every 1 week(s) on:

☐ Sunday ☐ Monday ☐ Tuesday ☑ Wednesday
☐ Thursday ☐ Friday ☐ Saturday

Range of recurrence

Start: Wed 3/7/07   ○ End after: 17 occurrences
                     ● End by: Wed 6/27/07

Calendar for scheduling this task

Calendar: None   ☐ Scheduling ignores resource calendars

Help   OK   Cancel

Figure 3-17 Specify the name and scheduling details of your recurring task.

5.   Under Recurrence Pattern, specify how often the task is to be scheduled; that is, daily, weekly, or monthly.

6.   Specify the details of when the task is to take place during that frequency, for example, every other Thursday or the first Monday of every month.

7.   Under Range Of Recurrence, specify when the recurring task is to start and end.

8.   If this recurring task is to be scheduled according to a base calendar that's different than the project calendar, in the Calendar box, select the name of the base calendar to be used.

9.   When finished, click OK.

     The recurring task is marked with a recurring task indicator. It's represented with a summary task with all occurrences of the task as subtasks. Click the + icon next to the recurring summary task to see each occurrence of the recurring task.

Recurring indicator

Note
Review the recurrence range by resting your pointer over the recurring task indicator. Double-click the recurring task to open the Recurring Task Information dialog box.

TROUBLESHOOTING

You enter project information in Gantt Chart view and your menus and toolbars have all turned gray

When you're in the middle of entering a task or any other task information in a Gantt Chart, the menus and toolbars become temporarily unavailable and are therefore dimmed.

Finish entering the task by pressing Enter. If you want to do something to that task, click it to select it again and then choose the command or button you want.

Sequencing and Organizing Tasks

With the Gantt Chart in your project file now full of tasks, it's time to put these tasks in a logical order. It's also time to add any forgotten tasks or delete duplicated ones.

Moving Tasks

To move a task from one row to another, follow these steps:

1. In the table portion of the Gantt Chart, select the entire task row by clicking the gray row heading, which includes the task number.

2. With your mouse pointer still over the row heading (the pointer should appear as a black crosshair), drag the task to the location in the Gantt Chart where you want to place it.

   A gray line along the row border follows your mouse movements, indicating where the task will be inserted when you release the mouse button.

3. Release the mouse button to insert the task in the new location.

> **Note**
> Dragging tasks is the best method for reordering tasks in your project plan. If you use the Cut and Paste commands, the Task Unique ID field for the tasks is renumbered. This can cause problems if you integrate the project with other applications, including third-party timesheet systems.

Inserting Additional Tasks

To add a new task to other existing tasks, follow these steps:

1. In the table portion of the Gantt Chart, click anywhere in the row above which you want the new task to be inserted.

2. Click Insert, New Task. (You can also simply press the Insert key.)

3. Click in the Name field for the new row, type the name of the new task, and then press Enter.

Chapter 3

Copying Tasks

You can copy one or more tasks to use as the basis for other tasks. The following list describes the various copy techniques:

Copy Cell

- **Copy a single task name** Click in the Task Name field and then click Copy Cell on the Standard toolbar. Click the Task Name field in a blank row and then click Paste on the Standard toolbar.

Paste

- **Copy multiple adjacent task names** Click the first task name you want to select, hold down the Shift key, and then click the last task name. All task names between the first and last are selected. Click Copy Cell. Click the first Task Name field where you want the selected tasks to be pasted and then click Paste. You can also simply drag to select the tasks. If you want to copy the selected tasks to empty rows directly under a particular task, drag the fill handle in the lower-right corner of the cell into those empty rows (see Figure 3-18).

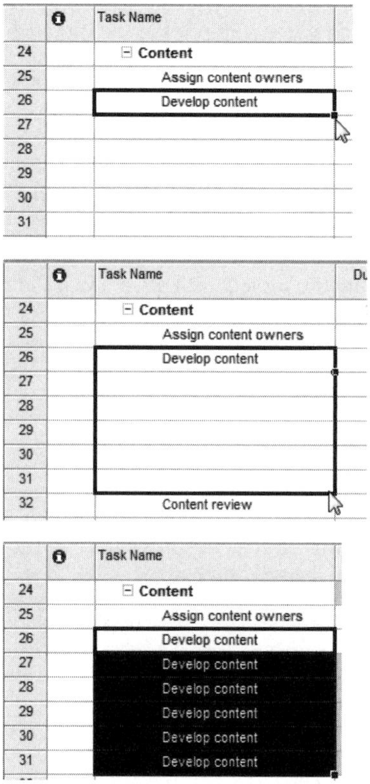

Figure 3-18 Copy tasks using the fill handle.

- **Copy multiple nonadjacent task names** Click the first task name you want to select, hold down the Ctrl key, and then click any additional task names you want to add to the selection (see Figure 3-19). Click Copy Cell. Select the Task Name field where you want the selected tasks to start to be added and then click the Paste button. The tasks are added in the order that you selected them.

	❶	Task Name	Duration
16		⊟ **Hardware and Software**	**56 days**
17		Perform system needs analysis	10 days
18		Evaluate equipment requirements	15 days
19		Evaluate software requirements	15 days
20		Order equipment	3 days
21		Order software	3 days
22		Install and configure equipment	5 days
23		Install and configure software	5 days

Figure 3-19 Copy multiple task names at once to save yourself some keyboard entry.

- **Copy a single task and its task information** Click the row heading of the task you want to copy, which selects the entire task and its associated information. Click Copy Task. To add the task into an empty row, select the row and then click Paste. To insert the task between two existing tasks, select the lower task and then click Paste. The copied task is pasted into a new row inserted above the selected task.

- **Copy multiple adjacent tasks and their task information** Click the row heading of the first task you want to copy. Hold down the Shift key and then click the row heading of the last task (see Figure 3-20). Click Copy Task. Select the task above which you want the copied tasks to start to be added and then click Paste.

	❶	Task Name	Duration
1		⊟ **Web Structure**	**18 days**
2		Brainstorm content categories	3 days
3		Hold user meetings	5 days
4		Develop Web structure	3 days
5		Web structure review	5 days
6		Finalize Web structure	2 days

Figure 3-20 Copy multiple tasks along with all their associated information.

- **Copy multiple nonadjacent tasks and their task information** Click the row heading of the first task you want to copy. Hold down the Ctrl key and then click the row headings of all the tasks you want to copy. Click Copy Task. Select the task above which you want the copied tasks to be added. Click Paste. The tasks are added in the order that you selected them.

Deleting Tasks

To delete a task you don't need, select the row heading and then press the Delete key.

When you click a task name (rather than the row heading) and then press the Delete key, the Delete indicator appears in the Indicators column. Choose whether to delete the entire task or just the task name (see Figure 3-21).

Chapter 3

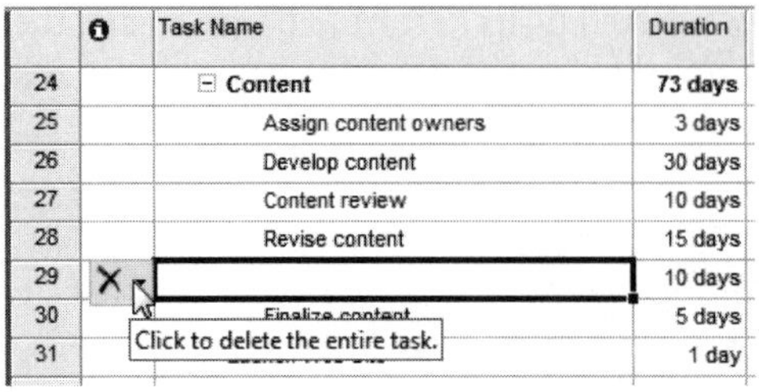

	❶	Task Name	Duration
24		⊟ **Content**	**73 days**
25		Assign content owners	3 days
26		Develop content	30 days
27		Content review	10 days
28		Revise content	15 days
29	✗		10 days
30		Finalize content	5 days
31			1 day

Click to delete the entire task.

Figure 3-21 Click the down arrow next to the Delete indicator to choose what you want to delete.

If you want to delete the entire task, click the indicator. If you simply want to clear the task name, press Enter or click elsewhere in the view.

Undoing Multiple Edits

With previous versions of Microsoft Project, you can undo only the last edit. New in Microsoft Office Project 2007 is the ability to undo multiple edits. To undo recent edits, press the Undo button on the Standard toolbar. Each time you press the Undo button, the previous edit is undone in the reverse order it was done.

Other ways to work with the Undo command are as follows:

- You can click Edit, Undo or press Ctrl+Z to reverse the last edit.

Undo

- To undo a series of edits all at once, click the arrow next to the Undo button on the Standard toolbar. Select the point to which you want to undo. All edits between the current state and the selected edit are undone.

- To redo an edit that you've undone, press the Redo button on the Standard toolbar.

- You can also click Edit, Redo or press Ctrl+Y to redo undone edits.

Redo

- To redo a series of undone edits all at once, click the arrow next to the Redo button on the Standard toolbar. Select the point to which you want to redo the edits. All edits between the current state and the selected edit are redone.

  You can redo only edits that you have previously undone. The Redo command does not repeat commands or edits.

- You can set the maximum number of undo operations. Click Tools, Options and then click the General tab. Under General Options For Microsoft Office Project, enter the maximum number of undo operations you want in the Undo Levels box. The default is 20 and the maximum is 99.

Organizing Tasks into an Outline

Now that your task list is sequenced to your satisfaction, you're ready to organize the tasks into a structure representing the hierarchy of tasks from the broader perspective to the deep and detailed perspective where the real work actually takes place.

A task at a higher outline level than other tasks is called a summary task; the tasks beneath that summary task are called subtasks (see Figure 3-22). Summary tasks typically represent phases in a project. For example, in a new business startup project, you might have summary tasks for developing the strategic plan, defining the business opportunity, planning for action, and proceeding with the startup plan.

Summary tasks

	ⓘ	Task Name	Duration	Start	Finish
0		⊟ WebDev5	74 days?	Mon 3/5/07	Thu 6/14/07
1		⊟ Web Structure	18 days	Mon 3/5/07	Wed 3/28/07
2		Brainstorm content categories	3 days	Mon 3/5/07	Wed 3/7/07
3		Hold user meetings	5 days	Thu 3/8/07	Wed 3/14/07
4		Develop Web structure	3 days	Thu 3/15/07	Mon 3/19/07
5		Web structure review	5 days	Tue 3/20/07	Mon 3/26/07
6		Finalize Web structure	2 days	Tue 3/27/07	Wed 3/28/07
7		⊟ Web Design	33 days?	Mon 3/5/07	Wed 4/18/07
8		⊟ Interior Pages	25 days?	Mon 3/5/07	Fri 4/6/07
9		Design interior pages	7 days	Mon 3/5/07	Tue 3/13/07
10		Interior page design review	5 days	Wed 3/14/07	Tue 3/20/07
11		Finalize interior page design	4 days	Wed 3/21/07	Mon 3/26/07
12		Develop style sheets	4 days	Tue 3/27/07	Fri 3/30/07
13		Develop page templates	5 days	Mon 4/2/07	Fri 4/6/07
14		Home Page	1 day?	Mon 3/5/07	Mon 3/5/07
15		⊟ Design Home page	8 days	Mon 4/9/07	Wed 4/18/07
16		Home page design review	5 days	Mon 4/9/07	Fri 4/13/07
17		Finalize Home page design	3 days	Mon 4/16/07	Wed 4/18/07
18		⊟ Hardware and Software	56 days	Mon 3/5/07	Mon 5/21/07
19		Perform system needs analysis	10 days	Mon 3/5/07	Fri 3/16/07
20		Evaluate equipment requirements	15 days	Mon 3/19/07	Fri 4/6/07

Subtasks

Figure 3-22 Use summary tasks and subtasks to combine related tasks into manageable chunks.

The subtasks under those phases can be actual tasks that are assigned to resources. Or they could be another set of summary tasks. For example, the "Define the business opportunity" summary task could have subtasks such as "Define the market," "Identify needed materials and supplies," and "Evaluate potential risks and rewards." These subtasks in turn can be summary tasks to still more subtasks.

> **Note**
>
> In previous versions of Microsoft Project, you could create up to nine outline levels. Microsoft Office Project 2007 has no such limit.

Chapter 3

Many project managers use the outline levels to correspond to their WBS, in which the lowest-level subtask corresponds to the work package.

For more information about WBSs in Microsoft Project, see the section titled "Setting Up Your Work Breakdown Structure" later in this chapter.

As you create the outline structure in your task list, you might find that you need to refine the task list even more by inserting, moving, and deleting tasks.

All your tasks are initially at the first outline level. To make a summary task, you need to indent subtasks beneath it. The following list describes various outlining techniques:

Indent

- **Make a task a subtask** Click the task. On the Formatting toolbar, click Indent. The task is indented, and the task above it becomes its summary task. Summary tasks are highlighted in bold in the table portion of the Gantt Chart and are marked with a black bar spanning the summary tasks in the chart portion of the Gantt Chart.

- **Create a subtask under a subtask** Click a task under a subtask. Click Indent twice. It's now in the third outline level, as a subtask of a subtask.

Outdent

- **Move a subtask to a higher level** Click a subtask and then click Outdent.

- **Indent several tasks at one time** Drag the mouse pointer across several adjacent tasks to select them and then click Indent. Use the Ctrl key to select several non-adjacent tasks at once and then click Indent. This method also works for tasks that will become subtasks to different summary tasks.

Show

- **Show the tasks at a specified outline level** If you want only tasks at the first and second outline levels to be visible throughout your entire project plan, for example, on the Formatting toolbar, click Show and then click Outline Level 2. You can select any outline level you want. You can also click All Subtasks to see all outline levels.

Show Subtasks

Hide Subtasks

- **Hide or show the subtasks for a selected summary task** Next to each summary task is a plus or minus sign. The plus sign indicates that there are hidden subtasks for this summary task. Click the plus sign, and the subtasks appear. The minus sign indicates that the subtasks are currently displayed. Click the minus sign, and the subtasks will be hidden. You can also use Show Subtasks and Hide Subtasks on the Formatting toolbar to do the same thing.

Summary tasks show rolled-up task information that is an aggregate of the information in the associated subtasks. For example, if there are four subtasks, each with a duration of two days, the summary task shows the total of eight days. You can also see rolled-up summary information for costs, start dates, finish dates, and more.

You can also display a summary task for the project as a whole. The project summary task shows rolled-up summary information for the project as a whole; for example, total costs, total duration, project start, and project finish. To show the project summary task, follow these steps:

1. Click Tools, Options.

2. On the View tab, under Outline Options, select the Show Project Summary Task check box.

The project summary task name is adopted from the project file name. You can change this summary task name if you want.

Setting Up Your Work Breakdown Structure

As mentioned earlier in this chapter, many project managers and organizations use a WBS as an essential element of their project management methodology. Similar to the outline structure of your project task list, the WBS is a hierarchical chart view of deliverables in a project in which each level down represents an increasingly detailed description of the project deliverables.

WBS levels can be associated with a particular code set, such as 2.1.3.a. Levels in the hierarchy represent summary tasks, subtasks, work packages, and deliverables. You can define a project's scope and develop its task lists with the WBS.

Industries, application areas, and organizations experienced with a particular type of project tend to have WBSs developed to represent the life cycles of their typical types of projects, for example, the design of a new vehicle or the construction of an office building.

Understanding Work Breakdown Structure Codes

Each item and level in a work breakdown structure is described by a unique WBS code. Each digit in the code typically represents a level in the structure's hierarchy, such as 2.1.4.3 or 5.B.c.3. A WBS code such as 1.2.3 might represent the third deliverable for the second activity in the first phase of the project.

> **Note**
>
> In some industries or application areas, the work breakdown structure is also known as the *project breakdown structure*, or *PBS*.

Chapter 3

In Microsoft Project, any outline structure you set up for your tasks is assigned a set of unique outline numbers. The outline number for the first summary task is 1; the outline number for the first subtask under the first summary task is 1.1 (see Figure 3-23).

	❶	Outline Number	WBS	Task Name	Duration
1		**1**	**1**	**⊟ Web Structure**	**18 days**
2		1.1	1.1	Brainstorm content categories	3 days
3		1.2	1.2	Hold user meetings	5 days
4		1.3	1.3	Develop Web structure	3 days
5		1.4	1.4	Web structure review	5 days
6		1.5	1.5	Finalize Web structure	2 days
7		**2**	**2**	**⊟ Web Design**	**33 days?**
8		**2.1**	**2.1**	**⊟ Interior Pages**	**25 days?**
9		2.1.1	2.1.1	Design interior pages	7 days
10		2.1.2	2.1.2	Interior page design review	5 days
11		2.1.3	2.1.3	Finalize interior page design	4 days
12		2.1.4	2.1.4	Develop style sheets	4 days
13		2.1.5	2.1.5	Develop page templates	5 days
14		2.1.6	2.1.6	Home Page	1 day?
15		**2.2**	**2.2**	**⊟ Design Home page**	**8 days**
16		2.2.1	2.2.1	Home page design review	5 days
17		2.2.2	2.2.2	Finalize Home page design	3 days
18		**3**	**3**	**⊟ Hardware and Software**	**56 days**
19		3.1	3.1	Perform system needs analysis	10 days
20		3.2	3.2	Evaluate equipment requirements	15 days

Figure 3-23 The outline number specifies the task's position in your project plan's task outline hierarchy.

By default, Microsoft Project creates WBS codes that are derived from these outline numbers, and you can't change the code scheme of the outline numbers. However, if you and your organization have a specific WBS coding scheme, you can change the WBS numbering. When working with WBS codes, keep the following in mind:

- You can have only one set of WBS codes. However, if you use additional coding schemes, you can create up to ten sets of outline codes and then sort or group your tasks by those codes.

> **Note**
>
> Certain project management methodologies use other structured and hierarchical codes that can describe your project from different viewpoints. Examples include the *organizational breakdown structure (OBS)*, the *resource breakdown structure (RBS)*, and the *bill of materials (BOM)*.
>
> For more information about outline codes, see the section titled "Working with Outline Codes" in Chapter 25.

- You can include ordered numbers, uppercase letters, and lowercase letters as part of your custom WBS code format. You can also include unordered characters in the code format.

- You can automatically generate your custom WBS codes for tasks as you add them.

Setting Up Work Breakdown Structure Codes

To set up your custom WBS code scheme, including any prefix and *code mask*, follow these steps:

1. Click Project, WBS, Define Code.

2. If you use a prefix for the project in front of the WBS code to distinguish it from other projects using the same code format, enter that prefix in the Project Code Prefix box.

3. In the Sequence field in the first row, select whether the first digit of the code (representing the first level of the hierarchy) is an ordered number, ordered uppercase letter, ordered lowercase letter, or unordered character.

4. In the Length field in the first row, specify whether there is a length limit for the first code.

5. In the Separator field in the first row, specify the character that separates the first and second code.

6. Repeat the procedure in the Sequence field in the second row.

   Continue these steps until all the levels of your custom WBS code are set up (see Figure 3-24). As you enter the code mask for each succeeding level, the Code Preview box shows an example of the code.

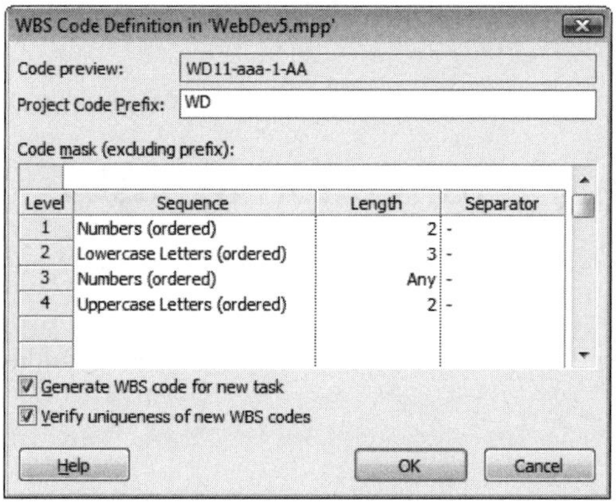

Figure 3-24 Define your organization's WBS code format.

7. When finished, click OK. The WBS codes for your tasks are reset to conform to your custom structure (see Figure 3-25).

	❶	Outline Number	WBS	Task Name	Duration
1		1	WD01	⊟ Web Structure	18 days
2		1.1	WD01-aaa	Brainstorm content categories	3 days
3		1.2	WD01-aab	Hold user meetings	5 days
4		1.3	WD01-aac	Develop Web structure	3 days
5		1.4	WD01-aad	Web structure review	5 days
6		1.5	WD01-aae	Finalize Web structure	2 days
7		2	WD02	⊟ Web Design	33 days
8		2.1	WD02-aaa	⊟ Interior Pages	25 days
9		2.1.1	WD02-aaa-1	Design interior pages	7 days
10		2.1.2	WD02-aaa-2	Interior page design review	5 days
11		2.1.3	WD02-aaa-3	Finalize interior page design	4 days
12		2.1.4	WD02-aaa-4	Develop style sheets	4 days
13		2.1.5	WD02-aaa-5	Develop page templates	5 days
14		2.2	WD02-aab	⊟ Design Home page	8 days
15		2.2.1	WD02-aab-1	Home page design review	5 days
16		2.2.2	WD02-aab-2	Finalize Home page design	3 days
17		3	WD03	⊟ Hardware and Software	56 days
18		3.1	WD03-aaa	Perform system needs analysis	10 days
19		3.2	WD03-aab	Evaluate equipment requirements	15 days

Figure 3-25 Your newly defined WBS codes replace the default WBS codes derived from the outline numbers.

> **Note**
>
> In Microsoft Project 2003, the Visio WBS Chart Wizard was available to display project information in a Visio WBS chart. In Microsoft Office Project 2007, this feature has been replaced by the visual reports created in Microsoft Office Visio.
>
> For more information about creating a visual report in Visio, see the section titled "Creating a Visual Report" in Chapter 12.

Adding Supplementary Information to Tasks

You can annotate an individual task by entering notes. To add a note to a task, do the following:

1. Click the task and then click Task Information on the Standard toolbar.

2. Click the Notes tab.

3. In the Notes area, type the note.

4. When finished, click OK.

You can insert an entire document as a note associated with an individual task. For more information, see the section titled "Copying a Document into Your Project File" earlier in this chapter.

If you want to change an existing note, double-click the note icon. Make the change you want. If you want to remove the note altogether, first select all contents in the Notes box by dragging across the content or by clicking in the Notes box and pressing Ctrl+A. Press the Delete key, and then click OK. The note is gone, along with the Note icon in the task's indicator field.

> **Note**
>
> You can also hyperlink from a task to a document on your computer or on a Web site. For more information, see the section titled "Hyperlinking a Document to Your Project File" earlier in this chapter.

Chapter 3

Viewing Project Information

Understanding Project Information Categories **106**

Accessing Your Project Information **107**

Rearranging Your Project Information **138**

Arranging Your Microsoft Project Window **147**

Navigating to a Specific Location in a View **152**

To plan, track, and manage your project with Microsoft Office Project 2007, you enter a variety of detailed information regarding tasks, resources, assignments, durations, resource rates, and more. Office Project 2007, in turn, calculates certain entries to create even more information, including start dates, finish dates, costs, and remaining work. In Microsoft Project, more than 400 distinct pieces of information, including your own custom information, are available for tasks, resources, and assignments. The more tasks, resources, and assignments you have in your project, and the more custom capabilities you use, the more these pieces of information are multiplied.

There's no way you could look at this mass of project information at one time and work with it in any kind of meaningful or efficient way. To solve this problem, Microsoft Project organizes and stores the information in a *database*. All information associated with an individual task, for example, is a single *record* in that database. Each piece of information in that record is a separate *field* (see Figure 4-1).

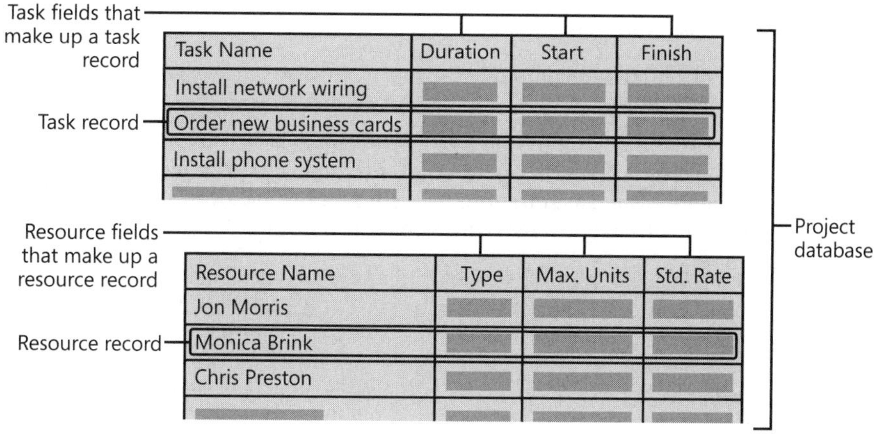

Figure 4-1 Each task represents a single record in your project database, with all associated information represented by individual fields.

> **Note**
>
> The project database is distinct from the SQL Server database that Microsoft Project uses to store data. In the SQL Server database, information about one task can actually be spread across multiple tables in multiple records.

When you need to look at or work with a particular set of information, you choose a particular *view* to be displayed in the Microsoft Project workspace. A view filters the project information in a specific way according to the purpose of the view and then presents that layout of information in the Microsoft Project workspace so you can easily work with it. More than 25 different views are built into Microsoft Project.

You can rearrange the project information presented in a view. You can sort information in many views by name, date, and so on. You can group information, for example, by complete versus incomplete tasks. You can filter information to see only the information you want, for example, only tasks that are assigned to a particular resource. These concepts and techniques are all presented in this chapter.

Understanding Project Information Categories

The means for organizing, managing, and storing the thousands of pieces of project information is the Microsoft Project database. There are three major categories in the project database:

- Task information
- Resource information
- Assignment information

When you start entering project information, typically you enter tasks and associated information such as duration, date constraints, deadlines, and task dependencies. These all fall under the task information category.

Then you enter resource names and associated information such as standard rate, overtime rate, and working times calendar. These all fall under the resource information category.

As soon as you assign a resource to a task, this creates a new entity—the assignment, which is the intersection of task and resource. Information associated with an assignment includes the amount of work, the assignment start and finish dates, the cost for the assignment, and so on. These fall under the assignment information category.

> **Note**
>
> There are also three subcategories of project information: task-timephased, resource-timephased, and assignment-timephased. These subcategories are covered in the section titled "Working with Usage Views" later in this chapter.

Understanding these three categories is important when viewing project information. There are task views and resource views. The individual fields that make up all views are also classified as task, resource, or assignment fields, and can only be seen in their respective views. Likewise, there are filters and groups designed just for task views and other filters and groups designed just for resource views.

Accessing Your Project Information

You view and work with information in Microsoft Project by selecting a specific view to be displayed in your Microsoft Project workspace. Of the many views built into Microsoft Project, some have to do with tasks, others with resources, and still others with assignments. Certain views are a spreadsheet of tables and columns. Others are graphs or forms. Other views are a blend, for example, the Gantt Chart includes both a sheet and a graph.

You can switch tables in a view, and add and remove fields shown in a view, and so modify these views to present your project information exactly the way you need.

Using Views

When you first start using Microsoft Project, typically the first view you use is the Gantt Chart, which is the default view. Here, you enter information such as tasks, durations, and task relationships. Then you might use the Resource Sheet, in which you enter resource information. As you continue to plan your project, your requirements become more sophisticated, and you find you need other views. For example, you might want to see all your tasks with their current percent complete, along with the critical path. Or you might need a graph showing a particular resource's workload throughout April and May.

> **Note**
>
> To change the view that opens when you first open Microsoft Project and create a new project file, click Tools, Options and then click the View tab. In the Default View box, click the view you want to appear by default whenever you create a new project file.
>
> This setting changes the view only for any new project files. For an existing project file, the last view shown when you saved and closed the file is the one that appears when you open it again.

Chapter 4

> **For more information about other view options, see the section titled "Arranging Your Microsoft Project Window" later in this chapter.**

The most commonly used views are available on the View menu. All views are available on the More Views submenu. To switch to a different view, do the following:

1. Click View and then look for the view you want.

2. If the view you want is listed, click its name. If the view is not listed, click More Views. The full list of available Microsoft Project views appears (see Figure 4-2).

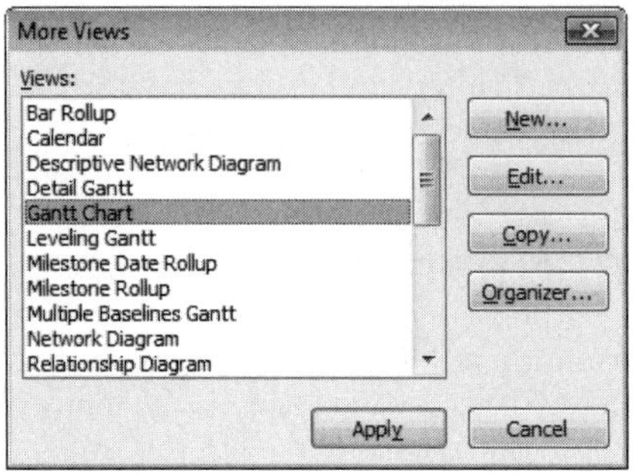

Figure 4-2 The More Views dialog box lists all available views in alphabetical order.

3. Double-click the view you want. It appears in your Microsoft Project workspace, replacing the previous view.

Keep in mind that when you switch from one view to another, you're not changing the data; you're just getting a different look at the data in your project database.

If you display the View bar, you can use it to quickly switch views. To show the View bar, do the following:

1. Click View, View Bar.

    The View bar appears on the far left edge of the Microsoft Project window (see Figure 4-3). The same views that appear on the View menu are listed on the View bar.

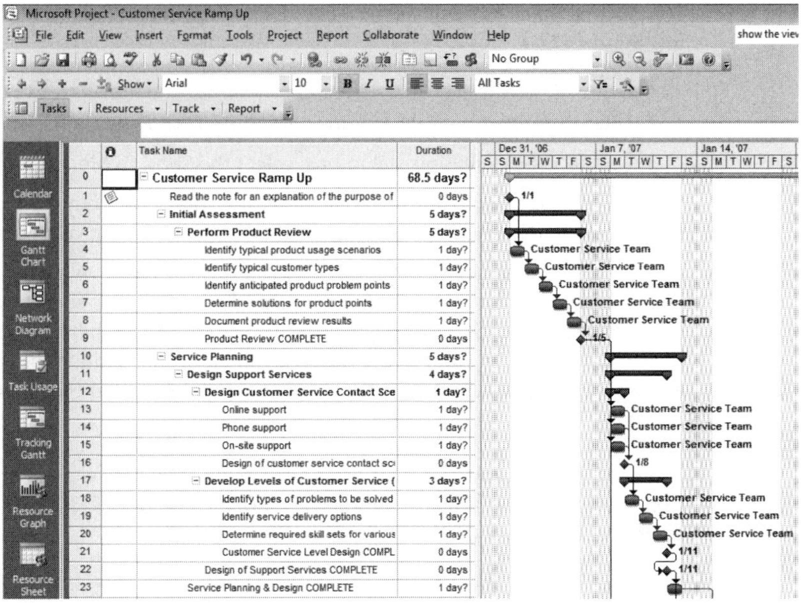

Figure 4-3 The View bar lists icons for the same views shown in the View menu.

2. Click a view's name or icon to switch to that view. If you can't see the view's name, click the arrow at the bottom of the list to see more views.

If the view isn't listed on the View bar, click More Views to see the full list.

Note

To hide a showing View bar, click View, View Bar. When the View bar is hidden, a blue vertical bar appears on the right edge of the current view. This is the Active View bar, and it shows the name of the current view. To change the current view, right-click the Active View bar. If the view you want appears in the shortcut menu, click it. Otherwise, click More Views to display the More Views dialog box and then click the view you want.

INSIDE OUT   **Add your favorite views to the View menu**

Although the most commonly used views are listed on the View menu and the View bar, they might not be *your* most commonly used views. For example, you might use the Task Entry view and the Detail Gantt daily, and you don't want to click More Views every time you need it.

You can add your frequently used views to the View menu and View bar. To do this, follow these steps:

1. Click View, More Views.

2. Click the view you want to add to the View menu and then click Edit.

3. In the View Definition dialog box, select the Show In Menu check box.

You can use this technique to remove views you never use from the View menu and View bar as well. Simply select the view, click Edit, and clear the Show In Menu check box.

You can also rearrange the order of views listed. The task views are listed first, in alphabetical order, and then the resource views are listed in alphabetical order. In the More Views dialog box, click the view you want to rearrange and then click Edit. In the Name box, add a number in front of the name; it is then brought to the top of its respective list. Prefix all the displayed views with a sequential number, and they'll appear in that sequential order.

You can fully customize your views and create entirely new views. For more information, see the section titled "Customizing Views" in Chapter 25, "Customizing Your View of Project Information."

You can think of Microsoft Project views in the following categories:

- Gantt charts
- Network diagrams
- Graph views
- Sheet views
- Usage views
- Forms
- Combination views

Working with Gantt Charts

Gantt charts are a special type of view used extensively in project management. The left side of a Gantt chart contains a sheet view and the right side contains a bar graph along a timescale (see Figure 4-4).

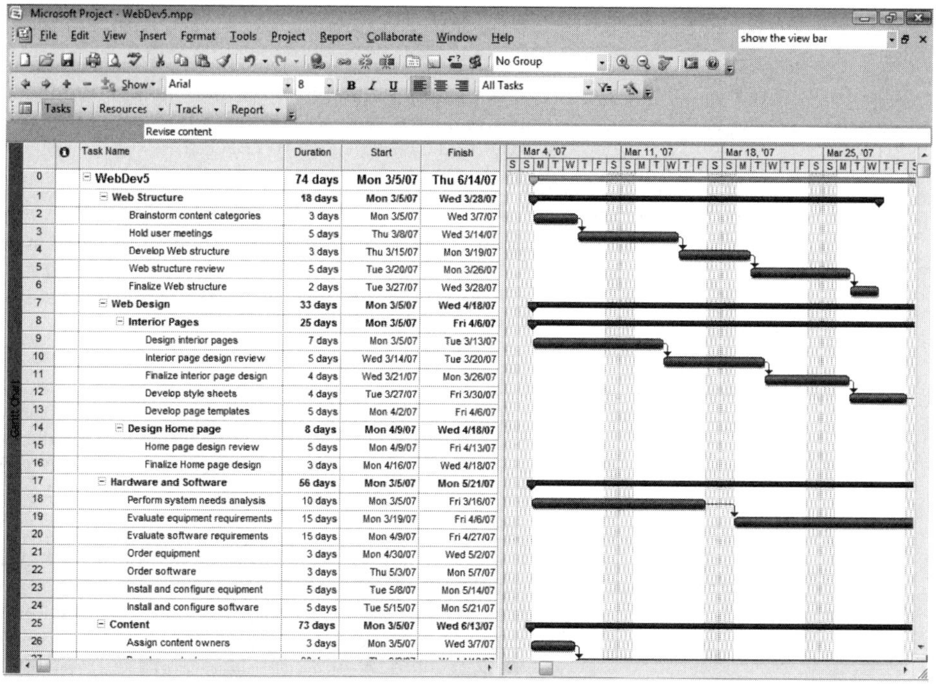

Figure 4-4 A Gantt chart shows task information in the sheet portion of the view; the corresponding bar graph shows the task's duration, start and finish dates, and task relationships.

While you can create custom Gantt charts, Table 4-1 describes the Microsoft Project Gantt charts that are built in to Microsoft Project.

Table 4-1 Microsoft Project Gantt Charts

Type of Gantt Chart	How you can use it	For more information
Bar Rollup (task view)	View summary tasks with labels for all subtasks. Use the Bar Rollup view with the Rollup_Formatting macro to see all tasks concisely labeled on summary Gantt bars.	"Organizing Tasks into an Outline" in Chapter 3
Detail Gantt (task view)	View tasks and associated information in a sheet and see slack and slippage for tasks over time in a bar graph on a timescale. Use the Detail Gantt to check how far a task can slip without affecting other tasks.	Chapter 9, "Checking and Adjusting the Project Plan"
Gantt Chart (task view)	View tasks and associated information in a sheet and see tasks and durations over time in a bar graph on a timescale. Use the Gantt Chart to enter and schedule a list of tasks. This is the view that appears by default when you first start Microsoft Project.	"Creating a New Project Plan" in Chapter 3

Chapter 4

Type of Gantt Chart	How you can use it	For more information
Leveling Gantt (task view)	View tasks, task delays, and slack in a sheet, and the before-and-after effects of the Microsoft Project leveling feature. Use the Leveling Gantt to check the amount of task delay caused by leveling.	"Balancing Resource Workloads" in Chapter 9
Milestone Date Rollup (task view)	View summary tasks with labels for all subtasks. Use the Milestone Date Rollup view with the Rollup_Formatting macro to see all tasks concisely labeled with milestone marks and dates on summary Gantt bars.	"Creating Milestones in Your Schedule" in Chapter 5
Milestone Rollup (task view)	View summary tasks with labels for all subtasks. Use the Milestone Rollup view with the Rollup_Formatting macro to see all tasks concisely labeled with milestone marks on the summary Gantt bars.	"Creating Milestones in Your Schedule" in Chapter 5
Multiple Baselines Gantt (task view)	View different colored Gantt bars for the first three baselines (Baseline, Baseline1, and Baseline2) on summary tasks and subtasks in the chart portion of the view. Use the Multiple Baselines Gantt to review and compare the first three baselines you set for your project.	"Saving Original Plan Information Using a Baseline" in Chapter 10
PA_Expected Gantt (task view)	View your schedule's expected scenario based on durations calculated from a PERT analysis.	"Calculating Your Most Probable Duration" in Chapter 5
PA_Optimistic Gantt (task view)	View your schedule's best-case scenario based on durations calculated from a PERT analysis.	"Calculating Your Most Probable Duration" in Chapter 5
PA_Pessimistic Gantt (task view)	View your schedule's worst-case scenario, based on durations calculated from a PERT analysis.	"Calculating Your Most Probable Duration" in Chapter 5
Tracking Gantt (task view)	View tasks and task information in a sheet, and a chart showing a baseline and scheduled Gantt bars for each task. Use the Tracking Gantt to compare the baseline schedule with the actual schedule.	Chapter 10, "Setting a Baseline and Updating Progress"

You can change the look and content of bars on a Gantt chart. You can:

- Change the pattern, color, and shape of the Gantt bar for a selected task.
- Change the text accompanying the Gantt bar for a selected task.
- Change the format and text for all Gantt bars of a particular type.

- Change the text style for all Gantt bars of a particular type.

- Change the layout of links and bars on a Gantt chart.

- Change the gridlines in the view.

TROUBLESHOOTING

You can't find the PERT analysis views

If you haven't used PERT (program evaluation and review technique) analysis since install-ing Microsoft Project 2007, you might not see the PA_Expected Gantt, PA_Optimistic Gantt, PA_Pessimistic Gantt, or PA_PERT Entry Sheet in the More Views dialog box. These views do not appear in the More Views dialog box until you select it on the PERT Analysis toolbar.

To do this, click View, Toolbars, PERT Analysis. On the PERT Analysis toolbar (see Figure 4-5), click the button for the PERT analysis view (for example, Optimistic Gantt) you need. From this point forward, that PERT analysis view is listed in the More Views dialog box.

Figure 4-5 A PERT analysis view does not become available in the More Views dialog box until you select it on the PERT Analysis toolbar.

For more information about changing the look and content of Gantt bars, see the section titled "Formatting a Gantt Chart View" in Chapter 25. To change the timescale in a Gantt Chart, see the section titled "Working with Timescales" later in this chapter. You can also change the content or look of the sheet portion of a Gantt chart. For details, see the section titled "Cus-tomizing Views" in Chpater 25. You can print views with the content and format you set up in the Microsoft Project window. For more information, see the section titled "Setting Up and Printing Views" in Chapter 12, "Reporting Project Information."

Working with Network Diagrams

Network diagrams are a special type of graph view that presents each task and associ-ated task information in a separate box, or *node*. The nodes are connected by lines that represent task relationships. The resulting diagram is a flowchart of the project. Net-work Diagram views (see Figure 4-6) are also referred to as PERT charts.

Chapter 4

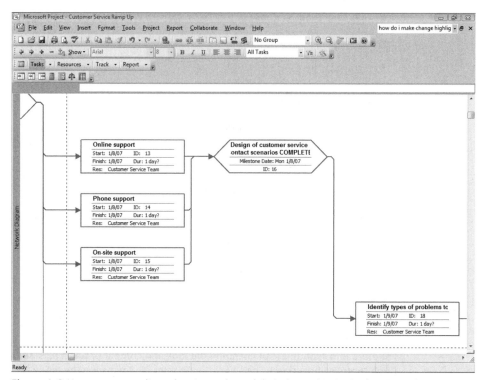

Figure 4-6 You can enter, edit, and review tasks and their dependencies in the Network Diagram view.

Table 4-2 describes the Microsoft Project network diagram views.

Table 4-2 Microsoft Project Network Diagram Views

Type of network diagram	How you can use it	For more information
Descriptive Network Diagram (task view)	View all tasks and task dependencies. Use the Descriptive Network Diagram to create and fine-tune your schedule in a flowchart format. This view is similar to the regular Network Diagram, but the nodes are larger and provide more detail.	"Establishing Task Dependencies" in Chapter 5
Network Diagram (task view)	Enter, edit, and review all tasks and task dependencies. Use the Network Diagram to create and fine-tune your schedule in a flowchart format.	"Establishing Task Dependencies" in Chapter 5

Type of network diagram	How you can use it	For more information
Relationship Diagram (task view)	View the predecessors and successors of a single selected task. In a large project or any project with more complex task linking, use this task view to focus on the task dependencies of a specific task.	"Establishing Task Dependencies" in Chapter 5

To learn about modifying the content or format of a network diagram, see the section titled "Modifying a Network Diagram" in Chapter 25.

Working with Graph Views

Graph views present project information in a pictorial representation that more readily communicates the data (see Figure 4-7).

Table 4-3 describes the Microsoft Project graph views.

Table 4-3 Microsoft Project Graph Views

Type of graph view	How you can use it	For more information
Calendar (task view)	View tasks and durations for a specific week or range of weeks in a monthly calendar format (see Figure 4-8).	Chapter 5, "Scheduling Tasks"
Resource Graph (resource view)	View resource allocation, cost, or work over time for a single resource or group of resources at a time. Information is displayed in a column graph format (refer to Figure 4-7). When used in combination with other views, the Resource Graph can be very useful for finding resource overallocations.	"Balancing Resource Workloads" in Chapter 9

Chapter 4

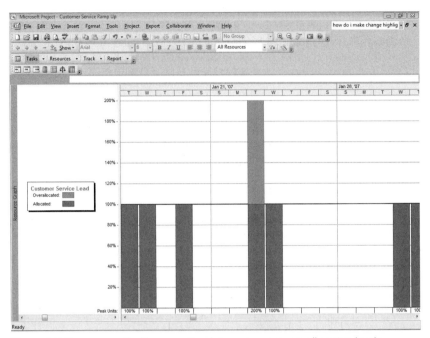

Figure 4-7 You can use the Resource Graph to review resource allocation levels.

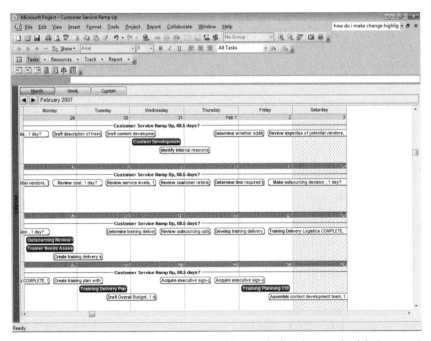

Figure 4-8 In the Calendar view, you can quickly see which tasks are scheduled on particular days, weeks, or months.

The Resource Graph shows peak units by resource, including the percentage of allocation and overallocation. You can change the type of information being shown in the Resource Graph by doing the following:

1. With the Resource Graph showing, click Format, Details.

   The Details submenu lists the various categories of information that the Resource Graph can chart, including Work, Percent Allocation, and Cost.

2. Click the category of information you want charted on the Resource Graph.

For information about modifying the format of the Resource Graph or Calendar view, see the section titled "Customizing Views" in Chapter 25.

Working with Sheet Views

Sheet views are spreadsheet-type views that are divided into columns and rows, and in which each individual field is contained in a cell (see Figure 4-9).

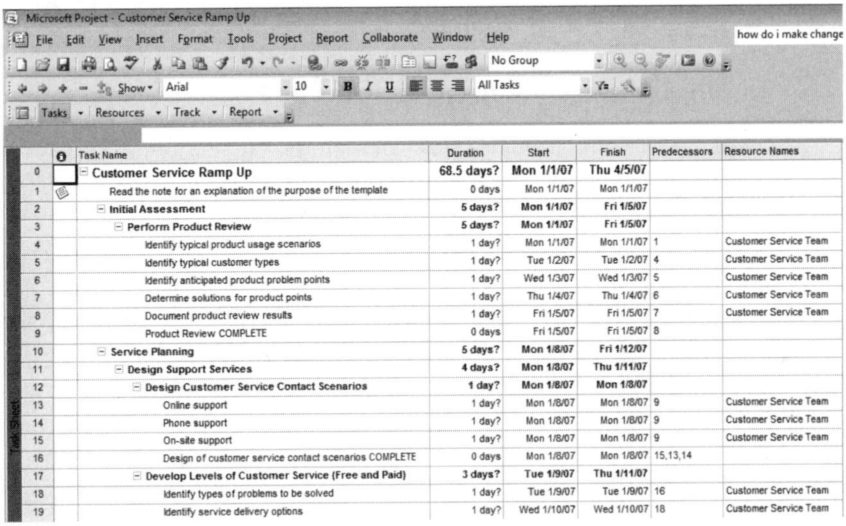

	Task Name	Duration	Start	Finish	Predecessors	Resource Names
0	Customer Service Ramp Up	68.5 days?	Mon 1/1/07	Thu 4/5/07		
1	Read the note for an explanation of the purpose of the template	0 days	Mon 1/1/07	Mon 1/1/07		
2	Initial Assessment	5 days?	Mon 1/1/07	Fri 1/5/07		
3	Perform Product Review	5 days?	Mon 1/1/07	Fri 1/5/07		
4	Identify typical product usage scenarios	1 day?	Mon 1/1/07	Mon 1/1/07	1	Customer Service Team
5	Identify typical customer types	1 day?	Tue 1/2/07	Tue 1/2/07	4	Customer Service Team
6	Identify anticipated product problem points	1 day?	Wed 1/3/07	Wed 1/3/07	5	Customer Service Team
7	Determine solutions for product points	1 day?	Thu 1/4/07	Thu 1/4/07	6	Customer Service Team
8	Document product review results	1 day?	Fri 1/5/07	Fri 1/5/07	7	Customer Service Team
9	Product Review COMPLETE	0 days	Fri 1/5/07	Fri 1/5/07	8	
10	Service Planning	5 days?	Mon 1/8/07	Fri 1/12/07		
11	Design Support Services	4 days?	Mon 1/8/07	Thu 1/11/07		
12	Design Customer Service Contact Scenarios	1 day?	Mon 1/8/07	Mon 1/8/07		
13	Online support	1 day?	Mon 1/8/07	Mon 1/8/07	9	Customer Service Team
14	Phone support	1 day?	Mon 1/8/07	Mon 1/8/07	9	Customer Service Team
15	On-site support	1 day?	Mon 1/8/07	Mon 1/8/07	9	Customer Service Team
16	Design of customer service contact scenarios COMPLETE	0 days	Mon 1/8/07	Mon 1/8/07	15,13,14	
17	Develop Levels of Customer Service (Free and Paid)	3 days?	Tue 1/9/07	Thu 1/11/07		
18	Identify types of problems to be solved	1 day?	Tue 1/9/07	Tue 1/9/07	16	Customer Service Team
19	Identify service delivery options	1 day?	Wed 1/10/07	Wed 1/10/07	18	Customer Service Team

Figure 4-9 Use the Task Sheet to enter tasks and durations, and to review calculated start and finish dates.

The Microsoft Project sheet views are described in Table 4-4.

Table 4-4 Microsoft Project Sheet Views

Type of sheet view	How you can use it	For more information
PA_PERT Entry Sheet (task view)	Enter your schedule's best-case, expected-case, and worst-case scenarios for a task's duration in preparation of calculating the most probable duration using a PERT analysis, which helps you consider and reconcile disparities between different task estimates.	"Calculating Your Most Probable Duration" in Chapter 5
Resource Sheet (resource view)	Enter, edit, and review resource information in a spreadsheet format.	Chapter 6, "Setting Up Resources in the Project"
Task Sheet (task view)	Enter, edit, and review task information in a spreadsheet format.	"Creating a New Project Plan" in Chapter 3

For information about modifying the content or format of a sheet view, see the section titled "Modifying a Sheet View" in Chapter 25.

Working with Usage Views

Usage views are made up of a sheet view on the left side and a timesheet on the right. Together with the timescale, the timesheet can show work, cost, availability, and other data broken out by time, that is, *timephased* (see Figure 4-10).

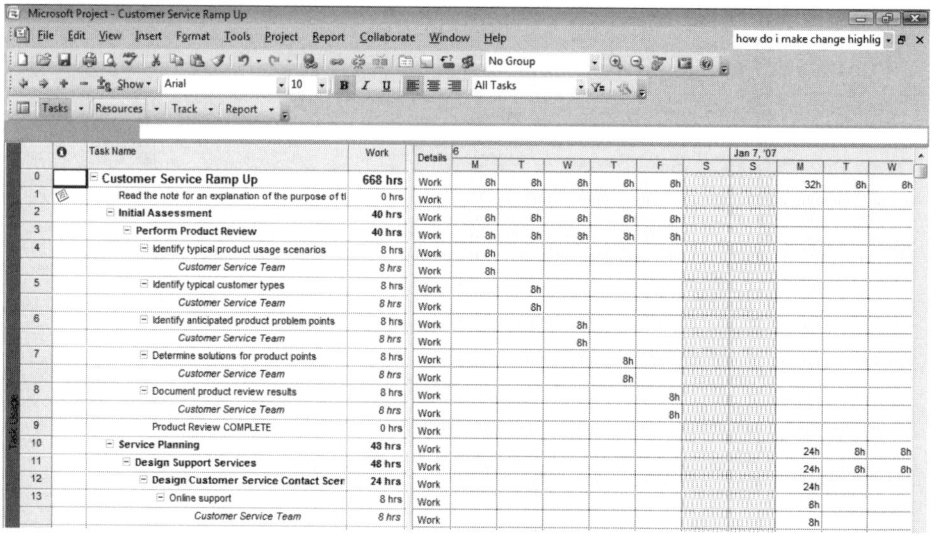

Figure 4-10 Display the Task Usage view to review assignments by task.

The Microsoft Project usage views are described in Table 4-5.

Table 4-5 Microsoft Project Usage Views

Type of usage view	How you can use it	For more information
Resource Usage (assignment view)	Review, enter, and edit assignments by resource. In the sheet portion of the Resource Usage view, each resource is listed with all associated task assignments indented beneath it (see Figure 4-11). In the timesheet portion of the view, information such as work or costs for the resource and the assignment is listed according to the timescale, for example, by week or month.	Chapter 7, "Assigning Resources to Tasks"
Task Usage (assignment view)	Review, enter, and edit assignments by task. In the sheet portion of the Task Usage view, each task is listed with the assigned resources indented beneath it (see Figure 4-12). In the timesheet portion of the view, information such as work or costs for the task and the assignment is listed according to the timescale, for example, by day or by week.	Chapter 7

Technology Lead	34 hrs
Build technology infrastructure plan (separate project plan required)	8 hrs
Determine technology budget	8 hrs
Design and develop technology solution (separate schedule required)	8 hrs
Test technology infrastructure	2 hrs
Deploy technology infrastructure	8 hrs

Figure 4-11 In the Resource Usage view, each resource is listed with its assigned tasks.

Build Technology Infrastructure	20 hrs
Design and develop technology solution (separate schedule required)	8 hrs
Technology Lead	8 hrs
Test technology infrastructure	12 hrs
Customer Service Team	2 hrs
Technology Lead	2 hrs
Content Developer	8 hrs
Technology Infrastructure Development COMPLETE	0 hrs
Customer Service Program Development	40 hrs
Build customer service programs	8 hrs
Customer Service Team	8 hrs

Figure 4-12 In the Task Usage view, each task is listed with its assigned resources.

Because the timesheet portion of the usage views breaks down information from certain fields and from specific time periods, there are three subcategories to the major field categories of tasks, resources, and assignments:

- Task-timephased
- Resource-timephased
- Assignment-timephased

You can review task-timephased and assignment-timephased fields in the timesheet portion of the Task Usage view. You can review resource-timephased and assignment-timephased fields in the timesheet portion of the Resource Usage view.

> **Note**
>
> Timephased information is used in many earned-value analysis calculations. For more information about earned value, see Chapter 13, "Analyzing Progress Using Earned Value."

The Work field is shown by default in the timephased fields in the timesheet portion of a usage view. Multiple fields of information can be "stacked" in the view at one time. To change the type of information shown, do the following:

1. With a usage view showing, click Format, Details.

    The Details submenu lists the different timephased fields that the timesheet portion of the usage view can display, for example, Actual Work, Baseline Work, and Cost. Any fields currently displayed are noted with a check mark.

2. Click the field you want to add to the timesheet. Another row of timephased information is added to the timesheet for each task.

3. To remove a row of information from the timesheet, click Format, Details and then click the item you want to remove.

For information about modifying the format of a usage view, see the section titled "Modifying a Usage View" in Chapter 25.

Working with Forms

Forms are specialized views that include text boxes and grids in which you can enter and review information in a way similar to a dialog box (see Figure 4-13). Although you can display a form on its own and click the Previous and Next buttons to cycle through the different tasks or resources in your project, a form is most useful when included as part of a combination view (see "Working with Combination Views" in the next section).

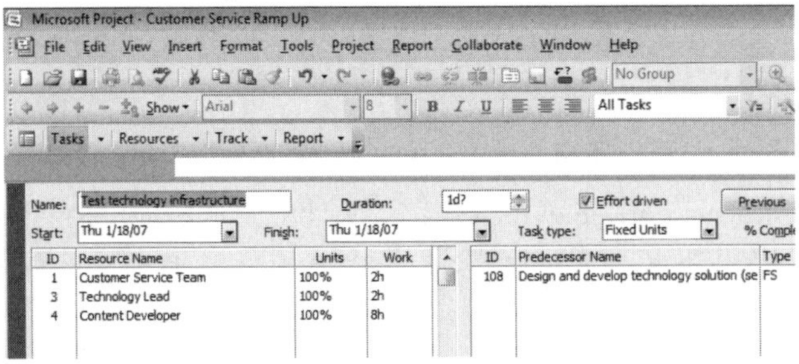

Figure 4-13 This Task Form shows fundamental information about the task, along with information about assigned resources and predecessor tasks.

The Microsoft Project forms are described in Table 4-6.

Table 4-6 Microsoft Project Forms

Type of form	How you can use it	For more information
Resource Form (resource view)	Enter, edit, and review all resource, task, and schedule information about a selected resource, one resource at a time. The grid area can show information about the resource's schedule, cost, or work on assigned tasks. It is most useful when used as part of a combination view (see Figure 4-14).	Chapter 7
Resource Name Form (resource view)	Enter, edit, and review the selected resource's schedule, cost, or work on assigned tasks. The Resource Name Form is a simplified version of the Resource Form.	Chapter 7
Task Details Form (task view)	Enter, edit, and review detailed tracking and scheduling information about a selected task, one task at a time. The grid area can show information about assigned resources, predecessors, and successors.	Chapter 5
Task Form (task view)	Enter, edit, and review information about a selected task, one task at a time. The grid area can show information about the task's assigned resources, predecessors, and successors.	Chapter 5
Task Name Form (task view)	Enter, edit, and review the selected task's assigned resources, predecessors, and successors. The Task Name Form is a simplified version of the Task Form.	Chapter 5

You can change the categories of information shown in a form view. To do this, follow these steps:

1. Click View, More Views. In the More Views dialog box, click the form you want. Click the Apply button.

2. Right-click the blank area on the form. A shortcut menu appears, which shows different types of information that can be shown in the form. A check mark appears next to the information currently shown in the form.

3. Click the information you want to display in the form. You can choose only one item from the shortcut menu at a time.

Working with Combination Views

Combination views are groupings of two views in a split screen. The information in one portion of the split screen controls the content in the other portion (see Figure 4-14).

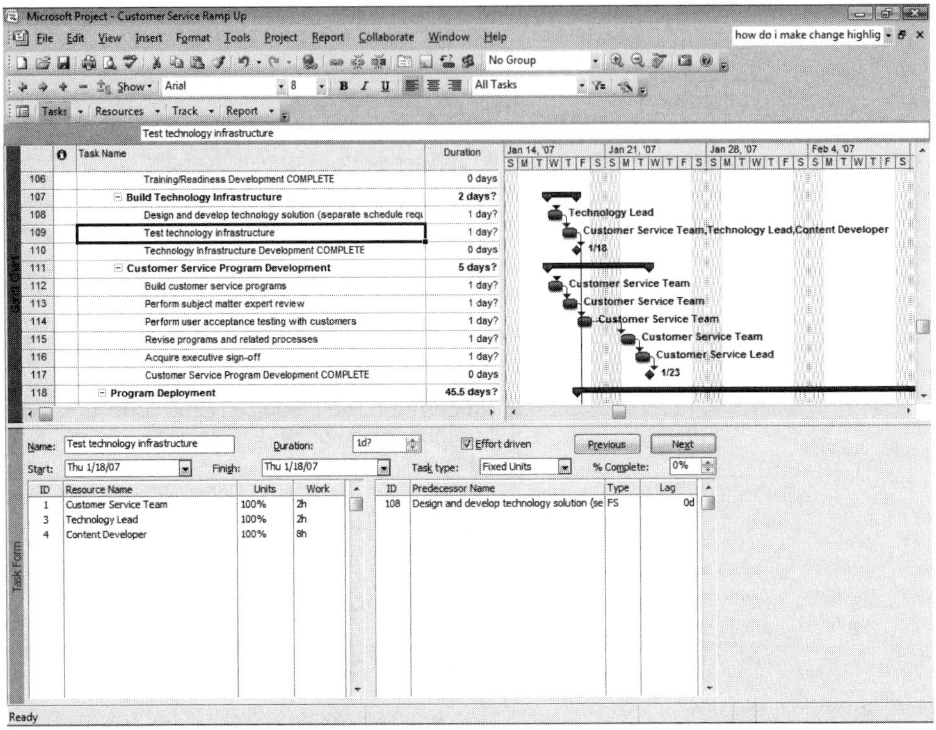

Figure 4-14 When you click a task in the upper Gantt Chart portion of the Task Entry view, the task, assignment, and predecessor information for that selected task appear in the lower Task Form portion of the view.

The predefined Microsoft Project combination views are described in Table 4-7.

Table 4-7 Microsoft Project Combination Views

Type of combination view	How you can use it	For more information
Task Entry (task view)	Enter, edit, and review detailed information about the task selected in the Gantt Chart. The Gantt Chart appears in the upper portion of the view, and the Task Form appears in the lower portion. The information shown in the Task Form corresponds with the task selected in the Gantt Chart.	Chapter 5

Type of combination view	How you can use it	For more information
Resource Allocation (resource view)	Review and resolve resource overallocations. The Resource Usage view appears in the upper portion of the view, and the Leveling Gantt appears in the lower portion. The information shown in the Leveling Gantt corresponds with the resource or assignment selected in the Resource Usage view.	"Balancing Resource Workloads," in Chapter 9

You can create your own combination view by simply splitting the view. For example, if you split the Gantt Chart view, the Task Form appears in the lower pane, instantly resulting in the Task Entry view. Likewise, if you split the Resource Sheet, the Resource Form appears in the lower pane.

The split bar is located in the lower-right corner of the Microsoft Project window, just below the vertical scroll bar. To split a view, drag the split bar up to about the middle of the view or wherever you want the split to occur. Or click Window, Split.

Split bar

TROUBLESHOOTING

The current view doesn't have a split bar

By their nature, graph views and forms do not have a split bar. However, you can still create a combination view with these views in the upper pane. Click Window, Split. The view splits, with the Task Form or Resource Form appearing in the lower pane. If necessary, apply the view you want to the newly revealed pane.

To remove the split and return to a single view, double-click the split bar, which is now the gray dividing bar between the two views. Or click Window, Remove Split.

Split bar

To modify a combination view, simply modify one component of the combination view as if it were in its own view.

For more information about combination views, see the section titled "Customizing Views" in Chapter 25.

TROUBLESHOOTING

You can't get the combination view to be a single view again

In a combination view such as Task Entry or Resource Allocation, one of the two views always has focus; that is, it's the currently active view. When you switch to another view, only the active view switches.

Before switching to another view, make the combination view a single view. To do this, click Window, Remove Split. Or double-click the split bar—the gray dividing bar between the two views. Then switch to the other view.

Working with Timescales

Many Microsoft Project views, including Gantt charts and usage views, use a timescale to indicate time in the project. The timescale appears above the chart or timesheet area of a view. You can display up to three timescales (see Figure 4-15), each timescale in a tier. The highest tier shows the broadest period of time, and the lowest tier shows the most detailed period of time. For example, you can show days within weeks within months, or you can show weeks within quarters.

Figure 4-15 You can zoom your timescales up or down while you're working.

The default timescale is two tiers: days within weeks. To set your timescale options, do the following:

1. Show a view that contains a timescale, for example, the Gantt Chart, Task Usage view, or Resource Graph.

2. Click Format, Timescale. The Timescale dialog box appears.

3. The Timescale dialog box has four tabs: Top Tier, Middle Tier, Bottom Tier, and Non-Working Time. The Middle Tier tab is displayed by default. In the Show box, click the number of timescale tiers you want to display (one, two, or three).

4. In the Units box, specify the time unit you want to display at the middle tier, for example, quarters, months, or weeks.

5. In the Label box, click the format in which you want to display the time unit, for example, January 27, Jan 27, Sun 27, and so on. If necessary, scroll to see more time unit formats to find the one you want.

6. If you chose to display more than one tier, click the Top Tier and/or Bottom Tier tabs and repeat steps 4 and 5.

Using Tables

Any sheet view, including the sheet portion of any Gantt chart or usage view, has a default table defined for it. You can change the table for these types of views. Or you can modify an existing table to add, change, or remove the fields in the columns.

Views That Use Tables

Table 4-8 shows the default table for each view.

Table 4-8 Default Table Views

View	Default table	View	Default table
Bar Rollup	Rollup Table	PA_PERT Entry Sheet	PA_PERT Entry
Detail Gantt	Delay	PA_Pessimistic Gantt	PA_Pessimistic Case
Gantt Chart	Entry	Resource Allocation	Usage (Resource Usage view) Delay (Leveling Gantt view)
Leveling Gantt	Delay	Resource Sheet	Entry
Milestone Date Rollup	Entry	Resource Usage	Usage
Milestone Rollup	Rollup Table	Task Entry	Entry
Multiple Baselines Gantt	Entry	Task Sheet	Entry
PA_Expected Gantt	PA_Expected Case	Task Usage	Usage
PA_Optimistic Gantt	PA_Optimistic Case	Tracking Gantt	Entry

Table 4-9 lists a description of the task tables and their default fields.

Chapter 4

Table 4-9 Task Tables and Their Default Fields

Information	Default fields included	For more information
Baseline		
Specific baseline values reflecting the schedule as originally planned	*ID, Task Name, Baseline Duration, Baseline Start, Baseline Finish, Baseline Work,* and *Baseline Cost*	"Saving Original Plan Information Using a Baseline" in Chapter 10
Constraint Dates		
The specific constraint types for each task, along with associated dates where applicable; you can use these fields to review or change the constraint type and date	*ID, Task Name, Duration, Constraint Type,* and *Constraint Date*	"Scheduling Tasks to Achieve Specific Dates" in Chapter 5
Cost		
Cost information for each task, helping you analyze various types of cost calculations	*ID, Task Name, Fixed Cost, Fixed Cost Accrual, Total Cost, Baseline, Variance, Actual,* and *Remaining*	"Monitoring and Adjusting Costs" in Chapter 11
Delay		
Information to help you determine how long it will take to complete your tasks, given the resources you have and the amount of time they have for a given task	*ID, Indicators, Task Name, Leveling Delay, Duration, Start, Finish, Successors,* and *Resources*	"Balancing Resource Workloads" in Chapter 9
Earned Value		
Earned value information that compares the relationship between work and costs based on a status date	*ID, Task Name, BCWS, BCWP, ACWP, SV, CV, EAC, BAC,* and *VAC*	"Analyzing Progress Using Earned Value" in Chapter 13
Earned Value Cost Indicators		
Earned-value cost information, including the ratio of budgeted to actual costs of work performed.	*ID, Task Name, BCWS, BCWP, CV, CV%, CPI, BAC, EAC, VAC,* and *TCPI*	"Analyzing Progress and Costs Using Earned Value" in Chapter 13

Information	Default fields included	For more information
Earned Value Schedule Indicators		
Earned-value schedule information, including the ratio of work performed to work scheduled	ID, Task Name, BCWS, BCWP, SV, SV%, and SPI	"Analyzing Progress and Costs Using Earned Value" in Chapter 13
Entry		
Fundamental information regarding tasks; this table is most useful for entering and viewing the most essential task information	ID, Indicators, Task Name, Duration, Start, Finish, Predecessors, and Resource Names	"Entering Tasks" in Chapter 3
Export		
A large set of fields from which to export task fields to other applications such as Microsoft Office Excel or Microsoft Access	ID, Unique ID, Task Name, Duration, Type, Outline Level, Baseline Duration, Predecessors, Start, Finish, Early Start, Early Finish, Late Start, Late Finish, Free Slack, Total Slack, Leveling Delay, % Complete, Actual Start, Actual Finish, Baseline Start, Baseline Finish, Constraint Type, Constraint Date, Stop, Resume, Created, Work, Baseline Work, Actual Work, Cost, Fixed Cost, Baseline Cost, Actual Cost, Remaining Cost, WBS, Priority, Milestone, Summary, Rollup, Text1–10, Cost1–3, Duration1–3, Flag1–10, Marked, Number1–5, Subproject File, Contact, Start1–5, and Finish1–5	"Importing and Exporting Information" in Chapter 16
Hyperlink		
Hyperlink information to associate linked shortcuts with your tasks	ID, Indicators, Task Name, Hyperlink, Address, and SubAddress	"Hyperlinking to Documents in Other Applications" in Chapter 16
PA_Expected Case		
Expected scheduling information based on PERT analysis of task durations	ID, Indicators, Task Name, Expected Duration, Expected Start, and Expected Finish	"Calculating Your Most Probable Duration" in Chapter 5
PA_Optimistic Case		
The best-case scheduling information based on PERT analysis of task durations	ID, Indicators, Task Name, Optimistic Duration, Optimistic Start, and Optimistic Finish	"Calculating Your Most Probable Duration" in Chapter 5

Chapter 4

Information	Default fields included	For more information
PA_PERT Entry		
The most probable duration information for a project, based on PERT analysis of task durations	ID, Task Name, Duration, Optimistic Duration, Expected Duration, and Pessimistic Duration	"Calculating Your Most Probable Duration" in Chapter 5
PA_Pessimistic Case		
The worst-case scheduling information based on PERT analysis of task durations	ID, Indicators, Task Name, Pessimistic Duration, Pessimistic Start, and Pessimistic Finish	"Calculating Your Most Probable Duration" in Chapter 5
Rollup Table		
Summarized task information that appears after you run the Rollup_Formatting macro	ID, Indicators, Task Name, Duration, Text Above, Start, Finish, Predecessors, and Resource Names	"Organizing Tasks into an Outline" in Chapter 3
Schedule		
Detailed scheduling information that can help you see when a task is scheduled to begin and how late it can actually begin without jeopardizing the project's finish date	ID, Task Name, Start, Finish, Late Start, Late Finish, Free Slack, and Total Slack	"Understanding Slack Time and Critical Tasks" in Chapter 9
Summary		
Overview of project information to analyze durations, dates, progress, and costs	ID, Task Name, Duration, Start, Finish, % Complete, Cost, and Work	"Bringing In the Project Finish Date" in Chapter 9
Tracking		
Actual progress and cost information, as contrasted with scheduled or baseline information	ID, Task Name, Actual Start, Actual Finish, % Complete, Physical % Complete, Actual Duration, Remaining Duration, Actual Cost, and Actual Work	"Updating Task Progress" in Chapter 10
Usage		
The most fundamental task schedule information	ID, Indicators, Task Name, Work, Duration, Start, and Finish	Chapter 5

Information	Default fields included	For more information
Variance		
Gaps between baseline start and finish dates and the actual start and finish dates, enabling a comparison between your original planned schedule and actual performance	ID, Task Name, Start, Finish, Baseline Start, Baseline Finish, Start Variance, and Finish Variance	Chapter 11, "Responding to Changes in Your Project"
Work		
A variety of measurements for analyzing the level of effort for each task	ID, Task Name, Work, Baseline, Variance, Actual, Remaining, and % Work Complete	"Updating Task Progress" in Chapter 10

Table 4-10 lists a description of all resource tables and their default fields.

Table 4-10 Resource Tables and Their Default Fields

Information displayed	Default fields included	For more Information
Cost		
Cost information about resources in a project	ID, Resource Name, Cost, Baseline Cost, Cost Variance, Actual Cost, and Remaining Cost	"Monitoring and Adjusting Costs" in Chapter 11
Earned Value		
Earned value information that compares the relationship between work and costs for resources based on a status date	ID, Resource Name, BCWS, BCWP, ACWP, SV, CV, EAC, BAC, and VAC	"Analyzing Progress Using Earned Value" in Chapter 13
Entry		
Essential information regarding resources; this table is most useful for entering and viewing fundamental resource information	ID, Indicators, Resource Name, Type, Material Label, Initials, Group, Maximum Units, Standard Rate, Overtime Rate, Cost/Use, Accrue At, Base Calendar, and Code	Chapter 6
Entry – Material Resources		
Essential information about consumable material resources	ID, Resource Name, Type, Material Label, Initials, Group, Standard Rate, Cost/Use, Accrue At, and Code	"Adding Material Resources to the Project" in Chapter 6

Chapter 4

Information displayed	Default fields included	For more Information
Entry – Work Resources		
Essential information about work (people and equipment) resources	ID, Resource Name, Type, Initials, Group, Maximum Units, Standard Rate, Overtime Rate, Cost/Use, Accrue At, Base Calendar, and Code	"Adding Work Resources to the Project" in Chapter 6
Export		
A large set of fields from which to export resource fields to other applications, such as Microsoft Excel or Access	ID, Unique ID, Resource Name, Initials, Maximum Units, Standard Rate, Overtime Rate, Cost Per Use, Accrue At, Cost, Baseline Cost, Actual Cost, Work, Baseline Work, Actual Work, Overtime Work, Group, Code, Text1–5, and Email Address	"Importing and Exporting Information" in Chapter 16
Hyperlink		
Hyperlink information to associate linked shortcuts with your resources	ID, Indicators, Resource Name, Hyperlink, Address, and SubAddress	"Hyperlinking to Documents in Other Applications" in Chapter 16
Summary		
Overview of resource information	ID, Resource Name, Group, Maximum Units, Peak, Standard Rate, Overtime Rate, Cost, and Work	Chapter 6
Usage		
The most essential resource scheduling information	ID, Indicators, Resource Name, and Work	Chapter 7
Work		
A variety of measurements for analyzing work, or the level of effort, for resources and their assigned tasks	ID, Resource Name, % Complete, Work, Overtime, Baseline, Variance, Actual, and Remaining	"Updating Progress Using Resource Work" in Chapter 10

> **Note**
> You can quickly see the name of the current table. Simply rest your mouse pointer in the All Cells box where the row and column headings intersect. The ToolTip containing the table name (and view name) appears.

Changing the Table in a View

To switch to a different table, follow these steps:

1. Display the view containing the table you want to change. This view could be theTask Sheet, Resource Sheet, Gantt Chart, Task Usageview, and so on.

2. Click View, Table.

3. If the table is listed on the submenu, click it. If the table is not listed on the submenu, click More Tables (see Figure 4-16) and then double-click the table you want.

    The table is replaced by the table you clicked.

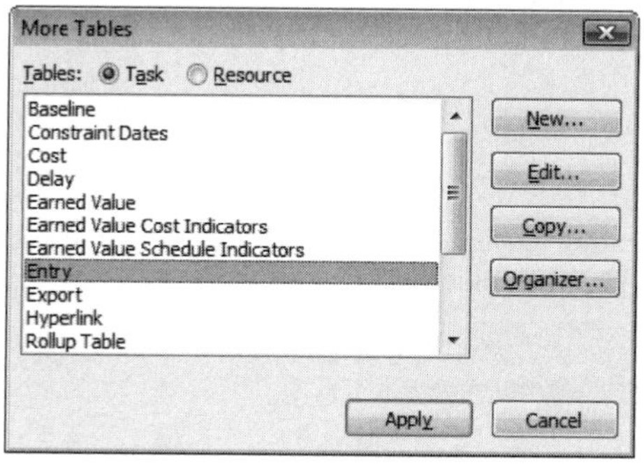

Figure 4-16 The More Tables dialog box contains the full list of built-in tables.

> **Note**
>
> If a task view is currently displayed, task tables are listed. If a resource view is currently displayed, resource tables are listed. You cannot apply a resource table to a task view, and vice versa.

> **Note**
>
> Another method for changing tables is to right-click the All Cells box where the row and column headings intersect. The Tables shortcut menu appears.

Modifying a Table

Suppose that the Entry task table provides all the information you need except baseline values. You can easily add another column to any table, and you can just as easily remove superfluous columns. You can also make certain changes to the columns themselves.

> **Note**
>
> When working with columns in a table, you're working with fields in your project database. Fields are discussed in more detail in the section titled "Using Fields" later in this chapter.

To add a column to a table, follow these steps:

1. Display the view and table to which you want to add a new column.

2. Right-click the column heading that will be to the right of the new column and then click Insert Column. The Column Definition dialog box appears.

> **Note**
>
> You can also open the Column Definition dialog box (see Figure 4-17) by clicking in a column and then clicking Insert, Column. 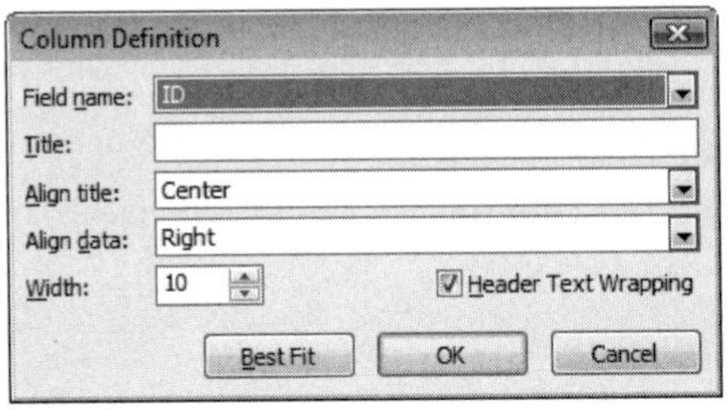
>
>
> **Figure 4-17** You can also open the Column Definition dialog box by clicking a column heading and then pressing the Insert key.

3. In the Field Name box, click the field representing the information you want in the new column.

> **Note**
>
> With the Field Name box selected, you can just type the first letter of the field's name to scroll close to its name in the list.

TROUBLESHOOTING

The field you're looking for is not in the Field Name list

When you display a task view and table, only task fields are listed in the Column Definition dialog box. Likewise, when you display a resource view and table, only resource fields are listed. Assignment fields are available only in the Task Usage and Resource Usage views.

To remove a column from a table, follow these steps:

1. Display the view and table from which you want to remove a column.

2. Right-click the heading of the column you want to remove and then click Hide Column.

   The column is removed. The field and its contents still exist in the database, however, and can be displayed again in this or other tables.

> **Note**
>
> You can also remove a column by selecting the column heading and then clicking Edit, Hide Column. Or simply select the column heading and press the Delete key.

Hiding and Showing Columns

You can hide a column in your table while keeping it in place. Position your mouse pointer over the right edge of the column heading border. The mouse pointer changes to a black crosshair. Drag the right border past the column's left border. The column disappears.

To show the column again, position your mouse pointer on the edge where your column is hidden. Drag to the right, and your column appears again.

Using this method is a bit tricky, however--you need to know where you hid the column because there's no visual indication that it's there.

You can change the title of the column to something other than the actual field name. You can also modify the column text alignment and the column width. To modify a column, follow these steps:

1. Display the view and table containing the column you want to modify.

2. Double-click the heading of the column you want to change. The Column Definition dialog box appears.

3. To change the field information appearing in the column, in the Field Name list, click the field you want.

4. To change the title of the column heading, type a new title in the Title box.

5. Use the Align Title list to change the alignment of the column title.

6. Use the Align Data list to change the alignment of the field information itself.

7. Enter a number in the Width box to change the column width.

> **Note**
>
> You can also change the column width directly on the table, exactly as you do in Excel. Click the column's heading to select the column. Then move the mouse pointer to the right edge of the column until the pointer changes to a black crosshair. Drag to the right to widen the column. Drag to the left to make the column narrower. Double-click the edge to widen the column to the same size as the longest entry in the column.

You can move a column to another location in the table simply by dragging. To move a column, follow these steps:

1. Display the view and table containing the column you want to move.

2. Click the heading of the column you want to move.

3. With the black crosshair mouse pointer over the column heading, drag to the new location for the column. As you drag, a gray line moves with the mouse pointer to indicate where the column will be inserted when you release the mouse button.

> **Note**
>
> In addition to adding and removing columns in existing tables, you can also create entirely new tables. For more information about tables, see the section titled "Customizing Tables" in Chapter 25.

Using Fields

Fields are the smallest piece of data in the vast collection of information that makes up your project database. For example, one task comprises a single record in this database.

This record consists of a number of task fields, such as the task name, duration, start date, finish date, assigned resource, deadline, and more.

Whether you see them in a view or not, there are numerous fields for your tasks, resources, and assignments, as well as for the project as a whole.

Some fields are entered by you, such as task name and duration. Other fields are calculated for you by Microsoft Project, such as start date, finish date, and total cost. Still other fields can either be entered by you or calculated by Microsoft Project.

From the discussion of views, tables, and the fields in those tables earlier in this chapter, you should already be familiar with the different field categories:

- Task fields
- Task-timephased fields
- Resource fields
- Resource-timephased fields
- Assignment fields
- Assignment-timephased fields

The timephased fields break down field information—such as work, costs, and availability—by time periods. This breakdown gives you more information to work with in your project. In the Task Usage and Resource Usage views, for example, you can see task cost by day or resource work by week. You can break either of those down further into the component assignments. The timephased fields also give you more tools for analysis through earned-value calculations.

> For more information about earned value analysis, see Chapter 13 titled "Analyzing Progress Using Earned Value."

Another way that fields are categorized is by *data type*. The data type indicates how a field can be used, for example, as a currency-type field, or a text-type field. The following are the field data types:

- **Currency.** Information is expressed as a cost.
- **Date.** Information is expressed as a date.
- **Duration.** Information is expressed as a span of time.
- **Enumerated.** Information is selected from a list of predefined choices.
- **Indicator.** Information is shown as graphical indicators, or icons, about a task, resource, or assignment.
- **Integer.** Information is expressed as a whole number.

Chapter 4

- **Outline code.** Information is defined with a custom tag for tasks or resources that enables you to show a hierarchy of tasks in your project.

- **Percentage/Number.** Information is displayed as a value that can be expressed as either a percentage or decimal number, such as 100 percent or 1.00.

- **Text.** Information is expressed as unrestricted characters of text.

- **Yes/No.** Information is set to either Yes or No, that is, a True/False or Boolean value.

Fields make up your project database, the whole of which you might never see, or even have a need to see. You do see various fields throughout your project plan, in the following locations:

- Columns in a table

- Rows in a timesheet

- Information in a network diagram node

- Gantt bars and associated text in a Gantt chart

- Fields in a form view

- Fields in a dialog box

Some of these locations, such as columns in a table and rows in a timesheet, can be changed to suit your needs. Others, such as the fields in a dialog box, are fixed.

You can create your own custom fields and add them to tables in your views. There are custom fields you can define for currency, dates, durations, finish dates, start dates, text, numbers, outline codes, and more. Microsoft Office Project Professional 2007 includes an additional set of enterprise custom fields as well, so an enterprise can design a robust set of fields that standardizes how the enterprise manages projects.

For more information about defining custom fields, see the section titled "Customizing Fields" in Chapter 25. For information about working with enterprise custom fields, see the section titled "Working with Custom Enterprise Fields" in Chapter 22, "Managing Enterprise Projects and Resources."

Learn More About Microsoft Project Fields

You can immediately get comprehensive information about any field in a table. Position
your mouse pointer over the column heading, and a ToolTip pops up that contains a link
to online Help for this field. Click the link, and the Help topic appears.

Duration	Start	Finish
18 days	Mon	/28/07
3 days	Mon 3/5/0	Wed 3/7/07
5 days	Thu 3/8/07	Wed 3/14/07

You can also get lists of field categories and find information about fields by following
these steps:

1. Click Help, Microsoft Office Project Help.

2. Under Browse Project Help, click Reference.

3. Click Fields Reference.

4. Click one of the field types, for example, Duration Fields. A complete list of fields
   of that type appears.

5. Click a field name, and its Help topic appears (see Figure 4-18).

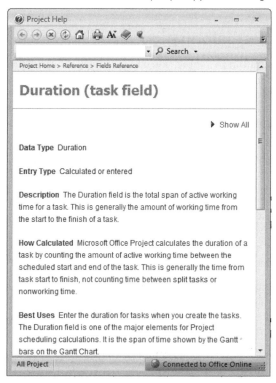

Figure 4-18 The Fields Reference Help topics contain comprehensive information about
the fields.

Chapter 4

These online Help topics about the fields contain the following information:

- Data type (duration, cost, text, and so on)
- Entry type (entered, calculated, or both)
- Description (a general overview of the field's function)
- How Calculated (for calculated fields)
- Best Uses (the purpose of the field)
- Example (how this field might be used to facilitate a project plan)
- Remarks (any additional information)

Rearranging Your Project Information

The ability to switch from one view to another, to switch tables in a sheet view, and to add or remove fields in a view gives you tremendous versatility in how you see your project information. You can take it a step further by sorting, grouping, and filtering the information in a view.

Sorting Project Information

By sorting information in a table, you can arrange it in alphabetical or numerical order by a particular field. For example, you might sort your tasks by start date so you can see tasks that are due to start next week. Or you might sort your tasks by duration so you can see the tasks with the longest durations and how you might break them up and bring in the project finish date.

You can also sort resources. For example, in the Resource Sheet, you might have originally entered all resources as they came on board, but they might be easier for you to manage if they were in alphabetical order. You can easily sort by the resource name. Better yet, you can sort by department or group name, and then by resource name.

To sort items in a sheet view, do the following:

1. Display the sheet view whose information you want to sort.

2. Click Project, Sort.

3. In the submenu that appears, commonly used sort fields are presented. For example, if you're working in the Gantt Chart, you can quickly sort by Start Date, Finish Date, Priority, Cost, or ID. If you're working in the Resource Sheet, you can quickly sort by Cost, Name, or ID.

4. If you want to sort by a different field than what's presented in the submenu, click Sort By. The Sort dialog box appears (see Figure 4-19).

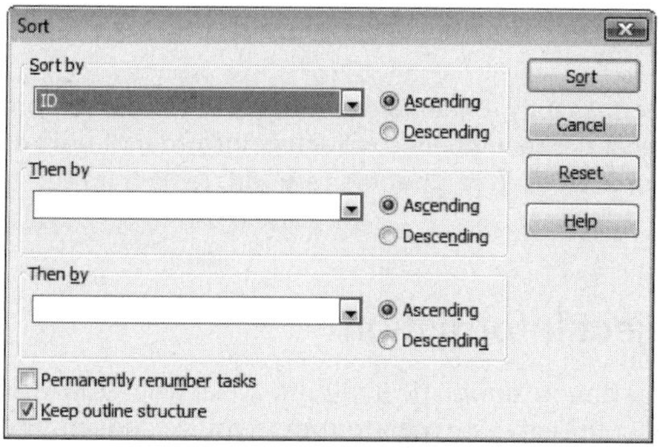

Figure 4-19 Use the Sort dialog box to choose the fields you want to sort by.

5. Under Sort By, click the name of the field you want to sort by and then specify whether you want the sort to be ascending (lowest to highest) or descending (highest to lowest). If you want to sort within the sort, add another field in one or both of the Then By boxes.

6. Make sure that the Permanently Renumber check box is cleared. You will likely want to clear this check box in the majority of the cases. However, if you really want this sort to be permanent, and you're certain that you won't ever want to return to the original order of the tasks or resources, go ahead and select this check box. The ID numbers for the tasks or resources are changed, and the tasks or resources will be sorted by order of the ID numbers when you don't have any other sort order applied.

7. Click Sort.

INSIDE OUT   Don't accidentally renumber tasks when sorting

If you select the Permanently Renumber Tasks or Permanently Renumber Resources check box for the current sort operation, the check box remains selected for your subsequent sort operations for this or any other project plans. This is true whether your next sort operation is for resources or tasks. This can be a problem if you want to do a temporary sort—which is likely to be the case most of the time—and you're not in the habit of looking at that check box.

To prevent unwittingly jumbling up your project plan, whenever you do a permanent renumber sort, immediately open the Sort dialog box again, clear the Permanently Renumber check box, and then click Reset.

To return a sorted sheet view to its original order, click Project, Sort and then click By ID.

> **Note**
>
> If you choose to permanently renumber your tasks or resources according to a new sort order, remember that this renumbering will affect the order of tasks and resources in all other task or resource views. This is not the case with temporary sorting operations.

Grouping Project Information

Think of grouping as a more sophisticated kind of sorting, in which a graphical layout is applied to the sheet to segregate the groupings you've chosen. For example, suppose you group your task sheet by complete and incomplete tasks. Tasks that are 0 percent complete (not started yet) are grouped first and marked by a yellow band (see Figure 4-20). Tasks that are 1–99 percent complete (in progress) are grouped next, bounded by another yellow band. Tasks that are 100 percent complete are grouped last.

	❶	Task Name	Duration	Start	Finish
		⊟ % Complete: 0%	58 days	Tue 3/27/07	Thu 6/14/07
6		Finalize Web structure	2 days	Tue 3/27/07	Wed 3/28/07
12		Develop style sheets	4 days	Tue 3/27/07	Fri 3/30/07
13		Develop page templates	5 days	Mon 4/2/07	Fri 4/6/07
15		Home page design review	5 days	Mon 4/9/07	Fri 4/13/07
16		Finalize Home page design	3 days	Mon 4/16/07	Wed 4/18/07
20		Evaluate software requirements	15 days	Mon 4/9/07	Fri 4/27/07
21		Order equipment	3 days	Mon 4/30/07	Wed 5/2/07
22		Order software	3 days	Thu 5/3/07	Mon 5/7/07
23		Install and configure equipment	5 days	Tue 5/8/07	Mon 5/14/07
24		Install and configure software	5 days	Tue 5/15/07	Mon 5/21/07
28		Content review	10 days	Thu 4/19/07	Wed 5/2/07
29		Revise content	15 days	Thu 5/3/07	Wed 5/23/07
30		Second content review	10 days	Thu 5/24/07	Wed 6/6/07
31		Finalize content	5 days	Thu 6/7/07	Wed 6/13/07
32		Launch Web Site	1 day	Thu 6/14/07	Thu 6/14/07
		⊟ % Complete: 1% - 99%	30 days	Thu 3/8/07	Wed 4/18/07
5		Web structure review	5 days	Tue 3/20/07	Mon 3/26/07
11		Finalize interior page design	4 days	Wed 3/21/07	Mon 3/26/07
19		Evaluate equipment requirements	15 days	Mon 3/19/07	Fri 4/6/07
27		Develop content	30 days	Thu 3/8/07	Wed 4/18/07
		⊟ % Complete: 100%	12 days	Mon 3/5/07	Tue 3/20/07
2	✓	Brainstorm content categories	3 days	Mon 3/5/07	Wed 3/7/07
3	✓	Hold user meetings	5 days	Thu 3/8/07	Wed 3/14/07
4	✓	Develop Web structure	3 days	Thu 3/15/07	Mon 3/19/07
9	✓	Design interior pages	7 days	Mon 3/5/07	Tue 3/13/07
10	✓	Interior page design review	5 days	Wed 3/14/07	Tue 3/20/07

Figure 4-20 Groups graphically separate categories of information in a view.

The grouping band shows the title of the group, for example, Percent Complete: 0% or 100% Complete. Where appropriate, the grouping band also rolls up information summarized from the group, such as the total duration for the grouping, the earliest start date for all tasks in the grouping, the latest finish date for all tasks in the grouping, and so on.

Built-in Task Groups

All built-in task groups appear on the Group By submenu on the Project menu when a task view is showing. The following is a complete list of these built-in task groups:

- Complete And Incomplete Tasks
- Constraint Type
- Critical
- Duration
- Duration Then Priority
- Milestones
- Priority
- Priority Keeping Outline Structure

You can also group resources in a resource sheet. For example, you might want to group resources by their department or code or by resource type (work or material).

Built-in Resource Groups

All built-in resource groups appear on the Group By submenu on the Project menu when a resource view is showing. The following is a complete list of these built-in task groups:

- Assignments Keeping Outline Structure
- Complete And Incomplete Resources
- Resource Group
- Standard Rate
- Work Vs. Material Resources

You can also group nodes in the Network Diagram view (see Figure 4- 21). To group task or resource information in a sheet view or Network Diagram, follow these steps:

1. Display the view whose information you want to group.

2. Click Project, Group By.

3. In the submenu that appears, click the grouping you want.

Chapter 4

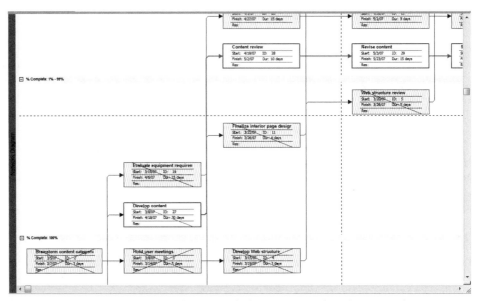

Figure 4-21 Nodes are collected and rearranged when you group them by a particular category.

To remove a grouping, click Project, Group By and then click No Group.

> **Note**
> You can also use the Group By tool on the Standard toolbar. With a sheet view displayed, click the grouping you want to apply. To restore the view to its original order, click the arrow in the Group By tool again and select No Group.

No Group
Group By

You can customize built-in groups and create entirely new groups as well. You can group by fields, including custom outline codes that you create.

For more information about groups, see the section titled "Customizing Groups" in Chapter 25.

Filtering Project Information

When you filter a view, you're excluding information you don't need to see so you can focus on what you do need to see. For example, if you want to see only tasks that use a particular resource so you can more closely analyze the workload, you can apply the Using Resource filter. Or if you're about to attend a status meeting and you want to discuss tasks that are either in progress or not started, you can apply the Incomplete Tasks filter to a task sheet.

Built-in Task Filters

The most commonly used task filters appear on the Filtered For submenu of the Project menu. All built-in filters are accessible in the More Filters dialog box. The following is a complete list of the built-in task filters:

- Completed Tasks
- Cost Greater Than
- Cost Overbudget
- Created After
- Critical
- Date Range
- In Progress Tasks
- Incomplete Tasks
- Late/Overbudget Tasks Assigned To
- Linked Fields
- Milestones
- Resource Group
- Should Start By
- Should Start/Finish By
- Slipped/Late Progress
- Slipping Tasks
- Summary Tasks
- Task Range
- Tasks With A Task Calendar Assigned
- Tasks With Attachments
- Tasks With Deadlines
- Tasks With Estimated Durations
- Tasks With Fixed Dates
- Tasks/Assignments With Overtime
- Top Level Tasks
- Unstarted Tasks
- Using Resource In Date Range
- Using Resource
- Work Overbudget

Chapter 4

Built-in Resource Filters

You can also apply filters to a resource sheet. If you want to examine all resources that are running over budget, for example, you can apply the Cost Overbudget filter. Or if you want to see only your material resources, you can apply the Resources – Material filter to a resource sheet.

The most commonly used resource filters appear on the Filtered For submenu of the Project menu. All built-in filters are accessible in the More Filters dialog box. The following is a complete list of the built-in resource filters:

- Budget Resources
- Cost Greater Than
- Cost Overbudget
- Created After
- Date Range
- Group
- In Progress Assignments
- Linked Fields
- Non-Budget Resources
- Overallocated Resources
- Resource Range
- Resources – Cost
- Resources – Material
- Resources – Work
- Resources With Attachments
- Resources/Assignments With Overtime
- Should Start By
- Should Start/Finish By
- Slipped/Late Progress
- Slipping Assignments
- Unstarted Assignments
- Work Complete
- Work Incomplete
- Work Overbudget

To filter information in a view, follow these steps:

1. Display the view whose information you want to filter. You can filter information in all views.

2. Click Project, Filtered For.

3. If the filter you want is listed on the submenu, click it. If the filter is not in the submenu, click More Filters and then find and click it in the More Filters dialog box (see Figure 4-22). Click Apply.

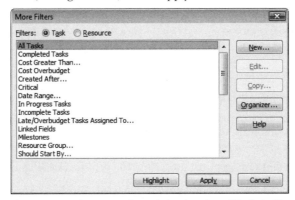

Figure 4-22 The More Filters dialog box lists all built-in filters.

4. Some filters require you to enter more information. For example, if you choose the Should Start/Finish filter, you need to enter start and finish dates and click OK.

> **Note**
>
> By default, a filter excludes tasks or resources that do not meet the conditions of that filter. If you prefer, you can instead have the filter highlight tasks or resources that do meet the filter conditions. Click Project, Filtered For, More Filters. Click the filter you want and then click the Highlight button instead of the Apply button.

To remove a filter and show all tasks or all resources again, click Project, Filtered For and then click All Tasks.

> **Note**
>
> You can also use the Filter tool on the Formatting toolbar. Display the view you want to filter; then use the tool to click the filter you want to apply. When finished, click the arrow in the Filter tool and select All Tasks (or All Resources).

All Tasks

Filter

Chapter 4

Using AutoFilter, you can quickly filter by a value in a particular field. To do this, follow these steps:

1. Display the sheet view whose information you want to autofilter.

AutoFilter

2. On the Formatting toolbar, click AutoFilter. The AutoFilter arrows appear in each column heading in the sheet view.

Task Name	Duratio▼	Start ▼	Finish ▼
⊟ **WebDev4-2**	**74 days**	**Mon 3/5/07**	**Thu 6/14/07**
⊟ **Web Structure**	**18 days**	**Mon 3/5/07**	**Wed 3/28/07**
Brainstorm content categories	3 days	Mon 3/5/07	Wed 3/7/07
Hold user meetings	5 days	Thu 3/8/07	Wed 3/14/07
Develop Web structure	3 days	Thu 3/15/07	Mon 3/19/07

3. Click the arrow in the column whose information you want to filter by and then click the value you want to filter by.

    For example, suppose you are displaying the Gantt Chart with the Entry table applied. If you want to filter for all tasks scheduled to start next month, click the AutoFilter arrow in the Start column and then click Next Month.

    When AutoFilter is applied, the text of the column heading changes color.

4. To show all tasks or resources again, click the AutoFilter arrow in the applied column heading and then click All.

> **Note**
>
> To show all tasks or resources again, you can also simply click the AutoFilter tool on the Formatting toolbar to turn it off. The AutoFilter arrows disappear and any filtered data is unfiltered again, that is, all data shows.

The AutoFilter arrows remain handy in the column headings for all views throughout your project plan until you turn AutoFilter off. With AutoFilter on, you can always quickly filter tasks or resources in a sheet. If you want to turn AutoFilter off, click the AutoFilter button again.

TROUBLESHOOTING

Some of your project information is missing

It's easy to apply a filter, work with your project information for a while, and then forget that the filter is applied. Then, when you look for certain tasks or resources that you know are there, you can't see them.

Check whether a filter is applied. Click the Project menu and look at the Filtered For command. If it says Filtered For: All Tasks Or All Resources, you know you're seeing all the information that's there. If, on the other hand, it says Filtered For: Critical, for example, you know you have a filter applied. Click All Tasks or All Resources to show your information again.

When you have an AutoFilter applied, the Project menu might still indicate that you're showing all tasks or resources. If the Project menu indicates that you're displaying everything (but you're not), check whether AutoFilter is on. If it is, review your column headings and find the one that's blue. Click the arrow and then click All to show all tasks or resources. Or, click the AutoFilter button on the Formatting toolbar.

You can customize built-in filters and create entirely new filters as well. You can also create custom AutoFilters. For more information, see the section titled "Customizing Filters" in Chapter 25.

Learn More About Microsoft Project Views, Tables, Filters, and Groups

In Microsoft Project online Help, you can get more information about all available views, tables, filters, and groups. To do this, follow these steps:

1. Click Help, Microsoft Office Project Help.

2. In the Project Help pane, click View Management.

3. Click the topic you want to read.

Arranging Your Microsoft Project Window

The more you work with Microsoft Project, the stronger your preferences become about how you want elements laid out in the application window. You can make changes to the Microsoft Project window that will persist across your working sessions with the project plan as well as to other projects you create. For example, you can reset which view should be the default when you first start a new project plan. You can also show or hide different elements in the default Microsoft Project window. In making these changes, you can set up your Microsoft Project window to be the most efficient for your own working methods.

On the other hand, sometimes you need to rearrange the Microsoft Project window temporarily to accomplish a specific task. For example, maybe you need to see the same window in two different panes. You can arrange open windows to do this. You can also easily switch among multiple open projects.

Setting Your Default View

The default view that appears whenever you start Microsoft Project or create a new project file is the Gantt Chart. This is because project managers use this view most often, at least as a starting point. However, if a different view is your favorite, you can make that one the default view. To do this, follow these steps:

1. Click Tools, Options.

2. Click the View tab.

3. In the Default View box, click the name of the view you want as your default view.

INSIDE OUT   Not always the default view

Setting the default view does not control the view that appears when you open an existing project plan. When you open an existing project plan, it displays the last view you were working with when you closed it. If you want your project plan to open in a particular view each time, make sure you end your working session in that view.

Showing and Hiding Screen Elements

Certain screen elements are displayed by default in the Microsoft Project window. To expand your working area, you can hide elements you don't use much. (You can still use these elements when you need them.) This also frees up more space if you want to add a different element in its place.

Table 4-11 lists the screen elements you can show or hide, along with the procedure for doing so.

Table 4-11 Screen Elements

Screen element	How to display or hide it
Project Guide	To close the Project Guide for the current project only, simply click the Close (X) button in the upper-right corner of the pane. When you want it to show again, click the Show/Hide Project Guide button on the Project Guide toolbar. To show or hide the Project Guide for all projects, click Tools, Options. On the Interface tab, under Project Guide Settings, select or clear the Display Project Guide check box.
View bar	Click View, View Bar.
Online Help	To show Help, click Help, Microsoft Office Project Help or press F1. The Project Help window appears. Browse through the list of topics displayed, enter a term or phrase in the Search box, or click the Table Of Contents button in the toolbar. To close the Project Help window, simply click its Close button.
Toolbars	Click View, Toolbars and then click the name of the toolbar you want to show or hide.
Entry bar (the bar above the view)	Click Tools, Options. On the View tab, under Show, select or clear the Entry Bar check box.
Scroll bars	Click Tools, Options. On the View tab, under Show, select or clear the Scroll Bars check box.
Status bar (the bar below the view)	Click Tools, Options. On the View tab, under Show, select or clear the Status Bar check box.

Show/Hide
Project Guide

Show Table of
Contents

Chapter 4

Splitting a Window

You might be familiar with the Split function in Microsoft Excel or Microsoft Office Word, in which you can divide a single window into two panes and scroll each pane independently. In Microsoft Project, you might need to refer to different parts of the same Microsoft Project view. Perhaps you want to show different parts of the same view in a split screen because you're modeling a new section of a project on an existing section farther up the view. Or maybe you want to see two different views at the same time.

The problem is that when you split a screen in Microsoft Project (using Window, Split), a form appears that gives you a combination view. You can switch to a different view, but the lower view is designed to show information relevant to the information selected in the upper view.

The solution is to open a second instance of the same window and then arrange them side by side in your Microsoft Project window. To see two independent panes of your project plan at the same time, follow these steps:

1. Click Window, New Window. In the New Window dialog box, click the name of your project plan and click OK. This opens a second instance of your project plan. The two instances are marked in the title bar with a "1" and "2," indicating that these are separate windows of the same project. Any changes you make in one window are simultaneously made in the other.

2. Click Window, Arrange All. Any open project plans are tiled in your project window (see Figure 4-23).

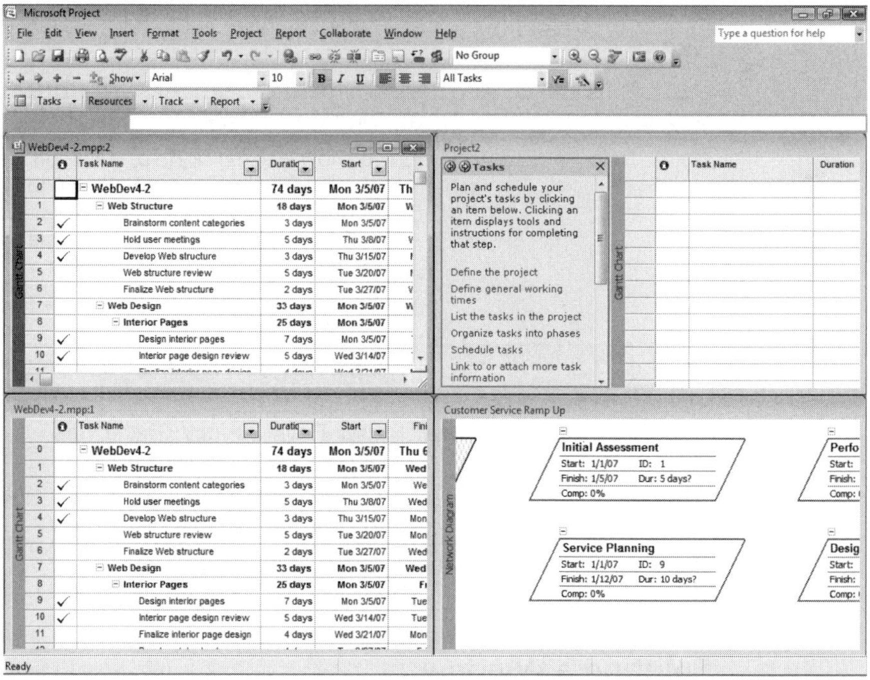

Figure 4-23   Clicking Arrange All makes all open projects visible.

3. If you have other project plans open besides the two you want to work with, either close them or select each one and click Window, Hide. When only the two instances of the project plan are displayed, click Window, Arrange All again. The two open projects are tiled horizontally: one above and the other below (see Figure 4-24). Now you can scroll the two windows independently of each other and also look at different views independently.

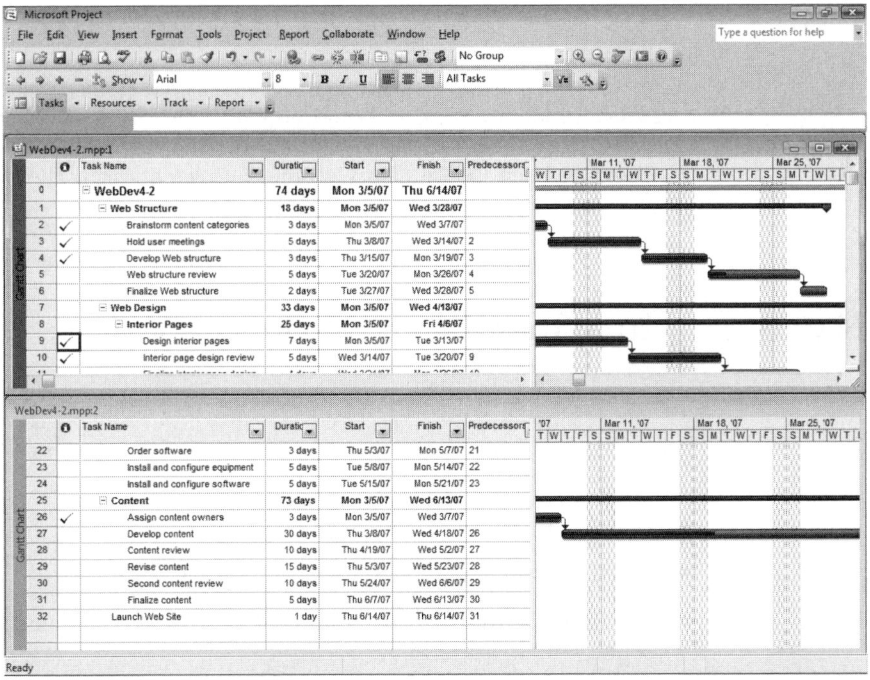

Figure 4-24 You can independently scroll or change views in the two tiled project windows.

> **Note**
>
> To give yourself more working space while viewing two project windows at one time, hide a toolbar or two. Click View, Toolbars and then click the name of the checked toolbar you want to hide. By default, the Standard, Formatting, and Project Guide toolbars are showing.

Switching Among Open Projects

If you have multiple projects open at the same time, there are several ways to switch among them. You can do the following:

- Click the project's button on the Windows taskbar
- Press Alt+Tab to cycle through all open programs and windows
- Press Ctrl+F6 to cycle through all open projects

> **Note**
>
> By default, multiple open Microsoft Project files are represented as individual buttons on the Windows taskbar. You can change this so that there's just a single Microsoft Project button on the taskbar, regardless of the number of open project files. Click Tools, Options and then click the View tab. Clear the Windows In Taskbar check box.

Navigating to a Specific Location in a View

With a long list of tasks, dozens of resources, and dates spanning months or even years, the different views in your project plan probably cover a lot of space. When you're trying to get to a specific place in a view, you can always scroll vertically or horizontally. But there are shortcuts, as follows:

- **Ctrl+Home** Moves to the first row in a sheet.

- **Ctrl+End** Moves to the last row in a sheet.

- **Alt+Home** Moves to the beginning of the project timescale (Gantt Chart, Resource Graph, usage view).

- **Alt+End** Moves to the end of the project timescale (Gantt Chart, Resource Graph, usage view).

Go To Selected Task

- **Go To Selected Task button, or Ctrl+Shift+F5** Moves the timescale portion of a view (Gantt Chart or usage view) to the location of the task or assignment selected in the sheet portion of the view.

- **F5, "Today"** Moves the chart portion of a timescaled view (Gantt Chart, usage view, or Resource Graph) to the location of today's date. You can either click today's date in the Date box or type the word **Today** in the box.

Scheduling Tasks

Setting Task Durations. 154

Establishing Task Dependencies. 167

Scheduling Tasks to Achieve Specific Dates 178

Setting Deadline Reminders. 186

Creating Milestones in Your Schedule. 188

Working with Task Calendars 192

Seeing Feedback on Scheduling Changes 195

Y ou've developed your work breakdown structure, and your task list is now sequenced and outlined. You have a good work breakdown structure now, but you
don't have a schedule...yet.

Although there are many knowledge areas (including scope management, cost management, and resource management) that contribute to successful project management,
time management is most related to development of your project schedule—your roadmap for completing tasks, handing off deliverables, passing milestones, and finally
achieving the goals of your project in a timely manner.

To develop an accurate and workable schedule that truly reflects how your project will
run, you need to do the following:

- Enter task durations.

- Identify the relationships, or dependencies, among tasks.

- Schedule certain tasks to achieve specific dates when necessary.

When you've done these three things, you begin to see the basic outline of a real project schedule. You have not yet added and assigned resources, which further influence
the schedule. Nor have you refined the project plan to make the project finish date and
costs conform to your requirements. However, at this point, you can start to see how
long certain tasks will take and how far into the future the project might run.

**To learn about adding and assigning resources, see Chapter 7, "Assigning Resources to Tasks."
For information about refining your project, see Chapter 9, "Checking and Adjusting the
Project Plan."**

You can use a variety of scheduling tools and cues to help keep you focused and on
track as you and your team work your way through the project. You can do the following:

- Create reminders to alert you as deadlines are approaching.

- Add milestones to your schedule as conspicuous markers of producing a deliverable, completing a phase, or achieving another major event in your project.

- Apply a calendar to a task that is independent of the project calendar or the calendars of resources assigned to the task, so that the task can be scheduled independently.

- See the effects of scheduling changes while you work, and review the factors that affect the scheduling of a task.

Setting Task Durations

When your task list is entered, sequenced, and outlined in Microsoft Office Project 2007 (see Figure 5-1), you're ready to start the work of creating a schedule.

	ⓘ	Task Name	Duration	Start	Finish
1		⊟ Web Structure	1 day?	Mon 3/5/07	Mon 3/5/07
2		Brainstorm content categories	1 day?	Mon 3/5/07	Mon 3/5/07
3		Hold user meetings	1 day?	Mon 3/5/07	Mon 3/5/07
4		Develop Web structure	1 day?	Mon 3/5/07	Mon 3/5/07
5		Web structure review	1 day?	Mon 3/5/07	Mon 3/5/07
6		Finalize Web structure	1 day?	Mon 3/5/07	Mon 3/5/07
7		⊟ Web Design	1 day?	Mon 3/5/07	Mon 3/5/07
8		⊟ Interior Pages	1 day?	Mon 3/5/07	Mon 3/5/07
9		Design interior pages	1 day?	Mon 3/5/07	Mon 3/5/07
10		Interior page design review	1 day?	Mon 3/5/07	Mon 3/5/07
11		Finalize interior page design	1 day?	Mon 3/5/07	Mon 3/5/07
12		Develop style sheets	1 day?	Mon 3/5/07	Mon 3/5/07
13		Develop page templates	1 day?	Mon 3/5/07	Mon 3/5/07
14		⊟ Design Home page	1 day?	Mon 3/5/07	Mon 3/5/07
15		Home page design review	1 day?	Mon 3/5/07	Mon 3/5/07
16		Finalize Home page design	1 day?	Mon 3/5/07	Mon 3/5/07
17		⊟ Hardware and Software	1 day?	Mon 3/5/07	Mon 3/5/07
18		Perform system needs analysis	1 day?	Mon 3/5/07	Mon 3/5/07
19		Evaluate equipment requirements	1 day?	Mon 3/5/07	Mon 3/5/07
20		Evaluate software requirements	1 day?	Mon 3/5/07	Mon 3/5/07
21		Order equipment	1 day?	Mon 3/5/07	Mon 3/5/07
22		Order software	1 day?	Mon 3/5/07	Mon 3/5/07
23		Install and configure equipment	1 day?	Mon 3/5/07	Mon 3/5/07
24		Install and configure software	1 day?	Mon 3/5/07	Mon 3/5/07
25		⊟ Content	1 day?	Mon 3/5/07	Mon 3/5/07
26		Assign content owners	1 day?	Mon 3/5/07	Mon 3/5/07
27		Develop content	1 day?	Mon 3/5/07	Mon 3/5/07
28		Content review	1 day?	Mon 3/5/07	Mon 3/5/07

Figure 5-1 Your project schedule displays all tasks starting on the project start date, each with an estimated duration of 1 day.

To create a realistic schedule, you can start by entering the length of time you believe each task will take to complete; that is, the task *duration*. As soon as you enter a task, Microsoft Project assigns it an estimated duration of 1 day, just to have something to draw in the Gantt Chart. You can easily change that duration.

Entering accurate duration estimates is very important for creating a reliable project schedule. Microsoft Project uses the duration of each task to calculate the start and finish dates for the task. If you will be assigning resources, the duration is also the basis for the amount of work for each assigned resource.

Developing Reliable Task Duration Estimates

As the project manager, you can start by entering a broad duration estimate based on your own experience. Then, you can refine the estimate by soliciting input from others who are more directly involved or experienced with the sets of tasks. There are four possible sources for developing reliable task durations, as follows:

- **Team knowledge** Suppose that you're managing a new business startup project, and you already have your team in place. The business advisor can provide durations for tasks such as creating a market analysis, researching the competition, and identifying the target market niche. The accountant can provide durations for tasks such as forecasting financial returns, setting up the accounting system, and obtaining needed insurance. Team members ready to work on the project can also provide duration estimates for tasks based on their previous experience as well as their projection of how long they expect the tasks to take for this particular project.

- **Expert judgment** If you have not yet assembled a team from whom you can obtain durations, or if you want reliable input from impartial specialists in the field, you might call upon experts such as consultants, professional associations, or industry groups. These can help you establish task durations for projects common to your field.

- **Past projects** Similar projects that have been completed in your organization can be a most excellent source of accurate durations. If Microsoft Project files are available, you can see the initial durations. If the project manager maintained the project plan by diligently tracking actual information throughout the life of the project, you have at your disposal invaluable information about how long certain tasks actually took, as well as any variances from their planned durations.

- **Industry standards** Historical duration information for tasks typical to an industry or discipline is sometimes available commercially through professional or standards organizations. You can adapt such information for tasks and durations to fit the unique requirements of your project.

You might use a combination of these methods to obtain durations for all the tasks in your project. It's often very useful to have durations based on established metrics. For example, suppose that you know the industry standard for the number of hours it takes to develop certain types of architectural drawings as well as the number of those drawings you need. You can multiply these figures to develop a reasonable duration for your specific task.

Chapter 5

> **Note**
>
> You can also use these methods to obtain work amounts for resources assigned to tasks. While duration is the span of time from task start to finish, work is the amount of time a resource has to complete the task. Sometimes duration and work are the same; many times they are not, depending on the type of task and then number and type of resources assigned.

> **Project Management Practices: Building in a Buffer**
>
> Building in a duration *buffer* is a method that many project managers use as a contingency against project risk. Some say that the durations should be as "real" and accurate as possible, already taking into account any possible risk. Others say it just isn't realistic to believe that you can account for all possible problems while you're still in the project planning processes. To build in a buffer, also known as *reserve time,* you can add a "buffer task" close to the end of the project, with a duration that represents either a percentage of the total project duration or a fixed work period, for example, two weeks.
>
> The reserve time can later be reduced or eliminated as more precise information about the project becomes available. For example, suppose you initially enter a duration of 5 days to set up the accounting system. Later on, more concrete information indicates that it will actually take 8 days. You can "transfer" that time from your buffer without pushing out your project finish date.

Understanding Estimated vs. Confirmed Durations

Any value in the Duration field that's followed by a question mark is considered a duration estimate. Technically, all planned durations are only estimates because you don't know how long a task takes until it's completed and you have an actual duration. However, the question mark indicates what you might consider an "estimate of a duration estimate." Estimated durations are calculated into the schedule the same as confirmed durations; they simply serve as an alert that a duration is still more of a guess.

> **Note**
>
> If you have no use for the estimated durations question mark, you can turn it off. Click Tools, Options and then click the Schedule tab. Clear the Show That Tasks Have Estimated Durations check box as well as the New Tasks Have Estimated Durations check box.
>
> This setting will take effect for the current project. If you want this setting to be in effect for all projects you create, click the Set As Default button.

By default, a duration estimate of 1 day is entered for any newly added task (**1d?**). Use this value as a flag to indicate that the duration still needs to be entered for this task. You can also enter a question mark (?) after a duration, for example, **2w?**. Any durations with question marks can serve as flags to indicate that the duration is still under consideration and might change after you receive more solid information. When you remove the question mark from a duration, the duration is confirmed; that is, you're now confident of this duration.

> **Note**
>
> You can sort, group, or filter tasks by whether a task has an estimated or confirmed duration. For more information, see the section titled "Rearranging Your Project Information" in Chapter 4, "Viewing Project Information."

Entering Durations

You can enter duration in different time period units, as follows:

- Minutes (m or min)

- Hours (h or hr)

- Days (d or dy)

- Weeks (w or wk)

- Months (mo or mon)

Whether you type **h**, **hr**, or **hour** in your duration entry, by default Microsoft Project enters "hr". You can change which abbreviation of the time unit appears in the Duration field. Click Tools, Options and then click the Edit tab. In each of the fields under View Options For Time Units, set the abbreviation of the time unit you want to see.

> **Note**
>
> This setting applies to the current project file only. If you want it to apply to all new projects you create, click the Set As Default button.

You can use different duration units throughout your plan. One task might be set with a duration of 2w, and another task might be set for 3d.

> **Note**
>
> If you don't specify a duration unit, by default Microsoft Project assumes that the unit is days and automatically enters "days" after your duration amount. If you want the default duration unit to be something different, such as hours or weeks, you can change it. Click Tools, Options and then click the Schedule tab. In the Duration Is Entered In box, select the time unit you want as the default.
>
> This setting applies to the current project file only. If you want it to apply to all new projects you create, click the Set As Default button.

To enter a duration, follow these steps:

1. Display the Gantt Chart.

2. In the Duration field for each task, type the duration, for example, *1w* or *4d*.

3. If a duration is an estimate, add a question mark after it, for example, *1w?* or *4d?*.

4. Press Enter. The Gantt bar is drawn to represent the time period for the task (see Figure 5-2). In addition, the Finish field is recalculated for the task. Microsoft Project adds the duration amount to the Start date to calculate the Finish date.

Confirmed durations

	ⓘ	Task Name	Duration	Start	Finish	Mar 4, '07	Mar
						F S S M T W T F S S	
1		⊟ **Web Structure**	**5 days**	**Mon 3/5/07**	**Fri 3/9/07**		
2		Brainstorm content categories	3 days	Mon 3/5/07	Wed 3/7/07		
3		Hold user meetings	5 days	Mon 3/5/07	Fri 3/9/07		
4		Develop Web structure	3 days	Mon 3/5/07	Wed 3/7/07		
5		Web structure review	5 days	Mon 3/5/07	Fri 3/9/07		
6		Finalize Web structure	2 days	Mon 3/5/07	Tue 3/6/07		
7		⊟ **Web Design**	**7 days?**	**Mon 3/5/07**	**Tue 3/13/07**		
8		⊟ **Interior Pages**	**7 days?**	**Mon 3/5/07**	**Tue 3/13/07**		
9		Design interior pages	7 days?	Mon 3/5/07	Tue 3/13/07		
10		Interior page design review	5 days?	Mon 3/5/07	Fri 3/9/07		
11		Finalize interior page design	4 days?	Mon 3/5/07	Thu 3/8/07		
12		Develop style sheets	4 days?	Mon 3/5/07	Thu 3/8/07		
13		Develop page templates	5 days?	Mon 3/5/07	Fri 3/9/07		

Figure 5-2 Confirmed as well as estimated durations are drawn with the Gantt bars.

> **Note**
>
> In a Gantt chart, you can also drag the right edge of a Gantt bar to change the task duration.

Task Information

Understanding How Durations Affect Scheduling

When you enter a duration, the task is scheduled according to its assigned calendar. Initially, this is the project calendar. When resources are assigned, the task is scheduled according to the resource's working times calendar. If a task calendar is applied, the task is scheduled according to the task's working times calendar.

For more information about task calendars, see the section titled "Working with Task Calendars" later in this chapter.

For example, suppose you enter a 2d duration for the "Create market analysis plan" task, and the task starts Monday at 8:00 A.M. Based on the default Standard calendar and its options, and assuming that the resource is assigned full-time to the task, Microsoft Project counts the 16 working hours in the 2-day duration to arrive at a finish date of Tuesday at 5:00 P.M.

Where Do Start and Finish Dates Come From?

Until you set task dependencies by linking predecessors and successors, the Start date of all your tasks is the same as the project start date by default.

You can make any new tasks adopt the current date (today) as the start date. Click Tools, Options and then click the Schedule tab. In the New Tasks box, click Start On Current Date.

In a schedule-from-finish project, the Finish date of all your tasks is the same as the Project finish date.

If you're working in a schedule-from-finish task and you enter a duration, Microsoft Project subtracts the duration amount from the Finish date to calculate the Start date.

If you want a task to take a set amount of time regardless of any working times calendars, you can enter an *elapsed duration*. An elapsed duration can be useful for tasks such as "Paint drying" or "Cement curing" that can't be stopped after they've started or that are independent of project schedules or resource assignments. Elapsed durations are scheduled 24 hours a day, 7 days a week, until finished. That is, one day is always considered 24 hours long (rather than 8 hours), and one week is always 7 days (rather than

5 days). To specify an elapsed duration, simply enter an **e** before the duration unit, for example, **3ed** for 3 elapsed days or **2ew** for 2 elapsed weeks (see Figure 5-3).

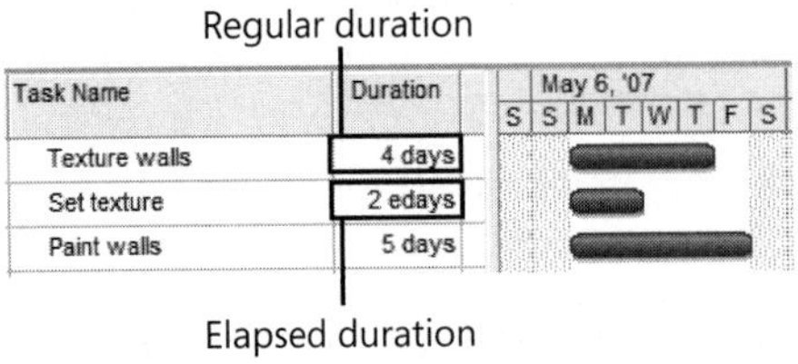

Figure 5-3 Regular durations are scheduled according to applied working times calendars, whereas elapsed durations are based on 24 hours per day, 7 days per week.

For regular (nonelapsed) durations, we need a way to specify the number of working hours in a day and week, the number of working days in a month, and so on. This way, when we specify 2 weeks as a duration, for example, we can be assured that this means the same thing as 80 hours, or 10 days. To set these options, follow these steps:

1. Click Tools, Options and then click the Calendar tab (see Figure 5-4).

   You can also click Tools, Change Working Time and then click the Options button.

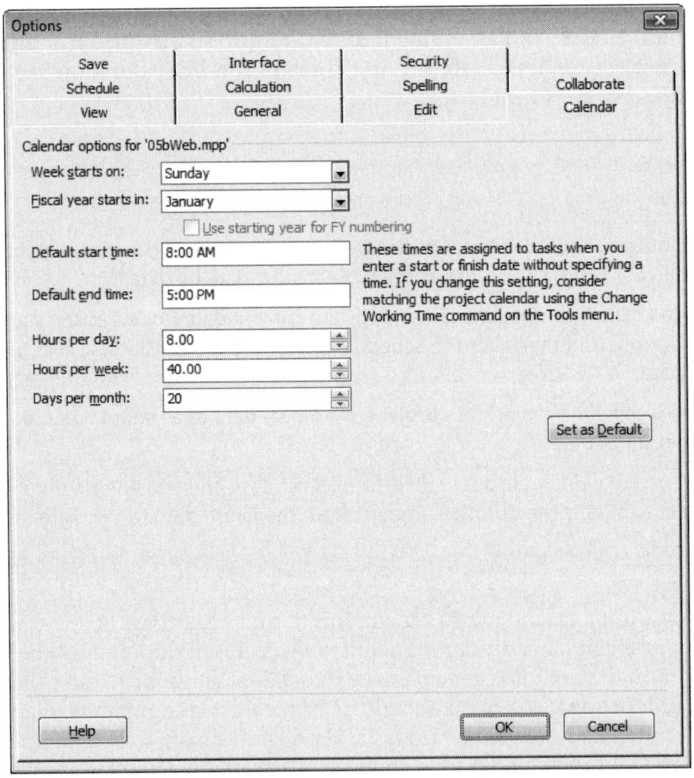

Figure 5-4 On the Calendar options tab, you can specify the details of your working time units, including the hours, days, and weeks.

2. Select the options on this tab to reflect the way your team works.

The Default Start Time (8:00 A.M.) and Default End Time (5:00 P.M.) are assigned to tasks when you enter a start or finish date without specifying a time.

The Hours Per Day, Hours Per Week, and Days Per Month values serve as your time unit specifications when needed. If you specify that a task has a duration of 1 month, does that mean 20 days or 30 days? These settings are used in conjunction with the working times calendars to dictate how your tasks are scheduled.

TROUBLESHOOTING

You set the calendar for 20 hours per week, but the tasks are still being scheduled for 40 hours per week

Or you thought you set the calendar for 8:00 A.M. to 12:00 P.M., for the project to be scheduled only in the mornings, but the tasks are still being scheduled 8:00 A.M. to 5:00 P.M.

Sometimes, the Calendar options tab confuses more readily than it assists. The Hours Per Day, Hours Per Week, and Days Per Month settings can easily be misinterpreted to make us think we're using them to set the schedule for the project. What we're actually doing is setting start and end times and specifying how duration entries are to be converted to assignment work.

Suppose you want to specify that work on this project is to be scheduled only in the mornings, from 8:00 A.M. until 12:00 P.M. To affect actual task scheduling in this way, you'd need to edit the working times for each day in the Change Working Time calendar. The Default Start Time field only specifies the time that Microsoft Project should enter if you enter a start date without a corresponding start time. The Default End Time field only specifies the time that Microsoft Project should enter if you enter a finish date without a corresponding finish time.

Also, suppose you want to specify that work on this project is to be scheduled only 20 hours per week because your team is working on another project at the same time. If you enter **20** in the Hours Per Week box and then enter a duration of 2 weeks, work on this project is scheduled for 40 hours—according to the project calendar. That means if the project's working times calendar is still set for Monday through Friday, 8:00 A.M. through 5:00 P.M., the 2 weeks is scheduled as two sets of 20 hours back to back, resulting in "2 weeks" taking place in 1 actual week in your schedule—probably not what you intended.

The solution is to make the corresponding change in the working times calendar. Set the working and nonworking times in the Change Working Time calendar so that there are 20 hours of working time per week. Then, when you enter 2 weeks as a duration, the first 20 hours are scheduled in the first week, and the second 20 hours are scheduled in the second week.

The settings in the Calendar Options tab also determine how durations are translated into work time units when you assign resources to tasks. Think of this as a "Conversions" tab, and it might be more clear.

Chapter 5

Reviewing Durations

Any Gantt chart view can give you a closer look at your task durations graphically across the timescale. The Calendar view also shows each task as a bar on the days and weeks in which it's scheduled.

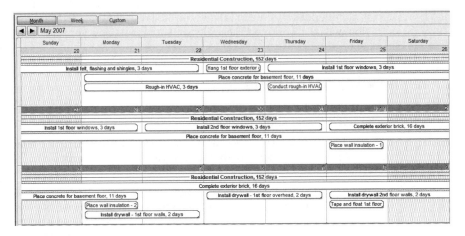

Calculating Your Most Probable Duration

In the course of researching task duration information, you might get conflicting results. Maybe the team member who will carry out a major task says it will take 3 weeks. Perhaps an expert stakeholder says it should take 2 weeks. And maybe the industry standard states that the same task should take 6 weeks. These are large discrepancies, and they're all coming from credible sources. How do you schedule a task with three possible durations?

Or imagine this situation—you have a single reliable duration or a duration range such as 2 weeks +/- 10 percent for all tasks in your task list, and you want your project plan to model a best-case scenario, a worst-case scenario, and an expected scenario for all durations. This way, you can learn the earliest possible project finish date, the latest possible date, and the most probable finish date.

To help resolve discrepancies or to model alternative scenarios, you can run a *PERT analysis*. A PERT (program evaluation and review technique) analysis uses a weighted average of optimistic, pessimistic, and expected durations to calculate task durations and therefore the project schedule. This analysis can be an effective risk management tool. It can also help if you're working out a project proposal or estimating time, cost, or resource requirements.

INSIDE OUT   **PERT analysis values placed in duration fields**

When you run a PERT analysis, the resulting calculated values are stored in certain custom fields, as follows:

- Optimistic Duration, Expected Duration, and Pessimistic Duration fields will be stored in the custom fields Duration1, Duration2, and Duration3, respectively.

- The optimistic start and finish dates are stored in the custom fields Start1 and Finish1.

- The expected start and finish dates are stored in the custom fields Start2 and Finish2.

- The pessimistic start and finish dates are stored in the custom fields Start3 and Finish3.

Any values in any of these custom fields are overwritten by the results of the PERT analysis. This can be significant if you were storing interim plan information in these fields or using these custom fields for any other purpose.

The good news is that when saving an interim plan, you can specify which sets of custom fields you want to use to store the interim plan data. You can do the same when you use custom fields for any other purpose, whether you want to use the Duration1 or Duration5 field, for example.

So if you ever think you might use PERT analysis, make a habit of using custom fields of Duration4 and higher, Start4 and higher, and Finish4 and higher. Then you won't have to worry about the PERT analysis process overwriting other information you wanted to keep.

For more information about interim plans, see the section titled "Saving Additional Baselines" in Chapter 10, "Setting a Baseline and Updating Progress." For more information about using custom fields, see the section titled "Customizing Fields" in Chapter 25, "Customizing Your View of Project Information."

To set up a PERT analysis, follow these steps:

1. Click View, Toolbars, PERT Analysis.

2. On the PERT Analysis toolbar, click PERT Entry Sheet.

PERT Entry Sheet

> **Note**
>
> The PA_PERT Entry Sheet does not appear in the More Views dialog box, and the PA_ PERT Entry table is not listed in the More Tables dialog box, until after the first time you click PERT Entry Sheet on the PERT Analysis toolbar. After that, the view and the table are listed and available.

Chapter 5

3. For each task, enter the optimistic, expected, and pessimistic durations in the appropriate fields (see Figure 5-5). You can also think of these fields as minimum, probable, and maximum durations for each task.

		Task Name	Duration	Optimistic Dur.	Expected Dur.	Pessimistic Dur.
	1	⊟ Web Structure	5 days	2 days	5 days	10 days
	2	Brainstorm content categories	3 days	1 day	3 days	5 days
	3	Hold user meetings	5 days	2 days	5 days	10 days
	4	Develop Web structure	3 days	1 day	3 days	5 days
	5	Web structure review	5 days	2 days	5 days	10 days
	6	Finalize Web structure	2 days	1 day	2 days	4 days
	7	⊟ Web Design	7 days	3 days	7 days	10 days
	8	⊟ Interior Pages	7 days	3 days	7 days	10 days
	9	Design interior pages	7 days	2 days	7 days	10 days
	10	Interior page design review	5 days	2 days	5 days	10 days
	11	Finalize interior page design	4 days	2 days	4 days	7 days
	12	Develop style sheets	4 days	2 days	4 days	5 days
	13	Develop page templates	5 days	3 days	5 days	6 days
	14	⊟ Home Page	5 days	2 days	5 days	7 days
	15	Design Home page	4 days	1 day	4 days	6 days
	16	Home page design review	5 days	2 days	5 days	7 days
	17	Finalize Home page design	3 days	2 days	3 days	4 days
	18	⊟ Hardware and Software	15 days	15 days	15 days	18 days
	19	Perform system needs analysis	10 days	4 days	10 days	12 days

Figure 5-5 Use the PERT Entry Sheet to specify the optimistic, expected, and pessimistic durations for each task.

If you do not expect a duration for a particular task to vary at all, enter the same value in all three fields.

Calculate PERT

4. On the PERT Analysis toolbar, click Calculate PERT.

The PERT Analysis message appears, which explains the Duration, Duration1, Duration2, and Duration3 fields.

5. Click Yes.

The estimated durations are calculated, and the results change the value in the Duration field (see Figure 5-6).

	Task Name	Duration	Optimistic Dur.	Expected Dur.	Pessimistic Dur.
1	⊟ Web Structure	5.33 days	2 days	5 days	10 days
2	Brainstorm content categories	3 days	1 day	3 days	5 days
3	Hold user meetings	5.33 days	2 days	5 days	10 days
4	Develop Web structure	3 days	1 day	3 days	5 days
5	Web structure review	5.33 days	2 days	5 days	10 days
6	Finalize Web structure	2.17 days	1 day	2 days	4 days
7	⊟ Web Design	6.67 days	3 days	7 days	10 days
8	⊟ Interior Pages	6.67 days	3 days	7 days	10 days
9	Design interior pages	6.67 days	2 days	7 days	10 days
10	Interior page design review	5.33 days	2 days	5 days	10 days
11	Finalize interior page design	4.17 days	2 days	4 days	7 days
12	Develop style sheets	3.83 days	2 days	4 days	5 days
13	Develop page templates	4.83 days	3 days	5 days	6 days
14	⊟ Home Page	4.83 days	2 days	5 days	7 days
15	Design Home page	3.83 days	1 day	4 days	6 days
16	Home page design review	4.83 days	2 days	5 days	7 days
17	Finalize Home page design	3 days	2 days	3 days	4 days
18	⊟ Hardware and Software	15 days	15 days	15 days	18 days
19	Perform system needs analysis	9.33 days	4 days	10 days	12 days

Figure 5-6 The recalculated durations based on the PERT analysis replace the values in the Duration field for each task.

INSIDE OUT   PERT analysis versus the critical path method

In addition to the PERT method for calculating task durations, there is the critical path method (CPM). In fact, standard Microsoft Project calculations are based on CPM. With CPM, project duration is forecasted by analyzing which sequence of project activities has the least amount of scheduling flexibility. An early start and early finish are calculated, as are a late start and late finish.

Sections later in this chapter discuss setting up task dependencies and task constraints. Both of these establish the amount of scheduling flexibility tasks have in relation to one another. Together with the duration, these elements go a long way toward determining the critical path of tasks through the project.

Many project managers use PERT analyses for their duration estimates and then use CPM to manage the importance of tasks in their schedule, given their level of scheduling flexibility.

For more information about the critical path method, see the section titled "Working with the Critical Path and Critical Tasks" in Chapter 9.

You can review Gantt charts using each of the three sets of durations, as follows:

- For the optimistic durations, click Optimistic Gantt on the PERT Analysis toolbar (see Figure 5-7).

Optimistic Gantt

Chapter 5

	❶	Task Name	Opt Dur	Opt Start	Opt Finish	Mar 4, '07
						F S S M T W T F S
1		⊟ **Web Structure**	**2 days**	**Mon 3/5/07**	**Tue 3/6/07**	
2		Brainstorm content categories	1 day	Mon 3/5/07	Mon 3/5/07	
3		Hold user meetings	2 days	Mon 3/5/07	Tue 3/6/07	
4		Develop Web structure	1 day	Mon 3/5/07	Mon 3/5/07	
5		Web structure review	2 days	Mon 3/5/07	Tue 3/6/07	
6		Finalize Web structure	1 day	Mon 3/5/07	Mon 3/5/07	
7		⊟ **Web Design**	**3 days**	**Mon 3/5/07**	**Wed 3/7/07**	
8		⊟ **Interior Pages**	**3 days**	**Mon 3/5/07**	**Wed 3/7/07**	
9		Design interior pages	2 days	Mon 3/5/07	Tue 3/6/07	
10		Interior page design review	2 days	Mon 3/5/07	Tue 3/6/07	
11		Finalize interior page design	2 days	Mon 3/5/07	Tue 3/6/07	
12		Develop style sheets	2 days	Mon 3/5/07	Tue 3/6/07	
13		Develop page templates	3 days	Mon 3/5/07	Wed 3/7/07	
14		⊟ **Home Page**	**2 days**	**Mon 3/5/07**	**Tue 3/6/07**	
15		Design Home page	1 day	Mon 3/5/07	Mon 3/5/07	
16		Home page design review	2 days	Mon 3/5/07	Tue 3/6/07	
17		Finalize Home page design	2 days	Mon 3/5/07	Tue 3/6/07	

Figure 5-7 The Optimistic Gantt shows the optimistic durations for the PERT Analysis.

Expected Gantt

- For the expected durations, click Expected Gantt on the PERT Analysis toolbar.

Pessimistic Gantt

- For the pessimistic durations, click Pessimistic Gantt on the PERT Analysis toolbar.

You can also display one of the PERT Analysis Gantt charts or the PERT Entry Sheet by clicking View, More Views and then selecting it in the dialog box. However, be aware that a PERT Analysis view does not appear in the More Views dialog box until you click the button for that view on the PERT Analysis toolbar the first time after installing Microsoft Project.

INSIDE OUT   Adjust PERT analysis weighting

Set PERT Weights

Sometimes, the PERT analysis results appear to be skewed or exaggerated. You can adjust how Microsoft Project weights duration estimates for the PERT analysis. On the PERT Analysis toolbar, click Set PERT Weights. Change the number in at least two of the three fields—Optimistic, Expected, and Pessimistic—so that the sum of all three numbers equals six (see Figure 5-8). Then, enter the durations in the PERT Entry Sheet as described previously. Finally, click Calculate PERT.

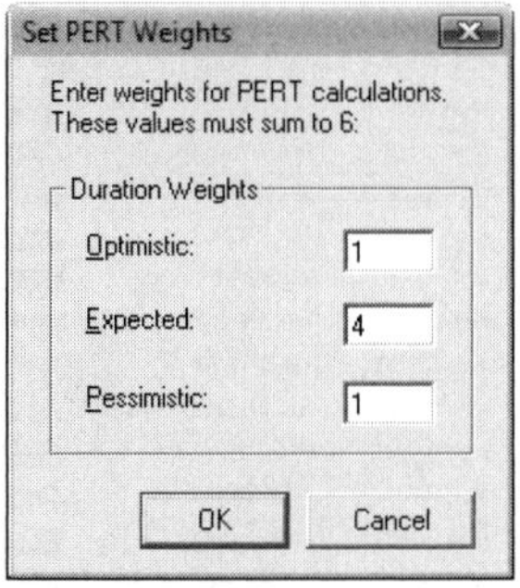

Figure 5-8 Use the Set PERT Weights dialog box to change the weighting of optimistic, expected, and pessimistic durations for the PERT Analysis calculation.

By default, the PERT weights are 1-4-1; that is, heavily weighted toward the expected duration, and lightly and equally weighted for the pessimistic and optimistic durations. Although 1-4-1 is the standard PERT weighting, 1-3-2 can build in a little more pessimism for better risk management.

Note

A good use of the PERT analysis is for a quick check of how your project is going. Has your critical path or resource leveling pushed the project schedule beyond your worst-case PERT analysis? If so, it can tell you it's time to replan your project.

Establishing Task Dependencies

At this point, your tasks all have what you hope are realistic durations. What is not realistic is that each task looks like it's starting on the project start date (see Figure 5-9).

Chapter 5

	❶	Task Name	Duration	Start	Finish	
1		⊟ **Web Structure**	**5.33 days**	**Mon 3/5/07**	**Mon 3/12/07**	
2		Brainstorm content categories	3 days	Mon 3/5/07	Wed 3/7/07	
3		Hold user meetings	5.33 days	Mon 3/5/07	Mon 3/12/07	
4		Develop Web structure	3 days	Mon 3/5/07	Wed 3/7/07	
5		Web structure review	5.33 days	Mon 3/5/07	Mon 3/12/07	
6		Finalize Web structure	2.17 days	Mon 3/5/07	Wed 3/7/07	
7		⊟ **Web Design**	**6.67 days**	**Mon 3/5/07**	**Tue 3/13/07**	
8		⊟ **Interior Pages**	**6.67 days**	**Mon 3/5/07**	**Tue 3/13/07**	
9		Design interior pages	6.67 days	Mon 3/5/07	Tue 3/13/07	
10		Interior page design review	5.33 days	Mon 3/5/07	Mon 3/12/07	
11		Finalize interior page design	4.17 days	Mon 3/5/07	Fri 3/9/07	
12		Develop style sheets	3.83 days	Mon 3/5/07	Thu 3/8/07	
13		Develop page templates	4.83 days	Mon 3/5/07	Fri 3/9/07	
14		⊟ **Home Page**	**4.83 days**	**Mon 3/5/07**	**Fri 3/9/07**	
15		Design Home page	3.83 days	Mon 3/5/07	Thu 3/8/07	
16		Home page design review	4.83 days	Mon 3/5/07	Fri 3/9/07	
17		Finalize Home page design	3 days	Mon 3/5/07	Wed 3/7/07	

Figure 5-9 Until you set up task dependencies, all tasks are shown as starting on the project start date.

Although many tasks in a project are likely to begin on the project start date, most other tasks cannot begin until another task has finished. Sometimes, several tasks are dependent upon the completion of one task; sometimes, several tasks must finish before a single later task can begin.

So, the next step in creating your schedule is to link tasks that are dependent upon each other. You can link the previous, or *predecessor* task, to its succeeding, or *successor* task, and thereby set up the *task dependency* between the two.

> **Note**
>
> A task dependency is also referred to as a *task relationship* or a *link*.

When you have your task dependencies combined with your durations in place, your project plan truly starts to look like a real schedule. You can begin to see possible start dates and finish dates, not only for the individual tasks, but also for major phases, milestones, and the project as a whole. When you create a link between two tasks, Microsoft Project calculates the successor's start and finish dates based on the predecessor's start or finish date, the dependency type, the successor's duration, and any associated resource assignments. There's still more information and refinement to be done, but you're getting closer to a schedule that starts to reflect reality.

Project Management Practices: Real vs. Preferred Task Dependencies

When building your project schedule, bear in mind whether the task dependencies you're creating are really required or whether they simply reflect a preference on your part.

For example, in a construction project, a task such as "Install siding" *must* be the predecessor to "Paint house." This is a true task dependency.

On the other hand, you might make a task such as "Finish interior" a predecessor to "Install landscaping." They don't need to be linked to each other, but might only reflect a preference you or your team has for a variety of reasons.

Be careful of these kinds of preferred but unnecessary dependencies because they can cause unnecessary problems later when you're trying to fine-tune the project plan or respond to problems that arise in the midst of tracking the project. At that point, you want as much scheduling flexibility in the project as possible. Any artificial task dependencies reduce that flexibility.

Creating the Finish-to-Start Task Dependency

The most typical link is the finish-to-start task dependency. With this link, the predecessor task must finish before the successor task can begin. To link tasks with the finish-to-start task dependency, follow these steps:

1. Display the Gantt Chart. You can set task dependencies in any task sheet, but you can see the effects of the links immediately in the Gantt Chart.

2. In the task sheet, select the two tasks you want to link. Drag from the predecessor to the successor task if they are right next to each other. If they are not adjacent tasks, click the predecessor, hold down the Ctrl key, and then click the successor.

Link Tasks

3. On the Standard toolbar, click Link Tasks. The tasks are linked in the chart portion of the Gantt Chart. In addition, the Predecessor field of the successor task lists the task number for its predecessor (see Figure 5-10).

		Task Name	Duration	Start	Finish
1		⊟ **Web Structure**	**18.83 days**	**Mon 3/5/07**	**Thu 3/29/07**
2		Brainstorm content categories	3 days	Mon 3/5/07	Wed 3/7/07
3		Hold user meetings	5.33 days	Thu 3/8/07	Thu 3/15/07
4		Develop Web structure	3 days	Thu 3/15/07	Tue 3/20/07
5		Web structure review	5.33 days	Tue 3/20/07	Tue 3/27/07
6		Finalize Web structure	2.17 days	Tue 3/27/07	Thu 3/29/07

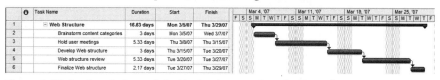

Figure 5-10 See how tasks are linked in the chart portion of a Gantt chart.

Tips and Techniques for Linking Tasks

- You can link multiple tasks at one time, as long as they all have the same type of task dependency. Select all the tasks that are to be linked, either by dragging across adjacent tasks or by clicking nonadjacent tasks while holding down the Ctrl key. On the Standard toolbar, click Link Tasks.

- You can have multiple links to and from a single task. One task might be the predecessor for several other tasks. Likewise, one task might be the successor for several tasks. There's no difference in how you set the links. Select the two tasks and click Link Tasks on the Standard toolbar. Or select the successor and then set the predecessor and link type on the Predecessors tab in the Task Information dialog box.

- In the chart portion of a Gantt chart, drag from the middle of the predecessor Gantt bar to the middle of the successor Gantt bar. Before you drag, be sure that you see a crosshair mouse pointer. As you drag to the successor, the mouse pointer changes to the link icon. This method creates a finish-to-start task dependency between them.

Note

When you edit the scheduling of a task—for example, its duration or a task dependency—you might affect other tasks that are linked with a task dependency to this task. When this happens, by default, the changed cells are temporarily filled with a background color so you can immediately see how your edit changed the scheduling for other tasks. This change highlighting changes or disappears when you make the next scheduling edit.

For more information about change highlighting, see the section titled "Highlighting the Ripple Effects of Schedule Changes" later in this chapter.

INSIDE OUT   Link in or out of order

When you drag across a series of tasks and then click Link Tasks, the tasks are linked in order from the task higher in the task list (lower Task ID number) to the task lower in the task list (higher Task ID number). It doesn't matter whether you drag from top to bottom or bottom to top—the resulting links are the same. This is also true if you select adjacent tasks using the Shift key—the order of selection does not matter.

However, if you hold down Ctrl and click each task, the tasks are linked in precisely the order in which you selected each individual task. Using this method, you can make a task lower in the list and the predecessor of a task higher in the list.

Understanding the Dependency Types

Although the finish-to-start task dependency is the most common, there are a total of four types of dependencies that help you model your task relationships. These dependency types are as follows:

- **Finish-to-Start (FS)** As soon as the predecessor task finishes, the successor task can start.

- **Finish-to-Finish (FF)** As soon as the predecessor task finishes, the successor task can finish.

- **Start-to-Start (SS)** As soon as the predecessor task starts, the successor task can start.

- **Start-to-Finish (SF)** As soon as the predecessor task starts, the successor task can finish. This type of link is rarely used, but still available if you need it.

> **Note**
>
> You can use the Project Guide to help you set task dependencies. On the Project Guide toolbar, click Tasks. In the Project Guide pane, click the Schedule Tasks link. Read the information and use the controls provided to link tasks. When finished, click the Done link.
>
> Tasks ▾

> **Note**
>
> By default, when you move a task from one location to another in your task sheet or when you insert a new task, that task is automatically linked like its surrounding tasks. You can control this setting. Click Tools, Options and then click the Schedule tab. Select or clear the Autolink Inserted Or Moved Tasks check box.

You've already seen that to quickly apply a Finish-To-Start task dependency, all you have to do is select the tasks in the task sheet and then click the Link Tasks button. But what about applying one of the other types of task dependencies?

You can still work directly in the Gantt Chart—you just need to take it a step further. After linking the tasks, double-click the task link line in the chart portion of the Gantt Chart. The Task Dependency dialog box appears, as shown in Figure 5-11. In the Type box, change the dependency type and then click OK.

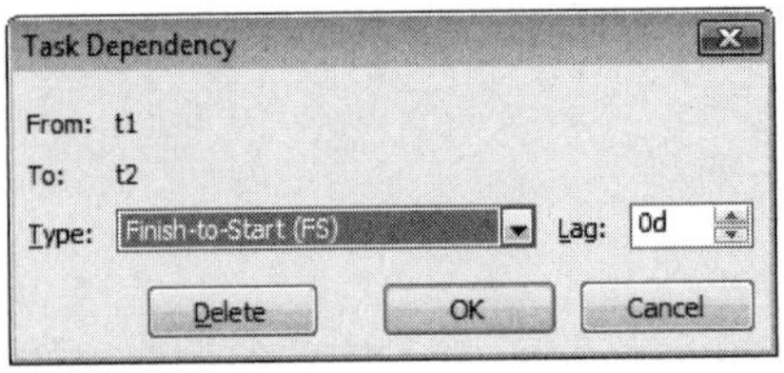

Figure 5-11 Double-click the task link line to open the Task Dependency dialog box and change the dependency type.

Another alternative, which doesn't require such a steady hand with the mouse, is to set up a task dependency using the Task Information dialog box. To do this, follow these steps:

1. Display the Gantt Chart or other task sheet view.

2. Click the task that is to become the successor in the dependency you will be setting.

3. On the Standard toolbar, click Task Information.

   You can also simply double-click a task to open the Task Information dialog box.

4. Click the Predecessors tab.

5. Click the first blank row in the Task Name field and then click the down arrow. The list of tasks in the project appears (see Figure 5-12).

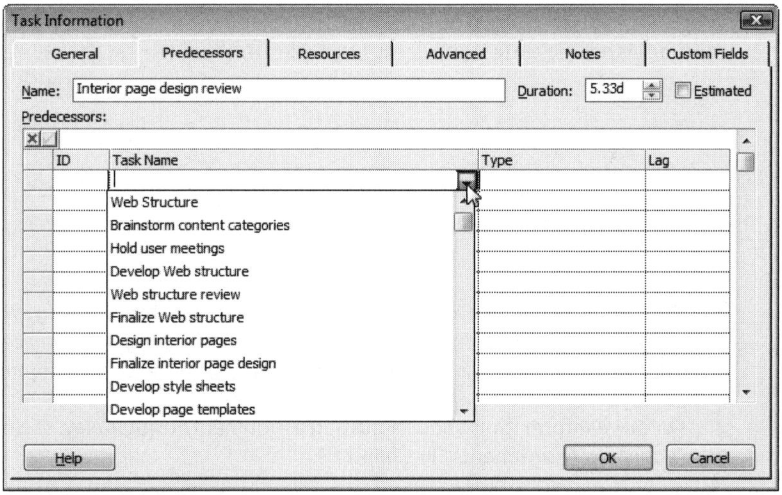

Figure 5-12 Use the Predecessors tab in the Task Information dialog box to set different types of task dependencies.

6. Click the task that is to be the predecessor to the current task.

7. Click the Type field and then select the type of task dependency: Finish-to-Start (FS), Start-to-Start (SS), Finish-to-Finish (FF), or Start-to-Finish (SF).

8. Click OK.

> **Note**
>
> Not only can you link tasks within one project, you can link tasks in different projects. For more information, see Chapter 15, "Exchanging Information Between Project Plans."

Delaying Linked Tasks by Adding Lag Time

Suppose you have a pair of tasks with a finish-to-start link. And then you realize that the successor really can't start when the predecessor is finished—there needs to be some additional delay. This is usually the case when something needs to happen between the two tasks that isn't another task.

For example, suppose the "Order equipment" task is the predecessor to the "Install equipment" task. Although the equipment cannot be installed until after the equipment is ordered, it still cannot be installed immediately after ordering. Some *lag time* is needed to allow for the equipment to be shipped and delivered. In such a case, the successor needs to be delayed, and you can enter lag time in the schedule to accurately reflect this condition.

Lag time can be expressed as a percentage of the predecessor, for example, **75%**. Or it can be a specific time period, for example, **16h** or **3ed**.

> ### Lag Time vs. Assignment Delay
>
> Don't confuse the delay afforded by lag time with *assignment delay*. With lag time, the delay is from the end of the predecessor to the beginning of the successor task. With assignment delay, there is a delay from the task start date to the assignment start date.
>
> **For more information about adjusting assignments using delay, see the section titled "Adjusting Assignments" in Chapter 9.**

To enter lag time for a linked task, follow these steps:

1. Display the Gantt Chart or other view with a task sheet.

2. Select the successor task that is to have the lag time.

3. On the Standard toolbar, click Task Information and then click the Predecessors tab.

4. In the Lag field for the existing Predecessor, type the amount of lag time you want for the successor. Use a positive number and enter the lag time as a percentage or duration amount.

Overlapping Linked Tasks by Adding Lead Time

One way to make your project schedule more efficient is to overlap linked tasks where possible. Suppose you have a task that isn't scheduled to begin until a previous task is finished. You realize that the predecessor doesn't actually have to be finished—the successor can really begin when the predecessor is only 50 percent complete. The successor essentially gets a 50 percent head start, hence the term *lead time*. For example, "Construct walls" is the predecessor to "Plaster walls." Although plastering cannot be done until the walls are constructed, the final wall does not need to be constructed before plastering of the first wall can begin. You can set an amount of lead time for the "Plaster walls" task.

Lead time is expressed as a negative value. If you think of it as reducing time in the schedule, the minus sign makes sense. Lead time can be expressed as a percentage of the predecessor, for example, **-25%**. Or, it can be a specific time period, for example, **-4d** or **-1ew**.

To enter lead time for a linked task, follow these steps:

1. Display the Gantt Chart or other view with a task sheet.

2. Select the successor task that is to have the lead time.

3. On the Standard toolbar, click Task Information.

4. In the Task Information dialog box, click the Predecessors tab.

5. In the Lag field for the existing Predecessor, type the amount of lead time you want for the successor. Use a negative number and enter the lead time as a percentage or duration amount.

Note

Although it might seem strange to use the Lag field to enter lead time, "lag time" and "lead time" are essentially the same idea. They express the amount of time that should pass before the successor task should start (or finish). Lag time adds time between the performance of predecessor and successor tasks, and so is expressed as a positive number. Lead time subtracts time between the performance of predecessor and successor tasks, hence the negative number.

Enter Lead or Lag Time Directly in the Gantt Chart

There are two other methods for entering lead or lag time for a pair of tasks that has you working directly in the Gantt Chart.

One method uses the sheet portion of the Gantt Chart. Click in the Predecessors field for the successor task. The field should already contain the Task ID of the predecessor task. After the Task ID, enter the code representing the link type and then enter the amount of lead time, for example, **9FS-1 day**, or **14FF-20%**; or lag time, for example, **9FS+1 day**, or **14FF+20%**.

The other method uses the chart portion of the Gantt Chart. Double-click the link line between the predecessor and successor tasks. In the Task Dependency dialog box, enter the lead or lag time in the Lag box. Remember to express lead time as a negative number and lag time as a positive number.

Chapter 5

Changing or Removing Links

To change or remove an existing task dependency, follow these steps:

1. Display the Gantt Chart or other view with a task sheet.

2. Select the successor task whose link you want to change.

3. On the Standard toolbar, click Task Information and then click the Predecessors tab.

4. Click in the Type field for the predecessor you want to change and then select the type of task dependency you want it to be: Finish-to-Start (FS), Start-to-Start (SS), Finish-to-Finish (FF), Start-to- Finish (SF), or None. If you select None, the link is removed entirely.

CAUTION!

Removing a link from a task can move the scheduling of the task way back to the project start date. Always check the new start and finish dates on a task when you have removed a link or changed the link type to be sure the task is being scheduled the way you expect.

Note

As with setting dependency types or entering lead or lag time, you can use the Predecessors field in the sheet portion of the Gantt Chart to change or remove a link. You can also double-click the link line in the chart portion of the Gantt Chart to use the Task Dependency dialog box to do the same thing.

TROUBLESHOOTING

You're trying to remove just the predecessor link from a task, but the successor link is removed at the same time

Unlink Tasks

When you click a task and then click Unlink Tasks, all links are removed: predecessor, successor, and any multiples. As a result, the scheduling of this task returns to the project start date or a start date entered as a constraint.

To remove just a single predecessor, click the task and then click Task Information on the Standard toolbar. In the Task Information dialog box, click the Predecessors tab. Click the task name of the predecessor you want to delete and then press the Delete key.

> **Note**
>
> In Microsoft Office Project 2007, you can now undo multiple edits. To undo recent edits, click Undo on the Standard toolbar. Each time you click Undo, the previous edit is undone in the reverse order it was done. You can also press Ctrl+Z or click Edit, Undo to reverse the last edit.
>
> To redo an edit that you've undone, click Redo on the Standard toolbar. You can also press Ctrl+Y or click Edit, Redo to redo undone edits.

Reviewing Task Dependencies

When needed, the following views can give you a closer look at the task dependencies in your project:

- The Gantt Chart shows task dependencies with link lines between the Gantt bars. In fact, all Gantt views show task dependencies this way.

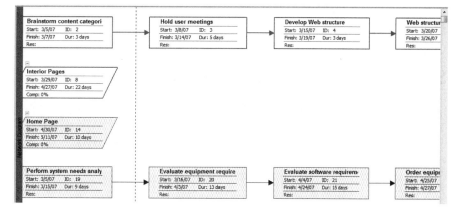

- The Network Diagram shows each task as an individual node with link lines between them. The Descriptive Network Diagram shows the same, but the nodes are larger and provide more detail.

- The Relationship Diagram shows the predecessors and successors of a single selected task. This view is particularly useful for a large project or any project with complex linking.

- The Task Details Form, Task Form, and Task Name Form can show predecessors and successors of a single selected task as part of a combination view. For example, you can display the Gantt Chart in the upper pane and one of the task forms in the lower pane. In fact, the Task Entry view is the built-in combination view of Gantt Chart and Task Form. By default, these forms show assigned resource information in the left grid and the predecessor information in the right grid. To show predecessor and successor information in the form, first click the form pane. Click Format, Details and then click Predecessors & Successors.

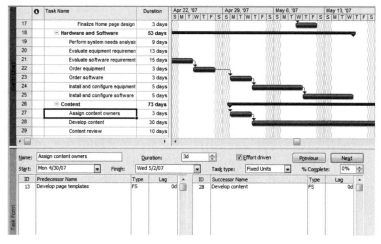

Scheduling Tasks to Achieve Specific Dates

With task dependencies established, your project schedule is taking shape and looking more and more realistic (see Figure 5-13).

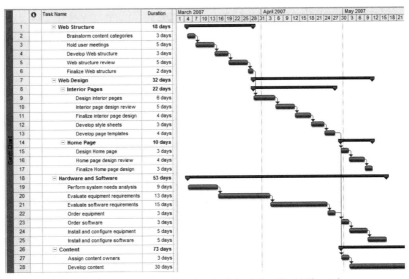

Figure 5-13 With durations entered and tasks linked, the Gantt Chart shows more meaningful schedule information.

Microsoft Project uses the task information and controls that you enter to schedule your project from start to finish. By default, Microsoft Project schedules each task to start "As Soon As Possible."

> **Note**
>
> For the standard project being scheduled from the project start date, Microsoft Project applies a default constraint of "As Soon As Possible." If you're scheduling from the project finish date, by default, Microsoft Project schedules each task to start "As Late As Possible."

However, you might have additional dates to consider. For example, maybe certain pivotal supplies will not be ready for use in the project until after April 6. Perhaps an important review meeting is taking place on June 29 that will set the stage for work toward the final milestones. Maybe one of your deliverables is a presentation at a key professional conference held on August 22.

To schedule around these important dates, you can set a *constraint*, which is a restriction on the start or finish date of a task. All tasks have a constraint applied—at the very least, the default As Soon As Possible constraint. The As Soon As Possible constraint indicates that the task should be scheduled according to its working times calendars, duration, task dependencies, and any resource assignments—without regard to any specific date.

Chapter 5

Understanding Constraint Types

The As Soon As Possible (ASAP) constraint is applied by default to all tasks in a project scheduled from the start date. In a project scheduled from the finish date, the As Late As Possible (ALAP) constraint is applied. The As Soon As Possible and As Late As Possible constraints are considered flexible constraints.

> **Note**
>
> Different types of constraints are applied in certain situations, depending on whether you're working with a project scheduled from the start date or from the finish date. For example, entering a date in the Start field of a project scheduled from the start date causes a Start No Earlier Than constraint to be applied. Doing the same thing in a project scheduled from the finish date causes a Start No Later Than constraint to be applied.

When a task needs to be scheduled in relation to a specific date, there are additional constraints you can apply, each of which is associated with a date. The following is a list of all the date constraints you can use to refine your project schedule:

- **Start No Earlier Than (SNET)** A moderately flexible constraint that specifies the earliest possible date that a task can begin. For projects scheduled from a start date, this constraint is automatically applied when you enter a start date for a task.

- **Finish No Earlier Than (FNET)** A moderately flexible constraint that specifies the earliest possible date that this task can be completed. For projects scheduled from a start date, this constraint is automatically applied when you enter a finish date for a task.

- **Start No Later Than (SNLT)** A moderately flexible constraint that specifies the latest possible date that this task can begin. For projects scheduled from a finish date, this constraint is automatically applied when you enter a start date for a task.

- **Finish No Later Than (FNLT)** A moderately flexible constraint that specifies the latest possible date that this task can be completed. For projects scheduled from a finish date, this constraint is automatically applied when you enter a finish date for a task.

- **Must Start On (MSO)** An inflexible constraint that specifies the exact date a task must begin. Other scheduling controls such as task dependencies become secondary to this requirement.

- **Must Finish On (MFO)** An inflexible constraint that specifies the exact date on which a task must be completed. Other scheduling controls such as task dependencies become secondary to this requirement.

INSIDE OUT   Beware of entering dates

If you enter a date in the Start field (in a project scheduled from the start date), the Start No Earlier Than constraint is applied. The finish date is recalculated based on the new start date and the existing duration.

If you then enter a date in the Finish field of the same task, the constraint changes to Finish No Earlier Than. The start date remains as you set it, but the duration is recalculated to reflect the difference between your entered start and finish dates.

These kinds of constraints can prevent your schedule from taking advantage of time saved by a task finishing earlier than expected. For example, suppose that the 8-day task "Construct walls" is scheduled to finish on October 3. It is the predecessor to the "Plaster walls" task which has a Start No Earlier Than constraint of October 4. If the "Construct walls" task finishes 2 days early, on October 1, the schedule for the "Plaster walls" task does not change to October 2, but maintains that the task not be started until October 4.

Always be aware that any dates you enter change the As Soon As Possible or As Late As Possible constraints to something more inflexible. If you enter both the start and finish dates for a task, Microsoft Project recalculates the duration.

Entering your own start and finish dates imposes often unnecessary restrictions on the capability of Microsoft Project to create the best possible schedule. It can also adversely affect results when you have Microsoft Project level overallocated resources. In the majority of cases, you get the best results when you enter durations and task dependencies and then let Microsoft Project figure out the best start and finish dates for tasks to be done as soon as possible. Use date constraints only when there is a specific calendar date that you must work toward, such as an event or a fixed deliverable due date that has no possibility of changing.

Project Management Practices: Working with Date Constraints

When developing your project schedule, you might contend with one of two major categories of date constraints: externally imposed dates and milestone dates.

An externally imposed date reflects situations outside the project that influence the project schedule. Examples include the following:

- A shipment of material needed for the project
- A market window for a new product
- A product announcement date at a trade conference
- Weather restrictions on outdoor activities
- A special event important to the project but scheduled by forces outside the project

You can reflect externally imposed dates as constraints on the tasks they affect. You can also add a task note as a reminder of the source of this date.

Milestone dates are typically dates set internally, often used to mark the end of phases or "chunks" of work in your work breakdown structure. As the project manager, you might set them yourself as goals to work toward. The project sponsor, customer, or other stakeholder might request certain dates for certain milestones, deliverables, or events being produced by the work of your project. You can set constraints on milestones as well as on regular tasks.

Changing Constraints

Remember, tasks always have a constraint applied—even if it's just As Soon As Possible or As Late As Possible. So we never think of *adding* or *removing* constraints. When making a change, we're typically changing a constraint from a flexible one to a more inflexible one or vice versa.

There are several methods for changing constraints, as follows:

- In the Gantt Chart or similar view with a task sheet, type or select dates in the Start or Finish fields. In a project scheduled from the start date, this causes a Start No Earlier Than or Finish No Earlier Than constraint to be applied. In a project scheduled from the finish date, this causes a Start No Later Than or Finish No Later Than constraint to be applied.

- In any task view, select the task whose constraint you want to change and then click Task Information on the Standard toolbar. In the Task Information dialog box, click the Advanced tab (see Figure 5-14). In the Constraint Type box, click the constraint type you want to apply to this task. If applicable, enter the date in the Constraint Date box.

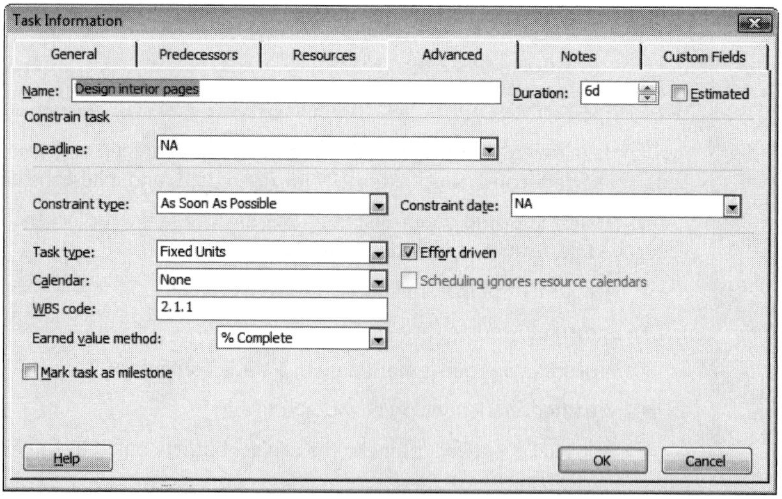

Figure 5-14 You can set constraints on the Advanced tab of the Task Information dialog box, in addition to deadlines, milestones, and task calendars.

- On the Project Guide toolbar, click Tasks. In the Project Guide pane, click the Set Deadlines And Constrain Tasks link. Read the information under Constrain A Task and use the controls that are provided to set constraints.

- In the Gantt Chart or other view with a task sheet, apply the Constraint Dates table. Click View, Table, More Tables. In the More Tables dialog box, click Constraint Dates and then click the Apply button. The table is applied to the view (see Figure 5-15). In the Constraint Type field, click the constraint type you want to apply to this task. If applicable, enter the date in the Constraint Date box.

	Task Name	Duration	Constraint Type	Constraint Date
1	⊟ **Web Structure**	**18 days**	**As Soon As Possible**	**NA**
2	Brainstorm content categories	3 days	As Soon As Possible	NA
3	Hold user meetings	5 days	As Soon As Possible	NA
4	Develop Web structure	3 days	As Soon As Possible	NA
5	Web structure review	5 days	Must Finish On	Mon 3/26/07
6	Finalize Web structure	2 days	As Soon As Possible	NA
7	⊟ **Web Design**	**32 days**	**As Soon As Possible**	**NA**
8	⊟ **Interior Pages**	**22 days**	**As Soon As Possible**	**NA**
9	Design interior pages	6 days	Start No Earlier Than	Thu 3/29/07
10	Interior page design review	5 days	As Soon As Possible	NA
11	Finalize interior page design	4 days	As Soon As Possible	NA
12	Develop style sheets	3 days	As Soon As Possible	NA
13	Develop page templates	4 days	Finish No Later Than	Fri 4/27/07

Figure 5-15 Apply the Constraint Dates table to review or change constraint types and dates.

CAUTION!

If a task has no predecessors, changing the constraint to an As Soon As Possible (or As Late As Possible) constraint can move the scheduling of the task back in time to the project start date. Always check the new start and finish dates on a task when you have changed constraint types to make sure the task is being scheduled the way you expect.

Change Constraints for Multiple Tasks at Once

In a task sheet, select all the tasks that will have the same constraint applied. Drag across adjacent tasks to select them or hold down Ctrl while clicking nonadjacent tasks. Click Task Information on the Standard toolbar and then click the Advanced tab in the Multiple Task Information dialog box. Change the Constraint Type and, if applicable, the Constraint Date. Click OK. The constraint is changed for all selected tasks.

This method works best if you're changing date constraints to As Soon As Possible or As Late As Possible because it's rare for multiple tasks to have the same constraint date.

TROUBLESHOOTING

You can't delete a constraint

By their nature, constraints are not deleted. A constraint is applied to every task. If you're thinking of deleting a constraint, what you probably want to do is change it from a date constraint such as Must Start On or Finish No Later Than to a flexible constraint such as As Soon As Possible.

Double-click the task to open the Task Information dialog box and then click the Advanced tab. In the Constraint Type box, click As Soon As Possible or As Late As Possible.

Working with Flexible and Inflexible Constraints

Three levels of flexibility are associated with task constraints: flexible, moderately flexible, and inflexible.

Flexible Constraints

The flexible constraints are As Soon As Possible and As Late As Possible. These constraints work with task dependencies to schedule a task as soon or as late as the task dependency and other scheduling considerations will accommodate. These default constraints give Microsoft Project maximum flexibility in calculating start and finish dates for the tasks. For example, a task with an As Soon As Possible constraint and a finish-to-start dependency is scheduled as soon as the predecessor task finishes.

Moderately Flexible Constraints

The moderately flexible constraints—Start No Earlier Than, Start No Later Than, Finish No Earlier Than, and Finish No Later Than—have a range of dates to work within. That is, the task is restricted to starting or finishing before or after the date you choose, which provides some room for flexibility, even though a date is in place. For example, a task with a Start No Later Than constraint for November 14 and a finish-to-start dependency to another task can begin any time its predecessor is finished up until November 14, but it cannot be scheduled after November 14.

Inflexible Constraints

The inflexible constraints—Must Start On and Must Finish On—have an absolute single date that the schedule must accommodate, which means that other scheduling considerations must fall by the wayside if necessary to meet this date. By default, constraints take precedence over task dependencies when there's a conflict between the two. For example, a task with a Must Finish On constraint for April 30 and a finish-to-start dependency to another task is always scheduled for April 30, regardless of whether the predecessor finishes on time.

INSIDE OUT   **Conflicts between dependencies and constraints**

If you set a moderately flexible constraint, such as Start No Earlier Than, or an inflexible constraint, such as Must Finish On, you run the risk of a conflict with task dependencies. Suppose the "Hang wallpaper" task has a Must Finish On constraint for June 25. Because of various delays, the task's finish-to-start predecessor task, "Install drywall," actually finishes on June 29.

This situation creates a scheduling conflict. According to the task dependency, you can't hang wallpaper until the drywall is installed, which won't finish until June 29. But according to the constraint, the wallpaper must be hung by June 25.

By default, where there's a conflict like this between a task dependency and a constraint, the constraint takes precedence. In this case, there would be 4 days of *negative slack*, which essentially means that the predecessor task is running 4 days into the time allotted to the successor task. You might see a Planning Wizard message regarding this, especially if you're still in the planning processes and are setting up tasks with such a conflict before actual work is even reported.

To prevent this situation during the planning phase, review your project for places where predecessors and successors either overlap or have lag. In those cases, check to make sure there is a non-zero lag on that link. If there is not, then there is a potential constraint problem or conflict on that link.

To resolve the scheduling conflict, you can change the constraint to a more flexible one, such as Finish No Earlier Than. You can change the Must Finish On date to a later date that will work. You can also change the scheduling precedence option. If you want task dependencies to take precedence over constraints, click Tools, Options. In the Options dialog box, click the Schedule tab and then clear the Tasks Will Always Honor Their Constraint Dates check box, which is selected by default.

Reviewing Constraints

With the right constraints in place, you have the beginnings of a schedule. The Gantt Chart can provide a great deal of information about your constraints and other scheduling controls.

You can sort tasks by Start Date, Finish Date, Constraint Type, or Constraint Date. You can group tasks by Constraint Type. You can filter tasks by the Should Start By date or the Should Start/Finish By date.

Such task arrangements can provide overviews of the big picture of start and finish dates across many tasks at a time. If you want to review details, you can review the Task Information dialog box for a task. The General tab includes the scheduled start and finish dates, and the Advanced tab includes the constraint type and constraint date.

You can apply the Task Entry view. Though the Task Form does not reflect constraints, other task details for any task you select in the Gantt Chart in the upper pane are shown in the Task Form in the lower pane. The default Resources & Predecessors details show task dependencies as well as any lead or lag time (see Figure 5-16).

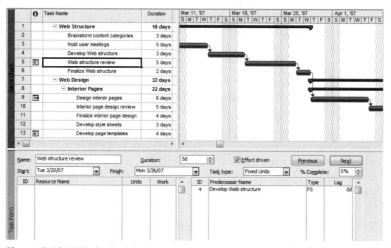

Figure 5-16 With the Task Entry view, you can review many details of an individual task selected in the Gantt Chart.

Setting Deadline Reminders

We are often tempted to enter a finish date on a task or a Must Finish On constraint when we want a task to be completed by a certain date. But instead of a date constraint, we really want a reminder or target to move our schedule toward.

Instead of setting a date constraint in such situations, set a *deadline* instead. A deadline appears as an indicator on your Gantt Chart as a target or goal, but does not affect the scheduling of your tasks.

To set a deadline, follow these steps:

1. Select the task for which you want to set a deadline.

2. On the Standard toolbar, click Task Information and then click the Advanced tab.

3. In the Deadline box, enter or select the deadline date.

    The deadline marker appears in the chart area of the Gantt Chart (see Figure 5-17). Repeat steps 1–3 to change or remove a deadline if necessary. If you're removing a deadline, select the date and press the Delete key.

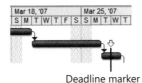

Deadline marker

Figure 5-17 The deadline provides a guideline for important dates.

Note

You can use the Project Guide to help you set deadlines. On the Project Guide toolbar, click Tasks. In the Project Guide pane, click the Set Deadlines And Constrain Tasks link. Read the information under Set A Deadline and use the controls provided to set deadlines.

Adjust Your Schedule to Hit Your Deadlines

When you have deadline flags set up in your project plan, you can graphically see the differences between your deadlines and the scheduled finish dates.

So what do you do when you have a discrepancy between the two?

The first thought is that the project schedule might simply give you the sanity check you needed to see whether your deadlines are realistic. If you think the task durations, dependencies, and constraints are all exactly as they should be, then the deadline might just need to be adjusted.

If you still really want to try to hit that deadline, there are various techniques in modifying scope, refining the schedule, and changing resource allocations to make the adjustments necessary to schedule the finish date closer to the desired deadline.

For more information about shortening the schedule for certain tasks or the project as a whole, see the section titled "Bringing in the Project Finish Date" in Chapter 9.

You can show deadlines in your task sheet as well, by adding the Deadline field as a column. Follow these steps:

1. Right-click the column heading to the right of where you want your new Deadline column to be inserted and then click Insert Column.

Or you can click the column heading and then click Insert, Column. The Column Definition dialog box appears.

Chapter 5

2. In the Field Name box, click Deadline. You can type the first one or two letters to go straight to it in the list.

The Deadline field shows any deadline dates that are already set and shows "NA" for tasks without deadlines. You can enter deadlines directly in this field.

If the schedule for a task moves beyond its deadline date, either because of normal scheduling calculations or because of actual progress information entered, an alert appears in the Indicators field, specifying that the task is scheduled to finish later than its deadline (see Figure 5-18).

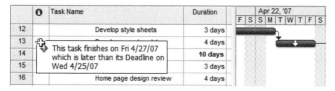

Figure 5-18 If a deadline will be missed, the deadline indicator provides the details.

You can set deadlines for summary tasks as well as individual tasks. If the summary task's deadline conflicts with the finish dates of any of the subtasks, the deadline indicator specifies a missed deadline among the subtasks. You can also set deadlines for milestone tasks.

INSIDE OUT   A deadline might affect scheduling after all

There are two instances in which a deadline can indeed affect task scheduling. The first is if you enter a deadline that falls before the end of the task's *total slack*. The total slack is recalculated using the deadline date rather than the task's late finish date. If the total slack reaches 0, the task becomes critical.

The second instance is if you set a deadline on a task with an As Late As Possible constraint. Suppose the task is scheduled to finish on the deadline date. However, if any predecessors slip, the task could still finish beyond its deadline.

For more information about the critical path, slack, and late finish dates, see the section titled "Working with the Critical Path and Critical Tasks" in Chapter 9.

Creating Milestones in Your Schedule

You can designate certain tasks as *milestones* in your project plan. Having milestones flagged in your project plan and visible in your Gantt Chart helps you see when you've achieved another benchmark. Milestones often indicate the beginning or ending of major phases or the completion of deliverables in your project. As you complete each milestone, you come ever closer to completing the project. Milestones are also excellent reporting points.

A milestone, as such, has no additional calculation effect on your schedule. However, you typically link a milestone to other tasks. You might also set a date constraint or deadline on a milestone.

The simplest method for entering a milestone is to create a task that's worded like a milestone (for example, "Web site launched") and enter a duration of 0. Any task with a 0 duration is automatically set as a milestone. The milestone marker and date are drawn in the chart area of the Gantt Chart (see Figure 5-19).

	❶	Task Name	Duration	Start	Fini
37		⊟ **System Cutover**	**5 days**	**Tue 8/21/07**	**Mon**
38		Update DNS	1 day	Tue 8/21/07	Tue
39		Final testing	2 days	Wed 8/22/07	Thu
40		Final bug fixes	2 days	Fri 8/24/07	Mon
41		Web Site Launched	0 days	Mon 8/27/07	Mon

Figure 5-19 Microsoft Project interprets any task with a 0 duration as a milestone.

However, a milestone doesn't have to have a 0 duration. You might want to make the final task in each phase a milestone, and these are real tasks with real durations.

CAUTION

Before you make tasks with durations into milestone tasks, be aware that you might be creating a new set of problems. The Gantt bar is replaced by a milestone marker at the finish date, so the duration is not shown unless you create a custom Gantt bar for this purpose. Also, if you export task data to other applications or copy task data between different projects, the milestone tasks are not likely to appear as expected.

To change a regular task into a milestone, follow these steps:

1. Select the task you want to become a milestone.

2. On the Standard toolbar, click Task Information and then click the Advanced tab.

3. Select the Mark Task As Milestone check box.

   The Gantt bar for the task changes to the milestone marker in the chart area of the Gantt Chart (see Figure 5-20).

	❶	Task Name	Duration	Start	Finish
22		Order equipment	3 days	Wed 4/25/07	Fri 4/27/07
23		Order software	3 days	Mon 4/30/07	Wed 5/2/07
24		Install and configure equipment	5 days	Thu 5/3/07	Wed 5/9/07
25		Install and configure software	5 days	Thu 5/10/07	Wed 5/16/07

Figure 5-20 You can set any task as a milestone.

Note

In previous versions of Microsoft Project, if you designate a task with duration as a milestone, by default the milestone marker sits at the task's start date in the chart portion of the Gantt Chart. This is misleading and potentially confusing, because the marker sits at the start date while the date label indicates the finish date.

In Microsoft Office Project 2007, the default milestone marker sits at the task's finish date, which makes much better sense.

INSIDE OUT Create Gantt bars to show milestones with duration

If all your milestones have a duration and if you never use a milestone with 0 duration, you might consider creating a milestone Gantt bar that shows duration from the start to the finish of the milestone task, with the milestone marker sitting on the finish date.

To do this, follow these steps:

1. Click Format, Bar Styles.

2. Click in the From field for the Milestone style and then click Start.

3. Make sure the To field shows Finish.

4. Below the grid, in the Bars tab, under Start, change the Shape box to show a blank instead of the diamond-shaped milestone marker.

5. Under Middle, select the shape, pattern, and color for the Gantt bar you want to represent the milestone bar.

6. Under End, change the Shape box to show the diamond-shaped milestone marker (see Figure 5-21).

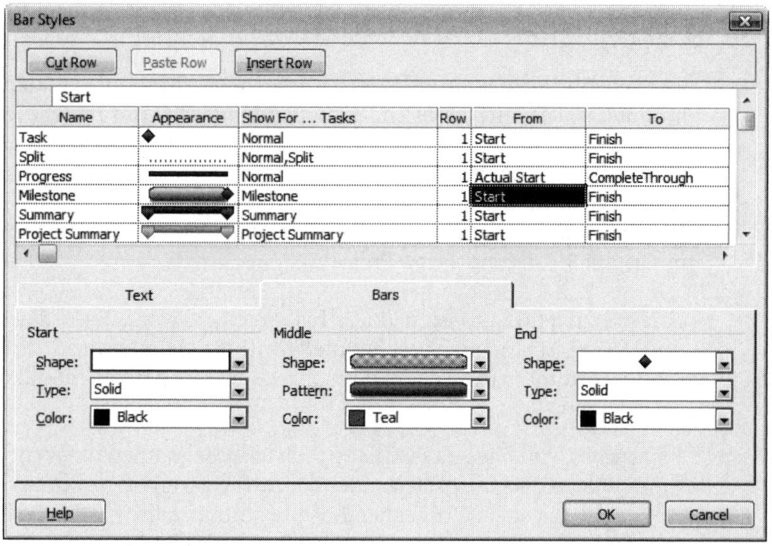

Figure 5-21 Change the settings for milestones in the Bar Styles dialog box.

The resulting Gantt bar appears in the Milestone row of the dialog box under Appearance. Click OK. This will produce a Gantt bar showing the duration of the milestone task as well as a symbol to mark the end of the task and the completion of the milestone (see Figure 5-22).

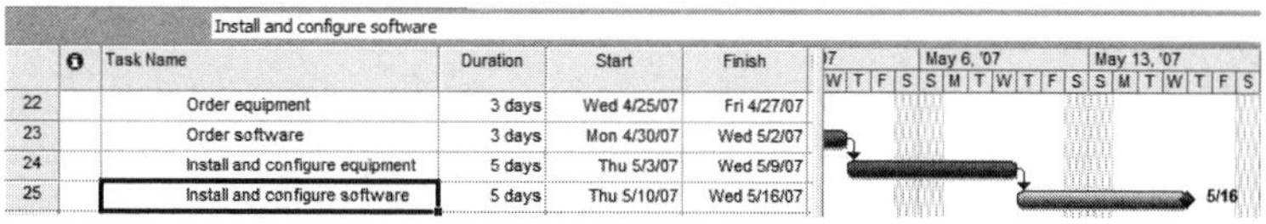

Figure 5-22 You can change the bar style for milestones from a single marker on the Start date to a Gantt bar with the diamond-shaped marker on the Finish date.

Remember, however, that if you create a milestone Gantt bar to show the start and finish date, there will be no marker if you create a milestone with 0 duration.

For more information about changing Gantt bar styles, see the section titled "Formatting the Appearance of Gantt Bars" in Chapter 25.

Chapter 5

Note

You can review specialized milestone Gantt Charts to take a closer look at project milestones. First, select the tasks you want to roll up. Click Tools, Macro, Macros. Click Rollup_Formatting and then click the Run button. Select the duration unit for tasks, for example, Days, and then click OK. Click View, More Views, Milestone Rollup or Milestone Date Rollup, and then click the Apply button.

Working with Task Calendars

The scheduling of your tasks is driven by task duration, task dependencies, and constraints. It's also driven by the project calendar. If your project calendar dictates that work is done Monday through Friday, 8:00 A.M. until 5:00 P.M., initially that's when your tasks are scheduled.

For more information about calendars, see the section titled "Setting Your Project Calendar" in Chapter 3, "Starting a New Project."

However, if a task is assigned to a resource who works Saturday and Sunday, 9:00 A.M. until 9:00 P.M., the task is scheduled for those times instead. That is, the task is scheduled according to the assigned resource's working times calendar rather than the project calendar.

Sometimes, you have a task that needs to be scheduled differently from the working times reflected in the project calendar or the assigned resource calendars. For example, you might have a task that specifies preventive maintenance on equipment at specified intervals. Or you might have a task being completed by a machine running 24 hours a day. In any case, the task has its own working time, and you want it to be scheduled according to that working time rather than the project or resource working time so it can accurately reflect what's really happening with this task.

> **Note**
>
> Unlike project or resource calendars, which are essential to the accuracy of your schedule, task calendars are more of an optional scheduling feature. Create and apply task calendars only in those special situations when a task has its own unique schedule that tends to be independent of the project or assigned resource calendar.

Setting Up the Task Calendar

To have a task scheduled according to its own working times, you must first set up the calendar. You can use or adapt a built-in base calendar, which is like a calendar template you can apply to the project as a whole, to resources, or in this case, to tasks. If the task's working times are quite different from anything available in the existing base calendars, you can create your own.

For specific procedures on modifying an existing base calendar, see the section titled "Modifying a Base Calendar" in Chapter 3. To create a new base calendar, see the section titled "Creating a New Base Calendar" in Chapter 3.

Note

When creating a base calendar to be used as a task calendar, give the new base calendar a specific name that indicates its role as a task calendar. This makes the differences among the base calendars very clear to you (and possibly other project managers) to prevent confusion and the application of the wrong calendars for the wrong purposes.

INSIDE OUT   Take care modifying a built-in base calendar

When you have the need for a task calendar, it's usually because the task has a schedule that's quite different from the project working times calendar or the assigned resource working times calendar.

Be careful when modifying an existing base calendar to use it for a task calendar. If that base calendar is used for a particular resource, for example, the scheduling of that resource will change to reflect what you were intending just for the task calendar.

If you're certain that the base calendar in question will not be used for anything except as the task calendar, then modify away. Otherwise, create a new base calendar. You can always base a new base calendar on an existing one. You can also name it in such a way as to make it crystal clear what your intentions are for this calendar.

Return a base calendar to its default settings

But suppose you inadvertently modified a base calendar being used to schedule resource working time, or even the entire project's working time. How do you return it back to its default settings? Follow these steps:

1. Click Tools, Change Working Time.
2. Click the Work Weeks tab and then click the Details button.
3. In the Select Day(s) box, in which Sunday is already selected, hold down the Shift key and click Saturday so that all seven days are selected.
4. Click the Use Project Default Times For These Days option and then click OK.

Note

If you have a set of tasks that are carried out entirely by equipment on the equipment's own schedule, an alternative to creating a task calendar is to set up the equipment as a work resource. You can then apply a working times calendar to the equipment resource and assign the equipment resource to the appropriate tasks.

For more information about creating work resources, see the section titled "Adding Work Resources to the Project" in Chapter 6, "Setting Up Resources in the Project."

Assigning a Base Calendar to a Task

To assign a base calendar to a task, follow these steps:

1. Select the task to which you want to assign a base calendar.

2. On the Standard toolbar, click Task Information and then click the Advanced tab.

3. In the Calendar box, click the name of the calendar you want to assign to this task. All base calendars are listed, including ones you have created yourself.

4. Click OK.

Task Calendar indicator

A task calendar icon appears in the Indicator column. If you rest your mouse pointer over the indicator, a ScreenTip displays the name of the assigned calendar (see Figure 5-23). Follow this same procedure to change to a different task calendar or to remove the task calendar.

	❶	Task Name	Duration
4		Develop Web structure	3 days
5		Web structure review	5 days
6		The calendar 'Review Task	2 days
7		Calendar' is assigned to the task.	32 days
8		⊟ Interior Pages	22 days

Figure 5-23 Assign a calendar to a task to schedule it independently from the project or resource calendars.

Don't confuse the task calendar with the Calendar view. A task calendar reflects working days and times for one or more selected tasks. The Calendar view is a graphical representation of tasks and durations in a monthly calendar format.

For more information about the Calendar view, see the section titled "Working with Graph Views" in Chapter 4.

TROUBLESHOOTING

You assigned a task calendar, but it's not scheduling tasks in all the times it should

The task probably also has a resource assigned, and the resource calendar is conflicting with what you want the task calendar to accomplish.

When you assign a task calendar, it takes the place of the project calendar. However, suppose resources are assigned to the task as well. Resources are all associated with their own resource calendars as well. Although a resource's calendar might be the same as the project calendar, it can be customized for the resource's specific working times.

When resources are assigned, the task is scheduled not just for the working times indicated in the task calendar. Instead, by default, Microsoft Project schedules the task according to the common working times between the task calendar and the resource calendar.

For example, suppose the 24-hour base calendar is assigned to a task that's also assigned to a resource who works Friday through Sunday, 9:00 A.M. until 7:00 P.M. The only times the two calendars have in common are Friday through Sunday, 9:00 A.M. until 7:00 P.M., so by default, those are the only times when work will be scheduled for this task.

If you apply a task calendar to a task with a resource assigned, and there are few to no common working times between the task calendar and the resource calendar, an error message appears, as shown in Figure 5-24.

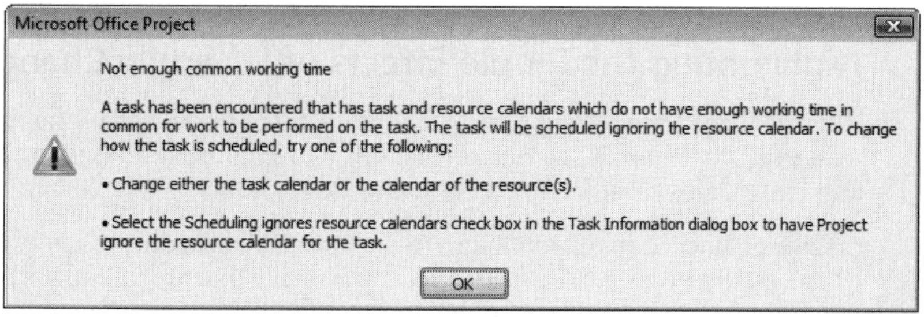

Figure 5-24 The Not Enough Common Working Time error message offers two suggestions for making sure your task is scheduled the way you want.

You can change the working times in the resource calendar to ensure enough common time. Or, you can change the working times in the task calendar. You might also remove the resource if that's possible for the task.

If you want the resource calendar to be ignored on a task, open the Task Information dialog box for the task and click the Advanced tab. Select the Scheduling Ignores Resource Calendars check box.

For more information about resource calendars, see the section titled "Setting Working Times and Days Off for Work Resources" in Chapter 6. For information about resource assignments, see the section titled "Assigning Work Resources to Tasks" in Chapter 7.

Seeing Feedback on Scheduling Changes

Sometimes you make a simple change to your project schedule, for example, you might increase a duration, change a task dependency, or add a date constraint, and something unexpected happens to the scheduling of the selected task. Sometimes there are several ripple-effect changes throughout the schedule. This can be a source of frustration for project managers, especially those new to Microsoft Project.

It's important to understand that one of the primary responsibilities of Microsoft Project is to handle all the schedule calculations so you don't have to. However, as the project manager, it's also important that Microsoft Project provide you with needed information when such recalculations are made or when you have choices as to how a change is to be interpreted in your schedule.

This is where Microsoft Project feedback information comes in handy. The new change highlighting and Task Drivers pane provide information to help you see exactly what is changing in your schedule and to help you make the decisions appropriate for your project.

For more information about changing your schedule, see Chapter 9.

Highlighting the Ripple Effects of Schedule Changes

When you change a duration in a task that is in the middle of a series of linked finish-to-start tasks, for example, that one task's change in duration is going to affect the start and finish dates for all of its successor tasks.

Likewise, other changes you might make to a task's schedule—such as a task dependency or a start date constraint—can affect other tasks that are linked with a dependency to this task. To make sure you see the impact of these kinds of changes on the rest of your schedule, by default, the changed cells are temporarily filled with a background color (see Figure 5-25).

Task Name	Duration	Start	Finish
⊟ **Web Design**	**34 days**	**Thu 3/29/07**	**Tue 5/15/07**
⊟ **Interior Pages**	**24 days**	**Thu 3/29/07**	**Tue 5/1/07**
Design interior pages	8 days	Thu 3/29/07	Mon 4/9/07
Interior page design review	5 days	Tue 4/10/07	Mon 4/16/07
Finalize interior page design	4 days	Tue 4/17/07	Fri 4/20/07
Develop style sheets	3 days	Mon 4/23/07	Wed 4/25/07
Develop page templates	4 days	Thu 4/26/07	Tue 5/1/07
⊟ **Home Page**	**10 days**	**Wed 5/2/07**	**Tue 5/15/07**
Design Home page	3 days	Wed 5/2/07	Fri 5/4/07
Home page design review	4 days	Mon 5/7/07	Thu 5/10/07
Finalize Home page design	3 days	Fri 5/11/07	Tue 5/15/07
⊟ **Hardware and Software**	**103 days**	**Mon 3/5/07**	**Wed 7/25/07**
Perform system needs analysis	9 days	Mon 3/5/07	Thu 3/15/07
Evaluate equipment requirements	13 days	Fri 3/16/07	Tue 4/3/07
Evaluate software requirements	15 days	Wed 4/4/07	Tue 4/24/07

Figure 5-25 See the ripple effects of scheduling changes you make by reviewing the highlighted cells in a task sheet.

New to Microsoft Office Project 2007, this change highlighting only shows in sheet views such as the Gantt Chart, the Task Usage view, or the Resource Sheet. There is no change highlighting for graphically oriented task views such as the Calendar view or Network Diagram.

The change highlighting remains in effect only until you make the next edit that affects scheduling, at which time the highlighting shifts to those cells affected by the new change. The last set of change highlighting is also cleared when you save the project.

By default, change highlighting is light blue in the Gantt Chart or Task Sheet, and light green in the Task Usage view and Tracking Gantt. To change the color of change highlighting, follow these steps:

1. Display the view whose change highlighting color you want to change.

2. Click Format, Text Styles.

3. In the Item To Change box, click Changed Cells (see Figure 5-26).

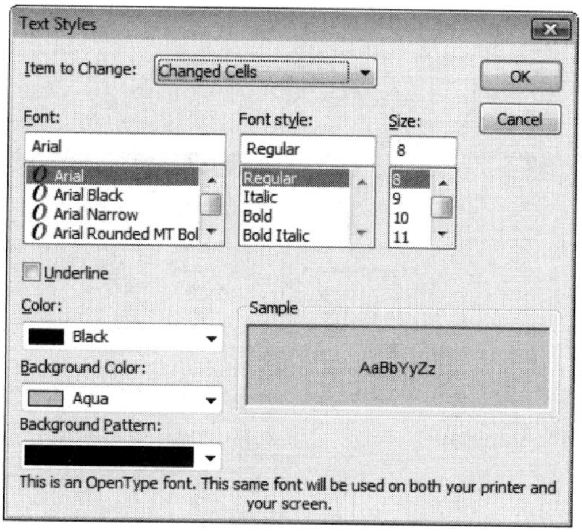

Figure 5-26 Change the color and pattern for change highlighting in a task sheet view using the Text Styles dialog box.

4. In the Background Color box, select the change highlighting color you want.

5. If you also want to change the background pattern, in the Background Pattern box, select the pattern you want.

6. Click OK.

If you don't want to use change highlighting, you can turn it off by clicking Hide Change Highlighting on the View menu. To turn it back on again, click View, Show Change Highlighting.

Reviewing the Factors That Affect a Task Start Date

When you first create your project schedule, you start by entering a project start date and setting up a project working times calendar. Then as you enter tasks to the project, you add scheduling information about those tasks such as task duration, dependencies, constraints, and task calendars.

Microsoft Project takes all this scheduling information and calculates the schedule of each task to ultimately build the full project schedule, complete with start dates and finish dates. Because you've entered this other information, you're freed up from having to figure out the start dates of each task yourself.

Chapter 5

If you're contemplating a change to a task schedule, particularly if you're trying to shorten the schedule of a particular task, a group of tasks, or the entire project schedule, it's tremendously helpful to understand which of these scheduling factors were instrumental in determining the start date of the tasks. You can now see this easily by reviewing the Task Drivers pane.

New in Microsoft Office Project 2007, the Task Drivers pane shows you the specific factors responsible for setting the start date of the selected task (see Figure 5-27).

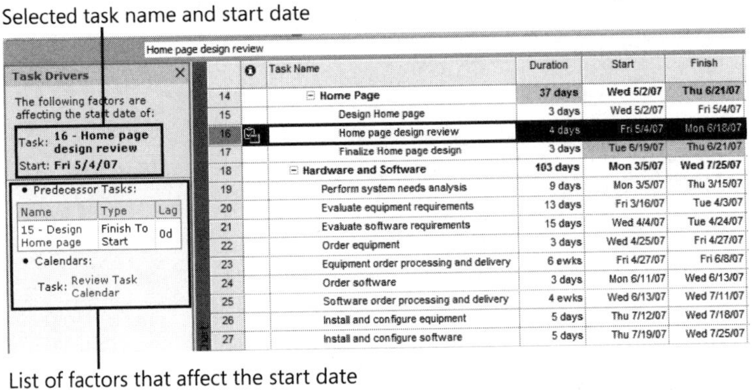

Selected task name and start date

List of factors that affect the start date

Figure 5-27 Show the Task Drivers pane to see a list of the factors responsible for setting a selected task's start date.

You can view the task driver for any task in your project. A task might have just a single task driver, or it might have three or four. Examples of common task drivers are:

- Project start date
- Project calendar
- Predecessor tasks
- Constraint date
- Resource calendar
- Task calendar
- Actual start date

To show the Task Drivers pane, follow these steps:

1. Display any task view, such as the Gantt Chart, Task Usage view, or Network Diagram.

2. Click Project, Task Drivers. Or, click Task Drivers on the Standard toolbar.

   The Task Drivers pane appears to the left of the view. The upper portion of the Task Drivers pane lists the name of the selected task and its start date. The lower portion lists the task drivers.

Task Drivers

You can click the name of a predecessor task to go to that task in the view and to see the task drivers for that task. You can click the name of a calendar listed in the Task Drivers pane to open that calendar in the Change Working Time dialog box.

Keep the Task Drivers pane open while you click different tasks and review their task drivers. When you're finished with the Task Drivers pane, click the X in the upper-right corner of the pane to close it.

Seeing Scheduling Feedback on Assigned Tasks

Another source of feedback in Microsoft Project is Microsoft Office Smart Tags technology. Microsoft Project Smart Tags appear only when you edit tasks that have resources assigned. When you make certain kinds of scheduling changes, a green triangle might appear in the corner of the edited cell of a sheet view such as the Gantt Chart or Task Usage view.

3 days	Thu 3/15/07
4 days	Tue 3/20/07
2 days	Mon 3/26/07

Scheduling feedback triangle

When you move your mouse pointer over the cell containing the feedback indicator, the Smart Tag icon appears.

	3 days	Thu 3/15/07
	4 days	Tue 3/20/07
	2 days	Mon 3/26/07

Smart tag icon

Click the Smart Tag icon. A message explains the scheduling ramifications of your edit. The message usually gives you the opportunity to change the edit so that the result is closer to your expectation.

	3 days	Thu 3/15/07	Mon 3/19/07	3	
	4 days	Tue 3/20/07	Fri 3/23/07	4	joe

You just decreased the duration of this task. Is it because the:

○ Work (person-hours) required to do this task has decreased, so it will take less time.

○ Resources will work more hours per day, so the task will take less time to complete.

Show me more details.

Feedback message

A Smart Tag usually appears after a potentially ambiguous edit and provides choices to ensure that you understand the schedule ramifications of the change you're making.

For more information about using Smart Tags for scheduling feedback, see the section titled "Changing Resource Assignments" in Chapter 7.

Chapter 5

Setting Up Resources in the Project

Understanding the Impact of Resources in the
Project Plan 202

Adding Resources to the Project 203

Removing a Resource from the Project 216

Identifying Tentative, Generic, or Budget Resources . . **216**

Setting When Resources Are Available for Work **220**

Adding Detailed Resource Information **228**

As soon as you're assigned as manager of the project, you might have certain resources in mind whom you know would be right for the project. As the scope becomes
more defined and as you develop the task list along with the milestones and deliverables, you're likely to have even more ideas. If you have specific people in mind, you
might start inquiring about their availability. You might also start investigating sources,
specifications, and prices for material and equipment. You're likely to have a particular
budget, and you might start thinking about the kinds of costs the tasks in your project
are likely to incur.

By the time you develop the durations of the tasks, you have very concrete information
in front of you—you now know exactly which tasks need to be done and what kinds of
resources you need to do them.

There might be a team in place already—the full-time members of a department who are
waiting to sink their teeth into a good project. There might be no team at all, and you'll
have to hire some people, borrow some from another group, and contract others. Or
you might have a core staff, but for this project you'll need to contract additional temporary workers to fill out the skills needed for the team.

You can add the names of resources who will be working on this project as you acquire
them. These might be the names of actual people. Or they might be generic resource
names that describe the skills and competencies needed to fulfill the task. Where applicable, you can enter the names of equipment or material resources that will also
help implement the project. You can specify cost resources such as equipment rentals
or travel fares. You can enter additional resource information, such as work schedule,
availability, cost, and notes.

How Many Resources Do You Need?

Although you know the tasks that need to be done and the kinds of resources you need
to be able to do them, you might not know how many of a particular type of resource
you need just yet.

Here's the process: First, identify the tasks that need to be done. Second, identify the resources needed to do those tasks. Third, assign resources to the tasks. At that point, you can see whether the resulting schedule meets your target date or target budget.

You need to have tasks in place to find out how many resources you need. You also need resources to assign to those tasks to create an accurate schedule and cost estimate. After assigning resources, if the schedule calculates a finish date later than the target finish date, you might have to go back and add more resources to your team. Or if the project costs are over budget and you haven't even started work yet, you might have to forego additional resources or scramble to replace expensive resources with less expensive ones.

As you can see, tuning your project plan to get the right number of resources to meet your schedule, costs, and workload requirements is an iterative process. You might need to go through several cycles of refinement before you arrive at the perfect plan.

For more information about refining the project plan to meet a target date or budget, see Chapter 9, "Checking and Adjusting the Project Plan."

Understanding the Impact of Resources in the Project Plan

Resources carry out the work of your project or model the expenditure of costs or consumption of materials. However, with your tasks defined and scheduled, why is it necessary to actually specify resources in your project plan? You could just print the schedule and tell people which tasks they're responsible for: Here are your due dates; now go make them happen.

This approach might seem like a simple way of managing a project, but if you do it this way, you'll miss out on the tremendous scheduling, tracking, and communication capabilities provided by Microsoft Office Project 2007. By adding resources to your project, you can do the following:

- Increase the accuracy of your schedule. Office Project 2007 already takes into account the project calendar, durations, task dependencies, and constraints to build an accurate model of your project. When you assign resources, Microsoft Project takes this schedule a significant step further by adding the working times and availability of your resources into the scheduling calculations.

- Know ahead of time whether any resources are overloaded with too much work in the allotted time. You can also see whether anyone is underallocated and shift responsibilities accordingly as you refine your schedule. Later, when work is being done and you're getting progress information on each task, you can find bottlenecks or any new overallocations or underallocations due to shifts in the schedule.

- Track progress according to resource work. Your resources can tell you how much time they've spent on their tasks for a given week and how much more time they will need. This tracking can help you make any necessary adjustments to keep the project moving in the right direction. Recording actual progress data also captures historical information that will be invaluable for future projects.

- Record the use, cost, and consumption of materials in your project. These details can help you monitor your budget performance as well as give you advance notice as to when you need to reorder supplies.

- Establish the means for tracking some of the largest costs in the project, including those costs for labor, equipment, materials, travel, rentals, software, and so on.

- Exchange task assignments, task updates, progress information, and status reports with your resources, via Microsoft Office Project Server 2007 and Microsoft Office Project Web Access.

- Make sure that all tasks are assigned to a responsible and accountable resource so nothing inadvertently slips through the cracks to be forgotten until it's too late.

Adding Resources to the Project

The following types of resources can be assigned to your tasks:

- People or equipment, or work resources

- Consumable materials, or material resources

- Cost items incurred in the performance of a task, or cost resources

Entering Resources in the Resource Sheet

To add resources to your project by simple data entry, follow these steps:

1. Click View, Resource Sheet to switch to the Resource Sheet view (see Figure 6-1).

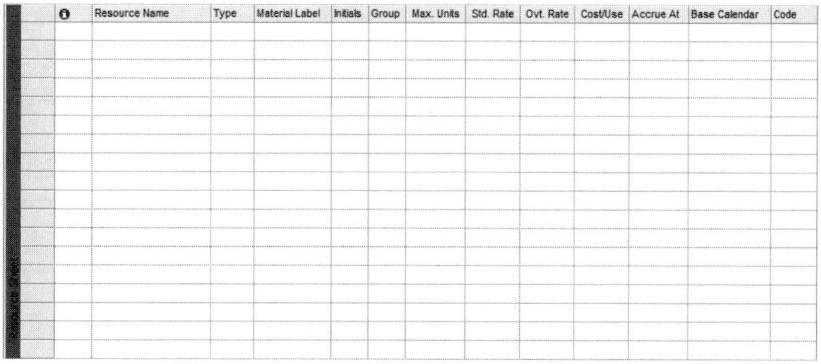

	❶	Resource Name	Type	Material Label	Initials	Group	Max. Units	Std. Rate	Ovt. Rate	Cost/Use	Accrue At	Base Calendar	Code

Figure 6-1 Enter resource information on the Resource Sheet.

2. Make sure the Entry table is applied. If necessary, click View, Table, Entry.

> **Note**
>
> You can always check which table is applied to a sheet view by resting your mouse pointer over the All Cells box where the row and column headings intersect. The ToolTip containing the table name (and view name) appears.

3. In the first Resource Name field, type the name of a resource and then press Enter.

4. Enter the names of other resources in the same way.

If a piece of equipment will be integral to the successful completion of a task, enter its name as a work resource, just as you would a human resource.

Sort Your Resource Names

When you have all the resources entered, you might want to sort them in a particular order and keep them in that order. In the Resource Sheet, click Project, Sort, Sort By. In the Sort By field, click the field you want the resources sorted by; for example, Name or Group. Select the Permanently Renumber Resources check box and then click Sort. This procedure makes this particular order permanent because it renumbers the unique identifier (Unique ID) for each resource.

Whenever you select the Permanently Renumber Resources check box and click Sort, it's a very good idea to open the Sort dialog box again, click Reset, and then click Cancel. This process clears the Permanently Renumber Resources check box. This way, the next time you sort your resources for some temporary need, you won't inadvertently renumber the resources again.

TROUBLESHOOTING

You have duplicate resource names, and information is being tracked separately for each instance

When you enter resource names, be aware that Microsoft Project allows duplicate entries of the same name. Through the use of a Unique ID for each resource record you enter, the duplicate entries appear unique to the Microsoft Project database. The problem is that when you assign tasks to a duplicated resource, you might assign some tasks to one instance of the resource and other tasks to the other instance. Microsoft Project tracks the resource and assignment information as if they are separate resources, so your information is skewed.

If you've entered a long list of resources, it's a good idea to sort the resource list and review the sorted list to check for duplicates. In the Resource Sheet, click Project, Sort, By Name.

Adding Work Resources to the Project

Work resources consist of people and equipment that use time as a measure of effort on a task. Add resources to your project simply by entering their names into your project plan as described in the previous section. To automate the process, you can select resource names from your company's e-mail address book. If you have a resource list in a Microsoft Office Excel 2007 workbook, you can import it into your project plan. After your resources are in place, you can add information regarding their availability, costs, notes, and more.

Note

If you're entering a significant number of work resources, or if you don't expect to enter any material resources, apply the Entry – Work Resources table. This table has only those resource fields applicable to work resources.

With the Resource Sheet showing, click View, Table, More Tables. Click Entry – Work Resources and then click Apply.

Project Management Practices: Staffing Management

Ongoing operations such as accounts payable or shipping and receiving always need to be staffed "forever." In projects, however, that's not the case: Because projects have a specific beginning and ending point, there's a definite starting point when you begin to need resources. There's also a definite ending point when resources are no longer needed because the project is complete. In between the start and finish dates, there are likely to be ramp-up and ramp-down periods, which often take place at a variety of times for different phases or functions.

Given this condition of project staffing, it's important to have a clear sense of when you actually need people to work on projects, what you need them for, at what point you don't need them anymore, and what happens to them after that point.

A staffing management plan is considered a subset of your project plan. It describes when and how your human resources will be brought on and taken off your project team. An excellent way to develop your staffing management plan is to develop your task list and preliminary schedule using generic resources, which can help you to determine your staffing needs based on specific tasks in the schedule.

Resources ▾

Resources

Add Resources Using the Project Guide

You can use the Project Guide to help add resources to your project plan. It can walk you through the steps to enter resources manually to add them from your company address book or directory, or to add them from Office Project Server 2007. To add resources using the Project Guide:

1. On the Project Guide toolbar, click Resources.

2. In the Project Guide pane, click the Specify People And Equipment For The Project link.

3. Read the succeeding panes and make choices as directed (see Figure 6-2).

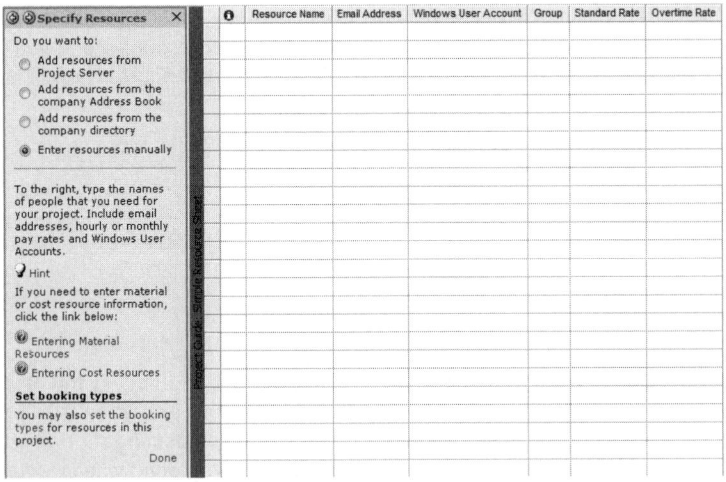

Figure 6-2 Make the choices you want, follow the directions, and click the controls provided. The Project Guide walks you through the process.

Adding Resources from Your E-Mail Address Book

If Microsoft Project is installed on the same computer as your organization's MAPI e-mail connection (for example, Microsoft Exchange Server 2007 or Microsoft Office Outlook 2007), you can add resources to your project plan from the e-mail address book. To do this:

1. Click Insert, New Resource From, Address Book.

   If the Choose Profile dialog box appears, click the profile name for your e-mail system.

   The Select Resources dialog box appears.

2. Click the resources you want and then click the Add button to add the selected resources to your project plan.

You can add all resources contained in a group or distribution list. Add the name of the group to your list, just as you would add an individual resource. When you click OK, Microsoft Project asks whether you want to expand the group to list the individual resources in the project plan.

> **Note**
> If you're connected to Project Server to use the enterprise features, you have access to all existing resources identified in the server. Click Insert, New Resource From, Microsoft Project Server. The Build Team dialog box appears. Under Enterprise Resource, select the team members you want to add to your project and then click Add. The names are added to the Team Resource table. When finished, click OK.

TROUBLESHOOTING

You get an error message when trying to display your e-mail address book

If you click Insert, New Resource From, Address Book, but get an error message instead of your address book listing, click OK in the error message. The Select Resources dialog box appears with no resources listed. Click the Show Names From The box to see what's available in the drop-down. If another Address Book or Contacts subfolder is listed, click it.

If you still do not see contacts from your address book, go to your e-mail system's online Help for other ideas. Remember that you can only import contact information from a MAPI-compatible e-mail program to your Microsoft Project resource sheet.

Using Resource Information from Office Excel

Suppose you have a list of resources in an Excel workbook. You can easily use it to populate your project's Resource Sheet. You can copy information or you can import the file.

To copy a resource list from an Excel workbook, follow these steps:

1. Open the Microsoft Office Excel workbook that contains the resource list.

2. Select the resource names. On the Home tab, in the Clipboard group, click Copy.

Copy

> **Note**
> If you're using Microsoft Office Excel 2003 or earlier, click Copy on the Standard toolbar.

3. Open the project plan. If necessary, click View, Resource Sheet.

    In the Resource Name column, click the cell where you want to begin inserting the copied resources.

Paste

4. On the Standard toolbar in Microsoft Office Project 2007, click Paste.

You can also use the Microsoft Project Plan Import Export Template to import resources from Excel to Microsoft Project. The standard Excel importing process involves mapping the Excel columns to the corresponding Microsoft Project columns to ensure that the right information ends up in the right locations in your Resource Sheet. The Microsoft Project Plan Import Export Template is set up to enter more detailed resource information in the format needed by Microsoft Project. To do this, make sure that Excel and the Microsoft Project Plan Import Export Template are installed on the same computer as Microsoft Project and then follow these steps:

1. Start Microsoft Office Excel.

2. Click the Microsoft Office Button and then click New.

The Microsoft
Office Button

3. In the New Workbook dialog box, under Templates, click Installed Templates (see Figure 6-3).

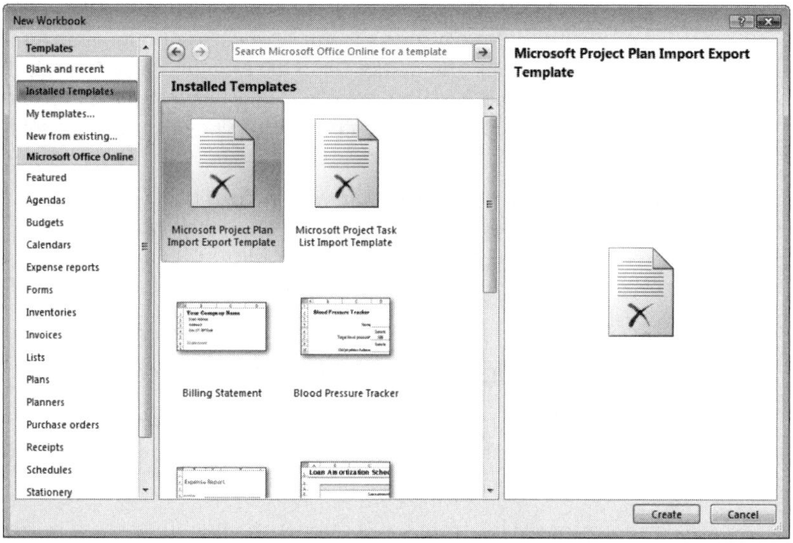

Figure 6-3 Two templates are available in Excel to facilitate entering information in Microsoft Project.

4. Double-click the Microsoft Project Plan Import Export Template.

    The template creates a new file with columns that correspond to the most commonly used fields in Microsoft Project.

5. At the bottom of the workbook window, click the Resource_Table tab.

Chapter 6

6. Enter resources and any other resource information in the columns provided (see Figure 6-4).

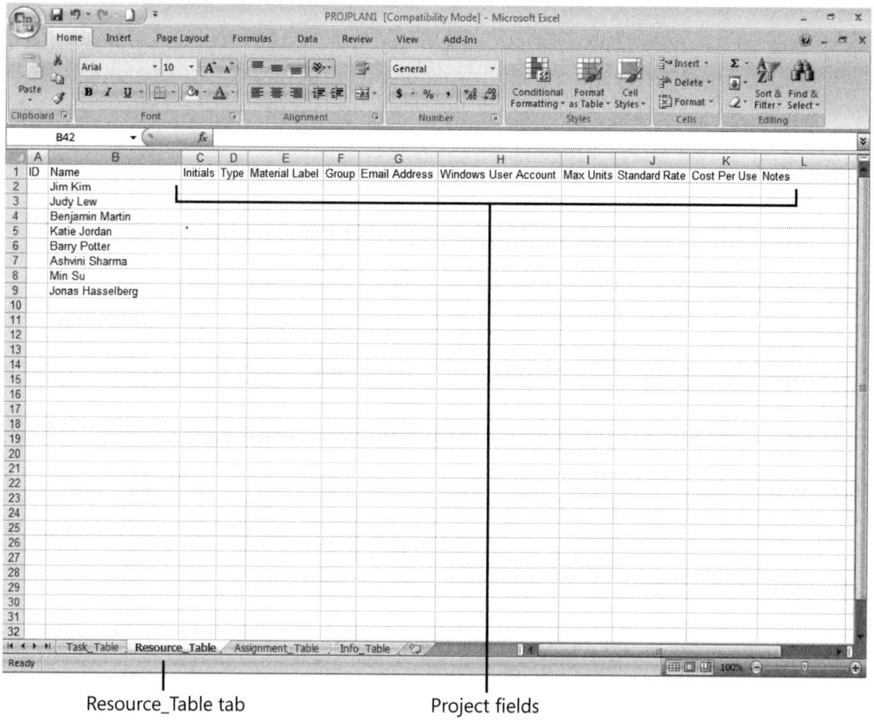

Resource_Table tab   Project fields

Figure 6-4 The Resource_Table sheet of the Microsoft Project Plan Import Export Template in Excel contains the most commonly used resource fields.

7. Click the Microsoft Office Button, point to Save As, and then click Excel 97-2003 Workbook. Browse to the location on your computer where you want to save the file, change the name from PROJPLAN1.xls if you like, and then click Save.

    You need to save the workbook as an .xls rather than an .xlsx file because Microsoft Office Project 2007 does not recognize the new Microsoft Office Excel 2007 format of .xlsx.

Save

> **Note**
>
> The xlsx file format was not finalized by the time the development work on Project 2007 was completed. It is expected that the xlsx file format will be a recognized file format in a future release of Microsoft Project.

> **Note**
> If you're working with a version of Microsoft Office Excel 2003 or earlier, you can still use the Microsoft Project Plan Import Export Template. Open Microsoft Office Excel 2003 and then click File, New. In the task pane, click the On My Computer link. Click the Spreadsheet Solutions tab. Double-click the Microsoft Project Plan Import Export Template.

When you're ready to import the resource list into your project plan, follow these steps:

1. If necessary, open the project plan.

Open

2. On the Standard toolbar, click Open.

3. Go to the location on your computer or network where the Excel workbook is saved.

4. Next to the File Name box, click the Microsoft Project Files (*.mp*) button.

   This button is the new incarnation of the Files Of Type list seen in previous versions of Microsoft Project.

5. In the list, click Microsoft Excel Workbooks (*.xls).

   The workbook appears in the list of folders and files.

6. Click the name of the workbook and then click the Open button.

   The Import Wizard appears (see Figure 6-5).

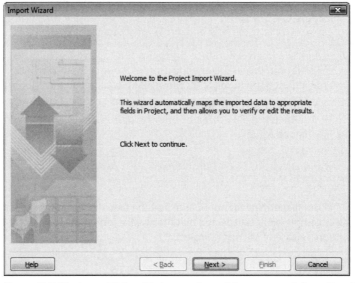

Figure 6-5 The Import Wizard helps you import the resource information from your Excel workbook into your project plan.

7. In the first wizard page, click Next.

8. Click Project Excel Template and then click Next.

9. Specify whether you want to import the file as a new project, append the resources to the currently active project, or merge the data into the active project.

10. Click Finish.

The resource information is imported (see Figure 6-6).

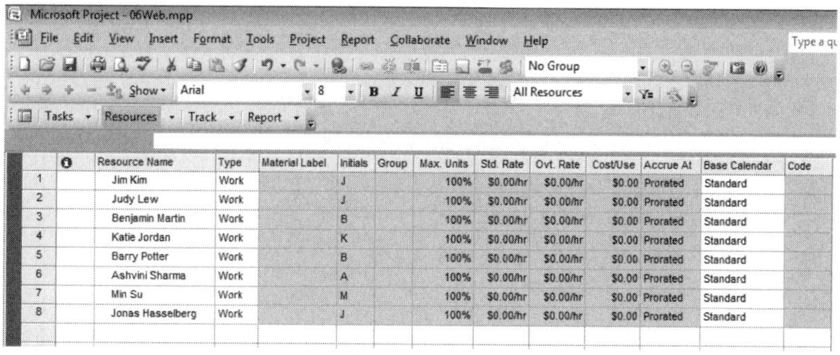

Figure 6-6 The resource information is imported into the Resource Sheet of Microsoft Project as you specified.

TROUBLESHOOTING

Microsoft Office Project 2007 will not let you import the older .xls file format

When you finish with the Import Wizard, you might see the following error message:

> **Microsoft Office Project**
>
> You are trying to open a file saved in an older file format. Your settings do not allow you to open files saved in older file formats.
>
> To change your setting, navigate to the "Security" tab in the Options dialog box.
>
> OK

If you see this message, click OK. Click Tools, Options, and then click the Security tab. Under Legacy Formats, select either the Prompt When Loading Files With Legacy Or Non Default File Format or the Allow Loading Files With Legacy Or Non Default File Formats option. Click OK.

Run through the Import Wizard process again. If you selected the Prompt When Loading Files With Legacy Or Non Default File Format option, you'll see the following prompt:

Click Yes. The information from the Excel Project template appears in your project file.

For more information about using Microsoft Office Project 2007 with other applications, see the section titled "Importing and Exporting Information" in Chapter 16, "Exchanging Information with Other Applications," and Chapter 17, "Integrating Microsoft Project with Microsoft Excel."

For more information about adding resources to your project plan from a shared resource pool file, see the section titled "Sharing Resources Using a Resource Pool" in Chapter 14, "Managing Master Projects and Resource Pools."

For more information about adding resources from the enterprise resource pool, see the section titled "Building Your Enterprise Project Team" in Chapter 22, "Managing Enterprise Projects and Resources."

Adding Material Resources to the Project

Material resources are consumable supplies that use quantity as a measure of effort on a task. Any supplies that are integral to completing tasks can be added to your project plan as material resources. Examples of such material resources might be steel for a building structure, roofing material for a home, and bricks for a landscaping project. You might have a task "Lay brick sidewalk," to which a bricklayer is assigned for a certain amount of time. You can also assign a quantity of bricks to the task. The bricklayer and the bricks are both essential resources to the completion of the task.

To enter a material resource:

1. Display the Resource Sheet with the Entry table applied.

2. In the next available Resource Name field, type the name of the material resource (for example, **Bricks**) and then press Tab.

3. In the Type field, click Material.

4. In the Material Label field, enter the unit of measurement for the material.

    This measurement will differ depending on the nature of the material. It might be tons, yards, feet, cartons, and so on.

When you specify that a resource is a material rather than a work resource, be aware of the following points:

- Maximum units (or resource units) and the associated variable availability are not applicable to material resources. You'll specify units (for example, 50 yards or 100 feet per day) when you assign the material resource to a task. With these assignment units, you can track the usage of materials and possibly the depletion rate of materials.

    For more information about material resource assignments, see the section titled "Assigning Material Resources to Tasks" in Chapter 7, "Assigning Resources to Tasks."

- Resource calendars are not available for material resources.

- Workgroup fields such as Workgroup and Windows Account are not available for material resources. The Overtime field is also disabled.

If you're entering a significant number of material resources, apply the Entry – Material Resources table. This table has only those resource fields applicable to material resources. With the Resource Sheet showing, click View, Table, More Tables. Click Entry – Material Resources and then click Apply.

> **Note**
> You can right-click the All Cells box that sits between the first column and first row. In the shortcut menu that appears, click More Tables, Entry – Material Resources, Apply.

Adding Cost Resources to the Project

In previous versions of Microsoft Project, you had work resources and material resources. A third resource type is new in Microsoft Office Project 2007—the cost resource. If you rely on Microsoft Project for tracking costs and adhering to your project budget throughout the life of the project, you'll find cost resources a most convenient tool.

What Are Cost Resources?

A cost resource is a cost item that contributes to the completion of a task but does not affect the duration or work of a task. When you include a cost resource with a task, or a set of tasks, you can be assured that not only are you tracking the cost of human resources or equipment resources with their cost per hour or per use, but you are also tracking any cost items incurred as a result of carrying out the task.

Suppose you have several tasks, such as "Hold user meetings," "Staff conference booth," or "Train trainers at client site." These might be at different locations and handled by different team members. However, they will all involve cost items such as airfare and lodging. They might also involve room rentals or equipment fees. You can create cost resources named Airfare, Lodging, Booth Rental, Conference Fees, Printing, and so on.

Unlike work or material resources, you do not enter a cost amount in the Resource Sheet or Resource Information dialog box. You only create the resource and identify it as a cost resource.

Only when you have assigned a cost resource to a task do you deal with the cost. At that point, you can enter the cost for the airfare, for example, as associated with the task to which the airfare cost resource is assigned.

For example, you might have the Airfare cost resource assigned to the "Hold user meetings" and the "Staff conference booth" tasks. The "Hold user meetings" task needs one person to travel from Portland to Chicago in the spring and costs $330. The "Staff conference booth" task needs three persons to travel from Raleigh to Las Vegas in the fall and costs $720 total. You're using the same cost resource, but entering different cost amounts on the different task assignments.

Identifying a Resource as a Cost Resource

To set up a cost resource, do the following:

1. Display the Resource Sheet.

2. In the next available Resource Name field, type the name of the cost resource. Good examples include Car Rental, Client Entertainment, Software Purchase, Airfare, Lodging, and so on.

Note

Make the cost resource name specific enough so that you can know what the resource is for when you get ready to assign it to a particular task. But make it general enough so that you can use it for multiple tasks. You might find it helpful to use your organization's budget category names. Later you can view information on how much you're spending throughout the project on all car rentals, for example.

3. In the Type field, click Cost.

Because cost resources do not rely on working time to accomplish their tasks, they are not associated with max units, base calendars, or availability dates. Also, because specific costs are entered on the task to which the cost resource is assigned, costs are not entered on the cost resource itself. Therefore, these fields in the Resource Sheet and Resource Information dialog box are not available for cost resources.

TROUBLESHOOTING

You can't enter costs for your cost resource

When you identify a resource as a cost resource, it might seem unexpected that the resource cost fields—Std. Rate, Ovt. Rate, and Cost/Use—suddenly become unavailable to you, both in the Resource Sheet as well as on the Costs tab of the Resource Information dialog box.

However, because cost resources are intended to be assigned to different tasks in which the cost amounts are likely to be different from assignment to assignment, the cost information is actually entered in the Assignment Information dialog box available from the Task Usage or Resource Usage view.

First, assign the cost resource to a task. Then open the Task Usage or Resource Usage view. Double-click the assignment of the cost resource on the task to open the Assignment Information dialog box. In the Cost box on the General tab, enter the cost for this cost resource as it pertains to the selected task assignment. You can also enter the cost in the Assign Resources dialog box or in the Cost field in the Task Usage or Resource Usage view.

For more information about working with cost resources, see the section titled "Assigning Cost Resources to Tasks" in Chapter 7, and "Entering Costs for Cost Resource Assignments" in Chapter 8, "Planning Resource and Task Costs."

Removing a Resource from the Project

If you've added a resource by mistake or have found duplicates of the same resource, you can delete a resource.

> **Note**
> If you're working with enterprise features using Microsoft Office Project Professional 2007 and Project Server, you cannot delete an enterprise resource from your project. Enterprise resources can be deleted only by the project administrator using Office Project Web Access.

To completely delete a resource:

1. Display the Resource Sheet.

2. Click somewhere in the row of the resource you want to delete.

3. Click Edit, Delete Resource.

    The resource row, along with any associated resource or assignment information, is removed from your project.

> **Note**
> You can also delete a resource by clicking the row header for the resource and then pressing Delete.

Identifying Tentative, Generic, or Budget Resources

As you add your work, material, or cost resources to the Resource Sheet, you can set these resources up with further characteristics that provide you with more flexibility in your resource management. You can identify any resource as a proposed rather than committed resource. You can specify that a resource is generic. You can set up a resource as a budget resource to help you compare your project costs against your established budget.

Proposing Tentative Resources

If you're using Office Project Professional 2007, you can specify that a resource be either proposed or committed to your project. Adding proposed resources and assigning them to tasks can help you decide whether a particular resource is needed without locking up their availability on other projects. You and other project managers and resource managers can search for resources and include or exclude proposed resources.

All resources you add are booked as committed to your project by default. To specify that a resource be proposed rather than committed, follow these steps:

1. Display the Resource Sheet.

2. Click the resource you want to specify as proposed.

3. On the Standard toolbar, click Resource Information (see Figure 6-7).

Resource
Information

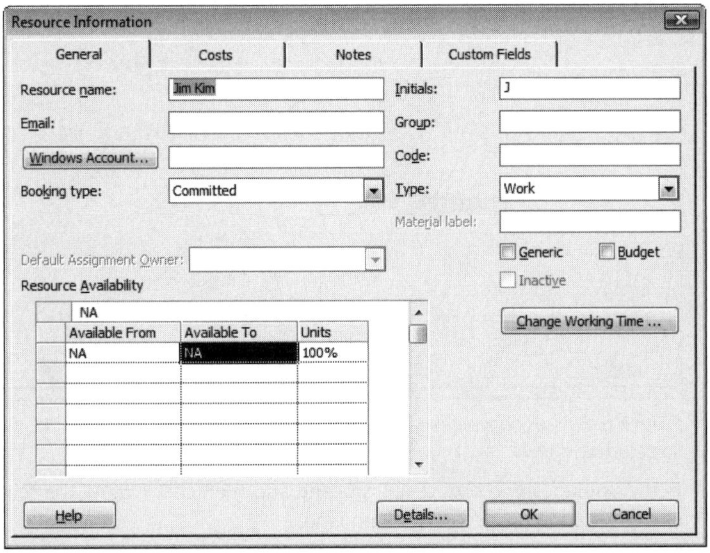

Figure 6-7 Use the Resource Information dialog box to view or enter details about a resource.

4. In the Resource Information dialog box, be sure that the General tab is showing.

5. In the Booking Type box, click Proposed.

6. Click OK.

Update Several Resources at Once

If you have several resources that you want to switch to the Proposed status, you can do this more quickly by selecting all the resources before opening the Resource Information dialog box.

Click the first resource you want to change, and then use Shift or Ctrl to select the other resources you want to change. On the Standard toolbar, click the Resource Information dialog box. The Multiple Resource Information dialog box appears. Only those fields that can be changed for multiple resources at once are available (see Figure 6-8).

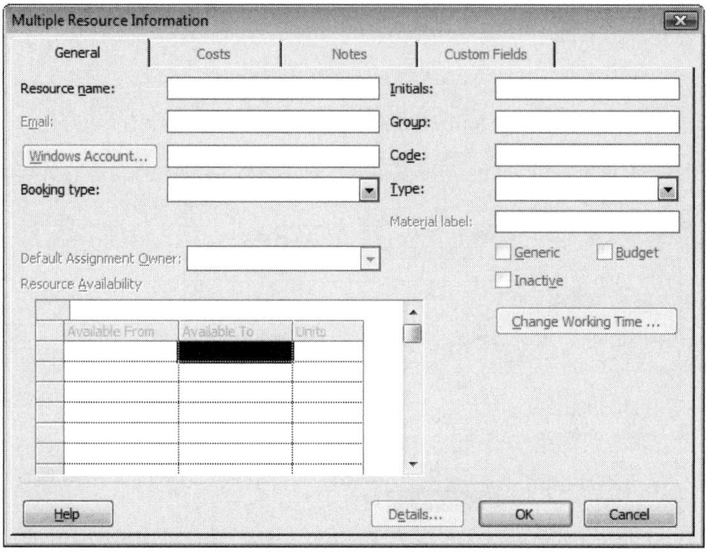

Figure 6-8 Use the Multiple Resource Information dialog box to make a global change to all selected resources.

In the Booking Type box, click Proposed and then click OK. All the selected resources are changed to the proposed booking status.

Using Generic Resources as a Placeholder

You can enter actual names of resources or you can enter *generic resources*. A generic resource is a title or other similar description of the resource instead of an actual name, for example, Accountant, Marketing Specialist, Sales Representative (see Figure 6-9).

Actual names

	ⓘ	Resource Name	Type	Material Label	Initials	Group	Max. Units	Std. Rate	Ovt. Rate	Cost/Use	Accrue At	Base Calendar	Code
1		Jim Kim	Work		J		100%	$0.00/hr	$0.00/hr	$0.00	Prorated	Standard	
2		Ashvini Sharma	Work		A		100%	$0.00/hr	$0.00/hr	$0.00	Prorated	Standard	
3		Katie Jordan	Work		K		100%	$0.00/hr	$0.00/hr	$0.00	Prorated	Standard	
4		Jonas Hasselberg	Work		J		100%	$0.00/hr	$0.00/hr	$0.00	Prorated	Standard	
5		Designer	Work		J		100%	$0.00/hr	$0.00/hr	$0.00	Prorated	Standard	
6		Product Engineer	Work		B		100%	$0.00/hr	$0.00/hr	$0.00	Prorated	Standard	
7		Drafter	Work		B		100%	$0.00/hr	$0.00/hr	$0.00	Prorated	Standard	
8		Editor	Work		M		100%	$0.00/hr	$0.00/hr	$0.00	Prorated	Standard	

Generic names

Figure 6-9 Use either actual resource names or generic categories of resources to get started.

As you bring resources into the project, you can either leave the generic names or you can replace the generic names with the actual names. Whenever you change resource names in the Resource Sheet, the names are changed on any assigned tasks automatically.

If you're using Project Professional, you can mark generic resources as such. Double-click the resource name to open the Resource Information dialog box. Make sure that the General tab is displayed and then select the Generic check box.

If you have a long list of resources to switch to or from a generic status, you can do this more quickly by adding the Generic column to the Resource Sheet. To do this, follow these steps:

1. Click the column head next to which you want the Generic column to be inserted.

2. Click Insert, Column.

3. In the Field Name box, type g to quickly go to Generic in the list.

4. Click Generic and then click OK.

    You can then go down the list in the Resource Sheet and select Yes or No in the Generic field.

Whether the Generic column is showing or not, you can use the Generic field to sort, group, or filter your resources to quickly find all your generic resources. This can help you determine any outstanding resource requirements.

For more information about sorting, grouping, or filtering resources by a particular field, see the section titled "Rearranging Your Project Information" in Chapter 4, "Viewing Project Information."

Estimating with Generic Resources

Entering generic resources can help you estimate which resources and how many of a type of resource you need to meet your project finish date within a targeted budget. Enter your generic resources in the Resource Sheet and then assign them to tasks.

For more information about associating resources with specific tasks, see Chapter 7.

Check the calculated project finish date to see if you need additional resources to meet the targeted project finish date. Check the total project costs to see if you need to change your resource mix to meet your budget.

When you finish tweaking your project plan to meet your requirements, you'll know which resources you need.

Specifying a Budget Resource

A budget resource is one that you will use specifically to capture a budget amount for a particular category related to the project as a whole. You create a resource that represents that project budget category, for example, Travel Budget, Equipment Cost Plan, or Project Materials. You can identify any work, material, or cost resource as a budget resource.

When you designate a resource as a budget resource, it can then only be assigned to the project summary task. This is because the purpose of a budget resource is to reflect the planned budget for that category for the overall project.

> **For more information about the project summary task, see the section titled "Showing the Project Summary Task" in Chapter 3, "Starting a New Project."**

You can then use this information to compare your planned budget amounts for both costs and amounts of work against what is being scheduled or carried out in your project.

> **For more information about your project budget, see the section titled "Setting Up and Reviewing a Project Budget" in Chapter 8.**

Setting When Resources Are Available for Work

It's likely that many of your work resources will work full-time on your project. However, you might have some who work part-time, or who work part-time on your project because they're being loaned from another group. You might have several individuals or machines (work resources) who perform the same function. You might also have a resource who will work full-time on your project until October, at which time she will be shared half-time with another project that is ramping up them. All of your work resources will take your designated holidays off, and most of them will take vacations and other days off throughout the year.

In Microsoft Project, you can account for all these different kinds of resource availability and working times to schedule resources most effectively and accurately for your project.

Setting Working Times and Days Off for Work Resources

The basis of setting the availability of resources on the project is the resource's working time calendar, also simply known as the *resource calendar*. Each work resource has an individual resource calendar, which is initially based on the project calendar. You can customize each resource calendar as necessary to reflect the individual resource's specific working times and days off. Because the resource calendar indicates when a resource is available to work on assigned tasks, it affects the manner in which tasks are scheduled.

For more information about the project calendar, see the section titled "Setting Your Project Calendar" in Chapter 3.

> **Note**
>
> If you're working with enterprise projects and enterprise resources, the calendars are set by the project administrator. Therefore, your ability to assign different calendars to resources might be limited.

Viewing a Resource Calendar

As soon as you create a resource, the project calendar is assigned by default as the resource's working time calendar. To view a resource's working time calendar:

1. Display the Resource Sheet or other resource view.

2. Click the resource whose working time calendar you want to view.

3. On the Standard toolbar, click Resource Information.

4. On the General tab in the Resource Information dialog box, click the Change Working Time button.

> **Note**
>
> In previous versions of Microsoft Office Project, the Resource Information dialog box had a Working Time tab. Now in Microsoft Office Project 2007, the Change Working Time button on the General tab opens the Change Working Time dialog box, which is the same as choosing Change Working Time on the Tools menu.

The working time calendar for the selected resource appears (see Figure 6-10). The resource calendar is identical to the project calendar until you change it.

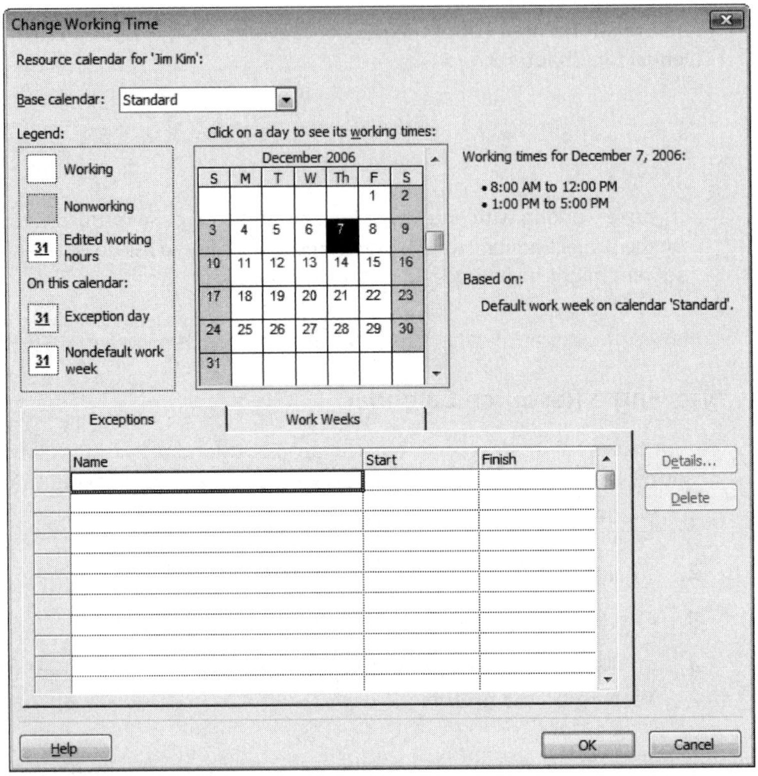

Figure 6-10 Use the Change Working Time dialog box to view or modify an individual re-source's working times. These are the days and times when assigned tasks can be scheduled for this resource.

5. To see the working times for a particular day, click on a date in the calendar thumbnail. The working times for that day appear to the right of the calendar.

6. To see the working times and days off for a typical week, click the Work Weeks tab. Make sure that the [Default] row is selected and then click the Details button. In the Select Day(s) box, click the day of the week to see the working times in the grid to the right. When finished, click OK or Cancel.

7. Click OK or Cancel in the Change Working Time dialog box and then click OK or Cancel in the Resource Information dialog box.

Applying a Different Base Calendar to a Resource

Microsoft Project comes with three *base calendars*: Standard, Night Shift, and 24 Hours. These base calendars are like calendar templates that you can apply to a set of resources, a set of tasks, or the project as a whole.

You can apply the base calendar you want for a resource. This can be useful if most of your team works the standard 8:00 A.M. to 5:00 P.M. day shift, but one or two of your resources work a graveyard shift. In that case, you can apply the Night Shift base calendar to those resources. To change which base calendar is applied to a resource, follow these steps:

1. In the Resource Sheet or other resource view, double-click the resource whose working time calendar you want to change.

2. On the General tab in the Resource Information dialog box, click the Change Working Time button.

3. In the Base Calendar box, click the name of the base calendar you want to make the origin of the current resource's calendar.

4. Click OK in the Change Working Time dialog box and then click OK in the Resource Information dialog box.

Modifying a Resource Calendar

You can change an individual resource's calendar to reflect a different work schedule from others on the project team. For example, most everyone on your team might work Monday through Friday, 8:00 A.M. until 5:00 P.M. But suppose one team member works just three days a week, and another team member works weekend nights. You can change their resource calendars to fit their actual work schedules. This way, their assigned tasks will be scheduled only when they're actually available to work on them.

A resource might need an alternative work week specified for a particular period of time. One example might be a trainer working a combination of day, swing, graveyard, and weekend shifts throughout the next two weeks to train individuals on those shifts.

You can also update resource calendars to reflect team member work week exceptions such as vacation time, personal time off, sabbaticals, and so on. Updating the resource calendars helps keep your schedule accurate.

For more information about changing base calendars, including specifying the normal work week, alternative work weeks, one-time calendar exceptions, and recurring calendar exceptions, see the section titled "Modifying a Base Calendar" in Chapter 3.

Creating a New Base Calendar for Resources

If you find you're making the same modifications to individual resource calendars repeatedly, you might do well to create an entirely new base calendar and apply it to the applicable resources. If you have a group of resources who work a different schedule, for example, a weekend shift or "four-tens," create a new base calendar and apply it to those resources.

For details, see the section titled "Creating a New Base Calendar" in Chapter 3.

When you create a new base calendar, it becomes available in any of the three calendar applications: project calendar, task calendar, or resource calendar. To apply the new base calendar to a resource, follow these steps:

1. Display the Resource Sheet or other resource view.

2. Double-click the resource to whom you want to assign the new base calendar.

3. In the Resource Information dialog box, click the Change Working Time button.

4. In the Base Calendar field, select the base calendar you want to apply to the selected resource.

5. Make any additional changes to the calendar as needed for this resource.

   These changes apply only to the selected resource; they do not change the original base calendar.

INSIDE OUT   You cannot apply a base calendar to multiple resources

You have to select each resource individually and then switch to the other base calendar you want. A faster way to do this is to work in the Resource Sheet. For each resource, select the new calendar in the Base Calendar field.

If you are changing the base calendar for many contiguous resources to the same base calendar, an even quicker method is to use the fill handle. Change the base calendar for the first resource. Then drag the fill handle in the lower right corner of the Base Calendar field for that resource and drag down through the fields of the other resources.

You can also set your resource working times using the Project Guide. On the Project Guide toolbar, click Resources. In the Project Guide pane, click the Define Working Times For Resources link. Read the succeeding panes and make choices as directed (see Figure 6-11).

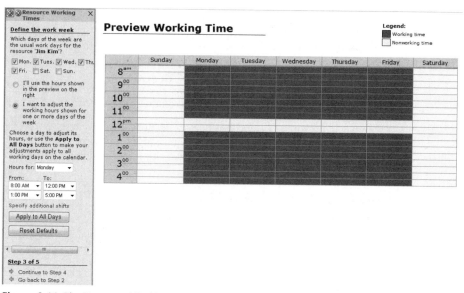

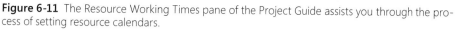

Figure 6-11 The Resource Working Times pane of the Project Guide assists you through the process of setting resource calendars.

Specifying Resource Availability with Max Units

Suppose that your team includes three full-time resources, one half-time resource, and another who is available three days each week or 60 percent of the time.

You can specify this kind of resource availability by setting the resource's *maximum units*, which you might also think of as *resource units*.

By definition, the full-time resources are each available at 100% max units. The half-time resource is available at 50% maximum units. The other part-timer is available at 60% max units. When you assign resources to tasks, those tasks are scheduled according to that resource's availability and indicates the point when the resource is considered overallocated.

But 100 percent or 50 percent of what, you might ask? The max units setting is multiplied by the availability shown in the resource calendar of working time and days off to determine the maximum level of availability of this resource on this project. If a resource calendar reflects a 40-hour work week, then 100% max units means a 40-hour work week for this project, while 50% max units means a 20-hour work week for this project (see Figure 6-12).

Resource Name	Max Units	Work	Details	M	T	W	T	F
⊟ Jim Kim	50%	20 hrs	Work	4h	4h	4h	4h	4h
Design interior pages		20 hrs	Work	4h	4h	4h	4h	4h
⊟ Katie Jordan	100%	40 hrs	Work	8h	8h	8h	8h	8h
Perform system needs analysis		40 hrs	Work	8h	8h	8h	8h	8h

Figure 6-12 Given the same 40-hour-per-week resource calendar, a 100% max units resource works 8 hours per day, while a 50% max units resource works 4 hours per day.

Likewise, if a resource calendar reflects a 20-hour work week, then 100% max units means a 20-hour work week while 50% max units for this resource would be a 10-hour work week. Again, max units plays against the resource calendar. Figure 6-13 illustrates the schedules for these two scenarios.

Resource Name	Max Units	Work	Details	M	T	W	T	F
⊟ Ashvini Sharma	100%	40 hrs	Work	4h	4h	4h	4h	4h
Develop Web structure		40 hrs	Work	4h	4h	4h	4h	4h
⊟ Jonas Hasselberg	50%	20 hrs	Work	2h	2h	2h	2h	2h
Design Home page		20 hrs	Work	2h	2h	2h	2h	2h

Figure 6-13 Given the same 20-hour-per-week resource calendar, a 100% max units resource works 4 hours per day, while a 50% max units resource works 2 hours per day.

Here's another scenario: Suppose that you have three engineers, two architects, and four drafters, all working a full-time schedule. Instead of naming them individually, you decide you want to name your resources by their functions and consolidate them into a single resource representing multiple individuals. You can do that with max units as well. The three engineers together are available at 300 percent, the two architects at 200 percent, and the four drafters at 400 percent.

If you have three full-time drafters and one half-time drafter, your *Drafter* resource is available at 350% max units.

To enter max units, simply type the percentage in the Max. Units field in the Resource Sheet (see Figure 6-14). The default for the Max. Units field is 100%.

	ⓘ	Resource Name	Type	Material Label	Initials	Group	Max. Units
1		Jim Kim	Work		J		50%
2		Ashvini Sharma	Work		A		100%
3		Katie Jordan	Work		K		60%
4		Jonas Hasselberg	Work		J		100%
5		Designer	Work		J		300%
6		Product Engineer	Work		B		200%
7		Drafter	Work		B		350%
8		Editor	Work		M		100%

Maximum units for resources

Figure 6-14 You can enter max units when you enter resource names, or come back to it later.

Now, suppose your staffing plan specifies that you'll start the project life cycle needing four drafters. After three months, you'll need only three drafters. Two months later, you'll need only one. To specify variable resource quantity or availability over time, follow these steps:

1. In the Resource Sheet, double-click the resource whose maximum units you want to adjust.

   The Resource Information dialog box appears. Make sure the General tab is displayed.

2. In the Resource Availability table, enter the first date range for the resource's first max units specification.

   That is, enter the beginning date in the first Available From field, the ending date in the first Available To field, and the max units that will be available during those dates in the Units field. For example, in the first row enter **4/2/07** under Available From; enter **6/29/04** under Available To; enter **400%** under Units.

3. In the second row, enter the second date range for the resource's max units specification.

   For example, enter **7/2/07** under Available From; enter **9/21/07** under Available To; enter **300%** under Units.

4. Continue in this manner until your entire resource availability specification is set.

   For example, enter **9/24/07** under Available From; enter **10/26/07** under Available To; enter **100%** under Units (see Figure 6-15).

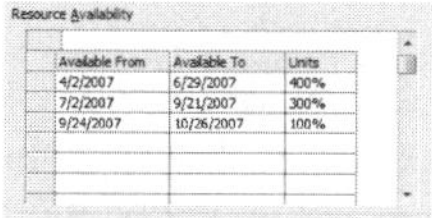

Figure 6-15 Use the Resource Availability table in the Resource Information dialog box to specify multiple levels of max units throughout the project.

Note

By default, maximum units are expressed as a percentage. You can represent them as a decimal if you prefer. Click Tools, Options and then click the Schedule tab. In the Show Assignment Units As A box, select Decimal. Now, instead of 100%, one full-time resource is shown as having 1 max unit.

INSIDE OUT   **Allow for non-project work**

It's a reality that your resources are not likely to spend every minute of every work day devoted to project tasks. To allow for department meetings, administrative tasks, and other nonproject work, you can adjust the project calendar, the resource calendar, or max units.

First, determine how much nonproject work there is. If you're thinking of the project as a whole, adjust the project calendar. If you think of nonproject work in terms of individual resources, adjust the individual resource calendars. For example, instead of defining a day as 8 hours long, you might define it as 6 or 7 hours. Changing the calendar directly affects the days and times when tasks are scheduled.

You can also adjust max units for resources. Instead of setting up full-time resources with 100% max units, set them up with 75% max units. This method distributes task scheduling over time, without regard to specific days and hours.

With either method, you can keep from having every single hour of the day being scheduled for project work and allow for the realities of daily overhead and administrative tasks.

If you're set up for enterprise project management using Project Professional and Project Server, you can use the timesheets and administrative time to formalize and track resources' non-project activities.

For more information about administrative projects, see the section titled "Reviewing and Approving Administrative Time" in Chapter 22.

Note

You can enter max units with varying availability and a customized resource calendar for equipment resources just as you can for human resources. Both equipment and human resources are considered work resources. Setting equipment working times and availability can help account for other projects using the same equipment at different times, and schedule downtime for preventive maintenance.

Adding Detailed Resource Information

Along with the basic resource information such as the resource name, type, units, and calendar, you can add supplementary information to work, material, or cost resources. This data can include additional fields of resource information, notes, or hyperlinks.

Working with Supplemental Resource Fields

You can add initials, group designations, or a code to a resource using the appropriate field in the Resource Sheet or the General tab in the Resource Information dialog box. The following list provides examples of how you might use these fields:

- **Initials.** If you want a resource's initials, rather than his or her entire name, to appear in certain fields in your project plan, enter the initials in the Initials field in the Resource Sheet or on the General tab in the Resource Information dialog box.

- **Group.** Use the Group field to specify any categories of resources that might be useful for sorting, grouping, or filtering. For example, you can specify the department the resources come from, such as Product Development or Marketing. If you are using contracted resources, you can enter their company's name in the Group field. Or you can use the Group field to specify the resource's title or skill set, for example, Engineer, Architect, or Designer.

> **Note**
>
> You cannot assign a group name to a task. The group simply provides more information about a resource so you can sort, group, or filter resources.

- **Code.** Enter any code meaningful to you or your company in the Code field. It can be any alphanumeric designation you want. In fact, you can use it the way you use the Group field. You can enter job codes or skill codes, for example. Like the Group field, you can then sort, group, or filter these codes.

Cost-related fields are an important part of the Resource Sheet. The Resource Information dialog box also includes a Costs tab.

For more information about resource cost information and using the cost fields in the Resource Sheet and the Resource Information dialog box, see the section titled "Planning Resource Costs" in Chapter 8.

In addition to the default Entry table on the Resource Sheet, other tables containing different collections of resource fields are available. To apply a different table to the Resource Sheet:

1. Display the Resource Sheet.

2. Click View, Table. Click the table you want.

   If the table you want is not listed, click More Tables. Click the table in the list (see Figure 6-16) and then click Apply.

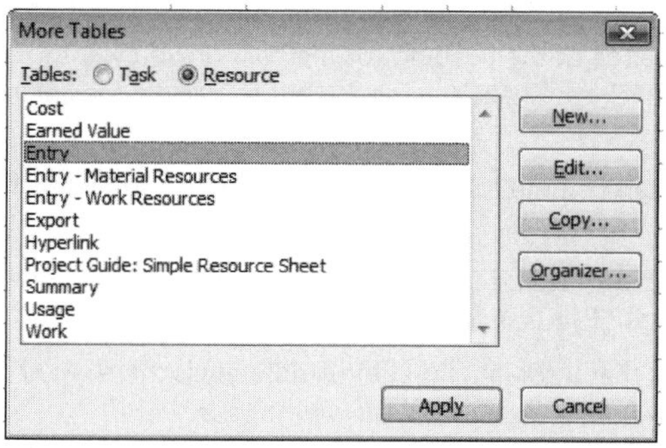

Figure 6-16 Apply any table that fits what you're trying to do.

Dozens of additional resource fields are available for you to add to your Resource Sheet. To add a new field to your current table:

1. Click the column heading next to where you want the new column to be inserted.

2. Click Insert, Column or simply press the Insert key.

   The Column Definition dialog box appears.

3. In the Field Name box, click the field you want to add.

   The fields listed are all resource fields. You can quickly move to a field by typing the first one or two letters of its name.

Note

A new Cost Center text field is available in Microsoft Project 2007. If your organization associates employees and other budget items such as materials, equipment, and travel with cost centers, you can add the Cost Center field to the Resource Sheet or Resource Usage view. After entering your cost center codes for resources, you can sort, group, or filter by cost center.

To hide a field you don't need, follow these steps:

1. Click the column heading you want to hide.

2. Click Edit, Hide Column or simply press the Delete key.

   The column is hidden, but the information is not deleted. It's still in the database and can be shown again whenever you display its column.

Hide a Column by Making It Very Narrow

You might frequently hide and insert certain columns, for example, when you print a view for presenting at a status meeting. If you're getting tired of constantly deleting and then inserting these columns, you can just make them very narrow. Position your mouse pointer on the right edge of the heading for the column you want to hide. When the pointer becomes a black crosshair, drag to the left to narrow the column until the contents cannot be seen.

If you drag past the left column edge, the column will be completely hidden, although it is actually still there.

When you're ready to display the narrow column again, drag the edge of the column heading to the right until you can read the contents of the column.

There's no indication that a column you hid completely is there—you just have to remember...and then be rather dextrous with your mouse.

Specifying Contact Information

If you will communicate project information electronically with resources, you might need to complete one or more of the following fields on the General tab in the Resource Information dialog box:

- **E-mail.** Specifies the resource's e-mail address, which is essential if you exchange e-mail messages, schedule notes, or project files with team members. If the resource is outside your company—that is, using a different e-mail system than you—be sure to specify the full e-mail address; for example, someone@microsoft. com. If you added resources from your MAPI address book using the Insert, New Resource From, Address Book command, the resources e-mail addresses are already filled in.

  For more information about communicating project information through e-mail, see Chapter 18, "Integrating Microsoft Project with Microsoft Outlook."

- **Windows Account.** Finds the resource's user account in the local address book and places it in that resource's Windows User Account field. Click the Windows Account button. In the alert that appears, click Yes. If there is more than one match, click the one you want in the Check Names dialog box. Click OK.

Adding a Note Regarding a Resource

Use notes to add comments regarding a resource. Notes might include information about the skills or experience of the resource or anything you believe is pertinent to this resource working on this project. To add a note to a resource:

1. Display the Resource Sheet or other resource view.

Resource Notes

2. Click the resource name and then on the Standard toolbar, click Resource Notes.

   The Resource Information dialog box appears with the Notes tab open (see Figure 6-17).

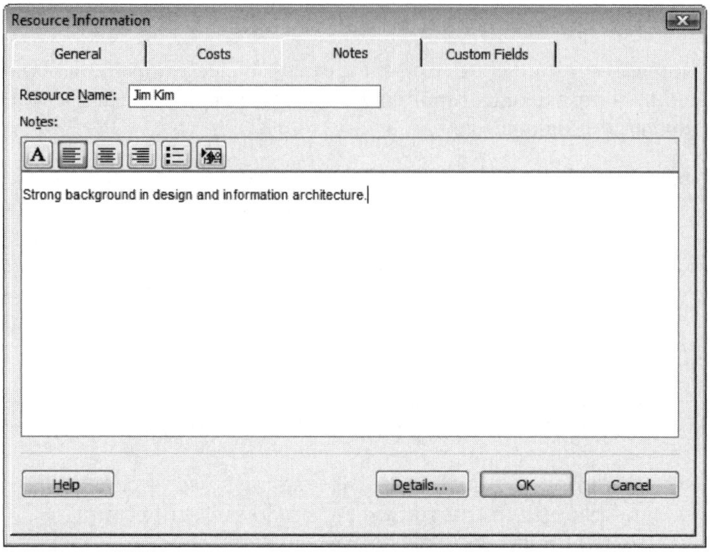

Figure 6-17 Enter relevant notes about a resource in the Notes tab of the Resource Information dialog box. You can also attach outside documents in the Notes tab.

3. In the Notes area, type the note.

4. When finished, click OK.

The Note indicator appears next to the resource name in the Indicators field of the Resource Sheet (see Figure 6-18). You can double-click this icon when you want to read the note.

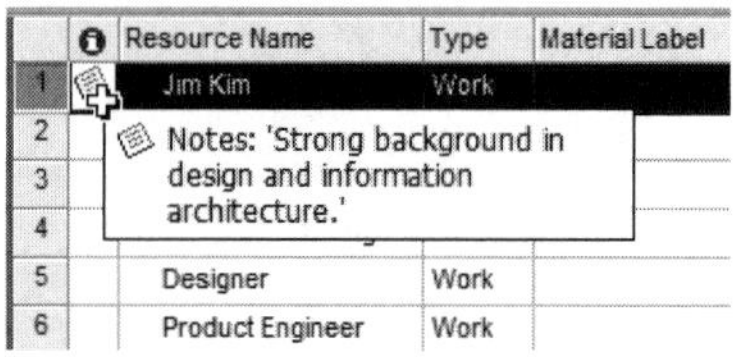

Figure 6-18 Position your mouse pointer over the Note indicator to read the note. Double-click the indicator to open the Notes tab in the Resource Information dialog box.

Hyperlinking to Resource Information

If there's a document or Web site relevant to a resource, you can create a hyperlink to reference it. This is a very efficient method of opening associated documents quickly. To insert a hyperlink, follow these steps:

1. Display the Resource Sheet or other resource view.

2. Click the resource to which you want to link an outside document or Web page.

3. On the Standard toolbar, click Insert Hyperlink.

4. In the Text To Display box, type a descriptive name for the document to which you are linking, for example, **Quarterly Goals**.

5. Find and select the document or site you want to link to your project file (see Figure 6-19).

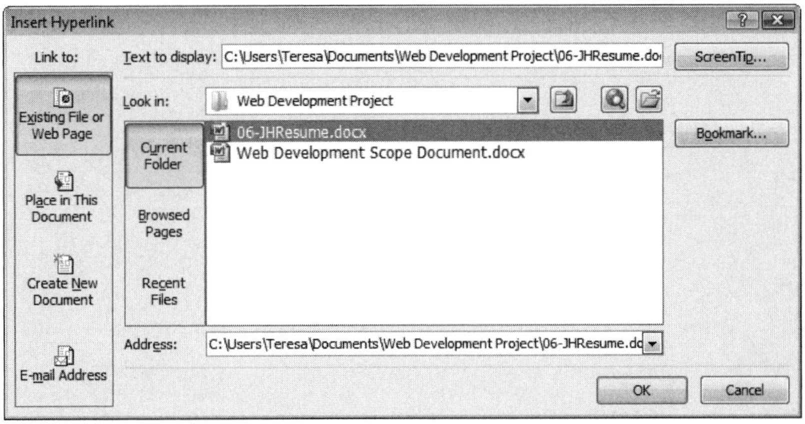

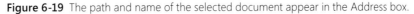

Figure 6-19 The path and name of the selected document appear in the Address box.

6. Click OK.

    The Hyperlink indicator appears in the Indicators field of the Resource Sheet (see Figure 6-20).

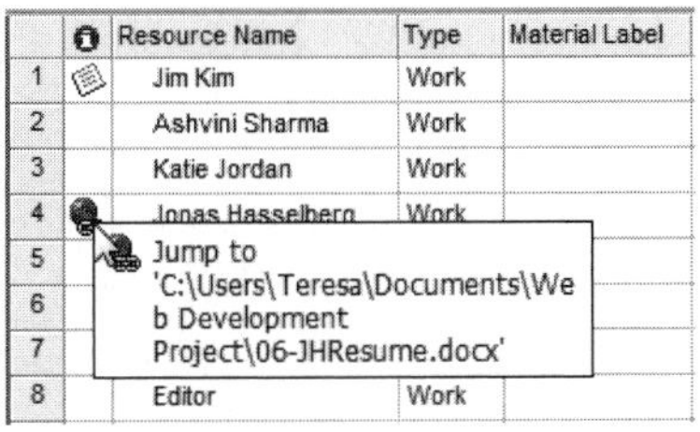

	ⓘ	Resource Name	Type	Material Label
1	📝	Jim Kim	Work	
2		Ashvini Sharma	Work	
3		Katie Jordan	Work	
4	🔗	Jonas Hasselberg	Work	
5		Jump to		
6		'C:\Users\Teresa\Documents\Web Development		
7		Project\06-JHResume.docx'		
8		Editor	Work	

Figure 6-20 Position your mouse pointer over the Hyperlink indicator to read the link. Click the indicator to jump to the link's location.

Whenever you need to review the target of the hyperlink, just click the Hyperlink indicator. The contents open in their own application window.

You can use the Project Guide to help you add notes or hyperlinks to resources. On the Project Guide toolbar, click Resources. In the Project Guide pane, click the Link To Or Attach More Resource Information link. Read the succeeding panes and make choices as directed.

Assigning Resources to Tasks

Assigning Work Resources to Tasks **235**

Assigning Material Resources to Tasks **251**

Assigning Cost Resources to Tasks. **253**

Reviewing Assignment Information **256**

Changing Resource Assignments. **261**

Contouring Resource Assignments **269**

Y ou have tasks. You have resources. Now you need to get them together. Tasks + resources = assignments. With human and equipment resources assigned to tasks, Microsoft Office Project 2007 can create a project schedule that reflects not only the project calendar, task durations, dependencies, and constraints, but also the calendars and availability of assigned resources. With material and cost resources assigned to tasks, you can track the depletion of project-related inventory as well as specific cost items to ensure you have what you need to accomplish tasks when you need them.

Assigning Work Resources to Tasks

When you assign a work resource, you are attaching the resource name to a task and then indicating how much of the resource's total availability is to be devoted to this task.

When you first add a resource to the project plan, through the use of maximum units (you might also think of them as *resource units*), you specify how available this resource will be to this project. For example, if the resource is available full time on the project, say, 40 hours a week, you would probably specify that the resource has 100% maximum units. If another resource is available 20 hours a week, you would probably specify that this resource has 50% maximum units. If you have three of the same type of resource (for example, three graphic designers), you could indicate that there are 300% maximum units.

When you assign these resources to tasks, you take the idea of availability a step further by using *assignment units*. With maximum units, you specify resource availability to the project as a whole. With assignment units, you specify resource allocation to the specific task to which the resource is assigned.

For example, one resource might be available full time to perform one task. When that's finished, she'll be assigned full time to the next task, and so on. Upon assigning this resource to the task, you indicate 100% assignment units for this resource.

You might have another full-time resource, however, who is spending 40 percent of his time on one task and 60 percent of his time on another task that takes place at the same time. For the first task, you specify 40% assignment units; and for the second task, 60%. The assignment units specify the percentage of the full 100% maximum units being used for the task in question.

Now, take the case of a half-time resource (50% maximum units) who is spending all available time on one task. The maximum assignment units you can have for this resource are 50%. If this resource is spending half her time on one task and half on another, the assignment units are 25% for each task.

> **Note**
>
> If this resource is assigned to other tasks at the same time, Office Project 2007 allows it, but flags the resource and the assignment as overallocated, that is, having more work than there is time, or availability, to do the tasks.

Finally, let's look at the case of the three graphic artists whose max units are 300%. When you start to assign tasks to a *consolidated resource* such as this one, Project 2007 does not assume that you want to use all three on one task. You can, but the default assignment units are 100%. You can change those units to any increment up to 300%.

INSIDE OUT   Max units vs. assignment units

Because maximum units and assignment units are both called "units," the terms can be confusing. They're related but different. It would be nice if the respective names were a little more different and a little more descriptive. However, they're vital to our assignment scheduling, and they're what we have to work with. So we need to keep them straight in our minds.

The Max. Units field applies to resources. Think of max units as total *resource units*. The value you enter in the Max. Units field tells Microsoft Project how much of a particular resource you have available for work on this project, whether it's half of full time (50%), full time (100%), or three full-time equivalents (300%). Also remember that this percentage is based on the available time reflected in the resource's working time calendar.

On the other hand, the Units field applies to assignments. Think of the Units field as *assignment units*. The value you enter in the Units field tells Microsoft Project how much of the resource you can use to work on this specific assignment.

Another way to differentiate the two kinds of units is to pay attention to the context in which you see them. If you see a Units field in the Resource Sheet, it's referring to the resource's availability on the entire project. If you see a Units field in the Assign Resources dialog box or the Assignment Information dialog box, it's referring to the resource's availability on the individual assignment.

Both kinds of units can be expressed in either percentages or decimals.

> **Note**
>
> By default, assignment units are expressed as a percentage, but you can express them as a decimal if you prefer. Click Tools, Options and then click the Schedule tab. In the Show Assignment Units As A box, click Decimal. A resource working full time on an assignment is shown as having 1 assignment unit instead of 100%. This setting also changes how maximum units are displayed in the Resource Sheet.

Creating Work Resource Assignments

By creating an assignment, you specify both the resources assigned to a task as well as their associated assignment units. Using the Assign Resources dialog box, you can assign one resource to a task, multiple resources to a task, or multiple resources to multiple tasks. To assign a work resource to a task, follow these steps:

1. In the Gantt Chart or other task sheet, click the task to which you want to assign resources.

Assign Resources

2. On the Standard toolbar, click Assign Resources.

   The Assign Resources dialog box appears (see Figure 7-1).

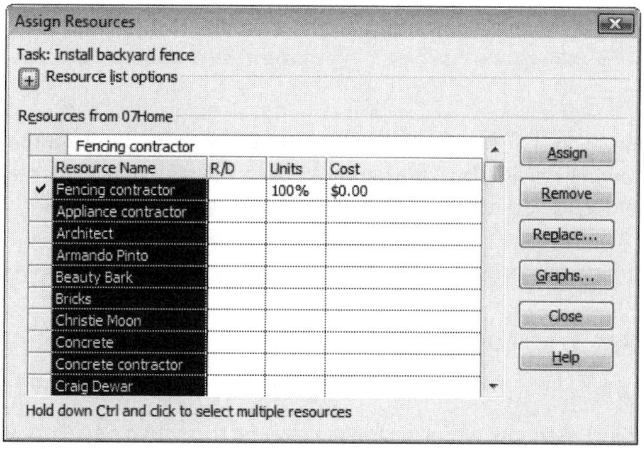

Figure 7-1 Use the Assign Resources dialog box to specify which resources are to be assigned to which tasks, and for how much of their available time.

3. In the dialog box, click the name of the work resource you want to assign to the task and then click the Assign button.

   The resource name moves to the top of the Resources list in the table, and a default percentage appears in the Units field for the resource. For individual resources, the default assignment units are the same as the resource's maximum units. For consolidated resources with more than 100% maximum units, the default assignment units are 100%.

4. If you want to assign a second resource, click that resource name and then click the Assign button.

5. Modify the Units field for any assigned resources as necessary. If you change the Units field, you need to press Enter or click another field. Pressing Enter ends the edit mode for the field, sets your change, and makes the Assign button available.

> **Note**
>
> You can select all resources to be assigned to a task and assign them at once. Click the first resource, hold down Ctrl, and then click all other resources. Click the Assign button.

6. Repeat steps 4 and 5 for all resources you want to assign to the selected task.

7. To assign resources to a different task, click the next task for which you want to make assignments.

   You don't have to close the Assign Resources dialog box to select a different task.

8. Repeat steps 3–6 to assign resources to all tasks as necessary.

9. When finished assigning resources to tasks, click the Close button.

> **Note**
>
> Unlike other dialog boxes, you can switch back and forth between the task sheet and the Assign Resources dialog box. It's handy to keep the dialog box open while you're working out all the details you need to finish making your assignments.

> **Project Management Practices: Assigning the Right Resources to Tasks**
>
> As the project manager, you consider several factors when deciding whom to assign to which tasks. One of the most important factors is the resource's skill set, competencies, and proficiencies. His or her ability to carry out the assigned task is essential to the success of the task. You can set up your resources in Microsoft Project so that you can find and assign resources based on their skill sets.
>
> Another important factor is the resource's availability. If the perfect resource is 100 percent committed to another project during the same timeframe as your project, you can't use this resource. Microsoft Project can help you find resources that are available to work on your project.

There are other factors as well:

- **Experience** Have the resources you're considering for the assignment done similar or related work before? How well did they do it? Perhaps you can use this assignment as an opportunity to pair a more experienced team member with one who has less experience. This pairing can set up a mentoring situation in which both team members can benefit, and your team is strengthened in the long run.

- **Enthusiasm** Are the resources you're considering personally interested in the assignment? A resource with less experience but more enthusiasm can often be more effective than a seasoned but bored resource.

- **Team dynamics** Do certain tasks require several resources to work together? If so, are the resources you're considering likely to work well together? Do they have a history of conflicts with each other? Do certain team members have good synergy with one another?

- **Speed** Is alacrity important to your project, all other things being equal? Some resources work faster than others. This speed can be a function of experience. Or it can be a function of working style or level of quality. Determine how important speed is to your project and assign tasks accordingly.

- **Cost** Are you hiring contractors for the project? If you have specific budget limitations, cost is definitely a factor. Sometimes, the rework required by an inexpensive resource can negate any cost savings. Conversely, sometimes more expensive resources can be a bargain, especially if they work faster than the norm.

- **Quality** What are your quality standards for the project? Try to assign resources who can match those standards.

Adding and Assigning Resources at the Same Time

Suppose that you want to assign a specific resource to a task, but that resource isn't listed in the Assign Resources dialog box because you haven't added him or her to your Resource Sheet yet. You can add new resources to your project plan while working in the Assign Resources dialog box and then immediately assign the newly added resource to tasks. You can then go to the Resource Sheet and complete any detailed resource information you want. To add new resources in the Assign Resources dialog box, follow these steps:

1. In the Gantt Chart or other task sheet, click the task to which you want to assign resources.

2. On the Standard toolbar, click Assign Resources to display the Assign Resources dialog box.

3. In the Resources table, type the resource name in the next available blank Resource Name field and then press Tab to enter the name and stay in the same field.

4. Click the Assign button.

   The resource name moves to the top of the Resources list in the table, and 100% appears in the Units field for the resource.

5. Adjust the assignment units if necessary. Assign any additional tasks you want.

6. When finished, click the Close button.

7. Click View, Resource Sheet.

   The new resource you added in the Assign Resources dialog box is listed. Modify any resource fields as necessary; for example, Group, Max. Units, Calendar.

> **Note**
>
> Double-click any resource name in the Assign Resources dialog box, and the Resource Information dialog box appears for that resource. Enter detailed resource information as you wish.

You can add an entire group of resources from your e-mail address book, Microsoft Office Project Server 2007, or your Windows Server Active Directory to the Assign Resources dialog box, just as you can in the Resource Sheet. To add resources from a server, follow these steps:

1. With the Gantt Chart or other task sheet open, click Assign Resources on the Standard toolbar.

2. If necessary, click the + Resource List Options button to expand the dialog box (see Figure 7-2).

Click this button to collapse or expand resource list options

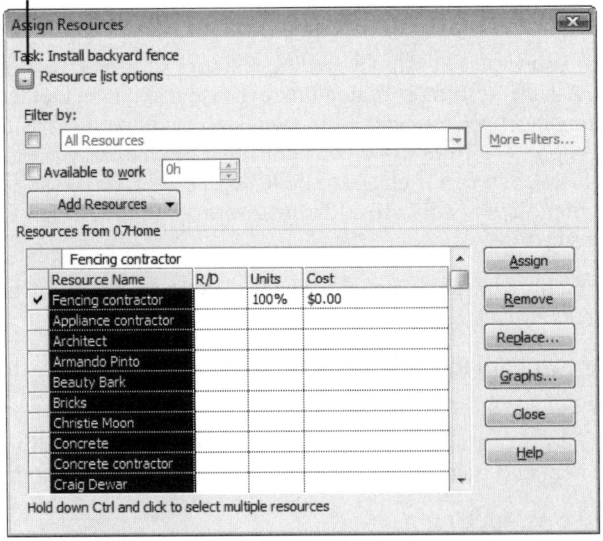

Figure 7-2 Click the Resource List Options button to collapse the Assign Resources dialog box; click the + Resource List Options button to expand it.

3. Click the Add Resources button.

4. Click From Active Directory if you are working with Microsoft Windows Server and want to add resources from the Active Directory directory service.

    Click From Address Book if you want to add resources from your e-mail program's address book.

    Click From Microsoft Project Server if you want to add the resources who are listed as Office Project Server 2007 users.

5. Click the resources you want from the source you chose and then click the Add button to add the selected resources to the Assign Resources dialog box.

6. After the resources are added, you can immediately assign them to tasks.

Avoid Assigning Resources to Summary Tasks

Be very careful about assigning resources to summary tasks. Technically you can do it, and in some cases it's beneficial. However, having resources assigned to summary tasks can cause confusion when reviewing rolled-up values for work, actual work, cost, and so on. By default, the summary task Gantt bar does not show the resource name, so that can cause still more confusion.

Also take care when you create additional tasks and make them subtasks under existing tasks that have resources assigned. This creates a situation where resources are now assigned to summary tasks.

Finding the Right Resources for the Job

You can use the Assign Resources dialog box to narrow your list of resources to only those who meet the criteria needed for the tasks you're assigning. For example, you can filter the resource list to show only those resources who belong to the marketing department, or only those resources who have a particular job code or skills definition. Using resource fields such as Group or Code comes in handy in these scenarios.

If you create and apply resource outline codes, you can also filter for a particular outline code level.

To find resources that meet certain criteria, follow these steps:

1. With the Gantt Chart or other task sheet open, click Assign Resources on the Standard toolbar.

2. If necessary, click the + Resource List Options button. The Assign Resources dialog box expands to show the Filter By box.

3. Select the check box immediately under Filter By.

4. Click the arrow in the All Resources box. Scroll to and click the filter that applies to the type of resource you want to find, for example, Group or Resources – Work (see Figure 7-3).

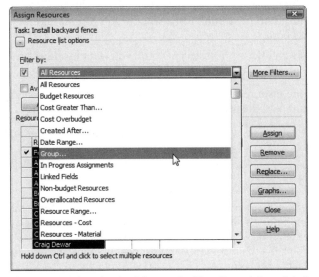

Figure 7-3 Select the check box under Filter By and then click the name of filter that describes the type of resource you're seeking.

Any filter that requires additional information includes an ellipsis (...) after its name. Click the filter, enter the requested information in the dialog box that appears, and click OK.

As soon as you select a filter, the list in the Resources table changes to show only those resources that meet the filter's criteria (see Figure 7-4).

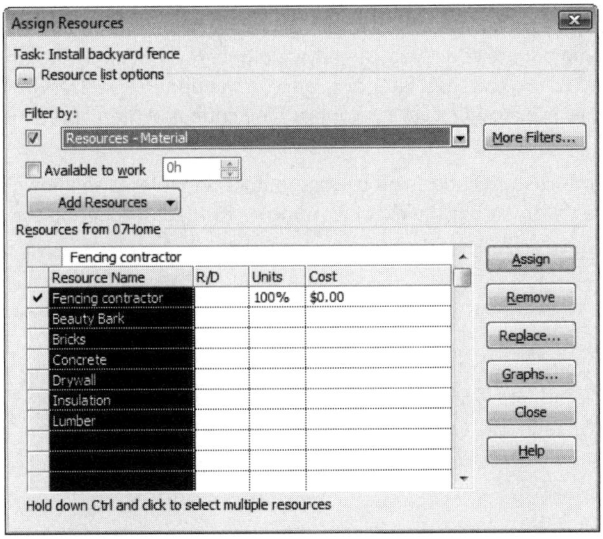

Figure 7-4 By filtering your resource list, you can choose from a set of targeted resources that meet the criteria for the tasks you are currently assigning.

5. Assign resources to tasks as usual.

6. When you want to review the full list of resources again, click All Resources in the Filter By list, or simply clear the Filter By check box.

Define a Resource Skill Set

If you set up a resource field that defines certain skill sets, you can use the Assign Resources dialog box to filter for resources with specific skills. For example, you can use the Group field in the Resource Sheet to specify the type of resource, for example, "Writer," "Editor," "Designer," or "Programmer." To assign writing tasks, you can filter for Writer in the Group field. To assign programming tasks, you can filter for Programmer in the Group field. Filtering by the Group field can be especially useful if you have a large number of resources.

Other fields you can use to define skill sets include Code and Outline Code. You can also use custom fields such as Text1 or Number1 to specify skills descriptions or numbers. The Code field is present by default on the Entry table of the Resource Sheet. You can enter any alphanumeric string you like in the Code field. Enter the set of skill codes that correspond with how you identify skills in your organization or develop your own scheme. For example, you can have a set of codes for Designer-1, Designer-2, Programmer-1, and so on. As long as you enter your codes consistently for your resources, you can successfully sort, group, and filter resources by their code.

For a more sophisticated and hierarchical code scheme, set up an outline code for skill sets. With an outline code, you can have a higher level, such as Designer, and sub-levels of 1, 2, and 3. You can then filter or group on the upper-level Designer or find just designers at level 3. You first set up your outline code and then apply the appropriate outline code to resources.

With all your custom codes, you can set up lookup tables (also known as pick lists), so you don't have to remember the exact wording or format for entering the code.

Note

For more information about working with fields, see the section titled "Customizing Fields" in Chapter 25, "Customizing Your View of Project Information." For more information about outline codes, see the section titled "Working with Outline Codes" in Chapter 25.

INSIDE OUT   Missing resource filters

There is no built-in resource filter for Code or Outline Code. You can create your own filters. To do this, click New in the More Filters dialog box and then specify the field name, test, and value that defines your new filter. For example, you can create a filter that finds all resources that have a Code field greater than 9100. Or you can create a filter that finds all resources that have an Outline Code equal to Engineer-1.

If you're using Microsoft Office Project Professional 2007, you might have added certain resources to your project as *proposed resources*. It would be nice, therefore, to have a filter to find only confirmed resources or to find just proposed resources when setting up assignments. But such filters are not built in, and you need to create them yourself.

For more information about adding proposed resources, see the section titled "Proposing Tentative Resources" in Chapter 6, "Setting Up Resources in the Project." For more information about creating your own filter, see the section titled "Customizing Filters" in Chapter 25.

You can filter your resources to see only those who actually have time to take on more work. For example, suppose that you assigned all your resources to tasks. Then you add several more tasks, and you want to assign only resources who have time for them. To filter for resources with a certain amount of available time, do the following:

1. With the Gantt Chart or other task sheet open, select the task to which you want to assign resources with available time.

2. Click Assign Resources on the Standard toolbar.

3. If necessary, click the + Resource List Options button. The Assign Resources dialog box expands.

4. Select the Available To Work check box.

   In the Available To Work box, enter the amount of time needed for the task you're about to assign. For example, if you need a resource with 4 days of available time, enter **4d** in the box.

   As soon as you enter the amount of time, the list in the Resources table changes to show only those resources who have the specified availability.

5. Assign resources to the selected task as usual.

6. If you click another task, the filter is applied to that task as well. The list of resources available to work for the specified amount of time might change, depending on the task dates and the resource availability during those dates.

7. When you want to see the full list of resources again, simply clear the Available To Work check box.

> **Note**
>
> You can find resources in the category you want who have the right amount of available time for your assignments. Under Resource List Options in the Assign Resources dialog box, select both check boxes under Filter By. First, select the resource filter you want to use in the first box and then enter the amount of time in the Available To Work box.

TROUBLESHOOTING

Your Filter By boxes are dimmed

It might look like the Filter By box and its More Filters button are unavailable to you because they're dimmed. They don't look available until you select the check box next to the Filter By box, which is also dimmed.

The same applies to the Available To Work box. It's dimmed until you select the dimmed Available To Work check box.

Selecting the check boxes is necessary because it helps you specify what kind of filter you want to apply. You can apply a resource filter only or just check for available time. And of course, you can combine the two—applying a filter to find only those resources who meet the filter criteria and have a certain amount of available time.

You can review graphs of resource availability from within the Assign Resources dialog box. This can help you decide which work resource should be assigned to a task. To review the resource availability graph, follow these steps:

1. With the Gantt Chart or other task sheet open, click Assign Resources on the Standard toolbar.

2. In the Assign Resources dialog box, click the work resource whose availability graph you want to view. Note that availability only applies to work resources—not material or cost resources.

3. Click the Graphs button. The Resource Availability Graph for the selected resource appears (see Figure 7-5). By default, the work graph is displayed.

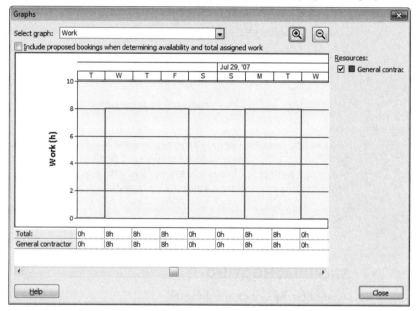

Figure 7-5 In the Work version of the Resource Availability Graph, you can review the selected resource's remaining availability over time.

4. To change the field on which the graph is based, click Remaining Availability or Assignment Work in the Select Graph list.

   The Work graph shows the total work for all the selected resource's assignments. The Assignment Work graph breaks down the work on the currently selected tasks in relation to the selected resource's total work assigned (see Figure 7-6). The Remaining Availability graph shows when the selected resource has any available time for more assignments.

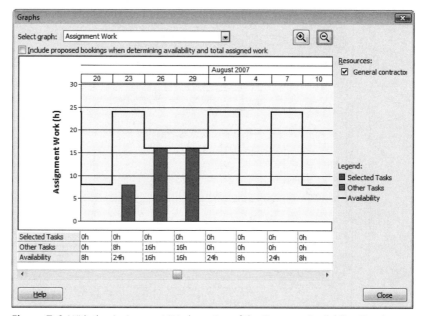

Figure 7-6 With the Assignment Work version of the Resource Availability Graph, you can compare the workload of selected tasks with those of other tasks.

5. To change the timescale for the graph, click the Zoom In or Zoom Out buttons.

The Zoom In button provides a closer look at a shorter time period. For example, it can change the graph from a view of weeks to a view of days. The Zoom Out button provides an overview of availability over a longer time period. For example, it can change the graph from a view of weeks to a view of months.

6. When finished reviewing the graph, click the Close button.

The Assign Resources dialog box appears again.

Review Availability Graphs for Multiple Resources

Select multiple resources in the Assign Resources dialog box and then click the Graphs button. The Resource Availability Graph shows graphs for each resource at the same time, using different colors for each resource (see Figure 7-7).

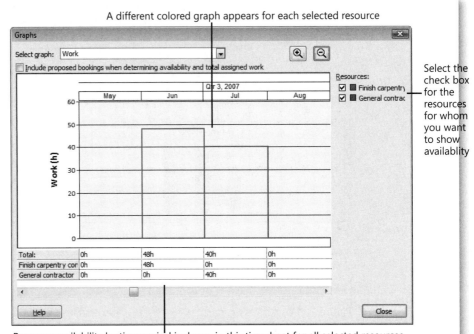

A different colored graph appears for each selected resource

Select the check box for the resources for whom you want to show availablity

Resource availability by time period is shown in this timesheet for all selected resources

Figure 7-7 View the availability graphs and timesheets for several resources at one time.

In the upper-right corner of the graph window, clear the check box for any resource whose graph you want to hide. The timesheet for all resources still shows below the graph.

Understanding Assignment Calculations

Work is the amount of effort it takes to complete a task. As soon as you assign a resource to a task, the duration is translated into work. A simple example: If you have a task with a 3-day duration, and you assign a single full-time resource to it, that resource now has an assignment with 24 hours of work spread across three days (assuming default calendar settings).

You can see this principle in action by adding the Work field to the Gantt Chart or other task sheet, as follows:

1. Display the Gantt Chart or other task sheet that contains the Duration field.

2. Click the heading of the column to the right of the Duration field. For example, if you are working with the default Gantt Chart with the default Entry table applied, click the Start column heading.

3. Click Insert, Column.

4. In the Field Name box, click Work. To move quickly to the fields that begin with W, type **W**.

5. Click OK.

    The Work field appears next to the Duration field, and you can see comparisons between the two (see Figure 7-8).

Task Name	Duration	Work	Resource Names
⊟ **Landscaping and Grounds Work**	**12 days**	**56 hrs**	
Pour concrete driveway and sidewalks	2 days	16 hrs	Concrete contractor
Install backyard fence	2 days	16 hrs	Fencing contractor
Sod and complete plantings - front yard	2 days	16 hrs	Landscape contractor
Sod and complete plantings - backyard	1 day	8 hrs	Landscape contractor

Figure 7-8 Adding the Work field to a task sheet shows the relationship of task duration to task work, based on how tasks are assigned to resources.

That task with a 3-day duration and a single full-time resource assigned translates (by default) to 24 hours of work. Another task with a 3-day duration and two full-time resources assigned translates to 48 hours of work. Another task with a 3-day duration and three full-time resource assigned translates to 72 hours of work.

Duration is the length of time it takes from the start to the finish of the task, but work equates to person-hours for the resources assigned.

These calculations are based on the *initial assignment*; that is, assigning one, two, or six resources at one time to a task that previously had no assigned resources. That is, if you assign two full-time resources to that same 3-day task, both resources are assigned 24 hours of work, also spread across 3 days (see Figure 7-9). When you assign multiple resources *initially*, Microsoft Project assumes that you intend for the resources to have the same amount of work across the original task duration.

Task Name	Work	Duration	Details	y 2007 2	5	8	11	14	17
⊟ Pour concrete driveway and sidewalks	24 hrs	3 days	Work	8h	16h				
Concrete contractor	24 hrs		Work	8h	16h				
⊟ Install backyard fence	48 hrs	3 days	Work				16h	16h	16h
Jon Morris	24 hrs		Work				8h	8h	8h
Thomas Andersen	24 hrs		Work				8h	8h	8h

Figure 7-9 In the first task with a single resource assigned, the total work is 24 hours. In the second task with two resources assigned, the total work is 48 hours.

> **Note**
>
> Instead of entering duration and having Microsoft Project calculate work amounts upon assigning tasks, you can do this the other way around. You can enter tasks, assign resources, and then enter work amounts from estimates those resources provide. From those work amounts, Microsoft Project can calculate duration.
>
> Just as work is calculated from the duration and assigned resource availability, duration can be calculated from work amounts and assigned resource availability.

Translate Duration to Work Amounts

You have some control over how Microsoft Project translates duration to work amounts. By default, if you specify a 1-day duration, Microsoft Project translates this to 8 hours of work. However, if you want 1 day to mean 6 hours to account for nonproject work, you can change your calendar options.

Click Tools, Options. In the Options dialog box, click the Calendar tab. Change the settings in Hours Per Day, Hours Per Week, or Days Per Month, as needed to fit your requirements.

If you want the project or resource calendar to reflect the changes you made to the duration to work-amount settings, you must change the appropriate working time calendars to match. If the calendars don't match the calendar option settings, you'll see odd results.

For more information about changing the project calendar, see the section titled "Setting Your Project Calendar" in Chapter 3, "Starting a New Project." For information about resource calendars, see the section titled "Setting Working Times and Days Off for Work Resources" in Chapter 6.

TROUBLESHOOTING

You assign two resources to a task, but the work is doubled rather than halved

When you assign multiple resources initially, Microsoft Project assumes that you intend for the same amount of work to be applied to all assigned resources across the time span represented by the task duration.

If you want the duration to be reduced because multiple resources are assigned, set the duration accordingly. Or start by assigning just one resource. Then assign the additional resources in a separate operation. As long as the task is not a *fixed-duration task*, the duration is reduced based on the number of additional resources added.

The calculations for work and duration can change if you assign one resource initially and then later assign a second resource. This might also be true if you initially assign two resources and later remove one of them.

For more information about these schedule recalculations, see the section titled "Changing Resource Assignments" later in this chapter.

Note

If you don't specify a work unit, by default Microsoft Project assumes the unit to be hours and automatically enters hrs after your work amount. You can change the default work unit if you like. Click Tools, Options and then click the Schedule tab. In the Work Is Entered In box, select the time unit you want as the default for this project.

Assigning Material Resources to Tasks

When you assign a material resource, you are attaching the material resource name to a task and then indicating the quantity of material to be used in fulfilling this task.

Material resources are supplies consumed in the course of fulfilling a task. As with work resources, there are units of measurement to specify how much of the resource is available to carry out the task. With work resources, this measurement is time: number of hours or days, for example. With materials, however, the measurement, and therefore the material resource assignment units, is quantity. When you assign a material resource to a task, you specify the quantity of resource that this task will consume.

For example, suppose that you have a landscaping project that includes the "Lay down beauty bark" task. The material resource for this task is obviously beauty bark. Because beauty bark is measured in cubic yards, you would have set the material's unit of measurement, or label, as *cubic yards* when you added beauty bark as a material resource in the Resource Sheet. Now, when you assign beauty bark as a material resource to the "Lay down beauty bark" task, you can specify the assignment units as **6**, to indicate 6 cubic yards of beauty bark.

Other examples of material labels include tons, linear feet, packages, cartons, pounds, crates, and so on.

The quantity of material consumed in the course of performing a task can be fixed or variable, based on duration. That is, if the same amount of material will be used whether the task takes 2 days or 2 weeks, the material is said to have a *fixed material consumption*. However, if more material will be used if the duration increases and less material used if the duration decreases, the material is said to have a *variable material consumption*. To specify variable material consumption, enter a per-time period specification in the assignment Units field: for example, 1/week or 3/day. This will be translated with the material's label: for example, 1 ton/week or 3 yards/day.

For more information on setting up a material resource, see the section titled "Adding Material Resources to the Project" in Chapter 6.

INSIDE OUT   Specify a variable consumption rate

You might think that a material with a variable consumption rate can be set as such in the Label field of the Resource Sheet. Not so. You can enter any string you want in the Label field, including something like **yards/day**. But when you assign the material to a task, the expected per-day calculations are not made.

To specify the variable consumption rate, always specify it in the Units field in the Assign Resources dialog box rather than in the Label field in the Resource Sheet.

To assign a material resource to a task, follow these steps:

1. In the Gantt Chart or other task sheet, click the task to which you want to assign a material resource.

2. On the Standard toolbar, click Assign Resources.

3. In the Assign Resources dialog box, click the name of the material resource you want to assign to the task and then click the Assign button.

    The material resource name moves to the top of the Resources list in the table, and the label appears in the Units field, defaulting to a quantity of 1, for example, **1 yards**.

4. Change the **1** in the Units field to the correct quantity for this assignment, for example, **3 yards** (see Figure 7-10).

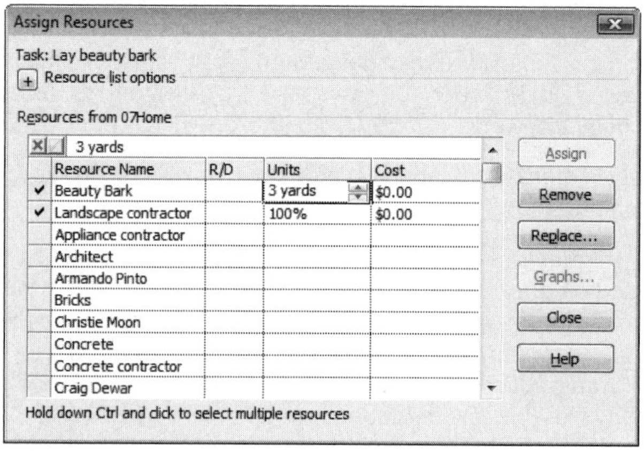

Assign Resources			
Task: Lay beauty bark			
+ Resource list options			
Resources from 07Home			

x	3 yards				Assign
Resource Name	R/D	Units	Cost		
✔ Beauty Bark		3 yards	$0.00		Remove
✔ Landscape contractor		100%	$0.00		
Appliance contractor					Replace...
Architect					
Armando Pinto					Graphs...
Bricks					
Christie Moon					Close
Concrete					
Concrete contractor					Help
Craig Dewar					

Hold down Ctrl and click to select multiple resources

Figure 7-10 Change the default of 1 unit to the appropriate quantity of material to be used to complete the selected task.

Enter icon

You might find it easier to change the quantity in the entry bar just above the resource table. Click the Enter (check mark) icon when finished.

If you change the quantity directly in the Units field, press Tab or Enter when you're finished, or click another field to enter the change and exit the edit mode.

5. If necessary, change the material from the default fixed consumption rate to variable consumption rate (see Figure 7-11). After the material's label, enter a slash and time period abbreviation, for example, **3 yards/d**.

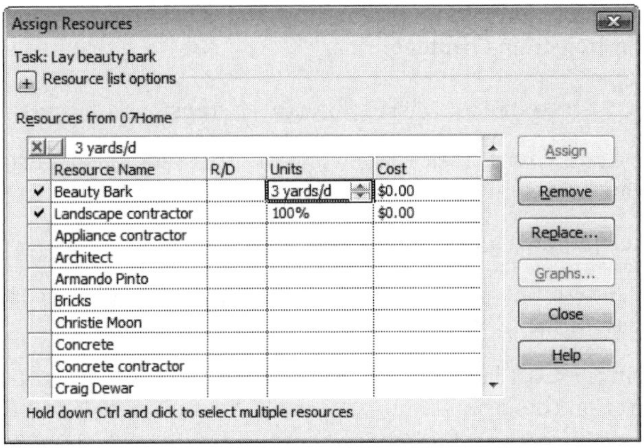

Figure 7-11 Use the standard time period abbreviations (h, d, w, and so on) to specify the quantity per time period for a material resource with a variable consumption rate.

6. If you want to assign another resource to the selected task, click the name and then click the Assign button. Modify the Units field as necessary.

   You can assign material and work resources in the same operation.

7. To assign material resources to a different task, click that task. You don't have to close the Assign Resources dialog box to select a different task.

8. When finished assigning resources to tasks, click the Close button.

Assigning Cost Resources to Tasks

When you assign a cost resource to a task, you are associating a cost item that must be incurred to complete that task. Entering costs for work resources, such as an hourly rate for a human resource or a cost per use for an equipment resource, certainly helps you track some of the biggest project costs you're likely to encounter. Cost resources, a new feature in Microsoft Office Project 2007, help you track those other nonlabor costs that are nonetheless significant. Examples of cost resources might be travel costs or facility rentals associated with the fulfillment of a task.

Unlike work or material resources, you do not enter a cost amount in the Resource Sheet or Resource Information dialog box. You only create the resource and identify it as a cost resource.

Only after you assign a cost resource to a task do you deal with the cost. At that point, you can enter the cost for the facility rental, for example, as associated with the task to which the facility rental cost resource is assigned.

For example, you might have the Facility Rental cost resource assigned to the "Conduct focus group meetings" and "Conduct usability tests" tasks. The facility used for the "Conduct focus group meetings" task costs $200 per day. The facility used for the "Conduct usability tests" task costs $400 per day. You're using the same cost resource but entering different cost amounts on the different task assignments.

For more information on setting up a cost resource, see the section titled "Adding Cost Resources to the Project" in Chapter 6.

To assign a cost resource to a task, follow these steps:

1. In the Gantt Chart, Task Usage view, or other task sheet, click the task to which you want to assign the cost resource.

2. On the Standard toolbar, click Assign Resources.

3. In the Assign Resources dialog box, click the name of the cost resource you want to assign to the task.

4. Click in the Cost field for the cost resource and type the cost amount for this resource on this task.

    For cost resources, the Units field is not available.

5. Click the Assign button.

6. To assign the same cost resource to a different task, click that task. Enter the cost for that cost resource on the newly selected task and then click the Assign button.

7. When finished assigning resources to tasks, click the Close button.

    By default, the name of the cost resource as well as the cost amount for the assignment is shown next to the Gantt bar for the task (see Figure 7-12).

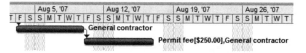

Figure 7-12 The default Gantt bar shows the name of the cost resource as well as the cost amount for the task to which the cost resource is assigned.

You can change the cost you entered on a cost resource assignment. This is helpful if the cost for the resource on the task has changed or if you didn't have that information at all when you first made the assignment. There are several ways to change the cost on a cost resource assignment:

- In the Gantt Chart or any other task sheet, select the task and then click Assign Resources on the Standard toolbar. Click in the Cost field for the cost resource and change the amount.

- In any task sheet, double-click the task to open the Task Information dialog box. Click the Resources tab. In the Cost field for the cost resource, change the amount (see Figure 7-13).

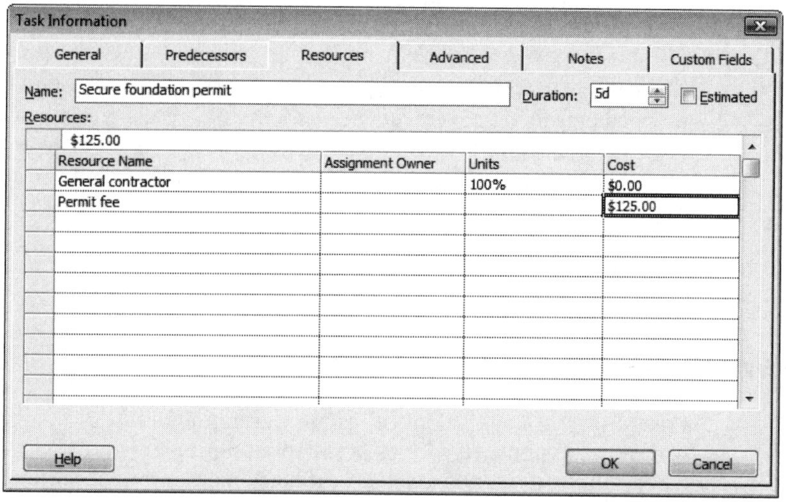

Figure 7-13 The Resources tab of the Task Information dialog box shows the cost amount for an assigned cost resource.

- In the Task Usage view, double-click the assignment, that is, the name of the cost resource under the task to which it is assigned. In the Assignment Information dialog box, on the General tab, change the amount in the Cost box.

- In the Resource Usage view, double-click the assignment, that is, the name of the task under the cost resource name assigned to that task. In the Assignment Information dialog box, on the General tab, change the amount in the Cost box.

- In either the Task Usage or Resource Usage view, add the Cost column to the sheet portion of the view. Right-click any column heading and then click Insert Column on the shortcut menu. In the Field Name box, type **cost** to move quickly to the Cost field. Click the Cost field and then click OK. The Cost field is entered next to the selected column heading. Change the amount next to the assignment (see Figure 7-14).

Task Name	Work	Cost
⊟ **Apply for Permits**	**40 hrs**	**$325.00**
⊟ Secure foundation permit	40 hrs	$125.00
General contractor	40 hrs	$0.00
Permit fee		$125.00
⊟ Secure framing permit	0 hrs	$200.00

Figure 7-14 Add the Cost field to the Task Usage or Resource Usage view to review or modify the amount for a cost resource assignment.

For more information about working with project costs, see the section titled "Reviewing Planned Costs" in Chapter 8, "Planning Resource and Task Costs."

> **Note**
>
> Also new in Microsoft Office Project 2007 are budget resources. Budget resources are assigned only to the project summary task for the express purpose of tracking project costs and project work for the overall project budget. For more information about working with budget resources, see the section titled "Setting Up and Reviewing a Project Budget" in Chapter 8.

Reviewing Assignment Information

There are several ways to look at resource assignments. You can switch to a usage view, which shows assignments for each task or assignments for each resource. You can also add a form to your Gantt Chart or other task view and review assignment information in relation to selected tasks.

Showing Assignments by Task or Resource

You can see work assigned to resources in either the Task Usage or Resource Usage views. The Task Usage view shows assignments by tasks (see Figure 7-15). The information for each assignment is rolled up, or summarized, in the row representing the task. To switch to the Task Usage view, click View, Task Usage.

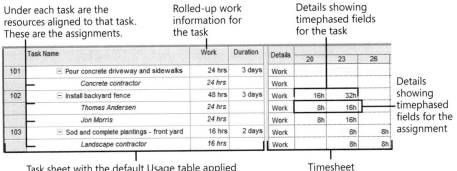

Figure 7-15 The Task Usage view shows task duration as well as assignment work.

The Resource Usage view shows assignments by resources (see Figure 7-16). The information for each assignment is rolled up, or totaled, in the row representing the resource. To switch to the Resource Usage view, click View, Resource Usage.

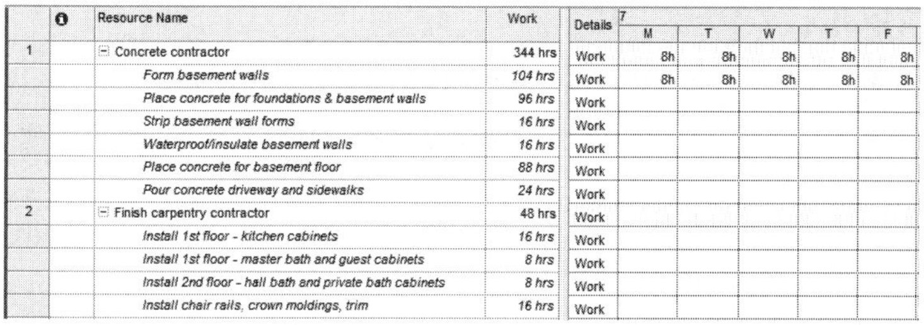

	ⓘ	Resource Name	Work	Details	7				
					M	T	W	T	F
1		⊟ Concrete contractor	344 hrs	Work	8h	8h	8h	8h	8h
		Form basement walls	104 hrs	Work	8h	8h	8h	8h	8h
		Place concrete for foundations & basement walls	96 hrs	Work					
		Strip basement wall forms	16 hrs	Work					
		Waterproof/insulate basement walls	16 hrs	Work					
		Place concrete for basement floor	88 hrs	Work					
		Pour concrete driveway and sidewalks	24 hrs	Work					
2		⊟ Finish carpentry contractor	48 hrs	Work					
		Install 1st floor - kitchen cabinets	16 hrs	Work					
		Install 1st floor - master bath and guest cabinets	8 hrs	Work					
		Install 2nd floor - hall bath and private bath cabinets	8 hrs	Work					
		Install chair rails, crown moldings, trim	16 hrs	Work					

Figure 7-16 The Resource Usage view focuses on resource and assignment work.

Either usage view is great for reviewing assignment information. Which one you use depends on whether you want to see assignments within the context of tasks or resources.

The usage views are the only two views in which you can see detailed assignment information. From these two views, you can also access the Assignment Information dialog box (see Figure 7-17). Just double-click the assignment whose information you want to see.

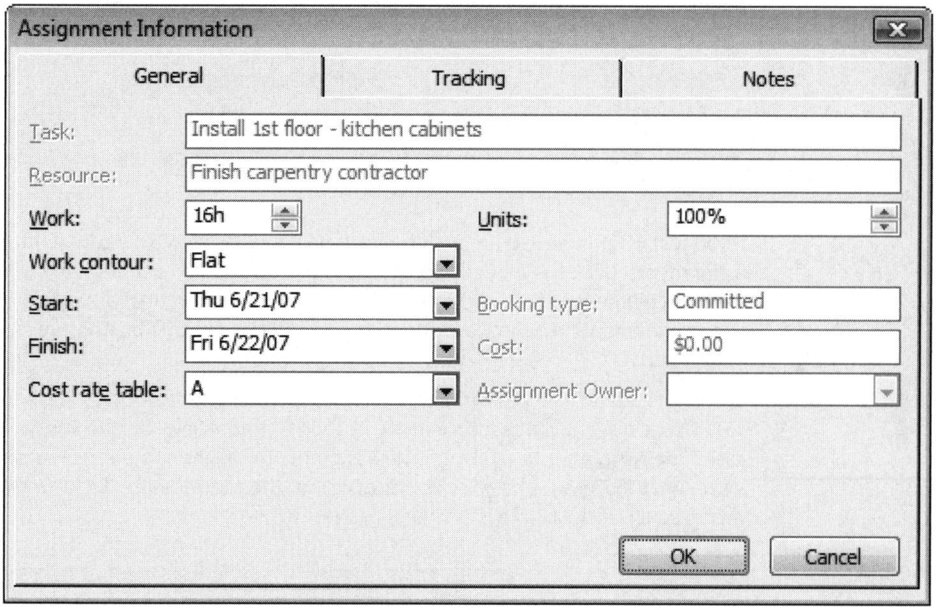

Figure 7-17 You can open the Assignment Information dialog box by double-clicking an assignment in the Task Usage or Resource Usage views.

> **Note**
>
> You can enter a note about an individual assignment. In the Task Usage or Resource Usage view, click the assignment and then click Assignment Notes on the Standard toolbar. The Notes tab in the Assignment Information dialog box appears. Enter the note and then click OK. The Notes icon appears in the Indicators column of the usage view.

Assignment
Notes

TROUBLESHOOTING

The Assignment Information dialog box does not open

If you're in the Task Usage view or Resource Usage view, and you want to open the Assignment Information dialog box, be sure that you actually have selected an assignment. In the usage views, the assignments appear under the task name or resource name. If you double-click the task or resource name at the summary level, the Task Information or Resource Information dialog box opens.

Instead, double-click the assignment under that summary level. In the Task Usage view, the summary level shows the task name, and the subordinate assignment level shows the resource names. Those are the resources assigned to the task; that is, the task's assignments. If you double-click a resource name in the Task Usage view, the Assignment Information dialog box appears.

In the Resource Usage view, the same principle applies. The summary level shows the resource name, and the subordinate assignment level shows the task names. Those are the tasks to which this resource is assigned; that is, the resource's assignments. If you double-click a task name in the Resource Usage view, the Assignment Information dialog box appears.

Show/Hide
Assignments

Show and Hide Assignments

If you just want to see summary information in a usage view, you can temporarily hide assignments. Click the All Cells box in the upper-left corner of the sheet view (between the first column and first row) to select the entire sheet. On the Formatting toolbar, click Hide Assignments. To show assignments again, click the same button, which is now Show Assignments.

You can hide and show assignments for individual tasks or resources. Click the task in the Task Usage view or the resource in the Resource Usage view. On the Formatting toolbar, click Hide Assignments. Clicking Hide Assignments has the same effect as clicking the – sign next to the summary task or resource for the assignments. To show the assignments again, click Show Assignments or the + sign.

Showing Assignment Information Under a Task View

You can use different types of forms under the Gantt Chart or other task view to see detailed information about assignment information. The easiest way to do this is to apply the Task Entry view, which is a built-in combination view made up of the Gantt Chart and the Task Form (see Figure 7-18).

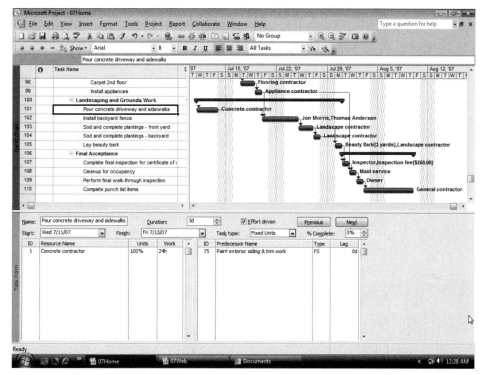

Figure 7-18 Detailed task and assignment information is shown in the Task Form in the lower pane for the task selected in the Gantt Chart in the upper pane.

With the Task Form, you can easily see all schedule-related information, including duration, task type, units, and work. Click the Previous or Next button to move to different tasks.

An abbreviated version of the Task Form is the Task Name Form, which dispenses with the task details and includes only the Task Name with the two tables of information (see Figure 7-19).

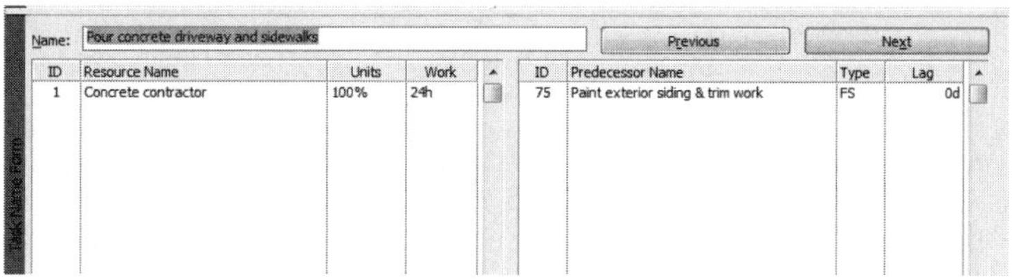

Name:	Pour concrete driveway and sidewalks				Previous			Next		
ID	Resource Name	Units	Work	▲	ID	Predecessor Name		Type	Lag	
1	Concrete contractor	100%	24h		75	Paint exterior siding & trim work		FS	0d	

Figure 7-19 Use the Task Name Form if you're interested only in the table information.

To apply the Task Name Form:

1. Click in the lower pane to make the form the active pane.

2. Click View, More Views, Task Name Form.

3. Click Apply.

In either the Task Form or the Task Name Form, the default table information includes resources on the left and predecessors on the right. You can change which categories of information are shown. To do this:

1. Click in the lower pane to make the form the active pane.

2. Click Format, Details.

You can also simply right-click in the form and then click the categories you want to see.

3. In the submenu, click the information you want to see in the form's tables.

You can see more detailed information about resources assigned to the selected task by applying the Resource Form or Resource Name Form as the lower pane under a task sheet.

To apply the Resource Form or Resource Name Form:

1. Click in the lower pane to make the form the active pane.

2. Click View, More Views.

3. In the submenu, click Resource Form or Resource Name Form.

4. Click Apply.

In the Resource Form, you can review detailed information about the resources assigned to the task selected in the task sheet in the upper pane (see Figure 7-20). This data includes availability and cost information.

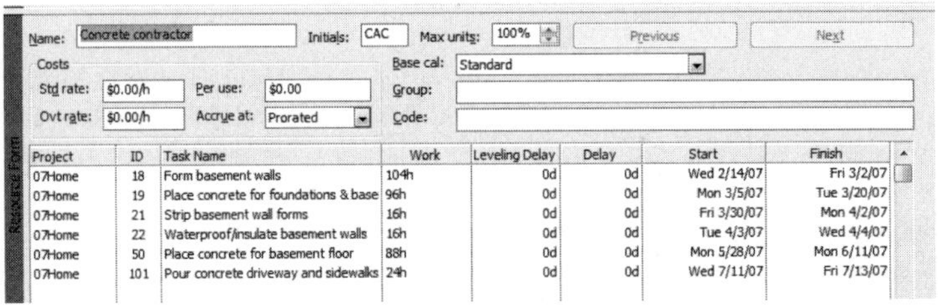

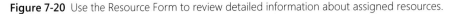

Figure 7-20 Use the Resource Form to review detailed information about assigned resources.

By default, schedule information is shown in the table area. To change the category of table information, right-click the form and then click one of the other categories, for example, Cost or Work. Click the Previous or Next button to move to the resources assigned to the current task.

The Resource Name Form is a condensed version of the form, showing just the Resource Name with the table of information.

> **Note**
> To return to a single-pane view, double-click the split bar dividing the two panes. Or click Window, Remove Split.

Changing Resource Assignments

You can make three types of changes to resource assignments:

- You can add more resources to the existing resources assigned to a task.
- You can replace one resource with another.
- You can remove a resource from a task.

To add more resources to the existing ones initially assigned to a task, follow these steps:

1. In the Gantt Chart or other task sheet, click the task to which you want to add more resources.

2. On the Standard toolbar, click Assign Resources. The Assign Resources dialog box appears, showing a check mark next to the names of resources already assigned.

   You can also open the Assign Resources dialog box by pressing Alt+F10.

3. Click the name of the resource you want to add to the task and then click the Assign button.

   The resource name moves to the top of the Resources list in the table, and the default percentage appears in the Units field for the resource.

4. Review the Units field and make sure that it's appropriate for this assignment.

   If you change the Units field, press Enter or click another field to set your change and exit the edit mode for the field.

5. When finished working with resource assignments, click the Close button.

In the task sheet, you'll see that the task has been updated to include the new resource. Depending on the task type (fixed units, fixed work, or fixed duration), you might see changes in the duration or work amount as a result of the newly assigned resource. You'll also see the green feedback triangle in the task cell. Position your mouse pointer over the triangle, and the Smart Tag icon appears in the Indicators field. Click the Smart Tag icon. A menu appears (see Figure 7-21).

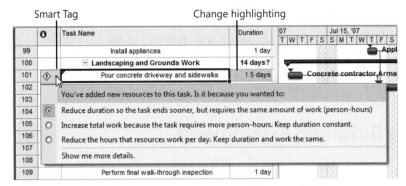

Figure 7-21 The Smart Tag informs you of the ramifications of adding a resource to the task. These results are based on the task type.

When you change a resource assignment, you'll also see certain cells highlighted so you can see which fields have changed as a result of the assignment change.

Get Feedback on Changes with Smart Tags

After you assign tasks to resources, Microsoft Project employs Microsoft Office Smart Tags technology to provide scheduling feedback. When you make certain kinds of changes that affect scheduling—such as changes to duration, start date, or finish date—a green triangle might appear in the corner of the edited cell in a Gantt Chart, task sheet, or usage view. A Smart Tag might also appear when you delete a task, assign an additional resource to a task, or remove a resource from a task.

When you move your mouse pointer over the cell containing the feedback indicator, the Smart Tag icon appears. Click the Smart Tag icon. A message explains the scheduling ramifications of your edit. The message usually gives you the opportunity to change the edit so that the result is closer to your expectation.

The indicator appears in the cell as long as the edit is available for an Undo operation. After you make a new edit, the indicator disappears.

Smart Tags provide feedback for users who are still getting used to the ways Microsoft Project schedules tasks. This feedback helps users understand the impact of their scheduling changes.

If you understand the impact of your scheduling changes, you might not need Smart Tags, and you can turn them off. To do this, click Tools, Options and then click the Interface tab. Clear any of the check boxes under Show Indicators And Options Buttons.

To replace one resource with another, follow these steps:

1. In the Gantt Chart or other task sheet, click the task for which you want to replace a resource.

2. On the Standard toolbar, click Assign Resources.

   The Assign Resources dialog box appears, showing a check mark next to the names of resources already assigned.

3. Click the name of the assigned resource you want to replace and then click the Replace button.

   The Replace Resource dialog box appears, showing the same resources that are displayed in the Assign Resources dialog box, according to any filters you might have applied.

4. Click the name of the replacement resource and then click OK.

   The name of the replacement resource moves to the top of the Resources list in the table, and the default percentage appears in the Units field for the resource.

5. Review the Units field and make sure that it's appropriate for this assignment.

6. When finished replacing resources, click the Close button.

To remove a resource assignment, follow these steps:

1. In the Gantt Chart or other task sheet, click the task from which you want to remove a resource.

2. On the Standard toolbar, click Assign Resources.

   The Assign Resources dialog box appears, showing a check mark next to the names of resources already assigned.

3. Click the name of the assigned resource you want to remove and then click the Remove button.

4. When finished working with resource assignments, click the Close button.

Note

When you remove a resource assignment, you're removing only the assignment, not the resource itself. The resource is still assigned to other tasks and is available for assignment to other tasks.

In the task sheet, you'll see that the task has been updated to exclude the deleted resource. If multiple resources were assigned, and you removed one of them but left others intact, you'll also see the green feedback triangle in the task cell. Position your mouse pointer over the triangle, and the Smart Tag icon appears in the Indicators field. Click the Smart Tag icon. A menu appears (see Figure 7-22).

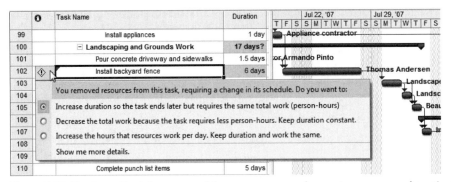

Figure 7-22 The Smart Tag informs you of the consequences of removing a resource from the task. These results are based on the task type.

> **Note**
>
> As an alternative to the Assign Resources dialog box, you can double-click a task to open the Task Information dialog box and then click the Resources tab. Although the Task Information dialog box doesn't have all the options of the Assign Resources dialog box, you can still assign, replace, and remove assigned resources (as well as set the assignment units) for a single task.

Controlling Changes with Effort-Driven Scheduling

When you assign an additional resource to a task that already has assigned resources, by default, the amount of work scheduled for each assigned resource decreases. Likewise, suppose that you remove a resource from a task, leaving at least one remaining resource assigned. By default, the amount of work scheduled for each remaining assigned resource increases.

These changes in work amounts are a function of *effort-driven scheduling*, which dictates that as more resources are added, there is less work for each resource to perform, although the total work to be performed by all resources stays constant. If resources are removed, each remaining resource needs to do more work—again, with the total work remaining constant.

The results of effort-driven scheduling operate in conjunction with the task type. If the task type is set to fixed units or fixed work, adding resources decreases the duration. If the task type is set to fixed duration, adding resources decreases the units for each assigned resource.

By default, effort-driven scheduling is enabled for all tasks. This makes sense because, in the majority of cases, the primary reason for adding resources to a task is to bring in its finish date.

However, you might have certain tasks whose work should not change regardless of the addition or removal of assigned resources. For example, you might have a 4-day document review task. You want all resources assigned to have 4 days to review the document. Suppose that you realize later that you forgot a resource who also needs to review the document. When you add this resource to the task, you wouldn't want the work to be reduced—you still want everyone to have 4 days. Because each resource is reviewing different aspects of the document, it isn't the type of task that can be completed more quickly if more resources are added. For such a task, it's best to turn off effort-driven scheduling.

To turn off effort-driven scheduling for selected tasks, follow these steps:

1. In the Gantt Chart or other task sheet, click the task for which you want to turn off effort-driven scheduling.

   If you want to turn off effort-driven scheduling for several tasks at one time, click the first task, hold down Ctrl, and then click the other tasks you want.

2. On the Standard toolbar, click Task Information.

3. In the Task Information dialog box, click the Advanced tab.

4. Clear the Effort Driven check box.

Task Information

To turn off effort-driven scheduling for all new tasks in this project plan:

1. Click Tools, Options and then click the Schedule tab.

2. Clear the New Tasks Are Effort Driven check box.

Controlling Schedule Changes with Task Types

Adding or removing resources after the initial assignment can change the task and assignment scheduling based on whether the task is effort-driven.

The scheduling for a task or assignment can also change when one of the following items is changed:

- Task duration
- Assignment units
- Work

Duration, units, and work are interrelated and interdependent. When you change one of the three, at least one of the others is affected. For example, by default, if you revise duration, work is recalculated. If you revise assignment units, duration is recalculated. This is based on the basic Microsoft Project scheduling formula:

Duration * Units = Work

> **Note**
>
> Along with the concept of effort-driven scheduling, this interrelationship between duration, units, and work is a major principle that drives how Microsoft Project schedules your project. Commit this formula to memory, write it on a yellow stickie on your computer's monitor, make it your screen saver marquee—anything to help you remember this concept as you work with your project.

You need to be able to control how the schedule is affected when you change duration, assignment units, or work. This control is the *task type*. Think of the task type as the one anchor among the three elements of duration, units, and work. When you make a change, the task type dictates which of the three elements must remain fixed, and which of the other two can flex to accommodate the change (see Figure 7- 23).

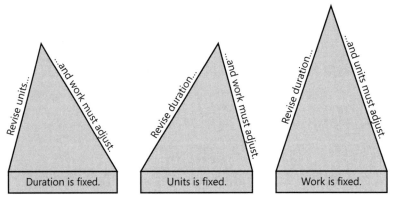

Figure 7-23 When you change one of the three elements, at least one of the others is affected, which changes your task or assignment scheduling.

Therefore, the three task types are as follows:

- Fixed Units
- Fixed Duration
- Fixed Work

Which task type you choose for your project default and change for individual tasks has to do with how you develop your project and the scheduling rules you have in mind as you set your task durations and assign your resources.

> **Note**
>
> When you change units, work, or duration, any cells containing fields with changed information are highlighted. In addition, the Smart Tag feedback icon appears in order to help you ensure you get the scheduling results you expect. Click the Smart Tag icon to read your options and then make any changes you want. If you click Show Me More Details, the Customize Assignment pane in the Project Guide appears.

Understanding the Fixed Units Task Type

When you assign a resource to a task, you specify the assignment units in the Units field of the Assign Resources dialog box. You can see the units in the chart portion of the Gantt Chart (see Figure 7-24). By default, the units appear with the resource name next to the Gantt bar if it's anything other than 100%.

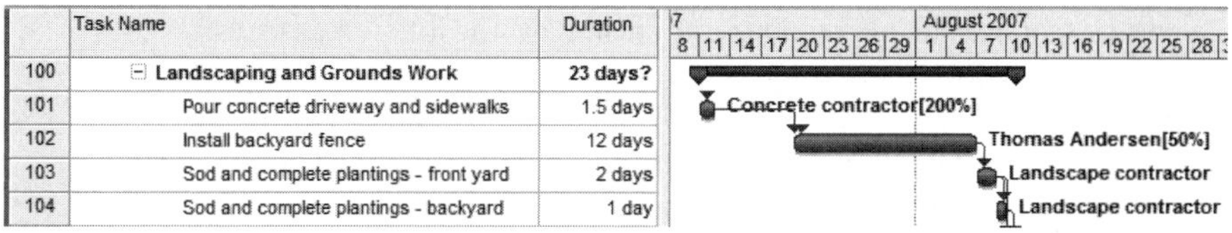

	Task Name	Duration	
100	⊟ Landscaping and Grounds Work	23 days?	
101	Pour concrete driveway and sidewalks	1.5 days	Concrete contractor[200%]
102	Install backyard fence	12 days	Thomas Andersen[50%]
103	Sod and complete plantings - front yard	2 days	Landscape contractor
104	Sod and complete plantings - backyard	1 day	Landscape contractor

Figure 7-24 Assignment units other than 100% are shown next to the relevant Gantt bars.

The Fixed Units task type dictates that the percentage of assignment units on an assignment should remain constant regardless of changes to duration or work. This is the default task type because it's the task type that fits the majority of project tasks. If you increase task duration, Microsoft Project shouldn't force you to find another resource or force a 50% resource to work 100% on the assignment.

Changes to a Fixed Unit task have the following results:

- If you revise the duration, work also changes, and units are fixed.

- If you revise work, duration also changes, and units are fixed.

- If you revise units, duration also changes, and work is fixed.

Understanding the Fixed Work Task Type

When you assign a resource to a task, the task's duration is translated into work. You can see the amount of work in the Task Usage or Resource Usage view.

The Fixed Work task type dictates that the amount of work on an assignment should remain constant regardless of changes to duration or units.

Changes to a Fixed Work task have the following results:

- If you revise the duration, units also change, and work is fixed.

- If you revise units, duration also changes, and work is fixed.

- If you revise work, duration also changes, and units are fixed.

Understanding the Fixed Duration Task Type

When you create a task, you specify the task's duration in the Duration field of the Gantt Chart or other task sheet. The Gantt bar for the task is drawn according to the duration you set.

The Fixed Duration task type dictates that the task duration should remain constant, regardless of changes to units or work.

Changes to a Fixed Duration task have the following results:

- If you revise units, work also changes, and duration is fixed.

- If you revise work, units also change, and duration is fixed.

- If you revise the duration, work also changes, and units are fixed.

Changing the Task Type

As you gain more experience working with Microsoft Project, you'll see the impact of the schedule recalculations engendered by the changes you make. You can control the way changes to the resource assignments of tasks are made by choosing a default task type, and you can make occasional exceptions when needed.

By default, all tasks are Fixed Units. To change the task type of selected tasks, follow these steps:

1. In the Gantt Chart or other task sheet, click the task for which you want to change the task type.

    If you want to change the task type for several tasks at one time, click the first task, hold down Ctrl, and then click the other tasks you want.

2. On the Standard toolbar, click Task Information.

3. In the Task Information dialog box, click the Advanced tab.

4. In the Task Type box, click the task type you want to apply to the selected tasks.

To set the default task type for all new tasks in this project plan, follow these steps:

1. Click Tools, Options. In the Options dialog box, click the Schedule tab.

2. In the Default Task Type box, click the task type you want to apply to all new tasks.

All the tasks in your schedule can have the same task type. As you come to appreciate the power of using different task types in different situations, however, you'll find that though the majority of your tasks are set at the default task type, you'll have a handful of tasks that use different task types, because they need to be scheduled differently.

Contouring Resource Assignments

When you assign a work resource to a task, typically the work time allotted for the task is spread equally across the task duration. For example, if Pat is the only resource assigned full-time to a 4-day task, Pat is assigned 8 hours of work in each of the 4 days.

If you want to adjust how the hours are assigned, however, you can shape the work amounts. You can assign 1 hour on the first day, 2 hours on the second day, 5 hours on the third day, 8 hours on the fourth and fifth day, 5 hours on the sixth day, 2 hours on the seventh day, and 1 hour on the eighth day. You still have 32 hours of work, but the duration has stretched to 8 days. The assignment is shaped like a bell: It has a ramp-up period, a full-on period, and a ramp-down period. A shape applied to the work is called a work *contour* (see Figure 7-25).

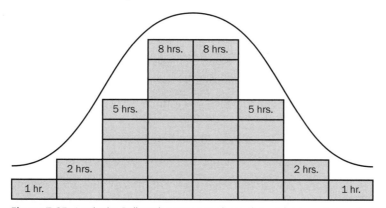

Figure 7-25 Apply the Bell work contour to shape the work amounts to reflect ramp-up, peak, and ramp-down periods, in the shape of a bell.

You can apply this shape by manually adjusting work amounts for the assignment in the timesheet portion of the Task Usage view. Or you can apply the built-in bell contour, which converts the default flat contour into different shapes of time, such as back loaded, front loaded, early peak, and more.

The available built-in work contours are the following:

- Flat (the default)
- Back Loaded

  ![Back Loaded contour icon]

- Front Loaded

  ![Front Loaded contour icon]

- Double Peak

  ![Double Peak contour icon]

- Early Peak

  ![Early Peak contour icon]

- Late Peak

  ![Late Peak contour icon]

- Bell

  ![Bell contour icon]

- Turtle

  ![Turtle contour icon]

To apply a built-in work contour to an assignment, follow these steps:

1. Display the Task Usage or Resource Usage view so you can see assignments.

2. Click the assignment to which you want to apply a work contour and then click Assignment Information.

   The Assignment Information dialog box appears.

3. If necessary, click the General tab.

4. In the Work Contour box, click the work contour you want to apply (see Figure 7-26).

   Work for the assignment is redistributed in the shape of the selected contour.

Assignment
Information

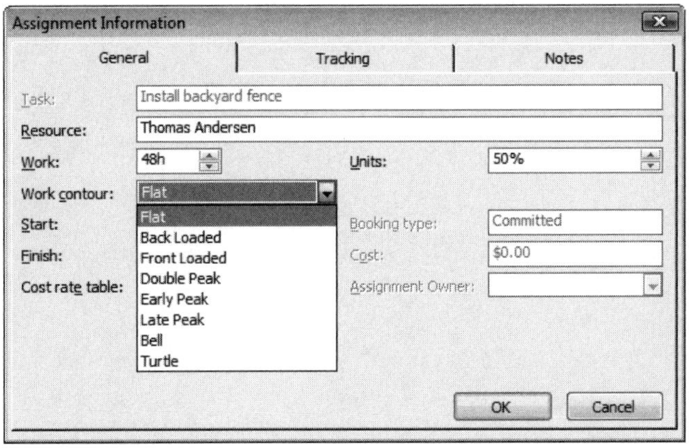

Figure 7-26 Use the General tab in the Assignment Information dialog box to set work contours.

You can also manually reshape the work for an assignment by editing work amounts in the timesheet portion of the Task Usage or Resource Usage view. When you do this, an icon appears in the Indicators column, alerting you to the fact that work amounts have been edited.

Edited work indicator

Any assignment with a work contour applied shows the specific contour icon in the Indicators field of the Task Usage or Resource Usage view.

> **Note**
>
> Although work contours do not apply to cost resources, you can apply a work contour to material resources. In this case, the quantity of material used is distributed over the task span according to the selected contour.

CHAPTER 8
Planning Resource and Task Costs

Working with Costs and Budgeting 274

Planning Resource Costs 275

Planning Fixed Task Costs 284

Reviewing Planned Costs 287

Setting Up and Reviewing a Project Budget 292

Setting a Different Currency 304

Microsoft Office Project 2007 can help you plan, forecast, and track costs associated with the performance of the project. The bulk of your costs is likely to be generated by the resources assigned to tasks. There might also be costs directly associated with tasks.

To set up your project plan so that it reflects costs incurred, you can:

- Enter unit costs for work and material resources and assign those resources to their tasks.

- Assign and quantify cost resources such as travel costs, facility rentals, permit fees, and equipment or software purchases.

- Specify any fixed costs for tasks.

When you have entered all applicable cost items and associated them with your project tasks, Office Project 2007 calculates the cost forecast for each assignment, each resource, each task, and the project as a whole. You can therefore see costs as granular or as high-level as you need for various purposes.

Because you are currently in the planning stage of the project, you can then use this cost forecast to develop your project's budget. If the budget has already been imposed on you, see whether the project plan is in line with the realities of the budget. You can use the new budget resource feature to help you compare your project's planned costs against your allocated budget.

If your planned costs go beyond your budget, use the data you have in Microsoft Project to lobby for additional funding or adjust project scope, schedule, or resources to match the cost forecast to the allocated budget.

As soon as you start executing the project, you start tracking and managing costs. At that point, you can compare actual costs to your original planned costs and analyze any variances between the two.

For more information about adjusting the project plan to conform to the budget, see the section titled "Reducing Project Costs" in Chapter 9, "Checking and Adjusting the Project Plan." For information about tracking costs, including setting cost baselines and entering actual costs, see Chapter 10, "Setting a Baseline and Updating Progress." For information about managing costs, see the section titled "Monitoring and Adjusting Costs" in Chapter 11, "Responding to Changes in Your Project."

Working with Costs and Budgeting

Project cost management is one of the many disciplines required for a successful project execution. Simply put, effective project cost management ensures that the project is completed within the approved budget. In fact, the benchmark of a successful project is its completion not only on time, but also within the allocated budget.

Processes associated with project cost management include the following:

- **Resource planning** After you determine the types and quantities of resources needed for the project, you can estimate costs for those resources. You obtain work resources by hiring staff through human resources processes. You obtain contract staff, material resources, and equipment resources through procurement processes. You then enter those resources into your project plan and assign them to tasks.

- **Cost estimating** *Top-down cost estimating* is the practice of using the actual cost of a previous similar project as the basis for estimating the cost of the current project. *Bottom-up cost estimating* involves estimating the cost of individual tasks and then summarizing those estimates to arrive at a project cost total. The estimate should take into consideration labor, materials, supplies, travel, fees, and any other costs. With Microsoft Project, you can see the planned costs of resources, as well as the fixed costs associated with tasks. Microsoft Project can total all costs to give you a reliable estimate of how much it will cost to implement the project.

- **Cost budgeting** The budget can allocate certain amounts to individual phases or tasks in the project. Or the budget can be allocated to certain time periods in which the costs will be incurred. The cost estimate and the project schedule—with the scheduled start and finish dates of the different phases, tasks, milestones, and deliverables—are instrumental to developing the project budget. In Microsoft Project, you can create budget resources that you can maintain as a fixed point of reference to compare against your planned and actual costs to see how well the project is performing against the budget.

- **Cost control** The cost control process manages changes to the project budget. Cost control addresses the manner in which cost variances will be tracked and managed, and how cost information will be reported. A cost management plan can detail cost control procedures and corrective actions.

Planning Resource Costs

The key to planning project costs is entering resource costs. Typically, the majority of your costs comes from resources carrying out their assignments. When you enter resource cost rates and assign resources to tasks, those resource cost rates are multiplied by the amount of work on assignments. The result is the cost of the assignment.

You can set costs for work resources as well as material resources. Cost rates might be variable, such as $40/hour, or $200/ton. Or they might be a fixed per-use cost, such as $300 per use.

You can also use cost resources, new in Microsoft Office Project 2007, to assign frequently used cost items—for example, facility rental, permit fees, or travel costs—to specific tasks and then specify the amount for that cost resource on that assigned task.

Chapter 8

Setting Costs for Work Resources

You can set pay rates for work resources: people and equipment. When these resources are assigned to tasks, Microsoft Project multiplies the pay rates by the amount of assigned work to estimate the planned cost for the assignment. You can also set per-use costs for work resources. If a resource has different costs for different types of assignments or during different periods of time, you can enter multiple costs for one resource.

> **Note**
>
> You can enter cost information for resources at the same time you add resources to the project. Simply complete all the fields in the Resource Sheet at the same time.

Specifying Variable Work Resource Costs

To set pay rates for work resources, follow these steps:

1. Click View, Resource Sheet.

2. If the Entry table is not already applied to the Resource Sheet, click View, Table, Entry.

3. Make sure that the work resource is set up.

   Work resources are designated with Work selected in the Type field.

   For more information about setting up work resources, see the section titled "Adding Work Resources to the Project" in Chapter 6, "Setting Up Resources in the Project."

4. In the Std. Rate field for the first work resource, enter the resource's standard pay rate, for example, **$30/hour**, or **$400/day**.

5. If the resource is eligible for overtime, enter the resource's overtime pay rate in the Ovt. Rate field (see Figure 8-1).

	❶	Resource Name	Type	Material Label	Initials	Group	Max. Units	Std. Rate	Ovt. Rate	Cost/Use	Accrue At
1	✎	Jim Kim	Work		JK		100%	$45.00/hr	$0.00/hr	$0.00	Prorated
2		Ashvini Sharma	Work		AS		100%	$45.00/hr	$0.00/hr	$0.00	Prorated
3		Katie Jordan	Work		KJ		100%	$500.00/day	$0.00/hr	$0.00	Prorated
4		Jonas Hasselberg	Work		JH		50%	$30.00/hr	$45.00/hr	$0.00	Prorated
5		Designer	Work		DE		200%	$60.00/hr	$90.00/hr	$0.00	Prorated
6		Product Engineer	Work		PE		300%	$75.00/hr	$0.00/hr	$0.00	Prorated
7		Drafter	Work		DR		350%	$20.00/hr	$30.00/hr	$0.00	Prorated
8		Editor	Work		ED		100%	$30.00/hr	$45.00/hr	$0.00	Prorated

Figure 8-1 Specify each work resource's standard pay rate and applicable overtime rate in the Resource Sheet.

Set Default Resource Cost Rates

You can set a default standard rate and overtime rate for all work resources in the current project. Click Tools, Options and then click the General tab. Enter values in the Default Standard Rate and Default Overtime Rate boxes.

Default rates ensure that there's at least an estimated value in the work resource rate fields, which can help you approximate project costs in broad terms until you have confirmed all resource rates.

These values take effect for any new resources you enter but do not change the standard or overtime rate for existing resources, even if their rates show $0.00/hr.

If you're working with Microsoft Office Project Professional 2007 in an enterprise environment, enterprise resource rate information can be updated by the project server administrator, portfolio manager, or other user with the proper permissions.

For more information about setting up enterprise resource information, see the section titled "Creating the Enterprise Resource Pool" in Chapter 21, "Administering Your Enterprise Project Management Solution."

INSIDE OUT   Specify overtime work yourself

Microsoft Project does not automatically assign the overtime pay rate when a resource's work exceeds 8 hours in a day or 40 hours in a week. Although it seems as if this overtime assignment would be the expected behavior, Microsoft Project can't make that assumption. If it did, you might end up with higher costs than you actually incurred.

For the overtime rate to be used, you must specify overtime work in addition to regular work for the resource. For example, if a person is scheduled to work 50 hours in a week, which includes 8 hours of regular work and 2 hours of overtime work per day, you should assign 10 hours of regular work per day and designate 2 hours of it as overtime work. The cost of the hours specified as overtime work is then calculated with the overtime rate you entered for the resource.

For more information about working with overtime, see the section titled "Balancing Resource Workloads" in Chapter 9.

Specifying Fixed Resource Costs

Some work resources incur a cost each time you use them. This *per-use cost* might be instead of or in addition to a cost rate and is often associated with equipment. It's a set, one-time fee for the use of the resource. For example, rental equipment might have a delivery or setup charge every time it's used, in addition to its day rate.

Per-use costs never depend on the amount of work to be done. They're simply one-time costs that are incurred each time the resource is used.

To specify a per-use cost, follow these steps:

1. Be sure that the Entry table is applied to the Resource Sheet. If it is not, click View, Table, Entry.

2. In the Cost/Use field for the work resource, enter the resource's per-use cost, for example, **$100**.

Setting Costs for Material Resources

To set resource costs for consumable materials, follow these steps:

1. Be sure that the Entry table is applied to the Resource Sheet. If it is not, click View, Table, Entry.

2. Make sure the material resource is set up in your Resource Sheet.

    Material resources are designated with Material selected in the Type field. Each material resource should also have a unit of measurement—such as yards, tons, or feet—in the Material Label field.

    For more information about setting up material resources, see the section titled "Adding Material Resources to the Project" in Chapter 6.

3. In the Std. Rate field for the material resource, enter the cost per unit.

    For example, if you have a material resource that is measured in tons, and each ton of this material costs $300, enter **$300** in the Std. Rate field.

4. If there's a per-use cost for the material, such as a setup fee or equipment rental fee associated with using the material, enter it in the Cost/Use field.

Project Management Practices: Procurement Management

When you need to hire contract staffing or use vendors for certain phases of your project, procurement management comes into play. Procurement is also necessary when you need to purchase materials and equipment from selected suppliers. Procurement might also be involved in travel planning.

You use procurement planning to identify which project requirements are best satisfied by purchasing products or services outside the project organization. Through procurement planning, you decide what you need, how much you need, when you need it, and who you're purchasing it from.

The procurement process includes the following:

- Bid solicitation planning
- Bid solicitation
- Vendor selection
- Contract administration
- Contract closing

Because contracting and procurement are specialized knowledge areas, it's best to enlist experts and get them involved with the project team as soon as possible.

Setting Multiple Costs for a Resource

Suppose that you know that certain work resources will get a 5 percent raise on September 1. Maybe the contract for an equipment resource stipulates a discount for the first month of use and then the cost returns to normal for the second month and beyond. Or perhaps a consultant has one rate for one type of work and another rate for another type of work. You can specify different costs at different times by using the *cost rate tables*. To specify different costs, follow these steps:

1. In the Resource Sheet, click the work or material resource for which you want to specify multiple cost rates.

2. On the Standard toolbar, click Resource Information.

3. In the Resource Information dialog box, click the Costs tab (see Figure 8-2).

Resource
Information

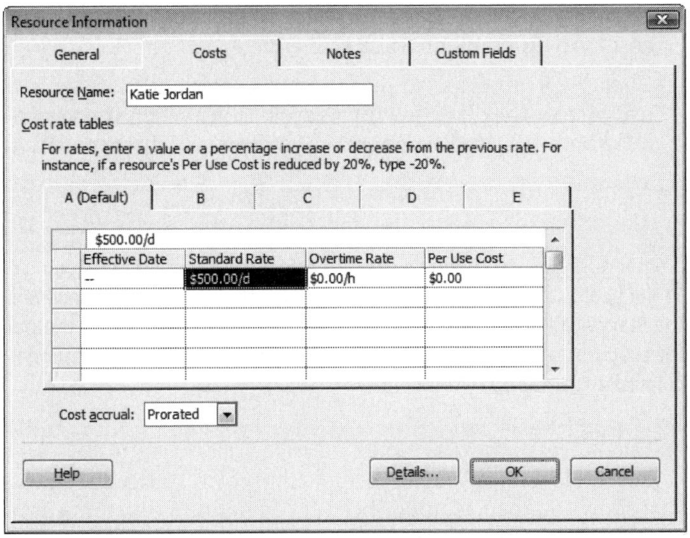

Figure 8-2 Use the cost rate tables in the Resource Information dialog box to specify different resource rates.

4. On the A (Default) tab, you see the standard rate, overtime rate, and per-use cost you might have already entered in the Resource Sheet.

5. To specify a change in rate after a certain period of time, click in the next blank Effective Date field and enter the date the change is to take effect. Enter the cost changes as applicable in the Standard Rate, Overtime Rate, and Per Use Cost fields (see Figure 8-3).

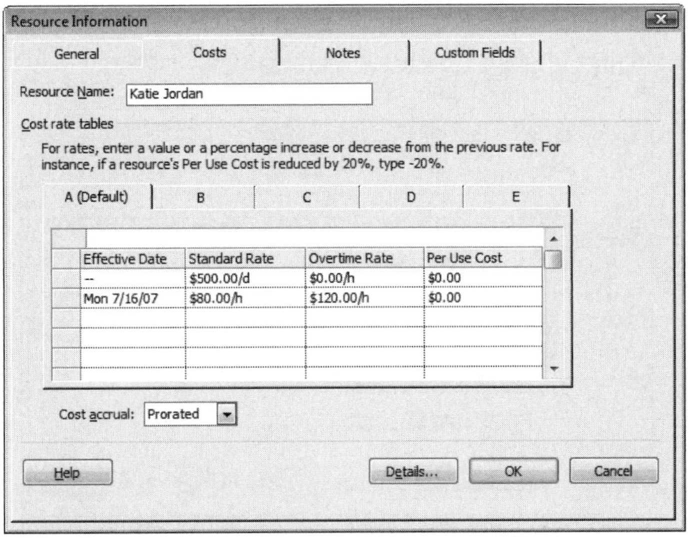

Figure 8-3 If new costs are to take effect on a certain date, add the date and costs in the A (Default) cost rate table.

Chapter 8

6. To specify different costs based on different types of activities, enter the different costs in a different tab, such as B or C.

Click the B tab, for example, and enter the standard rate, overtime rate, and per-use cost for the other activity as applicable. When you assign this resource to a task that uses the different rates, you can specify them with the assignment.

Note

If a percentage rate change goes into effect on a certain date, you can have Microsoft Project calculate the new rate for you. Enter the date in the Effective Date field. Then, in the Standard Rate, Overtime Rate, or Per Use Cost fields, enter the percentage change, for example, +10% or -15%. The actual rate representing that change is immediately calculated and entered in the field.

Cost Rate Table A for resources is applied to the resource's assignments by default and is what shows on the Resource Sheet. If you define a different cost rate table for another category of work, you can specify which cost rate table is to be used at the assignment level. To do this, follow these steps:

1. In a task view such as the Gantt Chart view, use the Assign Resources dialog box to assign the resource to the task.

2. Click View, Task Usage or View, Resource Usage to switch to an assignment view.

3. Click the assignment that needs a different cost rate table applied and then click Assignment Information on the Standard toolbar.

Assignment
Information

4. If necessary, click the General or Tracking tab.

5. In the Cost Rate Table list, click the cost rate table you want to apply to this assignment (see Figure 8-4).

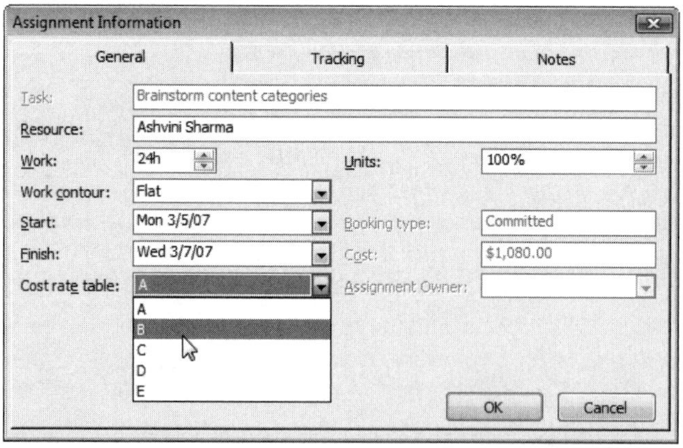

Figure 8-4   In the Assignment Information dialog box, select which cost rate table should be used for this assignment.

There is no way to enter a description for the different cost rate tables to explain what each one is to be used for. Because of this, it's a good idea to enter a resource note for any resource that uses multiple cost rate tables. Simply click the Notes tab in the Resource Information dialog box and enter the note.

Setting Cost Accrual

Cost accrual indicates the point in time when costs are incurred, or charged. You can have costs incurred at the beginning of the assignment or at the end of the assignment. Or you can have the costs *prorated* across the time span of the assignment, which is the default method. Specifying the cost accrual method isimportant for budget cash flow planning.

To specify the cost accrual method, follow these steps:

1. Be sure that the Entry table is applied to the Resource Sheet. If it is not, click View, Table, Entry.

2. In the Accrue At field for the work or material resource, click the method: Start, Prorated, or End.

You can also go to the Costs tab in the Resource Information dialog box to specify the cost accrual method for the resource.

> **Note**
> Although different resources can have different cost accrual methods, you cannot set different cost accrual methods for different cost rate tables.

> **Enter Cost Center Information**
>
> Your organization might associate employees and other budget items such as materials, equipment, and travel with certain cost centers. In Microsoft Office Project 2007, you can add the new Cost Center text field to the Resource Sheet or Resource Usage view.
>
> To do this, right-click the column heading to the right of where you want to insert the Cost Center field, and then click Insert Column on the shortcut menu. In the Field Name box, type **cos** to quickly move to the cost fields.
>
> Click the Cost Center field, and then click OK. You can enter your cost center code here. When the information is in place, you might find it useful to sort, group, or filter by cost center.

Entering Costs for Cost Resource Assignments

A cost resource is a cost item that contributes to the completion of a task but does not affect the schedule when assigned to that task. A cost resource represents a cost item other than a person, a piece of equipment, or a quantity of materials that is incurred in the performance of the task. Examples of cost resources can include airfare, lodging, and rentals.

When you create a cost resource, you do not enter the cost amount in the Resource Sheet as you do with work or material resources. The cost amount for that resource changes depending on the task to which it is assigned.

For example, suppose you have a cost resource named "Trade Show Registration." Your project plan includes participation in five different trade shows that each have differing registration fees. For the "Plan for Portland trade show" task, you can assign the "Trade Show Registration" cost resource and enter $975. For the "Plan for Las Vegas trade show" task, you can assign the same "Trade Show Registration" cost resource and enter $1,595 for the cost.

The advantage of using the same cost resource for different tasks is that you can summarize your total costs for a particular cost category, such as trade show registration, airfare, or permit fees.

> For more information about setting up cost resources, see the section titled "Adding Cost Resources to the Project" in Chapter 6.

To assign a cost resource to a task, follow these steps:

1. Make sure the cost resource is set up in your Resource Sheet.

   Cost resources are designated with Cost selected in the Type field.

2. In the Gantt Chart or other task sheet, click the task to which you want to assign the cost resource.

Assign Resources

3. On the Standard toolbar, click Assign Resources.

4. In the Assign Resources dialog box, click the name of the cost resource you want to assign to the task.

5. Click in the Cost field for the cost resource and type the cost amount for this resource on this task (see Figure 8-5).

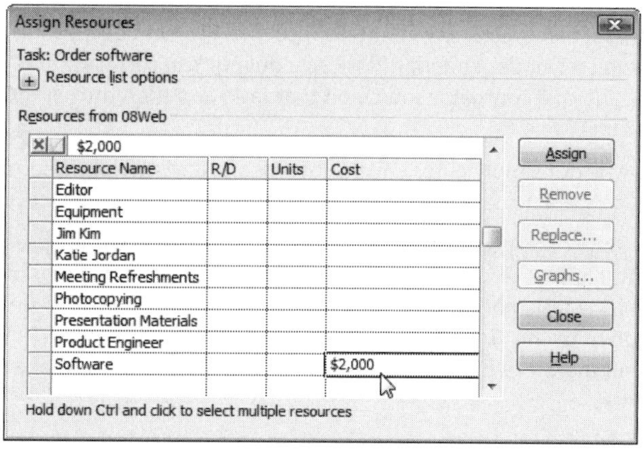

Figure 8-5 Enter the cost amount for this cost resource assigned to this particular task.

6. Click the Assign button.

7. To assign the same cost resource to a different task, click that task. Enter the cost for that cost resource on the newly selected task and then click the Assign button.

8. When finished assigning resources to tasks, click the Close button.

    By default, the name of the cost resource as well as the cost amount for the assignment is shown next to the Gantt bar for the task.

If you need to change the cost you entered on a cost resource assignment, double-click the task to open the Task Information dialog box. Click the Resources tab. In the Cost field for the cost resource, change the amount.

You can also assign cost resources on a timephased basis. Assign the cost resource using the Assign Resources dialog box as described above. Then go to the Task Usage or Resource Usage view. In the timephased portion of the view for the assignment, enter an amount for one time period, enter an amount for another time period, and so on. This can be useful if you want to show when the costs are incurred. For example, if you want to break down the daily costs on a Catering cost resource at a trade show, for example, you can enter $200 on one day, $150 on the second day, and $225 on the third day.

Why Use Cost Resources?

In previous versions of Microsoft Office Project, project managers sometimes created work resources called "Airfare" or "Lodging," and so on, with the cost entered in the Per-Use Cost field. However, the cost could only be a rough estimate if the same resource was to be used for multiple tasks. The alternative was to create a different "Airfare" resource for each instance in which it needed to be used. The other problem was that because it was a work resource, it affected scheduling. It had a work calendar, and adding or removing it to a task could affect duration or work.

Now with cost resources, new in Microsoft Office Project 2007, you can create a resource that is completely independent of task scheduling. You can assign the cost resource to a task, enter the cost for that resource on that task, and then track it thereafter very neatly and accurately.

But then, why not simply enter a fixed cost for a task? Entering fixed costs for tasks does not affect scheduling, and the costs roll up nicely into the project cost summary.

The advantage of using a cost resource instead of a fixed cost for a task is that you can assign multiple cost resources to a task, whereas you can only enter one amount as a fixed cost for a task. For example, you can assign the "Airfare," "Car Rental," and "Hotel" cost resources to the "Train customer service staff in Dayton" task. This gives you more control, and therefore more accurate cost information, when you apply different types of costs to tasks.

Entering a fixed cost is still quite useful when you want to enter a cost that doesn't need granular tracking or summarizing with others of its kind. If there's a one-off type of cost associated with the performance of a task, it's still a good technique. But if you have certain costs that you want to track individually, or that are used by different tasks throughout the project, the cost resource is the better alternative.

Planning Fixed Task Costs

You might have a task cost that is independent of any resource. For example, the performance of a task could include printing costs for reports for a customer review meeting task or it could include the purchase of a flash drive for transferring the files for the development of a deliverable from one resource to another. Such a task cost can be some kind of "miscellaneous" or incidental cost on the task. If the cost does not need to be tracked as its own category, or if it's only going to be incurred for a single task in the project, it might be a good candidate to be entered as a fixed cost for a task.

To enter a fixed cost for a task, follow these steps:

1. Display the Gantt Chart or other task sheet.

2. Click View, Table, Cost.

    The Cost table with the Fixed Cost and Fixed Cost Accrual fields is applied to the task sheet (see Figure 8-6).

	Task Name	Fixed Cost	Fixed Cost Accrual	Total Cost
1	⊟ **Web Structure**	**$0.00**	**Prorated**	**$7,895.00**
2	Brainstorm content categories	$0.00	Prorated	$1,440.00
3	Hold user meetings	$0.00	Prorated	$2,095.00
4	Develop Web structure	$0.00	Prorated	$840.00
5	Web structure review	$0.00	Prorated	$2,720.00
6	Finalize Web structure	$0.00	Prorated	$800.00
7	⊟ **Web Design**	**$0.00**	**Prorated**	**$13,020.00**
8	⊟ **Interior Pages**	**$0.00**	**Prorated**	**$9,500.00**
9	Design interior pages	$0.00	Prorated	$3,700.00
10	Interior page design review	$0.00	Prorated	$1,400.00
11	Finalize interior page design	$0.00	Prorated	$1,600.00
12	Develop style sheets	$0.00	Prorated	$1,200.00
13	Develop page templates	$0.00	Prorated	$1,600.00

Figure 8-6 Apply the Cost table to enter fixed costs for tasks.

3. In the Fixed Cost field for the task, enter the cost.

4. In the Fixed Cost Accrual field, specify when the cost should be accrued: at the beginning of the task, at the end, or prorated throughout the duration of the task. The planned fixed cost for the task is added to the planned cost for the task based on assigned resources and is shown in the Total Cost field.

> **Note**
>
> To set the default fixed cost accrual method, click Tools, Options and then click the Calculation tab. In the Default Fixed Costs Accrual list, select your preferred accrual method. This default accrual applies only to fixed costs for tasks, not resource costs.

You can also enter a fixed cost for the project as a whole. To do this, follow these steps:

1. Display the Gantt Chart or other task sheet.

2. Click View, Table, Cost.

The Cost table is applied.

3. Click Tools, Options and then click the View tab.

4. Under Outline Options, select the Show Project Summary Task check box and then click OK.

The project summary task row appears at the top of the view and includes rolled-up costs for tasks (see Figure 8-7).

	Task Name	Fixed Cost	Fixed Cost Accrual	Total Cost
0	⊟ **Web Site Development**	**$0.00**	**Prorated**	**$198,467.00**
1	⊟ **Web Structure**	**$0.00**	**Prorated**	**$7,895.00**
2	Brainstorm content categories	$0.00	Prorated	$1,440.00
3	Hold user meetings	$0.00	Prorated	$2,095.00
4	Develop Web structure	$0.00	Prorated	$840.00
5	Web structure review	$0.00	Prorated	$2,720.00
6	Finalize Web structure	$0.00	Prorated	$800.00
7	⊟ **Web Design**	**$0.00**	**Prorated**	**$13,020.00**
8	⊟ **Interior Pages**	**$0.00**	**Prorated**	**$9,500.00**
9	Design interior pages	$0.00	Prorated	$3,700.00

Figure 8-7 Add the project summary task to add a fixed cost for the entire project.

5. In the Fixed Cost field for the project summary task, enter the fixed cost for the project.

6. In the Fixed Cost Accrual field, specify when the cost should be accrued: at the beginning of the project, at the end, or prorated throughout the duration of the project.

   The planned fixed cost for the project is added to all other costs calculated for assignments and tasks throughout the project. This total is shown in the Total Cost field of the project summary task.

As you see, when you enter a fixed cost for either a task or the entire project, all you need to do is enter the amount and you're done. You're not asked to enter what the cost is for. Because of this, it's a good practice to document the fixed cost by entering a note. To enter a note about a fixed cost, follow these steps:

1. Select the task (or the project summary task) for which you have entered a fixed cost.

Task Notes

2. On the Standard toolbar, click Task Notes.

3. On the Notes tab in the Task Information (or Summary Task Information) dialog box, enter a note that explains the fixed cost.

Notes indicator

To review notes that have been entered on a task, select the task and then click Task Notes again. In many tables, including the default Entry table, the notes icon appears in the Indicators column. Rest your mouse pointer over the notes icon to read the note (see Figure 8-8). You can also double-click the notes icon to open the Notes tab in the Task Information dialog box.

2		Brainstorm content categories
3	📝	Hold user meetings
4	📝	Notes: 'Fixed cost is for the
5		printing of 40 handouts for the
6		series of meetings.'
7		⊟ **Web Design**
8		⊟ **Interior Pages**

Figure 8-8 Rest your mouse pointer over the notes icon to read the note explaining details about the fixed cost.

TROUBLESHOOTING

The rolled-up value for fixed task costs looks wrong

If you have fixed costs for individual tasks, and possibly a fixed cost for the project as a whole, these values are not rolled up into the project summary task or outline summary tasks.

Instead, the fixed costs for tasks and any resource costs are calculated and displayed in the Total Cost field for the individual tasks. In turn, the Total Cost field is rolled up in the project summary task, and that's where you can see project cost totals (see Figure 8-9)

	Task Name	Fixed Cost	Fixed Cost Accrual	Total Cost
0	⊟ **08Prototype**	**$500.00**	**Prorated**	**$800.00**
1	Identify resources	$0.00	Prorated	$0.00
2	Perform research	$100.00	Prorated	$100.00
3	Develop rough drawings	$100.00	Prorated	$100.00
4	Create samples	$100.00	Prorated	$100.00
5	Complete initial prototype	$0.00	Prorated	$0.00
6	Submit to stakeholders for review	$0.00	Prorated	$0.00

Figure 8-9 Fixed costs are not rolled up into summary tasks or the project summary task, enabling you to enter a fixed cost for a phase or the project as a whole.

The reasoning is that you might need to enter a fixed cost for a project phase, represented in a summary task. Likewise, you might need to enter a fixed cost for the project as a whole. Not rolling up totals in the Fixed Cost field makes it possible for you to do this, although at first glance it looks wrong. Keep your eye on the Total Cost field instead.

Reviewing Planned Costs

The planned costs for your project become reliable figures that you can use for a budget request or a project proposal when the following information is entered in your project plan:

- All required work and material resources, even if they're just generic resources

- Cost rates and per-use costs for all work and material resources

- Cost resources, assigned to tasks with their individual amounts

- All tasks, complete with reliable duration estimates

- Assignments for all tasks

- Any fixed costs for tasks

After this information has been entered, you can review planned costs by various categories, some granular and some high-level: assignment costs, resource costs, task costs, and total project costs.

Reviewing Assignment Costs

Review assignment costs by applying the Cost table to the Task Usage or Resource Usage view, as follows:

1. Click View, Task Usage or click View, Resource Usage to display one of the assignment views.

2. Click View, Table, Cost. The Cost table is applied to the view (see Figure 8-10).

	Task Name	Fixed Cost	Fixed Cost Accrual	Total Cost	Details	M	T	W	T	F
1	⊟ Web Structure	$0.00	Prorated	$7,930.00	Work	16h	16h	16h	8h	8h
2	⊟ Brainstorm content categories	$0.00	Prorated	$1,440.00	Work	16h	16h	16h		
	Ashvini Sharma			$840.00	Work	8h	8h	8h		
	Editor			$600.00	Work	8h	8h	8h		
3	⊟ Hold user meetings	$60.00	Prorated	$2,130.00	Work				8h	8h
	Designer			$2,000.00	Work				8h	8h
	Presentation Materials			$50.00	Work					
	Meeting Refreshments			$20.00	Work					
4	⊟ Develop Web structure	$0.00	Prorated	$840.00	Work					
	Jim Kim			$840.00	Work					

Figure 8-10   Apply the Cost table to the Task Usage view to see assignment costs.

In the Task Usage view, you can see individual assignment costs, as well as the total cost for each task. In the Resource Usage view, you can see individual assignment costs with the total cost for each resource.

You can review timephased costs by adding cost details to the timephased portion of the Task Usage or Resource Usage view, as follows:

1. Display either the Task Usage or Resource Usage view.

2. Click Format, Details, Cost. The Cost field is added to the Work field in the timephased portion of the view (see Figure 8-11).

	Task Name	Fixed Cost	Fixed Cost Accrual	Total Cost	Details	M	T	W
1	⊟ Web Structure	$0.00	Prorated	$7,930.00	Work	16h	16h	16h
					Cost	$480.00	$480.00	$480.00
2	⊟ Brainstorm content categories	$0.00	Prorated	$1,440.00	Work	16h	16h	16h
					Cost	$480.00	$480.00	$480.00
	Ashvini Sharma			$840.00	Work	8h	8h	8h
					Cost	$280.00	$280.00	$280.00
	Editor			$600.00	Work	8h	8h	8h
					Cost	$200.00	$200.00	$200.00

Figure 8-11   Review assignment costs over time by adding the Cost field to the Task Usage or Resource Usage timephased portion of the view.

Zoom In

To see more or less time period detail, click the Zoom In or Zoom Out buttons on the Standard toolbar.

Reviewing Resource Costs

You can review resource costs to see how much each resource is costing to carry out assigned tasks. To get total costs for a resource's assignments, add the Cost field to the Resource Sheet, as follows:

1. Click View, Resource Sheet.

2. Click the column heading to the right of where you want to insert the Cost field.

3. Click Insert, Column.

4. In the Field Name list, click Cost and then click OK.

   The Cost field is added to the table and shows the total planned costs for all assignments for each individual resource.

> **Note**
>
> Reviewing resource costs is a great way to see how much you're spending on different cost categories as represented by your cost resources. Suppose you have assigned the "Airfare" cost resource to three different tasks. For one task the airfare costs $200, for the second task it costs $500, and for the third task it costs $300. If you add the Cost field to the Resource Sheet, you see that the total cost for airfare in your project is $1,000.

You can sort, filter, and group resources by cost information. In the Resource Sheet with the Cost field added, you can rearrange the view by cost information as follows:

- Click Project, Sort, By Cost.

  To return your Resource Sheet to its original order, click Project, Sort, By ID.

- Click Project, Filtered For, More Filters. Click Cost Greater Than and then click the Apply button. Enter an amount and then click OK.

  To see all resources again, click Project, Filtered For, All Resources.

- Click Project, Group By, Standard Rate.

  To ungroup your resources, click Project, Group By, No Group.

If you want to see the total resource costs along with the assignments that contribute to that total, use the Resource Usage view with the Cost table applied. The Cost field next to the resource name shows the total cost for the resource, while the assignments listed under each resource name show the component cost for that assignment, or the amount that the resource costs for that particular task (see Figure 8-12).

Resource Name	Cost	Details	'07				Apr '07	
			4	11	18	25	1	8
2 ⊟ Ashvini Sharma	$4,152.00	Work	24h		32h			40h
Brainstorm content categories	$840.00	Work	24h					
Web structure review	$1,120.00	Work			32h			
Interior page design review	$1,400.00	Work						40h
Web Site Launched	$792.00	Work						

Figure 8-12 Review total resource costs along with the individual assignment costs that go into that total by applying the Cost table to the Resource Usage view.

Reviewing Task Costs

You can review task costs to see how much each task will cost to carry out. This cost is the sum of all the costs of resources assigned to this task, as well as any fixed costs for tasks. To view total costs for tasks, do the following:

1. Display the Gantt Chart or other task sheet.

2. Click View, Table, Cost.

3. Review the Total Cost field to see the cost for each task.

You can run one of two built-in reports that show planned costs: the Budget report and the Cash Flow report. To generate the Budget report, do the following:

1. Click Report, Reports.

2. Double-click Costs.

3. Double-click Budget.

   The Budget report appears (see Figure 8-13).

Budget Report as of Thu 1/11/07
Web Site Development

ID	Task Name	Fixed Cost	Fixed Cost Accrual	Total Cost
30	Develop content	$0.00	Prorated	$110,400.00
23	Equipment order processing and delivery	$0.00	Prorated	$15,120.00
25	Software order processing and delivery	$0.00	Prorated	$10,080.00
32	Revise content	$0.00	Prorated	$7,200.00
9	Design interior pages	$0.00	Prorated	$3,700.00
36	All pages test	$0.00	Prorated	$3,520.00
37	Link test	$0.00	Prorated	$3,520.00
22	Order equipment	$0.00	Prorated	$3,360.00
31	Content review	$0.00	Prorated	$2,800.00
33	Second content review	$0.00	Prorated	$2,800.00
5	Web structure review	$0.00	Prorated	$2,720.00
34	Finalize content	$0.00	Prorated	$2,400.00
38	Fix bugs	$0.00	Prorated	$2,400.00
24	Order software	$0.00	Prorated	$2,360.00
3	Hold user meetings	$60.00	Prorated	$2,130.00
43	Web Site Launched	$0.00	Prorated	$1,992.00
21	Evaluate software requirements	$0.00	Prorated	$1,800.00
11	Finalize interior page design	$0.00	Prorated	$1,600.00

Figure 8-13 The Budget report shows the task name, fixed costs, and total planned costs.

4. To print the report, click the Print button. To close the report, click the Close button.

To generate the Cash Flow report, do the following:

1. Click Report, Reports.

2. Double-click Costs.

3. Double-click Cash Flow.

    The Cash Flow report appears (see Figure 8-14).

Cash Flow as of Thu 1/11/07
Web Site Development

	3/4/07	3/11/07	3/18/07	3/25/07
Web Structure				
Brainstorm content categories	$1,440.00			
Hold user meetings	$852.00	$1,278.00		
Develop Web structure		$560.00	$280.00	
Web structure review			$2,720.00	
Finalize Web structure				$800.00
Web Design				
Interior Pages				
Design interior pages				$1,387.50

Figure 8-14 The Cash Flow report shows planned costs by task, with totals for tasks and for weekly periods.

4. To print the report, click the Print button. To close the report, click the Close button.

> **For more information about reports, see the section titled "Generating Reports" in Chapter 12, "Reporting Project Information."**

You can sort and filter tasks by cost. In the Gantt Chart or other task sheet, rearrange your view by cost information as follows:

- Click Project, Sort, By Cost.

    To return your task list to its sort original order, click Project, Sort, By ID.

- Click Project, Filter For, More Filters. Click Cost Greater Than and then click the Apply button. Enter an amount and then click OK.

    To see all tasks again, click Project, Filter For, All Tasks.

Reviewing the Total Planned Cost for the Project

You can see the total planned cost for the entire project. This cost is the sum of all task costs, as well as any fixed costs you might have entered for the project. To see the total cost for the project, apply the Cost table to the Gantt Chart or other task sheet and show the Project Summary Task, as follows:

1. Display the Gantt Chart or other task sheet.

2. Click View, Table, Cost.

    The Cost table is applied.

3. Click Tools, Options and then click the View tab.

4. Under Outline Options, select the Show Project Summary Task check box and then click OK.

   The project summary task row appears at the top of the view. The total project cost is displayed in the Total Cost field.

You can also see the total project cost in the Project Statistics dialog box. To display the Project Statistics dialog box, follow these steps:

1. Click Project, Project Information.

2. Click the Statistics button. The Project Statistics dialog box appears (see Figure 8-15).

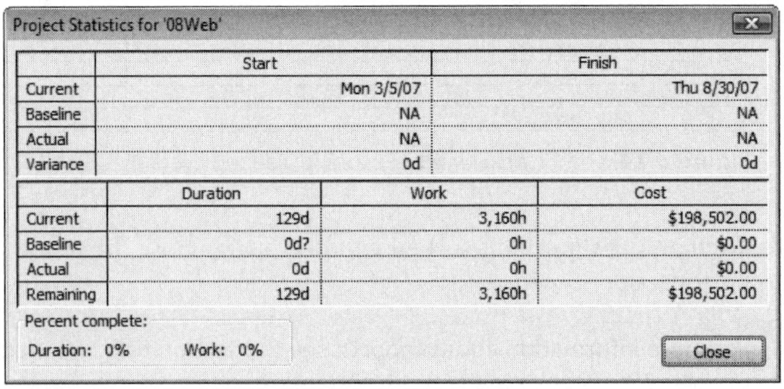
Project Statistics for '08Web'

	Start	Finish
Current	Mon 3/5/07	Thu 8/30/07
Baseline	NA	NA
Actual	NA	NA
Variance	0d	0d

	Duration	Work	Cost
Current	129d	3,160h	$198,502.00
Baseline	0d?	0h	$0.00
Actual	0d	0h	$0.00
Remaining	129d	3,160h	$198,502.00

Percent complete:
Duration: 0% Work: 0%
Close

Figure 8-15 The Project Statistics dialog box shows the overall project cost, as well as the project start and finish dates, total duration, and total work.

Setting Up and Reviewing a Project Budget

In previous versions of Microsoft Office Project, if you wanted to compare your planned costs in your project plan against your budget numbers for certain categories, you had to take numbers out of Microsoft Project, categorize them in ways that match your budget categories, calculate them, and then compare them. Much of this was likely done outside of Microsoft Project.

In Project 2007, there is a strategy to set up and enter values for budget categories within your project plan by using the new Budget Cost and Budget Work fields. You can identify which resources belong under which budget category. You can then group the resources by budget category and compare them against your budget amounts.

Although the initial setup is somewhat involved, you only have to do the setup once. After that, you can easily compare cost amounts against your budget amounts anytime you like.

Creating Budget Resources

Create budget resources that correspond with the budget line items you want to track and compare in your project. Examples of budget categories that might apply to a project plan include Employees, Vendors, Outside Services, Equipment Purchase, Equipment Rental, Materials Inventory, Travel Expenses, and Fees and Licensing. The majority of your costs will come from your resources: human, equipment, material, and cost resources.

> **Note**
>
> Some costs will come from fixed costs on tasks. This budget process does not factor in fixed costs.

To create budget resources, follow these steps:

1. Click View, Resource Sheet.

2. In the next available blank row, enter the name of the budget resource in the Resource Name field.

   Be sure to make the name of the budget resource easily distinguishable from the other resources. You might use all caps, for example, EMPLOYEES, if all other resource names are in lowercase letters or initial caps. You might use a budget number as a prefix to the budget resource name, for example, 6220-Vendors. Or, you can use Budget as part of the budget resource name, for example, "Budget-Equipment." This differentiation will become important later when you're looking at a view that compares the rolled-up numbers in your budget resources next to the numbers for the individual resources.

3. In the Type field, specify whether the budget resource is for work, material, or cost resources.

   For work resources, you will eventually express the target budget by the number of hours worked. For cost resources, you will express the target budget by the cost amount.

4. If you are creating a material budget resource, specify the unit of measurement in the Material Label field, for example, packages, pounds, or sets.

   For material resources, you will eventually express the target budget by the number of units. Because of this, create a different budget resource for each different material resource that you want to track against the budget.

5. Double-click the name of the new budget resource.

6. On the General tab of the Resource Information dialog box, select the Budget check box.

   Selecting this check box transforms a regular resource into the special budget resource.

7. Repeat steps 2–6 to create all the budget resources you intend to use with your project.

The Budget check box is not available in the Multiple Resource Information dialog box. However, if you have many budget resources, designate them more quickly by inserting the Budget column. To do this, follow these steps:

1. With the Resource Sheet showing, right-click the column heading to the right of where you want to insert the Budget column and then click Insert Column on the shortcut menu.

2. In the Field Name box of the Column Definition dialog box, type **bu** to quickly move to the Budget field.

3. Click the Budget field and then click OK.

4. For each of the budget resources, change the No in the Budget field to Yes. You can click in the field, type **y**, then move to the next field, type **y** again, and so on, until all the budget resources are so designated (see Figure 8-16).

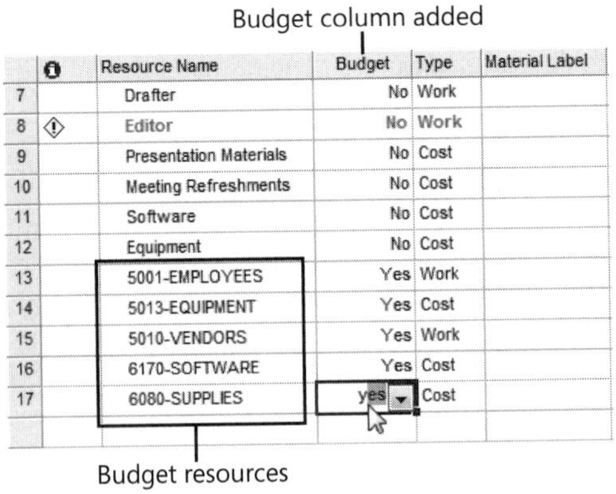

Budget column added

	ⓘ	Resource Name	Budget	Type	Material Label
7		Drafter	No	Work	
8	◈	Editor	No	Work	
9		Presentation Materials	No	Cost	
10		Meeting Refreshments	No	Cost	
11		Software	No	Cost	
12		Equipment	No	Cost	
13		5001-EMPLOYEES	Yes	Work	
14		5013-EQUIPMENT	Yes	Cost	
15		5010-VENDORS	Yes	Work	
16		6170-SOFTWARE	Yes	Cost	
17		6080-SUPPLIES	yes ▾	Cost	

Budget resources

Figure 8-16 You can quickly designate multiple budget resources as such by adding the Budget field to the Resource Sheet and then changing its value from No to Yes.

5. After you have designated all your budget resources using the Budget column, you can hide the column. Right-click the Budget column heading and then click Hide Column on the shortcut menu.

Assigning Budget Resources to the Project Summary Task

After you have created your budget resources, assign them all to your project summary task. The project summary task is the only task to which budget resources can be assigned. To assign budget resources to your project summary task, follow these steps:

1. Switch to the Gantt Chart or other task sheet.

2. Click Tools, Options and then click the View tab.

3. Under Outline Options, select the Show Project Summary Task check box and then click OK.

The project summary task now appears at the Task 0 position at the top of the sheet view.

4. Select the project summary task.

5. On the Standard toolbar, click the Assign Resources button.

6. Hold down the Ctrl key and click each of your budget resources. If necessary, scroll down through the list of resources to find them all.

If the list of resources is very long, you can click the + Resource List Options button to show the filter options. Click the check box under Filter By and then in the drop-down list, click Budget Resources. Make sure that all the budget resources are selected (see Figure 8-17).

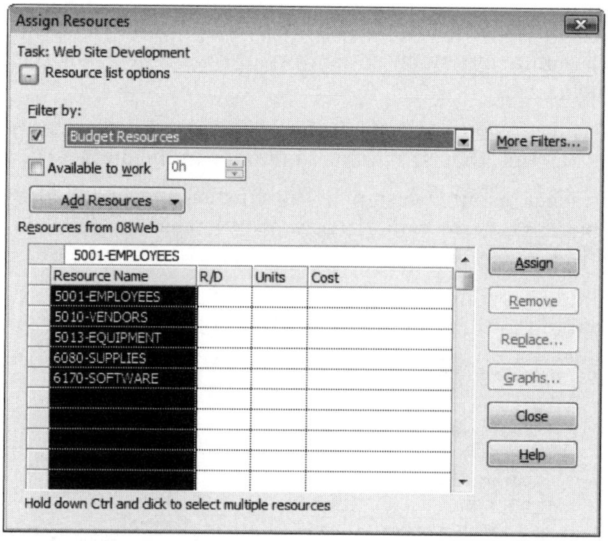

Figure 8-17 If necessary, filter the list of resources to show only budget resources.

7. Click the Assign button and then click the Close button.

TROUBLESHOOTING

The Assign button is unavailable for a budget resource

If you try to assign a budget resource, but the Assign (and Remove and Replace) buttons are dimmed in the Assign Resources dialog box, check the task that's currently selected. If it's any task other than the project summary task, the Assign button is unavailable. Select the project summary task, and the Assign button becomes available again.

Chapter 8

Entering Budget Values for the Budget Resources

Now that the budget resources are all assigned to the project summary task, you can enter the budget work amounts for work and material resources and budget cost amounts for cost resources. These values represent the cost targets against which you will be comparing project work and costs. To do this, follow these steps:

1. Switch to the Task Usage view or the Resource Usage view.

2. Right-click the column to the right of where you want to insert the Budget Cost column and then click Insert Column on the shortcut menu.

3. In the Field Name box of the Column Definition dialog box, type **bu** to quickly find the field.

4. Click the Budget Cost field and then click OK.

5. Repeat steps 2–4 to add the Budget Work field to the view.

6. In an assignment row, enter the work or cost value in the Budget Work or Budget Cost field.

   For a budget resource designated as a work resource, express the budget value as a work amount, that is, a number of hours, in the Budget Work field.

   For a budget resource designated as a material resource, also use the Budget Work field, but express the value according to the material label, for example, tons, board feet, yards, and so on.

   For a budget resource designated as a cost resource, express the budget value as a cost amount in the Budget Cost field (see Figure 8-18).

	ⓘ	Resource Name	Type	Budget Cost	Budget Work
13		⊟ 5001-EMPLOYEES	Work		2,000 hrs
		Web Site Development	Work		2,000 hrs
14		⊟ 5013-EQUIPMENT	Cost	$3,000.00	
		Web Site Development	Cost	$3,000.00	
15		⊟ 5010-VENDORS	Work		1,500 hrs
		Web Site Development	Work		1,500 hrs
16		⊟ 6170-SOFTWARE	Cost	$3,000.00	
		Web Site Development	Cost	$3,000.00	
17		⊟ 6080-SUPPLIES	Cost	$1,000.00	
		Web Site Development	Cost	$1,000.00	

Figure 8-18 Enter the work, material, and cost values for each of your budget resources. These values represent the target budget against which you will compare project costs.

TROUBLESHOOTING

You can't enter a value in the Budget Cost or Budget Work field

For budget resources designated as cost resources, you can only enter a value in the Budget Cost field, not the Budget Work field. Likewise, for budget resources designated as work or material resources, you can only enter a value in the Budget Work field, and not the Budget Cost field.

If you need to designate a certain budget within a specific period of time, for example, a month or a quarter, you can do so by adding the Budget Cost and Budget Work fields to the timephased portion of the Task Usage or Resource Usage view. To do this, follow these steps:

1. In the Task Usage or Resource Usage view, click Format, Detail Styles.

2. Under Available Fields, scroll down and click Budget Cost. Hold down the Shift or Ctrl key and also click Budget Work.

    Both fields are selected.

3. Click the Show button to add the two selected fields to the Show These Fields box.

4. Click OK. In the timephased portion of the view, double-click the right edge of the Details column heading to widen the column so you can see the full field names.

Zoom Out

5. On the Standard toolbar, click the Zoom Out or Zoom In button to see the time unit for which you want to enter timephased budget values.

6. In the assignment row under the budget resource for which you want to enter timephased budget values, enter the work or cost value in the Budget Work or Budget Cost field under the appropriate unit of time (see Figure 8-19).

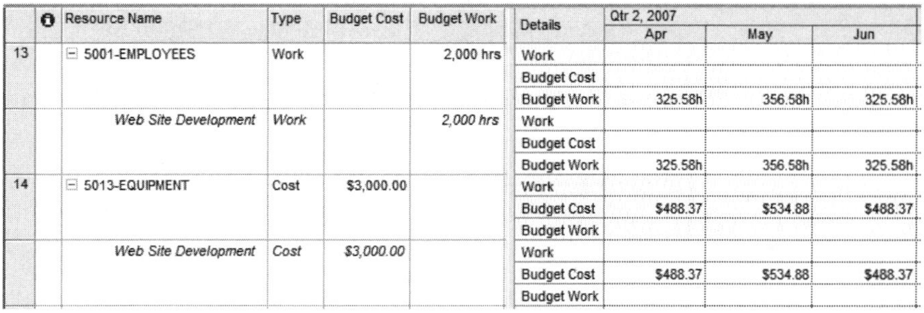

	❶	Resource Name	Type	Budget Cost	Budget Work	Details	Qtr 2, 2007 Apr	May	Jun
13		⊟ 5001-EMPLOYEES	Work		2,000 hrs	Work			
						Budget Cost			
						Budget Work	325.58h	356.58h	325.58h
		Web Site Development	Work		2,000 hrs	Work			
						Budget Cost			
						Budget Work	325.58h	356.58h	325.58h
14		⊟ 5013-EQUIPMENT	Cost	$3,000.00		Work			
						Budget Cost	$488.37	$534.88	$488.37
						Budget Work			
		Web Site Development	Cost	$3,000.00		Work			
						Budget Cost	$488.37	$534.88	$488.37
						Budget Work			

Figure 8-19 You can enter timephased budget resource values in the timephased portion of the Resource Usage view.

Note
Even though the Budget Cost and Budget Work fields appear next to all assignments in the view, remember that you can enter budget values only for the budget resources assigned to the project summary task.

Chapter 8

Aligning Resources with their Budget Resource Type

In this step of the process, you categorize the resources whose costs you want to compare with the budget resource values. You can use an existing text field that isn't doing anything else, such as the Group or Code field already in the Resource Sheet. Or, you can create a custom text field. Either way, you create your budget categories and then categorize the resources using the text field, including the budget resources themselves.

To create a custom text field for your budget categories, follow these steps:

1.   Switch to the Resource Sheet.

2.   Click Tools, Customize, Fields.

3.   Under Field, be sure that the Resource option is selected.

4.   In the Type box, select Text.

5.   In the Field box, select the custom text field you want to use, for example, Text1 or Text2.

6.   Click the Rename button and type the name you want for this field, for example, **Budget Category** or **Budget Group**. Click OK.

The renamed field appears in the Field box (see Figure 8-20).

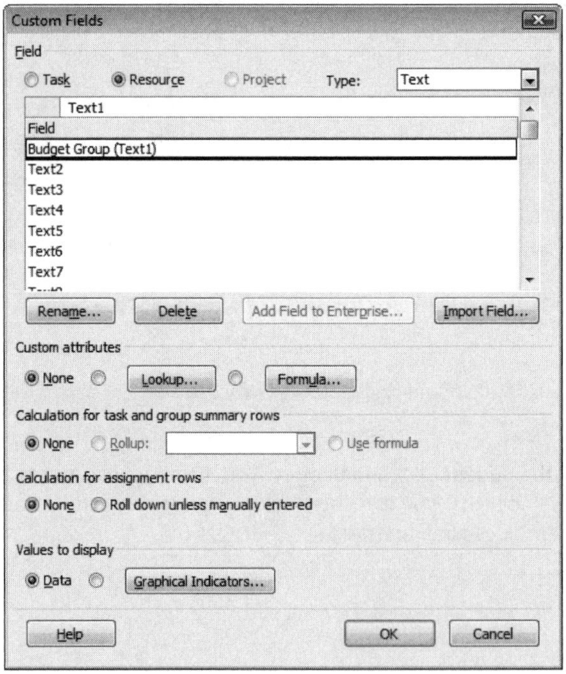

Figure 8-20   Create a custom text field to categorize your resources by their budget types.

7. Under Calculation For Assignment Rows, select the Roll Down Unless Manually Entered option. Click OK.

   This option, new in Microsoft Office Project 2007, specifies that the contents of your budget category field should be distributed across assignments in the Task Usage view or Resource Usage view unless you manually enter information in an assignment row.

To add your new text field to the resource sheet, follow these steps:

1. Right-click the column heading to the right of where you want to insert the text field and then click Insert Column on the shortcut menu.

2. In the Field Name box of the Column Definition dialog box, type **tex** or the first two or three letters of the name you gave to the text field to quickly find that field in the list.

3. Click the field name and then click OK.

   The text field appears in the Resource Sheet.

Now go down the list of resources and type a budget category for each resource you want to track against the budget. Be sure to also enter a budget category for the budget resources themselves (see Figure 8-21). The category names can be whatever you choose, for example, Employees, Vendors, or Equipment. Just be sure to use exactly the same names and same spelling for the same category. This will become important when you group the resources by their category names in the next step of the process.

	🛈	Resource Name	Type	Budget Group	Budget Cost	Budget Work	
1		Jim Kim	Work	Employees			
2		Ashvini Sharma	Work	Employees			
3		Katie Jordan	Work	Employees			
4		Jonas Hasselberg	Work	Vendors			
5		Designer	Work	Vendors			
6		Product Engineer	Work	Employees			
7		Drafter	Work	Vendors			
8		Editor	Work	Employees			
9		Presentation Materials	Cost	Supplies			
10		Meeting Refreshments	Cost	Supplies			
11		Software	Cost	Software			
12		Equipment	Cost	Equipment			
13		5001-EMPLOYEES	Work	Employees		2,000 hrs	
14		5013-EQUIPMENT	Cost	Equipment	$3,000.00		
15		5010-VENDORS	Work	Vendors		1,500 hrs	
16		6170-SOFTWARE	Cost	Software	$3,000.00		
17		6080-SUPPLIES	Cost	Supplies	$1,000.00		

Figure 8-21 Specify the budget category for each resource you want to track against your budget—possibly all your resources.

Chapter 8

Create a Lookup Table for Your Budget Types

You can enter your budget categories in a lookup table so that you can pick categories from a list rather than having to enter them for each resource. If you have a long list of resources you need to categorize, this can save you a lot of time. To create a lookup table for the custom text field you already created, follow these steps:

1. Click Tools, Customize, Fields.

2. Under Field, be sure that the Resource option is selected.

3. In the Type box, be sure that Text is selected.

4. In the Field box, select the custom text field you created previously.

5. Under Custom Attributes, click the Lookup button.

6. In the first row of the lookup table, type the first budget category name you want to use and then press Enter.

7. In the second row, type the second budget category name and press Enter.

8. Continue entering budget category names in different rows of the Value column, until all your categories are entered.

9. When finished, click Close. Click OK in the Custom Fields dialog box.

Now you can click in your custom text field, click the arrow that appears, and select a budget category from the list.

	❶	Resource Name	Type	Budget Group
1	◈ ▨	Jim Kim	Work	Employees
2	▨	Ashvini Sharma	Work	Employees
3		Katie Jordan	Work	Employees
4		Jonas Hasselberg	Work	Vendors
5		Designer	Work	Vendors ▾
6		Product Engineer		Employees
7		Drafter		Vendors
8	◈	Editor		Supplies
9		Presentation Materials		Software
10		Meeting Refreshments		Equipment

For more information about working with custom fields and lookup tables, see the section titled "Customizing Fields" in Chapter 25, "Customizing Your View of Project Information."

Note

If you're not using the Group or Code field on the Resource Sheet for any other purpose, you can use either of those fields to categorize your resources instead of going to the trouble of creating a custom text field. Like a custom text field, you can enter any information in the Group or Code field.

At this point, you've completed all the steps necessary for the initial setup of budget resources. Unless you find that you need new budget resources or new resources that you want to track against the budget resources, you're all set to compare project costs against your budget.

Comparing Resource Costs with Budget Resource Values

Now you can compare your resource costs against the values you've identified for your budget resources and see where you stand. This is useful in the planning stage. This will also be useful later when your project is in the monitoring stage, when tasks are being completed and actual costs are being incurred.

1. Switch to the Resource Usage view.

2. If they're not already showing, add the Budget Work, Budget Cost, Work, and Cost fields to the table (see Figure 8-22). Right-click the column to the right of where you want to insert the column and then click Insert Column on the shortcut menu. In the Field Name box, scroll to and select the field and then click OK.

	ⓘ	Resource Name	Budget Work	Budget Cost	Work	Cost
3		⊟ Katie Jordan			240 hrs	$96,000.00
		Develop content			240 hrs	$96,000.00
4		⊟ Jonas Hasselberg			1,080 hrs	$32,400.00
		Perform system needs analysis			36 hrs	$1,080.00
		Evaluate equipment requirements			52 hrs	$1,560.00

Figure 8-22 Show the columns necessary to be able to compare your planned costs against your budgeted costs.

3. Click Project, Group By, Customize Group By.

4. In the Group By field under Field Name, select the name of your custom text field (or Code or Group) that you used to categorize your resources (see Figure 8-23).

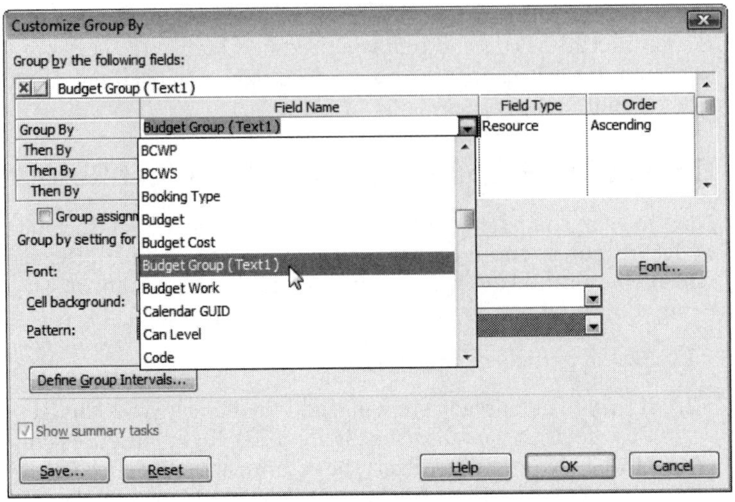

Figure 8-23 Use the Customize Group By dialog box to select the name of the field you used to categorize your resources by their budget type.

5. Click OK.

The resources in your project are grouped by the budget categories you assigned (see Figure 8-24). Each grouping includes one budget resource. The figures for the budget resource appear in the Budget Cost and Budget Work fields. The figures for all other resources appear in the Cost and Work fields. The total costs for the resources are rolled up in the grouping bar. Compare those rolled up values against the values for the budget resources to see how the costs in your project are faring against the budget for that category.

Compare this budget cost...

...with the rolled up cost for this category of resources.

ⓘ	Resource Name	Budget Work	Budget Cost	Work	Cost	Details	Qtr 3, 2007		
							Jun	Jul	Aug
	⊟ Supplies		$1,000.00		$70.00	Work			
						Budget Cost			
						Budget Work			
17	⊟ 6080-SUPPLIES		$1,000.00			Work			
						Budget Cost	$162.79	$170.54	$170.54
						Budget Work			
	Web Site Development		$1,000.00			Work			
						Budget Cost	$162.79	$170.54	$170.54
						Budget Work			
10	⊟ Meeting Refreshments				$20.00	Work			
						Budget Cost			
						Budget Work			
	Hold user meetings				$20.00	Work			
						Budget Cost			
						Budget Work			
9	⊟ Presentation Materials				$50.00	Work			
						Budget Cost			
						Budget Work			
	Hold user meetings				$50.00	Work			
						Budget Cost			
						Budget Work			
	⊟ Vendors	1,500 hrs		1,464 hrs	$51,600.00	Work	312h	168.5h	124h
						Budget Cost			
						Budget Work			
15	⊟ 5010-VENDORS	1,500 hrs				Work			
						Budget Cost			
						Budget Work	244.18h	255.82h	255.82h
	Web Site Development	1,500 hrs				Work			
						Budget Cost			
						Budget Work	244.18h	255.82h	255.82h
5	⊟ Designer			384 hrs	$19,200.00	Work			96h
						Budget Cost			

Compare this budget work value...

...with the rolled up work value for this category of resources.

Figure 8-24 When you group your resources by their budget categories, you can quickly compare the planned costs and planned work for the resources against the budgeted costs and work as shown by the budget resources.

Note

Your resources initially appear in the order in which they were entered in the project. If you want, click Project, Sort, By Name. It's easiest to analyze your budget performance if the budget resource appears at the top of each grouping, either because of its name or its ID, which reflects the order in which it was entered.

6. To ungroup the Resource Usage view, click Project, Group By, No Group. Or, on the Standard toolbar, in the Group By tool, click No Group.

Custom Group

Group By

INSIDE OUT

Create a budget resource view

If you expect to monitor your budget in this way rather often, consider creating a custom view. In this view, you could include a custom table that would always show the Budget Cost, Budget Work, Cost, and Work fields, along with the Resource Name. It would also always have the resources grouped the way you need to see the budget comparisons.

For more information about creating a view that would accomplish these tasks for you simply by applying the view, see the following sections in Chpater 25: "Creating a New Table," "Creating a New Group," and "Creating a New View."

Setting a Different Currency

The currency used in Microsoft Project is the one you have set in your computer system's regional and language options. However, you can set up your project to work with a different currency, or even to work with multiple currencies in a single plan. These capabilities facilitate cost planning and management for projects that span multiple countries and their currencies.

Setting Up a Different Currency in Your Computer

You can set up a different currency to take effect in all the applications you use on your computer by changing your computer's regional and language options. If you're using Windows Vista, follow these steps:

1. On the Windows taskbar, click Start, Control Panel.

2. Under Clock, Language, and Region, click Change Display Language and then click the Formats tab.

3. In the Current Format box, click the country whose currency you want to use throughout your computer system.

   The formats for numbers, currency, time, and date for the selected country are displayed.

4. Click OK.

If you're using Windows XP, follow these steps:

1. On the Windows taskbar, click Start, Control Panel and then double-click Regional And Language Options.

2. On the Regional Options tab, click the country whose currency you want to use throughout your computer system

   Under Samples, the formats for currency, time, and date for the selected country are displayed.

3. Click OK.

The new currency setting takes effect for any new projects that you create from this point forward. It does not change the currency settings for existing projects.

Setting Up a Different Currency in Microsoft Project

If you prefer, you can change the currency settings just in Microsoft Project, and not throughout your computer system. Currencies are set for individual plans, not for Microsoft Project globally. To apply a new currency in your project:

1. In Microsoft Office Project 2007, open the project in which you want to use the new currency.

2. Click Tools, Options and then click the View tab.

3. Under Currency Options, in the Currency box, select the currency you want to use (see Figure 8-25). You need to know the currency abbreviation, for example, GBP for British pounds, EUR for euros, or USD for American dollars.

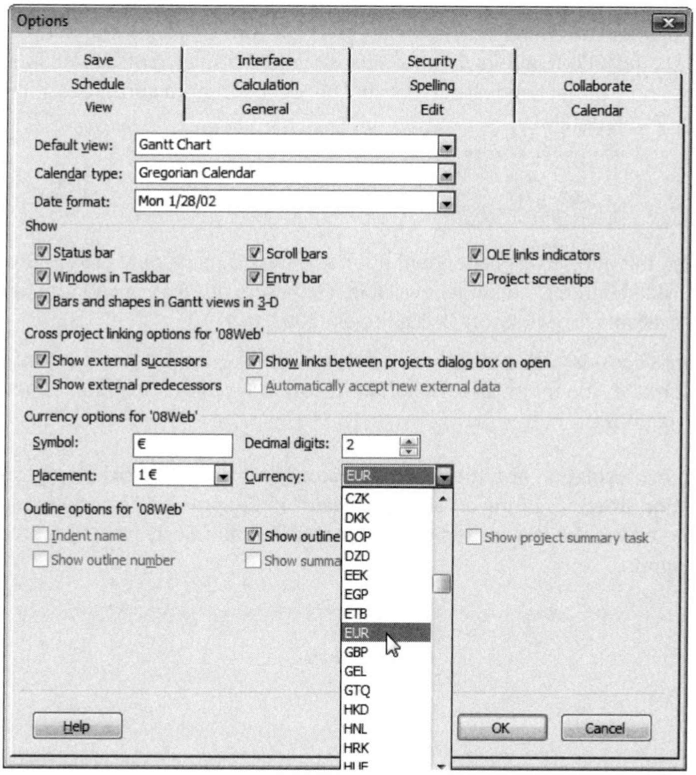

Figure 8-25 Use the View tab in the Options dialog box to specify the currency you want to use in this project plan.

The content of the Symbol, Placement, and Decimal Digits boxes change to reflect your chosen currency.

4. Make any necessary changes to the Placement or Decimal Digits box and then click OK.

Any currencies already entered in the project are changed to the new currency. Note, however, that currencies are not converted; the symbol is just switched.

Using this method, the one currency applies throughout the project plan. If you consolidate projects using different currencies, be sure to change the settings in each one to a common currency and make the necessary conversions to cost values. Although you can specify different currencies in different projects, only one currency can be in effect for any particular project.

INSIDE OUT   The Euro Converter is no longer available

In previous versions of Microsoft Office Project, a Euro Currency Converter Component Object Model (COM) add-in was available for you to display costs in multiple currencies in a single project and also to convert between different currencies in the European Monetary Unions (EMU).

However, this add-in was dependent upon a feature outside of Microsoft Project, and that outside feature is no longer available. Therefore, this add-in and functionality is no longer available for Microsoft Office Project 2007.

You might consider using custom cost fields that include a formula that represents the exchange rate. You might also use different cost rate tables for resources doing work in various countries.

For more information about creating a custom cost field that includes a formula, see the section titled "Creating a Calculated Field" in Chapter 25. For information about cost rate tables, see the section titled "Setting Multiple Costs for a Resource" earlier in this chapter.

Working with the Critical Path and Critical Tasks **309**

Bringing in the Project Finish Date **320**

Reducing Project Costs **331**

Balancing Resource Workloads **338**

Changing Project Scope **364**

Reviewing the Impact of Changes **364**

Obtaining Buyoff on the Project Plan **365**

In a perfect world, you'd define the project scope, schedule tasks, assign resources, and presto! The project plan would be finished and ready to execute.

In reality, however, this is rarely the case. After you've scheduled tasks and assigned resources, you generally need to check the results and see whether they meet expectations and requirements. Ultimately, you might need to answer one or all of the following questions to your satisfaction and to the satisfaction of your managing stakeholders:

- Will the project be finished on time?

- Is the project keeping to its budget?

- Do the resources have the appropriate amount of work?

If you get the wrong answers to any of these questions, you need to adjust your project plan until you get the right answers. For example, if the finish date is too far away, you can add more resources to major tasks.

After you make such adjustments, you need to check the project plan again. Adding resources to tasks might bring in the finish date, but it also might add cost if you have to hire additional resources or authorize overtime. And if you assign more tasks to existing resources, those resources might be overallocated.

To save time as well as money, you might decide to cut certain tasks, a deliverable, or a phase. But if this means you're cutting project scope, you probably need to get approval from your managing stakeholders.

This relationship between time, money, and scope is sometimes referred to as the project triangle (see Figure 9-1). Changing one side of the triangle affects at least one of the other sides of the triangle.

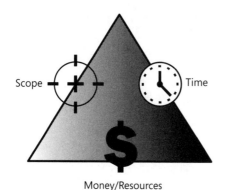

Figure 9-1 Managing your project requires balancing time, money, and scope.

You need to know which side of the triangle is your largest priority. Is it schedule—you definitely have to finish by October 26? Is it budget—there is absolutely $264,300 for this project, and not a penny more? Is it scope—it is imperative that each and every task in your project plan be implemented? Only one side of the triangle can be "absolute." The other two sides must be flexible so you can adjust the project plan to hit that one absolute.

Depending on which side of your project triangle is your absolute, you might adjust your project plan to do one of the following:

- Bring in the project finish date

- Reduce project costs

- Cut project scope

Although not strictly a part of your project triangle, it's likely that you also will check resource workloads. Resources are the biggest part of your project costs. If any resources are overallocated, you might be facing more overtime than your budget will allow. If resources are grossly overallocated, you run the risk that the tasks won't be done on time and the entire project will slip. If any resources are underallocated, you might be paying more for resources than you should, which also affects your budget.

After you make your adjustments and balance your project triangle to meet the project requirements, you'll be ready for stakeholder buyoff. After you have buyoff, you'll be ready to start the execution phase of the project.

Sources of your Scope, Finish Date, and Budget

Your project scope, finish date, and budget can be imposed on you for various reasons, depending on the type of project and the specific situation. The following are a few examples:

- You are a seller or potential subcontractor bidding on a project whose scope has been defined in the Request for Proposal (RFP). You need to provide the full scope, but your costs and finish date must be competitive with other bidders. If possible, you'll want to include value-added items to give your proposal an advantage while still making a good profit.

- You are a subcontractor and you have been awarded the contract based on a proposal including broad assumptions of scope, finish date, and cost. Having taken this risk, now you must create a detailed project plan that will actually implement that finish date, cost, and scope.

- You've been assigned as project manager of a project within your company. The scope, budget, or finish date have been handed down as one or more of the project assumptions. Your success is predicated upon your ability to implement the project within those limitations.

- You've been assigned as project manager of a project within your company. You and other stakeholders developed the scope to a fair level of detail. It's up to you to propose the budget and finish date for the project.

- You are the project manager, and you've balanced your project triangle the way you believe is best. However, after you submitted the project plan for client review, certain new project requirements or limitations surfaced. You have to readjust the project triangle to take the new limitations or requirements into account.

Working with the Critical Path and Critical Tasks

Most projects have multiple sets of tasks, which have task relationships with one another, taking place at any one time. In an office move project, for example, the facilities manager and her team might be researching new office sites and then working out the lease terms. At the same time, the office manager and his team might be ordering new office furniture and equipment and then arranging for movers. These two sets of activities are not dependent on each other and use different sets of resources. Therefore, they can be scheduled on parallel tracks (see Figure 9-2). The project can have any number of sets of tasks on these parallel tracks, or paths, depending on the size and complexity of the project, as well as the number of resources involved.

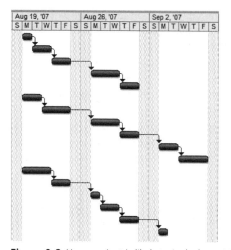

Figure 9-2 Your project is likely to include series of tasks on multiple parallel paths.

At any time, one task has the latest finish date in the project. This task, along with its predecessors, dictates the finish date of the project as a whole. The finish date of this path is critical to the finish date of the project itself; therefore, we call it the critical path. In turn, the tasks that make up each step along the critical path are called the critical tasks (see Figure 9-3). Because the critical path dictates the finish date of the project, we pay a tremendous amount of attention to it in project management.

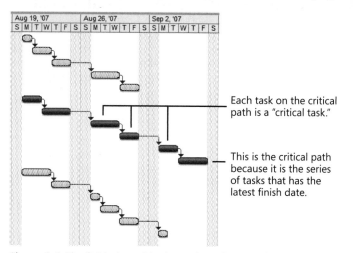

Each task on the critical path is a "critical task."

This is the critical path because it is the series of tasks that has the latest finish date.

Figure 9-3 The finish date of the last task on the critical path dictates the finish date of the entire project.

> **Note**
>
> The term *critical task* refers only to tasks that are on the critical path. These terms reflect the scheduling of the tasks, not their relative importance. There can be very important tasks that don't happen to be on the critical path.

In the planning phase, you identify a particular critical path. After you begin the execution phase and actual progress begins to be reported, the critical path might change from one set of linked tasks to another. For example, task progress is likely to differ in various ways from the original schedule. Perhaps one task in the critical path finishes early, but a task in a second path is delayed. In this case, the second path might become the critical path if that is now the path with the latest finish date in the project.

If you need to bring in the finish date, one of the most effective things you can do is focus on the critical path. If you can make critical tasks along that path finish sooner, you can make the project itself finish sooner.

For more information about strategies to bring in a project's finish date, see the section titled "Bringing In the Project Finish Date" later in this chapter.

Understanding Slack Time and Critical Tasks

Many tasks have some amount of scheduling buffer—an amount of time that a task can slip before it causes a delay in the schedule. This scheduling buffer is called **slack**, or **float**. The following describes the two types of slack:

- **Free slack** is the amount of time a task can slip before it delays another task, typically its successor task.

- **Total slack** is the amount of time a task can slip before it delays the project finish date (see Figure 9-4).

This task has 3 days of free slack—it can slip 3 days before delaying its successor task

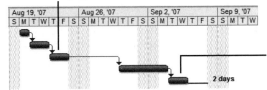

This task has 2 days of total slack—it can slip 2 days before delaying the project finish date.

Figure 9-4 Free slack and total slack show the amount of time a task can slip before it causes a scheduling problem.

Because critical tasks cannot slip without delaying the project finish date, critical tasks have no slack, and tasks with no slack are critical.

If a noncritical task consumes its slack time, it usually causes its successor to use some or all of its total slack time. The previously noncritical task becomes a critical task and causes its successor tasks to become critical as well.

Negative Slack Situations

Sometimes you run into a situation in which you have negative slack; that is, the opposite of slack time. Negative slack can occur in a task with a finish-to-start task dependency when a successor task is due to begin before the predecessor is finished. This can happen when the task duration of a predecessor task conflicts with a successor task that must begin on a date specified by an assigned constraint, for example (see Figure 9-5).

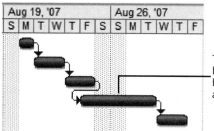

This task has negative slack because of a conflict between its predecessor and its date constraint.

Figure 9-5 In this example, the indicated task has negative slack because although it has a finish-to-start task dependency, its successor is scheduled to begin before the task is finished. As a result, all the task's predecessors also have negative slack.

Negative slack is a problem because it has tasks bunching up on each other, essentially indicating that to maintain the schedule, a task needs to start before it should. That is, the task has to be scheduled to start before the conditions of its task dependencies are fulfilled.

Maybe you don't want just those tasks with total slack of 0 to be critical. For example, perhaps you want your critical tasks to be those that still have 1 day of slack. In this case, you can change the definition of a critical task. To do this:

1. Click Tools, Options and then click the Calculation tab.

2. Near the bottom of the tab, enter your preference for a critical task in the Tasks Are Critical If Slack Is Less Than Or Equal To box (see Figure 9-6).

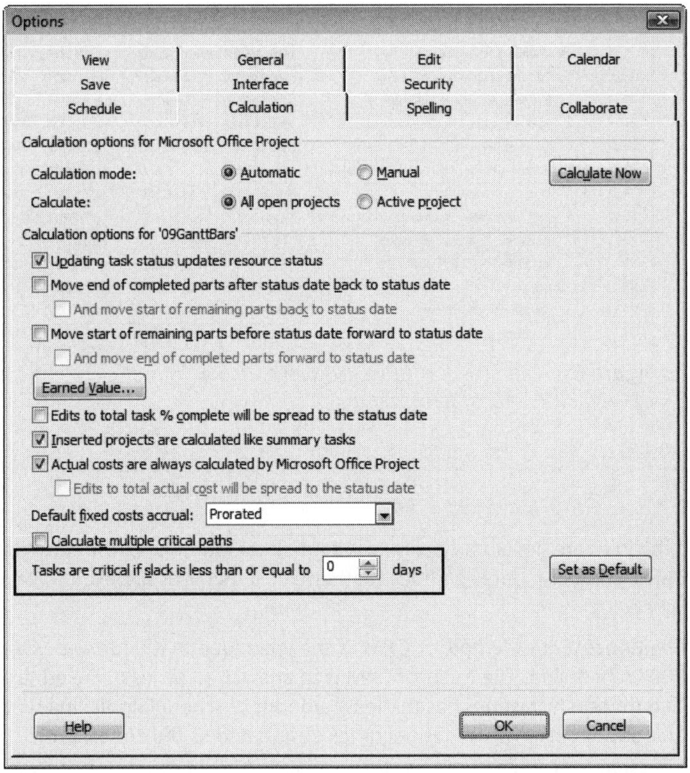

Figure 9-6 Specify the amount of slack that you want to define a critical task in your project plan.

To see how much free slack and total slack each task has, you can apply the Schedule table to a task sheet, as follows:

1. Click View, Gantt Chart. Or display any other task sheet you want.

2. Click View, Table, Schedule.

The Schedule table is applied (see Figure 9-7). You might need to drag the vertical divider to the right to see some of the columns in this table.

	Task Name	Start	Finish	Late Start	Late Finish	Free Slack	Total Slack
18	⊟ **Hardware and Software**	**Mon 3/5/07**	**Wed 7/25/07**	**Tue 4/10/07**	**Thu 8/30/07**	**26 days**	**26 days**
19	Perform system needs analysis	Mon 3/5/07	Thu 3/15/07	Tue 4/10/07	Fri 4/20/07	0 days	26 days
20	Evaluate equipment requirements	Fri 3/16/07	Tue 4/3/07	Mon 4/23/07	Wed 5/9/07	0 days	26 days
21	Evaluate software requirements	Wed 4/4/07	Tue 4/24/07	Thu 5/10/07	Wed 5/30/07	0 days	26 days
22	Order equipment	Wed 4/25/07	Fri 4/27/07	Thu 5/31/07	Mon 6/4/07	0 days	26 days
23	Equipment order processing and delivery	Fri 4/27/07	Fri 6/8/07	Tue 6/5/07	Tue 7/17/07	0.38 ewks	5.52 ewks
24	Order software	Mon 6/11/07	Wed 6/13/07	Tue 7/17/07	Thu 7/19/07	0 days	26 days
25	Software order processing and delivery	Wed 6/13/07	Wed 7/11/07	Fri 7/20/07	Fri 8/17/07	0.09 ewks	5.23 ewks
26	Install and configure equipment	Thu 7/12/07	Wed 7/18/07	Fri 8/17/07	Thu 8/23/07	0 days	26 days
27	Install and configure software	Thu 7/19/07	Wed 7/25/07	Fri 8/24/07	Thu 8/30/07	26 days	26 days
28	⊟ **Content**	**Tue 5/1/07**	**Thu 8/9/07**	**Tue 5/1/07**	**Thu 8/9/07**	**0 days**	**0 days**
29	Assign content owners	Tue 5/1/07	Thu 5/3/07	Tue 5/1/07	Thu 5/3/07	0 days	0 days
30	Develop content	Fri 5/4/07	Thu 6/14/07	Fri 5/4/07	Thu 6/14/07	0 days	0 days

Figure 9-7 The Schedule table shows the amount of free slack and total slack, as well as late start and late finish dates.

Critical Path Method (CPM)

Schedules are developed from task sequences, durations, resource requirements, start dates, and finish dates. Various mathematical methods are used to calculate project schedules.

The *Critical Path Method*, or *CPM*, is the technique that underlies Microsoft Office Project 2007 scheduling. The focus of CPM is to analyze all series of linked tasks in a project and determine which series has the least amount of scheduling flexibility; that is, the least amount of slack. This series becomes designated as the critical path.

Four date values are part of the slack calculation for each task:

- Early start
- Early finish
- Late start
- Late finish

The difference between the late start and early start dates is compared, as is the difference between late finish and early finish. The smaller of the two differences becomes the value for total slack.

Viewing the Critical Path

The easiest way to see the critical path in a Gantt chart is to click View, Tracking Gantt. The Tracking Gantt highlights the critical path in red in the chart portion of the view (see Figure 9-8). The Entry table is applied by default to the Tracking Gantt, just as in the regular Gantt Chart.

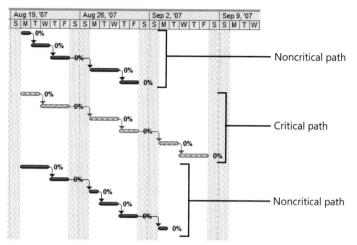

Figure 9-8 The Tracking Gantt highlights the critical path.

> **Note**
>
> When you first open a Gantt chart, the timescale is at today's date. If the tasks you're reviewing are in the past or future, you might not see the Gantt bars in the chart. Click a task whose Gantt bar you want to see. On the Standard toolbar, click Go To Selected Task.

Go To Selected Task

You can also use the Gantt Chart Wizard, which formats the chart portion of any Gantt Chart view to highlight the critical path. To do this, follow these steps:

1. Click View, Gantt Chart.

   If you want to modify another Gantt chart view, such as the Leveling Gantt or Tracking Gantt, display that view instead.

2. On the Formatting toolbar, click Gantt Chart Wizard.

   Gantt Chart Wizard

3. On the first page of the Gantt Chart Wizard, click Next.

4. On the second page, select the Critical Path option (see Figure 9-9). Then click Next.

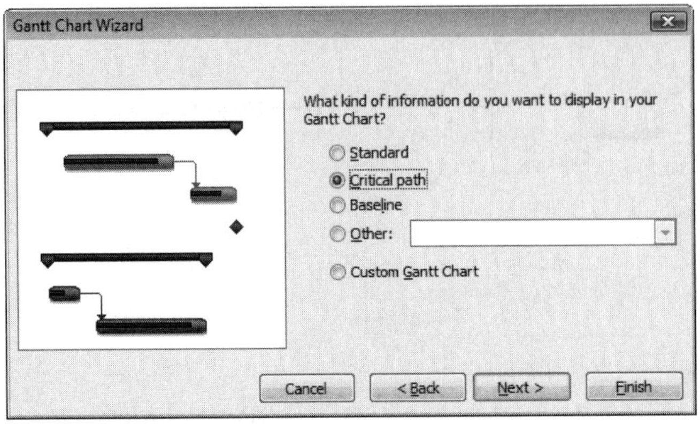

Figure 9-9 To highlight the critical path Gantt bars, select the Critical Path option.

5. On the third page, select the option for any text you want to accompany the Gantt bars, such as resource names, dates, and so on. Click Next.

6. On the fourth page, select whether you want the link lines for task dependencies to show. Click Next.

7. On the final page, click the Format It button.

    Office Project 2007 formats your Gantt chart according to your specifications.

8. Click the Exit Wizard button to view your new Gantt chart format, which displays red Gantt bars for critical tasks.

INSIDE OUT   Alternatives to the Gantt Chart Wizard

The Gantt Chart Wizard is convenient for quickly changing the Gantt bar format of certain types of tasks. However, if you use the wizard to do your formatting, you might lose certain standard Gantt bar formatting that you want to preserve. For example, the Deadline bar style is lost.

If you want to see only critical tasks in a Gantt chart view, switch to the Detail Gantt or the Tracking Gantt.

If you want to highlight critical tasks in the Gantt Chart, customize the bar styles using Format, Bar Styles.

For more information, see the section titled "Formatting a Gantt Chart View" in Chapter 25, "Customizing Your View of Project Information."

Although displaying the Detail Gantt or using the Gantt Chart Wizard can display the Gantt bars for the critical path at a glance, you can also look at the details for individual critical tasks. The following list details different methods for viewing critical tasks:

- **Display the Detail Gantt.** Click View, More Views, Detail Gantt. This view shows the critical path tasks in red Gantt bars (see Figure 9-10). By default, the Delay table is applied to the sheet portion of the view.

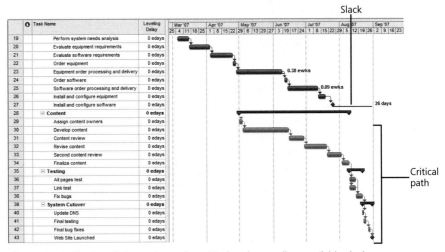

Figure 9-10 The Detail Gantt shows the critical path as well as available slack.

- **Review the Critical Tasks report.** Click Report, Reports. Double-click Overview and then double-click Critical Tasks.

- **Generate the Critical Tasks Status Report.** Click Report, Visual Reports. Click the Task Summary tab and then double-click either Critical Tasks Status Report (Metric) or Critical Tasks Status Report (US). Microsoft Office Visio 2007 opens to show the project's critical tasks in an Office Visio PivotDiagram (see Figure 9-11).

Chapter 9

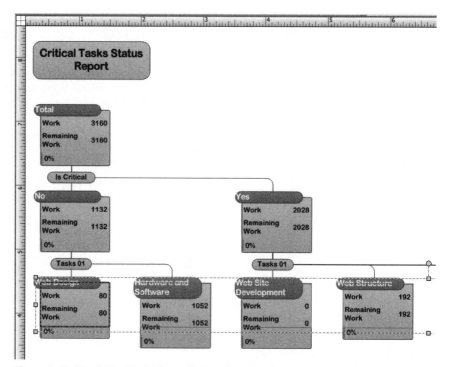

Figure 9-11 The Critical Tasks Status Report diagrams the project's critical tasks in Visio.

- **Group tasks by critical and noncritical tasks.** Click Project, Group By, Critical. Tasks are grouped by whether they are critical or noncritical (see Figure 9-12). To return tasks to their original order, click Project, Group By, No Group. You can also use the Group By tool on the Standard toolbar.

	ⓘ	Task Name	Duration	Start	Finish
		⊟ **Critical: No**	**103 days**	**Mon 3/5/07**	**Wed 7/25/07**
15		Design Home page	3 days	Tue 5/1/07	Thu 5/3/07
16		Home page design review	4 days	Fri 5/4/07	Wed 5/9/07
17		Finalize Home page design	3 days	Thu 5/10/07	Mon 5/14/07
19		Perform system needs analysis	9 days	Mon 3/5/07	Thu 3/15/07
20		Evaluate equipment requirements	13 days	Fri 3/16/07	Tue 4/3/07
21		Evaluate software requirements	15 days	Wed 4/4/07	Tue 4/24/07
22		Order equipment	3 days	Wed 4/25/07	Fri 4/27/07
23		Equipment order processing and delivery	6 ewks	Fri 4/27/07	Fri 6/8/07
24		Order software	3 days	Mon 6/11/07	Wed 6/13/07
25		Software order processing and delivery	4 ewks	Wed 6/13/07	Wed 7/11/07
26		Install and configure equipment	5 days	Thu 7/12/07	Wed 7/18/07
27		Install and configure software	5 days	Thu 7/19/07	Wed 7/25/07
		⊟ **Critical: Yes**	**129 days**	**Mon 3/5/07**	**Thu 8/30/07**
2		Brainstorm content categories	3 days	Mon 3/5/07	Wed 3/7/07
3		Hold user meetings	5 days	Thu 3/8/07	Wed 3/14/07
4		Develop Web structure	3 days	Thu 3/15/07	Mon 3/19/07
5		Web structure review	4 days	Tue 3/20/07	Fri 3/23/07
6		Finalize Web structure	2 days	Mon 3/26/07	Tue 3/27/07
9		Design interior pages	8 days	Wed 3/28/07	Fri 4/6/07
10		Interior page design review	5 days	Mon 4/9/07	Fri 4/13/07
11		Finalize interior page design	4 days	Mon 4/16/07	Thu 4/19/07

Figure 9-12 Use the Critical grouping to group critical tasks together and noncritical tasks together.

- **Filter for critical tasks.** Click Project, Filtered For, Critical. Only critical tasks are shown. To show all tasks again, click Project, Filtered For, All Tasks. You can also use the Filter tool on the Formatting toolbar.

- **Use the Project Guide.** On the Project Guide toolbar, click Report. Click the See The Project's Critical Tasks link. The view changes to a Critical Tasks Gantt generated by the Project Guide. Additional information is provided in the Project Guide task pane.

Work with Multiple Critical Paths

By default, you have one path through your project that constitutes your critical path. That one critical path constitutes the series of tasks whose end date is closest to affecting the end date of the project. When the last task is completed, the project is completed.

However, you can display multiple critical paths if you like. Although they might finish earlier than the one "real" critical path, each critical path can show the different networks of tasks throughout your project, for example, for different phases or parallel efforts. To do this, follow these steps:

1. Click Tools, Options and then click the Calculation tab.
2. Select the Calculate Multiple Critical Paths check box.

To create multiple critical paths, Microsoft Project changes the calculation of the critical path so that any task without a successor (that is, the last task in any series of linked tasks) becomes a critical task. The task's late finish date is set to be the same as its early finish date. This setting gives the task 0 slack, which in turn makes it a critical task. Any series of predecessors before this final task becomes a critical path, thereby providing multiple critical paths.

This calculation contrasts with that of a single critical path, in which a task without a successor has its late finish date set to the project finish date. This gives the task slack and therefore makes it a noncritical task.

Bringing in the Project Finish Date

A *time-constrained project* is one in which the project finish date is the most important factor in your project plan. Although you still need to balance budget constraints and satisfy the project scope, the finish date reigns supreme as the primary priority.

If your project plan calculates that your finish date will go beyond your all-important target finish date, focus on the critical path. Shorten the critical path and you bring in the finish date.

INSIDE OUT   Save an interim plan before making changes

Consider saving an interim plan before making changes that affect your project finish date. An interim plan saves a snapshot of the start and finish dates for all your tasks. After you've made some of the changes suggested in this section, you can add these interim start and finish fields as Gantt bars in your Gantt Chart to see the effects of your changes.

For more information about interim plans, see the section titled "Saving Additional Schedule Start and Finish Dates" in Chapter 10, "Setting a Baseline and Updating Progress." For information about creating custom Gantt bars, see the section titled "Formatting the Appearance of Gantt Bars" in Chapter 25.

Viewing Finish Dates and the Critical Path

Before you analyze the critical path, you just need to see your bottom line: What's the project finish date? Follow these steps:

1. Click Project, Project Information.

2. In the Project Information dialog box, click the Statistics button.

The Project Statistics dialog box appears. The current, or scheduled, finish date appears in the Finish column (see Figure 9-13).

Project Statistics for '09Web'

	Start		Finish	
Current		Mon 3/5/07		Thu 8/30/07
Baseline		NA		NA
Actual		NA		NA
Variance		0d		0d

	Duration	Work	Cost
Current	129d	3,160h	$198,502.00
Baseline	0d?	0h	$0.00
Actual	0d	0h	$0.00
Remaining	129d	3,160h	$198,502.00

Percent complete:
Duration: 0%   Work: 0%   Close

Figure 9-13 The Project Statistics dialog box shows overall project information: project start date, project finish date, total duration, total work, and total cost.

Another way to keep your eye on the project finish date at all times is to add the project summary task row to your project plan, as follows:

1. Click Tools, Options and then click the View tab.

2. Select the Show Project Summary Task check box.

The project summary task appears at the top of any task sheet view, including the Gantt Chart (see Figure 9-14). Task information is rolled up for the entire project and its summary total is displayed in the project summary row. Specifically, the Finish field in the project summary row shows the latest finish date in the project.

	ⓘ	Task Name	Duration	Start	Finish
0		⊟ **Web Site Development**	**129 days**	**Mon 3/5/07**	**Thu 8/30/07**
1		⊟ **Web Structure**	**17 days**	**Mon 3/5/07**	**Tue 3/27/07**
2		Brainstorm content categories	3 days	Mon 3/5/07	Wed 3/7/07
3	📖	Hold user meetings	5 days	Thu 3/8/07	Wed 3/14/07
4		Develop Web structure	3 days	Thu 3/15/07	Mon 3/19/07
5		Web structure review	4 days	Tue 3/20/07	Fri 3/23/07
6		Finalize Web structure	2 days	Mon 3/26/07	Tue 3/27/07
7		⊟ **Web Design**	**34 days**	**Wed 3/28/07**	**Mon 5/14/07**
8		⊟ **Interior Pages**	**24 days**	**Wed 3/28/07**	**Mon 4/30/07**
9		Design interior pages	8 days	Wed 3/28/07	Fri 4/6/07

Figure 9-14 The Project Summary row rolls up task information to display the totals for the entire project.

To see the critical path, click View, Tracking Gantt. By viewing the finish date or the critical path, you can easily see whether you're hitting your target finish date. If you need to bring in the finish date, you might want to focus on the critical tasks. You can filter your task sheet to show only critical tasks by clicking Project, Filtered For, Critical. To show all tasks again, click Project, Filtered For, All Tasks.

For more information about viewing the critical path, see the section titled "Viewing the Critical Path" earlier in this chapter.

What if You Have More Time Than Needed?

You reviewed your finish date and got a happy surprise—you have more time available than your schedule says you need. What to do? It depends, of course, on the type of project, the situation, and the amount of surplus time. You can:

- Use the extra time as buffer against potential risks.

- Add scope. Add tasks you were hoping to include, but thought you wouldn't have sufficienttime. Build in a higher level of quality. Increase quantities being produced, if applicable to your project.

- Use the extra time to save money. For example, you might be able to hire two designers instead of three and have those two designers carry out the design tasks in the longer amount of time that's available.

- Inform your manager or client that you can complete the project sooner than expected.

Checking Your Schedule Assumptions

If you've determined that you need to bring in the finish date, look first at the schedule itself. Make sure that all the scheduling controls you put into place are accurate and required. The fewer controls you impose, the more flexibility Microsoft Project can have with scheduling, and that added flexibility can give you an earlier finish date. In the Gantt Chart or other task sheet, review and update the following:

- Date constraints

- Task dependencies

- Durations

- Task calendars

You can look at all tasks in the project, but to affect the finish date, you need only make adjustments to critical tasks. If you shorten the sequence of critical path tasks to the point at which a different sequence is now the critical path, check to see if that path finishes before your target finish date. If it does, switch your focus to that new critical path until you achieve the planned project finish date you need.

In fact, as you make adjustments to tasks and enter actual progress information for tasks, the critical path is likely to change several times throughout the span of the project. Keep a close eye on the critical path as part of your monitoring activities. It's a good idea to apply the Schedule table or show the Total Slack and Free Slack fields in your favorite everyday table. This way you can see how close tasks are to becoming critical.

> **Note**
>
> If you change aspects of your schedule to bring in the finish date, the good news is that you probably won't adversely affect your project triangle. That is, adjusting your schedule to meet your schedule requirements affects only the schedule side of the triangle. Costs and scope will probably stay as they are.

Checking and Adjusting Date Constraints

First, look at any date constraints you've set in your schedule, particularly for your critical tasks. This is where you can potentially make a significant impact on your finish date. To look at the constraints you've applied, follow these steps:

1. Display the Gantt Chart or other task sheet.

2. Click View, Table, More Tables.

3. In the More Tables dialog box, click Constraint Dates and then click Apply.

   The table shows the constraint type and constraint dates for all tasks.

If you have the tasks sorted by Task ID—that is, in their outline sequence—you can review constraints for each task within the context of its surrounding tasks. If you like, you can sort the tasks by constraint type, as follows:

1. Apply the Constraint Dates table to the Gantt Chart or other task sheet.

2. Click Project, Sort, Sort By.

3. In the Sort By dialog box, click Constraint Type and then click Sort.

   The tasks are sorted by constraint type, so you can see where you might have applied a Must Finish On or Start No Later Than constraint, for example. You can also see their associated dates.

To see only the constraints for critical tasks, follow these steps:

1. Apply the Constraint Dates table to the Gantt Chart or other task sheet.

2. Click Project, Filtered For, Critical.

   Only critical tasks are shown. When you want to see all tasks again, click Project, Filtered For, All Tasks.

Make sure that the constraint types and dates you have applied are truly necessary. Wherever you can, change a date constraint to a flexible one such as As Soon As Possible or As Late As Possible. Even changing an inflexible date constraint such as Must Start On or Must Finish On to a moderately flexible date constraint such as Start No Later Than or Finish No Earlier Than can improve your schedule. To change the constraint, do the following:

Chapter 9

1. Apply the Constraint Dates table to the Gantt Chart or other task sheet.

2. Click the Constraint Type field, click the arrow, and then click the constraint you want in the list.

Task Information

Change All Constraints at One Time

Maybe you applied too many date constraints to too many tasks and you just want to start fresh. Select all tasks in the project, either by dragging them or by clicking the Select All box just above the row 1 heading in the upper-left corner of the table. On the Standard toolbar, click Task Information and then click the Advanced tab. In the Constraint Type box, click As Soon As Possible or As Late As Possible. The constraints on all selected tasks are changed.

For more information about constraints, see the section titled "Scheduling Tasks to Achieve Specific Dates" in Chapter 5, "Scheduling Tasks."

Note

New to Microsoft Office Project 2007 is *change highlighting*. When you make a change that causes other fields to be recalculated, the changed cells are temporarily filled with a background color so you can see the ripple effects of the change you've just made. The highlighting remains in effect only until you make the next edit that causes a recalculation, or when you save the project.

Checking and Adjusting Task Dependencies

The second place to check your schedule for critical path–shortening opportunities is your task dependencies. Gantt Chart is the best view for reviewing task dependencies and their impact on your schedule. To see critical tasks highlighted, view the Tracking Gantt or Detail Gantt. Focusing on the task dependencies of critical tasks helps you bring in the finish date.

Specifically, examine whether the task dependencies are required. If two tasks don't really depend on each other, remove the link. Or consider whether two tasks can begin at the same time. If so, you can change a finish-to-start dependency to a start-to-start dependency. Change a task dependency as follows:

1. Click the successor task.

2. On the Standard toolbar, click Task Information and click the Predecessors tab.

3. To change the link type, click in the Type field for the predecessor.

4. Click the arrow and then click the link type you want in the list.

To remove the link entirely, click anywhere in the predecessor row and press the Delete key.

Unlink Tasks

Remove All Links

If you want to start over with your task dependency strategy, you can remove all links in the project. Be sure that this is really what you want to do because it can erase a lot of the work you've done in your project plan. A safe thing to do is make a backup copy of your project before you remove all the links...just in case.

Click the Select All box just above the row 1 heading in the upper-left corner of the table. On the Standard toolbar, click Unlink Tasks. All links on all tasks are removed.

For more information about task dependencies, see the section titled "Establishing Task Dependencies" in Chapter 5.

Checking and Adjusting Durations

After adjusting date constraints and task dependencies, if the finish date is still beyond your target, look at task durations. However, be aware that it's risky to be too optimistic about durations, especially if you used reliable methods such as expert judgment, past project information, industry metrics, or program evaluation and review technique (PERT) analysis to calculate your current durations.

You can look at durations in the Gantt Chart or most task sheets. If your tasks are sorted by Task ID (that is, in their outline sequence), you can review durations for each task within the context of its surrounding tasks. However, you can also sort tasks by duration so you can see the longer durations first. These longer durations might have more buffer built in, so they might be a good place to trim some time. To sort tasks by duration, follow these steps:

1. Display the Gantt Chart with the Entry table applied, or display another task sheet that includes the Duration field.

2. Click Project, Sort, Sort By.

    The Sort dialog box appears.

3. In the Sort By list, click Duration and then click Sort.

    The tasks are sorted by duration.

4. To see only the durations for critical tasks, click Project, Filtered For, Critical.

    When you want to see all tasks again, click Project, Filtered For, All Tasks.

5. To change a duration, simply type the new duration into the task's Duration field.

    The schedule is recalculated with the new duration.

6. To return to the original task order, click Project, Sort, By ID.

For more information about duration, see the section titled "Setting Task Durations" in Chapter 5.

Undo

In Microsoft Office Project 2007, you can now undo multiple edits. To undo recent edits, click Undo on the Standard toolbar. Each time you click Undo, the previous edit is undone. You can also click Edit, Undo, or press Ctrl+Z to reverse the last edit. The series of operations you can undo goes back to the last time you saved your project.

> **Note**
>
> To redo an edit that you've undone, click Redo on the Standard toolbar. You can also click Edit, Redo, or press Ctrl+Y to redo undone edits.

> **Project Management Practices: Duration Compression**
>
> In project management, there are two commonly used methods of shortening a series of tasks without changing the project scope. These two *duration compression* methods are as follows:
>
> - **Crashing the schedule** The schedule and associated project costs are analyzed to determine how a series of tasks (such as the critical path) can be shortened, or *crashed*, for the least additional cost.
>
> - **Fast tracking** Tasks normally done in sequence are rescheduled to be done simultaneously (for example, starting to build a prototype before the specifications are approved).
>
> By their nature, both of these methods are risky. It's important to be aware that these methods can increase cost or increase task rework.

Checking Task Drivers

Along with durations, dependencies, and constraints, a number of other factors determine the schedule of any given task. A new tool available in Project 2007 is the Task Drivers pane. The Task Drivers pane lists the specific factors responsible for setting the start date of the selected task, for example, the project calendar, a predecessor task, or a constraint date.

To show the Task Drivers pane, follow these steps:

1. Open a task view, such as Gantt Chart or Network Diagram.

2. Select the task whose task drivers you want to review.

3. On the Standard toolbar, click Task Drivers.

Task Drivers

The Task Drivers pane appears. You can click the name of a predecessor task to go to that task in the view and to see the task drivers for that task. You can click the name of a calendar listed in the Task Drivers pane to open that calendar in the Change Working Time dialog box.

4. Keep the Task Drivers pane open while you click different tasks and review their task drivers. When you're finished with the Task Drivers pane, click the X in the upper-right corner of the pane to close it.

> **Note**
>
> If you use task calendars in your schedule, examine the tasks and the task calendars to make sure they're accurately reflecting reality and not holding upprogress. Tasks with task calendars assigned display a calendar icon in the Indicators column next to the task name. Place the mouse pointer over the icon to see more information.
>
> **For more information about task calendars, see the section titled "Working with Task Calendars" in Chapter 5.**

Chapter 9

Adjusting Resource Settings to Bring in the Finish Date

Another way to bring in the finish date is to adjust your resource settings. You can check that the resource availability affecting assigned task scheduling is accurate. You can also add resources to tasks to decrease task duration. Be aware that increasing resource availability as well as adding resources to tasks usually means an increase in costs.

Checking and Adjusting Resource Availability

The more availability your resources have, the sooner their assigned tasks can be completed. For example, a 4-day task assigned to a resource who works a regular 5-day week will be completed in 4 days. The same 4-day task assigned to a resource who works a 2-day week will be completed in 2 weeks. For resources assigned to critical tasks, review and update the following:

- Resource calendars

- Maximum (resource) units

- Assignment units

The Task Entry view is best for checking these three items. Apply the view, set the Task Form to show the resource information you need, and filter for critical tasks, as follows:

1. Click View, More Views.

2. In the More Views dialog box, click Task Entry and then click Apply.

3. To view critical tasks, click in the Gantt Chart (upper) portion of the view. Click Project, Filtered For, Critical.

Only critical tasks are displayed. You can also click View, Tracking Gantt. Critical tasks are shown in red.

4. Click in the Task Form (lower) portion of the view. Click Format, Details, Resource Work. The Task Form changes to show availability information (see Figure 9-15).

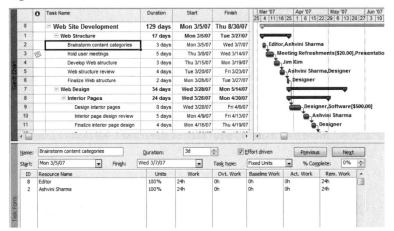

Figure 9-15 The Task Entry view is now set up to check resource and assignment availability.

5. Click a critical task in the Gantt Chart portion of the view.

The resources assigned to the selected task are listed in the Task Form portion of the view.

6. To check the resource calendar for this assigned resource, double-click the resource name. The Resource Information dialog box appears. On the General tab, click the Change Working Time button. Check the working times set for this resource and make sure they're correct. When finished, close the Change Working Time dialog box.

> For more information about resource calendars, see the section titled "Setting Working Times and Days Off for Work Resources" in Chapter 6, "Setting Up Resources in the Project."

7. To check resource units, return to the General tab in the Resource Information dialog box. Under Resource Availability, check the resource units and associated dates, if applicable, and make sure they're correct. Make any necessary changes and then click OK.

> For more information about resource units, see the section titled "Specifying Resource Availability with Max Units" in Chapter 6.

8. To check assignment units, review the Units field next to the resource name in the Task Form and make sure the setting is correct.

9. To switch the Task Entry combination view to a single-pane view of the Gantt Chart, click Window, Remove Split. To show all tasks again, click the Filter tool on the Formatting toolbar and then click All Tasks.

> **Note**
>
> You can check your resources' working time calendar, their resource units, and their assignment units—and everything might look correct. A great technique is to scan your project for any assignment units of less than 100%. Find out if the assigned resources can provide any more time on these tasks, especially the critical tasks, to help bring in the finish date. It doesn't hurt to ask, at least.

Adding Resources to Decrease Duration

A key method of shortening the critical path and bringing in the project finish date is to add resources to critical tasks in such a way as to decrease the task's duration. For example, two people working together might be able to complete a development task in half the time it takes either of them individually. For this to be the case, the tasks must be either fixed-units and effort-driven tasks or fixed-work tasks. Obviously, they cannot be fixed-duration tasks.

With fixed-units effort-driven scheduling, which is the default, when you assign an additional resource to a task that already has assigned resources, the amount of work scheduled for each assigned resource decreases. Likewise, when you remove a resource from an effort-driven task, the amount of work scheduled for each assigned resource increases.

The same is true for fixed-work tasks, which are effort-driven by definition. When you add or remove resources (that is, assignment units) on a fixed-work task, duration changes but work remains fixed, of course.

For more information about effort-driven scheduling, see the section titled "Controlling Changes with Effort-Driven Scheduling" in Chapter 7, "Assigning Resources to Tasks." For more information about task types, see the section titled "Controlling Schedule Changes with Task Types" in Chapter 7.

To check the task type of an individual task, follow these steps:

1. In a task sheet, such as the Gantt Chart, double-click the task.

2. In the Task Information dialog box, click the Advanced tab.

3. Review the Task Type list and the Effort Driven check box. Make any necessary changes.

Chapter 9

You can add the task type and effort-driven fields to a task sheet so you can see the scheduling methods for all tasks at a glance, as follows:

1. Display the task sheet to which you want to add the new columns.

2. Click the column heading to the right of where you want the new column to be inserted.

3. Click Insert, Column.

4. In the Field Name box, select Type.

   You can type **ty** to move quickly to the Type field in the list.

5. Click OK, and the task types are shown in the task sheet.

   You can use this Type field to quickly change task types.

6. Follow steps 1–5 to add the Effort Driven field to the task sheet.

   This field displays Yes or No, indicating whether the task is effort-driven.

When you assign additional resources to your fixed-units and effort-driven or fixed-work critical tasks, the duration of those critical tasks is reduced, and therefore the length of the critical path is reduced.

> **Note**
>
> Be aware that as you add resources to critical tasks, you run the risk of reduced productivity. Additional overhead might be associated with bringing on additional resources. More support might be needed to get those resources up to speed on the tasks, and you might lose whatever time savings you thought you might gain. Take care to add resources who are experienced enough to hit the ground running so your efforts don't backfire on you.

> **Project Management Practices: The Right Resources for Critical Tasks**
>
> Having overallocated resources assigned to critical tasks can push out your finish date. If you level overallocated resources, their assignments are rescheduled to times when they can perform them. Even if you do not level overallocated resources, and even if your schedule shows that there's no slip, this doesn't mean it will not happen. An overallocated resource has to let something slip. By leveling, you can see realistically when tasks can be done and make the necessary adjustments to make sure critical tasks are not late.
>
> As much as possible, shift assignments to evenly distribute the resource workload and to ensure that resources working on critical tasks are not overallocated.
>
> For more information about leveling, see the section titled "Leveling Assignments" later in this chapter.

If you have an overallocated resource assigned to critical tasks and an underallocated resource with the right skills and availability, you can switch to or add the underallocated resources to the critical tasks to shorten their durations.

Also, check that the fastest and more experienced resources are assigned to the longer or more difficult critical tasks. Although adjusting assignments might or might not actually reduce the duration, it significantly reduces the risk of critical tasks needing rework or being otherwise delayed.

You can also adjust scope to bring in the finish date. For more information about cutting scope, see the section titled "Changing Project Scope" later in this chapter.

Reducing Project Costs

A budget-constrained project is one in which costs are the most important factor in the project plan. Although you still need to balance schedule requirements and satisfy the project scope, in such a project the costs are at the forefront of your decision-making processes as you plan and execute the project.

If your project plan calculates that your total costs are above the allowed budget, you need cost-cutting strategies. Your best approach will involve cutting resources because resources and costs are virtually synonymous in projects. As described in the previous section, when you want to bring in the finish date, you focus on tasks in the critical path. In the same way, when you want to cut costs, you focus on resources to gain the biggest cost savings.

Viewing Project Costs

Review your cost picture first, compare it with your budget, and then make any necessary adjustments.

Reviewing Total Cost Using Project Statistics

To review total project costs using Project Statistics, do the following:

1. Click Project, Project Information.

2. In the Project Information dialog box, click the Statistics button.

   The Project Statistics dialog box appears. The current or scheduled total project cost appears in the Cost column.

Reviewing Costs with the Cost Table

You can review costs for tasks and summary tasks when you apply the Cost table to a task sheet. If you show the project summary task to a sheet with the Cost table applied, you can see the total project cost as well. To apply and analyze costs in the Cost table, follow these steps:

Chapter 9

1. Display the Gantt Chart or other task sheet.

2. Click View, Table, Cost. The Cost table is applied.

3. Click Tools, Options and then click the View tab.

4. Under Outline Options, select the Show Project Summary Task check box and then click OK.

   The project summary task row appears at the top of the task sheet. The total project cost, as currently scheduled, is displayed in the Total Cost field.

5. Review the Total Cost field for summary tasks. This is the rolled-up total of all assigned resource costs and fixed costs for the subtasks.

6. Review the Total Cost field for individual tasks. This is the sum of all assigned resource costs as well as fixed costs for tasks.

Comparing Resource Costs Against Budget Resource Values

If you are using the new budget resource type with the new Budget Work and Budget Cost fields, you can group and review predetermined budget values against your planned project costs.

> **For information about how to create and assign budget resources, enter budget values, and align resources with their corresponding budget resources, see the section titled "Setting Up and Reviewing a Project Budget" in Chapter 8, "Planning Resource and Task Costs."**

To group and compare resource costs against budget values, follow these steps:

1. Switch to the Resource Usage view.

2. Add the Budget Work, Budget Cost, Work, and Cost fields to the table. Right-click the column to the right of where you want to insert the column and then click Insert Column on the shortcut menu. In the Field Name box, scroll to and select the field and then click OK.

3. Click Project, Group By, Customize Group By.

4. In the Group By field under Field Name, select the name of the text field that you're using to categorize your resources. Depending on how you set up your budget categories, this could be a custom text field, the Code field, or the Group field.

5. Click OK.

   The resources in your project are grouped by the budget categories you assigned. Each grouping includes one budget resource. The figures for the budget resource appear in the Budget Cost and Budget Work fields. The figures for all other resources appear in the Cost and Work fields. The total costs for the resources are rolled up in the grouping bar. Compare those rolled up values against the values for the budget resources to see how the costs in your project are faring against the budget for that category.

6. To ungroup the Resource Usage view, click Project, Group By, No Group. Or, on the Standard toolbar, in the Group By tool, click No Group.

Generating Cost Reports

Five cost reports can help you analyze planned project costs, as follows:

- **Budget report** Click Report, Reports. Double-click Costs and then double-click Budget. The Total Cost column is a summary of the resource costs and fixed costs for each task (see Figure 9-16).

Budget Report as of Sat 1/13/07
Web Site Development

ID	Task Name	Fixed Cost	Fixed Cost Accrual	Total Cost
30	Develop content	$0.00	Prorated	$110,400.00
23	Equipment order processing and delivery	$0.00	Prorated	$15,120.00
25	Software order processing and delivery	$0.00	Prorated	$10,080.00
32	Revise content	$0.00	Prorated	$7,200.00
9	Design interior pages	$0.00	Prorated	$3,700.00
36	All pages test	$0.00	Prorated	$3,520.00
37	Link test	$0.00	Prorated	$3,520.00
22	Order equipment	$0.00	Prorated	$3,360.00
31	Content review	$0.00	Prorated	$2,800.00
33	Second content review	$0.00	Prorated	$2,800.00
5	Web structure review	$0.00	Prorated	$2,720.00
34	Finalize content	$0.00	Prorated	$2,400.00
38	Fix bugs	$0.00	Prorated	$2,400.00

Figure 9-16 Run the Budget report to view costs for each task.

- **Cash Flow report** Click Report, Reports. Double-click Costs and then double-click Cash Flow. This report forecasts the funding needed for each period of time, enabling you to see whether budgeted costs will be exceeded at a particular point.

- **Cash Flow visual report in Excel** Click Report, Visual Reports. In the Task Usage tab, double-click Cash Flow Report. Microsoft Office Excel 2007 opens to show the project's cash flow in a column chart (see Figure 9-17).

Chapter 9

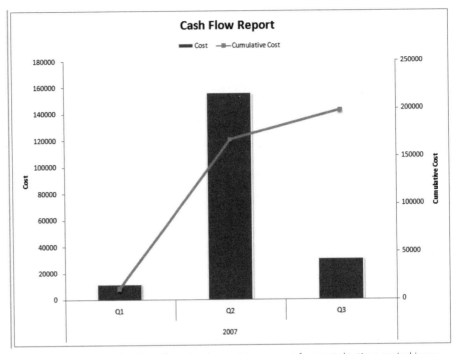

Figure 9-17 Generate the Cash Flow visual report to see cost forecasts by time period in an Office Excel 2007 column chart.

- **Cash Flow visual report in Visio** Click Report, Visual Reports. In the Resource Usage tab, double-click Cash Flow Report (Metric) or Cash Flow Report (US). Visio opens to show the project's cash flow in a Visio PivotDiagram (see Figure 9-18).

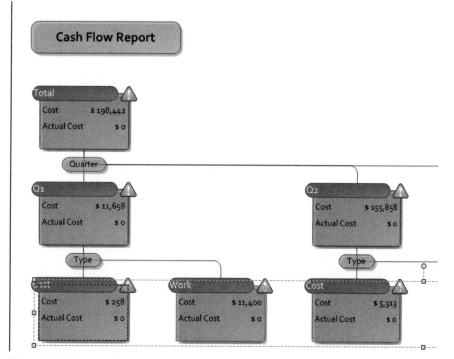

Figure 9-18 Run the Visio Cash Flow visual report to see cost forecasts by time period in a Visio PivotDiagram.

Sorting Tasks or Resources by Cost

You can sort a sheet view by costs. To review task or resource costs in order of amount, do the following:

1. Display a task sheet or resource sheet, depending on whether you want to see costs by resource or by task.

2. Click View, Table, Cost.

3. Click Project, Sort, By Cost.

   The sheet is sorted by the Total Cost field. To return to the original sort order, click Project, Sort, By ID.

Filtering Tasks or Resources by Cost

You can filter a sheet view to display only tasks or resources that have costs exceeding a specified amount. To do this, follow these steps:

1. Display a task sheet or resource sheet, depending on whether you want to see costs by resource or by task.

2. Click View, Table, Cost.

3. Click Project, Filtered For, More Filters.

4. In the More Filters dialog box, click Cost Greater Than and then click Apply.

5. In the Cost Greater Than dialog box, enter the amount (see Figure 9-19).

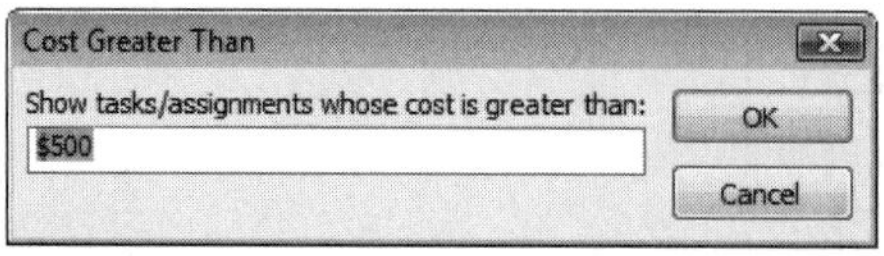

Figure 9-19 To see only those tasks or assignments that have a scheduled cost exceeding a certain amount, enter the amount in this dialog box.

To see all tasks or all resources again, click Project, Filtered For, All Tasks or All Resources.

What if You Have More Money Than You Need?

If you investigate your total project costs and discover that you have more budget than costs, you have some decisions to make. Depending on the type of project, the situation, and the amount of extra budget, you can:

- Reserve the buffer. Use the extra funds as insurance against potential risks.

- Add resources. Use the money to hire resources and take some of the load off overallocated resources or bring in the finish date.

- Add scope. Add tasks you were hoping to include, but thought you wouldn't have enough money to do. Build in a higher level of quality. If applicable, increase quantities being produced.

- Inform your manager or client that you can complete the project well under budget.

Checking Your Cost Assumptions

If you find that your scheduled costs are higher than your budget, first review the individual costs themselves. Check the resource rates as well as fixed costs for tasks and make sure they're accurate.

To check resource rates, review the Resource Sheet with the Entry table applied. With the default fields in the Entry table, you can see each resource's standard rate, overtime rate, and cost per use.

To check fixed costs for tasks, review a task sheet such as the Gantt Chart with the Cost table applied. The Fixed Cost field displays any costs associated with the tasks that are independent of resource costs.

Adjusting the Schedule to Reduce Costs

If many of your resource costs are based on time periods such as an amount per hour or per day, you might be able to cut costs if you can reduce task durations. For example, suppose you have a 2-day fixed-units task assigned to a $100/hour resource. By default, this resource is assigned to 16 hours of work, for a cost of $1,600. If you reduce the duration to 1 day, the work is reduced to 8 hours, and the cost is reduced to $800.

When you reduce task duration in a fixed-units or fixed-duration task, the amount of work is also reduced. However, if you reduce duration for a fixed-work task, work stays the same and assignment units increase. In this case, resource costs would not be reduced.

For more information about changing durations, see the section titled "Checking and Adjusting Durations" earlier in this chapter.

Adjusting Assignments to Reduce Costs

Another way to reduce work and therefore cut costs is to reduce work directly. In effect, you're cutting the amount of time that resources are spending on assigned tasks.

The manner in which a work reduction affects your task and resource scheduling depends on the individual task types. When you decrease work in a fixed-units or fixed-work task, duration is reduced. When you decrease work in a fixed-duration task, units are decreased.

To change work amounts for individual resources, display the Task Usage view or Resource Usage view. Then edit the Work field for the assignment.

Adjusting Cost Resources

You might be using cost resources in your project; that is, those cost items that contribute to the completion of a task but—unlike work or material resources—do not affect the schedule when assigned to that task. The ability to integrate cost resources is a new feature in Project 2007. Examples of cost resources include airfare, lodging, and rentals.

To review the amounts planned for cost resources, switch to the Resource Usage view. Apply the Cost table by clicking View, Table, Cost. If you only want to see cost resources, click Project, Filtered For, Resources – Cost.

You can now review the costs for each cost resource. If you need to make any adjustments, you can change the Cost field for the assignment under the cost resource.

Chapter 9

Strategies for Reducing Resource Costs

The following are suggestions for reducing resource costs by adjusting assignments:

- If you have assignments with multiple resources assigned, reduce the work for the more expensive resources and assign the work to less expensive resources. By shuffling work around on an assignment, you won't risk inadvertently changing duration or units.

- If you have resources with the same skills and availability, replace the more expensive work or material resources with less expensive ones. Although this replacement can introduce some risk into your project, it can also ensure that you're using your expensive resources where you really need them.

- If you have resources with the same skills and availability, replace slower work or equipment resources with faster ones. If one resource is faster than another, you might save money, even if the faster resource's rate is higher.

- If you have material resources whose costs are based on assignment units, for example, 3 tons or 100 yards, decrease the assignment units; that is, use less of the material.

- Review your cost resources and see if you can realize any savings there. For example, perhaps you can reduce the amount or cost of travel. Maybe you can try to get discounts on equipment or software that must be purchased for the project.

Note

You can also adjust scope to cut costs. For more information about cutting scope, see the section titled "Changing Project Scope" later in this chapter.

Balancing Resource Workloads

Although most projects are focused primarily on the finish date or the budget, sometimes a project is defined by its resource limitations, and the use of resources becomes the most important priority in the management of that project. In the resource-constrained project, you need to make sure that all the resources are used well, are doing the right tasks, and are neither underallocated nor overallocated. That is, you need to examine workloads and allocations and then fix any problems you find. You still need to keep your eye on the schedule and your costs, but schedule and costs are secondary to resource utilization in this type of project.

Balancing resource workloads isn't really part of the project triangle. However, you can adjust scope—add or remove tasks—to balance workload. You can also adjust the schedule—split or delay tasks until resources have time to work on them. Finally, you can adjust costs—add more money to pay for additional resources to help balance the workload.

Viewing Resource Workloads

When you analyze resource workloads, you're actually reviewing the way resources are assigned. The optimum situation is when all resources in your project are assigned at their full availability, no more and no less, throughout their time on the project.

However, there might be resources for whom you are not able to fill every hour. These resources are said to be *underallocated*. You might have to pay for these resources' time even when they're not directly carrying out project tasks, and this can adversely affect your project budget.

Other resources might consistently have more work than time. These resources are *overallocated*. Such a situation represents risk to the project. If there's more work than available time, it's highly probable that deadlines will be missed, quality will suffer, costs will increase, or scope will have to be cut.

At this point in the project, just before work actually begins, you can look at scheduled underallocations and overallocations, make the necessary changes to maximize your resource contributions, and reduce your risk from overallocation. The goal is to balance the workload as much as possible so that you're not wasting resource dollars and burning out a handful of key resources.

TROUBLESHOOTING

Tasks scheduled at the same time are causing overallocations

You influence how tasks and assignments are scheduled by specifying resource availability through their working time calendars, resource units (maximum units), and assignment units. Within those limitations, however, Microsoft Project might still schedule multiple tasks for the same time frame, which can cause overallocations.

For example, suppose a resource has a working time calendar specifying that she works on this project only on Tuesdays. When you assign a task to her, that task is scheduled to accommodate the fact that work will be done only on Tuesdays. When you assign a 5-day task to her, by default, this assignment will take 40 hours, which will stretch across 5 weeks.

Likewise, suppose another resource works half-time. His resource units are 50 percent. When you assign a task to him, by default, his assignment units are also 50 percent. So by default, a 5-day task does not translate to 40 hours in a week, but rather 20 hours.

However, if you have two 1-day tasks assigned to the same resource at the same time, both assignments will be scheduled for the resource at the same time, and therefore that resource will be overallocated.

You can resolve overallocations by following the strategies outlined in the section titled "Adjusting Assignments" and the section titled "Leveling Assignments" later in this chapter.

You can use one of several Microsoft Project views to review how much work is assigned to a resource in any selected time period, as follows:

- **Resource Graph**   Click View, Resource Graph (see Figure 9-20). In the default Peak Units format, the Resource Graph displays how much the resource is being utilized, in terms of maximum units, for the time period specified in the timescale.

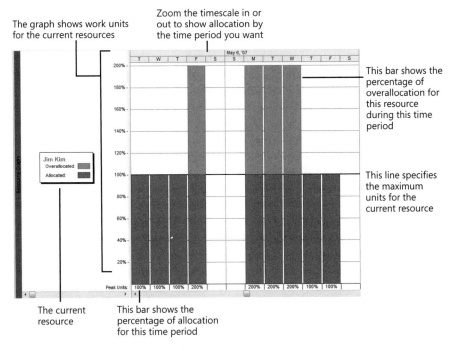

Figure 9-20 The Resource Graph displays resource utilization, one resource at a time.

Zoom In

To see resource allocation information by different measures, click Format, Details and then pick a different format such as Overallocation or Percent Allocation.

To change the timescale, click the Zoom In or Zoom Out buttons.

Zoom Out

To see information for a different resource, press the Page Down or Page Up buttons.

- **Resource Usage view**   Click View, Resource Usage. Each resource is listed with all assigned tasks (see Figure 9-21). The timephased portion of the view shows how work is allocated over the selected time period. As in all resource views, overallocated resources are shown in red. In the timephased portion, any work that exceeds the resource availability for the time period is also shown in red.

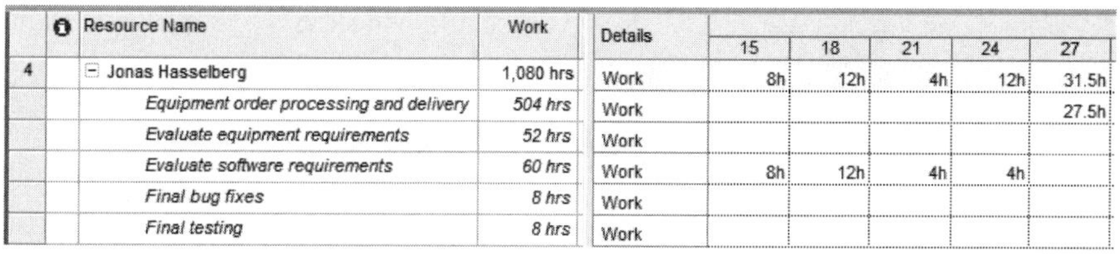

❶	Resource Name	Work	Details	15	18	21	24	27
4	⊟ Jonas Hasselberg	1,080 hrs	Work	8h	12h	4h	12h	31.5h
	Equipment order processing and delivery	504 hrs	Work					27.5h
	Evaluate equipment requirements	52 hrs	Work					
	Evaluate software requirements	60 hrs	Work	8h	12h	4h	4h	
	Final bug fixes	8 hrs	Work					
	Final testing	8 hrs	Work					

Figure 9-21 The Resource Usage view can help you find periods of overallocation.

- **Resource Allocation view** Click View, More Views and then click Resource Allocation. This is a combination view, with the Resource Usage view in the upper portion of the view and the Leveling Gantt in the lower portion (see Figure 9-22).

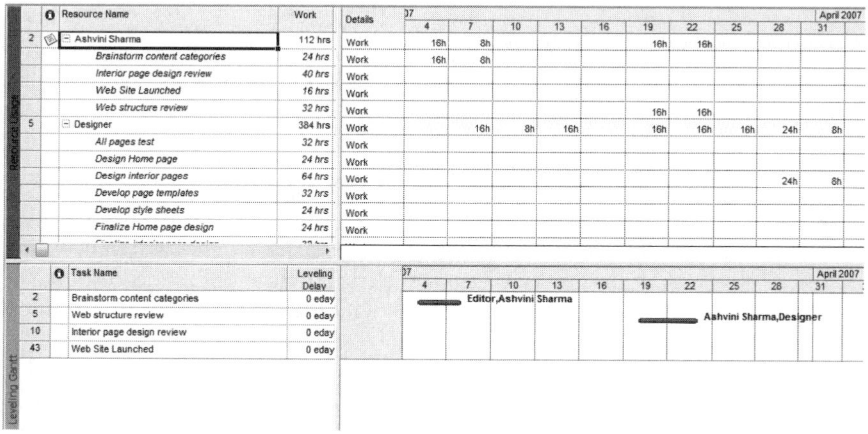

Figure 9-22 The Leveling Gantt portion of the Resource Allocation view displays details about the tasks assigned to the resource selected in the Resource Usage view.

Go To Next
Overallocation

Use the Resource Management Toolbar

The Resource Management toolbar (see Figure 9-23) includes a variety of functions that help you work with your resources. To show this toolbar, click View, Toolbars, Resource Management. As you're analyzing resource overallocations, click the Go To Next Overallocation button to find and review the assignments for each overallocated resource in turn.

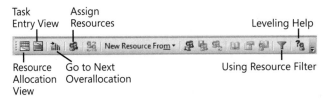

Figure 9-23 The Resource Management toolbar includes a variety of functions that help you work with your resources.

> **Note**
>
> When you want to switch to another view from a combination view, remember to first remove the split in the window. Click Window, Remove Split, or double-click the split bar. When you switch to the view you want, it will appear in the full screen the way you expect.

- **Resource Form** With a resource sheet view displayed, such as the Resource Sheet or Resource Usage view, click Window, Split. The Resource Form appears in the lower portion of the view, with the resource sheet in the upper portion (see Figure 9-24).

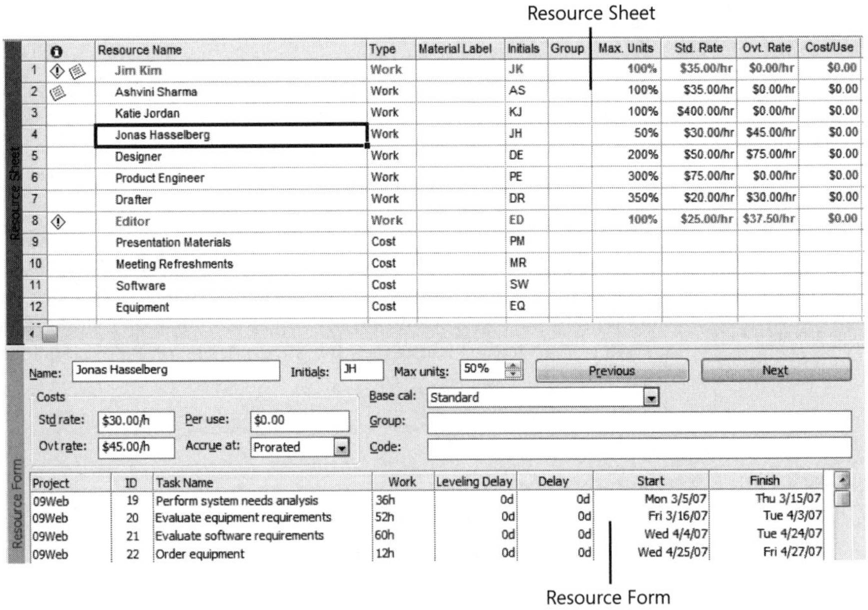

Resource Sheet

	①	Resource Name	Type	Material Label	Initials	Group	Max. Units	Std. Rate	Ovt. Rate	Cost/Use
1	◇ ✎	Jim Kim	Work		JK		100%	$35.00/hr	$0.00/hr	$0.00
2	✎	Ashvini Sharma	Work		AS		100%	$35.00/hr	$0.00/hr	$0.00
3		Katie Jordan	Work		KJ		100%	$400.00/hr	$0.00/hr	$0.00
4		Jonas Hasselberg	Work		JH		50%	$30.00/hr	$45.00/hr	$0.00
5		Designer	Work		DE		200%	$50.00/hr	$75.00/hr	$0.00
6		Product Engineer	Work		PE		300%	$75.00/hr	$0.00/hr	$0.00
7		Drafter	Work		DR		350%	$20.00/hr	$30.00/hr	$0.00
8	◇	Editor	Work		ED		100%	$25.00/hr	$37.50/hr	$0.00
9		Presentation Materials	Cost		PM					
10		Meeting Refreshments	Cost		MR					
11		Software	Cost		SW					
12		Equipment	Cost		EQ					

Name: Jonas Hasselberg   Initials: JH   Max units: 50%   Previous   Next

Costs   Base cal: Standard

Std rate: $30.00/h   Per use: $0.00   Group:

Ovt rate: $45.00/h   Accrue at: Prorated   Code:

Project	ID	Task Name	Work	Leveling Delay	Delay	Start	Finish
09Web	19	Perform system needs analysis	36h	0d	0d	Mon 3/5/07	Thu 3/15/07
09Web	20	Evaluate equipment requirements	52h	0d	0d	Fri 3/16/07	Tue 4/3/07
09Web	21	Evaluate software requirements	60h	0d	0d	Wed 4/4/07	Tue 4/24/07
09Web	22	Order equipment	12h	0d	0d	Wed 4/25/07	Fri 4/27/07

Resource Form

Figure 9-24 The Resource Form displays details about the resource selected in the upper portion of the view.

INSIDE OUT   **Task views give you no clue about overallocations**

Task views do not indicate when resources are overallocated, which can be a problem because you assign tasks in a task view. Even the Assign Resources dialog box doesn't give an indication unless you apply the Available To Work filter.

To see which resources have too much work assigned, switch from a task view to a resource view. Overallocated resources are highlighted in red.

To see at a glance which tasks have been assigned overallocated resources, add the Overallocated column to a task sheet. To do this, click the column heading to the right of where you want to insert the Overallocated column. Click Insert, Column. In the Field Name box, click Overallocated and then click OK.

The Overallocated field is a Yes/No field. Any tasks that have been assigned overallocated resources display a Yes. You can sort by the Overallocated field so you can better focus on balancing the assignments for those tasks. Be aware that by default, even resources overallocated by a couple hours in just one week are marked as overallocated.

Another means of seeing how your resources are allocated is to run assignment-related reports, as follows:

- **Who Does What When report** Click Report, Reports. Double-click Assignments and then double-click Who Does What When. This report displays the amount of work for each resource by day and by assignment (see Figure 9-25).

Who Does What When as of Mon 1/15/07
Web Site Development

	3/5	3/6	3/7	3/8	3/9	3/10	3/11	3/12	3/13	3/14	3/15	3/16
Jim Kim											8 hrs	8 hrs
Develop Web structure											8 hrs	8 hrs
Home page design review												
Assign content owners												
Develop content												
Content review												
Revise content												
Second content review												
Finalize content												
All pages test												
Link test												
Final testing												
Final bug fixes												
Web Site Launched												
Ashwini Sharma	8 hrs	8 hrs	8 hrs									
Brainstorm content categories	8 hrs	8 hrs	8 hrs									
Web structure review												
Interior page design review												
Web Site Launched												
Katie Jordan												
Develop content												
Jonas Hasselberg	4 hrs	4 hrs	4 hrs	4 hrs	4 hrs			4 hrs	4 hrs	4 hrs	4 hrs	4 hrs
Perform system needs analysis	4 hrs	4 hrs	4 hrs	4 hrs	4 hrs			4 hrs	4 hrs	4 hrs	4 hrs	
Evaluate equipment requirements												4 hrs
Evaluate software requirements												

Figure 9-25 Run the Who Does What When report to see assignment details by day.

- **Overallocated Resources report** Click Report, Reports. Double-click Assignments and then double-click Overallocated Resources. This report displays only overallocated resource information (see Figure 9-26). If no resources are overallocated, no report is generated.

Figure 9-26 Run the Overallocated Resources report to see assignment information about units and work for each overallocated resource.

- **Resource Usage report** Click Report, Reports. Double-click Workload and then double-click Resource Usage. This report displays the amount of work each week by resource and assignment. Totals are included for the resource, assignment, and week (see Figure 9-27).

Figure 9-27 Run the Resource Usage report to see assignment details by week.

- **Resource Availability visual report** Click Report, Visual Reports. Click the Resource Usage tab and then double-click the Resource Availability Report (Metric) or Resource Availability Report (US). Visio opens to show how much time each resource is working throughout the project and how much time the resource has available (see Figure 9-28). A red flag appears next to any overallocated resources.

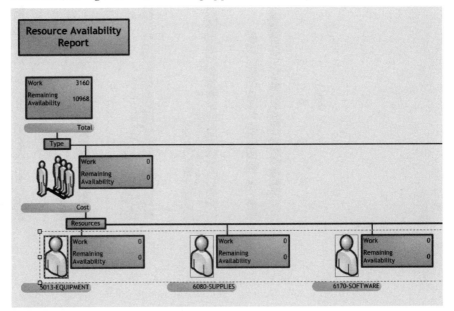

Figure 9-28 The Resource Availability Report diagrams resource usage, availability, and overallocation in a Visio PivotDiagram.

- **Resource Work Availability visual report** Click Report, Visual Reports. Click the Resource Usage tab and then double-click the Resource Work Availability Report. Excel opens to show a column chart of collective resource work, availability, and remaining availability in your project.

- **Resource Work Summary visual report** Click Report, Visual Reports. Click the Resource Usage tab and then double-click the Resource Work Summary Report. Excel opens to show work, work availability, and remaining availability for each resource in the project (see Figure 9-29). A red flag appears next to any overallocated resources.

Chapter 9

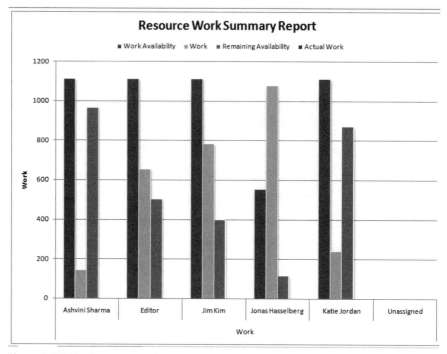

Figure 9-29 The Resource Work Summary Report uses an Excel column chart to show work and availability for each resource in your project.

Reports are particularly useful for resource management meetings or team status meetings. Remember that you can also print views for hardcopy distribution.

You can filter a view to examine task allocation, as follows:

- In a resource sheet like the Resource Usage view, click Project, Filtered For, Overallocated Resources.

- In a task sheet like the Gantt Chart, click Project, Filtered For, Using Resource. Enter the name of the resource whose tasks you want to see.

- When you want to see all resources or tasks again, click Project, Filtered, For, All Resources or All Tasks.

> **Note**
>
> You can use the Project Guide to review resource allocation. On the Project Guide toolbar, click Report. Click the See How Resources' Time Is Allocated link. The view changes to a combination view, including the Resource Usage view and Gantt Chart. Additional information is provided in the Project Guide task pane.

> ### What if You Have More Resources Than You Need?
>
> If you have more resources than needed for the project, you should determine whether this is a help or a hindrance. Depending on the type of project, the situation, and the number of extra resources, you can do one of the following:
>
> - If the underallocated resources have the same skills and availability as other resources that are overallocated, you can use them to balance the workload.
>
> - Even if you have no overallocations, consider assigning multiple resources to tasks to shorten the schedule.
>
> - If you can't use the resources, find another project for them. Having extra people without work can get in the way of progress on the project. It can also place an unnecessary burden on your budget.

Adjusting Resource Availability

If you find that resources are overallocated or underallocated, check with the resources to see whether their availability can be modified to reflect how they're needed on the project. For example, if a full-time resource is consistently 50 percent underallocated throughout the life of the project, you might consider changing his units to 50 percent and making him available as a 50 percent resource on another project. Or if a part-time resource is consistently 20 percent overallocated, ask her if she can add more time to her availability on the project.

To change resource units, in a resource sheet, double-click the resource name to open the Resource Information dialog box. Click the General tab. In the Resource Availability table, specify the units in the Units field. If necessary, enter the starting and ending dates of the new levels of availability.

To change a resource's working time calendar, click the Working Time tab in the Resource Information dialog box. Make the necessary changes to increase or decrease the resource's working time on the project.

Adjusting Assignments

You can shift assignments around to fix overallocations and underallocations. This shifting assumes, however, that you have resources with similar skills and availability who can fulfill the necessary tasks.

If you can't add or replace resources to take the burden off overallocated resources, you might be able to delay tasks or assignments until the resources have time to work on them. Or you can simply add overtime work to account for the overallocation.

Adding More Resources to Tasks

You can add underallocated resources to tasks to assist overallocated resources. Depending on the task type, you can distribute the work or the assignment units among the assigned resources, thereby better balancing the workload.

For more information about adding resources to tasks, including the impact of effort-driven scheduling and the different task types, see the section titled "Adjusting Resource Settings to Bring in the Finish Date" earlier in this chapter.

Replacing Overallocated Resources

On an assignment, you can replace an overallocated resource with an underallocated one as long as they have the same skills and availability. To replace a resource on a task, do the following:

1. In a task sheet such as the Gantt Chart, select the task for which you want to replace resources.

2. On the Standard toolbar, click Assign Resources.

Assign Resources

3. In the Assign Resources dialog box, click the resource you want to replace.

The currently assigned resources are at the top of the list and have check marks next to their names.

4. Click the Replace button.

The Replace Resource dialog box appears (see Figure 9-30).

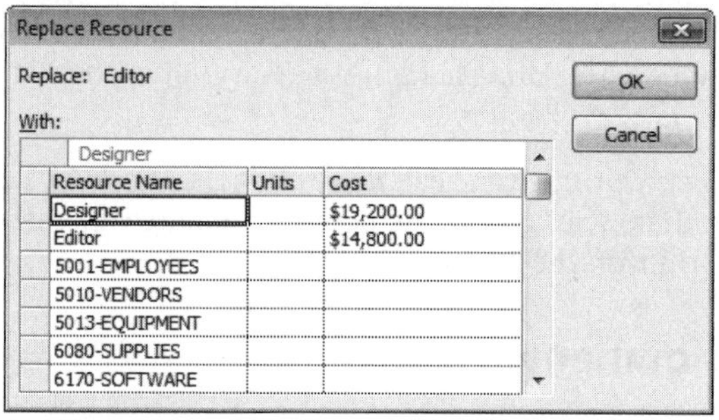

Figure 9-30 Use the Replace Resource dialog box to remove one resource and add a different one in a single operation.

5. Click the resource you want to add to the task and then click OK.

The old resource is replaced with the new one.

Delaying a Task or Assignment

You can delay a task or assignment until the assigned resource has time to work on it, as follows:

- **Leveling delay** This is a *task delay*—the amount of time that should pass from the task's scheduled start date until work on the task should actually begin. It delays all assignments for the task. *Leveling delay* can also be automatically calculated and added by the Microsoft Project leveling feature.

  For more information about leveling, see the section titled "Leveling Assignments" later in this chapter.

> **Note**
> Don't confuse lag time with task delay. Lag time is the amount of time to wait after the predecessor is finished (or has started, depending on the link type) before a successor task should start. For more information about lag time, see the section titled "Delaying Linked Tasks by Adding Lag Time" in Chapter 5.

- **Assignment delay** This is the amount of time that should pass from the task's scheduled start date until the assignment's scheduled start date (see Figure 9-31).

Figure 9-31 Assignment delay is the amount of time from the start date of the task and the start date of the assignment.

Because it's best to delay within available slack time, review the tasks or assignments in context of their slack time and then add delay as time is available. Otherwise, you could push out the finish date of the task (or even of the project) if it's a critical task. To check available slack, do the following:

1. Click View, More Views. In the More Views dialog box, click Resource Allocation and then click Apply.

2. Click the Resource Usage portion of the view and then click the resource or assignment for which you want to examine slack and possibly delay.

3. Click the Leveling Gantt portion of the view.

4. Click View, Table, Schedule.

Chapter 9

5. Review the Free Slack and Total Slack fields to find tasks that have slack (see Figure 9-32).

You need to drag the vertical split bar to the right to see these fields.

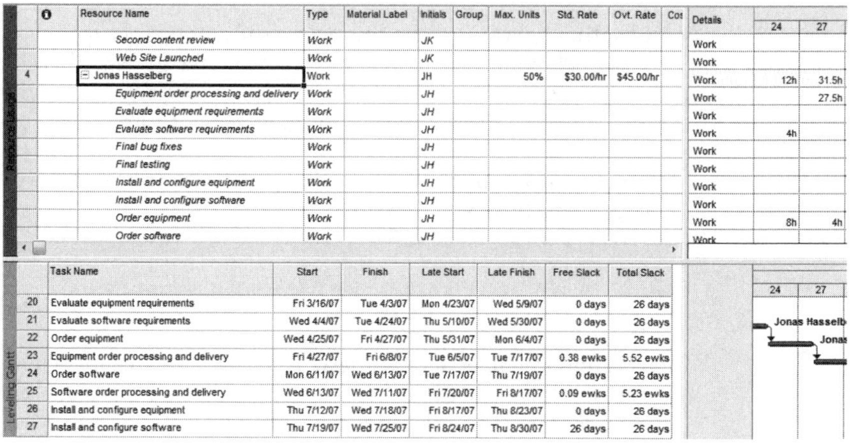

	0	Resource Name	Type	Material Label	Initials	Group	Max. Units	Std. Rate	Ovt. Rate	Cos	Details		24	27
		Second content review	Work		JK						Work			
		Web Site Launched	Work		JK						Work			
4		⊟ Jonas Hasselberg	Work		JH		50%	$30.00/hr	$45.00/hr		Work		12h	31.5h
		Equipment order processing and delivery	Work		JH						Work			27.5h
		Evaluate equipment requirements	Work		JH						Work			
		Evaluate software requirements	Work		JH						Work		4h	
		Final bug fixes	Work		JH						Work			
		Final testing	Work		JH						Work			
		Install and configure equipment	Work		JH						Work			
		Install and configure software	Work		JH						Work			
		Order equipment	Work		JH						Work		8h	4h
		Order software	Work		JH						Work			

	Task Name	Start	Finish	Late Start	Late Finish	Free Slack	Total Slack		24	27
20	Evaluate equipment requirements	Fri 3/16/07	Tue 4/3/07	Mon 4/23/07	Wed 5/9/07	0 days	26 days			
21	Evaluate software requirements	Wed 4/4/07	Tue 4/24/07	Thu 5/10/07	Wed 5/30/07	0 days	26 days		Jonas Hasselb	
22	Order equipment	Wed 4/25/07	Fri 4/27/07	Thu 5/31/07	Mon 6/4/07	0 days	26 days		Jonas	
23	Equipment order processing and delivery	Fri 4/27/07	Fri 6/8/07	Tue 6/5/07	Tue 7/17/07	0.38 ewks	5.52 ewks			
24	Order software	Mon 6/11/07	Wed 6/13/07	Tue 7/17/07	Thu 7/19/07	0 days	26 days			
25	Software order processing and delivery	Wed 6/13/07	Wed 7/11/07	Fri 7/20/07	Fri 8/17/07	0.09 ewks	5.23 ewks			
26	Install and configure equipment	Thu 7/12/07	Wed 7/18/07	Fri 8/17/07	Thu 8/23/07	0 days	26 days			
27	Install and configure software	Thu 7/19/07	Wed 7/25/07	Fri 8/24/07	Thu 8/30/07	26 days	26 days			

Figure 9-32 Use the Schedule table in the Leveling Gantt portion of the Resource Allocation view to find available slack in which to add task delay.

6. Also review the chart portion of the Leveling Gantt. The thin bars to the right of the regular Gantt bars show any available slack (see Figure 9-33).

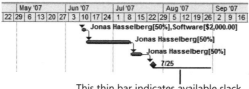

This thin bar indicates available slack.

Figure 9-33 Use the Leveling Gantt portion of the Resource Allocation view to find available slack in which to add task delay.

After you find tasks with slack that you can use, add leveling delay as follows:

1. With the Resource Allocation view displayed, click the Leveling Gantt portion of the view.

2. Click View, Table, More Tables. In the More Tables dialog box, click Delay and then click Apply.

3. In the Resource Usage portion of the view, click the assignment whose task you want to delay.

4. In the Leveling Gantt portion of the view, in the Leveling Delay field, enter the amount of time you want to delay the task.

If you want to delay an individual assignment for a task that has multiple resources assigned, add assignment delay instead of leveling delay, as follows:

1. With the Resource Allocation view displayed, click the Resource Usage portion of the view.

2. Click the column heading to the right of where you want to insert the Assignment Delay column.

3. Click Insert, Column.

4. In the Field Name box, click Assignment Delay and then click OK.

5. In the Assignment Delay field of the assignment you want to delay, enter the length of the delay.

   This entry indicates how much time after the task's start date the resource is to wait before starting work on this assignment.

Specifying Overtime Work to Account for Overallocations

Often, you can't reassign overallocated work to other resources or delay a task until later. In this case, overtime might be the answer.

Microsoft Project does not automatically assign overtime or the associated overtime pay rate when a resource's work exceeds your definition of a normal workday (for example, 8 hours) or a normal workweek (for example, 40 hours). You need to specify overtime work, in addition to total work, for the resource.

For example, suppose a resource is assigned to 10 hours of work in a day. You can specify 2 of those hours as overtime work. The work still totals 10 hours, but 8 hours are regular work and 2 hours are overtime.

Regular Work, Overtime Work, and Total Work

When working with overtime, it's important to keep your work terminology straight; otherwise, it can get confusing. The Work field is actually *total work*; that is, the total amount of time that this resource is assigned to this task.

When you add overtime on an assignment, that amount is stored in the Overtime Work field, and the (total) Work amount stays the same.

Another field, Regular Work, contains the amount of regular (nonovertime) work, based on your amount of total work and overtime work, according to the following calculation:

Regular Work + Overtime Work = (total) Work.

You can add the Regular Work field to a sheet view if you want to see the amount of regular work scheduled for a resource, in relation to overtime work and (total) work.

To specify overtime work for overallocated resources, first set up a view containing overtime work fields, as follows:

1. Click View, Resource Usage.

2. Click the column heading for the Work field.

3. Click Insert, Column.

4. In the Field Name box, click Overtime Work. Click OK.

   The Overtime Work field is added to the Resource Usage view.

5. Click Format, Detail Styles.

   The Detail Styles dialog box appears.

6. In the Available Fields box, click Overtime Work and then click Show (see Figure 9-34).

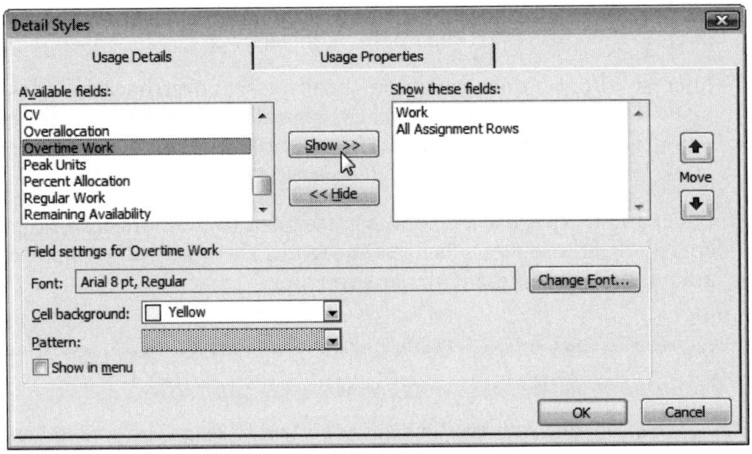

Figure 9-34 Use the Detail Styles dialog box to add another row of timephased information to the timephased portion of the Resource Usage or Task Usage view.

The Overtime Work field appears in the Show These Fields box.

7. Click OK.

   The Overtime Work field is added to the timephased portion of the view (see Figure 9-35).

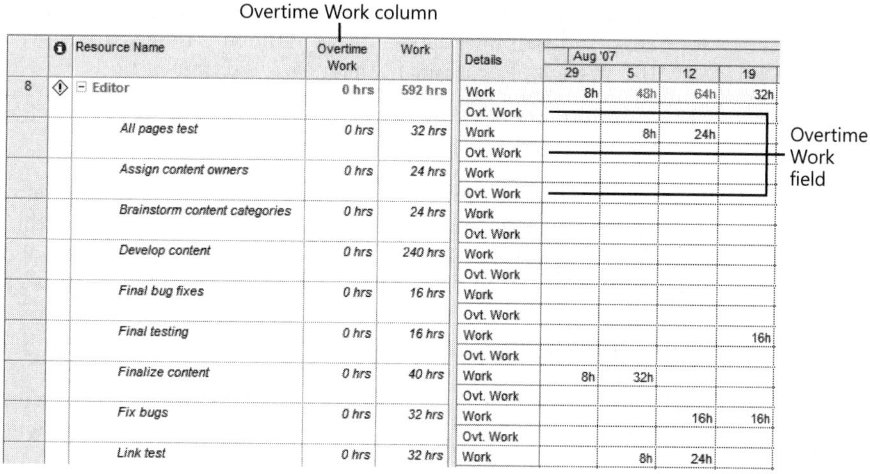

Overtime Work column

❶	Resource Name	Overtime Work	Work	Details	Aug '07			
					29	5	12	19
8 ⟐	⊟ Editor	0 hrs	592 hrs	Work	8h	48h	64h	32h
				Ovt. Work				
	All pages test	0 hrs	32 hrs	Work			8h	24h
				Ovt. Work				
	Assign content owners	0 hrs	24 hrs	Work				
				Ovt. Work				
	Brainstorm content categories	0 hrs	24 hrs	Work				
				Ovt. Work				
	Develop content	0 hrs	240 hrs	Work				
				Ovt. Work				
	Final bug fixes	0 hrs	16 hrs	Work				
				Ovt. Work				
	Final testing	0 hrs	16 hrs	Work				16h
				Ovt. Work				
	Finalize content	0 hrs	40 hrs	Work	8h	32h		
				Ovt. Work				
	Fix bugs	0 hrs	32 hrs	Work			16h	16h
				Ovt. Work				
	Link test	0 hrs	32 hrs	Work		8h	24h	

Overtime Work field

Figure 9-35 Add the Overtime Work field to the sheet and timephased portion of the Resource Usage view.

> **Note**
>
> You might also find it helpful to add the Regular Work field to the sheet portion of the Resource Usage view. Click the Work field and then click Insert, Column. In the Field Name box, click Regular Work and then click OK.

To specify overtime work for overallocated resources, follow these steps:

1. In the Resource Usage view containing the Overtime Work field, find the first overallocated resource (highlighted in red) for whom you want to add overtime work.

2. Under the overallocated resource, review the assignments and the hours in the timephased portion of the view. Find the assignments that are contributing to the overallocated work amounts.

3. In the sheet portion of the view, in the Overtime Work field for the assignment, enter the amount of overtime you want to designate.

   You do not change the work amount because the overtime work amount is a portion of the total work. The amount you enter in the Overtime Work field is distributed across the time span of the assignment, which you can see in the timephased portion of the view. For example, if an assignment spans 3 days, and you enter 6 hours of overtime, an amount of overtime is added to each day for the assignment.

In the timephased portion of the view, you can view how the overtime work you enter is distributed across the assignment's time span. However, you cannot edit the amount of overtime in the individual time periods.

4. Repeat this process for any other assignments causing the resource to be overallocated.

When you enter overtime work, the duration of the task is shortened. Overtime work is charged at an overtime rate you enter for the resource, either in the Resource Sheet or in the Resource Information dialog box. The resource name is still shown in red as overallocated, but now you've accounted for the overallocation using overtime.

Splitting Tasks

Sometimes a resource needs to stop working on one task, start work on a second task, and then return to the first task. This can happen, for example, when an overallocated resource needs to work on a task with a date constraint. In this situation, you can split a task. With a *split task*, you can schedule when the task is to start, stop, and then resume again. As with delay, splitting a task can ensure that resources are working on tasks when they actually have time for them.

> **Note**
>
> In a split task, the task duration is calculated as the value of both portions of the task, not counting the time when the resource is working on something else. However, if you split a task with an elapsed duration, the duration is recalculated to include the start of the first part of the task through the finish of the last part of the task.

To split a task, follow these steps:

1. Display the Gantt Chart by clicking View, Gantt Chart.

2. On the Standard toolbar, click Split Task. Your mouse pointer changes to the split task pointer, and a small pop-up window appears.

Split Task

3. In the chart portion of the view, position your mouse pointer on the Gantt bar of the task you want to split, on the date when you want the split to occur.

4. Drag the Gantt bar to the date when you want the task to resume (see Figure 9-36).

   While you drag, the pop-up shows the start and finish dates.

Figure 9-36 Drag the Gantt bar to represent when the task stops and when it resumes again.

You can split the task multiple times. Click Split Task on the Standard toolbar to activate each new split.

To remove the split in a split task, drag the right portion of the split Gantt bar toward the left portion until both sides of the bar touch and join.

> **Note**
>
> After you begin the execution and tracking phase of the project, you can also split a task on which a resource has started working. For more information on rescheduling, see the section titled "Rescheduling the Project" in Chapter 10.
>
> **You can also adjust scope to balance the workload. For more information about cutting scope, see the section titled "Changing Project Scope" later in this chapter.**

Leveling Assignments

The previous sections described how you can delay and split tasks to balance or **level** resource assignments according to your own date calculations. Microsoft Project can balance the workload for you with the leveling feature, which calculates and implements delay and splits in your project plan according to general specifications that you set.

You can have Microsoft Project level assignments whenever you give the command. You also have the option to keep the leveling feature on all the time. If you leave leveling on all the time, whenever you change the schedule in some way, Microsoft Project levels assignments at that time.

Note that leveling does not reassign tasks or units. It does not change work amounts. It causes the start date to move later by adding delays, or it splits a task so that it finishes later when the assigned resources have available time. Also, leveling works only on existing work resources—not generic resources, material resources, or cost resources.

When you level resources, you carry out some or all of these major process steps, which are detailed in the following sections.

Setting Leveling Priorities

You can set a priority for each task if you like. Priorities range from 0 (the lowest priority) to 1,000 (the highest). All tasks start with a default priority of 500; that is, they are all equal in priority. Microsoft Project uses the task priority setting as a leveling criterion. If you have certain tasks that are so important that you never want the leveling feature to split or delay them, you should set them at a priority of 1,000, which ensures that Microsoft Project will never level resources using that task. You might have other tasks that, although important, enjoy more potential flexibility as to when they can be completed. Those tasks can be set at a lower priority, such as 100. Having tasks set at lower priorities gives Microsoft Project the flexibility it needs to effectively level resource assignments.

To change the priority of an individual task, do the following:

1. In the Gantt Chart or other task sheet, double-click the task whose priority you want to change from the default of 500.

2. In the Task Information dialog box, click the General tab.

3. In the Priority box, enter the number representing the priority you want for this task.

INSIDE OUT   Priorities apply only to resource leveling and substitution

Although it seems that priorities can help influence the way that Microsoft Project schedules tasks throughout your project, priorities are actually used only in the context of leveling. (If you're working with Office Project Professional 2007, priorities also play a part in the Resource Substitution Wizard.) When Microsoft Project is determining whether to split or delay one task versus another to level resources, it can use priority as one of its criteria, in addition to the other criteria you have set in the Resource Leveling dialog box.

You can still use priorities in your own ways. You can sort and group tasks by priority. You can also create a filter to see only tasks above a certain priority.

Suppose there are ten tasks throughout your project that you want to set at a higher priority than the average. You can select those tasks and then change their priority in one operation, as follows:

1.   In the Gantt Chart or other task sheet, select all the tasks whose priority you want to change to the same number.

2.   On the Standard toolbar, click Task Information.

3.   In the Multiple Task Information dialog box, click the General tab.

4.   In the Priority box, enter the number representing the priority you want for all selected tasks.

You can add the Priority field to a task sheet and change the priority for tasks individually throughout the sheet. To do this, follow these steps:

1.   In the Gantt Chart or other task sheet, click the column to the right of where you want the new Priority column to be inserted.

2.   Click Insert, Column.

3.   In the Field Name box, click Priority and then click OK. The Priority column appears in your sheet (see Figure 9-37).

	❶	Task Name	Duration	Priority	Start
7		⊟ **Web Design**	**34 days**	**500**	Wed 3/28/07
8		⊟ **Interior Pages**	**24 days**	**500**	Wed 3/28/07
9		Design interior pages	8 days	500	Wed 3/28/07
10		Interior page design review	5 days	500	Mon 4/9/07
11		Finalize interior page design	4 days	500	Mon 4/16/07
12		Develop style sheets	3 days	500	Fri 4/20/07

Figure 9-37 Type or select the priority you want in the Priority field.

4.   For any task whose priority should be other than the default, enter the number in the Priority field.

Leveling Resources with Standard Defaults

You use the Resource Leveling dialog box to set your leveling preferences and give the command to level. The default settings of the dialog box work for the majority of resource-leveling needs. It's a good idea to try leveling with those settings first and see how they work for you. Then you'll have a better idea of the kinds of controls you want to impose on the leveling operation. Follow these steps to level resources by using the default settings:

1.   If you want to level only selected resources rather than all resources, switch to a resource sheet and select the resource(s) you want to level.

To select multiple adjacent resources, drag from the first to the last resource.

To select multiple nonadjacent resources, click the first resource, hold down the Ctrl key, and then click each of the others.

2.   Click Tools, Level Resources.

The Resource Leveling dialog box appears (see Figure 9-38).

Chapter 9

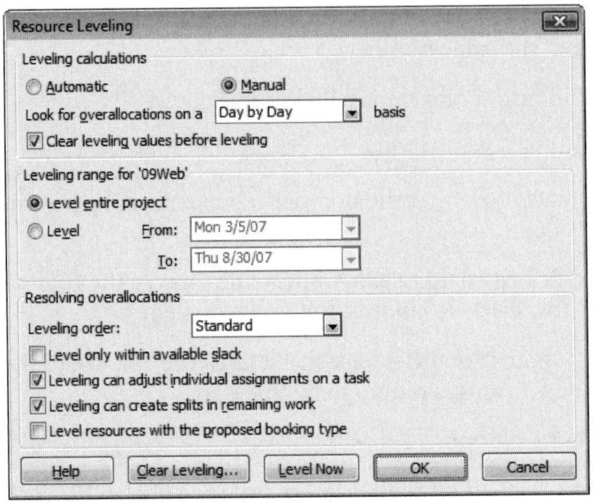

Figure 9-38 You can do a standard leveling operation using the defaults, or you can set your own options.

3. Click the Level Now button.

4. If you selected resources, the Level Now dialog box appears (see Figure 9-39). Select the Entire Pool or Selected Resources option and then click OK.

Figure 9-39 Specify whether you want to level all or selected resources.

This dialog box does not appear if you had a task selected. In that case, all resources are leveled for the entire project.

Your resources are leveled according to the default dialog box settings.

> **Note**
>
> Remember, leveling does not reassign tasks or units. It does not change work amounts. It causes the start date to move later by adding delays, or it splits a task so that it finishes later when the assigned resources have available time.
>
> To see the changes that leveling has made, see the section titled "Checking the Results of Leveling" later in this chapter.

INSIDE OUT   **Rein in the extent of resource leveling**

By default, Microsoft Project levels on a day-by-day basis. That means even if resources are assigned to a task that goes just one minute over their availability in a day as determined by their resource calendar or maximum units, their assignments will be leveled.

You might think this is somewhat nitpicky, and maybe you'd rather not split tasks or add delays unless there are larger overallocations. In this case, click Tools, Level Resources. Then under Leveling Calculations, change the Day By Day setting to Week By Week or Month By Month.

If you set leveling to Week By Week, for example, a resource set up with a 40-hour workweek is only leveled if she is assigned more than 40 hours in a week. However, her assignments are not leveled if she is assigned 14 hours in a single day, as long as the weekly total stays at or below 40 hours.

Setting Leveling Options

If you've leveled your project a few times and want to take more control over how Microsoft Project levels, click Tools, Level Resources and then, in the Resource Leveling dialog box, change the options you want. The following list describes the available options:

- **Calculate automatically or manually.** Under Leveling Calculations, be sure that the Manual option is selected. This ensures that resources are leveled only when you give the Level Now command.

  The Automatic option is available if you want Microsoft Project to level resources whenever you make a change that affects scheduling. However, be aware that this setting can cause Microsoft Project operations to become sluggish and therefore this option is not recommended. If you do select the Automatic option, clear the Clear Leveling Values Before Leveling check box to improve performance.

- **Specify the overallocation leveling time period.** Resources are considered overallocated if they have even one minute of work scheduled beyond their availability, as determined by their resource calendars and maximum units. You can set the time period at which leveling is triggered in the Look For Overallocations On A Basis box. By default, the time period basis is a day, so if resources are overallocated by a minute within a day, they'll be leveled. If you set the overallocation leveling time period basis to the week, resources that are scheduled for more work than can be accomplished by their weekly availability will be leveled. The choices are Minute By Minute, Day By Day (the default), Week By Week, and Month By Month.

- **Clear leveling.** The Clear Leveling Values Before Leveling check box is selected by default. This setting specifies that any delays previously entered as a result of leveling or as a result of manually entering leveling delay are to be cleared before the next leveling operation is performed. The Clear Leveling button does the same thing. Use the check box if you're about to level again and you want to start fresh. Use the button if you're not planning to level right now, but want to remove any leveling delay from your project plan.

- **Level certain tasks or the entire project.** Under Leveling Range, you can specify that only those tasks falling within a date range you enter should be leveled. This can be particularly useful in projects that take place over a long period of time or that are subject to many changes. The default is for all tasks in the project to be leveled.

- **Set the order of leveling operations.** The first part of the leveling process is to determine which tasks are causing overallocations. Then Microsoft Project works through the project, splitting tasks and adding delays to remove the overalloca-tion. You can control the order in which Microsoft Project levels through the proj-ect by setting the leveling order. By default, Microsoft Project uses the Standard leveling order, which looks at task relationships, slack, start dates, priorities, and constraints to determine whether and how tasks should be leveled (see Table 9-1). If you choose the ID Only leveling order, Microsoft Project delays tasks with the higher ID numbers before considering any other criteria. If you choose the Prior-ity, Standard leveling order, Microsoft Project first looks at any priorities you've set and then all the factors of the Standard leveling order.

- **Level within available slack.** By default, the Level Only Within Available Slack check box is cleared. Select this check box if you need to ensure that leveling will not push out the finish date. However, unless your project has a fair amount of built-in slack, if this check box is selected, you might not see many changes to your project.

  Selecting this check box, at least for your first try, can be a good way to see what adjustments can be made by delaying assignments and splitting tasks without pushing out the project finish date. If you don't see many changes as a result, you might realize that you indeed need to add resources, cut scope, or extend the proj-ect finish date.

- **Adjust individual assignments on a task.** By default, the Leveling Can Adjust Individual Assignments On A Task check box is selected. This setting controls adjustments to when a resource works on a task, independent of other resources working on the same task.

- **Create splits in remaining work.** By default, the Leveling Can Create Splits In Remaining Work check box is selected. This means that not only can leveling split tasks that haven't started yet, it can also split tasks that are currently in prog-ress.

- **Level proposed resources.** If you're working with Project Professional, you can add resources tentatively to your project and assign them to tasks. Such resources have a *proposed* booking type. By default, proposed resources are not included in a leveling operation; only committed resources are. If you want to include proposed resources in the leveling operation, select the Level Resources With The Proposed Booking Type.

For more information about working with proposed and committed resources, see the section titled "Proposing Tentative Resources" in Chapter 6. If you're working with proposed enterprise resources, see the section titled "Building Your Enterprise Project Team" in Chapter 22, "Managing Enterprise Projects and Resources."

After you change the leveling options to your satisfaction, level the resources in your project plan by clicking the Level Now button.

Table 9-1 explains the order in which resource leveling is carried out.

Table 9-1 Order of Operations for Resource Leveling

With this leveling order...	These fields are examined...
Standard	*Task relationships* *Slack* *Start date* *Priority* *Constraint*
ID Only	*Task ID*
Priority, Standard	*Priority* *Task relationships* *Slack* *Start date* *Constraint*

INSIDE OUT   Understanding delay in projects scheduled from the finish date

If you level tasks in a project scheduled from the finish date, negative delay values are applied from the end of the task or assignment, which causes the task or assignment's finish date to happen earlier.

Also, if you switch a project to be scheduled from the finish date from one to be scheduled from the start date, any leveling delays and splits are removed.

TROUBLESHOOTING

Leveling delay you entered manually has disappeared

Suppose you entered leveling delay to manually delay tasks. When you use the Microsoft Project leveling feature, by default, any previously entered leveling delay is removed. This is true whether the delay was entered automatically or manually.

To prevent manual leveling delay from being removed in the future, always clear the Clear Leveling Values Before Leveling check box in the Resource Leveling dialog box. And don't click the Clear Leveling button.

You might also consider entering assignment delay rather than leveling delay when manually entering delay values. Whereas leveling delay values delay all assignments on a task, assignment delay values delay individual assignments. Therefore, it might be a little more cumbersome and repetitive to enter initially, but you never have to worry about losing the values to a new leveling operation.

To get your leveling back, click the Undo button on the Standard toolbar as many times as necessary until you get to the point where you have reversed the leveling operation. You can undo operations until the point when you last saved the project file. If you cannot undo, you might need to enter the leveling delay again or use a backup project file.

For more information about manually entering delay, see the section titled "Delaying a Task or Assignment" earlier in this chapter.

Checking the Results of Leveling

To see the changes made to your project plan as a result of leveling, use the Leveling Gantt. Display the Leveling Gantt as follows:

1. Click View, More Views.

2. In the More Views dialog box, click Leveling Gantt.

    The Gantt bars in this view display the task schedule as it looked before the leveling operation in addition to the task schedule as it looks after leveling, so you can compare the changes made (see Figure 9-40). It also shows any new task delays and splits.

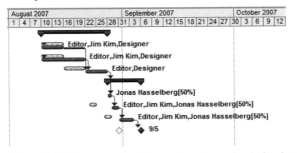

Figure 9-40 The green Gantt bars show the preleveled task schedule; whereas the blue bars, delays, and splits show the results of the leveling operation.

3. If you don't like the results of leveling, click Tools, Level Resources and then click Clear Leveling.

TROUBLESHOOTING

Microsoft Project performance has slowed since you last leveled

You probably set resource leveling to Automatic. Every time you make a scheduling change that affect assignments, Microsoft Project automatically levels resources. Although this is a nice feature and is often what we expect Microsoft Project to do for us, it can significantly slow down performance in larger or more complex projects.

To resolve the slowdown, in the Resource Leveling dialog box, select the Manual option under Leveling Calculations. Then click Level Now whenever you want resources to be leveled.

Note

If you go to the Leveling Gantt first and then level your project, you can see the results immediately in the Leveling Gantt. If you don't like the results, you can immediately click Undo on the Standard toolbar to reverse the changes made by leveling.

TROUBLESHOOTING

You told Microsoft Project to level your resources, but nothing changed

One reason this might happen is that the setting under Leveling Calculations might be too broad. If the setting is Look For Overallocations On A Month By Month basis, for example, a resource could be scheduled for 16-hour days in the first two weeks of the month with little to nothing scheduled in the last two weeks, and this resource would not be leveled. Change the setting to a narrower leveling trigger such as Week By Week.

Another reason this might happen is that you chose to level only within available slack. If there is little to no slack in your schedule, then little to no leveling can be done. In the Resource Leveling dialog box, clear the Level Only Within Available Slack check box and try again.

A third reason nothing changed when you gave the leveling command is that you might have clicked OK instead of Level Now. If your leveling calculations selection is set to Manual, you need to click Level Now..

Remember, leveling does not reassign tasks or units, and it does not change work amounts. It causes the start date to move later by adding delays, or it splits a task so that it finishes later when the assigned resources have available time.

Changing Project Scope

In the course of checking and adjusting your project plan, you might need to cut scope. For example, to meet the finish date, you might need to cut tasks you perceive as optional. To bring project costs in line with your allotted budget, you might cut tasks associated with increased quality or quantity that you think you can live without. Or maybe you need to cut an entire phase or deliverable to alleviate resource overallocation.

> **Note**
> Your task list is likely based on the scope statement that all the stakeholders, including customers, originally approved. If you need to cut scope, you might have to go back and obtain stakeholder approval for these changes.

To delete a task, simply click its row heading and press the Delete key.

> **CAUTION**
> If you delete a task that includes links to predecessors or successors, make sure that the scheduling for the tasks still in place are not adversely affected. If you delete a predecessor, for example, the successor could end up being scheduled back at the project start date unless you link it to a different predecessor.

You can also delete a summary task that represents an entire phase or group of related tasks. To delete a summary task, click its row heading and press the Delete key. A message appears and warns you that deleting the summary task will delete all of its subtasks as well. Click OK to confirm that you want to do this.

Reviewing the Impact of Changes

After you adjust your project plan to bring in your finish date, reduce costs, or balance your workload, check that you've succeeded in hitting your target. Look at the Project Statistics dialog box or review the project summary task, as described earlier in this chapter.

If you had created an interim plan to save the task start and finish dates as they were before you started making changes, you can add the interim start and finish fields as Gantt bars in your Gantt Chart to compare them against your new start and finish fields.

> For more information about interim plans, see the section titled "Saving Additional Schedule Start and Finish Dates" in Chapter 10. For information about creating custom Gantt bars, see the section titled "Formatting the Appearance of Gantt Bars" in Chapter 25.

When you're content with one aspect of your project plan, such as your finish date, it's a good idea to see whether you've "broken" any other aspect of your project, such as your costs. Keep an eye on your finish date, total project costs, and resource allocation while always remembering your highest priority of the three. Continue to adjust and balance until all aspects of the project are just the way you want them.

Obtaining Buyoff on the Project Plan

Typically, before you even start working with Microsoft Project, you have a defined scope for your project. This scope drives the development of deliverables, milestones, phases, and tasks; and it was also probably developed in conjunction with various stakeholders.

If you were forced to cut scope as a result of adjusting the project plan to meet finish date, cost, or resource requirements, you need to go back to those stakeholders and get their approval for your scope changes.

You might need to justify your changes and specify the tradeoffs that are being made to meet the finish date, reduce costs, or balance workload to a reasonable level. You can also point out that the scope is now defined more precisely, based on the project limitations. With this more precise definition, you lower potential risks. The plan is solid and realistic. The project is now less apt to incur unexpected delays, costs, or other changes that can disrupt the project, cause rework, or lower productivity.

As soon as you obtain buyoff from your stakeholders, you have officially completed the planning phase of your project. You're finally ready to tell your team "Go!" and enter the execution phase of the project.

PART 3

Tracking Progress

CHAPTER 10

Setting a Baseline and
Updating Progress. 369

CHAPTER 11

Responding to Changes in Your Project. . . . 401

Setting a Baseline and Updating Progress

Saving Original Plan Information Using a Baseline ... **370**

Updating Task Progress. **382**

Updating Actual Costs **397**

By now, you've completed the planning phase of your project. The scope is set, along with the project goals and objectives. The tasks and deliverables are scheduled. The budget is approved, and you've procured the necessary human, equipment, and material resources. Your project plan reflects all these details and has been signed off by upper management or by your customers.

After all this, you're ready to charge forward with your team and actually start doing the work prescribed by the project. You are now leaving the planning phase and entering the execution phase.

The execution phase consists of four major activities:

- **Tracking** You track progress on tasks so you know when tasks are actually completed by their assigned resources.

- **Analyzing** You examine any differences between your original plan and how it's actually progressing. You monitor the differences in schedule or cost to anticipate any potential problems.

- **Controlling** You take any necessary corrective actions to keep the project on a steady course toward completion by its deadline and on its budget.

- **Reporting** You keep stakeholders informed. Whether you're providing the big picture to your team members or presenting high-level progress information to executives, you regularly report various aspects of project information.

You used Microsoft Office Project 2007 in the planning phase to organize, schedule, and budget your project. Now you can use it in the execution phase to enter progress information, analyze performance, and generate status reports. With a close eye on progress and performance, you can adjust the project plan as necessary to ensure that your scope, schedule, costs, and resources are all balanced the way you need.

To execute your project with Office Project 2007, do two things:

- Set baseline information on your project as planned.

- Enter progress information as your resources complete their assigned tasks.

With both baseline and progress information in hand, you can use the power of Microsoft Project to execute your project toward a successful outcome.

INSIDE OUT Are you a charter or a tracker?

Some project managers set up a project plan, painstakingly enter tasks, and create a schedule with meticulously accurate durations, task dependencies, and constraints. They acquire and assign exactly the right resources and calculate costs to the last penny. However, after they have their plan perfected, they execute the project and leave the project plan behind. What started out as an excellent roadmap of the project is now little more than a bit of planning history.

To graduate to the next level of project management, take your project plan with you as you move to the execution phase. This means maintaining the plan and entering actual progress information as tasks are being worked on. By tracking progress in this way, your schedule and costs are updated so you know what to expect as you traverse the weeks and months of your project. Use the calculating power of Microsoft Project to:

- Calculate variances between your original baseline plan and your current schedule and use these variances to help you adjust tasks later in the project.

- Perform earned value analyses to measure your progress against where you expected to be at this point in time.

- Compare resource costs as they are being incurred against your project budget to see whether you are on track or if overruns are on the horizon.

- Generate reports you can share at status meetings to communicate the appropriate level of information.

By entering tracking data in your project plan, you'll always have the up-to-date details you need at your fingertips. If you need to adjust the plan, either to recover a slipping phase or to respond to a directive to cut 10 percent of the project budget, Microsoft Project serves as your project management information system to help you quickly and accurately make those adjustments.

Saving Original Plan Information Using a Baseline

The project plan, having been adjusted to perfection, is considered your baseline. Think of it as your original plan. It represents the most ideal balance between scope, schedule, and cost.

The project plan, at this point in time, is also your scheduled plan. Think of it as your current plan. This is the only point in the project when the original plan and the current plan are exactly the same.

They're identical only at this time because the current project plan is fluid. As soon as you enter progress information, such as one task's actual start date or another task's percentage complete, your project plan is recalculated and adjusted to reflect the new information from those actuals.

For example, suppose that Task A has a scheduled finish date of May 3. It's linked with a finish-to-start task dependency to Task B, so Task B's scheduled start date is also May 3. However, Task A finishes 2 days early on May 1. So after entering the actual finish date of Task A, the scheduled start date of Task B, which has the default ASAP constraint, changes to May 1. The scheduled start dates of any other successor tasks are recalculated as well.

This constant recalculation is essential for you to always know where your project stands in the current reality. But what if you want to know what your original start dates were? What if you want to compare the original baseline plan with the current schedule to analyze your progress and performance?

The answer is to save baseline information. By setting a baseline, you're basically taking a snapshot of key scheduling and cost information in your project plan at that point in time; that is, before you enter your first actuals and the scheduled plan begins to diverge from the original baseline plan. With fixed baseline information saved, you'll have a basis for comparing the current or actual project plan against your original baseline plan.

The difference between baseline and current scheduled information is called a variance. Baselines, actuals, and variances are used in a variety of ways, including earned value analyses, to monitor project schedule and cost performance. In fact, you cannot perform earned value analyses at all unless you have first set a baseline.

Saving a baseline is not the same as saving the entire project plan. When you set a baseline, you copy the contents of the following specific fields for all tasks, resources, and assignments into their corresponding baseline fields:

- Cost, in the Baseline Cost field
- Duration, in the Baseline Duration field
- Finish, in the Baseline Finish field
- Start, in the Baseline Start field
- Work, in the Baseline Work field

These are the fields that will give you a good basis for schedule and budget performance as you execute your project.

New in Microsoft Office Project 2007 are additional baseline fields for specialized purposes, as shown in Table 10-1.

Table 10-1 New Baseline Fields in Project 2007

If you have set up this...	Then baseline information is copied here...	For more information, see...
Project budget resources that use the Budget Cost and Budget Work fields	Baseline Budget Cost Baseline Budget Work	The section titled "Setting Up and Reviewing a Project Budget" in Chapter 8
Deliverables with linked projects	Baseline Deliverable Finish Baseline Deliverable Start	The section titled "Depending on Deliverables in Other Linked Projects" in Chapter 22
Fixed costs on any tasks	Baseline Fixed Cost Baseline Fixed Cost Accrual	The section titled "Planning Fixed Task Costs" in Chapter 8

Setting a Baseline

To save the first set of baseline information for your project plan, follow these steps:

1. Click Tools, Tracking, Set Baseline.

   The Set Baseline dialog box appears (see Figure 10-1).

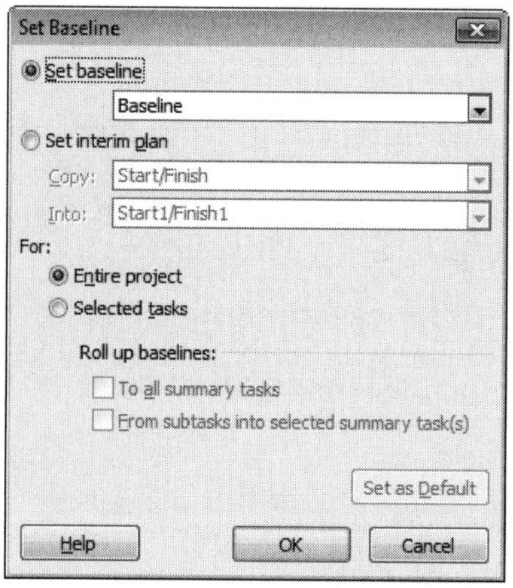

Figure 10-1 Use the Set Baseline dialog box to save up to 11 baselines and 10 interim plans.

2. Make sure that the Set Baseline option is selected.

3. In the box under the Set Baseline option, make sure that Baseline (not Baseline 1 or Baseline 2) is selected.

4. Under For, make sure that the Entire Project option is selected.

5. Click OK.

Although nothing appears to happen, as soon as you click OK, all your scheduled fields are copied into their corresponding baseline fields. The value stored in the Cost field is copied into the Baseline Cost field. The value stored in the Work field is copied into the Baseline Work field, and so on.

But what if you set a baseline and later add another set of additional tasks? Even after you initially set the baseline, you can still add tasks to it, as follows:

1. In the Gantt Chart or another task sheet, select the tasks that you want to add to the baseline.

2. Click Tools, Tracking, Set Baseline to display the Set Baseline dialog box. Make sure that the Set Baseline option is selected.

3. Under the Set Baseline option, make sure that Baseline is selected.

   The Baseline box lists the date you last set the baseline. If you want to add tasks to a different baseline, for example, Baseline 1 or Baseline 2, click that baseline in the list.

4. Under For, select the Selected Tasks option.

   When you select the Selected Tasks option, the Roll Up Baselines check boxes become available (see Figure 10-2). This option ensures that the summarized baseline data shown in summary tasks is accurate and rolled up the way you expect.

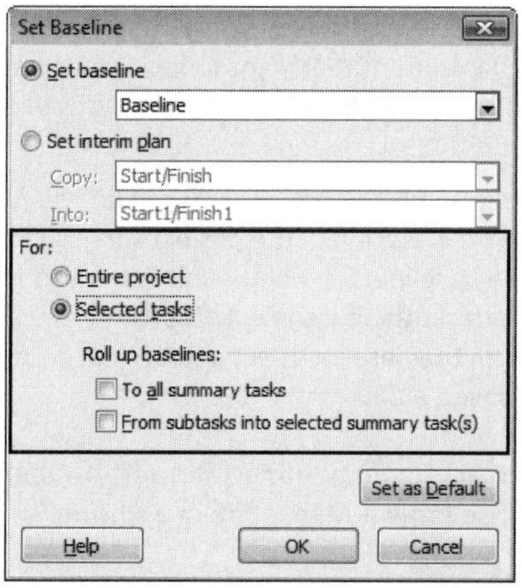

Figure 10-2 When you set a baseline for selected tasks, you can choose how to update the corresponding baseline data on summary tasks.

5. Select the check box that reflects how you want the baseline information of the selected task to be rolled up to summary tasks.

   By default, after the initial baseline is set, a summary task is not updated when a subtask is modified, added, or deleted.

   ❏ If you want the selected tasks to be rolled up to all associated summary tasks, select the To All Summary Tasks check box.

   ❏ If you want the selected tasks to be rolled up only to a selected summary task, select the From Subtasks Into Selected Summary Task(s) check box.

6. Click OK and then click Yes to confirm that you want to change the existing baseline.

Chapter 10

Note

When setting a baseline, click the name of the baseline that has a Last Saved date. Under For, select Entire Project or Selected Tasks to specify whether you want to overwrite the baseline information of the entire project or only of selected tasks. The current schedule information in your project plan overwrites the baseline information in the selected baseline.

Protecting Baseline Information

If you're using Microsoft Office Project Professional 2007 with Microsoft Office Project Server 2007 and the enterprise project management features, your project server administrator grants or denies the ability to set baselines in enterprise projects. Only those who have the Save Protected Baseline or Save Unprotected Baseline permission set by the administrator can set or potentially overwrite a baseline in your project. This baseline protection feature is used by organizations that want to lock down baseline information and ensure it's never changed through the life of the project without the proper stakeholder approvals.

For example, the project manager builds the project and obtains buyoff from all managing stakeholders. When that buyoff is achieved, the project server administrator might check out the project and set the baseline. Or the administrator might temporarily grant the project manager permission to set the baseline. After it's set, the administrator removes that permission. Either way, the baseline is set and cannot be edited or changed. Additional baselines cannot be saved either.

For more information about project server administrator responsibilities, see Chapter 21, "Administering Your Enterprise Project Management Solution."

Reviewing Baseline Information

After you save baseline information, you can review it in various ways. Initially, baseline information is identical to the scheduled information. As your team starts to complete work on the project, the two might diverge. It is this deviation, and the amount of it, that you'll be interested in as you monitor and control the project.

The following lists methods of reviewing baseline information:

- **Apply the Tracking Gantt.** Click View, Tracking Gantt. The Tracking Gantt shows the baseline Gantt bars underneath the scheduled Gantt bars (see Figure 10-3).

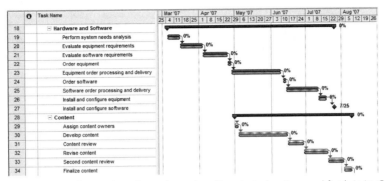

Figure 10-3 The Tracking Gantt shows baseline start, duration, and finish in its Gantt bars, in relation to the scheduled Gantt bars.

- **Apply the Baseline table to a task sheet.** Click View, Table, More Tables. Click Baseline and then click Apply. This table shows baseline information for duration, start, finish, work, and cost (see Figure 10-4). This table is also useful if you ever need to edit baseline information.

Task Name	Baseline Dur.	Baseline Start	Baseline Finish	Baseline Work	Baseline Cost
⊟ **Hardware and Software**	**103 days**	**Mon 3/5/07**	**Wed 7/25/07**	**1,052 hrs**	**$36,560.00**
Perform system needs analysis	9 days	Mon 3/5/07	Thu 3/15/07	36 hrs	$1,080.00
Evaluate equipment requirements	13 days	Fri 3/16/07	Tue 4/3/07	52 hrs	$1,560.00
Evaluate software requirements	15 days	Wed 4/4/07	Tue 4/24/07	60 hrs	$1,800.00
Order equipment	3 days	Wed 4/25/07	Fri 4/27/07	12 hrs	$3,360.00

Figure 10-4 The Baseline table shows many of the baseline fields.

> **Note**
>
> Technically, a baseline field should never be edited. The baseline information is a snapshot of the project plan information at a particular point in time. When you change a baseline field, you're probably changing a variance or results of an earned value analysis.

If you need different values in baseline fields because of changed circumstances, set a new baseline, for example, Baseline 1 or Baseline 2. You can retain the values in your original baseline and choose which baseline is to be used for earned value analyses.

- **Add baseline fields to an existing table.** You might like to add a baseline field next to the equivalent scheduled field in the Entry table, for example (see Figure 10-5). You can add the Baseline Duration field next to the Duration field and the Baseline Start field next to the Start field. Click Insert, Column. In the Field Name box, click the baseline field you want to add. The names of all baseline fields begin with the word Baseline.

Chapter 10

Task Name	Baseline Duration	Duration	Baseline Start	Start	Baseline Finish	Finish
⊟ **Hardware and Software**	**103 days**	**103 days**	**Mon 3/5/07**	**Mon 3/5/07**	**Wed 7/25/07**	**Wed 7/25/07**
Perform system needs analysis	9 days	9 days	Mon 3/5/07	Mon 3/5/07	Thu 3/15/07	Thu 3/15/07
Evaluate equipment requirements	13 days	13 days	Fri 3/16/07	Fri 3/16/07	Tue 4/3/07	Tue 4/3/07
Evaluate software requirements	15 days	15 days	Wed 4/4/07	Wed 4/4/07	Tue 4/24/07	Tue 4/24/07
Order equipment	3 days	3 days	Wed 4/25/07	Wed 4/25/07	Fri 4/27/07	Fri 4/27/07
Equipment order processing and delivery	6 ewks	6 ewks	Fri 4/27/07	Fri 4/27/07	Fri 6/8/07	Fri 6/8/07

Figure 10-5 Showing baseline fields next to the equivalent scheduled fields in a table can help you see at a glance whether and how much of a variance exists.

Note

Open the Project Statistics dialog box to compare current schedule information with baseline information in terms of Start, Finish, Duration, Work, and Cost. Click Project, Project Information and then click the Statistics button.

TROUBLESHOOTING

You see nothing in the baseline fields

Baseline fields show a value of 0 or NA until you set a baseline. If you add baseline fields to a table, apply the Baseline table, or show the Tracking Gantt before you have set a baseline, you'll see no information. Click Tools, Tracking, Set Baseline and then click OK. The baseline fields are now populated.

For more information about using baseline information to analyze variance and monitor progress, see Chapter 11, "Responding to Changes in Your Project." For more information about earned value, see Chapter 13, "Analyzing Progress Using Earned Value."

TROUBLESHOOTING

Your baseline information doesn't roll up

When you first set your baseline, any baseline fields you display show the proper rollup amounts, whether it's duration, start date, finish date, cost, and so on.

As you adjust the schedule or enter tracking information, your scheduled information changes, whereas the baseline information remains the same. It's supposed to stay the same. The job of the baseline is, of course, to always show information from your original plan so you can make the necessary comparisons.

Now suppose that you edit a baseline field, even if you know you shouldn't. Although Microsoft Project enables you to edit an individual baseline field, its associated summary tasks are not recalculated to reflect your edit. Every change that's made to the baseline chips away at the integrity of the baseline information and dilutes the purpose of having the baseline in the first place.

A more likely scenario is that you've added or removed tasks in the plan, and these changes are not reflected in the baseline. Strictly speaking again, such changes are not supposed to be in the baseline because it is a different state from your original plan.

In any case, if you do have a legitimate reason for updating baseline information, you can add selected tasks to the baseline and have the summary information recalculated, as follows:

1. Select the tasks with the changed information. If applicable, select the summary task(s) you want updated as well.

2. Click Tools, Tracking, Set Baseline. Make sure the Set Baseline option is selected, and that the baseline you want to use is selected in the box.

3. Under For, click the Selected Tasks option.

   The Roll Up Baselines section becomes available.

4. Select the To All Summary Tasks check box if you want all changed information in the selected tasks to roll up to all associated summary tasks.

   Select the From Subtasks Into Selected Summary Task(s) if you want the changed information in selected subtasks to roll up only into your selected summary tasks.

Saving Additional Baselines

Sometimes, you track your project for a period of time and then a big change occurs. Maybe your company undergoes a major shift in priorities. Maybe an emergency project comes up that takes you and your resources away from this project. Maybe funding was stalled and then started up again. In such cases, your original baseline might not be as useful a tool as it once was. And although you don't want to replace it entirely, you want to use another more up-to-date baseline for your everyday tracking requirements.

Even if nothing catastrophic happened to your project, you might still have good uses for multiple baselines. In addition to taking that snapshot at the beginning of your execution phase, you might want to take another snapshot at the end of each month or each quarter. This snapshot can show more exact periods of time when you experienced greater variances between baseline and scheduled information.

You can save up to 11 different baselines. If you use earned value analyses, you can select any of 11 saved baselines for the earned value calculations.

To set an additional baseline, do the following:

1. Click Tools, Tracking, Set Baseline.

2. Make sure that the Set Baseline option is selected.

3. In the Set Baseline list, click Baseline 1, for example (see Figure 10-6).

Chapter 10

Figure 10-6 To set an additional baseline, choose any of the baselines in the list.

If a baseline has a Last Saved date after it, you already saved information in that baseline. If you select a baseline with a Last Saved date, you'll overwrite the previous baseline information with current schedule information.

4. Under For, make sure that the Entire Project option is selected.

To review the contents of additional baseline fields, click Insert, Column in a task sheet. In the Field Name box, click the name of the additional baseline field you want to add to the table, for example, Baseline1 Duration or Baseline5 Start. The column and the contents of the field for each task are displayed in the table.

Reviewing Multiple Baselines

Using the Multiple Baselines Gantt, you can view Gantt bars reflecting different baselines. Showing stacked and differentiated Gantt bars for all the baselines you've set provides you with a visual representation of schedule changes from one set of baseline information to another.

Click View, More Views and then click Multiple Baselines Gantt. Each baseline is represented as a different color Gantt bar (see Figure 10-7).

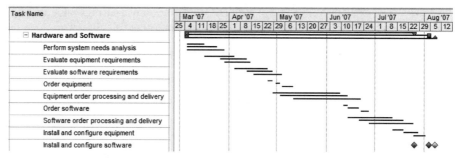

Figure 10-7 Apply the Multiple Baselines Gantt to show all the baselines you have set.

Project Management Practices: Working with the Baseline

The first baseline you set is the approved project schedule. This plan has been adjusted and refined to the point where it meets the scope, the targeted finish date, and the budget of the project. The baseline plan has been deemed technically feasible given available resources. The baseline plan has been approved as the plan of record by the managing stakeholders.

This baseline plan is a component of the overall project plan. It provides the basis for measuring the schedule and cost performance of the project. In turn, any variances found can drive decisions about whether corrective actions should be taken and what those corrective actions should be.

In the course of project execution, if the schedule variance becomes very large, perhaps because of major scope changes or lengthy delays, rebaselining might be needed to provide realistic information from which to measure performance. Prior to Microsoft Office Project 2002, rebaselining was a painful decision for project managers using Microsoft Project because only one set of baseline information could be saved. However, now project managers can save up to 11 baselines. There should always be a single primary baseline, however, to serve as the definitive baseline to be used for analysis and authoritative historical data.

Saving Additional Scheduled Start and Finish Dates

When you set a baseline, remember that it saves duration, work, and cost information, as well as the start and finish information for each task. Because of this, be aware that each baseline you save significantly increases the size of your project file. Setting the first baseline can nearly double the file size. Setting the second baseline can add another third on top of that.

If you have certain situations in which you don't need to save the entire baseline, but could just use a quick snapshot of your start and finish fields at a certain point in time, consider saving an interim plan instead. An interim plan is similar to a baseline plan in that it saves task information at a certain point in time for you to use for comparison purposes later. It differs from a baseline in that it saves only the start and finish fields, and therefore doesn't create such a big hit on your project file size.

You can save up to 10 different sets of start and finish dates with 10 different interim plans. Think of these interim plans as mini-baselines. An interim plan saves the current start and finish dates and stores them in the custom Start1-10 and Finish1-10 fields.

An interim plan is best used as a quick tool for seeing the effects of a series of changes, for example, a set of progress updates or adjustments to bring in the project finish date. Save an interim plan just before making such changes. Make the changes you want, and then set up a Gantt chart view showing the current start and finish Gantt bars with the Start1 and Finish1 Gantt bars so you can easily see the differences your changes made to the task dates.

Chapter 10

To set an interim plan, follow these steps:

1. Click Tools, Tracking, Set Baseline.

2. Select the Set Interim Plan option.

3. By default, the Copy box displays Start/ Finish.

   This display indicates that the dates in the currently scheduled Start and Finish fields will be saved as this interim plan. You can copy from a different set of Start and Finish fields. In the Copy list, click the set you want.

4. By default, the Into box displays Start1/ Finish1.

   This display specifies where the start and finish dates of this interim plan will be stored. You can copy the Start and Finish fields into a different set of Start and Finish fields. In the Into box, click the set you want.

5. Under For, click Entire Project or Selected Tasks.

You can copy start and finish dates from other baselines into an interim plan. This process can be useful if you have an old baseline you want to reuse, but you want to retain the start and finish dates. To do this, click the old baseline in the Copy list and then click the set of Start and Finish fields in the Into list.

You can also copy start and finish dates from an interim plan to one of the baselines, which can be useful if you used interim plans as a substitute for baselines in the past. Now that multiple baselines are available, you can take advantage of them by using your interim plan information. To do this, click the interim plan containing the start and finish dates in the Copy list. Then in the Into list, click the baseline to which you want the information to be moved.

Rename the Fields Used in Your Interim Plan

If you set an interim plan using the Start1 and Finish1 fields, for example, remember that you cannot then use the Start1 and Finish1 fields for any other purpose. It's a good idea to give the fields a name so you don't forget and create another use for them. To name the custom fields used in an interim plan, follow these steps:

1. Click Tools, Customize, Fields.

2. In the Type field, click Finish.

3. In the Field list, click the custom finish field, for example Finish1 or Finish4, that you are using for your interim plan.

4. Click the Rename button and then enter a name for the custom finish field, for example, Interim Plan2 (see Figure 10-8).

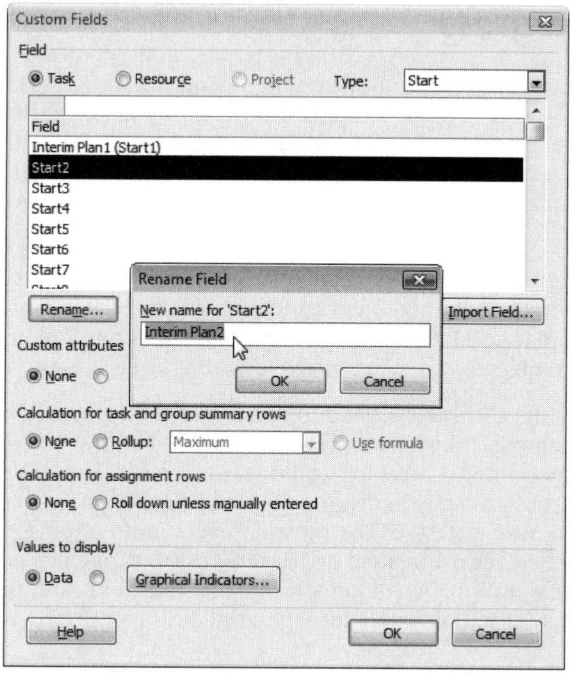

Figure 10-8 To prevent confusion, rename the custom start and finish fields you are using for interim plans.

5. Click OK in the Rename Field dialog box.

6. In the Type field, click Start.

7. Repeat steps 3–5 for the custom start field you are using for your interim plan.

Clearing a Baseline

You can clear baseline and interim plan fields, as follows:

1. Click Tools, Tracking, Clear Baseline.

The Clear Baseline dialog box appears.

2. Select the Clear Baseline Plan or Clear Interim Plan option.

3. In the corresponding box, click the name of the sets of fields you want to clear; for example, Baseline 3, or Start5/Finish5.

4. Select the Entire Project or Selected Tasks option.

5. Click OK.

The selected fields are cleared.

Updating Task Progress

So the resources are digging into their assignments and progress is being made. At regular intervals, you want to record their progress in Microsoft Project. Depending on how much time you want to spend entering progress information (and how much time you want your team members to spend doing that), you can choose a simple, high-level method; a comprehensive, detailed method; or something in between.

Entering actual progress information into Microsoft Project ensures that you'll always know how the project's going. You can keep an eye on the critical path and your budget. You can monitor key tasks and know exactly when you'll be handing off an important deliverable. With actual information coming into your project plan, you can also anticipate potential problems and take corrective actions as necessary.

If you're using Office Project Server 2007 with Microsoft Office Project Web Access, updating task progress can become highly automated. You set up the types of progress information you want to receive from your team members, and that information is integrated with the assignments in the progress tracking Web page that team members use in Office Project Web Access. Every week (or however often you specify), team members send you an update regarding their actual progress toward completing tasks. You can have the progress information automatically integrated into your project plan, or you can review the information before incorporating it.

For more information about exchanging task updates using Project Web Access, see Chapter 22, "Managing Enterprise Projects and Resources."

> ## Project Management Practices: Scope and Quality Verification
>
> As you meet milestones in your project and hand off deliverables, be sure to obtain formal acceptance of the project scope from the appropriate stakeholders, for example, the sponsor or customer. The sponsor reviews the deliverables and signs off that they're completed to his or her satisfaction.
>
> At the same time, the sponsor should also check the correctness, or quality standards, of the work results.
>
> It's important to have this acceptance process at various intermediate stages throughout the project—for each deliverable or at the end of each major phase, for example—rather than waiting until the end of the project.

Whether you're exchanging updates electronically, getting a status update in a weekly meeting, using paper timesheets, or making the rounds to hear team members' progress, you can enter the following actual progress information in your project plan:

- Percentage complete
- Actual duration and remaining duration

- Actual start and actual finish

- Percentage work complete

- Actual work complete and remaining work

- Actual work complete by time period

> **Note**
>
> When you enter actuals in your project plan, bear in mind that you're not just keeping your schedule up to date. You're also building historical information that you can use as metrics for other similar project plans. You're recording solid, tested data about how long these tasks actually take.

When you enter one piece of status information, Microsoft Project often calculates other pieces of information. Certainly the schedule and costs are automatically recalculated.

Choosing the Best Method for Entering Actuals

You have several ways to track actual progress information in your project plan. How do you decide which method to use?

The first consideration is the level of detail you need. Your managing stakeholders might expect you to report a certain level of detail at the weekly status meetings. Or you might need reliable historical information from this project because it's serving as a benchmark for similar future projects.

The second consideration is time. Will you have time to enter detailed progress information, or will you be so busy managing the project and perhaps working on your own assigned tasks that you won't be able to keep track of everything with an adequate amount of detail? What about your team members? Are they going to be too stretched to complete an electronic or paper timesheet? If you're using Project Server and Project Web Access, certain processes are automated for you, but they still take time for your team members.

The third consideration is whether you've assigned resources to tasks in your project plan. Obviously, resources will carry out the tasks one way or another. But if you've chosen not to include resources in your project plan, you have fewer available tracking methods.

A fourth and very important consideration is the accuracy and completeness of your progress tracking data. While you can choose a single method such as entering percentage complete or actual start and actual finish, it's really a combination of methods that will result in the most reliably updated project. Whatever combination of methods you choose, make sure you record each of the following types of information:

- Actual start date

- A value of actual work completed, such as percentage complete or actual work

- A value indicating the amount of work yet to be completed, such as remaining duration or remaining work

The following are recommended methods which include these three values:

- Actual start, percentage complete, and remaining duration

- Actual start, actual work, and remaining work

- Actual work and remaining work in the timephased portion of the Task Usage or Resource Usage view

Tailor Project Web Access Progress Fields

If you're using Project Server and Project Web Access to collaborate with your team members, your project server administrator can tailor the fields shown in the team members' electronic task progress pages and timesheets. Depending on the progress information your organization wants to track, any of the following fields can be added:

- % Work Complete

- Actual Work Complete

- Actual Duration

- Remaining Duration

- Actual Finish

- Remaining Work

- Actual Start

These fields are task progress fields, so they can be most useful for helping you and team members track and update assignments. However, any task or assignment field available in Microsoft Project can be added. The updated progress information becomes part of the periodic task update that the team members send you.

For more information about how the project server administrator sets up progress fields and timesheets in Project Web Access, see the section titled "Setting Up Team Member Work Pages" in Chapter 21.

Using one primary method of tracking actuals does not prevent you from using other methods for other tasks. Although you might achieve more consistent results if you stick to one method, sometimes other tasks simply lend themselves to a different type of progress information. Certain tasks are so important that you want to track them very closely. You can do that—you're never locked into a single tracking method.

Use the Tracking Toolbar

Many of your tracking functions are available on the Tracking toolbar (see Figure 10-9). To display the Tracking toolbar, click View, Toolbars, Tracking. You can also right-click an empty spot in the toolbars area and then click Tracking.

Update as   Add   0%   Update   Collaborate
scheduled   Progress   Complete   Tasks   Toolbar
               Line

Project   Reschedule   100%   Set
Statistics   Work   Complete   Reminder

Figure 10-9 The Tracking toolbar includes buttons for setting percentage complete, updating multiple tasks at once, and more.

Depending on how you update progress in your schedule, consider continuously display the Tracking toolbar, which contains tools to review and update task status throughout the life of the project.

The following list describes the functions available on the Tracking toolbar:

- **Project Statistics** Opens the Project Statistics dialog box, which shows the current, baseline, actual, variance, and remaining information for overall project start, finish, duration, work, and cost.

- **Update As Scheduled** Enters actual information to show that the selected tasks are proceeding exactly as planned. This is a shortcut to using the Update Project dialog box with the default settings.

- **Reschedule Work** Reschedules the entire project to start any uncompleted work after the current date. This is a shortcut to using the Update Project dialog box to reschedule uncompleted work.

- **Add Progress Line** Changes your cursor to a selection tool for you to select the status date for the progress line. Click the date in the chart portion of the Gantt Chart, and the progress line is drawn according to that date. This is a shortcut to using the Progress Lines dialog box.

- **0% Complete through 100% Complete** Specifies that the selected tasks should be set to the selected percentage complete. This is a shortcut to entering numbers in the % Complete field in the Update Tasks dialog box.

- **Update Tasks** Opens the Update Tasks dialog box so you can enter percentage complete, actual or remaining duration, or actual start or finish dates.

- **Set Reminder** Opens the Set Reminder dialog box. If you work with Microsoft Office Outlook 2007, you can have a reminder appear a specified amount of time before the start or finish date of selected tasks.

- **Collaborate Toolbar** Displays the Collaborate toolbar, which you can use to publish assignments, update project progress, request progress information. You can also use various features associated with Project Server, Project Web Access, and enterprise project management.

Chapter 10

Updating Progress with Task Scheduling Controls

You can update progress by entering actual information from task scheduling controls such as percentage complete, duration, start date, and finish date. You can use these methods whether or not resources are assigned in Microsoft Project.

Entering Percentage Complete

One of the simplest methods of tracking task progress is to specify percentage complete. When you enter percentage complete, Microsoft Project calculates actual duration and remaining duration.

To enter percentage complete for one or more tasks, do the following:

1. In a task sheet view, such as Gantt Chart or Tracking Gantt, select the task(s) whose percentage complete you want to update.

   If you are updating multiple tasks at one time, make sure they all have the same actual start date and the same percentage complete.

2. Click Tools, Tracking, Update Tasks. The Update Tasks dialog box appears (see Figure 10-10).

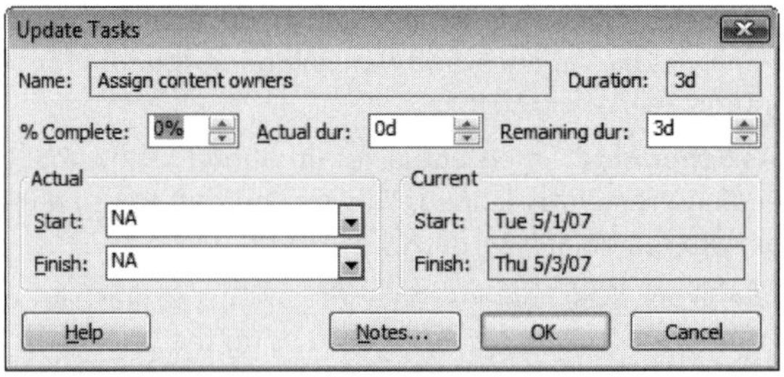

Figure 10-10 Use the Update Tasks dialog box to enter different types of progress information for one or more selected tasks.

3. In the % Complete box, enter the percentage complete that applies to all selected tasks.

4. Note the start date date under Current. If the actual start date for the selected task(s) is different from the current start date, enter that date in the Start box under Actual.

   If you do not change this start date, the actual start date is recorded as the current or scheduled start date. If you do change the actual start date, that becomes the new current, scheduled start date.

   The tasks are updated to reflect the actual start date and percentage complete. In the Gantt Chart, the percentage complete is represented as a thin black line within Gantt bars (see Figure 10-11). If you changed the actual start date, the Gantt bar shifts to the new start date, and any successor tasks are also adjusted accordingly.

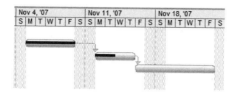

Figure 10-11 Gantt bars display how much of the task has been completed.

By default, when you enter percentage complete for a task, this percentage is distributed evenly across the actual duration of the task. You can change this to distribute to the status date instead. Click Tools, Options and then click the Calculation tab. Select the Edits To Total Task % Complete Will Be Spread To The Status Date check box.

Entering Actual and Remaining Duration

If you enter the actual duration of a task, Microsoft Project calculates the percentage complete. You can change remaining duration, if necessary.

To enter actual duration of one or more tasks, do the following:

1. In a task sheet view, such as the Gantt Chart or Tracking Gantt, select the task whose actual duration you want to update.

2. Click Tools, Tracking, Update Tasks.

3. In the Actual Dur box, enter the actual duration value.

    Note that when you change a value in the Actual Dur box, the value in the Remaining Dur box is not automatically recalculated unless you click OK and close the dialog box. For example, suppose you're entering your first actuals for a 4-day task. When you enter 2d in the Actual Dur box, the Remaining Dur box still shows 4d. If you leave the Remaining Dur box as is and click OK, when you open the Update Tasks dialog box again, the Remaining Dur box now shows 2d.

4. If you expect the task to take more or less time than currently scheduled, update the remaining duration in the Remaining Dur box.

5. Note the start date date under Current. If the actual start date for the selected task(s) is different from the current start date, enter that date in the Start box under Actual.

    If you do not change this start date, the actual start date is recorded as the current or scheduled start date for the task. If you do change the actual start date, that becomes the new current, scheduled start date for the task.

    The tasks are updated to reflect the actual start date and actual duration, including the calculated percentage complete.

Chapter 10

> **Note**
>
> By default, when you enter progress information for tasks, Microsoft Project automatically calculates the actual and remaining work and cost for assigned resources. This is the case when you update percentage complete, actual duration, or remaining duration of tasks or assignments.
>
> If you prefer to enter values for actual and remaining work and cost yourself rather than have Microsoft Project calculate it for you based on entered task progress, you can turn this option off. Click Tools, Options and then click the Calculation tab. Clear the Updating Task Status Updates Resource Status check box.

Entering Actual Start and Actual Finish

When you enter actual start and finish dates for tasks, you can better monitor the finish date of the project as whole, especially when working with critical tasks. When you enter an actual start date, the scheduled start date changes to match the actual start date. Likewise, when you enter an actual finish date, the scheduled finish date changes to match the actual finish date. Any successor tasks are rescheduled as needed.

To enter an actual start or finish date for one or more tasks, do the following:

1. In a task sheet view, such as the Gantt Chart or Tracking Gantt, select the task(s) whose actual start or finish date you want to update.

2. Click Tools, Tracking, Update Tasks.

3. Under Actual, enter the actual start date in the Start box or the actual finish date in the Finish box.

    The scheduled start and finish dates are shown under Current.

TROUBLESHOOTING

Your scheduled start and finish dates change when you enter actuals

When you enter actual start or actual finish dates, your scheduled (current) start or finish dates change to match. Microsoft Project recalculates the scheduled dates so that you can see any effects the change might have on the rest of your schedule. For example, if Task A were scheduled to finish on May 14 but it finished on May 18 instead, you'd need to know how its successor Task B is now scheduled. This update is especially important when critical tasks are involved.

If you want to keep your scheduled start and finish dates for comparison purposes, set a baseline or interim plan before you enter the actuals. With a baseline, not only can Microsoft Project remember the original start and finish dates; it can also calculate the differences between the original and scheduled information. These differences are stored in the Variance fields, which are empty until you set a baseline and start entering progress information.

Design a Custom Tracking View

Use the Project Guide to help you set up a custom tracking view tailored to work-related progress information and how you're receiving it. The tracking wizard facilitates your tracking efforts, whether progress information comes in automatically through Project Server and Project Web Access or you're entering information manually. Either way, the wizard helps you set up the tracking of work-related progress information.

To start, click Track on the Project Guide toolbar and then click the Prepare To Track The Progress Of Your Project link. Read the information in the Project Guide pane and work through the steps, clicking the Continue link at the bottom of the page when you're ready to move to the next step. When finished, click the Save And Finish link (see Figure 10-12).

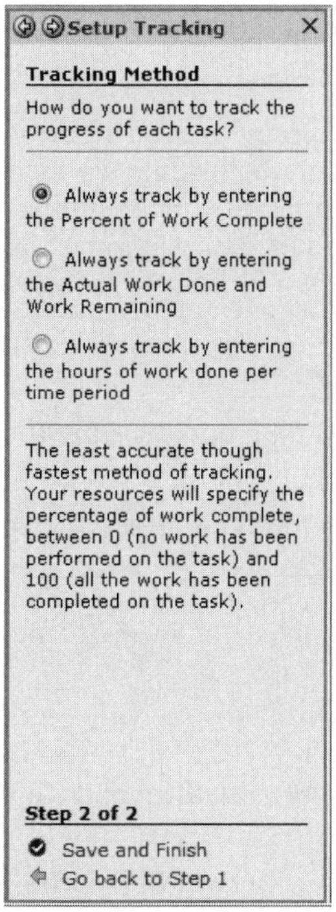

Track ▾

Track

Figure 10-12 The wizard in the Project Guide walks you through the steps for setting up a custom tracking view.

When you want to enter progress information, click Track on the Project Guide toolbar. Click the Incorporate Progress Information Into The Project link. Your custom view appears, and the Project Guide pane provides guidelines and controls to help you through the process.

You can also access your custom tracking view on the View menu.

Chapter 10

Using Resource Work to Update Progress

If resources are assigned in Microsoft Project, you can update progress information based on work for the task or the assignment. Work doesn't exist in your project plan unless you assign resources, at which time task duration is translated into assignment work time. Work can be further divided among multiple assigned resources, depending on the task type. Using work to update progress can be more precise than updating with percentage complete or actual duration.

The following work tracking methods are listed in order from the quickest and simplest to the most sophisticated. Remember that for the most accurate and complete updates of project information, be sure that the method you use includes the actual start date, some indication of actual work completed, and some indication of the remaining work.

Entering Percentage Work Complete

If human resources are assigned in Microsoft Project, you can enter their reports of what percentage of work they've completed so far. Remember, work comes into existence only when work resources (people or equipment) are assigned to tasks. To enter percentage work complete for a task (rather than for an assignment), follow these steps:

1. Display a task sheet view, such as the Tracking Gantt or Task Usage.

2. Click View, Table, Work to apply the Work table.

3. In the % W. Comp. field of the task you want to update, enter the value of percentage work complete.

For better progress tracking results, also make sure that the Actual Start field for this task is updated.

Follow these steps to enter percentage work complete for an assignment (rather than for a task):

1. Display the Task Usage view.

2. Select the assignment (the resource name beneath the task) whose percentage work complete you want to update.

   If you want to update several assignments at once with the same percentage work complete, select them all.

Assignment
Information

3. On the Standard toolbar, click Assignment Information and then click the Tracking tab (see Figure 10-13).

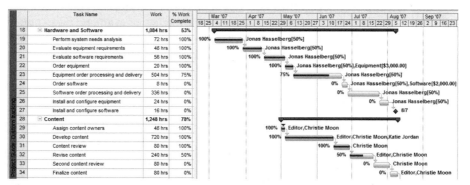

Figure 10-13 Use the Tracking tab in the Assignment Information dialog box to update progress for an assignment.

4. In the Actual Start box, enter the date that work on this assignment began.

5. In the % Work Complete box, enter the percentage complete for this assignment.

If entering percentage work complete will be your primary method of updating progress information, use the Project Guide to create a custom tracking view. A view similar to the Tracking Gantt is created with the % Work Complete field added as a column in the sheet portion of the view (see Figure 10-14).

Figure 10-14 The Project Guide can create a custom view for updating percentage work complete, which is considered the quickest method of entering work-related actuals.

Update Progress Around a Status Date

As you enter actual progress, you can choose the status date to be the reference point for actual and remaining portions of the task. Changing the status date can be helpful if you received actuals on Friday, but you don't enter them into the project plan until the next Wednesday. If you were to use Wednesday's date as the status date, some of your actuals could be skewed. By default, the status date is the current date; that is, today. To set the status date, do the following:

1. Click Project, Project Information.

2. In the Status Date box, enter the status date you want to use for the actual progress information you're about to enter.

You have additional options about how actual progress is to be entered in your project plan. Click Tools, Options and then click the Calculation tab. Under Calculation Options for your project file, a series of four check boxes provides options for handling actual and remaining task information in your schedule in relation to the status date. These options are as follows:

- Move End Of Completed Parts After Status Date Back To Status Date

- And Move Start Of Remaining Parts Back To Status Date

- Move Start Of Remaining Parts Before Status Date Forward To Status Date

- And Move End Of Completed Parts Forward To Status Date

Entering Actual Work Complete and Remaining Work

If resources are assigned in Microsoft Project, you can enter their reports of actual work completed. If they believe that there is more or less work (than originally scheduled) remaining to be done, you can adjust remaining work as well.

If you have multiple resources assigned to a task, and you enter actual work completed for the task, the work amounts are evenly distributed among the assigned resources. To enter total amounts for actual work completed on a task (rather than for an assignment), do the following:

1. Display a task sheet, such as the Task Usage view or Tracking Gantt.

2. Click View, Table, Work.

3. If necessary, drag the divider bar to see the Actual (work) field (see Figure 10-15).

	Task Name	Work	Baseline	Variance	Actual	Remaining	% W. Comp.
18	⊟ Hardware and Software	1,084 hrs	1,052 hrs	32 hrs	574 hrs	510 hrs	53%
19	Perform system needs analysis	72 hrs	36 hrs	36 hrs	72 hrs	0 hrs	100%
20	Evaluate equipment requirements	48 hrs	52 hrs	-4 hrs	48 hrs	0 hrs	100%
21	Evaluate software requirements	56 hrs	60 hrs	-4 hrs	56 hrs	0 hrs	100%
22	Order equipment	20 hrs	12 hrs	8 hrs	20 hrs	0 hrs	100%
23	Equipment order processing and delivery	504 hrs	504 hrs	0 hrs	378 hrs	126 hrs	75%
24	Order software	8 hrs	12 hrs	-4 hrs	0 hrs	8 hrs	0%
25	Software order processing and delivery	336 hrs	336 hrs	0 hrs	0 hrs	336 hrs	0%

Figure 10-15 Use the Work table to update actual work on a task.

4. In the Actual (work) field of the task you want to update, enter the actual work value.

The values in the Remaining (work) and % W. Comp fields are recalculated.

For better progress tracking results, make sure that the Actual Start field for this task is updated.

To enter total amounts of actual work completed on an assignment (rather than for a task), do the following:

1. Display the Task Usage view.

2. Click View, Table, Work.

3. If necessary, drag the divider bar to see the Actual (work) field.

4. In the Actual (work) field of the assignment (the resource name under the task) you want to update, enter the actual work value.

    The values in the Remaining (work) and % W. Comp fields for the assignment are recalculated.

> **Note**
>
> Another way to update actual work is by using the Assignment Information dialog box. Double-click the assignment to open the Assignment Information dialog box. Click the Tracking tab. Update the value in the Actual Work box. This is also a good method of updating actual work for multiple assignments if they all have the same value.

If entering actual work will be your primary method of updating progress information, use the Project Guide to create a custom tracking view. A view similar to the Tracking Gantt is created with the Tracking table applied. You might consider adding the Actual Start field to the table. This method is considered a happy medium—moderately detailed and moderately time-consuming.

Chapter 10

> **Automate Tracking with Project Web Access**
>
> If you use Office Project Professional 2007 with Project Server and Project Web Access, you can automate the gathering and entry of actuals so you don't have to enter actuals on assignments yourself. Your project server administrator sets up your team members' task progress pages and timesheets in Project Web Access so they can periodically enter and submit their actuals.
>
> You can then review these actuals and accept them for incorporation into the project plan. If you prefer, you can set a rule to have these actuals automatically accepted and incorporated.
>
> **For more information about working with team member task updates and timesheets in Project Web Access, see the section titled "Collaborating with Your Project Team" in Cahpter 22.**

Entering Actual Work by Time Period

The most comprehensive method of updating actual progress information is to enter actual and remaining work on assignments by time period. This is the smallest unit of information you can enter because you're entering information about the assignment (rather than the task as a whole), and you're probably entering hours worked in a day.

To enter actual and remaining work in the timephased portion of the Task Usage view, follow these steps:

1. Display the Task Usage view.

2. Click Format, Details, Actual Work.

   The timephased portion of the view changes to include Act. Work as a row under (scheduled) Work.

3. If you also want to show rolled-up actual work totals for assignments, apply the Work table to the sheet portion of the view. Click View, Table, Work (see Figure 10-16).

Task Name		Work	Baseline	Variance	Actual	Remaining	% W. Comp.	Details	M	T	W	T	F
22	⊟ Order equipment	20 hrs	12 hrs	8 hrs	20 hrs	0 hrs	100%	Work	4h	4h	4h	4h	
								Act. Work	4h	4h	4h	4h	
	Jonas Hasselberg	20 hrs	12 hrs	8 hrs	20 hrs	0 hrs	100%	Work	4h	4h	4h	4h	
								Act. Work	4h	4h	4h	4h	
	Equipment			0			0%	Work					
								Act. Work					
23	⊟ Equipment order processing and delivery	504 hrs	504 hrs	0 hrs	378 hrs	126 hrs	75%	Work				3.5h	12h
								Act. Work				3.5h	12h
	Jonas Hasselberg	504 hrs	504 hrs	0 hrs	378 hrs	126 hrs	75%	Work				3.5h	12h
								Act. Work				3.5h	12h
24	⊟ Order software	8 hrs	12 hrs	-4 hrs	0 hrs	8 hrs	0%	Work					
								Act. Work					
	Jonas Hasselberg	8 hrs	12 hrs	-4 hrs	0 hrs	8 hrs	0%	Work					
								Act. Work					

Figure 10-16 Use the Task Usage view to enter daily values of actual work on assignments.

4. In the Act. Work field for the assignment and the day, enter the actual work value.

   If you want to enter actual work for different time periods, click Zoom Out or Zoom In on the Standard toolbar.

Zoom Out

Zoom In

5. If you want to enter timephased remaining work as well, click Format, Details, Remaining Work and enter values as needed.

If entering actual work by time period will be your primary method of updating progress information, use the Project Guide to create a custom tracking view. A view similar to the Task Usage view is created with the Act. Work field added as a row in the timephased portion of the view and the Work and Actual Work fields added as columns in the sheet portion of the view.

Protect Actuals Information

Using Project Professional, Project Server, and Project Web Access to automatically gather and enter actuals, you can protect the integrity of actuals submitted by team members. Maintaining true actuals can be crucial if those actuals are directly submitted to your organization's general ledger system to produce customer invoices.

Your project server administrator first sets up the Project Web Access progress method to track hours of work per day or per week. Then the administrator sets the open reporting time period. Team members can enter actuals only during the open reporting period, not long after the period is past.

Furthermore, options can be set so that if the project manager or another user changes actual hours that have been submitted and incorporated into the project plan, those changes can be audited against what was originally submitted by the team member.

You can review the protected actuals submitted by the team member by adding the Actual Work Protected and Actuals Overtime Work Protected fields to a task sheet. You can also return actuals edited in the project plan back to their value as submitted and stored on Project Server. To do this, click Tools, Tracking, Sync To Protected Actuals.

For more information about working with actuals from team members in Project Web Access, see the section titled "Exchanging Task Progress Requests and Updates" in Chapter 22.

Rescheduling the Project

Suppose that you and your team started executing a project a few months ago. Some tasks were completed and some were in progress when your team's efforts were redirected to a different urgent priority. Now, you're all back to work on this project again, ready to pick up where you left off.

What do you do with your project plan? The scheduled dates of tasks you need to work on now are two months old. Do you have to readjust all the tasks to align them with the current calendar?

No, you just need to reschedule incomplete tasks for the current date. Microsoft Project will shift any incomplete tasks forward to a date you specify, and you can continue forward from there.

This can also work with shorter periods of time, whether it's a few weeks or even a few days on selected tasks (see Figure 10-17).

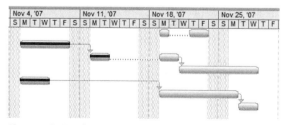

Figure 10-17 This project stalled for a few days and then was rescheduled to continue on November 19.

Chapter 10

> **Note**
>
> In a situation like this, it might be a good idea to set a new baseline. Keep the old one, but use the new baseline for your everyday variance measurements.

To reschedule uncompleted tasks, follow these steps:

1. Click Tools, Tracking, Update Project.

2. Select the Reschedule Uncompleted Work To Start After option.

3. Enter the start after date in the box.

   By default, today's date appears.

You can use this method to reschedule the entire project or just selected tasks. Select either the Entire Project or the Selected Tasks option to specify your choice.

By default, any tasks that were in progress are split so that remaining work is scheduled after the date you specify. If you don't want in-progress tasks to be split, click Tools, Options and then click the Schedule tab. Clear the Split In-Progress Tasks check box.

Any uncompleted tasks that have a date constraint (such as Must Start On or Finish No Earlier Than) are not rescheduled, which preserves the constraint and gives you the option of deciding how to handle it.

You can enter any reschedule date you want, even one in the past. If a task is in progress, the date does need to be after the task's existing stop date or actual start date.

INSIDE OUT   Update the project as scheduled

Because most tasks and projects in the real world do not run according to even the "best-laid plans," you typically would not have much use for the Update Work As Complete Through function, at least not if you want to maintain accurate progress information about the project.

However, if you have neglected entering progress information in your plan which is currently well on its way, you can use this function to help you "catch up" to where the project is now.

Using today's date or another date as the reference complete through date, you can update tasks as scheduled by following these steps:

1. Click Tools, Tracking, Update Project.

2. Make sure that the Update Work As Complete Through option is selected.

3. Enter the complete through date in the box. By default, today's date appears.

4. Select the Set 0% - 100% Complete option if you want Microsoft Project to calculate whether the task is not started, 100% complete, or in progress.

- ❑ If a task's scheduled start date is after your complete through date, the task remains 0% complete.

- ❑ If a task's scheduled finish date is before your complete through date, the task is set to 100% complete.

- ❑ If a task's scheduled start date is before your complete through date, and the scheduled finish date is after your complete through date, Microsoft Project calculates a percentage complete value.

5. Select the Set 0% Or 100% Complete Only option if you want in-progress tasks to remain at 0%. That is, any tasks whose scheduled finish date is after your complete through date do not have any progress entered for them.

You can use this method to update the entire project or selected tasks. Select the Entire Project or Selected Tasks option to specify your choice.

Updating Actual Costs

When you enter progress information for tasks or assignments, by default, the costs associated with those tasks and assignments are calculated accordingly.

Updating Actual Costs for Work Resources

If your assigned work resources (people and equipment) are associated with cost rates or per-use costs, when you enter progress information on their tasks or assignments, not only is actual work calculated, but actual costs are as well.

Updating Actual Costs for Material Resources

If you have entered costs for material resources, actual costs are also calculated based on the completion of the task.

If you need to, in the Actual Work field, you can change the value for the material by specifying the amount of material actually used. Material is measured by its material label, for example, board feet, cubic yards, or cartons, while the Work and Actual Work fields use a time unit such as hours or days for work resources. However, you can edit the Work or Actual Work fields for material resource assignments in the Task Usage view, Resource Usage view, or Tracking tab on the Assignment Information dialog box (see Figure 10-18).

Chapter 10

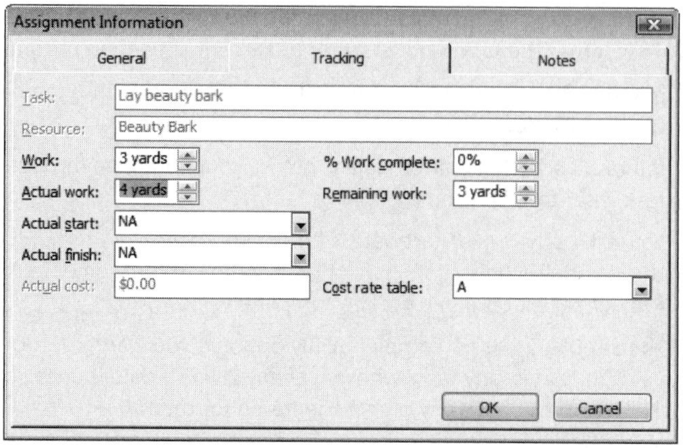

Figure 10-18 You can enter the actual amount of material used or the actual cost for the material on the Tracking tab in the Assignment Information dialog box.

Updating Actuals for Cost Resources

When you specify a percentage complete for a task, the work amount and costs for any assigned work and costs for any material resources are calculated automatically. So are any fixed costs associated with the task.

However, any assigned cost resources are not included in this automatic calculation of actual costs. You can only enter progress for cost resources on the assignment level. To do this, follow these steps:

1. In the Task Usage or Resource Usage view, double-click the assignment of the cost resource to the task.

2. In the Assignment Information dialog box, click the Tracking tab.

3. Even though cost resources are not associated with work, you can enter a percentage in the % Work Complete field, and an actual cost amount will be calculated.

    For example, if a cost resource assigned to a task is set to $100, and you enter 50% in the % Work Complete field, the actual cost will be calculated as $50.

4. If the task is 100% complete and the total cost for the cost resource has been incurred, enter that cost in the Actual Cost field.

Updating Actuals for Fixed Costs on Tasks

When you enter progress information on a task that includes a fixed cost, the actual fixed cost is calculated with the progress according to the accrual method you selected (start, finish, or prorated).

If a fixed cost has changed from your original setting, simply change the amount. In a task sheet, apply the Cost table and then change the amount in the Fixed Cost field for the task.

Manually Updating Project Costs

If resources are assigned to tasks in your project plan, and those resources also have their costs entered in Microsoft Project, costs are updated whenever you enter actual progress information. For example, suppose that a $25/hour resource is assigned to 8 hours of work on a task. When you enter that the task is 50 percent complete, $100 of actual cost is recorded for this task.

If you do not want Microsoft Project to calculate costs for you in this manner, you can turn off this option and enter costs yourself. To turn off automatic cost calculation, follow these steps:

1. Click Tools, Options and then click the Calculation tab.

2. Clear the Actual Costs Are Always Calculated By Microsoft Office Project check box.

3. By default, any edits you make to cost will be distributed evenly across the actual duration of a task.

   If you would rather distribute the costs to the status date, select the Edits To Total Actual Cost Will Be Spread To The Status Date check box.

To enter task costs manually, display a task sheet and click View, Table, Cost to apply the Cost table. Enter total actual costs in the Actual field for the task.

To manually enter timephased costs for tasks or assignments, display the Task Usage view. Click Format, Details, Actual Cost to add the Actual Cost field to the timephased portion of the view.

> **Note**
>
> It can be cumbersome and tricky to update costs manually. You'll experience more accurate results if you enter work resources and their costs in your project plan, along with any cost resources and fixed costs of tasks. When you assign those resources to tasks, costs are forecasted. When you enter progress on tasks, actual costs are calculated.

Monitoring and Adjusting the Schedule . . . . **403**   Monitoring and Adjusting Resource Workload **424**

Monitoring and Adjusting Costs **415**

During the execution phase of your project, your resources are working on their tasks, and you're tracking their progress by entering actuals into your project plan. Those actuals, combined with your baseline information, give you the means to compare your current progress against your original plan. As part of your project control responsibilities, you use this information to keep an eye on project progress. In this way, you can analyze project performance, see how you're doing, and take any corrective action that you might deem necessary.

As you monitor and analyze project performance day to day, occasionally you'll need to make adjustments. Perhaps one task finishes a few days early, and this affects its successors and their assigned resources. Maybe another task took longer than expected and went over budget. Suppose that various changes in the schedule caused a resource to become overallocated and another one to be underutilized.

You might need to adjust your project plan to account for such variances. Sometimes, the differences work in your favor, as when a task finishes early. Other times, the differences point to a potential problem, which you can prevent if you catch it soon enough.

The nature of the changes you make to your project plan depends on your project priorities. Remember the one fixed side of your project triangle (finish date, budget/resources, or scope) and adjust your project accordingly.

For more information about the project triangle, see Chapter 9, "Checking and Adjusting the Project Plan."

In addition to the day-to-day monitoring and adjusting of a project in progress, sometimes larger modifications are needed because of external changes imposed on the project. For example, your customers might announce that you must move the finish date up six weeks. Or a new corporate edict might cut $8,000 from your budget or reduce your staff by 10 percent.

Sometimes, wholesale changes to the project are needed because the scheduled finish date, overall cost, or resource allocation has somehow gotten way off track. In this case, radical measures might be needed to bring the project into conformance again.

With large, externally imposed changes or a temporarily derailed project, you might need to *replan* or reschedule the project. The techniques used are similar to those you used to hit your targets when you were first planning the project. In your project plan, you make adjustments to the schedule, costs, resources, or scope; and Microsoft Office Project 2007 recalculates your schedule so you can quickly see the results of your replanning.

Baseline, Scheduled, and Actual Project Information

In the course of monitoring project performance, you should keep in mind four terms:

- **Baseline** Baseline dates, costs, durations, and work are your project plan's values at the time you saved baseline information, typically just after you have refined the project to reflect all the elements you need and just before the project begins and you start tracking progress. This is also referred to as *planned* information.

- **Scheduled** The current project combines the project's *actual* performance on past and current tasks with the *planned schedule* for current and future tasks. The combination of the actual and scheduled information forms the current plan as scheduled. In other words, Actual + Remaining = Scheduled. Once you start entering actual progress information, the scheduled information becomes a forecast based on what has already taken place and what's expected to happen from this point forward.

- **Actual** Actual progress information reflects real data about task status. *Actuals* include data such as percentage complete, actual work, actual finish date, and actual costs.

- **Variance** The difference between baseline information and scheduled information is the *variance*. Office Project 2007 subtracts the baseline value from the scheduled value (which incorporates any actuals you have entered) to calculate the variance. Therefore, a positive work variance means more work is scheduled. A positive finish or duration variance indicates you're behind in your schedule. A positive cost variance signifies that the project is over budget. On the other hand, a negative variance means you're ahead of the game—finishing faster or under budget. A variance of zero indicates that your baseline and scheduled values are exactly the same. If actuals have been entered, this means that everything went exactly according to plan. If the task is still in the future, this means that projections forecast that the task will still go according to plan.

Whether you're making large adjustments to respond to large issues or small adjustments to keep a healthy project well on its way, you can always keep a close eye on progress. You can analyze the current status of the project and decide on any corrective actions necessary.

INSIDE OUT **Variances are calculated from scheduled values**

It might seem odd that variances are calculated from scheduled values rather than actual values. However, because the scheduled values incorporate any actual values, it makes sense. And by not requiring actual values to make the calculation, you can see variances in future tasks as well. If you see any large variances projected for future tasks or for the project as a whole, you'll still have time to take corrective action and head off the problems.

Note

Now that you're in the execution phase of your project, you might find it convenient to display the Tracking toolbar. It contains many of the tools you need to quickly review and update task status. Click View, Toolbars, Tracking. You can also right-click an empty spot in the toolbars area and then click Tracking.

Monitoring and Adjusting the Schedule

If you're managing a time-constrained project, you'll want to keep a close eye on a few pieces of task information, including the following:

- Project finish date

- Critical path

- Start and finish dates of critical tasks

- Current progress of critical tasks

If actuals have changed task scheduling to the point where your target project finish date is projected to be late, you'll need to adjust the schedule to bring that finish date back in line.

Project Management Practices: Schedule Control

It would be a safe bet to say that no project runs precisely as planned. Tasks take more or less time than planned, resources discover new information, forgotten tasks are remembered, and outside forces influence the project implementation. When changes to the project schedule take place, you might have to revise durations, rearrange task sequences, or analyze what-if scenarios for your project.

Microsoft Project is an excellent tool for schedule control because it can calculate and predict the effects of any schedule changes, whether the change comes as a result of entering actual information or what-if information. Microsoft Project tracks your planned dates against your actual dates (and other schedule information). This variance analysis is key to schedule control. Analyzing variances in dates, durations, and other schedule information helps you detect where the project is diverging from your original plan. You can then predict possible delays in the schedule further down the line and take corrective actions now to offset those delays.

Monitoring Schedule Progress

Use one or more of the following techniques to help you monitor progress and make adjustments to achieve your finish date:

- Review finish dates and the critical path to see whether you're still on track, or whether the project is slipping behind.

- Check and adjust task constraints, dependencies, and durations as necessary to have the project still finish on time.

- Add resources to tasks to shorten the duration of tasks.

For more information about monitoring and adjusting the schedule to achieve a specific finish date, see the section titled "Bringing In the Project Finish Date" in Chapter 9.

Another method for monitoring schedule progress is to set a baseline and then compare it against the current schedule. For example, you can see baseline finish dates for tasks next to their scheduled finish dates, based on actuals you entered. Then, you can look at the variances between the baseline and scheduled finish. The finish date variance, for example, is calculated as follows:

(Scheduled/Current) Finish − Baseline Finish = Finish Variance

> ### Note
>
> You can use earned value calculations, such as the Schedule Performance Index (SPI) and Schedule Variance (SV) earned value fields, to analyze your project performance so far.
>
> For more information on examining project performance, see Chapter 13, "Analyzing Progress Using Earned Value."

Set a Baseline Early On

Because baseline information is vital to tracking and analyzing progress on your project, be sure to set a baseline early in the project. The ideal time to set a baseline is after you build your project plan and adjust all values to hit your target finish date, budget, and resource workload levels.

Even if you're well into tracking progress when you realize you haven't set a baseline, go ahead and set a baseline at that time. Better late than never.

For more information about setting a baseline, see the section titled "Saving Original Plan Information Using a Baseline" in Chapter 10, "Setting a Baseline and Updating Progress."

Reviewing Overall Schedule Progress

Review your project statistics to get a broad view of how your project status compares with your baseline. Project statistics show your currently scheduled start and finish dates, along with their baseline, actual, and remaining values. To review your project statistics, follow these steps:

1. Click Project, Project Information.

   The Project Information dialog box appears.

2. Click the Statistics button.

   The Project Statistics dialog box appears. The current (scheduled) finish date appears in the Finish column (see Figure 11-1).

Project Statistics for '11NewBiz'

	Start			Finish
Current		Mon 5/7/07		Thu 10/25/07
Baseline		NA		NA
Actual		NA		NA
Variance		0d		0d

	Duration	Work	Cost
Current	124d	1,368h	$0.00
Baseline	0d?	0h	$0.00
Actual	0d	0h	$0.00
Remaining	124d	1,368h	$0.00

Percent complete:

Duration: 0%   Work: 0%   Close

Figure 11-1 The Project Statistics dialog box shows overall project information with its currently scheduled values, baseline values, actual values, and more.

Note

You can also use the Tracking toolbar to quickly open the Project Statistics dialog box. On the Tracking toolbar, click Project Statistics.

Project Statistics

Another way to keep your eye on the schedule at all times is to add the project summary task row, as follows:

1. Display the Gantt Chart or other task sheet.

2. Click Tools, Options and then click the View tab.

3. Select the Show Project Summary Task check box.

The project summary task appears at the top of any task sheet view, including the Gantt Chart (see Figure 11-2). Task information is rolled up for the entire project, and its summary total is displayed in the project summary row. Specifically, the Finish field in the project summary row shows the latest finish date in the project. If you added additional fields or applied different tables, information is also rolled up for those fields as appropriate.

	❶	Task Name	Duration	Start	Finish	May 6, '07	May 13, '07	May 20, '07
0		☐ 11NewBiz	124 days	Mon 5/7/07	Thu 10/25/07			
1		☐ Phase 1 - Strategic Plan	23 days	Mon 5/7/07	Wed 6/6/07			
2		☐ Self-Assessment	3 days	Mon 5/7/07	Wed 5/9/07			
3		Define business vision	1 day	Mon 5/7/07	Mon 5/7/07	Manager		
4		Identify available skills, information and support	1 day	Tue 5/8/07	Tue 5/8/07	Business advisor,Manager		
5		Decide whether to proceed	1 day	Wed 5/9/07	Wed 5/9/07	Manager		
6		☐ Define the Opportunity	10 days	Thu 5/10/07	Wed 5/23/07			
7		Research the market and competition	1 day	Thu 5/10/07	Thu 5/10/07	Business advisor		
8		Interview owners of similar businesses	5 days	Fri 5/11/07	Thu 5/17/07	Owners		

Figure 11-2 The Project Summary row rolls up task information to display the totals for the entire project.

By default, the regular Gantt Chart shows progress as a thin black line through the Gantt bar. To also see percentage complete next to the Gantt bars, apply the Tracking Gantt. Click View, Tracking Gantt (see Figure 11-3).

	❶	Task Name	May 20, '07	May 27, '07	Jun 3, '07
9	✓	Identify needed resources	100%		
10	✓	Identify operating cost elements	100%		
11		☐ Evaluate Business Approach		38%	
12		Define new entity requirements	75%		
13		Identify on-going business purchase opportunities	75%		
14		Research franchise possibilities	0%		
15		Summarize business approach	0%		
16		☐ Evaluate Potential Risks and Rewards			28%
17		Assess market size and stability	75%		
18		Estimate the competition	0%		

Figure 11-3 The Tracking Gantt shows the progress, the percentage complete, the baseline, and the critical path in the chart area of the view.

Reviewing Schedule Variances

To review the differences between your original baseline plan values and your currently scheduled values, apply the Variance table, as follows:

1. Display the Gantt Chart or other task sheet.

2. Click View, Table, Variance.

The Variance table is applied to the current view (see Figure 11-4).

	Task Name	Start	Finish	Baseline Start	Baseline Finish	Start Var.	Finish Var.
1	⊟ Phase 1 - Strategic Plan	Mon 5/7/07	Wed 6/6/07	Mon 5/7/07	Wed 6/6/07	0 days	0 days
2	⊟ Self-Assessment	Mon 5/7/07	Tue 5/8/07	Mon 5/7/07	Wed 5/9/07	0 days	-1 day
3	Define business vision	Mon 5/7/07	Mon 5/7/07	Mon 5/7/07	Mon 5/7/07	0 days	0 days
4	Identify available skills, information and	Mon 5/7/07	Mon 5/7/07	Tue 5/8/07	Tue 5/8/07	0 days	-1 day
5	Decide whether to proceed	Tue 5/8/07	Tue 5/8/07	Wed 5/9/07	Wed 5/9/07	0 days	-1 day
6	⊟ Define the Opportunity	Mon 5/7/07	Wed 5/23/07	Thu 5/10/07	Wed 5/23/07	-3 days	0 days
7	Research the market and competition	Mon 5/7/07	Wed 5/9/07	Thu 5/10/07	Thu 5/10/07	-3 days	-1.75 days
8	Interview owners of similar businesses	Tue 5/15/07	Mon 5/21/07	Fri 5/11/07	Thu 5/17/07	2 days	2 days
9	Identify needed resources	Fri 5/18/07	Mon 5/21/07	Fri 5/18/07	Mon 5/21/07	0 days	0 days

Figure 11-4 The Variance table shows the currently scheduled start and finish dates as compared with the baseline start and finish dates (including the differences between them).

> **Note**
>
> To quickly change to a different table, right-click the Select All box in the upper-left corner of the table in a sheet view. The list of tables appears.
>
> To quickly see the name of the current view and table, position your mouse pointer over the Select All box. A ScreenTip lists the name of the current view and table.

TROUBLESHOOTING

Your scheduled values change whenever you enter actuals

Whenever you enter actual progress information, Microsoft Project recalculates your scheduled information based on these actuals, so you can see any effect the actual progress information has on the rest of your schedule. This also enables you to continue to see scheduled projections for the project finish date and total cost, based on performance to this point. For example, if Task A was scheduled to finish on May 15, but it finishes on May 20 instead, you'd need to know how its successor, Task B, is now scheduled. This information is especially important if these are critical tasks.

If you want to keep your original start and finish dates for comparison purposes, save a baseline or interim plan before you enter the actuals. Then, add the Baseline Start and Baseline Finish fields to a task sheet, perhaps right next to your scheduled Start and Finish fields. If you're using start and finish dates saved with your interim plan, add Start1 and Finish1 (or whichever custom fields you used for your interim plan) to a task sheet.

For more information about setting baselines, setting interim plans, and adding original field information to your task sheet, see the section titled "Saving Original Plan Information Using a Baseline" in Chapter 10.

Reviewing the Critical Path

By viewing the finish date or the critical path, you can easily see whether you're still scheduled to hit your target finish date, given the actuals you've entered. To see the critical path, click View, Tracking Gantt. If you need to bring in the finish date, you might want to focus on the critical tasks.

You can filter your task sheet to show only critical tasks by clicking Project, Filtered For, Critical. To show all tasks again, click Project, Filtered For, All Tasks.

Another way to select a filter is to click the Filter tool on the Formatting toolbar. In the Filter list, click Critical. When finished, click All Tasks in the Filter list.

All Tasks
Filter

> **Note**
>
> After a critical task is completed, it becomes noncritical because it can no longer affect the completion of future tasks.
>
> For more information about viewing the critical path, see the section titled "Viewing the Critical Path" in Chapter 9.

Reviewing Task Progress

Reviewing the progress of critical tasks is the most effective means of quickly learning whether your project is staying on track to meet its target finish date. The following filters can help you focus on any potential problems with task progress:

- Late/Overbudget Tasks Assigned To
- Should Start By
- Should Start/Finish By
- Slipped/Late Progress
- Slipping Tasks (see Figure 11-5)
- Tasks With Deadlines
- Tasks With Fixed Dates

	Task Name	Start	Finish	Baseline Start	Baseline Finish	Start Var.	Finish Var.
0	⊟ 11NewBiz	Mon 5/7/07	Thu 10/25/07	Mon 5/7/07	Thu 10/25/07	0 days	0 days
1	⊟ Phase 1 - Strategic Plan	Mon 5/7/07	Wed 6/6/07	Mon 5/7/07	Wed 6/6/07	0 days	0 days
6	⊟ Define the Opportunity	Mon 5/7/07	Wed 5/23/07	Thu 5/10/07	Wed 5/23/07	-3 days	0 days
7	Research the market and competition	Mon 5/7/07	Fri 5/11/07	Thu 5/10/07	Thu 5/10/07	-3 days	0.25 days
16	⊟ Evaluate Potential Risks and Rewards	Sat 5/26/07	Tue 6/5/07	Fri 5/25/07	Mon 6/4/07	1 day	0.75 days
18	Estimate the competition	Fri 6/1/07	Fri 6/1/07	Tue 5/29/07	Tue 5/29/07	3 days	3 days
19	Assess needed resource availability	Wed 5/30/07	Mon 6/4/07	Wed 5/30/07	Thu 5/31/07	0 days	2 days
20	Evaluate realistic initial market share	Fri 6/1/07	Tue 6/5/07	Fri 6/1/07	Fri 6/1/07	0 days	1.75 days

Figure 11-5 Apply the Slipping Tasks filter to quickly see which tasks are in jeopardy (the summary tasks provide context for the tasks).

To apply one of these filters, follow these steps:

1. Display the Gantt Chart or other task sheet you want to filter.

2. On the Formatting toolbar, click the arrow in the Filter tool.

3. In the Filter list, click the filter you want.

4. When you want to show all tasks again, in the Filter list, click All Tasks.

You can also run text-based and visual reports that provide information about the progress of tasks, such as the following:

- Unstarted Tasks

- Tasks Starting Soon

- Tasks In Progress

- Completed Tasks

- Should Have Started Tasks

- Slipping Tasks

- Critical Tasks Status Report (visual report in Microsoft Office Visio 2007)

- Task Status Report (visual report in Office Visio 2007)

To run a text-based report, follow these steps:

1. Click Report, Reports.

2. Double-click Current Activities.

3. Double-click the report you want.

4. If a dialog box appears asking for more information, enter the information and then click OK.

   The report appears in a preview window. You can zoom or print the report for a closer look.

To run a visual report, follow these steps:

1. Click Report, Visual Reports.

2. On the All tab, double-click the name of the report you want.

   The report is generated from Microsoft Project data and displayed in a Visio Pivot-Diagram.

Chapter 11

Display Status Icons

You can add the Status Indicator field to any task sheet. This field displays icons that indicate whether a task is completed, on schedule, or behind schedule.

Select the column heading to the right of where you want to insert the Status Indicator column. Click Insert, Column. In the Field Name list, click Status Indicator.

If you prefer to show current task status as text rather than icons, insert the Status column instead. For every task, the status of "Future Task," "On Schedule," "Late," or "Complete" appears.

	Status Indicator	Status	Task Name
4	✓	Complete	Identify available skills, information and support
5	✓	Complete	Decide whether to proceed
6	⊘	**Late**	⊟ **Define the Opportunity**
7	⊘	Late	Research the market and competition
8	✓	Complete	Interview owners of similar businesses
9	✓	Complete	Identify needed resources
10	✓	Complete	Identify operating cost elements
11	⊘	**On Schedule**	⊟ **Evaluate Business Approach**
12	⊘	On Schedule	Define new entity requirements
13		Future Task	Identify ongoing business purchase opportunities
14		Future Task	Research franchise possibilities

Showing Progress Lines

You can add *progress lines* to your Gantt Chart that provide a graphic means of seeing whether tasks are ahead of schedule, behind schedule, or exactly on time. Progress lines are shown for tasks that have been completed, are in progress, or are currently due. They are not shown for tasks in the future.

For any given progress date, which you can set as the status date, you can have Microsoft Project draw a progress line connecting in-progress tasks and tasks that should have started (see Figure 11-6). You can set the progress date to be the current date, the project status date, or any other date you select. You can also set multiple progress dates at recurring intervals, for example, on the first Monday of every month.

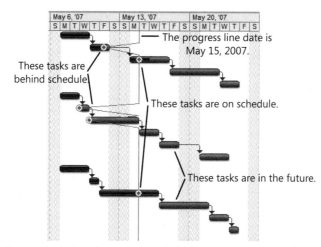

Figure 11-6 The left-pointing peaks indicate a negative schedule variance, whereas straight lines show tasks that are on or ahead of schedule as of the progress line date.

Progress lines create a graph on the Gantt Chart that provides valuable progress information, as follows:

- A progress line angled to the left indicates work that's behind schedule as of the progress line date.

- A straight progress line indicates a task on schedule as of the progress line date.

- Tasks untouched by the progress line are tasks scheduled to start in the future from the progress line date.

To add a progress line to a Gantt chart:

1. Display the Gantt Chart, Tracking Gantt, or any other Gantt view.

2. Click Tools, Tracking, Progress Lines.

    The Progress Lines dialog box appears (see Figure 11-7).

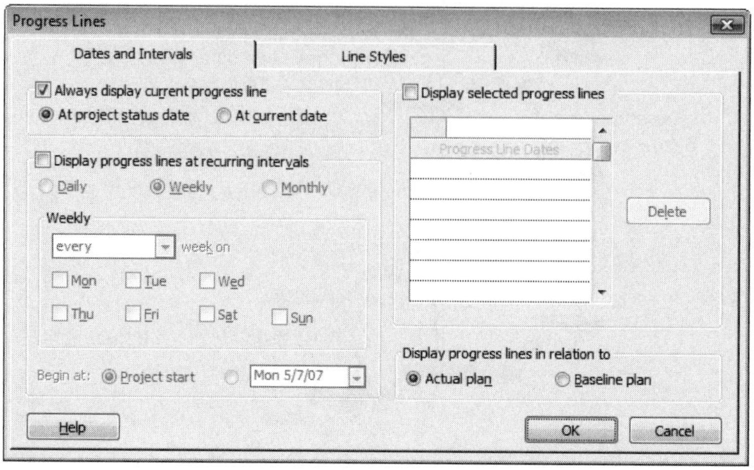

Figure 11-7 Set progress lines in the Gantt Chart using the Progress Lines dialog box.

3. On the Dates And Intervals tab, select the Always Display Current Progress Line check box. Then select whether you want the progress line to be displayed at the project status date or the current date.

The project status date, as well as the current date, is set in the Project Information dialog box (Project, Project Information). If no status date is set there, the current date (today) is used instead.

4. Under Display Progress Lines In Relation To, select whether you want progress lines to reflect the actual plan or your baseline.

5. Set any other preferences for the way you want dates and intervals of dates to be represented with your progress lines.

You can enter specific progress line dates, display progress lines at selected date intervals, and so on.

6. Click the Line Styles tab and set your preferences for how you want the progress lines to appear in the Gantt Chart.

You can specify the line type and color and the progress point shape and color for the current progress line and other progress lines (see Figure 11-8).

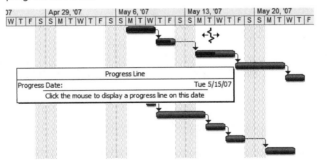

Figure 11-8 Use the Line Styles tab in the Progress Lines dialog box to customize how progress lines appear in your Gantt Chart.

Quickly Add a Progress Line

You can use the Tracking toolbar to quickly add a progress line. On the Tracking toolbar, click Add Progress Line. A ScreenTip appears, and the mouse pointer changes to the progress line icon:

In the chart area of the Gantt Chart, click where you want the progress line to be added. The Progress Line ScreenTip shows the exact date you're pointing at. The date you click becomes the status date on which the resulting progress line is based.

Add Progress Line

If you have defined progress line dates in addition to the status date or current date, you can choose to show them only when you want. For example, you might want to show progress lines in a printed view for a status meeting, but hide them while updating progress. To temporarily hide progress lines:

1. Click Tools, Tracking, Progress Lines.

2. On the Dates And Intervals tab, clear the Display Selected Progress Lines check box.

   The defined progress lines are removed from your Gantt Chart, but the dates remain in the Progress Lines dialog box for when you want to show them again.

You can remove one or more of your defined progress lines. To delete a progress line:

1. Click Tools, Tracking, Progress Lines.

2. Make sure the Dates And Intervals tab is showing.

3. Under Progress Line Dates, select the progress line you want to remove from the Gantt Chart and then click the Delete button.

To hide the current progress line reflecting the project status date or the current date:

1. Click Tools, Tracking, Progress Lines.

   The Progress Lines dialog box appears.

2. On the Dates And Intervals tab, clear the Always Display Current Progress Line check box.

Correcting the Schedule

Suppose that you reviewed your schedule details and found that your project isn't going as quickly as planned and the finish date is in jeopardy. Or perhaps upper management has imposed a schedule change, and you need to work toward a different finish date.

If you need to take corrective actions in your project plan to bring in the scheduled finish date, you can do the following:

- Check schedule assumptions—such as duration, constraints, and task dependencies—to see whether any adjustments can be made.

- Add resources to recover a slipping schedule (this will likely add costs).

- Cut scope to recover a slipping schedule (this will probably require stakeholder approval).

For more information about using any of these techniques to adjust the schedule to meet the current or new finish date, see the section titled "Bringing In the Project Finish Date" in Chapter 9.

Create a What-If Project

Suppose that an external change is being proposed, or you just want to see the effect of a potential change to your project plan. You can save another version of your project plan and make the necessary adjustments to reflect the potential change. You can then examine specifically what the imposed changes will do to your project plan in terms of schedule, cost, and resource allocation.

To save a separate what-if project, first save the project to capture any recent changes. Then click File, Save As. In the File Name box, enter a name for the what-if project and then click OK.

You can change the what-if project as much as you like. Because you saved it under a different file name, your working version of the project plan remains intact, but you gained valuable information about the impact of potential change.

If you or other stakeholders decide to go ahead with the change, you can adopt the what-if project as your new working project.

When you adjust your project plan to achieve the finish date you need, be sure to check costs, resource allocation, and scope. You need to know how your changes affect other areas of the project plan.

You might also need to set a new baseline, especially if there have been major schedule changes.

For more information on new baselines, see the section titled "Need a New Baseline?" later in this chapter.

Monitoring and Adjusting Costs

If your project is primarily constrained by budget, you'll want to keep a close eye on the resource and task costs, and on estimated costs for the project as a whole. You'll also want to adjust your project plan if you receive any actuals that are likely to blow the budget.

Project Management Practices: Cost Control

Cost control enables a project to stay within the bounds of the prescribed project budget. It involves continual monitoring of the project plan, tracking actual work and cost information, and taking corrective action where needed. If a task early in the project costs more than expected, costs might have to be trimmed in later tasks. In addition, outside forces might affect the project budget. For example, certain material costs might have gone up from the time you developed your plan to the time you're actually procuring the material. Or your company might undertake a cost-cutting initiative that requires you to cut all project costs by 15 percent.

When changes to project costs take place, you might have to adjust assignments or scope to bring costs in line with the budget. If you have a positive cost variance, the scheduled or current cost is more than your planned baseline cost. If you have a negative cost variance, the scheduled cost is less than your baseline cost. Although you certainly need to know why costs are higher than planned, you also should look into costs that are lower than planned. Lower costs can point to potential problems with increased risk, and perhaps with quality issues.

Earned value analysis is particularly useful for cost control. With variances and earned value analysis, you can assess the differences between planned and scheduled costs, determine their causes, and decide whether corrective actions are needed.

Monitoring Project Costs

Use one or more of the following techniques to monitor and adjust costs so you can continue to work within your budget:

- Display specialized views and tables to review project costs.

- Adjust the schedule to reduce costs.

- Adjust assignments to reduce costs.

For more information about monitoring and adjusting costs to achieve a specific budget, see the section titled "Reducing Project Costs" in Chapter 9.

Using baseline information you saved, you can review your current costs and compare them with baseline costs. For example, you can see baseline costs for tasks (including their resource costs) next to their scheduled costs, based on actuals you entered. Then, you can review the variances between the baseline and scheduled cost. The cost variance is calculated as follows:

(Scheduled/Current) Cost − Baseline Cost = Cost Variance

> **Note**
>
> You can use earned value calculations, such as the Budgeted Cost of Work Scheduled (BCWS) and Cost Variance (CV) earned value fields to analyze your project performance against the budget so far.
>
> For more information, see the section titled "Generating Earned Value Data" in Chapter 13.

Reviewing Overall Cost Totals

There are two ways to review your overall cost totals, as follows:

- **Review project statistics.** Click Project, Project Information and then click the Statistics button. Under Cost, review the current, baseline, actual, and remaining cost for the project. You can also click Project Statistics on the Tracking toolbar.

- **Add the project summary task row.** In the Gantt Chart or other task sheet, click Tools, Options and then click the View tab. Select the Show Project Summary Task check box. Summary totals for task information in the current table are displayed in the project summary task row at the top of the sheet. If a table containing cost information is applied, the project summary task row shows project cost totals.

Reviewing Cost Variances

Use the Cost table to review the differences between your original baseline costs and your currently scheduled costs. The Cost table includes fields containing baseline costs, total scheduled costs, actual costs, remaining costs, and cost variances. To apply the Cost table, follow these steps:

1. Display the Gantt Chart or other task sheet.

2. Click View, Table, Cost.

   The Cost table is applied to the current view (see Figure 11-9).

	Task Name	Fixed Cost	Fixed Cost Accrual	Total Cost	Baseline	Variance	Actual	Remaining
0	⊟ 11NewBiz	$0.00	Prorated	111,098.00	$0.00	111,098.00	$12,564.50	$98,533.50
1	⊟ Phase 1 - Strategic Plan	$0.00	Prorated	$19,130.00	$0.00	$19,130.00	$11,524.50	$7,605.50
2	⊟ Self-Assessment	$0.00	Prorated	$3,672.00	$0.00	$3,672.00	$528.00	$3,144.00
3	Define business vision	$0.00	Prorated	$528.00	$0.00	$528.00	$528.00	$0.00
4	Identify available skills, information and support	$0.00	Prorated	$3,144.00	$0.00	$3,144.00	$0.00	$3,144.00
5	Decide whether to proceed	$0.00	Prorated	$0.00	$0.00	$0.00	$0.00	$0.00
6	⊟ Define the Opportunity	$0.00	Prorated	$7,630.00	$0.00	$7,630.00	$7,337.50	$292.50
7	Research the market and competition	$650.00	Prorated	$1,170.00	$0.00	$1,170.00	$877.50	$292.50
8	Interview owners of similar businesses	$0.00	Prorated	$2,640.00	$0.00	$2,640.00	$2,640.00	$0.00
9	Identify needed resources	$0.00	Prorated	$1,920.00	$0.00	$1,920.00	$1,920.00	$0.00
10	Identify operating cost elements	$300.00	Prorated	$1,900.00	$0.00	$1,900.00	$1,900.00	$0.00

Figure 11-9 Apply the Cost table to a task sheet to see the most important cost data for tasks.

With the project summary task row applied, you can also review rolled up cost totals.

There's also a cost table for resources, which includes cost information for all a resource's assignments. With the Resource Sheet or Resource Usage view displayed, apply the Cost table. The Resource Cost table includes the baseline cost, scheduled cost, actual cost, remaining cost, and cost variance for all the resource's assignments (see Figure 11-10). Cost information is shown for all types of resources—work, material, and cost resources.

Chapter 11

	Resource Name	Cost	Baseline Cost	Variance	Actual Cost	Remaining
1	Business advisor	$28,080.00	$0.00	$28,080.00	$4,420.00	$23,660.00
2	Peers	$880.00	$0.00	$880.00	$880.00	$0.00
3	Lawyer	$24,480.00	$0.00	$24,480.00	$0.00	$24,480.00
4	Government agency	$2,080.00	$0.00	$2,080.00	$0.00	$2,080.00
5	Manager	$37,488.00	$0.00	$37,488.00	$2,112.00	$35,376.00
6	Owners	$2,640.00	$0.00	$2,640.00	$2,640.00	$0.00
7	Accountant	$11,200.00	$0.00	$11,200.00	$1,600.00	$9,600.00
8	Banker	$2,000.00	$0.00	$2,000.00	$0.00	$2,000.00
9	Information services	$800.00	$0.00	$800.00	$0.00	$800.00
10	Travel	$1,300.00	$0.00	$0.00	$0.00	$1,300.00
11	Marketing collateral	$500.00	$0.00	$500.00	$0.00	$500.00

Figure 11-10 Apply the Cost table to a resource sheet to see summarized cost data for resources based on their task assignments.

Review Costs Using Budget Resources

If you are using the new budget resource type with the new Budget Work and Budget Cost fields, you can group and review predetermined budget values for work and cost against your planned project costs.

Note, however, that the figures for work will be expressed as periods of time, such as hours, days, or weeks, rather than dollars. The budget costs apply only to cost resources, not work or material resources.

For information about how to create and assign budget resources, enter budget values, and align resources with their corresponding budget resources, see the section titled "Setting Up and Reviewing a Project Budget" in Chapter 8, "Planning Resource and Task Costs."

To group and compare resource costs and work against budget costs and work, see the section titled "Comparing Resource Costs Against Budget Resource Values" in Chapter 9.

Reviewing Overbudget Costs

You can apply a filter to a task or resource sheet to see only those tasks or resources associated with overbudget costs, as follows:

1. Display the view and apply the table that contains the information you want to review in the context of overbudget costs.

2. Click Project, Filtered For, More Filters.

3. In the More Filters dialog box, click Cost Overbudget and then click Apply.

   If you prefer to see all tasks or resources, but have the overbudget tasks or resources highlighted, click Highlight instead.

Microsoft Project filters for any tasks or resources whose scheduled or actual costs are higher than the baseline costs.

4. Review the tasks or resources to analyze the extent of the cost overages.

5. When you finish, show all tasks again by clicking the Filter tool on the Formatting toolbar and then clicking All Tasks.

Reviewing Cost Performance by Using Earned Value Analysis

If you set a baseline and are entering actuals, you can evaluate current cost and schedule performance using earned value calculations. To generate most earned value information, you must have the following items in your project plan:

*   A saved baseline

*   Resources assigned to tasks

*   Costs associated with assigned resources

*   Actual progress information

To review earned value information, follow these steps:

1. Display the Gantt Chart or other task sheet.

2. Click View, Table, More Tables.

3. Click Earned Value, Earned Value Cost Indicators, or Earned Value Schedule Indicators, depending on the type of earned value information you want to review.

    The table is applied to the task sheet (see Figure 11-11).

	Task Name	Planned Value - PV (BCWS)	Earned Value - EV (BCWP)	CV	CV%	CPI	BAC	EAC	VAC	TCPI
0	⊟ 11NewBiz	$0.00	$0.00	($8,261.50)	0%	0	$0.00	113,748.00	13,748.00)	0
1	⊟ Phase 1 - Strategic Plan	$0.00	$0.00	($8,261.50)	0%	0	$0.00	$21,780.00	($21,780.00)	0
2	⊟ Self-Assessment	$0.00	$0.00	($528.00)	0%	0	$0.00	$3,672.00	($3,672.00)	0
3	Define business vision	$0.00	$0.00	($528.00)	0%	0	$0.00	$528.00	($528.00)	0
4	Identify available skills, information	$0.00	$0.00	$0.00	0%	0	$0.00	$3,144.00	($3,144.00)	0
5	Decide whether to proceed	$0.00	$0.00	$0.00	0%	0	$0.00	$0.00	$0.00	0
6	⊟ Define the Opportunity	$0.00	$0.00	($7,337.50)	0%	0	$0.00	$9,130.00	($9,130.00)	0
7	Research the market and competiti	$0.00	$0.00	($877.50)	0%	0	$0.00	$2,670.00	($2,670.00)	0
8	Interview owners of similar busine:	$0.00	$0.00	($2,640.00)	0%	0	$0.00	$2,640.00	($2,640.00)	0

Figure 11-11 The Earned Value Cost Indicators table displays earned value fields related to budget performance.

You can see a list of all earned value fields available in Microsoft Project. In the Type A Question For Help box, type **fields** and then press Enter. Click Earned Value Fields. The list of all available earned value fields appears in a separate Help window.

Click a field name to open a Help topic that gives a description of each field, how it's calculated, its best uses, and an example of its use.

Table 11-1 lists the default contents of each of the three earned value tables.

Chapter 11

Table 11-1 Earned Value Tables

Table name	Included fields
Earned Value	*BCWS (Budgeted Cost of Work Scheduled)*, also known as *Planned Value* or *PV*
	BCWP (Budgeted Cost of Work Performed), also known as *Earned Value* or *EV*
	ACWP (Actual Cost of Work Performed), also sometimes referred to as *AC*
	SV (Schedule Variance)
	CV (Cost Variance)
	EAC (Estimate At Completion)
	BAC (Budget At Completion)
	VAC (Variance At Completion)
Earned Value Cost Indicators	*BCWS (Budgeted Cost of Work Scheduled)*, also known as *Planned Value* or *PV*
	BCWP (Budgeted Cost of Work Performed), also known as *Earned Value* or *EV*
	CV (Cost Variance)
	CV% (Cost Variance Percent)
	CPI (Cost Performance Index)
	BAC (Budget At Completion)
	EAC (Estimate At Completion)
	VAC (Variance At Completion)
	TCPI (To Complete Performance Index)
Earned Value Schedule Indicators	*BCWS (Budgeted Cost of Work Scheduled)*, also known as *Planned Value* or *PV*
	BCWP (Budgeted Cost of Work Performed), also known as *Earned Value* or *EV*
	SV (Schedule Variance)
	SV% (Schedule Variance Percent)
	SPI (Schedule Performance Index)

For more information about analyzing project performance with earned value, see the section titled "Reviewing Earned Value Data" in Chapter 13.

TROUBLESHOOTING

Your earned value fields all show $0.00

If you applied an Earned Value table or inserted an earned value field only to find all the values to be $0.00, it's likely that you're missing one or more of the pieces of information needed by Microsoft Project to calculate earned value fields.

For earned value to be calculated, you must have all the following items in your project plan:

- A saved baseline
- Resources assigned to tasks
- Costs associated with assigned resources
- Actual progress information
- A status date

Reviewing Budget Status

The following filters can help you focus on any potential problems with project costs and budget:

- Cost Greater Than (see Figure 11-12)
- Cost Overbudget
- Late/Overbudget Tasks Assigned To
- Work Overbudget

	Task Name	Fixed Cost	Fixed Cost Accrual	Total Cost	Baseline	Variance	Actual	Remaining
81	⊟ Establish the Operating Control Base	$0.00	Prorated	$16,560.00	$16,560.00	$0.00	$0.00	$16,560.00
83	Obtain required licenses and permits	$0.00	Prorated	$7,840.00	$7,840.00	$0.00	$0.00	$7,840.00
90	⊟ Provide Physical Facilities	$0.00	Prorated	$12,224.00	$12,224.00	$0.00	$0.00	$12,224.00
91	Secure operation space	$0.00	Prorated	$7,200.00	$7,200.00	$0.00	$0.00	$7,200.00
97	⊟ Provide Staffing	$0.00	Prorated	$21,120.00	$21,120.00	$0.00	$0.00	$21,120.00
98	Interview and test candidates	$0.00	Prorated	$7,392.00	$7,392.00	$0.00	$0.00	$7,392.00
100	Train staff	$0.00	Prorated	$8,448.00	$8,448.00	$0.00	$0.00	$8,448.00

Figure 11-12 The Cost Greater Than filter has been applied to this table to focus on those tasks that have the highest costs.

Apply a filter by clicking the arrow beside the Filter tool on the Formatting toolbar. In the Filter list, click the name of the filter you want. To show all tasks again, in the Filter list, click All Tasks.

You can also run text-based and visual reports that provide information about costs and budget status, as follows:

- Cash Flow
- Budget
- Overbudget Tasks
- Overbudget Resources
- Earned Value
- Baseline Cost Report (visual report in Microsoft Office Excel 2007)
- Baseline Report (visual report in Visio)
- Budget Cost Report (visual report in Office Excel 2007)
- Cash Flow Report (visual reports in Excel or Visio)
- Earned Value Over Time Report (visual report in Excel)
- Resource Cost Summary (visual report in Excel)

To run a text-based cost report, click Report, Reports. Double-click Costs and then double-click the report you want. If a dialog box asks for more information, enter the information and then click OK. The report appears in a preview window in which you can go on to print the report or study the details (see Figure 11-13).

Resource Name	Cost	Baseline Cost	Variance	Actual Cost	Remaining
Manager	$48,048.00	$45,408.00	$2,640.00	$2,112.00	$45,936.00
Business advisor	$31,590.00	$30,550.00	$1,040.00	$4,420.00	$27,170.00
	$79,638.00	$75,958.00	$3,680.00	$6,532.00	$73,106.00

Overbudget Resources
11NewBiz

Figure 11-13 Run the Overbudget Resources report to see which resource costs are greater than the baseline resource costs.

To run a visual report, follow these steps:

1. Click Report, Visual Reports.
2. On the All tab, double-click the name of the report you want.

The report is generated from Microsoft Project data and displayed in Visio or Excel (see Figure 11-14 for an example of a chart displayed in Excel).

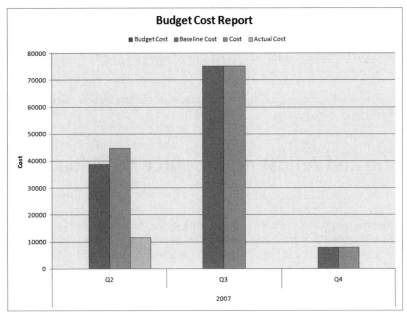

Figure 11-14 Run the Budget Cost visual report in Excel to generate a column chart showing a comparison of budgeted, baseline, scheduled, and actual costs over time.

Realigning the Project with the Budget

Suppose that you reviewed your budget details against the current project costs and found that you will end up significantly over budget. Or perhaps upper management has asked you to cut costs by 10 percent, and you need to work toward a different total project cost.

If you need to take corrective actions in your project plan to reduce project costs, you can do the following:

- Recheck your basic cost assumptions such as resource rates, per-use costs for resources, amounts for cost resources assigned to tasks, and fixed costs for tasks.

- Adjust the schedule to reduce costs. Reducing task durations and adjusting task dependencies can help reduce costs.

- Adjust assignments to reduce costs. Add, remove, or replace resources on assignments as appropriate to cut costs.

- Cut scope to reduce costs (which will probably require stakeholder approval).

When you adjust your project plan to achieve the budget you need, be sure to check your finish date, resource allocation, and scope. You need to know how your changes affect other areas of the project plan.

> **For more information about using any of these strategies to trim project costs, see the section titled "Reducing Project Costs" in Chapter 9.**

You might also consider setting a new baseline, especially if there have been major cost changes or changes that have affected the schedule.

> **For more information on setting a new baseline, see the section titled "Need a New Baseline?" later in this chapter.**

Monitoring and Adjusting Resource Workload

If you're a resource manager, or if your biggest project priority is to maintain a balanced workload among your resources, monitor your resources' workload and see if anyone is unexpectedly overallocated or underallocated. As you receive information from resources about their assigned tasks and enter actuals, you can see whether you need to take any action to prevent potential resource allocation problems in the near future.

Monitoring Resource Workload

Do one or more of the following to help you monitor and adjust the schedule to achieve a balanced resource workload:

- Review resource workloads.

- Adjust resource availability.

- Adjust assignments.

- Split tasks to reschedule remaining work for when resources have available time.

- Level assignments.

Because work (in hours, days, weeks, and so on) is the measure of resource effort on tasks, you can use the baseline value for work to help review how well resources are utilized according to actual and scheduled values. For example, you can see Maureen's baseline work for tasks next to her values for scheduled work, based on actuals she has submitted regarding her progress. Then, you can review the variances between the baseline and scheduled work. Work variance is calculated as follows:

(Scheduled/Current) Work − Baseline Work = Work Variance

If actual work values are considerably higher than originally planned, you can anticipate some problems with resource overallocation now or in the near future.

> **For more information about balancing the resource workload, see the section titled "Balancing Resource Workloads" in Chapter 9.**

You can use earned value calculations, such as the Budgeted Cost of Work Scheduled (BCWS) and Actual Cost of Work Performed (ACWP) earned value fields, to analyze project performance based on resource work. For more information, see Chapter 13.

Reviewing Overall Work Totals

There are two ways to review your overall work totals, as follows:

- **Review project statistics.** Click Project, Project Information and then click the Statistics button. Under Work, review the current, baseline, actual, and remaining work for the project. You can also click Project Statistics on the Tracking toolbar.

- **Add the project summary task row.** In the Gantt Chart or other task sheet, click Tools, Options and then click the View tab. Select the Show Project Summary Task check box. Summary totals for task information in the current table are displayed in the project summary task row at the top of the sheet. If a table containing work information is applied, the project summary task row shows project work totals.

Reviewing Work Variances

To review the differences between your original baseline work and your currently scheduled work, apply the Work table, as follows:

1. Display the Gantt Chart or other task sheet.

2. Click View, Table, Work.

    The Work table is applied to the current view (see Figure 11-15).

	Task Name	Work	Baseline	Variance	Actual	Remaining	% W. Comp.
0	⊟ **11NewBiz**	**1,606 hrs**	**1,550 hrs**	**56 hrs**	**172 hrs**	**1,434 hrs**	**11%**
1	⊟ **Phase 1 - Strategic Plan**	**478 hrs**	**422 hrs**	**56 hrs**	**156 hrs**	**322 hrs**	**33%**
2	⊟ **Self-Assessment**	**104 hrs**	**104 hrs**	**0 hrs**	**8 hrs**	**96 hrs**	**8%**
3	Define business vision	8 hrs	8 hrs	0 hrs	8 hrs	0 hrs	100%
4	Identify available skills, information and support	96 hrs	96 hrs	0 hrs	0 hrs	96 hrs	0%
5	Decide whether to proceed	0 hrs	0 hrs	0 hrs	0 hrs	0 hrs	100%
6	⊟ **Define the Opportunity**	**112 hrs**	**96 hrs**	**16 hrs**	**94 hrs**	**18 hrs**	**84%**
7	Research the market and competition	24 hrs	8 hrs	16 hrs	6 hrs	18 hrs	25%
8	Interview owners of similar businesses	40 hrs	40 hrs	0 hrs	40 hrs	0 hrs	100%
9	Identify needed resources	32 hrs	32 hrs	0 hrs	32 hrs	0 hrs	100%
10	Identify operating cost elements	16 hrs	16 hrs	0 hrs	16 hrs	0 hrs	100%

Figure 11-15 Apply the Work table to a task sheet to see scheduled, baseline, and actual work—along with any variances.

With the project summary task row applied, you can also review rolled up work totals.

Reviewing Overbudget Work

You can apply a filter to a task or resource sheet to see only those tasks or resources who have more actual work reported than was planned, as follows:

1. Display the view and apply the table that contains the information you want to review in the context of overbudget work.

2. Click Project, Filtered For, More Filters.

3. In the More Filters dialog box, click Work Overbudget and then click Apply.

If you prefer to see all tasks or resources, but have the overbudget tasks or resources highlighted, click Highlight instead.

Microsoft Project filters for any tasks or resources whose actual work reported is higher than the baseline work.

4. Review the tasks or resources to analyze the extent of the work overages.

5. When you finish, show all tasks again by clicking the Filter tool on the Formatting toolbar and then clicking All Tasks.

Reviewing Resource Allocation

If a resource is overallocated, his or her name appears in red in any resource view. In resource sheets, a leveling indicator is also displayed next to the resource name, recommending that the resource be leveled.

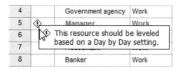

To see the extent of overallocation or underallocation for a resource, use the Resource Graph, as follows:

1. Click View, Resource Graph.

The Resource Graph appears (see Figure 11-16).

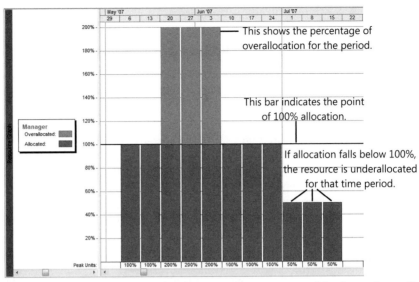

Figure 11-16 The Resource Graph can show whether a resource is fully allocated, overallocated, or underallocated for a selected period of time.

2. Review the allocation for the first resource.

By default, the Resource Graph shows *peak units* for each time period, including the percentage allocated and the percentage overallocated. You can show different types of information in the Resource Graph. Click Format, Details and then click another type of information (for example, Work or Remaining Availability).

Zoom Out

3. On the Standard toolbar, click the Zoom Out button to see the Resource Graph for a longer period of time. Click the Zoom In button to see details about a shorter period of time.

Zoom In

4. To see information for the next resource, press the Page Down key or click in the horizontal scroll bar in the left pane of the view.

> **Note**
> Adding the Resource Graph as the lower pane in a combination view can be very useful in finding resource overallocations.

Chapter 11

INSIDE OUT   Relieve the leveling hair-trigger

The leveling indicator often suggests that the resource be leveled on a Day By Day basis because Microsoft Project has found that this resource is overallocated by at least one minute over the resource availability for a day.

You might find that level of detail too fine for your purposes. It might be more effective to level resources on a Week By Week basis or a Month By Month basis. Although the overallocation is still detected when you're overallocated by just one minute, looking at the entire week or the entire month instead of just one day provides more of a buffer for overallocations to take care of themselves.

To change the leveling trigger, click Tools, Level Resources. In the Look For Overalloca-tions On A Basis box, click Week By Week or Month By Month. Click OK.

You can also see the details about which assignments are causing resource overalloca-tions (or underallocations) by using the Resource Usage view, as follows:

1. Click View, Resource Usage.

    The Resource Usage view appears (see Figure 11-17.

Resource Name	Work	Details	Jun '07			
			20	27	3	10
⊟ Manager	728 hrs	Work	30h	50h	64h	40h
Define business vision	8 hrs	Work				
Identify available skills, information and support	48 hrs	Work	8h			
Decide whether to proceed	0 hrs	Work				
Define new entity requirements	48 hrs	Work	16h	32h		
Identify ongoing business purchase opportunities	64 hrs	Work	6h	8h	40h	10h
Research franchise possibilities	32 hrs	Work		2h	0h	30h

Figure 11-17 The Resource Usage view shows how resources are allocated for each time period, as well as the specific assignments that contribute to that allocation.

Any resource whose name appears in red or with a leveling indicator is overallo-cated.

2. Review the timephased portion of the view to see where the overallocation occurs.

    You might need to scroll to move to a different time period.

3. On the Standard toolbar, click the Zoom Out button to see the Resource Usage view for a longer period of time. Click the Zoom In button to see details about a shorter period of time.

4. Review the sheet portion of the view to see the assignments for each resource.

5. You can add the Overallocation field to the timephased portion of the view, which you can use to learn how many hours or days, for example, a resource is overallocated. To do this, click Format, Details, Overallocation.

    The Overallocation field is added as a new row in the timephased portion of the Resource Usage view (see Figure 11-18).

Resource Name	Work	Details				Jun '07
			13	20	27	3
⊟ Manager	728 hrs	Work	40h	30h	50h	64h
		Overalloc.			10h	24h
Define business vision	8 hrs	Work				
		Overalloc.				
Identify available skills, information and support	48 hrs	Work	40h	8h		
		Overalloc.				
Decide whether to proceed	0 hrs	Work				
		Overalloc.				
Define new entity requirements	48 hrs	Work		16h	32h	
		Overalloc.				
Identify ongoing business purchase opportunities	64 hrs	Work		6h	8h	40h
		Overalloc.				

Figure 11-18 Add the Overallocation field to the Resource Usage view to see the number of hours (or other time period) by which each resource is overallocated.

6. To see underallocations or the amount of time that a resource is available for more assignments, add the Remaining Availability field to the timephased portion of the view. Click Format, Details, Remaining Availability.

Note

If you apply the Work table to the Resource Usage view, you can see work details and tracking information for each resource and assignment—including baseline work, the variance between the baseline and scheduled work, any actual work reported, remaining work, and percentage complete.

Use the Resource Allocation view to see the Resource Usage view in combination with the Leveling Gantt. This view helps you see which resources are overallocated in conjunction with the tasks that are causing the overallocation. Click View, More Views. In the More Views dialog box, click Resource Allocation and then click Apply (see Figure 11-19 for an example).

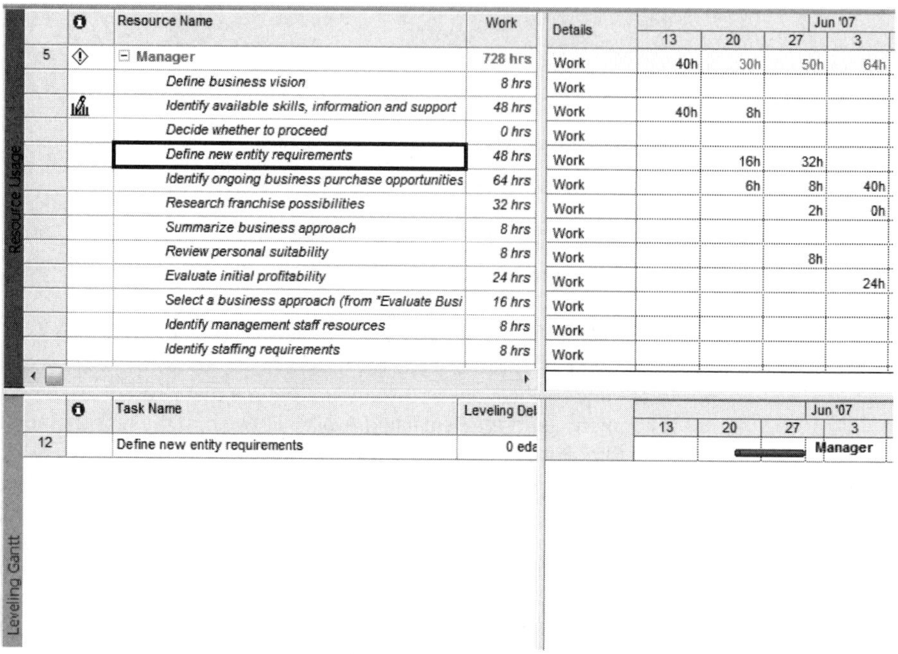

Figure 11-19 With the Resource Allocation view, you can see task information in the lower pane for any assignment you click in the Resource Usage view in the upper pane.

With the Summary table applied to a resource view, you can see the Peak field, which can quickly tell you whether resources are allocated to their maximum availability (100 percent), overallocated (more than 100 percent), or underallocated (less than 100 percent). Click View, Table, Summary (see Figure 11-20 for an example).

	Resource Name	Group	Max. Units	Peak	Std. Rate	Ovt. Rate	Cost	Work
1	Business advisor		100%	200%	$65.00/hr	$0.00/hr	$31,590.00	486 hrs
2	Peers		100%	0%	$55.00/hr	$0.00/hr	$880.00	16 hrs
3	Lawyer		100%	100%	$180.00/hr	$0.00/hr	$24,480.00	136 hrs
4	Government agency		100%	100%	$65.00/hr	$0.00/hr	$2,080.00	32 hrs
5	Manager		100%	200%	$66.00/hr	$0.00/hr	$48,048.00	728 hrs
6	Owners		100%	0%	$66.00/hr	$0.00/hr	$2,640.00	40 hrs
7	Accountant		100%	100%	$100.00/hr	$0.00/hr	$11,200.00	112 hrs
8	Banker		100%	100%	$50.00/hr	$0.00/hr	$2,000.00	40 hrs
9	Information services		100%	100%	$50.00/hr	$0.00/hr	$800.00	16 hrs
10	Travel			0%			$1,300.00	
11	Marketing collateral			1 pieces/day	$1.00		$500.00	500 pieces

Figure 11-20 By reviewing resources' Peak fields, you can quickly see how many resources are allocated and whether they're available to take on more assignments.

The following filters can help you focus on any potential problems with overallocated resources:

- Overallocated Resources (see Figure 11-21)

- Work Overbudget

- Resources/Assignments With Overtime

- Slipping Assignments

	Resource Name	Group	Max. Units	Peak	Std. Rate	Ovt. Rate	Cost	Work
1	Business advisor		100%	200%	$65.00/hr	$0.00/hr	$31,590.00	486 hrs
5	Manager		100%	200%	$66.00/hr	$0.00/hr	$48,048.00	728 hrs

Figure 11-21 Apply the Overallocated Resources filter to a resource view to quickly see a list of resources who have more work assigned than time available for that work.

With a resource view displayed, apply a filter by clicking the Filter tool on the Formatting toolbar. In the Filter list, click the name of the filter you want.

You can also generate and print a report. The following reports provide information about resource usage:

- Who Does What

- Who Does What When

- To-Do List

- Overallocated Resources

- Task Usage

- Resource Usage

- Baseline Work Report (visual report in Excel)

- Budget Work Report (visual report in Excel)

- Resource Availability Report (visual report in Visio)

- Resource Remaining Work Report (visual report in Excel)

- Resource Status Report (visual report in Visio)

- Resource Work Availability Report (visual report in Excel)

- Resource Work Summary Report (visual report in Excel)

To run a text-based report about assignments or workloads, click Report, Reports. Double-click Assignments or Workload and then double-click the report you want. If a dialog box asks for more information, enter the information and then click OK. The report appears in a preview window from which you can print the report or study the details (see Figure 11-22).

Overallocated Resources
11NewBiz

❶	Resource Name				Work

❂	Business advisor				486 hrs
ID	Task Name	Units	Work	Delay	Start
4	Identify available skills, information and support	100%	46 hrs	0 days	Wed 6/6/07
7	Research the market and competition	100%	24 hrs	0 days	Mon 6/7/07
9	Identify needed resources	100%	16 hrs	0 days	Fri 6/15/07
17	Assess market size and stability	100%	16 hrs	0 days	Sat 6/26/07
18	Estimate the competition	100%	12 hrs	0 days	Fri 6/1/07
19	Assess needed resource availability	100%	16 hrs	0 days	Wed 6/30/07
20	Evaluate realistic initial market share	100%	16 hrs	0 days	Fri 6/1/07
21	Determine financial requirements	100%	16 hrs	0 days	Tue 6/19/07

Figure 11-22 The Overallocated Resources report shown here is one of many text-based reports you can generate to see information about resource usage.

To run a visual report, follow these steps:

1. Click Report, Visual Reports.

2. On the All tab, double-click the name of the report you want.

   Microsoft Project data is gathered and the report is built and displayed in Visio or Excel.

Balancing the Resource Workload

Suppose that you reviewed information about assignments and workload throughout your project plan and found that some resources are overallocated and others are underallocated. Or perhaps your company had a reduction in force, and your project staffing was reduced by 15 percent.

If you need to take corrective actions in your project plan to balance the resource workload, you can:

- Adjust resource availability.

- Adjust assignments, for example, add resources, replace resources, delay a task or assignment, or specify overtime.

- Split tasks to balance the workload.

- Use the Microsoft Project leveling feature to balance the workload.

- Adjust scope (this will probably require stakeholder approval).

   For more information about using any of these strategies to better allocate your resources, see the section titled "Balancing Resource Workloads" in Chapter 9.

When you adjust your project plan to achieve the resource allocation levels you need, be sure to check the scheduled finish date, costs, and scope. You need to know how your changes affect other areas of the project plan.

Need a New Baseline?

If you made substantial changes to the schedule or costs in your project plan, consider whether you should set a new baseline. Your decision depends on how you intend to use baseline information, in terms of variance monitoring, earned value calculations, and archival data. Which will give you the more meaningful data: the original baseline or a new one based on recent changes?

You can retain the original baseline (usually the best idea in terms of project data integrity) and save the new information as Baseline 1, for example.

Another alternative is to copy the original baseline information to Baseline 1, for example, and then make the new baseline the primary. The primary baseline (that is, Baseline—rather than Baseline 1 or Baseline 2) is always used for earned value calculations.

For more information about copying baseline fields, see the section titled "Saving Additional Baselines" in Chapter 10.

PART 4

Reporting and Analyzing Project Information

CHAPTER 12
Reporting Project Information 437

CHAPTER 13
Analyzing Progress Using Earned Value. . . . 489

Reporting Project Information

Establishing Your Communications Plan **438**

Using Views to Report Project Information **440**

Generating Text and Visual Reports **445**

Running Reports for Your Requirements **452**

Revising a Built-In Report **474**

Building a Custom Report **478**

Saving Project Data Fields **484**

By this stage of the game, you've built your project plan and you're using it to track progress and display project information. Because you're now in the execution and control processes of the project, you'll need to share important data with stakeholders. For example, your new test procedure might have worked better than expected, but your materials testing ran into some unanticipated slowdowns. All this information is reflected in the project plan. However, for different audiences and different purposes, you want to highlight certain information and filter out other information to present a particular focus with professional panache.

You can print views and generate reports built in to Microsoft Office Project 2007 and use them as an integral part of your project communication plan. These views and reports leverage the power of Office Project 2007 by presenting the specific focus and clarity required by corporate and program departments. By tailoring the views and reports to the interests of different groups (finance, human resources, and procurement, among others), you can feed the right information to the right people, avoid misunderstandings, and mitigate problems. Microsoft Project views and reports are often used for:

- Weekly project team meetings

- Monthly department status conferences

- Quarterly or annual executive reviews

In addition to printing views and generating built-in reports, you can design custom reports to meet your specific project communication needs. Many of these are tabular text-based reports. Now in Microsoft Office Project 2007, you have a new set of visual reports available that use project data for graphical display in Microsoft Office Excel 2007 or Microsoft Office Visio 2007.

Establishing Your Communications Plan

Reports are instrumental in effective project management. As part of the initial project planning, you'll determine the requirements for reporting, including:

- **Report recipients** Who needs to see the reports? Stakeholders throughout the organization and within the project team need to see certain reports tailored to their areas of responsibility. For example, you might generate one report for your team members, another one for team leads and resource managers, and yet another for executives and customers.

- **Specific content of the reports** What type of information is included? The reports can focus on any aspect of the project, for example, tasks, resource allocation, assignments, costs, and so on. Reports might focus on past successes or current progress. They can provide a forecast of upcoming tasks, costs, or workloads. They might present a high-level summary. They can point out areas of risk or current problems that need resolution.

- **Frequency of report publication** How often should you generate reports? Regularly scheduled project meetings or status reporting often drive the generation of reports. Certain important issues that are being closely watched might warrant report generation more frequently than usual. Be sure to strike a balance between providing up-to-date information often enough and overloading a stakeholder with too detailed or too frequent reporting.

Establishing your communications strategy for a project helps you effectively communicate realistic progress and estimates. You can point to unexpected changes that present risks. You can avoid larger problems and understand root causes. Specifically, with reports you can:

- Review status.

- Compare data.

- Check progress on the schedule.

- Check resource utilization.

- Check budget status.

- Watch for any potential problems looming in the future.

- Help stakeholders make decisions affecting the project.

Using the appropriate Microsoft Project views and reports on a regular basis for progress analysis and communication is a key component of effective project management. By implementing a communications plan, including regular presentations of reports to stakeholders, you can keep interested parties aware of crucial information and trends.

Project Management Practices: Communications Management

Communication is a vital element of successful project management. Effective project communication ensures that the appropriate information is generated, collected, and distributed in a timely manner to the appropriate project stakeholders. Different stakeholders need different kinds of project information—from the team members carrying out the project tasks, to customers sponsoring the project, to executives making strategic decisions regarding the project and the organization. Your stakeholders don't just receive project information; they also generate it. When all your stakeholders share project information, people are linked and ideas are generated—all of which contributes to the ultimate success of the project.

The first stage of effective project communications management is communications planning. This stage should take place in the initiating and planning processes for the project, in conjunction with scope and activity development. As you develop and build your project plan, you also need to determine what types of communication will be necessary throughout the life of the project.

Determine what tools you have at your disposal and how your project team communicates most effectively. You might have weekly meetings and weekly status reports. Perhaps you'll also have monthly resource management and cost management reviews. Other possible communication vehicles include presentations, e-mail, letters, and an intranet site. You'll likely use a combination of these vehicles for different aspects of project management and different audiences.

If you're using Microsoft Office Project Server 2007 and Microsoft Office Project Web Access, you have a very effective means of communicating electronically with your team members and other stakeholders. You can automate the flow of progress information about the project, including progress updates, timesheets, and narrative status reporting. Stakeholders can also review major project views. Because Windows SharePoint Services is integrated with Office Project Server 2007, you can store reports, manage risks, and track issues.

While the project is being executed, you'll be executing your communications plan. You'll report on current project status, describing where the project stands at that point in time, especially as it relates to the schedule, budget, scope, and resource utilization. You'll also report on overall progress, describing the accomplishments of the project team to date and what is yet to be done. Finally, you'll make forecasts by using project plan information to predict future progress on tasks and anticipating potential problems.

Tasks will be completed, milestones met, deliverables handed off, and phases concluded. Your communications management strategy provides the means for documenting project results and the receipt of deliverables as each stage of the project is completed.

Chapter 12

Using Views to Report Project Information

Suppose that you've been tracking and managing your project for some time now by using the Gantt Chart, the Resource Sheet, and other Microsoft Project views. You can set up one of these views to contain exactly the fields of information you need and then print it to create a kind of interactive report. By printing views, you can share pertinent information with team members and stakeholders. You can include printed views in project status reports and in progress meetings.

> **Note**
> Form views, such as the Task Form or Resource Form, cannot be printed. Neither can combination (split-screen) views. You can print one part of a split screen at a time, but if one part of the split screen is a form (such as Task Entry), the form portion is not printed.

Setting Up and Printing Views

To set up and print a view, follow these steps:

1. Open the view and arrange the data as you want it to appear when printed.

For more information about available views and arranging information in those views, see Chapter 4, "Viewing Project Information."

2. Click File, Page Setup to display the Page Setup dialog box (see Figure 12-1).

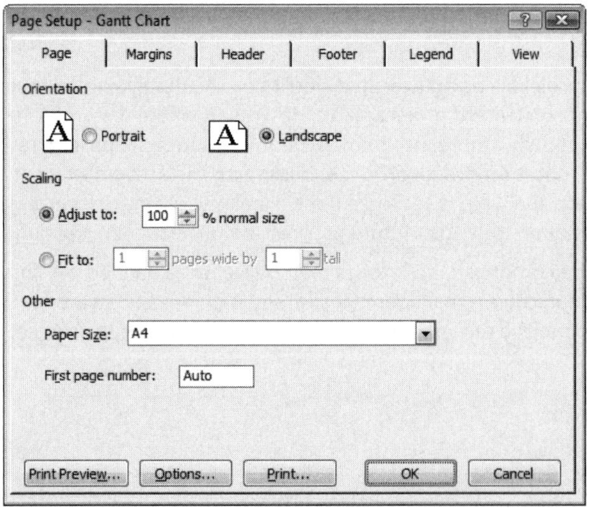

Figure 12-1 Use the Page Setup dialog box to set your margins, legend, headers, and more.

3. Specify the options you want for the printed view by using controls on the different tabs of this dialog box.

You can adjust the view orientation, page scaling, margins, header and footer, and so on. When finished, click OK.

Print Preview

4. On the Standard toolbar, click Print Preview.

A picture of the view as it will be printed appears, reflecting your Page Setup options (see Figure 12-2).

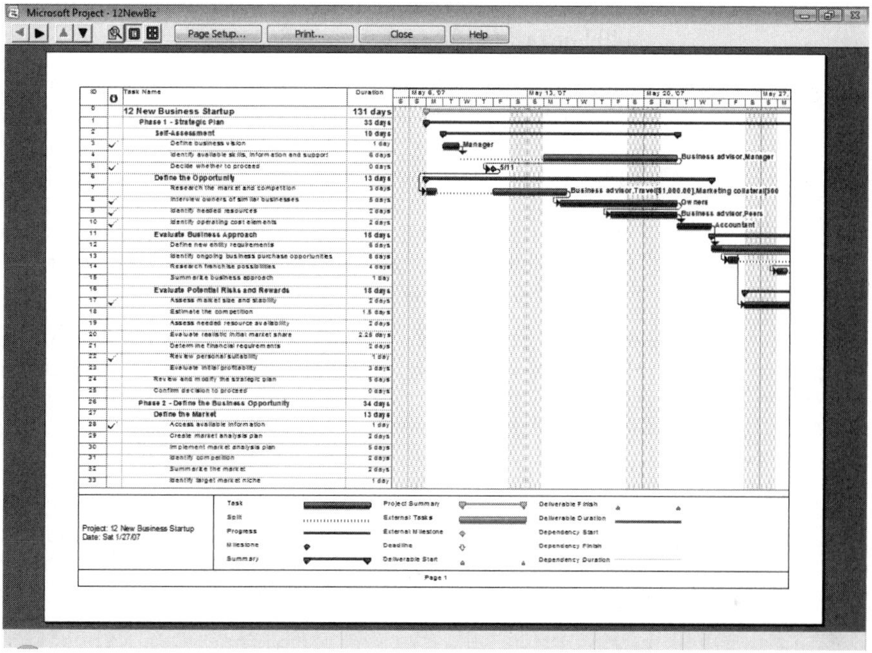

Figure 12-2 The Print Preview window shows the printable layout of the current view.

5. To make further adjustments to the print options, click Page Setup at the top of the Print Preview window.

6. To make further adjustments to the view itself, click Close on the Print Preview toolbar and work in the view again.

Print

7. When finished with your adjustments, print the view by clicking Print on the Standard toolbar.

Set Options for Printed Views

The following list describes the options available on the six tabs of the Page Setup dialog box, which controls how your view looks when printed. To display this dialog box, click File, Page Setup.

- **Page tab** Specifies whether the view should be printed in portrait or landscape orientation, and whether the view should be scaled up or down to fit on a page.

- **Margins tab** Specifies the size of each of the four margins and whether a border should be printed around the page.

Insert File Name

- **Header tab** Specifies the content and location of header information. You can add the page number, current date and time, or the file name. You can also add a picture (such as a company or project logo) as part of your left, center, or right header. For example, next to Alignment, click the Center tab and then click Insert File Name to display the project file name at the center top of every page. You can also specify that a project field should be part of the header. You can enter your own text as well. Simply click the Left, Center, or Right tab and then click the text box and type the text you want.

Insert Current Date

- **Footer tab** Specifies the content and location of footer information. The same information available for headers is also available for footers. For example, click the Left tab in the Alignment area and then click Insert Current Date to display the date in the lower-left corner of every page. The Preview box shows what your footer will look like.

- **Legend tab** Specifies the content and location of a view's legend, which specifies what symbols or bars on the view represent. For example, when printing the Gantt Chart, the legend includes a key for the task bars, summary bars, deadlines, and milestone symbols. By default, the legend appears on the bottom 2 inches of every page and includes the project's title and the current date. The same information available for headers and footers is available for legends. You can also enter your own information.

- **View tab** Specifies which elements you want printed on each page, for example, notes, blank pages, or sheet columns.

Note

Divided views, such as Task Usage, have a table on the left and the timephased information sheet on the right. Such divided views are not split screens, so you can print both sides of these views.

INSIDE OUT

Be careful when inserting the current date and time on a printed view

Insert Current Time

The Insert Current Date and Insert Current Time buttons take their information from your computer's system clock. This date and time will change to reflect the date and time that you print the view. However, you might prefer to print a fixed date or time, perhaps one that specifies when the project was last updated, rather than last printed. In this case, in the Alignment area of the Page Setup dialog box, simply type the date or time on the Left, Center, or Right tab text box itself.

Getting Assistance from the Report Project Guide

Report ▾

Report

Use the Report Project Guide to help you set up key views presenting important progress and cost information. On the Project Guide toolbar, click Report. The Report pane appears.

Note

If your Project Guide toolbar is not showing, click View, Toolbars, Project Guide. If the Project Guide toolbar is not listed on the Toolbars menu, click Tools, Options, Interface and then select the Display Project Guide check box.

The Report Project Guide includes steps and controls for setting up your project to view specific types of information, such as critical tasks, risks and issues, resource allocation, project costs, and so on.

The Report Project Guide focuses on view setup and printing options. Click the Print Current View As A Report link to start the Print Current View Wizard. This wizard provides options for printing the current view, with optimum print spacing and scaling (see Figure 12-3).

Chapter 12

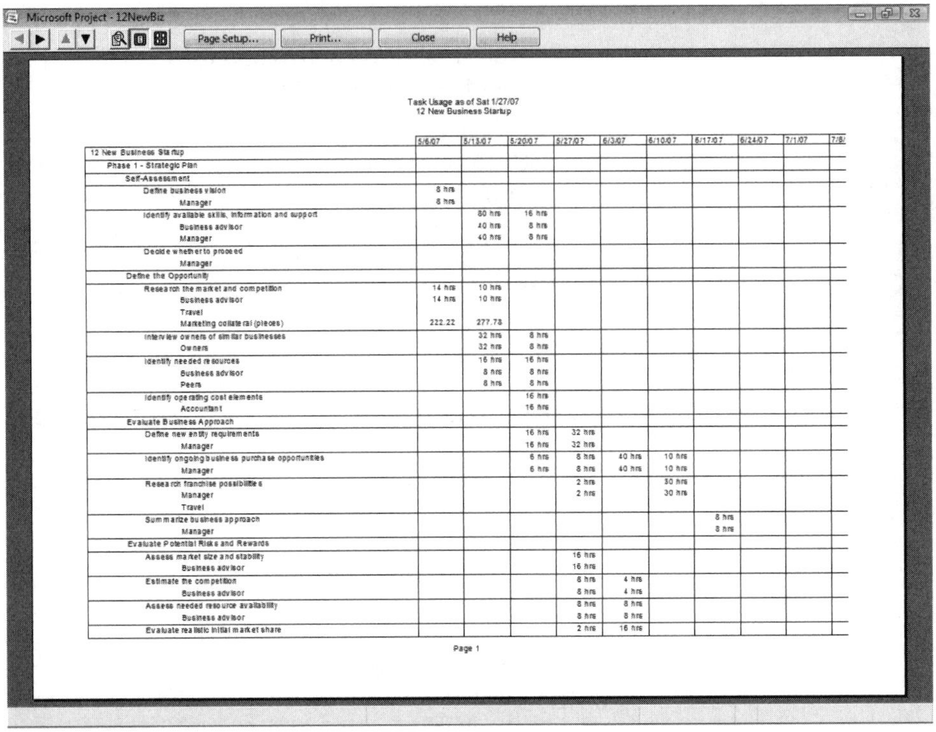

Task Usage as of Sat 1/27/07
12 New Business Startup

	5/6/07	5/13/07	5/20/07	5/27/07	6/3/07	6/10/07	6/17/07	6/24/07	7/1/07	7/8/
12 New Business Startup										
Phase 1 - Strategic Plan										
Self-Assessment										
Define business vision	8 hrs									
Manager	8 hrs									
Identify available skills, information and support		80 hrs	16 hrs							
Business advisor		40 hrs	8 hrs							
Manager		40 hrs	8 hrs							
Decide whether to proceed										
Manager										
Define the Opportunity										
Research the market and competition	14 hrs	10 hrs								
Business advisor	14 hrs	10 hrs								
Travel										
Marketing collateral (pieces)	222.22	277.78								
Interview owners of similar businesses		32 hrs	8 hrs							
Owners		32 hrs	8 hrs							
Identify needed resources		16 hrs	16 hrs							
Business advisor		8 hrs	8 hrs							
Peers		8 hrs	8 hrs							
Identify operating cost elements			16 hrs							
Accountant			16 hrs							
Evaluate Business Approach										
Define new entity requirements			16 hrs	32 hrs						
Manager			16 hrs	32 hrs						
Identify ongoing business purchase opportunities			6 hrs	8 hrs	40 hrs	10 hrs				
Manager			6 hrs	8 hrs	40 hrs	10 hrs				
Research franchise possibilities				2 hrs		30 hrs				
Manager				2 hrs		30 hrs				
Travel										
Summarize business approach							8 hrs			
Manager							8 hrs			
Evaluate Potential Risks and Rewards										
Assess market size and stability				16 hrs						
Business advisor				16 hrs						
Estimate the competition				8 hrs	4 hrs					
Business advisor				8 hrs	4 hrs					
Assess needed resource availability				8 hrs	8 hrs					
Business advisor				8 hrs	8 hrs					
Evaluate realistic initial market share				2 hrs	16 hrs					

Page 1

Figure 12-3 Use the Print Current View Wizard to set options for printing the current view.

For more information about the Project Guide, see the section titled "Working with the Project Guide" in Chapter 1, "Introducing Microsoft Office Project 2007."

Copy a Picture of a View

You can copy a view in Microsoft Project and paste it as a graphic file into a Microsoft Office Word 2007 document or a Microsoft Office PowerPoint 2007 presentation slide. If you're copying to Office Word 2007, Office PowerPoint 2007, or Office Visio 2007, you can use the Copy Picture To Office Wizard. For these or any other application, you can use the Copy Picture function.

For more information about copying a view and using the graphic in another application, see the section titled "Copying a Picture of a View" in Chapter 16, "Exchanging Information with Other Applications."

Generating Text and Visual Reports

In addition to the ability to print views, Microsoft Project comes with more than 40 built-in reports that you can simply select, preview, and print. These reports compile the most commonly used sets of information needed to manage a project, coordinate resources, control costs, analyze potential problems, and communicate progress.

When you select and generate a report, information is drawn from selected fields throughout your project. That information is laid out in the predetermined report design or template, in either discrete or summarized form, depending on the specific report. You can generate an up-to-date report mere minutes before the start of a meeting, and the report instantly reflects the very latest changes you made or that team members have submitted.

You can generate two categories of reports: text-based reports and visual reports. The text-based reports compile information into a tabular format within Microsoft Project. Visual reports, which are new in Microsoft Office Project 2007, automatically compile and export project information to either Excel or Visio, where it is presented in a graphic such as a column chart or flow diagram.

INSIDE OUT   The Report Project Guide helps print views, not reports

The Report Project Guide is somewhat misnamed: it really is the Printed View Guide—only one link takes you to a built-in generated report. The rest of the links display views displaying certain types of information often needed in progress reports or status meetings. These links display various guides which walk you through setting up the view for optimum printing.

However, there's nothing here that tells you the best report to use or how to customize it for your own purposes.

The Report Project Guide does get you to the point of opening the Reports dialog box. On the Project Guide toolbar, click Report. In the Project Guide pane, click Select A View Or Report, click Print A Project Report, and then click Display Reports.

Working with Text-Based Reports

To see the list of available text-based reports, click Report, Reports. The Reports dialog box appears, showing six report categories (see Figure 12-4).

Figure 12-4 There are five categories for 22 built-in text-based reports, plus a Custom category for designing your own report.

The text report categories are:

- Overview
- Current Activities
- Costs
- Assignments
- Workload
- Custom

Each category focuses on a specific type of information. You might find that certain reports are best-suited to one type of audience, whereas other reports are better for another type of audience. For example, Cost reports might be most appropriate for meetings with the finance department, whereas you might prefer to distribute Assignment reports to team leads.

To generate these reports, Microsoft Project gathers information from a particular time period, from certain tables, and with a particular filter applied as appropriate for the requirements of the specific report. Information is formatted with bands, highlights, fonts, and other professional layout considerations.

To select and print a text report, follow these steps:

1. Click Report, Reports.

2. In the Reports dialog box, double-click the category you want.

   A dialog box appears, showing the available reports in that category (see Figure 12-5).

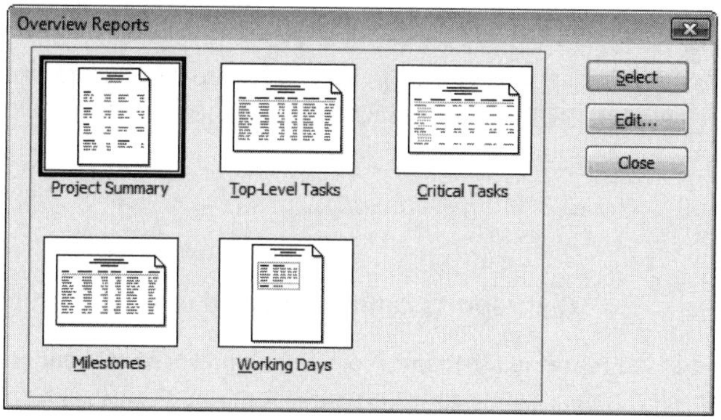

Figure 12-5 The Overview Reports dialog box shows the available summary reports.

3. Double-click the report you want.

4. If a dialog box prompts you for more information, such as a date range, enter it and then click OK.

The report appears in a Print Preview window (see Figure 12-6). Click any portion of the report to zoom in on it. Click a second time to zoom back out again. On the Print Preview toolbar, click Page Setup to change the page orientation, scaling, margins, header, or footer.

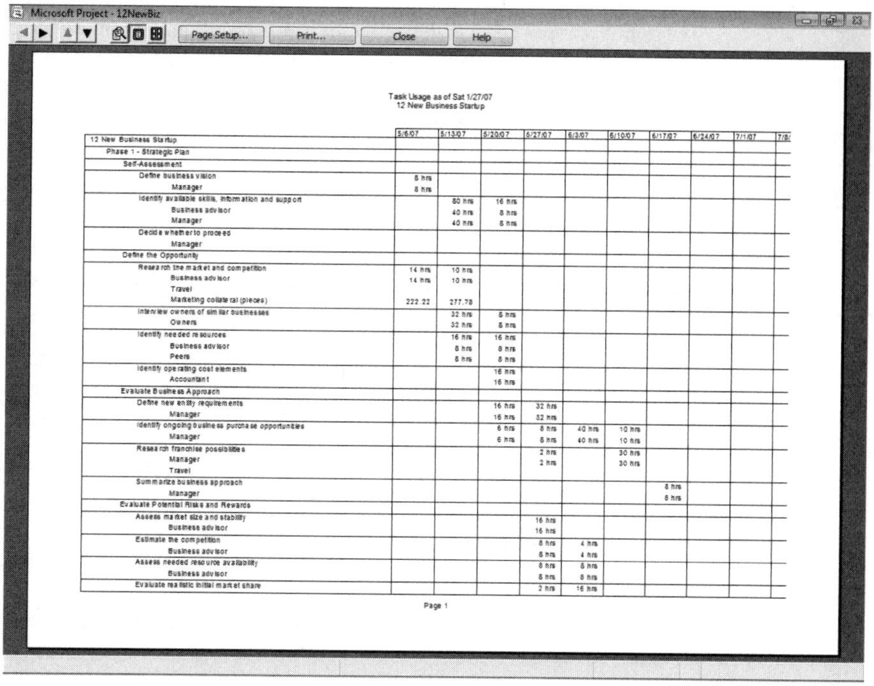

Figure 12-6 A picture of the report shows how it will look when printed.

5. When you're ready to print the report, click Print on the Print Preview toolbar.

6. In the Print dialog box that appears, select the page range and number of copies you want to print and then click OK.

INSIDE OUT   Text reports cannot be saved or published to the Web as is

Each text-based report in Microsoft Project has a preset format and is generated from current project data, so you cannot save a built-in report as such. Essentially, it's already saved. As long as your project file is saved, you can always quickly generate the report again using current information.

For the same reasons, project text reports cannot be converted to HTML or XML format because the reports are designed only for previewing and printing, and cannot be saved as a discrete unit.

However, if you do want to save an instance of a report, perhaps for an historical record of a moment in time or for a series of certain reports throughout the project life cycle, you can apply the table on which the report is based and then click Copy Picture on the Standard toolbar. Select the To GIF Image File option, and then click Browse to select the location and enter the file name. Another good option is to use a third-party application to print the report as a PDF file. If your weekly routine has you generating a particular report and saving it as a GIF file, consider creating a macro to do this for you each week.

For more information about creating macros, see Chapter 27, "Automating Your Work with Macros."

Working with Visual Reports in Excel and Visio

Just as text reports present project information in a tabular format, visual reports present project information, well, visually. When you generate a visual report, specific project data is compiled and sent to Excel or Visio. A PivotTable or PivotDiagram structure specifies how the data is to be displayed in the chart or diagram.

For an Excel visual report, a PivotTable is generated, from which a chart, such as a column or pie chart, is drawn.

A Visio visual report generates a PivotDiagram, a collection of boxes or other shapes arranged in a tree structure.

In either case, you can change the arrangement of the source data to display the information from different perspectives as needed.

To see the list of built-in visual reports, click Report, Visual Reports. The Visual Reports – Create Report dialog box appears (see Figure 12-7).

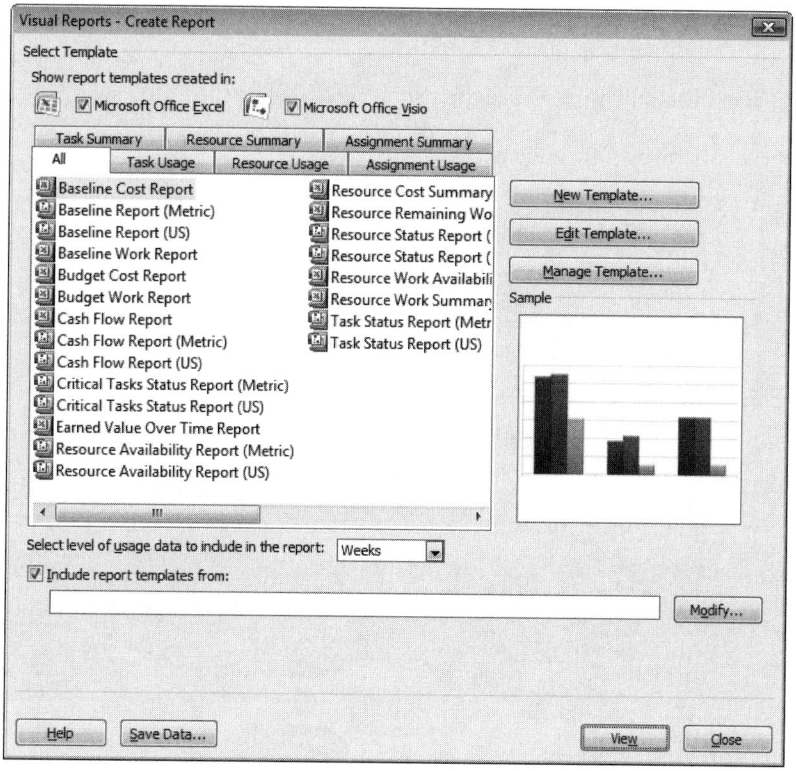

Figure 12-7 There are six categories for 22 built-in visual reports.

The visual report categories are:

- Task Summary

- Resource Summary

- Assignment Summary

- Task Usage

- Resource Usage

- Assignment Usage

The summary reports are more high-level, while the usage reports have specific detail.

To generate a visual report, follow these steps:

1. Click Report, Visual Reports.

2. In the Visual Reports – Create Report dialog box, click the tab for the report category you want.

You might find it easier to simply click the All tab and see the list of all 22 visual reports in one place.

3. If you only want to see the list of Excel visual reports, clear the Microsoft Office Visio check box. If you only want to see the list of Visio reports, clear the Microsoft Office Excel check box.

4. Click the report you want. Icons next to each report name indicate whether it's an Excel or Visio report template.

An icon representing the report appears in the Sample box.

5. In the Select Level Of Usage Data To Include In The Report box, select the period of time you want to use. The default is Weeks.

6. Click View.

Microsoft Project gathers the information required by the selected report template, builds the OLAP (Online Analytical Processing) cube (the set of fields that will be used), opens the template in the target application—either Excel or Visio—and finally displays the visual report in that application (see Figure 12-8).

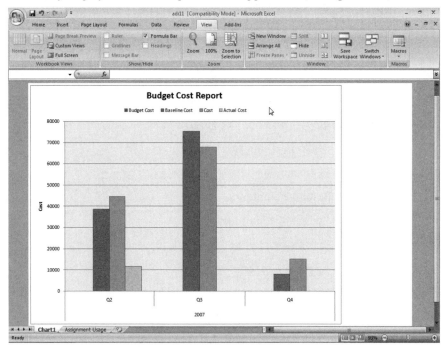

Figure 12-8 When you run an Excel report template, the resulting report is displayed in Excel.

7. In Excel, if you want to view or change the PivotTable on which the report is based, click the second tab below the worksheet. It's named something like Assignment Usage or Task Summary (see Figure 12-9).

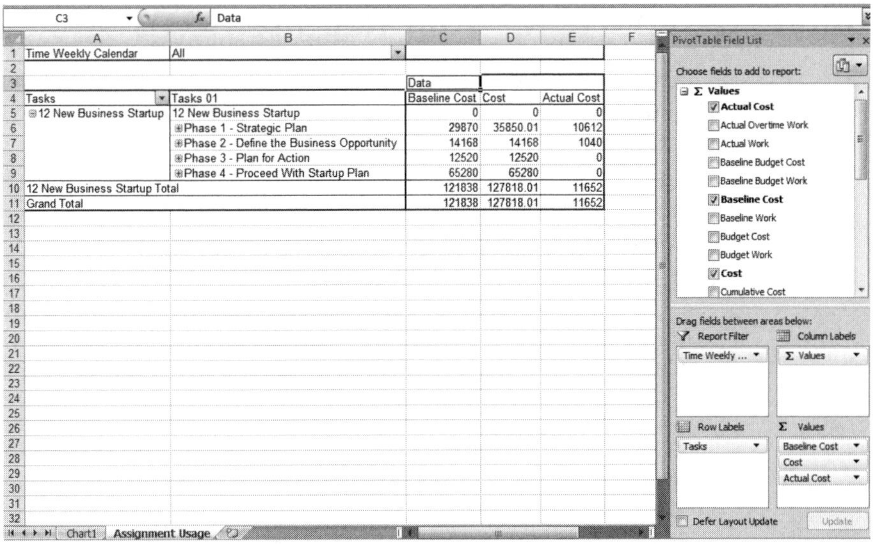

Figure 12-9 The Assignment Usage tab displays the crosstab table on which the Excel chart is based.

8. To print a report in Excel 2007, click the Microsoft Office Button and then click Print.

To print a report in Excel 2003 or in Visio, click Print on the Standard toolbar.

Office

Save

9. If you want to save an Excel 2007 report, on the Quick Access Toolbar next to the Microsoft Office Button, click Save.

If you want to save an Excel 2003 or Visio report, click Save on the Standard toolbar.

The XML Reporting Wizard Is No Longer Needed

The XML Reporting Wizard, available in Microsoft Office Project 2003, is not available in Microsoft Office Project 2007. Between the ability to save a project as an XML file in the Save As dialog box as well as the new visual reports functionality, the wizard is no longer needed. When you generate a visual report, you're essentially saving specific project information as XML data, exporting it to Excel or Visio, porting that XML data into a preset template, and then generating the chart or diagram for the report.

Running Reports for Your Requirements

This section categorizes each of the built-in text and visual reports by the activities or requirements that dictate the different ways you might need to present your project information. There are overview reports, reports about current activities, reports about costs, and reports about resource allocation. These groupings can help you determine which report would best suit your needs in a specific situation.

Remember, to generate a text report, click Report, Reports. To generate a visual report, click Report, Visual Reports. Each report description in this section indicates whether the report is a text or visual report, and also specifies the category in which the report is found.

> **Note**
>
> In many cases throughout this section, there is no illustration of a report with its description. This is because many of the reports are so dense with information that to shrink them to illustration size would render them illegible. The best idea is for you to open a project, either a real project or a sample, and generate the reports yourself while you read about them here. You'll see the details of what each report can provide for you, and therefore understand how you might actually use a given report.

Summarizing with Overview Reports

Overview reports are well-suited for executives and members of upper management who need more generalized project information and status. Overview reports provide summary project information at a glance.

Using the Project Summary Report

The Project Summary text report, in the Overview category, focuses on the most important information in the project plan and is particularly useful to upper management because of its concise presentation of overall project data.

The information in the Project Summary report is the same as that available in the Project Statistics dialog box. It includes a high-level summary of rolled-up dates, duration, work, costs, work and resource status, and notes. The format is designed for easy comparison of baseline (planned) versus actual data.

> **Note**
>
> To enter project properties, click File, Properties. Complete the information on the Summary tab.

Using the Top-Level Tasks Report

The Top-Level Tasks text report, in the Overview category, presents information about the project plan's summary tasks. It displays the results of the top summary tasks, rolling up all the data from any subtasks. This is most useful for organizations that are clearly divided into functional groups. If each group has its own section at the same level in the project plan, the Top-Level Tasks report quickly shows the status of each group's efforts (see Figure 12-10).

Top Level Tasks as of Sat 1/27/07
12 New Business Startup

Task Name	Duration	Start	Finish	% Comp.
12 New Business Startup	131 days	Mon 5/7/07	Mon 11/5/07	10%
Phase 1 - Strategic Plan	33 days	Mon 5/7/07	Wed 6/20/07	32%
Phase 2 - Define the Business Oppo	34 days	Thu 6/7/07	Tue 7/24/07	6%
Phase 3 - Plan for Action	21 days	Wed 7/25/07	Wed 8/22/07	0%
Phase 4 - Proceed With Startup Plan	53 days	Thu 8/23/07	Mon 11/5/07	0%

Figure 12-10 The Top-Level Tasks report shows summary task information.

The Top-Level Tasks report is based on the Summary table for tasks, with the Top Level Tasks filter applied. The report includes the top-level summary tasks and their rolled-up durations, start and finish dates, percentage complete, cost, and work.

Using the Critical Tasks Report

The Critical Tasks text report, in the Overview category, filters your project information to show only those tasks that are most likely to affect the project finish date; that is, critical tasks. In addition to displaying task notes, this report provides a subtable containing successor task information under each task, which shows the other tasks that will be affected by progress on the critical task.

Because task information is always changing, it's a good idea to print the Critical Tasks report very shortly before presenting it for review. This report also lists any summary tasks to the critical tasks and any indicators from the Task Entry view.

The Critical Tasks report is typically used to explain why problems are occurring in a project. If the list becomes too lengthy, you can filter it down further:

1. In the Overview Reports dialog box, click Critical Tasks and then click Edit.

2. Be sure that the Definition tab is showing in the Task Report dialog box.

3. In the Filter list, click any of the filters to define the type of critical tasks you want to see in the report.

The Critical Tasks report is based on the task Entry table with the Critical filter applied. The report includes durations, start and finish dates, indicators, notes, and successor fields for all critical tasks.

For more information about critical tasks, see the section titled "Working with the Critical Path and Critical Tasks" in Chapter 9, "Checking and Adjusting the Project Plan."

Chapter 12

INSIDE OUT   **Decipher subtables in a text report**

Certain text reports include additional task, resource, or assignment information. For example, the Critical Tasks report adds successor information after each critical task listed in the table. The Tasks Starting Soon report adds assignment schedule information after each upcoming task listed.

At first, this additional detail looks like so much clutter in the report. The details are in italics in a subtable below the name of the associated task or resource. This format takes some getting used to, but it's worth the time because it contains such pertinent and useful information.

If you really hate the additional detail, however, you can get rid of it. Click the report name, click Edit, and then click the Details tab. Under Task, Resource, or Assignment, clear the check box that represents the additional detailed information you want to remove.

Using the Critical Tasks Status Report in Visio

The Critical Tasks Status Report is a Visio visual report in the Task Summary category. It displays a PivotDiagram showing scheduled work and remaining work for critical and noncritical tasks (see Figure 12-11). The data bar at the bottom of each node specifies the percentage of work complete.

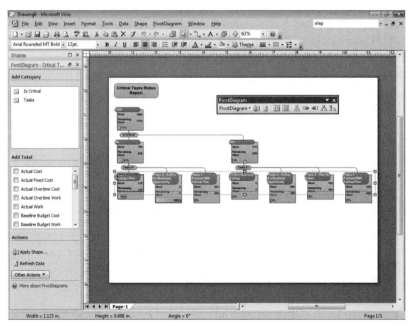

Figure 12-11 The Critical Tasks Status Report shows scheduled work, remaining work, and percentage of work complete for critical and noncritical tasks.

Using the Milestones Report

The Milestones text report, in the Overview category, filters your project tasks to show only milestone tasks and associated information. This high-level report helps you focus on key events and dates in your project.

The Milestones report is based on the task Entry table with the Milestone filter applied. The report includes durations, start and finish dates, indicators, and notes for all milestone tasks.

For more information about milestones, see the section titled "Creating Milestones in Your Schedule" in Chapter 5, "Scheduling Tasks."

Using the Working Days Report

The Working Days text report, in the Overview category, specifies which days are working days and which are nonworking days for each base calendar used in the project (see Figure 12-12). You might use several base calendars to reflect the scheduled working days of different functional groups or to reflect working times specified by labor contracts.

Base Calendar
12 NewBusiness Startup

BASE CALENDAR:	Standard
Day	Hours
Sunday	Nonworking
Monday	8:00 AM - 12:00 PM, 1:00 PM - 5:00 PM
Tuesday	8:00 AM - 12:00 PM, 1:00 PM - 5:00 PM
Wednesday	8:00 AM - 12:00 PM, 1:00 PM - 5:00 PM
Thursday	8:00 AM - 12:00 PM, 1:00 PM - 5:00 PM
Friday	8:00 AM - 12:00 PM, 1:00 PM - 5:00 PM
Saturday	Nonworking
Exceptions:	None

Figure 12-12 The Working Days report shows working days for each base calendar used in the project.

The Working Days report shows working and nonworking time for each base calendar as well as any exceptions to the norm. For more information about calendars, see the section titled "Setting Your Project Calendar" in Chapter 3, "Starting a New Project."

Focusing on Tasks with Schedule Progress Reports

Reports that focus on the schedule and current progress of tasks are useful for everyday or weekly checks to make sure that tasks are moving along according to plan. Such reports are designed for more frequent usage and geared toward audiences more directly involved with the work of the project. For example, project teams can use these reports at weekly status meetings. Functional groups in a project can use these reports to quickly check how they are measuring up against the project plan. You might rely on these reports toward the end of projects, when current task status must be monitored frequently.

Chapter 12

Text reports specializing in schedule progress are found in the Current Activity Reports dialog box. There are six text reports in the Current Activity Reports category (see Figure 12-13).

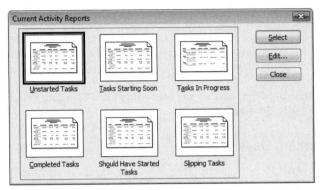

Figure 12-13 The Current Activity Reports dialog box shows the available text reports for this category.

Visual reports specializing in schedule progress are found in the Assignment Summary and Assignment Usage categories.

Using the Unstarted Tasks Report

Tasks in the project that have not had any actual progress reported are displayed in the Unstarted Tasks text report, in the Current Activities category. Generally, the number of tasks displayed decreases as the project progresses, so this report can be especially useful toward the end of the project. This information can help with planning expenditures, deploying tools and materials, and quickly assessing the amount of work yet to be done. This report is also effective at showing functional leads and team members the scope of their required efforts.

The Unstarted Tasks report is based on the Entry table with the Unstarted Tasks filter applied. The report includes the task duration, start and finish dates, predecessors, and indicators. Assigned resource information is listed in a subtable under the associated task.

Using the Tasks Starting Soon Report

The Tasks Starting Soon text report, in the Current Activities category, is actually a subset of the Unstarted Tasks report. The format is similar to the Unstarted Tasks report. The difference is that the Date Range filter is applied. You specify the dates for the tasks you want to see in the report.

Using the Tasks In Progress Report

The Tasks In Progress text report, in the Current Activities category, is a handy tool that enables you to keep close track of work currently being done. This report quickly shows the amount of work that has started; it also points out tasks that are behind schedule. The in-progress tasks are grouped by month.

Grouping tasks by the month of their start dates helps managers see the longest ongoing tasks that are still unfinished. Using this report regularly helps prevent managers from overlooking (or forgetting) the status updates and long-overdue tasks.

The Tasks In Progress report is based on the Entry table with the Tasks In Progress filter applied. The report includes the task duration, start and finish dates, predecessors, indicators, and assignment schedule information.

Using the Completed Tasks Report

The other end of the spectrum of status reports about current progress is the report showing all 100% completed tasks, grouped by month (see Figure 12-14).

Completed Tasks as of Sat 1/27/07
12 New Business Startup

ID	Task Name	Duration	Start	Finish	% Comp.
May 2007					
3	Define business vision	1 day	Tue 5/8/07	Tue 5/8/07	100%
5	Decide whether to proceed	0 days	Fri 5/11/07	Fri 5/11/07	100%
8	Interview owners of similar businesses	5 days	Tue 5/15/07	Mon 5/21/07	100%
9	Identify needed resources	2 days	Fri 5/18/07	Mon 5/21/07	100%
10	Identify operating cost elements	2 days	Tue 5/22/07	Wed 5/23/07	100%
17	Assess market size and stability	2 days	Sat 5/26/07	Tue 5/29/07	100%
June 2007					
22	Review personal suitability	1 day	Fri 6/1/07	Fri 6/1/07	100%
28	Access available information	1 day	Thu 6/7/07	Thu 6/7/07	100%

Figure 12-14 The Completed Tasks report shows all tasks that are reported as complete so far.

The Completed Tasks text report, in the Current Activities category, is significant for both historical reference and as a record of the team's accomplishments. It provides real data about "lessons learned," helps estimate task durations for future projects, and gives you a general idea of how much work is left to do in the current project. Another important use of this report is to boost team morale, increase motivation, and foster pride in team accomplishments. Although the project goal is paramount, accomplishments and successes to date can be recognized.

The Completed Tasks report is based on the Summary table with the Completed Tasks filter applied. The report includes the task duration, start and finish dates, total cost, and total work.

Using the Should Have Started Tasks Report

The Should Have Started Tasks text report, in the Current Activities category, is most effective when used regularly. This report alerts you to all tasks whose scheduled start dates have passed but for which no progress information has been reported to indicate that work on the task has begun. Sometimes, the data shown in this report reflects missing status updates, making this report an effective tool for optimizing the flow of communication on project progress.

When you select this report, you're prompted to enter a Should Start By date. Any tasks that do not have an actual start date entered and that are scheduled to start on or before a given date (usually the current date) are displayed in this report.

The Should Have Started Tasks report is based on the Variance table with the Should Start By filter applied. Tasks are sorted by start date. The report includes the baseline and scheduled start and finish dates, along with the start variance field. It also includes task notes and subtables for successor task to show the tasks immediately affected by those starting late.

Using the Slipping Tasks Report

The Slipping Tasks text report, in the Current Activities category, can only be generated for projects with a baseline saved. The focus of this report is the list of tasks that have started but that will finish after their baseline finish date. This slipping of the finish date can be caused by the start date occurring later than originally planned or by an increase in the duration.

The Slipping Tasks report is based on the Variance table with the Slipping Tasks filter applied. Tasks are sorted by start date. The report includes the baseline and scheduled start and finish dates, along with the start variance field. It also includes task notes and subtables for successor task to show the tasks immediately affected by the slipping tasks.

For more information about setting and using a baseline, see Chapter 10, "Setting a Baseline and Updating Progress."

TROUBLESHOOTING

You can't adjust text report column sizes

When you generate a text report, you see the report in a preview window in which you have no control over column widths. There you can specify the content, change font sizes of report elements, adjust the timescale, and modify the headers and footers. This is true whether you're generating a built-in or custom text report.

If you want to change the width of a column in a report, you can do so by changing the width of the column in the table on which the report is based. To find the name of this table, in the Reports dialog box box, double-click the category, and then click the name of the report you want to run. Instead of clicking Select, click Edit. On the Definition tab, the Table box shows the name of the table on which the report is based. Apply that table to a task or resource sheet as applicable, and then change the column width of the field by dragging the edges of the column headings. Generate the report, and you'll see that the column width in the report reflects your change.

Remember that you can add and remove fields in a table and such changes are also reflected in any reports based on that table.

If you find it easier, you might also consider manipulating and printing the sheet view with your table applied.

> **For more information about printing views, see the section titled "Setting Up and Printing Views" earlier in this chapter.**

You can also adjust the scale of the report so you can fit more columns on a page, or switch the report between portrait and landscape page orientation.

> **For more information on changing page setup options, see the section titled "Adjusting the Page Setup of a Report" later in this chapter.**

For example, suppose that you want to generate the Unstarted Tasks report, but you don't like that it goes across two pages. You can change the page setup to reduce the left and right margins to 0.5 inch each, and the scaling to 80 percent.

Using the Baseline Report in Visio

The Baseline Report is a Visio visual report in the Assignment Usage category. It displays a PivotDiagram of the project broken down by quarter, and then by task. The diagram compares scheduled work and cost to baseline work and cost for each task. Icons show when scheduled values for work and cost exceed the baseline values.

Using the Baseline Work Report in Excel

The Baseline Work Report is an Excel visual report in the Assignment Usage cateogry. It displays a column chart showing baseline, scheduled, and actual work for each task.

Using the Task Status Report in Visio

The Task Status Report is a Visio visual report in the Assignment Summary category. It displays a PivotDiagram showing work and percentage of work complete for all tasks in the project (see Figure 12-15). Icons show when baseline work exceeds scheduled work, when baseline work equals scheduled work, and when scheduled work exceeds baseline work. The data bar at the bottom of each node indicates the percentage of work complete.

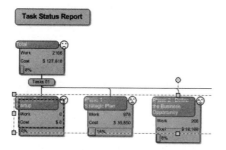

Figure 12-15 The Task Status Report is a Visio diagram that shows work and percentage of work complete for all tasks in the project.

Using the Budget Work Report in Excel

The Budget Work Report is an Excel visual report in the Assignment Usage category. It displays a column chart showing budget, baseline, scheduled, and actual work over time.

Analyzing Budget Status with Cost Reports

Microsoft Project cost reports are a powerful and effective means of tracking the fiscal health of a project. By using these reports, you can quickly and accurately focus on the pressing cost issues and catch potential problems early. Because the costs are directly tied to the tasks and the resources assigned to those tasks, you can generate these reports without having to rekey or recalculate values—Microsoft Project does it all for you.

Text reports specializing in costs are found in the Cost category, where five reports are available for reviewing your project's costs and budget (see Figure 12-16).

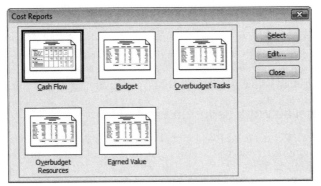

Figure 12-16 Choose one of the available cost-related reports in the Cost Reports dialog box.

Visual reports specializing in costs are found in the Task Usage, Resource Usage, and Assignment Usage categories.

Using the Cash Flow Report

The Cash Flow text report, in the Costs category, is a *crosstab* report that displays total scheduled costs by each task and by each week in the project timespan (see Figure 12-17).

Cash Flow as of Sat 1/27/07
12 New Business Startup

	5/6/07	5/13/07	5/20/07
12 New Business Startup			
Phase 1 - Strategic Plan			
Self-Assessment			
Define business vision	$528.00		
Identify available skills, information and support		$5,240.00	$1,048.00
Decide whether to proceed			
Define the Opportunity			
Research the market and competition	$2,652.22	$1,057.78	
Interview owners of similar businesses		$2,112.00	$528.00

Figure 12-17 The Cash Flow report shows costs for each task by each week in the project.

Use this report to see the costs that go into the performance of tasks (assigned human resources, materials, equipment, fees, and fixed costs) per time period. The information shown also enables quick comparisons with baseline budgets or projections, especially when used in conjunction with others, such as the Overbudget Tasks Report, the Tasks In Progress Report, and the Slipping Tasks Report—both to show cost impacts and to clarify budget and earned value figures.

The tasks are listed in order, along with their summary tasks. Rolled-up costs for the summary tasks are included so you can see interim totals for phases or types of work. The costs for each week and each task are totaled.

For more information about establishing project costs, see Chapter 8, "Planning Resource and Task Costs."

Using the Cash Flow Report in Excel

The Cash Flow Report in Excel is a visual report in the Task Usage category. Use this report to generate a bar graph with cost and cumulative cost amounts shown over time. This report is based on timephased task data.

Using the Cash Flow Report in Visio

The Cash Flow Report in Visio is a visual report in the Resource Usage category. Use this report to produce a diagram that shows planned and actual costs for your project over time. Costs are broken down by resource type (work, material, cost). An icon displays next to any node in which planned costs exceed baseline costs.

Using the Baseline Cost Report in Excel

The Baseline Cost Report is an Excel visual report in the Assignment Usage category. It displays a column chart comparing baseline, scheduled, and actual costs in groupings by task (see Figure 12-18).

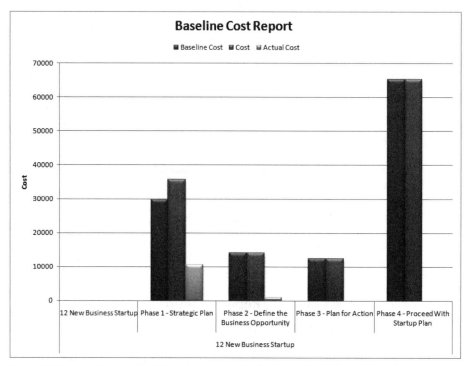

Figure 12-18 The Baseline Cost Report shows an Excel column chart of costs by task.

Using the Budget Report

The Budget text report, in the Costs category, lists all project tasks in order of total cost. Use the Budget report to quickly focus on your "big ticket" tasks.

The Budget report is based on the Cost table for tasks. The total scheduled costs for each task are listed, sorted from highest to lowest cost. The total costs include forecasted costs as well as any actual costs that have accrued as a result of tasks started, in progress, or completed. Also included are any task fixed costs and fixed cost accrual (start, end, prorated). The baseline costs and variances between baseline and total costs show whether you're over budget or under budget, or exactly as originally planned. The actual and remaining cost fields show costs for completed and in-progress tasks. Each column of cost data is totaled.

Using the Budget Cost Report in Excel

The Budget Cost Report is an Excel visual report in the Assignment Usage category. It displays a column chart showing groupings of budget, baseline, scheduled, and actual costs over time.

Using the Resource Cost Summary Report in Excel

The Resource Cost Summary Report is an Excel visual report in the Resource Usage category. It displays a pie chart showing the distribution of resource costs among the work, material, and cost resources assigned to tasks in the project (see Figure 12-19).

Resource Cost Summary Report

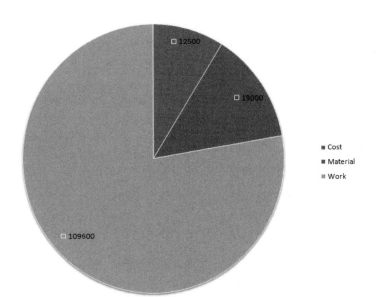

Figure 12-19 In this Resource Cost Summary Report, an Excel pie chart shows that $12,500 is being spent on cost resources, $19,000 on material resources, and $109,600 on work resources.

Using the Overbudget Tasks Report

The Overbudget Tasks text report, in the Costs category, provides a quick look at all tasks in the project whose actual or scheduled costs are higher than their baseline costs. This includes costs associated with resources assigned to these tasks as well as any fixed costs for tasks. Obviously, this report can be used only for projects with saved baselines. The columns of data are the same as those in the Budget report, but the report filter selects only those tasks whose costs are higher than the baseline.

The Overbudget Tasks report is based on the Cost table with the Cost Overbudget filter applied. The amount of cost variance is listed, and the tasks are sorted in order of the highest variance first. This report is most useful for analyzing the extent of cost overruns for specific tasks.

For more information about adjusting costs to conform to your budget, see the section titled "Reducing Project Costs" in Chpater 9.

Using the Overbudget Resources Report

Like the Overbudget Tasks report, the Overbudget Resources report shows the resources whose actual costs exceed those in the baseline plan.

The Overbudget Resources text report, in the Costs category, is based on the Cost table for resources with the Cost Overbudget filter applied. Tasks are sorted by cost variance. The Cost, Baseline Cost, Variance, Actual Cost, and Remaining Cost columns are included and totaled for all overbudget resources.

Usually, the reason these resources are over budget is that their tasks are requiring more work than originally planned. This report is most useful for analyzing the extent of cost overruns for specific resources.

For more information about reviewing and controlling costs in your project, see the section titled "Monitoring and Adjusting Costs" in Chapter 11, "Responding to Changes in Your Project."

TROUBLESHOOTING

Microsoft Project says there is no data to print

If you try to generate a text report, and you get a message saying that there is no data to print, it typically means that the filter that the report is based on is not returning any fields.

Single-click the name of the text report you want and then select Edit. The dialog box that appears shows how the report is defined, including the fields and filters the report is based on. If there is no data in those fields, or if the applied filter finds no match in your project, this might explain why the report is not generated on your project data.

If you get this message when you're trying to generate the Overbudget Tasks or Overbudget Resources reports, either all your tasks and resources are under budget or right on target. It can also indicate that:

- You haven't entered costs for assigned resources. These costs become a part of your baseline to determine your target budget figures. Display the Resource Sheet and enter costs for resources in the Std. Rate field. You might need to set a new baseline.

- You haven't entered fixed costs for tasks. These costs become a part of your baseline to determine your target budget figures. Apply the Cost table to a task sheet and make any necessary entries in the Fixed Cost field for the tasks. You might need to set a new baseline.

- You haven't set a baseline yet. The baseline determines your target budget figures. Click Tools, Tracking, Set Baseline.

- You haven't entered any tracking data for in-progress or completed tasks. Select the task(s) and then click Tools, Tracking, Update Tasks.

The Should Have Started Tasks and Slipping Tasks reports are also based on variances between the current scheduled start dates and the baseline start dates. If no baseline has been saved, or if there is no variance between the baseline start and scheduled start, there is no data to print for this report.

Using the Earned Value Report

The Earned Value text report, in the Costs category, is based on the concept of comparisons between planned and actual costs. More specifically, *earned value* is the analysis of cost performance based on comparisons between the baseline and actual costs and between the baseline and actual schedule.

The earned value analysis always uses a specific date as the reference point for the comparisons being made. This date is referred to as the *status date*, or sometimes the *cutoff date*. To set a status date that's different from today's date, click Project, Project Information and then enter a date in the Status Date box.

The Earned Value report is based on the Earned Value table for tasks. Every nonsummary task is listed along with its earned value calculations for BCWS (Budgeted Cost of Work Scheduled), BCWP (Budgeted Cost of Work Planned), ACWP (Actual Cost of Work Performed), SV (Schedule Variance), CV (Cost Variance), EAC (Estimate At Completion), BAC (Budget At Completion), and VAC (Variance At Completion).

> **Note**
>
> By default, the EAC, BAC, and VAC columns of the table flow over onto a second page, even though the report is set up to print in landscape orientation. To adjust the layout so that all columns fit on a single page, click Page Setup in the report preview window. On the Page tab, under Scaling, change the Adjust To percentage to a smaller value, for example **75**. The Fit To option is not available for this report.
>
> For more information about working with the report layout, see the section titled "Adjusting the Page Setup of a Report" later in this chapter. For more detailed information, including the underlying calculations, about earned value analysis, see Chapter 13, "Analyzing Progress Using Earned Value."

Using the Earned Value Over Time Report in Excel

The Earned Value Over Time Report is an Excel visual report in the Assignment Usage category. It displays a line chart that plots a line each for Actual Cost of Work Performed (ACWP or AC), Budgeted Cost of Work Performed (BCWP or planned value), and Budgeted Cost of Work Performed (BCWP or earned value). Based on timephased task data, the lines are plotted over time.

Evaluating Resource Allocation with Assignment Reports

Reports that focus on resource assignment work and resource allocation are useful for generating to-do lists for resources and their assigned tasks, to follow up with resources and their current task progress, or to determine who has too many assignments in the available time.

Four text reports relate to resource assignments (see Figure 12-20).

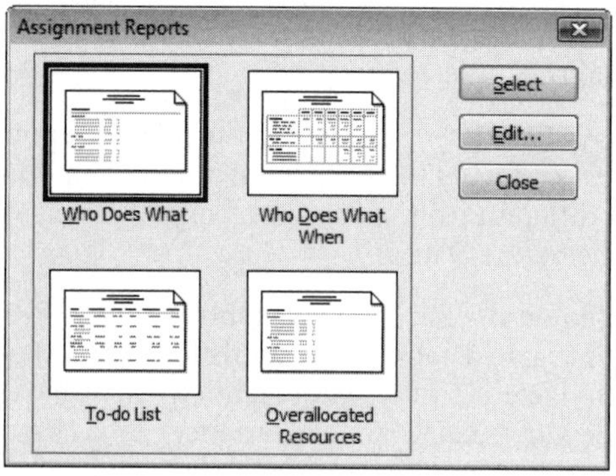

Figure 12-20 The Assignment Reports dialog box lists the reports for resources and their assigned tasks.

Two additional text reports in the Workload report category show assignment work over time either by task or by resource (see Figure 12-21). These reports are excellent tracking tools for seeing the amount of work per task or per resource, on a weekly basis. Both are crosstab reports, showing a tabular presentation of assigned work by assignment along the left and by week across the top.

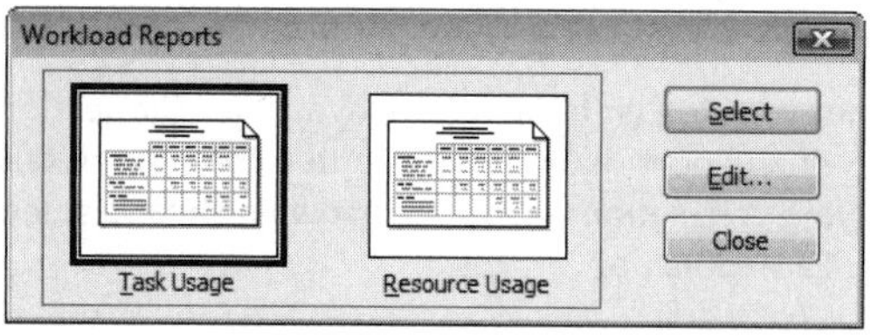

Figure 12-21 The Workload Reports dialog box shows the available reports in this category.

Visual reports specializing in assignments and resource usage are found in the Resource Usage, Resource Summary, and Assignment Summary categories.

Using the Who Does What Report

The Who Does What text report, in the Assignments category, lists the tasks assigned to each resource. It clearly shows the relative number of assignments for all the project resources. This report can also help you or a resource manager plan for coverage when a resource becomes unavailable.

The Who Does What report is based on the Usage table for work resources, and it also shows assignment schedule information.

For more information about making and changing resource assignments, see Chapter 7, "Assigning Resources to Tasks."

Using the Who Does What When Report

The Who Does What When text report, in the Assignments category, is an amplification of the information given in the Who Does What report, adding the daily breakdown of hours of work assigned. Who Does What When is a crosstab report that shows a tabular presentation of work assigned by resource, by assignment, and by day (see Figure 12-22).

Who Does What When
12 New Business Startup

	9/1	9/2	9/3	9/4	9/5	9/6
Interview owners of similar businesses						
Accountant					8 hrs	8 hrs
Identify operating cost elements						
Forecast financial returns						
Confirm decision to proceed						
Estimate sales volume during startup period						
Forecast operating costs						
Select business tax-basis category					8 hrs	8 hrs
Choose and set up the accounting system						
Obtain needed insurance						
Banker			8 hrs			
Establish accounts						
Establish line of credit			8 hrs			

Figure 12-22 The Who Does What When report is a daily accounting of resources and their assigned tasks.

Down the left side, you see a list of all resources with all their assigned tasks. Across the top is each day in the project. All work hours for each of those assignments are listed by resource and by day. Not only does this show you how resources are assigned, but you can also easily see when a resource is assigned to excessive amounts of work on a given day.

INSIDE OUT   Manage the voluminous Who Does What When report

Because it is so detailed, the Who Does What When text report requires a lot of paper to print. Also, generating the data needed to create the report might take some time. Thus, it might be best to use this report less frequently than others or to view it in Print Preview rather than printing it.

Chapter 12

You cannot print a date range with this report unless you create a new custom report based on the data this report generates. However, you can easily modify the report to show work amounts by weeks or by months rather than by days. To do this, follow these steps:

1. Click Report, Reports.

2. Double-click Assignments.

3. Click Who Does What When and then click Edit.

   The Crosstab Report dialog box appears.

4. Next to Column, change Days to Weeks or Months, for example.

   You can also change the number next to Column to indicate that data should be shown for every two weeks, for example.

5. Click OK.

6. Double-click the Who Does What When report, and you'll see that your changes have taken effect.

Who Does What When
12 New Business Startup

	Aug 26, '07	Sep 2, '07	Sep 9, '07	Sep 16, '07
Interview owners of similar businesses				
Accountant				
Identify operating cost elements		16 hrs	16 hrs	24 hrs
Forecast financial returns				
Confirm decision to proceed				
Estimate sales volume during startup period				
Forecast operating costs				
Select business tax-basis category		16 hrs		
Choose and set up the accounting system			16 hrs	
Obtain needed insurance				24 hrs
Banker	32 hrs	8 hrs		
Establish accounts	32 hrs			
Establish line of credit		8 hrs		

The changes you made to this report are saved with this project file.

Using the To-Do List

Use the To-Do List to generate a list of tasks to provide to assigned resources. This can be especially useful if you're not using Project Server and Office Project Web Access to exchange assignment information electronically with your resources.

The To-Do List, a text report in the Assignments category, is based on the Entry table for tasks, with the Using Resource filter applied. It's grouped by week and sorted by task start date. The To-Do List shows the names of all tasks to which the selected resource is assigned, the task durations, and the start and finish dates.

INSIDE OUT   Reports can't be e-mailed

It would be nice to be able to e-mail a report like the To-Do List to team members or a report like the Project Summary to your boss. But that capability is not available (for many of the same reasons you can't save a report from a moment in time).

Note

Consider using the Copy Picture button on the Standard toolbar to save the table on which the report is based as a GIF, JPG, or other image file. Or, you can use a third-party application to print the report as a PDF file. Either way, you can then e-mail that file to team members or other stakeholders.

What you can do, however, is e-mail selected tasks or selected resources from your project plan to your team members. This works if you're using a MAPI-compliant 32-bit e-mail application such as Microsoft Office Outlook. You must also have your resources' e-mail addresses entered in the Resource Information dialog box.

To e-mail selected tasks or resources, follow these steps:

1. Display a sheet view that contains the list of tasks or resources you want to send in an e-mail message.

2. If necessary, apply a filter to show just the tasks or resources you want.

3. Select the tasks or resources whose information you want to send in an e-mail message.

4. Click File, Send To, Mail Recipient (As Schedule Note).

5. In the Send Schedule Note dialog box, select the Resources check box.

6. Click the Selected Tasks or Selected Resources option.

7. Under Attach, select the Picture Of Selected Tasks or Picture Of Selected Resources check box.

8. Click OK. Your e-mail program's message form appears with address information filled in and the picture of tasks or resources already attached.

9. Adjust the recipients of the message, add a comment if you like, and then click Send.

For more information about using e-mail to exchange project information, see the section titled "Sending Project File Information" in Chapter 18, "Integrating Microsoft Project with Microsoft Outlook."

Using the Overallocated Resources Report

The Overallocated Resources text report, in the Assignments category, lists only the resources that have been assigned work in excess of their availability, as reflected in their resource calendars. For example, if a resource's availability is based on the default Standard calendar, the resource will become overallocated when scheduled for more than 8 hours per day or more than 5 days per week.

The list includes every task assigned to a resource, not just the tasks for which the resource is overallocated. Overallocated resources have an overallocated indicator by their name, but the report does not show which specific tasks are actually causing the overallocation. Analyze the task start and finish dates and the amount of work scheduled during those timespans to find the periods of overallocation.

The Overallocated Resources report is based on the Usage table for resources, with the Overallocated Resources filter applied. This report includes the resource's name and total work hours on the summary level and the resource's assignment schedule information in a subtable.

For more information about resolving overallocated resources, see the section titled "Balancing Resource Workloads" in Chapter 9.

Reports That Identify Problems

Various reports can help you identify problems in the project so that you can mitigate issues before they become disasters. The following reports help you look at potential or current problems:

- Critical Tasks text report (Overview category)
- Critical Tasks Status report (Visio visual report)
- Should Have Started Tasks text report (Current Activity category)
- Overbudget Tasks text report (Cost category)
- Overbudget Resources text report (Cost category)
- Earned Value text report (Cost category)
- Earned Value Over Time report (Excel visual report)

- Overallocated Resources text report (Assignment category)
- Resource Work Summary Report text report (Excel visual report)

For more information about resolving project problems, see Chapter 9 and Chapter 11.

Using the Resource Availability Report in Visio

The Resource Availability Report is a Visio visual report in the Resource Usage category. It displays a PivotDiagram that shows scheduled work and remaining availability for all project resources, broken down by work, material, and cost resources.

A red flag is displayed next to any work resource that is overallocated.

Using the Resource Work Availability Report in Excel

The Resource Work Availability Report is an Excel visual report in the Resource Usage category. It displays a column chart showing total capacity, work, and remaining availability for work resources over time (see Figure 12-23)

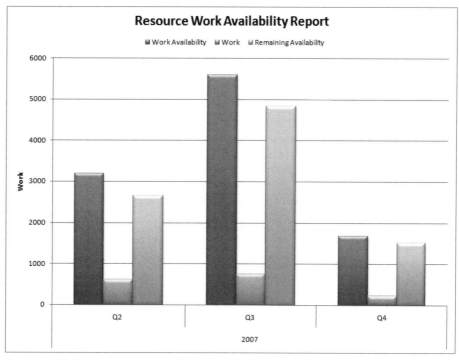

Figure 12-23 The Resource Work Availability Report generates an Excel column chart of work resources over time.

Using the Task Usage Report

The Task Usage text report, in the Workload category, emphasizes assignment hours by task and by week. Under the task names are the assignments, shown as the names of the assigned resources (see Figure 12-24).

Task Usage
12 New Business Startup

	5/6/07	5/13/07	5/20/07
12 New Business Startup			
Phase 1 - Strategic Plan			
Self-Assessment			
Define business vision	8 hrs		
Manager	8 hrs		
Identify available skills, information and support		80 hrs	16 hrs
Business advisor		40 hrs	8 hrs
Manager		40 hrs	8 hrs
Decide whether to proceed			
Manager			
Define the Opportunity			
Research the market and competition	14 hrs	10 hrs	
Business advisor	14 hrs	10 hrs	
Travel			
Marketing collateral (pieces)	222.22	277.78	

Figure 12-24 The Task Usage report shows assignments by task.

The Task Usage report is very similar to the Task Usage view. Summary tasks are shown so the logical groupings of tasks within the project are easy to follow. Totals are shown for each week and each task. This is a clear way to show the full extent of how work and material resources are assigned to every task.

Using the Resource Usage Report

The Resource Usage text report, in the Workload category, emphasizes assignment hours by resource and by week. Under the resource names are the assignments, shown as the names of the tasks to which the associated resource is assigned.

The Resource Usage report is very similar to the Resource Usage view. For each resource, all assigned tasks are listed along with weekly totals of the hours of work assigned for that task. The report layout is the same as the Task Usage report (see Figure 12-24).

Using the Resource Work Summary Report in Excel

The Resource Work Summary Report is an Excel visual report in the Resource Usage category. It displays a column chart showing total capacity, work, remaining availability, and actual work by work units (days, weeks, months, and so on) for each work resource assigned to tasks in your project.

Using the Resource Remaining Work Report in Excel

The Resource Remaining Work Report is an Excel visual report in the Resource Summary category. It displays a column chart showing actual work and remaining work for each work resource by work units (days, weeks, months, and so on).

Using the Resource Status Report in Visio

The Resource Status Report is a Visio visual report in the Assignment Summary category. It displays a diagram of the work and cost for each resource in the project (see Figure 12-25). The percentage of work complete is indicated by shading in each of the nodes, with the shading growing darker as the resource nears completion of total assigned work.

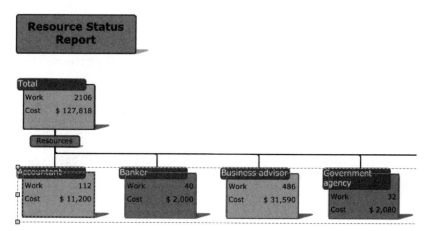

Figure 12-25 The Resource Status Report shows resource work and cost in a Visio diagram.

> ### More Built-In Text Reports
>
> If these reports weren't enough, several more available text reports aren't listed in the Reports dialog box. These additional reports are as follows:
>
> - Base Calendar
> - Resource
> - Resource (material)
> - Resource (work)
> - Resource Usage (material)
> - Resource Usage (work)
> - Task
>
> To generate these reports, follow these steps:
>
> 1. Click Report, Reports.
> 2. In the Reports dialog box, double-click Custom.
>
>   The Custom Reports dialog box appears, showing a single list of all built-in reports.
>
> 3. In the Reports box, scroll to and select the report you want to use.
> 4. Click Preview.

Revising a Built-In Report

After using the standard built-in text and visual reports for several reviews and meetings, you might come up with some new ideas for customizing your presentation and content. You can tweak a built-in report a little (or a lot) to make it better suit your needs. You can either change an existing report or create an entirely new report.

Modifying a Text Report

You can create a new text report by basing it on a copy of an existing report, leaving the original version intact. You can directly modify an existing report. You can also change the page layout of a report so that it prints the way you want.

Copying an Existing Text Report

Copying an existing text report and modifying the copy is the easiest and safest method for creating a new report. The original report remains unfettered, and you can feel free to go wild with the copy. It will probably turn out great, but it's good to know you can experiment without dire consequences. If you get into any trouble, you can always delete the copy and start over again with a fresh copy.

To copy and modify an existing text report, follow these steps:

1. Click Report, Reports.

2. Double-click Custom.

   The Custom Reports dialog box appears (see Figure 12-26).

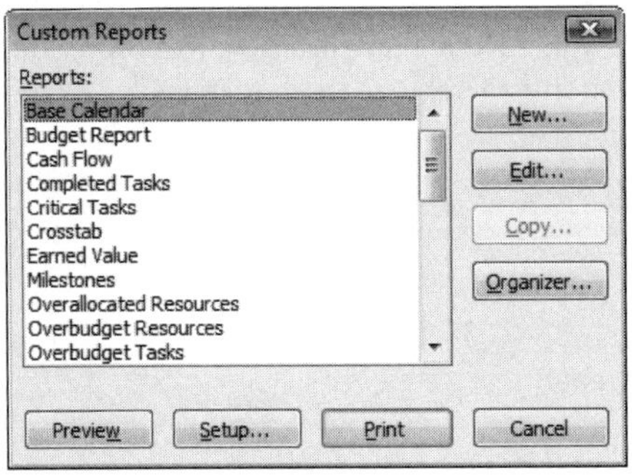

Figure 12-26 The Custom Reports dialog box shows all built-text in reports and text report formats.

3. In the Reports box, click the report you want to copy and then click Copy.

   One of three possible dialog boxes appears, depending on the format of the report you're copying: Task Report, Resource Report, or Crosstab Report (see Figure 12-27).

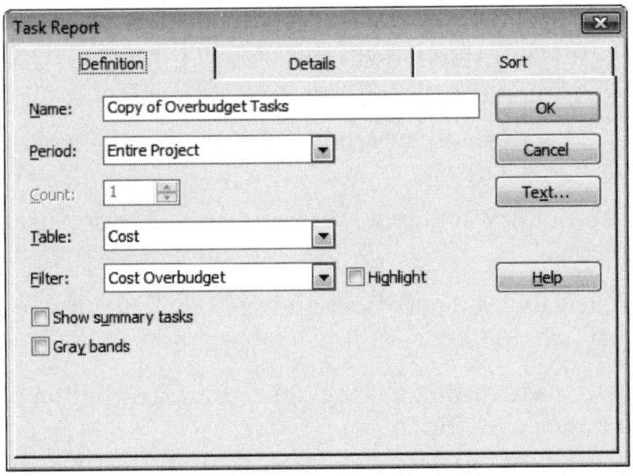

Figure 12-27 The Task Report dialog box appears for any report based on task information.

4. In the Name box, which shows Copy Of <Report Name>, enter the name of your new custom report.

   Make sure it's a name that's different than those already in the Reports list.

5. In the other fields and tabs of the dialog box, make any changes you want to the report content.

   Use the Definition tab to set the fields, time periods, and filters to be used. Use the Details tab to specify additional information you want to add to the report. Use the Sort tab to specify which field should dictate the order of information in the report.

6. Make any changes you want to the report fonts by clicking the Text button.

   The Text Styles dialog box appears (see Figure 12-28).

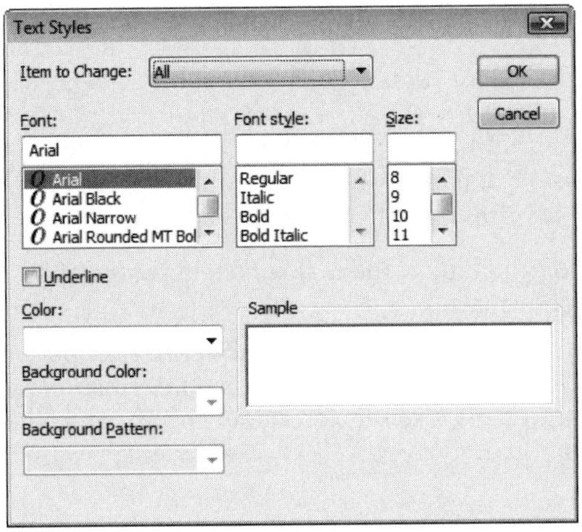

Figure 12-28 Change the font of various items in the report using the Text Styles dialog box.

In the Item To Change box, click the report element whose text you want to format and then specify the changes throughout the rest of the dialog box. When finished, click OK.

7. When finished with your new report's definition and changes, click OK in the report definition dialog box.

   The name of your new text report appears in the Reports list in the Custom Reports dialog box.

8. Select your new report if necessary and then click Preview to generate the report and see what it looks like.

9. If you want to make further changes, click the Close button in the Preview window and then click Edit.

   The report definition dialog box appears again.

Your new report is saved with your project file and is available whenever you work in this particular project.

Modifying an Existing Text Report

You can directly edit the definition properties of a built-in text report. The elements available for editing vary by report. In some reports, all you can change is the font. In other reports, you can change the reporting period, filter for specific types of information, specify that information be drawn from a specific table, and more.

When you change an existing report, your changes are saved only with the project file. If you open the same text report in any other project file, the original default report properties will still be present there.

To edit a text report, follow these steps:

1. Click Report, Reports.

2. In the Reports dialog box, double-click the report category you want.

3. Click the report you want and then click Edit.

   One of four possible dialog boxes appears, showing the options available for this report: Task Report, Resource Report, Crosstab Report, or Report Text.

4. In the other fields and tabs of the dialog box, make the changes you want to the report content or format.

   If available, use the Definition tab to set the fields, time periods, and filters to be used. Use the Details tab to specify additional information you want to add to the report (see Figure 12-29). Use the Sort tab to specify which field should dictate the order of information in the report.

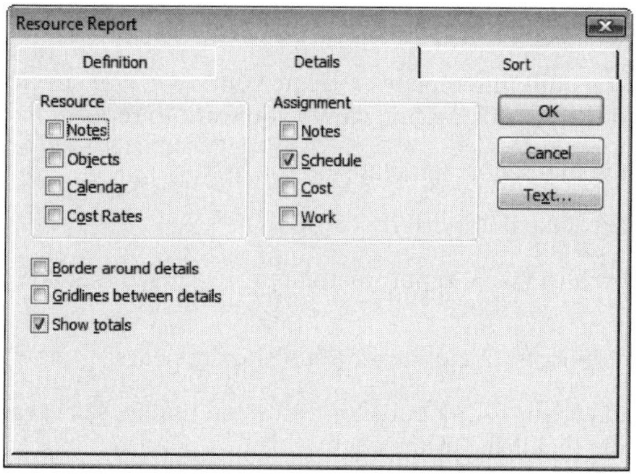

Figure 12-29 You can edit different types of information depending on the report you choose.

5. Make any changes you want to the report fonts by clicking the Text button.

6. When finished editing the report, click OK in the report definition dialog box.

7. Select the edited report if necessary and then click Preview to generate the report and see what it now looks like.

8. If you want to make further changes, click the Close button in the Preview window and then click Edit again to reopen the report definition dialog box.

Adjusting the Page Setup of a Report

You can modify the header, footer, page numbering, and other general page setup elements of a built-in report, a copied report, or a brand-new report. To do this, follow these steps:

1. Click Report, Reports.

2. Double-click Custom.

3. In the Custom Reports box, click the report whose page setup you want to modify and then click Page Setup.

4. Use the options on the Page, Margins, Header, and Footer tabs to make the changes you want.

> For more information about page setup options, see the sidebar titled "Set Options for Printed Views" earlier in this chapter, in Chapter 12, "Reporting Project Information."

The changes you make apply to the selected report in the current project and are saved with the project for the next time you need to print this report.

Modifying a Visual Report

Whether you edit a built-in template or create your own, you specify the fields you want to work with and the type of data on which you want to report.

To edit a built-in visual report template, do the following:

1. Click Report, Visual Reports.

2. Click the built-in visual report template you want to edit and then click Edit Template.

   The Visual Reports - Field Picker dialog box appears.

3. To add fields to the OLAP cube for the visual report, select the fields you want in the Available Fields list. Then click Add.

   The fields appear in the Selected Fields list.

4. To remove fields from the Selected Fields list, select the fields and then click Remove.

   You can select multiple fields to add or remove by holding the Ctrl key and clicking the fields.

5. Click the Edit Template button.

   Microsoft Project builds the OLAP cube based on the fields you selected. Depending on the type of report, Excel or Visio generates the report based on your modified template.

6. Make the changes you want to the settings in Excel or Visio.

7. In Excel or Visio, save the template.

   The changes you've made to the template are saved for future use, replacing the previous version of the template. This modified template is available to any Microsoft Project file you use.

   For more information, see the section titled "Configuring a Visual Report in Excel" in Chapter 17, "Integrating Microsoft Project with Microsoft Excel," and the section titled "Configuring a Visual Report in Visio" in Chapter 19, "Integrating Microsoft Project with Microsoft Visio."

Building a Custom Report

You might have a specialized report requirement that none of the built-in text or visual reports fulfills. The following sections describe how to create a new text report and a new visual report from scratch.

Creating a New Text Report

When you create a new text report, you start with a report template that gives you the framework within which to build a good report. There are four text report templates, or *report types*:

- Task

- Resource

- Crosstab

- Monthly Calendar

If you've edited or copied any existing text reports, or just looked at a report's definition out of curiosity, you're probably already familiar with at least some of these report types. They're also the basis for all the built-in text reports. You can preview any of these report formats. In the Custom Reports dialog box, select its name and click Preview.

To build a custom report, follow these steps:

1. Click Report, Reports.

2. In the Reports dialog box, double-click Custom.

3. In the Custom Reports dialog box, click New.

    The Define New Report dialog box appears (see Figure 12-30).

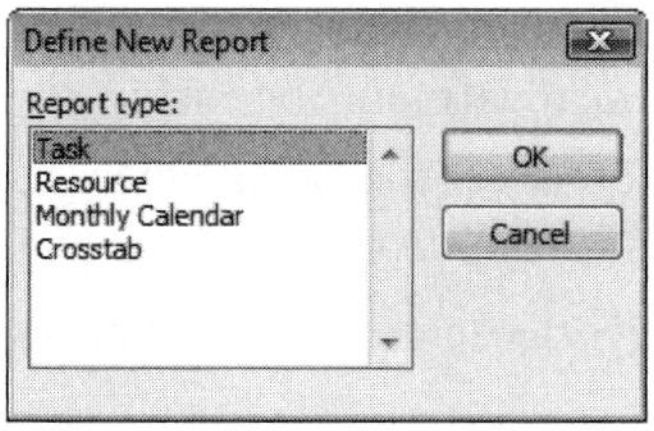

Figure 12-30 Select the format for your new report.

4. In the Report Type box, select the type of report you're creating and then click OK.

    The report definition dialog box appears. The dialog box you see depends on the report type you select (see Figure 12-31).

Chapter 12

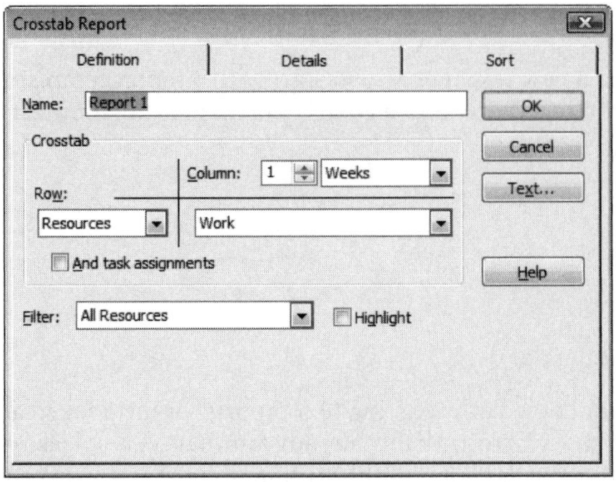

Figure 12-31 The Crosstab Report dialog box appears for any report that displays a tabular format of intersecting information along vertical and horizontal fields of information.

5. In the Name box, enter the name of your new custom report.

   Make sure that it's a unique name in the Reports list.

6. Define your report. Specify any fields, filters, or formatting as the report definition.

   If you're defining a task, resource, or crosstab report, also use the Details tab to specify additional information you want to add to the report. Use the Sort tab to specify which field should dictate the order of information in the report.

7. Make any changes you want to the report fonts by clicking the Text button.

   In the Item To Change box, click the report element whose text you want to format and then specify the changes you want. When finished, click OK.

8. When finished with your new report's definition and changes, click OK in the report definition dialog box.

   The name of your new report appears in the Reports list in the Custom Reports dialog box.

9. Select your new report if necessary and then click Preview to generate the report and see what it looks like.

10. If you want to make further changes, click the Close button in the Preview window and then click Edit.

    The report definition dialog box appears again.

Your new report is saved with your project file and is available whenever you work in this particular project.

Creating a New Visual Report Template

When you create a new visual report, you specify the data type, or OLAP cube, such as Task Usage or Assignment Summary. This provides the basis for the visual report, whether it's to be generated in Excel or Visio.

To create a visual report template from scratch, do the following:

1. Click Report, Visual Reports.

2. Click New Template.

   The Visual Reports – New Template dialog box appears (see Figure 12-32).

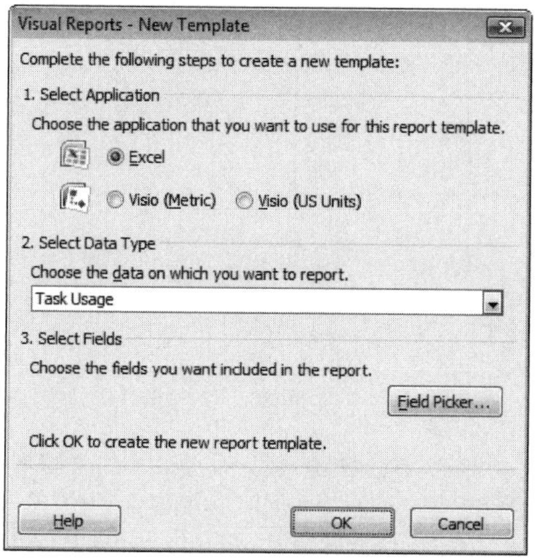

Figure 12-32 When you create a new visual report template, you must specify the application, the data type (OLAP cube), and the fields to be included.

3. Under Select Application, select Excel if you want to create an Excel chart from Microsoft Project data. Select one of the Visio options if you want to create a flow diagram from Microsoft Project data.

4. Under Select Data Type, choose the type of data you want to use as the basis for your report.

   Visual reports are based on six different sets of information: Task Summary, Task Usage, Resource Summary, Resource Usage, Assignment Summary, and Assignment Usage. These data types determine the fields that Microsoft Project adds to the OLAP cube, but you can add or remove fields as well.

5. To modify the fields to be used in the template, click Field Picker and add or remove fields in the Available Fields list.

   To add fields to the new visual report's OLAP cube, select the fields you want from the Available Fields list. Then click Add.

To remove fields from the Selected Fields list, select the fields and then click Remove.

6. Click OK in the Visual Reports – Field Picker dialog box and then click OK in the Visual Reports – New Template dialog box.

For an Excel template, Excel launches and opens a blank PivotChart (see Figure 12-33).

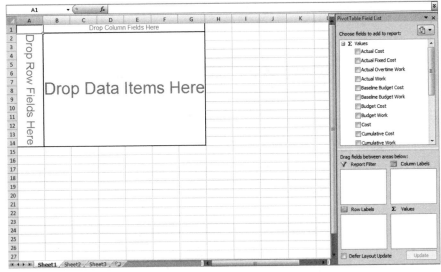

Figure 12-33 Drag fields onto the PivotTable to build your report.

For a Visio template, Visio launches and opens a blank PivotDiagram (see Figure 12-34).

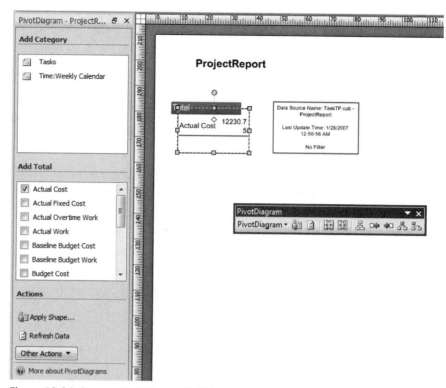

Figure 12-34 Create a PivotDiagram in Visio to use as a custom project visual report.

For details on building a new PivotTable in Excel for a Microsoft Project visual report, see the section titled "Creating and Editing Visual Report Templates in Excel" in Chapter 17. For details on building a new PivotDiagram in Visio for a Microsoft Project visual report, see the section titled "Creating and Editing Visual Report Templates in Visio" in Chapter 19.

7. When you have configured the PivotTable or PivotDiagram, save the template. In the Save As dialog box, make sure that the template is being saved to the folder where all the other templates are located, for example, the Documents and Settings\user\Application Data\Microsoft\Templates folder.

   Saving the template in this folder ensures that the template will appear in the Visual Reports – Create Reports dialog box.

   If you save the template in a location other than the default Microsoft templates folder, you can still have it included in the list of visual reports. On the Visual Reports – Create Report dialog box, click the Include Report Templates From check box, click the Modify button, and then browse to the location of your new template. Select the template and then click OK.

> ## Make New or Changed Reports Available to Other Projects
>
> When you change or create new text reports, they exist only within the current project file. If you want your changed or newly created text reports to be present in all your project files, you can use the Organizer to copy those reports from your current project to your *global.mpt* project template.
>
> You can go the other direction as well. If you've changed a built-in text report and want to return to the original default report, you can copy it from global.mpt back into the project file.
>
> For more information about copying project elements by using the Organizer, see the section titled "Sharing Customized Elements Among Projects" in Chapter 25, "Customizing Your View of Project Information."
>
> When you change or create a new visual report, its Excel or Visio template is saved as a separate file. These reports are therefore available to any project file without your needing to use the Organizer.

Saving Project Data Fields

You can save sets of fields or all fields in the current project file. This can be useful if you want to display or analyze project data in another application such as Excel or Microsoft Office Access 2007.

Saving the Reporting Cube

Six OLAP cubes contain combinations of field data for the current project file. These OLAP cubes are:

- Task Usage
- Resource Usage
- Assignment Usage
- Task Summary
- Resource Summary
- Assignment Summary

If you customize an OLAP cube with a different set of field data, you can save it as a separate cube file. To save a cube file, follow these steps:

1. Click Report, Visual Reports.

2. Click the Save Data button at the bottom of the Visual Reports – Create Report dialog box.

    The Visual Reports – Save Reporting Data dialog box appears (see Figure 12-35).

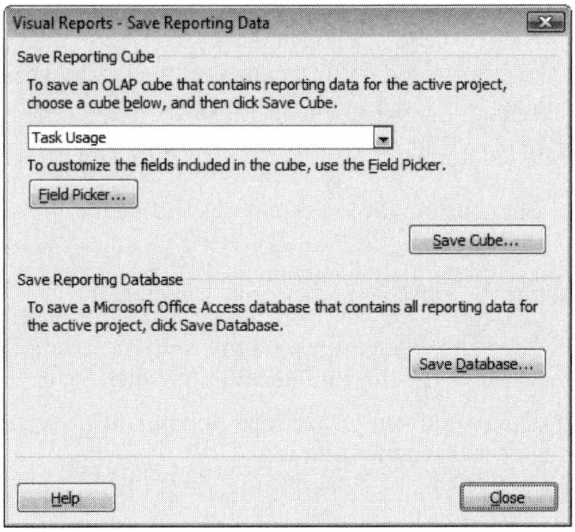

Figure 12-35 Use the Visual Reports – Save Reporting Data dialog box to save a customized OLAP cube.

3. Under Save Reporting Cube, click the cube you want to save.

4. If you want to change any of the fields in the cube you have selected, click the Field Picker button.

    The Selected Fields box lists all fields in the selected cube.

5. Change the fields included in the cube as needed.

    ❑ To add fields to the cube, select fields in the Available Fields box and then click the Add button.

    ❑ To remove fields from the cube, select fields in the Selected Fields box and then click the Remove button.

    ❑ To add custom fields to the cube, select fields in the Available Custom Fields box and then click the Add button.

6. Click OK.

7. In the Visual Reports – Save Reporting Data dialog box again, click Save Cube.

8. In the Save As dialog box, browse to the location where you want to save the cube file. Give the file a name if necessary and then click Save.

    The data in your selected fields are gathered, the cube is built, and the cube file is saved. You can open a cube file (with the .cub file name extension) in Excel, where you can then create a PivotTable with the imported fields.

Chapter 12

Saving the Reporting Database

In Microsoft Office Project 2007, the ability to save project fields to a database has been removed from the Save As dialog box. Saving a project file in XML format essentially saves all contents of all fields that make up the project file database.

However, you can save reporting data from a project file as an Access MDB file through the Visual Reports dialog box. To do this, follow these steps:

1. Click Report, Visual Reports.

2. Click the Save Data button at the bottom of the Visual Reports – Create Report dialog box.

3. Under Save Reporting Database, click Save Database.

4. In the Save As dialog box that appears, browse to the location where you want to save the database. Give the file a name and then click Save.

   The reporting data in your project file are gathered and saved as an Access (MDB) file. You can then open the file in Access.

TROUBLESHOOTING

You can't save project information as a Web page

In previous versions of Microsoft Project, you could save selected project information as a Web page—that is, an HTML file—for subsequent posting to a Web site.

This functionality was essential for posting project information to your organization's intranet or other Web-based project information system to allow for communication with stakeholders.

In Microsoft Office Project 2007, the Save As Web Page command is gone. However, it has been replaced by the ability to save the project as an XML file, which is more flexible to use. You can then apply your XSL style sheet to the XML file and post it to your Web site.

To save your project as an XML file, follow these steps:

1. Open the project plan you want to save as an XML file.

2. Click File, Save As.

3. In the Save As Type field, click XML Format.

4. In the Save As dialog box, navigate to the location where you want to save the new XML file.

5. In the File Name box, type the name for your new XML file.

6. Click Save.

The file is saved. You can now open it in a markup language editor, apply style sheets, and prepare the information for publication on the Web.If you simply want to publish a particular view to the Web, click Copy Picture on the Standard toolbar. Make sure that the For Screen option is selected. Specify the details about what you want to be copied and then click OK. Open a graphics application such as Microsoft Paint and click Edit, Paste. The picture of the Microsoft Project view appears. Manipulate the image further as needed, and save it as a JPG file, or whatever format you prefer. You can then publish the image to the Web page.

If you use an application which creates PDF files, you can print a view or report as a PDF and make it available for download from the Web page.

Chapter 12

Generating Earned Value Data. . . . . **489**   Reviewing Earned Value Data **492**

A s part of your efforts in tracking and controlling your project, you might want to analyze certain aspects of project performance. Project analysis, which you might think of as "project data crunching," can give you a closer look at the overall execution of the project. For first-time efforts at managing a particular kind of project or for new variations on an established project theme, you and your stakeholders might want to see performance indicators and estimates for the remainder of the project. These indicators help assess the effectiveness of the plan and define the amount of corrective action needed to make actual performance in the project conform to the baseline.

A good method for such an examination of project performance is *earned value* analysis, which is a systematic method of measuring and evaluating schedule, cost, and work performance in a project. A set of calculations is performed on certain types of project data. The result of these earned value calculations allows you then to do your earned value analysis. Earned value provides a variety of comparisons between baseline and actual information. The basis of earned value calculations are the following:

- The project baseline, including schedule and cost information for assigned resources

- Actual work and costs reported

- Variances between actuals and baseline information

- A status date

As soon as you set a baseline, Microsoft Office Project 2007 begins calculating and storing earned value data. You can use three earned value tables and an earned value report to view this data.

Generating Earned Value Data

Earned value data begin to be generated as soon as you set a project baseline. Then as you start entering progress information, such as actual start or finish dates, actual percentage completed, and so on, Office Project 2007 compares the actuals against the baseline, calculates variances, and plugs those variances into earned value calculations. There are three categories of earned value fields, each with a different focus:

- Cost

- Schedule

- Work

Setting the Baseline

Set the project *baseline* when you have built and refined the project plan to your satisfaction and just before you start entering progress information against tasks. The project plan should show all tasks and resources assigned, and costs should be associated with those resources. The project plan should reflect your target schedule dates, budget amounts, and scope of work.

To set a baseline, click Tools, Tracking, Set Baseline.

You can now save up to 11 different baselines. However, earned value is calculated on only a single baseline. To specify which baseline should be used for earned value analyses, follow these steps:

1. Click Tools, Options and then click Calculation.

2. Click the Earned Value button.

    The Earned Value dialog box appears (see Figure 13-1).

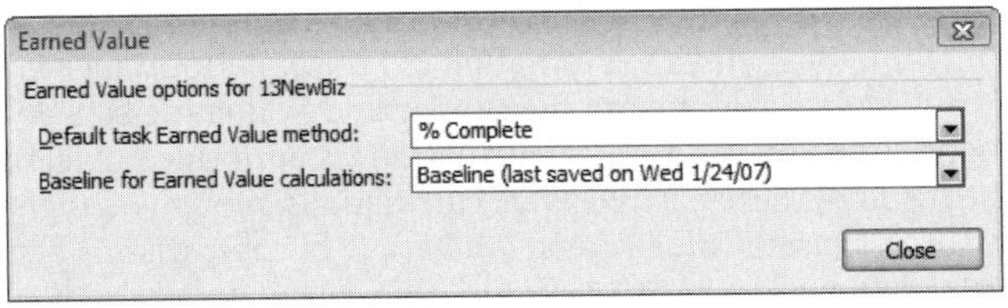

Figure 13-1 Specify which of 11 possible saved baselines should be used for the earned value calculations.

3. In the Baseline For Earned Value Calculations list, click the baseline you want to use.

> For a complete discussion of baselines, see the section titled "Saving Original Plan Information Using a Baseline" in Chapter 10, "Setting a Baseline and Updating Progress."

Entering Actuals

The counterpart to baseline information for earned value calculations is the *actuals* information. To enter task progress information manually, click Tools, Tracking, Update Tasks and then complete one or more of the progress fields indicating percentage complete, actual and remaining duration, or actual start and finish dates.

If you want to enter true timephased actuals, that is, the actual amount of work performed per day or other period of time, record them in the timephased portion of the Task Usage or Resource Usage view. Otherwise, Microsoft Project derives timephased actuals by dividing any total amount entered into the timespan of the assignment.

If you're set up for enterprise project management using Microsoft Office Project Professional 2007 and Microsoft Office Project Server 2007, progress information can be updated in your project plan as team members submit task updates via Microsoft Office Project Web Access.

If you and your project server administrator have set up Office Project Web Access to record actual work performed per time period (days or weeks), you'll receive true time-phased actuals from team members. However, if Project Web Access records actuals by percentage complete or total actual work and remaining work, again, Microsoft Project derives timephased actuals by dividing any total amount entered into the timespan of the assignment.

For more information about manually entering progress information, see the section titled "Updating Task Progress" in Chapter 10.

Microsoft Project can calculate *variances* as soon your project plan contains baseline as well as actuals information. With variances, the earned values fields begin to populate.

Specifying the Status Date

Earned value data is calculated based on a particular cutoff date, or *status date*. Unless you specify otherwise, the status date is today's date. However, you are likely to specify a different status date, for example, if you want to see figures based on the end of the month, which was last Thursday. Also, the status date is typically the date up to which you have collected status information. There is almost always a lag between the date of the latest status information and the date when you are running your earned value reports.

To enter a status date, do the following:

1. Click Project, Project Information.

2. In the Status Date box, enter the status date you want.

Because Microsoft Project stores *timephased* data for values such as baseline and actual work, cost, and so on, earned value can be calculated based on the specified status date.

Base Earned Value on Physical Percentage Complete

By default, earned value calculations are based on percentage complete which in turn is based on task duration or work. However, if your project is geared toward the usage of material, the number of units produced, or some other physical measurement that is not based on the amount of duration or work expended, then it might make more sense for your earned value calculations to be based on physical percentage complete.

For example, suppose your project includes the building of a product and then several follow-on support tasks. If you want the earned value to be calculated on the completion of the product itself and not the support tasks, you could use the physical percentage complete method to enter the percentage complete of the product up to the status date. If you specify that the project has a physical percentage complete value of 50 percent, earned value is calculated on how much money you should have spent on getting the product to 50 percent versus how much you have actually spent to get it to this point.

To set the project to the physical percentage complete method, click Tools, Options and then click Calculation. Click the Earned Value button. In the Default Task Earned Value Method list, click Physical % Complete.

Reviewing Earned Value Data

To study and analyze project performance, you can apply one of three earned value tables to a sheet view. You can run the Earned Value reports. You can also add selected earned value fields to any sheet view.

Working with Earned Value Tables

With a baseline set and actuals entered, you can evaluate current cost and schedule performance through earned value. To review your earned value information in a view, do the following:

1. Click View, More Views. Click Task Sheet and then click Apply.

2. Click View, Table, More Tables.

   The More Tables dialog box appears.

3. In the Tables list, click Earned Value and then click Apply.

   The earned value data for your project displays (see Figure 13-2).

	Task Name	Planned Value - PV (BCWS)	Earned Value - EV (BCWP)	AC (ACWP)	SV	CV	EAC	BAC	VAC
0	⊟ 12 New Business Startup	$74,262.00	$11,572.65	$12,229.50	($62,689.35)	($656.85)	$131,183.90	$124,138.00	($7,045.90)
1	⊟ Phase 1 - Strategic Plan	$30,870.00	$10,532.65	$11,189.50	($20,337.35)	($656.85)	$34,176.22	$32,170.00	($2,006.22)
2	⊟ Self-Assessment	$6,816.00	$528.00	$528.00	($6,288.00)	$0.00	$6,816.00	$6,816.00	$0.00
3	Define business vision	$528.00	$528.00	$528.00	$0.00	$0.00	$528.00	$528.00	$0.00
4	Identify available skills, information and suppc	$6,288.00	$0.00	$0.00	($6,288.00)	$0.00	$6,288.00	$6,288.00	$0.00
5	Decide whether to proceed	$0.00	$0.00	$0.00	$0.00	$0.00	$0.00	$0.00	$0.00
6	⊟ Define the Opportunity	$8,130.00	$6,628.24	$7,012.50	($1,501.76)	($384.26)	$9,659.30	$9,130.00	($529.30)
7	Research the market and competition	$1,670.00	$168.24	$552.50	($1,501.76)	($384.26)	$8,768.52	$2,670.00	($6,098.52)
8	Interview owners of similar businesses	$2,640.00	$2,640.00	$2,640.00	$0.00	$0.00	$2,640.00	$2,640.00	$0.00
9	Identify needed resources	$1,920.00	$1,920.00	$1,920.00	$0.00	$0.00	$1,920.00	$1,920.00	$0.00
10	Identify operating cost elements	$1,900.00	$1,900.00	$1,900.00	$0.00	$0.00	$1,900.00	$1,900.00	$0.00

Figure 13-2 Use the Earned Value table to review earned value fields.

Note

To analyze earned value data by resources instead of tasks, show the Resource Sheet. Click View, Table, More Tables and then click Earned Value.

Make Earned Value Tables and Views More Available

If you review the earned value table often, you might do well to add it to the Table menu. To do this, follow these steps:

1. Click View, Table, More Tables.

2. In the More Tables dialog box, click Earned Value or one of the other earned value tables you want to add to the Table menu.

3. Click Edit.

4. At the top of the Table Definition dialog box, select the Show In Menu check box.

   The selected table is now listed in the Table menu in the current project, and you can get to it with fewer clicks.

You can also create a custom earned value view, perhaps with the Earned Value table applied to the Task Sheet. You can then add your new view to the Views menu as well.

For information about creating a custom earned value view, see the section titled "Customizing Views" in Chapter 25, "Customizing Your View of Project Information."

Although the Earned Value table shows the majority of the earned value fields, two other tables help you focus on specific types of earned value information. Apply the Earned Value Cost Indicators table to analyze your project for budget performance. Apply the Earned Value Schedule Indicators table to analyze schedule and work performance. The fields included by default in each of the three earned value tables are shown in Table 13-1.

Table 13-1 Earned Value Tables

Table name	Included fields
Earned Value	Planned Value (PV), also known as BCWS (Budgeted Cost of Work Scheduled)
	Earned Value (EV), also known as BCWP (Budgeted Cost of Work Performed)
	Actual Value (AC), also known as ACWP (Actual Cost of Work Performed)
	SV (Schedule Variance)
	CV (Cost Variance)
	EAC (Estimate At Completion)
	BAC (Budget At Completion)
	VAC (Variance At Completion)

Table name	Included fields
Earned Value Cost Indicators	Planned Value (PV), also known as BCWS (Budgeted Cost of Work Scheduled)
	Earned Value (EV), also known as BCWP (Budgeted Cost of Work Performed)
	CV (Cost Variance)
	CV% (Cost Variance Percent)
	CPI (Cost Performance Index)
	BAC (Budget At Completion)
	EAC (Estimate At Completion)
	VAC (Variance At Completion)
	TCPI (To Complete Performance Index)
Earned Value Schedule Indicators	Planned Value (PV), also known as BCWS (Budgeted Cost of Work Scheduled)
	Earned Value (EV), also known as BCWP (Budgeted Cost of Work Performed)
	SV (Schedule Variance)
	SV% (Schedule Variance Percent)
	SPI (Schedule Performance Index)

Note

Add one or more earned value fields to other task or resource tables if you want to keep a close eye on one or two calculations without having to apply an entire earned value table. Display the view and table you want and then click the column header where you want the earned value field to be added. Click Insert, Column. In the Field Name box, click the earned value field you want and then click OK.

Understanding the Earned Value Fields

Measuring earned value helps you see the adherence to the baseline plan or deviation from it, in terms of cost and schedule. But when you review these numbers, what are you actually looking at? Are they good numbers or bad numbers? Or are they just right?

As a general rule, when you see positive numbers in the variance columns of the Earned Value table (that is, the SV, CV, and VAC columns), you're ahead of schedule or under budget so far. When you see negative numbers in these columns, the task is behind schedule or over budget. When you see $0.00 in the SV, CV, or VAC columns, the associated task is exactly on target with the schedule or budget.

The following list can help you interpret, in a general way, the calculations you see in your Earned Value report. Two names in a field indicates that this one calculation can be referred to by these two different names or initials.

The following list can help you understand how earned value fields are calculated in Microsoft Project and can also help you interpret the data as part of your analysis. A listing with two names indicates that this one calculation can be referred to by either of these two names or initials.

- **Planned Value (PV) or Budgeted Cost of Work Scheduled (BCWS)** The original planned cost of a task, up to the status date. BCWS indicates the amount of budget that should have been spent by now on this task (or for this resource). For example, if a task should be 50 percent finished according to the schedule, the BCWS would be 50 percent of the original planned cost of that task. Microsoft Project determines the values by adding the timephased baseline dates for the task up to the status date. Review this amount in conjunction with the BAC and EAC.

- **Earned Value (EV) or Budgeted Cost of Work Performed (BCWP)** The baseline cost of a task, multiplied by the calculated percentage complete, up to the status date. This reflects the cost of the task work actually done, according to the original budget. BCWP indicates the amount of budget that should have been spent by now on this task (or this resource), based on the amount of actual work reported by this date. If the task is actually 50 percent complete, the BCWP will be the originally planned cost of the work on the task multiplied by 50 percent. Because this is a measure of actual work costs incurred, BCWP is sometimes called the **earned value** of a task. Compare this amount with the EV/BCWS and AC/ACWP.

- **Actual Cost (AC) or Actual Cost of Work Performed (ACWP)** The sum of all costs actually accrued for a task to date. It includes standard and overtime costs for assigned resources, any per-use costs, cost resources, and fixed costs for tasks. ACWP indicates the amount of budget that should have been spent by now on this task (or this resource), based on the actual work reported by this date. Compare this amount with the EV/BCWS and AC/BCWP.

- **Cost Variance (CV)** The difference between the budgeted costs and the actual costs of a task (BCWP − ACWP). The CV dollar amount indicates the difference between the baseline and actual costs for tasks. A positive CV means that the task is currently under budget. A negative CV means that the task is currently over budget. A CV of $0.00 means that the task is exactly on budget. Compare this figure with SV and VAC.

- **Schedule Variance (SV)**   The measure of the difference between the cost as planned and the cost as performed (BCWP − BCWS). Even though it's called schedule variance, the variance really calculated is the cost resulting from schedule considerations. The SV dollar amount indicates the difference between the baseline costs for scheduled tasks and actual progress reported on those tasks. A positive SV means that the task is ahead of schedule in terms of cost. A negative SV means that the task is behind schedule in terms of cost. An SV of $0.00 means that the task is exactly on schedule in terms of cost. SV does not necessarily indicate whether you're under or over budget; however, it can be an indicator that budget should be looked at more closely. SV clearly shows how much schedule slippage and duration increases affect cost. Compare this figure with CV and VAC.

- **Estimate At Completion (EAC)**   The projected cost of a task at its completion, also known as Forecast At Completion (FAC). EAC is the amount calculated from the ACWP, BCWP, and the Cost Performance Index (CPI), resulting in a composite forecast total of costs for the task upon completion. This dollar amount indicates the current best guess of what this task will cost by the time it's finished. The projection is based on current schedule performance up to the status date. Compare this amount with the BAC.

- **Budgeted At Completion (BAC)**   The baseline cost of a task at its completion. BAC is the cost for the task as planned. BAC is exactly the same as the baseline cost, which includes assigned resource costs and any fixed costs for the task. The budgeted cost is based on the baseline planned schedule performance.

- **Variance At Completion (VAC)**   The difference between actual cost at completion and baseline cost at completion, or BAC − EAC. VAC is the cost variance for a completed task. A negative VAC indicates that the forecasted cost for the task is currently over budget. A positive VAC indicates that the forecasted cost for the task is currently under budget. A VAC of $0.00 indicates that the task is right on budget. Compare this figure with SV and CV.

- **Cost Performance Index (CPI)**   The ratio of budgeted to actual cost of work performed. CPI is also known as Earned Value for Cost. When the CPI ratio is 1, the cost performance is now exactly as planned, according to current work performance. A ratio greater than 1.0 indicates that you're under budget; less than 1.0 indicates that you're over budget. CPI is calculated by dividing BCWP by ACWP.

- **Schedule Performance Index (SPI)**   The ratio of budgeted cost of work performed to budgeted cost of work scheduled. SPI, which is also known as Earned Value for Schedule, is often used to estimate the project completion date. When the SPI ratio is 1.0, the task is precisely on schedule. A ratio greater than 1.0 indicates that you're ahead of schedule; less than 1.0 indicates that you're behind schedule. SPI is calculated by dividing BCWP by BCWS.

- **Cost Variance Percent (CV%)** The difference between how much a task should have cost and how much it has actually cost to date, displayed in the form of a percentage. CV is calculated as follows: [(BCWP – ACWP)/BCWP] * 100. A positive percentage indicates an underbudget condition, whereas a negative percentage indicates an overbudget condition.

- **Schedule Variance Percent (SV%)** The percentage of how much you are ahead of or behind schedule for a task. SV is calculated as follows: (SV/BCWS) * 100. A positive percentage indicates that you're currently ahead of schedule, whereas a negative percentage indicates that you're behind schedule.

- **To Complete Performance Index (TCPI)** The ratio of the work yet to be done on a task to the funds still budgeted to be spent on that task. TCPI is calculated as follows: (BAC – BCWP)/(BAC – ACWP). TCPI helps you estimate whether you will have surplus funds or a shortfall. Values over 1.0 indicate a potential shortfall. Increased performance for remaining work would be needed to stay within budget.

- **Physical Percent Complete** This is a user-entered value that can be used in place of % Complete when calculating earned value or measuring progress. It represents a judgment that overrides the calculations based on actual duration. To use this option, click Tools, Options and then click Calculation. Click the Earned Value button. In the Default Task Earned Value Method list, click Physical % Complete.

> **Note**
>
> You can see a list of all earned value fields available in Microsoft Project. In the Type A Question For Help box in the upper-right corner of the Microsoft Project window, type **fields** and then press Enter. Click Earned Value Fields. The list of all available earned value fields appears in a separate Help window.
>
> Click a field name to open a Help topic that gives a description of each field, how it's calculated, its best uses, and an example of its use.

Generating the Earned Value Text Report

The Earned Value text report is based on the Earned Value table for tasks. Every nonsummary task is listed, along with its earned value calculations for BCWS, BCWP, ACWP, SV, CV, EAC, BAC, and VAC. To run the Earned Value report, follow these steps:

1. Click Report, Reports.

2. Double-click Costs.

3. Double-click Earned Value.

   A preview of the Earned Value report appears (see Figure 13-3).

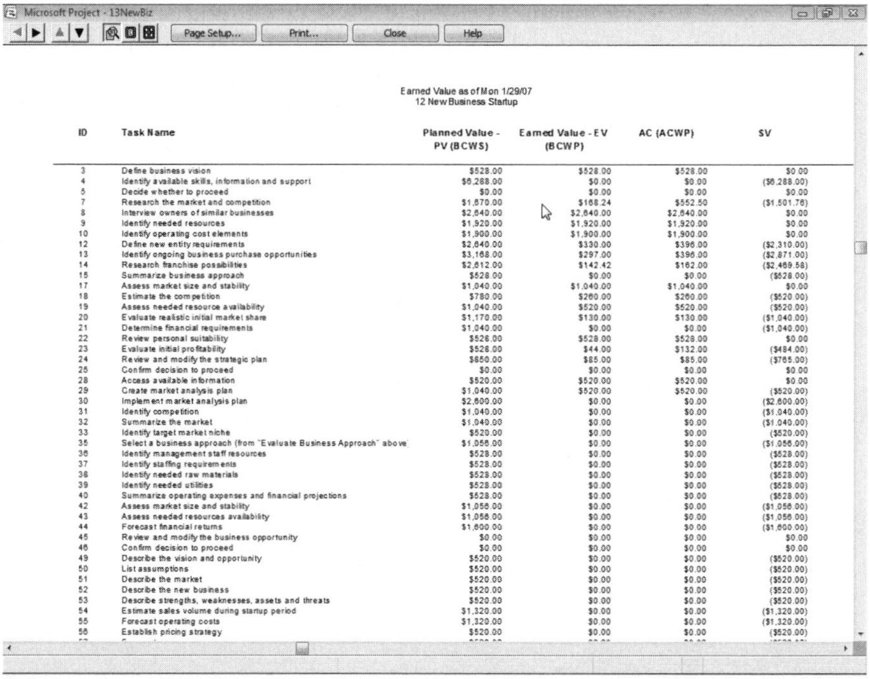

ID	Task Name	Planned Value - PV (BCWS)	Earned Value - EV (BCWP)	AC (ACWP)	SV
3	Define business vision	$528.00	$528.00	$528.00	$0.00
4	Identify available skills, information and support	$6,288.00	$0.00	$0.00	($6,288.00)
5	Decide whether to proceed	$0.00	$0.00	$0.00	$0.00
7	Research the market and competition	$1,670.00	$168.24	$552.50	($1,501.76)
8	Interview owners of similar businesses	$2,640.00	$2,640.00	$2,640.00	$0.00
9	Identify needed resources	$1,920.00	$1,920.00	$1,920.00	$0.00
10	Identify operating cost elements	$1,900.00	$1,900.00	$1,900.00	$0.00
12	Define new entity requirements	$2,640.00	$330.00	$396.00	($2,310.00)
13	Identify ongoing business purchase opportunities	$3,168.00	$297.00	$396.00	($2,871.00)
14	Research franchise possibilities	$2,612.00	$142.42	$162.00	($2,469.58)
15	Summarize business approach	$528.00	$0.00	$0.00	($528.00)
17	Assess market size and stability	$1,040.00	$1,040.00	$1,040.00	$0.00
18	Estimate the competition	$780.00	$260.00	$260.00	($520.00)
19	Assess needed resource availability	$1,040.00	$520.00	$520.00	($520.00)
20	Evaluate realistic initial market share	$1,170.00	$130.00	$130.00	($1,040.00)
21	Determine financial requirements	$1,040.00	$0.00	$0.00	($1,040.00)
22	Review personal suitability	$528.00	$528.00	$528.00	$0.00
23	Evaluate initial profitability	$528.00	$44.00	$132.00	($484.00)
24	Review and modify the strategic plan	$850.00	$85.00	$85.00	($765.00)
25	Confirm decision to proceed	$0.00	$0.00	$0.00	$0.00
28	Access available information	$520.00	$520.00	$520.00	$0.00
29	Create market analysis plan	$1,040.00	$520.00	$520.00	($520.00)
30	Implement market analysis plan	$2,600.00	$0.00	$0.00	($2,600.00)
31	Identify competition	$1,040.00	$0.00	$0.00	($1,040.00)
32	Summarize the market	$1,040.00	$0.00	$0.00	($1,040.00)
33	Identify target market niche	$520.00	$0.00	$0.00	($520.00)
35	Select a business approach (from "Evaluate Business Approach" above)	$1,056.00	$0.00	$0.00	($1,056.00)
36	Identify management staff resources	$528.00	$0.00	$0.00	($528.00)
37	Identify staffing requirements	$528.00	$0.00	$0.00	($528.00)
38	Identify needed raw materials	$528.00	$0.00	$0.00	($528.00)
39	Identify needed utilities	$528.00	$0.00	$0.00	($528.00)
40	Summarize operating expenses and financial projections	$528.00	$0.00	$0.00	($528.00)
42	Assess market size and stability	$1,056.00	$0.00	$0.00	($1,056.00)
43	Assess needed resources availability	$1,056.00	$0.00	$0.00	($1,056.00)
44	Forecast financial returns	$1,600.00	$0.00	$0.00	($1,600.00)
45	Review and modify the business opportunity	$0.00	$0.00	$0.00	$0.00
46	Confirm decision to proceed	$0.00	$0.00	$0.00	$0.00
49	Describe the vision and opportunity	$520.00	$0.00	$0.00	($520.00)
50	List assumptions	$520.00	$0.00	$0.00	($520.00)
51	Describe the market	$520.00	$0.00	$0.00	($520.00)
52	Describe the new business	$520.00	$0.00	$0.00	($520.00)
53	Describe strengths, weaknesses, assets and threats	$520.00	$0.00	$0.00	($520.00)
54	Estimate sales volume during startup period	$1,320.00	$0.00	$0.00	($1,320.00)
55	Forecast operating costs	$1,320.00	$0.00	$0.00	($1,320.00)
56	Establish pricing strategy	$520.00	$0.00	$0.00	($520.00)

Figure 13-3 The Earned Value report shows earned values for all tasks, based on your specified status date.

4. To print the report, click the Print button at the top of the report preview window.

Generating the Earned Value Over Time Visual Report

The Earned Value Over Time Report is an Excel visual report that plots a line each for Actual Cost of Work Performed (ACWP or AC), Budgeted Cost of Work Performed (BCWP or planned value), and Budgeted Cost of Work Performed (BCWP or earned value). Based on timephased task data, the lines are plotted over time.

To run the Earned Value Over Time Report, follow these steps:

1. Click Report, Visual Reports.
2. On the All tab or the Assignment Usage tab, click Earned Value Over Time Report.
3. Click View.

   Microsoft Project gathers the earned value information from your project and sends it to Microsoft Office Excel 2007. There it plots the information in a line chart for your analysis.

TROUBLESHOOTING

Your earned value fields are all $0.00

If you applied an earned value table or inserted an earned value field only to find all the values to be $0.00, it's likely that you're missing one or more of the pieces of information needed by Microsoft Project to calculate earned value fields.

For an earned value to be calculated, you must have all of the following items in your project plan:

- A saved baseline
- Resources assigned to tasks
- Costs associated with assigned resources
- Actual progress information
- A status date

If you set a baseline and you're seeing all zeros except in the EAC and BAC columns, you're probably close to the beginning of your project and haven't entered any tracking information yet. As time goes by and you start entering task progress data, those numbers will start changing to reflect the schedule and current progress.

Another reason for all zeros can be that the status date is set too far in the past.

If you set a baseline and you're seeing all zeros in the SV, CV, and VAC columns, your project is running exactly as planned, with no positive or negative variances recorded at all. Make sure that all your tracking information is entered and up to date. If it is, and you're still seeing all those zeros, you're precisely on schedule and on budget—great job!

PART 5

Managing Multiple Projects

CHAPTER 14

Managing Master Projects and
Resource Pools 503

CHAPTER 15

Exchanging Information Between
Project Plans 529

Structuring Master Projects with Subprojects. . . . . . . **503**   Sharing Resources by Using a Resource Pool **517**

Consolidating Project Information **513**

A s a project manager, you juggle time, money, resources, and tasks to carry out and complete a project successfully. Often, however, you're juggling not only multiple elements of a single project, you're also juggling multiple projects—each with its own associated challenges. The following are three typical scenarios involving multiple projects:

- Katherine manages a large project containing many phases or components for which other project managers are responsible. In Microsoft Office Project 2007, she can set up a master project with subprojects representing those subphases. She can keep an eye on the overall picture while the project managers responsible for the individual phases have complete control over their pieces of the project.

- Frank manages several unrelated projects and keeps the information for each in separate project files. Occasionally, however, he needs to see information about all of them together, perhaps to get accurate availability information about shared resources or to see whether milestone dates in the various projects are coinciding with one another. He might need to print a view or report that temporarily combines the projects. With Office Project 2007, Frank can consolidate information from multiple related or unrelated projects and can do so either temporarily or permanently.

- Sarah, Dennis, and Monique are project managers in the same organization. Although they manage different projects, they use many of the same resources. Sometimes, their projects conflict with one another because of demands on the same resources at the same time. In Microsoft Project, they can create a resource pool file that contains the resources they all use. They can then link their individual project files to that resource pool. The resource availability and usage information is available through that resource pool. When one project assigns tasks to a resource in the resource pool, the resource pool is updated with that resource's allocation information.

Structuring Master Projects with Subprojects

With Microsoft Project, you can insert one project into another. By default, inserted projects look and act like summary tasks in any task view, with their subordinate tasks readily available. You can view and change all tasks within that inserted project. The task information is changed in the source project file as well, because the two projects are linked by default.

Although you might insert projects for a variety of reasons, the most effective use of this capability is to create a *master project* structure with *subprojects* inserted within that master project. This structure is most useful when you have a large project containing a number of subcomponents, especially if those subcomponents are managed by other project managers. If you're managing the overall project, your master project can give you the view you need into the planning and execution of all the subprojects.

Even if you're the sole project manager, you might find the master project–subprojects structure helpful for alternating between project details and the overall project picture.

Information in the master project and subprojects are interactively linked to each other. When project managers of the subprojects make changes, by default, you see those changes reflected in your master project. The reverse is true as well—you can change subproject information in your master project, and those changes are updated in the source subproject.

Your master project can also contain regular tasks. Tasks and subprojects can be organized in relation to one another, and your inserted subprojects can be part of an outline structure and have dependencies, just like regular "native" tasks.

> **Note**
>
> Instead of inserting and linking projects together, you might need to just link an individual task in one project to a task in another project.
>
> **For information about linking tasks between projects, see the section titled "Linking Information Between Project Plans" in Chapter 15, "Exchanging Information Between Project Plans."**

Setting Up a Master Project

When you want to set up a master project with subprojects, first decide where all the files are going to reside. If you're the sole user of the projects and subprojects, the files can all be stored on your own computer. If you're handling the master project, and other project managers are responsible for subprojects, you'll need to store the projects on a central file server or in a shared folder to which all the managers have access.

Inserting Projects into a Master Project

Creating a master project is simply a matter of inserting subordinate projects into what you're designating as the central controlling project; that is, the master project. To insert a subproject into a master project, follow these steps:

1. Open the project that you want to become the master project.

2. Display the Gantt Chart or other task sheet.

3. Click the row below where you want to insert the project.

You can insert the project at any level in an existing outline structure. The inserted project adopts the outline level of the task above the location where it's inserted.

4. Click Insert, Project.

The Insert Project dialog box appears (see Figure 14-1).

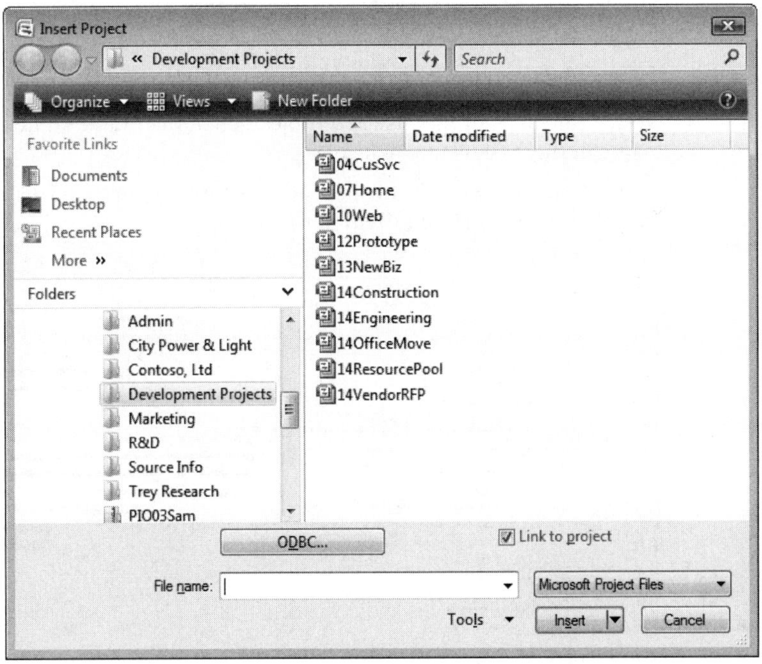

Figure 14-1 Browse in the Insert Project dialog box to find the project you want to insert.

5. Browse to the drive and folder in which the project to be inserted is stored.

6. Click the name of the project file that you want to become a subproject and then click the Insert button.

The project is inserted and its file name appears as a collapsed summary task name in the selected row. The inserted project icon appears in the Indicators field (see Figure 14-2).

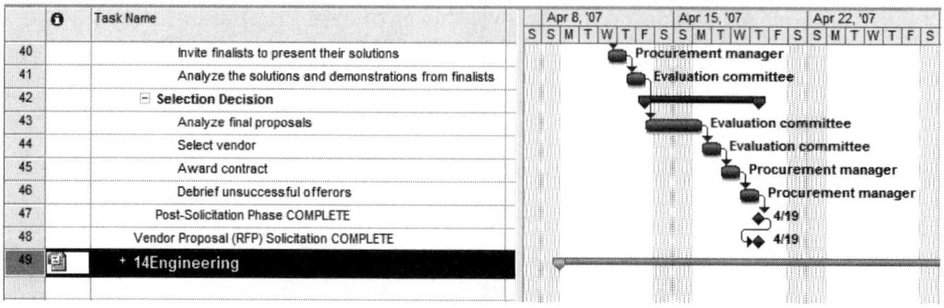

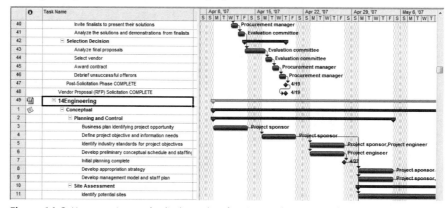

Figure 14-2 The inserted project looks like a summary task among your regular tasks.

7. To see the tasks in the inserted project, click the plus sign next to the project name in the Task Name field.

The subproject expands to show all tasks (see Figure 14-3). They look and behave exactly as if you created them in this project.

Figure 14-3 You can view and edit the tasks of an inserted project in the same way as those that were originally created in the master project.

To hide the tasks in the inserted project, click the minus sign next to the project name.

8. Repeat steps 3–6 for any other projects you want to insert into your master project (see Figure 14-4).

If you're inserting a project immediately after another inserted project, collapse the tasks of the latter subproject before inserting the next one. Otherwise, the newly inserted project will become a subproject within the previous inserted project, instead of standing on its own.

	❶	Task Name	Apr 8, '07	Apr 15, '07	Apr 22, '07
			S M T W T F S	S M T W T F S	S M T W T F S
41		Analyze the solutions and demonstrations from finalists		Evaluation committee	
42		⊟ **Selection Decision**			
43		Analyze final proposals		Evaluation committee	
44		Select vendor		Evaluation committee	
45		Award contract		Procurement manager	
46		Debrief unsuccessful offerors		Procurement manager	
47		Post-Solicitation Phase COMPLETE		4/19	
48		Vendor Proposal (RFP) Solicitation COMPLETE		4/19	
49	🗐	⊞ **14Engineering**			
50	🗐	⊞ **14Construction**			
51	🗐	⊞ **14OfficeMove**			

Figure 14-4 This master project contains three subprojects, each one containing the plan for a major project phase.

9. Indent or outdent the inserted project as appropriate. Also link inserted projects or tasks to native tasks as needed to reflect task dependencies.

In the Network Diagram view, the summary task representing the subproject is formatted differently from other tasks and includes the path and name of the source project file. The subproject tasks themselves look the same as regular tasks.

In the Calendar view, the name of the subproject appears with the individual subproject tasks. If you don't see the subproject name, drag the bottom edge of a calendar row to increase its height.

Breaking a Large Project into Subprojects

You might know during the preplanning stage of your project that you want your project set up as a master project with subprojects, which makes things easier. On the other hand, you might not know until you're in the middle of project execution that a master project is just the solution you need. You can still set it up without having to significantly rework your project files.

If you already have multiple project files that you want to bring together with a master project, it's pretty simple. Create a new project file, insert the projects, and you're all set.

If you have a single large project file and you want to break it up into more manageable subproject files, it's a little trickier, but still very doable. In this case, you need to do some reverse engineering. The overall process for doing this is as follows:

1. Create a new project file for each new subproject you want to insert.

2. In each new file, set the project start date (or project finish date if you're scheduling from the finish date) for the project.

   Set the project start date to the current start date of the first scheduled task in the set of tasks you will be moving into the new file.

3. Set the project calendar to match the project calendar in the original file.

> **For information about copying calendars and other project elements from one project file to another, see the section titled "Copying Project Elements Using the Organizer" in Chapter 15.**

4. Use the Cut and Paste commands to move tasks from the large project file into the subproject file.

Be sure to select all task information by selecting the row headers, not just the task names. When just the cell is selected, the command name is Copy Cell; when the entire row is selected, the command name is Copy Task, which is what you want. Selecting and copying the entire task copies all necessary task information, including any actual progress information, to the new project file.

> **For more information about moving project information, see the section titled "Copying and Moving Information Between Projects" in Chapter 15.**

5. After you have all your separate project files set up, as well as the proper project start and finish dates and calendars, you can insert those files as subprojects into your master project.

New in Microsoft Office Project Professional 2007 and Microsoft Office Project Server 2007 is the ability to insert one enterprise project into another to create a master project-subproject relationship between projects. Using this technique, you can model a program of projects, reflecting all the projects that are being implemented under a specific program in your organization. The overarching program can be represented as the master project, with all the projects within that program set up as subprojects within the master project.

> **For more information, see the section titled "Working with Enterprise Projects" in Chapter 22, "Managing Enterprise Projects and Resources."**

Working with Subproject Information

You can edit any task, resource, or assignment in a subproject. By default, any change you make to subproject information is instantly made in the source project file. Likewise, any change made in the source project file updates the information in your master project because the subproject and source project are *linked*. This updating is convenient because you never have to worry about whether you're synchronized with the most current subproject information.

TROUBLESHOOTING

Your master project has duplicate resource names

Often, your master project contains a set of tasks and a set of resources assigned to those tasks. When you insert a project, the resources from that inserted project are added to your master project. Resource information appears in the resource views, and task information from the subproject appears in the task views just as if you had entered it in the master project originally. You can review and edit the information normally.

If you inserted a project that contains some of the same resources as your master project, you see the names listed twice in your resource sheets. One instance of the resource name is associated with the master project, and the other instance is associated with the subproject. If that resource is a part of other projects you insert, that name can appear additional times.

You can assign resources from a particular subproject to tasks only in that subproject. That is, you cannot assign resources from one subproject to tasks in a different subproject.

To see which resources are associated with which project, add the Project column to the Resource Sheet or Resource Usage view.

If you want to work with a single set of resources across all your projects, consider setting up a resource pool.

For more information, see the section titled "Sharing Resources by Using a Resource Pool" later in this chapter.

Chapter 14

Changing Subproject Information to Read-Only

In some cases, you might not want subproject information to be changed from the master project. Maybe you want to view it only in the master project—which might be the case when you have several project managers in charge of their own subprojects—and you need to see only the high-level view of all integrated project information. In this case, you can change a subproject to be read-only information in your master project, as follows:

1. Display the Gantt Chart or other task view.

2. Click the subproject summary task name.

3. On the Standard toolbar, click Task Information.

Task Information

4. In the Inserted Project Information dialog box, click the Advanced tab (see Figure 14-5).

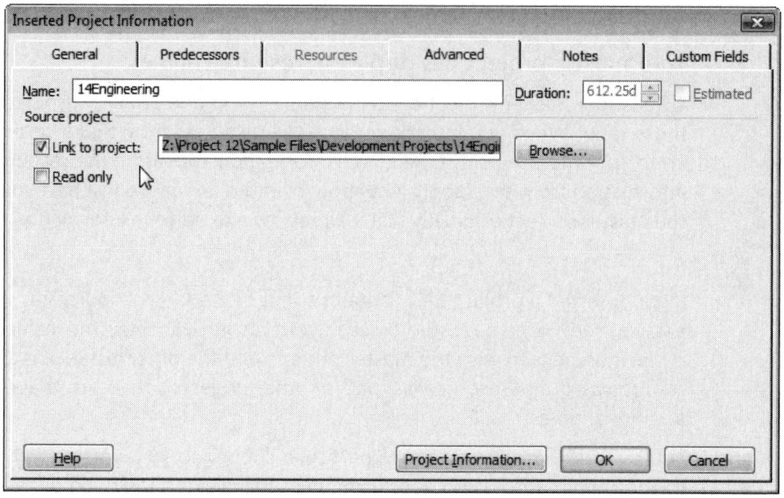

Figure 14-5 Use the Advanced tab in the Inserted Project Information dialog box to change a subproject to read-only or to remove the link to the subproject.

5. Select the Read Only check box.

Now, if you make changes to any subproject information and then try to save the master project, you'll see a message reminding you that the subproject is read-only.

Whether you make a subproject read-only or not, whenever you change subproject information in a master project and save the master project, you are given the choice to save the subproject information to the subproject file. You can always discard those changes.

INSIDE OUT   Is the subproject read-only or isn't it?

If you set your subproject as read-only in your master project, be aware of certain exceptions to read-only subproject enforcement.

If you work in the master project without opening the subproject file, everything behaves as expected: If you change subproject information in the master project, when you try to save the file, Microsoft Project reminds you that the subproject is read-only. It also gives you the opportunity to save the subproject as a new file or discard the changes. You can still save changes to other tasks in the master project that are not read-only.

But suppose that you want to open both the master project file and subproject file. The enforcement of the read-only setting depends on which file you open first. If you open the subproject file first and then the master project file, you can make changes to subproject information in the master project. The changes are reflected in the subproject file, and you can save them.

To be sure that your read-only settings are enforced, therefore, open only your master project, or open the master project first and then the subproject file. In this case, not only can you not save subproject information changed from the master project, you can't save edits made directly in the subproject file.

Chapter 14

Work with Subproject-Related Fields

You might find it helpful to add certain subproject-related fields to a task sheet or resource sheet. You can add the Project, Subproject File, and Subproject Read Only fields to a task sheet. In addition, if you want to know which project a resource is associated with, add the Project field to the Resource Sheet.

	❶	Task Name	Project	Subproject File	Subproject Read Only
44		Select vendor	14VendorRFP		No
45		Award contract	14VendorRFP		No
46		Debrief unsuccessful offerors	14VendorRFP		No
47		Post-Solicitation Phase COMPLETE	14VendorRFP		No
48		Vendor Proposal (RFP) Solicitation COMPLETE	14VendorRFP		No
49	📑	⊟ **14Engineering**	**14VendorRFP**	**14Engineering.mpp**	**No**
1	📝	⊟ **Conceptual**	**14Engineering**		**No**
2		⊟ **Planning and Control**	**14Engineering**		**No**
3		Business plan identifying project opportunity	14Engineering		No
4		Define project objective and information needs	14Engineering		No
5		Identify industry standards for project objectives	14Engineering		No

To add a field, click the column heading to the right of where you want the new field to be inserted. Click Insert, Column. In the Field Name list, click the field you want.

If you make a subproject read-only, and you add the Subproject Read Only column to a task sheet, you'll see that the subproject summary task is marked Yes, whereas the subtasks are marked No. However, they're all read-only.

You can also sort, group, or filter tasks or resources by these fields.

For more information about the ways you can view project data, see the section titled "Rearranging Your Project Information" in Chapter 4, "Viewing Project Information."

Viewing the Critical Path in a Master Project

By default, Microsoft Project calculates a single critical path across all your projects. If you prefer, you can change your settings to see the critical path for each subproject, as follows:

1. In your master project, click Tools, Options and then click the Calculation tab.

2. Clear the Inserted Projects Are Calculated Like Summary Tasks check box.

   This procedure results in a critical path being calculated for the master project independent of the subprojects. In addition, the critical path for each subproject is shown.

You can easily see the critical path(s) in the Tracking Gantt chart.

Review Overall Project Information for an Inserted Project

You can review project information and statistics for a subproject in a master project. Double-click the subproject summary task. The Inserted Project Information dialog box appears. Click the Project Information button. The Project Information dialog box appears for the inserted project, showing the project start, finish, and status dates, as well as the name of the project calendar.

To see overall project information for the inserted project—including the project start, finish, and cost—click the Statistics button in the Project Information dialog box.

TROUBLESHOOTING

You lose text and bar formatting when you insert projects

The formatting of the master project is adopted by any inserted projects, so if you changed the styles for text, Gantt bars, or Network Diagram nodes in the subproject, you won't see those customizations in the master project. However, any formatting changes you made to the master project are adopted by subprojects that are inserted. Also, any formatting changes are retained in the subproject file, even if the subproject and master project are linked.

Unlinking a Subproject from Its Source File

You can keep a subproject in a master project but unlink the subproject from its source project file. When you unlink a subproject from its source project file, changes to the source file won't affect the subproject in the master project, and vice versa. To disconnect a subproject from its source, follow these steps:

1. Display the Gantt Chart or other task view.

2. Double-click the subproject summary task.

3. In the Inserted Project Information dialog box, click the Advanced tab.

4. Clear the Link To Project check box.

5. Click OK.

6. If a message asks if you want to save changes to the subproject, click Yes or No as appropriate.

The subproject is now disconnected from its source, and all the tasks are adopted as native to the master project. The inserted project icon is removed from the Indicators field. Although the project file name still appears in the summary task name field, it's now just a regular summary task—not an inserted project (see Figure 14-6).

	ⓘ	Task Name	Project
44		Select vendor	14VendorRFP
45		Award contract	14VendorRFP
46		Debrief unsuccessful offerors	14VendorRFP
47		Post-Solicitation Phase COMPLETE	14VendorRFP
48		Vendor Proposal (RFP) Solicitation COMPLETE	14VendorRFP
49		⊟ **14Engineering**	**14VendorRFP**
50	🗒	⊟ **Conceptual**	**14VendorRFP**
51		⊟ **Planning and Control**	**14VendorRFP**
52		Business plan identifying project opportunity	14VendorRFP
53		Define project objective and information needs	14VendorRFP
54		Identify industry standards for project objectives	14VendorRFP
55		Develop preliminary conceptual schedule and staffing	14VendorRFP

Figure 14-6 The tasks from the disconnected subproject remain in the project, but they no longer have a link to the source project file.

Removing a Subproject from the Master Project

You can completely delete a subproject from the master project and keep the subproject file intact. To remove a subproject from the master project:

1. Display the Gantt Chart or other task view.

2. Select the heading of the row containing the subproject summary task.

3. Click Edit, Delete Task. Or simply press the Delete key.

    A Planning Wizard message reminds you that you're about to delete a summary task along with all of its subtasks.

4. Make sure that the Continue option is selected and then click OK.

    The subproject is removed from the master project. However, the source file for the subproject is still intact.

Consolidating Project Information

You can join information from multiple projects into a *consolidated project*, which can be useful if you're managing several unrelated projects at one time. Sometimes you need to see information from several projects in relation to one another, particularly when you want to view, organize, or work with project information from all projects as a single unit.

You can consolidate projects temporarily, for example, to print a specific view based on information in the projects. You can sort, group, or filter the tasks or resources of the combined projects. If this is a combination you use frequently, you can make it permanent and save the consolidated file for future use.

What's the Difference Between a Consolidated Project and a Master Project?

A consolidated project is simply another implementation of the Insert Project feature. The differences are as follows:

- The consolidated project is not necessarily structured as a hierarchy, as are the master project and subprojects. With a consolidated project, you might bring all the projects together at the same outline level. With subprojects, some projects might be subordinate to others, and you're likely to need them to be laid out in a specific sequence.
- The projects might be completely unrelated to one another. The consolidated project might simply be a repository for multiple project files.
- The consolidation of projects in a single file might be temporary—just long enough for you to review certain information or generate a report.

To combine multiple projects into a single consolidated project file, follow these steps:

New

1. On the Standard toolbar, click New.

   A new project window appears.

2. Click Insert, Project.
3. Select the project files you want to include in the consolidated project.

   If the project files are all stored on the same drive and in the same folder, open that location. Use the Shift key to select multiple adjacent project files. Use the Ctrl key to select multiple nonadjacent project files.

4. Click the Insert button. The projects are inserted into the new file (see Figure 14-7).

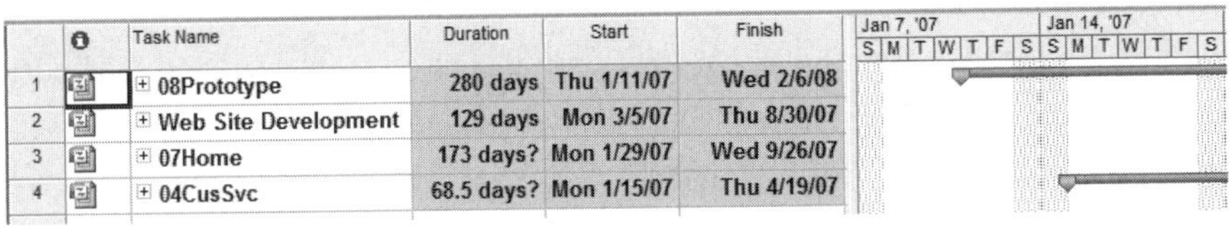

		Task Name	Duration	Start	Finish
1		08Prototype	280 days	Thu 1/11/07	Wed 2/6/08
2		Web Site Development	129 days	Mon 3/5/07	Thu 8/30/07
3		07Home	173 days?	Mon 1/29/07	Wed 9/26/07
4		04CusSvc	68.5 days?	Mon 1/15/07	Thu 4/19/07

Figure 14-7 The selected projects are inserted into a new window.

5. If you need to consolidate project files located on other drives or folders, repeat steps 2–4 until all the files you want are consolidated into your new project file.
6. To keep this file permanently, click File, Save. Select the drive and folder in which you want to store the consolidated file. Enter a name for the consolidated file in the File Name box and then click the Save button.

   If you're just using this file temporarily, you don't need to save it.

If the project files are already open, you can use the following alternative method to consolidate them:

1. Make sure that all the project files you want to consolidate are open.
2. Click Window, New Window.
3. In the Projects list, click the names of the project files you want to consolidate (see Figure 14-8).

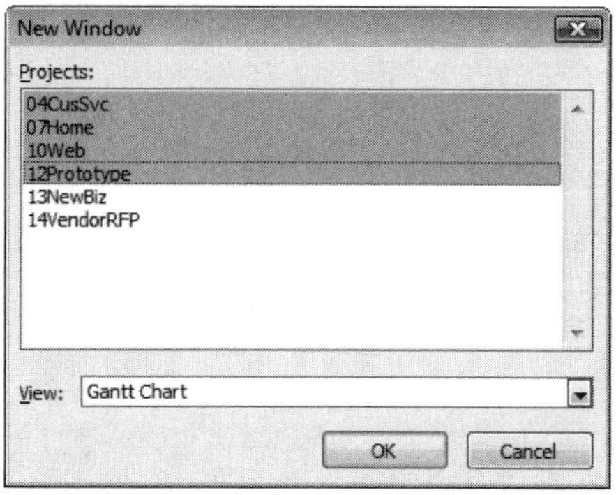
New Window
Projects:
04CusSvc
07Home
10Web
12Prototype
13NewBiz
14VendorRFP
View:
Gantt Chart
OK
Cancel

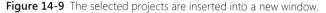

Figure 14-8 In the New Window dialog box, select the projects you want to consolidate.

4. In the View list, click the view in which you want to initially display the consolidated information.

   After you click OK, a new project window appears with the multiple project files inserted in alphabetical order and expanded to show all tasks (see Figure 14-9).

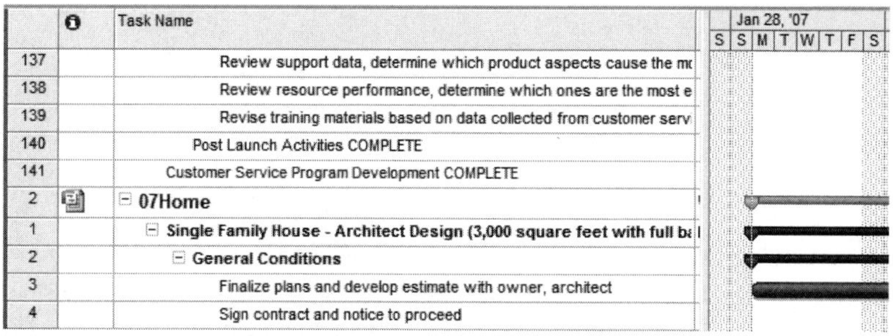
Task Name
Jan 28, '07
S S M T W T F S
137 Review support data, determine which product aspects cause the mc
138 Review resource performance, determine which ones are the most e
139 Revise training materials based on data collected from customer serv
140 Post Launch Activities COMPLETE
141 Customer Service Program Development COMPLETE
2 07Home
1 Single Family House - Architect Design (3,000 square feet with full ba
2 General Conditions
3 Finalize plans and develop estimate with owner, architect
4 Sign contract and notice to proceed

Figure 14-9 The selected projects are inserted into a new window.

Opening Multiple Project Files as a Set

If you always open the same set of project files, you can put those files together in a project *workspace*. Without creating a master project or consolidating the files into a single project file, you can simply associate the projects together. When you open the workspace file, all projects that are a part of that workspace open at once.

Updating Security Settings to Allow a Workspace to Be Saved

When you save a workspace, it is saved under an older Microsoft Project file format, MPW. However, new default security settings in Project 2007 block the opening or saving of legacy or nondefault file formats.

Therefore, you cannot save a workspace until you have changed your Microsoft Project security. To do this, follow these steps:

1. Click Tools, Options and then click the Security tab.

2. Under Legacy Formats, select either the Prompt When Loading Files With Legacy Or Non Default File Format option (medium security) or the Allow Loading Files With Legacy Or Non Default File Formats (low security).

Creating the Project Workspace File

To save a project workspace, follow these steps:

1. Open all project files you want to be a part of the workspace.

2. Close any project files you do not want to save in the workspace.

3. Click File, Save Workspace.

The Save Workspace As dialog box appears.

4. Select the drive and folder in which you want to save the workspace file and then enter the name for the workspace in the File Name box.

5. Click the Save button. Workspace files are saved with the *.mpw* extension.

Now whenever you open the workspace file, all files that are a part of that workspace are opened at the same time.

Sharing Resources by Using a Resource Pool

Typically, when you create a project file, you set up and schedule your tasks and then add resources and assign tasks to them. Often, however, resources are assigned to tasks in multiple projects. You might be the manager of these different projects and use the same resources in all of them. Or multiple project managers might share the same resources for their projects.

To prevent conflicts between projects and avoid resource overallocation among multiple projects, you can create a resource pool. A *resource pool* is a project file that's devoted to maintaining information about resources, including their availability, costs, and current usage or allocation.

Any project manager who wants to use the resources in the resource pool file can link the project file to the resource pool file and make the project file a *sharer file*. When you link a project file to the resource pool file, the resource names and other information appear in your project file. You can then assign those resources to tasks as if you originally created them in this project file.

The Enterprise Resource Pool

Using this local resource pool for multiple projects is similar in concept to using the enterprise resource pool. If you're set up for enterprise project management using Office Project Professional 2007 and Office Project Server 2007, your enterprise resource pool consists of all resources identified as part of the organization. With the enterprise resource pool, you can check skill sets, availability, costs, and other resource information to find the right resources for your project.

Because of this access to the enterprise resource pool, local resource pool functionality is disabled whenever you work with enterprise projects.

For more information for the project administrator setting up the enterprise resource pool, see the section titled "Creating the Enterprise Resource Pool" in Chapter 21, "Administering Your Enterprise Project Management Solution." For information for project managers using the enterprise resource pool, see the section titled "Building Your Enterprise Project Team" in Chapter 22.

Setting Up a Resource Pool

Resource pools are easier to manage in the long run if you have a project file whose only job is to serve as the resource pool file. However, if all the resources you need for the pool are already in a project you're executing, you can use that as your resource pool file as well.

To create a resource pool in its own dedicated project file, follow these steps:

1. On the Standard toolbar, click New.

    A new project window appears.

2. Click View, Resource Sheet.

3. Enter the information for all work or equipment resources you want to be included in the resource pool.

    This information should include at least the resource name, maximum units, and standard rate. If different from the default, also enter the cost per use, cost accrual method, and calendar. Enter the initials, group, and overtime rate if such information is applicable to your projects.

4. If you want material resources to be a part of your resource pool, enter at least the material resource names, identify them as material resources, and then enter the material labels and the unit costs.

5. If you want cost resources to be a part of your resource pool, enter at least the cost resource names and identify them as cost resources.

6. On the Standard toolbar, click Save. Select the drive and folder in which you want to store the resource pool file.

Save

If other project managers will be using this resource pool, make sure that you save the file in a location to which you all have access, such as a central file server or a shared folder.

7. Enter a name for the resource pool file in the File Name box and then click the Save button.

Give the resource pool file a name that identifies it as such, for example, **ResPool. mpp** or **Marketing Resources.mpp**.

For more information about entering resource information, see Chapter 6, "Setting Up Resources in the Project."

If you already have resource information in an existing project file, you can use it to create your resource pool file and cut down on your data entry. One method for doing this is to copy the existing project file and then delete the task information from the new copy. To do this, follow these steps:

1. Open the project file that contains the resource information you want to use.

2. Click File, Save As.

3. Select the drive and folder in which you want to store the resource pool file.

4. Enter a unique name for the resource pool file in the File Name box and then click the Save button.

5. Display the Gantt Chart or other task sheet.

6. Click the Select All box in the upper-left corner of the sheet, above the row 1 header.

The entire sheet is selected.

7. Press the Delete key.

All task information is deleted.

8. Display the Resource Sheet and check the resource information.

Update any information as necessary, including adding or removing resources.

9. On the Standard toolbar, click Save.

Another method of using existing resource information is to copy and paste information from the existing project files to the new resource pool file. To do this, follow these steps:

1. Open the project file that contains resource information you want to copy.

2. Display the Resource Sheet.

3. Select resource information by selecting the row headers.

To select adjacent resource rows, drag from the first to the last row header. Or click the first row, hold down the Shift key, and then click the last row.

To select nonadjacent resource rows, click the first row header. Then hold down the Ctrl key and click all other rows you want to select.

Be sure to select the row headers, not just the task names. Selecting row headers copies all the necessary information—including maximum units and costs—associated with the resource, even if that information isn't displayed in the sheet.

4. On the Standard toolbar, click Copy.

Copy

5. On the Standard toolbar, click New.

A new project window appears.

6. Display the Resource Sheet.

7. On the Standard toolbar, click Paste.

Paste

The resource information you copied from the other project file is inserted into the appropriate fields in the Resource Sheet.

8. Click File, Save As.

9. Select the drive and folder in which you want to store the resource pool file.

Enter a name for the resource pool file in the File Name box and then click Save on the Standard toolbar.

Linking a Project to Your Resource Pool

After the resource pool is set up, you can link project files to it. The project file that uses a resource pool is called the sharer file. As long as the resource pool and the sharer file are open at the same time, the resources in the resource pool file appear in the sharer file as if they were originally entered there. Even if you have resources in your project file, you can still use resources from the resource pool.

To link your project to a resource pool, follow these steps:

1. Open the resource pool file.

2. Open your project file that you want to share resources from the resource pool.

In this project file, click Tools, Resource Sharing, Share Resources.

The Share Resources dialog box appears (see Figure 14-10).

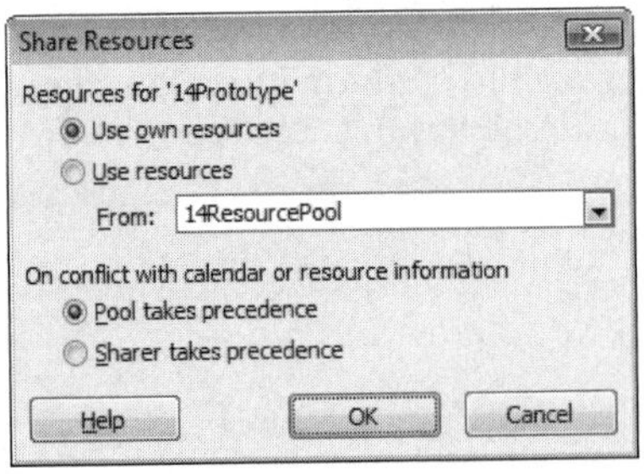

Figure 14-10 Use the Share Resources dialog box to specify that you want your project file to use the resource pool.

3. Select the Use Resources option.

4. In the From list, click the name of the resource pool file. All open files are displayed in this list.

5. Specify how you want any resource information conflicts to be handled.

   If you want the resource pool information to be the final authority in a conflict, select the Pool Takes Precedence option. This is the default, and it is the recommended option.

   If you want the resource information in the sharer file (your project file) to be the final authority, select the Sharer Takes Precedence option.

6. Click OK. Your project file is now designated as a sharer file of the resource pool, thereby linking the two.

   Now all resource information in the resource pool appears in your project file (see Figure 14-11), and any resource information in your project file is added to the resource pool.

	❶	Resource Name	Type	Material Label	Initials	Group	Max. Units	Std. Rate
1		Molly Clark	Work		MDC		100%	$35.00/hr
2		Craig Dewar	Work		CAD		100%	$55.00/hr
3		Denise Smith	Work		DNS		100%	$45.00/hr
4		Katherine Berger	Work		KRB		100%	$45.00/hr
5		Suchitra Mohan	Work		SCM		100%	$50.00/hr
6		Zheng Mu	Work		ZGM		100%	$60.00/hr
7		Christie Moon	Work		CTM		100%	$50.00/hr
8		Armando Pinto	Work		ARP		100%	$65.00/hr
9		Thomas Andersen	Work		TJA		100%	$40.00/hr
10		Hardware	Cost		H			
11		Supplies	Material	each	S			$200.00

Figure 14-11 With the resource pool and sharer file linked, the resource information for both files is merged.

TROUBLESHOOTING

The resource sharing commands are dimmed

If the Resource Sharing and Share Resources commands are unavailable, it indicates that you are working with an enterprise project through Project Professional 2007 and Project Server 2007. Enterprise projects do not use local resource pools. They use the enterprise resource pool instead.

To access the enterprise resource pool, click Tools, Build Team From Enterprise.

For more information about working with the enterprise resource pool, see the section titled "Building Your Enterprise Project Team" in Chapter 22.

TROUBLESHOOTING

You don't see an open project file in the Share Resources dialog box

Typically, any open project files are shown in the Use Resources From list in the Share Resources dialog box. Sharer files are the exception, however. You are never given the choice to use a sharer file as a resource pool.

You can now work with your project file and the resources as usual, including assigning resources from the pool to tasks. Be sure to save both the sharer file and the resource pool file because you're saving the link between the two. You're also saving any resource information from your sharer file as additional resources in the resource pool.

> **Note**
>
> You can make a regular project file into a resource pool file. Open the project file you want to use as a resource pool file. Also open the project file that is to become the sharer file. In the sharer file, click Tools, Resource Sharing, Share Resources. Select the Use Resources option and then select the other project file in the From list.
>
> Although making a regular project file into a resource pool can be convenient at first, keep in mind that when the project ends, the assignments will still be a part of the resource pool file, even though they're no longer relevant.

The next time you open your sharer file, you'll be prompted to open the resource pool also (see Figure 14-12).

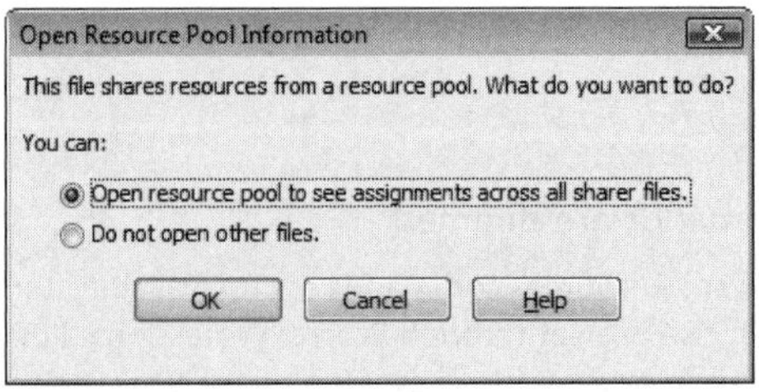

Figure 14-12 If you choose to open the resource file, you'll be able to see all resources, including their assignments, in your sharer file.

Click OK to open the resource file. It's opened with read-only privileges. If you select the Do Not Open Other Files option, the resources you're using from the resource pool do not appear.

If you open a resource pool file before opening any of its sharer files, you are prompted to select whether you want read-only or read-write privileges in the resource pool file (see Figure 14-13).

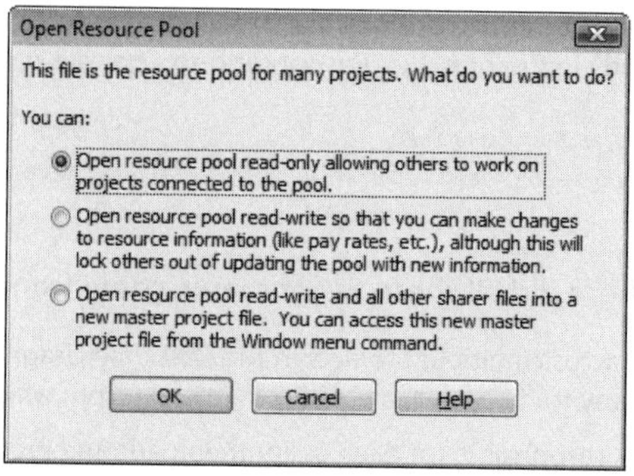

Figure 14-13 You see this alert whenever you directly open a resource pool file. Specify whether you want to open the resource pool as read-only or read-write.

Select the first option to open the resource pool as a read-only file. This is the default, and you should use this option in most cases. You can still update assignment information when working with a read-only resource pool.

Select the second option to open the resource pool as a read-write file. Choose this option when you need to explicitly change basic resource information such as cost or group information. Only one user can open a resource pool as a read-write file at one time.

Select the third option to open the resource pool as a read-write file along with all of its sharer files. These files will be combined into a master project file.

TROUBLESHOOTING

The resources are missing from your sharer file

Suppose that you already linked your project file to a resource pool, thereby making the file a sharer file. But when you close the resource pool, the resources no longer show up in your sharer file.

Open the resource pool, and because the two files are linked, the resources appear again in the sharer file.

Checking Availability of Resource Pool Resources

Display the Resource Usage view or the Resource Graph in the resource pool file to check the availability of resources across all sharer projects. In these views, you can see all the assignments for all the resources in the resource pool. You can see the amount of time they're assigned, if they're overallocated, or if they have time available to take on more assignments.

For more information about checking resource allocation, see the section titled "Monitoring and Adjusting Resource Workload" in Chapter 11, "Responding to Changes in Your Project."

INSIDE OUT   Where did all these assignments come from?

When reviewing assignments across multiple projects in the Resource Usage view of the resource pool file, there's no way to discern which assignments are from which projects.

If you want to see the projects responsible for each assignment, add the Project field to the sheet portion of the Resource Usage view. Click the Work column heading, for example, and then press the Insert key. In the Field Name box of the Column Definition dialog box, click Project and then click OK. The Project field is listed. The project file name for each assignment is listed.

	❶	Resource Name	Project	Work	Details	M	T
2		⊟ Craig Dewar	14ResourcePool	480 hrs	Work		
		Make final decision on office space	14OfficeMove	80 hrs	Work		
		Finalize lease on office space	14OfficeMove	80 hrs	Work		
		Develop rough drawings	14Prototype	320 hrs	Work		
3		⊟ Denise Smith	14ResourcePool	480 hrs	Work		
		Create samples	14Prototype	480 hrs	Work		
4		⊟ Katherine Berger	14ResourcePool	80 hrs	Work		
		Submit to stakeholders for review	14Prototype	80 hrs	Work		
5		Suchitra Mohan	14ResourcePool	0 hrs	Work		
6		Zheng Mu	14ResourcePool	0 hrs	Work		
7	⚠	⊟ Christie Moon	14ResourcePool	640 hrs	Work	16h	16h
		Identify potential office sites	14OfficeMove	160 hrs	Work	8h	8h
		Identify major tenant improvement needs	14OfficeMove	120 hrs	Work		
		Obtain estimates from contractors for major tenant	14OfficeMove	40 hrs	Work		
		Perform research	14Prototype	320 hrs	Work	8h	8h
8		⊟ Armando Pinto	14ResourcePool	152 hrs	Work		
		Make list of key needs that must be met by new offi	14OfficeMove	56 hrs	Work		

When assigning resources to tasks, you can also use the filters in the Assign Resources dialog box to find resources with the right skills and availability (see Figure 14-14).

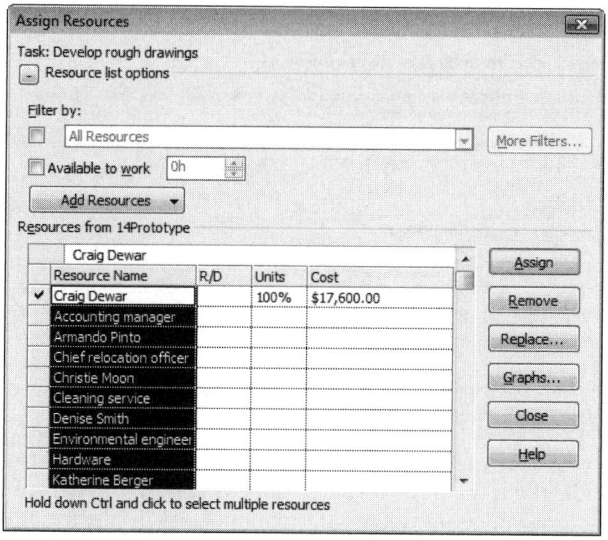

Figure 14-14 Use the Assign Resources dialog box to check resource availability while making assignments.

For example, you can find only those resources from the resource pool who are associated with a particular defined group. Or you can list only material resources. You can also specify that you just want to see a list of resources who have at least 16 hours of availability across all the projects to which they're assigned.

For more information about filtering resources and reviewing availability graphs, see the section titled "Assigning Work Resources to Tasks" in Chapter 7, "Assigning Resources to Tasks."

You can see more availability information about a resource by selecting the name in the dialog box and then clicking the Graphs button. Review the Work, Remaining Availability, or Assignment Work graphs.

Updating Resource Pool Information

If you need to change resource-specific information—such as cost information, notes, maximum units, or working time calendar—you need to open the resource pool file with read-write privileges and change the information. After you save these changes, the next time any users of the sharer files open the resource pool or refresh their resource pool information, they'll see the updated information.

If you're changing resource assignments, there's more flexibility. You can open the resource pool file with read-only privileges, access all your resource information, and change assignment information as needed. When you start to save the sharer file, a message appears, asking if you want to update the resource pool with your changes (see Figure 14-15). Click OK. Even though the resource pool is read- only, it's updated with your changes at that moment. Any other users of the resource pool will see the changes the next time they open the resource pool or when they refresh the open resource pool.

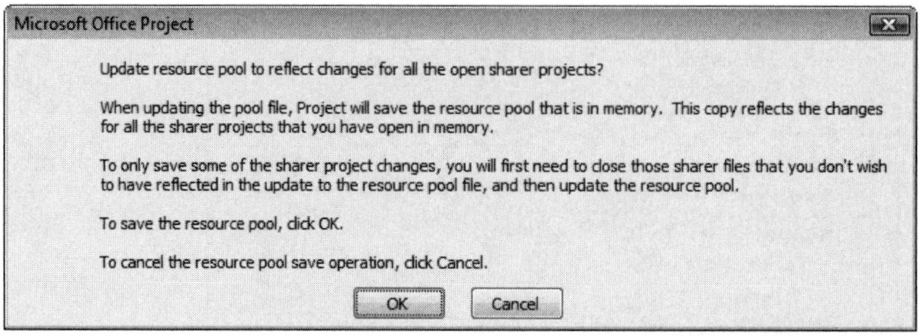

Figure 14-15 This message appears when you're working with a read-only resource pool and you make changes that affect resources in the pool.

Another way to update the resource pool after making assignment changes is to click Tools, Resource Sharing, Update Resource Pool.

If you're working with a sharer file and the resource pool that others also use, it's a good idea to periodically refresh the resource pool to make sure that you have the latest changes to resource and assignment information. Click Tools, Resource Sharing, Refresh Resource Pool.

INSIDE OUT The resource pool and system performance

Sometimes project managers find that Microsoft Project runs slower when large resource pools are linked with large or complex project files.

If you experience system performance problems such as these, open the sharer file without the resource pool file. If you can get by without the resource information, you'll be able to work faster.

Another alternative is to divide your project into a master project with subprojects. Then, link the resource pool with the smaller subprojects.

Disconnecting a Resource Pool from a Project Plan

If you no longer need the resource pool and the sharer file to be linked, you can disconnect them, as follows:

1. Open both the resource pool and the sharer file.

2. Display the sharer file.

3. Click Tools, Resource Sharing, Share Resources.

4. Select the Use Own Resources option.

The resources assigned to tasks in the sharer project remain in the project file. Any assignment information for these resources is removed from the resource pool file.

You can also disconnect the link from within the resource pool, as follows:

1. Open the resource pool.

2. Click Tools, Resource Sharing, Share Resources. The Share Resources dialog box opens (see Figure 14-16).

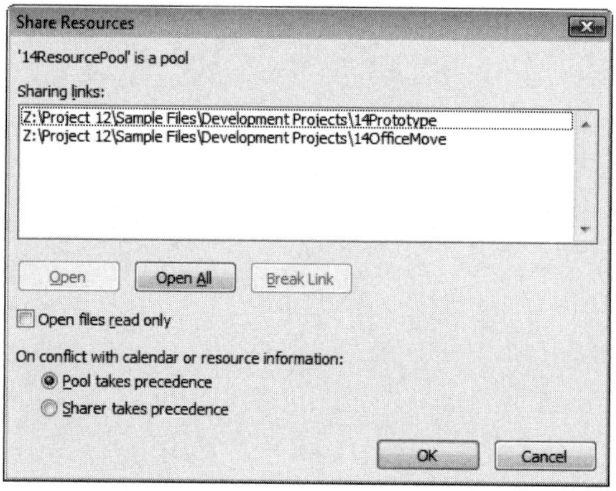

Figure 14-16 In the resource pool, the Share Resources dialog box shows the path of all sharer files.

3. In the Sharing Links box, click the name of the sharer file that you want to disconnect from the resource pool.

4. Click the Break Link button.

CHAPTER 15

Exchanging Information Between Project Plans

Linking Information Between Project Plans. **529**

Copying and Moving Information Between Projects . **538**

Copying Project Elements by Using the Organizer . . . **542**

You might occasionally find it necessary to share information between project plans, especially when you're working with multiple projects or adapting information from an old, finished project to a new project you're beginning to plan. There are a variety of situations in which you might need to share information, as follows:

- A task in one project might depend on the start or finish of a task in another project.

- Task or resource information or specific fields might need to be copied or moved from one project to another.

- Customized project elements, such as views, reports, or calendars, might need to be copied from one project to another.

With Microsoft Office Project 2007, you can easily exchange different types of information between project plans, enabling you not only to model your project appropriately, but also to increase your efficiency by decreasing duplicated entries or development.

Linking Information Between Project Plans

When you link two tasks, you're creating a task dependency or task relationship between them. In the most common link type (finish-to-start), as soon as a predecessor task finishes, its successor task can start.

Tasks don't have to be in the same project to be linked. You can have *external links*. An *external predecessor* is a task in another project that must be finished (or started) before the current task can start (or finish). Likewise, an *external successor* is a task in another project that cannot start (or finish) until the current task is finished (or started). Creating task relationships with external tasks like these is also referred to as *cross-project linking*.

Linking Tasks Between Different Projects

There are two methods for linking tasks between different projects. One method uses a temporarily consolidated project. The other has you typing a path.

To link tasks between temporarily consolidated projects:

1. Open both projects.

2. Click Window, New Window.

3. Under Projects, select the two projects that you want to link.

   Use the Ctrl or Shift key to select them both at the same time.

4. In the View list, click the name of the view you want the consolidated projects to appear in.

   The Gantt Chart is the default.

5. Click OK.

   The two projects are temporarily consolidated into one.

6. Click the task in the project you want to become the external predecessor.

7. Scroll to the task in the other project that you want to become the external successor.

8. When you find the task, hold down Ctrl and click the task.

   Now both the predecessor from one project and the successor from the other project are selected.

Link Tasks

9. On the Standard toolbar, click Link Tasks.

   The tasks are linked with a Finish-To-Start task dependency (see Figure 15-1). You can change the dependency type later.

	❶	Task Name	Duration
90		⊟ **Provide Physical Facilities**	**15 days**
91		Secure operation space	5 days
92		Select computer network hardware	1 day
93		Select computer software	1 day
94		Establish utilities	3 days
95		Provide furniture and equipment	4 days
96		Move in	1 day
97		⊞ **Provide Staffing**	**40 days**
101		Start up the business	0 days
2	📄	⊟ **15OfficeMove**	**127 days**
1		⊟ **Office Move**	**127 days**
2		⊟ **Two To Six Months Before Moving Day**	**77 days**
3	📝	Make list of key needs that must be met by new offi	7 days
4		Identify potential office sites	20 days
5		Make final decision on office space	10 days
6	📝	Finalize lease on office space	10 days
7	📝	Identify major tenant improvement needs	15 days

Figure 15-1 By consolidating projects, you can use the mouse to link tasks in different projects.

10. Close the consolidated project without saving it.

Review the two projects that are still open. You'll see that they now have external predecessors and external successors, as shown by the gray tasks in both projects (see Figure 15-2).

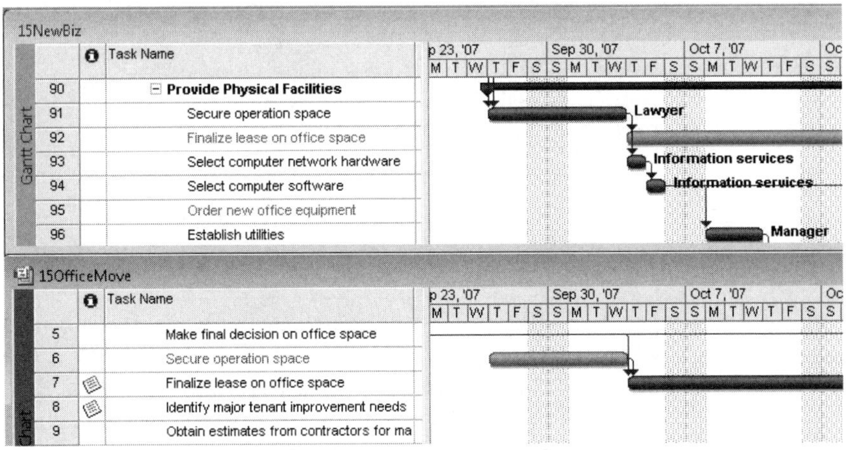

Figure 15-2 Any external predecessors or external successors are displayed in gray.

To link a task in one project to a task in another project by entering a path name:

1. Open both projects.

   Close any other projects.

2. Click Window, Arrange All.

   This isn't required to link, but it enables you to see the tasks in both projects.

3. In the Task Name field, double-click the task that is to be the successor to the external predecessor.

4. In the Task Information dialog box, click the Predecessors tab.

5. In the ID field, type the project path name and task ID of the external predecessor, separated by a backslash (see Figure 15-3).

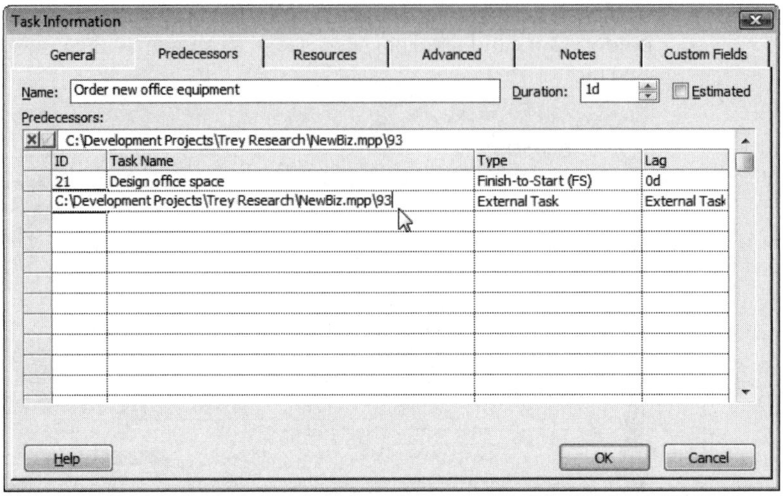

Figure 15-3 On the Predecessors tab in the Task Information dialog box, enter the path, name, and task ID of the external predecessor in the ID field.

For example, suppose that the path name of the project containing the predecessor is C:\Development Project\Trey Research\15NewBiz.mpp, and the ID for the predecessor task is 93 (see Figure 15-4). In the ID field of the Predecessor tab, you'd type **C:\Development Project\Trey Research\15NewBiz.mpp\93** and then press Enter.

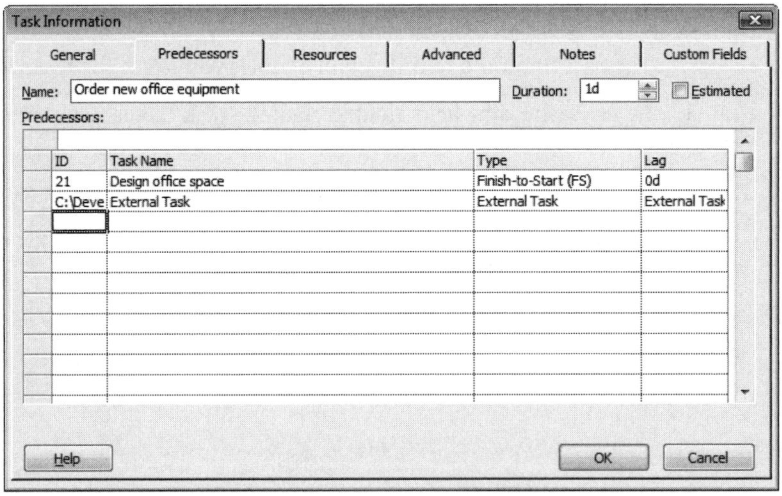

Figure 15-4 After you enter the name and ID of the external task, the other fields contain the words External Task and are temporarily not editable.

If you're linking tasks between two enterprise projects, the projects must both be of the same enterprise *version*, for example, "published" or "published1," according to the enterprise version control protocol. In addition, you need to precede the string with two angle brackets: <>, for example, **<>\15NewBiz.mpp.published\93.**

> For more information about enterprise project versions, see the section titled "Creating a New Enterprise Project" in Chapter 22, "Managing Enterprise Projects and Resources."

6. Click OK.

The name of the external predecessor appears in the current project just above the successor task. By default, table text, Gantt bars, and Network Diagram nodes of external predecessors are formatted in gray.

Just as with regular predecessors, you can change the link type from the default finish-to-start to any of the other three link types (finish-to-finish, start-to-start, or start-to-finish). You can also enter lead time or lag time. Use the Predecessors tab in the Task Information dialog box to do this, as follows:

Task Information

1. In the Task Name field, click the successor task to the external predecessor and then click Task Information on the Standard toolbar.

2. In the Task Information dialog box, click the Predecessors tab.

The name of the external task appears in the Task Name field, and the Type and Lag fields are now editable (see Figure 15-5).

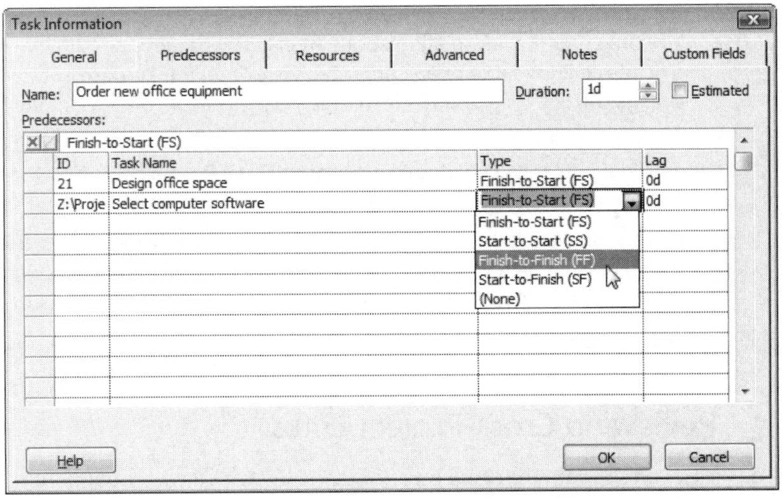

Figure 15-5 The second time you open the Task Information dialog box, the name of the external task appears in the Predecessors table.

3. To change the task dependency to a type other than finish-to-start, select it in the Type field.

4. To enter any lead or lag time for the dependency, enter the value in the Lag field.

Lag time is entered as a positive number, whereas lead time is entered as a negative number.

For more information about task dependencies in general, including lead and lag time, see the section titled "Establishing Task Dependencies" in Chapter 5, "Scheduling Tasks."

INSIDE OUT — Change a link: open, close, and open

When you first enter an external predecessor in the Task Information dialog box, you can't immediately change the link type or enter lead or lag time. Those fields contain the words External Task and are not editable.

Click OK to close the dialog box and then open it again. When you click OK, Microsoft Project finds the external task information and checks that it's valid. When you open the dialog box again, the name of the external task appears on the Predecessors tab, and the Type and Lag fields are now editable.

Enter External Link Information in the Predecessor field of the Entry table

You can enter the information about an external predecessor directly in the Predecessor field of the Entry table or any other table showing the Predecessor field. If you want to change the link type or enter lead or lag time, you can do it all in one step.

For example, for an external task with a finish-to-finish task link and 2 days of lead time, you could enter **C:\Development Project\Trey Research\15NewBiz.mpp\93FF-2d.** There are no spaces between the task ID, link type, and lead time.

Be very careful when entering cross-project links manually like this. Because it's typically a long path name with a cryptic code, a single typo can render your link ineffectual. After entering the predecessor information, be sure to test it and make sure it works.

Reviewing Cross-Project Links

You can see your external links in the different views throughout your project. Whether they're external predecessors or external successors, by default external tasks are highlighted in gray in sheets. External tasks are also represented with gray Gantt bars and gray Network Diagram nodes.

If you double-click an external task, the project containing that task opens, and the task is selected. You can then review its task information and current schedule. The other project is still open, and you can return to it by double-clicking the corresponding external task in the second project.

> **Note**
>
> If you don't want external tasks to be visible in your project, you can hide them. Click Tools, Options and then click the View tab. Under Cross Project Linking Options, clear the Show External Successors and the Show External Predecessors check boxes. This setting applies only to the current project.

To review the details about links throughout your project, click Tools, Links Between Projects. The External Predecessors tab in the Links Between Projects dialog box shows information about all external predecessors (see Figure 15-6). Likewise, the External Successors tab shows information about all external successors.

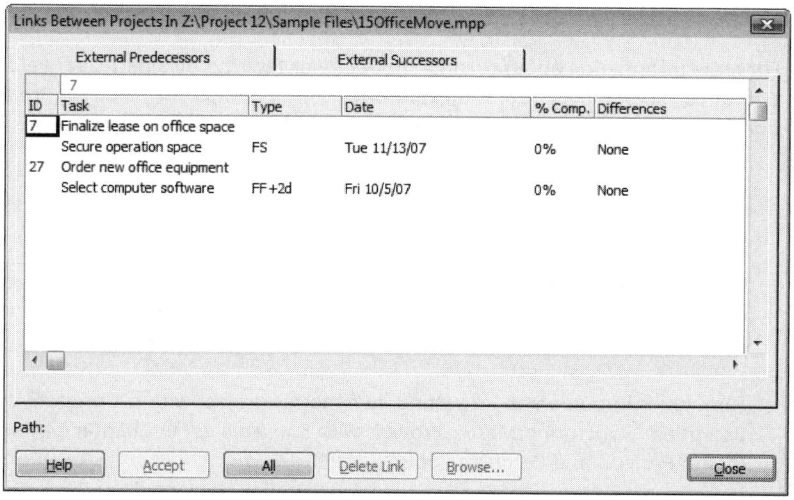

Figure 15-6 The Links Between Projects dialog box shows the pairs of linked tasks along with their link types, finish dates, current percentage complete, along with any available updates.

To see the path and name of an external task, click the task name in the Task field. The path and name appear in the lower-left corner of the dialog box.

There are two fields related to external tasks that you can add to a table or use for sorting, grouping, or filtering. The External Task field, which is a Yes/No (Boolean) field, simply indicates whether the task is external. The Project field contains the name of the project to which this task belongs. For external tasks, the Project field also contains the full path (see Figure 15-7).

	❶	Task Name	External Task	Project
90		⊟ **Provide Physical Facilities**	**No**	**15NewBiz**
91		Secure operation space	No	15NewBiz
92		Select computer network hardware	No	15NewBiz
93		Select computer software	No	15NewBiz
94		Order new office equipment	Yes	Files\15OfficeMove.mpp
95		Establish utilities	No	15NewBiz

Figure 15-7 You can add the External Task or Project fields to a task table to provide information about your cross-project linking.

To add a field to a task table, click Insert, Column and then click the field in the Field Name column.

Whether you add the External Task or Project fields to a table or not, you can sort, group, or filter by these fields. This capability can be handy when you want to see all your external tasks together.

For more information about sorting, grouping, or filtering by a particular field, see the section titled "Rearranging Your Project Information" in Chapter 4, "Viewing Project Information," and Chapter 25, "Customizing Your View of Project Information."

Linking Projects

Sometimes, an entire project cannot start or finish until another entire project has finished or started. You can set up this relationship between projects by using a master project and subprojects.

For more information about setting up a master project with subprojects, see the section titled "Structuring Master Projects with Subprojects" in Chapter 14, "Managing Master Projects and Resource Pools."

You can also simply create a task dependency between key tasks in the two projects. For example, if Project1 can't start until Project2 is completely finished, set up a finish-to-start task dependency from the final task or milestone in Project2 with one of the first tasks in Project1.

Updating Cross-Project Links

By default, the Links Between Projects dialog box appears whenever you open a project file that contains external links that have changed since the last time you opened the file. The Differences field alerts you to any changed information, such as a changed name, schedule change, or new progress information (see Figure 15-8).

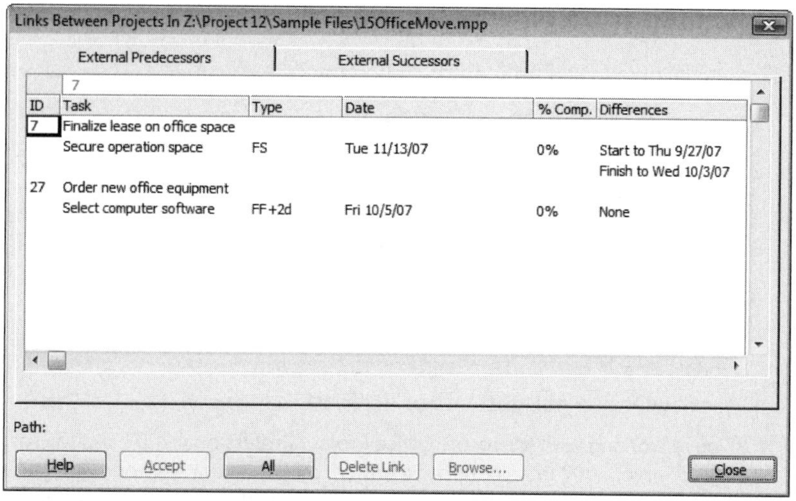

Figure 15-8 The Links Between Projects dialog box appears when you open a project whose external links have changed, and the change is noted in the Differences field.

To incorporate a change from an external task into your project plan, follow these steps:

1. In the Links Between Projects dialog box, review the change in the Difference field.

2. Click the name of the task that has changed and then click the Accept button.

   To incorporate multiple changes all at once, click the All button.

3. When finished accepting changes, click the Close button.

   If you click the Close button without accepting the changes, the changes are not yet incorporated into the project. As long as there are differences between the linked task information in the two projects, this dialog box will appear every time you open the project.

You can modify the way differences between projects are updated, as follows:

1. Open the project containing external links.

2. Click Tools, Options and then click the View tab.

3. Under Cross Project Linking Options, clear the Show Links Between Projects Dialog On Open check box.

   If this check box is cleared, the Links Between Projects dialog box does not appear when you open the project. Whenever you want to synchronize information between the two projects, you'll need to click Tools, Links Between Projects and then update links.

4. If you want external task changes to automatically be updated in your project, select the Automatically Accept New External Data check box.

Chapter 15

Removing Cross-Project Links

To remove an external link, do the following:

1. Click Tools, Links Between Projects.

2. In the Links Between Projects dialog box, click the External Predecessors tab or External Successors tab.

3. Click the link you want to remove.

4. Click the Delete Link button.

Identify Deliverables in Other Projects

If you're working with Microsoft Office Project Professional 2007 and Microsoft Office Project Server 2007 in an enterprise project management environment, you have the capability to identify deliverables in other projects that affect activities in the current project. You can then set up dependencies to those deliverables in such a way that the deliverable dependency is visible in the current project, but scheduling in this project is not affected.

For more information, see the section titled "Depending on Deliverables in Other Projects" in Chapter 22.

Copying and Moving Information Between Projects

Suppose that a project you just finished has a set of resources you want to use in a new project you're starting to plan. You can copy the resource information from one project to another using the Copy and Paste commands.

Maybe you're working with a huge project, and you need to break it up into a master project and subprojects. Or maybe several people are managing different pieces of a single project, and you're trying to pull together fragments of different project files related to that one project. You can move task information from one project to another using the Cut and Paste commands.

You can copy or move entire sets of task or resource information. You can also copy individual fields of information, such as task names and durations, or resource names.

Copying and Moving Task and Resource Information

When you want to copy or move all task information—including the task name, duration, predecessors, dates, notes, progress information, resource assignments, and so on—you need to select the entire task. Likewise, you can copy or move all resource information—including maximum units, availability dates, costs, and calendars—by selecting the entire resource, not just the resource name.

To copy or move task or resource information from one project to another, follow these steps:

1. In the source project, apply a task sheet or resource sheet.

   It doesn't matter whether the sheet contains all the information fields you want to copy or move. All information associated with the task or resource will be copied or moved.

2. Click the row heading for all tasks or resources you want to copy or move.

   If the tasks or resources are adjacent, simply drag across the row headings to select them. Or click the first row heading, hold down the Shift key, and then click the last row heading (see Figure 15-9).

	ⓘ	Task Name	Duration	Start	Finish
33		Order new address labels for notification	1 day	Mon 12/17/07	Mon 12/17/07
34		Obtain estimates from signage companies	7 days	Mon 12/17/07	Tue 12/25/07
35		Order signage for new location	1 day	Wed 12/26/07	Wed 12/26/07
36		Order phone system	1 day	Tue 1/1/08	Tue 1/1/08
37		Order phone lines	1 day	Wed 1/2/08	Wed 1/2/08
38		Order internet phone lines	1 day	Wed 1/2/08	Wed 1/2/08
39		Arrange internal maintenance service	1 day	Wed 12/26/07	Wed 12/26/07
40		Arrange external maintenance service	1 day	Wed 12/26/07	Wed 12/26/07

Figure 15-9 Drag or use the Shift key to select adjacent tasks or resources.

If the tasks or resources are nonadjacent, click the row heading of the first task or resource you want to select, hold down the Ctrl key, and then click the row headings of all other tasks or resources to be copied or moved (see Figure 15-10).

	ⓘ	Resource Name	Type	Material Label	Initials	Group	Max. Units	Std. Rate
1		Molly Clark	Work		MDC		100%	$35.00/hr
2		Craig Dewar	Work		CAD		100%	$55.00/hr
3		Denise Smith	Work		DNS		100%	$45.00/hr
4		Katherine Berger	Work		KRB		100%	$45.00/hr
5		Suchitra Mohan	Work		SCM		100%	$50.00/hr
6		Zheng Mu	Work		ZGM		100%	$60.00/hr
7		Christie Moon	Work		CTM		100%	$50.00/hr
8		Armando Pinto	Work		ARP		100%	$65.00/hr
9		Thomas Andersen	Work		TJA		100%	$40.00/hr

Figure 15-10 Use the Ctrl key to select nonadjacent resources or tasks.

Copy

3. On the Standard toolbar, click Copy.

   If you're moving rather than copying the information, click Cut on the Standard toolbar.

Cut

4. Open the destination project.

5. Display a view compatible with the information you've copied or cut.

   That is, if you're copying or moving task information, display a task sheet view, such as the Gantt Chart or Task Usage view. If you're copying or moving resource information, display a resource sheet view, for example, the Resource Sheet or Resource Usage view.

Chapter 15

6. Click anywhere in the row where you want the first of your selected tasks or resources to be pasted.

   When you paste full rows of task information or resource information, they are inserted among any existing tasks or resources. No information will be overwritten.

Paste

7. On the Standard toolbar, click Paste.

   The copied or cut information is pasted into the cells, starting at your anchor cell.

Copying Fields Between Projects

Instead of copying all information about tasks and resources, you can simply copy the contents of a field, such as task names, resource names, or a custom text field. This procedure can be handy if you just need to copy a set of resource names, for example, or a set of task names with their durations.

> **Note**
>
> Although you can move (rather than copy) fields from one project to another, it isn't all that useful to do so. For example, if you were to cut resource names from one project, you'd be left with a set of resource information that has no names associated with it.

To copy the contents of a field, do the following:

1. In the source project, apply the view containing the fields you want to copy.

2. Select the fields.

   If the fields are adjacent, simply drag to select them. Or click the first field, hold down the Shift key, and then click the last field (see Figure 15-11).

	❶	Resource Name	Type	Material Label	Initials
6		Zheng Mu	Work		ZGM
7		Christie Moon	Work		CTM
8		Armando Pinto	Work		ARP
9		Thomas Andersen	Work		TJA
10		Hardware	Cost		H
11		Supplies	Material	each	S
12		Chief relocation officer	Work		C

Figure 15-11   Drag or use the Shift key to select adjacent fields.

   If the fields are nonadjacent, click the first field, hold down the Ctrl key, and then click all other fields to be copied (see Figure 15-12).

	❶	Task Name	Duration
27		Order new office equipment	5 days
28		Obtain estimates from moving companies	12 days
29		Hire movers	1 day
30		Evaluate server room needs	2 days
31		Evaluate computer networking needs	2 days
32		Order change of address labels for notification	1 day
33		Order new address labels for notification	1 day
34		Obtain estimates from signage companies	7 days
35		Order signage for new location	1 day

Figure 15-12 Use the Ctrl key to select nonadjacent fields.

3. On the Standard toolbar, click Copy.

4. Open the destination project.

5. If necessary, apply a table that contains the same or compatible field as the information you're pasting.

For example, if you're pasting text information, such as task names, make sure that the Task Name or other editable text field is available. If you're pasting cost information, you need to paste it into an editable currency field, such as Standard Rate or Cost1. If necessary, add a field to a current table. Click a column heading and then press the Insert key. In the Field Name list, click the name of the field you want.

6. Click the anchor cell, which is the cell in which you want the first of your selected fields to be pasted.

7. On the Standard toolbar, click Paste. The copied information is pasted into the cells, starting at your anchor cell.

The information overwrites any existing information; it does not insert new cells. Because of this, be sure that you have the right number of blank cells in which to paste your information.

TROUBLESHOOTING

Your pasted information deleted existing information

When you paste selected fields of task or resource information, those fields flow into any existing cells, starting with the anchor cell and continuing into the cells below. If any of those cells contain information, that information is overwritten.

Undo

If this wasn't your intention, and if you haven't saved your file since you did this, click Undo on the Standard toolbar to undo the paste operation. If you have done other operations since you pasted the fields, repeatedly click Undo until your overwritten information returns.

You cannot undo operations done before the last time you saved the file. If you saved your file after you pasted the fields, then you might have to re-create the overwritten information or use your backup project file.

> **Tip**
>
> You can copy and paste project information into other applications and paste information from other applications into your project plan. For more information about this, see the section titled "Copying Information" in Chapter 16, "Exchanging Information with Other Applications."

Copying Project Elements by Using the Organizer

In the course of working on a project over a year or so, you might have created a number of efficiencies for yourself. For example, you might have modified and saved a view to display all key cost information at a glance or created a report for a specific meeting you have every other week. Maybe you've created a set of macros to automate a number of repetitive task-tracking activities.

When you start a new project and you're looking at your new project file, you might think you need to do all that modifying, customizing, and creating all over again. Not so. Just as you can copy task information from one project to another, you can copy customized project elements such as tables, calendars, and fields from one project to another. You do this with the Organizer.

Some elements you change in your project also change your Microsoft Project global template, which is applied to all projects on your computer system. Many other elements just stay in the current project. You can use the Organizer to copy elements to the project global template, thereby making them available to all projects. You can also use the Organizer to copy elements from one project to another.

For information about the project global template, see the section titled "Working with the Project Global Template" in Chapter 28, "Standardizing Projects Using Templates." Project managers creating new projects based on the enterprise global template can refer to "Creating a New Enterprise Project" in Chapter 22.

With the Organizer, you can copy the following project elements:

- Views
- Custom fields and outline codes
- Tables
- Toolbars
- Groups
- Forms
- Filters
- Microsoft Visual Basic for Applications (VBA) modules and macros

- Reports

- Import/export maps

- Base calendars

No matter which type of element you copy, the procedure is the same. You select a source file that contains the element that you want to copy, select a destination file into which you want to copy the element, and then copy the element.

Copying an Element from a Project to the Global Template

To copy an element from a project to the project global template, follow these steps:

1. Open the project that contains the element you want to copy.

2. Click Tools, Organizer. The Organizer dialog box appears (see Figure 15-13).

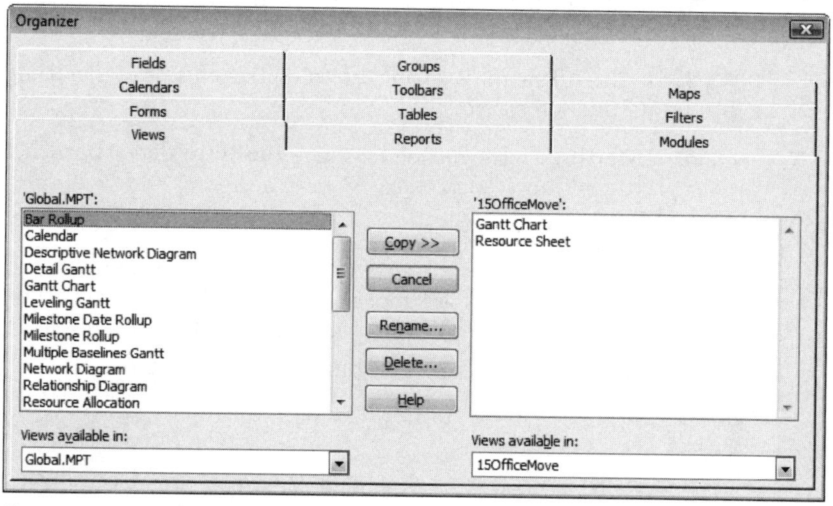

Figure 15-13 Use the Organizer to copy, rename, or delete customized elements between projects or between a project and the project global template.

3. Click the tab for the type of element you want to copy, for example, Views or Reports.

4. In the <Element> Available In list on the right side of the dialog box, click the project that contains the element that you want to copy.

<Element> stands for the name of the current tab.

5. In the list of elements on the right side of the dialog box, click the name of the element you want to copy.

6. Click the Copy button.

If an element with the same name already exists in the project global template, a confirmation message appears. Click Yes if you want to replace the element in the project global template with the one from the source project.

To copy the element with a different name, click the Rename button and then type a new name.

Copying an Element Between Two Projects

To copy an element between two projects, follow these steps:

1. Open both the source and destination projects.

2. Click Tools, Organizer.

3. In the Organizer dialog box, click the tab for the element you want to copy.

4. In the <Element> Available In list on the right side of the dialog box, click the source project.

5. In the <Element> Available In list on the left side of the dialog box, click the destination project.

6. In the list of elements on the right side of the dialog box, click the name of the element you want to copy.

7. Click the Copy button.

   If an element with the same name already exists in the project global template, a confirmation message appears. Click Yes if you want to replace the element in the project global template with the one from the source project.

   To copy the element with a different name, click the Rename button and then enter a new name.

PART 6

Integrating Microsoft Project with Other Programs

CHAPTER 16

Exchanging Information with
Other Applications. 547

CHAPTER 17

Integrating Microsoft Project with
Microsoft Excel. 581

CHAPTER 18

Integrating Microsoft Project with
Microsoft Outlook. 639

CHAPTER 19

Integrating Microsoft Project with
Microsoft Visio. 653

Exchanging Information with Other Applications

Copying Information 549

Embedding Information 557

Linking Information 568

Hyperlinking to Documents in Other Applications . . . 571

Importing and Exporting Information 573

You can exchange data in Microsoft Office Project 2007 with other applications. This capability can save everyone involved an immense amount of time and effort and can also provide for the flexibility of information so essential in an efficient project.

For example, you might want to provide a set of data from your project plan to a stakeholder who doesn't have access to Office Project 2007 but does have another compatible application such as Microsoft Office Excel 2007 or Microsoft Office Word 2007.

You might want to send project data to a spreadsheet or database application to manipulate the information in ways that those applications specialize in.

In the same way, you can easily bring information into Microsoft Project from other applications. If someone has a list of tasks or resources along with associated information that you need in your project plan, copying or importing this information can save you from rekeying existing data.

> Note
>
> When referring to the exchange of data between applications, we use the terms source and target to mean the originating application and the receiving application, respectively.

There are several techniques for exchanging information between applications. The method you use depends on what you're trying to accomplish with the information. Table 16-1 provides some basic guidelines.

Table 16-1 Appropriate Methods for Information Exchange

To do this	Use this method
Copy static text or numbers between Microsoft Project and another application. The information usually appears as if it were created originally in the target application.	Copy
Copy pictures between Microsoft Project and another application.	Copy Picture

To do this	Use this method
Add data along with its source application to another program. When you double-click the embedded information, the source application opens and you can work with it there.	Embed
Create a dynamic connection between the information in the source and target applications. When the information is updated in one, it's updated in the other as well.	Link
Reference a document at its source, whether it's a Web site or file location. Clicking the hyperlink finds and launches the document in its native application.	Hyperlink
Bring information into Microsoft Project from another application or another file format, making the information appear as if it were created in Microsoft Project to begin with. Similar to copying, but typically used with entire files.	Import
Convert Microsoft Project information into a file format able to be used by another application, making the information appear as if it were created in that other application to begin with. Similar to copying, but typically used with entire files.	Export
Convert Microsoft Project information into XML format for use in Web pages or any other application that reads or is based on XML.	Export Microsoft Project data as XML

It's important to keep in mind that some methods of exchanging data move the data and then freeze it, so the information transferred cannot be altered after the exchange. Other methods move the data into the other application and allow it to be dynamically manipulated.

> ### Note
>
> Microsoft Project has particularly robust methods for exchanging information with Office Excel 2007, Microsoft Office Outlook 2007, and Microsoft Office Visio 2007.
>
> These methods are covered in their own chapters: Chapter 17, "Integrating Microsoft Project with Microsoft Excel"; Chapter 18, "Integrating Microsoft Project with Microsoft Outlook"; and Chapter 19, "Integrating Microsoft Project with Microsoft Visio."

> ### Integrate with Other Business Applications
>
> If you're set up for enterprise project management using Microsoft Office Project Professional 2007 and Microsoft Office Project Server 2007, your organization might take advantage of additional means for working with other applications. Through the Project Server Interface, you can integrate information between Office Project Server 2007 and other organizational systems that interact with project management processes, such as accounting, procurement, and human resources.
>
> **For more information about working with the Project Server Interface, see the section titled "Integrate Project Information with Business Processes" in Chapter 21, "Administering Your Enterprise Project Management Solution."**

Copying Information

You can copy textual as well as graphical data between Microsoft Project and other applications. With one method, you simply use the Copy and Paste commands. With another method, you use a wizard.

Copying from Microsoft Project to Another Application

You can copy field information, such as from a task sheet or resource sheet, to another application, such as Office Word 2007 or Microsoft Office Access 2007. When you need a subset of project information in another application, the best transfer method is usually to simply copy and paste. To copy and paste data from Microsoft Project to another application, follow these steps:

1. In Microsoft Project, display the view and table that contains the information you want to copy. If necessary, insert other columns of information by clicking Insert, Column.

2. Select the data you want to copy to the other application (see Figure 16-1). You can drag across adjacent items (columns, rows, or fields) or hold Ctrl while clicking multiple nonadjacent items.

	❶	Task Name	Duration	Start	Finish
75		Draft Proxy Statement information	1 day	Mon 2/5/07	Mon 2/5/07
76		Financial Statement Notes and SEC document drafts Complete	0 days	Mon 2/5/07	Mon 2/5/07
77		− **Perform External Audit**	**4 days**	**Wed 2/14/07**	**Mon 2/19/**
78		Conduct Foreign and Subsidiary Financial Audits	1 day	Wed 2/14/07	Wed 2/14/07
79		Conduct Corporate Financial Audit	1 day	Thu 2/15/07	Thu 2/15/07
80		External Audit Complete	0 days	Thu 2/15/07	Thu 2/15/07
81		Review and Finalize Audit Results with Audit Committee	1 day	Fri 2/16/07	Fri 2/16/07
82		Sign off on Financial Statements/Obtain Senior Management Certifications	1 day	Mon 2/19/07	Mon 2/19/07
83		External Audit Complete	0 days	Mon 2/19/07	Mon 2/19/07
84		− **Perform Internal Legal Review**	**6 days**	**Tue 2/6/07**	**Tue 2/13/07**
85		Coordinate and review key significant events for inclusion in Annual Repor	1 day	Tue 2/6/07	Tue 2/6/07

Figure 16-1 Select the fields you want to copy to the other application.

3. On the Standard toolbar, click Copy Cell.

    Copy Cell

    A copy of the selected data is placed on the Clipboard.

4. Open the application into which you want to paste the project information. Select the area in which you want the data to begin being inserted.

5. In the target application, click the application's Paste command.

    Paste

    If you are pasting into a Microsoft Office 2007 application that uses the Ribbon, on the Home tab, in the Clipboard group, click Paste.

    Your copied data is inserted at the selection.

> **Note**
> When copying data without column headers, leave room in the target file to add them.

If the workspace of the target application is laid out in columns and rows like the Microsoft Project tables, as is the case with spreadsheet applications, the pasted project information flows easily into columns and rows.

However, if the workspace is open, as in a word processing program, the incoming project information comes in looking like a jumbled mess (see Figure 16-2). The information is tab-delimited, though, so it should be fairly easy to switch to a table format.

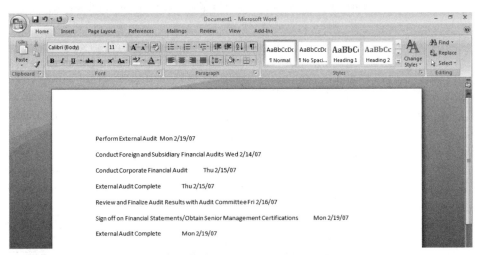

Figure 16-2 Your project data is pasted into the target application.

In such an application, you need to reformat the text to restore the columns and rows of your project data. To convert column and row information from Microsoft Project to a table in Word, follow these steps:

1. In Word, select the project data.

2. Click Table, Convert, Text To Table.

   If you are using Microsoft Office Word 2007, on the Insert tab, in the Tables group, click the arrow under Table and then click Convert Text To Table. In the dialog box, specify the number of columns and the separator.

   The project information is converted to a table, with the columns and rows separated as they were in Microsoft Project (see Figure 16-3).

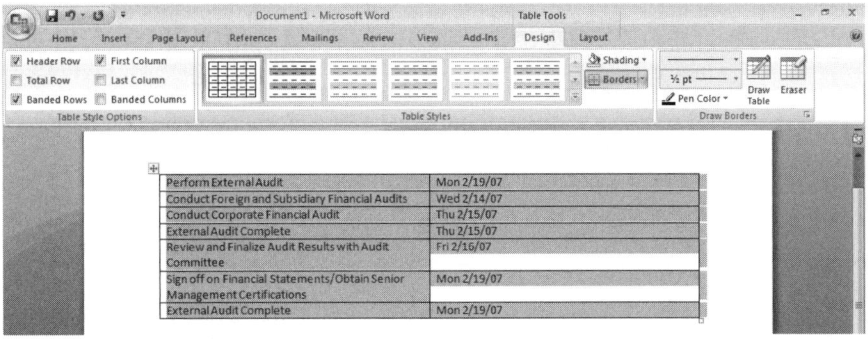

Figure 16-3 Your project data is converted to a table in Word.

INSIDE OUT   Paste directly into a Word table

You can create a Word table ahead of time with the right number of columns and rows. When you're ready to paste the information in, however, it's different from copying into a spreadsheet.

In a spreadsheet, you select the cell in the upper-left corner, and the information flows into as many rows and columns as it needs.

However, when you paste into a Word table, you need to select exactly the right number of rows and columns ahead of time; then click the Paste button. If you select too few, only the information that is supposed to occupy those cells will be pasted. If you select too many, the information will be repeated.

Copying from Another Application to Microsoft Project

You can copy table-based or listed information from another application—for example, Office Access 2007 or Word—and insert it into Microsoft Project. You select and copy the source data, select the cell in Microsoft Project in which you want the data to start being inserted, and then paste the data. This is a good way to get project-related information that was created by others in another application into your Microsoft Project file. For example, suppose that you asked your manufacturing manager to put together a detailed task list of the process that will be used to manufacture your new product. He completes the list, including tasks and resource assignments, using Access.

If you are copying multiple columns or tabs of information, you do need to be mindful of the order in which data is being pasted and inserted into the project table. The type of data you're pasting must match the field type in which the data is being pasted, or you'll get a series of error messages. For example, if you copy a column of text next to a column of numbers, in Microsoft Project the columns must be pasted into a text field column that's next to a number field column. To make sure the fields match, you can either set up the source information in the proper order or you can rearrange columns in a Microsoft Project table.

To copy table or list information from another application into Microsoft Project, follow these steps:

1. Open the source application and file.

2. Select the rows or columns you want to copy and then click the application's Copy command.

   If you are copying in a Microsoft Office 2007 application that uses the Ribbon, on the Home tab, in the Clipboard group, click Copy.

3. Open Microsoft Project and the project plan in which you want to insert the copied information.

4. Apply the view and table that represent the closest match to the types of information you'll be pasting.

   If you need to add any columns to match the incoming information, click the column to the left of where you want to insert the new field. Click Insert, Column. In the Field Name list, click the name of the field you want and then click OK.

5. Click the cell in which you want the incoming information to begin to be pasted.

6. On the Standard toolbar, click Paste.

   The copied information is pasted into the columns you've prepared.

   Pasting data into Microsoft Project overwrites data in the target cells. If this is not your intention, insert the appropriate number of empty rows in the sheet before selecting the Paste command.

Based on the newly inserted information, other project data might be automatically populated and calculated. Review other fields on this and other tables. Make any necessary adjustments to ensure that your project data is accurate.

> **Note**
>
> Any information that can be moved to the Clipboard by using the Copy command can be pasted into Microsoft Project, but not all views accept all types of data. For example, you can paste objects such as pictures only into the chart portion of the Gantt Chart. Nothing can be pasted into the Network Diagram.

TROUBLESHOOTING

Data doesn't paste into the target file correctly

When you use the Copy and Paste commands to exchange data, it's important to remember that fields and columns of data will stay in the order and format of their source file. Before you paste data from another application into your project file, first set up the columns in the source file in the order of the corresponding columns into which they'll be pasted in your project file.

Also be careful that data formats, particularly numbers and dates, are the same in the source file as in your project file. If you want to copy and paste data from another application into a project file that has no project field equivalent, insert columns of generic custom fields (for example, Text1 or Number1) to hold the new type of data. These extra columns must match the column order in the source file. This matching of compatible columns is called manual data mapping and must be done before you select the Paste command. If you paste inappropriate data into Microsoft Project fields, a pasting error message alerts you that a mismatch has occurred.

You'll repeatedly see a separate pasting error for every mismatched field in the paste operation.

For information about copying information from Excel to Microsoft Project, see the section titled "Copying Information from Excel" in Chapter 17.

Copying a Picture of a View

Suppose that you're creating a formal narrative project status report or preparing a presentation for a high-profile project status meeting. You can copy information from a view in Microsoft Project and paste it as a graphic file into a Word document or a Microsoft Office PowerPoint 2007 presentation slide. You can do this either with the Copy Picture function or the Copy Picture To Office Wizard.

Capturing a View for Word, PowerPoint, or Visio

With the Copy Picture To Office Wizard, you can configure and copy the information from a view in Microsoft Project and paste that information into a file in Word, Office PowerPoint 2007, or Office Visio 2007.

With this wizard, you can do so much more than simply capture the view as shown on your screen. Instead, you can specify options about the outline levels, the rows to be shown, the timescale, the image size, and even the fields to be included.

To use the Copy Picture To Office Wizard, you must have a 2000 or later version of Word, PowerPoint, or Visio installed on your computer.

To configure and copy a Microsoft Project view to Word, PowerPoint, or Visio, follow these steps:

1. Click View, Toolbars, Analysis.

Copy Picture To
Office Wizard

2. On the Analysis toolbar that appears, click Copy Picture To Office Wizard.

3. Read the first page of the wizard and then click Next.

4. If you are copying a picture of a task sheet view, the Select An Outline Level page appears. Select the outline level you want to copy in the picture and then click Next.

5. On the Specify Image Creation Options page, select options regarding which rows to copy, the timescale, and the image size to reflect how you want the Microsoft Project view to appear in the Office application (see Figure 16-4).

These options differ depending on the type of view. For example, a Gantt Chart presents different options from the Resource Graph.

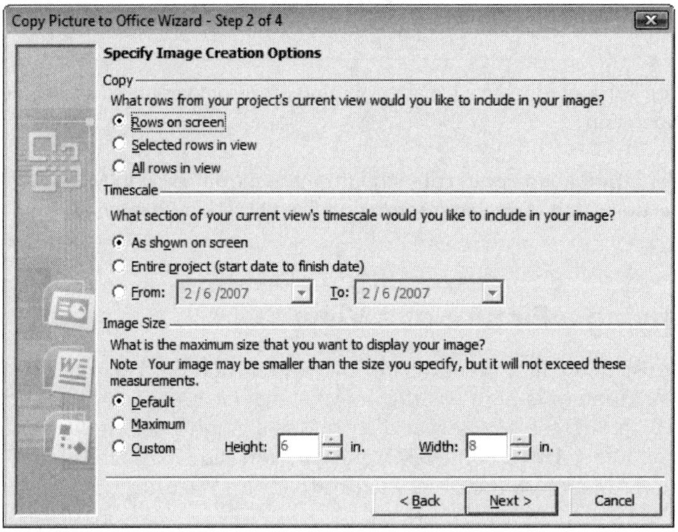

Figure 16-4 Specify options in the Copy Picture To Office Wizard to indicate how you want the picture of the Microsoft Project view to appear.

6. Click Next to see the Preview Image And Select Application And Orientation page.

7. Click the Preview button.

A picture of the view is exported and saved according to the options you selected. A Web browser window appears, showing the generated picture (see Figure 16-5). You might need to click the Web browser button on the task bar to show the window.

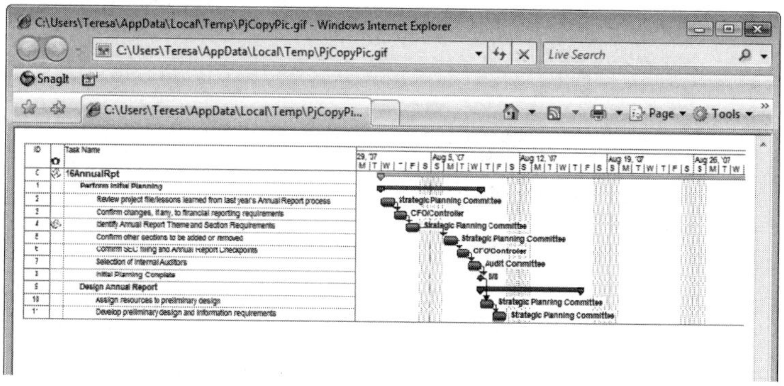

Figure 16-5 In your browser's window, preview the picture of project information you're specifying.

8. Return to Microsoft Project and the wizard. Under Application, select the option next to the name of the Office application to which you want to copy the project picture. If necessary, select whether the picture should be presented in portrait or landscape orientation. Click Next.

The option for any program not installed on your computer is dimmed.

Move up

Move down

9. In the Select Microsoft Office Project Fields To Export page, select any additional Microsoft Project fields you want to export along with the picture of the view. The available fields are listed in the Microsoft Office Project Fields box. Click one or more fields (using Shift or Ctrl to select multiple fields) and then click the Add button. Click the Move buttons if necessary to rearrange the positions of selected fields listed in the Fields To Export box. Then click Finish.

The picture of the Microsoft Project view with any selected fields is exported and saved to the selected Microsoft Office application.

10. In the final wizard page, click Close.

The selected Microsoft Office application opens and displays the picture (see Figure 16-6). You can now manipulate the picture object as needed in the application.

Chapter 16

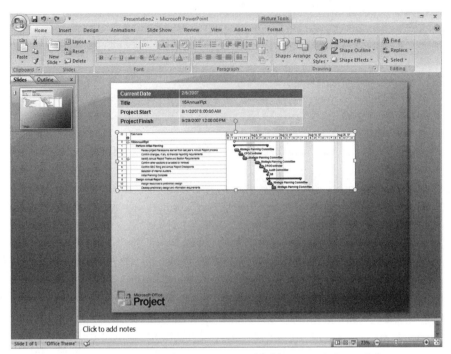

Figure 16-6 The selected Microsoft Project view and fields appear in PowerPoint.

Capturing a View for Other Applications

If you simply want to capture a view and use it in Word, PowerPoint, or Visio without having to go through the wizard steps to configure your options, or if you're copying to a different application, you can use the Copy Picture function.

With the Copy Picture function, you are taking a snapshot of the current view that you can use in whichever application you choose. This is also a good way to quickly create a simple picture of a view for use on a Web site or in a report. You can still make choices about the image output, the rows to be copied, and the timescale as appropriate to the current view.

To copy and paste a picture of a Microsoft Project view for use in another application, follow these steps:

1. In your project plan, display the view you want to copy to the other application.

2. Manipulate the view to show the information the way you want it to appear in the target application.

Copy Picture

3. On the Standard toolbar, click Copy Picture.

   You can also click Report, Copy Picture.

4. In the Copy Picture dialog box, select the options you want (see Figure 16-7).

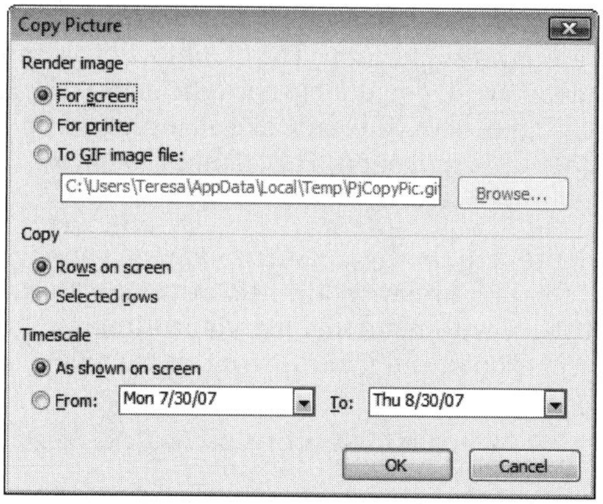

Figure 16-7 Choose the options you want for the picture you're copying.

- ❑ In the Render Image section, select whether the image is to be viewed on a computer screen (the default), to be printed, or to be used in a GIF image file.

- ❑ In the Copy section, select the Rows On Screen option (the default) if you want the rows currently showing on the screen to be copied, or if only selected rows should be copied.

- ❑ In the Timescale section, select the As Shown On Screen option (the default) if you want the timescale to be represented as set in the current view. Select the From and To boxes if you want to specify the timescale and date range now.

- ❑ When finished setting the Copy Picture options, click OK.

5. Open the target application. Click the place on the page where you want to paste the object.

6. Click Edit, Paste.

If you are pasting into a Microsoft Office 2007 application that uses the Ribbon, on the Home tab, in the Clipboard group, click Paste.

A static picture of the Microsoft Project view as you had set it up is pasted into the target application. If needed, you can resize the image by dragging any of the edges.

Embedding Information

An object is a class or a group of data that gets its format from another application. When you embed an object in one application that originated in a different application, you're basically inserting an entire file, with all of its source application's capabilities, into the target application.

For example, suppose that in Microsoft Project you embed a graphics illustration object originally created in a graphics application. The graphics object appears in Microsoft Project as if you created it there. If you double-click the object, the graphics application in which it was created is launched; you can make changes to the illustration on the spot, save them, and close the application. The changes you made are reflected instantly in the illustration in Microsoft Project.

For embedding to work properly, both the source and target applications must be installed on the same computer or have ready network access to it. Also, because embedding inserts an entire file within another file, embedding uses a large amount of memory while the project is open and makes the target file much larger.

> **Note**
>
> Embedding objects between different applications is made possible by the OLE technology. Any application that employs the OLE standard can embed and link information from another application that employs that standard.

Embedding from Microsoft Project to Another Application

You can embed the Microsoft Project file in another application, for example, Word or PowerPoint. When you double-click the object in the target application, Microsoft Project is launched on the spot, and you can switch views and manipulate data.

Embedding an Existing Microsoft Project File

To embed an existing Microsoft Project file in another application, follow these steps:

1. Open the target application and the file in which you want to embed the existing Microsoft Project file.

2. Select the location where you want the Microsoft Project object to be embedded.

3. Click Insert, Object.

   If you're embedding into a Microsoft Office 2007 application that uses the Ribbon, on the Insert tab, in the Text group, click Object.

   If the target application does not have an Insert Object command, embedding is probably not supported. Look in the application's online Help or other documentation to see if the command is called something else.

4. In the dialog box, click the Create From File option or tab.

5. Click the Browse button.

The Browse window appears. Navigate through your computer's filing system (and onto your network if applicable) to find the drive and folder in which the project file is located.

6. Find and double-click the file.

Its path and name are entered in the File Name box in the dialog box (see Figure 16-8).

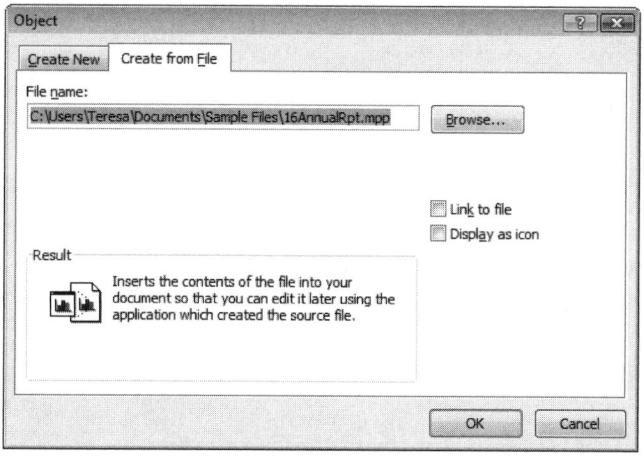

Figure 16-8 Select the project file you want to embed into another application's file.

7. If you want the embedded object to be linked to the source, select the Link To File check box.

 ❏ If you link the object, any changes in the original update the embedded object. Likewise, any changes made in the embedded object are reflected in the original.

 ❏ If you don't link the object, you're essentially making a copy of the original object, which becomes a separate entity from the original. You can change the embedded version without affecting information in the original.

8. If you want the embedded project to be displayed as an icon in the target application, rather than showing as a Gantt Chart or other view, select the Display As Icon check box.

9. Click OK.

Part of a view of the selected project file appears in the location you selected (see Figure 16-9).

Chapter 16

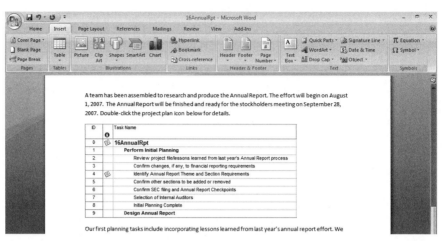

Figure 16-9 The selected project is embedded in the other application, in this case, Word.

If you selected the Display As Icon check box, the embedded project file appears as the Microsoft Project icon (by default) in the selected location (Figure 16-10).

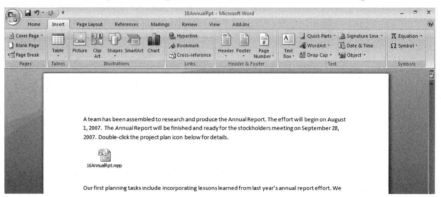

Figure 16-10 The selected project is embedded in PowerPoint, displayed as an icon.

Note

The Display As Icon check box in the Object dialog box is useful when you are embedding a large document. When the object is displayed as an icon, you just double-click the icon to open the linked file. This might be the most efficient way for you to embed a Microsoft Project object into another application. The file name is included with the icon, as is the shortcut arrow symbol.

Creating a New Microsoft Project File as an Embedded Object

You can create a new Microsoft Project file as an embedded object in another application. In this case, the object exists only within the target application. To create a new Microsoft Project file within another application, follow these steps:

1. Open the target application and the file in which you want to create a new Microsoft Project file as an embedded object.

2. Select the location in which you want the new Microsoft Project object to be embedded.

3. Click Insert, Object.

   If you're embedding into a Microsoft Office 2007 application that uses the Ribbon, on the Insert tab, in the Text group, click Object.

4. In the Insert Object dialog box, click the Create New option or tab.

5. Scroll through the list and click Microsoft Office Project Document (see Figure 16-11).

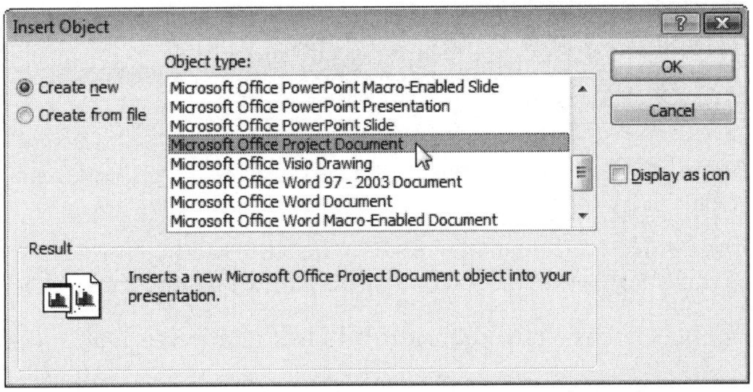

Figure 16-11 Use the Insert Object dialog box to create a new Microsoft Project file as an embedded object.

6. If you want the embedded project to be displayed as an icon in the target application rather than showing as a Gantt Chart or other view, select the Display As Icon check box.

7. Click OK.

   Part of a view of the new project file appears (see Figure 16-12).

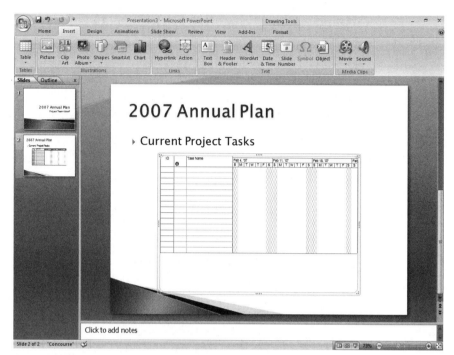

Figure 16-12 The new project is embedded in the target application, in this case Power-Point.

If you selected the Display As Icon check box, the embedded project file appears as the Microsoft Project icon (by default) in the selected location.

8. Double-click the new project to add information to it on the spot.

Working with the Embedded Microsoft Project File

Whenever you want to work with the embedded project file, just double-click the object. Microsoft Project launches, and the embedded project file appears. You can use Microsoft Project as normal, switching views, applying tables and filters, changing data, running calculations, and so on.

For information about embedding a Microsoft Project file in Excel, see the section titled "Embedding Between Microsoft Project and Excel" in Chapter 17.

Embedding from Another Application to Microsoft Project

Objects can be embedded into Microsoft Project from other applications, but only in a limited number of places, as follows:

- The chart portion of the Gantt Chart
- The Notes portion of the Task Form or Task Information dialog box

- The Notes portion of the Resource Form or Resource Information dialog box

- The Notes tab in the Assignment Information dialog box

- The Objects box in the Task Form

- The Objects box in the Resource Form

- Headers, footers, and legends of printable pages

For the best visibility, project managers often embed objects in the chart portion of the Gantt Chart.

Embedding an Object in the Gantt Chart

Objects you might find useful for embedding in the Gantt Chart include graphic charts of the data, symbols to show significant points, and even simple drawings. Other media forms can be embedded as appropriate, such as sounds and video.

> **Note**
>
> If you want to add an icon or other graphic to the Gantt Chart, it needs to be in the BMP image format. Other image formats—including TIF, GIF, and JPG—only appear in the Gantt Chart as icons.

To embed an object from another application into the chart portion of the Gantt Chart, follow these steps:

1. Open Microsoft Office Project 2007 and the project plan in which you want to embed the object.

2. Display the Gantt Chart and click in the chart portion of the view to make it active.

3. Click Insert, Object.

4. In the Insert Object dialog box, select the Create From File option.

5. Click the Browse button and find the location of the object you want to embed. Double-click the file.

   The file's path and name are entered in the File box in the Insert Object dialog box.

6. If you want the embedded object to be linked to the source, select the Link check box.

   If you link the object, any changes in the original update the embedded object. Likewise, any changes made in the embedded object are reflected in the original.

Chapter 16

If you don't link the object, you're essentially making a copy of the original object, which becomes a separate entity from the original. You can change the embedded version without affecting information in the original.

7. If you want the embedded object to be displayed as an icon in your project rather than showing as the item itself, select the Display As Icon check box.

8. Click OK.

The object appears in the upper-left corner of the Gantt Chart. Move the object to the location you want on the Gantt Chart and resize the image as needed.

Add an Icon to a Printed View

You can add an object (for example, a company or project logo) to the project file header, footer, or legend so the object appears when you print a view.

1. Click File, Page Setup.

2. In the Page Setup dialog box, click the Header, Footer, or Legend tab.

3. Select the location (Left, Center, Right) for the object.

4. Click Insert Picture. Find and double-click the picture.

Now when you print the view, the object appears in the location you specified.

Insert Picture

For more information about specifying headers and footers for printed views, see the section titled "Setting Up and Printing Views" in Chapter 12, "Reporting Project Information."

Embedding an Object in a Note

If the object you want to embed is associated with a particular task, resource, or assignment, you might prefer to embed it in a note. To do this, follow these steps:

1. Display a view that contains the task, resource, or assignment you want to associate with an object.

For example, for tasks, display the Gantt Chart. For resources, display the Resource Sheet. For assignments, display the Task Usage or Resource Usage view.

2. Double-click the task, resource, or assignment to which you want to associate the object.

   The Task Information, Resource Information, or Assignment Information dialog box appears.

3. Click the Notes tab.

Insert Object

4. Click the Insert Object button.

5. In the Insert Object dialog box, select the Create From File option.

6. Click the Browse button, find the file you want to embed as an object in the note, and double-click its name.

7. Specify whether you want the embedded object to be linked to the source or displayed as an icon and then click OK.

   The object appears in the upper-left corner of the notes area (see Figure 16-13).

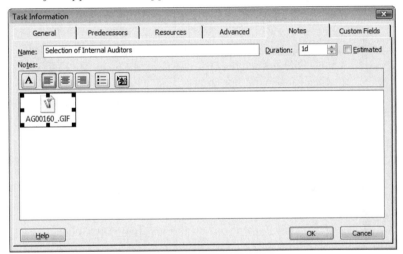

Figure 16-13 Embed an object in a task note, resource note, or assignment note.

Depending on the object's file type and where you're inserting it, it might be displayed as the file itself, for example, the actual image or the first page of a presentation. Or it might just show the file name. Either way, the object is embedded in your project and is associated with the selected task, resource, or assignment. When you double-click the object, the source application opens and the object is displayed.

Notes

As with any note, the Notes indicator appears in the indicators column in a sheet view when a note is present. Double-click the Notes indicator to quickly open the Notes tab and see the object.

Chapter 16

> **Note**
>
> You can embed an object in a note associated with the project as a whole. First, add the project summary task by clicking Tools, Options, View and then selecting the Show Project Summary Task check box.

Double-click the project summary task. In the Summary Task Information dialog box, click the Notes tab. Click the Insert Object button and add the object.

INSIDE OUT   Bury an object in a form

You can embed an object associated with a task or resource into the Task Form or Resource Form.

Select the task or resource in the form. Click Format, Details, Objects. Click Insert, Object and then find and add the object as usual. The object appears in the upper-left corner of the object area in the Task Form.

However, be aware that objects in a form are not as flexible as those inserted in the Gantt Chart or in a note. The object cannot be moved or resized. Plus, it takes a lot of clicks to get to it, so it's pretty buried.

Creating a New Object to Embed in the Project

You can create a new file as an embedded object in your project. In this case, the new object exists only within your project file. To do this, follow these steps:

1. In your project plan, go to the location where you want to embed the object, for example, the Gantt Chart or the Notes area of the Resource Information dialog box.

2. Click Insert, Object.

3. In the Insert Object dialog box, be sure that the Create New option is selected.

4. Scroll through the Object Type box and click the name of the application with which you want to create the new object, for example, Microsoft Equation 3.0 or Paintbrush Picture.

5. Specify whether you want the new object to be displayed as an icon in the project and then click OK.

Depending on your choice, either a miniature version of the application appears in the location you selected, or the application launches immediately (see Figure 16-14).

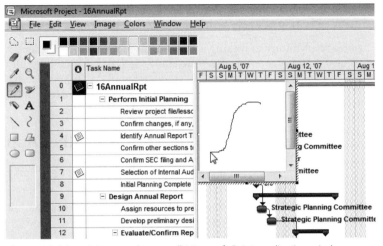

Figure 16-14 In this example, a small Microsoft Paint application window appears as an object embedded within your project.

6. Start creating the new file on the spot.

If necessary, double-click the application to launch it.

Working with the Embedded Object in the Project

If an object embedded in your project is a graphic that's displayed in its proper place, you might never need to do anything with it. With other objects, however, you need to open and work with them. This is particularly true of new objects you created within the project file. They contain nothing until you add your own data.

To open and work with an embedded object, simply double-click the object. The source application opens, and you can use its commands and tools to work with the object as needed. When finished, on the File menu, click the Close or Exit command. The source application closes, and the object appears in your project file showing the changes you just made.

> **Note**
> To delete an embedded object anywhere in your project plan, simply click it and press Delete.
>
> For information about embedding information from Excel to Microsoft Project, see the section titled "Embedding Between Microsoft Project and Excel" in Chapter 17.

Chapter 16

Linking Information

Linking is another method of exchanging data between applications. By linking information, you maintain a connection to the source application. When a change is made to the information, it's reflected in the target application.

A major advantage of linking is that the file size is much smaller than it would be if the information in the linked file were embedded. A potential difficulty with linking is that you always need to know the current location of the linked file and its update status. If the linked file is moved, the link is broken. If the information in the linked file becomes obsolete, the linked information also becomes out of date.

Linking from Microsoft Project to Another Application

You can create a link from Microsoft Project information in another application using the Copy and Paste Special commands. Follow this procedure:

1. In Microsoft Office Project 2007, display the view that contains the information you want to copy and link to another application.

    If it's text-based information—such as tasks, resources, or assignment fields—select the information. If it's graphical information—such as a Gantt Chart, Resource Graph, or Network Diagram—arrange the view to contain the information you want represented in the other application.

2. Click Edit, Copy.

    The Copy command changes based on the type of view you're copying and what is currently selected:

    - If you're in a sheet view with an individual cell selected, click Edit, Copy Cell.
    - If you're in a task sheet view with a row selected, click Edit, Copy Task.
    - If you're in a resource sheet view with a row selected, click Edit, Copy Resource.

3. Open the target application, for example, Word. Place the cursor where you want the information to be inserted.

4. In the target application, click Edit, Paste Special.

    If you're linking into a Microsoft Office 2007 application that uses the Ribbon, on the Home tab, in the Clipboard group, click the arrow under Paste. In the menu that appears, click Paste Special.

5. In the Paste Special dialog box, select the Paste Link option (see Figure 16-15).

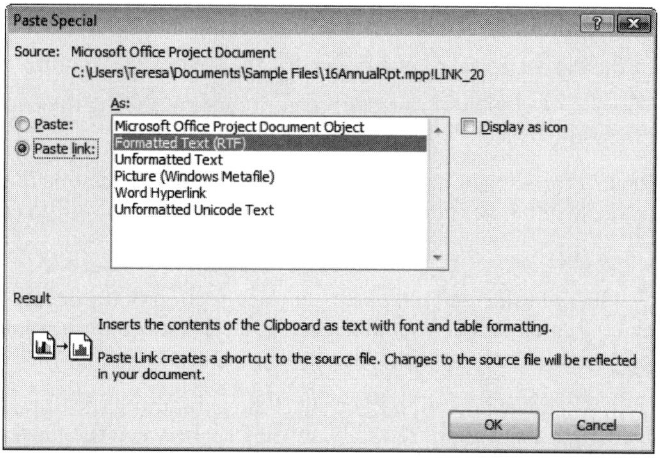

Figure 16-15 Use the Paste Special dialog box to create a link from Microsoft Project.

6. Review the choices available in the As box. Click each one to read its description in the Result box and then select the one that meets your needs.

The choices vary depending on the type of information that was copied in Microsoft Project. One of the choices is always Microsoft Office Project Document Object, which creates an embedded object that's linked.

7. Click OK.

The linked information appears in the target application. When changes are made to the information in Microsoft Project, those changes are reflected in the target application.

For information about linking information from Microsoft Project to Excel, see the section titled "Linking Between Microsoft Project and Excel" in Chapter 17.

Linking from Another Application to Microsoft Project

You can link a source object from another application into a target area in Microsoft Project. Linked graphical information can be pasted only in select locations in Microsoft Project, for example, the Gantt Chart, Notes areas, and the Task and Resource Forms. Linked textual information can also be pasted into a table cell.

To link data from another application, follow these steps:

1. In the source application, select the information to be linked in Microsoft Office Project 2007 and then click Edit, Copy.

If you want to copy and link information from a Microsoft Office 2007 application that uses the Ribbon, on the Home tab, in the Clipboard group, click Copy.

2. In Microsoft Office Project 2007, display the view and select the location to contain the linked information.

3. Click Edit, Paste Special.

4. In the Paste Special dialog box, click the Paste Link option.

The As box changes to present the options for linking the copied information into Microsoft Project.

5. Review the choices available in the As box. Click each one to read its description in the Result box and then select the one that meets your needs.

6. Click OK.

The linked information appears at the selection point in your project. When changes are made to the information in the source application, those changes can be reflected in this project file.

By default, whenever you open the project file containing the link, a message appears, asking whether you want to re-establish the link between the files (see Figure 16-16). Clicking Yes re-establishes the link and updates any changed information.

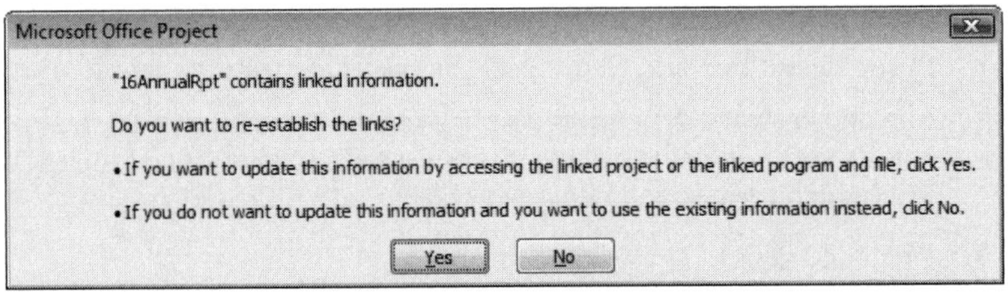

Figure 16-16 Each time you open a linked project, you are prompted to re-establish the link.

If you do not want to see this alert each time you open the project, click Tools, Options and then click the View tab. Under Show, clear the OLE Links Indicators check box.

To review and work with links in your project, follow these steps:

1. Click Edit, Links.

The Links dialog box appears, showing all links existing in your project file (see Figure 16-17).

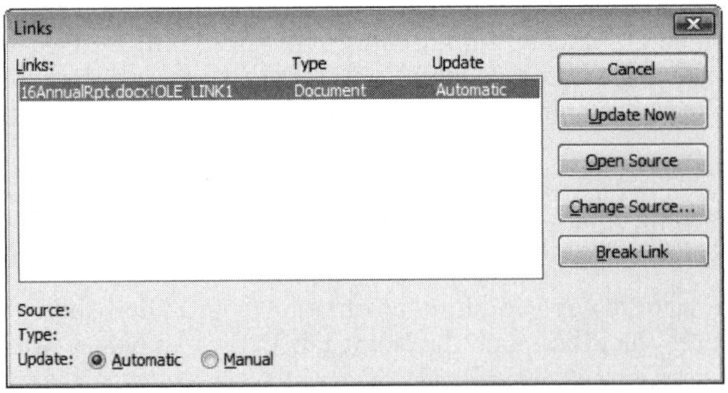

Figure 16-17 Review the status of links in your project file.

2. If you chose not to update a link when opening the project file or if you're not prompted, you can select a link and click Update Now.

3. If the linked document location has changed, you can update the information in the project by clicking Change Source.

4. To break the link with the source application, click Break Link.

> **For information about linking information from Excel to Microsoft Project, see the section titled "Linking Between Microsoft Project and Excel" in Chapter 7.**

Hyperlinking to Documents in Other Applications

In your project file, you can insert a hyperlink to jump to a Web site or another file on your computer or network. Inserting a hyperlink can be useful for including relevant reference material for tasks and resources in your project plan. It's also useful for linking project-related documents, such as the scope document and bill of materials, to your project plan.

> **Note**
>
> Although it's called a hyperlink, the item you're linking to does not have to be a Web page, and it does not have to be in HTML or XML format. It can be any document in any file format. You do need to have the application for that file on your computer, and it does need to be in a stable location.To create a hyperlink in your project:
>
> 1. In Microsoft Office Project 2007, display the view that contains the task, resource, or assignment to which you want to add a hyperlink.
>
> 2. Click the task, resource, or assignment name to select it.
>
> 3. On the Standard toolbar, click Insert Hyperlink.
>
>   The Insert Hyperlink dialog box appears.
>
> 4. In the Text To Display box, type a short description of the page you're linking to.
>
> 5. In the Look In list, locate and select the source file (see Figure 16-18).

Insert Hyperlink

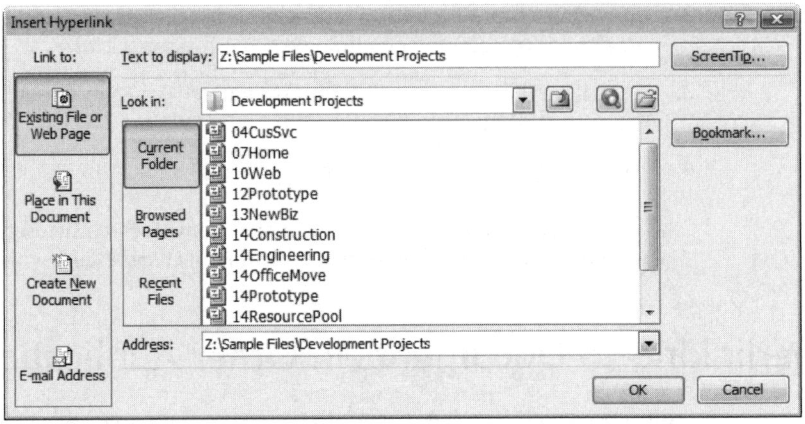

Figure 16-18 The path and name of the selected document appear in the Address box.

6. Click OK.

Hyperlink
indicator

The Hyperlink indicator appears in the Indicators column of the current view. If you rest your mouse pointer over the Hyperlink indicator, the name of the link appears.

> **Note**
>
> If you want to review all your hyperlink information in a table, apply the Hyperlink table. There's a version for task hyperlinks and another one for resource hyperlinks.

7. Apply a sheet view, such as the Gantt Chart or the Resource Sheet. Click View, Table, Hyperlink. Whenever you want to review the file pointed to by the hyperlink, simply click the Hyperlink indicator. The hyperlinked document appears in its own application window.

Set Up a Document Library

If you're using Office Project Professional 2007 with Project Server and Microsoft Office Project Web Access for enterprise project management, the preferred method for keeping all project documents together is the document library. In Office Project Web Access, you can set up and maintain a Windows SharePoint Services document library. This way, all your team members and other stakeholders can view the documents through their Web browsers. They can also check documents in and out, providing vital version control.

For information about setting up a document library, see the section titled "Controlling Project Documents" in Chapter 22, "Managing Enterprise Projects and Resources."

Importing and Exporting Information

When you import or export information between Microsoft Project and other applications, you're transferring information so that it appears as if the source information were originally created in the target application. Importing and exporting essentially converts the information from the file format of the source application to that of the target application.

Updating Security Settings to Allow Data Import and Export

When you import and export data from other applications in and out of Project 2007, files are often saved as an earlier version of whatever file format you're working with. However, new default security settings in Microsoft Office Project 2007 block the opening or saving of legacy or nondefault file formats.

Therefore, in most cases you will not be able to finish the import or export operation until you have set your Microsoft Project security appropriately. To do this, follow these steps:

1. Click Tools, Options and then click the Security tab (see Figure 16-19).

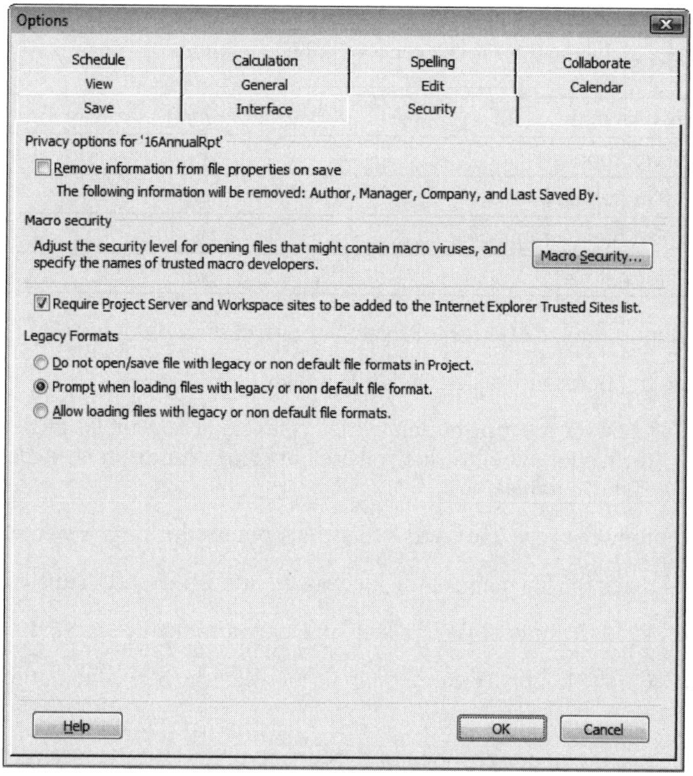

Figure 16-19 Use the Security tab to allow Microsoft Project to export information as an older Excel file.

Chapter 16

2. Under Legacy Formats, select either the Prompt When Loading Files With Legacy Or Non Default File Format option (medium security) or the Allow Loading Files With Legacy Or Non Default File Formats (low security) option.

Importing Information into Microsoft Project

You can bring information into Microsoft Project from another application and another file format by importing it. Importing converts another application's file format into the Microsoft Project file format. You start an import process by simply using the File, Open command.

You can import the file formats shown in Table 16-2.

Table 16-2 Supported Import File Types

File format	File name extension
Project files (for Project 1998 through 2007)	.mpp
Project templates	.mpt
Project databases	.mpd
Project workspaces	.mpw
Project Exchange (for Project versions 4.0 and 98)	.mpx
Access databases	.mdb
Excel workbooks	.xls
Text files (tab delimited)	.txt
CSV Text files (comma delimited)	.csv
XML format files	.xml

To import data to Microsoft Project, follow these steps:

1. In Microsoft Project, click File, Open.

2. Click the file type button, which is labeled Project Files by default, and then click the file format of the file you are importing, for example, Access Databases or Text (Tab Delimited).

3. Browse to the drive and folder that contain the file you want to import.

4. Click the file name of the file you are importing and then click the Open button.

5. Read the Import Wizard welcome page and then click Next.

6. On the Import Wizard – Map page, select the New Map option. Click Next.

7. On the Import Mode page, select whether you want to import the file as a new project, to be appended to the current project, or to be merged with the current project. Click Next.

8. On the Import Wizard – Map Options page, under Select The Types Of Data You Want To Import, click the Tasks, Resources, or Assignments check box as appropriate (see Figure 16-20). Click Next.

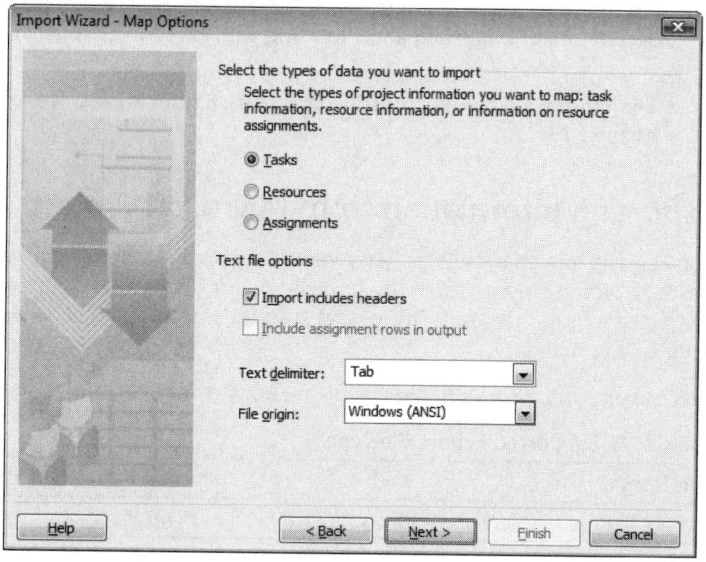

Figure 16-20 Use the Map Options page of the Import Wizard to specify the types of data you are importing.

You will see a separate Mapping page for each data type you select on this page, for example, Task Mapping, Resource Mapping, or Assignment Mapping.

9. On the Mapping page, complete the fields to specify the information to be imported. In the To: Microsoft Office Project Field column of the table, specify how fields from the source application are to map to specific Microsoft Project fields. Any unmapped data appears in red and will not be imported. Click Next.

10. If, on the Map Options page, you selected multiple types of data to import (for example, Tasks and Resources), click Next to proceed to the Mapping page for the next data type. Repeat step 9 for each additional data type.

    You can potentially work through a Task Mapping, Resource Mapping, and Assignment Mapping page.

11. On the Import Wizard – End of Map Definition page, click Save Map if you want this import map you just defined to be saved for future use.

    In the Map Name box of the Save Map dialog box, type a name for the map and then click Save.

12. Click Finish.

    The imported data appears in your project plan as you specified. This process might take a few minutes, depending on the source of the information and the speed of your computer. However, after the information is imported, it's set in

Chapter 16

your project plan. Save the project, and the information is there for you to work with instantly, as if you had originally created it in Microsoft Project.

> For information about importing information from Excel to Microsoft Project, see the section titled "Importing and Exporting with Excel" in Chapter 17.

> For information about importing information from Microsoft Project to Visio, see Chapter 19.

Exporting Information from Microsoft Project

You can use information from Microsoft Project in another application and another file format by exporting it. Exporting converts your Microsoft Project information into the file format of another application. You start an export process by simply using the File, Save As command.

You can export a project file to the file formats shown in Table 16-3.

Table 16-3 Supported Export File Types

File format	File name extension
Project files (for Project 1998 through 2007)	*.mpp*
Project templates	*.mpt*
Excel workbooks	*.xls*
Excel PivotTables	*.xls*
Text files (tab delimited)	*.txt*
CSV Text files (comma delimited)	*.csv*
XML format files	*.xml*

TROUBLESHOOTING

File formats I used to export to are no longer available

In Microsoft Office Project 2007, you can no longer use the Save As dialog box to save a project as a Microsoft Project database (.mpd), an HTML file, an Access (.mdb) file, or an Open Database Connectivity (ODBC) file for Microsoft SQL Server or Oracle Server.

Instead of saving your project as an MPD or HTML file, you can save your project as an XML file through the Save As dialog box.

> For more information about saving project information to XML and working with it in that format, see the section titled "Working with Microsoft Project and XML Files" later in this chapter.

To export data from Microsoft Project, follow these steps:

1. In Microsoft Office Project 2007, open the project that contains the information you want to export.

2. Click File, Save As.

3. In the Save In list, select the drive and folder where you want to save the new exported file.

4. In the File Name box, enter the name for the new exported file.

   By default, the name of the project is adopted, and the extension representing the new file format will be added.

5. In the Save As Type list, click the file format to which you want to export your project information. For example, if you want to export your project information to XML, click XML Format (*.xml).

6. Click the Save button.

   The Export Wizard opens and guides you step-by-step through the specifics of data mapping the information you want from Microsoft Project to the target file (see Figure 16-21). Some steps and choices of the Export Wizard vary depending on the file type you are exporting to.

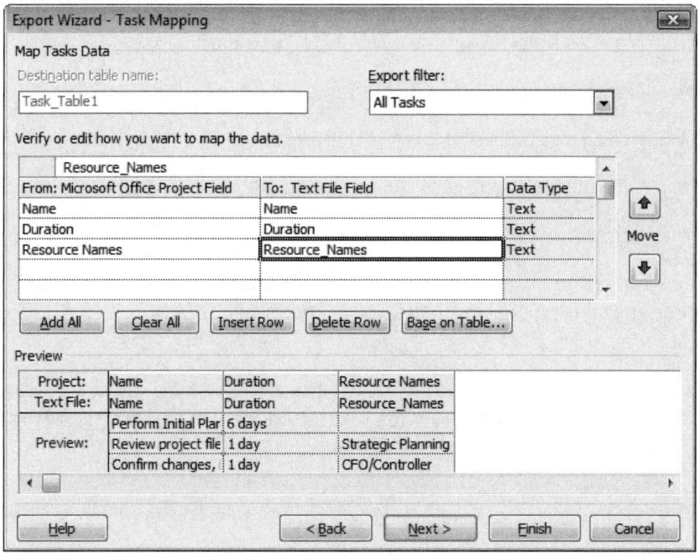

Figure 16-21 Work through the Export Wizard to define the project information to be made available to the target application.

7. Work through each page of the Export Wizard, clicking Next after making your selections on each page.

8. On the final page, click Finish. Microsoft Project exports your project information to the selected file format.

Note

If you want to export a wide and representative range of fields, click in the Export Wizard Task Mapping or Resource Mapping page, click the Base On Table button, and then click Export. The task Export table contains more than 70 task fields. The resource Export table contains more than 20 resource fields.

For information about exporting information from Microsoft Project to Excel, see the section titled "Importing and Exporting with Excel" in Chapter 17.

For information about exporting information from Microsoft Project to Visio, see Chapter 19.

Working with Microsoft Project and XML Files

Microsoft Project plans can be saved in XML format. XML is a self-defining, adaptable language that's used to define and interpret data between different applications, particularly in Web documents. With XML, you can:

- Define the structure of data used.

- Make your data platform-independent.

- Automatically process data defined by XML.

- Define your own unique markup tags that hold your data elements.

The simple and consistent nature of XML makes it very useful for exchanging data between many types of applications. You can use this project XML data in any application that recognizes XML.

By creating and applying an XSL template to the XML data, you can determine which project data is used and how it's formatted for use in a particular application, to generate a report, or to publish to a Web site.

Note

In Microsoft Office Project 2007, you can no longer save a project as an HTML or HTM file for an instant Web page. Instead, save the project as an file and then apply an XSL style sheet.

To save your project as an .XML file, follow these steps:

1. Open the project plan you want to save as an XML file.

2. Click File, Save As.

3. In the Save As Type field, click XML Format.

4. In the Save As dialog box, navigate to the location where you want to save the new XML file.

5. In the File Name box, type the name for your new XML file.

6. Click Save.

   The file is saved. You or your organization's Webmaster can now open it in a markup language editor, apply style sheets, and prepare the information for publication on the Web.

> **Note**
>
> If you just want to show a view of project information in a report or on a Web site, you can simply copy a picture of the view using the Copy Picture function. This creates a GIF graphic file, which you can insert into a report or on a Web page. For more information, see the section titled "Capturing a View for Other Applications" earlier in this chapter.

Importing and Exporting Database Information

In Microsoft Office Project 2007, the ability to save project fields to a database has been removed from the Save As dialog box. This includes the Microsoft Project database (.mpd file), and the ODBC file for SQL Server or Oracle Server. The ability to save a project file in XML format replaces this functionality, because saving the file to XML essentially saves all contents of all fields that make up the project file database.

Although you cannot export to these database formats, you can still open Microsoft Project database and ODBC files to import them into your project plan. ODBC is the protocol used to access data in SQL database servers. With ODBC drivers installed, it is possible to connect a Microsoft Project database to SQL databases.

To open an ODBC-compliant database file in Microsoft Project, follow these steps:

1. Click File, Open.

2. In the Open dialog box, click the ODBC button.

3. In the Select Data Source dialog box, browse to locate and select the file data source for the ODBC driver you want to connect to.

CHAPTER 17

Integrating Microsoft Project with Microsoft Excel

Copying Between Microsoft Project and Excel....... **584**

Embedding Between Microsoft Project and Excel.... **593**

Linking Between Microsoft Project and Excel........ **600**

Importing and Exporting with Excel **606**

Producing a Visual Report of Project Data in Excel ... **628**

A lthough the schedules you build with Microsoft Office Project 2007 contain much of the information you need to manage your projects, some crucial details are easier to deal with in other formats, such as databases, text documents, or Microsoft Office Excel spreadsheets. For example, information about product defects, their causes, and their resolutions is best suited to a spreadsheet or database file. Even so, you might want some of this type of information available in your project schedule.

Sometimes the information you use to build a schedule to begin with might start in Office Excel 2007. For example, team leaders might build task lists for their portion of a project in Excel. Or, detailed information about available resources might be listed in an Excel workbook. Regardless of whether you want to move a little or a lot of data from Excel, you can use the Excel-to-Project templates to import information into Office Project 2007.

Going the other direction, you'll find plenty of reasons to transfer some of your Project data into Excel. For example, you can export project cost and earned value data to Excel, where you can create graphs—such as S-curves—to analyze project performance. You can even link Excel information in Microsoft Project to automatically update when that information changes, for example, to update status for change requests that you've added to your schedule. If you are spoiled by the power of PivotTables for other kinds of management reporting you do, you can export Project information to Excel and pivot to your heart's content. In Project 2007, the new visual reports are built-in templates designed to help you choose which Project data to display in Excel and how that data should be presented.

For information about exchanging information with other applications besides Excel, see Chapter 16, "Exchanging Information with Other Applications."

Whether you want to integrate Excel information into your project plan or feed information from Microsoft Project to an Excel workbook, there are several methods for exchanging information. Transferring data between these two programs can simplify aspects of project planning, progress tracking, status reporting, and stakeholder communication.

The methods for transferring information between Microsoft Project and Excel, which are described in deatil throughout this chapter, are as follows:

- Copy and paste sheet or graphic information.

  You could paste the payment milestones from a Project schedule into the project's capital budgeting Excel workbook or paste the Excel cells that summarize software defect status in the Project Gantt Chart near the testing and debugging tasks.

- Insert, or embed, a Microsoft Project file into an Excel file.

  For example, you could embed a Project file into the Excel file you use to select or prioritize projects.

- Insert, or embed, an Excel workbook or chart into a Microsoft Project file.

  For example, this is helpful if you want to review pending change requests in an Excel file while you scan your Project schedule for resources with available time.

- Link information dynamically between the Microsoft Project and Excel files, so that when that information changes in one file, the same information in the other file automatically updates to reflect that change.

  Linking information is ideal when information changes frequently. For example, if you store risk analysis data in Excel, linking current cost projections in Excel to Project cost fields keeps your estimated project costs up to date automatically.

- Open, or import, an Excel file as a Microsoft Project file, or import a Microsoft Project file as an Excel file.

  This method comes in handy when you have schedule-related data in Excel that you want to use in Project, such as an initial task list or a resource list. Similarly, importing a Project file to Excel means you can use Excel's data analysis and formatting to analyze project information, which is particularly helpful if you don't have access to Microsoft Project Server and its enterprise project management features.

- Save, or export, a Microsoft Project file as an Excel file. The file is converted to the Excel file format so it can simply be opened in Excel. You can also export an Excel file as a Microsoft Project file.

  Saving a Project file as an Excel file, or vice versa, is equivalent to importing. Your choice to import or export hinges on which program you are more familiar with or perhaps, which one is open at the time.

INSIDE OUT
Switch from Excel to Microsoft Project for managing projects

Many project managers get their start building simple project schedules in Excel. Sometimes, not having a copy of Microsoft Project is the reason for using Excel. Other times, the magnitude of the features available in Microsoft Project is too daunting. As it turns out, you can get started with Microsoft Project by sticking to its basic features; the increase in productivity you obtain quickly pays back the purchase price of the software.

Although you have to invest some time learning to use the program, you'll recoup that time as well once Project starts handling the tasks—and the calculations—you had to perform manually before.

In Excel, it's easy enough to type task names into the cells in the first column of a worksheet. Then, if you type the weeks or months in the first row, you can create something akin to a Gantt chart by highlighting the cells when work is supposed to take place. The problems arise when the project plan changes—and of course, it always does. For example, because Excel doesn't track task dependencies, you have to manually reschedule your tasks if the project starts late or a task takes longer than you estimated. In addition, if you want to track durations, costs, or other project information, you have to craft your own formulas to do so. Then, if you consider the difficulty of using an Excel worksheet to assign resources to work on tasks, using Project starts to look like a better and better idea.

Moving Schedule Information from Excel to Microsoft Project

After you decide to use Microsoft Project to plan and track projects, the next step is to decide how best to make the transition from Excel to Microsoft Project. If you manage projects of short duration, the easiest approach is to manage new projects with Microsoft Project and continue using your old approach until the projects in progress are complete. However, if your projects run longer, or you can't abide your manual management approach one more day, you can transfer some, if not all, of your project information from Excel to Microsoft Project. How much you can move over depends on how you represented project data in Excel.

Your Excel file most likely includes a column with task names. At the very least, you can import those task names into Microsoft Project to set up your task list, as described in the section titled "Importing and Exporting with Excel" later in this chapter. If you also include columns for task duration and assigned resources, you can import those fields as well.

Importing Task Dates

In your Excel file, suppose you include columns for start and finish dates. Microsoft Project is a powerful scheduling tool because you don't have to specify when tasks start and finish. Instead, you define how tasks depend on each other, and Microsoft Project handles the start and end date calculations. However, when you import start and finish dates from Excel, the imported tasks include built-in date constraints, resulting in an over-restricted schedule and possible scheduling conflicts.

As it turns out, it's easier to build task dependencies and remove the date constraints in Project. For example, after you import the tasks, link the tasks as described in the section titled "Establishing Task Dependencies" in Chapter 5, "Scheduling Tasks." Then, insert the Constraint Type column into the table area of the Gantt Chart view. To remove all the date constraints, in the first Constraint Type cell, choose As Soon As Possible. Then, drag the small black square at the bottom right corner of the cell over all the other Constraint Type cells.

For more information about task constraints, see the section titled "Scheduling Tasks to Achieve Specific Dates" in Chapter 5.

Chapter 17

Linking Imported Tasks

After you import tasks from an Excel file into a Microsoft Project file, your first step is to create links (dependencies) between the tasks. For example, the "Paint Wall" task has a Finish-to-Start dependency with the "Paint Window Trim" task. If the tasks you import include durations, all you have to do is set the start date for the project, and— based on the project start date, the task dependencies, and their durations—Microsoft Project calculates the start and end dates for all the tasks.

For more information about linking tasks, see the section titled "Establishing Task Dependencies" in Chapter 5.

Copying Between Microsoft Project and Excel

By using the Copy and Paste commands, you can easily exchange sheet data and static graphics between Microsoft Project and Excel. For example, if you have an Excel file with a proposed list of tasks (with estimated durations) for a project, you can copy the cells for the tasks into a Microsoft Project Task Sheet to get your project schedule started. Similarly, the Copy and Paste commands work well if you want to display a graphic from one program in the other, for example, to show an Excel graph of sensors installed each week within the Gantt Chart of an equipment deployment project.

You can also use the Copy command to insert an embedded object. The benefit of embedding an Excel file within a Microsoft Project schedule, or vice versa, is that you can open the embedded object without switching programs and without having to access the original file.

See the section titled "Embedding Between Microsoft Project and Excel" later in this chapter.

Copying Information from Excel

You might want to copy two types of information from Excel worksheets:

- Data from Excel worksheet cells into cells in a sheet view in Microsoft Project.

   Copying data from Excel cells to Microsoft Project cells is a wonderfully simple way to import data from Excel to Microsoft Project–as long as the columns of information in Excel and Microsoft Project line up.

- Images of Excel graphs in graphically oriented areas in Microsoft Project.

   Excel is the program of choice when you want to graph numeric data. If you want to display a graph within your Microsoft Project file, for example, a pie chart or a histogram, you can copy the graph from Excel to the chart area of a Gantt Chart view or certain other nontable areas in Microsoft Project.

Copying Sheet Information from Excel

Anything in Excel worksheet cells can easily be copied and pasted into a Microsoft Project table. However, the order and data type of the columns of information must match, so some up-front preparation is needed in either the Excel workbook or the Microsoft Project table.

Match the Columns

Copying and pasting information is one of the easiest ways to get information from Excel to Microsoft Project. However, copy and paste success depends on the correct match-up of the columns of Excel information you're copying and the Microsoft Project columns into which you're pasting.

For example, suppose that your Excel worksheet contains four columns you want to copy to your project plan: Task Name, Resource, Duration, and Fixed Cost. To copy these columns from Excel to Microsoft Project, you must first add, remove, and rearrange columns in a Microsoft Project task table so that the corresponding four Microsoft Project columns appear next to each other (see Figure 17-1).

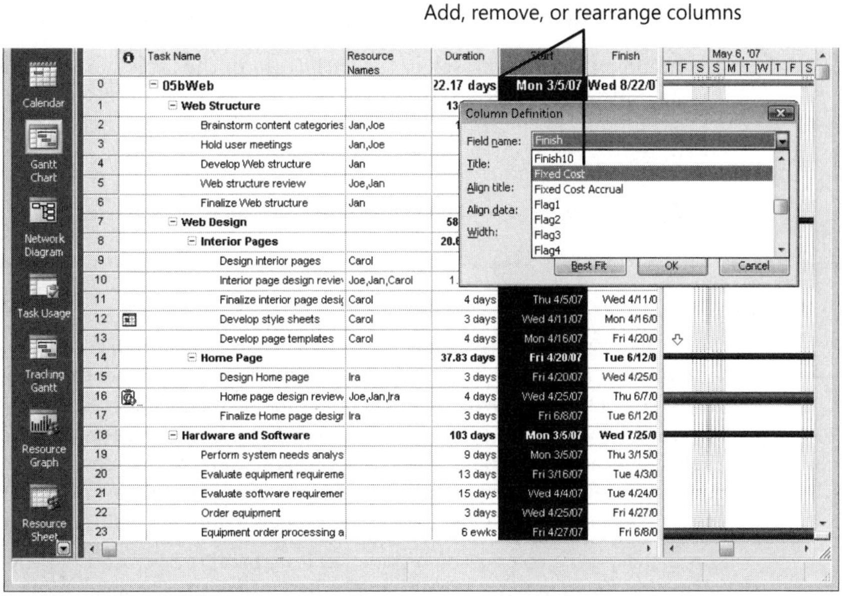

Add, remove, or rearrange columns

Figure 17-1 Insert columns in Microsoft Project so that the table columns match the order and type of the Excel data being copied and pasted.

The following are techniques you can use to arrange your Microsoft Project view to match the incoming Excel data:

- Apply a different table to a Microsoft Project sheet view. Click View, Table and then click the table you want.

- Add a column to a Microsoft Project table. Click in the column to the right of where you want the new column to appear. Click Insert, Column. In the Field Name box, click the field you want to add and then click OK.

- Remove a column from a table. Click the column heading and then click the Delete key.

- Move a column to a different location. Click the heading to select the entire column. When the mouse pointer changes to a four-headed arrow, drag to the location you want.

  A vertical gray marker appears to show where the column will be moved.

To copy and paste Excel worksheet cells into Microsoft Project, do the following:

1. Arrange the source Excel columns to match the target Microsoft Project field order and data type. Or, arrange the target columns in Microsoft Project to match the incoming Excel data.

2. In Excel, select the set of cells to be copied.

Copy

3. On the Home tab of the Ribbon, in the Clipboard group, click Copy.

4. In Microsoft Project, select the *anchor cell* in the table where you want the incoming information to begin to be pasted.

   This anchor cell will become the location of the upper-left cell of data selected in Excel.

Paste

5. On the Standard toolbar in Microsoft Project, click Paste.

Match the Data Types

As far as Microsoft Project is concerned, you can paste a set of resource names into any column that represents a text field, such as the Task Name field, the Group field, the Contact field, or even the WBS field. As long as the data type (such as text, date, or number) for the data you are pasting into a field matches the data type for the Microsoft Project field, the program obligingly pastes the information. For this reason, you could not paste that same set of resource names into the Work field or the Start field, for example, because they are incompatible data types. Work is a *duration field*, and Start is a *date field*.

So, matching the columns of information from Excel to Microsoft Project really means matching the data types—that is, the kind of information that can be stored in a field, for example, text, number, or date; and the format that information can take, for example, **14d** for a duration field, **6/29/07** for a date field, or **$35.90** for a currency field.

If you are pasting estimated task duration into Microsoft Project, chances are you want to use the Duration field. However, if you don't want to use the exact Microsoft Project fields, custom fields that are of the matching *data type* work just as well. For example, if you estimate optimistic, most likely, and pessimistic durations, you can paste that data into any custom duration fields, such as Duration 5, Duration 6, and Duration 7.

To add a custom field to a Microsoft Project table, click the column to the right of where you want the new column to appear. Click Insert, Column. In the Field Name box, click the field you want to add and then click OK.

For more information about working with custom fields, see the section titled "Customizing Fields" in Chapter 25, "Customizing Your View of Project Information." For a list of custom fields available in Microsoft Project, type fields in the Type A Question For Help box, and then press Enter. Click one of the field types, for example, Duration Fields. A complete list of fields of that type appears in the Help pane.

Copying Graphics from Excel

Copying an Excel graph and pasting it into specific areas of Microsoft Project as a picture is the most obvious application of copying Excel graphics into Microsoft Project. However, you can also paste Excel worksheet cells as a picture in Microsoft Project, instead of pasting those cells into table cells.

To paste Excel information as a static picture, do the following:

1. In Excel, select the chart or other data you want to insert as a picture in Microsoft Project.

2. On the Home tab of the Ribbon, in the Clipboard group, click Copy.

3. In your Microsoft Project file, display the location at which you want to place the picture. The following locations in Microsoft Project can accept pictures:

   ❑ Chart area of a Gantt chart

   ❑ Notes tab in the Task Information, Resource Information, or Assignment Information dialog box

   ❑ Objects box in the Task Form or Resource Form

   ❑ Notes box in the Task Form or Resource Form

   ❑ Header, footer, or legend of a printable view or report

4. Click Edit, Paste Special.

   The Paste Special dialog box appears.

5. Select the Paste option.

6. In the As box, click Picture or Picture (Bitmap), as illustrated in Figure 17-2.

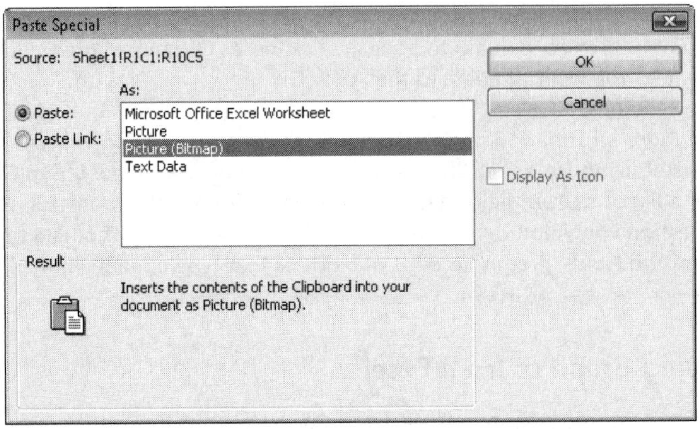

Figure 17-2 Use the As box in the Paste Special dialog box to specify that you want to insert the Excel information as a picture.

This option ensures that the data, whether it's a chart or a set of worksheet cells, is pasted as a graphic rather than as an embedded graphic or straight text.

> **Note**
>
> If the Paste Special command is not available for the location at which you want to paste the picture, press Ctrl+V instead.

7. Click OK.

The new picture is pasted in Microsoft Project at your selected location (see Figure 17-3).

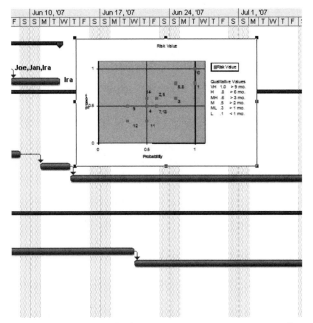

Figure 17-3 The Excel information appears as a picture in the Microsoft Project location you selected.

Although static pictures look like embedded objects, you cannot open or edit them. However, you can drag the entire object or a side to move or resize them.

For more information about embedded objects, see the section titled "Embedding an Excel Object in Microsoft Project" later in this chapter.

Copying Information to Excel

Copying information from Microsoft Project and pasting it into Excel worksheets is one solution when you need to process project data in a way that Microsoft Project doesn't handle easily. Likewise, if you're more comfortable with Excel's sorting, grouping, and formatting features, you can copy data from Microsoft Project to Excel to quickly obtain the results you need, for example, when you're rushing to prepare for a hastily convened meeting.

Copying Sheet Information to Excel

Copying and pasting data from a Microsoft Project table to Excel worksheet cells is actually easier than the reverse process. Unlike copying from Excel to Microsoft Project, the columns or data types don't have to match, because all Excel fields can accept any data type.

Chapter 17

To copy Microsoft Project table cells and paste them into Excel worksheet cells, follow these steps:

1. In Microsoft Project, display the view that contains the information you want to copy to Excel.

   If necessary, apply a different table or add columns that contain the information you need.

2. Select the cells or columns you want to copy.

   To select a column, click its heading. Select multiple adjacent columns by dragging across the column headings. Select multiple nonadjacent columns by holding down Ctrl while you click each column heading.

3. On the Standard toolbar, click Copy Cell or press Ctrl+C.

4. In Excel, select the anchor cell in the worksheet where you want the incoming information to begin to be pasted.

   This anchor cell will become the location of the upper-left cell of data selected in Microsoft Project.

5. On the Home tab of the Ribbon, in the Clipboard group, click Paste.

   The selected project data appears in the Excel worksheet starting at the anchor cell. Adjust column widths in the worksheet as necessary to see the data (see Figure 17-4).

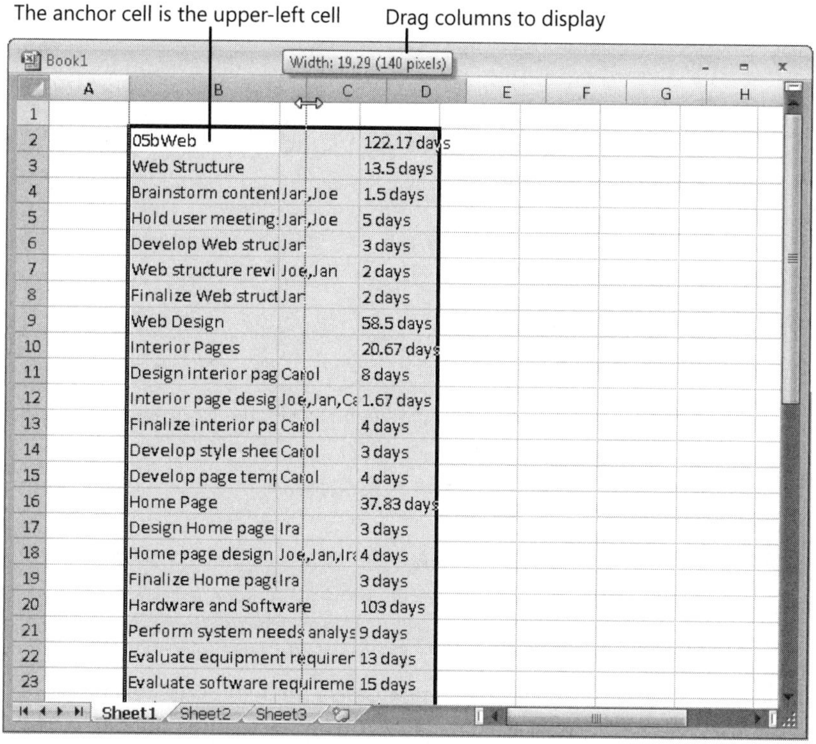

The anchor cell is the upper-left cell   Drag columns to display

Figure 17-4 Your project data is pasted into the Excel worksheet.

TROUBLESHOOTING

You can't find the Analyze Timescaled Data function

Previous versions of Microsoft Project include a button on the Analysis toolbar called Analyze Timescaled Data. This function, which copied task usage or resource usage over time from Microsoft Project to Excel has been replaced by visual reports in Project 2007. Visual report templates for assignment usage can produce reports based on assignments over a period of time. In fact, whenever you want to copy time-phased data such as resource usage or assignment usage, you can use a visual report to do so.

For more information about visual reports in Excel, see the section titled "Producing a Visual Report of Project Data in Excel" later in this chapter.

Copying Graphics to Excel

You can copy a picture of any Microsoft Project view and then paste it into Excel. To do this, follow these steps:

1. In Microsoft Project, display the view you want to capture as a picture for Excel.

2. Manipulate the view to show the information the way you want it to appear in Excel.

Copy Picture

3. On the Standard toolbar, click Copy Picture.

> **Note**
>
> You can also create a picture to copy by clicking Copy Picture To Office Wizard on the Analysis toolbar.

4. In the Copy Picture dialog box, select the options you want.

    - In the Render Image section, select the option for the most likely method for viewing the image: on a computer screen (the default), printed, or a GIF image file (ideal for pictures published to the Web).

    - In the Copy section, select the Rows On Screen option (the default) if you want the rows currently showing on the screen to be copied. The Selected Rows option copies the currently selected rows whether or not they appear on the screen.

    - In the Timescale section, select the As Shown On Screen option (the default) if you want the timescale to be represented as set in the current view. Select the From and To boxes if you want to specify a timescale and date range different than what appears on the screen.

    When you've finished setting the Copy Picture options, click OK.

5. In Excel, select the location in the worksheet where you want to paste the picture of the view.

6. On the Home tab of the Ribbon, in the Clipboard group, click Paste.

    A static picture of the Microsoft Project view appears on the Excel worksheet (see Figure 17-5). You can move the image by dragging it. You can also resize the image by dragging any of the edges.

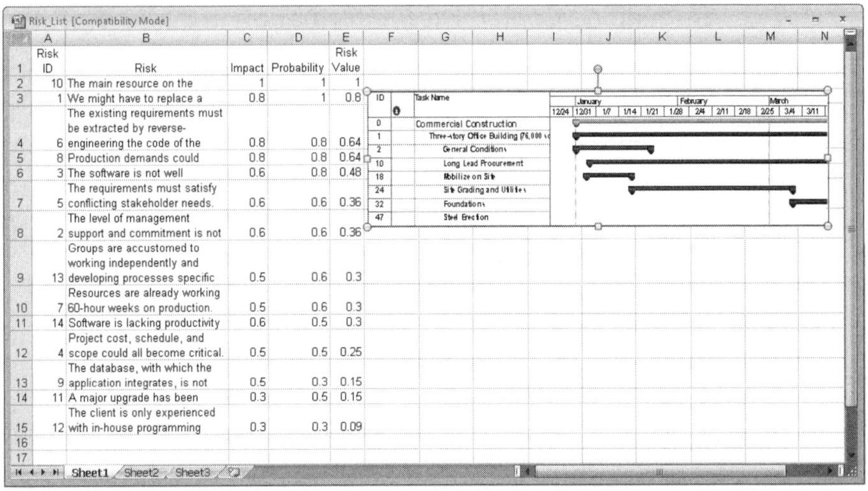

Figure 17-5 The copied picture of your Microsoft Project view appears at the position you select in Excel.

Embedding Between Microsoft Project and Excel

You can integrate information from Microsoft Project and Excel by embedding a source file from one application as an *embedded object* in a file in the target application. When you embed an object in an application, you're basically inserting an entire file, along with all of its source application's capabilities, into the target application file.

Therefore, not only can you have a picture of a Gantt chart in an Excel worksheet, but you can double-click that picture of the Gantt chart to access Microsoft Project commands and change the Gantt chart data. You can even switch to a different Microsoft Project view, such as the Resource Sheet, and change information there as well. Likewise, in Microsoft Project, you can have a picture of an S-curve graph generated by Excel and also double-click it to launch Excel and edit the format of the graph or even the underlying data for the graph.

Embedding an Excel Object in Microsoft Project

Whether you insert all or part of an Excel worksheet or chart into Microsoft Project as an embedded object, when you double-click the object, you can access the entire Excel workbook. The benefit of inserting a portion of an Excel worksheet or chart is that the portion you select is what appears in the embedded object. If you insert an entire file, you can drag its edges to change the portion of the embedded object that's visible.

Chapter 17

Embedding Copied Excel Information in a Microsoft Project File

To copy and paste selected Excel information as an embedded object, follow these steps:

1. In Excel, select the data or chart you want to insert as an embedded object in Microsoft Project.

2. On the Home tab of the Ribbon, in the Clipboard group, click Copy.

3. In your Microsoft Project file, display the location where you want to place the object.

   Only the chart area of a Gantt chart and the Objects box in the Task Form or Resource Form can accept a chart or worksheet fragment as an embedded object.

> **Note**
> To apply the Objects box in the Task Form or Resource Form, click in the form area to make it active (if it's part of a combination view such as the Task Entry view). Click Format, Details, Objects.

4. Click Edit, Paste Special.

5. In the Paste Special dialog box, select the Paste option.

6. In the As box, click Microsoft Excel Worksheet or Microsoft Excel Chart.

7. Click OK.

   The data or chart is embedded in Microsoft Project.

Embedding an Entire Excel File in a Microsoft Project File

To embed an entire existing Excel file into a Microsoft Project file, follow these steps:

1. In Microsoft Project, open the project plan in which you want to embed the Excel file.

2. Display the location at which you want to insert the file.

   Only the chart area of a Gantt chart, the Objects box in the Task Form or Resource Form, and the Notes tab in the Task Information, Resource Information, or Assignment Information dialog box can accept an Excel file as an embedded object.

3. Click Insert, Object.

   To insert an object onto the Notes tab of one of the Information dialog boxes, click the Insert Object button above the Notes area in the dialog box. (You can't click Insert, Object while the dialog box is open.)

4. In the Insert Object dialog box, select the Create From File option.

5. If you want the embedded Excel file to be linked to the source, select the Link check box.

   If you link the file, any changes to the file in Excel update the embedded object in Microsoft Project. If you try to change the embedded object, you'll see a message indicating that the object is linked, and if you change information, the link will be removed. In this way, the linked information is protected.

   If you don't link the object, you're essentially making a copy of the original object, and it becomes a separate entity from the original. You can change information in the embedded version without affecting the source data.

6. If you want the embedded object to be displayed as an Excel icon in your project, rather than showing as part of the worksheet, select the Display As Icon check box.

7. Click the Browse button and find the location of the Excel file you want to insert. Double-click the file.

   The file's name appears in the File Name box in the Insert Object dialog box.

8. Click Insert.

9. In the Insert Object dialog box, click OK.

   The Excel file appears in the area you selected. Drag to move or resize the object as needed (Figure 17-6).

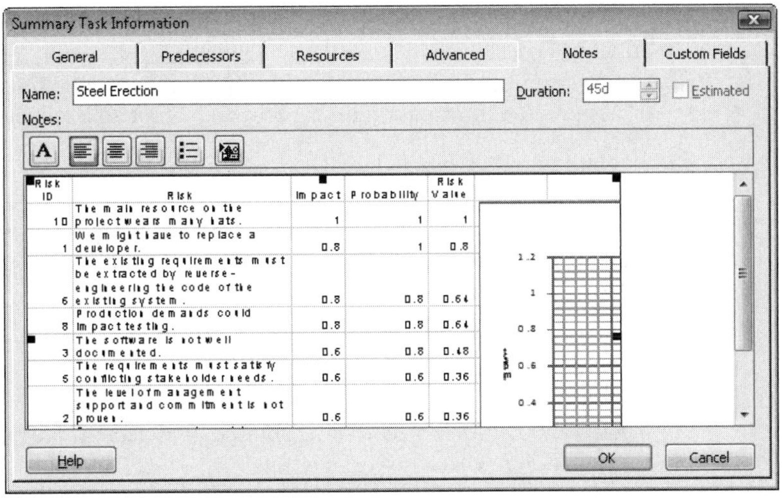

Figure 17-6 The selected Excel file appears embedded in the area you select, such as the Notes tab in the Task Information dialog box.

Chapter 17

> **Note**
>
> You can embed an Excel file in a note associated with the project as a whole. First, display the project summary task by clicking Tools, Options, View and then selecting the Show Project Summary Task check box. Click OK.
>
> Double-click the project summary task. In the Summary Task Information dialog box, click the Notes tab. Click the Insert Object button and add the Excel file.

Creating a New Excel Object in Microsoft Project

You can create a new Excel workbook or chart as an embedded object in your project. In this case, the new Excel object exists only within your project file.

> **Note**
>
> If you think you would ever want to work on the Excel file outside of Microsoft Project, you should instead create the file in Excel and embed or link it within Microsoft Project.

To create an embedded Excel file within Microsoft Project, follow these steps:

1. In your project plan, display the location at which you want to embed the object.

    Only the chart area of a Gantt chart, the Objects box in the Task Form or Resource Form, and the Notes tab in the Task Information, Resource Information, or Assignment Information dialog box can accept an Excel file as an embedded object.

2. Click Insert, Object.

    To insert an object into the Notes tab of one of the Information dialog boxes, click the Insert Object button above the Notes area in the dialog box. (You can't click Insert, Object while the dialog box is open.)

3. In the Insert Object dialog box, select the Create New option.

4. In the Object Type box, click Microsoft Excel Chart or Microsoft Excel Worksheet.

5. If you want the new object to be displayed as an icon in the project, select the Display As Icon check box.

6. Click OK.

    An Excel worksheet or chart appears in the location you selected. Double-click the Excel object to start adding your information.

Working with an Embedded Excel Object

Microsoft Office
Button

To open and work with an embedded Excel object, simply double-click the object. Excel launches and opens the embedded Excel object. When finished editing the Excel object, click the Microsoft Office Button and then click Exit Excel. The Excel window closes, and the modified Excel object appears in Microsoft Project.

> **Note**
>
> To delete an embedded object anywhere in your project plan, click it and then press the Delete key.

Embedding a Microsoft Project File in Excel

You can embed a new or existing Microsoft Project file as an object in an Excel worksheet. When you double-click the Microsoft Project object in Excel, Microsoft Project menus and commands temporarily replace those of Excel so that you can create or edit project information without leaving the Excel file.

Embedding an Existing Microsoft Project File in Excel

To embed an existing Microsoft Project file in Excel, follow these steps:

1. Open the Excel file in which you want to embed the existing Microsoft Project file.

2. Select the location at which you want the Microsoft Project object to be embedded.

3. On the Insert tab of the Ribbon, in the Text group, click Object.

4. In the Object dialog box, click the Create From File tab.

5. Click the Browse button to open the Browse window. Navigate through your computer's filing system (and onto your network if applicable) to find the drive and folder where the project file is located.

6. Double-click the file.

    The file's path and name appear in the File Name box in the Object dialog box.

7. If you want the embedded Microsoft Project object to be linked to the source file, select the Link check box.

    If you link the object, any changes in the source project plan update the embedded object. If you try to change the embedded object, you'll see a message indicating that the object is linked, and you cannot change the information. This protects the integrity of the source information.

Chapter 17

If you don't link the object, you're making a copy of the original object, which becomes a separate entity from the original. You can change the embedded project without affecting information in the original project.

8. If you want the embedded project to be displayed as a Microsoft Project icon in Excel, rather than showing a part of the Gantt Chart or other view, select the Display As Icon check box.

9. Click OK.

Part of a view of the selected project file appears in the location you selected (see Figure 17-7).

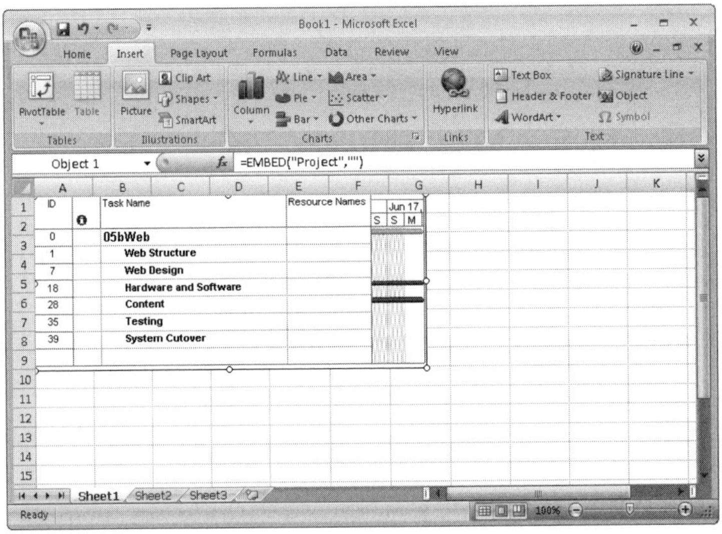

Figure 17-7 The selected project is embedded in Excel.

If you selected the Display As Icon check box, the embedded project file appears as the Microsoft Project icon (by default) in the selected location. This is particularly useful when empty areas on your Excel worksheet are hard to find.

Creating a New Microsoft Project File in Excel

Although you can create a new Microsoft Project file as an embedded object in Excel, you should avoid doing so because the Microsoft Project object would exist only within the Excel file. Opening Excel to access a Microsoft Project object would quickly grow tiresome as you work with your schedule throughout the life of the project. However, if you do decide to create a new Microsoft Project file within Excel, follow these steps:

1. Open the Excel file in which you want to create a new Microsoft Project file as an embedded object.

2. Select the location at which you want the new Microsoft Project object to be embedded.

3. On the Insert tab of the Ribbon, in the Text group, click Object.

4. In the Object dialog box, click the Create New tab, if necessary.

5. In the Object Type box, click Microsoft Office Project Document (see Figure 17-8).

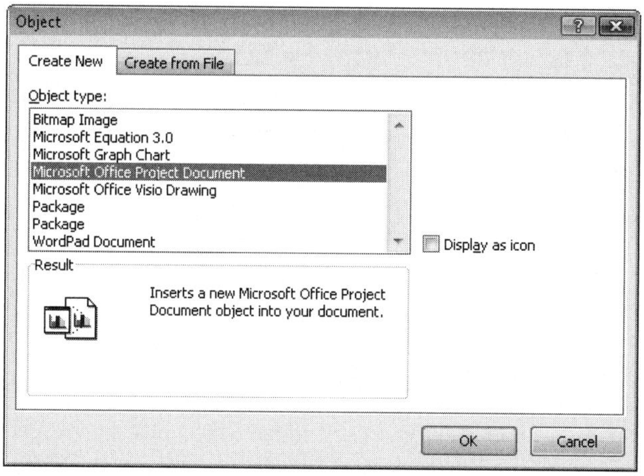

Figure 17-8 Use the Object dialog box to create a Microsoft Project file as an embedded object.

6. If you want the embedded project to be displayed as an icon in Excel, rather than showing a part of the Gantt Chart or other view, select the Display As Icon check box.

7. Click OK.

Part of a view of the new project file appears.

If you selected the Display As Icon check box, the embedded project file appears as the Microsoft Project icon (by default) in the selected location.

8. Double-click the new project to add information to it on the spot.

Working with the Embedded Microsoft Project File

Whenever you want to work with the embedded project file, just double-click the object. The Excel menus change to reflect the relevant Microsoft Project menus (see Figure 17-9). You can use Microsoft Project in the usual way: switch views, apply tables and filters, change data, run calculations, and so on.

Chapter 17

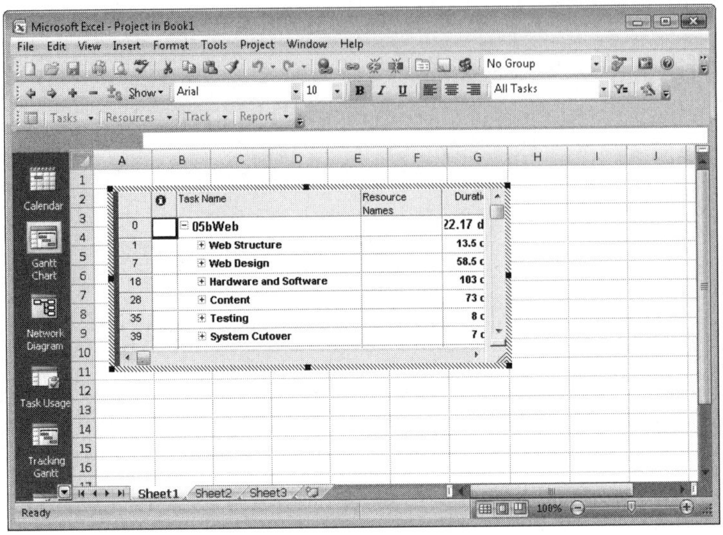

Figure 17-9 When you double-click an embedded Project object, the Excel menus and toolbars change to those of Microsoft Project.

Linking Between Microsoft Project and Excel

You can take the use of embedded objects one step further—by *linking* them to their source. With a dynamic link between source and target, your embedded object updates whenever the source changes. When linked, the source and target information are essentially the same file, rather than just a separate copy of one another, which is the case when they are not linked. The advantage of linking objects is that you don't have to worry about maintaining multiple copies of the same information. When you change the original file, those changes appear anywhere that file is linked. The disadvantage is that it's more difficult to distribute file with links. You must remember to send the linked files as well as the file that contains the links. Depending on where your recipients save the files, they might have to rebuild the links.

Creating a link to embedded objects is as easy as selecting a check box when you're embedding the object, whether it's a fragment you're inserting using the Paste Special dialog box or an entire file you're embedding using the Insert Object command.

Be aware that when you link information between Microsoft Project and Excel, you always need to know the current location of the linked file and its update status. If the linked file is moved, the link is broken. If the information in the linked file becomes obsolete, the linked object becomes outdated too. However, when the conditions are right, linking is an excellent way to maintain current information.

Linking from Excel to Microsoft Project

In Microsoft Project, you can link an Excel worksheet fragment or chart. To do this, follow the steps in the section titled "Embedding Copied Excel Information in a Microsoft Project File" earlier in this chapter. In the Paste Special dialog box, select the Paste Link option.

If you want to link an entire existing Excel file, follow the steps in the section titled "Embedding an Entire Excel File in a Microsoft Project File" earlier in this chapter. In the Insert Object dialog box, select the Link check box.

You can also copy worksheet cells and link them into Microsoft Project table cells. The data looks as if it were originally typed in Microsoft Project, but it's actually linked to Excel data. To link worksheet cell data in a Microsoft Project table, follow these steps:

1. In Excel, select the first column of information to be linked in Microsoft Project and then, on the Home tab of the Ribbon, in the Clipboard group, click Copy. By copying and pasting one column at a time, the Excel columns don't have to be in the same order as the Microsoft Project columns. In addition, the paste links will remain in place even if the columns in the Excel worksheet change or move.

2. In Microsoft Project, display the view and click the cell that is to become the anchor cell for the linked information.

    This anchor cell becomes the location of firstt cell of data selected in Excel.

3. Click Edit, Paste Special.

4. In the Paste Special dialog box, click the Paste Link option.

5. In the As box, click Text Data (see Figure 17-10).

    If you select Microsoft Excel Worksheet, an object of the selected cells is embedded and linked, rather than flowing the values into the table cells as text.

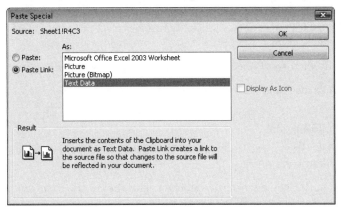

Figure 17-10 Choose these options in the As box in the Paste Special dialog box to link worksheet data with project table data.

6. Click OK.

   The linked information appears at your selection point in your project. When changes occur in the information in the source application, this project file reflects those changes.

7. Repeat steps 1 through 6 for each column in Excel that you want to link to a column in Microsoft Project.

TROUBLESHOOTING

You're getting paste error messages

Paste error messages are the result of a mismatch between the data type of the incoming Excel data and the Microsoft Project columns into which you want them to go. Click through the paste error messages to dismiss them.

Then review the order and type of the Excel data and the order and type of the Microsoft Project sheet and see where the problem is. Make any necessary corrections and repeat the Copy and Paste Special operation.

See the sidebar "Match the Data Types" earlier in this chapter to learn more about Microsoft Project data types.

Linking from Microsoft Project to Excel

In Excel, you can link to an embedded Microsoft Project file. To do this, follow the steps in the section titled "Embedding an Existing Microsoft Project File in Excel" earlier in this chapter. In the Object dialog box, select the Link To File option.

You can also copy a set of table cells in Microsoft Project and link them into Excel worksheet cells. The data looks as if it were originally typed in Excel, but it's actually linked to Microsoft Project data. To link Microsoft Project table data to Excel worksheet cells, follow these steps:

1. In Microsoft Project, select the table data to be linked in Excel.

2. On the Standard toolbar, click Copy.

3. In Excel, click the cell that is to become the anchor cell for the linked information.

   This anchor cell becomes the location of the upper-left cell of data selected in Microsoft Project.

4. On the Home tab, click the down arrow below the Paste button in the Clipboard group. Then click Paste Special.

5. In the Paste Special dialog box, click the Paste Link option.

6. In the As box, click Text.

If you select Microsoft Office Project Document Object, an object with the selected project data is embedded and linked, rather than flowing the values into the table cells as text.

7. Click OK.

The linked information appears at the worksheet selection (see Figure 17-11). When changes occur to the data in the project plan, those changes appear in this linked data in Excel.

Excel cells contain links to fields in Microsoft Project

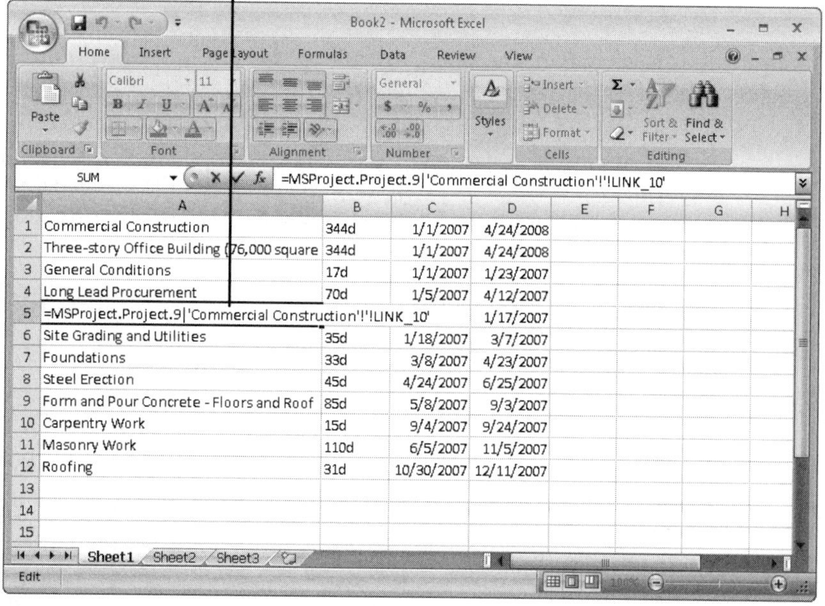

Figure 17-11 When you link Microsoft Project data into Excel cells, the cells contain links to fields in Microsoft Project.

Working with a Linked Object

After you have linked information in Microsoft Project or Excel, you can manipulate the information in a few ways. You can edit the source information and then accept updates in the target file from the source. You can review a list of all linked information in the file and then redirect or break the link if needed.

Editing Linked Information

If you try to change information in a linked object, a message indicates that you cannot do so from within the target application without breaking the link. This behavior protects the integrity of the information in the source file. However, you can double-click a linked object to launch the source file in the source application so you can make the changes you want. When finished updating the source, click Save and then return to the target application to see the changes reflected there.

Chapter 17

CAUTION

Double-clicking a linked object to launch the source file in the source application is different from working with an unlinked embedded object. When you work on an unlinked embedded object, you are working with a copy of the information, not the source file. With linked information, you always need to work in the source because the source updates the target through the link. There is one exception to linked objects: If you copy text from Microsoft Project and create the link as text, Microsoft Project simply copies the text into Excel cells.

Updating Linked Objects

In both Microsoft Project and Excel, when you open the file that contains links, by default you see a dialog box prompting you to update the file by using the link (see Figure 17-12). Click Yes to re-establish the link and update any information that has changed since the last time you opened and updated this file.

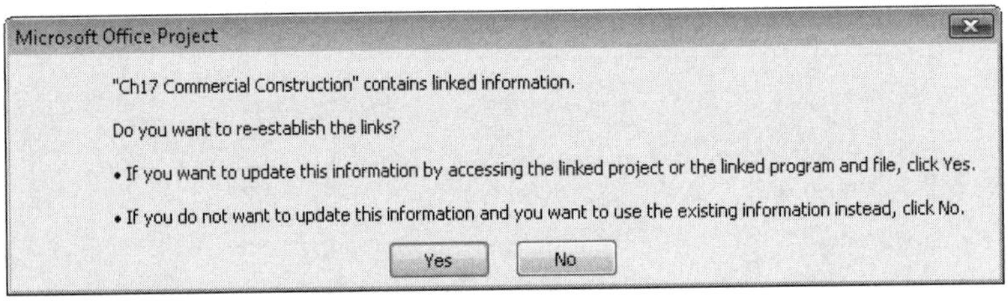

Figure 17-12 When you open a project plan or workbook that contains links, you'll see a message like this.

Showing and Hiding the Update Link Prompt

In Microsoft Project, if you do not want to see the Update Link alert each time you open the project containing links, click Edit, Links. In the Links dialog box, be sure to select the link and then select the Automatic option so that the links update automatically.

In Excel, if you do not want to see the Update Link alert each time you open the workbook, click the Microsoft Office Button and then click the Excel Options button at the bottom of the menu. In the Excel Options dialog box, click Advanced. Scroll down to the General section and then clear the Ask To Update Automatic Links check box. Click OK.

You can further specify when you want the Excel alert to appear. When you open the Edit Links dialog box and select a link, click Startup Prompt. In the Startup Prompt dialog box, choose an option to automatically update links without prompting, leave the links as they are without prompting to update, or let the user choose whether to display the alert.

Viewing Links

In Microsoft Project, to review and repair links in your project, follow these steps:

1. Click Edit, Links.

   The Links dialog box appears, showing all links existing in your project file.

2. If you know that linked data has changed, and you want to update the link immediately, select a link and click Update Now.

3. If the location of the linked workbook has changed, update the location information in the project by clicking Change Source.

   In the Change Source dialog box, type the full path to the source information and click OK. Alternatively, you can click Browse to locate the file.

4. To break the link with the source application, click Break Link.

   When you break a link, the information remains in the project file as a separate embedded object. You can still view and edit the Excel information; it's simply no longer linked.

To review and work with links in Excel, follow these steps:

1. In Excel, open the workbook containing the links.

2. Click the Data tab on the Ribbon. In the Connections group, click Edit Links.

   The Edit Links dialog box appears, showing all links existing in the workbook (see Figure 17-13).

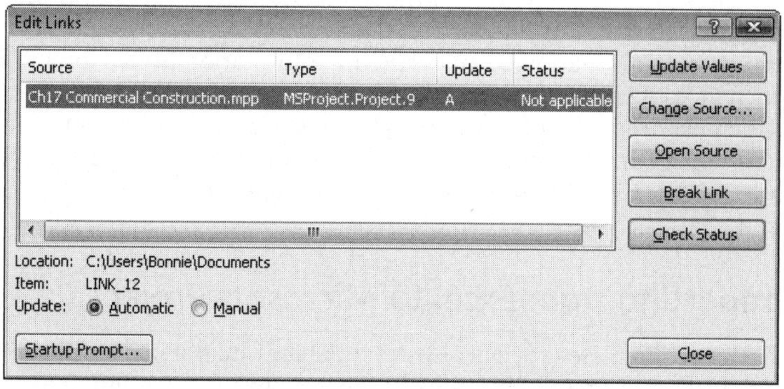

Figure 17-13 Use the Edit Links dialog box in Excel to review and update the links in the current workbook.

3. If you want to update a link immediately, particularly if you have set a link to be updated manually, select it and click Update Values.

4. If the location of the linked project has changed, update the location information in the workbook by clicking Change Source.

5. To break the link with the source application, click Break Link.

When you break a link, the project information remains in the workbook file as a separate embedded object. The link disappears from the list, but you can still view and edit the project information; it's simply no longer linked.

> **Note**
>
> If you create a link to another Excel file or a file built with another Microsoft Office application, you can check the status of the link by clicking the Check Status button. When you first open the Excel file, the status for the link shows up as Unknown.
>
> When you click the Check Status button, you might see a status of "Warning: value not updated" to remind you to update values. Or, you might see a status of "Source open" to inform you that the source file is open and might be edited.
>
> However, if the link is to a Microsoft Project file, the status shows as "Not applicable." In this case, clicking Check Status does nothing.

Importing and Exporting with Excel

Suppose you want to move larger quantities of information between Microsoft Project and Excel, or you don't like having to jockey columns around to make sure data transfers to the right place. For these situations, you can *import* or export information in either direction—from Microsoft Project to Excel or from Excel to Microsoft Project. Importing information means bringing information from a foreign file format into the current application (for example, from the Excel XLSX file format to Microsoft Project, which uses the MPP file format). When you export information, you're saving information in the current application in a different file format so that it can be opened by another application. In both cases, the information will look as if it were originally created in the target application.

Importing from Excel to Microsoft Project

With two templates specifically designed for integration, Excel gives you a head start on importing information for tasks, resources, and even assignments from Excel to Microsoft Project. These templates include commonly used fields, and the fields are already mapped to the corresponding fields in Microsoft Project. All you have to do is open the Excel file and make a few choices, and the data is imported into your project plan.

One template is designed for importing basic task information into a Gantt Chart. Another template allows for more detailed project information, including resources and assignments.

If a team member or other stakeholder has created project information in Excel without using one of these templates, never fear. You can still import an Excel workbook into Microsoft Project the "old way."

Importing a Project Task List from Excel

Building a project plan doesn't have to be a solitary activity. You might ask others on the project team to create task lists for their portion of a project and then incorporate their work in an Excel workbook into Microsoft Project. The Microsoft Project Task List Import template in Excel, introduced back in Project 2002, simplifies this process.

The standard Excel importing process involves mapping the Excel columns to the corresponding Microsoft Project columns to ensure that the right information ends up in the right places in your Gantt Chart task sheet. The Microsoft Project Task List Import template has columns set up to work with Microsoft Project's Import Wizard to handle that aspect of the process for you. For example, suppose that the marketing department suggests an addition to the project plan that clarifies their test marketing efforts, but they want to develop the list of detailed tasks in Excel. Have them use the Microsoft Project Task List Template in Excel, as follows:

1. In Excel, click the Microsoft Office Button and then click New.

2. In the New Workbook window, click Installed Templates.

3. In the Installed Templates list, click Microsoft Project Task List Import Template and then click Create.

    Excel creates a new file that contains columns corresponding to fields in the default Gantt Chart in Microsoft Project.

    The columns in this Excel template are specifically designed for integration with Microsoft Project. For example, the ID, Duration, Start, and Deadline fields are all set up to flow into their corresponding Microsoft Project fields.

    The second worksheet, labeled either Info_Table or "Microsoft Project, contains a brief explanation of how Microsoft Project can use and augment the template.

4. Enter the task information in the Task_Table sheet (see Figure 17-14).

    In the template, the columns are labeled so you know where to enter each piece of information. The columns are also formatted to fit the type of data they are to contain. Be sure to enter data valid to the data type that's expected for each column. For example, the Start cells are already set up to display values as dates, but you still must type valid dates. The Duration field must contain values that represent a length of time. You can type a value, such as **2d** or **2w**, to represent the duration, but typing words or a date will generate an error when you try to import the file.

ID	Name	Duration	Start	Deadline	Resource Names	Notes
1	Identify market segment	2d	7/1/2007		Tom	
2	Prepare market survey	5d	7/6/2007		Dale	
3	Identify survey recipients	3d	7/12/2007		Pat	
4	Distribute surveys	1d	7/15/2007		Maureen	
5	Collate survey results	10d	7/16/2007		Dale	
6	Prepare survey report	5d	7/31/2007		Pat	

Task_Table / Info_Table

Figure 17-14 Share the Microsoft Project Task List Import template with your team to help build your project plan.

5. When you finish entering task information, click the Microsoft Office Button, click Save, and give the file a name.

   Make sure that you're saving the new task list as an Excel workbook, rather than overwriting the template (Excel Template).

6. Close the file.

TROUBLESHOOTING

You can't find the Excel Task List template

There are two reasons why the Task List template might not be available in the Templates dialog box.

If you are working with Microsoft Excel 2000 or earlier, the template is stored in a different location. In Excel, click File, New. Click the 1033 or Spreadsheet Solutions tab. Double-click Microsoft Project Task List Import Template.

If you still can't find it, click the Microsoft Office Button and then click Open. Browse to the Office template directory, which is typically \Program Files\Microsoft Office\Templates\1033. Double-click the Tasklist.xlt file.

The other reason you might not see the Task List template is that the computer you're working on might not have Microsoft Project installed on it. Although the Task List template is an Excel template, it is installed with Microsoft Project. If you have Excel installed on the same computer as Microsoft Project, the Excel-to-Project templates become available in Excel.

On a computer running Microsoft Project and Excel, use Windows Explorer to find the template file. Its typical location is \Program Files\Microsoft Office\Templates\1033. Copy the file to a disk or network location so that you can make it available to team members and other stakeholders who would rather use Excel to build their parts of the project schedule.

At this point, the new Excel task list is ready to be imported into Microsoft Project, as follows:

1. In Microsoft Project, open the project plan into which you want to import the Excel task list.

Open

2. On the Standard toolbar, click Open.

3. In the Open dialog box, browse to the location on your computer or network where the Excel task list is saved.

4. Click the arrow on the button that indicates the current file type, which is set to Microsoft Project Files by default, and click Microsoft Excel Workbooks.

   The file for the task list, along with other Excel workbooks, appears in the list.

> **CAUTION**
>
> If you don't see Excel workbooks that you've created, the problem is that choosing Microsoft Excel Workbooks as the file type does not display Excel 2007 workbooks, unless you save them with the Excel 97-2003 Workbook format. Compounding the problem, Microsoft Project sets a Security option by default that doesn't open or save files creating in Excel 97-2003 format. To open Excel workbooks created in Excel 2007, be sure to save them with the Excel 97-2003 Workbook format. In Project, choose Tools, Options. In the Options dialog box, click the Security tab and select the Allow Loading Files With Legacy Or Non Default File Formats options.

5. Click the task list workbook and then click Open.

   The Import Wizard appears.

6. On the Welcome page of the Import Wizard, click Next.

7. On the Data Type page, select the Project Excel Template option and then click Next.

8. On the Import Mode page, specify whether you want to import the file as a new project, append the tasks to the currently active project, or merge the data into the active project (see Figure 17-15).

   If you built an entire task list in the Excel template, select As A New Project. To add new tasks to the end of the current file, select Append The Data To The Active Project. If you plan to insert the imported tasks somewhere within the Project task list, select Merge The Data Into The Active Project.

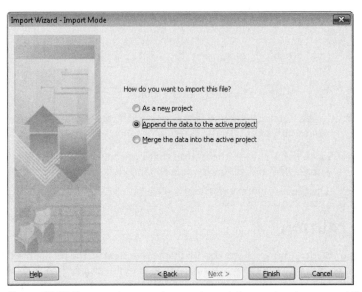

Figure 17-15 You can choose to import the task list template into a new Microsoft Project file or the active one.

9. Click Finish.

The values from the Excel columns are imported into the corresponding Microsoft Project fields, for example, the value in the Duration column imports into a task Duration field. If you scroll to the right, you see that the resource names appear in the Resource Names column, but the Predecessors column is still empty. The imported tasks still need to be organized, outlined, and linked.

For more information about inserting and organizing tasks, see Chapter 3, "Starting a New Project."

INSIDE OUT   Remove the SNET constraints

All tasks imported from the Excel task list template come in to the project file with a Start No Earlier Than (SNET) constraint. If the workbook's Start field contains a date, that becomes the SNET constraint date. If no date was entered, the SNET date is today's date.

Be sure to review those imported start dates. If any dates besides today's date are entered, check with the person who provided the task list to see if the SNET constraint was intentional. Unless you explain to the people who use the template that Microsoft Project figures out start dates for them, they might think they're supposed to enter a start date.

To make a schedule flexible so that you can respond quickly to the inevitable changes, you need to change those imposed (and arbitrary) date constraints to the most flexible As Soon As Possible constraint. To change the constraints all at once, do the following:

1. In the Gantt Chart, select the names of all tasks with date constraints.

   You can select the Start column if you're changing all tasks in the project to an ASAP constraint.

   If you want to change only certain tasks, click their row headings while holding the Ctrl key.

2. On the Standard toolbar, click Task Information.

3. In the Multiple Task Information dialog box, click the Advanced tab. In the Constraint Type box, click As Soon As Possible.

Task Information

When asking others to enter task information by using the Excel Task List template, ask them to enter any important finish dates in the Deadline column and any important start dates in the Notes column. By doing this, you can change all the SNET constraints to ASAP without having to examine every imported date to see whether it's a real date constraint.

For more information about setting constraints, see the section titled "Scheduling Tasks to Achieve Specific Dates" in Chapter 5.

Importing Detailed Project Information from Excel

If some team members or project stakeholders are doing more than just building a task list in Excel, have them use the Microsoft Project Plan Import Export Template. This Excel template includes columns for building a project with tasks, resources, and assignments.

The standard Excel importing process involves mapping the Excel columns to the corresponding Microsoft Project columns to ensure that the right information ends up in the right locations in your Resource Sheet, for example. The Microsoft Project Plan Import Export Template is set up to enter more detailed resource information in the format needed by Microsoft Project. To use this template, make sure that Excel is installed on the same computer as Microsoft Project and then follow these steps:

1. In Excel, click the Microsoft Office Button and then click New.

2. In the New Workbook window, click Installed Templates.

3. In the Installed Templates list, click Microsoft Project Plan Import Export Template and then click Create.

Chapter 17

> **Note**
>
> If the template is not in the Templates dialog box (which might be the case if you're working with Excel 2000 or earlier), close the dialog box and then click File, Open. Browse to the Office template directory, which is typically \Program Files\Microsoft Office\Templates\1033. Double-click the Projplan.xlt file.

The template creates a new file with columns that correspond to many commonly used fields in Microsoft Project. There is one worksheet each for tasks, resources, and assignments. A fourth worksheet, labeled Info_Table, provides general information on how to use the template.

The data fields are set up so that when you fill in the worksheets and import them into Microsoft Project, you don't need to map your data. If you decide to include additional columns (fields) of data, Microsoft Project maps that data to appropriate fields in the Microsoft Project data tables for you.

4. At the bottom of the workbook window, click the tab for the worksheet you want to use.

5. Enter the data in the fields you want. You don't have to use all the fields in all the sheets; just the ones you need (see Figure 17-16).

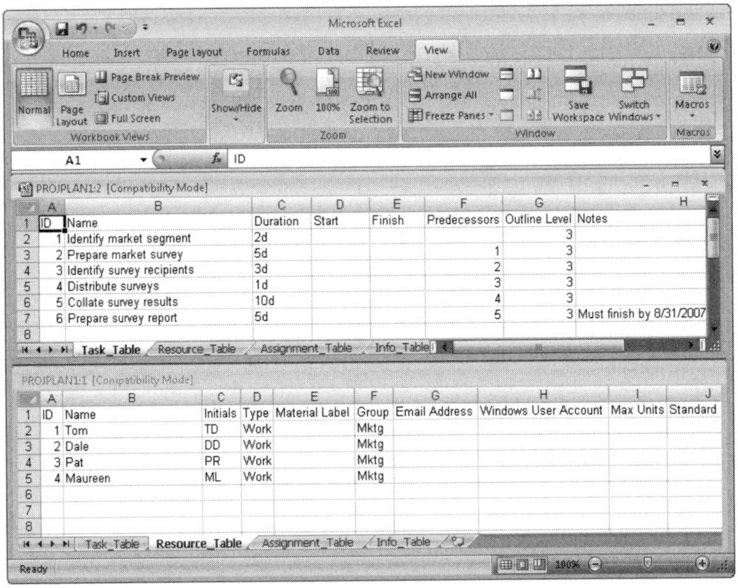

Figure 17-16 Use the Microsoft Project Plan Import Export Template to develop task, resource, and assignment information in Excel.

6. When finished, click Save on the Standard toolbar and give the file a name.

Make sure you're saving the new file as an Excel workbook, rather than overwriting the template.

7. Close the file.

This workbook is ready to import into Microsoft Project.

To import the information from this new Excel workbook into Microsoft Project, do the following:

1. On the Standard toolbar in Microsoft Project, click Open.

2. Go to the location on your computer or network where the Excel workbook is saved.

3. In the Files Of Type list, click Microsoft Excel Workbooks.

The workbook appears in the list of folders and files. Remember, choosing Microsoft Excel Workbooks as the file type does not show Excel workbooks saved in Excel 2007 format. To use an Excel 2007 file, save it with the Excel 97-2003 format.

4. Click the workbook file and then click Open.

The Import Wizard appears.

5. On the Welcome page, click Next.

6. On the Data Type page, click Project Excel Template and then click Next.

7. On the Import Mode page, specify whether you want to import the file as a new project, append the resources to the currently active project, or merge the data into the active project.

8. Click the Finish button.

The new project opens with all the data populated from the template (see Figure 17-17).

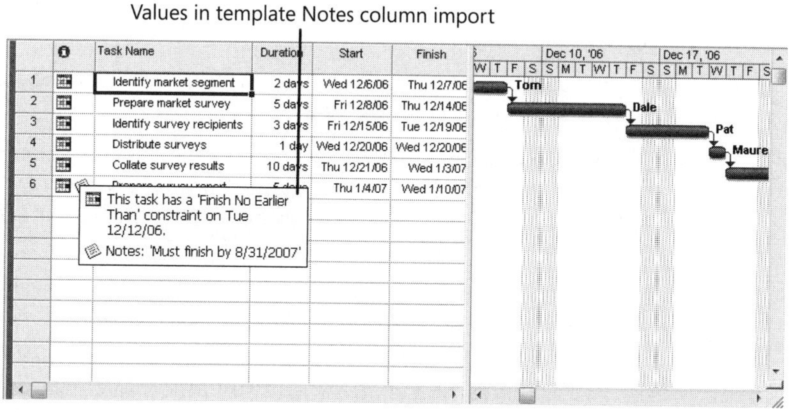

Figure 17-17 Using the template, you can import the project information from Excel to Microsoft Project without having to map individual fields.

Importing from Excel Without a Template

If you or your team members created an Excel workbook containing project information before you knew of the existence of the templates, you can still import Excel worksheets. The only difference is that you must map the columns in the workbook to fields in Microsoft Project, so your information imports to the appropriate fields.

To do this, follow these steps:

1. On the Standard toolbar in Microsoft Project, click Open.

2. Go to the location on your computer or network where the Excel workbook is saved.

3. In the Files Of Type list, click Microsoft Excel Workbooks.

   The workbook appears in the list of folders and files.

4. Click the workbook file and then click Open.

   The Import Wizard appears.

5. Read the Welcome page and then click Next.

6. On the Data Type page, select Only Selected Data and then click Next.

7. On the Map page, select New Map and then click Next.

> **Note**
>
> If you are a veteran data importer, you might have maps that you created in the past. If the Excel workbook you want to import conforms to the settings in an existing map, select Use Existing Map and then click Next. On the Map Selection page, select the name of the map you want to use and click Next.

8. On the Import Mode page, specify whether you want to import the file as a new project, append the resources to the currently active project, or merge the data into the active project. Click Next.

9. On the Map Options page, select the types of data you want to import. You can select one or more types depending on what you want to import. If your workbook file includes column headings, select the Import Includes Headers check box. Click Next.

10. On the Mapping page, under Source Worksheet Name, select the sheet that contains the data you're importing, even if it's just **Sheet1**.

    The fields from the selected Excel sheet appear in the From: Excel Field column. If there is an obvious match to a Microsoft Project field, it appears in the To: Microsoft Office Project Field column. If Microsoft Project cannot identify a matching field, the field name appears as **(Not Mapped)**.

11. For any fields that are not mapped, click the box and select the Microsoft Project field in which you want to store the corresponding imported field. Scroll through the entire table and make sure that all the Excel fields you want to import are mapped to a Microsoft Project field.

The Preview area shows a sample of how your table data is mapped (see Figure 17-18).

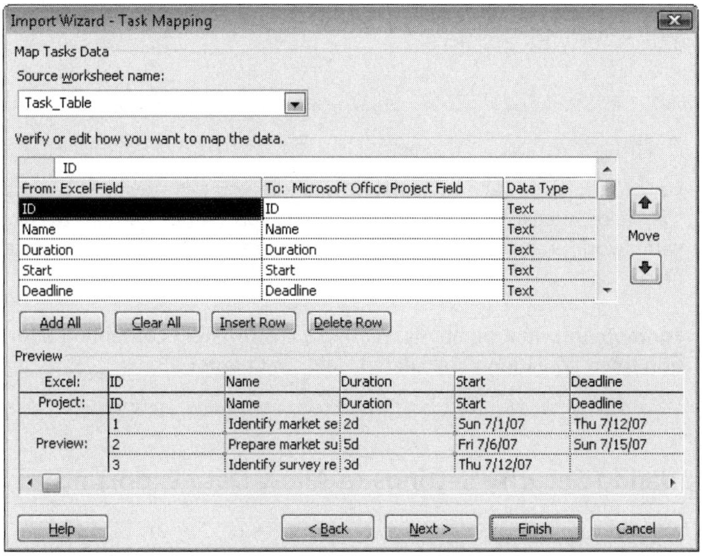

Figure 17-18 Use the Mapping page to match columns in an Excel worksheet with the corresponding Microsoft Project fields.

12. If, on the Map Options page, you selected multiple types of data to import (for example, Tasks and Resources), click Next to proceed to the Mapping page for the next data type. Repeat steps 10 and 11 for that data type.

You can potentially work through a Task Mapping, Resource Mapping, and Assignment Mapping page.

13. When finished mapping, click Next.

14. On the End Of Map Definition page, click Save Map if you want to save the map for future use.

In the Save Map dialog box, in the Map Name box, type a name for the map and then click Save.

15. Click Finish.

Microsoft Project creates a new project file if you specified that and imports the data from the workbook into the fields you specified.

Chapter 17

Exporting from Microsoft Project to Excel

Suppose that your company's accounting department wants to analyze your project cost information in conjunction with those of other projects taking place throughout the company. The department uses Excel to analyze project cost data, so you'll need to export your Microsoft Project information to an Excel workbook.

With the Export Wizard, you can export information you select or export key information from the entire project.

Calculating Project Information by Using Custom Formulas

For certain types of calculation and analysis, you can stay in Microsoft Project. With custom fields, such as Cost1 or Number3, you can set up formulas to calculate specified data within your project plan. The formula operates on the data in or related to your custom field.

For more information about creating a custom field containing a formula, see the section titled "Creating a Calculated Field" in Chapter 25.

Updating Security Settings to Allow Data Exporting

When you export data as an Excel file, it is saved as an Excel 5.0/95 workbook. However, new default security settings in Microsoft Project 2007 block the opening or saving of legacy or nondefault file formats.

Therefore, you cannot save an Excel export map until you have set your Microsoft Project security appropriately. To do this, follow these steps:

1. Click Tools, Options and then click the Security tab (see Figure 17-19).

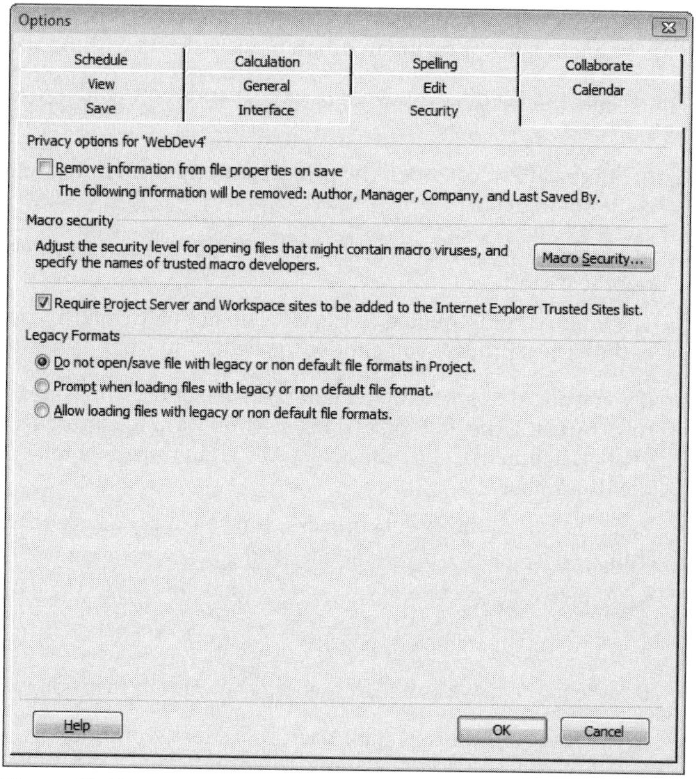

Figure 17-19 Use the Security tab to allow Microsoft Project to save your Excel export map.

2. Under Legacy Formats, select either the Prompt When Loading Files With Legacy Or Non Default File Format option (medium security) or the Allow Loading Files With Legacy Or Non Default File Formats option (low security).

Exporting Selected Data to Excel

Although you can export most information types from Microsoft Project to Excel, it's most useful to export numeric data for further analysis in Excel. *Numeric data* is any data that can be used in calculations and mathematical operations. Examples of such data include cost and work data. Work data (such as hours) can be converted to numeric fields, but it is stored in Microsoft Project as text because of the unit labels such as hours, days, or weeks. On the other hand, dates are not considered numeric data, even though they consist mostly of numbers.

When preparing to export information from Microsoft Project to Excel for numerical analysis, first decide which tasks, resources, and fields you want to export to Excel. You can export certain selected or filtered tasks or resources to Excel. You can export the same fields you see in a given table—such as the Earned Value, Cost, or Tracking table—or you can export just three or four fields that you select. You can export a large representation of all your project data with the different types of project, task, resource, and assignment data appearing in different worksheets within the Excel workbook.

To specify the project data you want to export and then send it to Excel, follow these steps:

1. In Microsoft Project, open the project plan that contains the project information you want to export.

2. Apply the view that contains the task, resource, or assignment information you want to export.

    The table or fields applied to the view do not matter at this point because as part of the export process you choose the fields you want.

3. If you want to export only certain tasks, resources, or assignments, select their rows by using the Shift or Ctrl keys. If you want to export all tasks, all resources, or all assignments, click the Select All cell in the upper-left cell in the view, above the ID number.

    Later, as part of the export process, you can apply a task or resource filter if you want.

4. Click File, Save As.

    The Save As dialog box appears.

5. Browse to the drive and folder where you want to save your information.

6. In the Save As Type list, click Microsoft Excel Workbook.

7. In the File Name box, enter a name for your new Excel file.

    By default, the project file name is adopted with the *XLS* extension.

8. Click Save.

9. On the Welcome page of the wizard, click Next.

10. On the Export Wizard – Data page, be sure that the Selected Data option is selected and then click Next.

11. On the Export Wizard – Map page, be sure that the New Map option is selected and then click Next.

12. On the Export Wizard – Map Options page, select the check box for each type of data you want to map and export: Tasks, Resources, or Assignments. Under Microsoft Office Excel Options, be sure that the Export Includes Headers check box is selected (see Figure 17-20). Click Next.

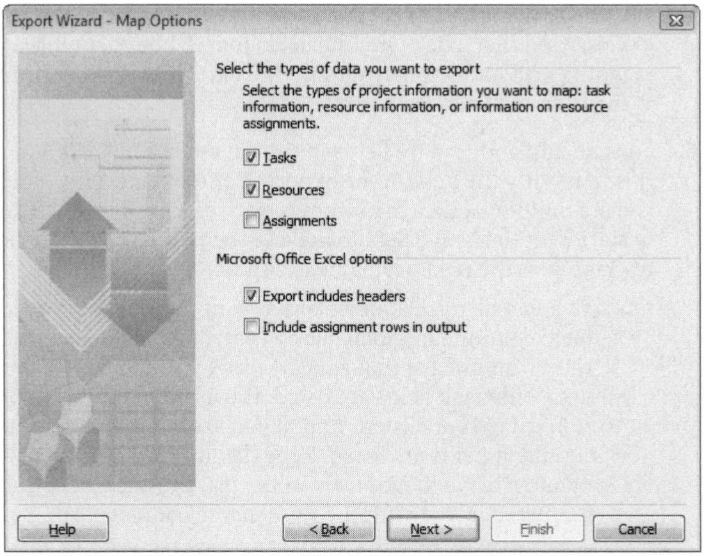

Figure 17-20 In the Export Wizard, select the type of data you're exporting to Excel.

13. On the Mapping page of the wizard, in the Destination Worksheet Name box, you can enter a name for the target worksheet within the workbook you're creating.

You can also just use the default name provided, for example, Task_Table1.

14. In the Export Filter box, click any filter you want to apply to the tasks or resources you're exporting.

15. If a particular Microsoft Project table—for example, the Entry table, the Cost table, or the Earned Value table—includes most or all of the fields you want to export, it's best to simply base the data mapping on that table. To do this, click the Base On Table button. The Select Base Table For Field Mapping dialog box appears (see Figure 17-21).

Figure 17-21 Select the Microsoft Project table that contains the fields you want to use as your export data source.

Click the Microsoft Project table you want to export (for example, Earned Value or Cost) and then click OK. The fields that define that table appear in the data mapping grid under Verify Or Edit Microsoft Project's Assumptions For How You Want To Import The Data.

16. You can add and remove fields in the data mapping grid one at a time as well. Do this to modify the fields to be exported or to create a list of fields from scratch. If you are building a data map from scratch rather than starting with a table, be sure to start with the Name field to include the task name, or the Resource Names field to make sure the resource name is exported.

❑ To add a field, click in a blank row in the From: Microsoft Office Project Field column, and then click the arrow that appears. Select the field you want from the list that appears (see Figure 17-22). If you are mapping tasks data, only task fields are listed. If you are mapping resource data, only resource fields are listed. And, if you are mapping assignment data, only assignment fields are listed. Type the first two or three characters of the field name to move to it quickly in the list. Press Enter or Tab, and the field name is entered, along with the Excel name counterpart.

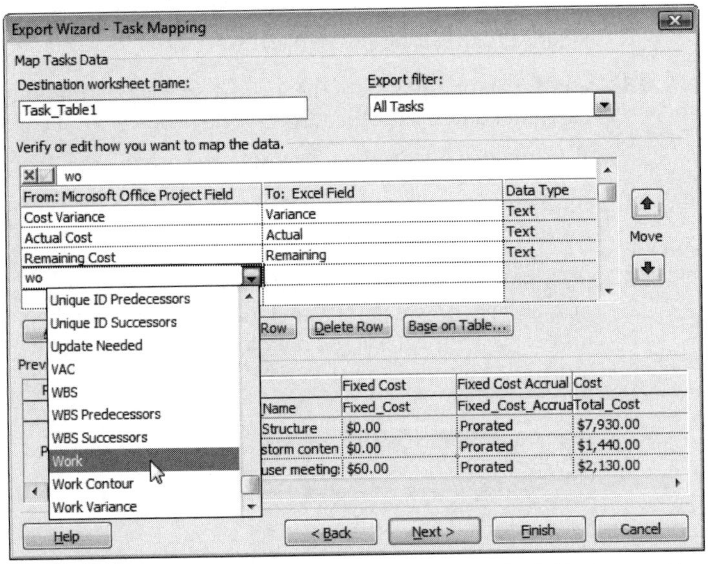

Figure 17-22 On the Mapping page, select the specific fields you want to export.

❑ To remove a field from the list, click the field name and then click Delete Row.

If you want to export just numeric project data, you can use this table to select only those fields containing numeric values. For example, you might select Name, Cost, and Duration.

17. In the table, specify how each field of data should be defined when it is exported to Excel.

As soon as you enter a field in the From column, its default equivalent appears in the To: Excel Field column, showing the name of the field as it will appear in the Excel workbook column heading (see Figure 17-23). You can change the Excel column heading here if you want (for example, from Baseline Cost to **Task Budget**).

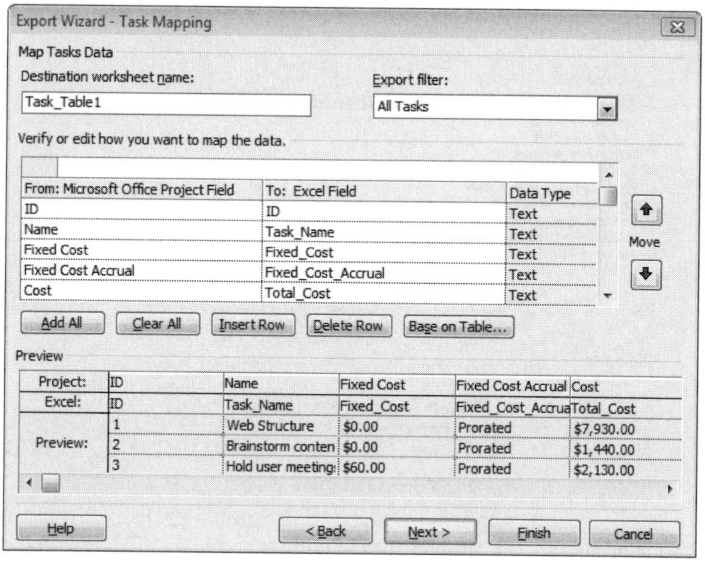

Figure 17-23 The Microsoft Project field, its Excel equivalent, and the data type as exported show in the table.

The Data Type column shows the data type of the field. Incidentally, this data comes in as Text fields, even though it might really be number, date, or currency fields in Microsoft Project. To simplify the export process, all fields are changed to text fields. Then you can easily convert the data type for any of these fields in Excel, which is especially important for numeric data on which you want to run calculations.

Use the Move up and down buttons to the right of the table to rearrange the order of the fields, which represents the order in which the columns will appear in Excel.

In the Preview area at the bottom of the Mapping page, a preview of the data shows how it will appear in Excel. Use the scroll bar to view all the columns.

18. When the map is the way you want, click Next.

19. If you had specified on the Map Options page that you want to export more than one type of data—tasks, resources, and assignments, for example—the Export Wizard – Resource Mapping page appears again for the next data type. Repeat steps 13–18 for that data type.

Each additional type of data will result in a separate worksheet in the Excel workbook.

When you have defined the data maps for each type of data, the Export Wizard – End Of Map Definition page appears.

20. If you expect to export this same information again, click the Save Map button. In the Save Map dialog box, give your map a name (see Figure 17-24). Click Save.

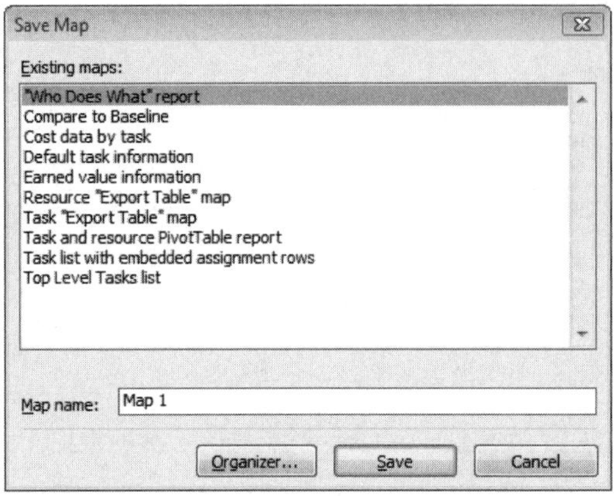

Figure 17-24 The Save Map dialog box shows all built-in export maps and any additional maps that you have created.

Your export map is now saved in the global project template (Global.mpt), so it's available in any project file on your system.

21. Click Finish.

Your specified project data is exported and saved as a complete Excel workbook in the Excel 97-2003 format and in the exact layout you defined.

TROUBLESHOOTING

You can't find a field you want in the Mapping table

The list of Microsoft Project fields changes depending on whether you're exporting tasks or resources. Tasks and resources have different fields associated with them.

Also, several earned value fields go by different names for the same calculation. Table 17-1 lists these name equivalents and the name you will find in the list of fields.

Table 17-1 Earned Value Field Names

If you want this earned value field	Select this equivalent
Budgeted At Completion (BAC)	Baseline Cost
Planned Value (PV)	Budgeted Cost Of Work Scheduled (BCWS)
Earned Value (EV)	Budgeted Cost Of Work Performed (BCWP)
Actual Cost (AC)	Actual Cost Of Work Performed (ACWP)

If you're looking for a Variance field, look for the specific type of variance—for example, Cost Variance or Earned Value CV (Cost Variance). There's also Work Variance, SV (Schedule Variance), and VAC (Variance At Completion).

TROUBLESHOOTING

Microsoft Project is not exporting to Excel because of security settings

You might define all your fields in the export map, only to click Finish, see a security error message, and lose all your mapping work.

Because of new default security settings in Microsoft Project 2007, you cannot save an export map until you have set your security to allow loading of files with legacy or non-default file formats. This is because Microsoft Project saves the Excel file to a Microsoft Excel 5.0/95 workbook to ensure that you can read the exported project data in whatever recent version of Excel you have installed on your computer.

To change your security setting, follow these steps:

1. Click Tools, Options and then click the Security tab.

2. Under Legacy Formats, select either the Prompt When Loading Files With Legacy Or Non Default File Format option (medium security) or the Allow Loading Files With Legacy Or Non Default File Formats option (low security).

To open and review your exported project data in Excel, follow these steps:

1. In Excel, click the Microsoft Office Button and then click Open.

2. In the Open dialog box, browse to the drive and folder in which you saved your exported Excel workbook.

3. Double-click the workbook.

   Your project data appears in the workbook, using the tasks (or resources or assignments), filter, and table or fields you selected in the export process (see Figure 17-25).

Chapter 17

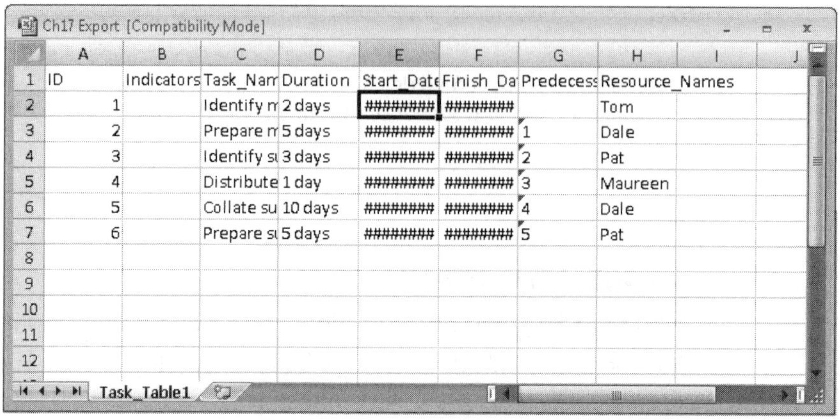

Figure 17-25 View and manipulate your project data in Excel.

4. Adjust columns, change data types, and do any additional reformatting needed. If you're analyzing numerical data, you can now set up the formulas or charts you want.

   Sometimes, Smart Tags appear on some cells, for example, when the export transfers numbers into fields formatted as text. Click a Smart Tag and, if necessary, click a command to correct an error.

5. Click the Microsoft Office Button and then click Save.

Change the Data Type in an Excel Column

After exporting your project information to Excel, if you need to, you can change the data type of a field of information from text, for example, to numbers. For example, Duration fields are exported as text. You can easily change that text to numbers so that you can run calculations on them.

In Excel, select the column heading. On the Home tab, in the Cells group, click Format and then click Format Cells. Click the Number tab if necessary. Under Category, select General, Number, or Currency, as appropriate (see Figure 17-26). Set any number attributes you want and then click OK.

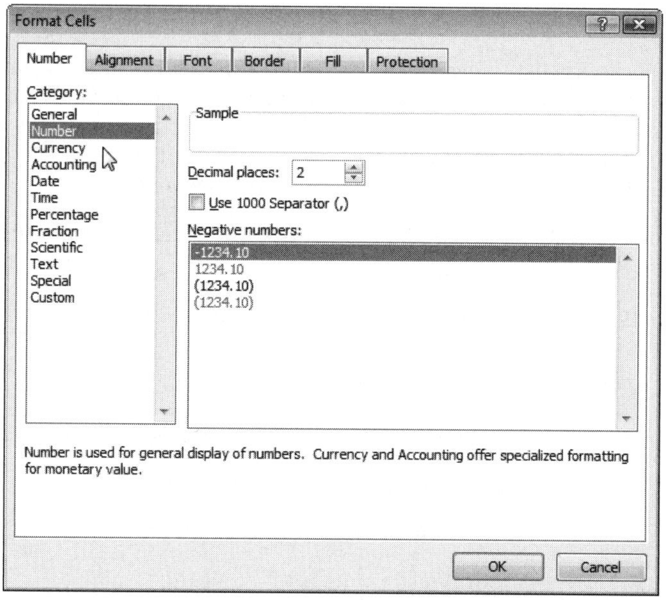

Figure 17-26 Use the Number tab in the Format Cells dialog box in Excel to change the data type or number format of a set of exported project fields.

Even though the Task Mapping page of the Microsoft Project Export Wizard says they're Text fields, currency fields (such as Cost and Actual Cost) and earned value currency fields (such as BCWS and VAC) are automatically formatted as currency in Excel.

INSIDE OUT   Overwrite Excel Format

Suppose that you changed information or formatting in your new Excel workbook that contains your exported project information, and now you're ready to save your changes. After you click the Save button, you might get a prompt asking whether you want to overwrite the older Excel format with the current format.

To ensure compatibility with older versions of Excel, Microsoft Project exports to the Microsoft Excel 5.0/Excel 95 file format. When you begin the process of saving the new Excel file the first time, Excel prompts you to update the format to the current version you have installed on your computer, which might be Excel 2003 or Excel 2007, for example.

Click Yes to update the workbook format, which ensures that you can use the latest features of your current Excel version on your exported project data.

Exporting Complete Project Data to Excel

Just as you can import information about tasks, resources, and assignments, the Export Wizard helps you export complete project information, organized by Task, Resource, and Assignment data types, which in turn are presented in their own separate worksheets in a single Excel workbook. However, this export procedure does not export timephased information, such as resource usage over time.

To create a complete Excel workbook of project information from your project file, follow these steps:

1. In Microsoft Project, open the project whose complete information you want to export to Excel.
2. Click File, Save As.
3. Browse to the drive and folder where you want to save your information.
4. In the Save As Type list, click Microsoft Excel Workbook.
5. In the File Name box, enter a name for the Excel file and then click Save.
6. In the Export Wizard Welcome page, click Next.
7. In the Export Wizard – Data page, click Project Excel Template and then click Finish.

   Your data is saved as an Excel workbook in the Excel 97-2003 format.

To open and review your exported project data in Excel, follow these steps:

1. In Excel, open the Excel file.

   The workbook contains four worksheets of discrete information: Task_Table, Resource_Table, Assignment_Table, and Info_Table (see Figure 17-27). Info_Table provides general instructions for using this workbook.

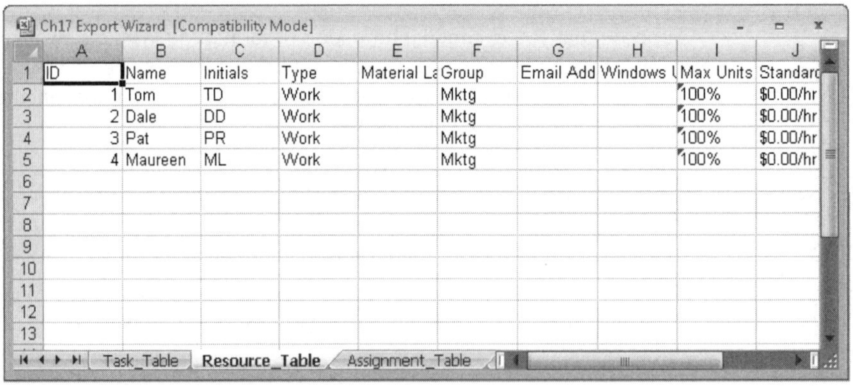
Ch17 Export Wizard [Compatibility Mode]

	A	B	C	D	E	F	G	H	I	J
1	ID	Name	Initials	Type	Material La	Group	Email Add	Windows U	Max Units	Standard
2	1	Tom	TD	Work		Mktg			100%	$0.00/hr
3	2	Dale	DD	Work		Mktg			100%	$0.00/hr
4	3	Pat	PR	Work		Mktg			100%	$0.00/hr
5	4	Maureen	ML	Work		Mktg			100%	$0.00/hr
6										
7										
8										
9										
10										
11										
12										
13										

Task_Table | Resource_Table | Assignment_Table

Figure 17-27 By exporting tasks, resources, and assignments to Excel, separate worksheets are created to hold key task, resource, and assignment information from the selected project.

2. Resize and reformat the date fields as necessary.

3. Click the Microsoft Office Button and then click Save.

> **Note**
>
> When you export date fields from Microsoft Project to Excel, the Excel date fields also include the time. If you prefer, you can change the Excel date format. To do this, first click the column headings for the date fields. On the Home tab, in the Cells group, click Format and then click Format Cells. In the Format Cells dialog box, click the Number tab if necessary. Under Category, click Date. Click the date format you prefer and then click OK.

Re-Using a Previously Saved Export Map

If you frequently use the same Microsoft Project data in Excel to, for example, run a monthly report, you would benefit from saving the export map and re-using it each time, rather than having to re-create it each time you need it. At the end of the export map definition step in the export data process, you click the Save Map button and give your map a name. Then you can call the map up in the future when you need to export the same Microsoft Project fields again. To do this, follow these steps:

1. Open the project that contains the data you want to export with your saved export map.

2. If you want to export only certain tasks, resources, or assignments, use the Shift or Ctrl keys to select their rows. If you want to export all tasks, all resources, or all assignments, click the Select All cell in the upper-left cell in the view, above the ID number.

3. Click File, Save As.

The Save As dialog box appears.

4. Browse to the drive and folder where you want to save your information.

5. In the Save As Type box, select Microsoft Excel Workbook.

6. In the File Name box, enter a name for your new Excel file.

By default, the project file name is adopted with the *XLS* extension.

7. Click Save.

The first page of the Export Wizard appears.

8. On the Welcome page of the wizard, click Next.

9. On the Export Wizard – Data page, be sure that the Selected Data option is selected. Click Next.

10. On the Export Wizard – Map page, select Use Existing Map. Click Next.

11. In the Export Wizard – Map Selection page, click your export map from the list (see Figure 17-28).

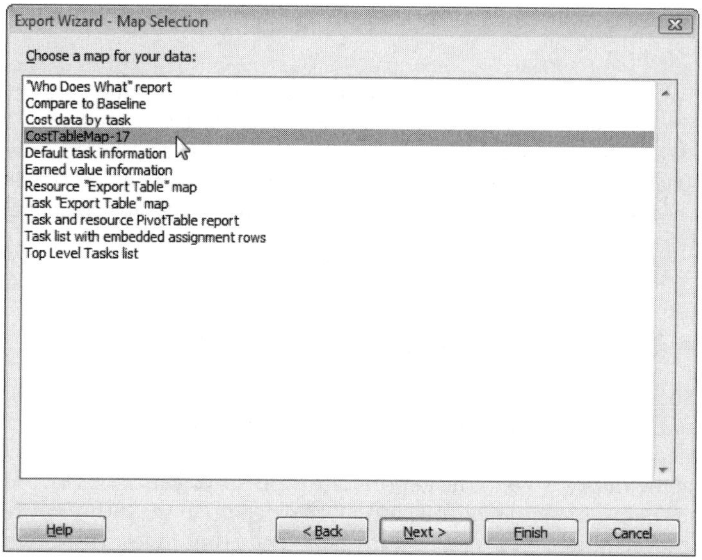

Figure 17-28 The Export Wizard – Map Selection page lists built-in export maps as well as any export maps you have previously saved.

12. Click Next.

The Export Wizard – Map Options page appears with selections as defined by your saved export map.

13. Click Next.

The Export Wizard – Task Mapping page appears with the fields already defined as you had saved them.

14. Click Finish.

Your project data is exported as an Excel file.

Producing a Visual Report of Project Data in Excel

Visual reports are new in Microsoft Office Project 2007 and are easy-to-build report templates that use Microsoft Office Excel 2003 or later (as well as Microsoft Office Visio Professional 2007) to transform Microsoft Project task, resource, and assignment information into charts and graphs that communicate your project information more effectively. For example, in earlier versions of Microsoft Project, displaying an Excel graph of earned value required special toolbars and numerous steps to produce the earned value status you wanted. In Microsoft Project 2007, you simply choose the Earned Value Over Time report, and the graph appears in Excel.

When you first start generating an Excel visual report, Microsoft Project gathers the information requested for the selected template and stores it in a database. Then, the visual report template calls on an Excel template to generate the report in an Excel PivotChart. Unlike Microsoft Project's text-based reports, once data is set up for a visual report, you can configure the report to examine different fields over different time periods without generating a brand new report each time. For example, you could begin by analyzing cost overruns for each fiscal quarter and then drill down to view overruns by each week of the project. In addition, you can add, remove, or rearrange the fields you want to analyze.

You can modify existing visual reports or create your own report templates to do exactly what you want. You can use them on your own projects as well as publish them for other team members or project managers to use.

What Are PivotTables?

A powerful method for analyzing project data in Excel is to use *crosstab tables* of information, which are tabular presentations of intersecting information along vertical and horizontal fields of information. In Excel, these crosstabs are known as *PivotTables*. PivotTables are a flexible way to reorganize data in comparative form, with one category of information being filtered and populated into another category of information.

For example, you can use an Excel PivotTable to analyze information regarding the relative cost performance of different groups of team members and to also see how that performance varies according to the different phases of your project.

You can use one of two methods to export Microsoft Project data to an Excel PivotTable: You can create a visual report template, or you can create an export map to an Excel PivotTable file. They both create PivotTables, although a visual report creates a PivotTable that's linked to an OLAP cube file. Using an export map creates a PivotTable that contains the data from your Microsoft Project file.

To create a visual report template that sets up an Excel PivotTable you can then configure, see the section titled "Creating and Editing Visual Report Templates in Excel" later in this chapter.

Generating a Visual Report from a Built-In Template

Unlike the text reports that are available in Microsoft Project 2007 and in earlier versions, visual reports transfer data to Excel and use Excel's PivotTable feature to categorize and collate results. For example, suppose the executives on your project selection team ask to see cash flow by quarter for potential projects. Rather than use the text report of cash flow, which displays values for cash spent by time period, the Visual Cash Flow report generates an Excel chart that shows cash flows by quarter more clearly, as illustrated in Figure 17-29.

Chapter 17

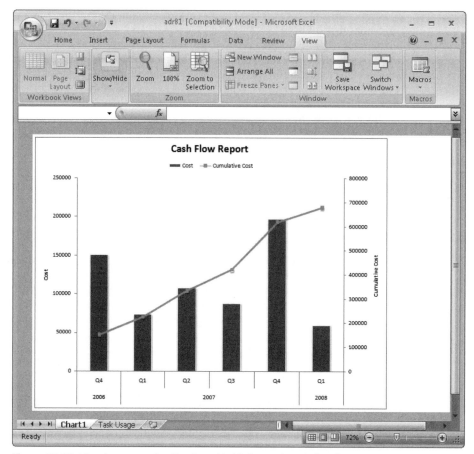

Figure 17-29 Visual reports using Excel can highlight results graphically.

To generate a built-in visual report, do the following:

1. In Microsoft Project, click Reports, Visual Reports.

2. To view only those visual report templates that use Excel, clear the Microsoft Office Visio check box and be sure to select the Microsoft Office Excel check box.

3. To view all the visual report templates that come with Microsoft Project, regardless of the category to which they belong, click the All tab (see Figure 17-30).

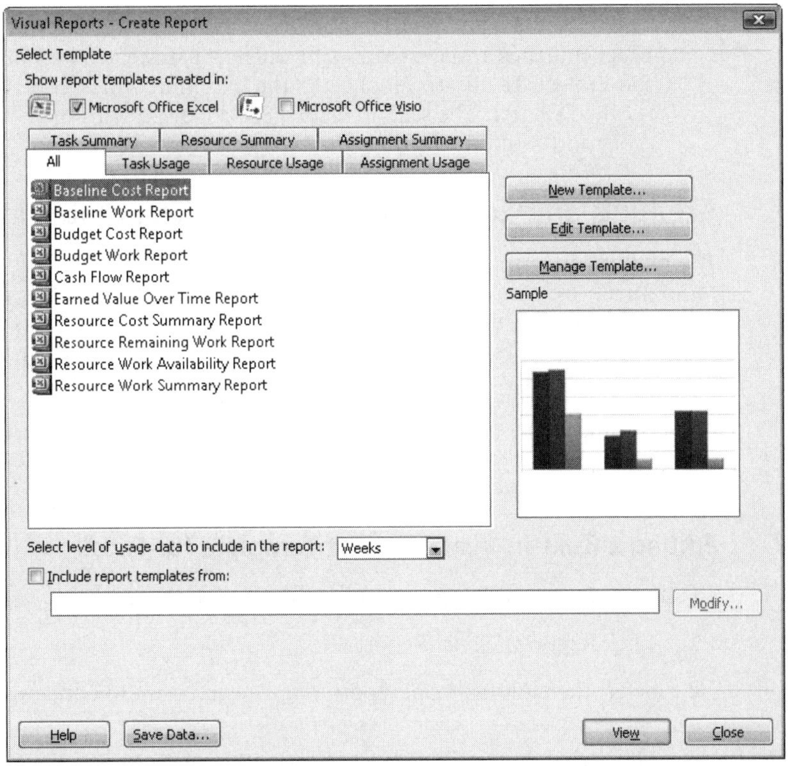

Figure 17-30 Specify whether you want to see report templates based on Excel or Visio and then select the report you want to generate.

Unless you create numerous custom visual report templates, it's easy to find the reports you want on the All tab. However, if the list of reports grows unwieldy, select a category tab to see only the reports in that category. For example, the Task Usage category includes the Cash Flow Report template, whereas the Assignment Usage category includes templates for reporting baseline and budgeted costs and work as well as earned value over time.

4. To specify the level of detail that Microsoft Project transfers to Excel, click a time period (Days, Weeks, Months, Quarters, or Years) in the Select Level Of Usage Data To Include In The Report box.

For projects with shorter durations, choose Days or Weeks. If a project spans a year or more, consider using Months, Quarters, or even Years.

> **Note**
> If you want to save an OLAP (Online Analytical Processing) cube that contains the data for the report, click Save Data. This can save you time generating additional reports because Microsoft Project doesn't have to gather the reporting data required or transfer it to Excel.

5. To generate the report, click View.

Excel launches and generates a PivotChart using the data transferred from Microsoft Project. The first worksheet in the Excel file, which contains the PivotChart, is called Chart1. The second worksheet is labeled with the name of the report category and contains the data for the report.

Creating and Editing Visual Report Templates in Excel

The built-in visual report templates cover many of the project status and performance topics that project managers need, such as baseline cost and work, cash flow, earned value, and resource availability. If none of the built-in reports do exactly what you want, you can edit a template to fit your requirements or create a new custom template.

Because visual reports use Excel PivotCharts or Visio Pivot Diagrams to do the heavy report lifting, visual report templates are either Excel or Visio templates. Whether you edit a built-in template or create your own, you specify the fields you want to work with and the type of data on which you want to report.

Editing a Built-In Visual Report Template for Excel

To edit a built-in visual report template, do the following:

1. Click Reports, Visual Reports.

2. Select the built-in visual report template you want to edit and then click Edit Template.

The Visual Reports Field Picker dialog box appears (see Figure 17-31).

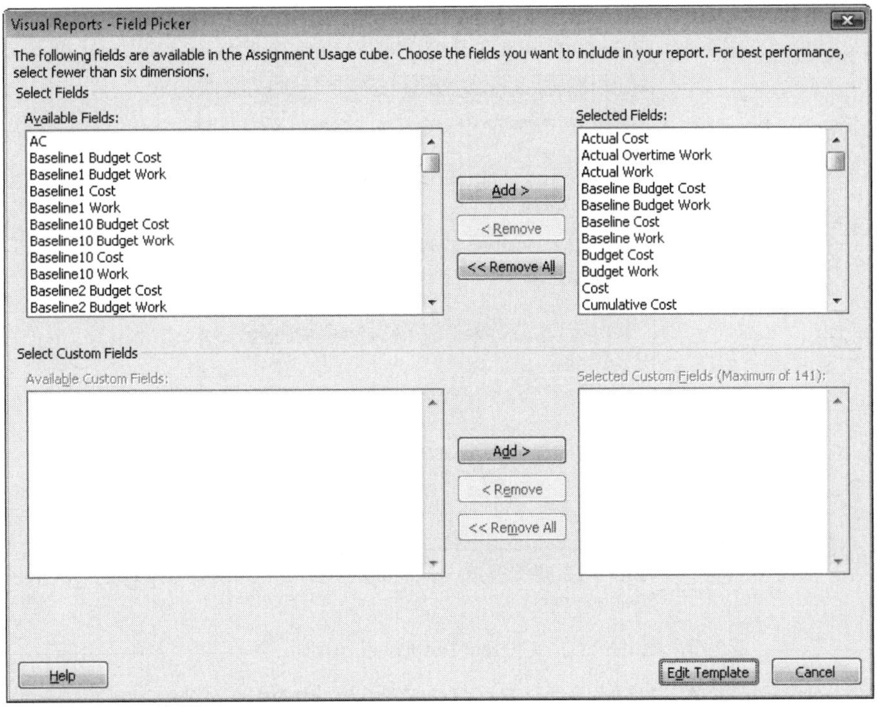

Figure 17-31 You can specify the Microsoft Project fields to include in the data cube for a visual report.

3. To add fields to the OLAP cube for the visual report, in the Available Fields list, select the fields you want and then click Add.

   The fields appear in the Selected Fields list. Remove fields from the Selected Fields list by selecting the ones you want to remove and then clicking Remove. You can select multiple fields to add or remove by holding the Ctrl key and clicking the fields.

4. Click the Edit Template button.

   Microsoft Project builds the OLAP cube based on the fields you selected. Excel launches using the built-in Excel template.

5. Make the changes you want to the settings in Excel and then save the Excel template.

Creating a New Visual Report Template for Excel

To create an Excel visual report template from scratch, do the following:

1. Click Reports, Visual Reports.

2. Click New Template.

Chapter 17

The Visual Reports New Template dialog box appears with the three basic selections you must make to build a template (see Figure 17-32).

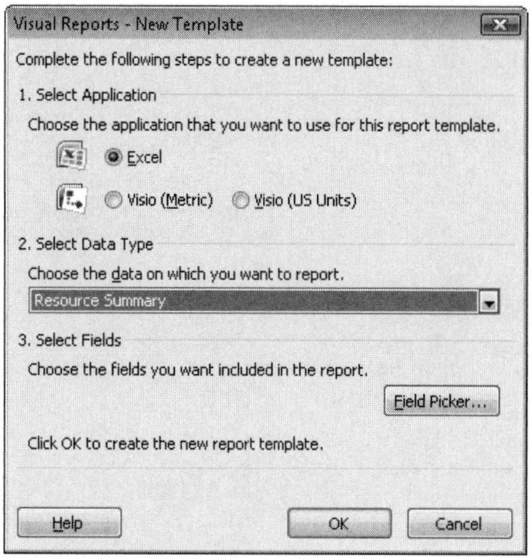

Figure 17-32 When you create a new visual report template, you must specify only a few basic elements.

3. If necessary, select the Excel option.

4. Under Select Data Type, choose the type of data you want to use as the basis for your report.

   Visual reports are based on six different sets of information: Task Summary, Task Usage, Resource Summary, Resource Usage, Assignment Summary, and Assignment Usage. These data types determine the fields that Microsoft Project adds to the OLAP cube, but you can add or remove fields as well.

5. To modify the fields for the template, click Field Picker and add or remove fields in the Available Fields list.

   ❑ To add fields to the new visual report's OLAP cube, select the fields you want in the Available Fields list and then click Add.

   ❑ To remove fields from the Selected Fields list, select the fields and then click Remove.

6. Click OK in the Visual Reports – Field Picker dialog box and then click OK in the Visual Reports – New Template dialog box.

   Excel launches and opens a blank PivotChart (see Figure 17-33).

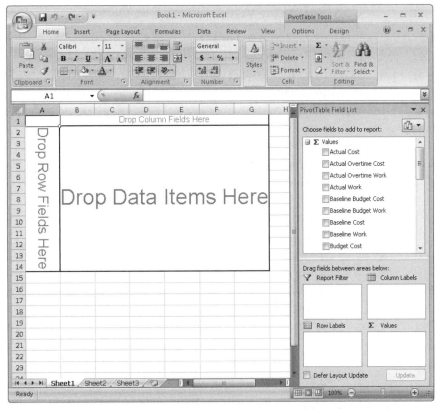

Figure 17-33 Drag fields onto the PivotTable or into the PivotTable configuration boxes to build your report.

7. To build the PivotTable, drag the field you want to use for rows in the table to the area labeled Drop Row Fields here. For example, to produce a resource report, drag the Resources field. Drag the field that you want to use for columns to the area labeled Drop Column Fields here, such as a time period for an earned value report.

8. Drag the Microsoft Project fields on which you want to report to the area labeled Drop Data Items Here.

9. When finished configuring the PivotTable, click the Microsoft Office Button and then click Save. In the Save As dialog box, make sure that the template is being saved to the folder where all the other templates are located. By default, this is in the \Users\username\AppData\Roaming\Microsoft\Templates\1033 folder.

Saving the template in this folder ensures that the template will appear in the Visual Reports – Create Reports dialog box.

10. If you'd rather save your custom template in another location, you can still make it appear in the Visual Reports dialog box. In that dialog box, select the Include Reports Template From check box and click Modify to specify the path that contains your custom templates.

Configuring a Visual Report in Excel

When Excel is open and displays one of your visual reports, you can use Excel PivotTable tools to configure what you see in the report. For example, you can change the time periods you see, add or remove fields in the chart, or display additional calculations.

Use one or more of the following techniques to change a visual report:

- To control the totals that appear in the chart, click the tab for the data worksheet, such as Task Usage for the Cash Flow Report, and then expand or collapse the groupings in the table.

  When data in the worksheet is collapsed as it is by default, you see plus signs to the left of collapsed groupings. For example, for a time-based report, Q1, Q2, Q3, and Q4 for each year are collapsed, but the years are expanded (indicated by a minus sign to the left). To show more detail for some or all of the report, click the plus sign next to the group you want to expand (see Figure 17-34).

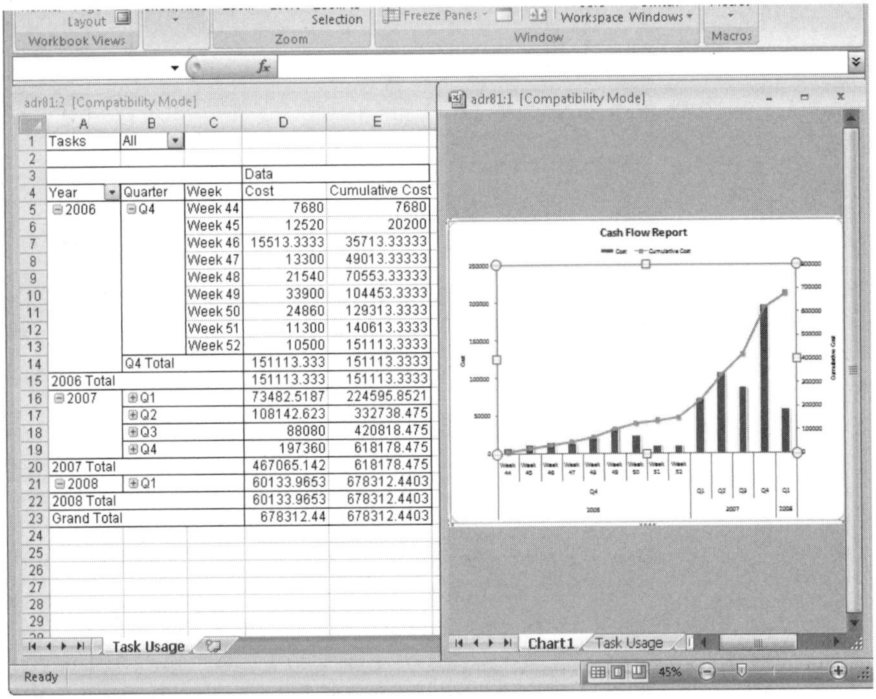

Figure 17-34 Expanding or collapsing time periods or other groups on the data worksheet controls the time periods or groups that appear in a visual report.

- To add fields within the chart, in the PivotTable Field list, select the check box for the field you want to add.

  To remove a field, clear its check box.

- To filter the tasks, resources, or assignments included in the report, in the worksheet, click the down arrow in the first row. Expand the dropdown list to the level you want to see and then select the items you want to include (see Figure 17-35).

Figure 17-35 Select the tasks, resources, or assignments you want the report to include.

- To change the calculation that appears in the chart, in the $\sum$ Values section, right click a field and then click Value Field Settings. In the Value Fields Settings dialog box, in the Summarize Value Field By list, click the type of calculation you want, such as the sum, average, minimum value, maximum value, and so on.

CHAPTER 18

Integrating Microsoft Project with Microsoft Outlook

Exchanging Task Information with Outlook **639**

Building Your Resource List with Outlook **643**

Sending Project File Information **644**

Microsoft Office Project 2007 and Microsoft Office Outlook 2007 are partners well-suited for one another. An Office Project 2007 plan is made up of tasks, and Office Outlook includes the Tasks list. Microsoft Project schedules when tasks should be started and finished; Outlook has its Calendar. You use Microsoft Project to set up resource information; Outlook has its Address Book listing information about people in your organization and beyond. You need to communicate project information with team members and other stakeholders; Outlook can send messages and files to these people.

When you use Microsoft Project and Outlook together, you can do the following:

- Add tasks from your Outlook Tasks list to your Microsoft Project plan

- Add resource information to your project plan from your Outlook address book

- Send or route an entire project file to others

- Publish a project file to an Exchange folder

Some of these techniques work only with Outlook. With other techniques, you can use any 32-bit Messaging Application Programming Interface (MAPI)–based e-mail system. These distinctions are made throughout the chapter.

Exchanging Task Information with Outlook

You can bring tasks into your project plan from your Outlook Tasks list. You can also copy a task from your project plan and add it as a task in your Outlook To-Do List.

Integrate Project Web Access Tasks with Outlook

If you're working in an enterprise project management environment with Microsoft Office Project Professional 2007 and Microsoft Office Project Server 2007, your team members can bring nonproject tasks from their Outlook Calendar into their task list in Microsoft Office Project Web Access. This process works the other way as well: Team members can send assigned tasks from Office Project Web Access to their Outlook Calendar and work with them there.

For more information about how team members using Project Web Access in an enterprise environment can integrate their Outlook calendar with their assigned tasks, see the section titled "Working with Project Tasks in Your Outlook Calendar" in Chapter 23, "Participating on a Team Using Project Web Access."

Adding Outlook Tasks to Your Project Plan

You might have started brainstorming tasks for a new project in your Outlook Tasks list, and you're now ready to import them into Microsoft Project (see Figure 18-1).

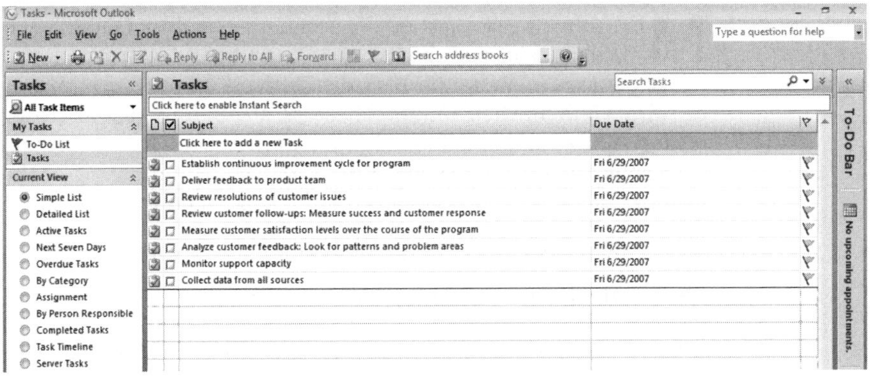

Figure 18-1 Tasks entered in your Outlook Tasks view can be imported to your project plan.

To import Outlook tasks into your project plan, follow these steps:

1. In Microsoft Office Project 2007, open the project plan in which you want to import the Outlook tasks.

2. Click Tools, Import Outlook Tasks.

3. If a security alert appears, click Allow.

    The Import Outlook Tasks dialog box appears (see Figure 18-2). Outlook does not necessarily need to be already running. However, at least one incomplete task must be present in your Outlook Tasks list. Any tasks marked complete in Outlook are not made available for import into Microsoft Project.

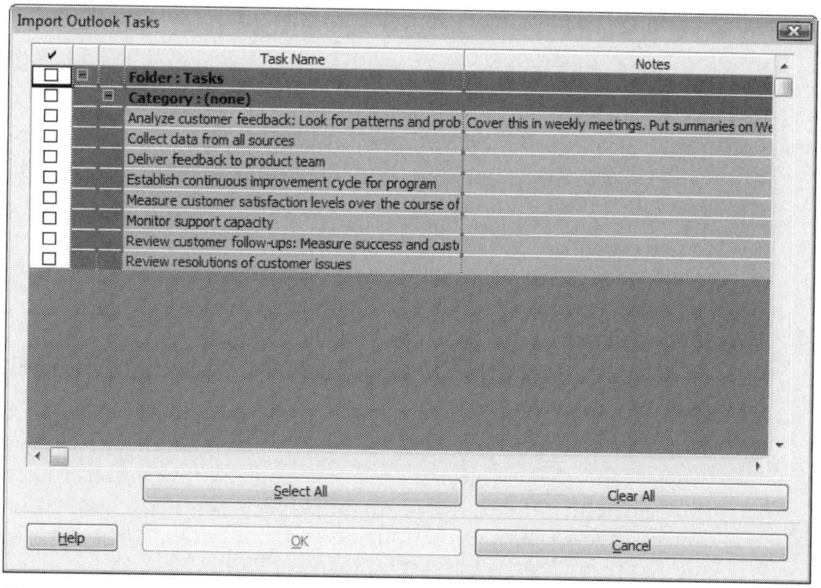

Figure 18-2 Use the Import Outlook Tasks dialog box to copy tasks from Outlook to your project plan.

4. Select the check box for each task you want to import. Click the Select All button to select all tasks.

Items listed with the darker background are folders or summary tasks, and you might not want to import them. If the same tasks are saved in multiple folders, be careful to select just one instance of the task for import. Clear the check box for any Outlook tasks not relevant to your project plan.

5. After selecting the tasks you want, click OK.

The tasks you selected are appended after the last task in your project plan (see Figure 18-3).

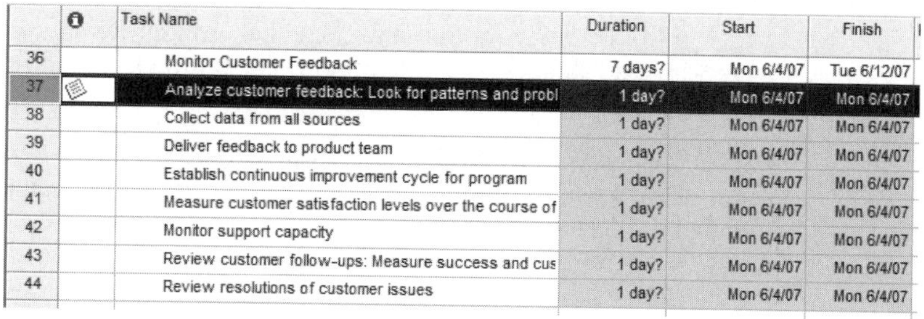

Figure 18-3 The selected Outlook tasks and associated notes are appended to the current project plan.

The imported Outlook tasks have the following characteristics:

Note

- Any notes entered in Outlook become task notes. Double-click the Note icon in the indicator column to review the note.

- Durations entered in Outlook are not copied into Microsoft Project. The imported Outlook tasks revert to the default estimated duration of 1 day.

- The start date of all imported tasks adopts the project start date, with the ASAP constraint.

- There are no links, predecessors, or assigned resources.

Adding Microsoft Project Tasks to Outlook Tasks

Although adding Outlook tasks to your project plan can help you track tasks necessary to your project, going the other direction—that is, adding key project tasks from your project plan to your Outlook Tasks list—can also be a big advantage. Adding such tasks can be helpful if there are certain tasks that you want to keep a closer eye on, for example, critical tasks or milestone tasks. Or, they might be tasks that you're assigned to, and you're tracking your own tasks in Outlook.

New in Project 2007 is the ability to send several tasks and some of their associated information to your Outlook Tasks list by using the new Set Reminder button on the Tracking toolbar. To do this, follow these steps:

1. Open the project plan that contains the tasks you want to track in Outlook.

2. Select the tasks you want to send to Outlook.

   Drag to select multiple adjacent resources or hold down the **Ctrl** key to select multiple nonadjacent resources.

3. Show the Tracking toolbar by clicking View, Toolbars, Tracking.

4. On the Tracking toolbar, click Set Reminder.

   If the Set Reminder button is not showing, click Toolbar Options at the far right edge of the Tracking toolbar and then click Add Or Remove Buttons. Point to Tracking and then click Set Reminder. The button is added to the Tracking toolbar and the Set Reminder dialog box appears.

Set Reminder

5. Specify when you want the reminder to alert you. You can set the reminder for a number of minutes, hours, days, or other period of time before the start or finish date of the selected tasks.

6. Click OK.

   The selected tasks are added to your Tasks list in Outlook. The start date, reminder time, and due date (finish date) are included.

Another way to add project tasks to Outlook is to use the Copy and Paste commands. However, you can only copy the task name, and you have to copy the tasks one at a time. To copy and paste a task name to your Outlook task list, follow these steps:

1. In your project plan, display a task view such as Gantt Chart.

2. Select the name of the task you want to copy to Outlook.

   You can copy and paste only one task at a time from your project plan to Outlook. Also, it's best to only select the task name. If you select multiple fields, the information is all pasted together in the task's Subject field in Outlook.

3. On the Standard toolbar, click Copy.

Copy

4. Switch to Outlook and display the Tasks view or the To-Do List.

5. Click in the Subject entry box labeled Click Here To Add A New Task.

6. Click Edit, Paste.

   The copied task from your project plan appears in the box (see Figure 18-4).

	Tasks
	Click here to enable Instant Search
☐ ☑	Subject
☐	Acquire executive sign-off on plan and budget
☐	Establish continuous improvement cycle for program
☐	Deliver feedback to product team
☐	Review resolutions of customer issues
☐	Review customer follow-ups: Measure success and customer response
☐	Measure customer satisfaction levels over the course of the program
☐	Analyze customer feedback: Look for patterns and problem areas
☐	Monitor support capacity
☐	Collect data from all sources

Figure 18-4 Use Copy and Paste to add a project task to Outlook.

7. Press Enter.

   The task is added to the Tasks list.

8. Repeat steps 2–7 for any additional tasks you want to copy to Outlook.

Building Your Resource List with Outlook

You can quickly and accurately add resource names and e-mail addresses to your project plan by pulling them into your project plan from your Outlook Address Book or Contacts list.

> **Note**
>
> If you're set up for enterprise project management using Office Project Professional 2007 and Office Project Server 2007, don't use the Outlook Address Book or Contacts list to build your resource list. Use the enterprise resource pool instead.

To import resource names from Outlook into your project plan, follow these steps:

1. In Microsoft Office Project 2007, open the project to which you want to add resources from Outlook.

2. Click View, Resource Sheet. Select the row in which you want the new resources to start being added.

3. Click Insert, New Resource From, Address Book. The Select Resources dialog box appears (see Figure 18-5). Under Address Book, select Outlook Address Book, Contacts, or any other folder where you might have the resources you need stored.

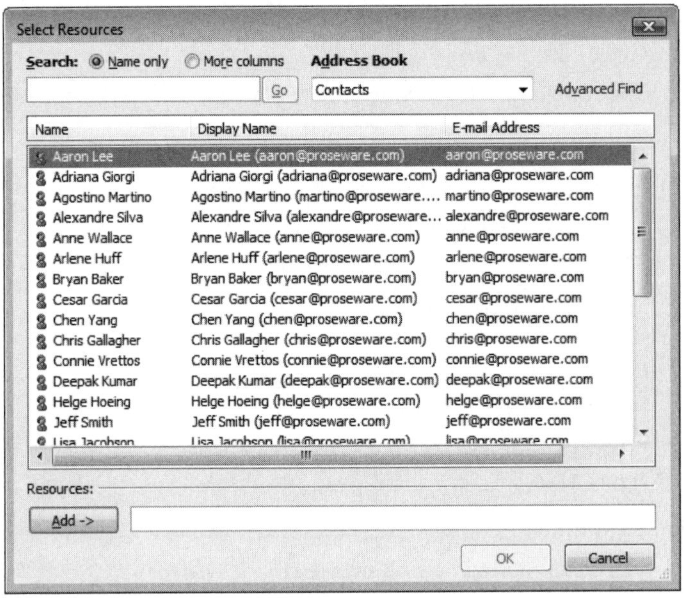

Figure 18-5 Use the Select Resources dialog box to select resources from your e-mail address book.

4. Select the names of resources you want to add to your project. Drag to select multiple adjacent resources or hold down the **Ctrl** key to select multiple nonadjacent resources.

5. Click the Add button and then click OK.

The selected resources are added to your project and listed in the Resource Sheet.

Sending Project File Information

You can send information from your project file to others using Outlook or any other MAPI-based e-mail system, including Microsoft Exchange, Microsoft Mail, Novell GroupWise, Eudora, or Lotus Notes. You can send project file information in the following ways:

- Send the entire project file as an attachment.

- Send a selected set of tasks or resources as a Microsoft Project file attachment.

- Send a set of tasks or resources as a picture to a set of predefined recipients.

- Route a project file to a group of recipients to obtain their input.

- Publish a project file to a Microsoft Exchange public folder.

Sending an Entire Project File

You can quickly send an entire file to selected recipients directly from within your project file. To do this, follow these steps:

1. In Microsoft Office Project 2007, open the project file you want to send.

2. Click File, Send To, Mail Recipient (As Attachment).

Your MAPI e-mail application is launched, if necessary. The new e-mail message form appears, showing your project file already attached and the name of the project in the Subject field.

3. In the To box (and Cc box, if necessary), add the e-mail addresses of the recipients.

4. In the message area, add any necessary comments regarding the project file.

Your resulting e-mail message should look similar to the example in Figure 18-6).

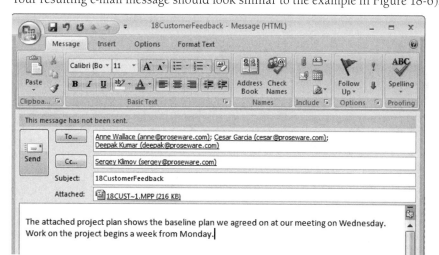

Figure 18-6 Quickly send the project file as an e-mail attachment.

5. Click the Send button.

Your message and the attached project file are sent to the specified recipients.

Chapter 18

Send a Project File to Predefined Recipients

You can also send the project file by clicking File, Send To, Mail Recipient (As Schedule Note). Under Attach, select the File check box. Clear the Picture Of Selected Tasks check box. Under Address Message To, specify the group of recipients associated either with the entire project or the currently selected tasks.

If you're using a non-MAPI e-mail program, you can still send a project file as an attachment. You just can't do so from within Microsoft Project. Start your e-mail program, select the attachment function, and then select the Microsoft Project file.

Sending Selected Tasks or Resources

Note

You can send a schedule note if you're using Outlook or any other 32-bit MAPI-based e-mail program.

You can send a picture of selected tasks or resources in any given view to the assigned resources and other associated contacts by using the Send Schedule Note dialog box. Send a Schedule Note when you want to do the following:

- Send information about critical tasks to the assigned resources.

- Send information about tasks leading up to a major milestone to the assigned resources.

- Ask assigned resources about progress on late tasks.

- Ask assigned resources to report on the status of current tasks.

- Alert contacts in human resources, procurement, or accounting about their responsibilities related to a set of resources.

- Report current status of selected tasks to a managing stakeholder.

To send a schedule note, do the following:

1. In Micrsoft Office Project 2007, open the project file that contains the information you want to send.

2. Display the view, including the table and fields, you want to send.

3. Select the tasks or resources whose information you want to send.

4. Click File, Send To, Mail Recipient (As Schedule Note).

The Send Schedule Note dialog box appears (see Figure 18-7).

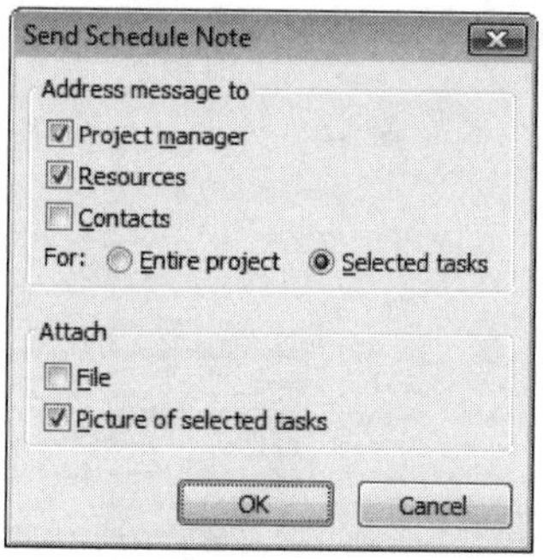

Figure 18-7 You can transmit selected project information with a schedule note.

5. Under Address Message To, select the Resources check box.

   The e-mail addresses for resources must be identified. This can be done by adding the Email Address field to the Resource Sheet or by entering it in the Resource Information dialog box.

   If you are using the Contacts field in a task view to include the e-mail addresses of stakeholders or other individuals associated with tasks, you can also select the Contacts check box to send a schedule note to them.

6. Under Attach, be sure that the Picture Of Selected Tasks check box is selected.

   If you also want to send the entire project file, select the File check box.

7. Click OK.

   Depending on the settings in your e-mail program or virus protection program, you might see a message specifying that an outside program is attempting to access your e-mail addresses. Specify that you do want to allow this. You might see this message for each recipient of your schedule note.

   Your MAPI e-mail application is launched, if necessary. The new e-mail message form appears with address information filled in and the title bar reflecting the name of the project file. The specified attachment is included. If you are sending a picture of selected tasks or resources, a BMP file is attached. If you are sending the entire project file, an MPP file is attached.

8. In the To and Cc boxes, add any additional recipients as necessary.

9. In the Subject box, enter a subject.

10. In the message area, type a message to inform your recipients of your intentions with the project attachments.

11. Click Send.

If your schedule note consists of a picture of selected tasks or resources, recipients can double-click the BMP attachment to open it (see Figure 18-8).

Chapter 18

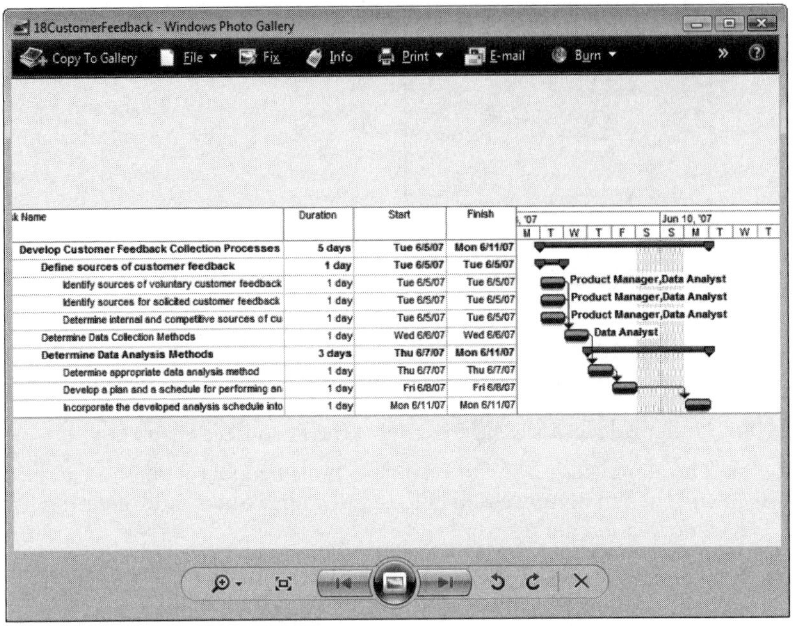

Figure 18-8 When recipients double-click a graphic attachment sent in a schedule note e-mail, the picture of selected tasks or resources appears.

If your schedule note consists of the project file, recipients can double-click the MPP attachment to open the project file, as long as they have Microsoft Project installed on their computer.

INSIDE OUT   Send filtered task lists

It would be nice to be able to e-mail a text report like the To-Do List to team members or a report like the Project Summary to your boss. But that capability is not available, for many of the same reasons that you can't save a report from a moment in time.

What you can do, however, is use your MAPI-compliant e-mail application to send selected tasks or selected resources from your project plan to your team members. Apply the Using Resource filter to see a list of tasks assigned to a particular resource. Apply the Summary Tasks or Critical Filter to see a list of high level tasks to send to your manager. You can then select those filtered tasks to be sent as an e-mail attachment.

For more information about filters, see the section titled "Filtering Project Information" in Chapter 4, "Viewing Project Information."

TROUBLESHOOTING

Only a fragment of the project file is being sent

Suppose that you're using the Send Schedule Note dialog box to send a project file, but only a few of the tasks or resources are showing up in the e- mail attachment.

When you select the Entire Project option in the Address Message To section, this refers to the recipients associated with the entire project. This does not indicate that the entire project is being sent.

Check the setting under Attached. By default, the Picture Of Selected Tasks check box is selected. If you want to send the entire project, select the File check box.

Routing a Project File

Note

You can route a project file if you're using Outlook or any other 32-bit MAPI-based e-mail program.

Sometimes you need specific information from certain individuals regarding the project plan. Maybe one team member is developing the task list, someone else is adding the resources, and someone else is assigning those resources to tasks. Or perhaps you want various leads to update progress on their segments of the project. One very effective way to give a comprehensive picture of your work is to route your project plan through e-mail to a list of individuals. You can specify whether your addressees receive your e-mail message one at a time or all at once. To route a project file, follow these steps:

1. In Microsoft Office Project 2007, open the project file you want to route.

2. Click File, Send To, Routing Recipient.

    The Routing Slip dialog box appears.

3. Click the Address button.

    The Address Book dialog box appears.

4. Click the names of the individuals you want on the distribution list and then click the To button. Click OK.

    Note that to open the project file, each individual on the distribution list must have access to Microsoft Project on their computer.

5. If you're routing the project one recipient at a time, use the Move buttons to designate the order of recipients by rearranging their names on the list.

Chapter 18

6. In the Subject field, change the subject if necessary.

7. In the Message Text box, enter any comments or instructions to accompany the attached project file (see Figure 18-9).

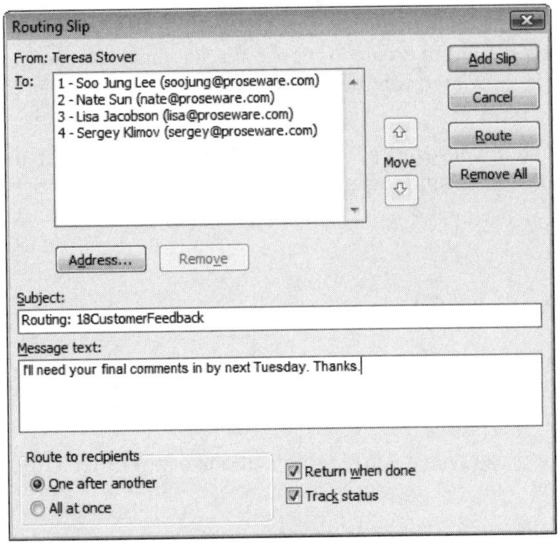

Figure 18-9 Complete the Routing Slip dialog box to send the project file to multiple recipients.

8. Under Route To Recipients, select the One After Another option (the default) or the All At Once option.

   Although sequential routing can be time-consuming and impractical for urgent information, it can work well for review and evaluation, especially when reviewers are in widely dispersed locations. Each recipient edits the project file and adds comments to the routing message. To send it to the next designated addressee, the recipient clicks File, Send To, Next Routing Recipient.

9. Select the Track Status check box to keep an eye on the progress of the project routing and make sure it doesn't get stuck too long with any one recipient. Select the Return When Done check box to make sure the file comes back to you so that you can see everyone's changes and comments.

10. Click the Route button.

    The message with the project file is routed to your designated recipients through e-mail.

The routing e-mail will provide instructions for the recipients as well as the attached project file (see Figure 18-10). When the recipient is finished reviewing the project and has entered his or her comments in the routing slip, he or she clicks File, Send To, Next Routing Recipient. When all recipients have reviewed the project, the e-mail message with the attached project and routing slip full of comments returns to you.

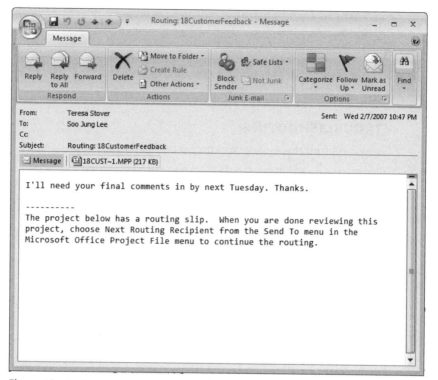

Figure 18-10 The routing e-mail provides instructions to each recipient, along with the attached project file.

Publishing the Project File to an Exchange Folder

> **Note**
> You can publish a project file to an Exchange folder if you're using Microsoft Exchange Server and if you have permission to use public folders.

You can send your project file to an Exchange folder, which is most useful for making the project file available to a large number of stakeholders. To send the file to an Exchange folder, do the following:

1. In Microsoft Office Project 2007, open the project file you want to publish to an Exchange folder.

2. Click File, Send To, Exchange Folder.

The Send To Exchange Folder dialog box appears, displaying the folders available to you.

3. Click the folder to which you'd like to send the project file and then click OK.

Your project file is copied into the selected folder.

TROUBLESHOOTING

You can't find the e-mail workgroup messaging functions

In past versions of Microsoft Project, an e-mail workgroup messaging solution existed in which users of 32-bit MAPI-based e-mail systems could exchange project workgroup messages, including task assignments and progress updates, with project team members. E-mail workgroup messaging started out as a forerunner to Project Web Access, and ended up being a simple, low-end method for team collaboration on a project more and more on the periphery of Microsoft Project with each succeeding version.

In Microsoft Project, e-mail workgroup messaging is no longer available in any form. With the advent and increasing acceptance of Project Server and Project Web Access, e-mail workgroup messaging became woefully outmoded. Even small project management teams in small companies have found Project Server and Project Web Access to be the right collaboration solution, which can be scaled to their size and purpose.

CHAPTER 19

Integrating Microsoft Project with Microsoft Visio

Creating a Visual Report of Project Data in Visio **654**

Presenting Project Data with Visio **661**

Exporting Data from Visio to Microsoft Project **666**

Representing Project Data in a Visio Diagram **668**

Many of the processes and structures reflected in your project plan can be represented in a graphical format and illustrated to help others better visualize them. In Microsoft Office Project 2007, you are already using a Gantt Chart and Network Diagram to depict your project plan. By using the Microsoft Office Visio 2007 diagramming software, you can create more extensive visual representations of the flows, concepts, structure, and organization involved with your project. The unique capabilities of Office Visio 2007 make it a great tool to use in conjunction with Office Project 2007.

As a project management tool, Microsoft Project represents your project by calculating task dates, establishing resource usage, and maintaining a database of the thousands of pieces of data that make up your project plan and keep it moving along. As a diagramming tool, Visio can take information you select from your project plan and represent it in an easy-to-understand graphic that can clearly communicate project information to wider audiences.

With Microsoft Office Project 2007, your favorite integration between Microsoft Project and Visio is likely to be the new visual reports feature. Choose a visual report, and Microsoft Project transfers the appropriate data to a Visio template, ready for viewing. The Visio templates include commands for configuring which results you see, which is indispensible when stakeholders question you about different aspects of project performance.

In addition to visual reports, you'll find other reasons to transfer data between Microsoft Project and Visio. Sometimes, the easiest way to summarize project status or highlight problem areas is to export key project information to a Visio timeline or Gantt chart. If the copy of Microsoft Project that you requested for your birthday hasn't arrived, you can start building projects using the Visio Timeline, Gantt Chart, and PERT Chart templates. When you switch to Microsoft Project, you can export your Visio timelines and Gantt charts and start up in Microsoft Project where you left off in Visio.

You can exchange information between Microsoft Office Project 2007 and Visio in several ways:

- Use a visual report in Microsoft Project to analyze data with a Visio PivotDiagram. Each visual report specifies the data to transfer for the report and the Visio PivotDiagram template to use to communicate project information. By swapping which fields you use to summarize or total results, Visio PivotDiagrams are perfect when you want to be ready to answer any questions that arise.

- Import a Microsoft Project file to a Visio timeline or Gantt chart. Importing a Microsoft Project file into Visio is helpful when you want to take advantage of the presentation features in Visio to present project highlights.

- Import a Visio timeline or Gantt chart into a Microsoft Project file. You might not use this method as frequently as you transfer in the other direction, but it's ideal when you want to bring an initial task list into Microsoft Project for full-blown project management.

> ### Embed and Link Between Microsoft Project and Visio
>
> You can embed or link a Microsoft Project file within Visio, and embed or link a Visio file within certain areas of Microsoft Project. For more information, see the sections titled "Embedding Information" and "Linking Information" in Chapter 16, "Exchanging Information with Other Applications."

Creating a Visual Report of Project Data in Visio

New in Microsoft Office Project 2007, visual reports use Microsoft OfficeVisio Professional 2007 or Microsoft Office Excel 2003 or later to transform Microsoft Project data into easy-to-understand charts and graphs. Microsoft Project 2007 comes with numerous built-in report templates for communicating task, resource, and assignments information.

A visual report assembles the data it needs and stores that data in a database. Then, it applies a Visio (or Office Excel 2003 or later) template to the data to generate the report in a Visio PivotDiagram (or Excel PivotChart). Once you generate the visual report, you can configure the report using Visio or Excel pivot tools to examine different fields over different time periods—without generating a brand new report. For example, you might begin by analyzing cost flow for each fiscal quarter and then, when cash flow is tight, expand the report to view cash flow by week.

If necessary, you can modify any of the many existing visual reports or create your own report templates to do exactly what you want. You can add, remove, or rearrange the fields you want to analyze. In addition, you can publish your customized visual reports for team members or other project managers to use.

For more information about creating a visual report in Excel, see the section titled "Producing a Visual Report of Project Data in Excel" in Chapter 17, "Integrating Microsoft Project with Microsoft Excel."

Generating a Built-in Visual Report for Visio

Visual reports for Visio transfer data to a Visio PivotDiagram for analysis. For example, the Task Status report shows how much money has been spent and the percentage complete for the entire project. You can configure the report to analyze tasks at every layer of the work breakdown structure.

For more information about using the traditional Microsoft Project text-based reports, see the section titled "Working with Text-Based Reports" in Chapter 12, "Reporting Project Information."

To generate a built-in visual report for Visio, do the following:

1. In Microsoft Project, click Reports, Visual Reports.

2. To view visual reports that use Visio, clear the Microsoft Office Excel check box and be sure to select the Microsoft Office Visio check box (see Figure 19-1).

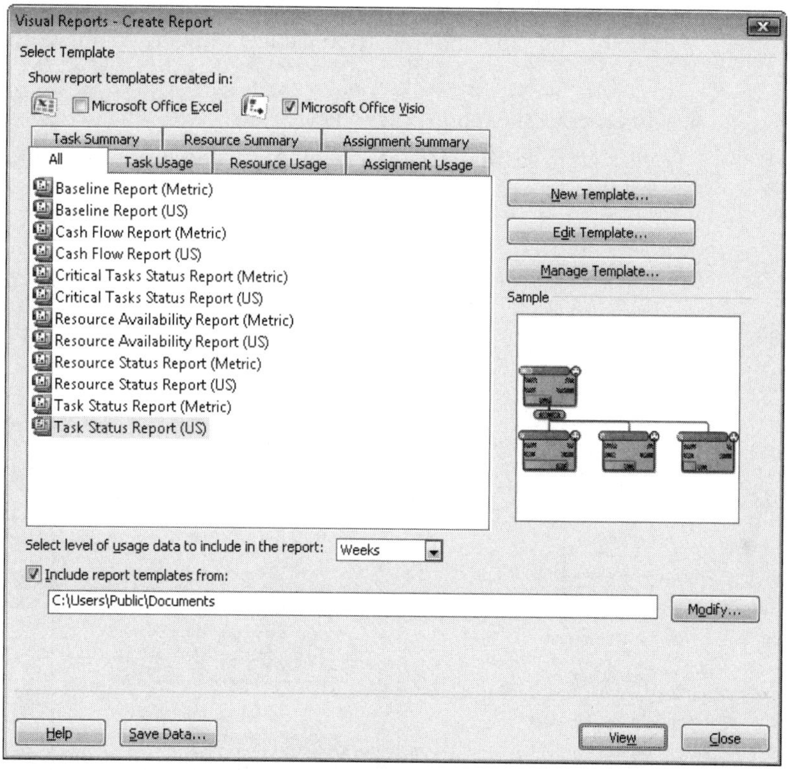

Figure 19-1 Microsoft Project comes with several built-in visual reports that use Visio Pivot-Diagrams.

3. To view all the visual reports that come with Microsoft Project, regardless of the category to which they belong, click the All tab.

Using the All tab is the easiest way to find the reports you want, unless you have created many of your own custom visual report templates. To see only the reports in a specific category, select the tab for that category. For example, the Task Usage category includes the Cash Flow Report template, whereas the Assignment Usage category includes templates for reporting baseline and budgeted costs.

4. To specify the level of detail that Microsoft Project transfers to Visio, click a time period (Days, Weeks, Months, Quarters, or Years) in the Select Level Of Usage Data To Include In The Report box.

   Although any time period can work with any project, Days or Weeks are better for shorter project, whereas Months or longer periods provide faster reporting for longer projects.

5. If you want to save an OLAP (Online Analytical Processing) cube of the data for the report, click Save Data.

   Saving an OLAP cube makes generating additional reports faster, because the step of gathering and transferring data is already complete and saved in the OLAP cube.

6. To generate the report, click View.

   Visio launches and creates a PivotDiagram that uses the OLAP cube of data transferred from Microsoft Project (see Figure 19-2).

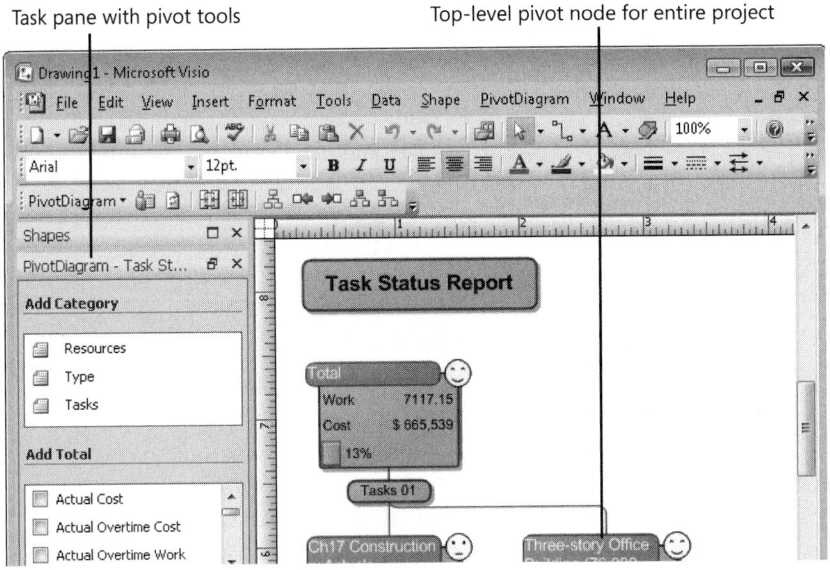

Figure 19-2 A PivotDiagram appears in Visio along with a task pane for further configuring the visual report.

Configuring a Visual Report in Visio

When a visual report first opens in Visio, the most detail you see is a box with data for the entire project (see Figure 19-2 in the previous section). The tools you need to view the data by different categories or with various calculations are all in the Visio PivotDiagram task pane. For example, you can change the category to view results by tasks, resources, or time periods, and you can add different total (such as work or cost) or group nodes in different ways.

To modify a visual report to show different results, use any of the following methods:

- Use a category to expand a node in the diagram. Right-click the node and then click the category you want for the next level on the shortcut menu (see Figure 19-3). You can also click the category you want in the PivotDiagram task pane.

Choose the category for the next level in the diagram

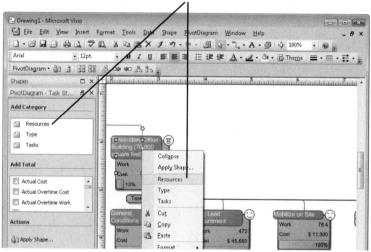

Figure 19-3 You can specify the category to use for the next level in the diagram with each level by using a different category.

- Filter the data that appears at a level. By default, a level in a PivotDiagram includes all the data in the OLAP cube. If you want to display information for only some parts of the project, right-click the Pivot Breakdown shape for that level (the small box that contains the category name, such as Tasks 02, shown in Figure 19-4) and click Configure Level on the shortcut menu. In the Configure Level dialog box (shown in Figure 19-4) in the Filter section, specify tests and values to filter the data.

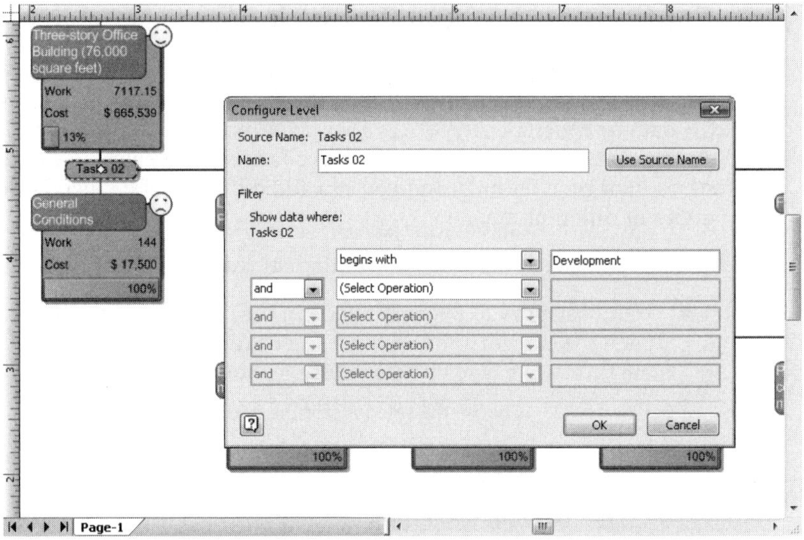

Figure 19-4 In the Configure Level dialog box, you can specify tests to filter the nodes that appear at a level of the diagram.

- Show different totals in nodes. The nodes for a visual report contain specific totals by default, but you can include other totals as well. In the PivotDiagram task pane, in the Add Total section, select the check boxes for the fields you want to total (see Figure 19-5).

Select a field total to add it to nodes

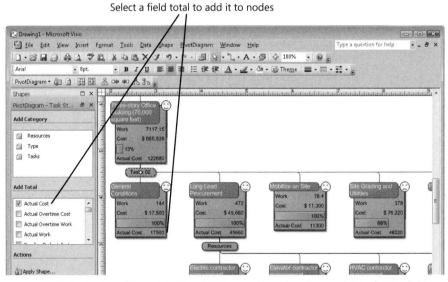

Figure 19-5 To display a field total in the diagram nodes, select the check box for the field in the Add Total section of the PivotDiagram task pane.

- Combine nodes in different ways. For example, to add the tasks for two summary tasks together, in the PivotDiagram task pane, click Other Actions and then click a command, such as Merge, Promote, or Collapse (see Figure 19-6).

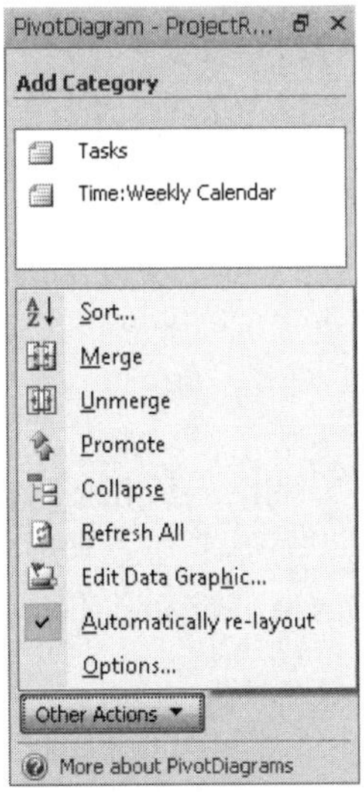

Figure 19-6 The Other Actions menu in the PivotDiagram task pane includes commands for fine-tuning the nodes in a PivotDiagram.

> **Note**
>
> For more information on working with Visio PivotDiagrams, in the Type A Question For Help box in the upper-right corner of the Visio window, type **PivotDiagram** and press Enter.

Creating and Editing Visual Report Templates in Visio

The built-in visual report templates cover many aspects of project performance, from baselines and cash flow to resource availability and task status. If none of the built-in reports do exactly what you want, you can edit a template to fit your requirements. You can even create a new custom visual report template from scratch, which involves only a few more steps than editing a built-in template.

When you choose a visual report template, you are in effect specifying the fields you want to work with and the type of data on which you want to report. Because Visio visual reports use PivotDiagrams, you can use pivot features to further fine-tune the report after it's built in Visio.

To edit a built-in visual report template, do the following:

1. Click Reports, Visual Reports.

2. Select the built-in visual report template you want to edit and then click Edit Template.

The Visual Reports Field Picker dialog box appears.

3. To add fields to the OLAP cube for the visual report, in the Available Fields list, select the fields you want and then click Add.

The fields appear in the Selected Fields list. Remove fields from the Selected Fields list by selecting the ones you want to remove and then clicking Remove. You can select multiple fields to add or remove by holding the Ctrl key and clicking the fields you want to select.

4. Click the Edit Template button.

Microsoft Project builds the OLAP cube based on the fields you selected and launches Visio with the built-in Visio template for the selected report.

5. Make the changes you want to the settings in Visio and then save the Visio template.

To create your own template, do the following:

1. Click Reports, Visual Reports.

2. Click New Template.

The Visual Reports - New Template dialog box appears with the three basic selections you must make to build a template (see Figure 19-7).

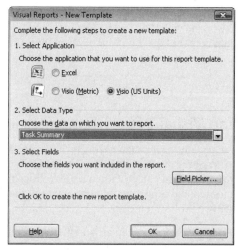

Figure 19-7 When you create a new visual report template, you must specify three aspects of the template.

3. To create a Visio-based report, select either the Visio (Metric) or Visio (US Units) option.

4. Under Select Data Type, choose the type of data you want to use as the basis for your report.

   Visual reports are based on six different sets of information: Task Summary, Task Usage, Resource Summary, Resource Usage, Assignment Summary, and Assignment Usage. These data types determine the fields that Microsoft Project adds to the OLAP cube, such as resource-related fields for resource reports. You can add or remove fields as well.

5. To modify the fields for the template, click Field Picker.

   You can add or remove fields for the template just as you would for a built-in template, as described earlier in this chapter.

6. Click OK.

   Visio launches and opens a PivotDiagram with a node for the entire project, and it sets up a few categories.

7. Configure the diagram using the techniques described in the section titled "Configuring a Visual Report in Visio" earlier in this chapter.

8. When the PivotDiagram looks the way you want, on the File menu, click Save. In the Save As dialog box, navigate to the folder in which you want to save the template, enter a name for the template, and click Save.

9. To see your custom templates in the Visual Reports dialog box list, select the Include Reports Template From check box and click Modify to specify the path that contains your custom templates.

Copy a Microsoft Project View for Visio

You can capture a view in Microsoft Project for use in a Visio diagram using either the Copy PictureTo Office Wizard or the Copy Picture feature. For more information, see the section titled "Copying a Picture of a View" in Chapter 16.

Presenting Microsoft Project Data with Visio

If you already have a project schedule built in Microsoft Project, the main reason to view that data in Visio is to present your project information more effectively. You can transfer all tasks in a project or only top-level tasks, summary tasks, milestones, or any combination of these. Then, you can use the shapes and formatting tools in Visio to highlight crucial information. Although Visio includes four templates for schedule-oriented information, only the Timeline and Gantt Chart templates include wizards for displaying the Microsoft Project data you export in Visio diagrams.

INSIDE OUT   Replace the Visio WBS Chart Wizard

A WBS is frequently shown as a hierarchy that looks like an organization chart. The Visio WBS Chart Wizard in Microsoft Project 2003 converted tasks in a Microsoft Project file into a hierarchical tree in Visio, but this handy tool is not available in Microsoft Project 2007. A visual report that uses a Visio PivotDiagram can generate a hierarchy of tasks similar to a WBS, but Project 2007 doesn't include a built-in visual report for this purpose.

As described in the section "Creating and Editing Visual Report Templates in Visio" earlier in this chapter, you can build your own visual report templates. To approximate a WBS hierarchy, you can set up a Visio PivotDiagram template to display task names and WBS codes in a hierarchical tree.

Showing Project Timeline Information in Visio

If you want to summarize project timeline information, for example, to show project phases and key milestones, you can display schedule information that you build in Microsoft Project in a Visio Timeline diagram. You don't have to export information from Microsoft Project. Instead, with the Import Timeline Data Wizard in Visio, you can select the tasks you want from a Microsoft Project file and display them as tasks and events along a horizontal or vertical bar in Visio.

To display Microsoft Project information in a Visio timeline, follow these steps:

1. Make sure that the Microsoft Project file that you want to present is not open in Microsoft Project.

2. In Visio, create a new Timeline drawing or open an existing one.

3. Choose Timeline, Import Timeline Data.

CAUTION!

If the Timeline menu in Visio doesn't include the Import Timeline Data command, Microsoft Project is not installed on the computer you are using.

4. On the first wizard screen, click Browse. Navigate to the Microsoft Project file that you want to display in Visio. Select the file and then click Open. Click Next to proceed to the next wizard screen.

5. On the Select Task Types To Include screen, select the type of tasks you want to display in Visio and then click Next.

By default, All is selected, which is perfect if you want to build a timeline of the entire project. For presentations, especially to upper management stakeholders who need a high-level view, you might choose Top Level Tasks And Milestones.

6. On the Select Shapes For Your Visio Timeline screen, select the shapes you want to use on the timeline if they differ from the ones selected by default (see Figure 19-8). Click Next.

The wizard transfers the overall project schedule information into a Timeline shape. Milestones in your Microsoft Project schedule (and any tasks with a duration of zero) become Visio Milestone shapes. Summary tasks in your project schedule become Interval shapes.

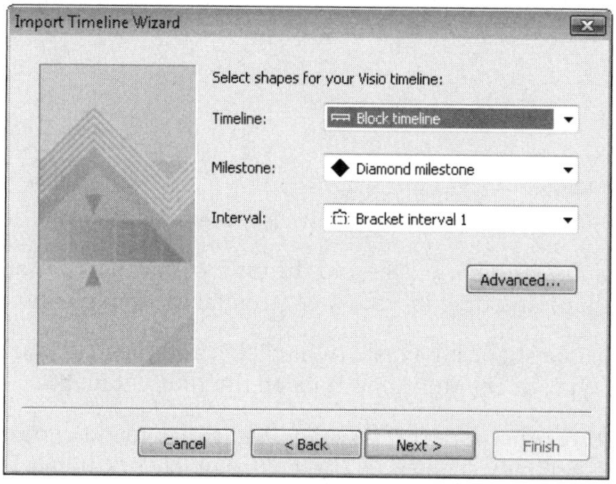

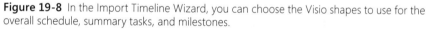

Figure 19-8 In the Import Timeline Wizard, you can choose the Visio shapes to use for the overall schedule, summary tasks, and milestones.

> **Note**
>
> If you're ready to specify the timescale and data settings for the timeline, click Advanced. However, you can set these options after the timeline is created and see right away whether the settings do what you want.

7. On the final wizard page, review the import properties you selected. If you decide to change any of the properties, click Back until you get to the appropriate screen.

8. When the import properties are set the way you want, click Finish.

Visio transfers the information from the selected Microsoft Project tasks (see Figure 19-9) into Visio shapes. If you opened an existing Timeline drawing, Visio creates the new timeline on a new page.

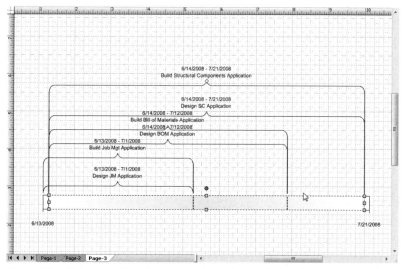

Figure 19-9 If shapes in the diagram overlap, select and drag them to another location.

9. If you display summary tasks and the intervals or their annotations overlap, select a shape and drag its yellow control handle to reposition the label.

10. To change the shape for a task, right-click it and then click Set Timeline Type, Set Interval Type, or Set Milestone Type on the shortcut menu.

11. To configure other aspects of a shape, right-click it and choose a command from the shortcut menu, such as Set Percent Complete or Change Date/Time Formats.

Displaying Project Information in a Visio Gantt Chart

To display Microsoft Project data in a Visio Gantt Chart, follow these steps:

1. In Visio, choose File, New, Schedule, Gantt Chart.

   In the Gantt Chart Options dialog box, click OK to close the dialog box. You can configure the Gantt Chart after you import the tasks from Microsoft Project.

   You can also import Microsoft Project data into an existing Gantt Chart drawing.

2. In the Visio menu bar, choose Gantt Chart, Import.

   The Import Project Data Wizard launches.

3. On the I Want To Create My Project Schedule From screen, select Information That's Already Stored In A File and then click Next.

4. On the Select The Format Of Your Project Data screen, select Microsoft Office Project File and then click Next.

5. On the Select The File Containing Existing Project Schedule Data screen, click Browse, navigate to the directory that contains the file you want to import, select the file, and click Open. Click Next.

6. On the Time Scale screen, specify the major and minor timescale units, as well as the time units you want to use for duration. Click Next.

> **Note**
>
> If you want to specify the shapes for the Gantt Chart, on the Time Scale screen, click Advanced. You can also change shapes after the schedule is imported.

7. On the Select Task Types To Include screen, select the type of tasks (All, Top Level Tasks Only, Milestones Only, Summary Tasks Only, or Top Level Tasks And Milestones) you want to import from Microsoft Project to Visio. Click Next.

8. On the final wizard screen, review the import properties you selected.

To change any properties, click Back until you get to the appropriate screen.

9. When the import properties are set the way you want, click Finish.

The selected tasks import into tasks in a Gantt Chart in Visio. If you import into an existing drawing, Visio creates a new page for the imported chart.

10. To configure the chart, click Gantt Chart, Options (see Figure 19-10), which opens the Gantt Chart Options dialog box.

You can specify the start and finish dates for the timescale, the units to use for duration, and the time units for the timescale. On the Format tab, you can specify the shapes for task bars, summary bars, and milestones, as well as the text that appears as labels on the bars.

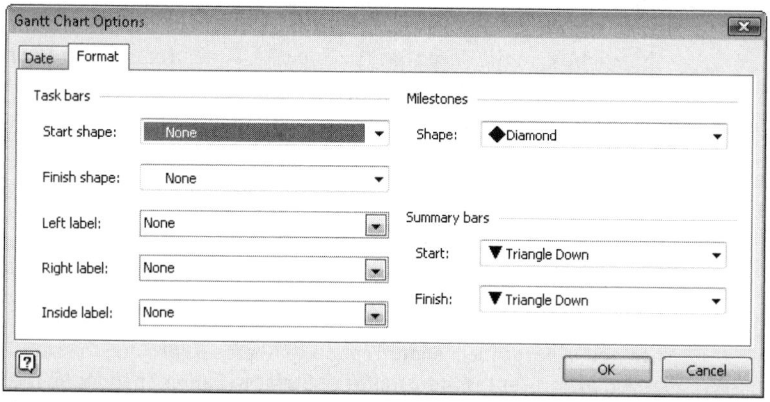

Figure 19-10 After you transfer the schedule information into a Visio Gantt Chart, you can set Visio Gantt Chart options to configure the appearance of the chart.

Exporting Data from Visio to Microsoft Project

Although you're not likely to transfer data from Visio to Microsoft Project as often, the process is even easier than going from Microsoft Project to Visio. If you build draft schedules in Visio as timelines or Gantt Charts, it's easy to bring that information into Microsoft Project for further work.

Exporting Timelines from Visio to Microsoft Project

As long as Microsoft Project and Visio are both installed on your computer, you can transfer timeline data from Visio to Microsoft Project or vice versa. For example, consider a simple project you built as a Visio timeline to present at a project selection committee meeting. The project was approved, and now you want to use the Visio timeline to build the basic schedule in Microsoft Project. When you export a timeline from Visio into Microsoft Project, intervals turn into tasks with start dates, finish dates, and durations.

To export information from a Visio Timeline to Microsoft Project, follow these steps:

1. In Visio, open the timeline drawing and select the timeline shape.

2. Choose Timeline, Export Timeline Data.

> **Note**
>
> If the timeline you select is associated with expanded timelines, Visio asks if you want to export markers on the expanded timelines. To export only the overview timeline, click No. To export all information, click Yes.

3. In the Export Timeline Data window that appears, navigate to the folder in which you want to save the exported project file, type the project file name in the File Name box, make sure that the Save As Type box is set to Microsoft Project File, and then click Save.

   A message box appears telling you that the project has been successfully exported. Click OK.

4. Open the exported file in Microsoft Project.

> **Note**
>
> When you export timeline information to Microsoft Project, the start and finish dates that you export set task constraints of Start No Earlier Than for all the tasks. The easiest way to change these to As Soon As Possible is to insert the Constraint Type column into the Task Sheet.

Right-click a column heading in the Task Sheet and then click Insert Column on the shortcut menu. In the Field Name box, click Constraint Type and then click OK. In the Constraint Type column for the first task, click As Soon As Possible. Then, drag that value down through the rest of the tasks.

Importing Visio Gantt Charts to Microsoft Project

To export project information from a Visio Gantt Chart into Microsoft Project, follow these steps:

1. In Visio, open the Gantt Chart drawing.

2. Select the Gantt Chart frame and then choose Gantt Chart, Export. The Export Project Data Wizard launches.

3. On the Export My Project Data Into The Following Format screen, select Microsoft Office Project File and then click Next.

4. On the Specify The File To Enter Project Schedule Data screen, click Browse, open the folder in which you want to save the exported project file, type the project file name in the File Name box, and click Save.

5. Back in the wizard, click Next.

6. On the final wizard screen, review the export properties and click Finish to export the data. A message indicates that the project has been successfully exported. Click OK.

    If you want to change any properties, click Back until you get to the appropriate screen.

7. In Microsoft Project, open the project file you just created.

Copy Elements Between Microsoft Project and Visio

As described in Chapter 16, you can copy Visio diagrams and paste them into Microsoft Project schedules or copy portions of a Microsoft Project schedule and paste them into Visio diagrams. For example, you could build a Visio organization chart to show the reporting structure of a team and embed it in the Notes box of the Resource Information dialog box for the resource who acts as the team lead. You could also take a picture of a Microsoft Project view and embed it in a Visio file, for instance, to show the high-level project schedules for each business unit in a Visio organization chart.

Using the Copy command in Visio in conjunction with the Paste Special, Paste As Picture command in Microsoft Project, you can embed a Visio diagram in a vacant area of your Gantt Chart or in the Notes box of the Task Information or Resource Information dialog boxes.

Representing Project Data in a Visio Diagram

If you decide to build a project directly in Visio, or if you plan to export Microsoft Project information to a Visio diagram, it's helpful to understand how the four Visio templates for schedules work. The templates that apply to projects or other date-related information include the following:

- **Timeline**   The Timeline template displays tasks and events in a way that Microsoft Project does not. It shows them along a horizontal or vertical bar. This can be useful, for example, to summarize the phases of a multiyear project and key milestones toward its completion.

- **Gantt Chart**   Although you can use Visio to build simple Gantt charts, it is more useful as a presentation tool when you're using data exported from Microsoft Project.

- **PERT Chart**   The Microsoft Project Network Diagram view is a much better option than its Visio PERT Chart counterpart, because Microsoft Project calculates start and finish dates for tasks in addition to showing the hierarchy of tasks.

> For more information about using the PERT Chart in Microsoft Project, see the section titled "Working with Network Diagrams" in Chapter 4, "Viewing Project Information."

- **Calendar**   Although the Calendar template is a member of the Schedule category in Visio, it doesn't integrate with Microsoft Project. You can build calendars for special events within a project, but, to show the work that's scheduled for a project, the Calendar view in Microsoft Project is a better tool.

> For more information about the Microsoft Project Calendar view, see the section titled "Working with Graph Views" in Chapter 4.

Using the Visio Timeline Template

The Visio Timeline template summarizes the time span for phases and tasks, and highlights milestones along the horizontal or vertical timeline. By expanding portions of a timeline, you can emphasize critical portions of a project.

Configuring the Time Period and Time Format

Configure the time period and time format for a timeline by doing the following:

1. Right-click a timeline shape, such as Block Timeline or Cylindrical Timeline, and then click Configure Timeline on the shortcut menu.

2. In the Configure Timeline dialog box (see Figure 19-11), under Time Period, type the start and finish dates for the time period that the timeline represents. If the timeline spans a short period, you can specify the start and finish times, too.

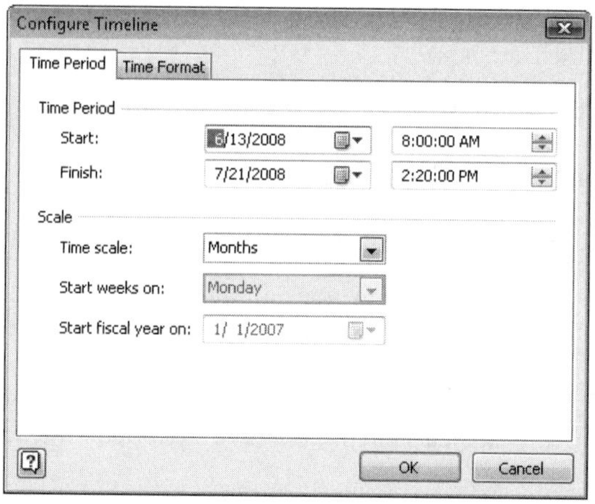

Figure 19-11 The Configure Timeline dialog box contains controls for specifying the start and finish dates and time intervals for a timeline.

3. In the Time Scale dropdown list, choose the time interval to show on the timeline, such as Months. When you select Quarters, you can also specify the Start Fiscal Year On date. For Weeks, you can specify the first day of the week.

4. Specify the date format by choosing a language in the Timeline Language box on the Time Format tab.

5. Control whether dates and times appear on a timeline by clicking the Time Format tab and selecting the check boxes that control whether the start date, finish date, and interim time scales appear. In addition, you can select the date format for dates and specify whether interim marks show the date or only tick marks.

Configuring a Timeline Interval

Configure an interval within a timeline, for example, to adjust the phases of a project or the duration of a task, by doing the following:

1. Right-click an Interval shape, such as Block Interval, and then click Configure Interval on the shortcut menu.

2. In the Configure Interval dialog box, specify the start date and finish dates, and optionally, the start and finish times.

3. In the Description box, type the text that you want within the interval.

Configuring Milestones

Configure milestones for events or key dates by doing the following:

1. Right-click a Milestone shape, such as Diamond Milestone, and then click Configure Milestone on the shortcut menu.

2. In the Configure Milestone dialog box, specify the date (and, optionally, the time) in the Milestone Date box.

3. In the Description box, type the text for the milestone.

Expanding a Portion of a Timeline

For a multiyear project, activities that span only a few days or weeks are barely visible in a timeline, but they might nevertheless be essential to success. By adding Expanded Timeline shapes to a timeline diagram, you can display more detail for a small portion of the total project. Furthermore, you can expand a timeline to more than one level.

To expand a timeline, follow these steps:

1. From the Timeline Shapes stencil, drag the Expanded Timeline shape onto the drawing.

2. In the Configure Timeline dialog box, specify the start and finish dates for the expanded timeline, and optionally, the start and finish times as well. The dates that you specify for the expanded timeline must be within the date range of the overview timeline.

3. In the Time Scale box, select the time intervals the expanded timeline covers.

4. Click OK to add the expanded timeline to the drawing. Visio adds milestones, intervals, and date markers that occur during the expanded time period.

Synchronizing Milestones and Intervals

Visio synchronizes milestones and intervals between higher-level and expanded time-lines, but you can synchronize milestones and intervals across any number of timelines on a page. To synchronize a milestone or interval with another, follow these steps:

1. Select the milestone or interval you want to synchronize or drag the Synchronized Milestone or Synchronized Interval shape onto the timeline.

2. Click Timeline, Synchronize Milestone or Timeline, Synchronize Interval.

3. In the Synchronize With dropdown list, select the other milestone or interval with which to synchronize.

4. Select the date format, if necessary, and click OK. A gray dotted line shows the synchronization between the milestones or intervals.

Using the Gantt Chart Template

Just as in Microsoft Project, in a Visio Gantt Chart, task data appears in both a table as well as a chart of task bars, milestones, and other symbols that represent the relationships and schedule of project tasks. The major difference, of course, is that a Visio Gantt Chart does not calculate start and finish dates, resource assignments, costs, and other project management information. For this reason, the Visio Gantt Chart template is best for presentations or status reports. If you don't have easy access to Microsoft Project, you can add shapes to a Visio drawing to build a Gantt Chart.

Whether you import a Visio Gantt Chart from Microsoft Project or build one from scratch, you can modify the Gantt Chart in Visio in the following ways:

- Add task bars and milestones by dragging Row, Task Bar, and Milestone shapes onto a Gantt Chart frame or by clicking Gantt Chart, New Task. Type the name of the new task along with the start date, finish date, duration, and any other task information.

- Delete tasks by selecting the tasks and then clicking Gantt Chart, Delete Task.

- Rename a task by double-clicking the task name, typing the new name, and pressing Esc.

- Add project fields, such as Resource Names or % Complete, in the table area of the Gantt Chart by right-clicking a Gantt Chart frame and then clicking Insert Column on the shortcut menu. In the Insert Column dialog box, click the field you want to add.

- Remove a column from the table by clicking anywhere in the column and then clicking Gantt Chart, Hide Column.

- Indent and outdent tasks to specify summary tasks and their subtasks.

- Link tasks by using the Link Lines shape to show dependencies between predecessor and successor tasks.

- Specify the working days and hours for your project team by clicking Gantt Chart, Configure Working Time. The Configure Working Time dialog box appears (see Figure 19-12). Then, select the check boxes for work days and click the times in the Start Time and Finish Time boxes.

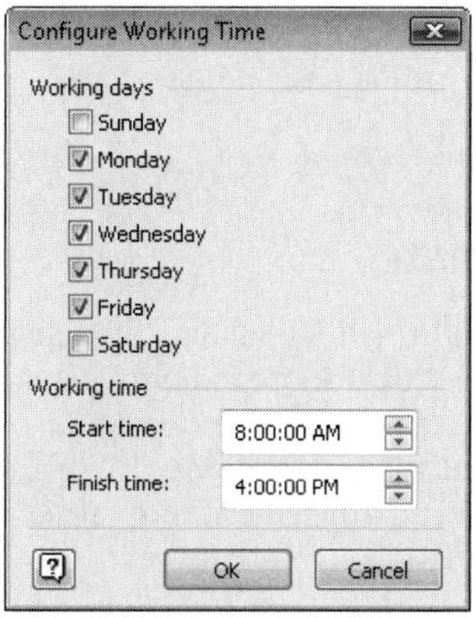

Figure 19-12 You can specify working days and times in the Configure Working Time dialog box.

- Annotate the Gantt Chart for presentations by adding Title, Legend, Text Block, and Horizontal Callout shapes.

- Configure the Gantt Chart time units, duration, and timescale by clicking Gantt Chart, Options, clicking the Date tab, and then choosing the settings you want, such as the start and finish dates for the Gantt Chart.

- Format task bars, milestones, and summary task bars by clicking Gantt Chart, Options and then clicking the Format tab.

- Change start date, finish date, and duration by typing values in the fields in the table within the Gantt Chart shape or by dragging task bars in the chart area. Dragging task bars is quick, but typically not as accurate as typing values. You can also show progress by dragging the yellow control handle on the left side of a task bar toward the right.

Navigating Within Visio Gantt Charts

The Gantt Chart toolbar, shown in Figure 19-13, includes commands for finding task bars and dates in a Gantt Chart. The following tools navigate within the chart area of your Visio Gantt Chart:

- **Go To Start** Jumps to the first task bar in the project
- **Go To Previous** Displays the time period immediately prior to the current period
- **Go To Next** Displays the time period immediately after the current period
- **Go To Finish** Jumps to the last task bar in the project
- **Scroll To Task** Displays the task bar for the selected task

Figure 19-13 The Gantt Chart toolbar offers a fast way to perform task-related functions: finding, indenting, outdenting, linking, creating, and deleting tasks.

Using the PERT Chart Template

Program Evaluation and Review Technique (PERT) charts display project tasks as a network or hierarchy of boxes, much like a work breakdown structure. However, always keep in mind that the Visio PERT Chart is primarily designed for presentation, not actual project management. It does not calculate start dates, finish dates, or durations. If you need to use a PERT Chart as a project management tool rather than just a communications tool, use the Network Diagram in Microsoft Project.

To build a PERT Chart in Visio, drag shapes onto the drawing and type values in the boxes. There's no wizard for transferring information between Microsoft Project and Visio PERT Charts. However, you can use the data features in Office Visio Professional to link boxes on a diagram to data in a Microsoft Project database.

PART 7

Managing Projects Across Your Enterprise

CHAPTER 20

Understanding Enterprise
Project Management. 675

CHAPTER 21

Administering your Enterprise
Project Management Solution. 691

CHAPTER 22

Managing Enterprise Projects
and Resources 753

CHAPTER 23

Participating on a Team Using
Project Web Access. 827

CHAPTER 24

Making Executive Decisions Using
Project Web Access. 865

Understanding Enterprise Project Management

Who's Who in Enterprise Project Management **677**

Understanding the EPM Workflow **684**

Understanding the Components of EPM **680**

E nterprise project management provides the means for dynamic project workgroup collaboration and project management throughout an entire organization.

Through the use of Microsoft Office Project Server 2007 working closely with Microsoft Office Project Professional 2007 and Microsoft Office Project Web Access, your organization has the capacity to set up powerful and fully customizable enterprise project management (EPM) functionality.

Using the Office Project Server 2007 EPM solution, all levels of project management information can be processed, stored, and viewed. Here are some examples of how various members of an organization might use tools within Project Server:

- The team member might use her task page to review current tasks (see Figure 20-1).

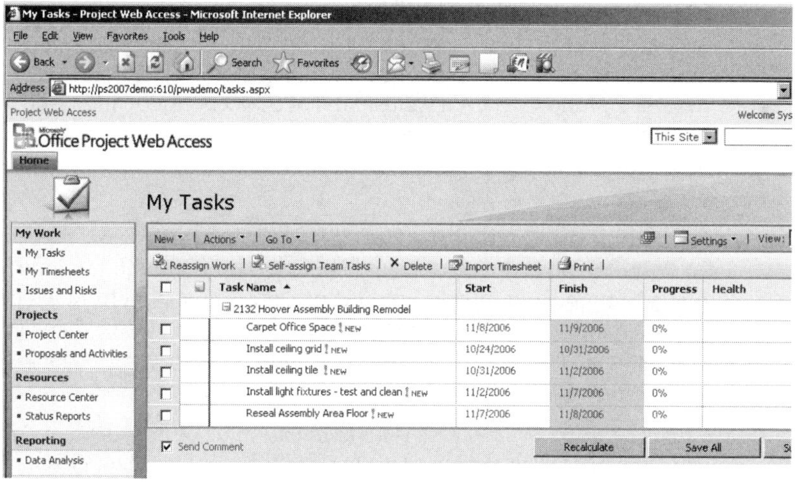

Figure 20-1 Team members often use the My Tasks page to see current assignments.

- The resource manager might perform a search for resources with specific skills and availability for possible use in an upcoming project.

- The project manager might collect and collate status reports for one of his projects and then generate a report for a meeting with stakeholders in the morning.

- The vice president of business development might analyze all the projects in a given portfolio to determine whether additional programs of this type are advantageous to the organization (see Figure 20-2).

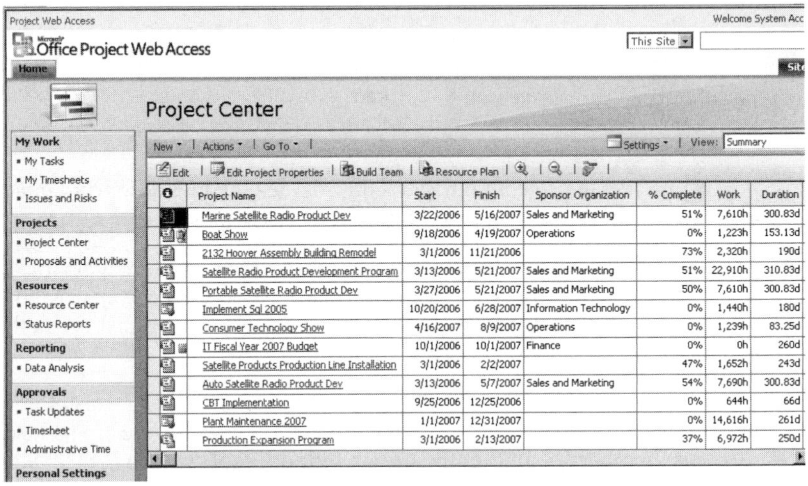

Figure 20-2 An executive can use the Project Center to see summary information about projects in progress throughout the organization.

Project Server facilitates communication of task assignments and actual progress among members of a project team, using Office Project Web Access as the Web-based interface. Hundreds, even thousands, of projects can be managed in a consistent manner throughout an organization. Microsoft Project elements such as views, toolbars, fields, and macros can be customized for the organization and standardized across all projects.

In addition, information about thousands of resources can be managed in Project Server. Resources and their associated skill, cost, and availability information can be built into a common and interactive enterprise resource pool from which all project managers can build their project teams. Team leads and resource managers can delegate tasks and manage resources as needed to accomplish the goals of the project and keep the project manager well-informed.

Because Project Web Access is an application of Windows SharePoint Services 3.0, the infrastructure is already in place for workgroup document check-in and checkout, issues tracking, and risk management.

Executives and other managing stakeholders can use Project Web Access to efficiently view and report on the portfolios of projects that make up a program or organizational initiative. They can do high-level modeling of analyses of tasks, resources, and costs across multiple projects and programs, including proposed projects.

Also available is the new Microsoft Office Project Portfolio Server 2007. Along with the companion Microsoft Office Project Portfolio Web Access, this product integrates with Project Server 2007 to provide a complete project portfolio management solution as part of your enterprise project management. It includes tools to help organizations identify, select, and manage portfolios in line with their business strategy.

Project Server 2007 has been re-architected to provide enhanced enterprise project management capabilities for managing complex programs and project portfolios with a large-scale globally distributed workforce. It is now easier for organizations to integrate their EPM solution with existing software and technologies having to do with human resources as well as organizational processes and policies. The new structure also provides for performance enhancements and other efficiencies.

Who's Who in Enterprise Project Management

Given the nature of project workgroups and enterprise project management, a variety of roles are played in project management, as follows:

- **Project manager** The traditional user of Microsoft Office Project, the project manager is still the hub around which all other roles revolve. The project manager primarily uses Office Project Professional 2007, but also typically uses Project Web Access as well. The project manager builds and adjusts the project, assigns resources, tracks progress, responds to changes, mitigates risks, and communicates progress throughout the project's life cycle (see Figure 20-3).

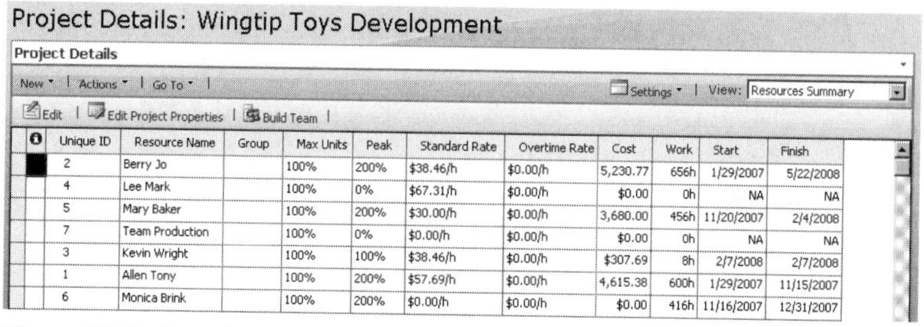

Unique ID	Resource Name	Group	Max Units	Peak	Standard Rate	Overtime Rate	Cost	Work	Start	Finish
2	Berry Jo		100%	200%	$38.46/h	$0.00/h	5,230.77	656h	1/29/2007	5/22/2008
4	Lee Mark		100%	0%	$67.31/h	$0.00/h	$0.00	0h	NA	NA
5	Mary Baker		100%	200%	$30.00/h	$0.00/h	3,680.00	456h	11/20/2007	2/4/2008
7	Team Production		100%	0%	$0.00/h	$0.00/h	$0.00	0h	NA	NA
3	Kevin Wright		100%	100%	$38.46/h	$0.00/h	$307.69	8h	2/7/2008	2/7/2008
1	Allen Tony		100%	200%	$57.69/h	$0.00/h	4,615.38	600h	1/29/2007	11/15/2007
6	Monica Brink		100%	200%	$0.00/h	$0.00/h	$0.00	416h	11/16/2007	12/31/2007

Figure 20-3 One of the many ways the project manager can use Project Web Access to collaborate with team members and other stakeholders is to provide access to detailed project information.

- **Resource manager** Although the project manager often plays the role of the resource manager, Project Web Access makes it easy for a separate resource manager to work with the project manager to assign tasks to the right people. The resource manager uses Project Web Access with special resource-related privileges. The resource manager can manage data about users in the enterprise resource pool, review timesheets, and create resource-related views (see Figure 20-4).

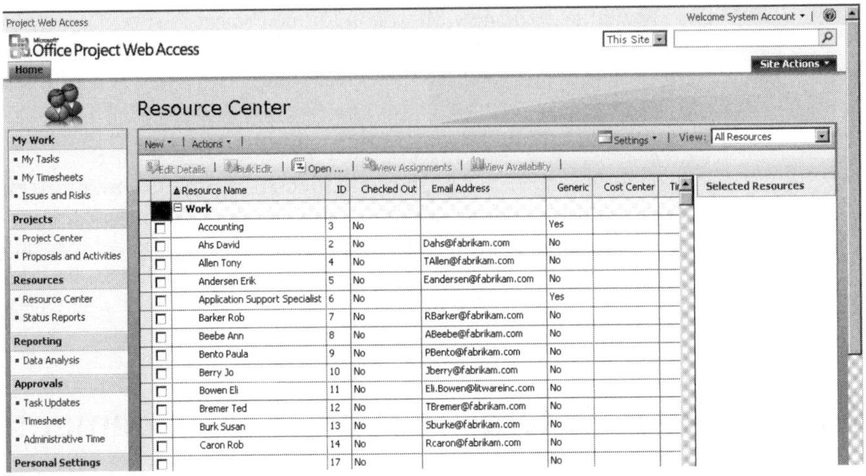

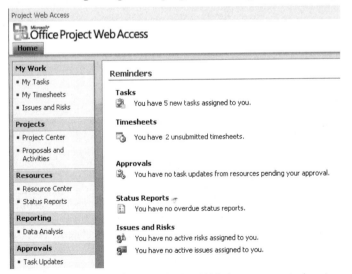

Figure 20-4 The resource manager can use tools to set up or view information about enterprise resources.

- **Team lead** A team member carrying out a set of project tasks can also be assigned to lead responsibilities for a small group of other team members. The team lead uses Project Web Access to manage both responsibilities.

- **Team member** Actually completing the tasks that contribute to the project's goal, team members implement the work of the project. Team members use Project Web Access to review, create, and update tasks and to see details of the project as a whole. Team members also use Project Web Access to enter and submit timesheet information regarding actual progress on assignments (see Figure 20-5).

Figure 20-5 Team members use Project Web Access to see task assignments, timesheets and status reports that are due, and other project-related information.

- **Proposal reviewer** Typically one of the managing stakeholders, the proposal reviewer is responsible for reviewing proposals submitted through Project Web Access. By viewing data about existing projects, running reports, analyzing resource availability, examining cost projections, and so on, the proposal reviewer can examine proposed projects and determine whether they are in line with the organization's strategic goals and worthy of pursuing.

- **Portfolio manager** The portfolio manager oversees the priorities and resource allocation for entire groups of projects. The portfolio manager can review information and run reports about all current and proposed projects and also create new proposals. This individual can also set up custom views, fields, and calendars for the entire enterprise.

- **Executive** Upper management, customers, or other managing stakeholders provide high-level direction for and support of a project, a portfolio of projects, or an entire program. These executives can keep an eye on progress of milestones, deliverables, costs, and other concerns through the use of specialized views in Project Web Access. They can also compare aspects of multiple projects against each other for sophisticated modeling or analysis leading to informed decisions for the organization.

- **Project server administrator** The project server administrator configures Project Server and Project Web Access to implement the features and permissions needed by the organization (see Figure 20-6). The administrator works mostly in Project Web Access and occasionally in Project Professional.

Server Settings

Security	Enterprise Data	Database Administration	Look and Feel
▪ Manage Users	▪ Enterprise Custom Field Definition	▪ Delete Enterprise Objects	▪ Manage Views
▪ Manage Groups	▪ Enterprise Global	▪ Force Check-in Enterprise Objects	▪ Grouping Formats
▪ Manage Categories	▪ Enterprise Calendars	▪ Schedule Backup	▪ Gantt Chart Formats
▪ Security Templates	▪ Resource Center	▪ Administrative Backup	▪ Quick Launch
▪ Project Web Access Permissions	▪ About Project Server	▪ Administrative Restore	

Cube	Time and Task Management	Queue	Operational Policies
▪ Build Settings	▪ Financial Periods	▪ Manage Queue	▪ Alerts and Reminders
▪ Configuration	▪ Timesheet Periods	▪ Queue Settings	▪ Additional Server Settings
▪ Build Status	▪ Timesheet Classifications		▪ Server-Side Event Handler Configuration
	▪ Timesheet Settings and Defaults		▪ Active Directory Resource Pool Synchronization
	▪ Administrative Time		▪ Project Workspaces
	▪ Task Settings and Display		▪ Project Workspace Provisioning Settings
	▪ Close Tasks to Update		

Figure 20-6 The project server administrator uses the Server Settings page to manage users, set up timesheets, configure standard reports, and customize views.

Although these roles are distinct, it's entirely possible for one person to fulfill two or more overlapping roles and have the permissions in Project Server that reflect these multiple responsibilities.

This chapter provides a broad overview of the Project Server workgroup collaboration and enterprise project management solution, providing the context for who is involved and how all the pieces work together. Succeeding chapters are designed for specific

Chapter 20

audiences who work with aspects of Project Server in their specialized ways according to their role in the organization. These chapters and their intended audiences are as follows:

- Chapter 21, "Administering Your Enterprise Project Management Solution," is written for the project server administrator. The chapter presents general guidelines on configuring and tailoring Project Server and Project Web Access for enterprise project management in a specific organization. This chapter also includes instructions for typical system administrator duties such as adding new users and setting user permissions. Creation of customized elements for standardization is covered, as is setup for the enterprise resource pool, timesheets, and reports. Chapter 21 can also be reviewed by project managers who want a clearer picture of capabilities that are implemented by the administrator.

- Chapter 22, "Managing Enterprise Projects and Resources," is the project manager's chapter. It details processes for creating an enterprise project, either from scratch or from an existing local project. It also discusses how to create a proposed project and activity plan. Building the project team from the enterprise resource pool is covered, as are details for team collaboration from the project manager's standpoint.

- Chapter 23, "Participating on a Team Using Project Web Access," is the chapter designed for the team member, team lead, and resource manager, who all work in Project Web Access. The chapter includes information on accepting and creating new task assignments, reporting on assignment progress, and viewing the overall project picture. Information on building project teams and reassigning tasks is for team leads and resource managers.

- Chapter 24, "Making Executive Decisions Using Project Web Access," is directed at the executive or other managing stakeholder who wants to review high-level project and resource information. Information about using the Cube Builder for portfolio analysis is included in this chapter.

Understanding the Components of EPM

There are different ways to look at the various pieces that contribute to the Project Server enterprise project management solution. You can look at it from an architecture standpoint or from a data flow standpoint. In this section, however, we'll review the components of Project Server enterprise project management from the point of view of the applications that the enterprise users interact with. These applications are Project Server, Project Professional, and Project Web Access.

For system requirements for Project Server and the enterprise features, see Appendix A, "Installing Microsoft Office Project 2007."

Understanding the Role of Project Server

Project Server is the server that manages all data associated with your enterprise projects, portfolios, and programs. It also manages the information related to user access, security settings, administrative settings, and so on.

Project Server sits atop the database that stores all project information generated either from Project Professional or Project Web Access (see Figure 20-7). This project database is powered by Microsoft SQL Server

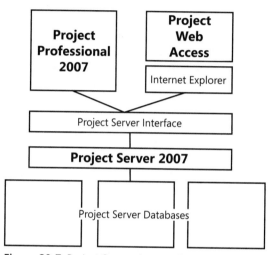

Figure 20-7 Project Server sits atop the project database, works with information from Project Professional, and provides a view to project information through Project Web Access.

In Microsoft Project 2003, the scheduling engine was available only in the Project Professional 2003 clients. However, Project Server 2007 includes a scheduling engine to enable project updates.

Project Server provides queuing services for efficient processing even at peak times. It also provides eventing services to enable updating of the database from either Project Professional or Project Server as well as integration with other applications. Project Server is built by using the Microsoft .NET Framework 2.0.

An available option is Project Portfolio Server, which works with Project Server to provide project portfolio management tools and services.

Project Server uses the Project Server Interface (PSI) as the application program interface (API), which is the means through which Project Professional and Project Web Access have a view into and interact with Project Server. The Project Server Interface enables tasks, resources, assignments, and entire projects to be manipulated—created, viewed, edited, or deleted programatically. The Project Server Interface replaces the Project Data Server (PDS) that was used in Project Server 2003.

In addition, developers can use the Project Server Interface to create methods for interacting with line of business applications (for example, human resources, procurement, and accounting systems) and other third-party applications.

Understanding the Role of Project Professional

As the project management application, Project Professional is the primary client of Project Server and the major source of project data, including projects, tasks, resources, assignments, scheduling dates, costs, and tracking information that is served by the project server.

When Project Professional is part of an enterprise project management solution, collaboration options become available (see Figure 20-8). These options make it convenient for project managers to move back and forth between the Project Professional environment and the Project Web Access environment.

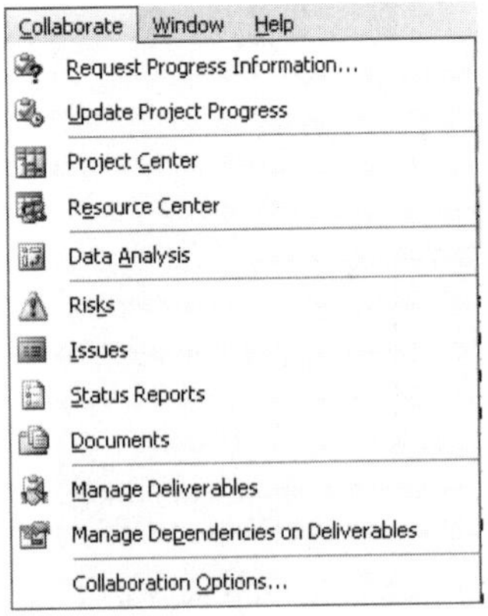

Figure 20-8 When Project Professional is connected to a project server, the Collaborate menu becomes available.

Another client of Project Server is Microsoft Internet Explorer. Other clients can include Microsoft Office Outlook, line of business applications, and third-party applications.

> **Note**
> Because of changes to the project server architecture, Project Professional 2003 cannot be used with Project Server 2007.

Understanding the Role of Project Web Access

Project Web Access is the Web-based source for project data, including tasks, resources, assignments, scheduling dates, costs, and tracking information. Project Web Access is a Web site running on at least Internet Explorer 6.0 with unique capabilities to work specifically with Project Server 2007 and display targeted project data. It is the view into the project server and the underlying project database.

This Web site typically lives on your organization's intranet or extranet and is accessed by project team members. A view into Project Web Access can also be accessed from within Project Professional.

Project Web Access is an application of Windows SharePoint Services 3.0, which provides the administrative and user interface framework, the infrastructure for user management, logon capabilities, team collaboration, and integration with the reporting features of Project Server.

Chapter 20

> **Note**
>
> Two other available components are Project Portfolio Server and Microsoft Office Project Portfolio Web Server. These work with Project Server and include tools to help organizations identify, select, and manage portfolios compatible with their organizational goals.

Putting the Project Server Components Together

Here's a simplified description of the sequenced interaction between the three Microsoft Project components in a little more detail:

1. Project data generated by either Project Professional or Project Web Access is saved to a project database that's part of your project server architecture.

2. When projects are published (rather than simply saved), their data is saved in the appropriate database: the working or draft database, the published database, or the reporting database. Whenever a project is saved, it is saved to the draft database. Whenever a project is published, it is also saved to the published database. The data in the published database is then transformed and added to the reporting database for analysis purposes.

3. When a user needs to see project, task, resource, or assignment information in Project Web Access or Project Professional, Project Server calls this information up from the appropriate database and displays it in pages created through the Project Server Interface (see Figure 20-9).

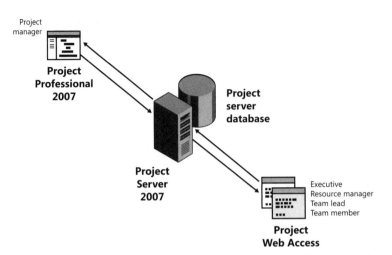

Figure 20-9 When project information is published, it is stored in the project database. Project Server and the Project Server Interface present project information in pages displayed in Project Web Access.

Understanding the EPM Workflow

The enterprise features of Project Professional scale up the power of Project 2007 beyond the individual project to multiple departments and groups in a mid- to large-size multiple-project business that can go as far as a complex program of projects that are distributed across various global locations. With enterprise project management, information stored in the project server database from every resource and every project in the entire company can be quickly collated and reported.

For any business that works on multiple projects, rich customization, resource management, reporting, and portfolio analysis capabilities become possible through enterprise project management. Executives, customers, and other managing stakeholders can review and analyze information on all projects and all resources in their organization, providing for a comprehensive understanding of the nature and progress of the activity within the organization. In addition, the enterprise features help individual project managers plan and control their projects within the context of their organization.

The following steps detail a typical process for working with multiple projects in an enterprise environment:

1. Early on, as part of the enterprise project management setup process, the project server administrator uses Project Professional to create the enterprise global template, the basis for all project plans to be created throughout the enterprise.

   This global template contains standardized project elements such as custom fields, currency format, tables, formulas, and Microsoft Visual Basic for Applications (VBA) modules created to reflect the organization's requirements. The use of the global template propagates the custom elements as the organizational standard for all projects.

2. The project server administrator or resource manager uses Project Professional to build and manage the enterprise-wide resource pool, which includes vital information such as resource skill sets, costs, and availability for project assignments.

3. Project managers throughout the organization use Project Professional to create and submit, or check in, brand new enterprise projects or existing projects that have been converted into enterprise projects.

    Project managers can also import existing local projects as enterprise projects.

    Project Server interfaces with SQL Server, which provides the project server database. Project Server also interfaces with Project Web Access, the Web-based view of project information.

4. Project managers use Project Professional to access the enterprise resource pool and find resources in the organization who have the right skill set and availability for their individual project requirements.

    Project managers can specify generic properties for required resources and then automatically build their team and assign real resources to tasks.

5. Executives can use Project Web Access to view multiple projects in the organization. Using the Project Center to see all projects, portfolio managers, program managers, and executives can review a high-level summary of projects throughout the enterprise, including information about scheduling, costs, resources, and more.

Collaborating as a Project Team

Communication is a critical component of effective project management. There's no question that establishing an effective two-way information flow prevents a host of problems.

Project Server and Project Web Access provide a highly efficient process for exchanging project information with team members. As the project manager working in Project Professional and Project Web Access, you can transmit project information through Project Server to do the following:

- Submit assignments and task changes to assigned resources.

- Request assignment actuals from assigned resources.

- Request, receive, and compile narrative status reports.

- Incorporate actuals submitted by assigned resources directly into the project plan.

- Publish the full project plan for review by team members and other stakeholders.

For details about workgroup collaboration information for the project manager, see Chapter 22.

Chapter 20

With Project Web Access, team members can see all the relevant project information for their assignments. The Web site that is their Project Web Access page (see Figure 20-10) has an easy-to-navigate layout that simplifies information flow.

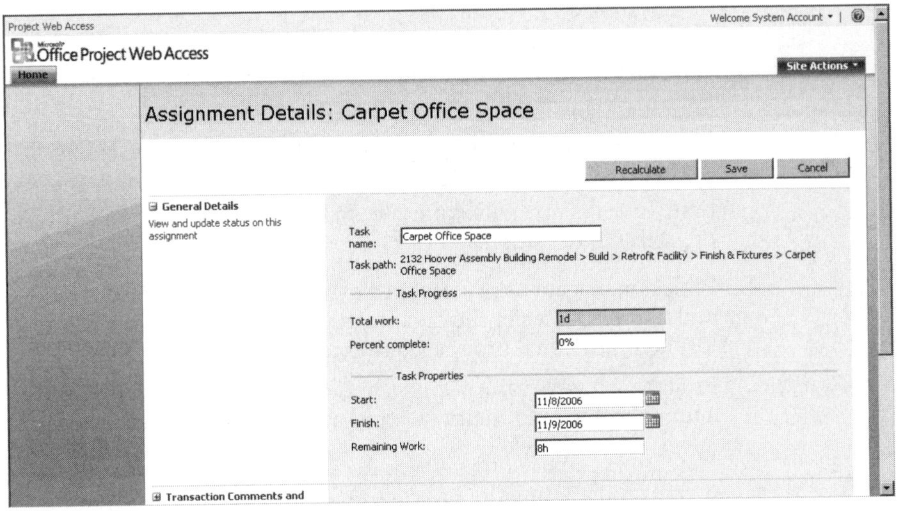

Figure 20-10 Team members use the Assignment Details page to review specifics about assigned tasks.

Using Project Web Access, team members can do the following:

- Accept (or reject) task assignments.

- Create and self-assign new tasks for addition to the project plan.

- Add comments to assignments that become part of the project task record.

- Update task information for incorporation in the project plan.

- Enter daily or weekly actuals, specify percentage complete, or indicate the amount of completed and remaining work to report progress on assignments and submit them to the project manager for incorporation into the project plan.

- Review assignments in different views, with applied filters, groups, and sorting.

- Review the entire project plan to see the context of individual assignments.

Information updated or changed by team members is stored in the project server database. As project manager, you can accept or reject changes. If you accept an update, you can incorporate it immediately into your project plan. The project server database is then updated to show that the change has been accepted, and team members who review the project plan through Project Web Access can see the updates (see Figure 20-11).

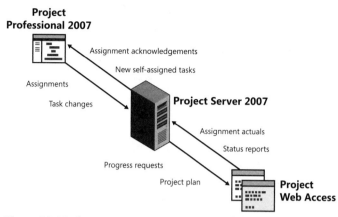

Figure 20-11 The project manager and team members exchange information via Project Server.

Within Project Web Access, team members can see different views of project data, review assignments, enter time reports, update tasks, view summary project plans, send information to the project manager, and more. Each of the Project Web Access users can individually customize their own views to enhance individual efficiencies.

For details about workgroup collaboration information for the team member, see Chapter 23.

Project Web Access is not just for team members, though. Any stakeholders—including functional managers, customers, human resources representatives, and finance managers—can be set up with a user name and a personalized set of permissions to access their view of Project Server through Project Web Access.

Because Project Web Access is a Windows SharePoint Services application, the following functions are built into the Project Web Access experience:

- **Document check-in and checkout** You can include project-related documents with the project, and even associate them with individual tasks or phases. You can implement version control through document check-in and checkout processes.

- **Issues tracking** You can record issues associated with a task or phase. You can then track the issues, assign responsibility, and close them when they're resolved. The issue becomes a part of the task history.

- **Risk tracking** You can record potential risks associated with a task or phase, along with mitigation plans should the risk become a reality. You can assign responsibility and track the risk, then close the risk record when appropriate. The risk information becomes a part of the task history, which can be especially helpful when planning another similar project.

Chapter 20

Standardizing Enterprise Projects

A key element of effective management and control systems is standardization. One purpose of standardization is to ensure that one project is operating with the same ground rules as any other project. Another is consistency throughout the organization.

You can standardize and customize the use of Microsoft Project for the way your enterprise specifically does business, as follows:

- Tailored fields, calendars, views, VBA modules, and other consistent Microsoft Project elements are applied throughout all projects through the use of the enterprise global template.

  Individual project templates are also available in Project Server.

- Your organization's project server administrator can use enterprise custom fields, create formulas and outlines, and pick lists for skill codes or titles.

  Project management efforts can therefore be tailored to the specific processes of the organization.

Managing Enterprise Resources

The lack of a skilled worker for a job can cause serious delays or loss of business. Likewise, having underutilized resources can be an unnecessary drain on the business treasury and can reduce profits.

Project Professional can provide valuable insight into resource utilization, allocation, and availability throughout the enterprise. Although it's not a human resources management tool, the Microsoft Project enterprise features help project managers, resource managers, and functional managers maximize their resource usage while keeping an eye on overallocations.

You can access, assign, and manage resources to leverage the many skill sets available throughout the enterprise. With Microsoft Project enterprise project management, you can obtain up-to-date information about the availability and utilization of thousands of resources in an enterprise as follows:

- All resource assignments throughout the enterprise are visible to project managers, resource managers, and other authorized stakeholders.

  This enterprise-wide visibility ensures that all parties have access to accurate information regarding resource availability. Resource assignments can be checked out, edited, and checked in again.

- The Team Builder helps you find resources throughout the enterprise who have the right skills and availability to work on your project.

  Filter and query the enterprise resource database to fine-tune your project for the right resources.

- Resource availability graphs enable project managers to quickly identify when and why resources might be underallocated or overallocated.

- With workgroup collaboration features, project managers and team members can automate their communications with each other and get the assignments and actuals they need.

> **For further information about managing projects with enterprise resources, see the section titled "Building Your Enterprise Project Team" in Chapter 22.**

Analyzing Project Portfolios

A key benefit of implementing Microsoft Project enterprise project management is that a view of all projects—that is, the organization's project portfolio—can be presented for a set of summary information that provides a unique view into multiple projects. In such a portfolio summary, executives can analyze schedules, costs, resource utilization, and other factors at a high level across all the projects taking place throughout the organization.

Through the Project Center, you can see summary information about all projects throughout the enterprise. You can drill down into any project to get the level of detail you want.

Through data analysis, you can build a PivotTable that shows the information you need. In this way, you can "mine" the portfolio data for specific kinds of information drawn from the entire organization.

If your implementation includes the new Project Portfolio Server 2007 and Project Portfolio Web Server 2007, you have additional sophisticated project portfolio management tools. With these tools, executives can make information decisions in support of enterprise priorities and initiatives.

> **For more information about project portfolio management, see Chapter 24.**

Logging On and Off **692**

Managing Users and Permissions **692**

Administering the Enterprise Resource Pool **704**

Establishing the Enterprise Portfolio **720**

Standardizing Enterprise Project Elements **721**

Setting Up Team Member Work Pages **732**

Managing Pages, Views, and Reports **741**

Managing and Maintaining the Server **751**

A fter the servers, database, and software are installed and working together properly, it is the job of the project server administrator to configure Microsoft Office Project Server 2007 so that it is ready for the users.

The project server administrator might be a portfolio manager with a good working knowledge of systems and databases. Or, the administrator can be an IT professional. In either case, the project server administrator needs to be dedicated and available when Office Project Server 2007 and Microsoft Office Project Web Access are first being set up. This person also needs to be available whenever project managers, team members, or other system users need to change their setup.

Specifically, the project server administration functions include:

- Adding users and setting their permissions.

- Establishing the enterprise resource pool and associated resource information.

- Standardizing project elements included in the enterprise global template.

- Customizing views and pages for the requirements of the enterprise or a particular project.

Although this chapter is targeted for project server administrators, it's a good idea for project managers to review this chapter as well. This chapter can help project managers understand the enterprise project management capabilities available, as well as the effort required to implement certain features.

Guidelines for Installing Project Server 2007

This chapter covers setup and administrative procedures performed by the project server administrator after the server equipment and software are set up, along with the operating system, database, and clients.

> For more information about system requirements and installation, including general guidelines for installing Project Server 2007 and enterprise project management, see Appendix A, "Installing Microsoft Office Project 2007."
>
> However, be aware that Appendix A only covers broad generalities of installation for Project Server 2007. Each organization has unique requirements for its enterprise project management configuration, and therefore the installation process must be customized to those requirements.
>
> For more detailed information, see the Office Project Server 2007 Technical Library. Go to *http://technet2.microsoft.com/Office* and then click Office Project Server 2007.

Logging On and Off

To log on to Office Project Web Access, follow these steps:

1. Open your Web browser. In the Address bar, enter the URL for the location of the project server.

2. On the logon page, enter the user ID and password that were set up for you as the administrator.

   The home page of Project Web Access appears.

To log off of Project Web Access, follow these steps:

1. In the upper-right corner of the Project Web Access window, click the Welcome button.

2. In the drop-down list that appears, click Sign Out.

Managing Users and Permissions

As the project server administrator, you configure enterprise project management options on the Server Settings page in Project Web Access. Links to all pages are listed on the left side of the Project Web Access window in the task pane, which is called the Quick Launch. Click Server Settings. The Server Settings page appears (see Figure 21-1). Only users with administrator permissions can open the Server Settings page in Project Web Access.

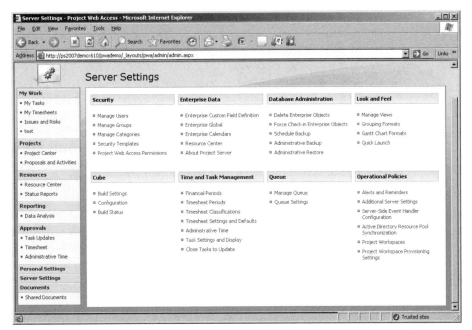

Figure 21-1 Set up enterprise project management options on the Server Settings page in Project Web Access.

Carry Out Administrative Duties

The Server Settings page in Project Web Access contains all the tools and commands you need to administer enterprise project management features for your organization, as follows:

- Security
- Enterprise data
- Database administration
- Look and feel
- Cube
- Time and task management
- Queues
- Operational policies

To allow people throughout the organization to use the Microsoft Office Project 2007 enterprise project management features they need, you first need to identify them as users of your project server. At the same time, you also specify the users' permissions that enable them to carry out their category of project responsibilities according to that user's role and responsibilities.

> **Note**
>
> If you ever need assistance while using Project Web Access, click Help in the upper-right corner of the Project Web Access page. Microsoft Project Web Access Help appears on the right side of the window.

Understanding Groups, Categories, and Permissions

Project Server 2007 is loaded with a set of built-in user groups, each of which is associated with a set of permissions having to do with various aspects of enterprise project management. Consider using the built-in groups and permission sets as a starting point. As you and your organization gain more experience with Project Server 2007 and start to get a better idea about how you want to implement enterprise project management features, you can make adjustments and customizations.

The built-in user groups, also known as roles, are as follows:

- Administrators
- Executives
- Portfolio Managers
- Project Managers
- Proposal Reviewers
- Resource Managers
- Team Leads
- Team Members

Each of the user groups can be associated with a security template that includes the set of permissions most likely to be needed by someone in that user group.

In addition to setting the permissions for a new user, you also set the categories of information that can be associated with a user group, to which users are then assigned. Although you can create your own categories, the built-in categories are as follows:

- My Direct Reports
- My Organization
- My Projects
- My Resources
- My Tasks

Creating a New User Account

To create a new user account in Project Web Access and set the user's permissions, follow these steps:

1. In the Project Web Access Quick Launch task bar, click Server Settings.

2. Under Security, click Manage Users.

    The Manage Users page appears (see Figure 21-2).

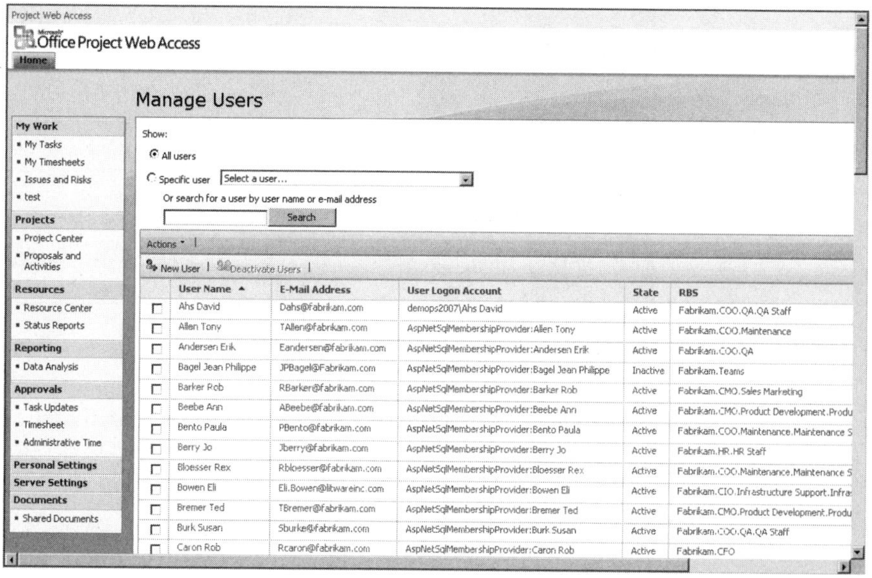

Figure 21-2 Open the Manage Users page to add a new user account.

3. Above the table, click New User.

    The New User page appears (see Figure 21-3).

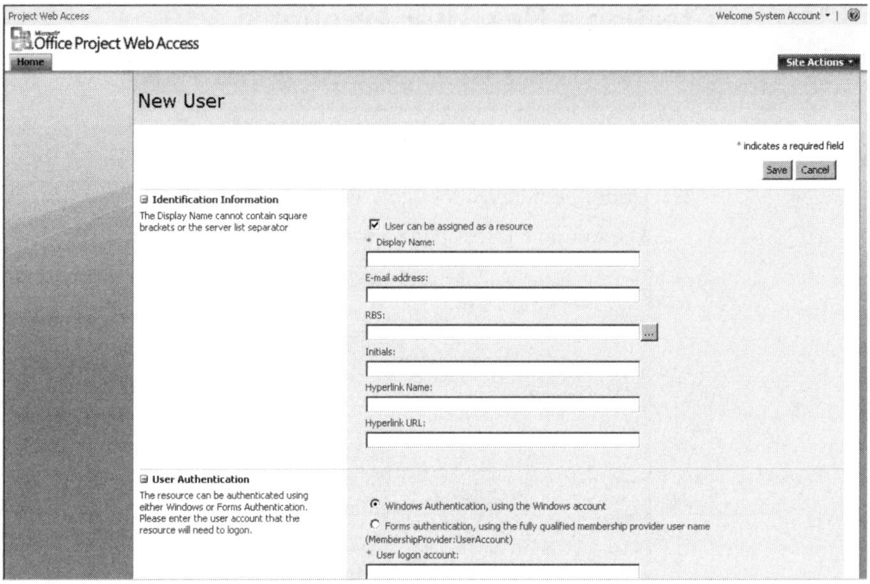

Figure 21-3 On the New User page, specify the new user's authentication, group, and permissions.

4. In the Identification Information section, make sure that the User Can Be Assigned As A Resource check box is selected if the user is to be part of your enterprise resource pool.

5. Enter at least the user's display name, typically the person's first and last names.

If you complete the E-mail Address box, type it in the format of someone@microsoft.com.

6. In the User Authentication section, select the option for this user's authentication method.

With Windows Authentication, users can log on to Project Web Access by using the same user ID and password they use to log on to your organization's Windows network.

With Forms Authentication, users log on to Project Web Access by using the user ID you set up on this page. They can then set their password in Project Web Access. If you have already added enterprise resources, they are automatically added as forms authentication users.

7. In the User Logon Account box, enter the user's account name.

If you're entering a Windows account, enter it in the format of domain\username.

If you're entering a Forms account, the name is typically in the form of MembershipProvider:UserAccount. The person who set up Project Server 2007 determined the exact form, so check with that person if you're not sure. The first time that forms authentication users log on to Project Web Access, they'll be prompted to set a password.

8. In the Assignment Attributes and Resource Custom Fields sections, make any necessary changes appropriate for this user.

    This section is available only for users identified as resources.

9. In the Security Groups section, click the group that this user belongs to and then click Add.

    A user can be a member of more than one group.

10. In the Group Fields, Team Details, and System Identification Data sections, make any necessary changes or entries appropriate for this user. Click the plus sign next to the section name if necessary to expand the section.

    The Team Details section is available only for users identified as resources.

11. When finished, click the Save button at the bottom of the page.

After you set up the user accounts, team members and other Project Web Access users just need to use their Web browser to go to the designated URL for your project server location. They enter their user name (and password if necessary), and their own view of Project Web Access appears.

Chapter 21

Note

You can see a list of all users and their permissions. In any page of Project Web Access, click Site Actions in the upper-right corner and then click Site Settings. Under Users And Permissions, click Advanced Permissions. A list of all users, their user names, and their permission group appears.

To return to the Project Web Access home page, click the Home tab in the upper-left corner.

Add Your Project Server Users as Enterprise Resources

When you add users to your project server, you have the choice of making them enterprise resources at the same time. On the New User page, make sure that the User Can Be Assigned As A Resource check box is selected. You can then enter resource and assignment information, as follows:

- **Resource Can Be Leveled** Specify whether this resource's assignments can be split or delayed to resolve overallocations. By default, this check box is selected.

- **Base Calendar** Select the base calendar to be used to schedule this resource's working and nonworking times. By default, the Standard calendar is selected.

- **Default Booking Type** Select whether this resource should show as a committed or proposed resource by default.

- **Timesheet Manager** Enter the name of the user responsible for receiving this resource's timesheets. You can click Browse to select a resource from a list.

- **Default Assignment Owner** Enter the name of the user who will be responsible for entering progress information for this resource's assignments. By default, the current resource is the assignment owner. You can click Browse to select another resource from a list.

- **Earliest Available** Enter the soonest date this resource will be available to accept assignments. If you leave this box blank, Office Project 2007 assumes that this resource is currently available.

- **Latest Available** Enter the latest date that this resource will be available to accept assignments. If you leave this box blank, Microsoft Project assumes that this resource has open-ended availability.

- **Resource Custom Fields** If any custom fields have been created for resources, they are listed here for you to enter the information appropriate for the current resource.

- **Team Assignment Pool** If the current resource is a member of a team that can carry out tasks assigned to that team, select this check box.

- **Team Name** If the Team Assignment Pool check box is selected, enter or click the name of the team to which the current resource belongs.

Project managers using enterprise project management features in Microsoft Office Project Professional 2007 and Project Web Access should refer to Chapter 22, "Managing Enterprise Projects and Resources."

Team members and resource managers needing information about using Project Web Access should refer to Chapter 23, "Participating on a Team Using Project Web Access."

Executives and other managing stakeholders using Project Web Access should refer to Chapter 24, "Making Executive Decisions Using Project Web Access."

Removing a User from Your Project Server

You can deactivate a user, for example, one who has left the company after working on several projects. When you deactivate a user, the information about that user's assignments remain intact. You can also delete a user. This should only be done if the user was added by mistake, or if no project information is associated with that user.

To deactivate a user, follow these steps:

1. On the Server Settings page, under Security, click Manage Users.

2. Select the check box next to the name of the user you want to deactivate. You can select several check boxes if you need to deactivate multiple users.

3. Above the table, click Deactivate Users.

4. In the alert that appears, click OK.

   The selected user is deactivated and can no longer log on to the project server.

To delete a user from the project server, follow these steps:

1. On the Server Settings page, under Database Administration, click Delete Enterprise Objects.

2. Under What Do You Want To Delete From Project Server, select the Resources And Users option.

   The page updates to show all users.

3. Select the check box next to the name of the user you want to delete. You can select several check boxes if you need to delete multiple users.

4. Click the Delete button.

5. In the alert that appears, click OK.

   The selected user is deleted from the project server. Any projects owned by that user are assigned to your account.

Viewing or Changing Permissions for User Groups

You can review the sets of permissions assigned to a particular user group. You can also modify the set of permissions used for a user group. To do this, follow these steps:

1. Open the Server Settings page of Project Web Access.

2. Under Security, click Security Templates.

3. Click the name of the template whose permissions you want to see, for example, Executives or Proposal Reviewer.

4. In the Add Or Edit Template page, scroll through the Category Permissions and the Global Permissions lists to see the permissions for the selected group.

5. Make any changes you want by selecting or clearing the Allow or Deny check boxes next to permissions. When finished, click Save at the bottom of the page.

> **Note**
>
> You can see a list of all available permissions. On the Server Settings page, click Project Web Access Permissions under Security.

Creating a New Security Template

A security template is a collection of permissions that can be associated with a user group or a category. Project Server 2007 comes with eight built-in security templates: one for each of the eight built-in user groups from Team Member to Administrator.

You can set up your own security templates with entirely different sets of permissions. You can then assign the new set of permissions to users, groups, and categories in a single step. To create a new security template, follow these steps:

1. Open the Server Settings page of Project Web Access.

2. Under Security, click Security Templates.

3. Above the table, click New Template.

   The Add Or Edit Template page appears.

4. In the Name section, enter at least a name in the Template Name box. You can also type a description.

5. If you want to base your new security template on an existing template, click a template in the Copy Template box.

6. In the Category Permissions section, make any changes needed to permissions by selecting or clearing the Allow or Deny check boxes next to permissions.

7. In the Global Permissions section, make any changes you want to permissions by selecting or clearing the Allow or Deny check boxes next to permissions.

8. When finished, click Save at the bottom of the page.

> **Note**
>
> To delete a security template, on the Server Settings page, under Security, click Security Templates. Select the check box next to the name of the security template you want to delete. Click Delete Template.

Creating a New Group

Each group, or role, defined in Project Web Access is identified by a set of permissions. You can specify which users belong to which group, the categories of information they have access to, and the permissions for what they can do with that information.

If your organization uses different roles from those identified as groups in Project Web Access (for example, Project Managers and Team Leaders), you can create your own. To do this, follow these steps:

1. Open the Server Settings page of Project Web Access.

2. Under Security, click Manage Groups.

   The Manage Groups page appears (see Figure 21-4)

Figure 21-4 Use the Manage Groups page to review, modify, add, or delete groups (roles) in your project server.

3. Above the table, click New Group.

   The Add Or Edit Group page appears.

4. In the Group Information section, enter the group name and description in the first two boxes.

5. In the Users section, click the users you want to add to the group and then click Add.

   You can also add users after you've finished defining the group.

6. In the Categories section, click any categories (for example, My Tasks or My Resources) that are appropriate to be accessed by members of this group and then click Add.

7. In the Selected Categories box, select each category in turn and then, in the Permissions box, set the permissions for the category. Repeat this process for each category in the Selected Categories box.

   If you want to use a security template to set permissions for a category, scroll to the bottom of the page, click the arrow in the Set Permissions With Template box, and then select the template. Click Apply. Make any adjustments to the permissions as necessary for the selected category.

8. Click the plus sign next to the Global Permissions label to expand the list. Specify the global permissions that you want to apply to your new group.

   If you prefer to use a security template to set global permissions for a category, scroll to the bottom of the page, click the arrow in the Set Permissions With Template box, and then select the template. Click Apply. Make any adjustments to the permissions as necessary for the selected category.

9. When finished defining the new group, click Save at the bottom of the page.

To edit an existing group, click Manage Groups under Security on the Server Settings page. In the table, click the group you want to change. The Add Or Edit Group page appears. Make the changes you want to add or remove users in the group, change the categories associated with the group, or change permissions for the group.

> **Note**
> To delete a group, on the Server Settings page, under Security, click Manage Groups. Select the check box next to the name of the group you want to delete. Click Delete Group.

> **Permissions Shown are Specific to the Group and Category**
> When you select a category in the Selected Categories box on the Manage Groups section, remember that the set of permissions displayed are specific to the group/category combination, and does not cover all the categories.
>
> Each category has its own set of permissions for this group. This concept is key to understanding Project Server security.

Customizing Categories

Categories are clusters of information, such as My Tasks, My Projects, or My Resources. Some user groups should have access to all categories, whereas other groups only need access to two or three categories.

If the built-in categories don't quite fit the way your organization works with projects, you can customize them or create entirely new ones. To create a new category, follow these steps:

1. Open the Server Settings page of Project Web Access.

2. Under Security, click Manage Categories.

    The Manage Categories page appears.

3. Above the table, click New Category to open the Add Or Edit Category page.

4. In the Name And Description section, enter a name and description for your new category.

5. In the Users And Groups section, select the users and groups you want to be a part of the category and then click the Add button.

6. Select the first user or group in the Users And Groups With Permissions box, and then in the Permissions box, specify the permissions that users in this category

should have. Repeat this process for each user and group you have added to the category.

7. In the Projects section, specify which projects the users in this category should be able to access: all projects in your project server database or just selected projects.

Select or clear the project-related check boxes to further define the category.

8. In the Resources section, specify which resources the users in this category should be able to view: all current and future resources in your project server database or just selected resources (see Figure 21-5).

Select or clear the resource-related check boxes to further define the category.

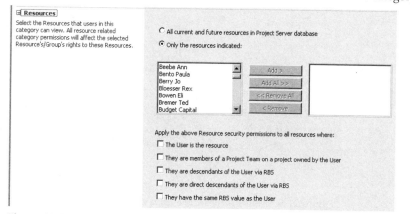

Figure 21-5 Specify the resources whose information can be accessed by users in this category.

9. In the Views – Add To Category section, select the check box for the views that the users in this category should be able to see. To select all views in a group of views, such as Project or Resource Center, select the check box next to that name, and all the views within that group are selected.

10. When finished, click Save at the bottom of the page.

Your new category is added to the table in the Manage Categories page.

To modify an existing category, click the category name in the Manage Categories page that you want to change, for example, My Direct Reports or My Tasks. Review the information in the Add Or Edit Category page and make the changes you want. When finished, click Save.

> **Note**
>
> To delete a category, on the Server Settings page, under Security, click Manage Categories. Select the check box next to the name of the category you want to delete. Click Delete Category.

Chapter 21

Sending Automated Alerts and Reminders to Users

You can have Project Server 2007 automatically send e-mail messages to team members and project managers to remind them about assignments and status reports that are due. To set up automated alerts and reminders, follow these steps:

1. On the Server Settings page, under Operational Policies, click Alerts And Reminders.

2. Complete the fields in the Notification E-Mail Settings section (see Figure 21-6).

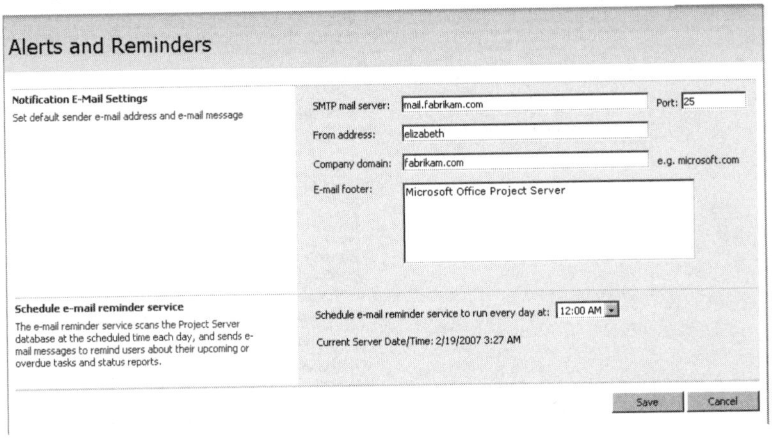

Figure 21-6 Use the Alerts And Reminders page to send e-mail reminders to users about their assignments and status reports.

3. In the Schedule E-Mail Reminder Service section, specify the time of day that the reminder should be sent.

4. Click Save.

Administering the Enterprise Resource Pool

The enterprise resource pool is the set of people, equipment, and materials available to be assigned to and carry out the work of projects throughout an organization. The organization can be as compact as a small department or as wide ranging as all employees in all regions of a worldwide corporation. The enterprise resource pool contains fundamental information about resources, such as skill sets and availability, which helps project managers find the right resources for their projects. The enterprise resource pool also contains cost information, which not only helps project managers work within their allotted budgets, but also helps accounting and human resources figure costs from their points of view.

With the enterprise resource pool, high-level visibility of resource availabilities, skills, roles, and utilization is now possible. Project managers as well as upper management can see when additional staff is needed and where there are underutilized resources. They also can view the basic data for all project resources in one place.

Furthermore, project managers can plan for project staffing needs with accurate and current resource information from the entire enterprise, instead of from just their own team or group. The advantages of the multiple project resource pool, such as resource sharing between project managers, are magnified when applied to the entire enterprise.

Resource managers can use the enterprise resource pool to staff, plan, and budget with more accuracy and confidence. They can see resources by skill level and definition, availability, and organizational hierarchy. In addition, they can assist project managers with current and anticipated resource requirements by analyzing the enterprise resource database. Together with the project managers, resource managers can work with generic resources in the enterprise resource pool to perform planning and contingency analyses.

The project server administrator is often the one who sets up and maintains the enterprise resource pool. However, because of the specialized information having to do with resource skills, costs, and availability, other specialists such as a portfolio manager or a human resources representative might be involved in the setup. By default, the project server administrator and portfolio manager are given the permission to add and edit enterprise resource data.

A user with the permission to edit enterprise resource data can do the following:

- Create and add users to the enterprise resource pool.

- Update information on resources in the enterprise resource pool.

- Customize resource fields for use in the enterprise resource pool.

- Specify multiple properties for resources in the enterprise resource pool.

Project managers working with enterprise projects connected to the project server cannot use the regular resource pool because it is replaced by the enterprise resource pool. However, the local resource pool features are available to users working with local, non-enterprise projects.

For more information about working with the resource pool, see the section titled "Sharing Resources by Using a Resource Pool" in Chapter 14, "Managing Master Projects and Resource Pools."

Creating the Enterprise Resource Pool

After you create the enterprise resource pool, project managers can access it and build project teams from it. If you can, add the bulk of your resources at one time. You can always add individual resources as time goes on. Project managers who have been working with their own resources can also import those local resources into the enterprise resource pool. Now in Project 2007, you can add a team resource, such as Accounting or Research. Any individual enterprise resource that's a member of that team can do the work on tasks assigned to the team resource.

Adding Multiple Enterprise Resources

If you want to add several resources at one time to your enterprise resource pool, along with information about each resource, you can use the Project 2007 Resource Sheet. To do this, follow these steps:

1. Make sure your user profile allows the Edit Enterprise Resource Data permission in your project server.

   If you are the project server administrator or portfolio manager, you have this permission by default.

2. In Office Project Professional 2007, click Tools, Enterprise Options, Open Enterprise Resource Pool.

   The Checked-Out Enterprise Resources window appears, showing the Resource Center (see Figure 21-7).

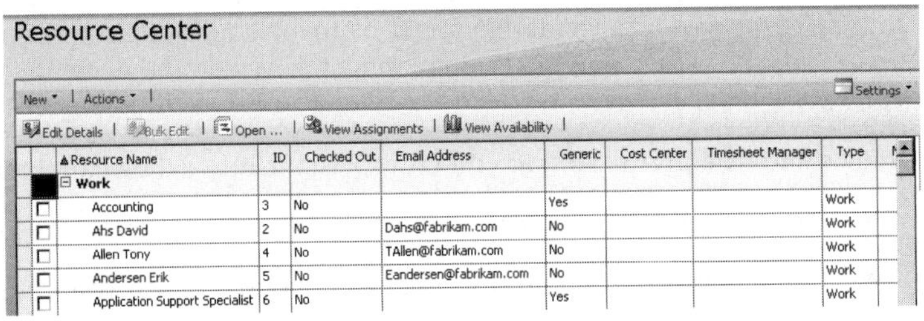

Figure 21-7 The Checked-Out Enterprise Resources window shows the enterprise resource pool in the Resource Center.

3. Above the table, click the Open button.

   Still in the Checked-Out Enterprise Resources window, the Resource Sheet appears. If you have not selected any resources in the Resource Center, the sheet is empty.

> **Note**
>
> When adding a new resource to an existing enterprise resource pool, it might seem odd to see a blank Resource Sheet, especially because you selected the Open Enterprise Resource Pool command.
>
> In reality, however, you never really check out the entire resource pool unless you select all resources and then click the Open button. Typically, you come here to add several new resources or edit information for a select group of resources, while the rest of the resources are still safely checked in.

4. In the Resource Name field, type the name of the resource. Enter any other information in the other fields, such as type, group, maximum units, cost rates, and base calendar.

Resource Information

If you want to add more complete resource information, click the Resource Information button on the Standard toolbar. The Resource Information dialog box appears. Enter information on the various tabs as appropriate to this resource. When finished, click OK.

> **Note**
>
> For more information about the different types of resource information that can be added to the Resource Sheet and Resource Information dialog box, see Chapter 6, "Setting Up Resources in the Project."

5. Repeat step 4 for all other resources you want to add (see Figure 21-8).

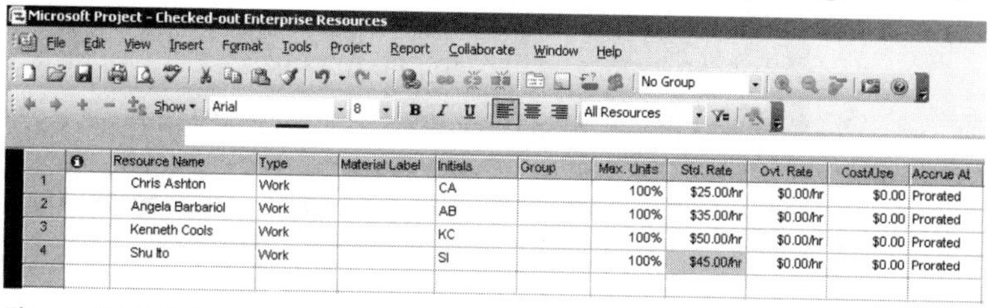

Microsoft Project - Checked-out Enterprise Resources
File Edit View Insert Format Tools Project Report Collaborate Window Help
No Group
Show
Arial
8
All Resources
Resource Name
Type
Material Label
Initials
Group
Max. Units
Std. Rate
Ovt. Rate
Cost/Use
Accrue At
1 Chris Ashton Work CA 100% $25.00/hr $0.00/hr $0.00 Prorated
2 Angela Barbariol Work AB 100% $35.00/hr $0.00/hr $0.00 Prorated
3 Kenneth Cools Work KC 100% $50.00/hr $0.00/hr $0.00 Prorated
4 Shu Ito Work SI 100% $45.00/hr $0.00/hr $0.00 Prorated

Figure 21-8 Enter resource names and associated information in Checked-Out Enterprise Resources.

Save

6. Whenever you want to save changes, just click Save on the Standard toolbar.
7. When you're finished adding resources, and you want to check the enterprise resource pool and its new information in to your project server, click File, Close.

   Don't press the Close (X) button in the upper-right corner, or Microsoft Project will try to close the application as well as any open projects. Clicking File, Close closes only the Checked-Out Enterprise Resources window.
8. If a prompt asks if you want to save your changes, click Yes.

When you return to Project Web Access and click Resource Center, you'll see that the new resources are now added to the enterprise resource pool.

> **Note**
>
> Another method for entering multiple resources is to add them from your e-mail program's address book. In Project Professional 2007, click Insert, New Resource From, Address Book.

TROUBLESHOOTING

Your new resources are not added as project server users

Although it might be convenient to quickly enter resources in the Resource Sheet of Project Professional 2007, the drawback is that resources entered in this manner are not added as project server users.

To add these resources as project server users, follow these steps.

1. In the Resource Center, select the check boxes next to the names of the resources you want to add as users.

2. Click Edit Details in the toolbar above the table.

   The Edit Resource page appears for the first resource.

3. In the Identification Information section, select the Resource Can Logon To Project Server check box.

4. Complete the User Authentication, Security Groups, Security Categories, and Global Permissions sections for this resource.

5. When finished editing the information for the first user, click the Save And Continue button.

   The second selected resource appears so you can repeat steps 3-5 for that resource.

Edit Details

Adding Resources by Synchronizing with Active Directory

If your organization uses Active Directory directory service, you have at your fingertips the easiest method for generating your enterprise resource pool. You can synchronize the Active Directory security groups with those in your project server. In this way, resources from a specific Active Directory group are instantly mapped to the enterprise resource pool. Not only does this add the resources to your project server, but the periodic synchronization helps keep your list of users and resources up to date. If the resource exists in Active Directory, the resource is automatically added to the enterprise resource pool upon the next scheduled Active Directory update to your project server. Any resources that no longer exist in Active Directory are likewise removed from your project server. This is a one-way synchronization, from Active Directory to your project server.

The Active Directory synchronization options are set as part of your project server configuration. These options can be set during initial configuration, or they can be set anytime afterward. To synchronize your project server with Active Directory, follow these steps:

1. Open the Server Settings page of Project Web Access.

2. Under Operational Policies, click Active Directory Resource Pool Synchronization.

   The Active Directory Enterprise Resource Pool Synchronization page appears (see Figure 21-9).

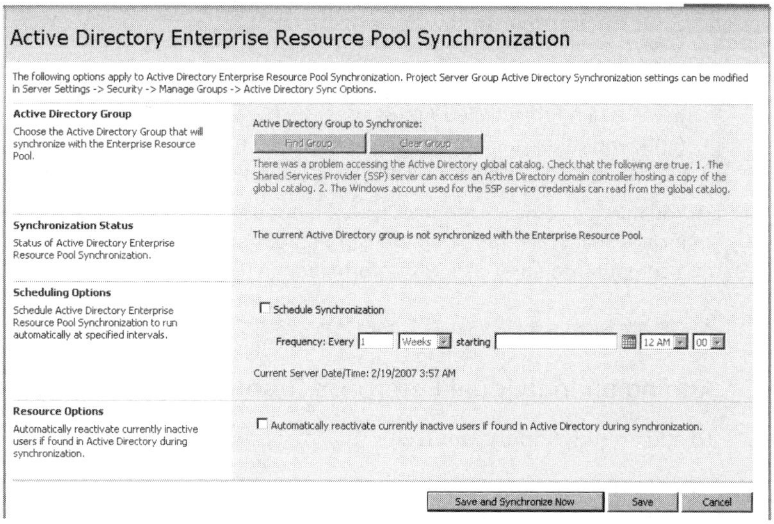

Figure 21-9 Set scheduling and resource options to synchronize an Active Directory group with your enterprise resource pool.

3. In the Active Directory Group section, select the Active Directory group you want to synchronize with your enterprise resource pool.

4. In the Scheduling Options section, select the Schedule Synchronization check box. Then specify the frequency at which your project server should be synchronized with your Active Directory, for example, every week or every 2 months. Specify the date when updates should begin and the time of day when updates should be done.

5. When finished, click Save And Synchronize Now or Save.

Note

Your organization might have information about your enterprise resource pool in another existing system, for example, your human resources or general ledger system. The Project Server Interface (PSI) can be used to develop an application program interface (API) that can interact with that other system to help you create your enterprise resource pool.

For more information, see the section titled "Integrating Project Information with Business Processes" later in this chapter.

Users and Resources Are Not Necessarily the Same

Project Web Access users are often enterprise resources, but not always. You are likely to have certain Project Web Access users such as executives, resource managers, accountants, and other managing stakeholders who need access to project information, but who are not themselves available to be assigned to a project team.

You might also have resources who are not users of Project Web Access. Examples might include team members who are carrying out project tasks but who do not have access to a computer to enter progress information in Project Web Access.

Adding an Individual Enterprise Resource

To add an individual resource to the enterprise resource pool, follow these steps:

1. In the Resource Center, click New, Resource.

   The New Resource page appears.

2. Complete all the sections on the page as they apply to the new resource you're creating.

3. If this resource is also to be a user of your project server, be sure that the Resource Can Logon To Project Server check box is selected.

4. When finished, click Save.

   The new resource is saved as a new member of the enterprise resource pool.

Add Enterprise Resources as Project Web Access Users

When you add work resources from within Project Web Access, you have the choice of making them project server users at the same time. On the New Resource page, in the Identification Information section, make sure that the Resource Can Logon To Project Server check box is selected. This check box is selected by default.

When this check box is selected, you can enter logon and permissions information, as follows:

- **User Authentication** Enter the user's logon account name.
- **Security Groups** Select and add the user group(s) that this user is to be a member of.

- **Global Permissions** In the Set Permissions With Template box, select the template that represents this user's role and then click Apply. In the Global Permissions list, select or clear individual check boxes as necessary to tailor the permissions for this user.

Adding a Team Resource

Suppose your organization has several resources in the product testing department who are all capable of carrying out the same tasks. The project manager could assign Chris to do one task, Sam to do another, and Maria to do a third. But it might be easier to assign all three tasks to a resource named "Product Testing Team" and let Chris, Sam, and Maria decide among themselves who should do what.

This is the idea behind team resources, new in Project 2007. You can create a resource that represents a group of resources, that is, a team. A project manager can then assign tasks to the team. Resources who are identified as part of that team can assign themselves to a team task, report on it, and complete it.

To create a team resource in Project Web Access, follow these steps:

1. In the Quick Launch task bar, click Resource Center.

2. Click New, Resource.

3. In the Type section, make sure that the Generic check box is cleared.

4. In the Identification Information section, clear the Resource Can Logon To Project Server check box.

5. Enter the name of the team resource, for example, Drafters or Writers.

6. In the Assignment Attributes section, specify the options for leveling, base calendar, default booking type, and availability dates as appropriate to the collective resources who will make up this team. Enter a resource in the Timesheet Manager and Default Assignment Owner boxes.

7. Complete the fields in the Resource Custom Fields and Group Fields as applicable to this team resource.

8. In the Team Details section, select the Team Assignment Pool check box. This identifies this resource as a team resource.

9. When finished, click Save.

   The team resource is created as part of your enterprise resource pool in your project server, and project managers can now assign tasks to this team resource.

> **Note**
> You can also create team resources in Project Professional. Add the Team Assignment Pool field to the Resource Sheet and change the field to Yes to mark your team resources.

To create the list of teams in your enterprise, you use a "built-in" custom field called Team Name. You create and associate a lookup table to the Team Name field. The lookup table of teams becomes available in the Team Name drop-down list in the Edit Users and Edit Resources pages in Project Web Access.

To create your list of teams for the Team Name field, follow these steps:

New Lookup Table

1. On the Server Settings page, under Enterprise Data, click Enterprise Custom Field Definition.

2. In the Lookup Tables For Custom Fields table, click New Lookup Table.

3. In the Name field, enter a name for your team lookup table, for example, Team Pools.

4. Scroll down to the Lookup Table section.

5. To define a new team, click an available row and then type the name of the team (see Figure 21-10).

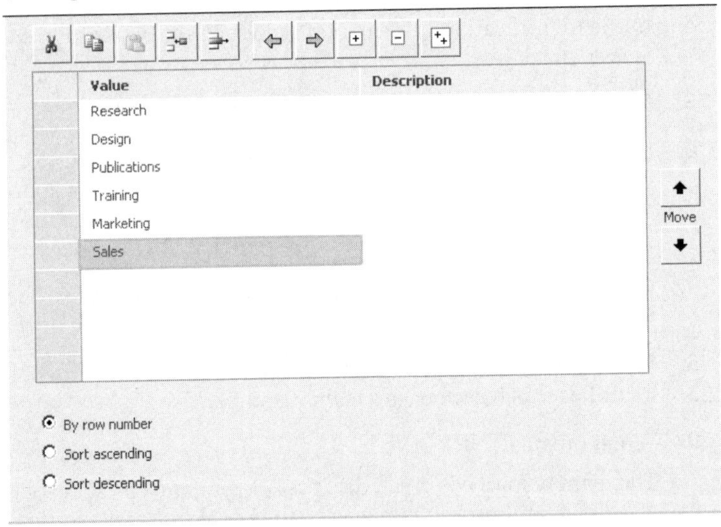

Figure 21-10 Define your teams on the New Lookup Table page and then associate that lookup table with the Team Name built-in custom field.

Insert Row

6. To insert a team name between two others, click the team name below where you want to insert a new team and then click the Insert Row button. Type the name of the team.

Outdent

Indent

Delete Row

7. To edit an existing team name, drag across a team name and then type to make the change you want.

8. Use the Outdent and Indent buttons to specify the team position in the hierarchy, if applicable.

9. Use the Move buttons to change the sequence of the team names as necessary.

10. To delete a team name, click in its row and then click Delete Row.

11. Click Save.

To associate the Team Name enterprise custom field with your team lookup table, follow these steps:

1. On the Custom Fields And Lookup Tables page, click Team Name in the Enterprise Custom Fields table.

Team Name is the "built-in" custom field designed for the team resource function.

2. In the Custom Attributes section, in the Lookup Table box, select the name of your team definition lookup table.

> **Note**
>
> Once you associate the team lookup table with the Team Name field, this association becomes permanent. However, you can always change the content of the lookup table.

3. Click Save.

After the team resources have been created and identified as such, you need to identify the resources who belong to each team. To do this in Project Web Access, follow these steps:

1. In the Resource Center, select the check boxes next to the names of the resources who are to be identified as members of a particular team.

2. Click Edit Details.

3. In the Edit Resource page for the first selected resource, scroll down to the Team Details section. In the Team Name box, select the name of the team to which this resource belongs.

4. Click the Save And Continue button.

The second selected resource appears.

5. Repeat steps 3–4 for that resource. Continue in this manner until the appropriate resources have been associated with their team resource.

Chapter 21

Resources who want to assign themselves to a team task follow these steps:

1. In the Quick Launch task bar, click My Tasks.

Self-Assign
Team Tasks

2. Click Self-Assign Team Tasks.

   Any tasks that have been assigned to the team to which you belong are listed in the table on the Team Tasks page.

3. Select the check box next to the team task to which you want to assign yourself.

4. Click Assign Task To Me.

> For more information about how team members work with tasks and assignments, see the section titled "Working on Your Assignments and Updates" in Chapter 23.

What's the Difference Between a Generic Resource and a Team Resource?

A generic resource is a placeholder for work or cost resources who will be added to a project at a later date, typically after the project has been approved and can be staffed up. The generic resource provides a means for estimating resource requirements and costs. Generic resources typically have job title names such as "Engineer," "Trainer," "Architect," or "Graphic Designer."

On the other hand, a team resource represents a group of people, each of whom are capable of carrying out tasks to which the team resource has been assigned. Use of the team resource provides the project manager or resource manager with more flexibility in making assignments. Use of the team resource method also provides members of the team with the freedom to choose which assignments they take on. Team resources typically have team or department names such as "Quality Assurance Team," "Maintenance Crew," or "Sales and Marketing."

Importing Existing Local Resources to the Project Server

A number of resources, complete with reliable availability and cost information, might already exist in enterprise and nonenterprise projects. You can easily open those projects and import the resources into the enterprise resource pool using the Import Resource Wizard.

Local Resource

Local resources are flagged with the Local Resource icon in the Indicators field of the Resource Sheet.

Follow these steps to import local (nonenterprise) resources from an existing project to the enterprise resource pool:

1. Be sure you're logged in to the project server through Project Professional 2007. It doesn't matter whether the project containing the local resources is open.

2. Click Tools, Enterprise Options, Import Resources To Enterprise.

The Open dialog box appears showing a list of projects.

3. If the resources you want to import are in an enterprise project, click the name of that project and then click Open.

If the resources are in a local project stored on your computer or network, find its general location in the Look In task pane. Browse to the file and then double-click to open it.

The Import Resources Wizard task pane appears (see Figure 21-11).

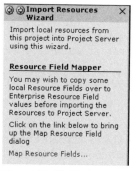

Figure 21-11 The Import Resources Wizard task pane appears.

4. If any custom resource fields in this project also need to be imported with the resources, click the Map Resource Fields link. Map any custom resource fields from the original project to the enterprise resource pool (see Figure 21-12). This ensures that all the necessary information associated with the resource is imported to the enterprise resource pool. When finished, click OK.

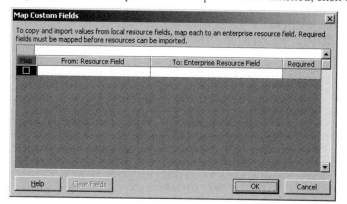

Figure 21-12 Map any custom resource fields to the enterprise resource pool.

5. Click the Continue To Step 2 link to open the Confirm Resources task pane.

This task pane lists the number of local resources to be imported and the number of import errors that are anticipated. The nature of any errors are listed in the Errors column next to the resource name in the Import Resource sheet.

6. If there are any resources you do not want to import, click No in the Import field for that resource.

7. To resolve any errors, double-click the resource name to make the necessary changes in the Resource Information dialog box.

8. To check for errors again, click the Validate Resources button in the task pane.

9. When all errors are resolved, click the Save And Finish link.

    The resources and their associated calendar, cost, and other information are imported to the project server to become part of your enterprise resource pool.

Import Projects and Resources at Once Using the Import Projects Wizard

If you want to import resources from a nonenterprise project that you need to import to the project server as an enterprise project, you can do both at the same time. The primary job of the Import Projects Wizard is to import tasks in an existing project into a new enterprise project. If you want, you can specify that the resources in that project also be added to the enterprise resource pool and assigned to the newly created enterprise project.

For more information about importing projects with their resources and custom fields, see the section titled "Importing a Local Project to the Server" in Chapter 20.

Updating Resource Information

Once resources are added to the enterprise resource pool, you can edit their resource information by making the necessary changes in the Edit Resource page in Project Web Access.

You can also edit resource information in the Project Professional Resource Sheet by checking the resources out, making the necessary changes, and then checking them in again.

Any resource information—such as base calendar, group name, and resource custom fields—can be edited this way. Some types of resource information are more readily available in the Project Web Access Edit Resource page, and others are more readily available in the Project Professional Resource Sheet or Resource Information dialog box. So depending on the nature of the changes you're making, you might equally use both methods.

> **Note**
>
> Assignment information is changed in the enterprise project itself, not in the enterprise resource pool.

Resource information cannot be changed casually by project managers. Only those granted the Edit Enterprise Resource Data permission can check out and edit this resource information. By default, the project server administrator and portfolio manager are the only ones granted this permission.

Finding and Selecting Resources

When working with an enterprise resource pool that supports even a handful of projects, you might soon find that your enterprise resource pool is quickly filled with dozens if not hundreds of resources. Because of this, it's important to be able to deftly find and select the resources you need in the Resource Center without too much scanning and scrolling.

The upper-right corner of the Resource Center contains controls for helping you find the resources you want to modify, as follows:

- **Select a view.** Click the arrow in the View box to see a list of resource views. You can create additional views. See the section titled "Creating and Managing Views" later in this chapter.

- **Filter for resources.** Click Settings, Filter to show filter controls above the toolbar. You can create a custom filter and add it to the Filter box. You can also apply the Auto Filter to filter by a particular value in a field in the resource table.

- **Group resources.** Click Settings, Group. Grouping controls appear above the toolbar. You can group up to three levels by fields. Groups are separated by a colored band in the table.

- **Search for resources.** Click Settings, Search to show the search controls above the toolbar.

Any resources whose check boxes are selected are listed in the Selected Resources box to the right of the resource table. To select all resources listed, click Actions, Select All Resources. To clear all selected resources, click Actions, Clear All Resources.

These controls are fairly standard throughout Project Web Access.

Modifying Enterprise Resource Information

To modify enterprise resource information in Project Web Access, follow these steps:

1. In the Resource Center, select the check boxes next to the resources whose information you want to change.

Bulk Edit

2. If you're changing the timesheet manager, default assignment owner, or the content of custom fields, click Bulk Edit. Make the changes in the Bulk Edit page, select the corresponding Apply Changes check box, and then click Save.

   You only need to make the change once on this page, and the change is applied to all selected resources.

3. For any other changes, click Edit Details.

4. In the Edit Resource page for the first resource, make your changes.

5. Click the Save And Continue button.

6. Repeat steps 4–5 for the second resource. Continue in this manner until you have changed the resource information for all selected resources.

7. When you finish the last resource, click Save.

If you prefer, or if it's easier given the accessibility of certain resource information fields, you can change resource information in Project Professional. To do this, follow these steps:

1. In Project Web Access, select the check boxes next to the resources whose information you want to change and then click the Open button on the toolbar.

   Alternatively, if you're already working in Project Professional, click Tools, Enterprise Options, Open Enterprise Resource Pool. Select the check boxes next to the resources whose information you want to change and then click the Open button on the toolbar.

   Either way, the selected resources are checked out and listed in a Resource Sheet in Project Professional.

2. On the Resource Sheet, make the changes you want to the enterprise resource.

3. If you need to work with additional resource information, double-click the resource name to open the Resource Information dialog box. Enter information on the various tabs as appropriate to this resource. When finished, click OK.

4. Whenever you want to save changes, just click Save on the Standard toolbar.

5. When you're finished modifying the resource information, and you want to check the enterprise resources back into your project server, click File, Close.

6. If a prompt asks if you want to save your changes, click Yes.

If an enterprise resource is checked out by another user, and you need to check the resource back into the enterprise resource pool (usually because of some extenuating circumstance), you can force a resource check-in as follows:

1. In the Project Web Access Quick Launch task bar, click Server Settings.

2. Under Database Administration, click Force Check-In Enterprise Objects.

3. In the Select The Type Of Object You Want To Force Check-In box, click Enterprise Resources.

    All resources that are currently checked out are listed in the table.

Check In

4. Select the check boxes for the resources you want to check in and then click Check-In.

Removing a Resource from the Enterprise Resource Pool

Although you can either delete or just deactivate a project server user, you can only deactivate resources because even obsolete resources are probably associated with assignments and actuals that are best retained for your archival project data. You can deactivate a resource by using the Edit Resources page in Project Web Access or by checking out the enterprise resource in Project Professional.

To deactivate a resource with Project Web Access, follow these steps:

1. In the Project Web Access Resource Center, select the check box next to the name of the resource you want to deactivate.

2. Click Edit Details.

3. In the Identification Information section, in the Account Status box, click Inactive.

4. Click Save.

    The selected resource is deactivated. The deactivated user cannot log on to the project server, and other users cannot send updates, tasks, or requests to the deactivated user. By default, the resource is still listed in the resource table, but its active flag has been changed from Yes to No. If you want, you can create a filter or autofilter that does not show inactivated users.

> **Note**
>
> When you deactivate a resource who is also a project server user, the person is also deactivated as a project server user.
>
> If you need to, you can retain a deactivated resource as an active user, as in the case when a resource stops working on project tasks but is still a project stakeholder. To do this, click Server Settings and then, under Security, click Manage Users. In the table, click the name of the inactive user/resource to open the Edit User page. In the Identification Information section, change the Account Status field to Active. Then clear the User Can Be Assigned As A Resource check box.

Chapter 21

To deactivate resources by checking them out in Project Professional, follow these steps:

1. In Project Web Access, select the check box next to the resource who you want to deactivate and then click the Open button on the toolbar.

2. In the Resource Sheet in Project Professional 2007, double-click the resource name to open the Resource Information dialog box.

3. On the General tab, select the Inactive check box and then click OK.

4. Click Save on the Standard toolbar.

5. When you're ready to check the deactivated resource back in to your project server, click File, Close.

> **Note**
>
> If you really must, you can still completely remove a resource, for example, to delete resources mistakenly added. To do this, click Server Settings in the Project Web Access Quick Launch task bar. Under Database Administration, click Delete Enterprise Objects. In the first section, select the Resources And Users option. Select the check boxes for the resources you need to delete. Click Delete and then click OK. If these resources own any projects, they will be assigned to your account.

Establishing the Enterprise Portfolio

The enterprise portfolio is the full set of projects that is stored on your project server. Individual project managers initially add their projects to the project server and then they check their own projects out and in. Team members might participate on one, two, or more projects in the enterprise portfolio at one time, or transition from one to another over time. Executives, portfolio managers, and other managing stakeholders can review aspects of some or all projects in the portfolio.

Individual project managers are responsible for adding projects to the project server. They can create a new enterprise project entirely from scratch. They can also import a local project; that is, one they've been working on that's stored on their own computer or elsewhere on the network. Importing a local project essentially copies the project to the project server, and that copy becomes the live enterprise version.

After a project is added to the project server, it is considered published to the enterprise. The new enterprise project becomes available to be viewed and checked out by users with the proper permissions.

Project managers needing more information about creating a new enterprise project can refer to the section titled "Saving a New Enterprise Project to the Server" in Chapter 22. For more information about importing an existing project, refer to the section titled "Importing a Local Project to the Server" in Chapter 22.

If a published project is checked out by a project manager or other user, and you need to check it in (usually because of some extenuating circumstance), you can force a project check-in as follows:

1. In the Project Web Access Quick Launch task bar, click Server Settings.

2. Under Database Administration, click Force Check-In Enterprise Objects.

3. In the Select The Type Of Object You Want To Force Check-In box, click Enterprise Projects.

   All projects that are currently checked out are listed in the table.

4. Select the check boxes for the projects you want to check in. Then click Check In.

Standardizing Enterprise Project Elements

As the project server administrator, you have the authority to define customizations needed by your organization and then propagate those customizations to all enterprise projects as the accepted project management standards.

To create and disseminate custom project elements, you use the enterprise global template, also simply known as the enterprise global. You check out the enterprise global and then customize any number of Microsoft Project elements as necessary. You can define views, tables, filters, toolbars, macros, custom fields, and more. When you check in the enterprise global with your changes, your changed elements become part of all projects throughout the enterprise.

Working with the Enterprise Global Template

When a project manager or other authorized user checks out an enterprise project, the latest update of the enterprise global is automatically attached. The enterprise global is akin to a global template, or the "global global" over the standard project global template. The enterprise global dictates standards being enforced and customizations made available to Microsoft Project interface elements in projects throughout the enterprise. These standards provide for customization and consistency across all projects in an organization. The standards propagated through the enterprise global template also make it possible for project information throughout the enterprise to be compared and analyzed in meaningful ways.

The following list contains examples of tailoring and standardizing you might do for projects in your enterprise:

- Define custom views.

- Design reports.

- Build and apply macros to enterprise data.

- Set up custom calendars.

- Define and customize information tables.

Chapter 21

Table 21-1 shows all the Microsoft Project elements that can be modified in the enterprise global and integrated with all enterprise projects. The table also provides cross-references to places on the Internet and sections in this book where you can find more information about customizing these interface elements.

Table 21-1 Customizable Microsoft Project Elements

Project element	For more information
Filters	"Customizing Filters" in Chapter 25
Forms	"Creating and Customizing Forms" in Chapter 26
Groups	"Customizing Groups" in Chapter 25
Import and export maps	"Importing and Exporting Information" in Chapter 16
Macros	"Automating Your Work with Macros" in Chapter 26
Reports	"Revising a Built-In Text Report" and "Building a Custom Report" in Chapter 12
Tables	"Customizing Tables" in Chapter 25
Toolbars	"Creating and Customizing Toolbars" in Chapter 26
VBA modules	Project 2007 Software Developer Kit (SDK) Documentation at *http://msdn2.microsoft.com/en-us/library/bb244260.aspx*
Views	"Customizing Views" in Chapter 25

Changing the Enterprise Global

By default, only the project server administrator and portfolio manager have permission to update the enterprise global. They do this through the Save Enterprise Global permission.

To use Project Professional 2007 to check out and change the enterprise global, follow these steps:

1. Be sure you're logged in to the project server through Project Professional 2007.

2. In Project Professional, click Tools, Enterprise Options, Open Enterprise Global.

   The enterprise global opens as a special project plan called Checked-Out Enterprise Global (see Figure 21-13)

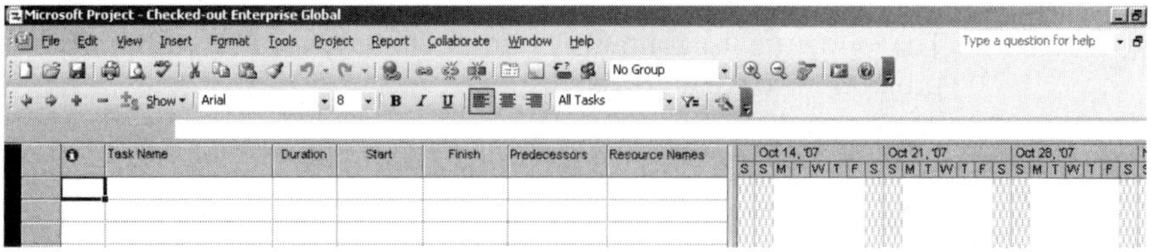

Figure 21-13 The Checked-Out Enterprise Global is a special project plan you use to standardize some elements of project plans to be used throughout your organization.

3. Define and customize the Microsoft Office Project 2007 elements for the enterprise as needed.

   Refer to Table 21-1 to find specific instructions for customizing a specific element.

4. When you're finished working with the enterprise global and you want to check it back in to the project server, click File, Close.

5. In the prompt that appears, click Yes to save your changes.

   The updated enterprise global is checked in to the project server and is now available to all project managers.

Note

You can also check out the enterprise global from within Project Web Access. On the Server Settings page, under Enterprise Data, click Enterprise Global. Click the Configure Project Professional button. The enterprise global is checked out to you and appears in Project Professional. You can now make the changes you need. When finished, save your changes and check the enterprise global back into the project server.

Create an Enterprise Global Change Process

It's likely that project managers will have a number of good ideas regarding items that should become part of the enterprise global. They are also likely to have thoughts on custom fields and calendars. Your organization might do well to develop a consistent process for handling such suggestions. It might be something as simple as having project managers submit a written suggestion to the project server administrator showing an example of the proposed change. The process might be as formal as a periodic change review meeting. It depends entirely on your organization.

Even if you can't implement a change right away (or at all), remind project managers that they can still create and use their own project global templates, as long as there's no conflict between elements in the project global and elements in the enterprise global.

For more information about working with the project global template, see Chapter 28, "Standardizing Projects Using Templates."

Copying a Custom Element from a Project to the Enterprise Global

You might find it a great idea to experiment with certain customized changes by using a regular enterprise project or even a local project before checking out the enterprise global and making the changes there. But you don't have to make the change twice. You can simply copy the custom change from the regular project to the enterprise global using the Organizer.

To copy custom elements from a regular project to the enterprise global, follow these steps:

1. Log in to the project server through Project Professional 2007.

2. Open the regular enterprise or nonenterprise project that contains the element you want to copy to the enterprise global.

3. In Project Professional 2007, click Tools, Enterprise Options, Open Enterprise Global.

    The enterprise global opens as Checked-Out Enterprise Global.

4. Click Tools, Organizer to open the Organizer dialog box (see Figure 21-14).

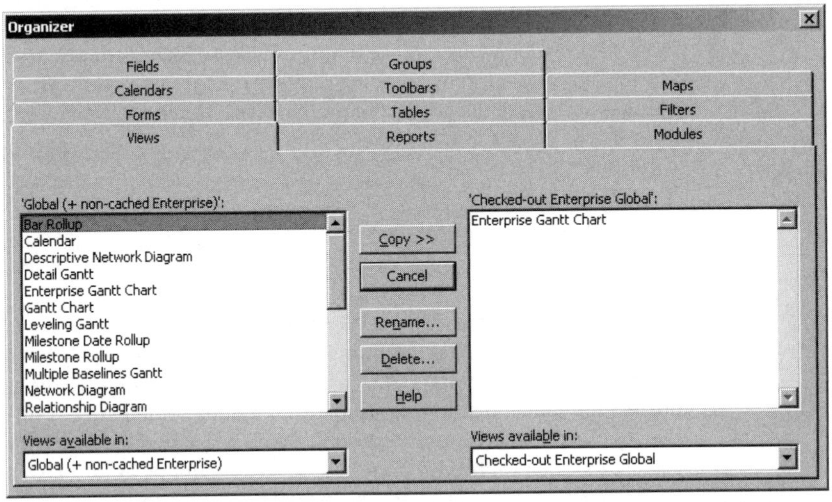

Figure 21-14 Copy customized elements from a project and the enterprise global.

5. Click the tab for the type of element you want to copy, for example, Views or Toolbars.

6. In the <Element> Available In box in the lower-right corner of the dialog box, click the project that contains the element you want to copy, if necessary. (<Element> stands for the name of the current tab.)

    The name of the project from which you want to copy the element might already be showing in the box.

7. Make sure the box in the lower left of the dialog box is labeled Global (+Non-Cached Enterprise).

    If it is not currently showing, select Global (+Non-Cached Enterprise) from the <Element> Available In box. This is the name of the enterprise global template.

8. From the list of elements on the right side of the dialog box, click the name of the element you want to copy.

9. Click Copy.

If an element with the same name already exists in the enterprise global, a confirmation message asks you to confirm that you want to replace the element in the enterprise global. Click Yes to replace the element in the enterprise global with the one from the source project.

To copy the element with a different name, click Rename and then type a new name.

10. Check the enterprise global to make sure that your new element is present.

11. When finished working with the enterprise global, click File, Close.

12. In the prompt that appears, click Yes to save your changes and check the enterprise global in to the project server.

Customizing Enterprise Project Fields

Another responsibility of the project server administrator is to set up any custom fields for enterprise projects as a whole as well as individual enterprise tasks, resources, and assignments. You can define these custom fields to hold special information—such as a specific category of costs, dates, or text that is not provided by built-in Microsoft Project fields. You can also create lookup tables for all custom fields except for the Yes/No field.

You can create a custom field in any enterprise project in Project Professional. You then give a command to add the field to the enterprise, and it becomes a part of the project global template. However, note that you cannot create fields in the checked-out global template itself.

Although local projects impose a limit on the number of custom fields you can create, new in Project Server 2007 is the ability to create an unlimited number of custom fields for enterprise projects. You might use Duration1 to create an enterprise task field, but as soon as you add the field to the project server, Duration1 becomes available again.

You can define the following custom field types for projects as a whole, tasks, resources, and assignments:

- Cost
- Date
- Duration
- Finish
- Flag
- Number
- Start
- Text

Establishing Custom Fields

For enterprise projects, you can create a wide range of custom fields. There are different sets of custom fields for the different types of project database information, as follows:

- **Project fields** Store summary project information. Custom project fields can be viewed as part of the project summary row in an individual project plan. They can also be viewed in conjunction with other projects by users of the Data Analysis cube reporting features.

- **Task fields** Store information about the tasks in a project. Similar to the other types of fields, this information can include, for example, cost, date, text, and number information.

- **Resource fields** Store information about the resources in a project.

Custom fields can be defined in Project Web Access or Project Professional.

To use Project Web Access to define a custom enterprise field, follow these steps:

1. On the Server Settings page, under Enterprise Data, click Enterprise Custom Field Definition.

2. To create a single-value custom field, click New Field under Enterprise Custom Fields. Enter your specifications for the new custom field and then click Save.

   If you want to create a custom field with a lookup table of multiple values, click New Lookup Table under Lookup Tables For Custom Fields. Enter your specifications for the lookup table and then click Save.

To use Project Professional 2007 to define a custom field for enterprise projects, follow these steps:

1. With Project Professional 2007 logged on to your project server, click Tools, Customize, Fields.

2. Under Field, click the Task, Resource, or Project option.

3. In the Type box, click the type of custom field you want to create, for example, Text, Cost, or Date.

4. In the Field box, click the next available custom text field, for example, Date1 (see Figure 21-15).

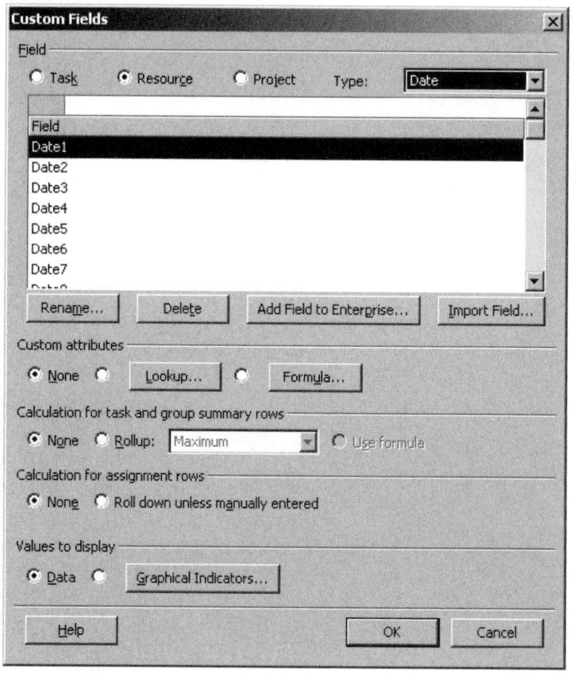

Figure 21-15 Use the Custom Fields dialog box to define enterprise resource fields.

5. Click the Rename button and then type a descriptive name for your new custom resource field. Click OK.

6. If you want to specify a formula or graphical indicator for the custom field, use the sections in the lower half of the dialog box.

7. If you want this custom field to include a lookup table, that is, a drop-down list of preset values, click the Lookup button under Custom Attributes. In the Value column of the table, enter the items that are to comprise the drop-down list (see Figure 21-16).

Chapter 21

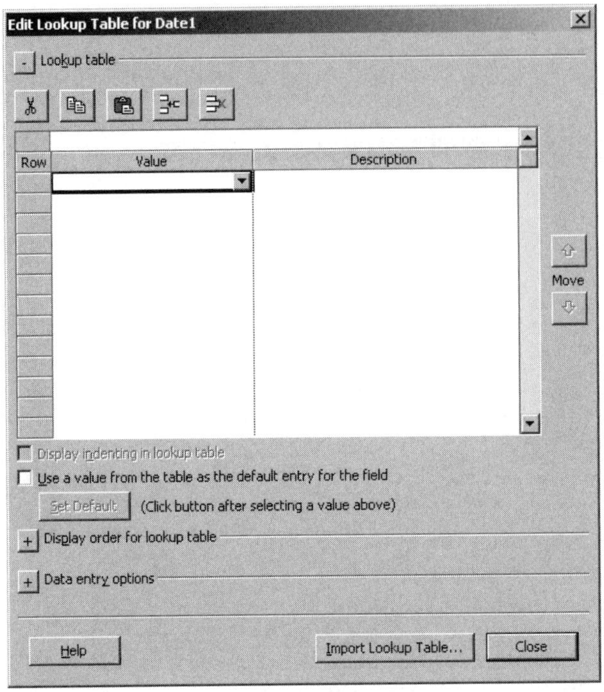

Figure 21-16 Use the Edit Lookup Table to define the items that should appear in a custom field's drop-down list.

8. Make any other changes you want to the definition of the lookup table for the new custom field, including a default value or the display order. When finished, click Close.

9. In the Custom Fields dialog box, click the Add Field To Enterprise button.

10. In the Field Name box, enter the name of the custom field as you want it to appear in a table in Project Professional 2007 or a custom view in Project Web Access. In the Lookup Table Name box, enter the name of the custom field as you want it to appear in a drop-down list of custom enterprise fields. Click OK.

11. In the alert that indicates that the field has been added to your project server, click OK.

    The new field does not appear in Project Professional 2007 until you restart the application. However, it does become available in Project Web Access immediately.

12. Click OK in the Custom Fields dialog box.

13. Restart Project Professional 2007 to see and use the new field.

For more information about defining custom fields and outline codes, including lookup tables, formulas, and graphical indicators, see the section titled "Customizing Fields" in Chapter 25, "Customizing Your View of Project Information."

Associating Resource Codes with Resources

After you have defined an enterprise resource custom field, associate the field and their values with enterprise resources by following these steps:

1. In the Resource Center of Project Web Access, select the check boxes next to the names of the resources for whom you want to enter resource custom fields and values.

2. Click Edit Details.

3. In the Resource Custom Fields section, enter the appropriate value in the custom resource field. If you had created a lookup table for the field, click the arrow in the field and then click an entry in the drop-down list. If there is no lookup table, simply type the value in the field.

4. Click the Save And Continue button.

5. Enter the value in the custom resource field for the next resource. Repeat steps 3–4 until you've entered the values in the custom resource fields for all selected resources.

> **Note**
>
> If you're making the same change to custom resource fields for multiple resources, you can select the resources and click Bulk Edit. Your custom fields appear in the Resource Custom Fields section. Enter the value in the custom resource field that applies to all selected resources. Select the Apply Changes check box next to the custom resource field and then click Save. The change is applied for all selected resources at once.

> **Use Regular Custom Fields**
>
> Only the project system administrator or another user with the proper permissions can create and save custom enterprise fields to the enterprise.
>
> If, for individual project plans, custom fields are needed that don't affect the enterprise, project managers can define custom fields for their own use in enterprise projects. Instead of using the enterprise custom fields such as Enterprise Cost1-10, they can use Cost1-10, Date1-10, Text1-30, and so on.
>
> For more information about regular custom fields, see the section titled "Customizing Fields" in Chapter 25.

Creating Calendars to Reflect Nonworking Times

In addition to standardizing elements such as views, toolbars, and fields to reflect the operations of your organization, you can also create enterprise-level working times calendars that dictate how projects and resources are scheduled. By default, resources are assigned to the Standard working times base calendar, which reflects a schedule of Monday through Friday, 8:00 A.M. to 5:00 P.M. with an hour off for lunch. You can customize the Standard calendar to reflect your organization's holidays, company meetings, offsite conferences, and other events to make sure that project tasks are not scheduled for work during those times.

You can create other base calendars as needed to reflect a different working times schedule for a project or for individual resources. In enterprise project management, only those with the Manage Enterprise Calendars privilege may create or modify base calendars because the calendar settings become part of the enterprise global. Users identified as the administrator or portfolio manager have the Manage Enterprise Calendars privilege by default. Project managers can view the working times calendars, but they cannot change them.

To change the Standard base calendar that is the starting point for working and nonworking times for all projects in your organization, follow these steps:

1. In the Quick Launch task bar, click Server Settings. Under Enterprise Data, click Enterprise Calendars.

2. Click Standard in the Enterprise Calendars table and then click Edit Calendar.

   The Change Working Time dialog box opens in Project Professional (see Figure 21-17).

Edit Calendar

Change Working Time   ✕

For calendar: Standard

Calendar 'Standard' is a base calendar.

Legend:

☐ Working

☐ Nonworking

31 Edited working hours

On this calendar:

31 Exception day

31 Nondefault work week

Click on a day to see its working times:

October 2007

S	M	T	W	Th	F	S
	1	2	3	4	5	6
7	8	9	10	11	12	13
14	15	16	17	18	19	20
21	**22**	23	24	25	26	27
28	29	30	31			

Working times for October 22, 2007:

• 8:00 AM to 12:00 PM
• 1:00 PM to 5:00 PM

Based on:

Default work week on calendar 'Standard'.

Exceptions | Work Weeks

Name	Start	Finish

Details...

Delete

Help   OK   Cancel

Figure 21-17   Use the Change Working Time dialog box to edit the enterprise calendar.

3. Change the Standard working time calendar the way you need, either by entering exceptions or by creating alternative workweeks.

> For detailed information about changing a working time calendar, see the section titled "Modifying a Base Calendar" in Chapter 3, "Starting a New Project."

4. When you've made all the changes you want, click OK.

The Standard working time calendar is applied and will be applied to projects the next time project managers check out any enterprise project that uses the Standard calendar.

Copy Calendar

You can create a new base calendar that uses an existing calendar as its starting point. In the table on the Enterprise Calendars page, click the name of the calendar that you want to copy. Click Copy Calendar. Enter the name for the new calendar and then click OK. The copied calendar appears in the list. Select it, click Edit Calendar, and make the changes you want.

New Calendar

You can also create a new base calendar from scratch, that is, with no exceptions or alternative workweeks defined other than the defaults. The new base calendar is essentially the built-in Standard base calendar, with working times of Monday through Friday, 8:00 A.M. to 5:00 P.M., with an hour off for lunch. To create a new calendar, on the Enterprise Calendars page, click New Calendar. In the For Calendar box in the Change Working Time dialog box, enter a name for your new calendar. Make the changes you want and then click OK.

To assign a base calendar to a resource, follow these steps:

1. In the Resource Center, click the check box next to the resource to which you want to apply a calendar.

2. Click Edit Details.

3. In the Assignment Attributes section, click the calendar you want in the Base Calendar box.

4. Click Save, or Save And Continue if you're editing multiple resources.

Setting Up Team Member Work Pages

Team members use Project Web Access primarily to track and update their tasks assigned from one or more projects. This is done on the My Tasks page.

Team members can also use the Windows SharePoint Services features built in to Project Web Access to manage issues and risks that have been assigned to them for resolution. This is done on the Issues And Risks page.

New in Project Server 2007 is the ability to submit timesheets that track different categories of time, for example, billable time, nonbillable time, billable overtime, and nonbillable overtime. This is done on the My Timesheets page.

These three pages are available under My Work in the Quick Launch task bar.

> **Note**
> In previous versions of Project Web Access, the task progress page was called the timesheet. Now in Project 2007, the timesheet is a different page and serves a different, but complementary, purpose to the task progress page.

What's the Difference Between My Tasks and My Timesheets?

Your organization might choose to use just the My Tasks page alone, or it might decide to implement the My Tasks page in conjunction with the timesheet. To use either or both of these pages successfully, you must understand the differences between the two as well as how they work together.

Understanding the My Tasks Page

The My Tasks page, also referred to as the task progress page, is the page that team members work with to track and update their tasks assigned from one or more projects (see Figure 21-18). As the project server administrator, you can customize the My Tasks page to suit the needs of your organization.

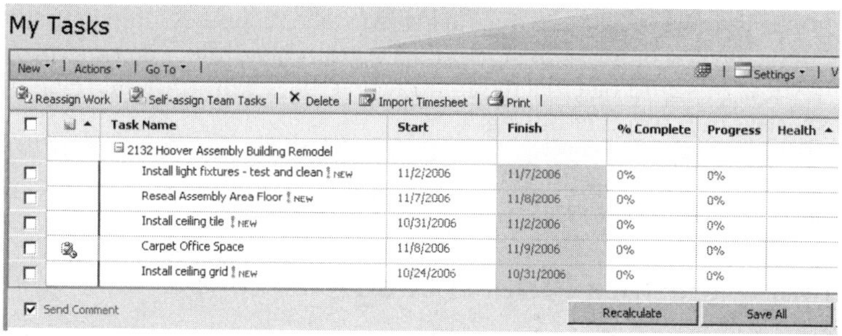

Figure 21-18 Design the task progress page to fit the requirements of your organization and its projects.

Team members use the My Tasks page to see the tasks they're assigned to, their scheduled start and finish dates, and other assignment information. They also use this page to periodically report on current progress, submitting this progress information to their project manager for incorporation into the project plan.

Understanding the My Timesheets Page

The My Timesheets page is used in organizations that have specific time reporting requirements. For example, use the timesheet when you want visibility into certain time categories, for example, billable and nonbillable time, scheduled and actual time, overtime, and so on. Default time categories are provided, but you can set up custom time categories as appropriate. The timesheet is especially useful when you need to integrate information about resource time with an accounting or general ledger system, particularly for client billing purposes.

In the timesheet, team members can also set up and use the administrative time feature, in which they can identify instances of nonproject working time or nonworking time.

Similar to task progress on the My Tasks page, team members submit timesheets to their designated timesheet managers on a periodic basis.

Working with Task Progress and Timesheets

You do not have to use both task progress and timesheets. If you do not have specialized time reporting needs outside the project plan, then just use the task progress page to update the project plan.

However, use both if you need to update the project plan as well as an accounting or general ledger system.

Remember that the task progress page indicates status on how complete a task assignment is, while the timesheet indicates the number of hours spent per day or per week doing various activities. The two are often, but not always, related.

For example, suppose the project team is working for a customer who is to be billed 8 hours per day (40 hours per week) for the contracted work. The timesheet would reflect this, and invoices would be generated for the customer from the timesheet showing 8 hours a day for 5 days a week. However, the resource might actually be working 10 hours a day to complete the tasks by a certain deadline. The task progress page would show this, and be reflected in project actuals, but would have no impact on the timesheet or the customer billing.

Team members can import information from their task progress page into their timesheet page and vice versa.

Defining the Task Progress Page

To set up the task progress page (the My Tasks page), you need to establish the update method and rules used by your organization. If you need to, you can also change the fields and the type of Gantt Chart used on the page.

> **Note**
> For more information about how team members work with the My Tasks page, see the section titled "Tracking Progress on Your Assignments" in Chapter 23.

Setting the Update Method and Restrictions

With your project server administrator privileges, you define the assignment progress tracking method that is then reflected on the My Tasks page. The tracking method can be as simple as noting whether an assignment is not started, in progress, or completed. It can also be as detailed as tracking every hour devoted to each assignment.

Depending on the level of project management control that your organization needs, you can set up a number of assignment update restrictions. You can specify whether time should be reported every day or just once a week. You can specify whether project managers have the capability to edit updates submitted by team members. You can close tasks to further update by anyone after a certain period of time.

Work with the project managers, the portfolio manager, and the requirements of the organization to determine the most appropriate default tracking method. After setting the default, project managers might still be able to switch to a different tracking method for their own projects, but only if you allow that possibility in your project server configuration.

The three tracking methods are as follows:

- **Percentage of work complete** This is the least restrictive and least time-consuming tracking method. The My Tasks page includes a field that team members use to update how far along they are with their assignments.

- **Actual work done and remaining work** This tracking method provides a medium level of detail. With this method, the My Tasks page includes fields for total actual work and remaining work for each assignment. Team members enter those total amounts for each progress update requested.

- **Hours of work done per time period** This is the most detailed tracking method. The My Tasks page includes a field for each time period, either days or weeks, for the duration of the project. Team members enter the number of hours worked per day or per week and submit this information with each progress update.

In addition to the default tracking method, you can also control when actuals are accepted and whether they can be changed after they've been submitted to the project server.

For more information about tracking actual work in Project 2007, see the section titled "Using Resource Work to Update Progress" in Chapter 10, "Setting a Baseline and Updating Progress."

To set the default tracking method and certain update restrictions, follow these steps:

1. On the Server Settings page, under Time And Task Management, click Task Settings And Display.

The Task Settings And Display page appears (see Figure 21-19).

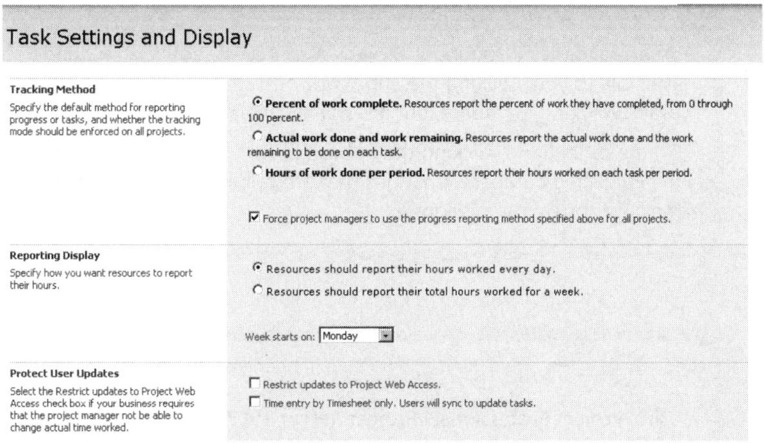

Figure 21-19 Use the Task Settings And Display page to set the default work tracking method for the team member task progress page.

2. In the Tracking Method section, select the option for the tracking method that represents the default for your organization: Percent Of Work Complete, Actual Work Done And Work Remaining, or Hours Of Work Done Per Period.

3. Select or clear the Force Project Managers To Use The Progress Reporting Method Specified Above For All Projects check box. If this check box is cleared, project managers are allowed to change the tracking method in their individual projects. If this check box is selected, project managers must always use the default method selected on this page.

   If you allow project managers to change the default tracking method, they can do so by clicking Tools, Options, Collaborate In Project Professional 2007.

4. Work through the other options on this page, reading the information in the left pane of each section for additional guidance. Options include whether team members should report their hours each day or at the end of the week, and whether the project manager is permitted to change actual time worked as reported by the team members.

5. When finished, click Save.

Closing Tasks Against Further Reporting

Another restriction you can apply to protect actual progress information is to close completed tasks to prevent any further updates from being submitted on them. This is also known as locking down the tasks. On the Server Settings page, under Time And Task Management, click Close Tasks To Update. In the Project section, select the project that contains the tasks you want to lock down. The tasks in that project are listed in the Select Tasks section. Select the check box next to the task you want to close. Click Publish or Submit.

What's the Difference Between Submit and Publish?

In several pages throughout Project Web Access, both Submit and Publish buttons are available to you. Clicking the Submit button saves the changes from that page in the Draft (Working) database, but are not available to others.

On the other hand, clicking the Publish button saves the changes and locks it down in the Published database. Changes that are published can be accessed by other users with the appropriate permissions.

Protecting Actuals Information

Using Project Professional , Project Server 2007, and Project Web Access to automatically gather and enter actuals, you can protect the integrity of actuals submitted by team members. This can be crucial if those actuals are directly submitted to your organization's general ledger system to produce customer invoices.

As the project server administrator, you first set up the Project Web Access progress method to track hours of work per day or per week. You also set whether team members can enter actuals only during the current reporting period, or for periods in the past or in the future.

Furthermore, you can set an option to prohibit project managers or other users from changing actual work figures.

You can also lock down tasks to ensure that no more reporting can be submitted on them.

Only actuals for enterprise resource assignments can be protected. Project managers can still edit actuals for tasks that have local or no resources assigned.

Setting the Fields

The My Tasks page is set up with a standard set of task and assignment fields. That set of fields changes according to the tracking method chosen. You can change the fields that the team members see on their task progress page. As the project server adminis-trator, you can choose from the full set of Microsoft Project fields to establish the set of available Timesheet fields.

> **Note**
>
> In Microsoft Office Project 2003 and earlier versions, the project server administrator could set a collection of available fields for the task progress page. Project managers then could select fields from this collection to tailor the task progress page for their indi-vidual projects.
>
> In Microsoft Office Project 2007, this functionality is no longer available. To provide for consistency among projects and better reporting, it's best for the task progress pages to all have the same fields.

If you have defined any custom enterprise fields, including custom fields with a drop-down "pick list" or lookup table, you can include them in the set of default task prog-ress fields as well.

For more information about defining custom enterprise task fields, including defining drop-down lookup tables, see the section titled "Customizing Enterprise Project Fields" earlier in this chapter on page 21xx.

To modify the set of default task progress fields, follow these steps:

1. On the Server Settings page in Project Web Access, under Look And Feel, click Manage Views.

   The Manage Views page appears (see Figure 21-20).

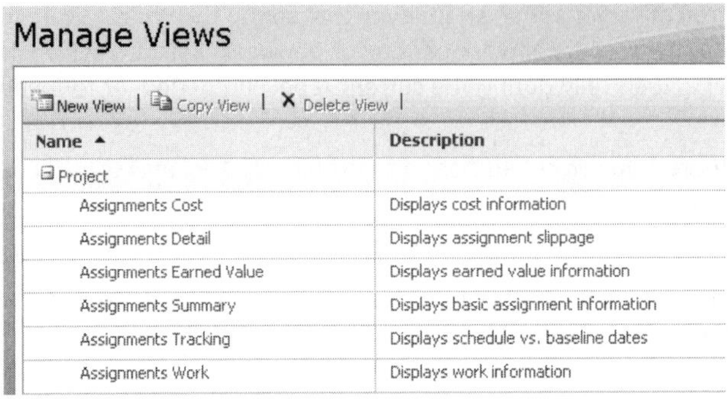

Figure 21-20 Use the Manage Views page to modify, add, or remove views in Project Web Access.

2. Scroll down the table, almost to the bottom, to find and click the My Assignments view under the My Work category.

   The Edit View: My Assignments page appears (see Figure 21-21).

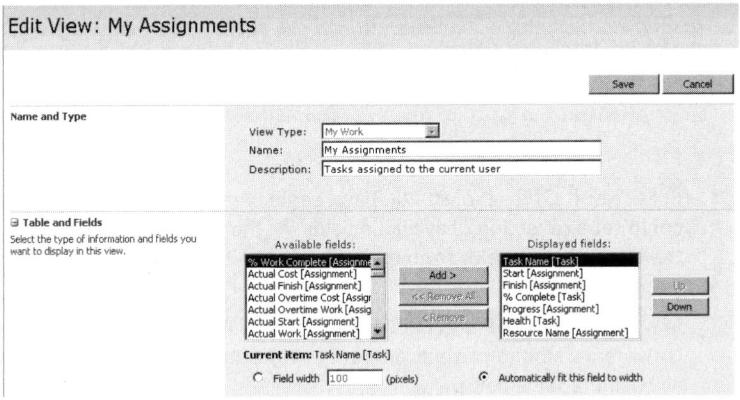

Figure 21-21 The details for the selected view appears on the Edit View page.

3. In the Table And Fields section, select one or more fields in the Available Fields box and then click Add to move them to the Displayed Fields box on the right.

   This process adds the selected fields to the task progress page.

   If you have defined any custom enterprise fields, they are also part of the list of available fields.

4. If you need to delete any fields from the view, select them in the Displayed Fields box on the right and then click Remove to delete them from the set of fields shown in the task progress page.

5. Use the Up and Down buttons to arrange the fields into the order you want them displayed in the view.

6. When finished, click Save.

   Your changes are saved to the project server. The next time any team member click My Tasks, they'll see your new version of the page.

Defining the My Timesheets Page

To set up the timesheet (My Timesheets) page, you establish the fiscal year and reporting periods for your organization. You set up the categories of time to be reported and set any necessary timesheet update rules.

> **Note**
>
> For more information about how team members work with the timesheet, see the section titled "Tracking Time in Your Timesheet" in Chapter 23.

Identifying the Reporting Periods

Because team members will be using the timesheet to report on their progress, you can be sure that the time periods on which they're reporting map not only to your organization's fiscal year but also to the reporting periods you need, whether it's weekly, biweekly, or monthly.

The first step is to set up your fiscal year and define your monthly periods within that year, whether they are calendar months, 4-week periods, or 4-week periods with a 5-week adjustment period. To set up your organization's fiscal year and the reporting periods within that year, follow these steps:

1. In the Project Web Access Quick Launch task bar, click Server Settings. Under Time And Task Management, click Financial Periods.

2. In the Manage Fiscal Period section, click the year you are defining and then click Define.

   The Define Fiscal Year Parameters page appears.

3. Follow the instructions in the left pane to complete this page and define the fiscal year start date, the fiscal period model, and the fiscal period naming conventions.

4. Click Create And Save.

   The Fiscal Periods page appears again, this time showing the table of fiscal periods you have just specified.

5. If you need to make any adjustments, click in the End Date field for a period. Using the date picker icon that appears, click the date for the fiscal period. Repeat this for any other fiscal periods you want to adjust.

6. Click Save.

Setting Timesheet Defaults and Update Restrictions

As the project server administrator, you are responsible for defining the defaults and updating rules for the resources' timesheets.

To set timesheet defaults and additional update restrictions, follow these steps:

1. On the Server Settings page, under Time And Task Management, click Timesheet Settings And Defaults.

2. Work through the options on this page, reading the information in the left pane of each section for additional guidance. Options include what information can be displayed in the Microsoft Office Outlook timesheet, whether the Project Web Access timesheet should include fields for overtime and nonbillable time, how timesheets are created, whether tracking units are days or weeks, and whether future time reporting is allowable.

3. When finished, click Save.

Setting Categories for Administrative Time

Team members are each associated with a working time calendar. However, they can also designate administrative time to schedule vacation or nonbillable working time, that is, time spent not working directly on project tasks. Project managers and resource managers can then approve and incorporate administrative time into the project scheduling.

As the project server administrator, you can set up categories for administrative time, for example, vacation, company meetings, and training. You specify whether the administrative time is a working or nonworking time, and whether it requires approval by the team member's manager.

To add a new administrative time category, follow these steps:

1. On the Server Settings page, under Time And Task Management, click Administrative Time.

The Edit Or Create Administrative Time page shows the list of categories. Default categories are Administrative Working Time, Sick Time, and Vacation Time.

2. Click New Category.

New Category

3. In the new row that's added to the table, type the name of the new category.

4. In the Status field, specify whether the category is Open or Closed. With an open category, team members can record time against the category. A closed category does not show in the team member's Administrative Time dialog box.

5. In the Work Type field, specify whether the category is Working or Non Work. For example, a category called Nonproject Meeting would be a Working type, while the Personal Time Off category would be Non Work.

6. In the Approve field, specify whether the category requires approval by the team member's manager.

7. In the Always Display field, select the check box if the category should appear in the team member's Administrative Time dialog box. Clear the check box if it should not appear.

Turning the Always Display field on or off can be useful if there is a category that your organization wants to make available only during a certain period of the year.

8. When finished, click Save.

To edit an existing category, simply click in the field and make the change you want. To delete an existing category, click the name of the category and then click Delete Category.

For more information about how project managers work with administrative time, see the section titled "Approving Administrative Time" in Chapter 22.

For information about how team members set up administrative time, see the section titled "Planning for Nonproject Working Time and Days Off" in Chapter 23.

Setting the Billing Categories

Built in to Project Server 2007 is a Standard billing category for project work, as well as three billing categories for administrative work (Administrative, Sick Time, and Vacation). You can add different billing categories as needed. To do this, follow these steps:

1. On the Server Settings page, under Time And Task Management, click Timesheet Classifications.

New
Classification

2. Click New Classification.

3. In the new row that's added to the table, type the name of the new billing category.

4. In the Description field, type an explanation for the use of this new category.

5. Click Save.

The new line classification becomes available in the timesheet. When a resource working in the timesheet clicks Add Lines to add an existing assignment or other item, the new category is listed in the Line Classification box. The selected category appears in the Billing Category field for the new line.

Managing Pages, Views, and Reports

As the project server administrator, you have the capability to create custom pages, views, and reports for your Project Web Access users. Do this to make Project Web Access clearly reflect your organization and also to provide users with information where and when they need it.

Pages are the major screens you see as you move from area to area within Project Web Access. For example, Server Settings is a page, Project Center is a page, and Resource Center is a page. You can add and remove elements on most pages by editing the page's Web Parts, which are the content components that make up the page.

Chapter 21

On the other hand, views are subsets of pages. Views specify a certain collection or format of information within a page. For example, the default view for the Project Center page is the Summary view. But you can switch to the Cost view or the Tracking view.

Reports in Project Web Access are PivotTables and PivotCharts that are built dynamically and displayed from selected fields of project information. As the project server administrator, you set up various groupings of project fields. These groupings, or cubes, are then made available to users such as portfolio managers and executives to select the information they want for their analyses and reports.

Creating and Managing Pages with Web Parts

Project Web Access is essentially a Web site made up of a series of pages. The elements on these pages come from a collection of predesigned Web Parts. Web Parts are self-contained, reusable components that consist of types of information varying from sophisticated dynamic Web page content embedded in a frame to simple concise text messages. Generally, most features and content that can be seen on a Web page can be included as a Web Part. Web Parts group and position all key information logically and consistently; the information is accessed through hyperlinks.

You can use Web Parts to develop Web page components in Project Web Access that convey key project information efficiently for your team or organization.

For example, the My Tasks page is made up of the My Tasks Web Part, and the Project Center is made up of the Project Center Web Part. But you could put the two together to create a new page that has both of these together. You can add the Reminders Web Part to the Timesheet page if you learn that's what your users need.

Web Parts are a function of Windows SharePoint Services, which is the basis for Project Web Access.

Modifying a Built-In Page

You can modify the structure and content category of any Project Web Access page, including the home page. To do this, follow these steps.

1. In Project Web Access, navigate to the page you want to change.

2. Click the Site Actions button in the upper-right corner of the window and then click Edit Page.

The page is redrawn with several Add A Web Part controls (see Figure 21-22). One is at the top of the page (header), one is at the bottom of the page (footer), and three are in a row (left column, middle column, and right column) in roughly the center of the page. In addition, a title bar is added to each Web Part element already existing on the page. An Edit and Delete control sits at the right edge of the title bar.

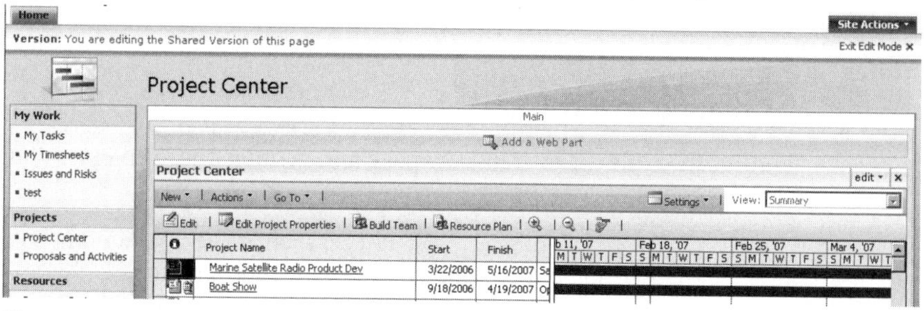

Figure 21-22 When you edit a page, Web Part controls appear directly on the page.

3. Using the Web Parts controls, edit the page:

   ❑ To add a new Web Part, click the Add A Web Part control that is closest to the area where you want the new Web Part to be positioned. In the Add Web Parts dialog box, select the check box next to the Web Part you want to add. Scroll through the list to see them all. Click Add. The Web Part is added to the page.

   ❑ To edit an existing Web Part, click the Edit button on the right edge of the Web Part's title bar and then click Modify Shared Web Part. A task pane appears on the right side of the window (see Figure 21-23). Specify how you want to modify the Web Part. The choices will be different depending on the nature of the Web Part. However, most Web Parts provide choices for Appearance, Layout, and Advanced. Click OK or Apply at the bottom of the Web Part pane to implement your changes in the page.

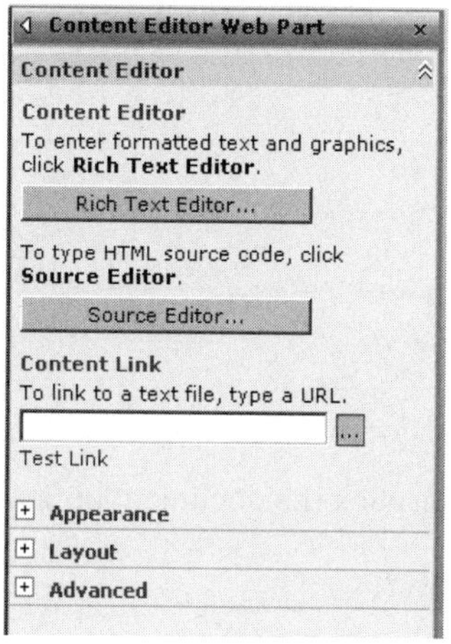

Figure 21-23 Use the Web Part task pane to edit an existing Web Part.

    ❑   To delete a Web Part on a page, click the Close (X) button on the right edge of the Web Part's title bar. The page is redrawn with that Web Part removed.

4. When finished making changes to Web Parts on the current page, click Exit Edit Mode in the upper-right corner of the page, just under Site Actions.

    The Web Parts controls disappear, and the changes you made are shown on the page.

Creating a New Page

You can create an entirely new page and arrange the Web Parts you want on it. To do this, follow these steps:

1. On any page in Project Web Access, click the Site Actions button in the upper-right corner of the window and then click Create.

2. On the Create page, under Web Pages, click Web Part Page.

3. On the New Web Part Page page, enter the name that you want to appear in headings and links throughout Project Web Access when referring to this new page.

4. In the Layout section, in the Choose A Layout Template box, click the page layout you want for the new page (see Figure 21-24).

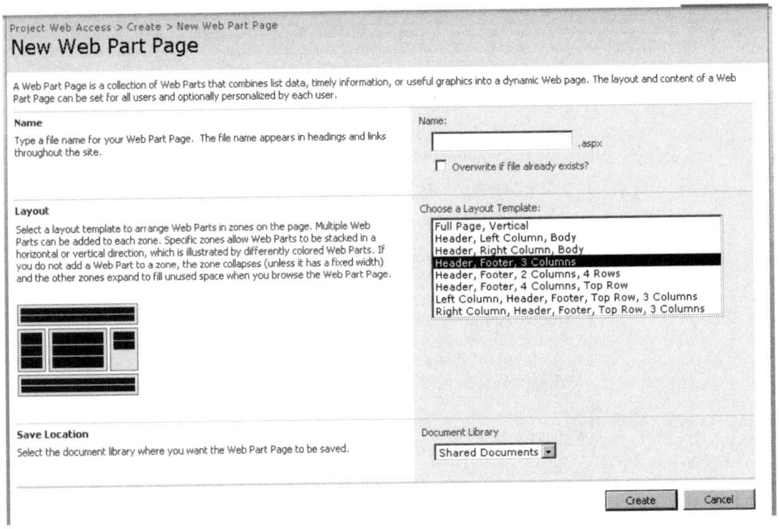

Figure 21-24 Specify the layout for your new page.

5. In the Save Location section, click the document library where this Web page is to be saved.

6. Click Create.

The page is created and appears as a page filled only with Web Parts controls (see Figure 21-25).

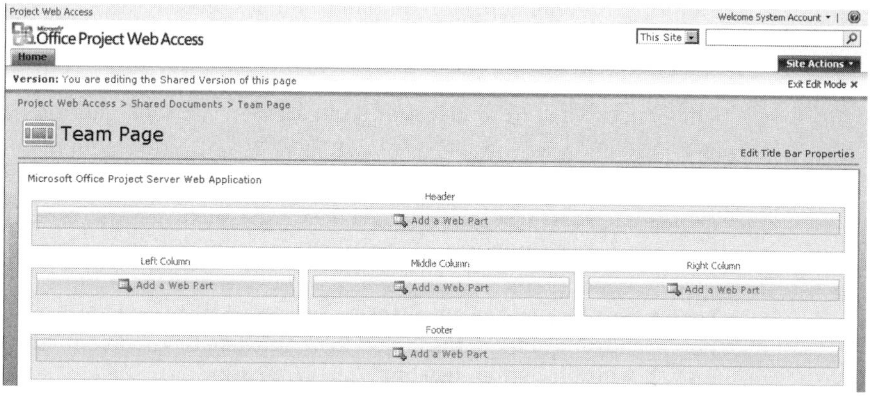

Figure 21-25 When you create a new Web Parts page, a series of Web Parts controls appears to help you start building the content on the page.

7. Click the Add A Web Part control that is closest to the area where you want the new Web Part to be positioned.

8. In the Add Web Parts dialog box, select the check box next to the Web Part you want to add. Scroll through the list to see them all.

9. Click Add.

The Web Part is added to the page.

10. Repeat steps 7–9 for any additional Web Parts you want to add to this new page.

11. When finished adding Web Parts to the new page, click Exit Edit Mode.

The new page appears according to your specifications.

Deleting a Custom Project Web Access Page

To delete an entire Web page in Project Web Access, in the Quick Launch task bar, click Shared Documents. Any pages you have created are listed. Click the arrow in the box that appears when you move the mouse over the name of the page. Then click Delete. To return to Project Web Access, click the Home tab in the upper-left corner.

For more information about working with Web Parts, Site Actions, project workspaces, and other aspects of Windows SharePoint Server, see the Windows SharePoint Services 3.0 Technical Library, available at go.microsoft.com/fwlink/?LinkId=81199.

Integrating Project Information with Business Processes

Project 2007 has a new method for extending functionality and integrating project information with other applications. Through the new application program interface (API) called the Project Server Interface (PSI), which works with the Windows Workflow Foundation, you can integrate information between your project server and other organizational systems that interact with project management processes, such as accounting, procurement, and human resources. In fact, the means through which Project Professional and Project Web Access interact with Project Server 2007 is solely through the Project Server Interface.

The Project Server Interface also provides the means for solutions built with the XML-based Project Data Service (PDS) methods in Project Server 2003 to be ported to Project Server 2007.

Depending on other resources in use by your organization, you can also integrate Outlook and Active Directory for additional functionality.

For information about the Project Server Interface, the Event Modeler, and Windows Work-flow Foundation, refer to the Project 2007 Software Development Kit, available at http://msdn2.microsoft.com/en-us/library/bb187382.aspx.

Creating and Managing Views

Many pages throughout Project Web Access only need to display a single view of project data. Examples of such pages include the home page, the Proposals And Activities page, and the Personal Settings page.

The use of other pages, however, benefit from the availability of different views of project data. Such pages include:

- My Tasks
- My Timesheets
- Project Center
- Resource Center
- Data Analysis

A view is a collection of selected fields filtered in a particular way, laid out in a certain format, with certain permissions applied. The Project Center page includes the Cost, Earned Value, Project Owner, Summary, Tracking, and Work views. To see the views available for one of these pages, the user selects from the View box in the upper-right corner of most pages throughout Project Web Access.

You can modify existing Project Web Access views or create new views to add to a page. When defining a view, you can specify the following types of information:

- View name and description
- The fields to be displayed in the view's table
- Formatting for the view, including Gantt Chart format if applicable, outline levels, grouping format, and sort order

- The filter to be applied to the view's information
- The security categories that the view belongs to

Modifying a Built-In View

To modify an existing view, follow these steps:

1. On the Server Settings page, under Look And Feel, click Manage Views.

   All views used throughout Project Web Access are listed under their categories.

2. Click the name of the view you want to change.

   The Edit View page appears.

3. Go to the section that contains the aspect of the view you want to change, for example, the fields included in the view are in the Table And Fields section, whereas the filter applied to this view is in the Filter section.

4. Click Save.

   The view is now changed for all Project Web Access users.

Creating a New View from a Copied View

You can create a new view that uses an existing view as its starting point. To do this, follow these steps:

1. On the Server Settings page, under Look And Feel, click Manage Views.

2. On the Manage Views page, click somewhere to the right of the name of the view you want to copy. Don't click the name of the view itself, or you'll open the Edit View page instead.

3. Click Copy View. Enter the name for the new view and then click OK.

   The copied view appears in the list.

4. Click the name of the copied view to open the Edit View page and then make the changes you want. Click Save when finished.

Creating a New View from Scratch

If you prefer, you can create a new view from a completely clean slate. To do this, follow these steps:

1. On the Server Settings page, under Look And Feel, click Manage Views.

2. Click New View.

3. In the Name And Type section, click the type of view you want from the View Type drop-down list.

   This view type determines the page on which your new view will become available.

4. Work through the sections of the New View page to define the view.

5. When finished, click Save.

   The new view is added to the list and is also now available to apply to the page you specified through the Views drop-down list.

Deleting a View

You can delete a view you have created. To do this, follow these steps:

1. On the Server Settings page, under Look And Feel, click Manage Views.

2. On the Manage Views page, click somewhere to the right of the name of the view you want to delete. Don't click the name of the view itself, or you'll open the Edit View page instead.

3. Click Delete View and then click OK in the alert that appears.

   The view is deleted from the list.

Customizing the Quick Launch Task Bar

To change the Quick Launch task bar to better suit the needs and preferences of your organization, follow these steps:

1. On the Server Settings page, under Look And Feel, click Quick Launch.

2. In the Configure Quick Launch Behavior section, specify how menu items should be expanded or collapsed within their sections.

3. In the Set Menu Item Details section, you can do the following:

   - Edit the name or Web address of a link in the Quick Launch task bar. Click the link name to open the Add Or Edit Link page. Enter a different name in the Custom Link Name field or enter a different URL in the Custom Web Address field.

   - Hide a link in the Quick Launch task bar. Click the link name to open the Add Or Edit Link page. In the Display Links In Quick Launch box, click No.

   - Change the order of links on the Quick Launch task bar. Click anywhere to the right of the link whose position in the list you want to change. Don't click the name of the item itself, or you'll open the Add Or Edit Link page. Click the Move Up or Move Down button until the link appears in the position you want.

   - Create a new link. Click New Link to open the Add Or Edit Link page. In the URL section, enter the name of the link as it should appear on the Quick Launch task bar. Also enter the Web address for the link. In the Heading section, select the location where the new link should appear on the Quick Launch task bar.

   - Delete a link you created. Click anywhere to the right of the link to select it and then click Delete Link.

4. When finished, click Save.

Move Up

Move Down

Delete Link

Setting Up Project Report Cubes for Data Analysis

Executives and other managing stakeholders can review aspects of all projects managed by the project server by using the Data Analysis services, which dynamically generate reports of summary or detailed project information needed for a single project or any collection of projects. These services providing reports in Project Web Access are also referred to as the Portfolio Analyzer.

Through the use of the Data Analysis services, managing stakeholders can review a high-level picture of tasks, resources, assignments, schedules, progress, costs, and other information across one, several, or all projects in the organization.

Data Analysis is implemented through the use of online analytical processing (OLAP) tools provided by SQL Server Analysis Services and the Cube Building Services in conjunction with Project Server 2007 and Project Web Access.

As the project server administrator, you must first configure the Data Analysis Services and create the OLAP cubes to then make these OLAP cubes available to users. The cubes, or dynamic reports, are added to the View list of the Data Analysis page for users to manipulate and view. Users can add, move, or delete fields in the resulting PivotTable or PivotChart.

For more information about how managing stakeholders use OLAP cubes configured for the Data Analysis page to analyze project information and generate reports, see the section titled "Analyzing Your Project Portfolio" in Chapter 24.

To specify the date range and update frequency for building the OLAP cubes, follow these steps:

1. On the Server Settings page, under Cube, click Build Settings.

2. In the Cube Build Settings page, make sure the Analysis Services Settings are complete.

   You might need to obtain some of this information from your SQL Server administrator.

3. In the Database Date Range section, indicate the date range of information for which the cube is to be built.

4. In the Cube Update Frequency section, indicate how often you want the cube to be refreshed.

   You can specify an automatic update at regular intervals or a manual update whenever you specify.

   Remember that frequent updates are important for the users generating reports from the cube. Balance this priority with the knowledge that building the cube takes project server resource time and can delay other processes in the queue if you specify that the cube be updated too often.

5. Click Save or Save And Build Now.

> **Note**
> If you ever want to check the status of your OLAP cubes, on the Server Settings page, under Cube, click Build Status.

You can build 11 cubes in Project Server 2007. These cubes are:

- Project Non-Timephased
- Resource Non-Timephased
- Resource Timephased
- Task Non-Timephased
- Assignment Non-Timephased
- Assignment Timephased
- Timesheet
- EPM Timesheet
- Issues
- Risks
- Deliverables

To build the cubes, follow these steps:

1. On the Server Settings page, under Cube, click Configuration.

2. In the Cube Dimensions section of the Cube Configuration page, select the cube (Project, Task, Resource, or Assignment) in the Cube box. From the list of available fields, select the fields that you want to make up the cube and then click Add. Select another cube in the Cube box and select the fields for that cube. Repeat this process until fields are identified as dimensions for each of the four cubes.

3. In the Cube Measures section, select the cube you want in the Cube box. In the Available Fields box, select the custom fields to be added. Repeat this process for all the cubes to which you want to add custom fields. If there are no custom fields for a cube, or if identified custom fields contain no data, the Available Fields box is empty.

Insert

4. If you want to further customize a cube with a Multiple Dimension Expression (MDX) script, you can do so in the Calculated Measures box. Select the cube and then click Insert in the table. Click under Member Name and type a name for the calculated member. Under MDX Expression, type the MDX script that defines the member. Repeat this process for all the cubes for which you want to identify MDX expressions.

5. Click Save.

> For more information about configuring your OLAP cubes for data analysis, see the article at *http://technet2.microsoft.com/Office/f/?en-us/library/5d90076f-bbcc-48c1-a569-bd236862d47c1033.mspx* in the Office Project Server 2007 Technical Library.

Managing and Maintaining the Server

Many of your responsibilities as the project server administrator have you doing specialized activities related to project management, for example, setting project-related permissions, creating custom fields and calendars, setting up the enterprise resource pool, customizing views, and so on. But you have regular system administrator responsibilities as well. Table 21-2 lists these responsibilities along with the links on the Server Settings page that will help you carry them out.

Table 21-2 System Administrator Responsibilities

To do this...	On the Server Settings page...
View the current status of queued jobs, for example, project check-in, proposal creation, timesheet reporting, and status updates	Under Queue, click Manage Queue or Queue Settings
Maintain the database, cleaning up items that are no longer needed, for example, projects, activities, resources, or status report messages	Under Database Administration, click Delete Enterprise Objects
Back up selected items in the project server database, for example, projects, custom fields, enterprise global, and view definitions	Under Database Administration, click Administrative Backup
Schedule regular backups for selected items in the project server database, for example, the enterprise resource pool and calendars, system settings, and category and group settings	Under Database Administration, click Schedule Backup
Restore selected items that were backed up from the project server database, for example, projects, view definitions, and system settings	Under Database Administration, click Administrative Restore

Chapter 21

Managing Enterprise Projects and Resources

Connecting to Your Project Server 754

Working with Enterprise Projects 763

Building Your Enterprise Project Team 780

Collaborating with Your Project Team 794

Creating Proposals and Activity Plans 820

As a project manager using Microsoft Office Project 2007, you have probably created projects, assigned resources, tracked progress, and generated your fair share of reports. If you're working with enterprise project management and collaborating with your project team through Microsoft Office Project Professional 2007, Microsoft Office Project Server 2007, and Microsoft Office Project Web Access, there are differences in how you work with your project and resources. This chapter covers these differences as they pertain specifically to the project manager.

Project server administrators and portfolio managers should see Chapter 21, "Administering Your Enterprise Project Management Solution." Resources can refer to Chapter 23, "Participating On a Team Using Project Web Access." Managing stakeholders can find pertinent information in Chapter 24, "Making Executive Decisions Using Project Web Access."

Chapter 23 and Chapter 24 are also provided as standalone e-chapters on the Bonus Content tab of the Companion CD.

Office Project 2007 enterprise project management coordinates multiple project managers in an organization, dealing with potentially hundreds of projects and thousands of resources. Different stakeholders can plug into the organization's project server to obtain whatever high-level or detailed view of project information they need for their varied functions. But at the heart of this system is the individual project plan—created and controlled by the individual project manager using Office Project Professional 2007.

To start using the Microsoft Office Project 2007 enterprise features, you log on to your project server, either from Project Professional 2007 or Office Project Web Access. Once you're logged on to one of these, you can go right into the other without having to log on again.

After your setup is configured and you can connect, you can create new enterprise projects or import existing projects to the project server. You can make full use of the enterprise resource pool to build your project team and assign those resources to the proper tasks based on their skills and availability. As you track progress, you can be in constant communication with your project resources, exchanging assignment and progress information through Office Project Server 2007. New in Project Server 2007 is the ability to create project proposals, activity plans, and resource plans.

> **Note**
>
> There are a variety of ways to review your project information in Project Web Access through the use of project workspaces, views, and filters. Project Web Access also provides new ways to generate reports. These methods are covered in the section titled "Analyzing and Reporting on Project Information" in Chapter 24.

> **Note**
>
> Your project server administrator is responsible for setting up the enterprise resource pool, the associated resource breakdown structure, and any other organizational customizations for project management. This should be done before you, as the project manager, start publishing any of your own projects to your project server.
>
> For more information about starting to create enterprise projects, talk with your project server administrator to learn more about your organization's processes and standards in implementing enterprise project management. Refer also to Chapter 21.

Connecting to Your Project Server

After your project server administrator adds you as a user with project manager permissions in your project server, you can configure your installation of Project Professional to connect to the server. Then you have all the allowed enterprise project management features at your disposal.

Setting Up Project Professional for Your Server

The first thing you need to do to get started with enterprise project management is make sure that the project server administrator has added you as a project server user. Then, set up your project server account in Project Professional by following these steps:

1. Start Microsoft Office Project Professional 2007.

2. Click Tools, Enterprise Options, Microsoft Office Project Server Accounts.

   The Project Server Accounts dialog box appears (see Figure 22-1).

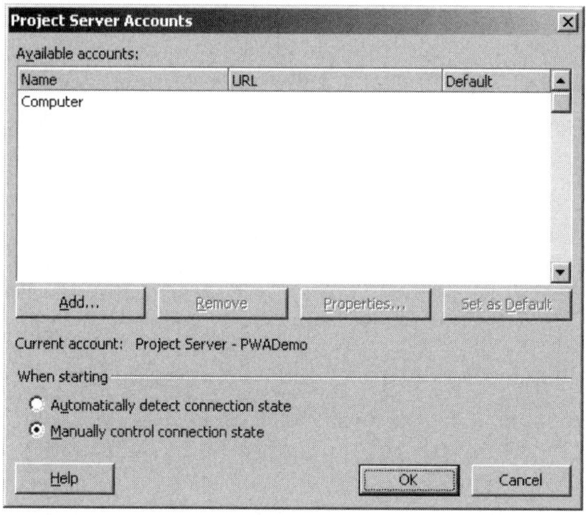

Figure 22-1 Add your project server location as an account for your installation of Project Professional.

3. In the Project Server Accounts dialog box, click Add.

The Account Properties dialog box appears (see Figure 22-2).

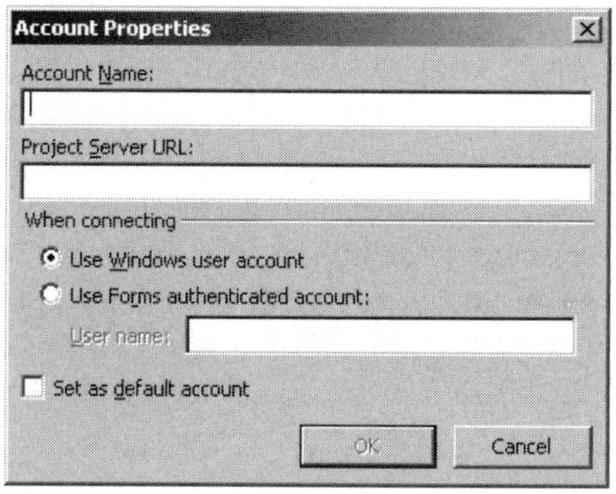

Figure 22-2 Enter the new account name and the project server URL.

4. In the Account Name box, enter the "friendly" name by which you want to identify the project server, for example, "Project Server" or "Corporate Group Project Server."

5. In the Project Server URL box, enter the address of your organization's project server, in the format of http:/ /servername/projectserver.

Obtain this address from your project server administrator.

6. Under When Connecting, specify whether you will be using your Windows account or Forms-authenticated account.

This account needs to match the way your project server administrator has already set up your user information. Find out from your project server administrator which type of authentication you are to use.

With Windows authentication, you can log on to Project Web Access using the same user ID and password you use to log on to your organization's Windows network.

With Forms authentication, you can log on to Project Web Access using the user ID the project server administrator has set up. If you will be using Forms authentication, enter the user name your project server administrator has set up for you.

7. Select the Set As Default Account check box if you want this account to be automatically selected for connection whenever you start Project Professional.

Setting the default account does not necessarily log you into this account when you start Project Professional; it's simply the account that's selected for logon.

8. Click OK.

The Project Server Accounts dialog box appears again, listing your new account in the Available Accounts box.

9. Under When Starting, specify whether you want to automatically connect to the server running Project Server as soon as you start Project Professional.

If you select Automatically Detect Connect State, upon startup, Project Professional will connect to the account you set as the default, which can be convenient if you know that you will always want to connect to a single project server and will rarely work offline.

If you select Manually Control Connection State, a dialog box will appear upon startup that gives you the choice of which account you want to use for this Project Professional session. This might the most appropriate choice if you sometimes expect to work offline. It is also the right choice if this computer is a shared network computer used by multiple users who have different user names and permissions.

10. When finished, click OK.

At this point, you are set up to log on to your project server through Project Professional. If you want to log on immediately, exit Project Professional and then start it up again.

Logging On via Project Professional

If you specified in the Project Server Accounts dialog box that you want to automatically connect to your project server, all you need to do to log on to your project server from Project Professional is to simply start Project Professional. The specified project server location is found, and Project Professional logs you on immediately.

Your user account must be set up by the project server administrator before you can successfully log on to the project server. If you have problems logging on, check with your administrator.

For more information about adding server accounts, see the section titled "Creating a New User Account" in Chapter 21.

If you specified that you want to manually connect to the project server, follow these steps:

1. Start Microsoft Office Project Professional 2007.

    If you are using forms authentication, the Login dialog box appears (see Figure 22-3).

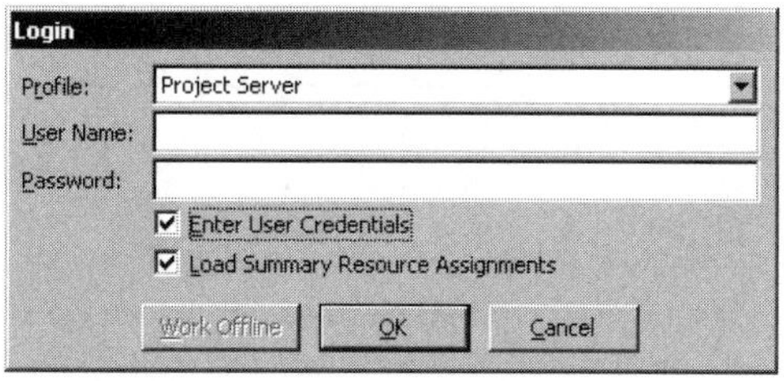

    Figure 22-3 Select your project server account.

2. In the Profile box, click the project server account you want to log on to.

    If you are set up to use your Windows account to log on, and your profile indicates to automatically connect without having to enter user credentials, then as soon as you select the project server and click OK, you are immediately authenticated and connected to the project server.

    If you are set up to use a Forms authentication account to log on, select the project server, enter your user name and password, and then click OK.

    If you ever want to work offline, or if there's a problem logging on to the project server, click the Computer account and then click Work Offline.

Logging On via Project Web Access

Many of your project management responsibilities are best carried out within your familiar Project Professional window. But other responsibilities are best done from within Project Web Access. Many tasks can be done in either place, and it's just a matter of which is more convenient at the time or which method you find more efficient.

As soon as you log on to the project server from Project Professional, you are automatically authenticated to work in Project Web Access without needing to log on again. Likewise, if you happen to log on to Project Web Access first, you can open Project Professional without needing to log on again there.

Chapter 22

To log on to Project Web Access, follow these steps:

1. Start Internet Explorer.

2. In the Address box, enter the URL for your project server and then click Go.

   This is the same URL you entered in the Account Properties dialog box in Project Professional. However, you do not need to have the account set up in Project Professional to log on to Project Web Access directly using Internet Explorer.

   If you are set up for forms authentication, the Project Web Access Sign In page appears (see Figure 22-4).

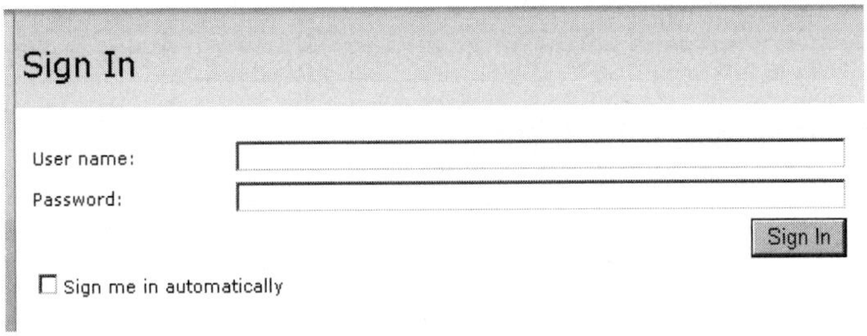

   Figure 22-4 If you are set up for forms authentication, you see the Sign In page whenever you start up Project Web Access.

3. Enter your user name and password as set up by the project server administrator and then click Sign In.

   This is the Forms account information set up by your project server administrator.

   If you are set up for Windows authentication, the Sign In page does not appear, and you are immediately connected to the project server.

   Your Project Web Access home page appears (see Figure 22-5). You can carry out many project management activities from within Project Web Access, and these responsibilities are described throughout the rest of this chapter.

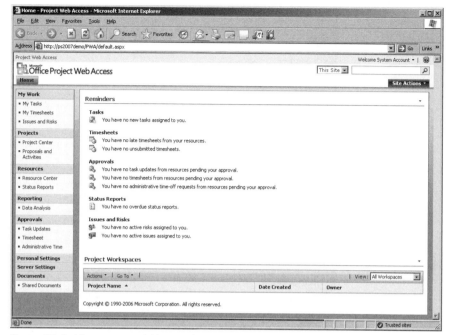

Figure 22-5 After a successful logon, the Project Web Access home page appears.

To log off of Project Web Access, follow these steps:

1. In the upper-right corner of any Project Web Access window, click the Welcome button.

2. In the menu that appears, click Sign Out.

Finding Your Way Around

Once you're signed on to Project Web Access, take a moment to click around and orient yourself to the content and controls. If you have used Microsoft Windows SharePoint Services, much of Project Web Access will feel familiar to you.

Using the Quick Launch Task Bar

The Project Web Access home page and other major pages show the Quick Launch task bar on the left side of the screen (see Figure 22-6). The Quick Launch task bar includes a list of links to all the major areas and functions throughout Project Web Access, for example, the Project Center, the Resource Center, and Shared Documents. Simply click a link on the Quick Launch task bar, and the page changes to show the item you clicked.

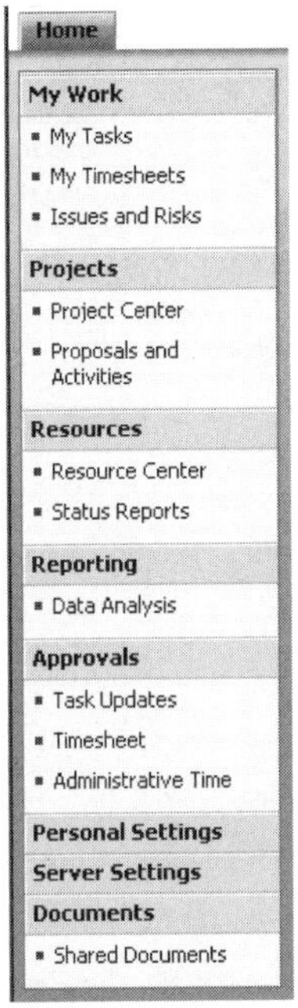

Home

My Work
- My Tasks
- My Timesheets
- Issues and Risks

Projects
- Project Center
- Proposals and Activities

Resources
- Resource Center
- Status Reports

Reporting
- Data Analysis

Approvals
- Task Updates
- Timesheet
- Administrative Time

Personal Settings

Server Settings

Documents
- Shared Documents

Figure 22-6 The Quick Launch task bar is your command center to all the areas of Project Web Access.

Working with Pages and Controls

The home page is the first Project Web Access page you see when you log on. By default, it includes a list of items that need your attention, for example, approvals you need to process or status reports that are coming due. It also lists the Web-based workspaces for the projects that have been set up for your enterprise. Your project server administrator can set up your home page to include the content most appropriate for your organization.

All pages throughout Project Web Access have certain standard controls, as follows:

- **Welcome button** In the upper-right corner of every page is a button that starts with Welcome. Click this button to see a menu that includes My Settings, Sign In As Different User, Sign Out, and Personalize This Page.

- **Help button** Next to the Welcome button is the Help button. If you ever need assistance while using Project Web Access, click the Help button. The Project Server Help window appears. A Help topic pertaining to the current page appears, but you can find other Help topics by typing a phrase or question in the Search For box or by clicking the Home button and then browsing through the Contents.

- **Enter Search Words** Under the Welcome and Help buttons is the Enter Search Words box. If your implementation of Project Web Access and Windows Share-

Help

Point Services has been indexed with keywords, you can search the site for a word or phrase. Type the word or phrase and then click the Go Search button.

- **Site Actions** The Site Actions tab is visible on every page and provides a menu for creating or editing Web pages or managing settings on the Project Web Access site. This is typically used by project server administrators or portfolio managers to customize Project Web Access.

- **Home** The Home tab is visible on every page. Click this tab to quickly move from an inside page on the Project Web Access site to the home page.

Most pages, such as the Project Center or Resource Center, have additional standard controls, as follows:

- **Select a view** Click the arrow in the View box to see a list of views. Views are different versions or layouts of content related to the current page. Some pages have just a single view, whereas others might have seven or eight views.

- **Filter** Click Settings, Filter to show filter controls above the toolbar. You can create a custom filter and add it to the Filter box. You can also apply the Auto Filter to filter by a particular value in a field in the table on the current page.

- **Group** Click Settings, Group. Grouping controls appear above the toolbar. You can group up to three levels by fields. Groups are separated by a colored band in the table on the current page.

- **Search** Click Settings, Search to show the search controls above the toolbar. The search tool finds information you specify in the table on the current page.

Working with Tables

Several pages throughout Project Web Access include a grid, or table, which lists information such as projects, tasks, or resources (see Figure 22-7).

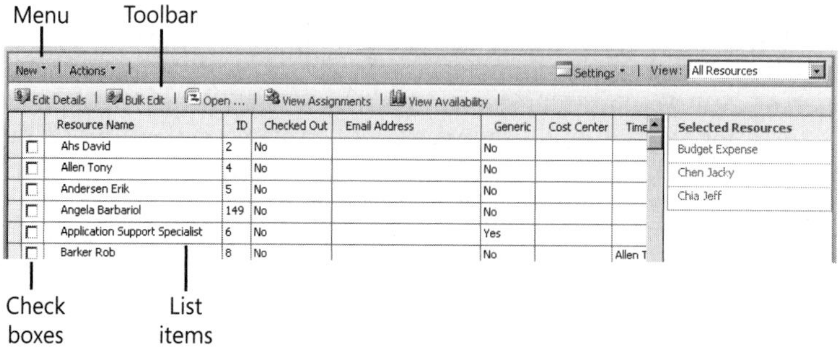

Menu   Toolbar

Check   List
boxes   items

Figure 22-7 You use tables throughout Project Web Access to view and edit project-related information.

The following elements are present in most tables:

- **List items** The main feature of a table is the list of items. In most cases, you can click an item to drill down to see more information, whether it's project or task details or resource information.

- **Check boxes** Some tables include check boxes next to each listed item. Clicking the check box selects the item for further action, typically with a menu item. Items that are selected can be viewed to the right of the table. To select all items in the table, click the Actions menu and then click the Select All command. To clear all selected items, click the Actions menu and then click the Clear All command.

- **Menus** Typically two or three menus are above a table. Click the menu name to view the drop-down menu of commands.

- **Toolbar** Several buttons are on a toolbar directly above the table. Typically, these are frequently used commands that are also available on a menu.

- **Print the table** You can print the My Tasks, Gantt view, Timesheet, Project Center, and Project Details pages, among others. Click Actions, Print Grid. A printable version of the table appears. Click Print Grid.

- **Export the table to Excel** You can export tables to Microsoft Office Excel 2007. On the page with the table, click Actions, Export Grid To Excel. The contents of the table appears in an Office Excel 2007 spreadsheet. Save the spreadsheet.

Working with Enterprise Projects

With your user account set up and Project Professional connected successfully to the project server, you're ready to get down to business and start creating enterprise projects. You can save a new project to the project server or import an existing local project to the project server. Either way, your new enterprise project is associated with the enterprise global template, which sets the project management standards for your organization.

You manage your enterprise project files in specific ways. You check out a project from the server, work on it, and then check it back in again. You can save your project file to the server as much as you like and only publish the project when you are ready to make the information available to assigned resources and other Project Web Access users.

After your enterprise projects are in place on the server, you can carry out your day-to-day project management tasks. With a project checked out, you can add new tasks, modify existing tasks, work with resources, update progress tracking information, review and add information in custom enterprise fields, generate reports, and more.

Creating a New Enterprise Project

You can choose one of two methods for creating an enterprise project. One way is to start a new project plan in Project Professional, make sure you're connected to the project server, and then save the project plan to the server. The other way is to open an existing local project and import it to the project server.

As soon as either type of project is saved to the project server, the enterprise global template is applied to the project, and accordingly, the enterprise standards apply.

Saving a New Enterprise Project to the Server

To create a brand new enterprise project, follow these steps:

1. Start Microsoft Office Project Professional 2007 and connect to the project server.

2. Click File, New.

3. In the New Project task pane, click Blank Project or the name of the existing project or template you want to use as the basis for the new project.

4. Enter tasks or adapt information for your new project.

For more information about creating a new project, see the section titled "Creating a Project File" in Chapter 3, "Starting a New Project."

5. Click File, Save As.

   The Save To Project Server dialog box appears (see Figure 22-8).

Chapter 22

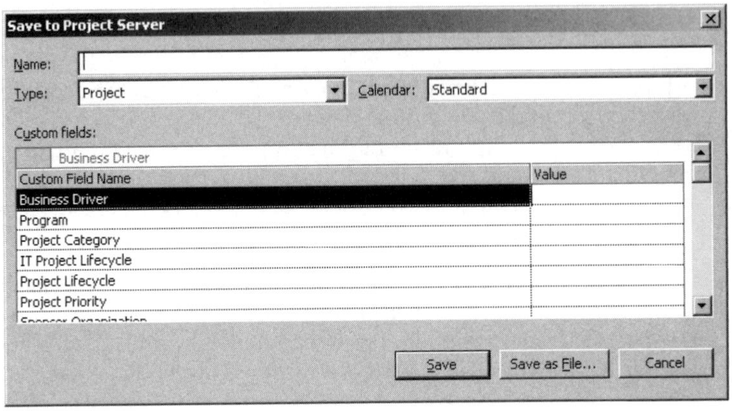

Figure 22-8   When you save a new file while connected to the server, the Save To Project Server dialog box appears.

6.   In the Name box, type the project file name.

7.   In the Calendar box, specify the base calendar being used as the project calendar. This project calendar is the one specified in the Project Information dialog box.

8.   Enter the value for any of the custom enterprise project fields listed in the Custom Fields table. These are fields that have been created for your organization to create standards and points of comparison among multiple projects.

9.   Click Save.

Your new project is saved as a new enterprise project on the project server.

> **Note**
>
> If you want to save the project but do not want to save it to the project server just yet, in the Save To Project Server dialog box, click Save As File then click OK. In the Save As dialog box, enter the file name and select the location on your hard drive where you want to save the project. Click Save. Later when you're ready, you can import the project to the server.

10.   As you begin the process of closing the new enterprise project, a message appears asking if you want to check the project in to the server. Click Yes to check the project in. Click No to keep the project checked out to you.

Importing a Local Project to the Server

To import an existing local nonenterprise project to your project server, follow these steps:

1. Make sure that Microsoft Office Project Professional 2007 is connected to the project server.

   The project you're importing may or may not be open; it doesn't matter to the process.

2. Click Tools, Enterprise Options, Import Project To Enterprise.

   The Open dialog box appears.

3. Navigate to the drive and folder containing the project you want to import to the project server. Click the name of the project and then click Open.

   The Import Project Wizard task pane appears (see Figure 22-9).

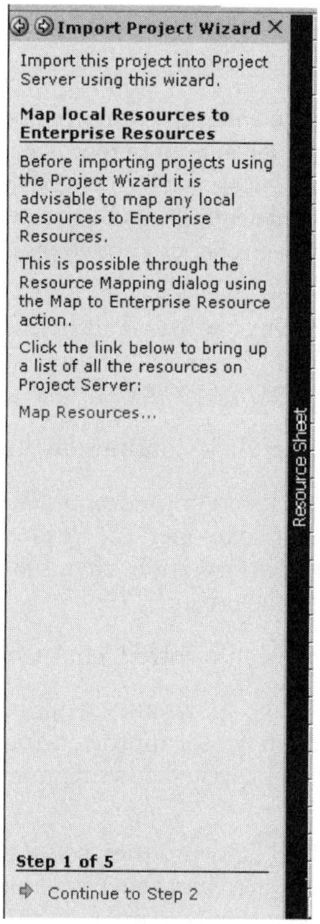

Figure 22-9 The Import Project Wizard walks you through the steps to save an existing local project to the project server.

4. If there are local resources to match with the enterprise resource pool, click the Map Resources link. Read the Map Project Resources Onto Enterprise Resources dialog box.

You can map your local resources to enterprise resources if you know that the resources have already been added to the enterprise resource pool. For each resource name that you want to map, click in the Action On Import field and then click Map To Enterprise Resource. In the Calendar Or Enterprise Resource field, click the down arrow and then select the name of the corresponding enterprise resource.

If you don't want to map or import the resource to the enterprise, retain the Action On Import field default of Keep Local With Base Calendar. If necessary, in the Action On Import field, click the name of the base calendar.

When finished mapping resources, click OK.

> **Note**
>
> When in doubt, don't import a resource to the enterprise resource pool. That is, if you're not sure whether certain resources belong in the enterprise resource pool or whether they're already there, bypass step 4 for now. Once a resource has been added to the enterprise resource pool, it's there semi-permanently. It can be deactivated, but only a database administrator can actually delete an erroneously added resource from the enterprise resource pool.
>
> As long as you have the proper permissions, you can always add a resource later.

5. In the Import Project Wizard task pane, click Continue To Step 2.

6. Review and resolve any errors that are listed in the Import Resource view. To resolve an error, double-click the resource to open the Resource Information dialog box. If you change any resource information, click the Validate Resources button to make sure you have cleared the errors.

7. When all resource import errors have been resolved, click Continue To Step 3.

8. Click the Map Task Fields link. This page shows any custom fields, such as Cost1 or Text3, that you might have defined in the local project. You can map these custom fields to any corresponding enterprise fields that might have been defined for your organization.

   Click the arrow in the From: Task Field field and then select the first field on the task sheet you are importing. Click the arrow in the corresponding To: Enterprise Task Field field and then select the field that is to map to the selected field. When finished mapping the custom fields, click OK.

9. Click Continue To Step 4.

10. Review and resolve any errors listed in the Import Task view. To resolve errors, double-click the task and then make the necessary changes in the Task Information dialog box.

11. When all task import errors have been resolved, click Continue To Step 5.

12. Click the Save As link. In the Save To Project Server dialog box, enter the name of the project in the Name box. Specify the calendar in the Calendar box and enter any values needed in the Custom Field Name table. When finished, click Save.

    The project is saved to the project server.

13. Click the Save And Finish link at the bottom of the Import Project Wizard task pane.

Managing Your Project Files on the Server

You need to be aware of three aspects of file management on the project server as you open, close, and save your project files:

- Project file checkout and check-in

- Saving changes in a project file

- Publishing project information to the project server

Checking Out an Enterprise Project

As soon as you give the command to save a project to the project server, it is saved and checked out to you. When you close the project, you are asked whether you want to check in the project.

It's good practice to check a project out of the server when you want to work on it and check it back in when you're done for the day

To check out an enterprise project, follow these steps:

1. With Microsoft Office Project Professional 2007 connected to the project server, click File, Open.

    The Open dialog box appears, showing the list of enterprise projects that have previously been opened on this computer and now have a copy in the local active cache (see Figure 22-10).

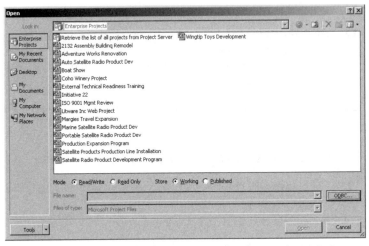

Figure 22-10 The Open dialog box presents a list of enterprise projects .

2. Click the name of the project you want to check out.

If the project you are looking for is not listed, double-click Retrieve The List Of All Projects From Project Server at the top of the list of files. The Group By control appears, and you can click the arrow in the Group By box to choose a property by which to categorize the projects so that you can more quickly find what you're looking for. Any project you open in Project Professional is copied into your active cache.

3. Make sure that the project you want to check out is not already checked out by someone else.

A project can be checked out by only one user at a time. To see whether a project is checked out, click Details in the Open dialog box.

4. Make sure that the Read/Write option is selected, which is the default.

If someone else has checked out the project you want, you can still open it if you select the Read Only option.

5. To see the list of published projects, select the Published option. To see the list of published as well as draft (nonpublished) projects to which you have access, select the Working option. The Working option is selected by default.

6. Click the project you want, and then click Open.

The project opens. The enterprise global template is attached to the template, and the enterprise resource pool is available for use in the project.

Saving Changes in Your Enterprise Project File

Whenever you save an enterprise project file, those changes are saved to the project server. Until you give the command to publish the project, it is considered a working draft, and no one but you can see it or work with it. You can build your draft project using the enterprise global template and the enterprise resource pool, but it's all your own business and no one else's...yet. The project is not listed in the Project Center, and assignments have not yet gone to their resources.

To create a working draft version of a project, simply click File, Save to save it to the project server.

Three Project Databases

Your project server maintains three project databases, or stores, each containing different versions of enterprise project files:

- **Draft** The Draft database, also known as the Working store, contains projects that have been saved to the project server but not yet published.

- **Published** The Published database contains projects that have been published. When you publish a project, it is listed on the Project Center for other users to view. Any task assignments are made available to the assigned resources. By default, a Web-based project workspace is created for the project.

- **Reporting** As soon as you publish your project, data from the project is added to the Reporting database in a format that in conducive to creating reports. As your project is updated, those updates are also reflected in the Reporting database. As reports and views are created, the most up-to-date information from your project is used.

Publishing Project Information to the Project Server

When your project is ready for public consumption and scrutiny by the rest of your organization, it's ready to be published to the project server.

As soon as you publish a new project, it is listed in the Project Center. Any task assignments are made available to the assigned resources. By default, a Web-based workspace is created to view the details of the newly published project.

Note

The workspace is a new feature in Project 2007 based on Windows SharePoint Services. In the workspace, team members and other project stakeholders can read announcements or calendar information. You can see any documents, issues, or risks associated with the project. You can view and participate in discussions about the project. To open a project workspace, from the Project Details page, click Go To, Project Workspace. The workspace opens in a separate Web browser.

Chapter 22

To publish a project for the first time, follow these steps:

1. Make sure that Microsoft Office Project Professional 2007 is connected to the server.

2. Click File, Save to save the project to the server.

3. Click File, Publish.

4. Review the Publish Project dialog box to make sure all the specifications are as they should be (see Figure 22-11).

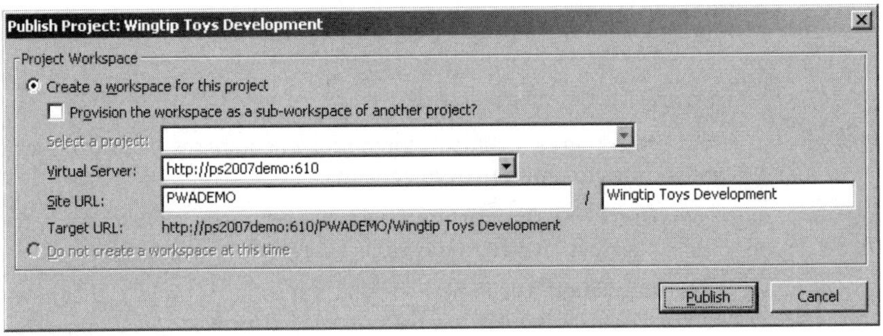

Figure 22-11 Use the Publish Project dialog box to make your project available to other enterprise users through Project Web Access.

5. Click Publish.

The project is now published to the project server and is available to other Project Web Access users.

Even after you first publish your project to the server, the changes you save and check in to the server are not automatically seen by other users. You always have choices as to whether any new changes you save are published to the server. To publish recent changes on an already-published project, click File, Publish. The latest version of your project is now made available to others viewing details about your project on Project Web Access.

Exclude Tasks from a Published Project

You can exclude selected tasks from being published to the project server. This means that even though you are publishing the rest of the project to the project server, the tasks you select are not published. This can be useful if you are working on some what-if scenarios with various tasks and are not ready to make those tasks known to the organization just yet.

To exclude tasks from being published to the server, follow these steps:

1. In a task sheet such as the Gantt Chart, right-click the column heading next to where you want to insert the Publish field.

2. In the shortcut menu that appears, click Insert Column.

3. In the Field Name box of the Column Definition dialog box, select Publish and then click OK.

The Publish field appears in the task sheet. By default, all tasks have a value of Yes in the Publish field.

4. For the tasks whose changes you do not want to publish to the project server, change the Publish field to No.

When you click File, Publish, all tasks that are marked Yes in the Publish field are published, whereas those that are marked No are not. However, you can still save and check in your file, and your changes are all intact.

Later, when you are ready to publish updates to those tasks to the project server, change the No to a Yes and then publish the project again.

Checking In Your Enterprise Project File

When you finish working with your enterprise project for the time being, you check it back in to the project server. Your organization might have specific rules for when you need to check in your projects.

To check in an enterprise project, follow these steps:

1. Make sure that Microsoft Office Project Professional 2007 is connected to the project server.

2. Click File, Save to save your final changes.

3. Click File, Close.

If you have made additional changes since the last time you saved the file, the Close dialog box appears, giving you the choice not only to save or discard your changes, but also to check in the file or not.

If the file is saved, a message asks if you want to check in the project.

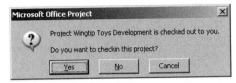

If you had not saved final changes, the Save And Check-In dialog box appears. Click Save Any Changes And Then Check-In. If you want to discard your changes, click Check-In Only.

> **Note**
>
> If there are any required custom enterprise fields whose values you have not completed, you'll see a prompt reminding you to do this. You must complete these fields before you can successfully check the project back in.
>
> See the section titled "Working with Custom Enterprise Fields" later in this chapter for more information.

After you check in your project, if it is published, other project server users with the proper permissions can edit it.

Working Offline with Enterprise Projects

You don't always need to be connected to the project server to work with projects. And you don't always need to work with enterprise projects when connected to the project server. Working offline is particularly helpful if you're traveling or in some other situation without easy Internet access and need to continue to work on your project files. This can also be handy if you want to try some contingency scenarios with an enterprise project.

The following is a list of possible ways you can work offline with an enterprise project:

- You can check out an enterprise project and then work offline. Click File, Work Offline. When ready to connect to the project server again, click File, Work Offline again to turn the offline mode off.

- You can be connected to the project server but also open a local nonenterprise project. To do this, click File, Open. In the Open dialog box, in the Look In box, click My Documents, My Computer, or another location that contains your local project. Browse to and select the local project and then click Open.

- You can open Project Professional without connecting to the project server, and open and work with a local nonenterprise project. To do this, you need to have Project Professional set up for manual connection. In the Login dialog box, click Computer in the Profile box and then click OK. Or click the name of the project server and then click Work Offline.

Refining Your Enterprise Projects

Now that your projects are stored on the project server, you can work with them as enterprise projects. What does that mean to you?

Essentially, it means that you're now using the enterprise global template, which contains any standard project elements that have been defined for your organization, including macros, views, toolbars, and so on. You also have access to enterprise resources and tools for working efficiently with those resources.

In the wider view, your enterprise projects can be reviewed and analyzed by others so that they can see the big picture of all projects taking place throughout the organization.

Reviewing the Enterprise Global Template

When you start Project Professional and connect to your project server, the latest update of the enterprise global template is automatically attached. The enterprise global template is akin to a global template or the "global global" over the standard project global template. The enterprise global template dictates standards being enforced and customizations made available to Project interface elements in projects throughout the enterprise. These standards provide for customization and consistency across all projects in an organization. The standards propagated through the enterprise global template also make it possible for project information throughout the enterprise to be compared and analyzed in meaningful ways.

By default, the portfolio manager and project server administrator are the only users with permission to modify the enterprise global template. However, project managers have permission to view the enterprise global template, so you can see the controls behind your individual enterprise projects. The following list details the project elements that can be modified and propagated as standards via the enterprise global template:

- Filters
- Formulas
- Forms
- Groups
- Import and export maps
- Macros
- Reports
- Tables
- Toolbars
- Microsoft Visual Basic for Applications (VBA) modules
- Views

Chapter 22

To review the enterprise global template and see the specific changes that are being enforced for your organization, follow these steps:

1. Make sure that Microsoft Office Project Professional 2007 is connected to the project server.

   As soon as you connect to the project server, the enterprise global template is loaded into memory for use with your enterprise projects.

2. Click Tools, Enterprise Options, Open Enterprise Global.

   A project plan, which appears to be empty, is displayed (see Figure 22-12).

Figure 22-12 Review features in the enterprise global template to see your organization's standards.

   Using the default project manager permissions, the enterprise global template is not checked out to you in the sense that you can make changes to it; but rather that you're using it as the foundation structure to your own checked-out enterprise projects.

3. You can browse around the various interface features—such as the view definitions, filter definitions, custom toolbars, and so on—to see how the enterprise global template has been customized.

4. When finished reviewing the enterprise global template, close it.

   Although you can inadvertently enter data in the enterprise global template, it is not saved when you close it. Only specific elements (views, macros, currency, and so on) are saved. Tasks or assignments are never saved with the enterprise global template.

   The global standards are still present in any enterprise projects you have currently checked out. In fact, if you browse the interface elements in your own enterprise project, you'll see that the same customizations are present there that are in the enterprise global template.

If the enterprise global template changes after you connect to the project server, you only see those changes after you close Project Professional and reconnect.

It's likely that your organization has a system—whether formal or informal—for project managers to suggest changes to the enterprise global template. Find out from the project server administrator or portfolio manager how you can suggest changes you want to see implemented. When the enterprise global template is updated, you see the changes take effect the next time you check out an enterprise project.

Even though the enterprise global template affects all your enterprise projects, this doesn't mean that you can't still use your own project global template, which is active on projects on your own computer. As long as there's no conflict between elements in the project global template and elements in the enterprise global template, you can create your own sets of standards for all your own projects. For example, you can create and use your own custom toolbar as long as it has a different name from any custom toolbars provided in the enterprise global template.

For more information about working with the project global template, see Chapter 28, "Starndardizing Projects Using Templates."

Finally, you can change interface elements to apply to an individual project without it being a part of the enterprise global template or your own project global template.

Working with Custom Enterprise Fields

Custom enterprise fields often constitute a major area of customization and standardization implemented via the enterprise global template. Custom fields can be designed to store a specific category of numbers, durations, or text not provided by built-in Microsoft Project 2007 fields. Different data types of custom fields are available for assignments, tasks, and entire projects. The portfolio manager or project server administrator defines these fields as part of the enterprise global template, and then they become part of your project.

Custom enterprise fields include the following:

- Custom enterprise project fields, such as Enterprise Project Cost or Enterprise Project Duration

- Custom enterprise task fields, such as Enterprise Date or Enterprise Flag

- Custom enterprise resource fields, such as Enterprise Text or Enterprise Number

Although local nonenterprise projects impose a limit on the number of custom fields you can create, new in Project Server 2007 is the ability to create an unlimited number of custom fields for each field type.

To add a custom enterprise field to your enterprise project, follow these steps:

1. With Microsoft Office Project Professional 2007 connected to the project server, check out the enterprise project to which you want to add the custom enterprise field.

2. Display the sheet view and table to which you want to add the custom enterprise field.

   If you're adding an enterprise task field, display a task view. If it's an assignment field, display the Task Usage or Resource Usage view.

   If you're adding an enterprise resource field, display a resource view.

Chapter 22

If you're adding an enterprise project field, display the project summary row. To do this, first display a task view. Click Tools, Options and then click the View tab. Select the Show Project Summary Task check box.

3. Right-click the column heading next to where you want the custom enterprise field to be inserted. Click Insert Column on the shortcut menu.

4. In the Field Name box, find and click the custom enterprise field.

    You'll know the name of the field from information you've received from your portfolio manager or project server administrator.

    You'll also know the name of the custom field because the word (Enterprise) appears after the field name, as in Project Cost Status (Enterprise).

5. In the Insert Column dialog box, click OK.

    A column containing the selected custom enterprise field appears in the sheet view.

Some custom fields are set up to be calculated from values in other fields in your project. If you added such a calculated field, it might already contain values.

Other custom fields are set up for you to simply add the appropriate data. For such entered fields, you might just type in data freeform. Entered fields can also be designed to contain a value list for you to choose from. If this is the case, click in the field. Click the arrow and select the appropriate choice for the task, resource, assignment, or project.

Setting Up a Program of Projects

You can insert one enterprise project into another to create a master project-subproject relationship between projects. Using this technique, you can model a program, reflecting all projects being implemented under a specific program in your organization. The overarching program can be represented as the master project, with all the projects within that program set up as subprojects within the master project. Therefore, as implemented through Project Server 2007, a program is a set of related projects that are often set up in a hierarchical relationship.

For more information about inserting one project into another, see the section titled "Structuring Master Projects with Subprojects" in Chapter 14, "Managing Master Projects and Resource Pools."

By contrast, a portfolio is simply a collection of enterprise projects being implemented by an organization as reflected in the project server. They might or might not be related to one another, and they might or might be set up in a hierarchical relationship.

All enterprise projects are listed on the Project Center page in Project Web Access, whether they are part of a program, and whether they are a master project or a subproject.

Setting up programs in Project Server through the use of master projects and subprojects supports large organizations implementing a number of large projects and subprojects, often taking place at various locations around the world.

When you open a master project, all the subprojects are listed (and checked out) as tasks in any task view. You can then drill down by clicking one of the subprojects to see the tasks within that project.

If you want to be able to distinguish between master projects and subprojects on the Project Center page, work with your project server administrator or portfolio manager to create and add a custom field to the table on the Project Center page. For example, a text field called "Master-Subproject" could be created in which project managers could indicate whether a project is a master project, a subproject, or neither. That field could then be added to a Project Center view. Another field for subprojects could specify the name of the master project.

You can set up dependencies and deliverables, or commitments, between the projects within a program, providing the visibility needed to know when a key deliverable that affects related project is coming due.

The program hierarchy can be maintained and statused in reports that are generated on the Data Analysis page using an OLAP cube.

Depending on Deliverables in Other Projects

New in Project Server 2007 is the ability to manage dependencies on deliverables among projects in your organization. By managing dependencies on deliverables in other projects, you can keep an eye on commitments in other projects without necessarily affecting the scheduling of your project.

Of course, you can still create links—task dependencies—from one project to another. This is still necessary when there is a true relationship between tasks, such as the common finish-to-start task relationship in which a task in one project cannot begin until a task in another project has been completed. This type of structure does affect scheduling, because if the predecessor task slips, the successor task slips as well.

For information about linking tasks between projects, see the section titled "Linking Information Between Project Plans" in Chapter 15, "Exchanging Information Between Project Plans."

However, if you're working in an enterprise project management environment, and you want to be alerted to the status of deliverables in one enterprise project that affect the outcome, but not necessarily the scheduling, of another enterprise project, then you might consider setting up deliverable dependencies.

Setting Up a Dependency on a Deliverable

To set up a dependency on a deliverable, follow these steps:

1. Make sure that Microsoft Office Project Professional 2007 is connected to your project server.

2. Open the enterprise project that is dependent on a deliverable in another enterprise project.

3. If you want to link a task to the deliverable in the other project, select the task.

Chapter 22

4. Click Collaborate, Manage Dependencies On Deliverables.

   The Dependency task pane appears.

5. Click Add New Dependency.

6. In the Select Project box, click the name of the project that contains the deliverable.

   The Select Deliverable pane appears. As you roll your mouse over each deliverable task, a pop-up shows the full name of the deliverable and its start and finish dates (see Figure 22-13).

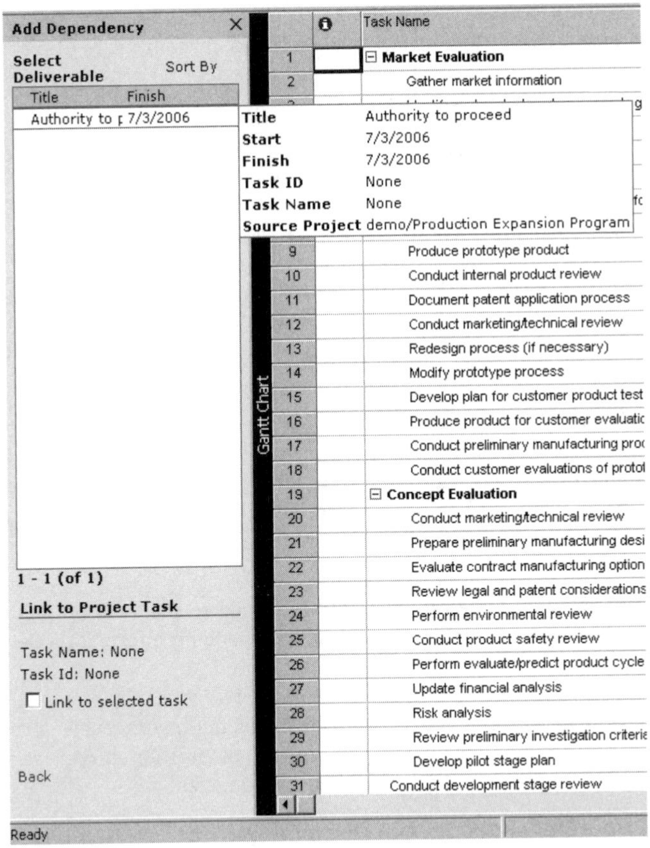

Figure 22-13 The Select Deliverable pane lists the deliverable tasks that have been identified in the other enterprise project.

7. Click the name of the deliverable you want to include as a dependency with the current project.

8. If you want to create a link (task dependency) with the deliverable, select the Link To Selected Task check box.

9. Click Done.

Checking the Status of a Deliverable

To see an update about a deliverable, follow these steps:

1. Make sure that Microsoft Office Project Professional 2007 is connected to your project server.

2. Open the enterprise project that is dependent on a deliverable in another enterprise project.

3. Click Collaborate, Manage Dependencies On Deliverables.

    The Dependency task pane appears, showing the names of the deliverables in other projects you have set up.

4. At the bottom of the Dependency task pane, click Accept All Server Changes if it's present. Also click Get Updates.

    Information about the deliverable's finish date is updated in the task pane.

Creating a Deliverable

In addition to creating dependencies to deliverables in other projects, you can create deliverables in your own projects. To do this, follow these steps.

1. Make sure that Microsoft Office Project Professional 2007 is connected to your project server and then open the enterprise project that is to contain the deliverable.

2. If the deliverable is a particular task, or if you want to associate a deliverable with a task in your project, select that task. However, the deliverable can be independent of any task in the project, associated only with the project as a whole.

3. Click Collaborate, Manage Deliverables.

    The Deliverables task pane appears.

4. Click Add New Deliverable.

5. Complete the fields in the Add Deliverable task pane.

6. If you are associating the deliverable with a selected task, select the Link To Selected Task check box.

    The fields under Deliverable Details are filled in with information from the selected task (see Figure 22-14).

Chapter 22

Figure 22-14 Create a deliverable associated with your enterprise project.

7. If the deliverable is to be associated with the project but not a particular task, enter a title for the deliverable, as well as a start and finish date.

8. Click Done.

Building Your Enterprise Project Team

Among the advantages of enterprise project management is the capability to work with the enterprise resource pool and its associated functions. The enterprise resource pool is the set of people, equipment, and materials available to be assigned and carry out the work of projects throughout an organization. It contains fundamental information about resources, such as skill sets and availability, which helps you find the right resources for your projects. The enterprise resource pool also contains cost information, which not only helps you work within your allotted budget, but also helps accounting and human resources figure costs from their points of view.

With the enterprise resource pool, comes a high level of visibility into resource availabilities, skills, roles, and utilization. Project managers as well as upper management can see when additional staff is needed and where there are underutilized resources. They also can view the basic data for all project resources in one place.

Resource managers can also use the enterprise resource pool to staff, plan, and budget with more accuracy and confidence. They can see resources by skill level and definition, availability, and organizational hierarchy. In addition, they can assist project managers with current and anticipated resource requirements by analyzing the enterprise resource database. Together with project managers, resource managers can work with generic resources in the enterprise resource pool to perform planning and contingency analyses.

The project server administrator is often the one who sets up and maintains the enterprise resource pool. However, because of the specialized information having to do with resource skills, costs, and availability, other specialists—such as the portfolio manager or a human resources representative—might be involved in the setup. By default, the project server administrator and portfolio manager are given permission to add and edit enterprise resource data.

For more information about enterprise resource pool setup, see the section titled "Administering the Enterprise Resource Pool" in Chapter 21.

> ### The Enterprise vs. Nonenterprise Resource Pool
>
> When you're working with enterprise projects and enterprise resources, your nonenterprise resource pool functionality is disabled. That is, when you click Tools, Resource Sharing, the commands on the submenu are dimmed. This is because using a local resource pool with an enterprise project can cause unnecessary confusion.
>
> However, if you ever work with nonenterprise projects, the nonenterprise resource pool commands and functionality are available to you.
>
> For more information about working with a nonenterprise resource pool, see the section titled "Sharing Resources Using a Resource Pool" in Chapter 14.

Finding Resources to Meet Your Needs

You can have Microsoft Project "mine" the entire enterprise resource pool to find resources who have the exact skills, availability, and other traits you need for your project. Specifically, in the planning processes of your project, when putting together the perfect team to carry out your project, you can:

- Find and add resources by name.

- Find resources associated with a certain title, code, skill set, or other attribute.

- Use a generic resource as a placeholder.

- Find resources who are available for work during a certain period of time.

- Replace a resource already on your team with another enterprise resource.

- Find more resources that have the same traits as a resource already on your team.

- Match and replace generic resources in your project with real enterprise resources.

- Propose tentative resources to your project.

You can use the Build Team dialog box to find enterprise resources and add them to your project team. The Build Team process adds resources to your project but does not

Chapter 22

necessarily assign tasks (unless you replace a resource who has already been assigned to tasks). After the resources are added, you use the Assign Resources dialog box, as usual, to assign tasks to project resources.

Adding Enterprise Resources by Name

You might already know exactly which enterprise resources you need to add to your team. If this is the case, find and add resources by name as follows:

1. Make sure that Microsoft Office Project Professional 2007 is connected to the project server and then check out the project to which you want to add resources.

2. Click Tools, Build Team From Enterprise.

If there are more than 1,000 resources in the enterprise resource pool, a dialog box appears to help you prefilter the enterprise resources. In the custom enterprise resource field that appears, select a code or other attribute to help define the list of resources you'll be working with. Click OK.

The Build Team dialog box appears (see Figure 22-15). The upper portion of the dialog box contains filters and options for finding resources that meet certain criteria. The Enterprise Resource table on the left contains the list of enterprise resources. When no filter is applied, the table lists all members of your organization's enterprise resource pool. The Project Resources table on the right lists any enterprise and nonenterprise resources you have already added to the current project.

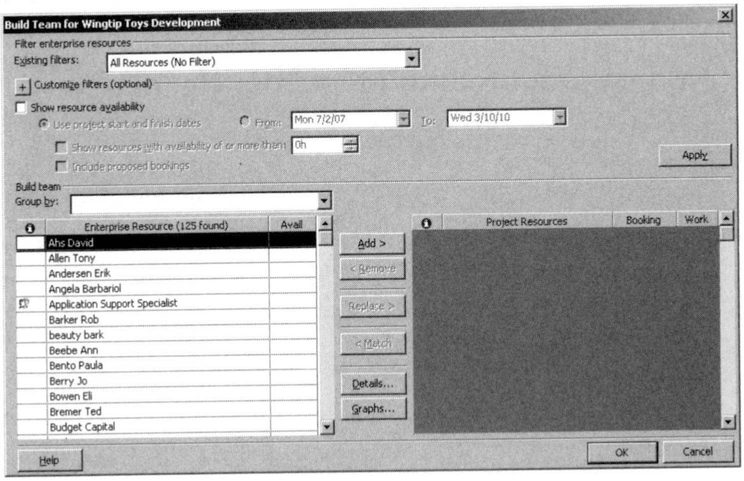

Figure 22-15 Use the Build Team dialog box to add enterprise resources to your project.

By default, the enterprise resources are listed alphabetically by name. To be certain, you can re-sort the list by clicking the Enterprise Resource column heading.

3. Scroll through the Enterprise Resource table to find and select a resource by name.

You can select multiple resources at once. Use Shift to select multiple adjacent resources; use Ctrl to select multiple nonadjacent resources.

4. Click the Add button.

The selected resources are added to the Project Resources table.

> **Note**
>
> You can learn more about a resource by clicking the resource name in either table and then clicking the Details button. The Resource Information dialog box opens. You can review information about this resource's availability, costs, and custom fields. This information is set up by users with special permission to edit resource information, as granted by the project server administrator.

Identifying Resource Attributes Using Custom Enterprise Fields

Custom fields for identifying enterprise resource attributes can be defined by your project server administrator or other user with the proper permissions.

After the custom resource fields are defined, the project server administrator (or other user) associates resources in the enterprise resource pool with the custom resource fields that define those resources. In this way, the enterprise resources are defined by their job code, qualifications, specialties, locations, or any other attributes needed by an organization.

For more information about custom enterprise fields, see the section titled "Working with Custom Enterprise Fields" earlier in this chapter.

You can use the custom enterprise resource fields to do the following:

- Match or replace resources in your project with others associated with the same values in their custom fields. You do this using the Build Team dialog box.

- Substitute generic or enterprise resources in your project with enterprise resources possessing matching values in their custom fields. You do this using the Resource Substitution Wizard.

- Arrange enterprise resources in your project by their custom fields so that you can review your project team by your organization's resource breakdown structure or other resource hierarchy. You do this by sorting, filtering, or grouping by the custom field.

Your project server administrator is responsible for setting up the custom enterprise resource fields according to the needs of your organization.

For more information, see the section titled "Customizing Enterprise Project Fields" in Chapter 21.

To add a custom enterprise resource field to your enterprise project, follow these steps:

1. With Microsoft Office Project Professional 2007 connected to the project server, check out the enterprise project to which you want to add the custom enterprise resource field.

2. Display the Resource Sheet and table to which you want to add the custom enterprise field.

3. Right-click the column heading where you want the custom enterprise field to be inserted. Click Insert Column on the shortcut menu.

4. In the Field Name box, find and click the custom enterprise resource field.

    You'll know the name of the field from information you've received from your project server administrator.

5. In the Insert Column dialog box, click OK.

    A column containing the selected custom enterprise resource field appears in the sheet view.

> **Note**
>
> In Microsoft Office Project 2003, certain enterprise resource outline codes could be used to define multiple traits within a single code. New in Microsoft Office Project 2007 is the ability for custom fields to represent multiple hierarchical values through the use of a lookup table. In fact, a lookup table can be defined for all the custom fields (Text, Number, Date, and so on) except for Flag, which by its nature is defined by Yes or No.

Using Generic Resources as Placeholders

You can use generic resources in Microsoft Project 2007 to help you define resources of a particular role or skill set, for example, VB Programmer Expert.

Generic resources can be created by the project manager. Generic resources can also be created and added to the enterprise resource pool by the project server administrator or other user with the proper permissions. For best results, an organization should define a generic resource for every classification in its resource breakdown structure. Project managers and resource managers can then use those generic resources in their projects for planning and modeling purposes.

Because generic resources are just placeholders for real resources, they are not associated with any availability status. They can be used in as many projects by as many project managers as needed.

Generic resources are invaluable for helping project managers identify team requirements and ultimately find real resources. Generic resources are typically defined by a job title or function, rather than a person's name. What makes generic resources truly useful is the association of custom enterprise resource fields, which go a long way toward defining the attributes of the resource.

With generic resources associated with custom fields that define resource attributes, you can populate your project team using the Build Team dialog box.

> **Note**
>
> Your organization might have established a set of generic resources as part of the enterprise resource pool. If this is the case, rather than create your own, use the Build Team dialog box to find the generic resources you want and then add them to your project team.
>
> If you're not sure whether generic resources have been defined for your organization, check with your project server administrator. Or, just filter and browse the enterprise resource pool in the Build Team dialog box.

Adding a Team Assignment Pool to Your Project Resource List

Sometimes you don't need to add specific enterprise resources to your project; sometimes you just need a collection of people from a particular department or group to carry out certain tasks. You can assign tasks to the group, and members of the group can assign themselves to the tasks, report on them, and complete them.

This is the idea behind team assignment pools, also known as team resources, a new feature in Project 2007. A team assignment pool might be a department such as Marketing, or a group of individuals doing the same job such as Editors.

> **Note**
>
> For you to be able to use team resources, your project server administrator needs to have defined the team assignment pool in the enterprise resource pool.

To find team assignment pools and add them to your list of project resources, do the following:

1. With Microsoft Office Project Professional 2007 connected to the project server, and your enterprise project open, click Tools, Build Team From Enterprise.

2. In the Build Team dialog box, click the plus button next to Customize Filters to expand the section.

3. Click in the Field Name column of the first row and select Team Assignment Pool. You can move to it quickly in the list if you type **te**.

Chapter 22

4. In the Test column, click Equals.

5. In the Value(s) field, click Yes.

6. Click the Apply button.

    All enterprise resources that are identified as team assignment pools, or team resources, are listed in the Enterprise Resource table.

7. Click a team resource you want and then click Add to add it to your project resource list (see Figure 22-16).

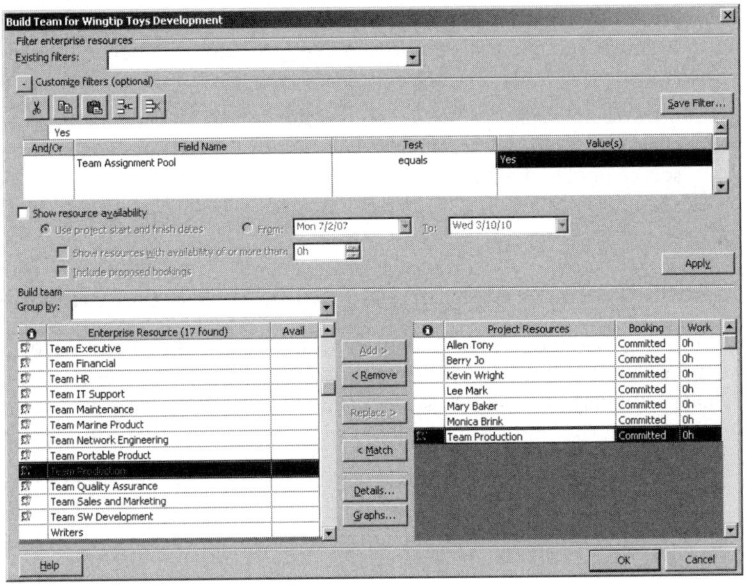

Figure 22-16 Build a custom filter to find all team assignment pools and then add the one you want to your project.

You can now assign tasks to the team assignment pool.

Finding Enterprise Resources That Meet Specific Criteria

If you're looking for a set of enterprise resources who fit a certain set of criteria, you can use the various built-in filters, groups, and other controls in the Build Team dialog box to narrow your search.

To find and add resources who possess certain attributes, follow these steps:

1. Click Tools, Build Team From Enterprise.

    The Build Team dialog box appears.

2. If you want to filter the enterprise resource list by using a built-in filter, under Filter Enterprise Resources, click the arrow in the Existing Filters box and then select the filter that describes the resources you're looking for, for example, material resources or group. Provide any additional information as applicable.

   Only those enterprise resources who meet the criteria of the filter are listed in the Enterprise Resource table. This not only reduces your choices to a more manageable level, but it also shows you just the resources that are most useful for your project's purposes.

3. If you need to find resources who have a certain amount of time available to work during a specific period of time, you can specify that with the Show Resource Availability controls. Select the Show Resource Availability check box.

   Specify whether you want to use the project start dates or other specific dates to indicate when you need the resources.

   If you want to filter for resources with a specific amount of available time, such as 180d or 40w, select the Show Resources With Availability Of Or More Than check box.

   Click the Apply button.

   The resources listed in the Enterprise Resource table change to show only those resources who meet the availability criteria you specified. The amount of availability shows in the Avail column.

4. If you want to group the resources in the table by a particular resource field, click the arrow in the Group By box and then click the field. For example, you might find it helpful to group resources by Standard Rate or Group.

   The list of enterprise resources is rearranged according to your selected group.

For more information about using existing filters and groups, see the section titled "Rearranging Your Project Information" in Chapter 4, "Viewing Project Information."

You can quickly create your own filter within the Build Team dialog box if you need to filter on a specific field (or two or three) that isn't provided for in the Existing Filters list. Creating your own Build Team filter is particularly useful if you want to find resources that are associated with a certain value in a custom enterprise field such as Enterprise Resource Text or Enterprise Resource Number. Likewise, if RBS codes have been set up and applied to enterprise resources, you can filter for a particular RBS code. If the filter is especially useful or one that you expect to apply often, you can save it.

To create a Build Team filter, follow these steps:

1. In the Build Team dialog box, click the plus button next to Customize Filters to expand the section.

   A filter definition table appears.

2. Click in the Field Name column of the first row and select the field you want to filter on (see Figure 22-17).

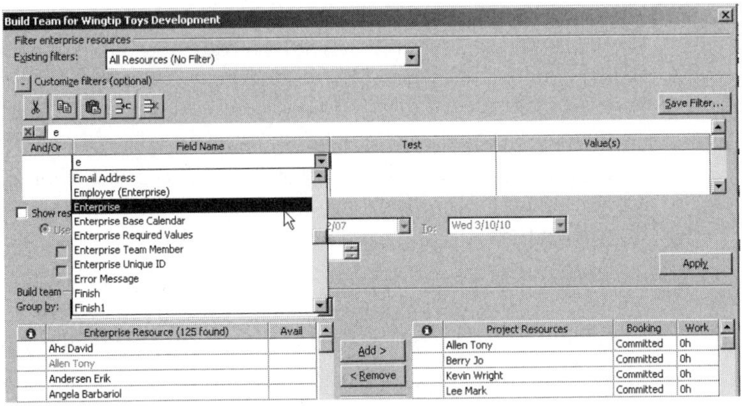

Figure 22-17 Create a filter to find those resources that meet your criteria.

3. In the Test column, click the test you want to use, such as Equals or Is Greater Than.

4. In the Value(s) field, enter the value that should be stored in the field for the resources found by the filter.

5. If you need to define another set of criteria, in the second row of the table, click in the And/Or field and then click And or Or.

6. In the rest of the row, select the field, test, and value for the second set of criteria.

7. When finished defining the filter, click Save Filter if you want to save it for future use. Otherwise, click the Apply button.

   You can combine the application of your filter with other criteria, including an existing filter or work availability criteria. When you click the Apply button, the list of enterprise resources changes to show only those resources who meet the criteria of your filter(s).

For more information about creating your own filters, see the section titled "Customizing Filters" in Chapter 25, "Customizing Your View of Project Information."

Replacing an Existing Project Resource with an Enterprise Resource

You can use the Build Team dialog box to replace a resource on your project team with one from the enterprise resource pool. This replacement is useful if you have a local resource in the project that you know has been added to the enterprise resource pool. It is also useful if you want to replace generic resources in your project with real enterprise resources.

To replace an existing project resource with an enterprise resource, follow these steps:

1. In the Build Team dialog box, apply any filters or groups you need to find the replacing resource.

2. In the Project Resources table, click the name of the resource you want to replace.

3. In the Enterprise Resource table, click the name of the replacing resource.

4. Click Replace.

   The resource selected in the Enterprise Resource table replaces the one selected in the Project Resources table. If the original resource had reported any actual work on assigned tasks, the original resource remains in the project plan as associated with those assignments. Any remaining work on any tasks assigned to the original resource is now assigned to the replacing resource.

Matching an Existing Project Resource

Suppose you have a resource who has the perfect combination of qualifications for certain tasks in your project, and everything is great—except that you need five more resources just like him. If the existing resource and enterprise resources have attributes defined for them—such as RBS codes, skill sets, or certifications—you can use the Build Team dialog box to find other resources who have the same attributes.

To find more enterprise resources whose defined traits match those of an existing project resource, follow these steps:

1. In the Build Team dialog box, apply any filters or groups you might need to define matching resources.

2. In the Project Resources table, click the name of the resource whose traits you want to match with additional enterprise resources.

3. Click Match.

   The list of filtered enterprise resources is searched for resource matches. The resulting list of resources represents resources whose attributes exactly match those of your selected resource.

4. If you want to add any of these resources, click their names and then click Add.

Chapter 22

Review a Resource's Availability Graphs

If you find a resource you want to add or replace in your project, you can get more information about that resource's availability and workload. This can help you decide whether this resource really has the time to work on your project.

Select the resource name in either table and then click Graphs. The Graphs dialog box appears. You can choose from three different graphs in the Select Graph box.

With the availability graphs, you can see timephased availability from different points of view:

- The Remaining Availability graph shows the amount of free time.
- The Work graph shows the amount of time taken by current assignments.
- The Assignment Work graph shows the amount of time taken by current assignments in the current project and other projects, and it also shows the remaining availability.

Each of these graphs shows assigned work or availability over time periods, which you can zoom in or out to the level of detail you want.

Matching and Replacing Generic Resources

You can combine the Match and Replace functions in the Build Team dialog box to help you find enterprise resources to replace generic resources, as follows:

1. In your project plan, click Tools, Build Team From Enterprise.

   The Build Team dialog box appears.

2. If necessary, apply any filters to better focus the list of resources.

3. In the Project Resources table, select your generic resource and then click Match.

   Microsoft Project 2007 finds all the resources in the enterprise resource pool that have the same attributes as the ones you defined in your generic resource. Those matching resources are listed in the Enterprise Resource table.

4. Select the matching resource you want to replace the generic resource and then click Replace.

   The matching enterprise resource is added to your project team. If you had assigned any tasks to the generic resource, the replacing enterprise resource is now assigned to those tasks.

5. Repeat steps 3–4 to match and replace any other generic resources in your project plan.

INSIDE OUT **Use the Build Team dialog box instead of the Resource Substitution Wizard**

Just as you can use the Build Team dialog box to match and replace generic or other placeholder resources in your project plan with real enterprise resources who have matching attributes, you can use the Resource Substitution Wizard to find, match, and replace placeholder resources that have been assigned to tasks.

However, the wizard is cumbersome to use and often does not provide satisfactory assignment results.

For more control over the outcome, use the match and replace feature in the Build Team dialog box to narrow down the list of resources in the enterprise resource pool. You can have the Build Team dialog box replace the generic resource, or you can do so manually.

Proposing Tentative Resources

As soon as you add enterprise resources to your project team and assign tasks to those resources, their availability information changes in the enterprise resource pool. This availability update ensures, for example, that a single resource is not inadvertently booked full-time to two or three different projects.

However, sometimes you need to build a project and its team as a proposal or estimate. You might want to show actual resources in the project, to demonstrate the skill level as well as calculate real costs. However, if the project is just an estimate or model, you probably wouldn't want to tie up the resource's availability in case the project does not actually happen.

In another scenario, you might be working with an approved project and want to run a what-if analysis on the impact of adding certain resources to the project.

For either of these cases, you can soft-book resources on your project by adding them as proposed, rather than committed resources on your team.

> **Note**
>
> The booking type, proposed or committed, applies to the resource as a whole on your project. The booking type does not apply to individual assignments within the project.

By default, all resources are booked as committed. To specify that a resource you're adding is to be booked as a proposed resource on your project team, do the following:

1. In the Build Team dialog box, apply any filters or groups you might need to find the resources you want.

2. In the Enterprise Resource table, click the name of the resource you want to add as a proposed resource.

3. Click Add.

4. In the Project Resources table, in the Booking field for the resource, change Committed to Proposed.

   This resource is now considered soft-booked. As you work through your project, you can choose to consider resources' booking types when assigning tasks to resources in your project and when leveling assignments to resolve overallocations.

Chapter 22

> **Note**
>
> When you're searching for resources who meet certain availability criteria, you can choose whether Microsoft Project should consider proposed resource information. In the Build Team dialog box, select or clear the Include Proposed Bookings check box.
>
> A resource's booking type becomes part of the resource information. When you're ready to confirm a resource's place in your project, display the Resource Sheet or other resource view. Double-click the proposed resource's name to open the Resource Information dialog box. On the General tab, in the Booking Type box, change Proposed to Committed.

Assigning Tasks to Enterprise Resources

Assign Resources

Once you have built your project team, you're ready to assign tasks to its members. You can assign tasks to regular resources, team resources, or generic resources. Use the Assign Resources button on the Standard toolbar to open the Assign Resources dialog box. Assign your project tasks to the resources in your list.

For more information, see Chapter 7, "Assigning Resources to Tasks."

Identifying Assignment Owners

When you assign a task to a work resource, by default, that resource becomes the assignment owner, that is, the person responsible for providing progress updates about the assignment. However, what if certain resources do not have Project Web Access readily available to them, or if there's some other reason they won't be able to provide progress updates? Or, what if the work resource is a piece of equipment?

In such cases, you can identify a different assignment owner. Even though the assigned resource is still responsible for carrying out the assignment itself, the assignment owner becomes responsible for the progress updates on the assignment.

> **Note**
>
> Assignments to material resources and generic resources are owned by the default assignment owner, which is typically the person who created the project plan. That's probably you. Cost resources do not have assignment owners.

To identify an assignment owner different from the assigned resource, follow these steps:

1. With Microsoft Office Project Professional 2007 connected to the project server, and your enterprise project open, make sure that the resource has been assigned to tasks.

2. Click View, Task Usage or View, Resource Usage to open an assignment view.

3. Click the assignment for which you want to designate a different assignment owner.

   In the Task Usage view, the assignment is the resource name under the task name. In the Resource Usage view, the assignment is the task name under the resource name.

4. On the Standard toolbar, click Assignment Information.

5. On the General tab, in the Assignment Owner box, select the name of the resource to be responsible for submitting status updates for this assignment.

   All enterprise resources added to this project, as well as the project manager who originally published this project, are listed as possible assignment owners.

6. Click OK.

   In Project Web Access, the assignment owner will receive the assignment information and the reminders to submit updates and status reports on this assignment.

Each work resource has a default assignment owner. Typically, that default is the resource himself or herself. Otherwise, the default assignment owner is the project manager who generated the current project. The default assignment owner for any enterprise resource can be changed to any work resource on your project team by the project server administrator or other user with the permission to edit enterprise resource information. This is done on the Edit Resource page in Project Web Access.

Although you cannot change the default assignment owner in Project Professional, you can see who it is on the General tab in the Resource Information dialog box.

Assigning Status Managers

The flip side of the assignment owner is the status manager. Just as a resource needs to be responsible for submitting status information about an assignment, another person needs to be responsible for receiving that status information. That person is the status manager.

The default status manager for a task is the person who originally published the task to the project server. There can be different status managers for different tasks. To see or change the status manager for tasks, add the Status Manager field to a task sheet in Project Professional, as follows:

Assignment
Information

Chapter 22

1. With Microsoft Office Project Professional 2007 connected to the project server, and your enterprise project open, switch to a task sheet such as the Gantt Chart.

2. Right-click the column heading next to where you want to insert the Status Manager field.

3. In the shortcut menu that appears, click Insert Column.

4. In the Field Name box of the Column Definition dialog box, select Status Manager and then click OK. To move to Status Manager quickly, type **stat**.

   The Status Manager field appears in the task sheet.

5. To change a status manager for a task, click in the field and then click the arrow. In the list of status managers for the current project, click the status manager you want for this task.

Collaborating with Your Project Team

After you set up your enterprise project team, you have powerful methods of project collaboration and communication at your fingertips. Using Project Professional and Project Web Access, you can assign tasks to resources, receive progress updates, and request narrative status reports—all electronically via publication of information to your project server.

This collaboration process automates the gathering and entry of actuals so that you don't have to enter actuals on assignments yourself. Your project server administrator or portfolio manager sets up your resources' task progress pages in Project Web Access so that they can enter and submit their actuals on a periodic basis. You can then review these actuals and accept them for incorporation into the project plan.

To keep a close eye on time usage and project availability, you can also track nonproject tasks and time through the use of timesheets and administrative time such as nonproject meetings, training, or nonworking time requested by resources.

Because Project Server is tightly integrated with Windows SharePoint Services, you can also control project-related documents, track project issues, and manage project risks.

Who Designs the My Tasks Page?

In Project Web Access, the My Tasks page, also known as the task update page, is the central view used by project resources. It contains the assignments for each individual resource. The My Tasks page also includes fields the resources use to enter progress information—their actuals—that they periodically submit to the project server for you to then incorporate into the project plan.

In previous versions of Microsoft Office Project, you have the ability to customize the fields that resources see on this page.

Now in Microsoft Office Project 2007, the project server administrator or portfolio manager is responsible for setting the fields used by resources. This simplifies tracking and also ensures that the same fields of information are available for all projects across the enterprise so that reliable reporting across multiple projects is made possible.

Work with your project server administrator to help determine the default timesheet fields and permissions so that your needs as a project manager are met while the organization's requirements are fulfilled as well.

For more information about administrator responsibilities in customizing the My Tasks page for resources, see the section titled "Setting Up Team Member Work Pages" in Chapter 21.

When collaborating with your resources on their project assignments, three basic activities are at work:

- You publish project information, thereby making project and assignment information available on the project server for resources and other Project Web Access users.

- You request information from resources, such as task updates and status reports.

- You review and accept information from resources, such as task updates and status reports, and then incorporate that information into the project plan.

Before you start doing any of these, it's a great idea to set up options that govern the details of how these activities are done.

Configuring Task Update Options

The project server administrator or portfolio manager often configures how progress reporting on team member task assignments are done throughout the enterprise. However, as the project manager, you have some choices in how to support your resources in their work as well as which efficiencies you need to help you manage the flow of information between you and your resources.

Changing the Method of Progress Reporting

Using the Collaborate tab in the Options dialog box, you can specify certain aspects of task assignment and tracking, as follows:

1. With Microsoft Office Project Professional 2007 connected to the project server, and your enterprise project open, click Collaborate, Collaboration Options. The Collaborate tab of the Options dialog box opens (see Figure 22-18).

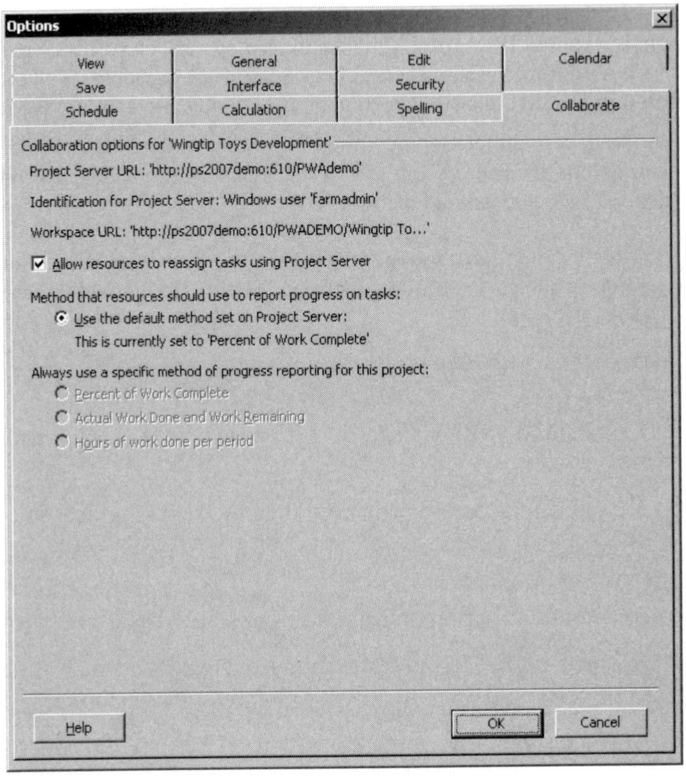

Figure 22-18 Use the Collaborate tab to specify your assignment and tracking options.

2. If it's acceptable for resources to reassign tasks to other resources, select the Allow Resources To Reassign Tasks Using Project Server check box.

   This is particularly useful if you have team leads or resource managers responsible for specific assignments or for delegating tasks as they see fit.

   This check box is selected by default.

3. If your project server administrator is allowing you to change the method of progress reporting, you can do so under Always Use A Specific Method Of Progress Reporting For This Project.

   ❑ If the options are available, then select the one you want to use for this project, or leave the selection at the Use The Default Method Set On Project Server.

   ❑ Select the Percent Of Work Complete option if you want resources to simply report percentage complete on each of their assignments, for example, 15%, 50%, or 100%. This is the least restrictive and least time-consuming tracking method. With this method, the My Tasks page includes a % Work Complete field that the resource uses for her assignment updates.

❑ Select the Actual Work Done And Remaining Work option if you want resources to report the total hours of work completed on an assignment so far as well as the number of hours remaining to complete the assignment. This tracking method provides a medium level of detail. The My Tasks page includes fields for total actual work and remaining work for each assignment. Resources enter those total amounts for each progress update requested.

❑ Select the Hours Of Work Done option if you want resources to report the number of hours of work completed per day or per week on each assignment. This is the most detailed tracking method and is required for any organization using the Managed Timesheet Periods feature of Project Server. The My Tasks page includes a field for each time period, either days or weeks, for the duration of the project. Resources enter the number of hours worked per day or per week and submit them with each progress update.

❑ If the options are dimmed, this means that you and your team are required to use the specific method of progress reporting imposed by the project server administrator.

Other Project Web Access task update and status options are set by the project server administrator or portfolio manager. Work with these individuals to set up the task update page you need for your project while at the same time adhering to your organization's standards (see Figure 22-19).

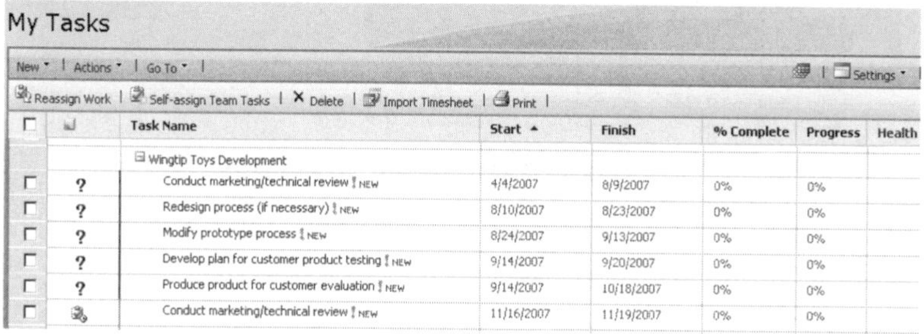

Figure 22-19 Project resources work with their individual assignment progress pages in Project Web Access.

Note

In previous versions of Microsoft Office Project, you could specify what information you wanted to publish to the project server whenever you saved your project. Now in Microsoft Office Project 2007, saving and publishing are separate operations.

For more information about saving, publishing, checkin, and checkout, see the section titled "Managing Your Project Files on the Server" earlier in this chapter.

Chapter 22

Setting Up E-Mail Notifications and Reminders

To help manage the flow of information between you and your resources, you can specify that alerts, reminders, and e-mail messages automatically be sent to you or your resources under certain conditions. Such conditions might include when a resource updates assignments, when a resource's assignment is coming about to start, or when a status report is due.

To set up automated alerts and reminders, follow these steps:

1. Start Microsoft Office Project Web Access and log on if necessary.

2. On the Quick Launch task bar, click Personal Settings.

3. On the Personal Settings page, click Manage My Resource's Alerts And Reminders.

4. On the page that appears, work through the fields to specify which alerts and reminders should be sent under which conditions (see Figure 22-20).

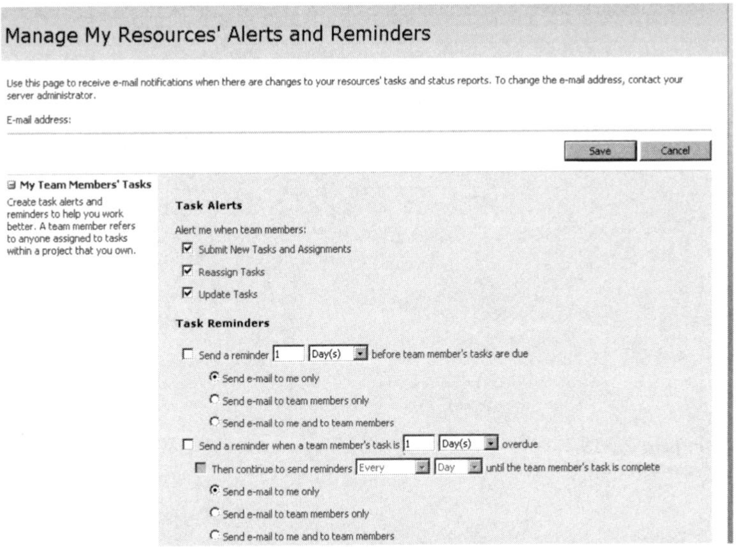

Figure 22-20 You can have alerts and reminders sent to your resources and to yourself regarding assignment updates and status reports.

5. Click Save.

Setting Rules for Accepting Updates

As resources work on, update, and complete their assigned tasks, they submit their task updates to the project server on a periodic basis. You can manually review each task update and accept the information into your project plan, or not. Or, you can set up rules to specify which updates are safe to automatically incorporate into your project plan. Using rules can help keep your project plan up-to-date while significantly reducing the number of updates you have to handle.

To set up rules for accepting changes to the project plan, follow these steps:

1. Start Microsoft Office Project Web Access and log on if necessary.

2. On the Quick Launch task bar, under Approvals, click Task Updates.

3. Click Actions, Manage Rules.

4. On the Rules page, click New Rule.

New Rule

5. On the Edit/Create Rule page, read the sections and make selections to set up the rules you want for managing assignments and updates (see Figure 22-21).

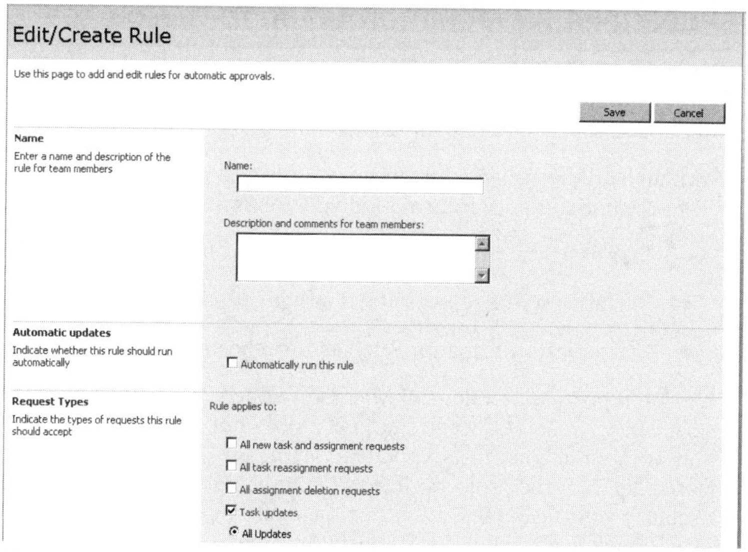

Figure 22-21 Specify the conditions under which updates can be automatically accepted.

6. When finished, click Save.

You can create different rules for different conditions. All the rules you create are listed on the Rules page.

Chapter 22

The Collaborate Toolbar

As you publish your project more and more frequently, update project progress with updates from your resources, or move back and forth between Project Professional views and Project Web Access pages, take advantage of the Collaborate toolbar. Click View, Toolbars, Collaborate to show the Collaborate toolbar. This toolbar makes your collaboration commands immediately accessible.

Publishing Project Information for Resources

Your enterprise project plan is built, resources are added, and tasks are assigned to those resources. Furthermore, your options for team collaboration using Project Web Access are set up. You're ready to start moving forward on your project.

Although all the information about your project is published on the project server, the three primary types of information you are exchanging with your resources are:

- Task assignments and progress updates on those assignments.

- Narrative status reports about assigned tasks.

- Nonproject information such as timesheets and administrative time.

Publish

Unlike in previous versions of Microsoft Office Project, merely saving a project to the server in Microsoft Office Project 2007 does not make it available for other users to see and work with. You must explicitly give the File, Publish command in Project Professional 2007 for the project information to be published to the server and therefore be usable to your resources and other users of the project server with the right permissions. You can also click the Publish button on the Collaborate toolbar.

When you publish your project, the changes you have made since the last time you published are made public on the server. Although you can explicitly exclude certain tasks from being published, typically all changes in your project are published at the same time. This includes new assignments, changed assignments, and any other information changed throughout the entire project.

> **Note**
>
> New in Microsoft Office Project 2007 are permanent assignment comments. If you create an assignment note and publish it, the assigned resource can see it and respond to it, and that response becomes part of the permanent comment as well. There can be as many additions to the comment as needed.

> **Changes to Publishing in Project 2007**
>
> In previous versions of Microsoft Office Project, saving the project initially also published the project. Now in Microsoft Office Project 2007, saving and publishing are two different steps, giving you more control over when information becomes available to Project Web Access users.
>
> Also, in previous versions of Microsoft Office Project, the project manager had to specify whether new assignments, changed assignments, or the entire project was being published. Now in Microsoft Office Project 2007, you publish the entire project with any new or changed assignments all at once. You can exclude the publication of certain marked tasks if you need to.
>
> **For more information about publishing your project and excluding certain tasks from being published, see the section titled "Managing Your Project Files on the Server" earlier in this chapter.**

! NEW
New

When you publish a project, assignments from the project appear on the Project Web Access My Tasks page for the assigned resources. By default, the assigned resources see an alert on their home page indicating that new tasks have been assigned to them. On their My Tasks pages, the new assignments are marked with the NEW icon. A resource can view details about the assignment, including the start and finish date, the amount of scheduled work, other resources assigned, predecessor and successor tasks, and notes.

Assignment
Updated

If you publish a project that includes changed assignments, those assignments are marked with the Assignment Updated icon in the assigned resources' My Tasks page.

Resources can also see details of the entire project by clicking its name in the Project Center. This is helpful for resources who want to see the overall context of their assignments.

For details about how resources and resource managers work with assigned tasks, see Chapter 23.

Exchanging Task Progress Requests and Updates

While your resources are working on their assignments, you periodically need progress updates of actual work on assignments. You can request progress updates, and then accept and incorporate those updates into your project plan.

Requesting Progress Updates

As soon as you publish assignments, your resources can submit updates. It's best for you and your project team to agree on when task updates should be submitted, for example, every Monday morning or every other Wednesday by noon. You might also want them to send you a task update whenever a task is completed, whenever a major milestone or deliverable has been fulfilled, or whenever there is a significant change or accomplishment.

However, you can explicitly request progress updates any time you want, as follows:

1. Make sure that Microsoft Office Project Professional 2007 is connected to the project server and that your project is checked out and open.

2. If you need information on only certain tasks, display a task view and select those tasks.

3. Click Collaborate, Request Progress Information.

   A message appears, stating that your project must be published before the update can be requested.

4. Click OK.

   The Request Progress Information dialog box appears (see Figure 22-22).

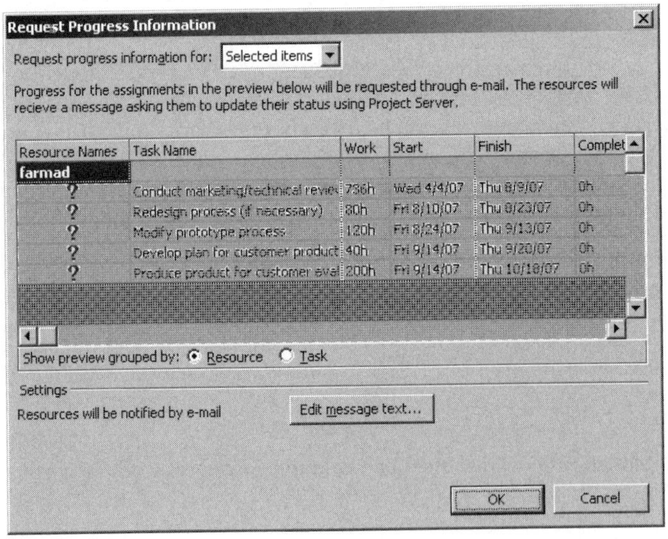

Figure 22-22 Request task updates from your resources about the entire project or just selected tasks.

5. In the Request Progress Information For box, select Entire Project, Current View, or Selected Items.

6. If you want the dialog box to group the assignments by task name, click the Task option. By default, the assignments are grouped by resource name.

7. If you want to edit the e-mail message text that will be sent along with this request, click the Edit Message Text button, make the changes you want, and then click OK.

8. Click OK in the Request Progress Information dialog box.

Your progress update request is published to the project server. Each of the tasks for which progress information is being requested is marked with the Request Progress Information icon in the indicators column.

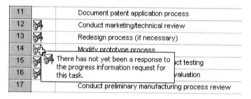

Your resources will receive the automated e-mail with your request. In addition, on their My Tasks page, the assignments for which you requested progress information are marked with an icon indicating that you have requested an update for this assignment.

Reviewing Task Updates from Resources

Just as you publish information for resources to see on the project server, resources submit information to keep you informed. Whenever they change a task assignment in some way—whether to update their progress, reassign it to someone else, or reject it—they can save it or they can submit it. When they submit it, the information is essentially published, and you are notified. Upon submitting the information, they can enter a comment about the transaction.

When your resources submit updates about their assignments, by default, you see a reminder item on your Project Web Access home page, for example, "You have 3 task updates from resources pending your approval."

You can click the link in that reminder to go to the Task Updates page in Project Web Access. You can also click Task Updates under Approvals on the Quick Launch task bar.

If you're working in Project Professional, you can open the Task Updates page from there. Click Collaborate, Update Project Progress. Or, on the Collaborate toolbar, click Update Project Progress. The Project Web Access Task Updates page appears in your Project Professional window. All updates submitted by resources are listed in the table.

On the Task Updates page, you can review the information resources are submitting and decide whether to accept the information and incorporate it into your project plan or whether you need to take some other action (see Figure 22-23).

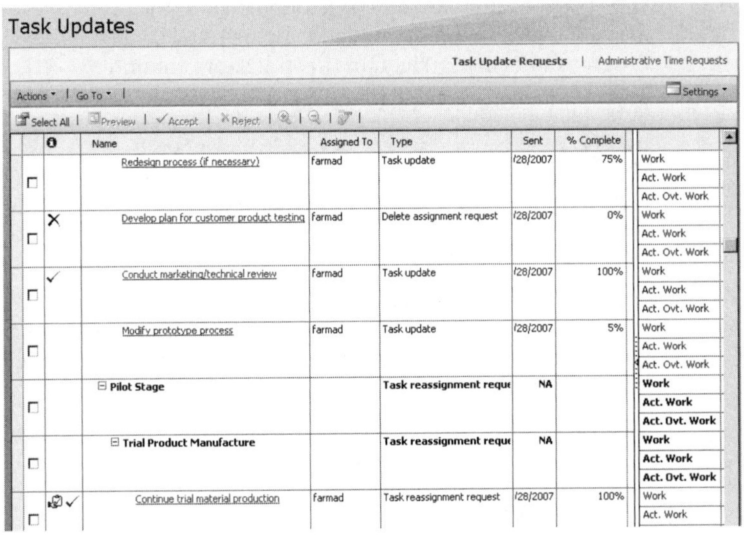

Figure 22-23 The Task Updates page shows any assignment information that has been submitted by a resource assigned to tasks in one of your projects.

Resources typically submit three types of information to the project server for you to review, accept, and incorporate as appropriate:

- **Rejected assignments** When you publish new assignments to the project server, resources see their assignments on their My Tasks pages. If necessary, resources can delete, or reject, an assignment. Project Web Access prompts resources to type a comment when they delete an assignment, generally to explain why they have to reject the assignment. You see any deleted assignments, along with the comment, listed on your Task Updates page (see Figure 22-24).

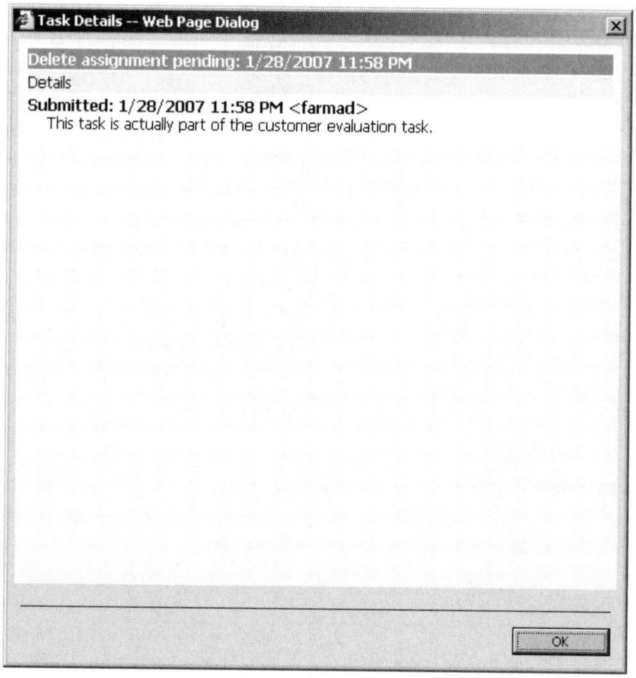

Figure 22-24 Click the assignment name to read the comment.

- **New self-assigned or reassigned tasks** From Project Web Access, resources can create new tasks, assign themselves to them, and submit them to the project server for inclusion in the project plan, if you approve. This is particularly helpful when you are relying on your resources to fill in the details of tasks that are needed for their areas of expertise.

  If your resources are members of a team assignment pool, they can assign themselves to a team task. If you allow it, your resources may reassign tasks to other resources.

  When resources assign themselves to newly created tasks, assign themselves to team tasks, or reassign tasks to other resources, you are notified on the Task Updates page. This way you always know of any new tasks and the specific resources working on those tasks.

- **Assignment progress updates** When you send a request for progress information, resources respond by updating their assignment-tracking information according to the tracking method set up by the project server administrator. They might update percentage complete on their current assignments, enter total work and remaining work hours on assignments, or enter the number of hours per day or per week they've spent on each assignment. Such updates are one of the primary reasons for using Project Web Access. They keep your project tracking up-to-date, and you always know the current status of tasks without having to collect and enter the information manually. Review the task update and any comments from your Task Updates page in Project Web Access.

Incorporating Task Updates into the Project

Once you have reviewed the task update information submitted by your resources, you can decide whether to incorporate the information into the project plan or to return it to the resource who sent the update.

To accept a task update, follow these steps:

1. On the Task Updates page, select the check box next to the name of the assignment(s) you want to accept and incorporate into your project plan.

Preview

If you're not sure whether you want to accept or reject an update, select the assignment in question and then click the Preview button. A separate Approval Preview window appears with a Gantt Chart showing how the schedule would look if you accepted the update (see Figure 22-25). Using this window, you can see the updated schedule in a Web browser before you commit to the changes the update would cause.

Approval Preview

This shows what the plan will look like if you accept the selected task update requests.

Actions ▼ | ☐ Settin

🔍 | 🔍 | 🔳 |

ⓘ ▲ ID	Task Name	Previous D	Duration	Previous	Start	Apr 1, '07 S M T W T F S	Apr 8, '07 S M T W
6	⊟ **Technical Product Evaluation**	**204d**	**204d**	**/29/2007**	**29/2007**		
7	Establish product characteristics (perfo	2d	2d	1/29/2007	1/29/2007		
8	Develop prototype process	10d	10d	1/31/2007	1/31/2007		
9	Produce prototype product	25d	25d	2/14/2007	2/14/2007		
10	Conduct internal product review	5d	5d	3/28/2007	3/28/2007		
11	Document patent application process	10d	10d	1/31/2007	1/31/2007		
12	Conduct marketing/technical review	92d	92d	4/4/2007	4/4/2007		
13	Redesign process (if necessary)	10d	10d	8/10/2007	8/10/2007		

Figure 22-25 Review the Approval Preview to see the potential impact of accepting the assignment update.

Accept

2. Click the Accept button on the toolbar.

3. In the dialog box that appears, you have another chance to view an approval preview. You can also enter a transaction comment that will become part of the assignment for the resource to see. Click Accept.

The information is submitted to the project server, and your project plan is updated accordingly. If the update was an assignment rejection, the resource is removed from the task. If the update was a reassigned task, the new resource is shown as assigned to the task in the project plan. If it was a progress update, the tracking information is incorporated into the project plan. The accepted task updates are removed from the Task Updates table.

To reject a task update, follow these steps:

1. On the Task Updates page, select the check box next to the name of the assignment you want to reject and send back to the resource who sent it.

Reject

2. Click the Reject button on the toolbar.

3. In the dialog box that appears, you can enter a comment for the resource who sent the update, explaining why you are rejecting the update. Click Reject.

Update rejected

Your project plan is unchanged, and the update is removed from the Task Updates table. The task is updated in the resource's My Tasks page, marked with an update rejected icon. Your comment appears in the assignment's transaction comments and task history, which can be viewed on the Assignment Details page.

If you want to see processed task updates that are waiting to be updated in the project plan, click Go To, Reviewed Requests. The Reviewed Task Update Requests page appears, listing updates you have recently processed (see Figure 22-26).

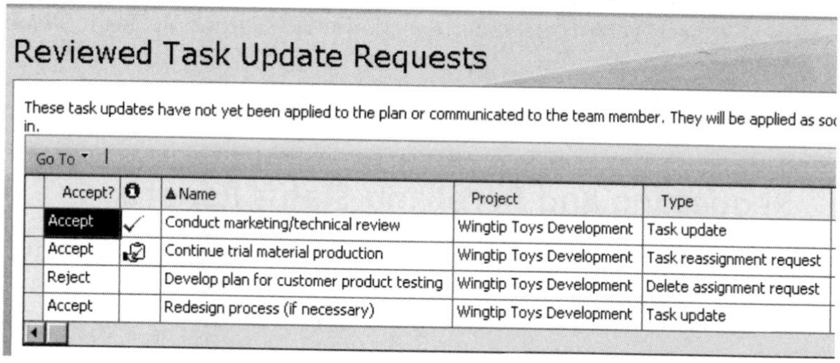

Reviewed Task Update Requests

These task updates have not yet been applied to the plan or communicated to the team member. They will be applied as soc in.

Go To ▾ |

Accept?	❶	▲ Name	Project	Type
Accept	✓	Conduct marketing/technical review	Wingtip Toys Development	Task update
Accept	🖼	Continue trial material production	Wingtip Toys Development	Task reassignment request
Reject		Develop plan for customer product testing	Wingtip Toys Development	Delete assignment request
Accept		Redesign process (if necessary)	Wingtip Toys Development	Task update

Figure 22-26 Review task updates that you have recently processed.

If you want to see processed task updates that have already updated the project plan, click Go To, Applied Requests And Errors. The Applied Task Update Requests And Errors page shows the list of updates that have already been implemented in the project server.

Chapter 22

> ### Locking Update Periods and Protecting Actuals
>
> Through the team collaboration features provided by Project Server, the integrity of actuals submitted by resources can be protected. This can be crucial if those actuals are directly submitted to your organization's general ledger system to produce customer invoices.
>
> Your project server administrator first sets up the Project Web Access progress method to track hours of work per day or per week. Then, the administrator sets the open reporting time period. Resources can enter actuals only during the open reporting period, not after the period is past.
>
> Furthermore, options can be set so that if the project manager or another user changes actual hours that have been submitted and incorporated into the project plan, those changes can be audited against what was originally submitted by the resource.
>
> For more information about setting up the task progress page for assignment tracking in Project Web Access, see the section titled "Setting Up Team Member Work Pages" in Chapter 21.

Requesting and Receiving Status Reports

It's great to get task updates specifying the percentage complete or the number of hours worked each day on a task. However, often you want more detail about task progress. That's where narrative status reports come into play. You can design a status report for resources to complete and submit to you periodically. You set up how often the status report should be submitted. You also set up the topics that the resources should report on. At the designated time periods, your resources write their status reports and submit them to the project server. When the resources' reports are in, the project server automatically compiles them into a full team status report.

You need to request the status report only when you first set it up. Resources see automated reminders on their Project Web Access home page when a status report is coming due.

Setting Up and Requesting Status Reports

To set up a narrative status report, follow these steps:

1. In Project Web Access, under Resources, click Status Reports.

   If you're working in Project Professional, you can open the Status Reports page from there. Click Collaborate, Status Reports. Or, on the Collaborate toolbar, click Status Reports. The Project Web Access Status Reports page appears in your Project Professional window.

2. Under Requests, click New, New Request.

   The Status Report Request page appears (see Figure 22-27).

Status Report Request

Report Title	
Name the status report request.	**Title:** New Status Report

Frequency
Indicate how often the report is due.

Recurrence:
- (•) weekly   ( ) monthly   ( ) yearly

Due [every ▼] week on:

☐ Sunday   ☐ Monday   ☐ Tuesday   ☐ Wednesday
☐ Thursday   ☐ Friday   ☐ Saturday

Start Date
When does the first reporting period begin?

Start:
1/29/2007

Resources
Select the resources who should respond to this status report request.

These resources' responses will be sent to you.

Available Resources:

Barker Rob
Beebe Ann
Bento Paula
Berry Jo
Bloesser Rex
Bowen Eli
Bremer Ted

[Add >]
[< Remove]

Resources who should respond:

Current item: Ahs David

Sections
Specify the status report sections.

Insert Section | Delete Section |

Figure 22-27 Use the Status Report Request page to design a periodic narrative status report.

3. Work through the page to specify the design and frequency of your status report.

4. In the Resources area, select the resources who are to receive this status report request and who will be responsible for submitting the status reports.

5. In the Sections area, specify the headings to be included in the status report under which your resources will report. To add a new heading, click Insert Section. A new row opens up. Click in the row and type the heading you want. To remove a heading, click it and then click Delete Section.

Insert Section

Delete Section

6. When finished, click Send.

The status report request, details, and schedule are sent to the selected resources. They will see reminders on their home page about status reports coming due. They will also see the name of the status report listed on their Status Reports pages.

When it's time for your resources to submit a status report, they'll click the name of your status report and complete the page. The page includes a box for each of the sections you identified in your request (see Figure 22-28).

Chapter 22

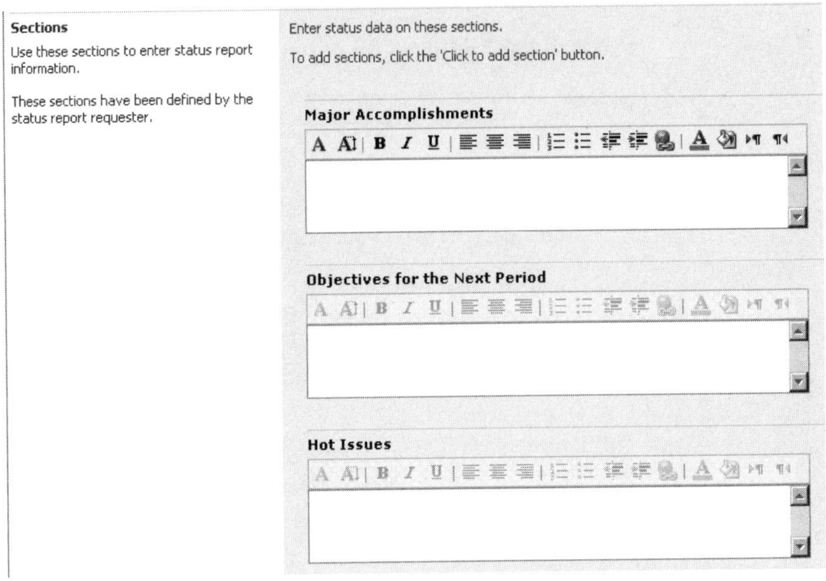

Figure 22-28 A box appears for each status report section you specified in your request.

Resources can add extra sections and send unrequested status reports outside the normal schedule if they want.

For more information about how resources work with their status reports, see the section titled "Submitting Text-Based Status Reports" in Chapter 23.

Reviewing Text-Based Status Reports

Project Web Access automatically merges the status reports from all resources for a given time period. To review the combined status reports that have been submitted, follow these steps:

1. In Project Web Access, under Resources, click Status Reports.

2. Under Requests, click the name of the status report whose responses you want to review.

   The View Responses page appears.

3. To specify the time period of status reports you want to see, set the dates in the View Status Reports From boxes and then click Apply.

4. Under Group Merged Reports By, select whether you want the merged report to be grouped by resource name or response date.

5. Click the Open button.

   The merged status report appears. The responses from each resource are grouped under the section headings you identified.

Open

6. If you want to include the status report in a Microsoft Office Word document for printing or for inclusion in a project status report, click Export To Word.

7. Click Yes in the ActiveX control alert that appears.

The report is formatted and exported to Office Word. You can save it or print it from there.

Tracking Billable and Nonbillable Time by Using Timesheets

Microsoft Office Project Server 2007 has a new method—timesheets—for tracking non-project working time and time off in conjunction with time spent on projects. With timesheets, an organization can essentially account for every hour of every resource's day, even time that's spent in meetings, in training, on different projects, or on time off.

Such detailed tracking is important in organizations that have specific time report-ing requirements. For example, certain organizations need visibility into certain time categories, for example, billable and nonbillable time, scheduled and actual time, or overtime. Default time categories are provided with the timesheet in Project Web Ac-cess, but your project server administrator can set up custom time categories as appro-priate. The timesheet is especially useful when you need to integrate information about resource time with an accounting or general ledger system, particularly for client billing purposes.

> **Note**
> In previous versions of Project Web Access, the task progress page is called the timesheet. Now in Microsoft Office Project 2007, the timesheet is a different page and serves a different, but complementary, purpose from the task progress page, which is also called the My Tasks page.

If your organization does not need such tight time tracking, it can simply ignore the timesheet feature and use just the My Tasks page to keep the project plan up to date. In fact, the project server administrator could set up Project Web Access in such a way as to remove the timesheet pages and links.

However, if you do use timesheets, here are some key points to understand:

- Your project server administrator or portfolio manager sets up the timesheet format. This includes the fiscal year and reporting periods, accounting classifica-tions, billing categories, and any rules and restrictions for how timesheets are updated.

> **Note**
>
> For information about what's involved in setting up the timesheet format, see the section titled "Setting Up Team Member Work Pages" in Chapter 21.

- Timesheets can be updated independently of the task progress page, or they can work together. Resources can incorporate assignments from the task progress page into the timesheet. Likewise, resources can import timesheet items into the task progress page.

- Resources can identify and report administrative time, which is used to account for nonproject working time such as meetings and classes. Administrative time can also be used to account for nonworking time such as vacations and personal time off.

> **Note**
>
> In Microsoft Office Project 2003, the administrative project was introduced, in which users could create non-project working time and nonworking time categories and then assign themselves to these categories. In Microsoft Office Project 2007, this feature has become a part of the timesheet as administrative time.

- If your organization uses timesheets, all resources using Project Web Access are associated with a timesheet manager. This could be the resource's supervisor, resource manager, or project manager. The timesheet manager is responsible for reviewing and approving the resource's periodic timesheets and any administrative time that requires approval. The project server administrator or other user with permissions to edit resource information identifies each resource's timesheet manager.

Reviewing and Approving Timesheets

Similar to task updates from the My Tasks page, resources submit timesheets to their designated timesheet managers on a periodic basis. If you are serving as a timesheet manager, you will receive timesheets for review and approval. Timesheets can be set up for automatic approval.

To review and approve timesheets, follow these steps:

1. On the Quick Launch task bar in Project Web Access, under Approvals, click Timesheet.

   The Timesheet Approvals page appears (see Figure 22-29).

My Tasks						
New ▾	Actions ▾	Go To ▾				⬛	☐ Settings ▾

Reassign Work | Self-assign Team Tasks | ✕ Delete | Import Timesheet | Print

☐		Task Name	Start ▲	Finish	% Complete	Progress	Health
☐		⊟ Wingtip Toys Development					
☐	?	Conduct marketing/technical review ⁞ NEW	4/4/2007	8/9/2007	0%	0%	
☐	?	Redesign process (if necessary) ⁞ NEW	8/10/2007	8/23/2007	0%	0%	
☐	?	Modify prototype process ⁞ NEW	8/24/2007	9/13/2007	0%	0%	
☐	?	Develop plan for customer product testing ⁞ NEW	9/14/2007	9/20/2007	0%	0%	
☐	?	Produce product for customer evaluation ⁞ NEW	9/14/2007	10/18/2007	0%	0%	
☐	⬛	Conduct marketing/technical review ⁞ NEW	11/16/2007	11/19/2007	0%	0%	

Figure 22-29 Your Timesheet Approvals page shows all timesheets submitted for your approval by resources for whom you are the timesheet manager.

2. If necessary, apply any filters to see just the timesheets you want.

   If the filter controls are not showing above the timesheet table, click Settings, Filter.

3. To approve a timesheet, select the check box next to the timesheet and then click Approve.

4. To reject a timesheet, select its check box and then click Reject.

> **Note**
>
> For information about how resources work with their timesheets, or if you need to submit timesheets yourself, see the section titled "Logging Time Using Timesheets" in Chapter 23.

Reviewing and Approving Administrative Time

No matter how dedicated and conscientious, no one can spend every minute of the workday or workweek devoted to project assignments. There is bound to be time taken for nonproject and nonbillable tasks such as handling e-mail, attending staff meetings, and participating in training workshops.

In addition, there is bound to be some nonworking time happening during the course of a project, such as sick time, vacation time, and holidays.

In past versions of Project Web Access, nonworking time was handled by the resource's working time calendar. Everyday administrative duties were not accounted for formally, although many project managers built in extra time for resources to handle them.

Now in Project 2007, through the use of timesheets, administrative time can be used to account for and even track nonproject time. Resources can assign themselves to an administrative time category in the timesheet.

Resources can also create additional administrative time categories as needed. New administrative time categories and sometimes the use of other categories set up by the project server administrator need to be approved by the resource's timesheet manager.

To review and approve administrative time, follow these steps:

1. On the Quick Launch task bar in Project Web Access, under Approvals, click Administrative Time.

   The Administrative Time page appears.

2. To approve administrative time, select its check box and then click Accept.

3. To reject administrative time, select its check box and then click Reject.

> **Note**
>
> For information about how resources work with administrative time, or if you need to use administrative time yourself, see the section titled "Requesting Nonproject or Nonworking Time" in Chapter 23.

Managing Documents, Risks, and Issues

Because Project Server is a Windows SharePoint Services application, you have the following collaboration features available in Project Web Access:

- Document control

- Risk management

- Issues tracking

Documents, risks, and issues can be added, tracked, linked with tasks, assigned responsibility, and eventually closed. These all become an important aspect of managing the project as well as capturing important project archival information for use in planning future projects.

Controlling Project Documents

Through Windows SharePoint Services and Project Server, you can establish a document library associated with your project. The Project Web Access document library can be an excellent repository for project-related documents, including needs analyses, scope definition, product specifications, deliverable documents, team contact information, change control plan, and status reports. By creating a central location for public documents related to the project, you can enhance collaboration and the project management process, ensuring that resources and other stakeholders have all essential information at their disposal.

Depending on permissions, you and your resources can add documents, view documents, and search for documents in the document library. When adding a new document, you enter the file name and location for the document, specify the owner and status (for example, Draft, Reviewed, Final), and enter any pertinent comments. You can also associate a document with specific tasks if you want.

Document versions can be controlled using check-in and checkout processes. If a document is checked out, only the user who has checked it out can save to it. Multiple versions of a document can be compared and archived separately. When a document is linked to a project or individual tasks, the most current version of the document is linked.

To work with the document library, follow these steps:

1. On the Quick Launch task bar in Project Web Access, under Documents, click Shared Documents.

   The Shared Documents page appears, showing documents that have been uploaded to this site.

2. Click a document name to open it in the Web browser.

3. Click the down arrow next to the document name to check out or edit the document.

4. Use the menus to add a new folder, create a new document, upload existing documents, set up e-mail notifications, and so on.

5. To return to Project Web Access, either click the Home tab or click Project Web Access above the table.

Documents

> **Note**
>
> You can also open the document library from within the Project Professional window. Click Collaborate, Documents. Or, on the Collaborate toolbar, click Documents.
>
> To return to your normal Project Professional view, click the Click Here To Close This View link in the upper-right corner.

You can also associate documents with projects and tasks. To do this, follow these steps:

1. On the Quick Launch task bar in Project Web Access, under Projects, click Project Center.

2. Click the name of the project to which you want to attach a document.
   The Project Details page appears.

3. Click Actions, Link Documents.
   The Link Risks, Issues And Documents page appears.

Chapter 22

4. In the Use The Following Lists To Link Items To This Task box, make sure Document Library is selected.

5. Click Upload.

6. On the Upload Document page, click Browse to navigate to the document you want to link to the project. Click the file and then click Open.

   If you're linking several files that are in the same folder, it's easier to click Upload Multiple Files. Browse to the folder and then click the check boxes next to the names of all the files you want to link. Click OK and then click Yes.

7. Click OK on the Upload Document page.

   The document is listed on the Link Risks, Issues And Documents page.

8. Click Save.

To see all documents for a project, open the project from the Project Center. Then on the Project Details page, click Actions, Link Documents. The Link Risks, Issues And Documents page appears.

Mitigating Project Risks

Risks are events or conditions that can have a positive or negative impact on the outcome of a project. Because of this, project management and risk management go hand in hand. Much of what we do in project management is essentially managing risk. Straightforward risk management functionality is provided in Project Web Access through Windows SharePoint Services integration. Users can record information about risks, update this information, and track the risk. Risks can be escalated to the right person for mitigation.

Risks can also be associated with specific tasks, resources, documents, issues, and other risks.

> **Note**
> Although the new risk management functionality enables you to attach risk assessments to tasks, it does not provide cross-project risk tracking, reporting, or sophisticated risk management, such as MonteCarlo analysis.

To log a risk against a project or even against a task within a project, follow these steps:

1. On the Quick Launch task bar in Project Web Access, under Projects, click Project Center.

2. Click the name of the project for which you need to log a risk.

   The Project Details page appears.

3. Click Actions, Link Risks.

    The Link Risks, Issues And Documents page appears.

4. Click New.

5. Complete the fields in the Risks: New Item page (see Figure 22-30). These include the owner of the risk, probability, impact and cost, description, mitigation plan, and contingency plan.

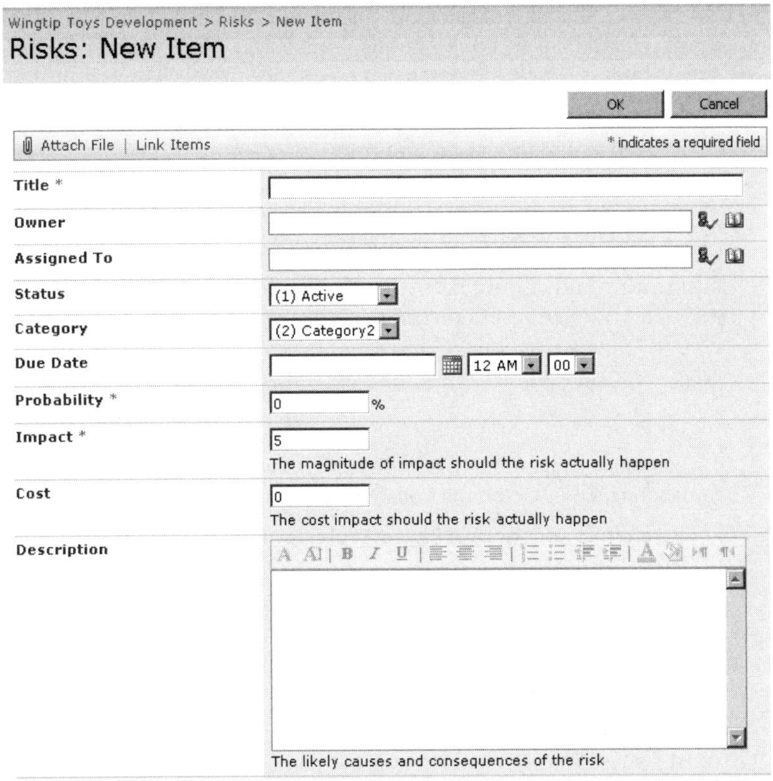

Figure 22-30 Use the Risks: New Item page to document all details about the risk.

6. To link the risk to one or more tasks in the project, click the Link Items button near the top of the page. All tasks in the current project are listed. Select the check box for the task(s) with which you want to associate this risk. In the Relation field, click the description of the relationship of the risk to the task, for example, Risk Affects Task or Task Triggers Risk. Click OK in the dialog box. The linked tasks are added to the Links section at the bottom of the page.

7. To attach a file related to the risk, click the Attach File button near the top of the page. Click the Browse button to navigate to the file location, select the file, and then click Open. Click OK. The file path is listed in the Attachments section at the bottom of the page.

8. When finished, click OK.

The new risk is saved and listed on the Link Risks, Issues And Documents page.

9. Click Save.

Although the risk is linked to the task, the task is not linked to the risk. There is no indication in the project plan about the risk. Because of this, it's worth your while to enter a task note referring to the risk.

To see all risks for a project, open the project from the Project Center and then on the Project Details page, click Actions, Link Risks. The Link Risks, Issues And Documents page appears. Click the name of a risk to see details. Click Edit Item if you want to make any changes to these details.

You can also review risks for a project by selecting (but not opening) the project from the Project Center and then clicking Go To, Risks. In a separate window, the Risks page opens, showing the list of risks for the project, who each risk is assigned to, and its status. Click the risk name to see details.

By creating and editing risks, you can make mitigation and contingency plans for the risk, and track progress on the risk until it is resolved.

Risks

> **Note**
>
> You can also open the risks page from within the Project Professional window. Click Collaborate, Risks. Or, on the Collaborate toolbar, click Risks.
>
> To return to your normal Project Professional view, click the Click Here To Close This View link in the upper-right corner.

Monitoring Project Issues

Issues tracking is integral to project management and team communication because most issues either arise from task activity or will affect task activity. By tracking issues related to a project, you can improve communication on project-related issues and ensure that problems are handled before they become crises.

With the issue tracker, resources can enter issues, assign ownership, track progress, record resolutions, and create related reports. The issues are stored on your project server and are accessible through Project Web Access.

Depending on permissions, you and your resources can create an issue, set its priority, and assign responsibility. The issue page includes a due date, discussion of the issue, and date of resolution. Issues can be associated with affected tasks, documents in the document library, or other related issues.

To log an issue against a project task, follow these steps:

1. On the Quick Launch task bar in Project Web Access, under Projects, click Project Center.

2. Click the name of the project for which you need to log an issue.

   The Project Details page appears.

3. Click Actions, Link Issues.

   The Link Risks, Issues And Documents page appears.

4. Click New.

5. Complete the fields on the Issues: New Item page (see Figure 22-31). These include the owner of the issue, status and priority, discussion of the issue, and resolution.

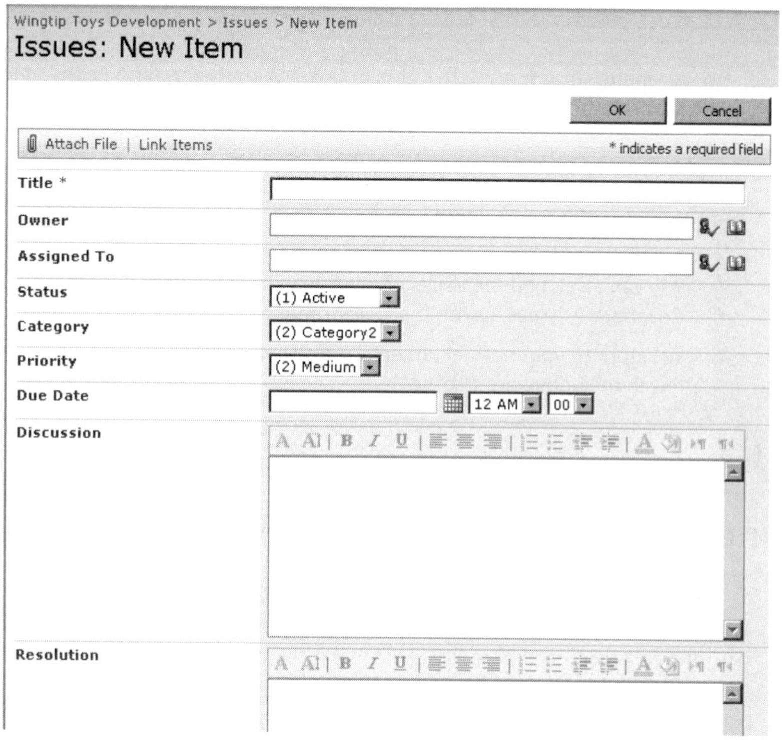

Wingtip Toys Development > Issues > New Item

Issues: New Item

	OK Cancel
⬚ Attach File | Link Items	* indicates a required field
Title *	
Owner	
Assigned To	
Status	(1) Active
Category	(2) Category2
Priority	(2) Medium
Due Date	12 AM 00
Discussion	A A| B I U | ≡ ≡ ≡ | ≣ ≣ ≣ ≣ | A 🎨 ◄¶ ¶►
Resolution	A A| B I U | ≡ ≡ ≡ | ≣ ≣ ≣ ≣ | A 🎨 ◄¶ ¶►

Figure 22-31 Use the Issues: New Item page to document all details about the issues.

6. If you want to link the issue to tasks other than the selected task, click the Link Items button near the top of the page.

   All tasks in the current project are listed. Select the check box for the task(s) with which you want to associate this issue. In the Relation field, click the description of the relationship of the risk to the task, for example, Issue Affects Task or Issue Resolves Task. Click OK in the dialog box. The linked tasks are added to the originally selected task in the Links section at the bottom of the page.

7. When finished, click OK.

The new issue is saved and listed on the Link Risks, Issues And Documents page.

8. Click Save.

Although the issue is linked to the task, the task is not linked to the issue. There is no indication in the project plan about the issue. Because of this, it's worth your while to enter a task note referring to the issue.

To see all issues for a project, open the project from the Project Center and then on the Project Details page, click Actions, Link Issues. The Link Risks, Issues And Documents page appears. Click the name of an issue to see details. Click Edit Item if you want to make any changes to these details.

You can also review issues for a project by selecting (but not opening) the project from the Project Center, and then clicking Go To, Issues. In a separate window, the Issues page opens showing the list of issues for the project, who each issue is assigned to, and its status. Click the issue name to see details. Click the Edit Item button to update these details.

> **Note**
>
> You can also open the issues page from within the Project Professional window. Click Collaborate, Issues. Or, on the Collaborate toolbar, click Issues.
>
> To return to your normal Project Professional view, click the Click Here To Close This View link in the upper-right corner.

Issues

Creating Proposals and Activity Plans

New in Microsoft Office Project Server 2007 is the means for using a simplified Web-based interface in Project Web Access to track activities throughout the entire project life cycle, that is, just before and just after the project itself is implemented.

With proposals, you can set up a preproject plan. You can create a resource plan to help you anticipate potential resource needs for the project without committing those resources to a project that might or might not be initiated. When the proposal is approved, the proposal can be converted into a project.

With activity plans, you can track the routine operations that typically take place after the completion of a project. You can also use activity plans to track maintenance activities or very small projects.

> **Note**
>
> Proposals, resource plans, and activity plans all operate only in Project Web Access; you cannot see these plans in Project Professional.

With both proposals and activity plans, you can use the views and reports in Project Web Access to do high-level or detailed analyses. This can be particularly useful with proposals. Portfolio managers and executives can review the proposals and evaluate feasibilities within the organization's strategic goals to help decide whether to move forward with a project.

You can also use timesheets and project workspaces with proposals and activity plans. Activity plans definitely work well with timesheets, because timesheets are designed to track various categories of time, whether related to a project or not.

Calendars and custom fields created in Project Web Access can also be used with proposals and activity plans.

Working with Proposals

A proposal is a simple way to list tasks and durations for a potential project without investing a lot of time in it. If the project is approved, you can then convert it into a real project plan that can be opened in Project Professional, and the groundwork is already laid. You don't need to do any converting or importing; you just need to add detail.

Creating a Proposal

To create a proposal, follow these steps:

1. On the Quick Launch task bar in Project Web Access, under Projects, click Proposals And Activities.

2. Click New, Proposal.

   The New Proposal page appears (see Figure 22-32).

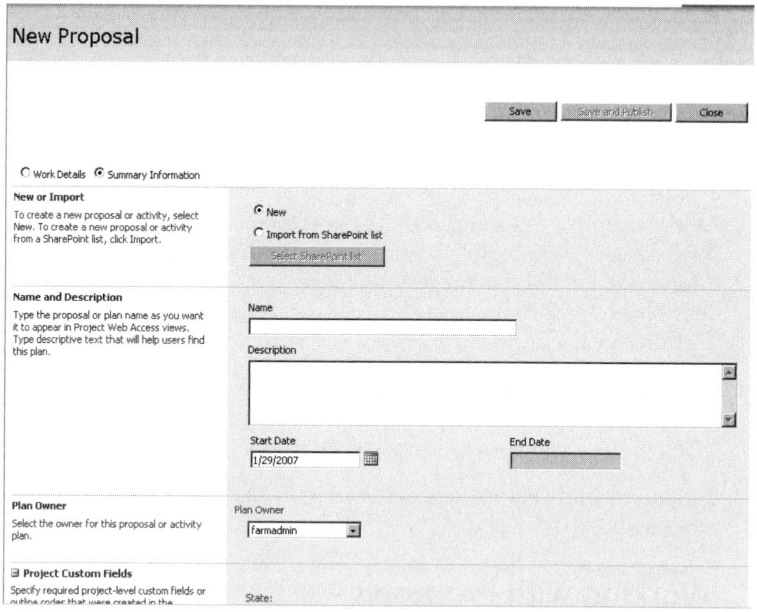

Figure 22-32 Start to create a proposal on the New Proposal page.

3. Near the top of the page, make sure that the Summary Information option is selected.

4. Work through the page, reading the section descriptions and completing the fields as appropriate.

5. If the Workflow Status section is present, click the link to the workflow status and activity pages.

The workflow status feature can be enabled or disabled as part of the customization done for your organization by your project server administrator.

6. Under Project Custom Fields, click the button next to the State box and then click Proposed.

The State field is a "built-in" custom field designed for use with proposals. The three enumerated states are Proposed, Approved, and Rejected.

7. When finished, click Save.

The new proposal is saved to your project server, and the Work Details view of your new proposal appears. Make sure that the Work Details option is now selected.

8. Enter the details of your new proposal. Enter task names and durations. Use the buttons on the toolbar to indent outline levels or insert new tasks.

Link Tasks

9. If you want to link tasks with a finish-to-start task relationship, select the predecessor task by clicking the row header. Hold down Ctrl and then click the row header for the successor task. Click the Link Tasks button.

   An icon in the indicators field shows that the two tasks are linked. You can only link tasks with a finish-to-start task relationship in a proposal.

10. Click Save to save the proposal to the project server but keep it to yourself. Click Save And Publish to save the proposal to the project server and also make it available for others to see and use.

    Your new proposal is listed on the Proposals And Activities page.

Viewing and Changing Proposal Information

To view your proposal information, change summary information, or change task details, follow these steps:

1. On the Quick Launch task bar in Project Web Access, under Projects, click Proposals And Activities.

2. On the Proposals And Activities page, click the name of the proposal.

   By default, the Work Details view of the proposal appears.

3. Make any changes you want to the task information and then click Save.

4. If you need to view or change summary information, above the table, select the Summary Information option.

   The Summary Information view of your proposal appears. In this view, you can review or change the proposal description, the proposal state, and so on.

5. When finished, click Save or Save And Publish. Click Close.

On the Proposals And Activities page, proposals are the items that have a state associated with them: Proposed, Approved, or Rejected. Activity plans are also listed on this page, but their state fields are blank. You can select a proposal without opening it by clicking anywhere in the row except on the proposal name itself.

Adding Resources to a Proposal

If you do not expect to create a resource plan to associate with your proposal, you can add resources to your proposal and assign them to tasks. Resources assigned to proposed tasks are not really assigned; that is, they do not see notifications of new assignments, even if the proposal is published. The purpose for doing this is to propose possible resources for if this proposal is approved and then converted to a project.

Chapter 22

To add resources to your proposal, follow these steps:

1. On the Quick Launch task bar in Project Web Access, under Projects, click Proposals And Activities.

2. On the Proposals And Activities page, click the name of the proposal to open its Work Details view.

3. If you make any other changes to the proposal, click Save.

4. Click Build Team.

Build Team

5. On the Build Team page, select the check boxes next to the resources you want to add to the proposal. Then click Add.

6. Click Save.

7. Click in the Resource Name field for a task, and you'll see a list of all the resources you just added. Click a resource to propose the assignment of that resource to the current task. You can only add one resource to a task.

8. When finished, click Save or Save And Publish. Then click Close.

Converting a Proposal to a Project

If it is determined that the proposal should become a project, you can easily convert it. To do this, follow these steps:

1. On the Quick Launch task bar in Project Web Access, under Projects, click Proposals And Activities.

2. On the Proposals And Activities page, click anywhere in the proposal's row except on the name to select the proposal but not open it.

3. Click Convert.

Convert

4. Read the alert that appears and then click OK.

   The proposal is submitted to the project server for conversion from a proposal to a project. When the conversion is finished, the Proposals And Activities page appears, and your proposal is no longer listed.

5. On the Quick Launch task bar, click Project Center.

   You'll see your former proposal, which is now a project, listed there.

6. Click the name of your newly converted proposal.

   You can now edit the proposal, which is now a project, in Project Web Access or Project Professional. If you had already added resources, when you publish the project, those resources will see their assignments for this project.

Creating an Activity Plan

Activity plans are designed to track routine operations or maintenance tasks that continue on after a project is complete. However, you can use activity plans as a simplified task list or for a very small project.

Activity plans are created and used in a manner nearly identical to proposals. To create an activity plan, click Proposals And Activities on the Quick Launch task bar and then click New, Activity. Follow the same process as for creating a new proposal. One difference is that for activities there is no Workflow Status section and no State field.

You can view and change activity plan information the same way as proposals, you can add resources to a proposal, and you can convert an activity plan to a project in the same way.

Creating a Resource Plan for a Proposal or Activity Plan

With a resource plan, you can estimate potential resource requirements for your proposal, activity plan, or project. A resource plan can also define the use of resources if you're using a proposal for a small task-only project.

Resource plans are always created within the context of a proposal or activity plan. The proposal or activity plan must be published before you can create its resource plan. To create a resource plan, follow these steps:

1. On the Quick Launch task bar, click Proposals And Activities.

2. On the Proposals And Activities page, click the name of the proposal or activity plan to open its Work Details view.

3. Be sure that your proposal or activity plan has been published. You can only create a resource plan for proposals or activity plans that have been published.

4. Click Resource Plan.

Resource Plan

5. Click Build Team and select the check boxes for the resources you want to add to your resource plan. Click Add and then click Save.

   The Resource Plan page for your proposal or activity plan appears, listing the resources you added from the Build Team page.

6. Click Settings, View Options.

   The Resource Plan page opens (see Figure 22-33).

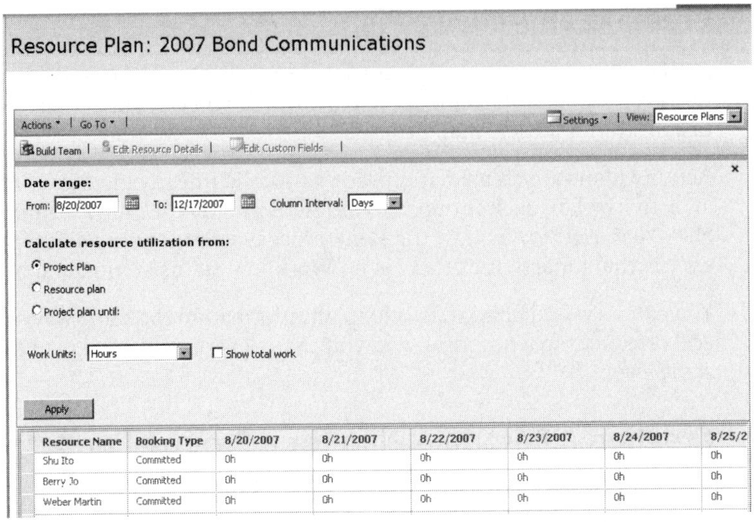

Figure 22-33   Create a resource plan to do preliminary resource planning for your proposal.

7. Under Date Range, set the options for how you want to view dates in the resource plan.

8. Under Calculate Resource Utilization From, select how resource availability should be calculated for reports generated from this resource plan, as follows:

   ❑ Select Project Plan to have availability calculated from all assignments in the proposal or activity plan, but not from the resource plan.

   ❑ Select Resource Plan to have availability calculated from resource information in the resource plan.

   ❑ Select Project Plan Until to have availability calculated from all assignments within this proposal or activity plan until the date you enter.

9. Click Apply. If you want, click Settings, View Options again to hide the view options.

10. In each time period for a resource, enter the amount of time that this resource should be shown as occupied. This will figure into the resource's availability data according to the calculations options you just set.

11. When finished, click Save or Save And Publish. Then click Close.

Getting Started with Project Web Access **828**

Working on Your Assignments and Updates **834**

Submitting Text-Based Status Reports **852**

Logging Time Using Timesheets **853**

Setting Up E-Mail, Reminders, and Calendars **858**

Managing Resources in Project Web Access **864**

A project plan might make an impressive report or boardroom presentation. But without resources to implement the tasks, that lovely project plan is nothing more than fiction. As a project team member, you know that it falls to you to help achieve the goals of the task. You also know that you must regularly inform the powers that be of your progress so that they know how the project is doing overall.

This is where you and Microsoft Office Project Web Access come on the scene. You use Office Project Web Access, the Web-based application for project team members that is a companion to Microsoft Office Project Professional 2007 (used by project managers). You use Project Web Access to maintain a detailed list of the tasks under your responsibility, to know when they're due, and to understand how they fit into the larger project picture. You also use Project Web Access to track your progress on assignments and submit that information to your project manager. If needed, you can use Project Web Access to log the amount of time you're spending for other tasks—project-related or not, billable or not.

Project Web Access doesn't limit you to just one project, either; rather, you can use it for as many projects as you're contributing to. And if you're working for two or three project managers at a time on these multiple projects, you can use Project Web Access to keep all this information straight and keep all project managers well-informed.

With project management more automated like this, you can spend more time working on your tasks and less time worrying about keeping management up to date. To this end, this chapter is designed for the project team members, team leads, and resource managers, all of whom use Project Web Access to carry out their project-related responsibilities.

To start using the Microsoft Project enterprise and team collaboration features, you use your Web browser to connect to your organization's installation of Microsoft Office Project Server 2007. You can then log on to Project Web Access.

If you're curious about the structure and flow of information among Project Web Access, Office Project Professional, and Office Project Server 2007, see Chapter 20, "Understanding Enterprise Project Management."

After your project manager publishes a project to the project server, you can see and work with the list of tasks to which you're assigned in Project Web Access. You can add more tasks and assign yourself to other tasks as needed. Project Web Access becomes the central location for all your project tracking activity.

With your assignments in place, your way is set to start working on those assignments, according to the established start and finish dates. While you work, you can record how far along you are on each assignment or even how much time you're spending on each assignment. You can make notes about any potential problems, significant accomplishments, issues, or potential problems. Then you have progress tracking information in place when your project managers ask for a progress update or status report.

The microcosm of your own tasks draws your focus most of the time. But sometimes it helps you to see the tasks that others on the project team are working on at the same time. You can use Project Web Access to review the full project schedule, which shows who's doing what when.

Through Project Web Access, you have access to collections of project-related documents, issues, and risks as well.

In addition to everything else you do, you might have resource management responsibilities. This might be something as simple as reassigning a few tasks to peers on your project team. Or, you might be the team lead or supervisor over a larger group of project team members. You might be a resource manager responsible for building teams and managing all resources on one, two, or many projects in your organization. Resource management features in Project Web Access make sure you have the tools you need.

Project server administrators and portfolio managers should see Chapter 21, "Administering Your Enterprise Project Management Solution." Project managers can refer to Chapter 22, "Managing Enterprise Projects and Resources." Managing stakeholders can find pertinent information in Chapter 24, "Making Executive Decisions Using Project Web Access." Chapter 24, along with this chapter, are provided as standalone e-chapters on the Bonus Content tab of the Companion CD.

Getting Started with Project Web Access

The first step, of course, is to start. You use your Web browser to connect to your organization's installation of Project Server. You then log on to the server from Project Web Access using the user identification established for you by the project server administrator.

After you're logged on, browse around to orient yourself to the layout of Project Web Access. This will give you some idea of how you can use Project Web Access as a partner in your assignment-tracking activities.

Logging On and Off

To log on to Project Web Access, follow these steps:

1. Start Microsoft Internet Explorer (at least version 6.0).

2. In the Address box, enter the URL for your organization's project server and then click Go.

   Your project manager or project server administrator provides you with the URL you need. Enter the URL exactly as provided, including any case sensitivity.

   If you are set up with a Forms account, the Project Web Access Sign In page appears (see Figure 23-1).

   ## Sign In

   | User name: | |
   | Password: | |

   □ Sign me in automatically

   Sign In

   Figure 23-1 If you are set up with a Forms account, you see the Sign In page whenever you start up Project Web Access.

3. Enter your user name and password as set up by the project server administrator and then click Sign In.

   Your user name here might be the same as for your corporate Windows account that you use to access your corporate network, e-mail, and so on. If your project server administrator set you up to use your Windows account, the Sign In page does not appear, and you connect to Project Web Access immediately.

   Alternatively, your project server administrator might have set you up with a separate project server account, called a Forms account. In this case, you'll need to enter that user name and the password that have been provided to you. You might need to add or change your password after you log on the first time.

   Your Project Web Access home page appears (see Figure 23-2).

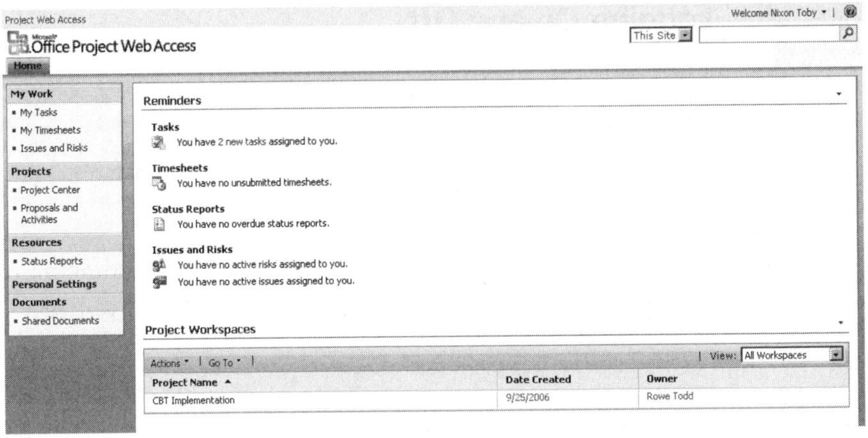

Figure 23-2 After a successful logon, the Project Web Access home page appears.

Create Shortcuts to Project Web Access

Because Project Web Access is your "command center" for project activities, it's a great idea to add the project server URL as a favorite Web site. When the Project Web Access Sign In page appears in Internet Explorer, click Favorites, Add To Favorites. Enter a name in the Name box and then click OK.

You might also consider adding a shortcut to Project Web Access on your Windows desktop. In Internet Explorer, click Favorites. Right-click the Project Web Access favorite you just created, point to Send To, and then click Desktop (Create Shortcut).

Note

If your project server administrator set you up with a separate project server Forms account, add a password the first time you log on to Project Web Access.

On the Quick Launch task bar, click Personal Settings. Click Change Password. Follow the instructions on the page that appears and then click Save.

When you are finished working with Project Web Access for the time being, it's important to log off. Because you have special permissions set up just for you in your Project Web Access user account, and you have access to possibly sensitive or proprietary project information and documents, it's important to practice your normal standards of corporate security.

To log off of Project Web Access, follow these steps:

1. In the upper-right corner of any Project Web Access window, click the Welcome button.

2. On the menu that appears, click Sign Out.

Finding Your Way Around

Working with Project Web Access is like working with most Web sites—you have content, links, and multiple pages.

On the page that's currently displayed, review what's available. Remember to use your scroll bar if it's showing. Click around and orient yourself to the content and controls. If you have used Microsoft Windows SharePoint Services or previous versions of Project Web Access, much of the site will seem familiar.

Using the Quick Launch Task Bar

The Project Web Access home page and other major pages show the Quick Launch task bar on the left side of the screen (see Figure 23-3). The Quick Launch task bar includes a list of links to all the major areas and functions throughout Project Web Access, for example, the Project Center, the Resource Center, and Shared Documents. Simply click a link on the Quick Launch task bar, and the page changes to show the item you clicked.

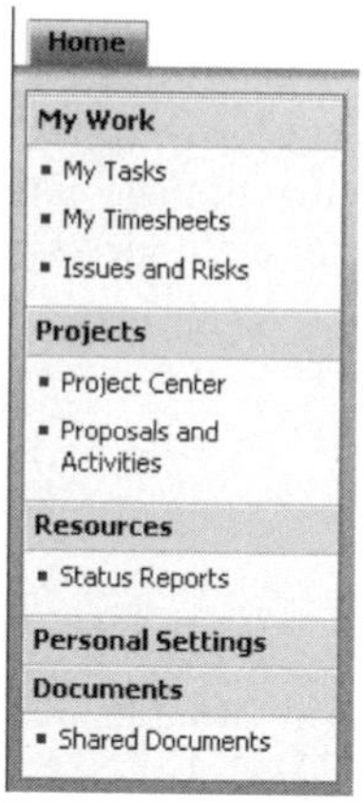

Figure 23-3 The Quick Launch task bar is your navigation center, taking you to all the areas of Project Web Access.

Working with Pages and Controls

The home page is the first Project Web Access page you see when you log on. By default, it includes a list of items that need your attention, for example, tasks that have been newly assigned or progress updates that are being requested by your project manager.

Chapter 23

Your project server administrator sets up your home page to include the content most appropriate for your organization.

All pages throughout Project Web Access have certain standard controls, as follows:

- **Welcome button** In the upper-right corner of every page is a button that says Welcome with your user name. Click this button to see a menu that includes My Settings, Sign In As Different User, Sign Out, and Personalize This Page.

- **Help button** Next to the Welcome button is the Help button. If you ever need assistance while using Project Web Access, click the Help button. The Project Server Help window appears. A Help topic pertaining to the current page appears, but you can find other Help topics by typing a phrase or question in the Search For box or by clicking the Home button in the Help window and then browsing through the Contents.

Help

Home

- **Home** The Home tab is visible on every page. Click this tab to quickly move from an inside page on the Project Web Access site to the home page.

On most pages, such as the My Tasks page or the Project Center, there are additional standard controls, as follows:

- **Settings** Click the Settings menu on the right side of the menu bar. On most pages, this menu includes View Options. This opens a pane that provides methods for you to control what you're seeing in the table, for example, a type of filter or a date range. On other pages, the Settings menus might also include commands to Filter, Group, and Search. Clicking one of these commandsalso open a pane providing the necessary controls.

- **Select a view** Click the arrow in the View box to see a list of views. Views are different versions or layouts of content related to the current page. Some pages have just a single view, whereas others might have seven or eight views.

Working with Tables

Several pages throughout Project Web Access include a grid, or table, which lists information such as tasks, timesheets, or projects (see Figure 23-4).

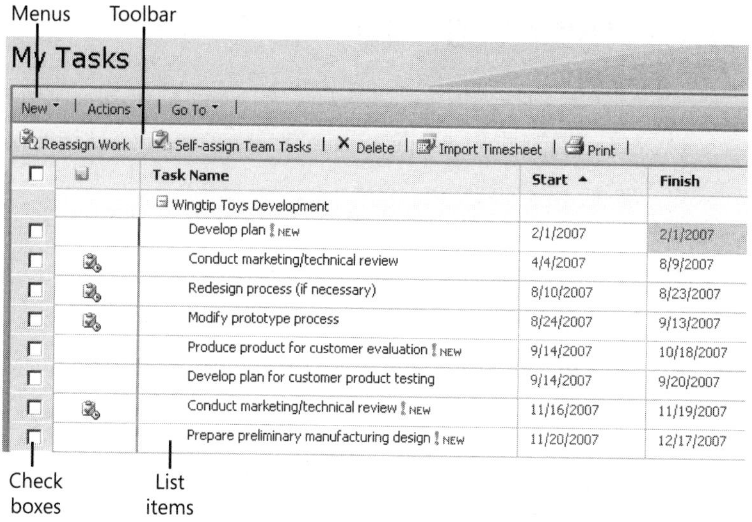

Menus   Toolbar

Check   List
boxes   items

Figure 23-4 You use tables throughout Project Web Access to view and edit project-related information.

The following elements are present in most tables:

- **List items** The main feature of a table is the list of items. In most cases, you can click an item to drill down, for example, to edit task details or review project details.

- **Check boxes** Some tables include check boxes next to each listed item. Selecting the check box marks the item for further action, typically with a menu item. Items that are selected can be viewed to the right of the table.

- **Menus** Two or three menus are typically above a table, for example, New, Actions, and Go To. Click the menu name to view the drop-down menu of commands.

- **Toolbar** Several buttons are on a toolbar directly above the table. Typically, these buttons are for frequently used commands that are also available on a menu. For example, the My Tasks page includes buttons for Reassign Work, Delete, and Print.

- **Print the table** You can print the My Tasks, Gantt view, Timesheet, Project Center, and Project Details pages, among others. Click Actions, Print or Print Grid. A printable version of the table appears. Use the Print command in your Web browser to print the table.

- **Export the table to Excel** You can export tables to Microsoft Office Excel. On the page with the table, click Actions, Export Grid To Excel. The contents of the table appear in an Office Excel spreadsheet. Save the spreadsheet.

Chapter 23

Working on Your Assignments and Updates

When the project plan is developed and tasks are assigned to resources, the project manager publishes the project plan to the project server. Then when you log on to Project Web Access, you see the tasks from that project that have been specifically assigned to you.

When working with your assignments, you can do the following:

- Review your new assignments and any changes to existing assignments
- Assign yourself to team tasks or reassign your tasks to other resources
- View the full project plan to see the context of your work
- Enter and submit progress information about your assignments

Reviewing New and Changed Assignments

As soon as you log on to Project Web Access, your home page lists any new notifications that require your attention. Notifications come from new or changed assignments or progress requests published to the project server for you by the project manager. The following are examples of notifications or reminders you might see in the Project Web Access home page (see Figure 23-5):

- New tasks have been assigned to you.
- Task information on an existing assignment has changed.
- The project manager is requesting a progress update on your assignments.
- A status report is coming due.

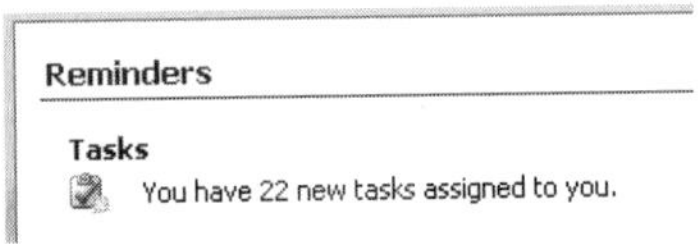

Reminders

Tasks
You have 22 new tasks assigned to you.

Figure 23-5 New assignments are posted on the home page.

When you want to see more details about one of the notifications, simply click the notification link. The page containing the details of the notification appears.

Reviewing New Assignments

The home page always includes notifications when a new task has been assigned to you. Click the notification link, and the My Tasks page appears. The other way to open the My Tasks page is to click My Tasks on the Quick Launch task bar.

The My Tasks page shows your list of tasks along with the fields appropriate to the progress tracking method that has been chosen by the project server administrator and your project manager. Typical fields might include the amount of scheduled work for each assignment, scheduled start date, scheduled finish date, and percentage complete.

When you receive new task assignments, they are marked with the !New assignment icon next to the task name. You don't need to take any further action to accept your new assignments. You can review the summary information on the page, or you can click the task name and review additional assignment details such as other resources assigned, predecessor and successor tasks, and notes (see Figure 23-6).

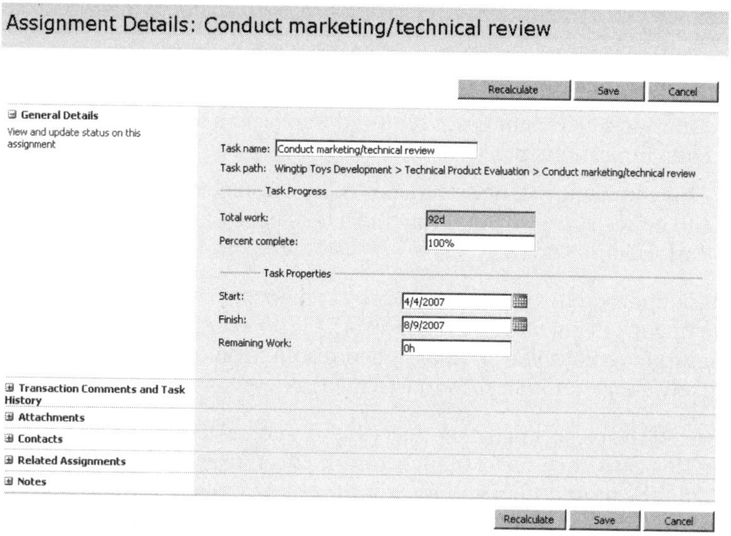

Figure 23-6 Click an assignment name to see additional information on the Assignment Details page.

All projects you are working on, even those owned by different project managers, show on your My Tasks page. By default, all your assignments are grouped by project.

Also by default, only assignments for the current period are listed. If you want to see all your assignments, first make sure that you have saved any changes to your assignments. Below the table, click Save All. click Settings, View Options. Clear the Show Only Current Tasks check box and then click Apply.

Rejecting an Assignment

On occasion, you might find it necessary to reject an assignment. Maybe the assignment is a duplicate of another one you already have. Maybe you feel you're not qualified to carry out the assignment. Maybe you have a scheduling conflict and cannot do it during the required time. Whatever the reason, if you need to reject an assignment, follow these steps:

1. On the My Tasks page, select the check box next to the assignment(s) you need to reject.

2. On the toolbar above the table, click Delete.

3. Click OK in the alert that appears.

   A strikethrough line appears through the assignment row.

4. Below the table, click Submit Selected.

   A dialog box prompts you to enter a comment about the task update you're about to submit.

5. Type a comment explaining to the project manager your reason for rejecting the assignment and then click OK.

   Entering a comment is not required to reject an assignment; however, it is a good communications practice.

   This comment will be stored as a transaction comment with the assignment and can be seen on your Assignment Details page in the Transaction Comments And Task History section.

This task update will appear on the project manager's Task Updates page, along with the comment you entered. If the project manager accepts your update, the project plan is changed to remove you as an assigned resource on the task. The project manager will then likely assign another resource to the task.

Update rejected

However, if the project manager rejects your update, the assignment will come back to you. In this case, the project manager is, in effect, rejecting your rejection of the assignment, and the project plan will remain unchanged in this regard. The strikethrough line is removed from the assignment on your My Tasks page, and the assignment is marked with the Update Rejected icon. If the project manager entered a comment about the reason for the rejection, you can read it on the Assignment Details page in the Transaction Comments And Task History section.

Reviewing Changed Assignments

Assignment
Updated

During the course of a project, task information often changes. New tasks are added, durations change, and then there is a ripple effect for related tasks throughout the project. When the project manager publishes the project with the changed tasks, if any of your assignments are affected, they are marked with the Assignment Updated icon in the indicators column on the My Tasks page.

Review the assignment information in the table—the cells of changed information are highlighted with another color. You can also click the assignment name to review the details.

Notes

If the Notes icon appears with an assignment, either you or the project manager has added a note about the task. Double-click the icon to read the note. You can respond to or add to the note by clicking in the lower pane. When you submit this task, the note appears on the project manager's Task Updates page. When the project manager accepts your task update, your note shows as a task note in the project plan.

Reassigning a Task to Another Resource

By default, resources can transfer an assignment to another resource. This can be useful in groups that are used to shifting workload according to the skills, availability, and preferences of members in the group. This can also be useful in organizations in which a team lead or resource manager decides who should handle a particular assignment. In such a case, the project manager can assign the task to the team lead or resource manager, and that individual then reassigns the task to the right person.

This function is made possible by permissions set by the project server administrator. The individual project manager can also allow or disallow task reassignment.

> **Note**
>
> In Microsoft Office Project 2003, you could delegate a task to another resource and choose whether you see update information about the task. In Microsoft Office Project 2007, a resource can reassign a task to another resource. Those with resource manager privileges can review task updates, status reports, and timesheets.

If you have the capability to reassign tasks, do so by following these steps:

Reassign Work

1. On the My Tasks page, click Reassign Work.

2. On the Task Reassignment page, in the Select New Resource(s) section, find the task you want to reassign.

3. Click in the Select Resource box to see the list of resources for this project (see Figure 23-7).

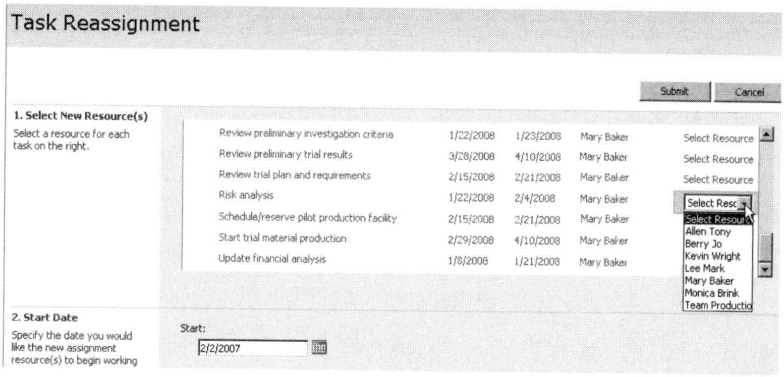

Figure 23-7 Use the Task Reassignment page to reassign tasks to other resources on the project

4. Change the Start Date or enter a comment if necessary.

    The project manager will see your comment when reviewing the task update reflecting this reassignment. Unless the reassignment is routine, it's a good idea to explain your reason for the reassignment.

5. Click Submit.

    This task update will appear on the project manager's Task Updates page as a task reassignment request. If the project manager accepts the update, the project plan is changed to show the reassigned resource on the task. If the project manager rejects the update, the assignment will return to you, and project plan remains unchanged.

Assigning Yourself to New Tasks

You can assign yourself to existing tasks you see in the project that you want to work on. If you're a member of a team assignment pool, you can assign yourself to a task assigned to a team of which you are a member.

You can also propose an entirely new task for a project you're working on and assign yourself to it. You can also create a mini-project or to-do list for your own personal use.

Assigning Yourself to an Existing Task

Your project manager might have published project information without assigning tasks to resources. By default, you can assign yourself to tasks in a published project in which you are a resource.

To see all the tasks in a project, first click Project Center on the Quick Launch task bar. Click the name of the project. The project details appear, including the task names. Take note of the summary task that contains the task you want to assign yourself to.

Once you have this information, you can assign yourself to the task by following these steps:

1. On the My Tasks page, click New, Task.

    The New Task page appears (see Figure 23-8).

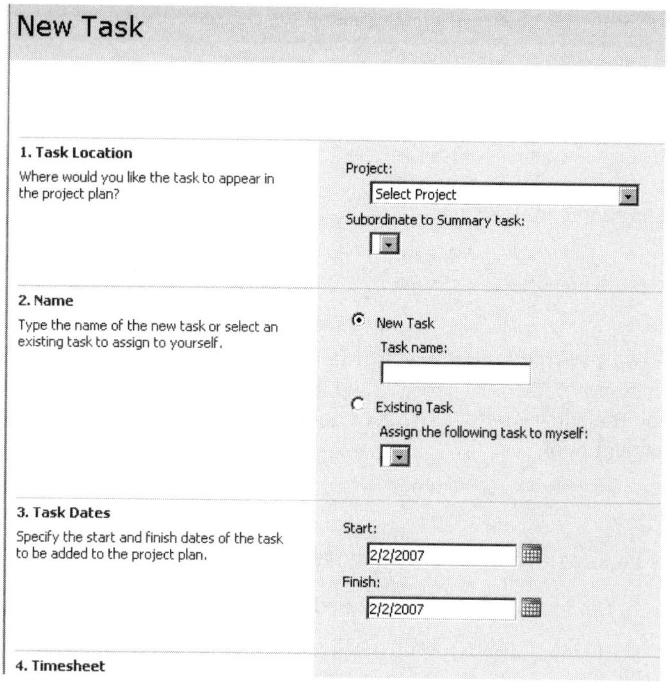

Figure 23-8 Use the New Task page to assign yourself to an existing task or to propose a new task in one of your projects.

2. In the Task Location section, click the project name.

The Project drop-down list includes all the projects in which you are a resource.

3. In the Subordinate To Summary Task box, click the name of the summary task that contains the task you want to assign yourself to.

4. In the Name section, select the Existing Task option.

5. In the Assign The Following Task To Myself box, click the task you want.

This box contains the list of tasks under the summary task you selected in step 3.

6. Complete the fields on the rest of the page as appropriate.

7. When finished, click Submit.

Your request will appear on the project manager's Task Updates page as a new assignment request. If the project manager accepts your request, the project plan is changed to show you as an assigned resource on the task.

Assigning Yourself to a Team Task

Instead of selecting and assigning an individual to a task, sometimes a project manager prefers to specify that a particular department or group be responsible for the task.

Chapter 23

Members of that group can then decide for themselves who will actually carry out the assignment.

This is the idea behind team assignment pools, also known as team resources, a new feature in Microsoft Office Project 2007. A team assignment pool might be a department, such as Business Development, or a group of individuals doing the same job, such as Analysts. When a project manager assigns a task to a team resource, that task is considered a team task.

> **Note**
>
> For you and your project manager to be able to use team resources, your project server administrator needs to have defined the team assignment pool in the enterprise resource pool. The administrator also needs to have identified you as a member of the team assignment pool.

To assign assign yourself to a team task, follow these steps:

Self-Assign Team Tasks

1. On the My Tasks page, click Self-Assign Team Tasks.

   Any tasks that have been assigned to the team to which you belong are listed in the table on the Team Tasks page.

2. Select the check box next to the team task to which you want to assign yourself.

3. Click Assign Task To Me.

Assign Task To Me

4. To return to the My Tasks page, click Go To, Tasks.

   The team task is now listed as one of your assignments. The project manager is notified on the Task Updates page.

Proposing a New Project Task

Suppose you're working on a project and you see that a task should be added. To propose the task to your project manager and to ensure that your work on the project is accounted for, you can create and submit a new task to the project manager.

To propose a new project task, do the following:

1. Identify where the new task might belong in the context of the whole project. Click Project Center on the Quick Launch task bar and then click the name of the project. On the Project Details page, take note of the summary task that should contain the new task you are proposing.

2. On the Quick Launch task bar, click My Tasks.

3. On the My Tasks page, click New, Task.

   The New Task page appears.

4. In the Task Location section, click the project name.

5. In the Subordinate To Summary Task box, click the name of the summary task under which your proposed task should be added.

6. In the Name section, be sure that the New Task option is selected.

7. Complete the fields on the rest of the page as appropriate.

8. When finished, click Submit.

   The new task appears in your task list. Your request also appears on the project manager's Task Updates page as a new task request. If the project manager accepts your request, the new task is added to the project plan with you as the assigned resource.

> **Note**
>
> Creating and assigning yourself to new tasks is a permission granted according to the user profile set up by your project server administrator.

Creating a To-Do List or Mini-Project Using an Activity Plan

In the course of carrying out your assignments, you might have a number of smaller activities that aren't big enough to be called tasks. With an activity plan, you can create a to-do list or mini-project for yourself to keep track of these kinds of tasks. Although an activity plan is stored on your project server, it has no connection to any project plan.

To create an activity plan, follow these steps:

1. On the My Tasks page, click New, Personal Activity.

   The New Activity page appears.

2. Near the top of the page, make sure that the Summary Information option is selected.

3. In the Name And Description section, enter a name for your activity plan. Type a description if you want and then enter the start date.

4. In the Project Custom Fields section, complete the field information for any custom fields you want to add to your activity plan.

5. When finished, click Save.

   The new activity plan is saved to your project server, and the Work Details view of your new activity plan appears. Make sure that the Work Details option is now selected (see Figure 23-9).

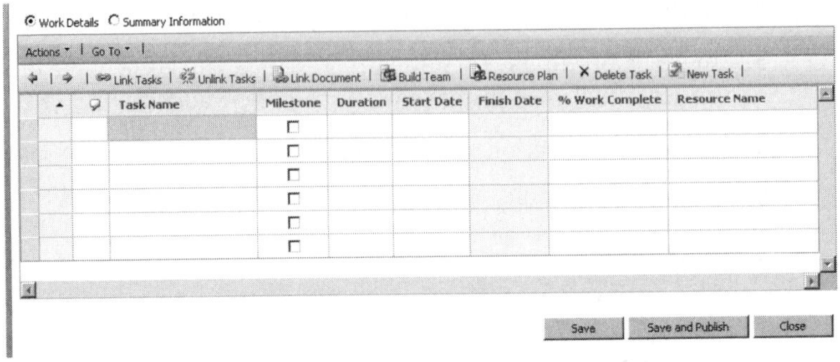

Figure 23-9 Specify the tasks for your to-do list or mini-project by using the New Activity page.

6. Enter the details of your activity plan. Enter task names and durations. Use the buttons on the toolbar to indent outline levels or insert new tasks as needed.

7. If you want to link tasks with a finish-to-start task relationship, select the predecessor task by clicking the row header. Hold down Ctrl and then click the row header for the successor task. Click the Link Tasks button.

An icon in the indicators field shows that the two tasks are linked. In an activity plan, you can only link tasks with a finish-to-start task relationship.

8. Click Save to save the activity plan to the project server but keep it to yourself. Click Save And Publish to save the activity plan to the project server and also make it available for others to see and use.

Unpublished activity plans are useful when you just need to keep a personal to-do list for yourself. Published activity plans are useful when used as a mini-project that you want to be able to share with other resources.

9. When finished working with your new activity plan, click Close.

Your activity plan is listed on the Proposals And Activities page. If you published the activity plan, others will be able to open it. If you only saved the activity plan without publishing it, only you can see it in the list.

To view and change summary information or change task details about your activity plan, follow these steps:

1. On the Quick Launch task bar in Project Web Access, under Projects, click Proposals And Activities.

2. On the Proposals And Activities page, click the name of your activity plan.

By default, the Work Details view of the activity plan appears.

3. Make any changes you want to the task information and then click Save.

4. If you need to view or change summary information, above the table, select the Summary Information option.

The Summary Information view of your activity plan appears. In this view, you can review or change the activity plan description, the start date, the activity plan owner, and so on.

5. When finished, click Save or Save And Publish. Click Close.

For information about adding resources to an activity plan or converting an activity plan to a project, see the section titled "Creating Proposals and Activity Plans" in Chapter 22.

Working with Your Assignment Information

The My Tasks page is your hub for your project assignment information and is likely the place where you spend the most time when working in Project Web Access.

On the My Tasks page, you can update progress information. You can show all your assignments or just the ones for the current period. You can switch to a Gantt Chart view and then view, filter, and group your assignments. You can print a table or export it to Excel.

> **Note**
>
> In Microsoft Office Project 2003 and earlier versions, the My Tasks page was is called the Timesheet. In Microsoft Office Project 2007, there is a new page with specific Timesheet functions separate from those on the My Tasks page.

Viewing or Updating Assignment Fields

Although the fields in the table of the My Tasks page show the summary information for your assignments, you can see and update specifics by clicking the assignment name to open the Assignment Details page. Here you can:

- Update progress information.
- Review the history of communications on this assignment between you and the project manager.
- Review any issues, risks, or documents associated with this task.
- See a list of and send e-mail to the other resources on this project.
- Review this task's predecessors and successors.
- Read and respond to task notes stored with this task in the project plan.

In certain fields in the My Tasks summary table, you can also enter progress tracking information, for example, % Complete or Remaining Work. You can simply double-click in the field and change the value.

Certain types of custom fields might have been created and added to your Tasks list by the project manager or project server administrator. Some of these custom fields can contain a value list from which you can choose an appropriate option. If such a custom field is part of your Tasks list, and if you have read-write permission, click in the field. A drop-down list shows all the choices. Click a choice, and that value now appears in the field. This procedure makes it easy for you to enter the correct form of information while maintaining project data integrity.

Arranging Information in the Table

You can customize your view of assignments to show, hide, or sort information, as follows:

- To show only tasks for the current time period in your Tasks list, click Settings, View Options. Select the Show Only Current Tasks check box. This check box is selected by default.

- To show all tasks to which you are assigned, clear the Show Only Current Tasks check box.

- You can sort assignments by a field in the Tasks table—for example, by Task Name or Finish Datemjn. To do this, click the heading of the field column you want to sort by. The field is sorted in either ascending or descending order. To sort in the other direction, click the column heading a second time.

Viewing Your Tasks in a Gantt View

You can switch to a Gantt chart view of your assignments. In the My Tasks page, click Go To, Tasks Gantt View. A Gantt chart showing your assigned tasks appears (see Figure 23-10).

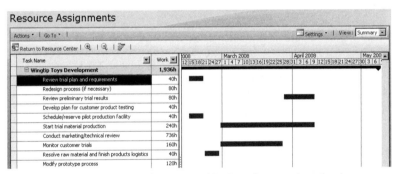

Figure 23-10   The Gantt view shows a graphic view of your assigned tasks.

On this page, you can:

Scroll To Task

Zoom In

Zoom Out

- Click a task and quickly display the Gantt bar for it by clicking Scroll To Task.

- Zoom the chart area in to expand the length of the Gantt bars and see shorter increments of time, for example, from days to hours.

- Zoom the chart area out to compress the length of the Gantt bars and see larger increments of time, for example, from days to weeks.

To return to the My Tasks page, click the Back button on your browser.

Rearranging Your Assignments

In the Gantt view, you can filter, group, or search your assignments by criteria you choose.

To filter assignments via a built-in filter, follow these steps:

1. On the Quick Launch task bar, click My Tasks.

2. Click Go To, Tasks Gantt View.

3. Click Settings, Filter.

4. In the filter pane that appears above the Gantt chart, click Custom Filter.

5. In the Define Custom Filter dialog box, in the Field Name box, click the field you want to filter by, for example, % Work Complete or Finish (see Figure 23-11).

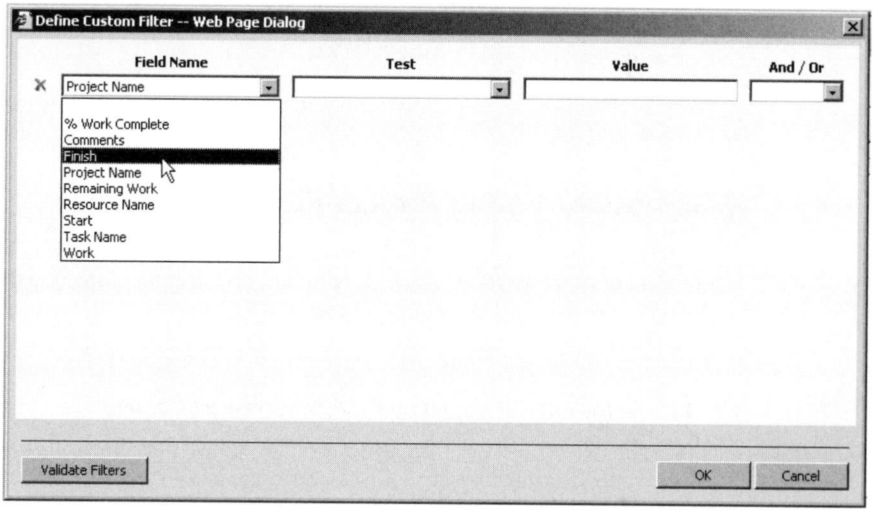

Figure 23-11 Click the field by which you want to filter your assignments.

6. In the Test field, enter the test criteria, for example, Equals or Contains.

7. In the Value field, enter the value for the field and then click OK.

   The task list changes immediately to show only those tasks that meet your filter criteria.

8. To see all tasks again, click All Assignments in the Filter box.

You can also select the AutoFilter check box to add the AutoFilter arrows to each column in the Tasks table. Click one of the arrows and then select a value by which to filter the list. To see all tasks again, click the AutoFilter arrow and then click (All).

To group assignments by a particular field, follow these steps:

1. On the Quick Launch task bar, click My Tasks.

2. Click Go To, Tasks Gantt View.

3. Click Settings, Group.

4. In the group pane that appears, click the arrow in the Group By box to see your grouping choices in the drop-down list.

5. Click the field you want to group by.

 The task list changes to reflect your grouping.

6. If you want a subgroup within the group, click the second field in the Then By box.

7. When you want to return to the original nongrouped order, click None in the Group By box.

To search for an assignment on this page, click Settings, Search. Search controls appear in a pane.

To close the Filter, Group, or Search pane, click the X (close) button in the upper-left corner of the pane.

Glimpsing the Big Project Picture

By default, you can review a list, the summary information, and component task information for all the published projects in which you're a resource. This is helpful to see the overall context of your assignments.

To review information about projects you're working on, follow these steps:

1. On the Quick Launch task bar, click Project Center.

 The Project Center page appears. The projects are listed in a summary project Gantt Chart (see Figure 23-12). Summary information typically includes the project start and finish dates, percentage complete, amount of work, and the owner or project manager.

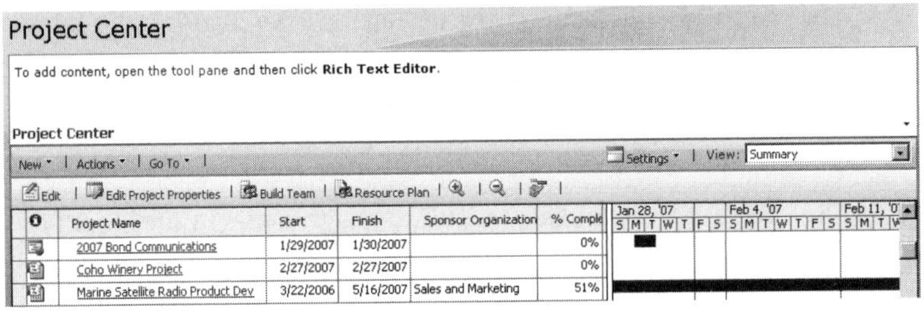

Figure 23-12 Go to the Project Center to review the list of your projects.

2. Click the link for the project whose tasks you want to review.

 The Project Details page appears (see Figure 23-13). The tasks, along with their durations, start and finish dates, and current progress are listed.

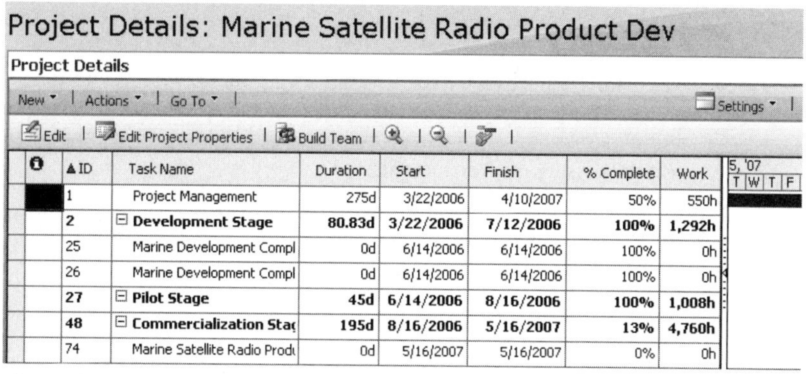

Figure 23-13 View the entire project schedule in Project Web Access.

> **Note**
>
> Whether you're reviewing a project summary or all the tasks within a project, you can set view options, sort, filter, group, and search. Click Settings and then click View Options, Filter, Group, or Search.

Depending on your user permissions and how your project server administrator has set up views, you might be able to review the project by different sets of information. In the upper-right corner of the Project Center or Project Details page, click the View box and review your choices.

You can also open the Web-based workspace for the project, a new feature in Project 2007 based on Windows SharePoint Services. In the workspace, you can read announcements or calendar information. You can see any documents, issues, or risks associated with the project. You can view and participate in discussions about the project. To open a project workspace, from the Project Details page, click Go To, Project Workspace. The workspace opens in a separate Web browser.

> **Project Documents, Issues, and Risks**
>
> Documents, issues, and risks can be added, tracked, linked with tasks, assigned responsibility, and eventually closed. They all become an important aspect of seeing the project through to a successful completion. They are also instrumental in capturing project archival information for use in planning future projects.

Chapter 23

> **Note**
>
> By default, Project Web Access resources are set up with the permission to view documents, issues, and risks. Depending on how the administrator has set up Project Server and Windows SharePoint Services, resources might also have the permission to add and edit risks, issues, and documents.
>
> **For more information, see the section titled "Managing Documents, Risks, and Issues" in Chapter 22.**

Tracking Assignments and Submitting Progress Updates

After your assignments are established, you're ready to work on those tasks. Of course, your project manager wants to be informed periodically of what you're accomplishing, as well as any snags you might be running into. You will provide up to three categories of progress information, depending on your organization's time and status tracking requirements:

- Specific work hours or percentage complete on your individual assignments, also known as actual work, or actuals

- Text-based status reports in a format set up by your project manager

- Hours or days spent on different categories, such as billable and nonbillable time, nonproject administrative time, nonworking time, and so on

> **Own Another Resource's Assignments**
>
> When the project manager assigns a task to a team member, by default, that resource becomes the assignment owner, that is, the person responsible for providing status updates about the assignment.
>
> However, certain resources do not have Project Web Access readily available to them or have some other reason they cannot provide status updates. Sometimes the resource responsible for carrying out a task is a piece of equipment, and status updates will be required on the progress of that equipment.
>
> In these cases, the project manager can designate an assignment owner who is different from the assigned resource. If you are designated as an assignment owner for another resource's assignments, those assignments appear on your My Tasks page. If the Resource Name field is present in the table, it shows the other resource name. Click an assignment name, and the Contact section in the Assignment Details page shows the name of the assigned resource.
>
> As the assignment owner, you are not responsible for carrying out the other resource's assignments, but you are responsible for progress updates and status reports to the project manager about these assignments.

Tracking Progress Information

While you work on your assignments, it's good practice for you to keep your My Tasks page updated. At the end of each day, for example, you can log the percentage complete, the remaining time on an assignment, or the number of hours worked on each task. Which of these three you update depends on how your My Tasks page has been set up by your project server administrator.

If all the fields you need to update are showing in the assignments table on the My Tasks page, you can double-click the value in a particular field and type the new value. Or, click the assignment name to open the Assignment Details page. In the General Details section, update the appropriate fields. When finished, click the Save All button below the table. This saves your information without submitting it for review by your project manager.

Keeping your assignment progress information up to date each day will make it all the easier for you to quickly send a progress update when your project manager asks for it.

Working with Progress Update Requests

As soon as you have assignments on your My Tasks page, you have the ability to submit progress updates. Your project manager and the rest of the project team might have agreed on when progress updates should be submitted, for example, every Friday at noon or the last day of each month. Your project manager might submit a project update request at those times or just expect you to submit a project update without a reminder. Your project manager can also explicitly request progress updates at any time. Either way, such requests appear as a reminder on your Project Web Access home page, and you also receive an automated e-mail notification.

Whenever your project manager submits a progress update request, a question mark icon appears next to the assignment on the My Tasks page.

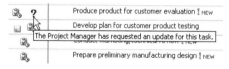

> **Note**
>
> The project manager who created the project is typically the project owner. By default, this project manager is also the status manager. A status manager different from the project manager can be designated for a project. This person is responsible for reviewing and accepting or rejecting progress updates and status reports for a project. You can see who the project manager and status manager are in the Contacts section of the Assignment Details page.

Submitting Progress Information

Submitting your progress updates, or actuals, on your individual tasks is the heart of the Project Web Access functions. Submitting your assignment actuals ensures that your project manager is well-informed about how you're doing on your tasks and also knows whether you have too much work or whether you need more time or assistance. In addition, the actuals you submit help everyone on the project team anticipate potential problems or bottlenecks and come up with solutions before they become crises.

You've already seen how you submit changes to your assignments, such as when you reassign a task to another resource, or when you create a new task for the project. The project manager is notified of your task update and decides whether to reject your change or accept it for incorporation into the project plan.

Submitting progress updates containing your actuals works the same way. You enter your actuals on your assignments and then submit them to the project server. Your project manager reviews your actuals and accepts them. This acceptance then updates the progress information in the project plan.

To enter and submit a progress update of assignment actuals, follow these steps:

1. On the My Tasks page, click the assignment name to open the Assignment Details page.

2. Under Task Progress or Task Properties, enter actuals for your assignments in the fields designated for this purpose by your project server administrator and project manager.

   If your project tracks percentage of work complete, the Task Progress section includes the Percent Complete field. Use this field to report percentage complete on each of your assignments at this point, for example, 15%, 50%, or 100% (see Figure 23-14).

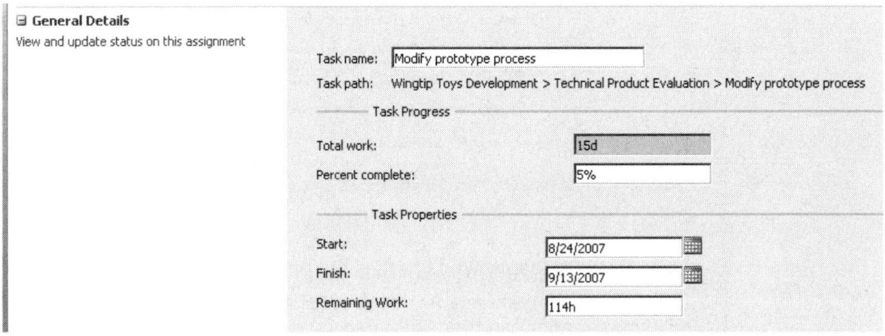

Figure 23-14 Enter actuals in the General Details section on the Assignment Details page.

   If your project tracks total actual work and remaining work for the reporting time period, the section includes the Actual Work and Remaining Work fields. In the Actual Work field, enter the amount of time you spent on each assignment. In the Remaining Work field, enter the estimated number of hours needed to complete the assignment.

If your project tracks hours of work done per time period, time periods such as days or week are provided. In the timephased fields for each time period (day or week), type the amount of time you spent on each assignment.

You might do this for all your current assignments or for those assignments marked with the update request (question mark) icon. It's perfectly fine to report on more assignments than the project manager requested. In fact, it's good practice to submit an update whenever there is a significant change or accomplishment on an assignment.

3. To save the changes you've made to your tasks while still updating your actuals, click Save.

4. To submit your progress updates, on the My Tasks page, select the check boxes for all the assignments you want to submit and then click the Submit Selected button below the table.

The Submit Changes dialog box appears, in which you can type a comment regarding the task update. The same comment will show for all assignments in this group you're submitting. Click OK.

The progress updates for your selected assignments are submitted to the project server and your project manager. When your project manager reviews and accepts your update, your actuals update the task progress information in the project schedule.

If you're updating assignments from multiple projects or multiple project managers, you don't need to do anything special. When you submit updates from multiple projects or for different project managers, the project server makes sure that the information is distributed to the correct managers and ultimately updates the correct project schedules.

Protecting Actuals

Depending on how your project server administrator has set Project Web Access options, the integrity of actuals that you and other resources submit can be protected. This is crucial if your actuals are directly submitted to your organization's general ledger system to produce customer invoices.

If your project tracks progress by hours of work per time period, your project server administrator can restrict when you can enter actuals on your My Tasks page. Locking the time periods ensures that you report hours only for current time periods, not for time periods in the past or future.

For more information about how the project server administrator sets up the My Tasks page, see the section titled "Setting Up Team Member Work Pages" in Chapter 21.

Submitting Text-Based Status Reports

Your project manager might design a status report for you and the other resources to complete and submit periodically. This is different from your progress updates, which deal strictly with assignment information such as actuals, new assignments, or reassigned tasks. Status reports are completely text-based and are not incorporated into the project plan. The project manager sets up the time period and the topic headings, such as "Accomplishments," "Goals," and "Potential Problems." At the designated time periods, you write your status report and submit it to the project server. When everyone's status reports are in, the project manager can review the compiled team status report.

After the project manager first sets up the status report, you'll see an automated reminder notification on your Project Web Access home page whenever a status report is coming due.

To create and submit your text-based status report, follow these steps:

1. On the Quick Launch task bar, under Resources, click Status Reports.

   The Status Reports page appears, showing a table of status reports for different projects (see Figure 23-15).

   Responses

   Responses are all Status Reports you need to submit that have been previously requested from your manager or another resource.

Actions ▾	Go To ▾

   🖹 Submit Unrequested Report |

Title ▲	Due to	Due on
Initiative 22 Status	Mary Baker	2/9/2007
Wingtip Toys Status Report	Mary Baker	4/6/2007

   Figure 23-15 The table on the Status Reports page shows all status reports for your various projects, which project manager receives them, and when the next one is due.

2. In the table, click the name of the status report you want to write.

   The Status Report Response page appears.

3. Change fields in the To and Period sections if needed.

4. In the Sections area, type your status report in the boxes provided.

   The headings of the boxes reflect the points that the project manager wants all resources to report on for each status report.

5. If you want to add another section of information, click the Click To Add Section button. Type a title for the section and then click OK. In the new box, enter your additional information.

6. If you just want to save your report and update the project server later, click Save.

   This option is useful if you're not quite finished with your status report, or if it's not time to submit the report yet. It's a good idea to enter status information whenever you have a significant accomplishment or encounter a possible blocking problem. Then when the status report comes due, you'll have most of your information in place already.

7. When you're ready to submit your status report to the project server and your project manager, click Send.

Your status report is submitted to the project server. The project server automatically merges your status report with the status reports from the other resources for the same time period for your project manager to view.

Submit
Unrequested
Report

You can also send a status report that's separate from the normal status report format or that's going to a different resource. You can specify your own status report title, the resources who should receive the status report, and which sections it should contain. To do this, on the Status Reports page, click Submit Unrequested Report. Complete the fields on the Unrequested Status Report page. In the Sections area, click the Click To Add Section button. Type a title for the section and then click OK. In the new box, enter your additional information.

Logging Time Using Timesheets

Not every minute of every day can be devoted to your project assignments. You know that you have to take time taken for nonproject tasks such as attending staff meetings and participating in training workshops. And then there are also vacations, holidays, and personal time off.

Project Web Access has a new method for tracking different categories of time— timesheets. With timesheets, you can log how you spend your time throughout the workday and the workweek, whether it's on project tasks, nonproject working, or nonworking time.

Such detailed tracking is important in organizations that have specific time reporting requirements, either for their own internal purposes or for working with their customers. For example, certain organizations need to see all billable and nonbillable time, scheduled and actual time, overtime, and so on. Your project server administrator sets up the format for the timesheet as it is to be used for your organization's needs.

> **Note**
>
> If your organization does not need such exact time tracking, it might not have implemented the timesheet feature. If this is the case, either you will not see it in Project Web Access, or it will be an empty page.

Chapter 23

Working with Your Timesheets

You submit timesheets to your timesheet managers on a periodic basis based on your organization's reporting period. Common reporting or fiscal periods include calendar months or 4-week periods. When you log on to Project Web Access, your list of reminders includes any timesheets that are coming due.

To see a list of timesheets for your reporting periods, click My Timesheets on the Quick Launch task bar and then click My Timesheets. The list of timesheets appears (see Figure 23-16).

My Timesheets

Timesheet Name	Period ▼	Total Hours	Status	Next Approver
My Timesheet	51 (4/16/2007 - 4/22/2007)	0h	In progress	
My Timesheet	50 (4/9/2007 - 4/15/2007)	0h	In progress	
Click to Create	49 (4/2/2007 - 4/8/2007)		Not Yet Created	
Click to Create	48 (3/26/2007 - 4/1/2007)		Not Yet Created	
Click to Create	47 (3/19/2007 - 3/25/2007)		Not Yet Created	

Plan Administrative Time | Surrogate Timesheet | Refresh

Figure 23-16 Timesheets for each of your organization's reporting periods are listed on the My Timesheets page.

To see a different set of timesheet periods, click the arrow in the View box and then click the set of timesheets you want.

The first time you open your list of timesheets, the entry in the Timesheet Name field for all of them might be Click To Create. Your project server administrator has already set up the information your timesheets are to include, as follows:

- Task assignments taking place during this reporting period

- The list of all projects to which you are assigned

- No tasks or projects; only the administrative time categories

In spite of this default, you can create your timesheet with the choice you want of these three. Rest your mouse pointer to the right of the Click To Create link until an arrow appear and then click the arrow. The drop-down list shows four options, the first one being to create with the default setting.

Timesheet Name	Period ▼
My Timesheet	51 (4/16/2007 - 4/22/2007)
My Timesheet	50 (4/9/2007 - 4/15/2007)
Click to Create	49 (4/2/2007 - 4/8/2007)
Click to Create	Create with Default Setting
Click to Create	Create with Tasks
Click to Create	Create with Projects
Click to Create	Do not Autopopulate
Click to Create	43 (2/19/2007 - 2/25/2007)

Make a selection and then the timesheet appears (see Figure 23-17).

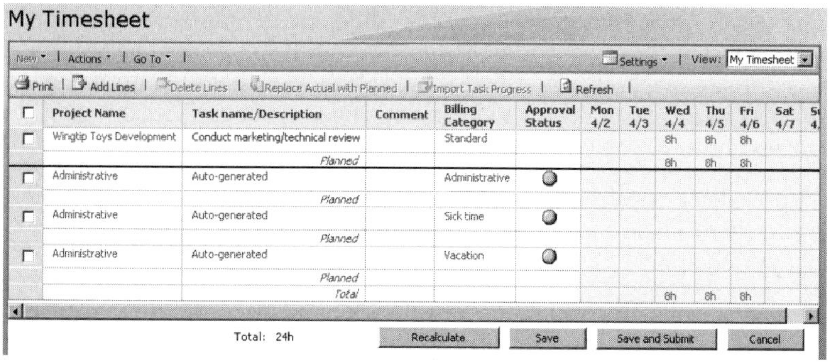

Figure 23-17 The timesheet for a particular period includes fields for each day in the reporting period.

To complete and submit your timesheet, follow these steps:

1. In the Timesheet Name column, click the name of the timesheet for the period for which you want to log your time.

2. To enter time on a day for a certain category, whether it's a project name, a task name, or administrative time such as Vacation, click in the day field for the timesheet item and then type the number of hours, for example, **8h**.

3. To save your changes to a timesheet, click the Save button. It's a good idea to keep your timesheet up to date as you work through the period. This way, when your timesheet comes due, it will be nearly complete and ready to submit.

4. When your timesheet is due and ready to submit to your timesheet manager, click the Save And Submit button.

5. In the Submit Timesheet dialog box, type a comment if you'd like, and then click OK.

   The timesheet is saved, and your timesheet manager will see a notification that your timesheet is available for review and approval.

   Your timesheet manager could be your supervisor, a resource manager, or other person in your organization who is responsible for reviewing and approving timesheets.

> **Note**
>
> In previous versions of Microsoft Office Project Web Access, the task progress page was called the timesheet. Now in Project 2007, the timesheet is a different page and serves a different, but complementary, purpose to the task progress page, which is now called the My Tasks page.

Chapter 23

Copying Items Between My Tasks and My Timesheets

Items in your timesheets can be used independently of the assignments on your My Tasks page, or they can work together. You can bring assignments from the My Tasks page into a timesheet. You can also bring timesheet items from the timesheet onto your My Tasks page. Doing this can help consolidate your time tracking for the different categories and save you some effort.

Import Task
Progress

If a timesheet has already been created without your tasks for that period and you want to add them, click Import Task Progress. In the alert that appears, click OK. Tasks for that period appear in your timesheet.

You can also use the Add Lines command to add any existing assignment or create an entirely new item as a line in your timesheet. To do this, follow these steps:

Add Lines

1. In the timesheet to which you want to add an assignment line, click Add Lines. The Select Task dialog box appears (see Figure 23-18).

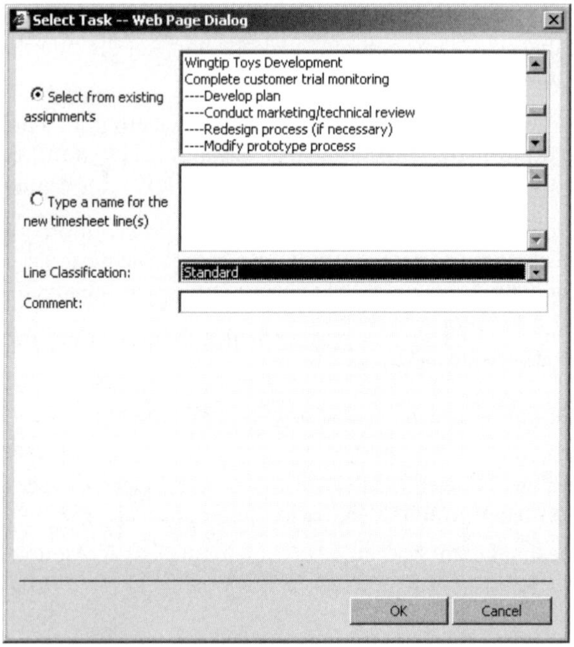

Figure 23-18 Specify whether you want to add a timesheet line from an existing assignment or create an entirely new line.

2. To add a line from one of your task assignments, make sure the Select From Existing Assignments option is selected and then click the name of the assignment in the box.

   To create a new line, select the Type A Name For The New Timesheet Line(s) option and then type the name for the line.

3. In the Line Classification box, select the billing category for the new line. These classifications are preset.

4. Enter a comment if necessary and then click OK.

    The new line appears in your timesheet.

5. Click Save.

To import timesheet items onto your My Tasks page, go to the My Tasks page and then click Import Timesheet. In the Timesheet field, select the reporting period of the timesheet you want to import. Click Import.

> **Note**
>
> Data already entered in the My Tasks page or the My Timesheet page can be overwritten by imported data.

Requesting Nonproject or Nonworking Time

If you are planning a vacation or an upcoming week of training, for example, you can account for this in your timesheet by requesting administrative time. Certain categories of administrative time are set up by your project server administrator to reflect common types of nonproject working time or nonworking time. You can specify when you plan to need administrative time, and it becomes a part of your timesheet. Some categories require management approval; others do not.

> **Note**
>
> In Project 2003, the administrative project was introduced, in which users could create nonproject working time and nonworking time categories and then assign themselves to these categories. In Project 2007, this feature has become a part of the timesheet as administrative time.

To specify administrative time, follow these steps.

Plan
Administrative
Time

1. In your list of timesheets, click Plan Administrative Time.

    The Administrative Time dialog box appears.

2. In the Category box, click the category for the administrative time you are planning, such as Vacation or Administrative (nonproject working time).

3. In the Period box, click the reporting period during which the event will take place.

    The timesheet updates to reflect your selected reporting period.

4. In the timesheet area, enter the number of working hours you will use for the event in the appropriate day. Notice that the timesheet area has a Committed and Planned field for each day. If the event is in the future, enter the number of hours in the Planned field for the day (see Figure 23-19). If the event is in the past, for example, for Sick Time, enter the number of hours in the Committed field.

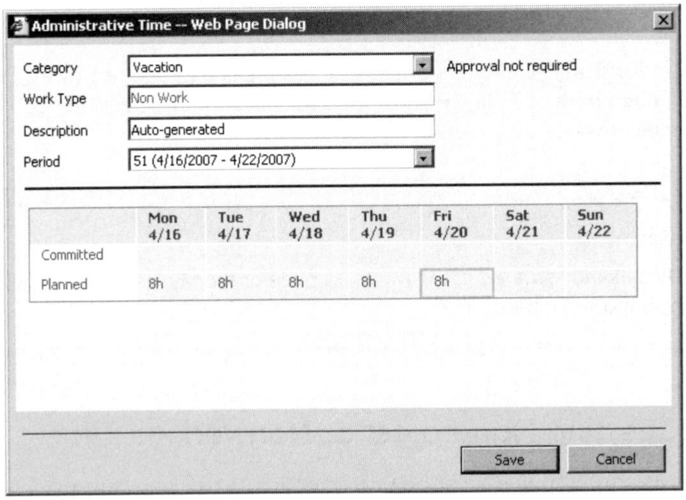

Figure 23-19 Identify vacation, sick time, or nonproject working time in the Administrative Time dialog box.

5. Click Save.

The administrative time is saved. When you open the timesheet for the time period in which you entered the administrative time, it reflects the hours you entered.

If you have chosen a category that requires management approval, your timesheet manager will get notification of it and then accept or reject your request.

Setting Up E-Mail, Reminders, and Calendars

Through Project Web Access, you have tools at your disposal for making your life a little easier. You can set up automated notifications so that you can receive e-mail reminding you about various aspects of your project and progress tracking. You can specify when you want to see reminders appear on your Project Web Access home page regarding your assignments and status reports. You can also integrate your project tasks into your Microsoft Office Outlook calendar.

Setting Your E-Mail Alerts and Home Page Reminders

To configure automated e-mail alerts and reminders to yourself, follow these steps:

1. On the Quick Launch task bar, click Personal Settings.

2. Click Manage My Alerts And Reminders.

3. Review the options in the Tasks and Status Reports sections, and select the check boxes and make further specifications for the events for which you want to be notified via e-mail (Task Alerts) and see reminders on the Project Web Access home page (Task Reminders).

   Clear the check boxes for events for which you do not want an e-mail notification or reminders.

   You can set up notification and reminder options for new or changed tasks, upcoming tasks, overdue tasks, and for status reports (see Figure 23-20).

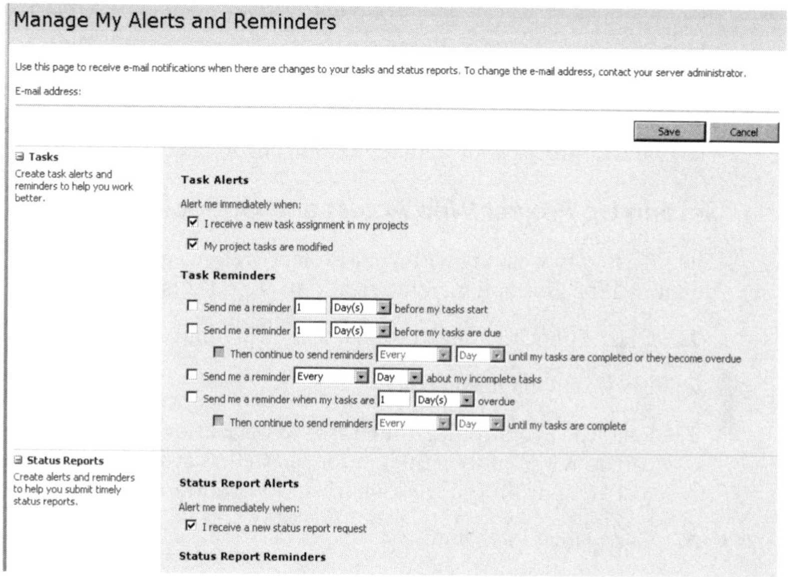

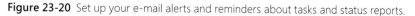

Figure 23-20 Set up your e-mail alerts and reminders about tasks and status reports.

4. When finished, click Save.

Working with Project Tasks in Outlook

If you use Office Outlook, you can keep track of your assigned tasks in your Outlook Calendar, along with your other appointments. You can update progress on your project assignments in the Calendar and report the status back to your project server directly from Outlook.

Project tasks can be displayed as free or busy time, just like any other Calendar entries.

As an alternative, you can also add your assigned project tasks to your Outlook Tasks list. Either way, you can get Outlook reminders for your project tasks, and report progress on them back to Project Web Access.

If you choose to integrate your project assignments with Outlook like this, your assignments are still published from Project Professional to the project server. At that point, your assignments appear in Outlook as well as in Project Web Access. You still use Project Web Access for the custom fields, project views, status reports, and other project-related features. However, you now have a choice to work in either Project Web Access or Outlook to review, track, and update your project assignments.

From Outlook, you can update your assignments and send actual progress information back to the project manager via the project server. As usual, the project manager reviews and approves your updates and incorporates them into the project plan.

Setting Up Project Web Access and Outlook Integration

The first step in working with your Project Web Access assignments in Outlook is to download the Outlook integration add-in. To do this, follow these steps:

1. On the Quick Launch task bar, click Personal Settings.

2. Click Set Up Outlook Sync.

3. Read the Synchronize Your Tasks With Outlook page, which explains what you can do with Outlook integration, as well as system requirements and download instructions for the Outlook integration add-in.

4. Click Download Now.

5. In the alert that appears, click Run (or Open).

6. In the security alert that appears, click Run.

7. Work through the Microsoft Office Project 2007 Add-In For Outlook Setup Wizard pages until the add-in is successfully installed.

To establish the connection between Outlook and Project Web Access, follow these steps:

1. In Outlook, click Tools, Options.

2. In the Options dialog box, click the Project Web Access tab.

3. Under Integrate With, select Outlook Tasks or Outlook Calendar.

4. Under Date Range, specify the time period from which you want assignments to be imported.

   If you want to import assignments from the standard reporting time period set up in Project Web Access, select the Project Web Access Date Range option.

   If you want to import assignments from a different time period (for example, the next 4 weeks), select the Next option and then select the date range.

5. Under Advanced, click the Advanced Options button.

6. Click the Enter Login Information button.

7. In the Project Web Access URL box, enter the address to your project server, for example, http://servername/projectserver.

   If you click the Test Connection button, Outlook tests the URL you entered and makes sure that it's a valid project server. If your project server account uses a Forms account for authentication (rather than Windows authentication), you will be prompted for your password.

8. Under When Connecting, specify whether you should be validated with your Windows user account or whether you're using a separate Project Server account name. If your project server account uses Forms authentication, click the Use A Project Server Account option and enter your user name if necessary. Click OK.

9. In the Advanced Options dialog box under Assignment Import, specify your availability for other appointments during the time of your assignments.

   Just as with other Outlook appointments, you can show your availability as free, busy, tentative, or out of the office. The setting you choose becomes the default for all project assignments in Outlook. You can still change the availability for individual assignments as needed.

10. Under When Importing From Project Web Access To Outlook, specify whether you want reminders. Click OK.

11. In the Options dialog box, click OK.

Chapter 23

Importing Project Assignments into Outlook

To import assignments from Project Web Access into Outlook, follow these steps:

1. Open the Outlook Calendar view or Tasks view.

   Which one you choose depends on whether you selected integration with Outlook Tasks or Outlook Calendar on the Project Web Access tab in the Options dialog.

2. If necessary, show the Project Web Access toolbar by clicking View, Toolbars, Project Web Access.

3. On the Project Web Access toolbar, click Import New Assignments.

   If the Enter Password dialog box appears, enter your Forms account password.

   The Import Assignments From Project Web Access dialog box appears, listing your project assignments (see Figure 23-21). These are the assignments within the date range you set previously in the Options dialog box.

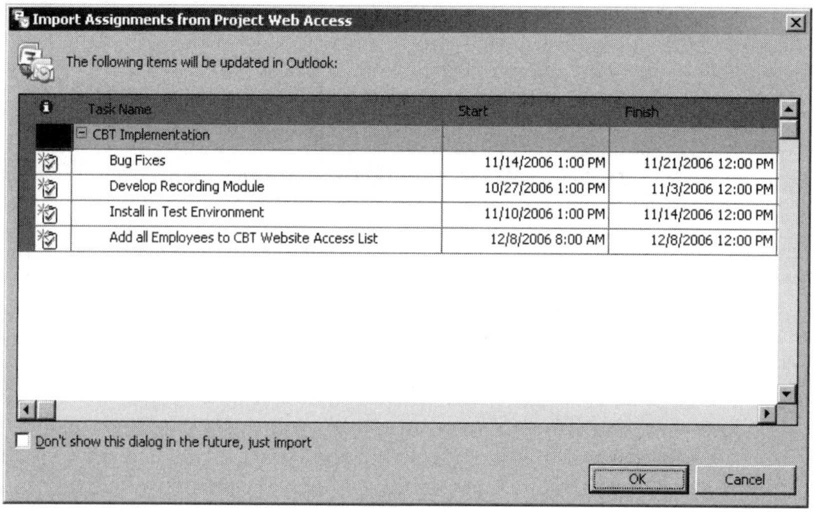

Import New Assignments

Figure 23-21 Review the assignments that will be imported from Project Web Access into Outlook.

4. Click OK.

   The listed assignments are imported into your Outlook Calendar or Tasks To-Do List.

Updating Assignments in Outlook

To record progress on a project assignment from Outlook, follow these steps:

1. Open the Outlook Calendar view or Tasks view.

    Which one you choose depends on whether you selected integration with Outlook Tasks or Outlook Calendar on the Project Web Access tab in the Options dialog.

2. Double-click the assignment for which you want to record progress.

    The appointment form appears, showing assignment details.

3. If you integrate with the Outlook Calendar, on the Project Web Access Appointment tab, in the Show group, click Project Web Access.

4. Depending on the tracking method configured for your project, enter the hours worked per time period, percentage complete, or actual work and remaining work (see Figure 23-22).

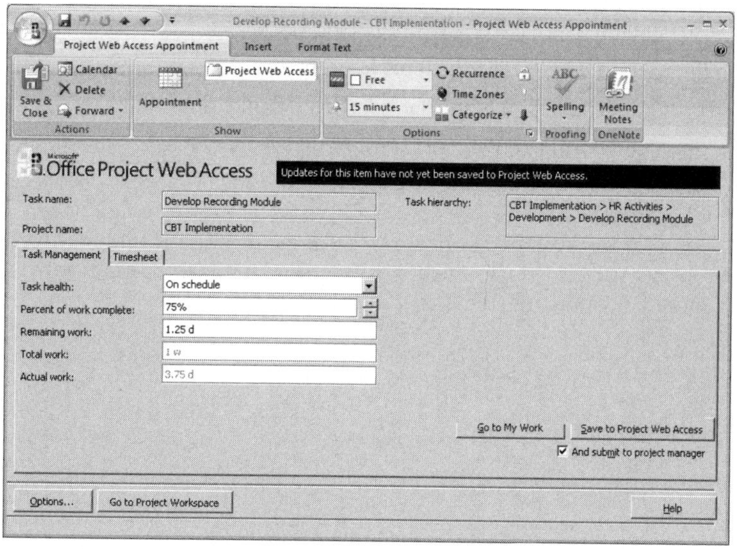

Figure 23-22 Enter progress information from within Outlook.

5. To save the updated information to your project server, click the Save To Project Web Access button.

    To also submit the information so that your project manager can see a progress update, select the And Submit To Project Manager check box.

Managing Resources in Project Web Access

If you're a resource manager supporting a project, you have additional capabilities available to you in Project Web Access. You can add to and edit the enterprise resource pool. You can build a project team based on skill sets. You can assign tasks to the right resources. You can review and approve task progress reports and timesheets.

For detailed information about the different resource management functions in Project Web Access and Project Professional 2007, refer to the appropriate section in Table 23-1.

Table 23-1 Resource Management References

Go to this section	In this chapter
"Creating the Enterprise Resource Pool"	Chapter 21
"Finding Resources to Meet Your Needs"	Chapter 22
"Finding Enterprise Resources that Meet Specific Criteria"	Chapter 22
"Assigning Tasks to Enterprise Resources"	Chapter 22
"Exchanging Task Progress Requests and Updates"	Chapter 22
"Requesting and Receiving Status Reports"	Chapter 22
"Tracking Billable and Nonbillable Time by Using Timesheets"	Chapter 22
"Creating a Resource Plan for a Proposal or Activity Plan"	Chapter 22
"Setting Up E-Mail Notifications and Reminders"	Chapter 22

Team leaders can also perform certain resource management functions, which include viewing resource assignments in assignment views, editing status report requests, and managing e-mail notifications and reminders.

CHAPTER 24

Making Executive Decisions Using Project Web Access

Getting Started with Project Web Access 866

Viewing Project Portfolio Information. 869

Working with the Project Portfolio 874

Working with Resource Information 883

Analyzing and Reporting on Project Information 891

Setting Your Alerts and Reminders 893

Executives and other managing stakeholders can use the enterprise features in Microsoft Office Project Web Access to monitor and measure projects and resources throughout the entire organization. They can see information about dozens of projects and thousands of resources, presented in a manner most relevant to their requirements.

When you are a managing stakeholder identified with executive-level permissions, you can log on to Office Project Web Access and see your entire portfolio of projects in one place, view all enterprise resource information, and arrange information in views or reports so that you can analyze, compare, and evaluate data.

You can compare one project against another, and look at overall resource allocation and availability throughout your organization. Your high-level views of the project portfolio and enterprise resources can be easily adapted and tailored to what you need to see for your particular focus, which can be quite different from what another managing stakeholder might need to see.

Because Microsoft Office Project Server 2007 is integrated with Microsoft Windows SharePoint Services, you have additional project collaboration and analysis information at your fingertips through workspace features that include discussion, calendars, risk management, issues tracking, and document control services.

Through all these, Project Web Access provides clear visibility into your organization's project efforts. You can access vital information that helps you prevent problems and ensure smooth operations. Through the Microsoft Office Project 2007 enterprise project management features, you can see the big project picture, use resources wisely, and make sound decisions for the future of your organization.

Project server administrators and portfolio managers should see Chapter 21, "Administering Your Enterprise Project Management Solution." Project managers can refer to Chapter 22, "Managing Enterprise Projects and Resources." Resources can find information designed for them in Chapter 23, "Participating on a Team Using Project Web Access."

Chapter 23, along with this chapter, are provided as stand-alone e-chapters on the Bonus Content tab of the Companion CD.

Getting Started with Project Web Access

Use your Web browser to connect to your organization's installation of Office Project Server 2007. You then log on to the server from Project Web Access by using the user identification established for you by the project server administrator.

After you're logged on, browse around to orient yourself to the layout of Project Web Access. This will give you some ideas of how you can use Project Web Access as a partner in your project analysis and decision-making.

Logging On and Off

To log on to Project Web Access, follow these steps:

1. Start Microsoft Internet Explorer (at least version 6.0).

2. In the Address box, enter the URL for your organization's project server and then click Go.

   The project server administrator provides you with the URL you need. Enter the URL exactly as provided, including any case sensitivity.

   If your project server administrator has set you up with a separate project server account, called a Forms account, the Project Web Access Sign In page appears (see Figure 24-1).

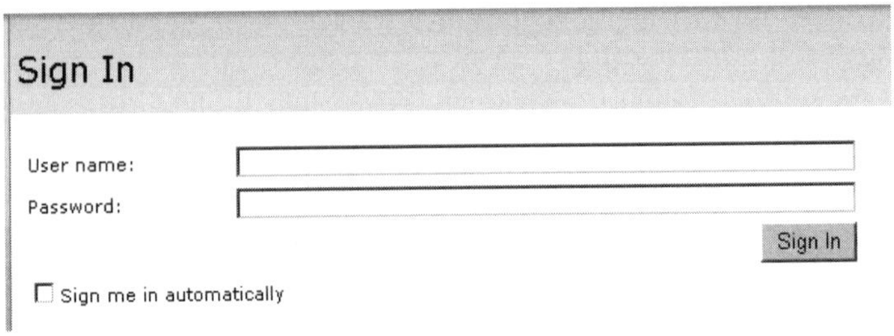

Figure 24-1 If you are set up with a Forms account, you see the Sign In page whenever you start up Project Web Access.

   Enter your user name and password as provided by the project server administrator and then click Sign In. You might need to add or change your password after you log on the first time.

   If your project server administrator has set you up to use your Windows account, the Sign In page does not appear, and you connect to Project Web Access immediately after you enter the Web address.

   Your Project Web Access home page appears (see Figure 24-2).

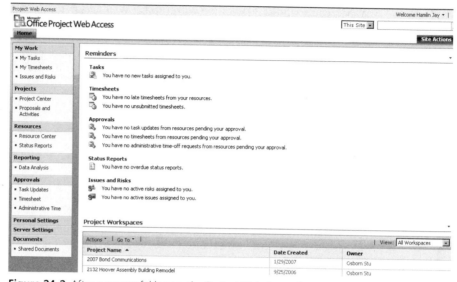

Figure 24-2 After a successful logon, the Project Web Access home page appears.

Create Shortcuts to Project Web Access

Because Project Web Access is your "command center" for project activities, consider adding it as a favorite Web site. When the Project Web Access Sign In page appears in Internet Explorer, click Favorites, Add To Favorites. Enter a name in the Name box and then click OK.

You might also consider adding a shortcut to Project Web Access on your Windows desktop. In Internet Explorer, click Favorites. Right-click the Project Web Access favorite you just created, point to Send To, and then click Desktop (Create Shortcut).

Note

If your project server administrator set you up with a separate project server Forms account, add a password the first time you log on to Project Web Access.

On the Quick Launch task bar, click Personal Settings. Click Change Password. Follow the instructions on the page that appears and then click Save.

When you are finished working with Project Web Access for the time being, it's important to log off. As a sponsor, customer, or other managing stakeholder, you have special executive permissions set up just for you in your Project Web Access user account. These permissions give you access to potentially sensitive or proprietary project information and documents, so it's important to practice your normal standards of corporate security.

To log off of Project Web Access, follow these steps:

1. In the upper-right corner of any Project Web Access window, click the Welcome button.

2. On the menu that appears, click Sign Out.

Finding Your Way Around

Browse around Project Web Access to get a feel for available features and how you might like to use them. You'll find Project Web Access similar to many Web sites, with information and links on multiple pages.

On the page that's currently displayed, review what's available. Remember to use your scroll bar as needed. Click around and orient yourself to the content and controls. If you have used Windows SharePoint Services or previous versions of Project Web Access, much of the site will seem familiar.

The Project Web Access home page and other major pages show the Quick Launch task bar on the left side of the screen (see Figure 24-3). The Quick Launch task bar includes a list of links to all the major areas and functions throughout Project Web Access, for example, the Project Center and the Resource Center. Simply click a link on the Quick Launch task bar, and the page changes to show the item you clicked.

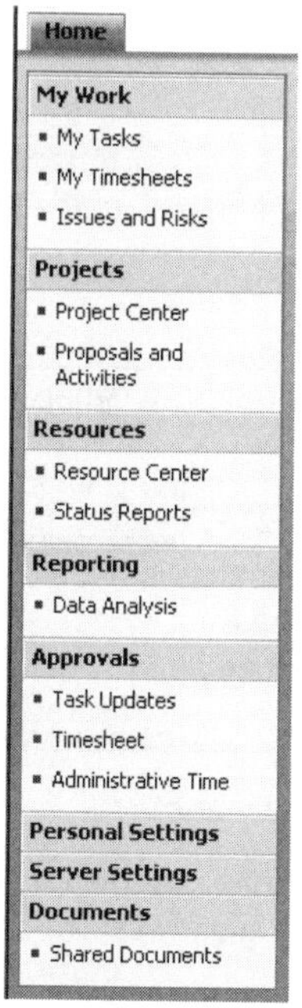

Figure 24-3 The Quick Launch task bar is your navigation center, taking you to all the areas of Project Web Access.

You are likely to spend most of your visits to Project Web Access in one of three key areas, as follows:

- **The Project Center** The list of all projects for your organization are listed in the Project Center. You can arrange and review summary information for various combinations of projects. You can also click a project to see its component tasks or to open it in Microsoft Office Project Professional 2007.

- **The Resource Center** The list of all resources in your organization's resource pool are shown in the Resource Center. You can review summary information for different groupings of resources. If you want, you can also drill down to see detailed assignment and availability information for an individual resource.

- **Data Analysis** You can use the Data Analysis page to build, view, and save reports generated from an online analytical processing (OLAP) cube. Your project server administrator or portfolio manager might create the cubes (sets of up to six fields) that you can use to dynamically generate a PivotTable or PivotChart.

Viewing Project Portfolio Information

As you navigate from page to page throughout Project Web Access to examine project, task, resource, and assignment information, you work with a number of different views, tables, and fields. For example, on the Quick Launch task bar, click Projects, and the

Chapter 24

Project Center view appears (see Figure 24-4). In this view is a table and probably also a Gantt chart, showing the portfolio of your enterprise projects.

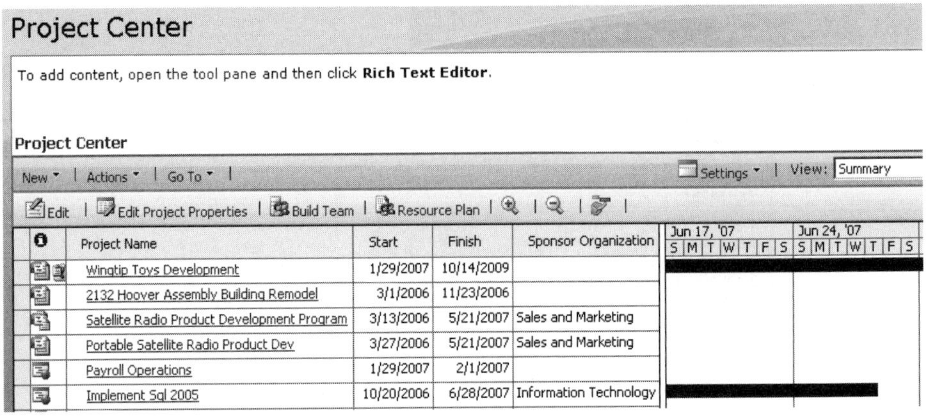

Figure 24-4   Go to the Project Center to review the list of enterprise projects.

The pages have certain controls to help you manage the information you want to see. Many pages give you choices for different views so that you can scrutinize different aspects of the information.

Certain commonly used pages—such as the Project Center and Resource Center—contain tables. There are certain techniques for working with those tables. Plus, those tables are made up of fields that you can also manipulate.

Working with Pages and Controls

The home page is the first Project Web Access page you see when you log on. By default, it includes a list of reminders, for example, issues or risks that require your attention. The home page also lists the Web workspaces for each of the enterprise projects. The project server administrator sets up your home page to include the content most appropriate for your organization.

All pages throughout Project Web Access have certain standard controls, as follows:

- **Welcome button**   In the upper-right corner of every page is a button that says Welcome with your user name. Click this button to see a menu that includes My Settings, Sign In As Different User, Sign Out, and Personalize This Page.

- **Help button**   Next to the Welcome button is the Help button. If you ever need assistance while using Project Web Access, click the Help button. The Project Server Help window appears. A Help topic pertaining to the current page appears, but you can find other Help topics by typing a phrase or question in the Search For box or by clicking the Help button in the Help window and then browsing through the Contents.

- **Home** The Home tab is visible on every page. Click this tab to quickly move from an inside page on the Project Web Access site to the home page.

Most pages, such as the My Tasks page or the Project Center, have additional standard controls, as follows:

- **Settings** Click the Settings menu on the right side of the menu bar. On most pages, this menu includes View Options. This opens a pane that provides methods for you to control what you're seeing in the table, for example, a type of filter or a date range. On other pages, the Settings menus might also include commands to Filter, Group, and Search. Clicking one of these commands also opens a pane providing the necessary controls.

- **Select a view** Click the arrow in the View box to see a list of views. Views are different versions or layouts of content related to the current page. Some pages have just a single view, whereas others might have seven or eight views.

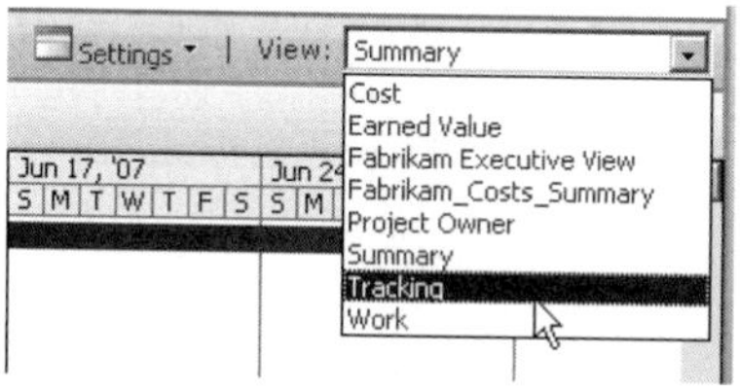

Working with Tables

Several pages throughout Project Web Access include a grid, or table, that lists information such as projects or resources (see Figure 24-5).

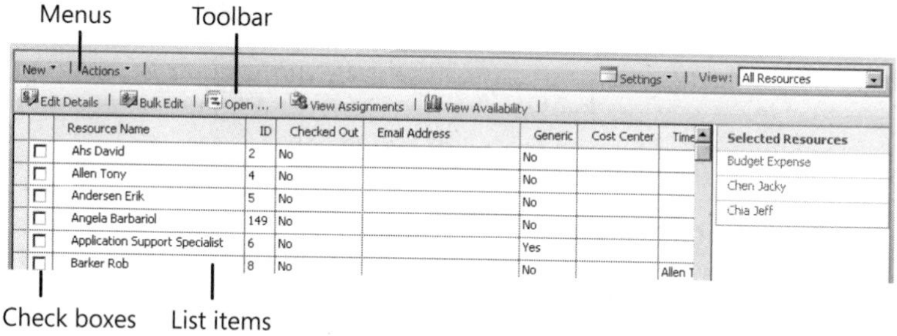

Figure 24-5 You use tables throughout Project Web Access to view and edit project-related information.

The following elements are present in most tables:

- **List items** The main feature of a table is the list of items. In most cases, you can click an item to drill down, for example, to edit task details or review project details.

- **Check boxes** Some tables include check boxes next to each listed item. Selecting the check box marks the item for further action, typically with a menu item. Items that are selected can be viewed to the right of the table.

- **Menus** Two or three menus are typically above a table, for example, New, Actions, and Go To. Click the menu name to view the drop-down menu of commands.

- **Toolbar** There are several buttons on a toolbar directly above the table. Typically, these buttons are for frequently used commands that are also available on a menu. For example, the Project Center page includes buttons for Edit Project Properties, Build Plan, and Scroll To Task.

- **Print the table** You can print the Project Center, Project Details, and Resource Center pages, among many others. Click Actions, Print Grid. A printable version of the table appears. Use the Print command in your Web browser to print the table.

- **Export the table to Excel** You can export tables to Microsoft Office Excel. On the page with the table, click Actions, Export Grid To Excel. The contents of the table appears in an Office Excel spreadsheet. Save the spreadsheet.

Understanding Fields

You can have either read-write or read-only access for the table fields in the view. Work with your project server administrator to make sure you have access to the fields you need in the views you use most often.

Certain types of custom fields might have been created and added to your views by the portfolio manager or project server administrator. Some of these custom fields can contain a value list from which users can choose an appropriate option. If such a custom field is part of a view that you are modifying, and if you have read-write permission, click in the field. A drop-down list shows all the choices. Click a choice, and that value now appears in the field. This makes it easy for you to enter the correct form of information while maintaining project data integrity.

Rearranging View Information

In many project and resource views, you can rearrange the order or information by sorting, grouping, or filtering information by criteria you choose.

Sorting Information

Sorting places information in alphabetical or numerical order, in either ascending or descending order. To sort items in a view by a particular field on a table, follow these steps:

1. In the table, click the heading of the field column you want to sort by.

   The field is sorted in either ascending or descending order.

2. To sort in the other direction, click the column heading a second time.

> **Note**
> Although not every table can be sorted like this, most of them can, including the tables on the Project Center, Project Details, and Resource Center pages.

Grouping Information

Grouping places information in categories relevant to the field you're grouping by. To group items by a particular field in a view, follow these steps:

1. In the view containing the table with fields you want to group, click Settings, Group.

2. In the group pane that appears below the menu bar, click the arrow in the Group By box to see your grouping choices in the drop-down list (see Figure 24-6).

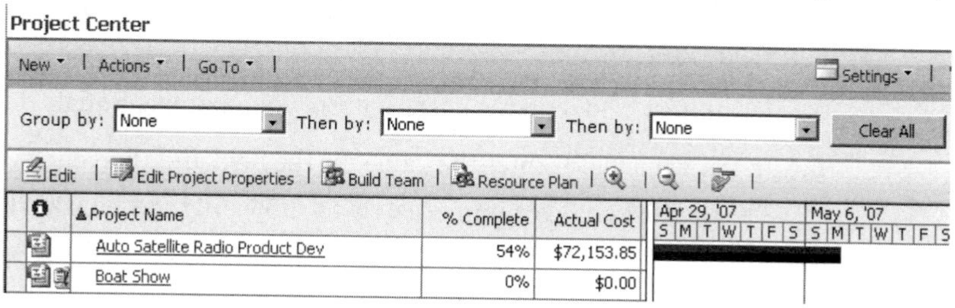

Figure 24-6 A pane with grouping controls appears when you click Settings, Group.

3. Click the field you want to group by.

   The task list changes to reflect your grouping.

4. If you want a subgroup within the group, click the second field in the Then By box.

5. When you want to return to the original nongrouped order, click None in the Group By box.

Filtering Information

Filtering removes information you don't want to view so that you see only the information that meets the conditions of the field(s) you are concerned with. To filter items by using a built-in filter in a view, follow these steps:

1. Display the view in which you want to filter information.

2. Click Settings, Filter.

3. In the filter pane that appears below the menu bar, click Custom Filter.

4. In the Define Custom Filter dialog box, click the field you want to filter by in the Field Name box, for example, % Complete or Finish (see Figure 24-7).

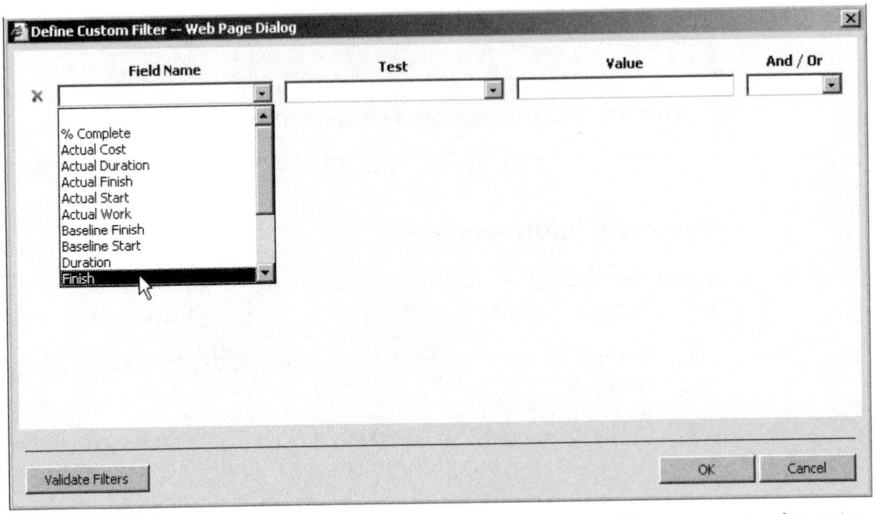

Figure 24-7 Use the Define Custom Filter dialog box to set up your filter for project information.

5. In the Test field, enter the test criteria, for example, Equals or Is Greater Than.

6. In the Value field, enter the value for the field and then click OK.

   The task list changes immediately to show only those tasks that meet your filter criteria.

7. To see all tasks again, click All Projects in the Filter box.

You can also select the AutoFilter check box to add the AutoFilter arrows to each column in the table. Click one of the arrows and then select a value by which to filter the list. To see all tasks again, click the AutoFilter arrow and then click (All).

To search for an assignment on your current page, click Settings, Search. Controls for search criteria appear in a pane.

To close the Filter, Group, or Search pane, click the X (close) button in the upper-left corner of the pane.

Working with the Project Portfolio

The Project Center is your hub of information for your project portfolio. This is where you can inspect the views of an individual project or analyze aspects of multiple projects to get the high-level picture of projects you need.

You can see the projects that are taking the bulk of your resources' time. This can help you determine whether you need to shift resource allocation and to ramp up or ramp down on hiring or the use of vendors.

You can use specialized views to look at overall costs of entire projects. You can combine projects in different ways to see those costs from various angles.

Most importantly, you can get that vital "view from 30,000 feet" into the collection of your organization's projects and gain insight into the key scope and activities of the organization. This can help you understand where your organization is now so that you can make strategic decisions about where you want it to go.

Viewing the Portfolio of Projects

You can see the summary list of all published enterprise projects and then drill down to examine the details of an individual project. To see the summary of enterprise projects, follow these steps:

1. On the Quick Launch task bar, click Project Center.

   The Project Center appears. The table lists all enterprise projects, with each project occupying a single row and showing summary data for that project in the table and in the Gantt Chart area.

   The Project Center also lists any published proposals and activity plans. These are discussed in the section titled "Creating Proposals and Activity Plans" later in this chapter.

2. Manipulate the Project Center table to see the information you want.

   In the View box, click the view that shows the best information. Different views can be created and added to the Project Center by the project server administrator or portfolio manager.

   You can also sort, filter, or group information to see it the way you need it. You can move the split bar between the table and chart to show more of one side or the other. Scroll through the table or chart. Compare values in a field of information among the various projects.

To see detailed information for any one of your enterprise projects, follow these steps:

1. In the Project Center, click the name of the project you want to review.

   The Project Details view appears, showing the component tasks of the selected project (see Figure 24-8)

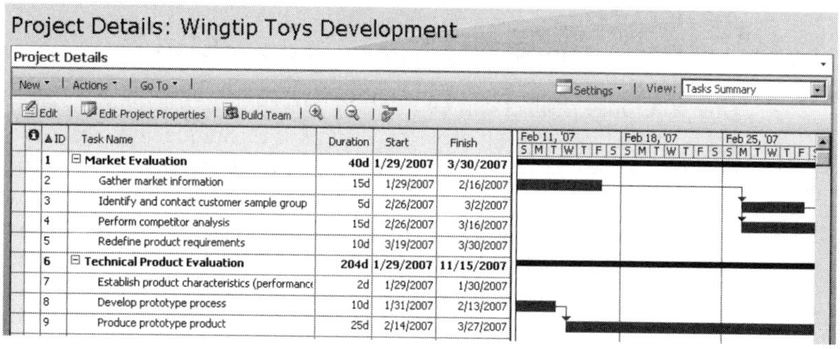

Figure 24-8 View individual project details.

2. Just as with the summary table, choose the view that shows the best information for your current purpose. Sort, filter, or group information. Scroll through the table or chart to find the information you're looking for. Compare values in a field of information among the various projects.

Zoom In

Zoom Out

Analyze Projects by Using a Gantt Chart

Whether you're working on the Project Center page or the Project Details page, the default view contains a Gantt chart. In a Gantt chart, the left side of the view is a table, and the right side displays the Gantt bars showing the start, duration, and finish of each item (project, task, or assignment) across the timescale. The current date is shown as a dashed vertical line.

You can click the Zoom In or Zoom Out buttons to see more or less detail in the time span shown in the chart area.

Opening a Project in Project Professional

Button Name

If you want to see the complete details for a project, you can open it in Office Project Professional 2007. On the Project Center page, click the Enterprise Project icon in the indicators column for the project you want to open in Project Professional 2007.

Depending on the logon method chosen by your project server administrator, you might need to enter your user name and password.

The selected project is now checked out to you and appears in Project Professional. You can view the project, resource, cost, and other information as needed. You can also make changes as your privileges allow.

For details about making changes to project information and publishing those changes to the project server, see the section titled "Managing Your Project Files on the Server" in Chapter 22.

INSIDE OUT   Projects, programs, and portfolios

One enterprise project can be inserted into another to create a master project–subproject relationship between projects. Using this technique, in Project Web Access a program can be modeled to reflect projects being implemented under a specific program in your organization. The overarching program can be represented as the master project, with all the projects within that program set up as subprojects within the master project. Therefore, as established through Project Server 2007, a program is a set of related projects that are often set up in a hierarchical relationship.

For more information about modeling programs in PWA, see the section titled "Setting Up a Program of Projects" in Chapter 22.

By contrast, a portfolio is simply a collection of enterprise projects being implemented as well as those currently under consideration by an organization as reflected in the project server. They might or might not be related to one another, and they might or might not be set up in a hierarchical relationship.

Either way, all projects are listed on the Project Center page in Project Web Access, whether they are part of a program, and whether they are a master project or a subproject.

Reviewing Program Information

Portfolio managers or project managers can set up programs in the project server through the implementation of master projects and subprojects. This structure supports large organizations implementing several large projects and subprojects, often taking place at various locations around the world.

When you open a master project, all the subprojects are listed (and checked out) as tasks in any task view. You can then drill down by clicking one of the subprojects to see the tasks within that project.

Dependencies and deliverables between the projects within a program can be identified by the project managers, thereby providing the visibility needed to know when a key deliverable that affects related project is coming due.

Project Portfolio Server 2007

New in Office Project 2007 is the option to configure and implement Microsoft Office Project Portfolio Server 2007, which can provide additional portfolio management services as part of your integrated enterprise project management solution. Office Project Portfolio Server 2007 is a separate product that also includes the Microsoft Office Project Portfolio Web Access client. Project Portfolio Server 2007 includes sophisticated tools to help organizations identify, select, and manage portfolios compatible with their business strategy. It also provides tools for resource management, billing, and invoicing.

For more information about Project Portfolio Server, go to the Microsoft Office Project Portfolio Server page on Microsoft Office Online at *www.microsoft.com/office /portfolioserver.*

Project Workspaces and Documents, Issues, and Risks

Documents, issues, and risks can be added, tracked, linked with tasks, assigned responsibility, and eventually closed. They all become an important aspect of seeing the project through to a successful completion. They are also instrumental in capturing project archival information for use in planning future projects.

For details about creating and viewing documents, risks, and issues, see the section titled "Managing Documents, Risks, and Issues" in Chapter 22.

The lists of documents, issues, and risks associated with a project are maintained in the project workspace. Typically, all projects have a Windows SharePoint Services workspace created for them. In addition to the documents, issues, and risks, the workspace can include announcements among team members, a calendar of upcoming events, a list of deliverables between related projects, and team discussions.

To open the workspace for a project, select the project either on the Project Center or Project Details page and then click Go To, Project Workspace. The workspace opens in a separate browser window (see Figure 24-9).

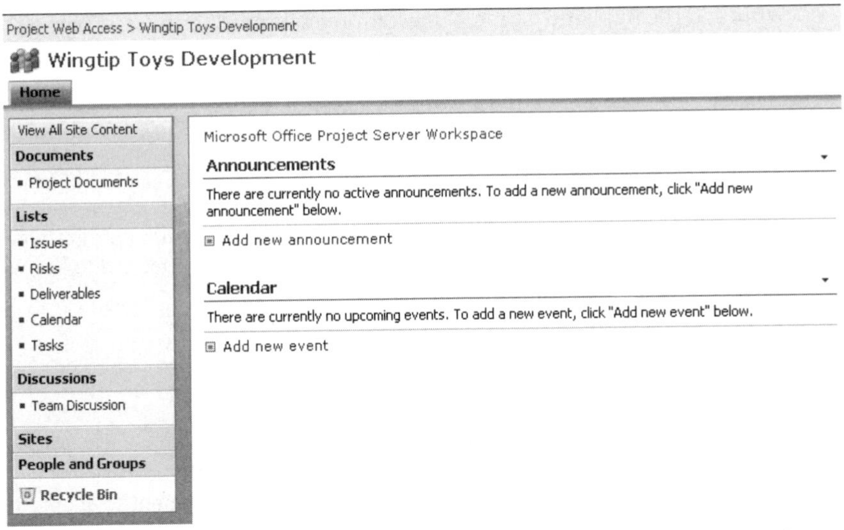

Project Web Access > Wingtip Toys Development

Wingtip Toys Development

Home

View All Site Content
Documents
- Project Documents

Lists
- Issues
- Risks
- Deliverables
- Calendar
- Tasks

Discussions
- Team Discussion

Sites

People and Groups

Recycle Bin

Microsoft Office Project Server Workspace

Announcements

There are currently no active announcements. To add a new announcement, click "Add new announcement" below.

Add new announcement

Calendar

There are currently no upcoming events. To add a new event, click "Add new event" below.

Add new event

Figure 24-9 By default, as soon as a new enterprise project is published, a new workspace is created for it.

A project team can use the workspace for communication and collaboration as well as the repository for project documents. It is also essential for tracking project issues and risks.

Creating a New Project

In addition to reviewing and editing existing projects, you can create new projects. This can be helpful if you want to share new project ideas with your staff, or if you want to set up the vision of a program that portfolio managers and project managers can then implement.

To create a new project, click New, Project on the Project Center page. The Project Professional window appears with a blank project (see Figure 24-10).

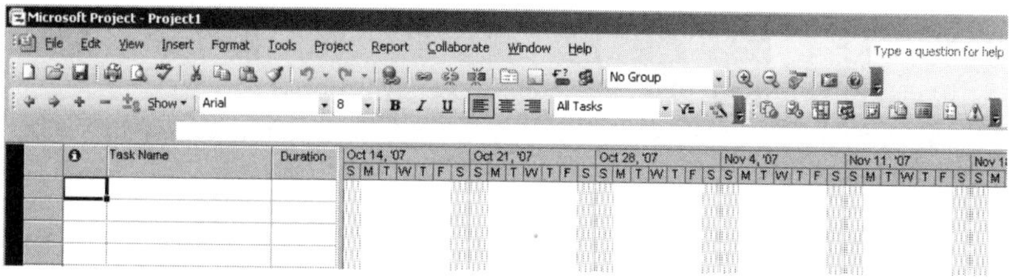

Figure 24-10 You can create a new enterprise project in Project Professional.

For more information about creating a new project, see the section titled "Creating a New Project Plan" in Chapter 3, "Starting a New Project." When you're ready to save, publish, and check in your new project, see the section titled "Managing Your Project Files on the Server" in Chapter 22.

Creating Proposals and Activity Plans

New in Microsoft Office Project Server 2007 is the means for using a simplified Web-based interface in Project Web Access to track activities throughout the entire project life cycle, that is, just before and just after the project itself is implemented.

With proposals, you can set up a preproject plan. This is useful if you have a vision for a new project with some high-level tasks, and you want to record these ideas without creating a new enterprise project. When the proposal is approved, it can be converted into a project.

Activity plans can best be used to track the routine operations that typically take place after the completion of a project. You can also use activity plans to track maintenance activities, very small projects, or your own personal to-do list.

> **Note**
> Proposals and activity plans all operate only in Project Web Access; there is no visibility to these plans in Project Professional. However, when they are published (rather than just saved), they do appear in the Project Center for all to see.

With both proposals and activity plans, you can use the views and reports in Project Web Access to do high-level or detailed analyses. This can be particularly useful with proposals. Portfolio managers and executives can review the proposals and evaluate feasibilities within the organization's strategic goals to help decide whether to move forward with a project.

Creating a Proposal or Activity Plan

To create a proposal or activity plan, follow these steps:

1. On the Quick Launch task bar in Project Web Access, under Projects, click Proposals And Activities.

2. To create a proposal, click New, Proposal.

   To create an activity plan, click New, Activity.

   The difference between the two is that the proposal might have a few more proposal-related fields than the activity plan (see Figure 24-11).

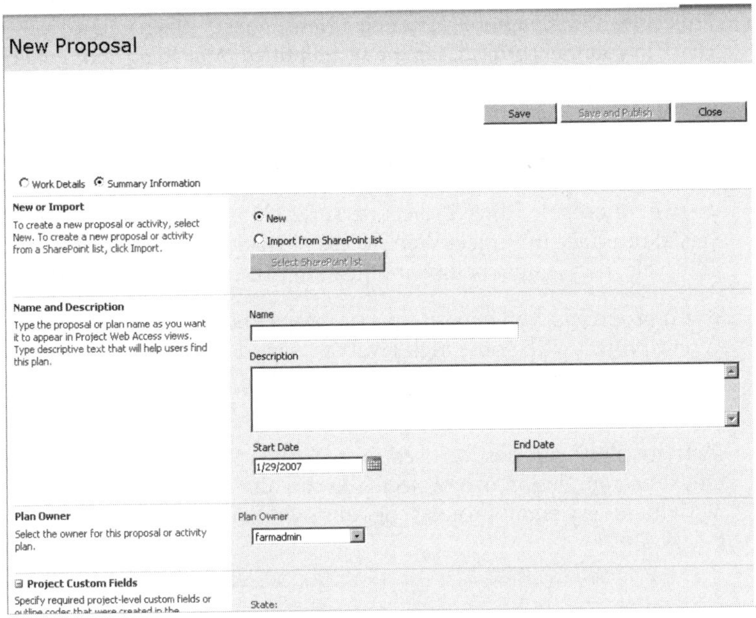

Figure 24-11 Start to create a proposal on the New Proposal page.

3. Near the top of the page, make sure that the Summary Information option is selected.

4. Work through the page, reading the section descriptions and completing the fields as appropriate.

5. If you're creating a proposal, and if the Workflow Status section is present, click the link to the workflow status and activity pages.

   The workflow status feature can be enabled or disabled as part of the customization done for your organization by your project server administrator.

6. If you're creating a proposal, under Project Custom Fields, click the button next to the State box and then click Proposed.

   The State field is a "built-in" custom field designed for use with proposals. The three enumerated states are Proposed, Approved, and Rejected.

7. When finished, click Save.

The new proposal or activity plan is saved to your project server, and the Work Details view of your new proposal or activity plan appears. Make sure that the Work Details option is now selected.

8. Enter the details of your new proposal or activity plan. Enter task names and durations. Use the buttons on the toolbar to indent outline levels or insert new tasks.

Link Tasks

9. If you want to link tasks with a finish-to-start task relationship, select the predecessor task by clicking the row header. Hold down Ctrl and then click the row header for the successor task. Click the Link Tasks button.

An icon in the indicators field shows that the two tasks are linked. You can only link tasks with a finish-to-start task relationship in a proposal or activity plan.

10. Click Save to save the proposal or activity plan to the project server but keep it to yourself. Click Save And Publish to save the proposal or activity plan to the project server and also make it available for others to see and use.

Unpublished proposals or activity plans are useful when you just need to keep a personal to-do list for yourself. Published proposals or activity plans are useful as a mini-project that you want to be able to share with other resources.

Your new proposal or activity plan is listed on the Proposals And Activities page. If you published the proposal or activity plan, others will be able to open it. If you only saved the proposal or activity plan without publishing it, only you can see it in the list.

Viewing or Changing a Proposal or Activity Plan

To view, change summary information, or change task details about your proposal or activity plan, follow these steps:

1. On the Quick Launch task bar in Project Web Access, under Projects, click Proposals And Activities.

2. On the Proposals And Activities page, click the name of the proposal or activity plan you want to view or change.

By default, the Work Details view of the proposal or activity plan appears.

3. Make any changes you want to the task information and then click Save.

4. If you need to view or change summary information, above the table, select the Summary Information option.

The Summary Information view of the proposal or activity plan appears. In this view, you can review or change the description, the proposal state, and so on.

5. When finished, click Save or Save And Publish. Click Close.

On the Proposals And Activities page, proposals are the items that have a state associated with them: Proposed, Approved, or Rejected. Activity plans are also listed on this page, but their state fields are blank. You can select a proposal or activity plan without opening it by clicking anywhere in the row except on the name itself.

Adding Resources to a Proposal or Activity Plan

You can add resources to your proposal or activity plan and assign them to tasks. Resources assigned to tasks in proposals or activity plan are not really assigned; that is, they do not see notifications of new assignments, even if the proposal or activity plan is published. The purpose for doing this is to suggest possible resources in the event that this proposal or activity plan is approved and then converted to a project.

To add resources to your proposal or activity plan, follow these steps:

1. On the Quick Launch task bar in Project Web Access, under Projects, click Proposals And Activities.

2. On the Proposals And Activities page, click the name of the proposal or activity plan to open its Work Details view.

3. If you make any other changes to the proposal or activity plan, click Save.

4. Click Build Team.

Build Team

5. On the Build Team page, select the check boxes next to the resources you want to add to the proposal or activity plan and then click Add.

6. Click Save.

7. Click in the Resource Name field for a task, and you'll see a list of all the resources you just added. Click a resource to suggest the assignment of that resource to the current task. You can only add one resource to a task.

8. When finished, click Save or Save And Publish and then click Close.

Converting a Proposal or Activity Plan to a Project

If it is determined that the proposal or activity plan should become a project, you can easily convert it. To do this, follow these steps:

1. On the Quick Launch task bar in Project Web Access, under Projects, click Proposals And Activities.

2. On the Proposals And Activities page, click anywhere in the row except on the name to select the proposal or activity plan but not open it.

3. Click Convert.

Convert

4. Read the alert that appears and then click OK.

The proposal or activity plan is submitted to the project server queue for processing. When it's finished, the Proposals And Activities page appears, and your proposal or activity plan is no longer listed.

5. On the Quick Launch task bar, click Project Center.

You'll see your former proposal or activity plan, which is now a project, listed there.

6. Click the name of your newly converted proposal or activity plan.

You can now edit the proposal or activity plan, which is now a project, in Project Web Access or Project Professional. If you had already added resources, when you publish the project, those resources will see their assignments for this project.

Working with Resource Information

The Resource Center is the key location for executives and resource managers who need to keep a close eye on the performance of resources in the organization. In the Resource Center, you can review resource skills and other identifying attributes, their current assignments, their current or future workload allocation, and their current or future availability for additional work.

Viewing the Enterprise Resource Pool

You can see the entire enterprise resource pool and then examine details for an individual resource. To see the enterprise resource pool, follow these steps:

1. On the Quick Launch task bar, click Resource Center.

The Resource Center appears, showing the enterprise resource pool. Each resource occupies a single row showing basic resource information in fields throughout the row (see Figure 24-12).

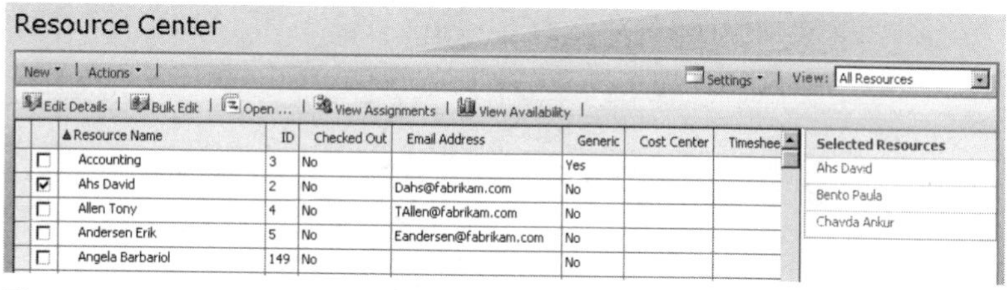

Figure 24-12 The Resource Center displays your enterprise resource pool.

2. Arrange the table to see the information you want.

In the View box, click the view that shows the information you want. The project server administrator or portfolio manager can create and add different resource views to the Resource Center.

You can also sort, filter, or group information to see it the way you need it. Scroll through the table to see more information.

Chapter 24

To see detailed information for any enterprise resource, follow these steps:

1. In the Resource Center, select the check box next to the name of the resource for which you want to see details.

   If you want to see details for multiple resources one after another, select the check boxes for all of them. Their names appear in the Selected Resources pane on the right side of the page.

Edit Details

2. Click Edit Details.

3. Scroll through the Edit Resource page, which shows the resource's contact information, assignment attributes, and availability dates, as well as the contents of any custom fields that have been designed.

   By default, executive privileges do not include the ability to edit resource information. However, if you need that capability, talk with your project server administrator.

4. If you selected multiple resources, when you're finished with the first resource, click the Save And Continue button.

   The Edit Resource page for your second selected resource appears. Continue in this manner until you get to the last resource. On the page for the last resource, click Cancel.

   The Resource Center showing the enterprise resources appears again.

Viewing Resources for Specific Projects

To see the resources assigned to specific projects, use the Project Center, as follows:

1. In the Project Center, click the project name to open the Project Details page.

2. In the View list, click the Resource Summary view or other view that shows the resources that are working on this project (see Figure 24-13).

Project Details: Wingtip Toys Development

O	Unique ID	Resource Name	Group	Max Units	Peak	Standard Rate	Overtime Rate	Cost	Work	Start	Finish
	2	Berry Jo		100%	200%	$38.46/h	$0.00/h	5,230.77	656h	1/29/2007	5/22/2008
	4	Lee Mark		100%	0%	$67.31/h	$0.00/h	$0.00	0h	NA	NA
	5	Mary Baker		100%	200%	$30.00/h	$0.00/h	3,680.00	456h	11/20/2007	2/4/2008
	7	Team Production		100%	0%	$0.00/h	$0.00/h	$0.00	0h	NA	NA
	3	Kevin Wright		100%	100%	$38.46/h	$0.00/h	$307.69	8h	2/7/2008	2/7/2008
	1	Allen Tony		100%	200%	$57.69/h	$0.00/h	4,615.38	600h	1/29/2007	11/15/2007
	6	Monica Brink		100%	200%	$0.00/h	$0.00/h	$0.00	416h	11/16/2007	12/31/2007

Figure 24-13 Apply a resource view to the Project Details page to see the resources on a specific project.

> **Note**
>
> If you want to see the resources assigned to specific projects, you can also open the project in Project Professional and then display the Resource Sheet.

Reviewing Resource Assignments

To review resource assignments, follow these steps:

1. In the Resource Center, select the check box next to the name of the resource whose assignments you want to see.

If you want to see assignments for multiple resources at once, select the check boxes for all of them.

🖼️ **View Assignments**

2. Click View Assignments.

The Resource Assignments page appears (see Figure 24-14). In a Gantt chart format, the assignments for the selected resources are listed, grouped by resource name and then by project name.

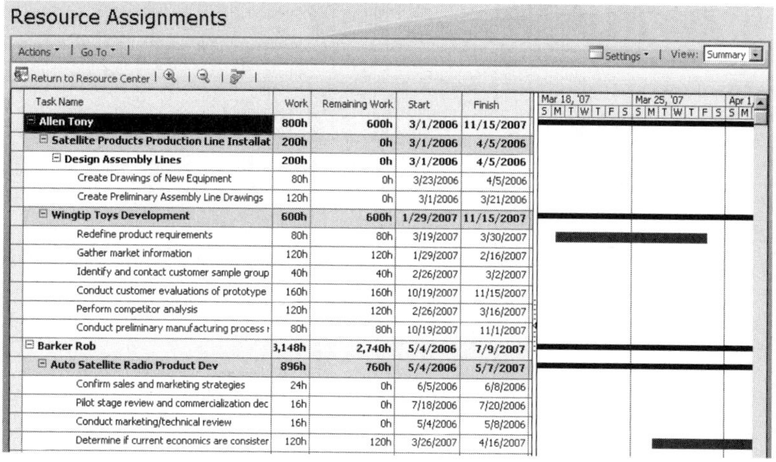

Figure 24-14 The assignments for the selected resources appear on the Resource Assignments page.

3. Scroll through the table and the chart to view the information you want.

🖼️ **Return To Resource Center**

4. When finished, click Return To Resource Center.

Reviewing Resource Availability

To review resource availability, follow these steps:

1. In the Resource Center, select the check box next to the name of the resource whose availability you want to see.

    If you want to see availability for multiple resources, select the check boxes for all of them.

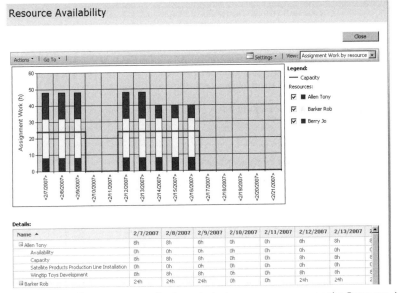

View Availability

2. Click View Availability.

    The Resource Availability page appears. The availability, as measured by work amounts over time, is drawn in a column chart for each selected resource (see Figure 24-15). Availability and capacity information are shown for each resource in a table below the chart.

Figure 24-15 The assignments for the selected resources appear on the Resource Assignments page.

3. If you want to hide a resource's availability information, clear the check box next to the resource's name in the legend. Select the check box to show the availability information again.

4. Click the View box for other ways to see resource availability, including Assignment Work By Project, Remaining Availability, and Work.

5. When finished, click Close.

    The Resource Center appears again.

Reviewing Resource Plans

With a resource plan, project managers and resource managers can estimate potential resource requirements associated with proposals or activity plans. A resource plan can also define the general use of resources if they're being used as part of a small task-only project described by an activity plan. You can review resource plans if you want to see how resources are being used for other nonproject activities.

For more information about resource plans, see the section titled "Creating a Resource Plan" in Chapter 22.

> **Note**
>
> By default, executive privileges do not include the ability to create or edit resource plans. However, if you need that capability, talk with your project server administrator.

To see a resource plan, follow these steps:

1. On the Quick Launch task bar, under Projects, click Proposals And Activities.

2. On the Proposals And Activities page, click somewhere in the row of a proposal or activity plan to select it. Don't click its name, or the proposal or activity plan will open.

3. Click Resource Plan.

   The resource plan for the selected proposal or activity plan appears.

4. When finished, click Close.

Resource Plan

Requesting and Responding to Status Reports

Suppose you want project managers or portfolio managers on your staff to submit narrative status reports to you every Monday morning so that you can be prepared with information for your Monday afternoon executive cabinet meeting. You can create and submit a status report format with the topics you need, for example, "Major Accomplishments," "Upcoming Milestones," and "Potential Problems."

In their home page Reminders section, your staff members are notified to submit their status reports on time. Their responses are compiled into a single report that you can then print or export to a Microsoft Office Word document.

Requesting a Status Report

To set up a narrative status report format, follow these steps:

1. In Project Web Access, under Resources, click Status Reports.

2. Under Requests, click New, New Request.

   The Status Report Request page appears (see Figure 24-16).

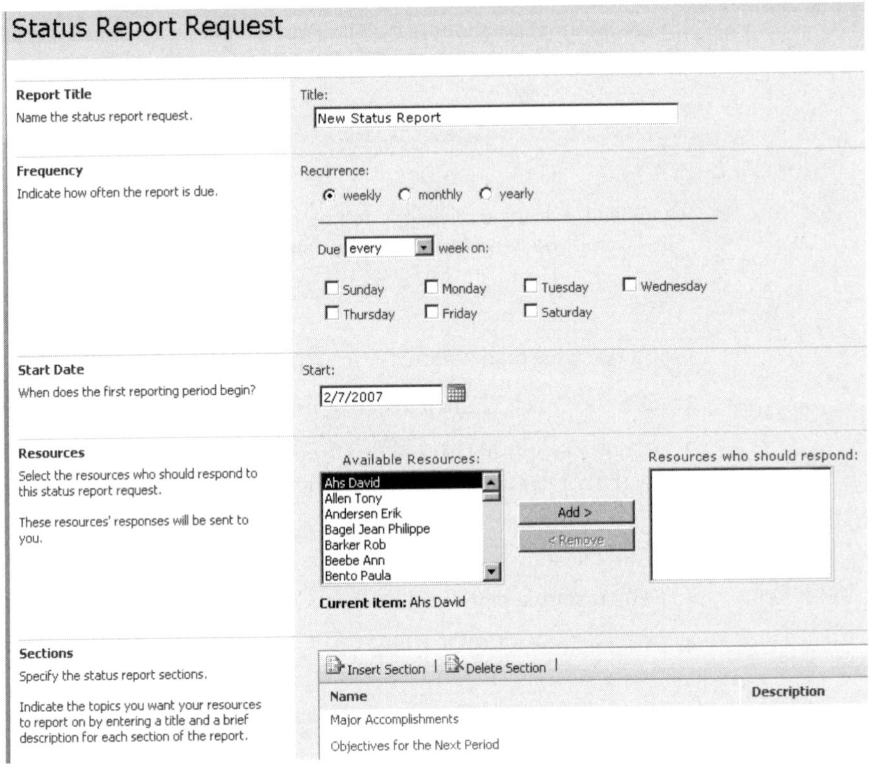

Figure 24-16 Use the Status Report Request page to design a narrative periodic status report.

3. Work through the page to specify the design and frequency of your status report.

4. In the Resources area, select the individuals who are to receive this status report request and who will be responsible for submitting the status reports.

5. In the Sections area, specify the headings under which your resources will report. To add a new heading, click Insert Section. A new row opens up. Click in the row and type the heading you want. To remove a heading, click it and then click Delete Section.

6. When finished, click Send.

Insert Section

Delete Section

The status report request, details and schedule are submitted to the selected resources. They will see reminders on their home page about status reports coming due. Their Status Reports page will present the name of the status report.

When it's time for your resources to submit status reports, they'll click the name of your status report and complete the page. The page includes a box for each of the sections you identified in your request (see Figure 24-17).

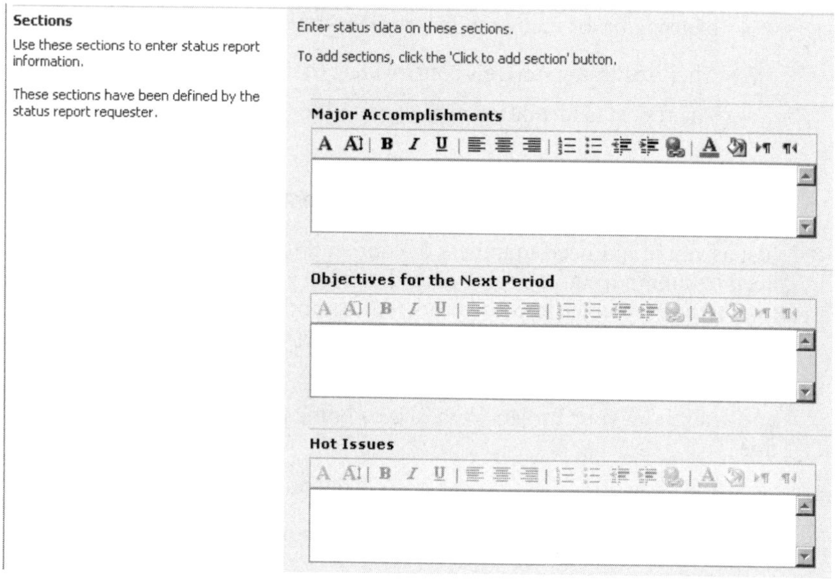

Figure 24-17 A box appears for each status report section you specified in your request.

Resources can add extra sections and send unrequested status reports outside the normal schedule if they want.

You request the status report only once—when you first set it up with a specified time period and frequency. Resources see automated reminders on their Project Web Access home page whenever a status report is coming due.

Reviewing the Compiled Status Report

The project server automatically merges the status reports from all resources for a given time period. To review the combined status reports, follow these steps:

1. In Project Web Access, under Resources, click Status Reports.

2. Under Requests, click the name of the status report whose responses you want to review.

    The View Responses page appears.

3. To specify the time period of status reports you want to see, set the dates in the View Status Reports From boxes and then click Apply.

4. Under Group Merged Reports By, select whether you want the merged report to be grouped by resource name or response date.

Open

5. Click the Open button.

The merged status report appears. The responses from each resource are grouped under the section headings you identified.

Export To Word

6. If you want to include the status report in an Microsoft Office Word document for printing or for inclusion in a project status report, click Export To Word.

7. Click Yes in the ActiveX control alert that appears.

The report is formatted and exported to Word. You can save it or print it from there.

Responding to a Status Report Request

Just as you might need members of your staff to submit status reports to you, you might need to submit a status report periodically to your manager. During the designated time periods, you write your status reports and submit them to the project server. When everyone's status reports are in, your manager can review the compiled status report.

After your manager first sets up the status report, you'll see an automated reminder notification on your Project Web Access home page whenever a status report is coming due.

To create and submit your status report, follow these steps:

1. On the Quick Launch task bar, under Resources, click Status Reports.

The Status Reports page appears, showing a table of status reports for different projects (see Figure 24-18).

Responses

Responses are all Status Reports you need to submit that have been previously requested from your manager or another resource.

Actions ▾ | Go To ▾ |

Submit Unrequested Report |

Title ▴	Due to	Due on
Initiative 22 Status	Osborn Stu	2/9/2007
Wingtip Toys Status Report	Osborn Stu	4/6/2007

Figure 24-18 The table on the Status Reports page shows all your different status report requests, which manager receives them, and when the next one is due.

2. In the table, click the name of the status report you want to write.

The Status Report Response page appears.

3. Change fields in the To and Period sections if needed.

4. In the Sections area, type your status report in the boxes provided.

The headings of the boxes reflect the topics that your manager wants all resources to report on for each status report.

5. If you want to add another section of information, click the Click To Add Section button. Type a title for the section and then click OK. In the new box, enter your additional information.

6. If you just want to save your report and update the project server later, click Save.

    Clicking Save is useful if you're not quite finished with your status report, or if it's not time to submit the report yet. It's a good idea to enter status information whenever you have a significant accomplishment or encounter a possible blocking problem. Then when the status report comes due, you'll have most of your information in place already.

7. When you're ready to submit your status report to the project server and your manager, click Send.

    Your status report is submitted to the project server. The project server automatically merges your status report with those from the other resources for the same time period.

Submit
Unrequested
Report

You can also send a status report that's separate from the normal status report format or to a different resource. You can specify your own status report title, the resources who should receive the status report, and which sections it should contain. To do this, on the Status Reports page, click Submit Unrequested Report. Complete the fields on the Unrequested Status Report page. In the Sections area, click the Click To Add Section button. Type a title for the section and then click OK. In the new box, enter your additional information.

Analyzing and Reporting on Project Information

One of the primary capabilities of the Project Server enterprise features is that it can show information about all projects, tasks, resources, and assignments in the entire enterprise. Although it's great to have all this data available, it's not practical to review the details of every project throughout the organization. However, it's highly advantageous to see a high-level summary of project schedules, costs, and resource utilization. It's also helpful to be able to roll information from multiple projects together and to make comparisons between them.

Using the Data Analysis services available in Project Server, you can analyze schedule performance or resource utilization for a single project, multiple projects, or even all projects in the enterprise portfolio. Such analysis can provide a wealth of usable information, from whether you're spending too much on material and equipment costs to whether it would make good business sense to follow through on your proposal for a new ambitious project.

Data Analysis dynamically generates reports in Project Web Access that provide summary or detailed project information necessary for a single project or any collection of projects.

Data Analysis is implemented through the use of online analytical processing (OLAP) tools provided by SQL Server Analysis Services and the Cube Building Services in conjunction with Project Server and Project Web Access.

Typically, the project server administrator or portfolio manager first configures the Data Analysis Services and creates the OLAP cubes, or dynamic reports, available to you and other users in the form of a spreadsheet (PivotTable) or column chart (PivotChart). These views are added to the View list of the Data Analysis page for you to select and manipulate. You can add, move, or delete fields in the resulting PivotTable or Pivot-Chart.

For more information about how the OLAP cubes are built by the project server administrator, see the section titled "Setting Up Project Report Cubes for Data Analysis" in Chapter 21.

When you want to see a PivotTable or PivotChart that analyzes various aspects of current enterprise project, resource, or portfolio data, follow these steps:

1. On the Quick Launch task bar, click Data Analysis.

   Data Analysis

   If you're working in Project Professional, you can open the Data Analysis page from there. Click Collaborate, Data Analysis. Or, on the Collaborate toolbar, click Data Analysis. The Project Web Access Data Analysis Updates page appears in your Project Professional workspace.

2. In the View box, click the view you want to use.

3. To change the fields used in the view, click Show Field List. Drag the fields you want from the list onto the appropriate areas of the view, as follows:

   Show Field List

   ❑ Drag a field you want for a PivotTable column into the area labeled Drop Filter Fields here.

   ❑ Drag a field you want for a PivotTable row into the area labeled Drop Row Fields Here.

   ❑ Drag a field you want for the Y-axis on a PivotChart to the area labeled Drop Filter Fields Here.

   ❑ Drag a field you want for the X-axis on a PivotChart to the area labeled Drop Category Fields Here.

The following are more methods for manipulating how you view the information in your PivotTable or PivotChart:

Expand

- Click Expand to increase the level of detail in the view.

Collapse

- Click Collapse to decrease the level of detail in the view.

Save

- Click Save PivotTable As Image to save the PivotTable as a GIF graphics image for use elsewhere, for example, in a Word report document.

- Click Save PivotChart As Image to save the PivotChart as a GIF graphics image for use elsewhere, for example, in a Microsoft Office PowerPoint presentation.

Get more options for manipulating your view with the PivotTable toolbar. Click Settings, View Options. In the pane that appears, select the Show PivotTable Toolbar. The PivotTable toolbar appears.

🔲
Help

For more information about working with PivotTables and PivotCharts, click the Help button on the PivotTable toolbar. Categories of topics include "Getting Started," "Using PivotTable List Tools," "Adding and Removing Fields," and "Filtering Data."

Work with your project server administrator or portfolio manager to learn how best to use the OLAP cubes that have been set up. Also let them know if you need different cubes designed that will help you analyze project and portfolio information in the way you need.

Setting Your Alerts and Reminders

Project Web Access provides tools to add a layer of efficiency to your project activities. You can set up automated notifications so that you can receive e-mail and see reminders about approvals, status reports, issues, and risks.

To configure automated e-mail alerts and Project Web Access home page reminders to yourself, follow these steps:

1. On the Quick Launch task bar, click Personal Settings.

2. Click Manage My Alerts And Reminders.

3. Review the options in the Tasks and Status Reports sections. Select the check boxes and make further specifications for the events for which you want to be notified via e-mail (Task Alerts) and see reminders on the Project Web Access home page (Task Reminders).

   Clear the check boxes for events for which you do not want an e-mail notification or reminder.

   You can set up notification and reminder options for upcoming tasks, status reports, and more.

4. When finished, click Save.

PART 8

Customizing and Managing Project Files

CHAPTER 25

Customizing Your View of
Project Information 897

CHAPTER 26

Customizing the Microsoft Project
Interface 967

CHAPTER 27

Automating Your Work with Macros 987

CHAPTER 28

Standardizing Projects Using
Templates 1003

CHAPTER 29

Managing Project Files 1021

Customizing Views 898
Customizing Tables 928
Customizing Fields 931
Working with Outline Codes 941

Customizing Groups 948
Customizing Filters 952
Sharing Customized Elements Among Projects 961

Organizations are as unique as people, and each project that an organization manages has its own particular needs. Each step in managing a project requires a specific set of information, as does responding to each new challenge that arises. In Microsoft Office Project 2007, you can control what information you see and how it is formatted, as well as whether to satisfy your own preferences or meet the specialized needs of a particular project or situation. Almost every aspect of viewing information in Office Project 2007 can be molded to your specifications, including the following:

- Views
- Tables
- Fields
- Groups
- Filters

You can also customize text-based and visual reports. For more information, see Chapter 12, "Reporting Project Information."

If you use codes to categorize information, such as accounting codes to assign tasks to lines in a budget or skill codes to identify resources, in Microsoft Project, customized outline codes can fulfill this purpose. You can adapt these codes to your organization's standards; apply them to project tasks and resources; and then use them to sort, group, or filter information.

When you customize Microsoft Project, you can choose to keep your customizations in one project or make them available to every project you create. In addition, with the Organizer, you can manage customized elements and copy them to share with others. This chapter describes how to customize all these features and use them in your projects.

Customizing Views

The right perspective on the right data can simplify your project management tasks, uncover potential problems, or show the way to potential solutions. Each view in Microsoft Project gives you a different perspective on project information. You don't have to stick with the views that come with the program. You can specify the views you want to see, change the tables and fields that a view displays, and control the organization and appearance of information to inspect your project information the way you want. Project 2007 introduces one additional way to customize views—Background Cell Highlighting. With this new feature, you can apply highlight colors or patterns to the cells in the view tables, similar to highlighting cells in a Microsoft Office Excel spreadsheet, for example, to make key tasks stand out.

For more information about working with built-in Microsoft Project views, see the section titled "Using Views" in Chapter 4, "Viewing Project Information."

Changing the Content of a View

Microsoft Project comes with numerous standard views that present task, resource, and assignment information. When these standard views don't meet your needs, you can customize their content or create new views that are more suitable. For example, if you like to take into account the amount of work that tasks require, you can change your Gantt Chart view to show a table with the Work field. In single-pane views, you can specify which screen, table, group, and filter to apply when the view appears. For combination views, you can designate the views that appear in the top and bottom pane.

> **Note**
>
> Even though views such as the Gantt Chart and Task Usage view are made up of two panes, one on the left and one on the right, they're still considered single-pane views.

> **Note**
>
> If you plan to use new tables, groups, or filters in a view, you must create those elements before you use them in a customized view. You must also create new single-pane views before you can include them in a combination view.
>
> For elements that already exist, it doesn't matter whether you customize them or assign them to customized views first.

To customize the content of an existing single-pane view—for example, the Gantt Chart, Resource Sheet, or Task Usage view—do the following:

1. Click View, More Views.

2. In the More Views dialog box, in the Views list, click the view's name (see Figure 25-1).

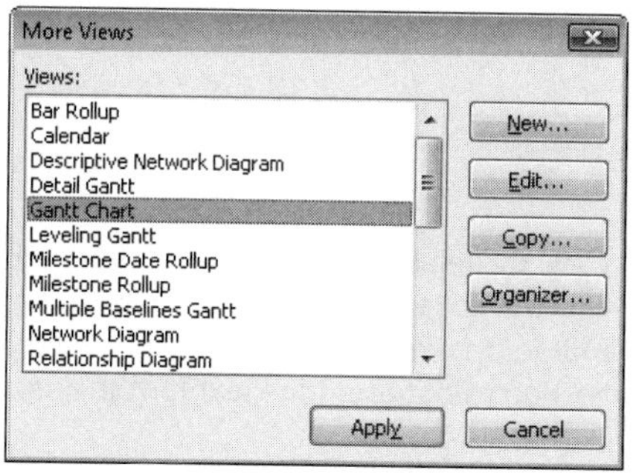

Figure 25-1 You can edit an existing view, copy an existing view, or create a completely new view.

3. Click the Edit button. The View Definition dialog box appears (see Figure 25-2). If you want to create a new view that is similar to the selected view, click the Copy button and type a new name in the Name box.

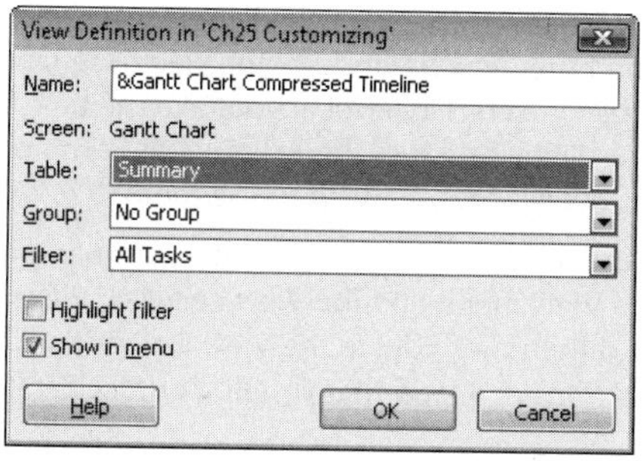

Figure 25-2 You choose a table, group, and filter when you customize a single-pane view.

Note

When you edit an existing single-pane view, the View Definition dialog box displays the screen used, such as Gantt Chart, but you can't modify it. When you create a new single-pane view from scratch, you can choose which type of screen to use.

4. In the Table box, click the table you want to appear in the customized view.

5. In the Group box, click the group you want to use.

    If you don't require a group, choose No Group.

6. In the Filter box, click the filter you want to apply.

    If you don't want a filter, choose All Tasks or All Resources (for a task or resource view, respectively).

Note

When you apply a filter to a view, by default, Microsoft Project hides the tasks or resources that don't meet the filter's criteria. If you want the view to show all tasks or resources, but emphasize the filtered tasks, select the Highlight Filter check box. This setting displays all tasks and resources but uses blue text for the ones that pass the filter tests.

INSIDE OUT   Tired of clicking More Views?

By default, the View menu and the View bar include the views used most frequently by the majority of Microsoft Project users. However, if you take the time to customize views or simply prefer other standard views such as the Task Details Form, you might get tired of clicking View, More Views every time you want to use them.

Fortunately, the views that appear on the View menu and View bar are within your control. To include a view on the View menu and the View bar, click View, More Views. Click the view you want to add and then click Edit. In the View Definition dialog box, select the Show In Menu check box. To remove a view that you don't use, clear its Show In Menu check box.

You can also modify the order in which views appear, for example, to relegate the Network Diagram to the bottom of the list while placing your customized Gantt Chart at the top. By default, task views appear first and in alphabetical order, followed by resource views in alphabetical order. In the More Views dialog box, click the view you want to move and then click Edit. In the Name box, add a number in front of the name to move it to the top of its respective list. If you precede all the displayed views with sequential numbers, the views will appear in numerical order.

Differentiating customized views from standard ones can help you select the view you want. For example, if you add the prefix C- at the beginning of the names of customized views, the View menu and View bar automatically segregate your customized and standard views.

To customize the content of an existing combination view—for example, the Task Entry view or Resource Allocation view—follow these steps:

1. Click View, More Views.

2. In the More Views dialog box, in the Views list, click the view's name.

3. To change the existing view, click the Edit button.

   To create a new view based on the existing view, click the Copy button. In the View Definition dialog box, in the Name box, type a new name for the view.

4. In the Top box, click the view that you want to appear in the top pane (see Figure 25-3).

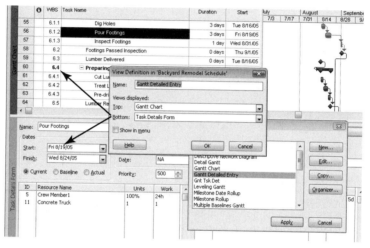

Figure 25-3 For combination views, you specify which single-pane views appear in the top and bottom panes.

5. In the Bottom box, click the view that you want to appear in the bottom pane.

INSIDE OUT   Change the table and view definition

When you're using a view, and you alter the table that is displayed, you have also altered the table in the definition of that view. This means the new table appears the next time you display that view. However, applying a group or filter to a view does not change the group or filter selected in the View Definition dialog box. The view steadfastly uses the group and filter you chose when you customized the view.

Creating a New View

If none of the existing views come close to meeting your needs, you can craft an entirely new single pane or combination view. To do this, follow these steps:

1. Click View, More Views.

2. In the More Views dialog box, click New.

3. In the Define New View dialog box, select either the Single View or Combination View option and then click OK.

   The View Definition dialog box for the type of view you selected appears and fills in the Name box with a default name, such as View 1.

4. If you are creating a new single-pane view, in the View Definition dialog box, choose the type of screen you prefer—a built-in view or form such as Gannt Chart or Task Form.

   When you customize a single-pane view, the View Definition dialog box displays the type of screen, but you can't modify it.

5. Specify the rest of the contents of the view, as described in the previous section, "Changing the Content of a View."

Apply a View Quickly

Keyboard fans can choose a view from the View menu by assigning a keyboard shortcut. In the View Definition dialog box for the view, type an ampersand (&) before the letter in the view name that you want to use for the shortcut and then save the customized view.

When you want to use your keyboard shortcut, press Alt+V to open the View menu and then press the shortcut letter to apply the view. This works for built-in views as well as your custom views.

Use a different letter for each keyboard shortcut. If you choose a letter that is already in use by another menu entry, you might have to press the letter more than once to apply the view you want.

Changing the Font for a View

By default, the font used throughout the Microsoft Project views is 8-point Arial. If your reading glasses nudge you toward a different font or larger size for text, you can adjust both the font and size for one or more elements in a particular view. To select the elements to change and the font and size to use, follow these steps:

1. Click Format, Text Styles.

2. To change the text characteristics for all text, in the Item To Change box, be sure that All is selected.

   This changes the font for all text elements in the current view in this project, including column and row headings, Gantt bar text, and all field data such as task and resource names. If you want to change the text for a specific element, such as Summary Tasks, in the Item To Change box, click the element.

3. In the Font list, choose the font you want.

4. To apply bold or italic to the text, in the Font Style list, choose the formatting you want.

5. In the Size list, choose the font size for the text.

   You can also apply a color to the text, which can emphasize important tasks. For instance, you might apply a bright blue or maroon color to the text for critical tasks so that they stand out in the task list as well as in the Gantt Chart.

6. To apply the changes, click OK.

INSIDE OUT   No way to set an overall default font style

Suppose you have used the Text Styles dialog box to apply specific fonts to row and column titles in the Gantt Chart view, another style to milestone tasks, and yet another to critical tasks. When you switch from the Gantt Chart to the Task Usage view, you find that the fonts revert to their default style in that view.

Text styles apply only to the current view in the current project. If you want those text styles to appear in other views, you need to make the same changes in each view in which you want them to appear.

If you take the time to make all those text style changes, you can increase the benefit by making them available to all your projects. To do this, use the Organizer to copy your modified views to the global template (global.mpt).

For information about copying views to the global template for use in other projects, see the section titled "Copying Customized Elements" later in this chapter.

Formatting a Gantt Chart View

The chart portion on the right side of the Gantt Chart view provides a graphical representation of your project schedule. You can emphasize information in your schedule by formatting individual Gantt bars or all Gantt bars of a certain type. Similarly, you can apply formatting to different categories of text or only to the text that is selected. Link lines and gridlines communicate important schedule information, but for high-level views, they might get in the way. Gantt Chart layout options and formatting for gridlines control how much you see of these elements.

> ### Quick Formatting with the Gantt Chart Wizard
>
> There's an easy way to format the primary elements in a Gantt Chart view. The Gantt Chart Wizard steps you through settings that specify the information you see in your Gantt Chart and how the elements are formatted. You can choose a standard type of Gantt Chart such as Critical Path or Baseline, choose from several predefined Gantt Chart styles, or create a custom Gantt Chart.
>
> If you opt for a customized Gantt Chart, you can control which types of Gantt bars appear and customize the color, pattern, and end shapes for each type. The customized settings in the Gantt Chart Wizard include whether to display resources and dates on the taskbars, exactly which fields to display, and whether to show or hide the link lines between dependent tasks.

Formatting the Appearance of Gantt Bars

The shape, fill pattern, and color of individual bars or types of Gantt bars are customizable. You can also customize the marks that appear at the beginning and end of those bars. For example, you can change the mark that designates milestone tasks, add color to summary task bars, or accentuate critical tasks that aren't complete by making them red with red stars at each end of task bars.

To change the appearance of all Gantt bars of a particular type, follow these steps:

1. Click View and then click the Gantt Chart view whose bars you want to customize.

   Your modifications will apply only to the Gantt bars in this specific Gantt Chart view.

2. Click Format, Bar Styles.

   The Bar Styles dialog box lists all the Gantt bar types for the current view with the settings for their appearance (see Figure 25-4). For example, Gantt bars appear blue for normal tasks, whereas summary Gantt bars are solid black with black end marks at both ends.

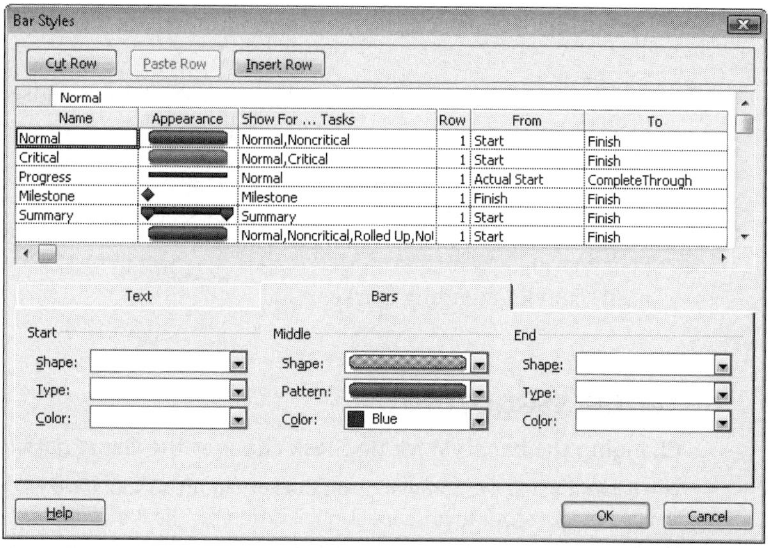

Figure 25-4 You can customize the appearance of the Gantt bar as well as markers at its start and end.

> **Note**
>
> The quickest way to open the Bar Styles dialog box is by double-clicking the background in the right pane of a Gantt chart view.

3. To select the Gantt bar to format, click its name in the table.

4. Click the Bars tab and then make the changes you want to the Start, Middle, and End of the bar.

   The settings for the start and end determine the appearance of the markers at the beginning and end of the bar, whereas the settings for the middle control the appearance of the bar itself.

5. For the start and end, begin with the Shape box and choose the mark to add to the start or end of the bar, such as the downward pointing arrows for summary tasks. Then, in the Type box, choose whether the mark should be a solid color, framed with a line, or outlined with a dashed line. Finally, choose the color for the mark.

6. For the bar itself, under the Middle heading, choose the shape of the bar, such as a full rectangle for regular tasks or a half-height rectangle to show progress. In the Pattern and Color boxes, select the pattern and color for the bar.

   For solid colors, in the Pattern box, choose the solid black entry.

To change the pattern, color, and shape of the Gantt bars for individual tasks (rather than all tasks of a particular type), do the following:

1. In the sheet portion of the view, click the task or tasks whose Gantt bars you want to change.

2. Click Format, Bar.

3. In the Format Bar dialog box, click the Bar Shape tab.

4. Make the changes you want to the Start (beginning marker), Middle (the bar itself), and End (ending marker).

TROUBLESHOOTING

Changing the bar style for one task changes the Gantt bars for all tasks

The Bar and Bar Styles commands on the Format menu sound similar and even perform similar functions, but their scope is quite different. The Bar command applies the changes you make to only the tasks that are currently selected. The Bar Styles command applies changes to all Gantt bars of a particular type, for example, critical tasks, incomplete tasks, or milestones.

This distinction is analogous to changing the formatting in a word processing document. You can select an individual paragraph and change the formatting to Arial 14, Bold. But if you want all headings to use this formatting, you can save time by creating a style and applying it to each heading paragraph.

Creating a Gantt Bar

In addition to changing the styles of Gantt bars, you can also define new types of Gantt bars. For example, if you use the Marked field to flag high-risk tasks, you can set up a special bar style to show marked tasks in lime green. To format your own type of bar, follow these steps:

1. Apply a Gantt Chart view.

2. Click Format, Bar Styles.

3. Scroll to the end of the list of Gantt bar types and click in the first blank row.

   If you want to insert the new Gantt bar type earlier in the list, click the row immediately below where you want to insert the type and then click Insert Row. Microsoft Project inserts a blank row above the selected row.

4. In the Name field, type the name of your new Gantt bar.

5. Click the cell in the Show For ... Tasks column.

6. Click the down arrow in the box and then click the category of task for which this bar should be displayed. For example, if you're creating a style for tasks that are not finished, click Not Finished.

> **Note**
>
> If you want a Gantt bar style to appear when a task satisfies more than one condition, click the first condition, type a comma, and then click the second condition, such as Critical, Not Finished. You can also create a Gantt bar that appears when a condition is not true. Type Not in front of a selected task condition, such as Not Milestone or Critical, Not In Progress.

7. In the From and To columns, click the date fields that determine the beginning and end of the Gantt bar. For example, you might draw a progress bar from the Start date to the Complete Through date, or a bar from the Actual Start date to the Deadline date for critical tasks that aren't yet finished.

8. Click the Bars tab and then specify the appearance for the Start, Middle, and End of the bar.

9. If you want to display text on the bar, click the Text tab and then click the box for the position where you want text to appear for the Gantt bar, such Left, Top, or Inside.

10. Click the down arrow in the box and then click the name of the task field whose content you want to appear for this Gantt bar type.

> **Note**
>
> If you want to call attention to tasks that don't meet any of the task conditions listed in the Show For... Tasks field, you can create a new bar style that applies only to marked or flagged tasks. When you set a task's Marked field or the appropriate flag field to Yes, its Gantt bar appears in that bar style.
>
> You can add the Marked field to the sheet portion of your Gantt chart and then set the value to Yes for each task you want to mark. If you are already using the Marked field, insert a column for one of the custom flag fields, such as Flag1, and set it to Yes for those tasks. In the Bar Styles dialog box, create a new bar style to specify the bar appearance and associated text for marked or flagged tasks.

TROUBLESHOOTING

A Gantt bar doesn't appear in the chart

Gantt chart views display bars in the order that they appear in the Bar Styles dialog box. If Gantt bar styles with a narrower shape, such as progress bars, appear above the full-height Gantt bars in the list, the wider Gantt bars hide the narrower ones.

To see all the bars, be sure to rearrange the order so narrower Gantt bars appear below the wider ones in the Bar Styles list.

INSIDE OUT   **Stack the Gantt bars**

Some tasks meet the conditions for several types of Gantt bars. For example, suppose that you have set multiple baselines and want to use the Multiple Baselines Gantt view to review trends in baseline dates. If you create a bar style for each baseline, Microsoft Project draws a Gantt bar for the task for each condition that it satisfies—in this example, for each baseline it contains.

Because multiple bars are likely to overlap each other, you can make them all visible at the same time by stacking up to four Gantt bars, one above the next. To do this, in the Bar Styles dialog box, in the Row field, specify 1, 2, 3, or 4 to indicate the position for that bar style in the stack.

Formatting the Appearance of Gantt Bar Text

Displaying task field values next to Gantt bars makes it easy to correlate task information with bars in the chart. In addition, displaying text next to Gantt bars might reduce the number of columns needed in the sheet portion of the Gantt chart, leaving more room on the screen to show the chart portion of the view.

To specify the text for all Gantt bars of a particular type, follow these steps:

1. Click Format, Bar Styles.
2. Click the name of the Gantt bar type whose text you want to change.
3. Click the Text tab.
4. Click the box for the position, such as Left or Right, at which you want the text to appear for the Gantt bar type.
5. Click the down arrow in the box and then click the name of the task field whose content you want to appear for this Gantt bar type (see Figure 25-5).

    For example, if you want the percentage of completion to appear to the right of the Gantt bar, click the Right box, click the down arrow, and then click % Complete. To remove text from a position, select the box for that position and then press Backspace.

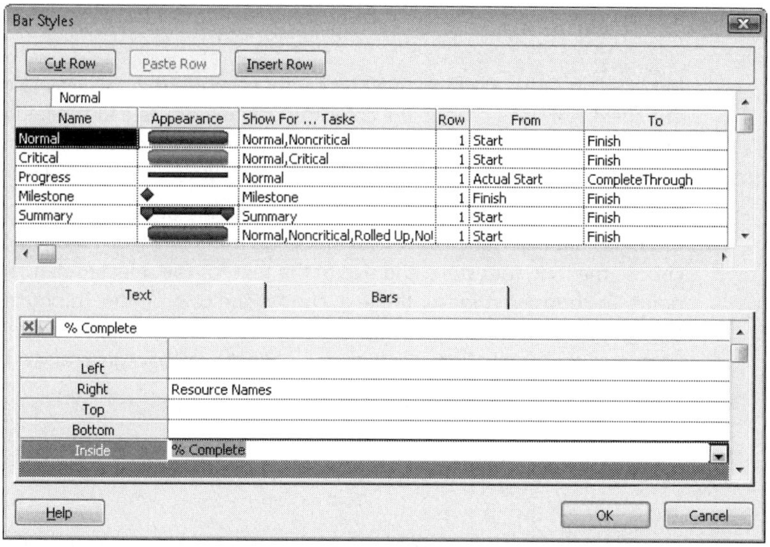

Figure 25-5 You can display project information to the left, right, top, bottom, and inside of Gantt bars by specifying fields to display as text.

6. When you're done, click OK to close the Bar Styles dialog box.

To change the text accompanying the Gantt bar for selected tasks, do the following:

1. In the sheet portion of the view, click the task or tasks whose Gantt bar text you want to change.

2. Click Format, Bar and then click the Bar Text tab in the Format Bar dialog box.

3. On the Bar Text tab, click the box for the position—such as Left, Right, Top, or Bottom—where you want the text to appear for the Gantt bar.

4. Click the down arrow to the right of the box and then click the name of the task field whose content you want to appear for this Gantt bar.

Although you can change the text position and content for individual Gantt bars, you can't change the font, style, or color of the text. Fortunately, you can change the text style for all Gantt bars of a particular type or the text style for the text at a specific position on a bar by performing the following steps:

1. Click Format, Text Styles.

2. In the Item To Change box, click the type of task whose text style you want to change.

   For example, if you want the text accompanying all critical tasks to be 16-point, red type, start by clicking Critical Tasks in the Item To Change box. To specify the text style for text at a specific position on all bars, in the Item To Change box, choose the position, such as Bar Text - Left or Bar Text - Inside.

3. Make the changes you want in the Font, Font Style, Size, and Color boxes.

Highlight the Background in Cells

In Microsoft Office Project 2003 and earlier versions, the only way to emphasize tasks in a sheet view is to change the color for task text or use a filter that highlights tasks. In Project 2007, you can now revise the background color of cells, for example, by choosing a light red background color to make critical tasks in a table stand out.

In the Text Styles dialog box, in the Item To Change drop-down list, choose the category of task to highlight, such as critical tasks, summary tasks, or changed cells. You can choose the font, font style, and size of the text for the selected item, such as Arial Italic 8-point. To choose a color for the text, choose the color in the Color drop-down list. Then, to highlight the cell background, in the Background Color drop-down list, choose the color you want, and Microsoft Project highlights cell backgrounds with that color.

Note

The Text Styles command on the Format menu formats the text for tasks of a particular type (such as critical tasks) or all text at the same position on all bars (such as text at the left end of all Gantt bars). To change the attributes of only the selected text, use the Font command instead. Click Format, Font and then choose the font, font style, size, and color.

Formatting the Layout of Gantt Bars

Link lines between dependent tasks show how tasks relate to each other. However, too many link lines can obscure the very information you are trying to communicate. If the schedule is too cluttered, you might want to modify the appearance of link lines, the height of Gantt bars, or whether splits and rolled-up bars are displayed. To change the layout of links and bars in a Gantt chart, do the following:

1. Click Format, Layout.

2. In the Layout dialog box, select the option for how you want the links between dependent tasks to appear.

   For example, you can hide the link lines, draw them as S shapes between the ends of tasks, or display them as L shapes from the end of one task to the top of another task.

3. If you display date fields on Gantt bars, choose a date format to use.

   For example, to keep text for dates to a minimum, choose a format that shows only the numeric month and day. If time or day of week is important, choose a format with these elements shown.

4. If you want to make Gantt bars thicker or thinner, in the Bar Height box, choose a number between 6 and 24, with 12 being the default thickness.

5. Choose other layout options to roll up Gantt bars, draw the bar length in increments of whole days, or show splits.

   For example, you typically want to select the Always Roll Up Gantt Bars check box so that summary tasks display information about their subordinate tasks. If you are fine-tuning your project schedule, you might want to view where splits occur or see the duration of tasks down to the hour.

Formatting the Appearance of Gridlines

Gridlines separate elements such as columns and rows in the sheet portion of a Gantt chart, or the dates and tasks in the chart portion. For example, you might want to add horizontal lines to the chart to help correlate Gantt bars with their associated tasks in the sheet portion. To change the gridlines in a Gantt chart, follow these steps:

1. Click Format, Gridlines.

2. In the Line To Change box, click the element for the gridlines you want to add, remove, or change.

3. Elements for both the sheet portion and chart portion of the Gantt chart appear in the Line To Change list.

   The current style appears in the Normal area.

4. In the Normal section, change the line type in the Type box and the color in the Color box.

5. If you want to display lines at certain intervals, such as after every fourth item, click the interval in the At Interval section.

> For information about modifying the timescale in the Gantt chart, see the section titled "Modifying the Timescale" later in this chapter.

Change the Format of a View

Formatting changes that you make within a view apply only to the active view. For example, modifications you make to bar or text styles, individual Gantt bars, or text formatting in the Tracking Gantt appear only when you display the Tracking Gantt. Although this separation means that you must repeat formatting in each view that you want to modify, the advantage is that you can customize the formatting for any view without worrying about modifying others.

Changes you make to views in one project file apply only to that project file. When you create a new project file, it uses the default views.

> If you want to make customized views available to other project files, see the section titled "Sharing Customized Elements Among Projects" later in this chapter.

Modifying a Network Diagram

Network diagrams display tasks as boxes, or nodes, with link lines showing the task dependencies. Because a network diagram doesn't include a task sheet like the Gantt chart, it's important to choose wisely when you select the fields that you want to appear inside the boxes. In addition, you can customize the appearance of the boxes and how they are arranged within the diagram.

Formatting the Content and Appearance of Boxes

Boxes in a network diagram are the equivalent of Gantt bars in a Gantt chart, so it should be no surprise that can change the appearance of boxes in a network diagram depending on the task type. Similar to selecting the fields that appear around or inside Gantt bars, the task fields that appear inside network diagram boxes are customizable as well.

To change the appearance and content for all boxes of a particular type, do the following:

1. Click View, Network Diagram.

2. Click Format, Box Styles.

   The Box Styles dialog box lists all the box types for the current view and the settings for their appearance (see Figure 25-6).

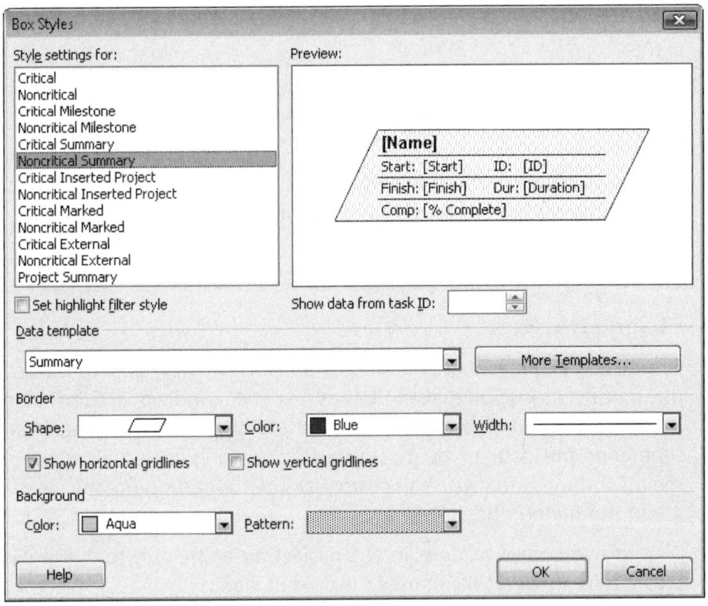

Figure 25-6 You can customize the appearance of a network diagram box as well as specify what task information appears inside each box.

3. To customize a specific type of box, click its name in the Style Settings For list.

4. To change the fields that appear within the box, in the Data Template box, click a data template.

    The Preview area shows the box with the fields that the selected data template specifies.

> **Note**
>
> To show exactly the fields you want, you can modify or create new data templates for the boxes in a network diagram. For example, you might want to include a custom field in a data template. Templates can contain fields that display graphical indicators.
>
> To modify or create a template, click More Templates, click a template name, and then click Edit or Copy. To create a new template, click New. To insert a field into the data template, in the Choose Cells section, click the cell where you want to insert the field, click the down arrow, and then click the name of the field in the list.

5. If you wish, in the Border area, change the shape, color, and width of the box border.

6. If you want to display horizontal or vertical gridlines between the fields inside a box, select the Show Horizontal Gridlines and Show Vertical Gridlines check boxes.

7. If you want a color or pattern other than the default, choose a background color and pattern.

CAUTION

> Although you can select different colors and patterns for the box background, dark colors make it difficult to read the task information.

To change the displayed fields and border appearance for individual boxes (rather than all boxes showing a particular type of project information), follow these steps:

1. Choose the boxes you want to format in the network diagram.

2. Click Format, Box.

3. In the Data Template box, click the data template you want to use.

    A preview of the box with the selected data template appears.

4. Make the changes you want to the shape, color, and width of the border.

5. Make the changes you want to the background color and pattern for the box.

> **Note**
>
> You can open the Format Box dialog box by double-clicking the border of a box. Double-clicking the background of a network diagram opens the Box Styles dialog box.

Changing the Layout of Boxes

The network diagram is much like a flowchart of the tasks in a project. The layout options for a network diagram control how boxes are positioned and aligned, the distance between the boxes, the appearance of links, and other settings.

To change the layout of a network diagram, do the following:

1. To open the Layout dialog box, click Format, Layout.

2. To position boxes manually by dragging, select the Allow Manual Box Positioning option.

   If you're happy to delegate layout to Microsoft Project, select the Automatically Position All Boxes option. The program uses the settings you choose to reposition the boxes in the network diagram.

3. In the Arrangement box, choose the order in which sequential boxes appear in the diagram.

   For example, you can arrange the boxes from the top left down to the bottom right of the diagram. Another popular choice is Top Down - Critical First, which arranges boxes from the top down but also places critical tasks before others.

4. With the Row and Column boxes, specify the alignment, distance between rows and columns, and the width and height of the boxes.

   The numbers in the Spacing boxes represent the number of pixels between boxes and must be between 0 and 200.

5. In the Link Style section, select how lines should be drawn between boxes, and whether arrows and link labels should be included.

6. If you want to show links in different colors, in the Link Color section, choose the colors you want for your links.

   By default, network diagrams display noncritical links in blue and critical links in red, similar to noncritical and critical bars in a Gantt chart.

> ### Fine-Tune the Display of the Network Diagram
>
> If you select the option to position boxes automatically, it's a good idea to also select the Adjust For Page Breaks check box in the Box Layout section. Otherwise, boxes located across a page break are printed on two pages in the diagram.
>
> Summary tasks are difficult to distinguish in a network diagram, so you might want to clear the Show Summary Tasks check box. If you display summary tasks, it's best to select the Keep Tasks With Their Summaries check box.

Modifying the Resource Graph

The Resource Graph shows resource allocation, cost, or work over periods of time. The horizontal axis represents time, and the vertical axis represents units such as resource availability, cost, or work. In addition to choosing the fields that appear in the graph, you can modify the appearance of bars and text of particular types as well as change the gridlines in the graph. Unlike Gantt charts, you cannot modify the appearance of individual bars or text.

Modifying the Appearance of Resource Graph Bars

The Bar Styles dialog box for the Resource Graph contains six areas, each of which controls the appearance of bars for different sets of information. For example, if you graph overallocations, the two top areas display overallocations, whereas the middle areas display allocations less than or equal to the maximum available units. The bottom areas show proposed assignments.

The areas on the left side of the dialog box control how data for an entire group appears. The areas on the right side of the dialog box control the appearance of data for a single selected resource.

Follow these steps to modify the appearance of Resource Graph bars of a particular type:

1. Click View, Resource Graph.

2. Click Format, Bar Styles.

    Because the bars in the Resource Graph represent information that you don't see in the Gantt chart, the Bar Styles dialog box for the Resource Graph, shown in Figure 25-7, contains a completely different set of choices than the Bar Styles dialog box for Gantt charts.

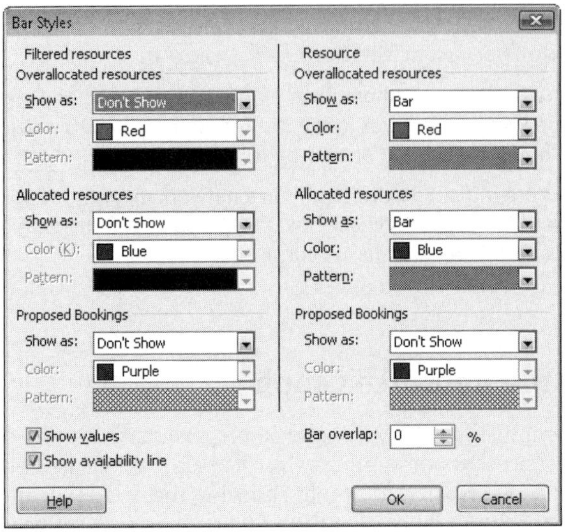

Figure 25-7 The Bar Styles dialog box for the Resource Graph includes choices for presenting allocations for individual resources and groups of resources.

3. In the Bar Styles dialog box, choose the types of data you want to show, for example, allocated resources or proposed bookings.

   For any information you do show, specify the color and pattern for its representative bars.

INSIDE OUT   Determine what the Resource Graph shows

When the Resource Graph appears in the bottom pane below a task view, the graph shows the values for only one resource, but for all tasks to which that resource is assigned. However, when the Resource Graph appears below a resource view or in the top pane, it displays the values for all tasks. It can display the data for one resource or a group of resources, or compare one resource's data to a group's data.

If you want to see the data for only the selected resource, click Don't Show in the Show As box for Filtered Resources. However, if you want to compare the values of the selected resource to other resources in a filter, in the Filtered Resources area, click one of the other graph methods, such as Bar or Step.

By default, the Resource Graph shows overallocations in red and regular assignments in blue, but you can change the methods, colors, or patterns for either. In addition, when you view any of the fields that relate to work or resource availability, you can select the Show Availability Line check box to display resource availability on the graph. Seeing the amount of time that a resource has available is helpful when you are trying to find someone to work on a task, or you want to know how much more you can assign to someone.

Changing the Fields That Appear in the Resource Graph

To choose which values appear in the Resource Graph, click Format, Details. On the shortcut menu that appears, choose the field you want to display:

- **Peak Units** Represents the highest percentage of units assigned to a resource during each period on the graph. Units that exceed the maximum units for the resource appear as an overallocation.

INSIDE OUT   Peak units can be misleading

Peak units are particularly helpful when you look at the allocation of a resource that represents more than one person, such as "Painters," which might have maximum units of 400 percent for a four-person painting team. Peak units show the highest allocation during a period. Suppose one resource is assigned concurrently to two 2-day tasks during one week. Peak Units equals 200 percent (two tasks multiplied by 100 percent allocation). However, by shifting one of the tasks, that person can complete 4 days of work during 1 week and would not use up more than 100 percent allocation during the period.

- **Work** Displays the amount of work assigned to a resource during the period. If the hours exceed the number of hours available for the resource, the excess hours appear as an overallocation. The hours available for a resource take into account both the resource calendar (working and nonworking time) and the resource's maximum units.

- **Cumulative Work** Displays the total work assigned to the resource since the project began.

- **Overallocation** Includes only the hours that the resource is overallocated during the period, not work hours that fit in the resource's workday.

- **Percent Allocation** Represents the work assigned to a resource as a percentage of his available time.

- **Remaining Availability** Shows the number of hours that the resource is available. This graph is helpful when you are trying to find someone to work on a new task.

- **Cost** Displays the labor cost and per-use cost of a resource for the period. The total cost of a task appears in the period in which the task begins or ends, depending on whether resource costs accrue at the start or end.

- **Cumulative Cost** Shows the running total of the cost since the start of the project. This choice shows the total cost of a project when you display the value for a group that includes all the project resources.

- **Work Availability** Represents the number of hours that a resource could work based on his or her maximum units and resource calendar. It doesn't take into account any existing assignments. This field is helpful for identifying whether you have correctly created a resource calendar.

- **Unit Availability** Displays the same information as Work Availability, formatted as a percentage.

> **Note**
>
> You can control how values are presented in the Resource Graph. To change the unit for work, click Tools, Options and then click the Schedule tab. In the Work Is Entered In box, select the time unit you want for work. For example, for large projects, you might choose Days, whereas for short projects, Hours might be more useful.
>
> To change the currency format for costs, click Tools, Options and then click the View tab. Under Currency Options, specify the currency format you want.

To modify which fields appear in the Resource Graph, follow these steps:

1. Right-click the background of the Resource Graph and then, on the shortcut menu, click the field to display in the Resource Graph.

   For example, if you are trying to eliminate overallocations for a resource, click Overallocation or Percent Overallocation. On the other hand, if you are looking for an available resource, click Remaining Availability.

2. If you want to format the bars in the view, right-click the background of the Resource Graph and then click Bar Styles to adjust the appearance of the information.

   For example, you can view overallocations for the selected resource and others in the same resource group (see Figure 25-8).

Chapter 25

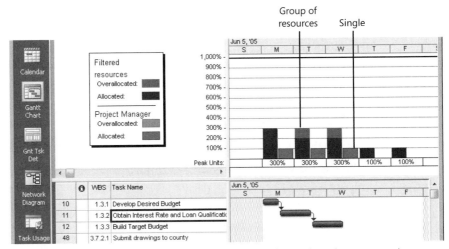

Figure 25-8 The Resource Graph can show information for a selected resource and a group of resources.

To modify the text styles or gridlines in the Resource Graph, follow the steps described in the sections titled "Formatting Text Styles and Individual Text" and "Formatting the Appearance of Gridlines" earlier in this chapter.

Modifying the Calendar View

You can change the Calendar view to display one week, several weeks, or a month. The bar styles, text styles, layout, gridlines, and timescale for task bars in the Calendar view are all customizable.

To choose the time period to display, use one of the following methods:

- On the Standard toolbar, click Zoom In or Zoom Out.

  By default, the Calendar view displays one month at a time. If you click Zoom In, Microsoft Project displays two weeks. Click Zoom In once more to show only one week. Click Zoom Out to switch from one week, to two weeks, to a full month.

- Above the Calendar, click the button for a time period.

  Click Month to display an entire month. Click Week to show one week. To show a specific time period, click Custom. In the Zoom dialog box, select the Number Of Weeks option and type the number in the box. You can also choose a start date and end date for the period.

> **Note**
>
> To navigate to the next or previous time period, above the Calendar, click the left arrow or right arrow. For example, if the Calendar shows one week, clicking the right arrow moves to the next week. Clicking the left arrow shows the previous week.

To display a monthly preview pane, do the following:

1. Right-click the Calendar and choose Timescale on the pop-up menu.

2. On the Week Headings tab, select the Display Month Pane checkbox.

3. Click OK.

   To the left of the Calendar, Microsoft Project displays a pane that displays the current, next, and previous month,

To modify the bar styles for a particular type of task, do the following:

1. Click View, Calendar.

2. Click Format, Bar Styles.

   Because the Calendar view presents information that you don't see in the Gantt chart, the Bar Styles dialog box for Calendars contains different settings from the Bar Styles dialog box for Gantt charts.

3. To change the appearance of a specific type of Calendar bar, in the Task Type list, click its name, for example, Noncritical or Marked.

4. In the Bar Shape section, specify the Bar Type, Pattern, Color, and Split Pattern for the Calendar bar.

5. In the Text section, in the Field(s) box, click the field that you want to appear inside the Calendar bar.

   If you want to show the contents of multiple fields with the Calendar bar, separate each field with a comma. For example, to see the task name and resource initials, select the Name field, type a comma, and then select Resource Initials (see Figure 25-9).

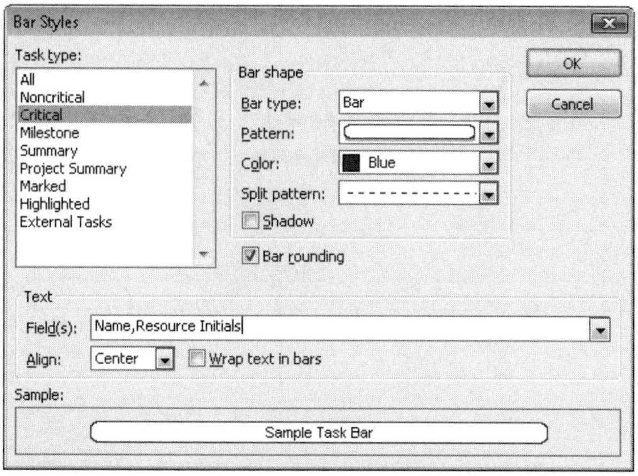

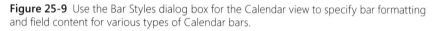

Figure 25-9 Use the Bar Styles dialog box for the Calendar view to specify bar formatting and field content for various types of Calendar bars.

To modify the arrangement of tasks in the Calendar, follow these steps:

1. Click Format, Layout.

   The Layout dialog box for the Calendar view appears.

2. To display as many tasks as you can in the Calendar boxes, select the Attempt To Fit As Many Boxes As Possible option.

   This option sorts tasks by Total Slack and then by Duration. Otherwise, tasks appear in the current sort order.

3. Select the Automatic Layout check box to reapply the layout options as you add, remove, or sort tasks.

To modify the timescale in the Calendar, do the following:

1. Click Format, Timescale.

2. In the Timescale dialog box, click the Week Headings tab and then choose the titles that you want to appear for months, weeks, and days in the calendar (see Figure 25-10).

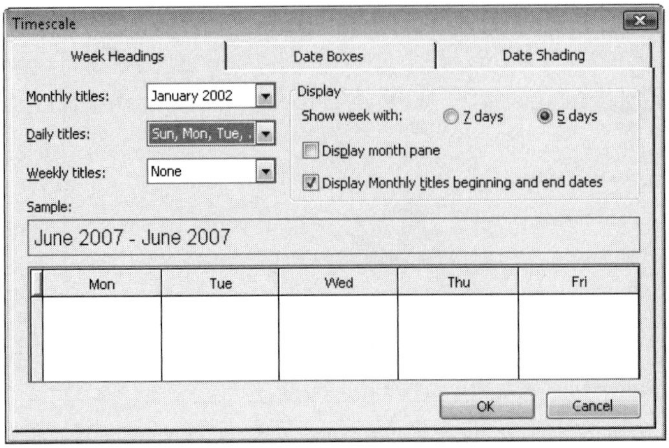

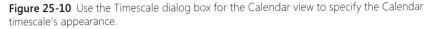

Figure 25-10 Use the Timescale dialog box for the Calendar view to specify the Calendar timescale's appearance.

3. Select the 7 Days option to display all days in a week. Select the 5 Days option to display only the workdays.

4. Select the Previous/Next Month Calendars check box to include a preview of the previous and following months in the view.

5. Click the Date Boxes tab to specify the information you want to appear in the heading for each date box.

   For example, by default, the day of the month appears at the top-right corner of the box, and the overflow indicator is in the top-left corner. You can choose the format for the date and display the date in a different corner. Altnernatively, you can show portions of the date in separate corners, such as the month in the upper-left and the day in the upper-right.

6. Click the Date Shading tab to customize how working and nonworking time for base and resource calendars appear on the calendar.

For information about modifying the text styles in the Calendar, refer to the section titled "Changing the Font for a View" earlier in this chapter. To change gridlines in the Calendar, follow the steps described in the section titled "Formatting the Appearance of Gridlines" earlier in this chapter.

Modifying a Sheet View

The Resource Sheet and the Task Sheet use a tabular layout to display information about your project resources and tasks. The Task Sheet appears as the sheet portion of a Gantt chart view. It's easy to change the table that appears in the sheet view along with the height of rows and width of columns.

For more information about customizing text, see the section titled "Changing the Font for a View" earlier in this chapter.

To change the table in the sheet view, use one of the following methods:

- Click View, More Views. In the More Views dialog box, click a sheet view, for example, Task Sheet or Resource Sheet, and then click Apply.

- Right-click the Select All box in the upper-left corner of the table (above row 1). A shortcut menu appears with tables for the sheet view. Click the name of the table that you want to appear.

  For example, to see costs in the Task Sheet, click Cost on the shortcut menu. If the table you want doesn't appear on the shortcut menu, click More Tables and then double-click the table you want in the Tables list.

To resize a column in the sheet, use one of the following methods:

- Position the mouse pointer between two column headings until it changes to a two-headed arrow and then double-click the column edge to resize the column to fit all the values in the column.

- Position the mouse pointer between two column headings until it changes to a two-headed arrow, and then click and drag until the column on the left is the desired width.

- Double-click the column heading to display the Column Definition dialog box. Click the column width in the Width box or click Best Fit.

> **Note**
>
> You can wrap text in a table's column headings by adjusting the column heading row height. To adjust the row height automatically to display the entire column title, click View, Table and then click More Tables. Click the table you want to modify and then click Edit. In the Table Definition dialog box, select the Auto-Adjust Header Row Heights check box. You can also drag to manually adjust the column heading row height.

You can change the height of one or more rows in a sheet. To change the height of a row, position the mouse pointer between the two row headings (beneath the row's ID number) until the mouse pointer changes to a two-headed arrow, and then click and drag upward or downward to make the row shorter or taller, respectively.

For information about resizing all rows in a table, as well as inserting, deleting, moving, and copying rows and columns in a table, see the section titled "Customizing Tables" later in this chapter.

Modifying a Usage View

Usage views, such as the Resource Usage and Task Usage view, display information divided across time periods. Usage views include a sheet view in the left pane and a timephased grid (the timephased portion of the view) with the field details in the right pane. You can customize the sheet and the timescale for the timephased portion as you can in the Gantt Chart and other views. You can also choose which fields you want to see in the timephased portion of the view.

To select and format the timephased fields shown in the timephased portion of a usage view, follow these steps:

1. Click View, Resource Usage or choose another usage view.

2. Right-click the timephased portion of the view, click Detail Styles, and then click the Usage Details tab.

    The Usage Details tab lists the different timephased fields that you can display in the timephased portion of the view, such as Work, Actual Work, Overtime Work, and Cost (see Figure 25-11).

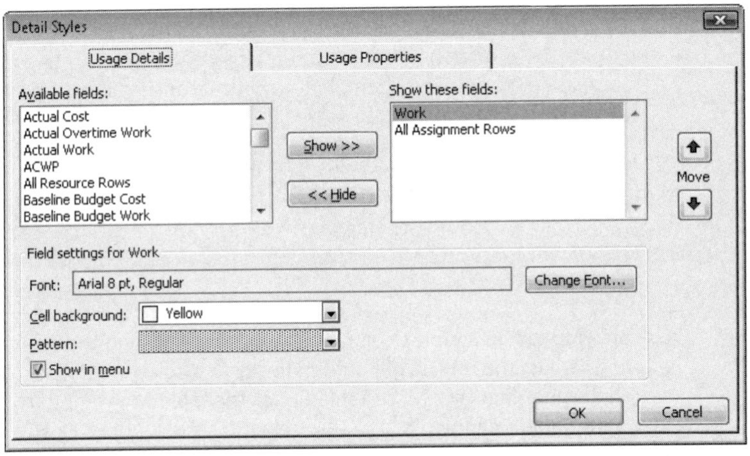

Figure 25-11 Choose the fields to display as well as their formatting in the Detail Styles dialog box.

3. In the Available Fields list, click the field you want to add to the timephased portion of the Usage View and then click Show.

    To include multiple fields, press Ctrl and then click each field to add it to the selection. Then click Show to add them all to the Show These Fields list.

4. To remove a field from showing in the timephased portion of the view, click its name in the Show These Fields list and then click Hide.

5. To change the order in which fields appear, click a field in the Show These Fields list and then click the Move up or down arrow buttons.

6. If you want to change a field's appearance in the timephased portion of the view, choose the font, color, and pattern for the selected field.

Move up

> **Note**
>
> To quickly add a field, right-click the timephased portion of the view and then, on the shortcut menu, click the field you want to add. A check box appears in front of the field name on the shortcut menu, and another row of timephased information appears in the timephased portion of the view for each task.
>
> To remove a field from the timephased portion of the view, right-click the timephased portion of the view and then, on the shortcut menu, click the field you want to remove.

The Usage Properties tab in the Detail Styles dialog box enables you to format the detail headers and the data within the timephased portion of the view:

- To align the data in the timephased cells, click Right, Left, or Center in the Align Details Data box.

- If you can't see the field names on the left side of the timephased portion of the view, click Yes in the Display Details Header Column box.

- If the field names are missing in some of the rows, select the Repeat Details Header On All Assignment Rows check box.

- If the field names take up too much space, select the Display Short Detail Header Names check box.

For information about modifying the text styles or gridlines in a Usage view, follow the steps described in the sections titled "Changing the Font for a View" and "Formatting the Appearance of Gridlines" earlier in this chapter. For information about formatting the sheet portion of the Usage view, see the sections titled "Modifying a Sheet View" earlier in this chapter and "Customizing Tables" later in this chapter. For information about formatting the timescale, see the section titled "Modifying the Timescale" later in this chapter.

The values in the timephased portion of the view often exceed the width of the columns. Instead of adjusting the width of columns in the Timescale dialog box, you can use the mouse to resize them in the timephased portion of the usage view timesheet. To resize columns in the timephased portion of the view, follow these steps:

1. Position the mouse pointer between two column headings in the timephased portion of the view until it changes to a two-headed arrow.

2. Click and then drag the pointer to the left or right until the columns are the desired width.

    If the usage view is part of a combination view that's displaying a timephased portion in both panes, changing the column width in one pane changes the width in the other pane so that the timephased columns always line up.

Modifying the Timescale

The timescale is a prominent feature in many Microsoft Project views, such as Gantt chart and usage views. A view can contain up to three timescales, for instance to show the fiscal year and fiscal quarters on two timescales; or to show the year, months, and days on three timescales. You can customize the units, the labels for time periods, and the label alignment for each timescale. In addition, you can choose how many timescales you want to use as well as the width of each period in the timescale.

Changes you make to the timescale apply only to the active view, but those changes become a permanent part of that view definition. Your timescale customizations appear each time you display that view.

To set the options for one or more tiers in the timescale, do the following:

1. Display a view that contains a timescale, such as Gantt Chart, Task Usage, or Resource Graph.

2. Right-click the timescale heading and then click Timescale on the shortcut menu.

   The Timescale dialog box appears.

3. The Timescale dialog box has four tabs (see Figure 25-12): Top Tier, Middle Tier, Bottom Tier, and Non-Working Time. The Middle Tier tab is displayed by default. In the Show list under Timescale Options, click the number of tiers you want to display (one, two, or three).

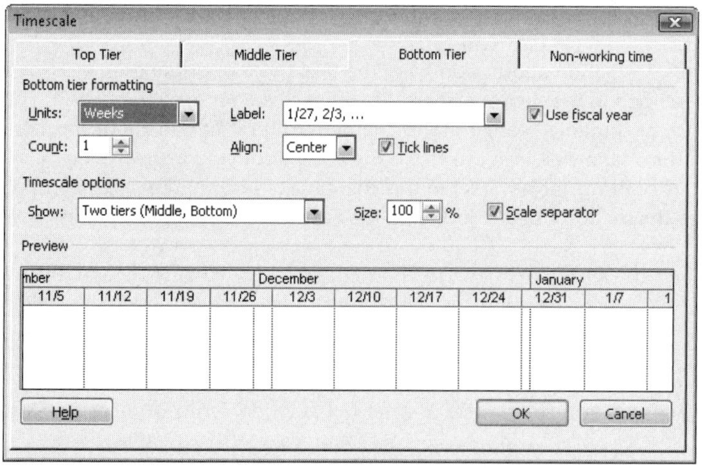

Figure 25-12 Customize the time periods that appear in a Gantt Chart, Task Usage, or Resource Graph view.

4. To change the width of the timescale columns, click a percentage in the Size box.

   If you use small time periods, choose a smaller percentage to fit a longer overall period in the view. If the values in the view appear as pound marks (#), choose a larger percentage to display the values.

5. Select the Scale Separator check box to draw lines between each timescale tier.

To set the options for each timescale tier, follow these steps:

1. In the Timescale dialog box, click the tab for the timescale tier you want to customize.

2. In the Units box, specify the time unit you want to display for the current tier. For example, you might choose Quarters for the top tier if your organization's financial performance depends on this project.

CAUTION

The time unit in a lower tier must be shorter than the unit for the tier above it. For example, if the top tier time unit is months, the middle tier can't be years.

3. To display the fiscal year in the timescale, select the Use Fiscal Year check box.

4. To display an interval of more than one unit, choose the number of units in the Count box.

   For example, to display two-week intervals, click Weeks in the Units box and 2 in the Count box.

5. To change the label format, choose a format in the Label box, for example, 1st Quarter, Qtr 1, 2004, or 1Q04.

6. To position the label in the timescale, click Left, Right, or Center in the Align box.

7. If you chose to display more than one tier, click the tabs for the other tiers and repeat steps 2–6.

CAUTION

When you click the Zoom In or Zoom Out buttons on the Standard toolbar or click Zoom on the View menu, changes you make to the labels in the timescales disappear.

You can also control how nonworking time appears in the timescale. To set the nonworking time options in the timescale, do the following:

1. In the Timescale dialog box, click the Non-Working Time tab.

2. To hide nonworking time, select the Do Not Draw check box.

3. If you display nonworking time, choose the color and pattern for the nonworking time shading.

4. Choose the calendar whose nonworking time you want to display in the Calendar box.

> **Note**
> The Non-Working Time tab in the Timescale dialog box changes only the appearance of nonworking time in the timescale. To modify the schedule for nonworking time, click Tools, Change Working Time. Alternatively, right-click the timescale heading and then click Change Working Time.

For more information about changing working and nonworking time, see the section titled "Setting Your Project Calendar" in Chapter 3, "Starting a New Project."

Customizing Tables

Sheet views—such as the Task Sheet, Resource Sheet, and Gantt Chart—display a table of data. If the information you want doesn't appear in the current table, you can switch tables or modify the table contents. You can customize the contents of a table directly in the view or through the Table Definition dialog box.

For information on switching the table applied to a sheet view, as well as working with tables in general, see the section titled "Using Tables" in Chapter 4.

INSIDE OUT   Permanent changes to table definition

Table changes you make in the view change the table definition. If you insert or remove columns, modify the column attributes in the Column Definition dialog box, or use the mouse to adjust the column width, the table definition changes to reflect those modifications.

Because it is so easy to make changes to a table in a view, it's important to remember that those changes become a permanent part of that table's definition. If you want to keep the current table the way it is, make a copy of it and then make your modifications to the copy.

Modifying the Columns in a Table

You can add, move, remove, or modify columns in any table. To modify the definition of an existing table, follow these steps:

1. Right-click the Select All cell in the upper-left corner of the sheet above row and then click More Tables on the shortcut menu.

   The More Tables dialog box appears with the current table selected.

2. Click the Edit button.

> **Note**
>
> To use the current table as a template for a new table, click Copy instead of Edit. To use a different table as a template, in the More tables dialog box, click that table's name and then click Copy.

3. The Table Definition dialog box, shown in Figure 25-13, appears. If necessary, type a descriptive name in the Name box.

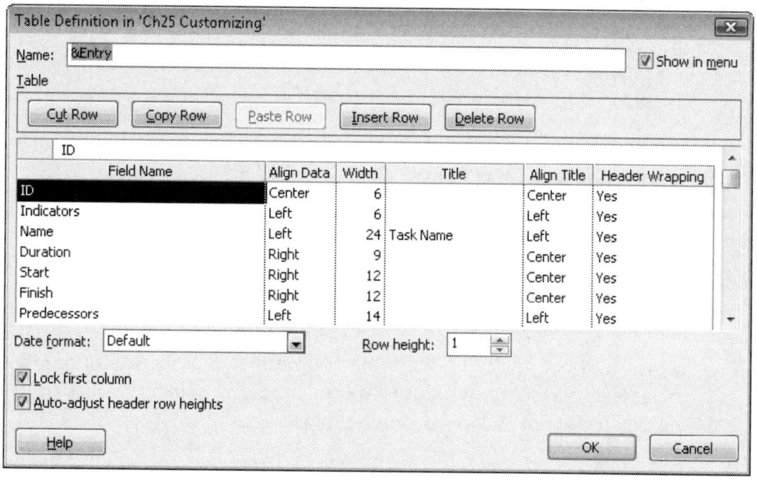

Figure 25-13 Use the Table Definition dialog box to customize the columns for a table.

If you want this table to appear on the Table menu, select the Show In Menu check box.

To move a column in the table, move fields in the rows in the Table Definition grid by doing the following:

1. Click the field name you want to move and then click Cut Row.

2. Click the row above where you want to insert the field.

3. Click Paste Row to insert the field at the new location.

You can add columns to the end of the table definition grid or insert them where you want. To insert a column into the table, follow these steps:

1. In the Table Definition dialog box, click the row in the grid above where you want to insert the field.

2. Click Insert Row to insert a blank row in the list.

3. Click the Field Name cell and then click the field name you want in the list.

CAUTION

Pressing Enter is the same as clicking OK—either action closes the Table Definition dialog box. To complete the row with default entries, press Tab or click another cell in the list.

4. Specify the alignment of the data and the column heading as well as the width of the column.

   If you want the column heading text to wrap, click Yes in the Header Wrapping cell.

5. To display text in the column header—other than the field name—in the Title cell, type the text you want to appear.

TROUBLESHOOTING

The Field Name list doesn't show the field you want to add

When you're editing a task table, only task fields appear in the Field Name list. Likewise, when you edit a resource table, you can add only resource fields. Assignment fields appear only when you edit Usage views.

Similarly, if you can't find the table you want to modify, you might have the wrong type of view displayed. In the More Tables dialog box, select the Task or Resource option to display the list of task or resource tables.

To remove a column from a table, follow these steps:

1. In the Table Definition dialog box, click the field name for the column you want to remove.

2. Click Delete Row.

Modifying Other Table Options

You can customize other properties of a table by using the Table Definition dialog box. For example, you can specify the format of dates or set a row height for all rows.

To set other table options, do the following:

1. In the Table Definition dialog box, in the Date Format box, click the format you want for any date fields.

   If you don't specify a format, the table uses the default date format for the entire project.

2. To change the height of the rows in the table, click a number in the Row Height box.

This number represents a multiple of the standard row height.

3. To adjust the height of the header row to make room for the full column title, select the Auto-Adjust Header Row Heights check box.

INSIDE OUT   Lock the first column for scrolling

If a table includes numerous columns, you might have to scroll in the sheet portion of the view to see them all. But it's difficult to enter data in the correct cells when you can't see the task name column. You can keep a column in view by moving it to the first column and then selecting the Lock First Column option in the Table Definition dialog box.

To lock the Task Name column, in the Table Definition dialog box, click Name in the Field Name column and then click Cut Row. Click the first row in the Field Name list and then click Paste Row to insert the Name field in the first row in the list. Select the Lock First Column check box and click OK. Task Name is the first column, shaded to indicate that it's locked in place. It does not disappear as you scroll.

Creating a New Table

If none of the existing tables even come close to meeting your needs, you can create a completely new table. To do this, follow these steps:

1. Click View, Table and then click More Tables.

2. In the More Tables dialog box, select the Task or Resource option to create a task or resource table, respectively.

3. Click New.

   The Table Definition dialog box appears with a default name in the Name box.

4. Enter a new descriptive name in the Name box.

5. If you want this table to appear in the View menu and View bar, select the Show In Menu check box.

6. Continue by adding the fields you want to appear in the table.

For information about how to add fields to a table, see the section titled "Modifying the Columns in a Table" earlier in this chapter.

Customizing Fields

Project 2007 comes with a robust set of fields of several data types. When you double-click a column heading in a task sheet or click Insert, Column, the Column Definition dialog box appears with a few modifiable attributes, such as the title or alignment. However, you cannot change what these built-in fields represent or how they are calculated. If you want to track information that Microsoft Project does not monitor, for example, defect rates during testing, you can create your own custom fields and add them to tables in your views.

For more information about adding fields to tables, see the section titled "Using Fields" in Chapter 4. For more information about Microsoft Project fields, type **fields** in the Type A Question For Help box, and then press Enter. Click one of the field types, for example, Duration Fields. A complete list of fields of that type appears in the Help pane.

Microsoft Project provides a set of several custom fields of each data type for tasks and another set of custom fields of each data type for resources. The number of custom fields varies for data type. For example, there are 10 fields for start and finish dates, 20 fields for flags and numbers, and 30 fields for custom text. In addition, there are sets of custom outline codes for both tasks and resources. Microsoft Office Project Professional 2007 provides similar sets of enterprise-level custom codes. With Office Project Professional 2007, you can define project-related custom fields in addition to task and resource fields.

The custom fields in both Project Standard and Project Professional are as follows:

- **Cost** Cost1 through Cost10 expressed in currency
- **Date** Date1 through Date10 expressed as a date
- **Duration** Duration1 through Duration10 expressed as time
- **Finish** Finish1 through Finish10 expressed as a date
- **Flag** Flag1 through Flag20 expressed as Yes/No flags
- **Number** Number1 through Number20 expressed as numeric data
- **Start** Start1 through Start10 expressed as a date
- **Text** Text1 through Text30 expressed as alphanumeric text up to 255 characters
- **Outline Code** Outline Code1 through Outline Code10 (the outline code format is defined by a code mask)

CAUTION

Even though the Start and Finish fields appear in the Custom Field list, Microsoft Project uses these fields to store the dates for interim plans. If you intend to save interim plans in your project, don't use the custom Start and Finish fields. Information in those fields will be overwritten when you save an interim plan. Instead, use custom Date fields for your customized dates.

Customizing a Field

Custom fields already exist; you can't introduce new fields into the Microsoft Project database. What you can do is modify the valid values for custom fields or specify how their values are calculated. You can control how their summary values are determined. If you don't want to display the values for a custom field, you can substitute graphical indicators.

> **Note**
>
> See the section titled "Working with Outline Codes" later in this chapter to learn how to create outline codes.

Follow these steps to customize a field of any type other than outline code:

1. Click Tools, Customize, Fields.

The Custom Fields dialog box appears (see Figure 25-14).

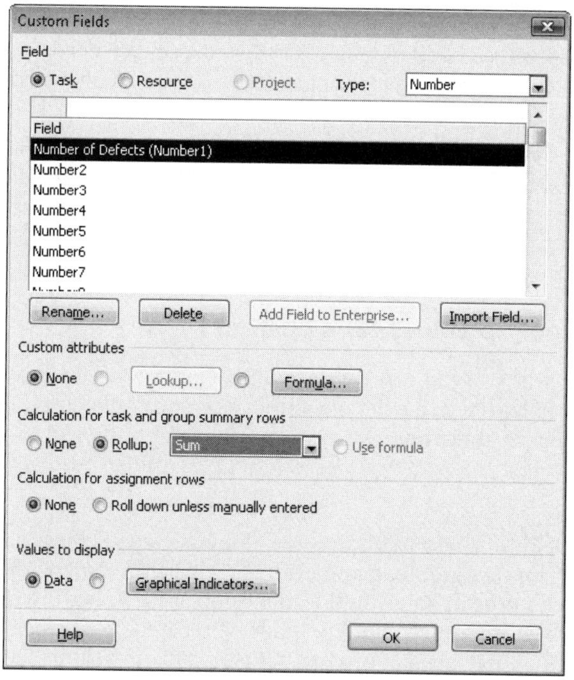

Figure 25-14 Create an alias, a list of values, or a formula for calculation. Or, set additional options for a custom field.

2. Select the Task or Resource option to specify whether this will be a task or resource field.

3. In the Type box, choose the type of custom field you want to customize.

> **Note**
>
> In Project 2003, outline codes had a separate tab in the Custom Fields dialog box. You clicked the Custom Fields tab to access all other types of fields, but clicked the Custom Outline Codes tab to customize outline codes. In Project 2007, the tabs are gone and instead, you choose the custom field data type in the Type box.

TROUBLESHOOTING

The custom field name isn't informative as a column heading in a table

Field names mainly tell you what type of field you're dealing with. To communicate the purpose of a field, you can change the title that appears in a column heading by clicking the heading and, in the title box, typing text for the heading. For example, you might use a title such as Overhead Cost instead of Cost1 in the column heading. Changing the title in this way affects the heading only in that table. If you include the Cost1 field in another table, the column heading reverts to the field name.

To create an alias for a custom field that appears instead of the field name each time you use the field, in the Custom Fields dialog box, click Rename. Enter a descriptive name for the field. The alias and the original field name both appear in field lists.

Specifying Lookup Values for a Custom Field

With custom fields, you can control the values that they accept, as well as whether those values are identified in a list of valid values or calculated by a formula. If you do not specify values in some way, the custom field accepts any entry as long as it meets the requirements for the data type, for example, a Number field accepts numbers, not text or dates.

Some custom fields are easy to fill in—Start, Finish, Date, Flag, and Cost are self-explanatory. However, for text, number, and outlice code fields, leaving the choice of values to the people who type in data could lead to gibberish. By setting up a list of values for people to choose from, called a lookup table, you can help them enter the right values. And, if valid values are specific, you can set up a custom field to accept only the valid values you specify. You can identify a lookup table for any custom field except for a Yes/No field.

To specify a list of values that appears in a custom field list, do the following:

1. In the Custom Fields dialog box, click Lookup. (In Project 2003, the button label was Value List.)

   The Edit Lookup Table dialog box appears (see Figure 25-15).

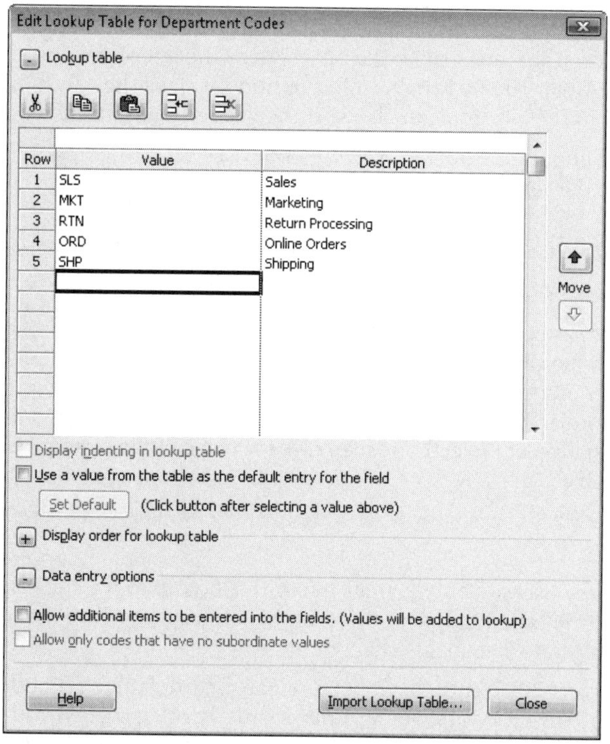

Figure 25-15 Specify the values to appear in a list for a custom field.

2. Click a blank cell in the Value column and then type the value. In the Description cell in the same row, add a description of what the value represents.

   For example, if you use a custom text field to store department abbreviations, the Description field can hold the full department name. When you display the drop-down list of values in a task sheet, the value and its description appear in the list.

> **Note**
>
> You can insert new values, remove existing values, or rearrange the values in custom fields by clicking Cut Row, Copy Row, Paste Row, Insert Row, or Delete Row. You can also rearrange the order of the values by clicking the up and down arrows to the right of the lookup table.

3. To specify one of the values as the default, select the Use A Value From The Table As The Default Entry For The Field check box. Click the cell that contains the default value and then click Set Default.

   The default value appears bolded and in blue.

4. To order the values, click the plus sign to the left of the Display Order For Lookup Table label. The By Row Number option displays the values in the order you enter them in the list. You can also sort the values in ascending or descending order.

   If you choose the Sort Ascending or Sort Descending options, click Sort to rearrange the rows.

> **Note**
> If another custom field (in the current project or another project) contains a lookup table with the entries you want, click Import Lookup Table. If the lookup table resides in another project, open the project file. Then, in the Import Lookup Table dialog box, click the project that contains the lookup table, select the option for the type of field (Task, Resource, or Project), and then click the name of the custom field that contains the lookup table.

5. To allow users to enter values not in the lookup table, click the plus sign to the left of the Data Entry Options label and select the Allow Additional Items To Be Entered Into The Fields check box.

   In Project 2007, this check box is cleared by default so that the lookup table values are the only valid values unless you say otherwise. If you allow other entries in the custom field, Microsoft Project adds those values automatically to the lookup table.

Creating a Calculated Field

Using formulas, you can set up a custom field to calculate its value with functions and other fields in the Microsoft Project database. For example, you might set up a field to show productivity by dividing the number of actual hours spent by the number of lines of code written (stored in another custom field).

To define a formula for a calculated field, follow these steps:

1. In the Custom Fields dialog box, click the Formula option.

   A message box appears telling you that any data in the field will be discarded because the formula will determine the field values. If the field is empty or contains data you don't care about, click OK to continue. To keep the data in the field, click Cancel and then choose a different field to customize.

2. Click the Formula button.

The Formula dialog box appears and displays the custom field name followed by an equal sign above the Edit Formula box.

3. To add a field to the formula, click Field, point to the field category, and then click the field you want to add (see Figure 25-16).

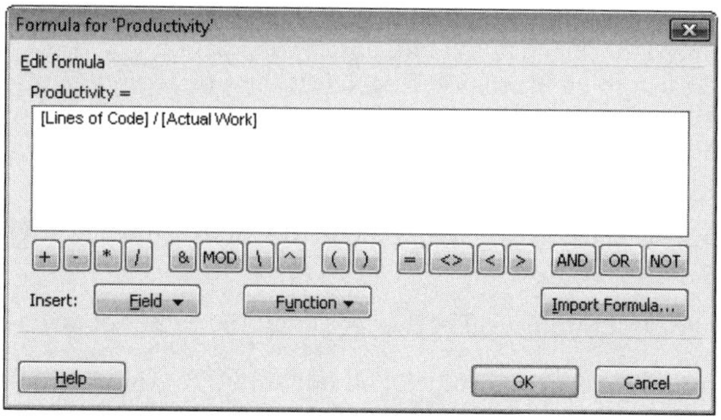

Figure 25-16 Build a formula by using functions, values, and any field in the Microsoft Project database.

4. To add a function to the formula, click one of the function buttons. Alternatively, click Function, point to the function category, and then click the function you want to add.

5. To type a value in the formula, click the location in the formula where you want to insert the value and then type the text or number.

6. To direct the order that functions execute, insert parentheses in the formula.

Share Formulas with Other Projects

You can share most customized elements between projects by copying them with the Organizer, but the Organizer doesn't include a tab for formulas. One way to copy a formula between projects is to copy the custom field whose definition contains the formula.

If you want to bring a formula into your current project from another one, you can also import the formula from a custom field in the other project. First, open the project that contains the custom field with the formula you want. Choose Tools, Customize, Fields and select the custom field to which you want to add the formula. Click Formula. In the Formula dialog box, click Import Formula. In the Import Formula dialog box, click the project that contains the formula, select the option for the type of field (Task, Resource, or Project), and then click the name of the custom field that contains the formula.

For more information about sharing elements, see the section titled "Sharing Customized Elements Among Projects" later in this chapter.

Calculating Group and Summary Values

By default, Microsoft Project does not calculate values for custom fields for summary tasks or for the rows containing rolled-up values for groups. However, if you want some type of calculation for summary tasks and group summary rows, you can choose the type of calculation or use the formula you defined for the field. To use the same formula that you defined for the custom field, under Calculation For Task And Group Summary Rows in the Custom Fields dialog box, select the Use Formula option.

If you select the Rollup option, you can choose from several built-in calculations in the Rollup drop-down list, including the following:

- **Average** The average of all nonsummary values underneath the summary task or group

- **Average First Sublevel** The average of all the values of tasks one level below

- **Maximum** The largest value of all nonsummary values

- **Minimum** The smallest value for all nonsummary values

- **Sum** The sum of all nonsummary values underneath the summary task or group

When you work with a custom number field, the following calculations also appear when you select the Rollup option:

- **Count All** The number of summary and nonsummary tasks one level below the summary task or group

- **Count First Sublevel** The number of nonsummary and summary tasks one level below the summary task or group

- **Count Nonsummaries** The number of nonsummary tasks below the summary task or group

Calculating Values for Assignment Rows

In Microsoft Office Project 2007, you can now control how values in a task custom field are distributed to the assignments within the task. For example, if you set up a number field, you can apportion the value to each assignment. Click the Roll Down Unless Manually Entered option to apportion the contents of the custom field to assignments. Microsoft Project divides the value across assignments unless you manually enter values into the custom field in an assignment row. Click the None option if you do not want to distribute the contents of the custom field to assignments.

Working with Graphical Indicators

Graphical indicators in place of custom field values can make values easier to interpret. At the same time, if you want your audience to see status without the actual results, you can use graphical indicators to hide the actual numeric values. For example, you might want to display a green light when a task is ahead of schedule, a yellow light when a task is slightly behind schedule, and a red light when a task is more than 2 weeks late.

To display graphical indicators instead of values, follow these steps:

1. Open the Custom Fields dialog box and choose the custom field to which you want to apply graphical indicators.

2. Under Values To Display, select the Graphical Indicators option and then click the Graphical Indicators button.

   The Graphical Indicators dialog box appears.

3. To assign graphical indicators to nonsummary rows, select the Nonsummary Rows option.

> **Note**
>
> By default, summary rows and the project summary row both inherit the same conditions that you specify for nonsummary rows. If you want to use different conditions for summary rows, select the Summary Rows option and then clear the Summary Rows Inherit Criteria From Nonsummary Rows check box. Define the tests and indicators for summary rows as you would for nonsummary rows. To specify different conditions for the project summary row, select the Project Summary option and then clear the Project Summary Inherits Criteria From Summary Rows check box. Define the tests and indicators for the project summary row.

4. In the table, click the first empty cell in the Test column, click the down arrow, and then click the test you want to apply for an indicator, for example, Equals or Is Less Than.

5. Enter the value for the test in the Value(s) cell.

   You can enter a number or other string, or you can select a field whose contents become the comparison value.

   For example, to display an indicator when a custom number field has a negative value, click Is Less Than in the list in the Test cell and then type 0 in the Value(s) cell. To display an indicator when a custom date field is greater than the baseline finish, click Is Greater Than in the Test cell and then click [Baseline Finish] in the Value(s) field.

6. Click the Image cell, click the down arrow, and then click the graphical indicator to display when the condition is true (see Figure 25-17).

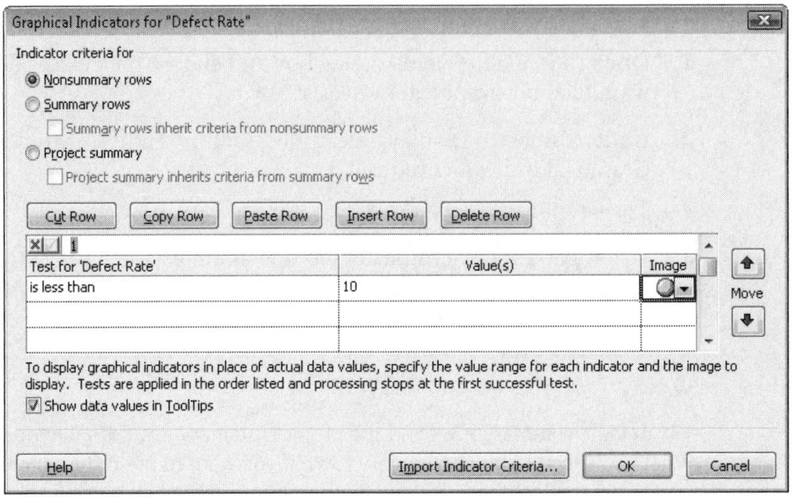

Figure 25-17 Set up criteria for displaying an icon that alerts you to specific conditions in the project.

7. To define graphical indicators when other conditions are true, repeat steps 4–6 in the next blank row in the table.

INSIDE OUT   Define graphic indicator tests carefully

With graphical indicators, Microsoft Project compares the field value against the first test you define. If the value passes the test, the graphical indicator for that test appears. If the value doesn't pass the test, Microsoft Project continues to check it against each subsequent test, until it passes.

You must be careful to set up your tests to include all possible outcomes. For example, if you have two "if greater than" tests, be sure to test for the largest value first, for example, values greater than 50 before values greater than 25. If you test for values greater than 25 first, values greater than 50 pass that test as well. Be careful to include "equal to" tests to ensure coverage for every value that occurs. For example, if you test for values less than 50, be sure to include a test for values greater than or equal to 50.

Working with Outline Codes

By default, the task outline delineates a hierarchy of tasks. A work breakdown structure (WBS) is a special hierarchy that separates the work for your project into manageable pieces that you can assign to project resources. But, you might need to structure your tasks according to different hierarchies. For example, the accounting department might have a set of codes for tracking income and expenses by business unit.

In addition, your organization might need one, two, or several ways of looking at resource hierarchies. For example, your organization's resource manager might want to review the resource breakdown structure, whereas the procurement manager might require a bill that itemizes the materials for the project.

Using custom outline code fields in Microsoft Project, you can create up to 10 sets of custom task codes and 10 sets of resource codes, in much the same way you set up WBS codes. You can then sort, group, or filter your tasks or resource by any of these outline codes to see the tasks or resources displayed in that structure.

For information about setting up a task outline of summary tasks and subtasks, see the section titled "Sequencing and Organizing Tasks" in Chapter 3. To set up and apply work breakdown structure codes, see the section titled "Setting Up Work Breakdown Structure Codes" in Chapter 3.

Setting Up Outline Codes

Outline codes are customizable alphanumeric codes that provide a method of categorizing tasks and resources in your project. Microsoft Project does not recalculate custom outline codes as you modify the location or indentation of a task or resource because only you know the structure of tasks or resources you want to represent. To help others use your custom outline codes properly, you can create a lookup table so that users can choose values from a list. You can eliminate invalid codes by restricting users to choosing only the predefined values.

An outline code can consist of several levels of uppercase or lowercase letters, numbers, or characters, along with a symbol to separate the levels of the code. The maximum length for an outline code is 255 characters.

Selecting the Outline Code

Follow these steps to select the custom outline code you want to start defining:

1. Click Tools, Customize, Fields.

2. Select the Task or Resource option to specify whether you're creating a task or resource outline code.

3. In the Type box, click Outline Code.

4. Click the name of the outline code that you want to modify in the code list, for example, Outline Code1 or Outline Code8.

5. To rename the custom outline code, click the Rename button and then type the new name in the Rename Field dialog box.

   This name and the original field name appear in lists where the outline code appears.

Defining a Code Mask

The code mask is the template that delineates the format and length of each level of the outline code as well as the separators between each level. For example, if your building name standard is a two character identifier followed by a hyphen and then a three digit number, the code mask identifies those criteria. To define the code mask, do the following:

1. In the Custom Fields dialog box, click the outline code for which you want to define a code mask.

2. Click the Lookup button.

   The Edit Lookup Table dialog box appears.

3. Click the + to the left of the Code Mask label to display the code mask options.

4. Click Edit Mask.

   The Code Mask Definition dialog box appears.

5. In the first row of the Sequence column, choose whether the first level of the code (or hierarchy) is a number, uppercase letters, lowercase letters, or alphanumeric characters.

6. In the Length field of the first row, specify the length of the first level of the code.

   A number in the Length cell indicates a fixed length for that level. If the level can contain any number of characters, click Any in the list.

7. In the Separator field of the first row, specify the character that separates the first and second levels of the code.

   You can use a comma, hyphen, plus sign, or forward slash as a separator.

8. Repeat steps 5–7 until all the levels of your custom outline code are set up (see Figure 25-18).

   As you enter the code mask for each succeeding level, the Code Preview box shows an example of the code.

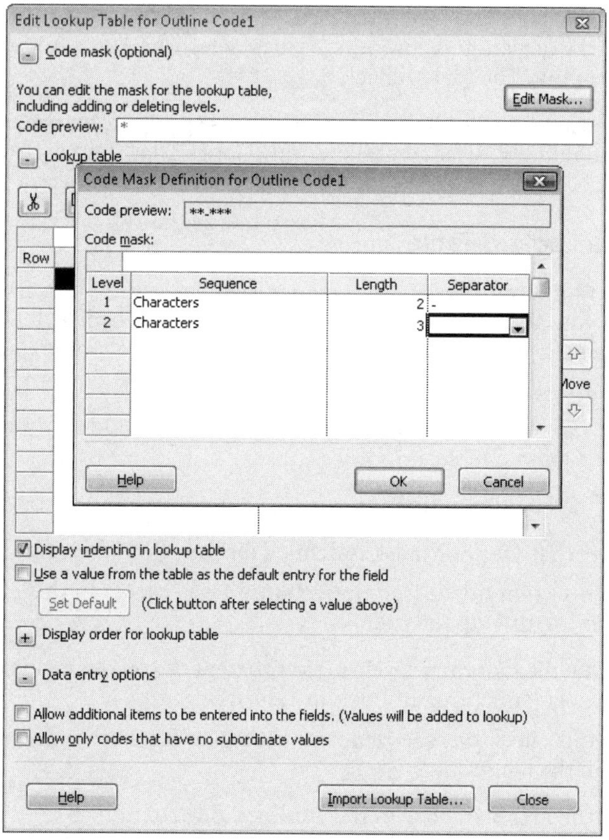

Figure 25-18 Open the Code Mask Definition dialog box to define the format of each component of an outline code.

With the code mask defined, your custom outline code is ready to use. If you click OK and then save the custom outline code, any sequence of characters that fits your code mask can be entered as a valid value for that outline code field.

Controlling Outline Code Values

To obtain the best results, providing users with some hints about correct values and format for outline codes is a good idea. And, if your custom outline code has specific valid values, you can ensure that users enter only those values. To do this, follow these steps:

1. Be sure that the Edit Lookup Table dialog box is open, and that the code mask is defined for the selected outline code.

   In the Edit Lookup Table dialog box, the Code Preview box shows a sample of the code mask set up for the field.

2. You don't have to do anything to restrict codes to only those listed in the lookup table. If you want to allow other values, select the Allow Additional Items To Be Entered Into The Fields check box.

3. To restrict codes to the ones with all levels specified, for example, both building ID and number, select the Allow Only Codes That Have No Subordinate Values check box.

Defining a Lookup Table

If you want more control over how you or other users enter information in the outline code fields, you can set up a lookup table for the outline code values. A lookup table comprises a list of values for the outline code. To define a lookup table, do the following:

1. In the Custom Fields dialog box, click the outline code for which you want to create a lookup table.

2. Click the Lookup button.

3. Be sure that the code mask is defined for the selected outline code.

   See the section titled "Defining a Code Mask" earlier in this chapter for instructions on setting up the code mask.

4. To make the hierarchy levels more apparent as you define lookup values, select the Display Indenting In Lookup Table check box.

   With this check box selected, the values you enter are indented according to their level in the hierarchy.

5. Click the first blank cell in the Outline Code column.

6. Type a value in the Outline Code cell.

   The format and length of this value must match the first level of your defined code mask. For example, if you specified that the first level in the outline code's hierarchy must be two characters in length, and you enter a three-character code, the entry appears in red.

7. Click the Description cell and type a meaningful description of the entry.

Indent

8. In the Outline Code cell in the second row, enter a value that conforms to the second level in the code mask. Click the Indent button to demote the entry to the next level of the code.

   The character types (number, uppercase letters, and so on) and length of each entry must match your code mask for the level. If the value you enter doesn't conform to the code mask defined for the outline level, the entry appears in red.

9. Repeat steps 5–8 to define additional values in the lookup table (see Figure 25-19).

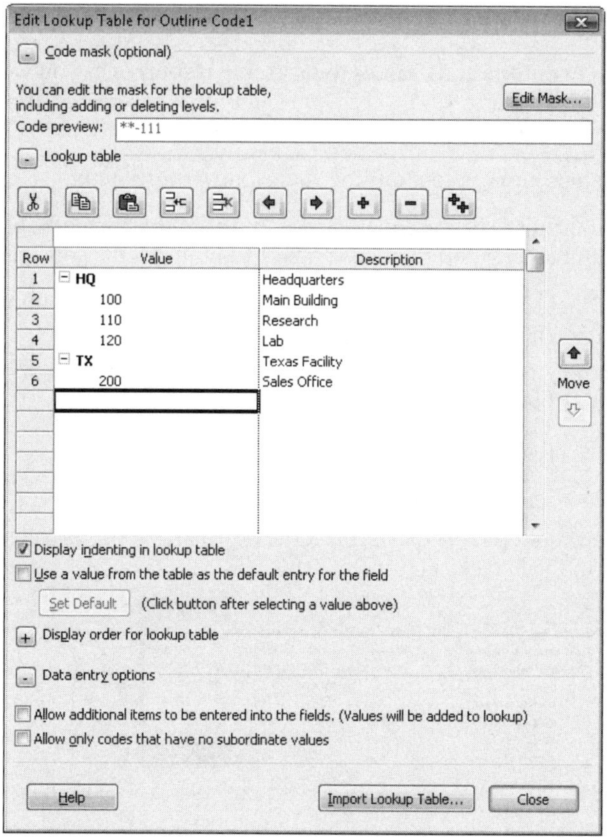

Figure 25-19 Define values in a lookup table to simplify outline code data entry.

10. To expand or collapse the outline levels, click the plus and minus signs that precede higher-level values.

11. To promote the entry one level higher in the code, click the Outdent button.

Outdent

12. When finished defining the lookup table, click Close.

The lookup table is saved with the outline code definition and code mask.

> **Note**
>
> To insert a value in the outline, click the Insert Row button. You can also use the Delete Row, Cut, Copy, and Paste buttons to edit the values that already exist in the list.

Assigning Outline Codes

You can assign outline code values to tasks and resources as you would enter values for any other fields in Microsoft Project. You can type the values or, if you created a lookup table, choose one from a list.

To assign values for a custom outline code, follow these steps:

1. If your custom outline code doesn't appear in the current table, right-click a column heading and then click Insert Column on the shortcut menu.

2. In the Field Name box, click the outline code field (for example, Outline Code1) and then click OK.

   If you renamed the outline code in the Custom Fields dialog box, you'll see your field listed both by its new name and its generic name.

3. Click a cell in the custom outline code column.

4. If no lookup table exists, type the value in the cell.

   When a lookup table exists, click the down arrow in the cell and then click an entry in the list (see Figure 25-20).

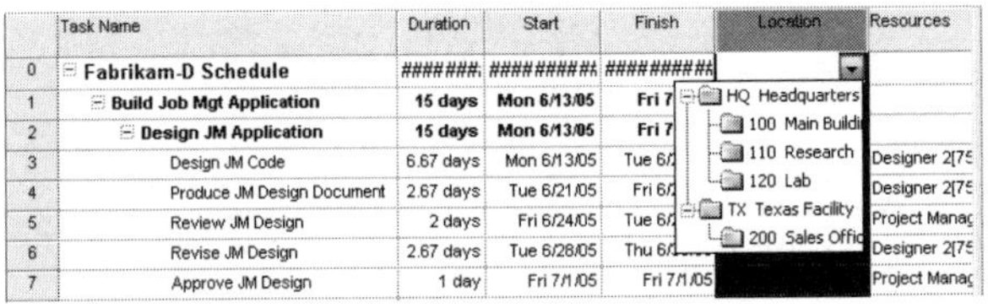

Figure 25-20 Click the down arrow in the outline code field to choose from the lookup table.

> **Note**
> Without a lookup table, there is no way to identify the format for the outline code. However, if you enter a value in a table cell that does not conform to the code mask, an error message appears that includes the correct format.

Reviewing Your Tasks or Resources by Outline Code

Grouping, filtering, and sorting by outline codes is similar to processing tasks and resources based on values in other fields. You simply apply a group, filter, or sort criterion that uses the custom outline code.

To quickly use a custom outline code to group tasks or resources, do the following:

1. Click Project, Group By, Customize Group By.

2. In the Customize Group By dialog box, click the down arrow in the Field Name cell and then click the name of the outline code.

3. If necessary, change the value in the Order cell, the color and pattern of the group, and other group settings.

For information about customizing a group, see the section titled "Modifying a Group" later in this chapter.

To quickly use a custom outline code to filter tasks or resources, follow these steps:

1. Display the sheet view whose rows you want to filter.

2. On the Formatting toolbar, click AutoFilter.

    The AutoFilter arrows appear in the column heading for each field in the sheet view.

3. Click the arrow in the outline code column.

4. Click the value by which you want to filter or click Custom if you want to create a custom filter based on the outline code.

> **Note**
> To turn off the AutoFilter arrows, click the AutoFilter button on the Formatting toolbar.

For information about customizing a filter, see the section titled "Customizing Filters" later in this chapter.

To use an outline code to sort your tasks or resources, do the following:

1. Click Project, Sort, Sort By.

2. In the Sort By dialog box, click the down arrow in the Sort By box and then click the name of the outline code in the list.

3. If necessary, select the Ascending or Descending option to change the sort order.

Customizing Groups

In Microsoft Project, groups can collate tasks, resources, or assignments that meet a set of conditions. For example, you might group tasks by their schedule variance so that you can concentrate on the ones furthest behind schedule. You might group resources by their level of availability so that you can assign the resources who have the most free time. You can also choose to group assignments instead of tasks or resources, for example, to see which assignments are running over on the targeted hours.

Group headings show subtotals for the values in the numeric fields for the group. For example, assignments grouped by salaried employees, hourly employees, and contractors can show the total hours of work performed by each group. When you group these elements, subtotals for the groups appear in the Task and Resource Sheet as well as in the timephased portion in usage views.

For information about applying built-in groups, see the section titled "Grouping Project Information" in Chapter 4.

Modifying a Group

If one of the existing groups doesn't meet your needs, you can modify a built-in group. If you want to keep the original group definition intact, simply copy an existing group and then modify the copy with the criteria you want. Do the following to customize a group:

1. Click Project, Group by, More Groups.

2. In the More Groups dialog box, click either the Task or Resource option to display the existing task or resource groups.

3. Click the group you want to modify in the list and then click Edit or Copy.

   The Group Definition dialog box appears.

4. If you have copied an existing group, in the Name box, change the name of the group.

5. Click the first empty cell in the Field Name column, click the down arrow, and then click the name of the field by which you want to group.

   The category for the field (Task, Resource, or Assignment) appears in the Field Type cell (see Figure 25-21).

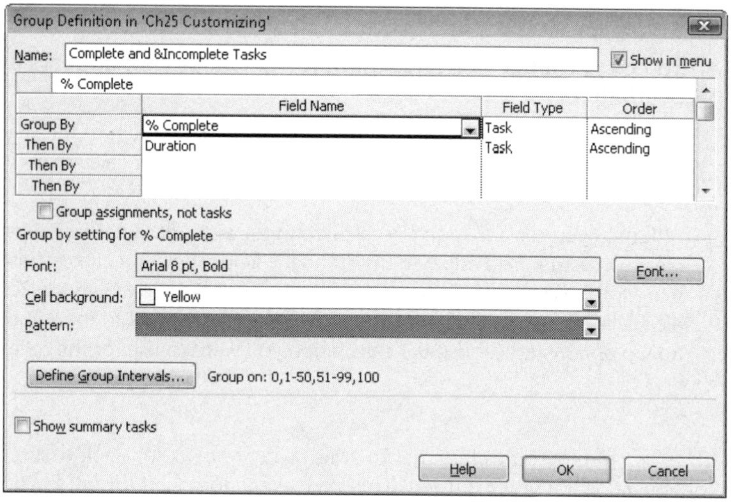

Figure 25-21 Group tasks, resources, or assignments by one or more fields.

6. If necessary, change the grouping order.

Choose Ascending to show the smallest numbers first, for example, to see the tasks that have the least amout of completed work as shown in the % Complete field. Descending order shows the largest values first, which is ideal for locating the resources with the most availability.

> **Note**
>
> For task usage views, you can group by tasks or assignments. Select the Group Assignments, Not Tasks check box for a task group, if you want to see groupings by individual assignments. For resource usage, you can group by resources or assignments by selecting the Group Assignments, Not Resources check box for a resource group.

7. To change the font for group rows, click Font. In the Font dialog box, choose a font, font style, font size, and color.

8. To change the background color for cells in group rows, click a color in the Cell Background box.

9. To change the pattern for the group headings, click a pattern in the Pattern box.

TROUBLESHOOTING

You can't change the calculation for the value that appears in the group heading row

The group heading rows for standard fields display the sum of the values for the entries in the group. However, you might want to use a different calculation for the group heading row, such as the largest value or the average.

Although you can't change the calculation for a standard field group summary, you can create a custom field equal to the standard field. Then you can calculate the group summary for the custom field by using the other summary calculations. To do this, first create a calculated custom field. Then set the custom field equal to the standard field. Select the Rollup option and choose the calculation you want to use for the rolled-up value.

Groups often display elements in small sets, one set for each discrete value that exists for the field that you grouped. This process works well for fields such as Milestones that have only two values. For groups based on cost or work, the number of discrete values can seem endless. The solution to this dilemma is to define intervals for groups, for example, to group tasks by % Complete equal to 0%, from 1% to 50%, from 51% to 99%, and finally 100%. To do this, follow these steps:

1. In the Group Definition dialog box, click the field for which you want to define intervals.

2. Click Define Group Intervals. The Define Group Interval dialog box appears (see Figure 25-22).

   The default selection for Group On is Each Value, which creates a separate group for each discrete value in the field.

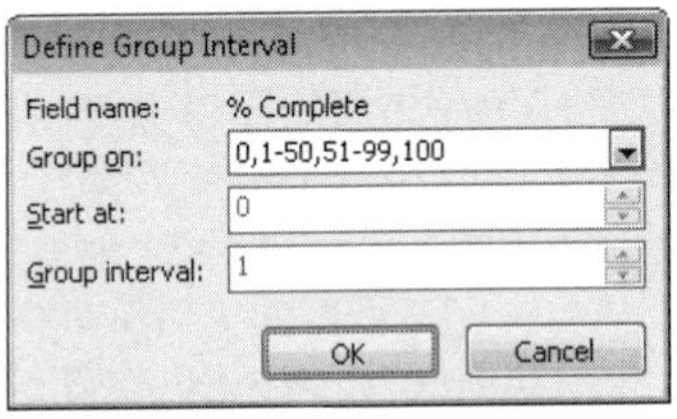

Figure 25-22 Set the starting value and size for group intervals.

3. Click the down arrow in the Group On box and then click the interval you want to use in the list.

   The intervals listed depend on the type of field. For example, the intervals for a field that represents work include units in which work is measured, such as hours, days, weeks, and months. For % Complete, the list includes several common sets of intervals.

4. To start the interval at a specific number, type the number in the Start At box.

5. To define the interval size, type the number in the Group Interval box. To group assignments in intervals of 2 weeks worth of work, type 2.

Creating a New Group

When no groups exist that are similar to what you want, you can create a new group. To create a new group, do the following:

1. Click Project, Group By, More Groups.

2. In the More Groups dialog box, select the Task or Resource option to specify whether you're creating a task or resource group and then click New.

3. In the Name box, type a descriptive name for the new group.

4. To define the group, follow the steps described in the section titled "Modifying a Group" earlier in this chapter.

Group Tasks with Overallocated Resources

You can create and apply a custom group that shows which tasks have overallocated resources assigned to them. This can help you determine which tasks are more at risk of missing their dates or generating overtime costs. To do this, complete these steps:

1. Click Project, Group By, More Groups.

2. In the More Groups dialog box, select the Task option and then click New.

3. In the Name box, type Overallocated.

4. Select the Show In Menu check box.

5. Click in the Group By row in the Field Name column, click the down arrow, and then type ov to scroll directly to the Overallocated field.

6. Click OK to save the group.

Your new group appears in the More Groups dialog box. Because the Overallocated field is a Yes/No field, the view is divided into two groups: those tasks that have overallocated resources assigned and those that do not.

7. Click Apply to initiate the Overallocated grouping to the current view. Click Close to close the dialog box without grouping.

Any time you want to apply the Overallocated grouping to a task view, click Group By on the Standard toolbar and then click Overallocated.

INSIDE OUT   Different "groups" in Microsoft Project

Microsoft Project uses the term group to represent several different features. Each feature serves a different purpose, so it's important to choose the correct one. A group resource represents several interchangeable resources. For example, you might define a resource called Carpenters, which represents five carpenters who can do basic carpentry. The Maximum Units for this resource would be the sum of the maximum units for each individual in the group resource, 500 percent in this example.

A resource group represents a category of individual resources. You might define a resource group for employees and another for contractors so that you can sort, filter, and view assignments that are performed in-house versus those that are outsourced.

Finally, a group that you apply using the Group By command on the Project menu categorizes and sorts tasks, resources, or assignments based on the values in any field in Microsoft Project.

Customizing Filters

Projects contain so much information that data that isn't pertinent can simply get in the way. Filters restrict the tasks or resources that appear so that you can more easily analyze a situation. Microsoft Project provides a number of standard filters that you can use as-is to hide certain kinds of information you don't need to see in a given situation. For example, the Incomplete Tasks filter displays only those tasks that are either in progress or not yet started so that you can focus on work yet to be done. These filters work equally well as templates for your own customized filters. You can create a filter based on the Incomplete Tasks filter to display incomplete tasks that are behind schedule. This enables you to see what kind of course correction you need.

For more information about working with the built-in Microsoft Project filters, see the section titled "Filtering Project Information" in Chapter 4.

Modifying a Filter

You can modify an existing filter, but it's better to keep the original filter intact by copying the filter and then modifying the copy. To customize a filter, follow these steps:

1. Click Project, Filtered For, More Filters.

2. In the More Filters dialog box, select the Task or Resource option to display the task or resource filters.

3. Click the filter you want to modify and then click Edit or Copy.

4. In the Name box, change the name to indicate what the filter shows.

5. Click the Field Name cell you want to change, click the down arrow, and then click the name of the field by which you want to filter (see Figure 25-23).

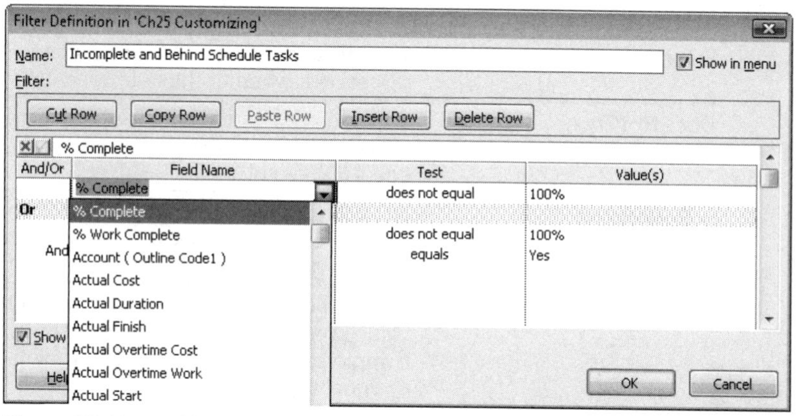

Figure 25-23 Modify the fields, tests, and values for a filter to display only the tasks that meet your criteria.

6. Click the Test cell, click the down arrow, and then click the name of the test you want to use for the filter.

7. In the Value(s) cell, specify the value you want to use for the filter test. You can type a value, click a field name from the list, or type a prompt to define an interactive filter.

> For information about creating an interactive filter, see the section titled "Creating Interactive Filters" later in this chapter.

8. To display the summary tasks for tasks that pass the filter criteria, select the Show Related Summary Rows check box.

TROUBLESHOOTING

A filter doesn't display the correct tasks

Making changes to your project can cause what appear to be incorrect filter results. If you make changes to your project after a filter is applied, elements that no longer meet the filter criteria don't disappear until you reapply the filter. The fastest way to reapply the current filter is by pressing Ctrl+F3.

Table 25-1 describes the tests you can use within a filter and provides an example of each.

Table 25-1 Filters

Filter test	How you can use it
Equals	The values must be equal. For example, to filter for milestones, test whether the Milestone field equals Yes.
Does Not Equal	The values are different. For example, to show tasks with overtime, test whether the Overtime Work field does not equal 0.
Is Greater Than	The value in the field is greater than the entry in the Value(s) cell. For example, to show tasks that are late, test for the Finish field greater than the Baseline Finish field.
Is Greater Than Or Equal To	The field value is greater than or equal to the entry in the Value(s) cell. For example, to show tasks at least 50 percent complete, test whether the % Complete field is greater than or equal to 50 percent.
Is Less Than	The field value is less than the entry in the Value(s) cell. For example, to show tasks that are ahead of schedule, test for the Finish field less than the Baseline Finish field.
Is Less Than Or Equal To	The field value is less than or equal to the entry in the Value(s) cell. For example, to show tasks that are within budget, test whether the Cost Variance field is less than or equal to 0.
Is Within	The Field Name value is between or equal to the boundary values in the Value(s) cell. For example, to find the tasks within a range, test whether the ID is within the range specified in the Value(s) cell. To specify a range, type the starting value, type a comma, and then type the last value, such as 100,200.
Is Not Within	The Field Name value is outside the boundary values in the Value(s) cell. For example, to find the tasks that are not in progress, test whether the % Complete value is not within 1%–99%.
Contains	The field value is text that contains the string in the Value(s) cell. For example, to find the tasks to which resources from any development group are assigned, test whether the Resource Group field contains the word *Development*.
Does Not Contain	The field value is text that does not contain the string in the Value(s) cell. For example, to find resources not in a resource group, check whether the Resource Group does not contain the name.
Contains Exactly	The field value is text that must exactly match the string in the Value(s) cell. For example, to find tasks to which only a particular resource is assigned, check whether the Resource Name field contains exactly the resource's name.

> **Note**
>
> When you use the Equals or Does Not Equal test, you can compare a text field value to a string with wildcard characters. Wildcard characters include the following:
>
> - * represents one or more characters.
>
> - ? represents any single character.
>
> For example, DB* matches DB Developer, DB Administrator, and DB Designer. Des??? matches Design, but does not match Describe.

Creating Filters

If you can't find a filter similar to what you want, you can create one and filter on any field or combination of fields in Microsoft Project, including custom fields that you defined. To create a new filter, follow these steps:

1. Click Project, Filtered For, More Filters.

2. In the More Filters dialog box, select the Task or Resource option to create a task or resource filter and then click New.

3. In the Filter Definition dialog box, type a descriptive name for the filter in the Name box.

4. If you want the new filter to appear on the Filtered For menu, select the Show In Menu check box.

5. Enter the field, test, and values that define your filter criteria.

6. To include the summary rows for the tasks or resources that meet the filter criteria, select the Show Related Summary Rows check box.

Create a Filter for Resource Booking Type

If you're using Project Professional, you might have added some resources to your project as proposed resources, that is, resources you would like to use but who haven't yet been committed to your project. You can create a filter to find proposed resources, for example, to see which managers you still need to convince, or just committed resources when you want to focus on fulfilled assignments. Creating such a filter can be particularly helpful when you're finalizing your project team or the task assignments.

To create a filter for a booking type, follow these steps:

1. Click Project, Filtered For, More Filters.

2. In the More Filters dialog box, select the Resource option and then click New.

3. In the Name box, type a descriptive name for the filter, for example, Proposed Resources or Committed Resources.

4. Select the Show In Menu check box.

5. Click in the first row of the Field Name column and then type bo to scroll quickly through the list of fields. Click Booking Type.

6. Click in the Test column and then click Equals.

7. Click in the Value(s) column and then click Proposed or Committed.

8. Click OK.

   Your new filter appears in the More Filters dialog box.

9. Click Apply or Highlight to apply your new filter to the current view. Otherwise, click Close.

Any time you want to apply your new filter to a resource view, click Filter on the Formatting toolbar and then click Proposed or Committed.

Creating Comparison Filters

Some of the handiest filters use criteria that compare the values in two different fields for the same task or resource. For example, to look for tasks that haven't started according to plan, you can filter for tasks in which the Actual Start date is greater than the Baseline Start date.

To define a test that compares two fields, do the following:

1. In the Filter Definition dialog box, click the Field Name cell, click the down arrow, and then click the name of the field by which you want to filter, for example, Actual Start.

2. Click the Test cell, click the down arrow, and then click the name of the test you want to use, "is greater than" in this example.

3. Click the Value(s) cell, click the down arrow, and then click the name of the field with which you want to compare the first field (see Figure 25-24)—in this example, [Baseline Start].

A field name in the Value(s) cell is enclosed in square brackets [ ].

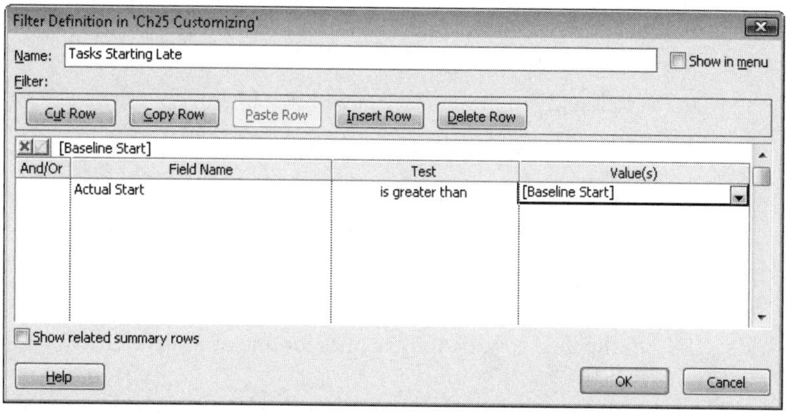

Figure 25-24 Create a filter that compares the value in one field against the value in another field.

Creating Filters with Multiple Tests

Sometimes it takes more than one or two criteria to filter the list to your satisfaction. You can create filters in which tasks or resources must meet at least one of the criteria or all of the criteria.

To define multiple filter criteria, follow these steps:

1. In the Filter Definition dialog box, in the Name box, type a descriptive name for the filter.

2. In the first row in the table, specify the field, test, and value for the first set of filter criteria.

3. In the second row, click the And/Or cell in the second row and then click And or Or.

   If you click And, the resulting filter displays only elements that meet both criteria. The filter displays tasks that meet one or both of the criteria when you click Or.

4. In the second row, specify the field, test, and values for the second set of filter criteria.

5. Repeat steps 2–4 for any additional tests you want to define for the filter, defining each test on a separate row in the table and relating them with an And or Or.

With more than one test, filters evaluate tests in the order in which they occur in the filter definition. The filter restricts elements to those that pass the first test and then compares those results to the outcome of the next test. The filter continues until there are no further tests to evaluate.

In some cases, you might want to adjust the order in which the tests are evaluated. For example, you might want to filter tasks first for those that use a particular resource and that aren't yet complete. Then you want to further filter the list for tasks that start and finish within a particular date range. You can control the order that Microsoft Project evaluates tests by clicking And or Or in the And/Or cell of an otherwise empty row. Including a test in an empty row is the equivalent of placing parentheses around the tests that occur before and after the empty row.

Do the following to group criteria within a filter:

1. Define one or more tests for the first group of filter criteria.

2. In the next blank row after the first group of criteria, click the And/Or cell and then click And or Or. Keep the rest of this row blank.

    This blank row containing only And or Or creates the grouping between the first set of filter criteria and the second set.

3. In the next row, define the tests for one or more additional filter criteria (see Figure 25-25).

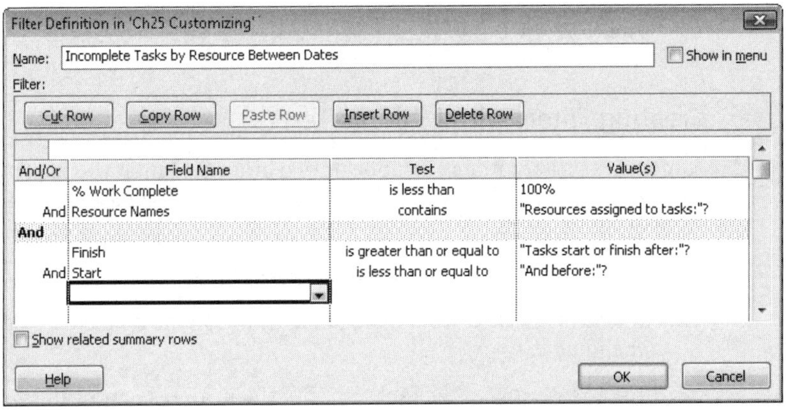

Figure 25-25 Use And or Or operators to control the order of test evaluation for a filter.

Creating Interactive Filters

In many cases, you want to supply different values each time you apply a filter. Interactive filters request values and then filter based on the values you provide.

To create an interactive filter, follow these steps:

1. In the Filter Definition dialog box for a new filter, in the Name box, type a descriptive name for the filter.

2. Click the field and test for the filter.

3. In the Value(s) cell, type a text string within quotation marks followed by a question mark (see Figure 25-25).

When you apply your new interactive filter, the text string you entered appears as a prompt in a dialog box (see Figure 25-26). The question mark instructs Microsoft Project to pause until the user enters the value.

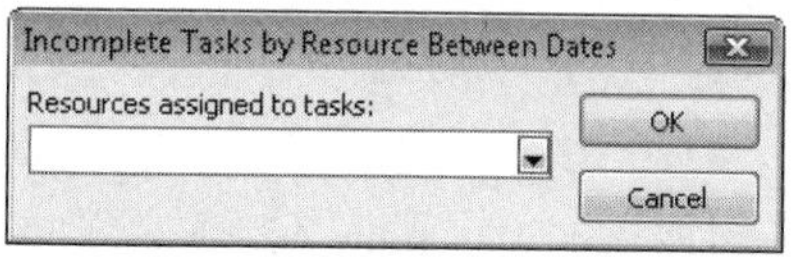

Chapter 25

Figure 25-26 When you create an interactive filter, a dialog box appears, asking for the information you specified.

Customizing AutoFilter Criteria

AutoFilter is an easy way to filter by values in a single field, for example, to show tasks assigned to a specific resource. In addition, you can quickly create custom filters by saving an AutoFilter test.

To use AutoFilter to create a custom filter:

1. Display the sheet view whose rows you want to filter.

2. Click AutoFilter on the Formatting toolbar.

AutoFilter

   The AutoFilter arrows appear in the column headings for each field in the sheet view (see Figure 25-27).

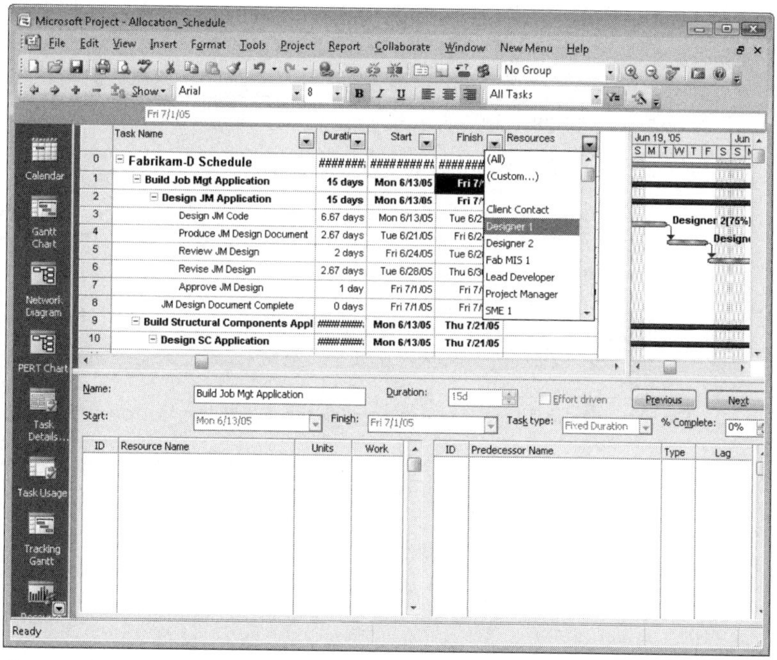

Figure 25-27 When you click the AutoFilter button, AutoFilter arrows appear in every column heading.

3. Click the arrow in the column whose information you want to filter by and then click Custom.

The Custom AutoFilter dialog box appears with the field set to the current column.

> **Note**
>
> If you want to filter by a specific value, click that value in the AutoFilter drop-down list. To remove the AutoFilter, click (All) in the drop-down list.

4. Click the arrow in the first test box and then click the criteria you want to apply.

5. In the first value box, click the arrow and then enter a value or field name.

6. To add a second test, select the And or Or option.

7. Click the test and value for the second test (see Figure 25-28).

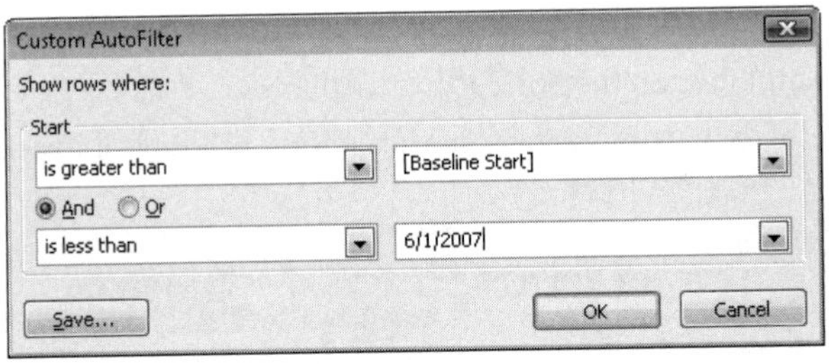

Figure 25-28 Customize and save an AutoFilter.

8. To save the AutoFilter test, click Save.

The Filter Definition dialog box appears with the tests that you defined via Auto-Filter. You can enter a filter name and make other changes before you click OK to save the filter.

> **Note**
>
> To turn off the AutoFilter arrows, click the AutoFilter button on the Formatting toolbar.

Sharing Customized Elements Among Projects

If you customize elements—such as tables, views, fields, or filters—in one project, you will probably want to use those elements in a new project. Some customized elements are stored in the project in which you create them, whereas others (menus and toolbars) are stored in the global template. In either case, you can copy elements to other projects or templates by using the Organizer. If you want a customized element available to every new project, use the Organizer to copy the element to the global template. In addition, you can use the Organizer to rename or remove elements from a project or template.

For information about using the global template, see the section titled "Working with the Project Global Template" in Chapter 28, "Standardizing Projects Using Templates." To use the enterprise global template, see the section titled "Standardizing Enterprise Project Elements" in Chapter 21, "Administering Your Enterprise Project Management Solution."

Working with the Organizer

The Organizer includes tabs for almost every type of customizable element in Microsoft Project (custom formulas belong to the custom fields in which you define them). By clicking a tab, you can see the elements of that type that are available in two project files. These project files can be active projects or templates, so you can copy customized elements between active projects or from a project to a template, or even restore the original element from a template to a project.

You can copy, delete, or rename customizable elements by including the following:

- Calendars of working time
- Filters
- Forms
- Fields
- Groups
- Maps for importing and exporting data
- Tables
- Toolbars
- Reports
- Modules of Microsoft Visual Basic for Applications (VBA) code and macros
- Views

To open the Organizer, click Tools, Organizer. An Organizer button to open the Organizer dialog box is also available in the following dialog boxes:

- More Views
- More Groups

- More Tables
- Custom Reports
- More Filters
- Customize Forms

Copying Customized Elements

No matter which type of element you copy, the procedure is the same. You choose a source file that contains the element you want to copy, choose a destination file into which you want to copy the element, and then copy the element.

Follow these steps to copy an element from a project to the global template:

1. Open the project that contains the element you want to copy.

2. Click Tools, Organizer to open the Organizer dialog box (see Figure 25-29).

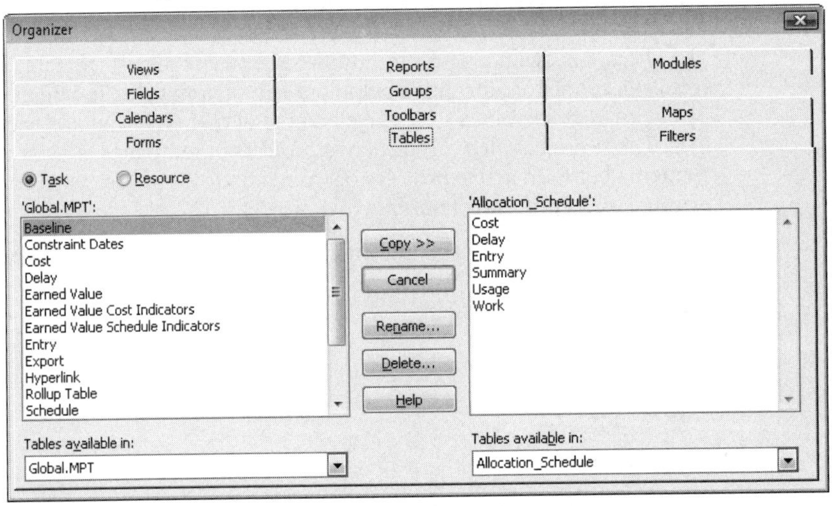

Figure 25-29 Copy customized elements between projects and templates, or rename and delete existing elements.

3. Click the tab for the type of element you want to copy.

4. In the <Element> Available In box on the right side of the dialog box, click the project that contains the element you want to copy.

   <Element> stands for the name of the current tab.

5. Click the name of the element you want to copy from the list of elements on the right side of the dialog box.

6. Click Copy. If an element with the same name already exists in the global template, Microsoft Project asks you to confirm that you want to replace the

element in the global template. Click Yes to replace the element in the global template with the one from the source project.

To copy the element with a different name, click Rename and then type a new name.

To copy an element between two projects, do the following:

1. Open both the source and destination projects.

2. Click Tools, Organizer to open the Organizer dialog box.

3. Click the tab for the type of element you want to copy.

4. In the <Element> Available In box on the right side of the dialog box, click the source project.

5. In the <Element> Available In box on the left side of the dialog box, click the destination project.

6. Click the name of the element you want to copy from the list of elements on the right side of the dialog box.

7. Click Copy. If an element with the same name already exists in the destination, Microsoft Project asks you to confirm that you want to replace the element in the destination project. Click Yes to replace the element in the destination project with the one from the source project.

   To copy the element with a different name, click No. Then click Rename and enter a new name.

CAUTION

You can't rename some built-in elements. In addition, you can't rename fields when you're working in the Organizer. You must change field names in the Custom Fields dialog box.

INSIDE OUT   Custom toolbars apply to the entire application

Microsoft Project treats toolbars differently from other customizable elements. Toolbars apply to the application instead of a particular project, so they are stored in the global template by default. When you modify a toolbar, the modified version appears, no matter which project you open.

If you want to share a customized toolbar with someone else, copy it from the global template to a project file and then send the project file to that person. They can use the Organizer to copy the toolbar to their global template.

Chapter 25

Removing Customized Elements

Although customized elements can simplify your work, extraneous elements in projects and templates can be distracting. When you copy a customized element to the global template, you no longer need it in the project in which you created it. Similarly, if you create a customized element by accident, you can remove it using the Organizer. To do this, follow these steps:

1. Open the project that contains the element you want to delete.

2. Click Tools, Organizer to open the Organizer dialog box.

3. Click the tab for the type of element that you want to delete.

4. In the <Element> Available In box on the right side of the dialog box, click the project that contains the element you want to delete.

   <Element> stands for the name of the current tab.

5. Click the name of the element you want to remove from the list of elements on the right side of the dialog box.

6. Click Delete. In the confirmation box, click Yes to delete the element.

Renaming Customized Elements

You can use the Organizer to rename customized elements. For example, you should re-name a customized element in your project if you want to copy it to the global template without overwriting the original element in the global template. You can't rename some built-in elements. Fields are renamed in the Custom Fields dialog box.

Do the following to rename a customized element:

1. Open the project that contains the element that you want to rename.

2. Click Tools, Organizer to open the Organizer dialog box.

3. Click the tab for the type of element that you want to rename.

4. In the <Element> Available In box on the right side of the dialog box, click the project that contains the element you want to rename.

   <Element> stands for the name of the current tab.

5. Click the name of the element in the list of elements on the right side of the dialog box.

6. Click Rename.

   The Rename dialog box appears.

7. Type the new name for the element.

Restoring Customized Elements to their Default State

If you forget that changes you make to a table in a view modify that table's definition, you might customize a standard table accidentally. You can reverse the changes you made, but if you made a lot of changes before you realized your mistake, it's easier to restore the standard table. You can restore standard elements by using the Organizer to copy them from the global template into your active project.

Follow these steps to restore a standard element:

1. Open the project to which you want to restore a standard element.

2. Click Tools, Organizer to open the Organizer dialog box.

3. Click the tab for the type of element that you want to restore.

> **Note**
> You can't restore a table if it appears in the current view. Either switch to a view that does not use that table or right-click the All Cells box (the blank cell above the ID numbebs) and click another table name on the shortcut menu.

4. In the <Element> Available In box on the right side of the dialog box, click the project to which you want to restore the standard element.

   <Element> stands for the name of the current tab. The global template appears on the left side of the dialog box by default.

5. Click the name of the element you want to restore in the list of elements in the global template on the left side of the dialog box.

6. Click Copy. When the confirmation dialog box appears asking you to confirm that you want to replace the element in the project, click Yes.

CHAPTER 26

Customizing the Microsoft Project Interface

Creating and Customizing Toolbars 967

Creating and Customizing Menus 977

Creating and Customizing Forms 979

Microsoft Office Project 2007 is loaded with features that help project managers pilot their projects to successful completion. Built-in menus, toolbars, and keyboard shortcuts provide easy access to commands commonly used by many project managers. Sometimes, the commands that you use frequently are not the ones on the built-in menus, or your favorites are scattered across several toolbars. As you use Office Project 2007 and begin to recognize commands you call on most often, you can customize menus and toolbars to gather your favorites in one place. If the keyboard is your tool of choice, you can also assign keyboard shortcuts to access commands without reaching for the mouse.

Microsoft Project also provides forms for entering data into fields. Although table views in Microsoft Project offer many convenient methods of data entry, forms provide more structure to the fields you fill in—perfect for folks who don't use Microsoft Project every day. Some forms, such as the Task Form and Task Details Form are off-limits—you can't change them. However, you can copy or alter some predefined forms to suit your data entry requirements or build your own.

> **Note**
>
> Although the interface for Microsoft Office programs—such as Microsoft Office Word and Microsoft Office Excel—has changed dramatically in the 2007 release, in Project 2007, the menu and toolbar interface looks comfortingly similar to its 2003 siblings.

Creating and Customizing Toolbars

Toolbars don't take up much space, but displaying several of them to see your shortlist of favorite commands consumes screen area that could be used for the Gantt Chart or other project information. By customizing existing toolbars or creating your own, you can both assemble your favorite commands in one place and minimize the space that open toolbars consume.

> **Note**
>
> You can squeeze both the Standard and Formatting toolbars along a single line to conserve space. This is the default. If some of the commands you want don't appear when these toolbars share a row, on the right end of the toolbar, click the Toolbar Options arrow and then click the toolbar button you want.
>
> If you would rather see your toolbars on two rows, which consequently give you more buttons showing at a time, right-click either toolbar and then click Customize. In the Customize dialog box, click the Options tab. Clear the Show Standard And Formatting Toolbars On Two Rows check box.

Customizing Toolbars

If a built-in toolbar has most of what you need, customizing it is easier than creating your own. For example, you might add a few buttons to the Standard toolbar from the Resource Management and Tracking toolbars. In addition to adding, removing, or rearranging toolbar buttons, you can specify how toolbars display their commands and the appearance of buttons.

Adding and Removing Buttons on a Toolbar

To add a button to an existing toolbar, follow these steps:

1.   If the toolbar you want to customize is not visible, click View, Toolbars and then click the name of the toolbar.

2.   To open the Customize dialog box, click Tools, Customize, Toolbars.

3.   Click the Commands tab.

   Categories of commands, such as File, Format, and Tracking, appear on the left side of the dialog box. The commands that belong to the selected category appear on the right side of the dialog box (see Figure 26-1).

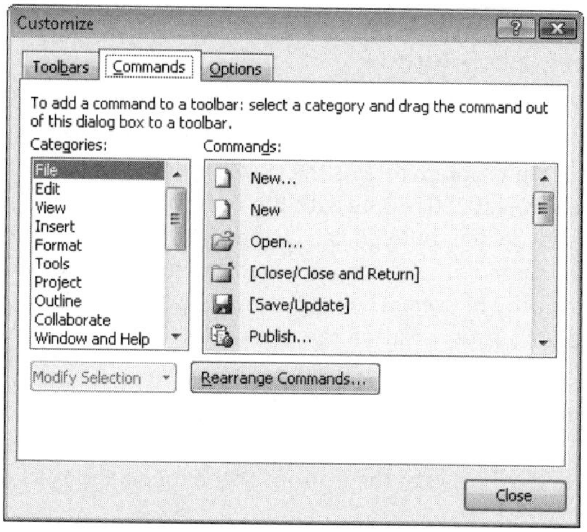

Figure 26-1 You can add commands to a toolbar or menu by dragging them from the list in the Customize dialog box.

4. Click the category of the command you want to add.

   If you don't know the category to which it belongs, select a generic or all-inclusive category, such as All Commands or All Macros.

5. Drag the command you want to add from the command list to the toolbar. The mouse pointer changes to an I-beam to indicate where the command will appear in the toolbar. Move the mouse pointer until the I-beam is in the location you want and then release the mouse button.

> **Note**
>
> A toolbar can offer even more commands when it contains a drop-down menu. To add a built-in menu to a toolbar, open the Customize dialog box and click the Commands tab. In the Categories box, click Built-In Menus and then drag the menu you want from the Commands box to its new position on the toolbar.
>
> To add a custom menu to a toolbar, click New Menu in the Categories box and drag the New Menu entry from the Commands box to the toolbar. Right-click the new menu on the toolbar, type a name in the Name box on the shortcut menu, and then press Enter. After naming the menu, you can drag commands or menus to it. Right-click a menu entry to modify the button images and text.

Chapter 26

Work with Personalized Toolbars

Microsoft Project can personalize toolbars and menus to display only the commands you use most frequently. If you upgrade to Microsoft Office Project 2007 from Microsoft Office Project 2003, the program retains the current setting for personalized menus. New installations of Project 2007 come with the personalized menu setting configured to show full menus by default, but you can change it to use personalized menus. With personalized menus turned on, the program loads menus and toolbars with commands popular with the majority of users. Then, as you select commands on menus and toolbars, those commands appear near the top of a menu, whereas commands you rarely use disappear.

If the toolbar buttons you want aren't visible, click the Toolbar Options button at the end of the toolbar and then click the button you want. To access hidden commands on a menu, click the double arrows at the bottom of the menu and then click the command you want.

To change the setting for personalized menus., right-click any menu or toolbar and click Customize on the shortcut menu. In the Customize dialog box, click the Options tab. Select the Always Show Full Menus check box to show all commands. Clear the check box to use personalized menus.

If you are patient, one way to obtain both personalized and full menus is to select the Show Full Menus After A Short Delay check box. This setting initially shows a personalized menu and then displays the full menu after a few seconds.

To remove a button from a toolbar, do the following:

1. If the toolbar you want to customize is not visible, click View, Toolbars and then click the name of the toolbar you want to customize.

2. In the Customize dialog box that appears, click Tools, Customize, Toolbars.

3. On the toolbar, right-click the command you want to remove and then click Delete on the shortcut menu.

   The command is removed only from the toolbar. It's still available in the Customize dialog box.

Quickly Customize Toolbars

You don't always need the Customize dialog box to customize toolbars. If you want to hide or display buttons that appear on a toolbar by default, click the Toolbar Options button, point to Add Or Remove Buttons, and then point to the name of the toolbar you want to customize. A list of all the buttons associated with the toolbar appears (see Figure 26-2).

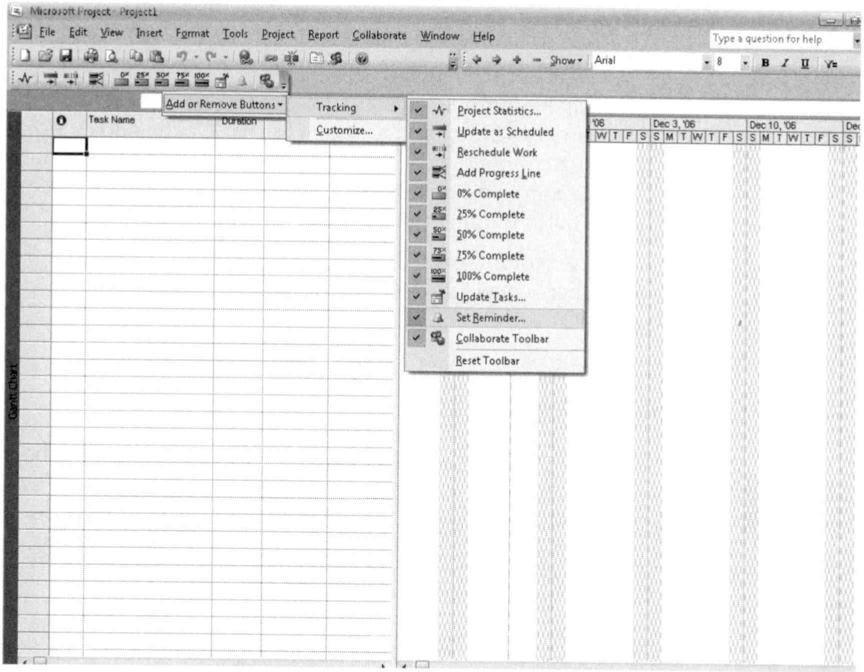

Figure 26-2 Click the Toolbar Options button on a toolbar to add or remove buttons on that toolbar.

The commands on the shortcut menu of toolbar buttons have the following characteristics:

- Commands that are preceded by a check mark currently appear in the toolbar.
- Commands that do not have a check mark are hidden.
- Commands that are dimmed are not on the toolbar by default.

Clicking a command in the list toggles the command between hidden and visible. If you add a button to a toolbar, you can remove it only by using the Customize dialog box.

To rearrange the buttons on a toolbar, follow these steps:

1. Click View, Toolbars and then click the toolbar's name to display the toolbar whose buttons you want to rearrange.

2. Click Tools, Customize, Toolbars.

    The Customize dialog box appears, which is the only result you need for rearranging—it doesn't matter which tab is showing.

3. On the toolbar, drag the button you want to move until the I-beam is in the location you want. Then release the mouse button.

TROUBLESHOOTING

You can't remove buttons on a toolbar

The Add Or Remove Buttons command doesn't remove custom buttons you add to a built-in toolbar or any buttons on a custom toolbar. On the Add Or Remove Buttons shortcut menu, a custom toolbar's name is dimmed, as are buttons you add to a built-in toolbar. The Customize dialog box must be open to remove buttons from a custom toolbar or custom buttons from a built-in toolbar.

To remove these buttons, right-click the toolbar and then click Customize. While the Customize dialog box is open, drag the buttons off the toolbar.

Changing the Properties of a Toolbar

When you right-click a toolbar button while the Customize dialog box is open, a shortcut menu with commands for changing the contents and properties of a toolbar appears. The commands on this shortcut menu include the following:

- **Reset** For a button on a built-in toolbar, this command restores the original button, command associated with the button, and settings.

- **Delete** Removes the button.

- **Name** Displays a box in which you can type the name that appears in the ToolTip for the button.

- **Copy Button Image** Copies the selected button image to the Clipboard so that you can paste it to another button.

- **Paste Button Image** Pastes the image on the Clipboard to the selected button. In addition to images from other buttons, you can paste graphics from other applications.

- **Reset Button Image** Restores the button image to the default.

- **Edit Button Image** Opens the Button Editor dialog box, in which you can edit the image.

- **Change Button Image** Displays a menu of predefined images that you can choose for the image.

- **Default Style** Displays only a button image on a toolbar and the button image and text on a menu.

- **Text Only (Always)** Displays only text for the command on toolbars and menus.

- **Text Only (In Menus)** Displays a button image on a toolbar and only text on menus.

- **Image And Text** Displays a button image and text on toolbars and menus.

- **Begin A Group** Adds a group divider to the toolbar.

- **Assign Macro** Opens the Customize Tool dialog box in which you can select a command for the button.

TROUBLESHOOTING

The toolbar doesn't appear where you want it

Toolbars can cling to the top, sides, or bottom of the screen; or they can nomadically float in their own window in the middle of the screen. To dock the toolbar in a location, drag the toolbar to the top, side, or bottom of the screen.

To float the toolbar, drag it to the location you want somewhere in the middle of the screen. Double-click a floating toolbar to dock it.

Creating Toolbars

If your favorite commands are scattered across several built-in toolbars, creating a custom toolbar might be the best solution. You can also use the Organizer to copy an existing toolbar to use as a template.

To create a new toolbar, follow these steps:

1. Click Tools, Customize, Toolbars.

   The Customize dialog box appears.

2. Click the Toolbars tab and then click New.

3. In the New Toolbar dialog box, type the name of the toolbar you're creating.

4. Click OK.

   In the Customize dialog box, the toolbar name appears in the toolbars list, and the empty toolbar appears on the screen (see Figure 26-3).

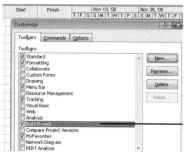

Figure 26-3 As soon as you name your new toolbar, it appears on the screen, ready to accept command buttons.

5. In the Customize dialog box, click the Commands tab.

6. Click the category of the command you want to add.

7. Drag the command you want to add from the command list to its location on the new toolbar.

 The icon for the command appears on the toolbar.

8. Repeat steps 6–7 for all the command buttons you want to add to your new toolbar (see Figure 26-4).

 The commands on a single toolbar can be from different categories.

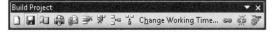

Figure 26-4 You can create a toolbar with the commands you use frequently regardless of which category holds them.

The Organizer is helpful if you want to make a copy of a toolbar so that you can modify it to meet your needs. Because Microsoft Project saves toolbars and menus in the global template by default, you must copy the toolbar to your active project, rename it, and then copy the new toolbar back into the global template for editing.

For more information about the global template, see Chapter 28, "Standardizing Projects Using Templates."

To use an existing toolbar as a template for a new toolbar, do the following:

1. Click Tools, Organizer.

2. In the Organizer dialog box, click the Toolbars tab.

 Elements in the global template appear on the left side of the dialog box.

3. In the list for the global template, click the name of the toolbar you want to use as a template.

4. Click Copy to copy the toolbar to your active project.

5. In the list for your active project, click the toolbar you just copied and then click Rename.

6. In the Rename dialog box, type a unique name for the toolbar and click OK.

 To make it easy to identify custom toolbars, add a special identifier to the toolbar name, such as preceding the name with C_ or your initials. To ensure that your custom toolbars appear at the beginning of any toolbar list, preface the name with A.

7. With the copied toolbar still selected, click Copy again to copy the renamed toolbar back to the global template.

8. In the list for your active project, click the toolbar and then click Delete so that the toolbar appears only in the global template list.

9. Close the Organizer.

10. To change your new toolbar, follow the steps in the section titled "Customizing Toolbars" earlier in this chapter.

TROUBLESHOOTING

You can't find the custom toolbar you built

Customized menus belong to Microsoft Project, not the active project file, and are stored in the global template so that they are available whenever you use Microsoft Project on your computer. For example, if you go to a different computer and open the project that was open when you created the custom toolbar, that toolbar does not appear on the Toolbars menu.

To use the custom toolbar on another computer, you must either copy the global template to that computer or use the Organizer to copy the toolbar. On the computer that contains the global template with the custom toolbar, open the Organizer and copy the toolbar from the global template to the project file itself. Then, on the other computer, open the project file, open the Organizer, and copy the custom toolbar to the global template on that computer.

Deleting Toolbars

You can't delete built-in toolbars, only custom toolbars that you created. Follow these steps to delete a user-defined toolbar:

1. Click Tools, Customize, Toolbars.

   The Customize dialog box appears.

2. Click the Toolbars tab and then click the name of the user-defined toolbar you want to delete.

3. Click the Delete button. Click OK in the dialog box that prompts you to confirm the deletion.

> **Note**
> To delete several toolbars without displaying each one, use the Organizer. Click Tools, Organizer. Click the Toolbars tab. Click the name of the custom toolbar and then click Delete.

TROUBLESHOOTING

You can't delete a toolbar

Although you can't delete the toolbars that are built into Microsoft Project, you can reset them to their original configuration. In the Customize dialog box, the Delete button is dimmed when you select a built-in toolbar. To reset a built-in toolbar, click the toolbar in the list and then click Reset. Click OK in the dialog box that prompts you to confirm your actions.

Resetting a toolbar removes any customizations you made, including any custom buttons you created. To save custom buttons, copy them to another toolbar before you reset the current one.

Modifying Button Images

You can modify the images that appear on toolbar buttons, whether to differentiate Print buttons for different printers or simply to satisfy your creative nature. You can move the image around within the boundaries of the button or change the colors of the cells that make up the image.

Do the following to modify a button image:

1. Right-click a toolbar and then click Customize.

   The Customize dialog box appears.

2. Right-click the button you want to edit and then click Edit Button Image.

   The Button Editor dialog box appears (see Figure 26-5).

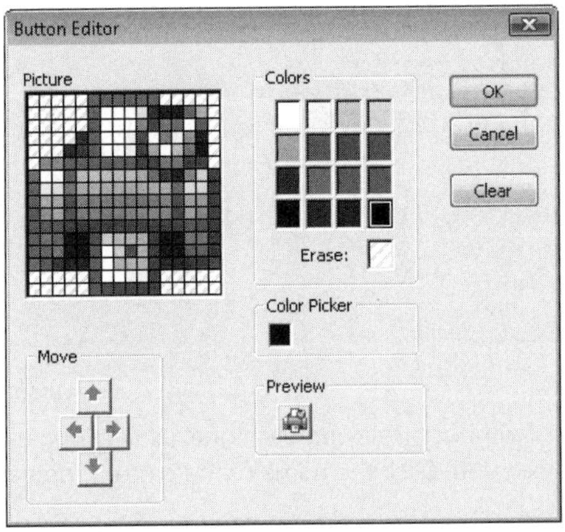

Figure 26-5 You can modify the image that appears on a toolbar button.

3. To choose a color to paint in the image, click a color in the Colors area. If you want to erase colored boxes in the image, click the Erase box.

4. In the Picture area, change the cell colors by clicking individual cells or dragging the mouse pointer over several cells.

    As you change the image, the Picture area shows what the image looks like.

5. To move the image within the Picture area, click a directional arrow in the Move area.

    If the image fills the Picture area in one or more directions, the directional arrows in those directions are dimmed.

Creating and Customizing Menus

Menus are simply toolbars with a different presentation style. Menus can contain commands or other menus, just like toolbars, but menus can also display a description of the commands or submenus.

> **Note**
>
> Toolbars and menus belong to the entire Microsoft Project application, not just to a particular project, which is why Microsoft Project stores them in the global template by default. When you modify a toolbar or menu, the modified version is available no matter which project you open.
>
> To share a customized toolbar with others, copy it from the global template to a project file and then send the project file to your colleagues. They can use the Organizer to copy the toolbar to their global templates.

You can add, remove, or rearrange commands and submenus on a menu. As you do for toolbars, you can also specify whether the menu displays buttons or text, and you can change the appearance of buttons.

To add a menu to another menu, follow these steps:

1. Click Tools, Customize, Toolbars.

    The Customize dialog box appears.

2. Click the Commands tab. Scroll to the bottom of the Categories list and click New Menu.

    New Menu is the only command in the New Menu category.

3. Drag the New Menu command to the location on a menu where you want to insert it (see Figure 26-6).

Figure 26-6 You can insert a menu on a menu bar or menu.

Create Keyboard Shortcuts

Keyboard shortcuts are a fast way to choose commands without switching between the keyboard and the mouse. You can assign a keyboard shortcut to any command on a menu. With the Customize dialog box open, right-click the menu or command for which you want to define a keyboard shortcut. In the Name box on the shortcut menu, type an ampersand (&) before the letter you want to use as the shortcut.

Take care to use a different letter for each keyboard shortcut on a menu. If you choose a letter that is already in use by another menu entry, you might have to press the letter more than once to select the command you want.

To choose a command by using a keyboard shortcut, click a menu to display its commands. Press the shortcut letter for the command you want to select.

To add a command to an existing menu, follow these steps:

1. Click the Commands tab in the Customize dialog box.

2. Click the category of the command you want to add to the menu.

3. Drag the command from the command list to its new location on the menu.

Note

When you drag any command from the Customize dialog box to a menu bar, an I-beam pointer appears. Drag the command until the I-beam is where you want to place the command or menu and then release the mouse button. If you want to insert a command in a menu, drag the command and point to the menu in which you want to insert it. When the commands for that menu appear, drag the mouse pointer to the new location and release the mouse button.

To remove a command from a menu, do the following:

1. Click Tools, Customize, Toolbars.

The Customize dialog box appears.

2. Right-click the command you want to remove from the menu bar and then click Delete. If you want to remove a command from a pull-down menu underneath the menu bar, navigate to the command you want to remove, right-click it, and then click Delete.

> **Note**
>
> You can rearrange the commands on a menu and modify their properties in the same way that you customize buttons on a toolbar. With the Customize dialog box displayed, drag a command or menu to its new location.
>
> To modify the properties of a command or menu, right-click it and then click the command you want on the shortcut menu, as described in the section titled "Changing the Properties of a Toolbar" earlier in this chapter.

Creating and Customizing Forms

Custom forms are simply dialog boxes containing Microsoft Project fields for data entry. Don't confuse custom forms with built-in form views such as the Task Entry view. Form views are built into Microsoft Project and show a set of predetermined fields. On the other hand, custom forms are dialog boxes in which you control the fields of information that appear on the form, where they appear, and whether they are editable or only viewable.

Before you dive into creating custom forms, keep in mind that entering field values in a table within a view is fast and easy. In a table, you can copy values to several tasks or resources at the same time by using the fill handle to drag values down the columns, as described on page 03xx. To enter the fields you want in a table, you might have to display a different table, insert the fields you want into the current table, or create a custom table with only the fields you want to enter.

The advantage of a custom form is that it presents only the information you want to enter, which comes in handy when you're not comfortable editing data directly in tables, or you delegate data entry to someone who doesn't use Microsoft Project regularly. When you choose values in the form fields, Microsoft Project takes care of assigning the values to the correct fields.

To use a custom form, you first select the tasks or resources you want to edit with the form. Then you open the form and enter values into the fields. When you click OK on the form, Microsoft Project applies the changes to the selected tasks or resources, and the form closes.

Chapter 26

Creating Forms

You can create a new custom form or copy an existing form and then edit it. With custom forms, you have the power to add fields, text, and buttons where you want them and group items within group boxes to visually separate them within the form.

Follow these steps to create a new form:

1. Click Tools, Customize, Forms.

The Customize Forms dialog box appears (see Figure 26-7).

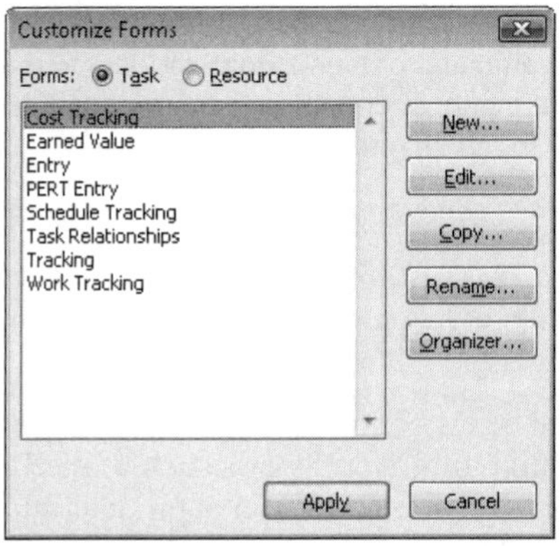

Figure 26-7 Use the Customize Forms dialog box to edit an existing form or create a new one.

2. To create a new custom form, click New.

To use an existing form as a template, click the form in the list and then click Copy. In the list of forms, the copy appears, which you can edit.

3. In the Define Custom Form dialog box, type a new name for the form. If you want to open the form with a keyboard shortcut, type the letter in the Key box.

CAUTION

Microsoft applications use many letters of the alphabet for keyboard shortcuts for other commands, such as C for Copy, X for Cut, and P for Paste. If you select one of these reserved characters for a shortcut key, a warning appears that instructs you to select another letter.

4. When you click OK, the Custom Form Editor opens (see Figure 26-8).

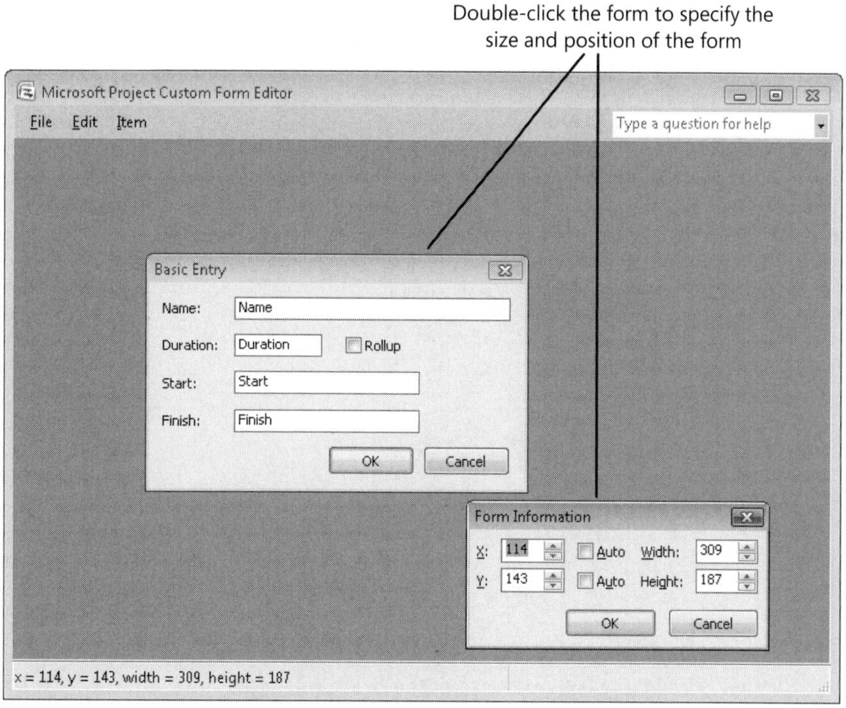

Double-click the form to specify the
size and position of the form

Figure 26-8 You can specify the size and position of the dialog box for a custom form as well as its contents.

5. To change the size of the form, drag a corner or one of its edges until the form is the size you want.

6. To change where the form appears when it loads, drag the title bar of the new form to the onscreen location you prefer.

   If you want to specify an exact size and location for the form, double-click the form. In the Form Information dialog box, enter values in the X and Y boxes to specify the form's location. Enter values in the width and height boxes to specify the form's size.

> **Note**
>
> In the Form Information dialog box, the values in the X and Y boxes represent pixels on the screen. If your screen resolution is 1280 by 1024, for example, a form with a width of 640 and height of 512 would take up half the screen.

7. To save your new form, click File, Save. To return to Microsoft Project, click File, Exit.

Adding Fields

Custom forms display fields that you can fill in to enter information about the selected tasks or resources. By default, you can view or edit any of the fields in a form. However, you can also restrict a field so that you can view it but not edit it.

To add a field to a form, follow these steps:

1. In the Microsoft Project Custom Form Editor window, click Item, Fields.

    The Item Information dialog box appears (see Figure 26-9).

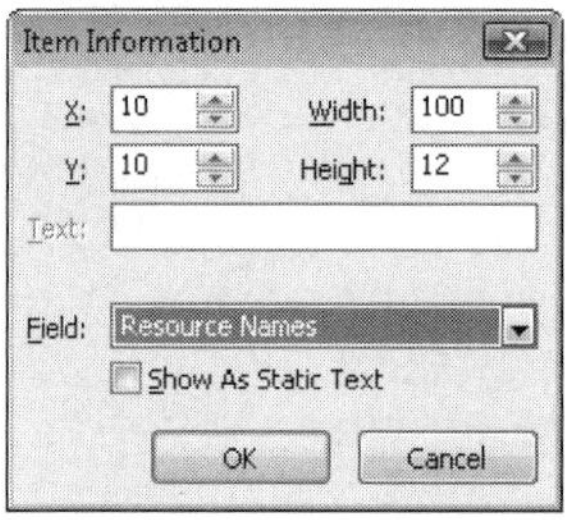

Figure 26-9 You can specify the size, position, and field name as well as whether users can edit the field value.

2. To specify the location of the field, enter values in the X and Y boxes.

3. To specify the size of the field box, enter values in the Width and Height boxes.

> **Note**
>
> After you add a field box to your form, you can easily resize it by dragging one of its edges or corners. You can also move the field box by dragging the center of the box to the new location.

4. In the Field box, click the field that you want to appear in the box.

    To quickly locate the field you want, click the down arrow and then type the first character or two of the field name.

5. To prevent users from editing the field, select the Show As Static Text check box. A value appears in the field, but users can't edit those values.

6. Click OK.

    The field box appears in the form as specified. Make any adjustments you want to the size and position of the field box.

7. Repeat this procedure for all field boxes you want to add to your custom form.

Adding Text

Entering data in the correct fields is difficult if you can't tell which field is which. You can add text to label the fields or display other information that makes the form easier to complete. To add text to a form, do the following:

1. In the Custom Form Editor window, click Item, Text.

A new blank text box appears as a dashed rectangle within the form you are editing.

2. Double-click the text box to display the Item Information dialog box.

3. In the Text box, type the text you want to appear on the form and then click OK.

The text appears in the form. If necessary, drag the text to the position you want.

Follow these steps to modify text:

1. To change the size of the text box, drag one of its edges or corners.

2. To reposition the text box in the form, drag the center of the text box to the location you want.

3. To change the text itself, double-click the text box and edit the text.

Adding Buttons

A new form includes OK and Cancel buttons by default. Because these are the only two buttons you can include in a custom form, the only time you need to add buttons is if you removed one of them earlier. To replace a button you removed, follow these steps:

1. In the Custom Form Editor window, click Item, Button.

The New Button dialog box appears.

2. Select the option for the button that you want to add to the form.

You can add only an OK or Cancel button.

3. Click OK in the New Button dialog box to add the button to the form.

4. Drag the button where you want it to appear in the form.

> **Note**
>
> A form includes an OK and Cancel button by default. You can't add another OK or Cancel button to the form. The only time you can exercise the Item, Button command is after you delete one of those buttons.

Chapter 26

Adding a Group Box

If a form contains a lot of fields, you can make the form more readable by grouping related fields. You can add a group box to the form and then move the items you want to group into it.

To add a group box to a form, do the following:

1. In the Custom Form Editor window, click Item, Group Box.

   The group box appears in the custom form.

2. Drag the group box to the location you want in the form.

3. To resize the group box, drag one of its edges or corners.

4. To change the text that appears at the top of the group box, double-click the group box. In the Item Information dialog box, type the new label in the Text box.

5. Move any other items you want into the group box.

TROUBLESHOOTING

I can't find the command to delete items in a custom form

Adding items to a custom form is easy, but you might have trouble figuring out how to delete items you don't want. None of the menus in the Custom Form Editor window contain a Delete command, and the old standby, Ctrl+X, doesn't work. If you added an item inadvertently, immediately pressing Ctrl+Z to undo the addition doesn't work either. In fact, Ctrl+Z doesn't undo any actions in the Custom Form Editor window.

The only way to delete an item on a custom form is to select the item and then press the Delete key on the keyboard. When you select an item, a dashed rectangle appears to show which item is selected.

Editing Forms

Follow these steps to edit an existing form in Microsoft Project:

1. Click Tools, Customize, Forms.

   The Customize Forms dialog box appears.

2. Click the name of the form you want to edit and then click Edit.

3. Make the changes you want in the Custom Form Editor window, as described in the section titled "Creating Forms" earlier in this chapter and the sidebar titled "Deleting Items in a Custom Form" earlier in this chapter.

4. When finished, click File, Save.

5. Click File, Exit to close the Custom Form Editor window and return to Microsoft Project and the Customize Forms dialog box.

Renaming Forms

Do the following to rename an existing form:

1. Click Tools, Customize, Forms.

2. In the Customize Forms dialog box, click the name of the form you want to rename and then click Rename.

3. In the Define Custom Form dialog box, type the new name and click OK.

Displaying Custom Forms

The Custom Forms toolbar includes an icon for every custom form. However, for a custom form you plan to use frequently, it's more convenient to add a button to a toolbar or assign a shortcut key to open it.

To open a custom form from the Microsoft Project menus, follow these steps:

1. Select the tasks or resources you want to edit.

2. To open a custom form, you can choose View, Toolbars, Custom Forms and then click the icon for the form (see Figure 26-10).

   If the toolbar doesn't include an icon for the form, click Tools, Customize, Forms. The Customize Forms dialog box appears. Click the name of the form you want to display and then click Apply.

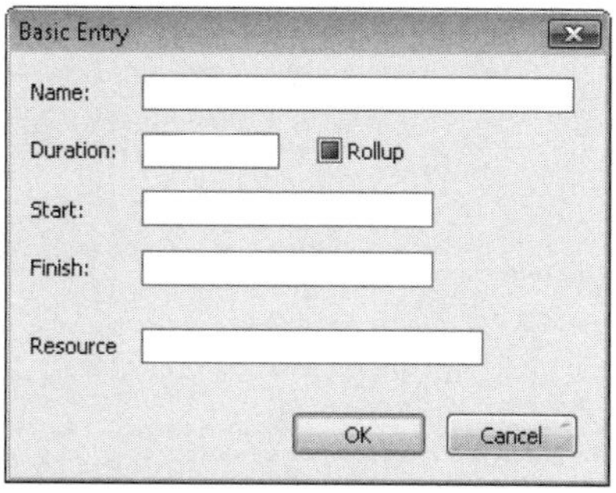

Figure 26-10 Select the task or resource form you want to edit and then click Apply to display the form.

To add a form as a toolbar button, follow these steps:

1. Click Tools, Customize, Toolbars.

   The Customize dialog box appears.

2. Click the Commands tab. Click the All Forms category.

3. Drag the form you want to add from the command list to the toolbar.

   For more information about adding buttons to toolbars, see the section titled "Adding and Removing Buttons on a Toolbar" earlier in this chapter. For information on defining a keyboard shortcut for a form, see the section titled "Creating and Customizing Forms" earlier in this chapter.

Automating Your Work with Macros

Understanding Macros 987

Creating Macros. 989

Running Macros. 998

One of the easiest ways to increase your day-to-day productivity with Microsoft Office Project 2007 is to use macros. Macros can automate repetitive, tedious, or complex tasks, freeing your time for more important tasks such as managing your projects.

This chapter focuses on macros you might use to automate tasks that you need to do frequently. Typically, macros are created by recording the steps in a task, which means that little (if any) programming is required.

Understanding Macros

Washing the dishes—what a chore. Pick up a dirty plate, wash it with soapy water, rinse it off, and then dry it. It's the same every time. But with a dishwasher, all the tedium of washing, rinsing, and drying is automatically handled by the machine, leaving you free to do better things with your time. Similarly, you don't want to perform the same tedious series of commands week after week; you just want a specially formatted report to print every Friday. What you need is a macro.

What Is a Macro?

Basically, a macro is a shortcut that performs a series of commands. Rather than manually performing each step necessary to complete a task, you simply tell the software what each step is, what needs to be accomplished in each step, and in what order the steps must occur. Then you designate some way to set this series of commands in motion.

To do this in Office Project 2007, you have Microsoft Visual Basic for Applications (VBA), a macro language that is not only powerful but easy to understand and use. A subset of the highly popular Microsoft Visual Basic programming language, VBA is both powerful and easy to understand. What's more, the tools available in Project 2007 make creating macros as easy as can be. Most macros can be created without ever seeing, much less writing, VBA code.

Why Use Macros?

When you use Microsoft Project (or any other business productivity software), you use it because it makes doing your job easier and more efficient. One of the reasons that software can make you more productive is that the features it has are, in a sense, a collection of macros that accomplish tasks that the software designers feel can be accomplished more effectively by using a computer. More importantly for this discussion, these "macros" perform tasks that the designers learned their customers want. But what the designers can't do is create all the features that every customer wants. This is where macros can prove so useful.

Because individual users can create a macro to accomplish some particular task, you can essentially customize the software by adding features that support the particular way you do your job.

For example, let's say that you do have to print a certain report every Friday. Before you can print anything, you have to do the following:

- Choose the right view of your project data.

- Choose among several filters to exclude unwanted tasks.

- Choose how you will sort the data.

- Choose the report format you need.

After you open the right project, you might have to click your mouse well over a dozen times before you can print the report. With a macro to perform all those steps for you, printing the report would be reduced to only a few mouse clicks.

Just because macros can be used to perform a complex series of steps doesn't mean that every macro has to be elaborate. Maybe you have certain simple things you do in Microsoft Project all the time, such as creating work breakdown structure (WBS) code masks. By recording a macro and creating a new toolbar button for it, you have a convenient one-click method for opening the WBS Code Definition dialog box.

> **Note**
> For more information about creating new toolbar buttons to run macros, see the section titled "Creating Toolbar Buttons" later in this chapter.

Creating Macros

The easiest and quickest way to create a macro, especially one that will be used to automate a lengthy series of steps, is to record the steps that make up a task. Recording a macro is just what it sounds like: Start the macro recorder, perform the series of actions you want the macro to do, and then stop the recorder. In most cases, there's no need to edit the VBA code generated by the recorder.

For more information about creating macros by writing VBA code directly, including how to edit macros, see the Microsoft Office Project 2007 Software Development Kit (SDK), available online at *http://msdn2.microsoft.com/en-us/library/aa568824.aspx*.

Understanding the Record Macro Dialog Box

Before you can record a macro, you must first prepare your project environment for recording by setting the conditions required for the steps in the macro to occur. Such conditions might include something obvious such as opening a particular project, but can also include steps such as selecting a certain task or resource. You should also have a clear plan for what you want to record. Any mistakes you make while the macro recorder is running will be included in the macro. After you have set the conditions and made your plan, you're ready to begin recording.

Click Tools, Macro, Record New Macro. The Record Macro dialog box appears (see Figure 27-1), in which you can enter information about the macro (such as a name and a description) and assign it a shortcut key.

Chapter 27

Figure 27-1 The decisions you make in the Record Macro dialog box determine not only when you can use a macro, but also aspects of how it will behave when it runs.

For more information about assigning keyboard shortcuts to macros, see the section titled "Creating Keyboard Shortcuts" later in this chapter.

Three settings in the Record Macro dialog box are even more important than the name of the macro or the keyboard shortcut you might use to run it:

- **Store Macro In**   Use the choices in the drop-down list to specify where the macro will be stored. If you choose This Project, the macro is stored in the file with the project that is currently open and will be available only when that project is open. If you choose Global File, the macro is stored in the global project template file (global.mpt) and is available whenever Microsoft Project is running, regardless of whether a particular project (or any project at all) is open.

  Store macro in: [Global File   ▾]

- **Row References**   Accept the default setting of Relative if you want Microsoft Project to record relative row references. Thus, when the macro is run, it will always attempt to move the same number of rows from the selected cell after the macro encounters the command to select a new cell.

  For example, suppose that a cell in row 1 is selected and you select a cell in row 4 while recording the macro. From then on, every time the macro is run and encounters the command to select a new cell, it always moves three rows from whatever cell was selected before the macro was run.

  Select the Absolute option if you want be certain that a particular row—based on the selected cell's row ID—will be selected when a macro runs. In the example just given, your macro will always select a cell in row 4, regardless of which cell is selected before the macro is run.

- **Column References**   Unlike row references, the default setting for column references is Absolute, based on the selected field. No matter where fields are positioned, absolute column references select the same column every time. Relative column references work just like relative row references.

Where the Macros Are: In the Project or the Global

When creating a new macro, you need to decide whether you will be storing the macro in the current project or in the project global file. Which is best? Well, that depends. Table 27-1 lays out the conditions and recommendations for different situations.

Table 27-1 Where to Store the Macros

Store the macro in the project if	Store the macro in the global if
Certain very specific conditions must be met in the project plan for the macro to run successfully. For example, you might need to select a particular task before running your macro, or you might need to select a varying group of resources.	Conditions aren't as stringent for the macros. Many formatting macros can fit this category.

Store the macro in the project if	Store the macro in the global if
You're distributing the project to others and want the project to be fully self-contained, without also having to provide the global project template.	The macro is entirely for your own use, for the use of individuals using the same project plan on the same computer, or for the use of individuals who all have access to the global project template, through a network share, for example.
You're not expecting to need to edit the macros.	The macro is used in multiple projects or by multiple users, and you know you might need to adjust the macros and want to make the change just once. When you edit a macro in the global project template, the change is implemented the next time any user accesses the global project template to open his project. That is, you don't have to edit the macro 30 times for 30 different users on 30 different computers.
You've set up a number of keyboard shortcuts, and you're concerned about the limited number of keyboard shortcuts in the global project template and keyboard shortcuts in the project getting in each other's way.	Keyboard shortcuts are not a big issue in your macros, or if you're certain that macros in the project plan and the global project template use different keyboard shortcuts.

Another note about keyboard shortcuts and the global file: Because all the macros in a particular project must share the available keyboard shortcuts, toolbar buttons, and names, only one macro in a project can use Ctrl+A as a keyboard shortcut, for example. This rule also applies to the Microsoft Project global file, which is open whenever Microsoft Project is running. If you use Ctrl+A as a keyboard shortcut in the global file, no other macro in the global file can use that shortcut. If you store your Ctrl+A macro in the project file, however, you can have another macro, stored in another project, which also uses Ctrl+A as its keyboard shortcut.

Absolute Column References Can Be Tricky

The decision to use absolute column references might seem like the best solution in all cases, but absolute column references are based on the selected field. Because fields can be moved, you might sometimes get unexpected results.

For example, suppose that you recorded a macro using absolute column references in a project you share with someone else. When you recorded the macro, you selected the third column, which contained the Start field. At some point, however, your co-worker opened the project and inserted the Duration field as the third column.

The next time you run the macro, the fourth column gets selected because that's the new location of the Start field. If you assumed that the third column would always be selected because absolute column references are "safe" and that's where you always put the Start field, your macro is now broken.

Knowing When to Say "When"

Knowing when to stop the recorder can be as important as the recording environment itself. For an automatic procedure like a macro to be truly trustworthy—and therefore useful—it should have an ending point that is intuitive, or at least easy to remember.

For example, the Bold button on the Formatting toolbar is basically a macro to auto-mate clicking Font on the Format menu and then clicking Bold in the Font Style list. If you have already selected a word, you know that clicking the Bold button formats the word a certain way and then stops. If you haven't selected a word, you know that the Bold button turns on a certain kind of formatting for anything you type until you click it again to turn that formatting off. Both endings are so easy to remember that they've probably become intuitive for you.

The same should be true for any macro you record. It should be easy for you to remem-ber what conditions must be met before you can run the macro, what the macro will do, and when it will stop. A macro that performs a 20-step procedure for you is no good if you're afraid to run it because you can't remember what it might do along the way.

Add the Visual Basic Toolbar

If you record new macros frequently or prefer to run macros by selecting them by name rather than using a keyboard shortcut or a toolbar button, you might find it convenient to use the Visual Basic toolbar:

To display the Visual Basic toolbar, click View, Toolbars, Visual Basic. You can also simply right-click in the toolbar area of the screen and then click Visual Basic on the shortcut menu. The same commands that are available by clicking Tools, Macro are available here on this toolbar.

Recording a Macro

Let's return to the idea of a weekly report, as described earlier in this chapter. The re-port that you print every Friday requires you to do the following:

- Change the view to the Tracking Gantt.

- Apply a filter to display only incomplete tasks.

- Sort the tasks by finish date in ascending order.

- Use the Slipping Tasks report to print the results.

> **Note**
>
> Before recording your macro, make sure that all your planned steps will take you successfully through to the end of the process you want to program.
>
> In the following example, you need to open a project that actually contains slipping tasks. If there are no slipping tasks, a report is not generated, and you can't record the steps for printing the report and closing the dialog boxes.

You've decided to automate the tasks needed to print your Friday report by recording them in a macro. Follow these steps to record the macro:

1. Click Tools, Macro, Record New Macro.

   The Record Macro dialog box appears.

2. In the Macro Name box, enter a name for your new macro, for example, Friday_ Report.

   A macro name cannot contain spaces, but you can use the underscore character to represent spaces if you want. Although the macro name can contain letters, numbers, and the underscore character, it must begin with a letter. Also, the macro name cannot use any word that Microsoft Project reserves as a keyword.

3. In the Store Macro In box, click This Project.

4. In the Description box, change the first line to a descriptive name, for example, Weekly task report.

5. Because the macro won't be selecting cells, make sure that the Row References option is set to Relative, and the Column References option is set to Absolute (Field).

6. Click OK to begin recording.

   If you are showing the Visual Basic toolbar, the Record Macro button changes to the Stop Recorder button. Otherwise, there's no indication that you're in the macro recording mode.

> **Note**
>
> Remember, everything you do when recording will be written into the macro that you are creating, including any mistakes.

7. Click View, Tracking Gantt.

8. Click Project, Filtered For, Incomplete Tasks.

9. Click Project, Sort, By Finish Date.

10. Click Report, Reports.

11. Double-click Current Activities, double-click Slipping Tasks, and then click Print.

12. Click OK in the Print dialog box and then click Close in the Reports dialog box.

13. Stop the recorder by clicking Tools, Macro, Stop Recorder. If you're showing the Visual Basic toolbar, you can click the Stop Recorder button instead.

Stop Recorder

> **Note**
>
> We chose to store this macro in the open project, but it's a good example of a macro that could be stored in the global file as well. Because all the macro does is change the way the data in a particular project is displayed and then print a report, you could record the steps to open the right project at the beginning of the macro. You could then print the report whenever Microsoft Project is running without having to manually open the project first.

TROUBLESHOOTING

Why doesn't your macro select the right cell?

If your macro is supposed to select cells as it runs, but it selects the wrong ones or even causes an error, one of the following items may be the cause:

- The macro was recorded using one combination of settings for absolute or relative column or row references, but the actual conditions under which the macro is run require a different combination.

  You can either re-record the macro by using a combination that better suits the situation under which the macro is run, or you can edit the macro code in the Visual Basic Editor (VBE) and then change it manually.

  Table 27-2 shows the different values that should be used when changing the type of column and row references, if you change the reference settings manually:

Table 27-2 Absolute and Relative References

Reference	Absolute	Relative
Column	The value for the Column argument is the name of the field in quotation marks.	The value for the Column argument is a positive number, indicating the number of the column.
Row	The value for the Row argument is a positive number, indicating the number of the row, and the RowRelative argument is False.	The value for the Row argument may be either a negative or positive number. The RowRelative argument is either True or is missing (the default value is True).

> **Note**
>
> The columns for the row number and the Indicators field (if showing) are both counted when using relative column references. The first "normal" column is actually column 3 when manually editing column references in a macro.

- The macro assumes that a particular cell or item has been selected before the macro is run.

  You could always try to remember that the proper cell is selected before running the macro, but re-recording the macro (or editing it in the Visual Basic Editor) to select the proper cell before it does anything else solves the problem and also makes the macro more robust.

- The column (or row, if it is for a subtask) containing the cell to select may have been hidden, or the row may have been deleted.

  Most of the solutions to this problem involve writing complicated Visual Basic code, so the best solution, until you're more comfortable working with the Visual Basic Editor to edit your macros, is to simply make sure that the proper conditions are met before running your macro. Using column references can also help you spot this problem early on because your macro will cause an error on the line that refers to the missing column and make it easier for you to guess what the problem is.

Looking at Macro Code

For many people, knowing how to record and play back a macro is sufficient for most of their needs. But what if you made a minor mistake while recording a macro? What if you recorded a complex macro that referenced a project by file name and then the file name was changed? Although you might not ever need to know how to write VBA code, much less create an entire macro with it, the first step to making simple changes or corrections is to understand how simple and logical the macro code can be.

For more information about the Visual Basic Editor, refer to its Help system. Click Tools, Macro, Visual Basic Editor. Click Help, Microsoft Visual Basic Help.

If you were to start the Visual Basic Editor that is included as part of Microsoft Project and open the Friday_Report macro, this is the code you would see:

```
Sub Friday_Report()

' Macro Weekly task report

' Macro Recorded Tue 2/5/07 by Steve Masters.

  ViewApply Name:="Tracking Ga&ntt"

  FilterApply Name:="I&ncomplete Tasks"

  Sort Key1:="Finish", Ascending1:=True

  ReportPrint Name:="Slipping Tasks"

End Sub
```

It's short and reasonably simple. You might already have made some guesses about what different sections of the code mean, such as information that also appears in the Microsoft Project interface. Table 27-3 gives descriptions of each line in the VBA code.

Table 27-3 Breakdown of Code in the Friday_Report Macro

Macro code	What it means
Sub Friday_Report()	It's the beginning of the macro. *Sub* is short for subroutine, which is what a macro really is. The text that follows is the name of the macro.
' Macro Weekly task report ' Macro Recorded Tue 3/5/02 by Steve Masters.	Any line that starts with an apostrophe is a comment and is ignored by Visual Basic. You can use comments anywhere in a macro to remind yourself of what the different parts do.
ViewApply Name:= "Tracking Ga&ntt"	This line changes the view to the Tracking Gantt. The ampersand (&) comes before the letter that acts as an access key on the View menu.
FilterApply Name:= "I&ncomplete Tasks"	This line applies a filter to display only incomplete tasks.

Macro code	What it means
Sort Key1:= "Finish", Ascending1:=True	This line sorts the tasks by finish date in ascending order.
ReportPrint Name:= "Slipping Tasks"	This line prints the Slipping Tasks report.
End Sub	It's the end of the macro, like the period at the end of a sentence.

If, after recording the macro, you decide that you prefer to sort the tasks in descending order, it doesn't take much time or trouble to record the macro all over again. But it takes even less time to simply edit the macro and change True to False in the line Sort Key1:= "Finish", Ascending1:=True.

Follow these steps to start the Visual Basic Editor so that you can edit the macro code:

1. Click Tools, Macro, Macros.

   Pressing Alt+F8 is another way to display the Macros dialog box.

2. In the Macro Name list, click the name of the macro you want to edit.

3. Click the Edit button.

   The Visual Basic Editor starts and displays your macro code (see Figure 27-2). You can now begin editing the macro code.

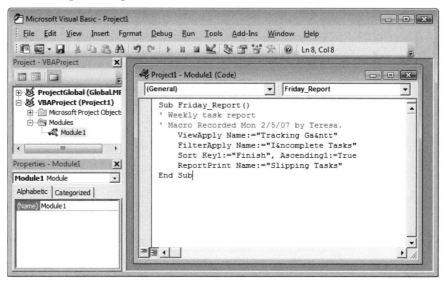

Figure 27-2 Open VBE to review and edit your macro code.

Running Macros

Run Macro

There are three standard methods for running a macro. First, you can run a macro by selecting it from the list of available macros in the Macros dialog box. In the Macros dialog box, select the name of the macro you want to run and then click the Run button.

The other two methods are to press a keyboard shortcut assigned to a macro and to click a toolbar button created for a macro.

Creating Keyboard Shortcuts

Key commands such as Ctrl+C are the oldest and most common shortcuts to access software features, especially for displaying dialog boxes or performing some quick action. Unfortunately, as more and more keyboard shortcuts are assigned to software features, fewer of these simple combinations are left over to be used for macros.

In Microsoft Project, a keyboard shortcut for a macro must be a combination of the Ctrl key and a letter. Because Microsoft Project has many built-in keyboard shortcuts, the only letters available for macro shortcuts are A, E, J, M, Q, T, and Y.

You can assign a keyboard shortcut to a macro when you record it, as described in the section titled "Creating Macros" earlier in this chapter. You can also assign a keyboard shortcut to a macro any time after you create it by using the Macro Options dialog box.

Follow these steps to open the Macro Options dialog box:

1. Click Tools, Macro, Macros.

2. In the Macro Name list, click the name of the macro you want to modify.

3. Click the Options button.

    The Macro Options dialog box appears (see Figure 27-3).

Macro Options
Macro name: Friday_Report
Description:
Weekly task report
Macro Recorded Mon 2/5/07 by Teresa.
Shortcut key: Ctrl + [   ]
OK   Cancel

    Figure 27-3 Change a macro's description or shortcut key with the Macro Options dialog box.

4. Add a shortcut key combination and then click OK.

    You can also edit the macro description if you want.

> **Note**
>
> To take the most advantage of the quick access provided by keyboard shortcuts, assign them to frequently used macros that perform simple tasks such as opening a dialog box.

Creating Toolbar Buttons

The most common shortcut for running a macro is to create a toolbar button for it. This is true for the following reasons:

- You don't have to memorize a key combination.
- You can display the name of the macro as part of the button.
- You can add it to both a menu and a toolbar, and you can group it with other buttons that are related in some way.

> **Note**
>
> Menus are treated just like toolbars—you can add, modify, or even delete menus and menu commands as you wish.

A macro is not associated with a toolbar button when you record it. Instead, you actually customize the Microsoft Project interface by using the Customize dialog box.

Follow these steps to create a new toolbar button for a macro:

1. Click View, Toolbars, Customize. You can also simply right-click in the toolbar area and then click Customize on the shortcut menu. The Customize dialog box appears.

2. Click the Commands tab and then click All Macros in the Categories list (see Figure 27-4).

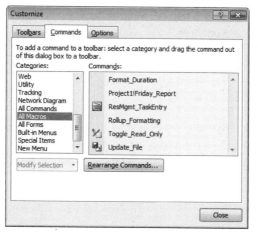

Figure 27-4 Open the Customize dialog box to choose a macro to add as a toolbar button.

Chapter 27

3. Click the name of a macro in the Commands list and then drag it to the desired location on any toolbar or menu (see Figure 27-5).

Project1!Friday_Report

Figure 27-5 Add your macro to any toolbar or menu in Microsoft Project.

When you create a toolbar button for a macro, the button initially displays just the name of the macro. You can modify the new button in many ways, including renaming it, assigning an image to it, or changing its display style. You can even edit the image used for a button or draw your own.

Follow these steps to assign an image to the button:

1. Click View, Toolbars, Customize.

2. While the Customize dialog box is open, click the toolbar button for which you want to display an image.

   When the Customize dialog box is displayed, clicking a toolbar button doesn't run the macro or command; instead, it selects the button. When selected, the button has a black border.

3. In the Customize dialog box, click the Commands tab.

4. Click the Modify Selection button.

5. Point to Change Button Image and then click the graphic you want to use for your selected toolbar button.

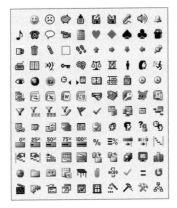

6. Click the Modify Selection button again and then click Default Style.

   The button displays the image you selected, but the name of the macro appears only as a ScreenTip when you move the mouse pointer over the button.

Note

The Name box on the Modify Selection menu is used for both the caption and the ScreenTip of the button you're modifying. You can change this text to whatever suits you without also changing the name of the macro itself.

For more information about customizing Microsoft Project toolbars and menus, see Chapter 26, "Customizing the Microsoft Project Interface."

Chapter 27

Standardizing Projects Using Templates

Understanding the Template Types. **1004**

Working with the Project Global Template **1005**

Working with Project Templates **1008**

Closing a Project **1018**

With each project you manage, you learn more and more. You practice effective project management methods and see what works and what doesn't, especially for your particular organization with your brand of projects. You gain more knowledge about project management in your specific discipline or industry. Likewise, as you continue to manage projects with Microsoft Office Project 2007, you increase your proficiency with it as a productivity tool for planning, tracking, and communicating your project information.

You can record some of the knowledge you gain from hard-won project management experience by using Office Project 2007 templates. As you enter the closing stages of a project, saving the project file as a template for future use can be one of your most valuable project closing activities because of the tremendous efficiencies it can create for future projects. Templates are special project files in which various types of project information can be stored for use with future projects, either by you or by other project managers.

You can also use templates to save yourself from reinventing that old wheel. Obtain project templates already developed by industry experts and adapt them for your own project requirements. This will likely save you time and give you a leg up on planning your next project. You might also find some new things to consider that you hadn't thought of before.

Whether a template is based on your own project experiences or someone else's, it can contain the following types of information:

- Tasks
- Durations
- Task sequencing
- Task dependencies
- Phases
- Deliverables
- Milestones

- Generic work, equipment, and cost resources

- Resource assignments

- Average resource rates

- Custom project, task, and resource fields

Templates are also a great means of setting standards. If your organization follows a specific methodology in each project, if certain review processes are required at certain stages, or if a specific format is mandated for deliverables, those requirements can all be reflected in the template. Similarly, any custom features—including custom fields, tables, views, filters, and so on—that reflect organization standards or that create project conveniences can also become a part of your template.

Understanding the Template Types

Microsoft Office Project 2007 has three types of templates:

- **Project template** The project template might contain task and resource information that you can use as a basis for starting a new project. It's often based on past project experiences in the organization or in the industry. For example, there are product development templates, commercial construction templates, software project templates, ISO 9000 management templates, and so on.

  A wide variety of project templates are available, both within Microsoft Project and from third-party sources. You can use such a project template as the basis for a new project you're creating. If you're closing a project, you can save and adapt your plan as a project template file for you or others to use and benefit from your experience.

- **Project global template** The project global template, also referred to as the global.mpt file, is a template that contains elements and settings pertinent to how you use Microsoft Project. Such elements include views, tables, groups, filters, and reports for customized ways of looking at project information. The project global template can include calendars, macros, and toolbars for specific methods of executing Microsoft Project commands and functions. The project global template can also include Microsoft Project program settings that define the defaults for editing, scheduling, and calculations, to name a few.

  The project global template is automatically attached to every project file you work with. As the user and project manager, you have control over the content of your project global template, and you can share it with others if you want.

- **Enterprise global template** If you're set up for enterprise project management using Microsoft Office Project Professional 2007 and Microsoft Office Project Server 2007, the enterprise global template is also automatically attached to every enterprise project you check out or create while Office Project Professional 2007 is connected to your project server. Think of the enterprise version as being the global template over the project global template, or the "global global."

This template dictates standards being enforced and customizations made available throughout the enterprise, for example, custom fields, views, and macros. These standards provide for customization and consistency across all projects in an organization. The standards propagated through the enterprise global template also make it possible for project information throughout the enterprise to be compared and analyzed in meaningful ways.

Because the enterprise global template affects all projects throughout the enterprise, only users who have certain permissions can check out and modify the enterprise global template. Many organizations give that responsibility to one or two project server administrators or portfolio managers.

The enterprise global template and your local project global template can work together. As long as there's no conflict between elements in your project global template and elements in the enterprise global template, you can create your own standards and customizations for all your own projects. If a conflict exists in such a situation, the enterprise global template takes precedence.

> **Note**
> For more information, see the section titled "Working with the Enterprise Global Template" in Chapter 21, "Administering Your Enterprise Project Management Solution."

Working with the Project Global Template

The project global template—global.mpt—is loaded every time Microsoft Project starts. Essentially, the project global template is a collection of custom elements and default settings throughout a project file. These elements include the following:

- Views
- Custom fields and outline codes
- Tables
- Toolbars
- Groups
- Forms
- Filters
- Macros and Microsoft Visual Basic for Applications (VBA) modules
- Reports
- Import/export maps
- Base calendars

As you alter settings in your project by customizing views and calendars, modifying tables, and creating sets of custom fields, for example, those changes initially apply to just the current project. If you want your custom settings available to any project opened on your local computer, you can add them to the project global template by using the Organizer (see Figure 28-1). Those new settings become your new defaults.

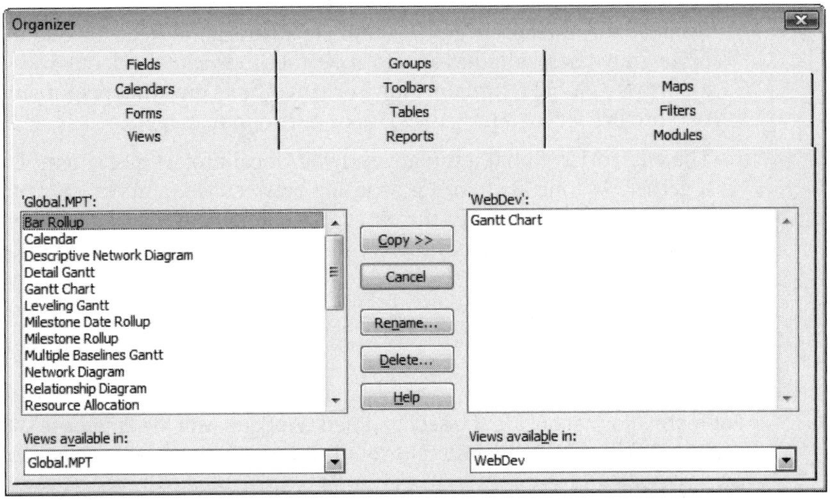

Figure 28-1 Use the Organizer to copy customized elements to the project global template and make those elements available to other projects.

For more information about the Organizer, see the section titled "Sharing Customized Elements Among Projects" in Chapter 25, "Customizing Your View of Project Information."

The project global template also contains your Microsoft Project-wide settings, which you access by clicking Tools, Options. In the Options dialog box, various categories of options are available—View, Schedule, Calculation, and so on. Certain settings apply just to the current project file; others apply to Microsoft Project as a whole and change the project global template. You can use the Set As Default button to add current project settings to your project global template (see Figure 28-2).

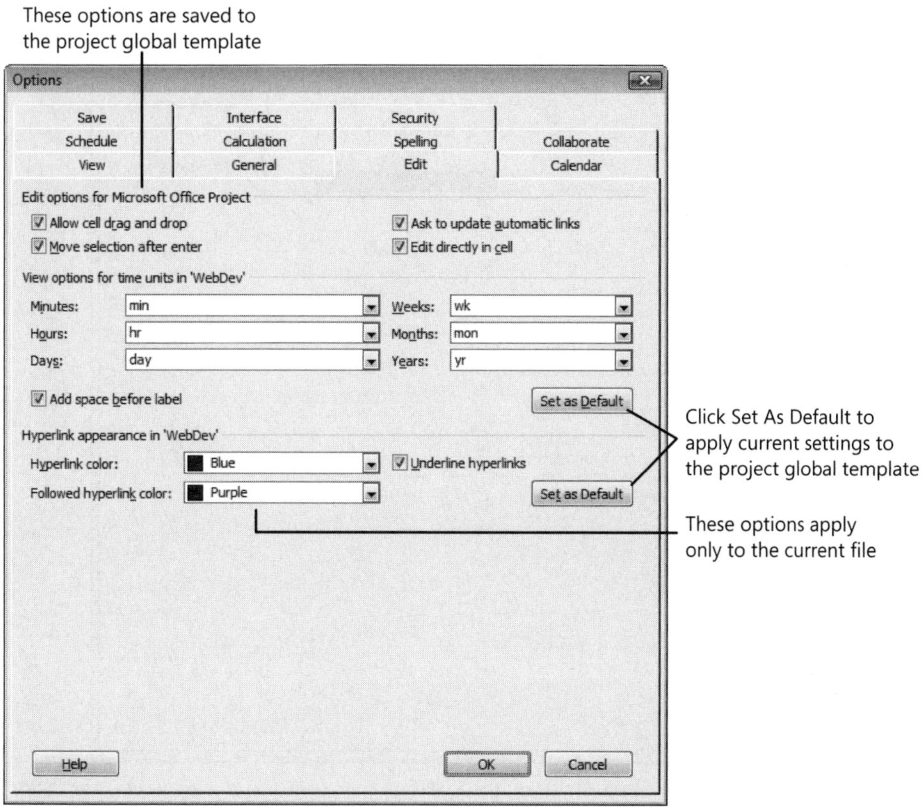

These options are saved to
the project global template

Click Set As Default to
apply current settings to
the project global template

These options apply
only to the current file

Figure 28-2 Any group of options specified as being for the current file applies only to that file unless you click the Set As Default button.

Settings that do not specify that they apply only to the current file apply to Microsoft Project in general (see Figure 28-3).

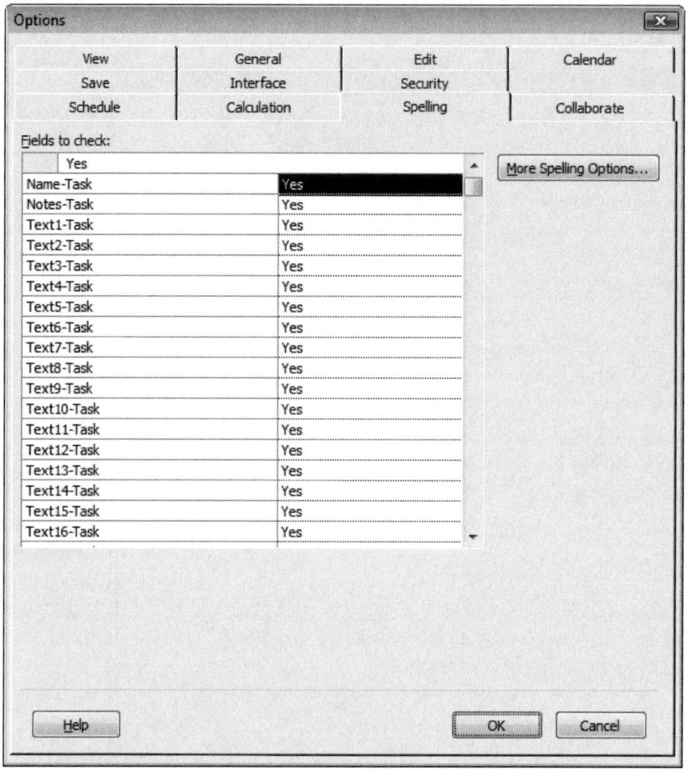

Figure 28-3 The settings on the Spelling tab apply to your spelling checker options in Microsoft Project in general. Changes here update the project global file.

When you change a Microsoft Project setting, every new file you open from that point on will reflect that change. When you change a local project setting and then set it as a default, it will apply to any new projects, but it will not change the setting for other existing projects.

Working with Project Templates

A project template is a standardized starting point for a new project. A template can contain task information, resource information, or both. It might be very broad in scope, showing just major phases and generic resource names, for example. Or, the template can be highly detailed, with multiple outline levels of tasks, their durations, task dependencies, and specific resource information.

Microsoft Project comes with a set of built-in templates for a variety of industries and applications. Microsoft Project templates are available from third-party sources as well, such as professional societies and standards organizations. You can create your own templates based on previous projects you have completed. It's good practice to adapt and save the plan of a completed project as a template for future use in your organization, either for yourself or for others.

For more information about using a project plan as template, see the section titled "Creating Your Own Project Template" later in this chapter.

A project template serves as a knowledge base for a certain type of project. It is meant to save you time when planning your new project and to let you build on past project experiences. The project template can also help set and enforce organizational standards. It can disseminate custom features and elements, such as specially designed reports, company-specific base calendars, and modified views.

Starting a New Project Using a Template

Whenever you start a new project, you're given the opportunity to choose a template. If you start a project with a template, your new project file is populated with information from that template. You then adapt that information to meet your project's specific requirements. When you save the file, you're saving a new project file, rather than overwriting the existing template file. This way, the template remains available for use in its more generic format.

Built-In Templates

Forty-one templates are supplied with Microsoft Office Project 2007—29 more than were built in to Microsoft Office Project 2003. The following are the categories of templates provided:

- Business development
- Customer service
- Construction and facilities
- Finance and accounting
- General business
- Human resources

Chapter 28

- Information technology
- Standards and process

Examples of new templates in Project 2007 include human resource information system implementation, insurance claim processing, ISO 9001 management review, marketing event planning and execution, Six Sigma DMAIC cycle, and vendor request for proposal solicitation.

For a complete list of the templates, see Table 3-1 in the section titled "Creating a Project File" in Chapter 3, "Starting a New Project." Or, click File, New. Click the On Computer link, and then click the Project Templates tab.

Creating a New Project with a Template

To create a new project from a template, follow these steps:

1. Click File, New.

Note

If you just click the New button on the Standard toolbar, you won't get the choices you need in the Project Guide.

2. In the New Project pane, under Templates, click the On Computer link.

3. In the Templates dialog box, click the Project Templates tab (see Figure 28-4).

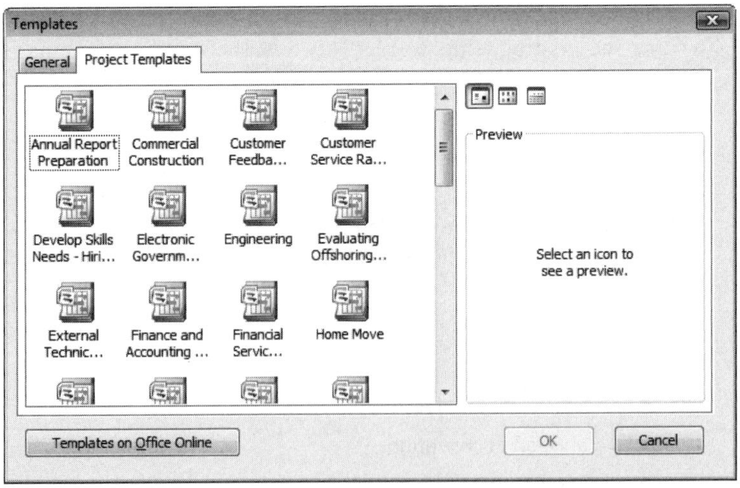

Figure 28-4 All built-in templates are listed on the Project Templates tab of the Templates dialog box.

4. Click the project template you want to use and then click OK.

A new project plan appears, based on the template you chose (see Figure 28-5).

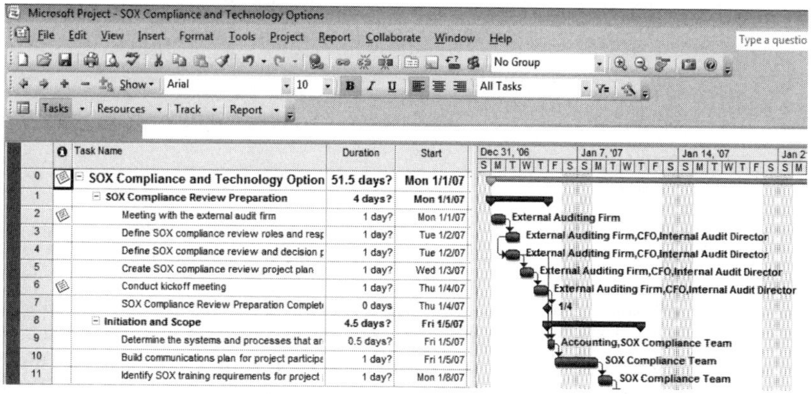

Figure 28-5 A new project file is created based on your selected template.

Saving Your New Project

The original template file has an extension of .mpt, indicating that it is a Microsoft Project template file type. When you save a new project file based on a template, by default, your new project file is saved as a normal MPP (Microsoft Project plan) file. To save a project based on a template, do the following:

1. On the Standard toolbar, click Save.

2. In the Save As dialog box, choose the drive and folder in which you want to save the new project.

3. In the File Name box, enter a descriptive name for your project and then click the Save button.

Adapting the Template to Your Project

Review your new project file for the types of information included and the level of detail. Review as follows:

- In the Gantt Chart or other task sheet, review the list of tasks. Determine whether you need to add more tasks or remove extraneous ones.

- Check to see whether durations are filled in for the tasks. If they are, see if they seem close to the durations you will expect in your new project. Most templates include durations as estimated durations, as indicated by the question mark (?).

- Examine the chart portion of the Gantt Chart or the Network Diagram and see whether task dependencies have been set up. Review their appropriateness and their complexity.

Save

Chapter 28

- Display the Resource Sheet. If generic resources are listed, start considering real resources who can replace the generics. If you're using a template generated within your organization, you might see names of actual individuals.

Based on this review, you can see how much adaptation you'll need to do to tailor this template to your project.

INSIDE OUT Create a new project from an existing one

You can use an existing project as the basis for a new project. To do this, click File, New. In the New Project pane, under New, click the From Existing Project link. Browse to find the project you want to use as the basis for your new project and then open it. When you save this file, Microsoft Project makes sure that you give it a different name, so the original file remains intact.

When you use an existing project file as the basis for a new project plan, you typically need to do a little more adaptation than with a regular template, because there is extraneous information, such as actuals, that you won't need in your new project.

A quick way to remove the bulk of this historical information while keeping the good stuff is to first save the file as a template, as follows:

1. Click File, Save As. Browse to the location where you want to save the new project and then give the new project a name. Then in the Save As Type list, click Template (*.mpt). Click Save.

2. In the Save As Template dialog box, select all the check boxes to remove baselines, actuals, and cost information. Then click Save.

   The file is saved as a template, minus the data that pertained only to the progress of that other project.

3. Click File, Save As again. This time save the file as a regular project file.

You're now set to go. There might be additional information yet to remove, such as date constraints or certain resource information, but you've already taken care of the majority.

If you're building a new project plan based on a template or on an existing plan, use the Adjust Dates tool to bring the scheduled project start date in the template to your own project's start date.

Click View, Toolbars, Analysis to show the Analysis toolbar. Click the Adjust Dates button on the Analysis toolbar. In the Adjust Dates dialog box, enter your project start date and then click OK.

Adjust Dates
Adjust Dates

Downloading a Project Template from the Web

You can download additional templates for different industries and endeavors from the Office Online Web site. To do this, follow these steps:

1. Click File, New.

2. In the New Project pane, click the Templates On Office Online link.

   Your Web browser launches and goes to the Templates page of the Office Online Web site.

3. In the Search Templates box, type **Microsoft Project** and then click Search.

   A list of Microsoft Project templates appears (see Figure 28-6). Some are created by Microsoft, others were suggested and added by project management experts in the field.

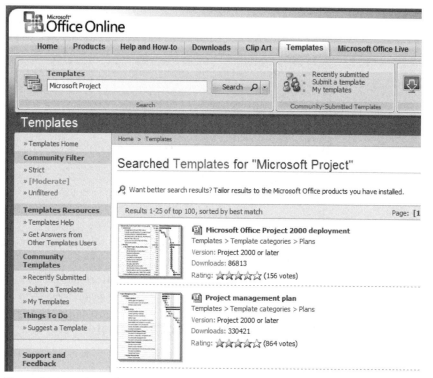

Figure 28-6 Find and download more project management templates.

Another way to find templates is to navigate through the lists of templates in the Browse Templates area. You can click a category, for example, Plans, to see the list of templates. To narrow that list to Microsoft Project templates, in the side pane, under Filter By Product, click Project.

4. To select or just preview a template you might want to download, click its name in the list.

A preview of the selected template appears (see Figure 28-7).

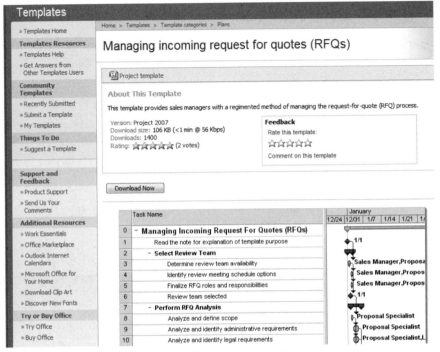

Figure 28-7 Preview a template to see if it meets your needs.

5. If you like the template, click Download Now.

6. In the Save As dialog box that appears, change the name if you want and then click Save.

The template is downloaded, saved, and appears in Microsoft Project. You can now adapt that template to the specifics of your project.

Creating Your Own Project Template

After you plan and track a few projects to completion using Microsoft Project, you'll see that you're recording valuable information in your project plans. Of course, you'll archive your project plan for historical purposes. However, you can also use an existing or completed project plan as the basis for a template that will save you and others a great deal of time when planning future projects.

By creating your own template, you can save task and resource information, format settings, project-specific options, calendars, macros, and other elements that you've used successfully in other projects. Any Microsoft Project file can be saved as a template.

To save an existing project file as a template for future use by you or other project managers, follow these steps:

1. Open the project file you want to save as a template.

2. Click File, Save As.

3. In the Save As Type list, click Template (*.mpt).

    The file name changes from the .mpp extension to .mpt, indicating that a copy of the regular project plan file will be saved as a template file. Also, the file is moved to the Templates folder. As long as your template is stored in this folder, it will appear in the Templates dialog box.

4. Click the Save button.

    The Save As Template dialog box appears (see Figure 28-8).

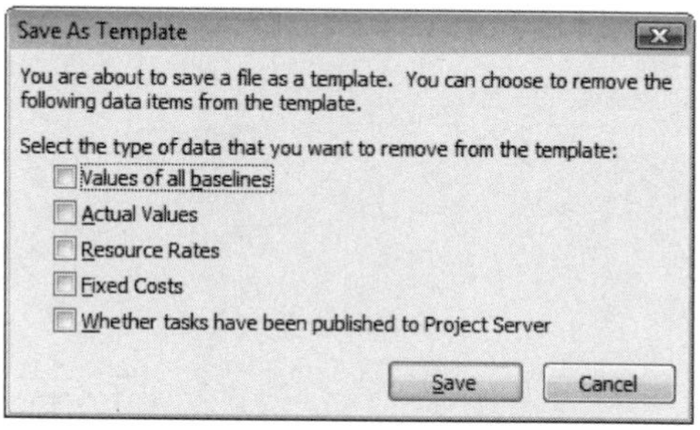

Figure 28-8 The file might include tracking and other specific information not appropriate for a template. Select the information you want to exclude from the template.

5. Select the check box for any item you do not want to be saved as part of the template and then click the Save button.

    The file is saved as a template in your Microsoft Templates folder on your computer's hard disk.

Copy Templates That Others Have Created

If you want to use templates that others in your organization have created, or if you obtain templates from a third-party source or an industry standards organization, copy the file into your Microsoft Templates folder. Storing the template in the right folder ensures that you'll see the templates listed in the Templates dialog box.

To see or change the default location that Microsoft Project is using to store templates, click Tools, Options and then click the Save tab. Under File Types, find the path for User Template.

For Microsoft Project running on Windows Vista, the default path is C:\Users\<Name>\AppData\Roaming\Microsoft\Templates.

For Microsoft Project running on Windows XP, the default path is C:\Documents and Settings \<Name>\Application Data\Microsoft\Templates.

By default, the Application Data folder is hidden in your Windows file system. To show hidden files and folders, open Windows Explorer. In Windows Vista, click Organize on the toolbar and then click Folder And Search Options. In Windows XP, click Tools, Options. In either Windows Vista or Windows XP, click the View tab. In the Advanced Settings box, double-click Hidden Files And Folders if necessary to show its options. Select the Show Hidden Files And Folders option. Click OK.

To check that your new template appears in the Templates dialog box, do the following:

1. Click File, New.

2. In the New Project pane, under Templates, click the On Computer link.

   Your new template should be listed on the General tab (see Figure 28-9).

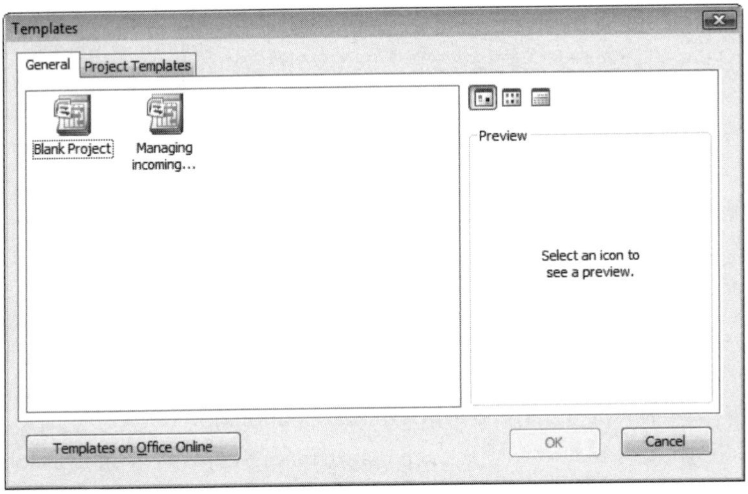

Figure 28-9 The General tab of the Templates dialog box contains any templates you've created.

Note

By default, templates stored in the Microsoft Templates folder appear in your Templates dialog box. You can store templates in a different folder, however, and direct the Templates dialog box to find them in the new location. Changing the location of the templates can be useful if a set of templates has been developed for your organization, and they've been placed on a file server for multiple project managers to use and perhaps update.

To change the location of the Microsoft Templates folder, click Tools, Options and then click the Save tab. Under File Locations, click User Templates and then click the Modify button. Browse to the new location and then click OK.

Review the new template file to see whether any other information should be removed. Here are some suggestions:

- Display the task sheet and apply the Constraints table. See if any date constraints should be changed to As Soon As Possible or As Late As Possible.

- Review the task dependencies shown in the template. Determine whether they're useful or should be removed.

- Review the Resource Sheet. Decide whether you want to keep specific resource information or replace it with generic resource names. Also decide whether you should change maximum units and other availability information, and whether the cost information should be retained or deleted.

- Review tasks, resources, and assignments to see whether any notes should be removed.

After you finish adapting the template, click Save on the Standard toolbar. Your changes are made to the template.

Updating an Existing Template

If you need to update the information in an existing template, you cannot simply open the template and save it. If you do, Microsoft Project will try to save a copy of the template as a regular project (MPP) file. To update and save information in the template itself, follow these steps:

1. Open the template you want to update.

2. Make the changes you want.

3. On the Standard toolbar, click Save to open the Save As dialog box.

4. In the Save As Type list, click Template.

   The current folder switches to the Templates folder. The template you just edited should appear in the list of files.

5. Click the template and then click the Save button.

   A prompt appears, indicating that you're about to replace the existing file. And that's exactly what you want to do.

6. Click OK. The Save As Template dialog box appears.

7. Click the Save button. Your changes are saved to the template file.

CAUTION!

If several project managers use the same project template, be careful when you're updating templates because your changes can affect many projects.

Chapter 28

Closing a Project

After the planning, executing, and controlling processes of the project, the final process is the closing of the project. At this point, you've fulfilled the goals of the project and it's now complete. In the closing stages of the project, you can analyze project performance with concrete data about schedule, cost, and resource use. You can also identify lessons learned and save acquired project knowledge.

Analyzing Project Performance

Review your overall project and compare your baseline plan to your actual plan. You can review variances in the schedule, in costs, and in assignment work. Any large variances can help point out problem areas in the project. Some helpful reports for such analysis include the following:

- Project Summary
- Overbudget Tasks
- Top-Level Tasks
- Overbudget Resources
- Milestones
- Earned Value
- Budget

To generate one of these reports, click View, Reports and then double-click Overview or Costs. Double-click the name of the report.

For more information about generating reports, see Chapter 12, "Reporting Project Information."

Recording Lessons Learned

Whether or not you will continue to be involved in this type of project, others are likely to benefit from the experience and knowledge you've gained. At the end of your project, gather your team together and conduct a "postmortem" session, in which you can objectively discuss what went well with the project and what could be improved next time.

It's often helpful to have team members prepare notes in advance. For larger projects, you might find it more practical to conduct a series of meetings with different groups of team members and stakeholders, perhaps those who were responsible for different aspects of the project.

Be sure to have a concrete method for recording the discussion points. After the session(s), compile the lessons learned report, including solutions to identified problem areas.

If the project plan is your repository for project-related documents, add your lessons learned report to the closed project. You can embed the document in the plan or create a link to the document. Or, if you're working in an enterprise environment with Office Project Server 2007, you can add it to the document library for the project.

For more information about adding a document to a project, see the section titled "Attaching Project Documentation" in Chapter 3. For information about using the document library,
see the section titled "Controlling Project Documents" in Chapter 22, "Managing Enterprise
Projects and Resources."

In addition to archiving the document with the rest of the project historical records, include it with your planning materials for the next project. Be sure to keep your solutions
in the forefront so that you can continue to improve your project management processes.

> ### Project Management Practices: Administrative Closure
>
> As you complete each major milestone or phase, you probably get formal acceptance of
> that phase by the sponsor or customer. The sponsor reviews the deliverables and checks
> that the scope and quality of work are completed satisfactorily, and then signs off the
> acceptance of that phase.
>
> When you reach the end of the project, you obtain your final acceptance and signoff,
> which at this point should be a formality because the sponsor has been involved and
> signing off on the interim deliverables all along.
>
> This final project acceptance is part of the administrative closure of the project. Admin-
> istrative closure also includes analyzing project success and effectiveness, and archiving
> documents and results. At this point, contracts are closed and budget records are ar-
> chived. Employees should be evaluated, and their skills in your organization's resource
> pool should be updated to reflect the increase in skills and proficiencies they've gained
> as a result of working on this project.
>
> A complete set of project records should make up the project archives, and these ar-
> chives should be readily available as a reference for future similar projects.

Saving Acquired Project Knowledge

Through the planning and tracking of your project, it's likely that you've recorded a
mass of valuable information about the following:

- Task durations
- Task and resource costs
- Work metrics (units per hour completed, and so on)

You might want to collect information about planned or actual durations, work, and
costs to use as standards for planning future projects.

These durations and work metrics can be included in a project template based on the
closing project. Save the project plan as a project template for future use by you or other
project managers in your organization who will be working on a similar type of project. In your template, you can remove actuals, resource names, and constraint dates,
for example. But the tasks, durations, task dependencies, base calendars, and generic
resources can be invaluable in a project template. In addition, any custom solutions
you've developed—such as views, reports, filters, and macros—can also become a part
of your template. Through the efficiencies you built into your project plan, you're laying
the groundwork for future efficiencies.

Opening Project Files **1021**

Saving Files. **1026**

Saving and Opening with Different File Formats **1030**

Safeguarding Your Project Files **1032**

I t's a very basic concept: When you save a project file, you're ensuring that it will be there when you need to open and work on it again. In a nutshell, managing project files involves saving and opening your project files. In addition to saving and opening project files for Microsoft Office Project 2007, you might need to search for a file you have misplaced. You might want to work with files that were created in earlier versions of Office Project 2007 or even files that were created in other applications.

You also want to guard against data loss in the event of a system crash by saving your file often enough and having a recent backup file handy. Another safeguard is password protection and security settings. These are all aspects of sound file management, which are covered in this chapter.

Opening Project Files

After you save a project, you can open it again and continue working. You can open a file stored on your own computer or on a network drive. If you're working in an enterprise environment, you can open your project file from the Microsoft Office Project Server 2007.

You can open many different types of files in Microsoft Project, including spreadsheet, text, and database files.

Opening a Saved Project

You can open files from your local machine as well as from a network drive. If you're running Microsoft Office Project Professional 2007, you can also open a project file from a project stored in the Office Project Server 2007 database.

Opening a Project from Your Local Computer or a Network Drive

To open a project from your local computer or a network drive, do the following:

Open

1. On the Standard toolbar, click Open.

The Open dialog box appears with your default folder selected (see Figure 29-1). You can also click File, Open to display the Open dialog box.

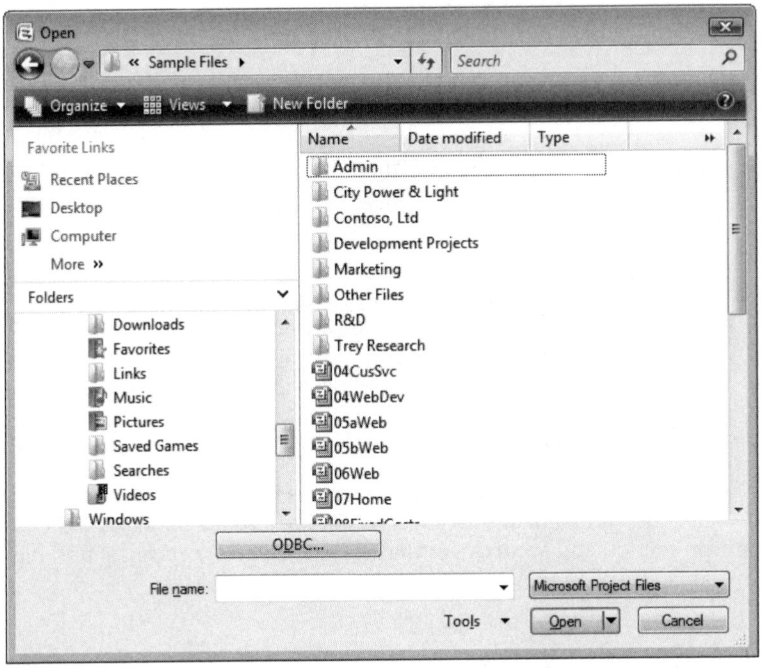

Figure 29-1 The Open dialog box shows the list of available project files in the selected location.

2. In the Folders or the Look In box, click the drive or folder where the project file resides.

3. If necessary, double-click the folder that contains the project file.

4. Double-click the project file you want to open. You can also click the project and then click Open.

Opening an Enterprise Project File

To open an enterprise project file, Office Project Professional 2007 must be connected to your project server.

> **Note**
> This section applies only if you're working with Project Professional 2007 set up for an enterprise environment.

To open an enterprise project stored in your project server database, follow these steps:

1. Start Microsoft Office Project Professional 2007 and connect to your project server.

If prompted, enter your user ID and password, and then click OK.

2. Click File, Open. The Open dialog box appears, showing the list of enterprise projects (see Figure 29-2).

By default, Enterprise Projects is selected. If you want to check out the file when you open it, make sure the Read/Write option below the list is selected. Checking out a file ensures that no one else can change the file while you are working on it. While you have the file checked out, however, others can still view the project in read-only file mode.

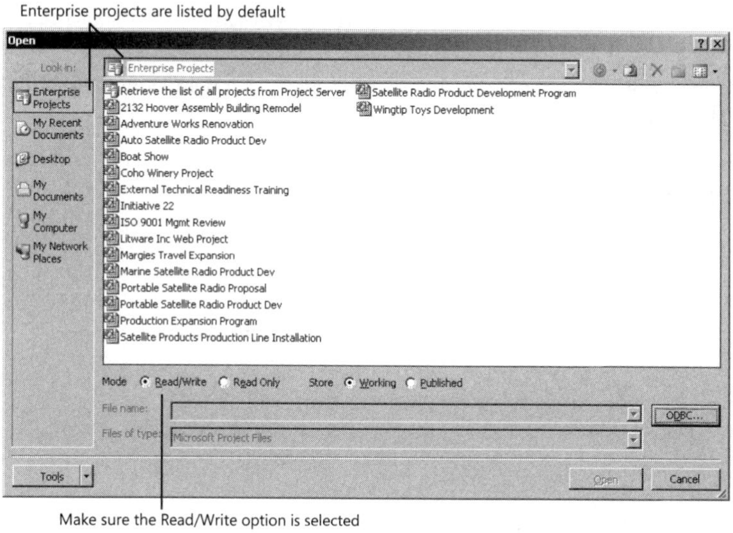

Enterprise projects are listed by default

Make sure the Read/Write option is selected

Figure 29-2 The Open dialog box shows the projects stored on the project server that you are authorized to check out or view.

3. Double-click the name of the project you want to open.

The project file opens in Microsoft Project.

> For more information about working with enterprise projects, see the section titled **"Creating a New Enterprise Project" in Chapter 22, "Managing Enterprise Projects and Resources."**

Opening Projects Created in Previous Versions of Microsoft Project

In Microsoft Office Project 2007, you can easily open project files created in earlier versions of Microsoft Project. If the file was created in Microsoft Office Project 2003, 2002, 2000, or Microsoft Office Project 98, it can be opened directly in Project 2007 with no additional steps required.

If the project file was created in a version of Microsoft Project earlier than Microsoft Project 98, it must first be saved as an MPX file before Microsoft Project 2007 can open it as a project file. The MPX file format is a record-based ASCII text file format available in Microsoft Project.

In addition to the MPX file format, you can open a variety of file formats other than the standard Microsoft Project Plan (MPP) file format.

For more information, see the section titled "Saving and Opening with Different File Formats" later in this chapter.

Searching for Files

Have you ever been unable to find a file? The search can be frustrating and painful, and it is often a big waste of time. Previous versions of Microsoft Project include a search tool in the Open dialog box. In Project 2007, that tool is gone because you can use the search tool in Windows Explorer instead to find those lost files.

To search for a file, do the following:

1. In Windows, click Start, All Programs, Accessories, Windows Explorer.

2. Start searching for the file.

   ❑ If you're working in Windows Vista, browse to the location where you want the search to begin. In the upper-right corner, type a portion of the file name you want to search for.

   For example, if you know that your file name contains the word software or deployment, as in Software Deployment Project, enter one or more of these words.

   As you type, results start to appear in the window. For more search options, click Search Tools on the toolbar.

   ❑ If you're working in Windows XP, click Search on the Windows Explorer toolbar. In the search pane that appears, click Documents. In the search box, type a portion of the file name you want to search for. Click any other options or links to help refine the search as you feel necessary.

   You can click Use Advanced Search Options and enter a key word in the A Word Or Phrase In The Document box. Here you can type a word from the project file's Properties dialog box, such as author, comments, company, manager, or subject. In the Look In box, you can specify the folder in which the search should be performed.

3. Click Search. Windows searches for your file using the criteria you set. Files found to meet your criteria are listed in the window.

Adding and Removing Project Summary Information

All projects can be associated with a title, subject, author, manager, and other information. As soon as you create a new file, some of these fields can be automatically filled in with your user information. When you add project summary information to your project, you are adding levels of detail that can be used for reports and searches. For example, if you search for a project's author, and the author has indeed been identified for a project, that project is returned as a result of the search.

You can also use these fields when creating customized reports. For example, if you want to create a set of reports about projects managed by a specific project manager, the Manager field needs to be completed for each project.

To add project summary information to your project, do the following:

1. Click File, Properties.

The Properties dialog box appears (see Figure 29-3).

Figure 29-3 Information you add to the Properties dialog box can be used in reports and searches.

2. If necessary, click the Summary tab.

3. Enter any summary information you want to maintain in the fields provided, for example, Title, Subject, Author, Manager, and Company.

Don't feel obligated to complete every field. Just fill in the fields you think you or others in your organization would find useful, either when searching for files or when using the information to format a report.

If you include content in these fields, and the file is about to go to a wider distribution, you might want to remove that content for security and privacy purposes. To remove that content all at once, click Tools, Options and then click the Security tab. Select the Remove Information From File Properties On Save check box and then click OK. The next time you save the file, the information in the Properties dialog box is removed.

Saving Files

Saving a project file ensures that it's stored on a hard disk for future access. The hard disk might be on your own computer or on your company's network. It can be your project server as an enterprise project. Saving files to a consistent location can make finding your primary and backup files easy.

Saving a New Project to Your Local Computer or Network Drive

Do the following to save a project file to a drive on your local computer or to a network drive:

1. On the Standard toolbar, click File, Save As.

The Save As dialog box appears (see Figure 29-4).

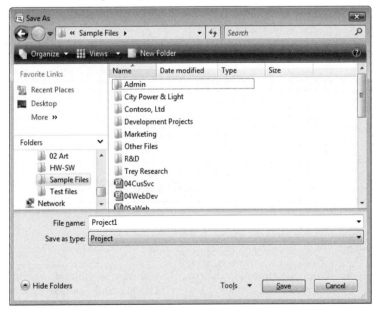

Figure 29-4 The Save As dialog box displays the contents of the default folder.

2. In the Folders or the Save In box, click the drive or folder where you want to save the file.

3. If necessary, double-click the folder in which you want to save the file.

4. In the File Name box, type the name of the file.

5. Click Save.

Save

After saving a file with a name and in a specific location, be sure to save continually during your work session. A good rule of thumb is to save about every five minutes, or whenever you make significant changes that you wouldn't want to lose in the event of a system failure or power outage. On the Standard toolbar, click the Save button or press Ctrl+S.

You can have Microsoft Project automatically and periodically save your file so that you don't have to remember to do so. See the section titled "Saving Project Files Automatically" later in this chapter.

Save Options

Depending on what you're trying to do, there are different ways to save your project file:

- **Save** When you click File, Save, you see the Save As dialog box. This is where you name the file and select the location where it is to be saved. For projects that are already saved, the Save command simply saves your changes to the existing file.

- **Save As** When you click File, Save As, the Save As dialog box appears. This is where you name the file and select the location where it is to be saved. Use this dialog box to save new project files as well as create an alternate or backup copy of your project. You can also save it as a different file type.

- **Save Workspace** When you open all the projects that you want to save and open together, and then click File, Save Workspace, you can combine individual projects into a group that's always opened together. The Save Workspace As dialog box appears with Workspace (*.mpw) selected as the file type. Select the location of the workspace to be saved, enter the name, and click Save. Now whenever you open a workspace file, all the projects saved in this workspace are opened at the same time.

Saving an Enterprise Project File

When working with an enterprise project, you first open the project from your project server. When you are finished with the project, you save and check in the file to the project server.

> **Note**
>
> This section applies only if you're working with Project Professional set up for an enterprise environment.

To create a working draft version of a project, simply click File, Save to save it to the project server. If this is the first time you're saving this project, the Save To Project Server dialog box appears (see Figure 29-5). Enter a name for the new project, specify that you're saving the file as a project (rather than as a template), and select the name of the calendar for the project. Complete any custom field values as needed and then click Save. The project is saved to the project server.

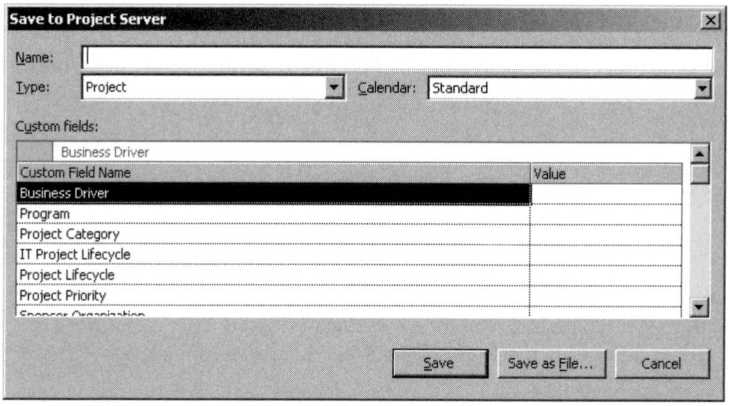

Figure 29-5 The Save To Project Server dialog box enables you to save project plans in the enterprise environment.

If you want to work with the enterprise project while not connected to the project server, click File, Save As. In the Save To Project Server dialog box, click Save As File. Specify the location where you want to save the project, give the file a name if necessary, and click Save.

Whenever you save an enterprise project file, those changes are saved to the project server. However, until you give the command to publish the project, the changes you have made since the last time the project was published are just part of the working draft of the project. No one but you can see or work with the changes you've made. The project is not listed in the Project Center, and assignments have not yet gone to their resources.

For more information about saving, publishing, and checking project files in and out of the project server, see the section titled "Managing Your Project Files on the Server" in Chapter 22.

What's in a File Name?

In Microsoft Project, you can name a project just about anything you want, as long as the name doesn't exceed 255 characters. Any combination of uppercase and lowercase letters can be used because Microsoft Project does not recognize case in file names. The following symbols cannot be used in a file name:

- Asterisk (*)
- Less-than symbol (<)
- Backward slash (\)
- Question mark (?)
- Colon (:)
- Quotation mark (")
- Forward slash (/)
- Pipe symbol (|)
- Greater-than symbol (>)
- Semicolon (;)

Specifying the Default Save Location

If you have a drive or folder dedicated to your project management files, you might want to make that your default save location. This default location will be the folder that is presented first whenever you open or save a project file. To set the default folder, do the following:

1. Click Tools, Options and then click the Save tab.

2. Under File Locations, click the Modify button.

3. In the Modify Location dialog box, browse to the drive and folder where you want your new project files to be saved by default. Click OK.

4. In the Options dialog box, click OK.

Note

If you regularly save your project files as something other than an MPP file (for example, a Microsoft Project 2002 file or a template), you can change the default file type from MPP to your file type of choice. Click Tools, Options and then click the Save tab. In the Save Microsoft Project Files As box, select the file type you want to use as the default.

Saving and Opening with Different File Formats

A file format is an arrangement of data in a file that specifies the file type and defines the file in a way that enables any application that can open the file to open it correctly. When you create and save a regular project file, it's saved as an MPP file. The file name's .mpp extension indicates that this is indeed a regular project file.

However, you can save project files in other file formats. You can also open files with other file formats in Microsoft Project. Table 29-1 details the file formats supported by Microsoft Project for saving, opening, or both.

Table 29-1 Supported File Formats

File format	Extension	Open or Save	Notes
Microsoft Project Plan	.mpp	Open Save	Opens or saves the file as a Microsoft Project Plan file, which is the default file type for projects being opened or saved.
Microsoft Project 2000-2003 Plan	.mpp	Open Save	Opens or saves the file as a Microsoft Project Plan file using the file format used by Microsoft Project 2000, 2002, and 2003.
Microsoft Project 98 Plan	.mpp	Open	Opens a project file that was saved using the file format used by Project 98.
Microsoft Project template	.mpt	Open Save	Opens a template file. You can change and save those changes to the template file. Saves the file as a Microsoft Project template file. The template can then be used as a basis for new projects.
Microsoft Project workspace	.mpw	Open Save	Saves all open project files as a Microsoft Project workspace file through the File, Save Workspace command. When you open an MPW file, all associated projects are opened in a single step.
Microsoft Project Exchange	.mpx	Open	Opens a file created in a version of Microsoft Project earlier than Microsoft Project 98. This is a record-based ASCII text file format that Project 2007 can read, allowing earlier Microsoft Project files to be converted to Project 2007 files.
Microsoft Project database	.mpd	Open	Opens a legacy Microsoft Project database.
Microsoft Access database	.mdb	.Open	Opens a Microsoft Access database file in Microsoft Project.
Open Database Connectivity		Open	Opens a database file created in ODBC-compliant Microsoft SQL Server databases. To open an ODBC file, click the ODBC button in the Open dialog box and follow the instructions in the Select Data Source dialog box.

File format	Extension	Open or Save	Notes
Microsoft Excel workbook	.xls	Open Save	Opens, through the import process, an Excel workbook in Microsoft Project. Saves certain fields as a Microsoft Excel data so the file can then be opened in Microsoft Excel.
Microsoft Excel PivotTable	.xls	Save	Saves selected field data to a Microsoft Office Excel PivotTable, which can then be opened in Microsoft Office Excel. A PivotTable is a table that combines and compares large amounts of data, and in which you can rotate columns and rows to modify the source data to create different views.
Text (Tab delimited)	.txt	Open Save	Opens information in a plain text file that uses tabs to separate fields of data. Saves fields from a single Microsoft Project table in the same way. This is ideal for using the project information in a third-party application or on another operating system.
Text (comma delimited)	.csv	Open Save	Opens a text file that uses commas to separate fields of data. Saves Microsoft Project data as a text file using commas to separate the data. This is ideal for using the project information in a third-party application or on another operating system.
Extensible Markup Language	.xml	Open Save	You can open an XML file in Microsoft Project. For Microsoft Project to understand and open it, an XML file must conform to the Microsoft Project XML schema. You can also save a project file as XML data. When Microsoft Project saves data as XML, the structure is determined by the Microsoft Project XML schema.

Opening a file from a different file format in Microsoft Project can be referred to as importing the file. Likewise, saving a project file with a different file format can be referred to as exporting the file. There's often more to the import and export process than simply opening or saving the file. Often you need to create an import/export map.

For more information about creating an import or export map, see the section titled "Importing and Exporting Information" in Chapter 16, "Exchanging Information with Other Applications."

Safeguarding Your Project Files

After you work hard creating, updating, and tracking your project file, you want to make the file as secure as possible. The further you get into the life cycle of the project, the more information you have in the project plan. The more information stored there, the more devastating a file loss can be.

Saving Project Files Automatically

Although it's not hard to remember to click the Save button every few minutes while working, you can also have Microsoft Project remember to save for you. You can set Microsoft Project to automatically and regularly save your file every few minutes. This can decrease your risk of losing recent work.

To have Microsoft Project automatically save active and open projects, follow these steps:

1. Click Tools, Options and then click the Save tab.

2. Under Auto Save, select the Save Every check box and then enter how often (in minutes) you want Microsoft Project to automatically save your active or open projects (see Figure 29-6).

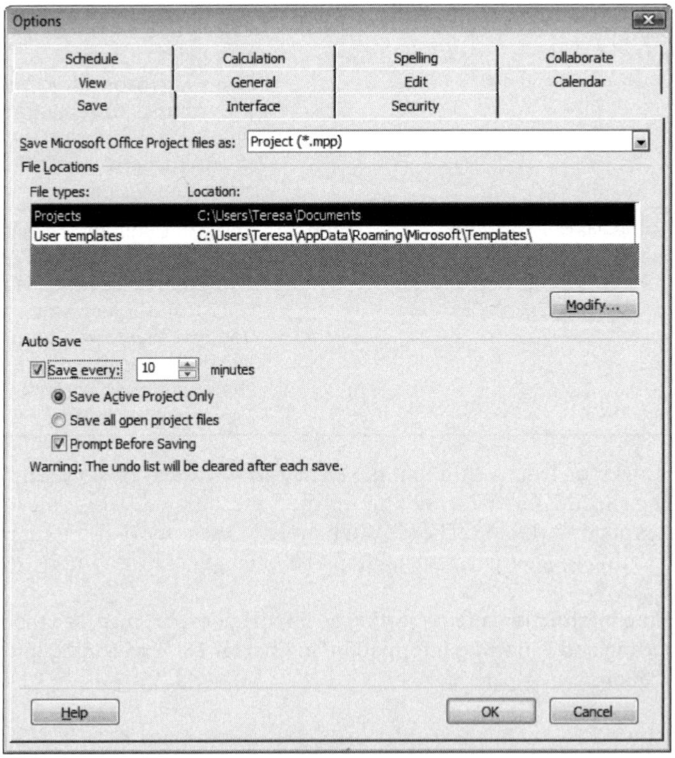

Figure 29-6 Use the Save tab in the Options dialog box to set your Auto Save preferences.

3. If you want Microsoft Project to save only the active project, select the Save Active Project Only option.

4. If you want Microsoft Project to save the active project along with any other open projects, select the Save All Open Project Files option.

INSIDE OUT   Turn off the autosave prompt

It can be handy to be notified when your application will perform an action that you might not otherwise be aware of. However, you might find the Prompt Before Saving feature annoying. You've already instructed Microsoft Project to save your file at a frequency that you specified. If you don't want to be asked at every specified interval whether you want to save, clear the Prompt Before Saving check box. However, if you frequently experiment with what-if scenarios in your project file, you might want to be prompted before Microsoft Project saves one of your experiments.

Backing Up Your Project Files

It's always a good policy to have at least two copies of any important computer file. This way, if the file is inadvertently deleted or somehow is corrupted (or if you get a little crazy with your what-if scenarios), you have another file to go back to.

Note
You cannot create backups of enterprise project files that are stored on your project server.

To automatically create backups of active project files, do the following:

1. Click File, Save As.

2. In the Save As dialog box, click Tools and then click General Options.

   The Save Options dialog box appears (see Figure 29-7).

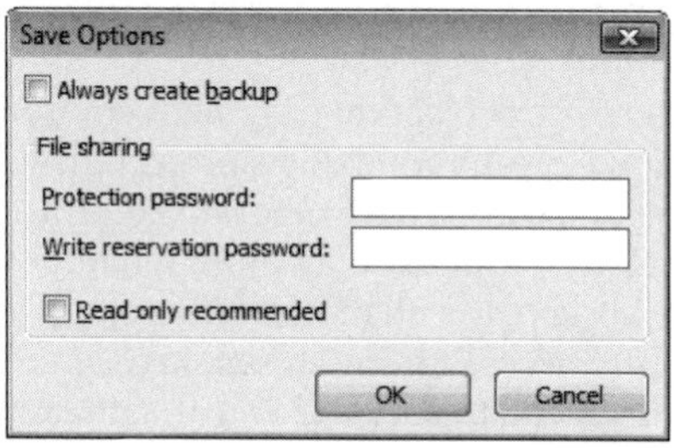

Figure 29-7 Use the Save Options dialog box to set up file backups and passwords.

3. Select the Always Create Backup check box.

The backup copy adopts the same file name as the original project file, but it has a different extension (.bak). For example, the backup file of deployment.mpp is deployment.bak.

To restore a backup file as a regular project file, follow these steps:

1. On the Standard toolbar, click the Open button.

2. In the Open dialog box, browse, if necessary, to the drive and folder where the backup file is stored.

3. Be sure that All Files (*.*) is selected in the Files Of Type box.

   Otherwise, files ending in .bak will not appear in the list.

4. Find the backup file and double-click it.

   Microsoft Project opens the backup file.

5. Click File, Save As.

6. The Save As dialog box appears.

   If necessary, browse to the location where you want to save the restored backup project file.

7. Enter a new file name for the restored backup file.

8. Make sure that Projects (*.mpp) is selected in the Save As Type box.

9. Click Save.

> **Note**
>
> Your project BAK file is a great contingency in case your project file is accidentally deleted or corrupted. However, if both the project and the backup are saved on the same drive and that drive crashes, your backup will be lost as well. Remember to periodically save a backup to an alternate drive.

Protecting Your Project Files with a Password

If you are not working in an enterprise project management environment that uses a project server as a central location for your company's project files, saving your project files to a public network folder is one way to have centralized project files. This enables your company to back up critical files more regularly and reliably. It also provides a convenient location for your co-workers to collaborate on projects. However, it can also enable unauthorized individuals to access files with sensitive or confidential information. Perhaps your project is in its initial phase, and you aren't ready to share it with the rest of the company. Or, maybe a project has information that should be seen only by a small group of people in your organization. If this is the case, consider assigning a password to prevent unauthorized access to sensitive project files.

> **Note**
>
> You cannot assign a password to an enterprise project file stored on the project server.

There are two types of passwords: Protection and Write Reservation. To assign a password to a project, do the following:

1. Click File, Save As.

2. In the Save As dialog box, click Tools and then click General Options.

3. In the Save Options dialog box, enter the password in either the Protection Password or Write Reservation Password text box.

   With a protection password, users can open the project file only if they know the password.

   With a write-reservation password, users can view the project file, but they cannot change it.

4. Click OK.

5. In the Confirm Password dialog box, type the password again. Click OK.

> **Note**
>
> If you want to remind users to open the project as Read-Only without locking out users who might have forgotten the password, consider the Read-Only Recommended check box. If you select this check box, the next time a user begins to open this file, a message suggests that the user open the file as read-only unless they need to save changes to the file. It then provides the option of opening the file as Read-Only.

Responding to a Microsoft Project Problem

If you encounter a problem with Microsoft Project, such as the program freezing or experiencing a "fatal error," you can send the details of the problem to the Microsoft Project development team. When the error happens, a dialog box is displayed, providing the option to restart Microsoft Project and view the details of the error report. If you want to provide information on the problem to Microsoft, click Send The Report To Microsoft. If you don't want to provide the information, click Don't Send.

Depending on the severity of the error, you might be able to continue working in Safe Mode, at least to get to the point where you can save your file.

INSIDE OUT **Don't send your proprietary project**

Depending on the nature of the error you encounter, your entire project file could be sent to the Microsoft Project development team. If your project contains confidential information, be sure to click Don't Send.

Opening Files Safely

New in Microsoft Office Project 2007 are security options regarding opening files from older file formats. By default, files from older file formats or nondefault file formats are not opened. If you need to open such a file, for example, when you're bringing older project files into Project 2007 or when you're importing an Excel file, you must change this security setting.

To do this, click Tools, Options and then click the Security tab. Under Legacy Formats, select the Prompt When Loading Files With Legacy Or Non Default File Format option or the Allow Loading Files With Legacy Or Non Default File Formats option.

You can also set the security level for opening files that contain macros. On the Security tab in the Options dialog box, click the Macro Security button. Select the security option you want on the Security Level tab.

Installing Microsoft Office Project 2007

This appendix describes system requirements, procedures, and guidelines for installing and activating the standalone desktop editions of Microsoft Office Project 2007.

This appendix also includes system requirements for implementing Microsoft Office Project Server 2007 for enterprise project management. It includes general guidelines to consider in planning an enterprise project management installation and provides resources for more detailed information.

Setting Up Project Standard or Project Professional 2007

You can install Microsoft Office Project Standard 2007 and Microsoft Office Project Professional 2007 as your standalone desktop project management solution. In the 2007 version, they have exactly the same desktop features.

When Office Project Professional 2007 is connected to Office Project Server 2007, additional features are made available to facilitate enterprise project management.

See the section titled "Understanding Issues for Project Server 2007 Setup" later in this appendix for more information.

Understanding System Requirements

Before you install Office Project Standard 2007 or Project Professional 2007, make sure that your system meets the minimum requirements. Table A-1 shows the minimum system requirements for a computer running Project Standard or Project Professional.

Table A-1 Minimum System Requirements for Project 2007

System requirement	Minimum specification
Processor speed	700 megahertz (MHz) or higher
Random access memory (RAM)	512 megabytes (MB)
Hard disk space	1.5 gigabyte (GB)
Media drive	CD-ROM or DVD drive
Monitor display	800 × 600 pixels, although 1024 × 768 pixels is recommended

System requirement	Minimum specification
Operating system	One of the following: ● Microsoft Windows XP with Service Pack (SP) 2 ● Microsoft Windows XP Tablet Editions 2005 SP2 ● Microsoft Windows Server 2003 with SP1 ● Microsoft Windows Vista
Internet	Internet access and a Web browser program such as Microsoft Internet Explorer (needed to use Internet functions such as Office Online or online activation and registration)
Microsoft Outlook	Microsoft Office Outlook 2003 SP2 (needed to use the Import Outlook Tasks feature)
Microsoft Office Excel	Office Excel 2003 SP2 (needed to use the Visual Reports feature with Excel Pivot-Tables)
Microsoft Office Visio	Office Visio Professional 2007 (needed to use the Visual Reports feature with Visio PivotDiagrams)

Setting Up Project 2007

To set up Project Standard or Project Professional on your computer, follow these steps:

1. Insert the Project Standard or Project Professional CD in your computer's CD or DVD drive.

   If the Project Setup program does not start automatically, click the Start button on the Windows taskbar and then click Run. Type X:\setup.exe (where X is the name of your CD-ROM drive) and then click OK. Or, use Windows Explorer to open the contents of the CD-ROM and then double-click the setup.exe file.

   If you are installing Office Project 2007 on Windows Vista, the AutoPlay window appears. Click Run Setup.exe. Then click Continue in the next security alert that appears.

   The Microsoft Office Project Professional 2007 window appears, asking for your 25-character product key.

2. Type your product key. It is either on the CD case, or it was provided as part of your license agreement.

   After you type the final digit, a check mark confirms the correct product key.

3. Click Continue.

4. On the next page, read the Microsoft software license terms and then select the I Accept The Terms Of This Agreement check box. Click Continue.

5. On the next page, choose the type of installation you want.

   ❑ If no previous version of Microsoft Project is present on your computer, the choices are Install Now or Customize. If you click Install Now, installation begins immediately.

   ❑ If you are upgrading from a previous version of Microsoft Project, the choices are Upgrade or Customize. If you click Upgrade, installation begins immediately.

   ❑ If you click Customize, a window with four tabs appears. The Upgrade tab gives you the choice between removing or keeping the previous version of Microsoft Project on your computer. The Installation Options tab lets you specify which individual features should be installed. The File Location tab lets you specify the location where the project program files should be installed. The User Information tab provides fields for you to enter your name, initials, and organization. When finished with your customized settings, click Install Now.

   The Installation Progress window shows the progress bar for the installation of Project 2007.

6. In the window that states that Project 2007 has been successfully installed, click Close.

7. Click Start, All Programs, Microsoft Office, Microsoft Office Project 2007.

Activating Project 2007

The activation process is designed to verify that your installation of Project 2007 is properly licensed. It checks that your product key is not in use on more computers than are permitted by the software license.

Project 2007 will open with full functionality 25 times before it requires activation—this is the activation "grace period." After this grace period expires, Project 2007 transitions to reduced functionality mode, in which Project 2007 operates like a viewer. You cannot create new projects or save changes to existing project files. When you obtain and enter your product key and activate Project 2007 after the grace period has expired, you can restore Project 2007 to full functionality again.

Until you activate, the Activation Wizard appears each time you open Project 2007. This wizard guides you through the activation process, which just takes a minute or so.

You can activate Project 2007 over the Internet or by phone. If you choose to activate by phone, the activation process could take longer.

To activate Project 2007, do the following:

1. Start Project 2007. The Microsoft Office Project 2007 Activation Wizard appears each time you start Project 2007 until you have activated it.

   You can also click Help, Activate Product.

If your installation of Project 2007 has already been activated, a message appears to this effect, in which case no further action is needed.

2. Follow the steps in the wizard to activate Project 2007. Select whether you want to activate over the Internet or by telephone. Click the Next button and follow the instructions.

3. On the next page, click Register Now to register your copy of Project 2007.

   Registering Project 2007 is an optional step. However, it is recommended so that you can be notified if there are any important patches or other product information that you need to know about.

4. Click Close to finish activating Project 2007.

Changing Your Project 2007 Setup

After Project 2007 has been installed successfully, you can add or remove optional features, repair any program files that might have become corrupted, or remove the entire application.

Adding or Removing Features

To add or remove Project 2007 features, do the following:

1. Insert your Project 2007 CD into your computer's CD or DVD drive.

2. Select the Add Or Remove Features option and then click Continue.

   The Installations Options window appears.

3. To add a feature, click the arrow next to the feature you want to add. Then change Not Available to Run From My Computer, Run All From My Computer, or Installed On First Use.

   Installed On First Use makes the feature available. The setup program would access your Project 2007 CD to install the added feature.

   Run From My Computer installs the feature on your computer's hard disk.

4. To remove a feature, click the arrow next to the feature you want to remove and change the Run From My Computer or Installed On First Use setting to Not Available. This will remove the feature from your setup.

5. Click Continue.

   The Configuration Progress window shows the current status of the changes that are being made.

6. When the changes have been completed, click Close.

Repairing Microsoft Project

If you notice that Microsoft Project isn't running as well as it should, or if a particular feature has stopped working correctly, you might need to repair some Project 2007 program files. To repair Project 2007 files by reinstalling them, follow these steps:

1. Insert your Project 2007 CD into your computer's CD or DVD drive.

2. Select the Repair option and then click Continue.

   The Configuration Progress window shows the status of repairs to the Project 2007 files. The setup file detects any problems with the files and replaces those files as needed.

3. When the repairs have been completed, click Close.

   In some cases, your system might need to be restarted to make the repairs take effect. In the message that appears, click Yes to restart your computer.

Removing Microsoft Project from Your Computer

Use the Project 2007 CD again if you ever need to uninstall Project 2007. To do this, follow these steps:

1. Insert your Project 2007 CD into your computer's CD or DVD drive.

2. Select the Remove option and then click Continue.

3. In the message that appears, click Yes to remove Project 2007.

   The Configuration Progress window shows the status of Project 2007 files being removed from your system.

4. When Project 2007 has been completely removed, click Close.

5. In the message that appears, click Yes to restart your computer. This completes the uninstall process.

Understanding Issues for Project Server 2007 Setup

This section includes general information and considerations for setting up Project Server 2007 in conjunction with Project Professional 2007 and Microsoft Office Project Web Access for enterprise project management.

The individuals responsible for installing and configuring Project Server 2007 and the enterprise project management solution should have a solid working knowledge of Microsoft SQL Server and skills and knowledge as a system administrator. In addition, your organization should commit resources—including project managers, resource managers, and portfolio managers—to planning your enterprise project implementation to ensure that you get the maximum benefit from your Project Server deployment.

Understanding the Components of Microsoft Enterprise Project Management

The following applications are used to implement the Microsoft enterprise project management solution, which runs on the Windows Server 2003 operating system.

- **SQL Server** As the foundation of Project Server and the enterprise project management solution, SQL Server is responsible for the project server databases. There are three project databases: Draft (or Working), Published, and Reporting.

- **Microsoft SQL Server Analysis Services and Cube Building Services** These applications, which are part of SQL Server, are installed to provide the data analysis features in Office Project Web Access and Project Professional. These applications provide for the online analytical processing (OLAP) tools required to create the views and reports needed to analyze projects and portfolios throughout the enterprise.

- **Project Server** Project Server is the server that manages all data associated with your enterprise projects, portfolios, and programs. Project Server provides timesheet, reporting, team collaboration, and data analysis tools. Project Server also manages the global settings and information related to user access, security settings, and other administrative settings.

  All this information, which is generated either in Project Professional or Project Web Access, is stored in the project databases powered by SQL Server.

  Project Server is protected by a security layer that restricts access to only those authorized to send and receive data from the database.

- **Microsoft Windows SharePoint Services** Project Server is now tightly integrated with Windows SharePoint Services 3.0, which provides the administrative and user interface framework, the infrastructure for user management, logon capabilities, layout and content of pages and views, team collaboration, and integration with the reporting features of Project Server.

  Specifically, the integration with Windows SharePoint Services enables the project collaboration workspace, document library, risk tracking, and issue tracking features of Project Web Access and Project Professional.

- **Project Server Interface** Project Server uses the Project Server Interface (PSI) as the application program interface (API), which is the means through which Project Professional and Project Web Access have a view into and interact with Project Server. The PSI enables tasks, resources, assignments, and entire projects to be manipulated—created, viewed, edited, or deleted. The PSI replaces the Project Data Server (PDS) that is used in Project Server 2003.

  In addition, developers can use the PSI to create methods for interacting with line of business applications (for example, human resources, procurement, and accounting systems) and other third-party applications.

- **Project Professional** Project Professional is the primary client application interface for Project Server. Users with appropriate permissions can use the enterprise global template and enterprise resource pool to build their projects and resource teams, publish project plans to Project Server, and perform other enterprise project and resource management tasks.

Project Professional is the major source of project data, including projects, tasks, resources, assignments, scheduling dates, costs, and tracking information that is served by the project server.

When Project Professional is part of an enterprise project management solution, collaboration options become available, making it convenient for project managers to move back and forth between the Project Professional environment and the Project Web Access environment.

- Project Web Access The Web-based source for project data, Project Web Access shows tasks, resources, assignments, scheduling dates, costs, and tracking information. Project Web Access is a Web interface running on Internet Explorer with unique capabilities to work specifically as a client to Project Server and display targeted project data. Project Web Access is the view into the project server and the underlying project database.

  Project Web Access is accessed by users who are authenticated either through Windows or through the project server. Such users can include team members, team leads, resource managers, project managers, portfolio managers, executives, and project server administrators.

> **Note**
>
> Also available to be integrated with the Microsoft enterprise project management solution is the new Microsoft Office Project Portfolio Server 2007. With its companion client Microsoft Office Project Portfolio Web Access, this product provides complete project portfolio management services that work with your enterprise project management solution through Project Server. It includes tools to help organizations identify, select, and manage portfolios in line with their business strategy.
>
> **For more information about the users, elements, and workflow of the Microsoft enterprise project management solution, see Chapter 20, "Understanding Enterprise Project Management."**

Analyzing Your Project Server Requirements

Before the enterprise project management components are installed, your organization needs to articulate how it manages projects, portfolios, and programs. It should also examine various line-of-business processes and determine how these interact with project management and resource management processes. This analysis will help you make the right decisions toward ensuring that the architecture and configuration of Project Server and its components correspond to the way your organization does business.

The following are some questions to consider:

- How many people do you expect to use Project Server, including from Project Professional and from Project Web Access?

- Will you be using Project Web Access for team collaboration?

- What are the roles that members of the project team play, and what kinds of responsibilities and privileges do they need?

- What types of projects does your organization implement?

- Do users from outside your corporate intranet require access to Project Web Access or Project Server?

- Which enterprise features do you expect to use?

- What categories of time-tracking information do you need employees to track and submit?

- How often do you want to build or update OLAP cubes?

For a series of worksheets that can help you and your organization answer these types of questions and more, go to Microsoft TechNet at www.microsoft.com/technet and then enter a search for Project 2007 Planning Worksheets. You should find an article titled "Planning Worksheets For Office Project Server 2007."

Understanding System Requirements for Enterprise Project Management

With the Microsoft enterprise project management capabilities afforded by Project Professional connected to Project Server, you have access to powerful standardization, customization, resource management, and executive analysis capabilities across your entire organization.

Project Server can be set up as a standalone server installation, as a single box installation, or as a farm deployment. Table A-2 lists the minimum server requirements for these three configurations.

Table A-2 Minimum Server Requirements for Project Server Configurations

Configuration type	Server requirements
Standalone installation	Server with a processor speed of at least 2.5 GHz, at least 1 GB of RAM capacity with 2 GB recommended, and at least 2 GB of disk space for installation
	SQL Server 2005 SP1 Express must be installed on the same server.
Single box installation	Server with a processor speed of at least 2.5 GHz, at least 1 GB of RAM capacity with 2 GB recommended, and at least 1 GB of disk space for installation
	At least SQL Server 2000 SP3a or SQL Server 2005 SP1 must be installed, with a processor speed of at least 2.5 GHz and at least 2 GB of RAM
Farm deployment	Web server with a processor speed of at least 2.5 GHz, at least 2 GB of RAM capacity, and at least 500 MB of disk space for installation
	Application server with a processor speed of at least 2.5 GHz, at least 2 GB of RAM, and at least 500 MB of disk space for installation
	At least SQL Server 2000 SP3a or SQL Server 2005 SP1 with a processor speed of at least 2.5 GHz, and at least 2 GB of RAM

In addition to these requirements, additional system requirements for a computer running Project Server are listed in Table A-3.

Table A-3 Project Server System Requirements

System requirement	Minimum specification
Server software and associated services	Windows Server 2003 SP1
	Microsoft .NET Framework 3.0
	Internet Information Services (IIS) 6.0
	ASP.NET 2.0
	ASP.NET Web services extensions (these extensions must be enabled in IIS)
	Microsoft SQL Server Analysis Services 2005 SP1 or later (these services, which are included with SQL Server, are required for the OLAP reports in the Data Analysis function)
	Windows Server System 3.0 (installed as part of Project Server, this system is required for opening documents from or saving documents to Project Server, publishing projects, Windows Workflow Foundation for proposals, and Project Tasks List)
Server software	Project Server 2007
Client software	Project Web Access
Client software	Project Professional
Messaging software	Internet Simple Mail Transfer Protocol/Post Office Protocol 3 (SMTP/POP3), Internet Message Access Protocol 4 (IMAP4), or MAPI-compliant messaging software (required for e-mail notifications)
Microsoft Outlook	Outlook 2003 SP2 or later for importing tasks to the Outlook calendar or tasks list
Media drive	DVD drive
Monitor display	At least 800 × 600, although 1024 × 768 is recommended
Internet	Internet access with at least Internet Explorer 6.0
Network connection	At least 100 megabits per second (Mbps)

Users such as project managers and resource managers who need to run Project Professional and Project Web Access should make sure their computers meet the minimum system requirements outlined in Table A-4.

Table A-4 Minimum System Requirements for Client Users of Project Professional with Project Web Access

System requirement	Minimum specification
Processor speed	700 MHz or higher
RAM	512 MB
Hard disk space	1.5 GB
Media drive	CD-ROM or DVD drive
Monitor display	800 × 600 pixels, although 1024 × 768 pixels is recommended
Operating system	One of the following: ● Windows XP with Service Pack (SP) 2 ● Windows XP Tablet Editions 2005 SP2 ● Windows Server 2003 with SP1 ● Windows Vista
Network connection	2 Mbps (required to connect to Project Server)
Internet	Internet access with Internet Explorer 6.0 (needed to use Project Web Access as well as other Internet features such as Office Online or online activation and registration)
Messaging software	Internet SMTP/POP3, IMAP4, or MAPI-compliant messaging software (required for e-mail notifications)
Microsoft Outlook	Office Outlook 2003 SP2 (needed to use the Import Outlook Tasks feature)
Excel	Excel 2003 SP2 (needed to use the Visual Reports feature with Excel Pivot-Tables)
Visio	Visio Professional 2007 (needed to use the Visual Reports feature with Visio Pivot-Diagrams)

Users such as team members and team leaders who are using Project Web Access but not Project Professional should make sure their computers meet the minimum system requirements outlined in Table A-5.

Table A-5 Minimum System Requirements for Client Users of Project Web Access

Processor speed	700 MHz or higher
RAM	128 MB (more RAM might be required, depending on the operating system)
Hard disk space	5 MB
Operating system	One of the following: • Windows XP with Service Pack (SP) 2 • Windows XP Tablet Editions 2005 SP2 • Windows Server 2003 with SP1 • Windows Vista
Monitor display	800 × 600 pixels, although 1024 × 768 pixels is recommended
Network connection	256 kB
Internet	Internet access with at least Internet Explorer 6.0
Messaging software	Internet SMTP/POP3, IMAP4, or MAPI-compliant messaging software (required for e-mail notifications)
Microsoft Outlook	Microsoft Office Outlook 2003 SP2 (needed to use the Import Outlook Tasks feature)

Finding Resources for Enterprise Project Management Setup

The following list includes articles and downloadable documents that can help you plan, configure, and install the hardware and software necessary to implement your organization's enterprise project management solution. Links to the Web pages and files for the downloadable books are also included on the Resources tab on the Companion CD to this book.

- Microsoft Office Project Server 2007 Product Guide
- Microsoft Office Enterprise Project Management Solution Product Guide
- Project Server TechNet Library
- Planning and Architecture for Office Project Server 2007 (downloadable book from TechNet)
- Deployment for Office Project Server 2007 (downloadable book from TechNet)
- Install Project Server 2007 to a Standalone Computer (TechNet)
- Install Project Server 2007 to a Server Farm Environment (TechNet)
- Migration Guide for Office Project Server 2007 (TechNet)
- Operations for Office Project Server 2007 (queuing system and disaster recovery from TechNet)
- Technical Reference for Office Project Server 2007 (permissions and categories from TechNet)
- Project 2007 Software Development Kit (MSDN)

This appendix includes a listing of resources on the World Wide Web related to Microsoft Office Project 2007 and project management.

If you'd rather not bother to type in the Web addresses yourself, these links are also provided on the Companion CD to this book.

Microsoft-Sponsored Resources

The following is a list of Microsoft Web sites that can provide further assistance and information in your work with Office Project 2007:

- **Microsoft Office Project Home Page** *www.microsoft.com/office/project* Official site for Microsoft Project. Includes sales information, product specifications, demonstrations, Help articles, templates, and downloads. It also includes links to other resources for Microsoft Project as well as project management and developer resources.

- **Microsoft Office Online** *http://office.microsoft.com* Official site for Microsoft Office. Contains step-by-step assistance, training modules, downloadable templates and clip art, articles, links, tools, and more for all Microsoft Office products, including Microsoft Project.

  To go to the Web site quickly, in Microsoft Project, click Help, Microsoft Office Online. Your Web browser launches and goes to the Microsoft Office Online Web site.

- **Office Online Templates** *http://office.microsoft.com/templates* In addition to the 41 project template files built in to Project 2007, additional project templates are continually being added to the Microsoft Office Online Web site. Some are created by Microsoft, others were suggested and added by project management experts in the field.

  To get to this Web site from Microsoft Project, click File, New. In the New Project pane, click the Templates On Office Online link. In the Search Templates box, type Microsoft Project and then click Search. In the list of templates that appears, click a template to see a preview. Click Download Now to copy the template onto your computer and into Microsoft Project.

- **Microsoft Project Knowledge Base** *http://support.microsoft.com/ph/11381* Microsoft Product Support Services maintains a knowledge base of articles about Microsoft Project. This Web site includes the latest news about Microsoft Project support issues, how-to articles, troubleshooting solutions, and articles categorized by Microsoft Project feature.

  You can also search the knowledge base to find answers to your specific questions about Microsoft Project or to troubleshoot a problem you're experiencing. In the Search Support (KB) box on the left side of the page, type your keyword, phrase, or question.

- **Microsoft TechNet** *http://technet.microsoft.com* Microsoft TechNet includes technical articles and resources designed specifically for information technology professionals and system administrators. In the left pane, click Office Systems and then click Desktop Applications or Project Server.

  You can also search on a particular topic. In the Search box at the top of the left pane, type a keyword, phrase, or question.

- **Microsoft Download Center** *www.microsoft.com/downloads* The Microsoft Download Center includes resources available for you to download. To find downloads available for Microsoft Project, in the Search box, click Office. In the second search box, type Project 2007, for example, and then click Go.

- **Microsoft Communities and Discussion Groups** *www.microsoft.com/communities* Join an online discussion group devoted to Microsoft Project or Microsoft Office Project Server 2007. Here you can find answers to your questions, learn from questions posed by other users, and answer questions yourself. In the left pane of the Communities page, click Newsgroups. Click Office, Microsoft Project and then General Questions, Server, or Developer. Current discussions are listed.

  Also on the Communities page are blogs written by Microsoft employees, forums, technical chats, user groups, Webcasts, and other resources.

- **Microsoft Project Solution Providers** *http://directory.partners.extranet.microsoft. com/project/ProjectPartners.aspx* Use this site to find companies worldwide that can help you develop and implement custom project management solutions for your organization, as well as project management training services. You can search this site for a specific solution provider by name, by country, or by solution category.

- **Microsoft Developer Network** *http://msdn.microsoft.com/project* The Microsoft Project center within the Microsoft Developer Network (MSDN) Web site contains programming guidelines, tips, and examples for developing solutions for Microsoft Project. The site includes articles of interest to developers, as well as code samples, downloads, blogs by Microsoft Project experts, and links to the Microsoft Project discussion groups. Also included are links to the Microsoft Project Software Development Kit (SDK).

- **Microsoft Office Project 2007 Software Development Kit (SDK)**
http://msdn.microsoft.com/project At this URL, click the Project 2007 SDK link. The Microsoft Office Project 2007 Software Development Kit contains tools and information for Microsoft Project solution providers, value-added resellers, and other developers interested in extending and customizing the features of Project 2007, Office Project Server, Microsoft Office Project Web Access, and the enterprise project management features.

- **Microsoft Office Project Portfolio Server 2007** *www.microsoft.com/office /portfolioserver* Find information about Microsoft Office Portfolio Server 2007 and its client application Microsoft Office Portfolio Web Access, separately licensed companion products to Project Server that provide complete portfolio management services as part of an integrated enterprise project management solution. On this Web site, get general information, watch an online demo, and download the product guide for more details.

The following are "semi-official" blogs produced by Microsoft employees.

- *http://blogs.msdn.com/chrisfie* A blog about deploying project server.

- *http://blogs.msdn.com/project/* The Microsoft Project product group blog.

- *http://blogs.msdn.com/Project_Programmability/* The blog of program managers in the Microsoft Project product group on topics about programming in Project and Project Server.

- *http://blogs.msdn.com/brismith/default.aspx* The blog of an individual in the Microsoft Project product support group which includes topics about Microsoft Project support issues.

- *www.projectified.com* A blog about Microsoft Project and Project Server.

Independent Resources

The following is a list of independent Web sites of organizations that can provide further assistance and information in your work with Microsoft Project and project management:

- **Project Management Institute (PMI)** *www.pmi.org* Project Management Institute is a nonprofit professional organization for project managers. PMI establishes industry-recognized project management standards and provides training. PMI also sponsors the Project Management Professional (PMP) certification, which is the most recognized professional credential for project managers. PMI publishes A Guide to the Project Management Body of Knowledge (PMBOK), which details generally accepted project management standards, practices, knowledge areas, and terminology.

- **MPA, The Official Industry Association for Microsoft Office Project** *www.mympa.org* MPA is an independent users group formed with the support and recognition of Microsoft. The Web site offers information about a variety of Microsoft Project and project management resources, with a goal to improve the understanding and use of Microsoft Project and related products. The site includes a calendar of MPA events, a directory of MPA chapters around the world, MPA blogs, and a job board.

- **Microsoft Project Most Valuable Professionals (MVPs)** *http://project.mvps.org* This is a Web site maintained by Microsoft Project MVPs, who are "super users" recognized by Microsoft as providing exceptional service to the Microsoft Project user community. The site includes frequently asked questions and links to information about third-party project management products, including Microsoft Project add-ons and templates.

For more Microsoft Project resources, Web sites, and third-party product demonstrations, see the Companion CD for this book.

Keyboard Shortcuts

This appendix lists Microsoft Office Project 2007 keyboard shortcuts for commonly used commands and operations you might otherwise carry out using the mouse. Table C-1 provides keyboard shortcuts for common file management commands. Table C-2 provides keyboard shortcuts for commands that control views and windows. Table C-3 lists keyboard shortcuts for commands that allow you to quickly move around a project view. Table C-4 lists keyboard shortcuts for commonly used editing commands. Table C-5 lists keyboard shortcuts for commands used while outlining project tasks. Table C-6 lists keyboard shortcuts for special-use commands.

Table C-1 Working with Files

Action	Keyboard shortcut
New	Ctrl+N or F11
Open	Ctrl+O
Print	Ctrl+P
Save	Ctrl+S
Save As	Alt+F2 or F12
Close	Ctrl+F4
Exit	Alt+F4

Table C-2 Working with Views and Windows

Action	Keyboard shortcut
Activate the other pane in a combination view	F6
Activate the next project window	Ctrl+F6
Activate the previous project window	Ctrl+Shift+F6
Activate the split bar	Shift+F6
Close the project window	Ctrl+F4
Zoom in (show smaller time units)	Ctrl+/
Zoom out (show larger time units)	Ctrl+Shift+*
Close the program window	Alt+F4
Open a new window	Shift+F11 or Alt+Shift+F1

Table C-3 Navigating in a Project View

Action	Keyboard shortcut
Move to the first field in a row	Home or Ctrl+Left Arrow
Move to the first row	Ctrl+Up Arrow
Move to the first field of the first row	Ctrl+Home
Move to the last field in a row	End or Ctrl+Right Arrow
Move to the last field of the last row	Ctrl+End
Move to the last row	Ctrl+Down Arrow
Move the timescale to the left	Alt+Left Arrow
Move the timescale to the right	Alt+Right Arrow
Move to the start of the timescale in a project	Alt+Home
Move to the end of the timescale in a project	Alt+End

Table C-4 Editing in a Sheet View

Action	Keyboard shortcut
Undo the last edit	Ctrl+Z
Redo the last item undone	Ctrl+Y
Cancel an entry	Esc
Clear or reset the selected field	Ctrl+Delete
Cut selected data	Ctrl+X
Copy selected data	Ctrl+C
Paste selected data	Ctrl+V
Delete selected data	Delete
Open the Find dialog box	Ctrl+F or Shift+F5
Find again	Shift+F4
Open the Go To dialog box	F5
Select a column	Ctrl+Spacebar
Select a row	Shift+Spacebar
Select all rows and columns	Ctrl+Shift+Spacebar

Table C-5 Outlining Tasks

Action	Keyboard shortcut
Indent	Alt+Shift+Right Arrow
Outdent	Alt+Shift+Left Arrow
Hide subtasks	Alt+Shift+Minus Sign
Show subtasks	Alt+Shift+=
Show all tasks	Alt+Shift+*

Table C-6 Giving Specialized Commands

Action	Keyboard shortcut
Link tasks	Ctrl+F2
Unlink tasks	Ctrl+Shift+F2
Reset sort to ID order	Shift+F3
Remove a filter and show all tasks or all resources	F3
Calculate scheduling changes in all open projects	F9
Calculate scheduling changes in the active project	Shift+F9
Switch between automatic and manual calculation	Ctrl+F9
Open Project Help	F1
Open the Help topic in a dialog box with a Help button	Shift+F1

> **Note**
>
> To find additional keyboard shortcuts, you can use Office Project 2007 Help. In the Type A Question For Help box in the menu bar, type **keyboard shortcuts** and then press Enter. Click the topic Keyboard Shortcuts For Microsoft Office Project 2007.

Index to Troubleshooting Topics

Topic	Description	Page
Address book error message	You get an error message when trying to display your e-mail address book	207
Analyze Timescaled Data	You can't find the Analyze Timescaled Data function	591
Assign button	The Assign button is unavailable for a budget resource	295
Assigning resources	You assign two resources to a task, but the work is doubled rather than halved	250
Assignment Information	The Assignment Information dialog box does not open	258
Bar Style commands	Changing the bar style for one task changes the Gantt bars for all tasks	906
Baseline problems	Your baseline information doesn't roll up	376
Calendar settings	You set the calendar for 20 hours per week, but the tasks are still being scheduled for 40 hours per week	161
Combination view	You can't get the combination view to be a single view again	124
Custom form deletions	I can't find the command to delete items in a custom form	984
Deleting constraints	You can't delete a constraint	184
Deleting toolbars	You can't delete a toolbar	976
Duplicate resource names	You have duplicate resource names, and information is being tracked separately for each instance	204
Earned value fields	Your earned value fields all show $0.00	421, 499
E-mail workgroup messaging	You can't find the e-mail workgroup messaging functions	652
Empty baseline fields	You see nothing in the baseline fields	376
Entering actuals	Your scheduled start and finish dates change when you enter actuals	388
Entering costs	You can't enter costs for your cost resource	215
Entering field values	You can't enter a value in the Budget Cost or Budget Work field	296
Field Name list	The field you're looking for is not in the Field Name list	133, 930
Filter By boxes	Your Filter By boxes are dimmed	245

Topic	Description	Page
Grayed toolbars in Gantt chart	You enter project information in Gantt Chart view and your menus and toolbars have all turned gray	92
Heading row calculations	You can't change the calculation for the value that appears in the group heading row	950
Importing files	Microsoft Office Project 2007 will not let you import the older .xls file format	211
Incorrect filter results	A filter doesn't display the correct tasks	953
Leveling delays	Leveling delay you entered manually has disappeared	362
Leveling problems	You told Microsoft Project to level your resources, but nothing changed	363
Locating custom toolbars	You can't find the custom toolbar you built	975
Loss of file formatting	File formats I used to export to are no longer available	576
Macro selections	Why doesn't your macro select the right cell?	994
Mapping table fields	You can't find a field you want in the Mapping table	622
Master project resources	Your master project has duplicate resource names	509
Missing Gantt bars	A Gantt bar doesn't appear in the chart	908
Missing resources	The resources are missing from your sharer file	523
Naming fields	The custom field name isn't informative as a column heading in a table	934
No data to print	Microsoft Project says there is no data to print	464
Overallocations	Tasks scheduled at the same time are causing overallocations	339
Paste error messages	You're getting paste error messages	602
Pasting causes deletions	Your pasted information deleted existing information	541
Pasting data	Data doesn't paste into the target file correctly	553
PERT analysis views	You can't find the PERT analysis views	113
Predecessor links	You're trying to remove just the predecessor link from a task, but the successor link is removed at the same time	176
Project Guide toolbar	The Project Guide toolbar is not available	27
Project Help pane	The Project Help pane is obstructing your work	30
Project information missing	Some of your project information is missing	147
Project server users	Your new resources are not added as project server users	708
Removing toolbar buttons	You can't remove buttons on a toolbar	972

Topic	Description	Page
Rolled-up values	The rolled-up value for fixed task costs looks wrong	287
Saving as Web page	You can't save project information as a Web page	486
Scheduled value changes	Your scheduled values change whenever you enter actuals	407
Scheduling tasks	You assigned a task calendar, but it's not scheduling tasks in all the times it should	194
Security settings	Microsoft Project is not exporting to Excel because of security settings	623
Sending project files	Only a fragment of the project file is being sent	649
Sharing commands	The resource sharing commands are dimmed	521
Slowed performance	Microsoft Project performance has slowed since you last leveled	363
Split bar missing	The current view doesn't have a split bar	123
Task List template	You can't find the Excel Task List template	608
Text and bar formatting	You lose text and bar formatting when you insert projects	512
Text report columns	You can't adjust text report column sizes	458
Toolbar placement	The toolbar doesn't appear where you want it	973
Viewing open projects	You don't see an open project file in the Share Resources dialog box	522

Index

A

Accrual of resource costs, 281
Active Directory synchronization, 708–710
Activity definition, 88. *See also* Task lists
Activity plans
  creating, 20
  in enterprise project management, 825–827
  in Project Web Access, 879–883
  to-do lists or mini-projects from, 841–843
Actual Cost of Work Performed (ABCWP), 465, 495
Actuals, 490–491, 736–737, 808, 851. *See also* Changes in projects; Updating progress
Analyze Timescaled Data function, 591
Analyzing. *See* Data Analysis Services; Earned value analysis; Updating progress
Application program interface (API), 25, 681
Applications, information exchange with, 547–579. *See also* Excel 2007; Outlook 2007; Visio 2007
  copying for, 549–557
    pictures of views, 553–557
    from Project 2007, 549–551
    to Project 2007, 551–553
  embedding for, 557–567
    from Project 2007, 558–562
    to Project 2007, 562–567
  hyperlinking for, 571–572
  importing and exporting for, 573–579
    from Project 2007, 576–578
    to Project 2007, 574–576
    security setting to allow, 573–574
    XML files for, 578–579
  linking for, 568–571
    from Project 2007, 568–569
    to Project 2007, 569–571
  purpose of, 547–548
As Late As Possible (ALAP) constraint, 180
Assignment delay, 174
Assignments. *See also* Resources assigned to tasks
  balancing resource workloads in, 347–354
  cost resource, 288, 295
  leveling, 355–363
  of outline codes, 946
  in Outlook 2007, 862–863
  overview of, 235–237
  owners of, 19, 698, 792–793, 848
  in Project Web Access, 885
    information on, 843–848
    reviewing, 834–836
    of tasks and resources, 837–842
  reducing costs and, 337
  reports on, 466–473
  in Resource Usage view, 524
  to team resources, 792–794
As Soon As Possible (ASAP) constraint, 179–180
Authentication of users, 710
Autofilter tool, 146–147, 959–960
Availability of resources
  adjusting, 327–329
  balancing workloads by, 347
  earliest and latest, 698
  graphs of, 247–248, 789–790
  max units for, 225–228
  Project Web Access information on, 886
  reports on, 471
  in resource graph view, 916–918
  in resource pools, 523–525
  working times in, 220–225

B

Backing up, 1033–1034
Base calendars, 72–81
  alternative work week in, 75–76
  in enterprise project management, 697
  holidays and one-time exceptions in, 76–78
  new, 80–81
  nonworking times on, 730–732
  normal work week in, 73–75

recurring exceptions in, 78–80
for resources, 223–225
task calendars from, 193–195
types of, 72–73
Baselines, 369–381
changes in projects and, 402, 405, 433
clearing, 381
earned value analysis and, 490–491
multiple, 377–379
for project execution, 369–370
in project management, 42–43, 48, 54
purpose of, 370–372
reports on, 459, 461–463
reviewing information in, 374–377
setting, 372–374
start and finish dates in, 379–381
Billable time, 22–23, 741
Bill of materials (BOM), 100
Booking types, 697, 791–792, 956
Brainstorming, 86
Budgeted at Completion (BAC), 465, 496
Budgeted Cost of Work Planned (BCWP), 50,
465, 495
Budgeted Cost of Work Scheduled (BCWS),
416, 465, 495
Budget resources, 220, 292–301. *See also* Costs,
planning for
budget values for, 296–297
creating, 293–294
project summary task and, 294–295
resource costs *versus,* 301–304, 332–333
review costs with, 418
sources of, 308–309
Budget tracking, 14–15
Buffer, duration, 156
Build Team dialog box, 782, 785, 788–791
Business process integration, 745–746

C

Calendars. *See also* Base calendars; Project
calendars; Resource calendars; Task
calendars
customizing views of, 919–922
on Project Web Access, 858–863
Cash flow report, 333, 460–461
Categories of project information, 106–107
Changes in projects, 401–433

cost adjustments in response to, 415–424
budget status for, 421–424
cost variances for, 417–418
earned value analysis for, 419–421
overall totals for, 417
overbudget costs for, 418–419
highlighting, 16, 324
overview of, 401–403
resource workload adjustments in response
to, 424–433
allocation review for, 426–432
balancing, 432–433
overall totals for, 425
overbudget work for, 426
work variances for, 425
schedule adjustments in response to, 403–
415
correcting, 414–415
critical path and, 408
Gantt Chart progress lines for, 410–414
schedule progress monitoring for, 403–406
schedule variances for, 406–407
task progress in, 408–410
Clipboard, 552
Closing projects, 44, 55, 1018–1019
Code
macro, 996–997
outline, 229, 243, 941–947
in WBS Code Definition dialog box, 988
Collaborate toolbar, 800
Combination views, 121–124
Communication, 8–9, 44, 438–439
Compression, duration, 326
Consolidated projects, 513–517
Constraints. *See also* Finish dates
changes in, 182–184
date, 42, 47, 323–324, 583
flexible *versus* inflexible, 184–185
in project scope, 61
reviewing, 185–186
scheduling from finish dates and, 71
types of, 179–182
Consultation, expert, 87
Contouring resource assignments, 269–271
Controlling projects, 44. *See also* Updating
progress
Copying
customized elements, 962–963

Excel 2007 information to Project 2007,
584–589
from Project 2007, 549–551
to Project 2007, 551–553
Project 2007 information to Excel 2007,
589–593
project templates, 1015–1016
Cost Performance Index (CPI), 496
Cost resources, 14–15. *See also* Changes in
projects
actual costs for, 398–399
adding to project, 214–215
in project management, 38, 40, 50
reducing costs and, 337–338
reports on, 460–466
in resource graph view, 917–918
task assignment of, 253–256
Costs, planning for, 273–306
actual, 397–399
budgeting as, 274
budget resources in, 292–301
assigning to project summary task, 294–
295
budget values for, 296–297
creating, 293–294
resource costs versus, 301–304
currency differences in, 304–306
fixed task, 284–287
reduction of, 331–338
of resources, 275–284
accrual of, 281
entering, 282–284
for materials, 277–278
multiple costs for, 278–281
for work, 275–277
reviewing, 287–292
Cost Variance (CV), 50, 416, 465, 495–496
Cost Variance Percent (CV%), 497
Crashing the schedule, 326
Critical Path Method (CPM), 309–320
changes in projects and, 408
critical tasks in, 330–331
finish dates in, 320–322
in master projects, 511–512
multiple critical paths in, 319–320
PERT analysis *versus,* 165–166
slack time and critical tasks in, 311–314
viewing critical paths in, 314–319

Cross-project linking, 529. *See also* Project
plans, information exchange between
Crosstab tables, 629. *See also* PivotTables and
PivotDiagrams
Cube Building Services, 25
Currency, different, 304–306
Customize dialog box, 978–979
Customizing, 8, 20. *See also* Views,
customizing
Cutoff date, in earned value analysis, 465

D
Data Analysis Services, 749–751, 869, 891–893
Databases, 24, 105–106, 769
Data types, 586–587, 624
Date constraints, 42, 47, 181–182
Deadlines, 47, 53, 186–188
Define the Project Wizard, 27–28, 70
Delays, 173–174, 349, 361–362
Deleting, 95–96, 184, 567
Deliverables, 18
entering tasks with, 86
of other projects, 538, 777–780
in project management, 41–42
in project scope, 62
Dependencies, 167–178
adjusting, 324–325
building, 583
changing, 176–177
constraints *versus,* 185
on deliverables, 18, 777–780
finish-to-start, 169–171, 312
lag time to delay, 173–174
lead time to overlap, 174–175
in project management, 43
reviewing, 177–178
scheduling from finish dates and, 71
types of, 171–173
Depletion of materials, 39
Discussion groups, 34–35
Documentation
attaching, 82–86
hyperlinking to, 103, 571–572
in Project Web Access, 847–848, 877–878
SharePoint Services for, 572
team control of, 814–816
Draft database, 24, 769

Drafter resource, 226
Durations, task, 47, 154–167
  actual and remaining, 387–388
  adjusting, 325–326
  calculating probable, 162–167
  decreasing, 329–331
  effects of, 159–161
  entering, 157–159
  estimates of, 88, 155–156
  estimates *versus* confirmed, 156–157
  fixed duration task type and, 268
  metrics for, 49
  work amounts and, 250

E

Earned value analysis, 50, 489–499
  calculations for, 416
  changes in projects and, 419–421
  fields for, 495–497
  generating data for, 489–492
  performance analysis by, 404
  reports on, 465–466, 497–499
  tables for, 492–494
Effort-driven scheduling, 264–265
Elapsed duration, 159
E-mail. *See also* Outlook 2007
  address book for, 206–207
  notifications by, 798
  Project Web Access setup of, 858–863, 893
Embedding to exchange information, 557–567
  Excel 2007 objects in Project 2007, 593–597
  to Project 2007, 562–567
  of Project 2007 files, 558–562
  Project 2007 files in Excel 2007, 597–600
  in Visio 2007 and Project 2007, 654
Enterprise global template, 768, 772–774
Enterprise project management, 6, 675–689
  components of, 680–684
  custom fields in, 20
  Data Analysis Services for, 891–893
  EPM workflow in, 684–689
  information exchange in, 548
  master and subprojects in, 18
  opening files in, 1022–1023
  Project 2007 in, 51–52
  roles in, 677–680
  saving files in, 1027–1029

Enterprise project management,
    administration of, 691–751
  business process integration with, 745–746
  Data Analysis Services for, 749–751
  enterprise portfolio in, 720–721
  enterprise resource pool in, 518, 704–720
    Active Directory synchronization with,
      708–710
    importing resources to, 714–716
    individual resources for, 710–711
    multiple resources for, 706–708
    nonenterprise resource pool versus, 781
    Project Web Access view of, 883–884
    removing resources from, 719–720
    team resource for, 711–714
    updating information to, 716–719
  logging on and off, 692
  Quick Launch task bar changes for, 748
  server management for, 751
  standardizing elements in, 721–732
    customized fields for, 725–730
    global template for, 721–725
    nonworking time on calendars for, 730–732
  team member work pages in, 732–741
    My Tasks versus My Timesheets in, 732–
      734
    My Timesheets page as, 739–741
    task progress page as, 734–738
  users and permissions in, 692–704
    automated alerts for, 704
    groups and categories in, 694, 700–703
    new accounts and, 695–698
    removing users in, 698–699
    security template for, 700
    viewing and changing, 699
  view management in, 746–748
  Web parts for page management in, 742–745
Enterprise project management, resources for,
    753–826
  for activity plans, 825–827
  creating new project in, 763–767
  custom enterprise fields in, 775–776
  deliverables of other projects and, 777–780
  enterprise global template in, 773–774
  pages and controls for, 760–761
  program of projects in, 776–777
  Project Professional setup for, 754–757
  Project Web Access logon for, 757–759

for proposals, 820–827
Quick Launch task bar for, 759–760
server project files in, 767–772
tables for, 761–762
team, 780–820
   assigning tasks to, 792–794
   assignment pool of, 785–786
   attributes of, 783–784
   criteria for, 786–788
   documents controlled by, 814–816
   enterprise versus project, 788–789
   generic, 784–785
   issues monitored by, 818–820
   matching, 789–791
   by name, 782–783
   publishing information by, 800–801
   risks mitigated by, 816–818
   status reports by, 808–811
   task update exchanges by, 802–808
   task update options for, 795–800
   tentative, 791–792
   timesheet for tracking, 811–814
Estimate at Completion (EAC), 465, 496
Estimating, 88, 155–157, 219, 274
Euro converter, 306
Excel 2007, 581–637
   cash flow report in, 333–334
   exporting tables to, 762
   Project 2007 embedded files in, 597–600
   Project 2007 embedded objects from, 593–597
   Project 2007 exports to, 17, 616–628
      complete data, 626–627
      export map for, 627–628
      security settings to allow, 616–617
      selected data, 617–625
   Project 2007 imports from, 606–615
      project information, 611–613
      project task lists, 607–611
      without templates, 614–615
   Project 2007 information copied from, 584–589
   Project 2007 information copied to, 589–593
   Project information exchange with, 548
   Project 2007 linked to, 600–606
   resource information from, 207–212
   switching to Project 2007 from, 582–584
   tables exported to, 833, 872

tasks imported from, 89–91
visual reports in, 628–637
   built-in templates for, 629–632
   configuring, 636–637
   editing templates for, 632–635
   types of, 448–451, 459–462, 466, 471–472, 478
Executing projects, 43
Executives, on project teams, 679. *See also* Project Web Access, executive decisions in
Expected duration, 163
External links, 529, 534
External predecessor task, 529, 534
External successor task, 529

F
Fast tracking, 326
Fields
   assignment, 843
   copying, 540–542
   on custom forms, 982
   for database records, 105
   duration, 163
   earned value analysis, 495–497
   enterprise
      customizing, 725–730
      to refine projects, 775–776
      for resource attributes, 783–784
   Field Name list of, 930
   Help for, 32
   on My Tasks page, 737–738
   predecessor, 89, 534
   in Project Web Access, 872
   resource, 228–230, 698
   on resource graph, 917
   saving data, 484–487
   Start and Finish, 89, 932
   subproject, 511
   troubleshooting, 133
   views of, 931–940
      accessing, 134–138
      calculated, 936–938
      graphical indicators in, 938–940
      lookup values for, 934–936
      setup process of, 933–934
      types of, 932
Files, project, 1021–1036

opening, 1021–1026, 1036
other formats for, 1030–1031
safeguarding, 1032–1036
saving, 1026–1029
Filtering information
 by cost, 335–336
 e-mailing, 648
 in Project Web Access, 873–874
 on resource booking types, 956
 on resources, 244–245
 views of, 900, 952–960
  autofilter criteria for, 959–960
  creating, 955–959
  description of, 142–147
  modifying, 952–955
Finish dates, 47, 320–331
 actual, 388–391
 in baselines, 379–381
 critical path and, 320–322
 resource settings and, 327–331
 schedule assumptions and, 322–327
 scheduling from, 70–72
 sources of, 308–309
Finish No Earlier Than (FNET) constraint,
  180
Finish No Later Than (FNLT) constraint, 180
Finish-to-finish (FF) dependencies, 171
Finish-to-start dependencies, 159, 169–171,
  312
Finish-to-start (FS) dependencies, 171
Fixed duration task type, 268
Fixed material consumption, 251
Fixed resource costs, 277, 293
Fixed task costs, 284–287, 398–399
Fixed units task type, 267
Fixed work task type, 268
Fonts, 902–903
Forms
 embedding objects in, 566
 in Project 2007 interface, 979–986
 resource, 342
 viewing, 120–121
Free slack time, 311, 350

G

Gantt Charts
 to analyze projects, 876
 assignments on, 844

 customizing views of, 904–911
 description of, 43
 Detail, 317
 embedding objects in, 553–554
 Gantt Chart Wizard for, 316, 904
 lag and lead time in, 175
 milestones on Gantt bars in, 190–191
 pasting to, 552
 progress lines in, 410–414
 tracking, 374
 troubleshooting, 92
 viewing, 64, 110–114
 in Visio 2007, 664–665, 667–668, 670–672
Generic resources, 218–219
Global permissions, 711
Global templates
 copying to, 543–544
 enterprise, 721–725, 768, 773–774, 1004–
  1005
 global.mpt as, 484
 project, 1004–1008
Graphical indicators, 938–940
Graph views, 115–117, 915–919
Grouping
 fields on forms, 984
 project information for viewing, 140–142
 in Project Web Access, 873
 resources, 229
 tasks, 318–319
Groups, 938, 948–952. *See also* Users and
  permissions

H

Headers and footers, 442
Help, Project 2007, 29–35
 browsing for, 31–32
 for dialog boxes, 33
 Project discussion groups for, 34–35
 for project fields, 32
 searching topics for, 29–31
 on Web, 33–34
Highlight Filter dialog box, 900
Hyperlinking
 to exchanging information, 571–572
 project files to documents, 84–86
 resource information, 232–233
 tasks to documents, 103

I

Importing and exporting. *See also* Excel 2007
  from Project 2007, 576–578, 762
  to Project 2007, 574–576
  security setting to allow, 573–574
  XML files for, 578–579
Import Project Wizard, 716, 765–766
Information exchange. *See* Applications,
    information exchange with; Project plans,
    information exchange between
Initial assignment, calculations on, 249
Interfaces. *See* Application program interface
    (API); Project 2007 interface; Project Server
    Interface (PSI)
Issues tracking, 818–820, 847–848, 877–878

L

Lag time, 173–174
Lead time, 174–175
Legends, 442
Leveling
  assignment units, 355–363
  delays, 349
  in enterprise project management, 697
  scheduling from finish dates and, 71
  timing of, 428
Limitations, in project scope, 61. *See also*
    Constraints
Links, task, 168, 170–171, 325. *See also*
    Dependencies
  to Excel 2007, 600–606
  external, 529
  imported, 585
  for information exchange, 529–534, 568–571
  to other projects, 504
  removing, 537
  to resource pools, 520–523
  reviewing, 534–536
  Update Link prompt for, 604
  updating, 536–537
Lookup tables, 300, 713, 944–945
Lookup values, 934–936

M

Macros, 987–1001
  code for, 996–997
  description of, 987–988

recording of, 992–995
  Record Macro dialog box for, 989–992
  running, 998–1001
  stopping recording of, 992
Mapping table, 622–623
Mask, code, 942–943
Master projects, 503–517
  consolidated projects *versus*, 513–517
  critical path in, 511–512
  duplicate resource names in, 509
  inserting projects into, 504–507
  in Project Web Access, 876–877
  subprojects in, 507–513
Material resources, 213
  actual costs for, 397–398
  assignment owners of, 792
  depletion of, 39
  planning for cost of, 277–278
  task assignment of, 251–253
Max units for resources, 225–228, 236
Milestones
  entering tasks with, 86
  in project management, 41, 43, 46–47
  reporting, 455
  in scheduling tasks, 188–191
  scope verification and, 382
  on Visio project timeline, 669–670
Model, of project, 46–49
More Views dialog box, 900
Must Finish On (MFO) constraint, 180
Must Start On (MSO) constraint, 180
My Tasks page, 732–734, 794–795, 856–857
My Timesheets page, 732–734, 739–741, 856–
    857

N

Negative slack situations, 312
Network diagram views, 43, 114–115, 912–915
Nodes, in network diagrams, 114
Nonbillable time, 22–23
Non-project work, in schedule, 227–228
Nonworking time, 12–13

O

Office Online, 32
Offline work, in enterprise project
    management, 772

OLAP (online analytical processing) cubes
  for Data Analysis Services, 749–751, 869,
    891–893
  interactive views and reports from, 24–25
  PivotTables linked to, 629
  reports from, 17, 450
  saving, 484–485, 631, 656
OLE technology, 558
Operations, projects *versus,* 37–38
Optimistic duration, 163
Organizational breakdown structure (OBS),
    100
Organizer, 542–544, 961–962
Outline, tasks in, 97–99
Outline codes, 243, 941–947
Outlook 2007, 639–652
  assignments in, 862–863
  integration with, 22
  Project 2007 information exchange with,
    548, 639–643
  Project Web Access integration with, 860–
    861
  publishing project files by, 651–652
  resource list building with, 643–644
  sending project files by, 644–651
Overallocated resources
  critical tasks and, 330–331
  group tasks with, 951
  leveling and, 359
  overtime work to account for, 351–354
  replacing, 348
  reports on, 470–471
  on resource graph, 917
  views of, 343–344
Overhead, 330
Overtime work, 276–277, 351–354

P
Passwords, 1034–1035
Pasting
  from Excel 2007 to Project 2007, 588
  to Gantt Charts, 552
  troubleshooting, 553, 602
  to Word 2007 tables, 551
PDF files, saving as, 487
Peak units, 427, 917
Percentage work complete, 391–392
Performance, 526, 1018

Permanently Renumber Task check box, 139
Permissions. *See* Users and permissions
PERT (program evaluation and review
    technique) analysis, 113
  critical path method *versus,* 165–166
  for probable durations, 162–164, 325
  in Visio diagram, 668, 672
  weighting adjustment in, 166–167
Pessimistic duration, 163
Phases in projects, 43, 46–47, 86
Physical percentage complete, 491–492
Physical Percent Complete, 497
PivotTables and PivotDiagrams, 17, 448, 629.
    See also Visio 2007
Planning
  in Professional edition, 18–19
  in project management, 41–43
  in Project Server and Project Web Access,
    20–21
  in Standard edition, 12–13
Portfolio managers, 52, 679, 772, 811. *See also*
    Project Web Access, executive decisions in
PowerPoint 2007, 444, 553–556
Predecessor tasks, 168, 176, 529, 534. *See also*
    Dependencies
Print Current View Wizard, 28
Printing, 440–443, 564
Problem statements, 39
Procurement management, 278
Productivity, 330, 582
Product *versus* project scope, 60–61
Professional edition of Project 2007, 6, 8–10,
    18–20, 682, 754–757. *See also* Enterprise
    project management; Project Web Access,
    executive decisions in
Progress, updating. *See* Updating progress
Progress lines, in Gantt Charts, 410–414
Project 2007, overview of, 3–36. *See also*
    Applications, information exchange with;
    Changes in projects; Project management
  Help in, 29–35
  Professional edition of, 6, 8–10, 18–20
  Project Guide of, 25–29
  Project Server 2007 of, 6, 10–11, 20–25
  Project Smart Tags of, 35–36
  Project Web Access of, 10, 20–25
  scheduling engine of, 7
  sections of, 4–6

Standard edition of, 8, 11–17
Project calendars, 81
Project Center, 868–869
Project files. *See* Files, project
Project Guide
  custom tracking view in, 389
  dependency setting in, 172
  description of, 25–29
  resource addition in, 206
  viewing critical path in, 319
Project 2007 interface, 967–986
  buttons on, 976–977
  forms for, 979–986
    creating, 980–984
    displaying, 985–986
    editing, 984–985
    renaming, 985
  menus for, 977–979
  toolbars for, 967–976
    creating, 973–975
    customizing, 967–973
    deleting, 975–976
Project management, 37–55. *See also* Changes
    in projects; Enterprise project management
  baseline setting in, 379
  closing projects in, 44, 1019
  communication planning in, 439
  controlling projects in, 44
  cost control in, 415–416
  of critical tasks, 330–331
  definition of, 37–41
  duration compression in, 326
  executing projects in, 43
  planning projects in, 41–43
  procurement in, 278
  Project 2007 in, 44–52
    capabilities of, 44–46
    in enterprise, 51–52
    project model from, 46–49
    team collaboration through, 49–51
  on resources assigned to tasks, 238–239
  schedule control in, 403–404
  scope and quality verification, 382
  staffing in, 205
  stakeholders of, 52–53
  successful, 53–55
Project managers, 677, 849
Project plans, adjusting, 307–365. *See also*
    Changes in projects

to balance resource workloads, 338–363
  by assignment changes, 347–354
  by availability changes, 347
  by leveling assignments, 355–363
  by splitting tasks, 354–355
  views of, 339–347
to bring in finish date, 320–331
  critical path and, 320–322
  resource settings and, 327–331
  schedule assumptions and, 322–327
buyoff of, 365
critical path for, 309–320
  multiple, 319–320
  slack time and critical tasks in, 311–314
  viewing, 314–319
disconnecting resource pools from, 526–527
impact of, 364–365
Outlook tasks in, 640–642
to reduce costs, 331–338
for scope changes, 364
Project plans, information exchange between,
    529–544
  copying and moving task and resource data
    for, 538–540
  copying fields for, 540–542
  cross-project links for, 534–537
  linking tasks for, 529–534
  Organizer for, 542–544
Project Portfolio Server 2007, 10–11, 689, 877.
    See also Enterprise project management;
    Project Web Access, executive decisions in
Project Server 2007, 6, 10. *See also* Enterprise
    project management
  components of, 683–684
  enterprise resource pool and, 518
  installing, 691–692
  master projects and, 508
  new features of, 20–25
  role of, 681–682
Project server administrators, 51–52, 679, 772,
    781, 785, 811
Project Server Interface (PSI), 25, 681
Project Smart Tags, 35–36
Project Statistics dialog box, 376, 385, 452
Project summary task, 82, 98, 294–295, 417,
    425
Project triangle *versus* rectangle, 40
Project Web Access, 6, 10, 827–864. *See also*
    Enterprise project management

assigning tasks and resources via, 837–842
assignment information on, 843–848
automated tracking in, 393
document library in, 85
e-mail, reminders, and calendars on, 858–863
logging on and off, 829–831
new features of, 20–25
pages and controls for, 831–832
progress fields in, 384
Quick Launch task bar for, 831
resource management in, 864
reviewing assignments via, 834–836
role of, 683
SharePoint Services integrated with, 9
status reports via, 852–853
tables for, 832–833
timesheets on, 853–858
updating progress via, 848–851
Project Web Access, executive decisions in, 865–893
alerts and reminders for, 893
analysis and reports for, 891–893
key areas for, 868–869
logging on and off in, 866–868
project portfolio information for, 869–883
arranging, 872–874
fields for, 872
new projects in, 878–879
opening in Project Professional, 876–877
page and controls for, 870–871
proposals and activity plans in, 879–883
tables for, 871–872
viewing, 875–876
workspaces, documents, issues, and risks in, 877–878
resource information for, 883–891
on assignments, 885
on availability, 886
on enterprise resource pool, 883–884
on plans, 887
on specific projects, 884–885
status reports as, 887–891
Project Working Times Wizard, 28
Proposals, 820–827
adding resources to, 823–824
creating, 20–21, 821–823
project conversion of, 824
in Project Web Access, 879–883

resource plan for, 825–827
reviewers of, 679
Proposed resources, 244
Prorating costs, 281
Publishing information
in enterprise project management, 800–801
in Outlook 2007, 651–652
published database for, 24, 769
saving *versus,* 19
to SharePoint Services, 769

Q

Quick Launch task bar, 748, 759–760, 821, 824, 831

R

Record Macro dialog box, 989–992
Records, database, 105
Relationships, task. *See* Dependencies
Reorder points, 39
Reporting, 437–487. *See also* Updating progress
assignment, 466–473
to balance resource workloads, 343–347
built-in reports for, 474–478
closing tasks and, 735–737
communications plan for, 438–439
to control projects, 44
cost, 333–335, 460–466
custom reports for, 478–484
database for, 769
on earned value analysis, 497–499
in Excel 2007
built-in templates for, 629–632
configuring, 636–637
editing templates for, 632–635
visual, 448–451
on My Timesheets page, 739
overview, 452–455
printing views for, 440–443
in Professional edition, 9, 19–20
in Project Server 2007 and Project Web Access, 23–25, 852–853, 891–893
Report Project Guide for, 443–444
saving data fields and, 484–487
schedule progress, 455–460
in Standard edition, 8, 15–17

on status
  on Project Web Access, 852–853, 887–891
  by teams, 808–811
text-based, 445–448
in Visio 2007, 448–451, 654–661
Report Project Guide, 443–445
Resource breakdown structure (RBS), 100, 754
Resource calendars, 81, 220–223
Resource Center, 868–869
Resource filters, 144, 244
Resource groups, 141
Resource managers, 677–678
Resource pools, 517–527. *See also* Enterprise project management, administration of
  availability of resources in, 523–525
  disconnecting project plan from, 526–527
  linking projects to, 520–523
  setting up, 518–520
  updating information on, 525–526
Resources, 201–233. *See also* Costs, planning for; Enterprise project management; Enterprise project management, resources for; Overallocated resources; Project plans, adjusting
  assigning tasks to, 837–838
  assignment owners of, 848
  balancing workloads of, 338–363
    by assignment changes, 347–354
    by availability changes, 347
    by leveling assignments, 355–363
    by splitting tasks, 354–355
    views of, 339–347
  booking types for, 697, 791–792, 956
  budget, 220
  contact information on, 231–232
  cost, 214–215
  duplicate names for, 509
  entering, 203–204
  exchanging information on, 538–540
  finish dates and, 327–331
  generic, 218–219
  graph views of, 915–919
  hyperlinking to information on, 232–233
  material, 213
  by outline codes, 947
  Outlook 2007 list of, 643–644
  in Professional edition, 8–9, 19

project plan impact of, 202–203
in Project Server 2007 and Project Web Access, 21–23
  on assignments, 885
  on availability, 886
  on enterprise resource pool, 883–884
  management of, 864
  on plans, 887
  on specific projects, 884–885
  status reports as, 887–891
  team, 837–842
removing, 216
setting availability of, 220–228
  max units for, 225–228
  working times in, 220–225
in Standard edition, 8
supplemental fields for, 228–230
tentative, 216–218
updating progress and, 390–395
work, 205–212
Resources assigned to tasks, 235–271
  changing, 261–269
    effort-driven scheduling for, 264–265
    instructions for, 263
    Smart Tags for, 262
    task types for, 265–269
  contouring, 269–271
  cost, 253–256
  material, 251–253
  showing, 256–258
  in task view, 258–261
  work, 235–250
    assignment calculations for, 248–250
    assignments of, 237–241
    job-specific, 241–248
Resources Management toolbar, 341
Resource Substitution Wizard, 790–791
Resource tables, 129–130
Resource units, 225, 235–236
Resource usage view, 924–925
Reverse time, in durations, 156
Ripple effects, of schedule changes, 196–197
Risks, 816–818, 847–848, 877–878

S

Scalability, of Project 2007, 8–9
Schedule Performance Index (SPI), 404, 496
Schedule Variance Percent (SV%), 497

Schedule Variance (SV), 50, 404, 465, 496
Scheduling. *See also* Base calendars
  effort-driven, 264–265
  engine for, 7
  in Professional edition, 18–19
  in project management, 42
  in Project Server 2007 and Project Web
    Access, 20–21
  in Standard edition, 12–13
  in starting projects, 70–72
Scheduling tasks, 153–199. *See also* Changes in
    projects
  calendars for, 192–195
  controls for, 385–389
  crashing, 326
  deadline reminders in, 186–188
  dependencies in, 167–178
    changing, 176–177
    finish-to-start, 169–171
    lag time and, 173–174
    lead time and, 174–175
    reviewing, 177–178
    types of, 171–173
  durations in, 154–167
    calculating probable, 162–167
    effects of, 159–161
    entering, 157–159
    estimates of, 155–156
    estimates versus confirmed, 156–157
  in Excel 2007 to Project 2007, 583
  feedback on changes in, 195–199
  finish dates and, 322–327
  milestones in, 188–191
  to reduce costs, 337
  reports on, 455–460
  for specific dates, 178–186
    constraint changes in, 182–184
    constraint flexibility in, 184–185
    constraint review in, 185–186
    constraint types in, 180–182
  in Standard edition, 8
Scope of project
  changes in, 364
  defining, 60–63
  description of, 38, 40, 43
  sources of, 308–309
  verification of, 382
Security
  groups for, 710

  for importing and exporting, 573–574, 616–
    617, 623
  for project files, 1032–1036
  saving workspaces and, 516–517
  templates for, 700
Servers. *See* Enterprise project management;
    Project Server 2007
Server-side scheduling, 20
Setup Tracking Wizard, 28
SharePoint Services. *See also* Enterprise project
    management
  for document libraries, 85, 572
  Project Web Access integrated with, 9
  project workspace in, 23–24
  publishing information to, 769
  reporting and, 439
Sharing resources. *See* Resource pools
Sheet views, 117–118, 922–923
Shortcuts
  for commands, 978
  to macros, 998–999
  to Project Web Access, 830, 867
  to views, 902
Skill sets, 243–244
Slack time, 311–314, 350, 360
Smart Tags, 35–36, 262
Sorting information, 138–140, 335, 872–873
Splitting Windows, 149–151
SQL Server database, 106
Staffing management, 205
Stakeholders, 43, 52–53, 365
Standard edition of Project 2007, 8, 11–17
Standardization, 8–9, 688, 721–732
  customized fields for, 725–730
  global template for, 721–725
  nonworking time on calendars for, 730–732
  templates for, 1003–1019
    closing projects and, 1018–1019
    creating, 1014–1017
    downloading, 1013–1014
    new projects by, 1009–1012
    project global, 1005–1008
    types of, 1004–1005
Start dates
  actual, 388–391
  in baselines, 379–381
  scheduling from, 70–72
Starting projects, 59–103
  base calendar in, 72–81

alternative work week in, 75–76
holidays and one-time exceptions in, 76–78
new, 80–81
normal work week in, 73–75
recurring exceptions in, 78–80
types of, 72–73
documentation in, 82–86
project file in, 63–69
saving project in, 69–70
scheduling decisions in, 70–72
scope in, 60–63
tasks in
 entering, 86–92
 notes for, 102–103
 outlining, 97–99
 sequencing, 93–96
work breakdown structure (WBS) in, 99–102
Start No Earlier Than (SNET) constraint, 180–
 181, 610–611
Start No Later Than (SNLT) constraint, 180
Start-to-finish (SF) dependencies, 171
Start-to-start (SS) dependencies, 171
Status date, in earned value analysis, 465,
 491–492
Status icons, 410
Status managers, 19, 793–794, 849
Subprojects
 in master projects, 507–508
 in Project Web Access, 876
 read-only information of, 509–511
 removed from master projects, 513
 unlinked from source files, 512–513
Subtables, 454
Successor tasks, 168, 176, 529. *See also*
 Dependencies
Summary task, 82, 98, 294–295, 417, 425

T
Tables. *See also* PivotTables and PivotDiagrams
 Baseline, 375
 cost, 331–332
 crosstab, 629
 customizing views of, 928–931
 earned value analysis, 420, 492–494
 for enterprise project management resources,
  761–762
 entry, 534
 lookup, 300, 944–945

mapping, 622–623
in Project Web Access, 832–833, 844, 871–
 872
report subtables as, 454
team lookup, 713
view definition and, 901
in views
 modifying, 131–134
 reviewing, 125–130
Word 2007, 551
Task calendars, 81
 adjusting, 327
 in scheduling, 192–195
 troubleshooting, 161
Task dates, 583
Task Drivers, 13, 29, 199, 326–327
Task filters, 143
Task groups, 141
Task lists. *See also* Costs, planning for;
 Critical Path Method (CPM); Project plans,
 adjusting; Resources assigned to tasks;
 Scheduling tasks; Updating progress
 copying and moving, 538–540
 critical tasks in, 330–331, 453–454
 grouping, 318–319
 by outline codes, 947
 progress tracking of, 43
 in project management, 41, 46–47
 project summary, 82, 98, 294–295, 417, 425
 on Project Web Access, 837–842
 sequencing of, 49
 sorting, 139
 splitting tasks in, 354–355, 360
 in starting projects
  entering, 86–92
  notes for, 102–103
  outlining, 97–99
  sequencing, 86, 93–96
Task tables, 126–129
Task types, 265–269
Task usage views, 924–925, 949
Team collaboration, 8–9. *See also* Enterprise
 project management, resources for; Project
 Server 2007; Project Web Access
 in entering tasks, 86
 lead and member roles in, 678
 lookup tables for, 713
 in project management, 49–51
 tasks of, 839–840

work pages for, 732–741
  My Tasks versus My Timesheets in, 732–734
  My Timesheets page as, 739–741
  task progress page as, 734–738
Templates. *See also* **Standardization**
  built-in Excel 2007, 629–632
  built-in Project 2007, 64–67
  creating projects with, 67–69
  enterprise global, 721–725
  for Excel 2007 reports, 632–635
  Excel Task List, 608
  global, 543–544
  global enterprise, 768, 773–774
  for network diagrams, 913
  for planning and scheduling, 12
  at project closing, 44, 49
  for reports, 481–484
  security, 700
  Visio Gantt Chart, 670–672
  Visio PERT Chart, 672
  Visio project timeline, 668–670
  visual report, 17
Tentative resources, 216–218
Timeline, project
  Visio diagram for, 668
  Visio display of, 662–664
  Visio exported, 666–667
  Visio template for, 668–670
Timephased data, 118, 925
Time resources
  lag, 173–174
  lead, 174–175
  nonproject or nonworking, 857–858
  in project management, 38, 40
  reverse, 156
  slack, 311–314, 350, 360
  tracking of, 8, 19, 21–23, 811–814
Timescales, 124–125, 591, 926–928
Timesheets
  for billable and nonbillable time, 22–23
  manager for, 698
  My Timesheets page as, 732–734, 739–741
  on Project Web Access, 843, 853–858
  for tracking team resources, 811–814
To Complete Performance Index (TCPI), 497
Total slack time, 311, 350
Tracking. *See also* **Updating progress**

automated, 393
custom view for, 389
fast, 326
issues, 818–820
in Professional edition, 19
progress, 54–55
in Project Server and Project Web Access, 21–23
in Standard edition, 8, 14–15
task progress, 43, 734–738
team resources, 811–814
Tracking toolbar, 385, 413
Troubleshooting
  Analyze Timescaled Data function, 591
  assignment information, 258
  baseline setting, 376–377
  budget resource assignment, 295
  combination views, 123
  cost resources, 215
  custom forms, 984
  deleting constraints, 184
  duplicate resource names, 204, 509
  earned value fields, 421, 499
  e-mail address book, 207
  e-mailing project files, 649
  e-mail workgroup messaging, 652
  entering values, 296
  Excel Task List template, 608
  Field Name list, 930, 934
  fields, 133
  Filter By boxes, 245
  filter display of tasks, 953
  fixed task costs, 287
  Gantt Charts, 92, 906, 908
  group heading values, 950
  Help pane, 30–31
  importing and exporting, 211–212, 576, 623
  leveling, 362, 363
  macros, 994
  Mapping table, 622–623
  missing project information, 147
  pasting, 541, 553, 602
  performance, 363
  PERT analysis views, 113
  predecessor links, 176
  printing, 464–465
  Project Guide toolbar, 27
  project server users, 708

report column sizes, 458–459
resources assigned to tasks, 250
resource sharing commands, 521–523
saving as Web pages, 486–487
schedule values *versus* actuals, 407
scheduling tasks, 339
start and finish dates, 388
task calendars, 161, 194
text and bar formatting, 512
toolbars, 972–973, 975–976
views, 123

U

Underallocated resources, 347
Undo and redo, multiple levels of, 16, 96
Update Link prompt, 604
Updating progress, 382–397
   actual costs in, 397–399
   entering actuals for, 382–385
   in Outlook 2007, 863
   in Project Web Access, 848–851
   reports on, 455–460
   rescheduling projects and, 395–397
   resource work for, 390–395
   task scheduling controls for, 385–389
   team exchanges for, 802–808
   team options for, 795–800
   work pages for, 734–738
Usage views, 118–120, 924–925
Users and permissions, 692–704
   automated alerts for, 704
   baseline information and, 374
   changing, 699
   groups and categories in, 694, 700–703
   new accounts and, 695–698
   removing users and, 698–699
   security template for, 700
   viewing, 699, 847

V

Variable material consumption, 251
Variable work resource costs, 275–277
Variance at Completion (VAC), 465, 496
Variances
   in cost, 417–418
   definition of, 402–403
   in project management, 48, 50

in schedule, 406–407
   Schedule Variance (SV) earned value field for, 404
   in work, 425
View Definition dialog box, 899–901
Views, 105–152
   of assignments on Project Web Access, 834–836, 843–848
   budget resource, 304
   of categories of project information, 106–107
   changing, 107–110
   combination, 121–124
   custom tracking, 389
   default, 64, 148
   in enterprise project management, 746–748
   of fields, 134–138
   filtering information for, 142–147
   of forms, 120–121
   Gantt Chart, 110–114
   graph, 115–117
   grouping information for, 140–142
   of links, 605–606
   navigation for, 152
   network diagram, 114–115
   PERT analysis, 113
   printing, 440–443
   in Professional edition, 19–20
   of project costs, 331–336
   in Project Server and Project Web Access, 23–25
   of resource workloads, 339–347
   sheet, 117–118
   sorting information for, 138–140
   in Standard edition, 15–17
   of tables
      description of, 125–130
      modifying, 131–134
   task, 343
   of timescales, 124–125
   troubleshooting, 123
   usage, 118–120
   Window preferences for, 147–152
Views, customizing, 897–965
   calendar, 919–922
   content changes as, 898–901
   of fields, 931–940
      calculated, 936–938
      graphical indicators in, 938–940

lookup values for, 934–936
process of, 933–934
types of, 932
of filters, 952–960
   autofilter criteria for, 959–960
   creating, 955–959
   modifying, 952–955
font changes as, 902–903
Gantt Chart, 904–911
of groups, 948–952
network diagram, 912–915
of outline codes, 941–947
resource graph, 915–919
restoring defaults to, 965
sharing among projects, 961–964
sheet, 922–923
of tables, 928–931
timescale, 926–928
usage, 924–925
Visio 2007, 653–672
   capturing views for, 553–556
   cash flow report in, 334–335
   copying pictures to, 444
   diagrams of, 668–672
   exporting data from, 665–667
   presenting data in, 661–665
   Project 2007 information exchange with, 548
   Project 2007 reports exported to, 17
   reporting in, 654–661
   visual reports in, 448–451, 454, 459, 461, 471, 473, 478
   WBS Chart Wizard in, 102, 662
Visual Basic for Applications (VBA), 684, 987, 992, 996

W

Web parts, 24, 742–745
"What-If" projects, 415
Windows, preferences for, 147–152
Windows Workflow Foundation, 25
Word 2007, 444, 551, 553–556
Work breakdown structure (WBS)
   in starting projects, 87, 99–102
   as task outline, 941
   Visio WBS Chart Wizard on, 102, 662
   WBS Code Definition dialog box for, 988

Working Days report, 455
Working time, 12–13
Work resources, 235–250. *See also* Changes in projects
   actual and remaining, 392–395
   actual costs for, 397
   assignment calculations for, 248–250
   assignments of, 237–241
   job-specific, 241–248
   percentage complete, 391–392
   planning for cost of, 275–277
   project additions of, 205–212
Workspaces
   features of, 769
   in Project Web Access, 877–878
   saving, 516–517, 1027
   viewing, 23–24
Work week. *See* Base calendars

X

XML files, saving as, 486, 579
XML Reporting Wizard, 451

About the Authors

Teresa S. Stover is a technical communications consultant who specializes in Microsoft Project and project management. She started up Stover Writing Services in 1987, and ever since she has been managing projects having to do with user assistance or instruction: online help, training curriculum, multimedia productions, and Web content. Clients have included Apple Computer, National Semiconductor, Boeing, MetLife, Unisys, and the Puyallup School District. Most significantly, she has worked with the Microsoft Project product team for every release since Project 4.0 in the early 1990s.

Having won several awards from the Society for Technical Communications, including a Best In Show, Teresa has written a number of other books including titles on Windows, Office, Team Manager, and Microsoft Money.

Teresa is typically planted in her Victorian home office in southern Oregon, but she sometimes tears herself away to conduct workshops on computer, business, and project management topics. She is also a disaster volunteer for the American Red Cross, participates in "disobedience" trials with Draco the wonder German Shepherd Dog, and plays store some Saturdays at her husband's shop, Stovepipe Antiques.

Learn more at Teresa's Web site *www.stoverwriting.com*. Teresa also welcomes e-mails from readers sent to teresa@stoverwriting.com.

Bonnie Biafore has always been good at getting things done, but a few decades passed before she realized that she was "Managing Projects." Now, with a Project Management Professional Certification (PMP) from the Project Management Institute (PMI), she runs her own company, MonteVista Solutions, Inc., offering project management and training services to clients in a variety of industries.

On a parallel course, writing and ferocious editing have been a lifelong habit. She's written award-winning books about project management, investing, and several commercial software programs (Microsoft Project, Quicken, QuickBooks, and Visio). Bonnie is also a regular contributor of project management articles to Microsoft's Work Essentials Web site.

When she isn't meeting deadlines, she cooks gourmet meals, hikes in the nearby mountains, or makes jewelry. You can learn more about Bonnie and her books at her Web site, *www.bonniebiafore.com*.

What do you think of this book?

We want to hear from you!

Do you have a few minutes to participate in a brief online survey?

Microsoft is interested in hearing your feedback so we can continually improve our books and learning resources for you.

To participate in our survey, please visit:

www.microsoft.com/learning/booksurvey/

...and enter this book's ISBN-10 number (appears above barcode on back cover*).
As a thank-you to survey participants in the United States and Canada, each month we'll randomly select five respondents to win one of five $100 gift certificates from a leading online merchant. At the conclusion of the survey, you can enter the drawing by providing your e-mail address, which will be used for prize notification only.

Thanks in advance for your input. Your opinion counts!

* Where to find the ISBN-10 on back cover

ISBN-13: 000-0-0000-0000-0
ISBN-10: 0-0000-0000-0

0 000000 000000

Example only. Each book has unique ISBN.

No purchase necessary. Void where prohibited. Open only to residents of the 50 United States (includes District of Columbia) and Canada (void in Quebec). For official rules and entry dates see:

www.microsoft.com/learning/booksurvey/